THE
FABULOUS
FIFTIES

THE
FABULOUS
FIFTIES

Edited by
Arleen Keylin

ARNO PRESS
NEW YORK • 1978

A Note to the Reader
Original copies of *The New York Times* were not available
to the publisher. This volume, therefore, was created from
35mm microfilm.

Library of Congress Cataloging in Publication Data
Main entry under title:

The Fabulous fifties.

    1.   United States—Social life and customs—
1945-1970—Sources. 2.   United States—Popular
culture—Sources. I. Keylin, Arleen. II. New
York times.
E169.02.F32   973.92   78-16393
ISBN 0-405-11518-0

Book design by Stephanie Rhodes

Editorial Assistant: Sandra D. Flamholtz

Manufactured in the United States of America

Contents

Introduction vii
1950 1
1951 29
1952 51
1953 81
1954 111
1955 137
1956 165
1957 189
1958 211
1959 235

Introduction

It's difficult to make a sweeping statement about such a complex matter as a decade. Yet, if one were to feel an urgent need to characterize the 1950s, it would be safe to state that they were groundbreaking. In many ways we are continuing along roads we began to travel in the 1950s. This applies to politics, entertainment, music, art, and literature—even to eating habits. And it isn't uniquely due to the American bent for nostalgia. True enough, the leather look and anklets may have found their way back again into today's fashion, and Elvis Presley's "ghost" is a winner on Broadway, but the important fact is that our way of life seems to have been reshaped in that turbulent, often crazy, span of ten years from 1950 to 1960. Americans woke up to the reality of a world far different from the one promised to them in the dramatic speeches of World War II's leaders. It was a world torn apart by the political rivalry of two superpowers operating under opposing political philosophies. It was a world threatened by unbelievably destructive weapons, and transformed through great technological skills and innovations perfected during the war years. This reality is still with us. Its character may have altered slightly in some respects, a great deal in others, yet basically it is a product of the Fabulous Fifties.

The most important pattern established in the 1950s is perhaps the most unpleasant. After fighting a bitter Second World War against totalitarian powers dedicated to a horrifying new world order, the Allies, strange political bedfellows at best, soon split into opposing blocs. Beginning in 1945 at Los Alamos, Hiroshima and Nagasaki, anxiety about the destruction of mankind through A-bombs and H-bombs lurked behind every political decision. When it was apparent that superweapons were also being developed by Soviet technology, anxieties increased to a feverish pitch. Americans were profoundly afraid that the conventional hostilities characterized by the conflict in Korea would soon develop into atomic warfare. The "Cold War" soon became the overriding consideration, its ominous pall hanging over everyone. Radioactive fallout, pre-fabricated bombshelters, air raid drills, and "end-of-the-world" forecasts became part and parcel of the daily lives of millions of Americans. When Stalin died in 1953, the Soviet Communist State did not die with him, as many believed—or hoped—it would. The Cold War took on new dimensions but still remained the primary factor behind most political decisions. Far from weakening, the Soviet bloc gained in power, and some responsible American leaders began to support perilous programs such as "brinkmanship." Quemoy and Matsu, obscure islands off the China coast were, in their opinion, as vital to American security as the waters off California. Reason reigned, luckily, and the reality of stalemate necessitated the more cautious policy of "containment," or holding even. In the 1960s and 70s, this evolved into "détènte."

Hand-in-hand with anxieties about nuclear confrontations, came an exaggerated fear about the fundamental strengths of Communism and its power to insidiously subvert the basic American social, political and economic structure. Champions of "Americanism" arose to thwart the Communist threat and to accuse those who had "sold America out!" Foremost among these frenzied fighters for the American way of life was Senator Joseph R. McCarthy who along with his young and staunch deputy, Roy Cohn, rose from relative obscurity to national attention. "Pinkos," witch-hunts, the Rosenbergs, anti-intellectualism (for weren't all Communists intellectuals?), and the Army-McCarthy hearings—all became nightly news themes of the newly expanded television networks. Until he was stopped, McCarthy had a good many Americans believing that only he, his committee and the F.B.I. stood between us and a nefarious Bolshevik conspiracy.

Perhaps it was this prevalent fear of intellectualism as a breeding ground for Communism that brought us President Dwight David Eisenhower. With military, not political, fame as a background, he won an easy victory over the "egg-heads." Yet even the easygoing Ike was forced to make some earth-shaking decisions. There was no way for him to escape the realities of his office and his time. As a reaction to the grim news of constant international strife, there was a bright side to the 1950s. It manifested itself in a mad dash to escape, and escape we did. We fled, if only for a brief time, to a new dimension—the 3-D movie. We sat there, row after row of us, with over-sized paper-framed glasses entranced by films of dubious artistic merit. When that became boring, we jammed into giant movie theaters to witness super-happenings in the form of cinerama and cinemascope. Perhaps the films were the same, but they spread before us like magical panoramas.

Our addictions took other forms and shapes. Crinolines became a fashion "must" for women of all ages. The younger set was gyrating indoors and outdoors encircled by hula-hoops while the fortunate manufacturers of these plastic sensations were reeling in dollars. The older set thought that these hoops were the key to physical fitness and the end to fat. Americans also found adventure in history—in Davy Crockett and the Alamo, and in science fiction fantasy—as flying saucers were spotted from coast to coast and "little green people" paid personal calls on obscure citizens. When the Russians launched Sputnik, we were "up there" with our galactic neighbors. The moon landing was still a score of years away, but the first giant step in its direction was taken.

One of the most profound changes in the American way of life came in the form of a technological innovation, television. Kids came to regard Howdy Doody and Kukla, Fran and Ollie as members of the family. Children were transfixed by the figures on the small black and white screens in the corner of the living room. Politicians were rapidly aware of their visual image as well as of their speaking potential. How many were defeated because they couldn't compete with the glamorous entertainment figures? "Your Show of Shows" with Sid Caesar, Imogene Coca, Carl Reiner and Howard Morris spoofed everything from "first dates" to foreign movies. Lucille Ball became the close "friend" of an entire nation. "Studio One" brought real drama into millions of households and Uncle Miltie—jolly Milton Berle with his blacked-out teeth—kept America laughing.

While the kids gyrated with hoops, Elvis Presley gyrated to "rock and roll" and millions of teenagers, sporting ducktails, pony tails, and poodle cuts, shouted and screamed and danced. They danced to the very beat that made a Donna Summer possible and set us all hustling on down the path to the disco to dance to the driving music of "Saturday Night Fever." Elvis was the favorite with the teenagers, but the more mature among us tingled when Peggy Lee sang "Fever," and let's not overlook Patti Page, Jo Stafford, Frankie Avalon, Rosemary Clooney, Pat Boone, the Everly Brothers, Ricky Nelson and Fabian. Today's T.V. commercials hawk trips into "nostalgia" by offering these "golden oldies." Paul Anka still draws enthusiastic crowds, and Dick Clark still holds sway over his "American Bandstand." Broadway featured such timeless hit musicals as "My Fair Lady," "The Music Man," "Bye Bye Birdie," and "West Side Story." The music of the 1950s is still being hummed and played by people all over again.

And then there was Hollywood. Hollywood in the Fifties was the Hollywood of the legendary Marilyn Monroe, of Debbie Reynolds, Burt Lancaster, Kim Novak, and Rock Hudson—not to forget Doris Day. As profoundly as young Americans were influenced by the Presley beat, they were guided by that "Rebel Without a Cause," James Dean. He was the symbol of their rebellion against the smugness of middle class suburbia and the world of kitchen gadgets, frozen food, and material consumption. And now even James Dean is having a revival!

Were the Fifties mindless? Far from it. The 1950s produced Jack Kerouac, Kenneth Rexroth, Allen Ginsberg and Gregory Corso, the literary rebels of one decade who became the standard bearers of the next. In art there were the Jackson Pollocks as well as those who painted by number. Philip Johnson's unique architectural style began to dominate metropolitan skylines all over America. James Jones, Mickey Spillane, James Baldwin—each one made a fresh and lasting contribution to American literary technique. Not idealistic? The 1950s provided the starting point of the agonizing journey of Dr. Martin Luther King through the obstacles of racial prejudice, a journey yet unended. Self-indulgent? It was a decade that gave rise to such penetrating, yet comic, critics of mores and standards as Mike Nichols and Elaine May, Mort Sahl and Lenny Bruce.

Times change, did you say? Well, Queen Elizabeth is still with us, and so are the civil rights movement, rivalry between the U.S.A. and the U.S.S.R., the crisis in the Middle East, the T.V. quiz show, junk foods, and a whole spectrum of ideas, items and cultural, social and economic phenomena that were born in the 1950s. After all, it was only the day before yesterday.

Sanford L. Chernoff

1950

"All the News That's Fit to Print"

The New York Times.

LATE CITY EDITION
Sunny and windy today; fair and colder tonight and tomorrow.
Temperature Range Today-Max.,50; Min.,36
Temperatures Yesterday—Max.,53; Min.,42
Full U. S. Weather Bureau Report, Page 47

Copyright, 1950, by The New York Times Company.

VOL. XCIX...No. 33,590 — Entered as Second-Class Matter. Postoffice, New York, N. Y. — NEW YORK, WEDNESDAY, JANUARY 11, 1950. — Times Square, New York 18, N. Y. Telephone LAckawanna 4-1000 — THREE CENTS IN NEW YORK CITY | FIVE CENTS ELSEWHERE

RUSSIAN QUITS U. N. COUNCIL ON CHINA RECOGNITION ISSUE; ACHESON IS FIRM ON POLICY

MALIK IN WALKOUT

Departs After Security Body Defers Motion to Oust Nationalists

ISSUE SET FOR TOMORROW

Soviet Delegate Is Expected to Return for Consideration of His Resolution

By THOMAS J. HAMILTON
Special to THE NEW YORK TIMES.

LAKE SUCCESS, Jan. 10—Jacob A. Malik, the Soviet representative, walked out of the United Nations Security Council this afternoon in protest against the Council's refusal to give immediate consideration to a Soviet resolution calling for the exclusion of Dr. T. F. Tsiang, the representative of Nationalist China.

Mr. Malik told the Council that for it to meet with Dr. Tsiang presiding would be a "parody" of a meeting, and announced his walkout with the following declaration:

"I, as representative of the Soviet Union, cannot participate in the work of this meeting of the Security Council until the representative of the Kuomintang has been removed from membership of the Security Council. This being so, I cannot remain at this table but shall leave the chamber."

Despite Mr. Malik's uncompromising statement, some delegates expressed their conviction after the meeting adjourned that he would be on hand Thursday afternoon, when the Council would meet to take up the Soviet resolution. Afterward the Council will consider a resolution adopted by the General Assembly last December on the disarmament question, which was the sole item on the agenda for today's meeting.

Tsiang Suggests Procedure

This procedure was suggested by Dr. Tsiang, who is President of the Council under its monthly rotation system, after Mr. Malik's walk out. As he strode to his waiting car Mr. Malik declined to answer inquiries from correspondents as to whether he would attend any more meetings as long as Dr. Tsiang sat at the Council table.

However, in an earlier statement to the Council, he said less uncompromisingly that "if the Security Council does not take suitable measures for the removal from the Security Council of the representative of the Kuomintang group, the Soviet Union delegation will not participate in the Security Council until the represent tive of the Kuomintang group is removed from membership in the Security Council."

It was assumed that, having at least brought it about that the Council should not take up any other business until it had disposed of the Soviet resolution, Mr. Malik would be on hand to vote for it, but would walk out again if, as is expected, it is rejected.

The Soviet Union, which supported Czechoslovakia, had previously announced that it would not recognize the election of Yugoslavia by the General Assembly as the representative of Eastern Europe on the Council. However, Mr. Malik did not challenge Dr. Ales Bebler's credentials today, and he is thus regarded as a fully accredited member of the Council.

Five Recognize Peiping

Of the eleven members of the Council only five — the Soviet Union, Britain, India, Norway and Yugoslavia—have recognized the "Central People's Government of the People's Republic of China," and this is two votes short of the majority required on any question.

Moreover, Sir Alexander Cadogan, the British representative, told the Council this afternoon that the Soviet resolution was "premature" in view of the fact that only a "small number" of the members of the United Nations had recognized the Communist regime, and British circles indicated they might abstain.

Since the United States, France and other countries that still recognize the Nationalist Govern-

Continued on Page 2, Column 2

A SOVIET PROTEST

Jacob A. Malik walking out of United Nations session at Lake Success yesterday.
The New York Times (by Fred Sass)

BARS MILITARY AID

Southeast Asia, as Well as Formosa Affected, Senate Unit Hears

ONLY POINT 4 HELP LIKELY

Secretary Silent on Military Advisers—U. S. Navy Assists Ship Shelled Off China

By WILLIAM S. WHITE
Special to THE NEW YORK TIMES.

WASHINGTON, Jan. 10—Secretary of State Dean Acheson stood unbendingly today before his Republican critics in a long closed conference with the Senate Foreign Relations Committee on the Administration's refusal to help Formosa militarily.

He was said also, by responsible Senators who heard him, to have offered no promise of substantial military aid to non-Communist lands anywhere in Southeast Asia. "About the most" that could be expected by such countries as Burma, Thailand, India, Indo-China, summed up the committee chairman, Senator Tom Connally, Democrat, of Texas, was "some aid under Point Four."

Point Four is the project of President Truman, yet to be approved by Congress, for economic help to the world's backward areas.

"Reportorial, Not Philosophical"

Another informant reported that the Secretary "gave a reportorial and not a philosophical" statement, and made no suggestion that a line would be drawn at any particular point in Asia beyond which communism would not be permitted to go.

[Under orders of the Defense Department two United States destroyers today were standing by to help the United States freighter Flying Arrow, shelled off China by Nationalist gunboats. A State Department spokesman said "nobody questions" that the Flying Arrow had been attacked in international waters.]

In a three-hour appearance before the committee Mr. Acheson defeated a Republican effort to force him to disclose the nature and source of all the military advice used by the Administration in adopting a hands-off policy for Formosa, the island headquarters of the Chinese Nationalist Government.

This attempt was particularly designed to determine whether General of the Army Douglas MacArthur in Tokyo, who has been represented by some Republicans as favoring the occupation of Formosa, had been consulted.

The intention also was to bring out the recommendations that had been made by the Joint Chiefs of Staff.

To questions along this line, it was reported later by Senator Connally, Mr. Acheson replied that he was not in position to speak for

Continued on Page 3, Column 5

JAPAN'S REDS OUST PRO-MOSCOW AIDE

Nakanishi, Legislator, Purged for Backing Cominform's Attack on Party Chief

By The Associated Press.

TOKYO, Jan. 10—Japan's Communists kicked out of the party today a prominent veteran member who supported the Communist Information Bureau attack against the Red leader Sanzo Nosaka.

Ko Nakanishi, member of the Parliament's House of Councilors, was read out of the party in a barren little room at Communist headquarters.

He told Japanese reporters later he would "make an effort outside the party to make the Japanese party a party based on Marxism."

Mr. Nakanishi himself had been called in by the party high command earlier in the day.

The expulsion order accused him of using recent dispatches dealing with the Cominform's blast from Bucharest, Rumania, to try to disrupt the Communist party of Japan.

Mr. Nosaka is accused not only by the Cominform, but by the Communist newspaper Pravda of Moscow of being anti-democratic, anti-socialist and anti-Japanese.

The Cominform accused Mr. Nosaka of deceiving the Japanese people in arguing that Japan could attain socialism under the occupa-

Continued on Page 2, Column 5

Truman to Seek Federal Grants To Help Worthy College Students

By JOHN D. MORRIS
Special to THE NEW YORK TIMES.

WASHINGTON, Jan. 10—President Truman is expected to recommend to Congress a program of aid to deserving college students calling for Federally financed scholarships and Federally-guaranteed loans on the basis of need and ability.

Without spelling out such details, the President notified Congress in the budget message yesterday of his intention to submit the draft of a bill to help worthy high school graduates continue their education to prepare for entrance to professional schools, obtain additional technical or vocational training or round out their general education.

He proposed the expenditure of $1,000,000 in the 1951 fiscal year, which begins next July 1, to establish the required organization and initiate the program.

The office of education and the Budget Bureau are now preparing the draft of a bill that probably will be introduced within a few months.

While firm decisions have not yet been made with respect to specific provisions, there is general agreement in the Administration on a two-part system of scholarships and loan guarantees.

The principal undecided point is the ultimate cost of the program, but Dr. Earl J. McGrath, Commissioner of Education, has suggested an annual appropriation of $300,000,000 for the Federally financed scholarships. He estimated that this would provide Federal scholarships for about 400,000 undergraduates and about 37,500 graduate and professional school students.

The scholarships, awarded and administered by state commissions, would give each student $600 a year, according to the present tentative form of the plan. State quotas of scholarships would be

Continued on Page 11, Column 2

INQUIRY DEMANDED ON PORT AUTHORITY; TOLLS, SALARIES HIT

Four Legislators From City Attack Agency's Practices, Ask Sifting of Powers

'SOVEREIGN SUPER-STATE'

Independent Status Declared to Have Been Abused, With Too Much Branching Out

By DOUGLAS DALES
Special to THE NEW YORK TIMES.

ALBANY, Jan. 10—Practices of the Port of New York Authority were denounced vigorously here today as New York City legislators moved for sweeping investigations into the powers of the bi-state body.

The Authority operates Hudson River crossings, including the George Washington Bridge and the Lincoln and Holland Tunnels, as well as airports and several other enterprises in New York City and northern New Jersey.

The attacks on the agency, made by both Republicans and Democrats, centered on the general allegation that it enjoyed virtual autonomy. The legislators also took the Authority to task for its schedule of tolls, the size of salaries paid to administrative officers, and the fact that it was not subject to court determinations.

Three Inquiry Proposals Made

Three separate proposals were made for joint legislative committees to inquire into the Authority's operations, two of them by Democrats and the third by a Republican.

Assemblyman Nathan Lashin, Democrat, of the Bronx, called for an investigating committee of six members to "revise the framework of the Authority in the light of its present operations."

Senator John M. Braisted Jr. and Assemblyman Edward V. Curry, Democrats, of Richmond, called for a similar investigation in companion resolutions, and attacked the Port Authority as "a sovereign super-state."

The Republican proposal, calling for a seven-man committee, was made by Assemblyman Samuel Roman of Manhattan, who assailed the contract-awarding policies of the Authority.

Efforts are under way to get similar resolutions introduced in the New Jersey Legislature, which convened at Trenton today.

The proposal of the Richmond legislators calls for an inquiry into the toll charges, but would not be limited to that subject. There has been agitation for several years from automobile associations for a reduction or elimination of toll charges for the Holland Tunnel, which is said to have paid for itself already.

Assemblyman Lashin said he was not concerned so much with the toll situation as he was with the policies and practices which he said had diverted the Authority from its original purpose of providing Hudson River crossings "into a self-perpetuating organization."

Contract Dispute Recalled

Lending additional interest to the proposals for legislative investigations of the Port Authority was the charge made last Thursday by the Merritt-Chapman & Scott Corporation that the authority had submitted incomplete information to Gov. Thomas E. Dewey and Gov. Alfred E. Driscoll of New Jersey to avoid their vetoes of a contract awarded for the Union Bus Terminal in New York City.

The Merritt-Chapman & Scott Corporation submitted the low bid of $8,938,617 for the bus terminal on Eighth Avenue between Forty and Forty-first Streets, but the contract was awarded to the second lowest bidder, the Turner Construction Company, whose bid was $9,194,759.

The Port Authority explained its award by saying it believed the greater experience of the Turner company in city building construction gave greater assurance that the terminal would be completed by next Nov. 1.

Assemblyman Roman asserted that the Authority had exceeded its powers in the matter of the award, and added:

"Complaints have been mounting from many quarters for many years over the Port Authority's conduct of its affairs, on the fixing of toll charges, the cost of its administration, the vast expenditures for consultation fees and its general relationship with the en-

Continued on Page 46, Column 2

FOR AN "ENCHANTING EVENING" (Times) S. Hurok presents Shankar Hindu Ballet, 48th St. Thea., Four More Days. Mat. TOMORROW. —Advt.

Republicans in Albany Deride O'Dwyer Gambling Proposal

But City Democrats Offer Bingo, Lottery and 'Horse Room' Bills—Chances Dim for Mayor's Plan to Legalize Bets

By LEO EGAN
Special to THE NEW YORK TIMES.

ALBANY, Jan. 10—Mayor O'Dwyer's proposal to legalize gambling produced a mixed reaction from legislators today, ranging from enthusiastic support to uncompromising opposition. Its chances of receiving serious consideration appeared dim.

Several new bills on the subject of gambling made their appearance today in the wake of the Mayor's statement. One by Assemblyman Alex Del Giorno, Queens Democrat, would legalize bingo if held under the auspices of a fraternal, religious, veterans or welfare society.

Another, sponsored jointly by Senator Alfred E. Santangelo and Assemblyman Louis A. Cioffi, both New York Democrats, would legalize lotteries in New York cities if proceeds were used for the support of schools or hospitals. A third, also by Mr. Santangelo and Mr. Cioffi, would legalize "horse rooms" in New York City under a taxing arrangement.

Senator James J. Crawford, Brooklyn Democrat, had previously introduced a bill to legalize off-track betting throughout the state. In all material respects it was identical with similar bills he has sponsored, without success, year after year in the past.

Oswald D. Heck, Republican Speaker of the Assembly, commented derisively on the O'Dwyer proposal: "That's a great subject. That's all I can say and I am not for it. I do not see a bright future for such legislation. We ought to study the results of such legislation in other countries before we consider it."

Senator Walter J. Mahoney, Republican, chairman of the Senate Finance Committee, said: "If the Mayor wouldn't object to setting up a horse room in City Hall, others would."

Assemblyman Harry A. Reoux, Republican, chairman of the Assembly Judiciary Committee, ob-

Continued on Page 18, Column 1

Up-State Users of City Water Urged to Observe 'Holiday'

By CHARLES G. BENNETT

As the city's Catskill and Croton reservoirs showed a reduced gain in water storage again yesterday, water officials asked the eighty up-state communities using city water to observe the same "water holiday" tomorrow that will be in effect here.

Meanwhile, in Poughkeepsie at a public hearing before the State Water Power and Control Commission, the city of Poughkeepsie failed in its initial attempt to block a project that would draw, in emergencies, 100,000,000 gallons of Hudson River water daily for New York. The commission denied motions to reject the project immediately and announced it would conduct further study of the project.

Stephen J. Carney, Commissioner of Water Supply, Gas and Electricity, called upon the city school system to make pupils especially "water conscious" tomorrow, both to educate them in the need for drastic saving and as a means of reaching parents and other adults in the children's homes.

The commissioner asked New Yorkers to make the same cuts in water uses that they made on "Dry Friday." Dec. 16. This means no baths, no shaves, combining dishwashing into one operation for the

Continued on Page 30, Column 2

The Water Situation

The following figures as of 8 A. M. yesterday give the number of gallons of water in the city's reservoirs. The difference in the two days is the net after intake and the day's consumption.

Monday	96,830,000,000
Yesterday	97,602,000,000
Net gain	772,000,000
Watershed rainfall	None

At normal consumption there remains about sixty days' supply before pressure fails.

At present consumption there remains about eighty-one days' supply before pressure fails.

Catskill and Croton reservoirs at capacity hold 253,136,000,000 gallons.

STATE VALIDATES RENT LAW OF CITY

Governor Signs Stopgap Bill, but Doubts Constitutionality—Asks Basic Legislation

Special to THE NEW YORK TIMES.

ALBANY, Jan. 10—Governor Dewey approved today stopgap legislation revalidating until May 1 the New York City rent and eviction control law that was voided by the Court of Appeals at the end of last month.

Earlier, the Senate had approved the bill, 37 to 12, with three New York City Democrats joining nine Republicans in opposition. The Assembly had approved the measure last night, 133 to 9, with one New York City Democrat joining eight upstate Republicans in voting against it.

The revalidated local law, known as the Sharkey Law, requires landlords to get the approval of the New York City Rent Commission before they may put into effect rent increases authorized by Federal authorities. Unless they do so, they are barred from evicting tenants for nonpayment of rent. The law also freezes rent as of last March 1.

In yielding to an urgent plea from Mayor William O'Dwyer for immediate approval of the measure, Governor Dewey voiced a fear that the revitalized law, like its predecessor, would be voided.

He urged the State Temporary Rent Commission, headed by Assemblyman D. Mallory Stephens, Putnam Republican, to propose for enactment at the present session

Continued on Page 9, Column 5

15,000 More Join Mine Walkout; Youngstown Slows Steel Output

By A. H. RASKIN

Fifteen thousand more miners joined yesterday in the series of "mystery" strikes that cast a pall of idleness over many areas of the country's soft-coal industry Monday. The new walkouts brought the number on strike to more than 60,000 and cut 400,000 tons of new production a day from the country's dwindling coal pile.

The strikes and the three-day work week enforced in other pits by John L. Lewis' United Mine Workers drew their first blood in the steel industry when the Youngstown Sheet and Tube Company at Youngstown, Ohio, announced that it was curtailing operations for lack of coal.

The company, which has been operating at 102 per cent of rated capacity and has a huge backlog of orders awaiting fulfillment, reduced operations at its two by-product coke plants last night and said it would begin banking blast furnaces early next week. The cuts will bring new unemployment to hundreds of steelworkers, who conducted a five-week strike of their own in October and November.

Although the "captive" mines owned by major steel companies are a prime target of the coal walkouts, most other steel companies have enough coal on hand to maintain full operating schedules for several weeks. United States Steel is understood to have about two months' supply of coal at most of its mills. Other companies have comparable stocks.

Robert N. Denham, general counsel of the National Labor Relations Board, conferred in Washington with Mr. Lewis on unfair labor practice charges filed against the union by the coal operators.

Also in Washington, the Senate Banking Committee recommended an early study to determine whether the anti-trust laws should be applied to labor unions.

No explanation of the spreading

Continued on Page 14, Column 3

ATTLEE SETS FEB. 23 AS ELECTION DATE; SOCIALISM IS ISSUE

More or Less Nationalization Is Held Supreme Question for Britons to Decide

LABOR, OPPOSITION READY

Dissolution of Parliament Feb. 3 to Launch Campaign—New House Meets March 6

By RAYMOND DANIELL
Special to THE NEW YORK TIMES.

LONDON, Jan. 10—Britain's election was fixed todady for Feb. 23. On that day the people of this country will decide whether they want more or less socialism. That is the great issue before them, overshadowing all personalities, but it may be obscured as the campaign progresses by more homely considerations, such as food, housing and the weekly pay envelope.

Both sides can be counted on to promise the best of two worlds—a capitalist paradise and a Socialist utopia. The Labor Government will point to its record of full employment and "fair shares for all" and the Conservatives will retort by saying that they approve all of this but could do it better for less.

Prime Minister Attlee, as is his right, chose the date and communicated it to his Cabinet and junior Ministers today. He had told the King on Sunday of his plans. The King, as was announced tonight, agreed to dissolve Parliament on Feb. 3. This, under the British constitution, makes the date of the general election fall on Feb. 23, as had been generally expected.

Parliament now stands adjourned until Jan. 24. But as soon as the King can summon a quorum of his Privy Counselors there will be a royal proclamation postponing the next sitting of Parliament until after the date of dissolution.

New Parliament Opens March 6

The new Parliament to be elected on Feb. 23 will be called into its first session for the swearing-in of members and the election of a Speaker on March 1. The King will open the new Parliament formally on March 6.

No one can tell now whether the new Parliament will be predominantly Labor or Conservative or, consequently, whether the King's opening speech will advocate more or less socialism. It may be, al-

Continued on Page 7, Column 1

JOHNSON DECLARES TIGHTENED BUDGET AMPLE FOR DEFENSE

Tells Reporters All Possible Economies Were Made, but Security Was Put First

SERVICE HEADS SATISFIED

But Symington Would Like 70 Air Groups—House Body Sets Armed Force Study

By AUSTIN STEVENS
Special to THE NEW YORK TIMES.

WASHINGTON, Jan. 10—Louis Johnson, Secretary of Defense, asserted today that the tightened budget of $13,545,000,000 for the armed services that President Truman submitted to Congress yesterday offered the country "an adequacy of defense for any situation that may arise in the next two years."

Mr. Johnson's remarks were made at a press conference, his first in several months, and it turned out to be a mass meeting. Ranged around him in a conference room in the Pentagon were the Secretaries of the Army, Navy and Air Force, the Chiefs of Staff of the Army and Air Force, the Chief of Naval Operations, the commandant of the Marine Corps, the three assistant Secretaries of Defense and other defense officials.

Mr. Johnson at the outset limited the session to questions on the budget. Attempts to change the subject were unavailing.

Coincidental with the Johnson press conference, the House Armed Services Committee announced that it would conduct a full dress study of the "true state of the national defense." The inquiry is expected to get under way in February.

Mr. Johnson's thesis on the budget was summed up in a prepared statement handed to reporters before the meeting. It was that the basic objective in adjusting the size of the armed forces had been "all possible economies," but that security had come first and economy second.

The proposed budget was hardly what the Joint Chiefs had wanted, he said, adding that if the requests of the three services had been granted "unilaterally," the budget would have been $7,000,000,000 higher.

However, also in statements prepared before the conference, the

Continued on Page 10, Column 3

World News Summarized

WEDNESDAY, JANUARY 11, 1950

Jacob A. Malik, the Soviet representative, walked out of the United Nations Security Council yesterday when it refused to consider immediately his resolution to expel Dr. Tsiang, representative of Nationalist China. Dr. Tsiang, presiding over the Council this month, called a meeting for tomorrow to consider both the Soviet motion and the regular agenda. [1:8.] Mr. Malik's walkout was carefully planned in advance. [3:1.]

During a three-hour closed session with the Senate Foreign Relations Committee, Secretary Acheson stood firmly on the Administration's China policy of no military aid to Formosa and refused to promise armed help to any non-Communist nation in Asia. Recognition of the Chinese Communists, he implied, will come eventually. [1:6.]

Three hundred tanks and armored cars ordered by the Nationalists with China-aid funds were loaded in Philadelphia for shipment to Formosa. The State Department moved four women from Formosa to other posts and advised families of diplomats to leave the island. [3:2.] Two United States destroyers were sent to help the Flying Arrow, shelled by Nationalists off Shanghai. [4:2.]

Japanese Communists, criticized by Moscow, expelled a veteran leader who supported the Cominform attack. [1:7.]

President Truman's military budget of $13,545,000,000 will provide adequate defense for the next two years, but the Joint Chiefs of Staff wanted a total $7,000,000,000 higher, Defense Secretary Johnson said. [1:5] A House committee, scheduling a full inquiry into the "true state of the national defense," unanimously dismissed all charges brought against the Air Force's B-36 bomber. [10:2.]

A general election will be held in Britain on Feb. 23. The present Parliament will be dissolved on Feb. 3 and the new one will sit on March 6. [1:4.] A shift in only a small percentage of the vote could unseat the Labor Government. [7:1.]

The Italian Cabinet is expected to resign this week, and Premier de Gasperi will in all probability be asked to form a new Government. [7:3.]

President Truman, it was said, will send to Congress a program of Federal scholarships and Government-guaranteed loans to college students. [1:6-7.] Strong opposition to Federal scholarships was voiced at the convention of college heads. [11:1.]

The wildcat soft-coal strike continued to spread and one steel mill cut production. [1:2-3.] A Senate committee, criticizing the three-day week in the mines, urged early study of the applicability of anti-trust laws to unions. [14:2.] In this city Mayor O'Dwyer sought to halt a strike of 1,200 coal and fuel-oil drivers scheduled for midnight tonight. [14:6.]

Governor Dewey, with doubt as to its legality, signed the bill revalidating this city's Sharkey rent and eviction law. [1:2.] Legislators of both parties from this city assailed the Port Authority's tolls and practices and introduced resolutions for broad investigations. [1:1.]

Albany reaction to Mayor O'Dwyer's proposal that the state legalize and control betting on sports was mixed. A number of bills dealing with gambling were introduced in the Legislature. [1:2-3.] Church groups vigorously opposed the Mayor's proposal. [18:1.]

Eighty up-state communities using this city's water were asked to observe tomorrow's water holiday. [1:2-3.]

A record $232,003,241 budget, with $13,000,000 for pay rises, will be asked by the Board of Education. [18:2.]

Index to other news appears on Page 24.

FIGHT TOOTH DECAY. Use PEB-AMMO ammoniated tooth paste for more effective, more lasting dental care. Triple-guaranteed to give complete satisfaction. 39c, 49c.—Advt.

Riesel, Brooks, McNeil and Davis comprised the panel of Meet the Press. The guest seen here with Spivak is James Roosevelt.

Marlin Perkins brought Zoo Parade to network television in 1950. It featured visits with animals behind the scenes at Chicago's Lincoln Park Zoo. It ran until 1957.

John Cameron Swayze, one of the first star personality newscasters.

Marilyn Monroe had a small part in All About Eve. She appears here in a scene with Gregory Ratoff, Anne Baxter, Gary Merrill, George Sanders and Celeste Holm.

Spencer Tracy takes his daughter, Elizabeth Taylor down the aisle in Father of the Bride.

Gregory Peck, Skip Homeier, and Karl Malden in The Gunfighter, an early "psychological western."

"All the News That's Fit to Print"

NEWS INDEX, PAGE 79, THIS SECTION

The New York Times.

LATE CITY EDITION
Cloudy, mild today and tomorrow, followed by clearing and colder.
Temperature Range Today—Max., 50; Min., 34
Temperatures Yesterday—Max., 40; Min., 24
Full U. S. Weather Bureau Report, Page 78

Section 1

VOL. XCIX..No. 33,601. Entered as Second-Class Matter. Postoffice, New York, N. Y. NEW YORK, SUNDAY, JANUARY 22, 1950. Including Magazine and Book Review. FIFTEEN CENTS New York City 50 Mile Zone } Elsewhere Twenty Cents

HISS GUILTY ON BOTH PERJURY COUNTS; BETRAYAL OF U. S. SECRETS IS AFFIRMED; SENTENCE WEDNESDAY; LIMIT 10 YEARS

TRUMAN, ACHESON DEMAND CONGRESS VOTE AID TO KOREA

Rayburn Says Bill Will Come to Floor Again, and It Is 'Going to Be Passed'

SPEEDY ACTION IS SOUGHT

Secretary of State Expresses 'Concern and Dismay'—Sees Threat to U. S. Policy

By JOHN D. MORRIS
Special to The New York Times.

WASHINGTON, Jan. 21—President Truman today deplored the House of Representatives rejection of the Korean aid bill, and called for "speedy rectification."

In a statement released by the White House along with a letter in which Dean Acheson, Secretary of State, expressed "concern and dismay" over the development, the President said he would take up the matter with Congressional leaders and urge immediate action.

Even before he spoke out, however, Speaker Sam Rayburn told reporters that a bill would be brought to the floor again, and "the House is going to pass it."

The measure authorizing $60,000,000 of appropriations to continue the $120,000,000 economic aid program for the infant Korean Republic, was killed in the House Thursday by a surprise vote of 193 to 191. The Senate had passed a separate bill last year.

"Important Foreign Policy"

President Truman called for early reversal of the House action "in order that important foreign-policy interests of this country may be properly safeguarded."

He expressed his entire concurrence in the views expressed by Mr. Acheson in a letter to the President dated yesterday.

The Secretary said the House action, if not quickly repaired, would have "the most far-reaching adverse effects upon our foreign policy, not only in Korea but in many other areas of the world" where "our encouragement is a major element in the struggle for freedom."

Mr. Acheson said our conduct in Korea was regarded by the world "as a measure of the seriousness of our concern with the freedom and welfare of peoples maintaining their independence in the face of great obstacles."

He suggested that failure to provide further aid would imperil Korea's survival as a free nation and be "disastrous" for this country's foreign policy.

Dr. John Myun Chang, the Korean Ambassador, said tonight he was gratified and "very much encouraged" by the Truman and Acheson statements.

The envoy expressed "deep gratitude" for the statements and added the hope that the United States could find a way to continue aid to Korea, which, he said, is "absolutely essential to the recovery of its domestic economy."

Parley on Another Vote

Congressional leaders have already conferred with Mr. Acheson and other State Department officials on the question of obtaining another House vote on the question.

They are now seeking to determine the best way of doing so. To bring the defeated measure up for reconsideration would require a two-thirds majority vote. Consequently, it is believed that some other method must be found.

The prevailing view appeared to be that the quickest way would be to take the Senate-approved Korean aid bill to the House floor. It would have to be reported first by the Foreign Affairs Committee, after being amended there to conform with the House bill.

Speaker Rayburn, indicating that he favored this method, said an attempt could then be made to obtain Rules Committee clearance and, if this failed, the measure could be called up under the "by-passing" procedure that the House retained yesterday.

Senator Tom Connally, Democrat, of Texas, chairman of the Senate Foreign Relations Committee, voiced his readiness to help with the problem, if necessary, by putting through a bill linking Korean aid with continuation of the authority to provide economic assistance to Nationalist China.

He said this might be done by revising a bill sponsored by Senators H. Alexander Smith of New Jersey and William F. Knowland of California, Republicans, now pend-

Continued on Page 4, Column 1

The New York Times Five Cents Tomorrow

Because of continued increasing costs in all phases of the operation of this newspaper, the newsstand price of THE NEW YORK TIMES *on weekdays in New York City will be five cents beginning tomorrow. The new price of* THE TIMES *will be the same as that of other standard-sized newspapers in New York and generally throughout the country.*

FULL ASIA VICTORY IS SEEN IN MOSCOW

Lenin Memorial Orator Says Capitalism Cannot Halt the Revolutionary Movement

By HARRISON E. SALISBURY
Special to The New York Times.

MOSCOW, Jan. 21—Top figures of the Soviet Government and the Communist party were told tonight that capitalism and imperialism were no longer capable of halting the mass revolutionary movement of millions of Asiatic peoples inspired by successes of communism in China and the Soviet Union.

This analysis of the contemporary situation in Asia was placed before leaders of the Soviet Union and Chinese Communist chiefs at the important annual memorial meeting held at the Bolshoi Theatre on the anniversary of Lenin's death twenty-six years ago.

The Lenin memorial oration is one of the year's most important Communist party declarations. Tonight as last year, it was given by P. N. Pospelov, editor of the party's newspaper Pravda.

[The Associated Press stated that among those reported present in the Bolshoi Theatre were Chinese Communist leader Mao Tse-tung and the regime's Premier and Foreign Minister, Chou En-lai. Mr. Mao received a special ovation at mention of his name by Mr. Pospelov.]

Chinese Leaders' Presence Cited

The leaders of the new Chinese Communist regime are in Moscow conferring upon the broadest kind of understandings with the Soviet leadership. Mr. Mao has been in Moscow for nearly five weeks. Last night he was joined by Mr. Chou, accompanied by a distinguished delegation including top figures in the new Northeast China Government established in Manchuria and most of the leading specialists of the new Chinese regime in trade, commerce and industry.

Mr. Pospelov's analysis of the revolutionary successes and possibilities in Asia was coupled with the sharpest denunciation of United States imperialists and a frank prediction that "capitalism will unavoidably be replaced by socialism."

The success of Communist construction in the Soviet Union, he declared, has become "an example for the people's democracies of Europe and Asia."

"The great victory of the Chinese people already has proved that imperialism is incapable of suppressing the forces of the people, that this struggle awakens and attracts into the struggle millions of toilers," he said. "The great teaching of Leninism shows the people of all countries the road of the fight against the unheard of calamities of imperialism, shows the road of liberation from the yoke of imperialism, the road to a new Socialist life."

He declared that the United

Continued on Page 5, Column 1

BERLIN RAIL OFFICE IS RETURNED BY U. S. TO EAST GERMANS

Commandant Says He Yielded to Avoid New Hardships in the Western Sectors

HITS SOVIET 'PROVOCATION'

Difficulties Following Seizure Outweighed the Gain of 600 Rooms, He Asserts

Special to The New York Times

BERLIN, Jan. 21—Maj. Gen. Maxwell D. Taylor, United States Commandant in Berlin, this afternoon ordered the State Railway Administration building in the American sector restored to East German custody. Western sector police were withdrawn at 5 o'clock.

At a press conference called simultaneously with the release of the building, General Taylor made it clear that the basis of his action was the reprisals already taken against the population of the Western sectors and the threats of further hardships through nonpayment of wages to railway employes living in those sectors.

Confiscation of the Reichsbahn structure had been ordered, General Taylor said, as part of a program to obtain the maximum use of office and housing space in the United States sector of this badly damaged city; only forty of its 600 rooms had been used recently.

"Far from sympathizing with this purpose," his prepared statement said, "the Soviet authorities have seized upon the affair as an excuse to harass the residents of West Berlin, to threaten fresh reprisals against Reichsbahn workers and generally to disturb the peace of the city. They have not attempted to conceal their intention to discharge additional railway workers, and threaten to make further reductions in their West mark salary payments.

Claim Termed Absurd

"On Jan. 20, representatives of the Berlin press were given a tour of the Reichsbahndirektion building, where they verified the absurdity of the claim that the communications of the Reichsbahn were being interfered with. They found the usual communications personnel on the job, coming and going in the same way as during the Reichsbahn occupation. Furthermore, they verified the extent of the building space standing vacant.

"It was the American intention to put this space to use for the benefit of Berlin. Unfortunately, the unreasonable and provocative attitude of the Soviets and of the Reichsbahn makes it appear probable that the hardships which they intend to impose outweigh the benefits arising from the American plan.

"Having regretfully reached this conclusion, I am suspending the notice of custody and withdrawing the West sector police from the interior of the building.

"We now know the facts about it and shall watch to see whether the Reichsbahn puts it to a remunerative use in providing transportation service to the city.

"If our action accomplishes this, it will have served its purpose."

Obviously taken by surprise, Communist propaganda agencies were unprecedentedly brief in their comment tonight on General Taylor's move. The Soviet-controlled Radio Berlin said that the United States had succumbed to "thousands of protests by workers."

Continued on Page 12, Column 3

CHURCHILL WARNS OF SOCIALIST DRIFT, ASKS END TO CURBS

Defines Big Election Issue as More Regimentation or a Return to Freedom

LABOR CLAIMS FLOUTED

Conservative Leader Credits Full Employment to Loans From U. S. and Dominions

By RAYMOND DANIELL
Special to The New York Times.

LONDON, Jan. 21—Striking the first blow for the Conservatives in the election campaign, Winston Churchill called upon the nation's voters to set Britain free of Socialist controls and restrictions.

"The main reason why we are unable to earn our own living and make our way in the world is because we are not allowed to do so," he declared in a radio speech from his home at Westerham in Kent.

The former Prime Minister's radio address was described as a "political" but not an "election" speech. The fact is that the campaign does not officially begin until Feb. 3 when Parliament is dissolved.

As the first step toward its dissolution, taken in the orderly process of British electoral machinery, King George VI issued a proclamation today postponing the next meeting of Parliament until after Jan. 24, the date on which it had been called to reconvene. This means that this Parliament, elected in 1945, will not meet again.

It was a good Churchillian speech, which "pinked" the Laborites where it hurt, on spending, housing and the high cost of living, but possibly because of the high standard of oratorical leadership that the wartime leader had set, it fell a little flat on British ears.

The first five persons this correspondent talked to after its delivery found it "disappointing." But Mr. Churchill was under the handicap of sounding a keynote for his party before his party has made known its election program. That will be issued in the coming week.

It would have been a tactical blunder for him to anticipate any surprises that this Conservative manifesto will contain. So his address to the electorate tonight was necessarily primarily a critique rather than a statement of policy, but he did manage to get across the idea that between the Laborites and the Conservatives there is no dispute about the virtue of a country's whole labor force being usefully employed.

The choice before the people on

Continued on Page 30, Column 1

PRINCIPAL FIGURES IN THE HISS PERJURY TRIAL

Alger Hiss leaving Federal Building. | Mrs. Ada Condell, foreman of the jury. | Judge Henry W. Goddard, who presided. The New York Times

JURY OUT 24 HOURS

Verdict Follows a Call on Judge to Restate Rulings on Evidence

CHAMBERS STORY UPHELD

Defendant Is Impassive—His Counsel Announces That an Appeal Will Be Taken

By WILLIAM R. CONKLIN

Alger Hiss, a highly regarded State Department official for ten of his forty-five years, was found guilty on two counts of perjury by a Federal jury of eight women and four men yesterday.

Nearly twenty-four hours after receiving the case, the jury reported its verdict at 2:50 P. M. The middle-aged jurors had begun their deliberations at 3:10 P. M. on Friday after ten weeks of testimony in the second perjury trial.

By convicting Hiss on both counts, the jury found that he had betrayed his trust by passing secret State Department documents to Whittaker Chambers. The former courier for a Communist spy ring was the Government's key witness against the former official. The verdict meant that the jury believed Mr. Chambers and the corroborating evidence produced by the Government.

The convicted defendant faces maximum penalties of five years' imprisonment and a $2,000 fine on each count, a combined total of ten years and $4,000. Federal Judge Henry W. Goddard continued his bail at $5,000 and set Wednesday at 10:30 A. M. for sentencing. Sentence will be passed in the same thirteenth floor courtroom of the United States District Court where Hiss was tried.

Lapsing of Espionage Charge

The case of "The United States of America versus Alger Hiss" rested on a two-count perjury indictment. Thomas F. Murphy, Government prosecutor, had taxed Mr. Hiss with treason and espionage against his country. However, any possible prosecution for espionage had been ruled out by a three-year statute of limitations, which conferred immunity after March, 1941.

Hiss was thus brought to trial on one count of perjury for denying that he ever gave secret documents to Mr. Chambers. The second count charged perjury for denying that he had seen the ex-Communist after Jan. 1, 1937. The Government contended that the documents were passed in February and March, 1938.

By its verdict the jury upheld the Government's contention that Priscilla Hiss, 46-year-old wife of the defendant, had typed copies of the documents for Mr. Chambers on the Hisses' Woodstock typewriter.

Mr. Chambers had told the jury that he had been a paid functionary of the Communist party in Washington and had collected secret information for Russia from 1935 to April, 1938.

Basis Laid for Appeal

Claude B. Cross and Edward C. McLean, defense attorneys, would not say at first whether they would appeal the verdict. They had established a basis for an appeal by taking exception to a part of the charge of Judge Henry W. Goddard.

"There won't be any statement," Mr. McLean said. "I do not wish to discuss the possibility of an appeal now. There is just no statement." But later Mr. Cross said that "you can be sure the verdict will be appealed."

After the jury had convicted on both counts, Mr. Murphy asked that Hiss' bail of $5,000 be increased in conformity with the custom for "all convicted defendants." After Mr. Cross protested, Judge Goddard permitted Hiss to remain at liberty under the same bail. Mr. Cross said he would make some motions on Wednesday, the day set for sentencing.

Should defense attorneys file an appeal, it would act as an automatic stay of sentence. If an appeal should reach the United States

Continued on Page 59, Column 7

EARLY 'RIGHTS' VOTE APPEARS UNLIKELY

Items of 'Unfinished Business' May Get Precedence Despite House Action on Rules

Special to The New York Times.

WASHINGTON, Jan. 21—Chances for consideration by the House of Representatives on Monday of the Administration's bill to establish a Federal Fair Employment Practices code were evaluated as practically nil at the Capitol today. Some proponents of the legislation had hoped a vote on it might be taken on that day.

Being the fourth Monday in the month, it will be in order for chairmen of committees that have favorably-reported bills pending before the Rules Committee for more than twenty-one days to move on the floor to proceed to their consideration. Such discharge motions

Continued on Page 37, Column 3

Senate to Sift R. F. C. Loans With View to Writing Curbs

By H. WALTON CLOKE
Special to The New York Times.

WASHINGTON, Jan. 21—The stage has been set for a full-scale Congressional investigation of the lending policy of the billion-dollar Reconstruction Finance Corporation. As a result of the inquiry, Congress is expected to set forth, once and for all, the terms on which it wants the RFC's lending operations to function.

Irritated by recent big loans that the RFC granted to several corporations, as well as some that were made in the earlier days of the agency, members on both sides of the aisle in Congress have been demanding a clarification of policy.

Leading this group is Senator J. William Fulbright, Democrat, of Arkansas, who recently lost a battle with the RFC over a loan to the Kaiser-Frazer Corporation.

The Senator, who has not forgotten the rather sharp rebuff, has started the wheels of Congressional investigation turning. On Tuesday he will ask the Senate Banking and Currency Committee, headed by Senator Burnet R. Maybank, Democrat, of South Carolina, to inquire into the RFC's action in granting the following loans:

Kaiser-Frazer Corporation..	$44,000,000
Northwest Air Lines........	12,000,000
Waltham Watch Co.........	6,000,000
Texmass Petroleum Co......	15,100,000

Financial observers here foresee nothing that would block the Senator's request for action. As head of the Senate Banking and Currency subcommittee on the RFC, he conducted a three-day inquiry into the loan policy of the agency last summer. It was at that time that the Senator questioned the wisdom of advancing additional funds to the Lustron Corporation, Columbus, Ohio, which is now in default on $37,500,000 of RFC loans.

Once the full committee ap-

Continued on Page 42, Column 2

MAYOR RIDICULES IDEA OF RESIGNING

Telephones From Florida That He Is Getting Rid of Virus and Will Return to Job

By JAMES A. HAGERTY

In a telephone message to THE NEW YORK TIMES from Key Largo, Fla., Mayor O'Dwyer declared yesterday that he had no intention of resigning.

In his telephone conversation, the Mayor appeared to be hearty of voice and very cheerful. Questioned about a report that he contemplated retirement, he said:

"It is utterly ridiculous. It touches my sense of humor."

The Mayor then laughed heartily and continued:

"I am down here to get the virus out of my system. I am going to stay till I've got it licked and I think I am well on the way to doing that. I feel much better. I want to get completely well so that I can return to the city and stay at my desk in City Hall to work uninterruptedly on my program."

The Mayor said that Dr. Edward M. Bernecker, who left Newark Airport by plane on Friday, had not arrived but was expected to reach Key Largo today. It is understood that he will have a series of talks with the Mayor and that

Continued on Page 37, Column 4

World News Summarized

SUNDAY, JANUARY 22, 1950

The jury of eight women and four men in the Alger Hiss trial yesterday found the former State Department official guilty of perjury on two counts. The jury reached this verdict nearly twenty-four hours after receiving the case and its decision meant that it had accepted the testimony of Whittaker Chambers, confessed former spy, over the denials by Mr. Hiss of having passed secret documents to Mr. Chambers. Federal Judge Goddard will pass sentence Wednesday. [1:8.]

Mayor O'Dwyer characterized as "utterly ridiculous" rumors that he might resign his office because of ill health. [1:7.]

Although some supporters of the Truman Administration's Federal Fair Employment Practices code had hoped that the House might vote on it tomorrow, there was little likelihood the measure would get to the House floor by that time. [1:5.]

Congress planned a sweeping inquiry into the lending policy of the Reconstruction Finance Corporation as a preliminary to fixing the terms on which the organization's lending may operate in the future. [1:6-7.]

President Truman urged "speedy rectification" in the House of its rejection by a narrow margin of the bill providing $60,000,000 for aid to Korea. Secretary of State Acheson asserted that failure to assist Korea would jeopardize her survival as a free nation. [1:1.]

The journey to Moscow of Communist China's Foreign Minister, Chou En-lai, was seen as an indication that the negotiations between the Chinese Communists and the Soviet Union had reached the decisive stage. Peiping vigorously denied Russia was "detaching" four north China areas as charged by Mr. Acheson. [7:1.]

The annual Lenin memorial meeting in Moscow was told that the mass revolutionary movement in Asia could not be stopped by capitalism. [1:2.]

Winston Churchill set the keynote for the campaign of the Conservative party for next month's general election by telling British voters that the "main reason why we are unable to earn our own living and make our way in the world is because we are not allowed to do so." Mr. Churchill said the choice was to regain freedom or plunge the nation deeper into socialism. [1:4.]

General Taylor, the United States commander in Berlin, ordered the seized Railway Administration building in the United States sector restored to East German custody. [1:3.]

Franco-German rapprochement was seen jeopardized as the result of an announcement by the West German republic that it was suspending trade talks with France. German officials cited France's attitude over the Saar as a reason for the suspension [1:2-3] and proposed an international Saar statute similar to that in the Ruhr. [3:1.]

The Allied High Commission, in a move intended as a public censure of the Bonn regime for "impudent" behavior, will demand that the Germans withdraw their announcement that gas rationing would end the end of this month. [2:2.]

Finland virtually rejected Moscow's demand that she extradite 300 "war criminals" who are said by the Russians to have found refuge among the Finns. [24:2.]

Bonn Halts French Trade Talks After Clash Over Policy on Saar

By HAROLD CALLENDER
Special to The New York Times.

PARIS, Jan. 21—A diplomatic crisis between France and Western Germany developed suddenly today when the French learned that, after challenging France's policy in the Saar, the Bonn regime had suspended negotiations for the trade treaty with France that was to have been signed a week ago.

French officials were angered by these German actions, which they considered as endangering the faint beginnings of a French-German rapprochement in the field of economic relations.

[In Bonn, it was reported that Chancellor Konrad Adenauer, in a parting conference with High Commissioner John J. McCloy, had proposed the creation of an international statute for the Saar that would be similar to the Ruhr statute now in force.]

When asked by the French Foreign Office for an explanation of their suspension of the negotiations, Bonn officials replied that they did not mean to go back on the trade pact but they must postpone its signature because of internal difficulties raised by German farmers and because of "the positions taken on the Saar question."

French officials said this reply surprised them because they considered the treaty would contribute to development of intra-European trade and desired to sign it as soon as possible.

This move by Bonn was regarded here as a maneuver to force reconsideration of the status of the Saar. Such was considered the purpose likewise of the statement that Dr. Konrad Adenauer, Chancellor

Continued on Page 3, Column 5

350,000,000-Gallon Water Loss In 24 Hours Largest Since Dec. 12

By PAUL CROWELL

The city's water storage reservoirs suffered a loss of 350,000,000 gallons in the twenty-four hours ended at 8 A. M. yesterday.

It was the first storage loss since Dec. 26 and the largest since Dec. 12. Officials of the Department of Water Supply, Gas and Electricity attributed the loss to a slightly increased consumption of water, coupled with the absence of appreciable rain or snowfall in the up-state watershed areas.

The city's reservoirs lost 103,000,000 gallons in the twenty-four hours ended at 8 A. M. on Dec. 27. In the twenty-four hours ended at 8 A. M. on Dec. 13 the storage loss was 692,000,000 gallons.

The reversal of the upward trend of water storage gave city officials serious concern and boosted to 1,121,000,000 gallons the aver-

Continued on Page 47, Column 1

The Water Situation

The following figures as of 8 A. M. yesterday give the number of gallons of water in the city's reservoirs. The difference in the two days is the net after intake and the day's consumption:

Friday	106,662,000,000
Yesterday	106,312,000,000
Net loss	350,000,000
Average daily storage gain needed to fill reservoirs by June 1	1,121,000,000
Watershed snowfall:	
Schoharie	.02 inch
Esopus	.04 inch
Croton	.02 inch

At present consumption there remains about ninety days' supply before pressure fails.

Catskill and Croton reservoirs at capacity hold 253,136,000,000 gallons.

"All the News
That's Fit to Print"

The New York Times.

LATE CITY EDITION
Fair and cold today. Partly
cloudy and milder tomorrow.

Temperature Range Today—Max.,38; Min.,25
Temperatures Yesterday—Max., 59; Min.,28
Full U. S. Weather Bureau Report, Page 30

Copyright, 1950, by The New York Times Company.

VOL. XCIX..No. 33,607.

Entered as Second-Class Matter,
Postoffice, New York, N. Y.

NEW YORK, SATURDAY, JANUARY 28, 1950.

Times Square, New York 18, N. Y.
Telephone Lackawanna 4-1000

FIVE CENTS

PAY RISES LIMITED TO MANDATORY ONES IN NEW CITY BUDGET

Facing $169,146,149 Increase in 1950-51, Patterson Intends to Hold to the Current Total

NO FURTHER CONCESSIONS

Director Stands by Warning as Parks Lead in Day's Calls for Greater Outlays

By THOMAS P. RONAN

Budget Director Thomas J. Patterson declared yesterday that he would not include in the 1950-51 finance budget any salary increases for city employes except those that are mandatory.

He said that if the requests already received from ninety city departments and agencies and those to be submitted by nineteen others were approved, the 1950-51 budget would be $169,146,149 above the current record of $1,198,-834,193. But he added that he intended, if possible, to keep the budget at the present level.

The budget Mr. Patterson is preparing must be submitted to the Board of Estimate by Mayor O'Dwyer by April 1. Some time after Feb. 3, when Mr. Patterson will end the hearings he is holding at the Municipal Building on departmental and agency requests, Mr. O'Dwyer will go into the traditional "retreat" with him to work out the final figures.

Last Say by Estimate Board

The Board of Estimate has the power to increase or decrease appropriations while the City Council, which receives the budget next, can only cut them. At hearings before the board large groups of city employes are expected to press for the across-the-board pay rises they already have demanded.

During the budget hearings held since Jan. 6 Mr. Patterson emphasized repeatedly that the city is not in a position to make concessions. In this connection it was recalled that the city used up all but $2,000,000 of its constitutional power to tax real estate to meet the requirements of the present budget and that there would be no material increase in this power this year.

Recently Mayor O'Dwyer appointed a fact-finding board to look into and report on the demand of the Transport Workers Union, CIO, for pay increases and a shorter work week for the 42,000 employes of the city transit lines. Among the other large groups that have asked salary rises are the policemen, firemen and teachers.

More Employes Sought

At yesterday's hearings the Park Department submitted a budget of $19,697,362, an increase of $2,647,-810 over the current allocation. The department requested an additional 421 seasonal employes and 446 year-round workers for new parks and playgrounds.

James A. Sherry, assistant executive officer of the department, said this budget could be pared $450,000 if the men now working in positions other than those for which they have qualified could be restored to their proper jobs and replacements assigned to the vacancies.

The Department of Public Works requested $51,135,638, with many new employes sought, among them engineers, bridge tenders and laborers.

Joseph A. McNamara, president of the Municipal Civil Service Commission, asked $1,243,090, an increase of $271,865.

Mr. McNamara asked a $5,000

Continued on Page 30, Column 7

Wild Hunt Bags Fox On Treasury Lawn

By The United Press.

WASHINGTON, Jan. 27—A fox hunt, minus pink coats and horses, raced through downtown Washington today and ended only when the wily beast was brought to bay on the lawn of the Treasury Building.

The animal, identified by a local farrier as a silver fox, might have attained the comparative refuge of the tree-lined White House grounds, across the street, had not his pursuers adopted such unsporting tactics as calling radio police cars.

Where the fox came from was a mystery. The National Zoo said all its silver foxes were in their cages. A Government wildlife expert speculated the creature emerged from wooded Rock

Continued on Page 7, Column 2

By Winston Churchill:

The Second World War

Volume III—The Grand Alliance
Book I—Germany Drives East

INSTALLMENT 3:

THE MEDITERRANEAN WAR

SINCE the days of Nelson Malta has stood a faithful British sentinel guarding the narrow and vital sea corridor through the Central Mediterranean. Its strategic importance was never higher than in this the latest war. The needs of the large armies we were building up in Egypt made the free passage of the Mediterranean for our convoys and the stopping of enemy reinforcements to Tripoli aims of the highest consequence. At the same time the new air weapon struck a deadly blow not only at Malta but at the effective assertion of British sea-power in these narrow waters. Without this modern danger our task would have been simple. We could have moved freely about the Mediterranean and stopped all other traffic. It was now impossible to base the main Fleet on Malta. The island itself was exposed to the threat of invasion from the Italian posts as well as to constant and measureless air attack. Hostile air-power also imposed almost prohibitive risks upon the passage of our convoys through the Narrows, condemning us to the long haul round the Cape. At the same time the superior Air Force of the enemy enabled them, by deterring our warships from acting fully in the Central Mediterranean except at much loss and hazard, to maintain a rivulet of troops and supplies into Tripoli.

About 140 miles from Malta, in the throat of the Western Narrows between Sicily and Tunis, lay the Italian island of Pantelleria, reputed strongly fortified and with an invaluable airfield. This place was important to the enemy's route to Tunis and Tripoli, and in our hands would markedly expand the air cover we could give around Malta. In September 1940 I had asked Admiral Keyes to make a plan for seizing Pantelleria with the newly-formed Commandos. The idea was to attach two or three troopships to the tail of one of our heavily-guarded convoys. While the main body was engaging the enemy's attention these would drop off in the darkness and storm the island by surprise. The project, which was called "Workshop," gained increasing support from the Chiefs of Staff. Keyes was ardent, and claimed to lead the assault in person, waiving his rank as an Admiral of the Fleet.

All agreements were obtained, but with our other affairs we could not meet the date at the end of January at which we had aimed. At a conference at Chequers on the morning of January 18 I agreed with the First Sea Lord and the other Chiefs of Staff to put it off for a month. I think I could have turned the decision the other way, but like the others was constrained by the pressure of larger business, and also by talk about the Commandos not being yet fully trained. Keyes, who was not present, was bitterly disappointed. The delay proved fatal to the plan. Long before the month had passed the German Air Force arrived in Sicily, and all wore a very different complexion. There is no doubt about the value of the prize we did not gain. Had we been in occupation of Pantelleria in 1942 many fine ships that were lost in our convoys, which we then fought through to Malta, might have been saved, and the enemy communications with Tripoli still further impaired. On the other hand, we might well have been overpowered by German air attack, lost our vantage, and complicated our defence of Malta in the interval.

* * *

OUR first serious naval encounter with the German Air Force occurred on January 10. The Fleet was engaged in covering a series of important movements, including the passage of a convoy through the Central Mediterranean from the west, the replenishment of Malta from the east, and various minor shipping movements to Greece. Early that morning the destroyer Gallant was mined in the Malta Channel while attending on the battle fleet. Presently shadowing aircraft appeared, and in the afternoon the severe attack of the German bombers began. The efforts were concentrated on the new carrier Illustrious, under Captain Boyd, and in three attacks she was hit six times with big bombs. Heavily damaged and on fire, with eighty-three killed and sixty seriously wounded, she successfully fought back, thanks to her armoured deck, and her aircraft destroyed at least five assailants. That night, under increasing air attack, and with disabled steering gear, Captain Boyd brought the Illustrious into Malta.

During the night Admiral Cunningham with the battle fleet escorted the east-bound convoy south of Malta unmolested. The next day the cruisers Southampton and Gloucester, by then well to the east of Malta, were hit by dive-bombers approaching unobserved down sun. The Gloucester was only slightly damaged by a bomb which failed to explode, but the Southampton was struck in the engine-room. A fire started which could not be controlled, and the ship had to be abandoned and was sunk. Thus, although the convoys passed on safely to their destinations the cost to the Fleet was heavy.

The Germans realised the desperate position of the wounded Illustrious in Malta, and made determined efforts to destroy her. However, our air-power in the island had already grown, and nineteen enemy planes were shot down in a single day during the contest. In spite of further hits while in the dockyard, the Illustrious was made capable of sailing on the evening of January 23. The enemy, seeing she was gone, tried hard to find her, but she reached Alexandria safely two days later.

By this time no fewer than 250 German aircraft were working from Sicily. Malta was attacked fifty-eight times in January, and thereafter till the end of May three or four times daily with only brief respites. But our resources mounted. By June the first fierce onslaught had been repulsed, and by the skin of its teeth the island survived. Its main ordeal was reserved for 1942.

* * *

Amid the stresses of the ever-expanding scale of events in the Mediterranean we tried to find means of bringing the war to the Italian mainland. The morale of the Italian people was said to be low, and a blow here would depress them still more and bring closer the collapse which we desired. On February 9 Admiral Somerville carried out a daring and successful raid on the port of Genoa. Force H, comprising the Renown, Malaya, and Sheffield, appeared off the town and subjected it to heavy bombardment for half an hour. At the same time aircraft from the Ark Royal bombed Leghorn and Pisa and laid mines off Spezia.

Continued on Page Fifteen

COAL PARLEY PLAN RELIEVES PRESSURE ON THE WHITE HOUSE

North-West Operators Accept Resumption of Negotiations After a Long Deadlock

SENATORS HOLD UP ACTION

N. L. R. B. Reported Surprised by Lewis Move but Is Ready to Push for an Injunction

By JOSEPH A. LOFTUS
Special to The New York Times.

WASHINGTON, Jan. 27—An agreement to resume coal negotiations eased pressure on the White House today.

President Truman at his news conference refused to talk about the coal shortage, except to say that he had read very carefully the report of Dr. James Boyd, Director of the Bureau of Mines.

An agreement between John L. Lewis and Northern and Western operators would mean a delay in any contemplated White House action.

In fact, this surprise development in the last twenty-four hours put a new face on the coal problem temporarily, although there is no evidence of any fundamental change.

It contributed to a decision of the Senate Labor and Public Welfare Committee to postpone indefinitely further consideration of a resolution calling on the President to recognize an emergency in coal so as to use his Taft-Hartley authority.

The United Mine Workers, it is expected, will seek further postponement of injunction proceedings on grounds that contract negotiations are being resumed. A hearing on the injunction petition of Robert N. Denham, general counsel of the National Labor Relations Board, is set for 10 A. M. Wednesday.

New ICC Action Deferred

The Interstate Commerce Commission put off until next Tuesday consideration of possible further cuts in coal-burning passenger service on the railroads. This decision was based on information that the carriers had added a day and a half supply to their stocks since last Tuesday. Meanwhile, railway labor executives charged that the first cut had been pushed through in an arbitrary manner.

Dr. Boyd's statement before the Senate committee on Wednesday implied that an emergency would have to be recognized unless there were immediate resumption of "substantially increased coal production."

In the present fight FEPC proponents have forced it back into weekly observance. On Wednesdays the chairman of the committee in alphabetical line for recognition.

In recent weeks President Tru-

Continued on Page 8, Column 3

World News Summarized

SATURDAY, JANUARY 28, 1950

Arms shipments from this country to its European associates under the North Atlantic Treaty may start about March 1 following the signing of bilateral agreements yesterday by eight nations that had requested such assistance. President Truman proclaimed as in effect the "integrated" mutual defense plan formulated in Paris last month by the Defense Committee set up under the pact. [1:8.]

The military position of France, and therefore of Western Europe, was seen as weakened by the continuing drain upon her resources because of the civil war in Indo-China. This result was considered a definite gain for communism. [4:2.]

Despite the Western Allies' plea to the Russians for a relaxation of the curbs on traffic between Berlin and Western Germany, more than 300 freight trucks were stalled for miles on both sides of the Berlin Autobahn check point of the Berlin Autobahn. They inched forward at a rate of a mile and a half an hour. [1:7.]

The press spokesman for Chancellor Adenauer of the Western German regime resigned. He said he objected to making repeated denials of published statements. [7:1.]

Prime Minister Attlee, the British Labor party's candidate for Parliament from the West Walthamstow district, will be opposed by candidates of three other groups. [3:6-7.]

Reports circulated in United Nations circles that two additional members of the Security

Council might withdraw recognition next month from the Chinese Nationalist Government, thus making it possible to seat a delegation representing the Communist regime. [4:6.]

President Truman said he had not made up his mind on whether this country should go ahead with the attempt to make a hydrogen atomic bomb. He said the final decision would be his responsibility. [1:6-7.]

The Chief Executive also made known that he intended to give his steadfast support to his civil rights program despite Congressional objections. Talk of a possible compromise with Southern Democrats over the proposal to establish a permanent Fair Employment Practice Commission persisted in the House. [1:5.]

There was a lessening of pressure on the White House for action in the coal argument as a result of an agreement between John L. Lewis and Northern and Western operators to resume negotiations on Wednesday. [1:4.]

In this city the Budget Director, citing requests for pay rises that would lift the 1950-51 budget $169,146,149, said he would not recommend any increases that were not mandatory. [1:1.] City officials expressed themselves as highly pleased by the results of "dry Thursday." New Yorkers consumed 832,000,000 gallons of water, or 5,000,000 less than was used on the water holiday last week. [30:4.]

A United States Air Force transport plane, with forty-four persons aboard, was reported lost on a trip from Alaska to Great Falls, Mont. [1:6-7.]

Index to other news appears on Page 14.

PRESIDENT REJECTS ANY COMPROMISE IN RIGHTS PROGRAM

He Declares He Stands Flatly on Ten Points of His Special Message of Feb. 2, 1948

F.E.P.C. PETITIONS STALLED

Republican Tears Up Letter by Powell—Cotton Aid Meets House Delaying Tactics

By C. P. TRUSSELL
Special to The New York Times.

WASHINGTON, Jan. 27—President Truman stood firmly behind his Civil Rights recommendations today in the face of Congressional battling over whether the House would consider establishment of a permanent Fair Employment Practice Commission, and amid continued talk, backstage, of possible compromise with Southern Democrats in an effort to get his program approved.

The President told his weekly news conference, as questions were posed, that his compromise (he used that word in a way that indicated that he meant no compromise) could be found in the special message on Civil Rights that he sent to Congress Feb. 2, 1948.

This message contained ten recommendations, included the FEPC, anti-lynching legislation, a wiping out of poll taxes, an end to discrimination based on race, creed or color in interstate transportation facilities and the setting up of civil rights commissions in the executive and legislative branches.

Makes Message His Answer

The President suggested that his questioners consult his message again. He said he knew nothing of any proposed compromises.

This was at a stage when the bitter House fight over the FEPC took a new turn. The commission provided in the FEPC bill would function to prevent racial or religious discrimination by employers.

It appeared tonight that, of the four highly complex parliamentary devices employed by sponsors of the FEPC to force the bill to a showdown, one, known as Calendar Wednesday, had the best chance of succeeding.

Calendar Wednesday comes potentially every week. However, since the Seventy-ninth Congress (the present one is the Eighty-first) it has been in operation only twice. At other times the House has dropped it by unanimous consent.

In the present fight FEPC proponents have forced it back into weekly observance. On Wednesdays the chairman of the committee in alphabetical line for recognition.

Continued on Page 8, Column 3

EIGHT ATLANTIC NATIONS SIGN ARMS AID PACTS AS TRUMAN PUTS DEFENSE PLAN IN FORCE

SIGNING DEFENSE AGREEMENT

French Ambassador Henri Bonnet, left, and Secretary of State Dean Acheson at ceremony in Washington yesterday.
The New York Times (by Bruce Hoertel)

Decision on Hydrogen Bomb Rests With Him, Truman Says

By WILLIAM S. WHITE
Special to The New York Times.

WASHINGTON, Jan. 27—President Truman indicated at his press conference today that no decision had been reached on whether and when this country would proceed with construction of a so-called "super" hydrogen bomb.

Nothing authoritative could yet be divulged on the subject, the President observed, and when any decision was made it would be made by him, and by no one else. This was his response when reporters recalled recent suggestions attributed to Bernard M. Baruch and others, that if the United States could make such a weapon it should do so at once.

[In New York Prof. Harold C. Urey Friday night became the first atomic scientist to speak out on the hydrogen bomb, saying that this nation had no choice but to go ahead with its development and perfection.]

Mr. Truman added that he was unable to comment now as to whether he was likely to make another try at international control of atomic energy, and to use the fact that a hydrogen weapon was in prospect. He had been working for control, he said, ever since he entered the White House.

Just before the President spoke, the principal Government authority directly in control of atomic energy had been in consultation over "plans for advances in the technological improvement of atomic weapons." These were the terms used by Senator Brien McMahon, Democrat, of Connecticut, chairman of the joint Congressional Atomic Energy Committee, to describe a long meeting between members of the committee and the Atomic Energy Commission.

The discussion obviously involved high policy considerations.

First recalling that the committee had the duty to keep "fully informed" as to the activities of the commission, Senator McMahon had this to say:

"We have had a number of

Continued on Page 6, Column 4

RUSSIANS CONTINUE BERLIN TRUCK JAM

300 Freight Vehicles Moving Toward Barrier at Rate of 1½ Miles an Hour

By KATHLEEN McLAUGHLIN
Special to The New York Times.

HELMSTEDT, Germany, Jan. 27—As twilight closed down tonight on this strategic spot on the superhighway between Berlin and Western Germany, more than 300 freight trucks remained stalled on either side of the Soviet zone border. Up hill and down, they spanned a length of highway approximately twelve miles long and were inching their way toward the barrier at the rate of about one and one-half miles an hour. Some had waited fifty hours.

At 6 o'clock this evening three times as many east-bound trucks waited for clearance to Berlin as were held up on the opposite side of the checkpoint bound for the West. From a tiny community called Baumke just west of Helmstedt the east-bound column was measured at more than eight miles.

The trucks carry cargoes both perishable and otherwise—milk, wine, poultry, meat, cheese, beer, fat, peas, beans, fish, iron and steel, machinery, carpets, paper, roofing tiles, tires and small hardware.

The points of origin of the various shipments are plainly labeled on most of the trucks: Brunswick,

Continued on Page 7, Column 3

C-54 With 44 Missing in Yukon; Balchen Heads U. S. Searchers

By The Associated Press.

EDMONTON, Alberta, Jan. 27—Forty-four persons are missing aboard a United States Air Force C-54 transport plane unreported since it was last heard from yesterday over the wild, blizzard-swept Yukon country.

Only slim clues, including reports of flares sighted along the route, were available for a vast search being conducted by United States and Canadian planes.

A famed polar flier, Col. Bernt Balchen, is in command of the over-all American search, with headquarters at Elmendorf Field, Alaska.

Aboard the ship which took off from Anchorage for Great Falls, Mont., were a mother and son, thirty-four military personnel and eight crewmen. The woman and child are dependents of military personnel.

Biggs Air Force Base officials at El Paso, Tex., said the following airmen left there as crewmen of the C-54. They said they did

not know if all of them made the return trip:

First Lieut. Kyle E. McMichael, 28 years old, plane commander. His wife, Mrs. Verda McMichael, lives in San Antonio.

Maj. Ashael F. Brittain, 36, pilot. His father, Fred Brittain, lives in Akron, Ohio.

First Lieut. Joseph W. Metzler, 31, navigator. His mother is Mrs. Josephine H. Metzler of St. Louis.

Staff Sgt. Clarence A. Gibson, 35, radio operator, whose father, James C. Gibson, lives in Gray, Ala.

Master Sgt. Clyde A. Streitmann, 29, engineer, whose mother, Mrs. Barbara Streitmann, lives in Renfrew, Pa.

Tech. Sgt. Harry W. McConegly, 30, engineer. His mother, Mrs. Berth McConegly, lives in Albion, Pa.

Staff Sgt. Raymond H. Snow, 24, engineer, whose mother, Mrs. Ida

Continued on Page 7, Column 6

SUPPLIES TO START

Shipments of Equipment From U. S. Scheduled to Begin March 1

PARIS PROGRAM APPROVED

Formal Ceremony Represents American Acceptance of Mutual Military Project

The texts of documents on arms aid are printed on Page 2.

By WALTER H. WAGGONER
Special to The New York Times.

WASHINGTON, Jan. 27—President Truman proclaimed the North Atlantic joint defense plan in effect today and eight Western European Governments immediately signed agreements enabling them to receive $1,000,000,000 in United States arms and equipment.

The President's statement, and an accompanying Executive order, signified his approval of an "integrated" mutual defense plan drawn up in Paris last month by the Defense Committee of the North Atlantic Treaty organization. The simultaneous action of the eight countries seeking military assistance under the program indicated their agreement to conditions imposed on the use of the forthcoming United States supplies.

The agreements require that the assistance be used in integration of defense of the North Atlantic area and according to defense plans under the North Atlantic Treaty organization. It could be used in colonies or for "other purposes" only with prior consent of the United States.

Today's formalities were the last organizational hurdles to putting the North Atlantic security plan into effect, and officials estimated that the first shipments of arms, bound from the United States to its friends in Europe, would get under way about March 1.

Conference Room Used

The twelve North Atlantic Treaty countries had asked their diplomats filed into the State Department's big international conference room this afternoon with Mr. Secretary of State Dean Acheson, the bilateral agreements controlling the use of the arms.

The eight countries were Belgium, Denmark, France, Italy, Luxembourg, the Netherlands, Norway and the United Kingdom. Secretary Acheson, in a brief statement at the end of the fifteen-minute ceremony, said that "the peoples of the North Atlantic community value peace and freedom above all things, and they are determined to take whatever measures may be required to preserve them."

"In the world today," he said, "this depends upon their being strong and joining their collective strength in support of the cause of peace and freedom."

Lessons of History Utilized

Wilhelm Munthe de Morgenstierne, Ambassador of Norway and dean of the diplomatic corps, responded with an expression of "deep satisfaction" to be taken from the conviction that the North Atlantic Treaty "means that in this instance, at least, we have profited by the lessons of history."

"We have refused to make all over again the fatal mistake of letting an aggressor pick some of us off one by one," he said.

"In accordance with the letter and spirit of the Charter of the United Nations we have decided to exercise our inherent right of individual and collective self defense if, God forbid, an armed attack should occur against any one of us."

President Truman, concerned more in his statement with the over-all objectives of the North Atlantic Treaty than with the specific arms agreements, said he approved the defense arrangements because they provided for a common defense based on the cooperative use of national resources and on individual national specialization.

He added, however, that the developments of today, resulting from close cooperation among free

Continued on Page 2, Column 6

An embarrassed William Holden listens as Gloria Swanson speaks of her past glories, in Sunset Boulevard.

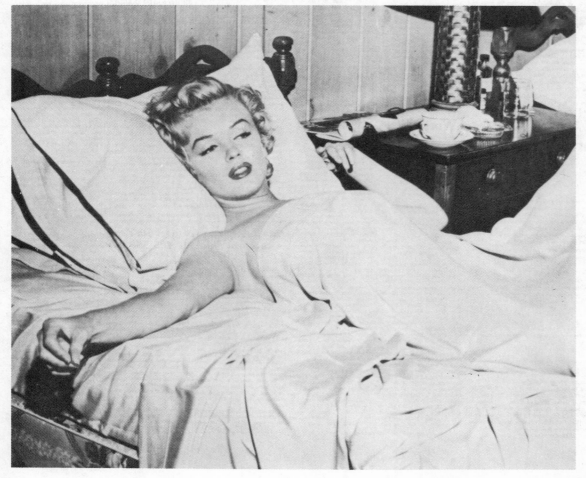

Marilyn Monroe, in a provocative scene from Niagara, in which she was given her longest part thus far.

"All the News That's Fit to Print"

The New York Times.

LATE CITY EDITION
A little rain and cold today. Cloudy, continued cold tomorrow.
Temperature Range Today—Max.,38; Min.,31
Temperatures Yesterday—Max.,37; Min.,32
Full U. S. Weather Bureau Report, Page 33

VOL. XCIX...No. 33,611. Entered as Second-Class Matter, Postoffice, New York, N. Y. NEW YORK, WEDNESDAY, FEBRUARY 1, 1950. Times Square, New York 18, N. Y. Telephone Lackawanna 4-1000 FIVE CENTS

TRUMAN ORDERS HYDROGEN BOMB BUILT FOR SECURITY PENDING AN ATOMIC PACT; CONGRESS HAILS STEP; BOARD BEGINS JOB

PRESIDENT SEEKS 70-DAY COAL TRUCE, FACT-FINDING BOARD

He Ignores Taft Law in Asking 5-Day Week at Old Wages Pending Study of Dispute

AVOIDS WORD 'EMERGENCY'

Operator Acceptance Is Seen Likely, but the Plan Holds Disadvantages for Lewis

Text of announcement by White House on coal, Page 22.

By JOSEPH A. LOFTUS
Special to THE NEW YORK TIMES.

WASHINGTON, Jan. 31—President Truman moved into the soft coal dispute today with a proposal that John L. Lewis and the operators call a seventy-day truce and submit their arguments to a fact-finding board. He asked for an answer by 5 P. M. Saturday.

Under the truce "normal" production of coal would be resumed. This was understood to mean a return to the five-day work week by the members of the United Mine Workers, headed by Mr. Lewis. The wage scale of the expired union contract would be paid. A board of three would make recommendations in sixty days, but the recommendations would not be binding.

President Truman thus used the approach he used in the steel dispute last summer. This avoids use of the Taft-Hartley Law and its injunctive authority, although the President said in November that if he acted in the coal case he would use that law.

"Grave Concern" Voiced

The President's message to Mr. Lewis and the operators spoke of the "grave concern" about the dispute, but avoided Taft-Hartley words, such as "emergency" and "health and safety."

The dispute in the anthracite industry was omitted from the proposal.

The President said that in the final analysis the parties themselves must write their own agreement. "Voluntary action, not compulsion, in these matters is not only my personal conviction but the national policy," he declared.

Aware that the miners and operators were to meet at 2 P. M. tomorrow to try bargaining again, the President said he did not want to interfere with that. He told them that if they could reach an agreement to resume full production next Monday they should disregard his proposal and let him know about it by noon Saturday.

Mr. Lewis' attorneys are due in court at 10 A. M. tomorrow to answer a petition for an injunction filed by Robert N. Denham, general counsel of the National Labor Relations Board. Mr. Lewis and the other officers of the union filed affidavits in the case today. They denied violating the Taft-Hartley Law in the coal negotiations which began last May and accused the operators of refusing to bargain.

Surmise on Board Make-Up

The make-up of the fact-finding board, if the President's truce proposal goes into effect, is a matter of conjecture. When the proposal was under consideration at the White House in November the three men who had been asked if they were available were David L. Cole, who was a member of the fact-finding steel panel; John Dunlop, Harvard economics professor, and Willard Wirtz of Northwestern University, former chairman of the National Wage Stabilization Board.

Neither side would say tonight

Continued on Page 22, Column 2

Melchior Threatens To Quit Opera Here

Lauritz Melchior stepped into the Metropolitan Opera dispute last night by saying that he would not return next season "unless indicated plans change materially." He would make no comment on the possible return of Kirsten Flagstad, but, like Helen Traubel, he indicated resentment at not being approached sooner by Rudolf Bing, who will be the general manager for 1950-1951.

"I would have assumed," Mr. Melchior said, "that the natural courtesy of the management for the Metropolitan would dictate a call to any leading artist who had appeared regularly with the company for twenty-four years to determine his position with

Continued on Page 24, Column 2

By Winston Churchill: *The Second World War*

Volume III—The Grand Alliance

Book I—Germany Drives East

INSTALLMENT 6:

THE JAPANESE ENVOY

THE New Year had brought disturbing news from the Far East. The Japanese Navy was increasingly active off the coasts of Southern Indo-China. Japanese warships were reported in Saigon harbour and the Gulf of Siam. On January 31 the Japanese Government negotiated an armistice between the Vichy French and Siam. Rumours spread that this settlement of a frontier dispute in South-east Asia was to be the prelude to the entry of Japan into the war. The Germans were at the same time bringing increased pressure to bear upon Japan to attack the British at Singapore.

* * *

About this time several telegrams arrived from our Commander-in-Chief in the Far East urging the reinforcement of Hong Kong. I did not agree with his views.

Prime Minister to General Ismay 7 Jan 41

This is all wrong. If Japan goes to war with us there is not the slightest chance of holding Hong Kong or relieving it. It is most unwise to increase the loss we shall suffer there. Instead of increasing the garrison it ought to be reduced to a symbolical scale. Any trouble arising there must be dealt with at the Peace Conference after the war. We must avoid frittering away our resources on untenable positions. Japan will think long before declaring war on the British Empire, and whether there are two or six battalions at Hong Kong will make no difference to her choice. I wish we had fewer troops there, but to move any would be noticeable and dangerous.

Later on it will be seen that I allowed myself to be drawn from this position, and that two Canadian battalions were sent as reinforcements.

* * *

IN the second week of February I became conscious of a stir and flutter in the Japanese Embassy and colony in London. They were evidently in a high state of excitement, and they chattered to one another with much indiscretion. In these days we kept our eyes and ears open. Various reports were laid before me which certainly gave the impression that they had received news from home which required them to pack up without a moment's delay. This agitation among people usually so reserved made me feel that a sudden act of war upon us by Japan might be imminent, and I thought it well to impart my misgivings to the President.

Former Naval Person to President Roosevelt 15 Feb 41

Many drifting straws seem to indicate Japanese intention to make war on us or do something that would force us to make war on them in the next few weeks or months. I am not myself convinced that this is not a war of nerves designed to cover Japanese encroachments in Siam and Indo-China. However, I think I ought to let you know that the weight of the Japanese Navy, if thrown against us, would confront us with situations beyond the scope of our naval resources. I do not myself think that the Japanese would be likely to send the large military expedition necessary to lay siege to Singapore. The Japanese would no doubt occupy whatever strategic points and oilfields in the Dutch East Indies and thereabouts they covet, and thus get into a far better position for a full-scale attack on Singapore later on. They would also raid Australian and New Zealand ports and coasts, causing deep anxiety in those Dominions, which have already sent all their best-trained fighting men to the Middle East. But the attack which I fear the most would be by raiders, including possibly battle-cruisers, upon our trade routes and communications across the Pacific and Indian Oceans. We could by courting disaster elsewhere send a few strong ships into these vast waters, but all the trade would have to go into convoy and escorts would be few and far between. Not only would this be a most grievous additional restriction and derangement of our whole war economy, but it would bring altogether to an end all reinforcements of the armies we had planned to build up in the Middle East from Australasian and Indian sources. Any threat of a major invasion of Australia or New Zealand would of course force us to withdraw our Fleet from the Eastern Mediterranean, with disastrous military possibilities there, and the certainty that Turkey would have to make some accommodation, for reopening of the German trade and oil supplies from the Black Sea. You will therefore see, Mr. President, the awful enfeeblement of our war effort that would result merely from the sending out by Japan of her battle-cruisers and her twelve 8-inch-gun cruisers into the Eastern oceans, and still more from any serious invasion threat against the two Australasian democracies in the Southern Pacific.

Some believe that Japan in her present mood would not hesitate to court or attempt to wage war both against Great Britain and the United States. Personally I think the odds are definitely against that, but no one can tell. Everything that you can do to inspire the Japanese with the fear of a double war may avert the danger. If however they come in against us and we are alone, the grave character of the consequences cannot easily be overstated.

The agitation among the Japanese in London subsided as quickly as it had begun. Silence and Oriental decorum reigned once more.

Former Naval Person to President Roosevelt 20 Feb 41

I have better news about Japan. Apparently Matsuoka is visiting Berlin, Rome, and Moscow in the near future. This may well be a diplomatic sop to cover absence of action against Great Britain. If Japanese attack which seemed imminent is now postponed, this is largely due to fear of United States. The more these fears can be played upon the better, but I understand thoroughly your difficulties pending passage of [Lend-Lease] Bill on which our hopes depend. Appreciation given in my last Personal and Secret of naval consequences following Japanese aggression against Great Britain holds good in all circumstances.

* * *

Behind the complex political scene in Japan three decisions seem to emerge at this time. The first was to send the Foreign Secretary, Matsuoka, to Europe to find out for himself about the German mastery of Europe, and especially when the invasion of Britain was really going to begin. Were the British forces so far tied up in naval defence that Britain could not afford to reinforce her Eastern possessions if Japan attacked them? Although he had been educated in the United States, Matsuoka was bitterly anti-American. He was deeply impressed by the Nazi movement and the might of embattled Germany. He was under the Hitler

Continued on Page 31,

FRANCE PROTESTS SOVIET RECOGNITION OF HO CHI MINH RULE

Note to Russia Asserts Action Could 'Gravely Impair' Paris-Moscow Ties

U. S. AND BRITAIN INFORMED

Government of North Korea Announces Acceptance of Viet Nam Rebel Regime

By LANSING WARREN
Special to THE NEW YORK TIMES.

PARIS, Jan. 31—France tonight delivered to the Soviet Embassy here a vigorous protest against Soviet recognition of Ho Chi Minh, the enemy of France in Indo-China. The note charged that the Soviet action was of a nature "gravely to impair French-Soviet relations."

In diplomatic circles here the Soviet Union's action was considered as a threat not only to the French position in Indo-China but as an effort to prevent the United States from building a policy of containment in Asia such as has been successful in Europe.

The text of the French note follows:

> The French Government has learned through publication of a communiqué by the Tass Agency that the Government of the U.S.S.R. has taken the decision of recognizing as the Government of the Viet Nam the insurrectional government of Ho Chi Minh. Such a decision violates the principles of international law, since the only regular government of the Viet Nam is the government constituted by His Majesty Bao Dai, to whom the French Government has transferred the rights of sovereignty which it previously held.
>
> In encouraging, as is the obvious intention of the Soviet Government, the insurrectional movement of Ho Chi Minh, this decision can only render more difficult the restoration of peace in Viet Nam. In taking the initiative which it has just announced, the Government of the U.S.S.R. is committing with regard to France an act whose character and consequences cannot be underestimated.
>
> For all these reasons the French Government raises a solemn protest against a decision which is of a nature gravely to impair Franco-Soviet relations.

The note was delivered by Alexander Parodi, general secretary of the French Foreign Ministry, after Soviet Ambassador Alexandre Bogomolov, who was invited to the Quai d'Orsay, had replied he could not come today but would present himself tomorrow.

Copies of the French protest to

Continued on Page 11, Column 1

DISCUSSING PLANS FOR MAKING HYDROGEN BOMB

Members of the Joint Congressional Atomic Energy Committee talk with Sumner T. Pike, right, acting head of the Atomic Energy Commission, after President Truman gave his approval. Seated are Chairman Brien McMahon, Representatives Carl T. Durham, Chet Holifield and W. Sterling Cole. Standing are Senator John W. Bricker, Representatives Paul J. Kilday, Melvin Price, Carl Hinshaw and Charles H. Elston. The New York Times (by George Tames)

HISTORIC DECISION

President Says He Must Defend Nation Against Possible Aggressor

SOVIET 'EXPLOSION' CITED

His Ruling Wins Bipartisan Support on Capitol Hill—No Fund Request Due Now

By ANTHONY LEVIERO
Special to THE NEW YORK TIMES.

WASHINGTON, Jan. 31—President Truman announced today that he had ordered the Atomic Energy Commission to produce the hydrogen bomb.

The Chief Executive acted in his role of Commander in Chief of the Armed forces, ordering an improved weapon for national security. Thus, from the domestic standpoint, he removed the question of producing the super-weapon as an issue that might be argued on moral grounds.

As for international statecraft, Mr. Truman, by treating the hydrogen bomb as an addition to the American armory, also removed it as an issue that might be interpreted as an advanced threat or inducement in seeking international control of atomic weapons.

Nevertheless, Mr. Truman said that his perseverance in providing for national defense would be matched by his efforts to seek international control of atomic weapons.

New Phase of Atomic Age

In his announcement, Mr. Truman regarded the hydrogen bomb as a progressive outgrowth of United States production of the uranium-plutonium atomic bomb. He put it this way: the commission was "to continue its work on all forms of atomic weapons, including the so-called hydrogen or super-bomb."

His use of the word "continue" was understood to imply that with national security the over-riding consideration, the chief factor guiding his decision was whether it was practicable to make the weapon. Scientists have said that it is.

In effect, the President's decision, which won wide acclaim in Congress, marked the advent of a new phase of the atomic age and a surge ahead of Russia in the race to retain military ascendancy:

The bombs that visited destruction on Hiroshima and Nagasaki split the atom. The new bomb would fuse atoms instead, but with a power 100 to 1,000 times greater than the improved fission bombs that have been developed since the Japanese cities were struck.

The President's Statement

The President made his decision known in the following brief statement:

"It is part of my responsibility as Commander in Chief of the armed forces to see to it that our country is able to defend itself against any possible aggressor. Accordingly, I have directed the Atomic Energy Commission to continue its work on all forms of atomic weapons, including the so-called hydrogen or super-bomb.

Continued on Page 3, Column 2

STIKKER IS NAMED E. R. P. CONCILIATOR

Council in Paris Accepts Dutch Leader Supported by Britain —E. C. A. Goals Unmet

By HAROLD CALLENDER
Special to THE NEW YORK TIMES.

PARIS, Jan. 31—Dr. Dirk U. Stikker, Foreign Minister of the Netherlands, was named today to the post of "political conciliator" of the European Marshall Plan Council instead of Paul-Henri Spaak, former Premier of Belgium, whose appointment was vetoed by the British Government. Paul G. Hoffman, Economic Cooperation Administrator, and W. Averell Harriman, ECA Ambassador in Europe, had desired that M. Spaak be chosen.

Dr. Stikker was elected by the Council. He was the candidate of the British who had first suggested Dr. Halvard M. Lange, Nor-

Continued on Page 14, Column 4

Truman Asks Utility Leader To Head Top Research Body

By JAMES RESTON
Special to THE NEW YORK TIMES.

WASHINGTON, Jan. 31—President Truman has offered the Government's top scientific job—chairmanship of the Research and Development Board in the Department of Defense—to William Webster of Boston, a vice president of the New England Electric System, it was learned today.

Mr. Webster, 49 years old, a graduate of the United States Naval Academy and former chairman of the Defense Department's Military Liaison Committee with the Atomic Energy Commission, would be largely responsible for preparing an integrated military research and development program so that weapons such as the new hydrogen bomb would take their proper place in a well-balanced defense policy.

The chairmanship of the Research and Development Board was held by Dr. Vannevar Bush from 1947 to 1948 and by Dr. Karl T. Compton, former president of Massachusetts Institute of Technology, from 1948 until Nov. 3, 1949. Since then the work of the board has been supervised by Dr. Robert F. Rinehart as deputy chairman.

Coincidental with his offer of the Government's principal scientific position to Mr. Webster, President Truman was reported to be working actively on selection of a successor to David E. Lilienthal as chairman of the Atomic Energy Commission. One person said to be under consideration is Carroll Wilson, present general manager of the AEC.

Mr. Lilienthal is reliably reported to have proposed that control of

Continued on Page 5, Column 3

IT'S A TRITON BOMB, MIGHTIEST POSSIBLE

Would Release Energy More Than Seven Times '45 Type —No Critical-Mass Limit

By WILLIAM L. LAURENCE

What President Truman referred to yesterday as "the so-called hydrogen bomb" is not a hydrogen bomb at all in the true scientific meaning of the term.

This, the most powerful super-bomb that can be built on earth, it can now be revealed, actually is the triton bomb, in which the basic element used is tritium, a hydrogen isotope (twin) of atomic mass 3. It is an element hardly known to the public but well known to nuclear physicists. A triton is the nucleus of tritium, composed of one proton and two neutrons.

The term hydrogen, as used by scientists, refers strictly to the common form of hydrogen of atomic mass 1, a mass that cannot be made into a bomb.

While the process responsible for the vast amounts of energy released by the sun every second is

Continued on Page 4, Column 4

World News Summarized

WEDNESDAY, FEBRUARY 1, 1950

President Truman, acting in his capacity of Commander in Chief of the Armed Forces, yesterday directed the Atomic Energy Commission "to continue its work on all forms of atomic weapons, including the so-called hydrogen or super-bomb." The work, he said, would go forward "on a basis consistent with the over-all objectives of our program for peace and security" and "until a satisfactory plan for international control of atomic energy is achieved." [1:8.]

Congressional opinion heavily supported the President, and demands for speeding the work were made. The Atomic Energy Commission reported to Congress that atomic weapons now were being made by the "industrial type" of production and stockpiles were growing rapidly. [3:5.]

New defense safeguards were thrown about the atomic plants at Oak Ridge, Tenn.; Los Alamos, N. M., and Hanford, Wash. Any plane approaching within 100 miles of the plants without prior identification and clearance will be intercepted by Air Force fighters. [1:8.]

The hydrogen bomb, it was disclosed, is really a triton bomb, the basic element of which is tritium, a hydrogen isotope. [1:7.]

William Webster has been asked to head the Research and Development Board of the Department of Defense as successor to Dr. Karl T. Compton, who resigned. [1:6-7.]

Dealing with the major domestic problem of coal, President Truman asked John L. Lewis and the operators to call a seventy-day truce and to submit the issues to a nonstatutory fact-finding board such as he had named in the steel dispute. The President asked for a full five-day week in the soft-coal mines during the truce. [1:1.] Leaders of more than 100,000 striking miners were divided over urging the men to return. Operators indicated an inclination to accept the plan. [22:5.]

This state paid $357,000,000 in jobless benefits last year, nearly twice the 1948 total, Albany reported. [21:1.]

A House committee reported, 17 to 1, a bill for economic aid to Korea and Nationalist China. [13:2.] The brutality of South Korean police was seen as a major problem of the Seoul Government. [13:4.]

France, in a strong note of protest, told Moscow that Soviet recognition of Ho Chi Minh in Indo-China "gravely" impaired French-Soviet relations. Washington called Moscow's action proof that the Ho regime was Communist. [1:4.]

Senator Connally said Britain's policy of extending her embargo on dollar oil to the Commonwealth was "an act of hostility to our economy." [15:2.]

Britain won a victory in the European Marshall Plan Council when Foreign Minister Stikker of the Netherlands was elected "political conciliator." [1:5.]

French Premier Bidault won five close votes of confidence on the budget. [14:3.]

This city's tentative realty value for tax purposes was set at $18,493,559,079. [1:6-7.]

Index to other news appears on Page 30.

City Realty Values Up for 6th Year; Assessment Total $18,493,559,079

By LEE E. COOPER

New York's taxable realty wealth has increased on the city's books for the sixth consecutive year, with the result that property owners are due to pay levies on the highest aggregate valuation in seventeen years, according to official figures made public yesterday.

In a report to Mayor O'Dwyer's office, William E. Boyland, president of the Tax Commission, set the total tentative assessed valuation of real estate in the five boroughs for 1950-51 at $18,493,559,079. This is $381,327,900 above the final valuation for 1949-50, which was $18,112,231,179.

The high mark in realty valuations here, including utility property and special franchises, was reached in 1932, with $19,616,935,429.

The report showed a net rise for this year of $316,525,750 in "ordinary" real estate, to $16,120,113,875, and of $64,802,150 in the holdings of utility corporations, which were listed tentatively for the new tax year at $1,655,893,290.

Added to these sums was $717,551,914 for special franchises, the exact amount of which will not be set by the State Tax Commission for another month. The figure used by the city officials is based on the 1949-50 records.

Although no particular area was found by the field assessors to have increased generally in value—in contrast to last year when sharp gains were listed for the land around Stuyvesant Town and the United Nations site—there were three times as many rises as there were decreases in the city as a whole.

Largely for purposes of "equalization," to bring properties in line with neighboring valuations, in-

Continued on Page 20, Column 4

Air Defense Mapped For Atom Projects

By AUSTIN STEVENS
Special to THE NEW YORK TIMES.

WASHINGTON, Jan. 31—The Air Force disclosed tonight that it planned to throw a protective aerial "wall" around key atomic installations of the country.

Under a plan worked out today at the Pentagon, the Air Force will insist on the positive identification of any airplane flying within 100 miles of three atomic plants and, failing to be advised of an aircraft's identity will send fighter planes aloft to observe its character and course.

The plan in effect is a revival of a wartime measure whereby in combat zones any aircraft picked up by radar or other means of detection was consid-

Continued on Page 8, Column 6

Fred Allen made the switch from radio to TV in 1950 as one of the stars in rotation on the Colgate Comedy Hour. He is seen here with Monty Woolley.

Wayne Howell, Jerry Lester, Milton Delugg and Dagmar were the regular cast of Broadway Open House, a show that made its debut in 1950 and aired at 11:30 P.M. live.

A popular show that originated in 1949 and lasted for three years of the decade was Man Against Crime, featuring Ralph Bellamy.

One of the finest musicals of the 50s was Guys and Dolls. *Vivian Blaine, Robert Alda (center, white tie) and Sam Levene (in pin stripe suit), were among the stars in this long-running and money-making Broadway production.*

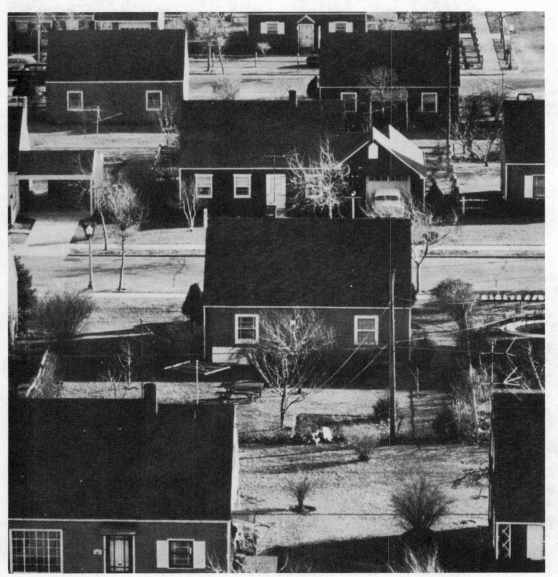

The move to suburbia was in full swing.

"All the News That's Fit to Print"

The New York Times.

LATE CITY EDITION
Drizzle and fog early today, fair later. Cloudy tomorrow.
Temperature Range Today-Max.,42; Min.,34
Temperatures Yesterday—Max.,41; Min.,33
Full U. S. Weather Bureau Report, Page 51

Copyright, 1950, by The New York Times Company.

VOL. XCIX..No. 33,617. | Entered as Second-Class Matter, Postoffice, New York, N. Y. | NEW YORK, TUESDAY, FEBRUARY 7, 1950. | Times Square, New York 18, N. Y. Telephone LAckawanna 4-1000 | FIVE CENTS

TRUMAN INVOKES TAFT-HARTLEY ACT IN COAL STRIKE, NAMES FACT BOARD; 370,000 MINERS OUT, VOICING DEFIANCE

RESORT TO THE LAW

President Acts Against Lewis, Chooses Inquiry Body Headed by Cole

ASKS A REPORT BY MONDAY

Injunction Move Is Due Then if the Operators and Miners Have Not Resumed Talks

By ANTHONY LEVIERO

Special to THE NEW YORK TIMES.

WASHINGTON, Feb. 6—President Truman invoked the Taft-Hartley Act against John L. Lewis and the United Mine Workers today as the soft-coal strike became almost complete and virtually ended bituminous production.

Simultaneously the Chief Executive appointed an emergency board of three seasoned labor arbitrators to study the dispute and report to him on or before next Monday.

This move under the law allowed the mine owners and the miners six days in which to seek again a basis for negotiation. Failing that, the real showdown should follow next week. Under the Taft-Hartley Law, the Government is compelled to apply for a court injunction that would require the miners to go back to work for eighty days pending a renewed search for a settlement.

David L. Cole, a lawyer of Paterson, N. J., and a veteran arbitrator with experience in coal disputes, was appointed chairman of the board. The other members were William Willard Wirtz, a Professor of Law at Northwestern University and former chairman of the National Wage Stabilization Board, and John Dunlop, associate professor of economics at the Harvard School of Business Administration.

Board Holds First Meeting

The board members arrived here tonight and had a session with Peter Seitz, general counsel of the United States Conciliation Service, who briefed them on the background of the dispute. Then they held an organization meeting and planned to begin their proceedings tomorrow.

Through a spokesman, Mr. Lewis blanketed the President's dramatic action with a "no comment" and then lapsed into silence. What his course might be was a riddle. There was no assurance that he would cooperate with the board or that his miners would heed the eighty-day injunction, if the proceedings went that far.

All that appeared certain tonight was that Mr. Lewis had created an imposing dilemma for his old antagonist, President Truman, who has made the repeal of the Taft-Hartley Act a major political issue for this year's Congressional election.

Unlike his unsuccessful action of last Tuesday, when he issued a conciliatory statement and sought to bring the operators and the miners before an extralegal board, Mr. Truman today said nothing. He did what the law required—issued an executive order creating the board.

In the order, phrased in legal language, Mr. Truman expressed the opinion that if the strike were allowed to continue it "will imperil the national health and safety." He acted under Section 206 of the Taft-Hartley Act, which provides for Presidential action when a strike threatens to reach emergency proportions.

Action Forecast for Days

His action was announced by Charles G. Ross, White House press secretary. It had been forecast for several days, and a large number of reporters had gathered in the lobby of the Executive offices. Mr. Ross called them in a little after noon and said:

"The President at 11:35 this morning signed an Executive order creating a board to inquire into a dispute in the bituminous coal industry. This board is to report not later than Feb. 13. Of course, it could report earlier, but that is the terminal date."

Earlier the reporters got an intimation of this action from Speak-

Continued on Page 12, Column 1

BITUMINOUS TIE-UP

Only 30,000 of 400,000 Diggers Stay on Job in Soft Coal Fields

TAFT ACT 'CLUB' ASSAILED

But Owners Hold Strikers Will Obey Writ to Work—Anthracite Mines Busy

By A. H. RASKIN

Special to THE NEW YORK TIMES.

PITTSBURGH, Feb. 6—A general strike in the country's soft coal fields was the reply given by members of the United Mine Workers today to President Truman's request for voluntary restoration of "normal" coal production.

Two hundred and seventy thousand miners who had been working a three-day week put aside their tools and joined 100,000 others who have been on a "no-day week" for the last month. Their walkout left some 30,000 UMW members at work in bituminous mines that have signed new contracts with John L. Lewis, president of the union, and in a handful of mines west of the Mississippi.

News that President Truman had put in motion the machinery for an eighty-day injunction under the national emergency provisions of the Taft-Hartley Act brought fresh expressions of defiance from the strikers. In Pennsylvania and West Virginia, where the tie-up has been in effect for a full month, local union leaders asserted that their men did not intend to go back without a contract, even if Mr. Lewis ordered them to do so.

Sabotage Is Predicted

These statements were discounted by mine owners. They voiced certainty that the miners would go back on Mr. Lewis' signal when an injunction was issued. However, some operators said they expected many locals might be slow to return and that the injunction period would be marked by "sabotage, slowdowns and sporadic stoppages" in many areas.

The first hint that the union would instruct its members to comply with a back-to-work order

Continued on Page 19, Column 4

Ching Asks a 16-Day Delay In Call for Telephone Strike

Union, Polling Leaders Across Nation, Will Reply Today—Mediator Gravely Warns the 320,000 Set to Quit Tomorrow

A sixteen-day postponement of the threatened strike affecting 320,000 telephone workers hung in the balance last night. Acting on a proposal of Cyrus S. Ching, Federal Mediation and Conciliation Service director, the executive board of the Communication Workers of America, CIO, was being polled across the country on whether to accept the delay.

The walkout, scheduled for 6 A. M. tomorrow, would affect directly 100,000 telephone employes represented by the CWA. Another 220,000 telephone workers probably would refuse to cross picket lines. The postponement sought by Mr. Ching would delay the strike call until Feb. 24.

Before the union can answer Mr. Ching, nine members of the executive board must indicate their position to Joseph A. Beirne, president of the CWA.

These include, beside Mr. Beirne, John J. Moran, John Crull and A. T. Jones, all vice presidents of the national union; C. W. Werkau, secretary-treasurer, and four regional directors, Mrs. Mary Hanscom, Eastern region, Newark; Ray Hackney, Southwestern, St. Louis; Joseph Deirdoroff, Western, Denver, and Ray Dreyer, Central, Chicago.

Mr. Ching will receive the union leaders' decision in Washington this morning. He formulated his proposal for delay while in New York, where he sought vainly for a break in the deadlocked negotiations between the CWA and the American Telephone and Telegraph Company. The negotiations resume at 10 A. M. today in the New Yorker Hotel.

Mr. Ching warned of the grave impact should the strike take place. He told both union and company spokesmen that "many of the freedoms which both sides presently enjoy, and are enjoyed by employers and unions generally, will be endangered by a demonstration of an absence of sound and stable management-labor relations in the critical communications industry."

Despite this warning, after the

Continued on Page 18, Column 5

TRANSIT INQUIRY ON; QUILL LEADS FIGHT

Mayor's Committee Hearings Open With Union Vigorously Pressing Its Demands

By ALEXANDER FEINBERG

The Transport Workers Union, CIO, got its long-sought opportunity yesterday to start presenting to Mayor O'Dwyer's fact-finding board its case for higher wages and improved working conditions.

At the first all-day session of the board, the union restated its demands for a wage increase of 21 cents an hour across the board for all of the city's 43,000 transit workers, along with forty-eight hours' pay for a five-day, forty-hour week. Other salient points among its demands called for the setting up of a grievance committee with recourse to impartial arbitration, and improved pension, vacation and holiday benefits.

John F. O'Donnell, union counsel, introduced voluminous exhibits tending to show that New York's transit workers were the lowest paid of any in twelve major cities, several of them with municipally operated systems. Other exhibits sought to show that they were paid less than railroad employes and truck drivers.

Through still other exhibits he sought to make the contrasting point that New York took good care of its policemen, firemen and

Continued on Page 17, Column 4

WATER SUPPLY DIPS 3D SUCCESSIVE DAY

Officials Call On the Public to Reduce Consumption in 'Every Possible Way'

By CHARLES G. BENNETT

As water shortage in the city's Catskill and Croton reservoirs dipped by 134,000,000 gallons yesterday, the third successive day of storage losses, water officials issued an urgent appeal to the public to reduce water use "in every possible way."

The new appeal was underscored by the weekly consumption report. This showed that last week's water consumption averaged 868,000,000 gallons daily, an increase of 8,000,000 gallons daily over use in the previous week. It was the first week since mid-November that consumption had not declined or at least done no worse than in the preceding week.

Stephen J. Carney, Commissioner of Water Supply, Gas and Electricity, noted that in spite of the one-week rise, New Yorkers still had maintained an over-all average daily reduction of 324,000,000 gallons in water consumption since the "base" week, Oct. 2 to 8, 1949.

The new series of daily storage losses, coming at a time of the year when normally the reservoirs are rising, Mr. Carney said, make it imperative that the public make even further savings.

Mr. Carney said that he thought

Continued on Page 17, Column 2

Port Body Urges Helicopter Lines; Offers Field Atop Its Bus Terminal

By FREDERICK GRAHAM

The Port of New York Authority told the Civil Aeronautics Board yesterday that it strongly recommended mail, passenger and express service by helicopters in the metropolitan area. It offered to provide a landing area atop the new bus terminal it is building on Eighth Avenue between Fortieth and Forty-first Streets.

The recommendation and offer were made by Fred M. Glass, director of airport development for the bi-state agency, at the opening session of a CAB hearing to determine whether the New York area is to have helicopter shuttle service. The hearing was held in the assembly room of the Commerce and Industry Association, 233 Broadway.

In addition to the Port Authority, representatives of five communities in New Jersey, Connecticut and New York appeared before Ferdinand M. Moran, CAB examiner, to urge authorization of helicopter shuttle service.

Representatives of helicopter manufacturing companies also testified as to the types, performance and availability of their equipment. The sum of their testimony was that dependable helicopters were now flying and had been extensively tested both by the armed services and in commercial operations. They added that larger and better helicopters were coming along.

After explaining that the Port Authority was appearing at the hearing because of its obligation to promote the full, efficient and economical development of transportation in its area, Mr. Glass said:

"With our greater population and more intensified commercial life, the New Jersey-New York Port District, more than any other area in the country, requires the best transportation services. The helicopter, with its unique ability to take off and land on small spaces, and to move passengers and

Continued on Page 23, Column 3

G. O. P. POSES ISSUE FOR '50 AS LIBERTY VERSUS SOCIALISM

FAIR DEAL IS TARGET

Republicans Want Cuts in Spending and Taxes, Revised Taft Law

BACK FOREIGN POLICY AID

But Hit Conduct of Program—Party Declaration Fails to Win United Support

Text of Republican party statement is printed on Page 20.

By W. H. LAWRENCE

Special to THE NEW YORK TIMES.

WASHINGTON, Feb. 6—The Republican party policy makers today proclaimed "Liberty Against Socialism" to be the major domestic issue of the 1950 Congressional elections.

But the party failed to achieve complete unity, either in its denunciation of the Truman Administration's program at home and abroad, or on the alternatives which it promised.

In all-day separate and closed meetings members of the Republican National Committee and the House and Senate Republican conferences finally gave their approval to a "statement of principles and objectives" designed to serve as a national platform for the months between now and the November elections.

Party chieftains had hoped that the declaration would demonstrate party unity and purpose and bring a new flow of financial contributions to defray campaign expenses, but a group led by Senator Henry Cabot Lodge Jr. of Massachusetts, Senator Margaret Chase Smith of Maine, Representative Jacob K. Javits of New York and Representative James G. Fulton of Pennsylvania promptly made known its dissatisfaction.

"Fair Deal" Vigorously Opposed

As was to be expected, the party declaration approved by the majority was vigorous in its opposition to enactment of the most of the Fair Deal program put before Congress by President Truman.

On foreign policy questions it found a middle ground, advocating continuance of a bipartisan attitude but sharply criticizing the administration of foreign policy with particular reference to "secret agreements" made at Yalta and Potsdam "which have created new injustices and new dangers throughout the world."

An effort made by Werner Schroeder, Illinois national committeeman, to put the party on record as opposed to continuance of the bipartisan foreign policy, was overwhelmingly defeated in the national committee. Members said that a voice vote showed support for Mr. Schroeder from only one or two others.

The party statement declared:

"We advocate a strong policy against the spread of communism or fascism at home and abroad, and we insist that America's efforts toward this end be directed by those who have no sympathy either with communism or fascism."

It asserted that "basic American principles are threatened by the Administration's program for a planned economy modeled on the Socialist Governments of Europe, including price and wage control, rationing, socialized medicine, regional authorites and the Brannan Plan with its controls, penalties, fines and jail sentences."

The Republican program "to rebuild a prosperous and progressive America" included these major planks:

A return to a balanced budget

Continued on Page 20, Column 3

11,000 Crowd Arena For $1 Party Supper

Special to THE NEW YORK TIMES.

WASHINGTON, Feb. 6 — The Republicans followed up their declaration of principles today with a box-supper party at Uline Arena. It was a noisy and crowded success. The scene was that of an old-fashioned political rally.

The crowd inside the building numbered about 11,000, it was estimated, with 2,000 more outside trying to get in. Only 7,000 supper boxes were on hand at the start.

Admission was $1.20 a person, the 20 cents being Federal tax. The guests good-naturedly seized upon the tax as an issue for impromptu and one-sided debate. Party officials stressed the price of their meal, comparing it with the Democrats' $100-a-plate fund-raising affairs.

There was a good deal of music, both professional and otherwise. Part of the celebration was broadcast over the American Broadcasting Company network, while various leaders made short speeches. The platform was studded with party stalwarts.

JAPAN SAID TO BACK GIVING BASES TO U.S.

Visit by Joint Chiefs Is Held to Have Convinced Most Party Heads on Move

By LINDESAY PARROTT

Special to THE NEW YORK TIMES.

TOKYO, Feb. 6—Leaders of Japan's major political parties with the exception of the extreme left have become convinced as a result of the visit here by the Joint Chiefs of Staff that this nation should grant air, naval and army bases to the United States in return for a protective guarantee under the peace treaty. There are indications they believe that the view would be supported by a large majority of the post-war Japanese electorate.

The conviction of the Japanese leaders, the importance of which it is difficult to overstress, comes as a result of the emphasis they believe was placed by the Joint Chiefs on big American installations already existing here.

The three generals and one admiral who compose the Joint Chiefs left Japan today for Okinawa after visiting the naval base at Yokosuka, Army installations in the Osaka region and the large Air Force base at Itazuke in Kyushu. They were prevented from inspecting the newly built major air base at Misawa in northeast Honshu by weather conditions.

Though no information was forthcoming, either from the chiefs or local United States military authorities, the Japanese were inclined to believe the principal point of the visit was evaluation of these and other bases and the

Continued on Page 11, Column 2

McCloy Warns the Germans Against a Revival of Nazism

At Opening of Amerika Haus in Stuttgart He Clarifies U. S. Policy, Declaring Its Chief Concern Is to Build Democracy

By DREW MIDDLETON

Special to THE NEW YORK TIMES.

STUTTGART, Germany, Feb. 6—The United States will use all its power to fight a revival of nazism in Germany, John J. McCloy, United States High Commissioner, asserted today.

The western Germans were bluntly warned to concentrate on internal problems, avoid "agitation" on foreign issues and to build democracy toward "unification of all Germany."

Speaking before an audience of 1,600 in the Stuttgart Opera House, Mr. McCloy turned the dedication of this city's Amerika Haus, an information center, into what was at once a major declaration of United States policy in Germany and an admission that the progress of Germany toward democracy had been neither as fast nor as complete as some officials had believed.

Mr. McCloy flatly told the Germans they would not be allowed a political position endangering the peace of Europe and "there will be no German army or air force."

Later at a press conference he declared he was not contemplating any changes in the occupation statute that defines the Allied powers at present and did not talk about such changes on his recent trip to Washington.

Shortly after his speech the High Commissioner intervened sharply and perhaps decisively in the denazification scandal currently shaking the government of Wuerttemberg-Baden by publicly

Continued on Page 4, Column 3

The text of the McCloy address is on Page 4.

WORLD ARMS TALK URGED BY TYDINGS TO END 'NIGHTMARE'

Senator Asks Call by Truman to Ease Fears by Reducing All Weapons Down to the Rifle

By WILLIAM S. WHITE

Special to THE NEW YORK TIMES.

WASHINGTON, Feb. 6—Senator Millard E. Tydings, Democrat, of Maryland, appealed to President Truman today to call a world conference for disarmament, in conventional as well as atomic weapons, to "end the world's nightmare of fear."

Mr. Tydings, a powerful figure as chairman of the Senate's Armed Services Committee and a member of its Foreign Relations Committee and the Joint Congressional Committee on Atomic Energy, asked the Senate to approve a resolution "authorizing and requesting" the President to summon such a meeting.

Lacking some such "fundamental" approach to peace, he asserted, "we are up against the possible extinction of all the human beings of this earth."

It would be "difficult" for Marshal Stalin or any other ruler, he argued, to "refuse an appeal by the President openly made on an honest and fair basis."

Senator Tydings' speech reopened a Senate debate on atomic policy, and weapons policy generally, which had been set off last week by Senator Brien McMahon, Democrat, of Connecticut, with the recommendation that this country at "almost any cost" seek an international arrangement neutralizing atomic and hydrogen weapons.

It appeared to reflect a considerable Congressional dissatisfaction at the fact that President Truman's recently announced decision to go ahead with the hydrogen bomb development was accompanied by no new approach to the Soviet Union toward atomic control.

Mr. Tydings contended that strict international inspection of

Continued on Page 3, Column 6

WEST GERMANS CUT SHIPMENT OF STEEL INTO RUSSIAN ZONE

Act After East Drops Far Below Pact Figure on Sending Grain to Western Areas

By JACK RAYMOND

Special to THE NEW YORK TIMES.

FRANKFORT, Germany, Feb. 6—The West German Government has decided to curtail steel shipments from the Ruhr to the Soviet zone, it became known today.

The reason to be given the East zone regime will be that terms of the interzonal trade agreement are in danger of being broken by Soviet zone failure to provide adequate shipments of grain. It may be assumed that recent transport difficulties imposed by the Soviet zone regime had no little to do with it.

[Monday night the Russians again delayed traffic at Helmstedt without explanation, slowing down the entry of Berlin-bound trucks to the point where a waiting line was established again, The Associated Press said. By midnight, with the entry rate cut to four or five trucks an hour, there was a line of fifteen trucks, the first such

Continued on Page 6, Column 5

Widnall, Jersey Republican, Wins Thomas Seat in Congress by 2 to 1

Special to THE NEW YORK TIMES.

HACKENSACK, N. J., Feb. 6—William B. Widnall, a Republican lawyer from Saddle River, tonight won a two-to-one victory in the special Seventh Congressional District election to choose a successor to J. Parnell Thomas, Republican, jailed for payroll padding.

Mr. Widnall received 31,754 votes against 15,370 for his Democratic opponent, former Mayor George T. English of East Paterson, a textile manufacturer.

The 43-year-old victor, a State Assemblyman from Bergen County, took the lead as soon as returns began to come in when the polls closed at 8 P. M. and maintained a wide margin from that time on.

A little more than two hours later Mr. English, who had predicted a "resentment vote" growing out of the Thomas scandal, conceded victory to Mr. Widnall.

"The victory is yours," he said at 10:10 P. M. in a telephone call to Mr. Widnall at the Republican campaign headquarters in Ridgewood. "My congratulations to you. Your support in the Seventh Congressional District apparently goes beyond partisan politics at this time."

On Mr. Widnall's invitation, Mr. English, accompanied by Mrs. English, then visited his opponent's headquarters, where a victory party was in the making. A momentary silence that greeted the Democrat and his wife when they walked in gave way immediately to a heavy burst of applause and cheers.

Mr. Widnall introduced his opponent to the gathering and read the message conceding victory. There was more applause and cheers.

The Republican said he hoped to offer a constructive program toward a better United States.

"It is my hope," he continued, "that this Republican victory is a forerunner of great Republican victories in November."

Mr. Widnall entered the primary fight for the candidacy without the

Continued on Page 35, Column 3

World News Summarized

TUESDAY, FEBRUARY 7, 1950

President Truman invoked the Taft-Hartley Act yesterday and named a three-man fact-finding board in the soft-coal dispute. The board was instructed to report not later than Monday, and if negotiations have not been resumed the President may seek an eighty-day injunction. It was the eighth time Mr. Truman had invoked the Taft-Hartley Act, which he strongly opposes, and the third time against the coal union. John L. Lewis made no comment. [1:8.] The miners, who went on a general strike, expressed defiance of an injunction. [1:5.]

Leaders of the CIO telephone union, who have called a nation-wide strike for tomorrow, were voting on a Government proposal to delay action sixteen days while Federal mediators sought a peace formula. [1:6-7.]

In this city, a fact-finding board opened hearings on demands by the transit workers for a pay increase, shorter hours and other changes in working conditions. [1:6.] The Continental Paper Company announced it was closing its $16,000,000 Ridgefield Park, N. J., plant, which has been strike-bound seven months. [17:1.]

Concern was expressed over the growing danger to peace resulting from the inability of the United States and the Soviet Union to agree on atomic control. Senator Tydings introduced a resolution calling on the President to convoke a world conference for disarmament of conventional as well as atomic weapons under constant world-wide inspection. [1:3.] A Senate group heard pleas for a "tyranny-proof" United Nations police force to be set up with or without Soviet consent. [3:4.] Some United Nations observers held direct Washington-Moscow talks might prove of value. [3:2-3.]

The FBI told a Congressional committee that Dr. Fuchs, British atomic scientist who had worked on bomb research in this country, had transmitted "vital secret information" to the Russians and had a long record of "sympathy with Communist ideology." Dr. Fuchs is under arrest in Britain. [3:1.] A Justice Department official told the jury in the Coplon-Gubitchev espionage trial how a decoy message had led to the arrest of the defendants. [14:2.]

Republican policy conference, with distinct rumblings of discontent, adopted a statement proclaiming "liberty against socialism" the keynote of this year's Congressional elections. [1:1.] In New Jersey, William B. Widnall, Republican, was elected representative to succeed J. Parnell Thomas. [1:2-3.]

"We Americans are not here exclusively to feed the German people and promote economic recovery, but to help the Germans establish a political democracy, regain economic health, rejoin the democratic world and stamp out every vestige of nazism," United States High Commissioner McCloy said in Stuttgart. [1:3-4.] His blunt speech, which was welcomed by the British and French, was said to reflect accurately this country's new policy of straight talking. [5:3.]

Western Germany has decided to cut steel shipments to the Soviet zone. [1:4.]

Premier Bidault formed a new French Cabinet without any Socialist Ministers. [7:1.]

Index to other news appears on Page 28.

By Winston Churchill:
The Second World War

Installment 11 of the excerpts from Mr. Churchill's memoirs of the war will be found today on
Page 29

1950

One of TV's first families of the 1950s was The Nelsons: Ozzie, Harriet, Ricky and David.

What's My Line *made its debut on the CBS network in 1950.*

The couple dancing is Arthur and Kathryn Murray on their show The Arthur Murray Party. *It commenced in 1950 featuring dance contests and instruction and was on the air through 1960.*

"All the News That's Fit to Print"

The New York Times.

LATE CITY EDITION
Sunny with pleasant temperatures today. Fair tomorrow.
Temperature Range Today-Max.,80; Min.,60
Temperatures Yesterday-Max.,90.3; Min.,69
Full U. S. Weather Bureau Report, Page 55

VOL. XCIX. No. 33,758. | Entered as Second-Class Matter. Post Office, New York, N. Y. | NEW YORK, WEDNESDAY, JUNE 28, 1950. | Times Square, New York 18, N. Y. Telephone LAckawanna 4-1000 | FIVE CENTS

TRUMAN ORDERS U. S. AIR, NAVY UNITS TO FIGHT IN AID OF KOREA; U. N. COUNCIL SUPPORTS HIM; OUR FLIERS IN ACTION; FLEET GUARDS FORMOSA

114 RESCUED HERE AS LINER GROUNDS AFTER COLLISION

Excalibur, With Hole 15 Feet Wide in Side, Settles on Mud Flat Off Brooklyn

FIRES START ON FREIGHTER

One Person Slightly Injured—Responsibility for the Crash Still to Be Decided

By WILLIAM R. CONKLIN

Thirty-five minutes after a gay departure for a Mediterranean cruise, the American Export Line's Excalibur was disabled in a collision yesterday with a Danish freighter in the Narrows, but all her 114 passengers were taken off safely.

The confetti-speckled cruise ship left Pier 4, Jersey City, at noon for a forty-three-day voyage. At 12:35 P. M. the collision with the inbound Colombia occurred off Sixty-ninth Street, Brooklyn.

The impact crushed the bow of the freighter and tore a hole fifteen feet wide in the port side of the Excalibur forward of the bridge. Fire broke out in the Colombia's forepeak in a paint storeroom.

While passengers and both crews remained calm, water quickly flooded the forward holds of the cruise ship. The Excalibur settled with her bow on a midstream mud bank, with her screw lifted in the air.

Passengers Taken Off by Tugs

Passengers on the sinking ship donned bright orange life preservers and were taken off by two tugs of the Moran Towing Company. Except for one woman who bruised three fingers of her left hand, all passengers were uninjured. They were returned to Pier 4, and the ship line arranged for hotel accommodations for them.

No official on the scene would assess responsibility for the collision. The Coast Guard required both captains to file written reports on the crash today. Under usual procedure, a Coast Guard board of inquiry hears evidence and fixes blame. Unofficially, it was said that a misunderstanding of whistle signals was the probable cause of the accident.

Capt. S. N. Groves of Brooklyn, a veteran of twenty-five years at sea, commanded the Excalibur, a ship of 9,644 gross tons with a top speed of seventeen knots. The Colombia, owned by the United Steamship Lines of Denmark, was commanded by Capt. Christian Mikkelsen of Copenhagen. The freighter was operated by the Scandinavian-American Steamship Company of 25 Broadway. Carrying cotton, wool and lubricating oils, she was bound from Philadelphia to Pier 24 at Congress Street, Brooklyn.

When the collision occurred there was good visibility despite a light haze over the lower bay. Persons in Shore Road Park saw the collision clearly, half a mile off the Brooklyn waterfront.

As the Excalibur's forward holds filled, her nose dropped into a mudbank and she swung to face upstream on the incoming tide.

2 Fireboats Help Freighter

The fireboats William J. Gaynor and Firefighter put lines on the 5,146-ton freighter to fight the fire on board. With the help of the ship's forty-two crewmen they subdued a fire in the forward hold. A collision bulkhead between that point and the forecastle prevented them from tackling another fire in the peak.

With Army, Navy, Coast Guard and Moran tugs helping, the burning vessel was moved into the north side of the Sixty-ninth Street ferry pier. John L. Holman, Deputy Fire Chief commanding the Marine Division, summoned a hook and ladder company to pour streams into the burning peak from the pier. Within an hour, the fire was extinguished.

Joseph H. Boggs, senior assistant purser of the Excalibur, said it was fortunate that the collision had occurred in shoal water.

"Immediately after the crash we

Continued on Page 29, Column 2

SANCTIONS VOTED

Council Adopts Plan of U. S. for Armed Force in Korea, 7 to 1

THE SOVIET IS ABSENT

Yugoslavia Casts Lone Dissent—Egypt and India Abstain

Mr. Austin's statement to the United Nations is on Page 6.

By THOMAS J. HAMILTON
Special to THE NEW YORK TIMES.

LAKE SUCCESS, June 27—The Security Council adopted tonight a United States resolution recommending that members of the United Nations use armed force in repelling the invasion of southern Korea and restoring international peace and security.

The vote on the resolution, which amounted to Security Council authorization for President Truman's decision to send United States naval and air units to the defense of the Republic of Korea, was 7 to 1, with Yugoslavia voting against.

The representatives of India and Egypt did not vote because they had not received instructions from their Governments. The Soviet Union was absent.

Representatives of Britain, France, Nationalist China, Cuba, Ecuador and Norway announced this afternoon that they would vote for the United States resolution without change. However the Council recessed at 5:12 P. M. to permit Sir Benegal Rau and Mahmoud Bey Fawzi, the representatives of India and Egypt, to try to reach their Governments by telephone.

The vote was finally taken at 10:45 P. M. after both said they had been unable to establish communication with responsible authorities. With Egypt and India not participating, the Council then rejected, seven to one, a Yugoslav resolution proposing that the Council renew its appeal for compliance with the cease-fire resolution it adopted Sunday, and request the two sides to agree to United Nations mediation.

The Council then recessed again while Sir Benegal and Fawzi Bey again attempted to obtain instructions. Apparently Fawzi Bey did so, but neither he nor Sir Benegal made any further statement, and the Council adjourned at 11 P. M.

Both Security Council members and other delegates who crowded around their table showed their realization that a historic decision for the United Nations and the world was being taken tonight. Warren R. Austin, the United States representative, was determined to avoid postponing a decision until tomorrow, and the Indian and Egyptian representatives cooperated by not requesting a postponement because of their failure to receive instructions.

Mr. Austin said after the meeting that the immediate effect of the resolution "should be to stop

Continued on Page 7, Column 1

President Takes Chief Role In Determining U. S. Course

Truman's Leadership for Forceful Policy to Meet Threat to World Peace Draws Together Advisers on Vital Move

By ARTHUR KROCK
Special to THE NEW YORK TIMES.

WASHINGTON, June 27—Some of those who participated in the meetings Sunday and Monday nights, at which the momentous decisions were taken to resist further Communist aggressions, beginning in the Far East, with the combat air and naval power of the United States, described the President to associates today as determined from the outset to adopt the forceful policy which was announced this morning.

As soon as the first meeting assembled, they said, Mr. Truman made it plain that these were to be the bases of his decision:

1. The situation created by Communist tactics at various points of the world, culminating in the attack of North Korea on South Korea, had been allowed to drift too long.
2. The entire Far East was deteriorating in a manner to threaten the peace of the world, a line had to be drawn at once, and the United States had to draw it.
3. National security was the primary interest, but embedded in this were world peace and the prestige and future effectiveness of the United Nations, which was the architect of the South Korean Government.
4. It was a time for courage, even boldness, and calculated risk, which other members of the United Nations would be invited to share as they saw fit.
5. It was not a time to give the slightest consideration to previous policies or to individuals associated with those policies. If, for example, the fundamental change in the Far Eastern sit-

Continued on Page 4, Column 3

MAINLAND ATTACKS ENDED BY FORMOSA

Chinese Nationalists Halt Air, Navy Forays in Accordance With Request by Truman

By The Associated Press

TAIPEI, Formosa, Wednesday, June 28—The Chinese Nationalists today ordered their Air Force and Navy to cease attacks on the Communist mainland in accordance with a United States request.

President Truman had ordered United States warships to protect Formosa against Communist attack and at the same time asked the Nationalists to cease offensive operations.

Nationalist Foreign Minister George Yeh hailed the President's order for warship protection as "a most welcome sign of comradeship in the fight against communism."

Generalissimo Chiang Kai-shek and his Cabinet had met after the United States note was delivered to the United States Embassy. It was understood the note carried with it instructions to see that it was brought personally to Generalissimo Chiang's attention.

Mr. Yeh translated the text to the Generalissimo last night in the presence of United States Charge d'Affaires Robert Strong.

Mr. Strong was with Generalissimo Chiang for about twenty minutes. After his departure the latter consulted with Mr. Yeh, Premier Chen Cheng and other officials.

The decision was announced after Generalissimo Chiang conferred with Gen. Chou Chih-jou, Chief of the Joint General Staff and other top Nationalist commanders.

The Nationalists were believed to have agreed to Washington's re-

Continued on Page 8, Column 4

HOUSE VOTES 315-4 TO PROLONG DRAFT

Korea Crisis Breaks Deadlock—Bill Expected to Be Sent to White House Tonight

Special to THE NEW YORK TIMES.

WASHINGTON, June 27—The House of Representatives today passed, by a vote of 315 to 4, an extension of the draft for another year.

The bill added authority for President Truman to call to active duty members of the National Guard and the reserve forces for periods not exceeding twenty-one months.

The Senate agreed to vote on the bill tomorrow afternoon. Swift passage is expected there so that the bill may reach President Truman for his signature tomorrow night.

As recently as yesterday the Senate and the House appeared to be in a hopeless deadlock over the manner in which the selective service system could be kept alive without much leeway for the President to put it to use. Today when

Continued on Page 16, Column 5

U. S. FORCE FIGHTING

MacArthur Installs an Advanced Echelon in Southern Korea

FOE LOSES 4 PLANES

American Craft in Battle to Protect Evacuation—Seoul Is Quiet

By LINDESAY PARROTT
Special to THE NEW YORK TIMES.

TOKYO, Wednesday, June 28—The United States is now actively intervening in the Korean civil war, an announcement from Gen. Douglas MacArthur's headquarters here made clear this morning.

[Gen. Douglas MacArthur announced Wednesday that the forces of South Korea now were holding the Communist Korean invaders, a United Press dispatch from Tokyo said. At the same time he reported that United States fliers had begun bombing and strafing missions against North Korean forces. Seoul was reported quiet.]

General MacArthur revealed that a "small advanced echelon" from his headquarters had been established in Korea, presumably cooperating with the United States Military Advisory Group, which has been in Korea since the republic was established there under President Syngman Rhee two years ago.

The MacArthur announcement stated that Far East air forces and elements of the naval forces under the general's command were "conducting" combat missions south of the Thirty-eighth Parallel—the dividing line between Communist North Korea and the United States-recognized Korean Republic. These operations, it was officially stated, are "in support of the Korean Republic," whose Government has now been reinstalled in the capital, Seoul, after isolation of the Northern armored spearheads that had penetrated to the outskirts of the city yesterday.

The announcement said that United States planes, which were providing air cover for the evacuation of women and children dependents of various United States missions, had shot down four North Korean fighters that were interfering with the operation of

Continued on Page 17, Column 3

World News Summarized

WEDNESDAY, JUNE 28, 1950

United States air and sea forces were ordered by President Truman yesterday to give Korean troops "cover and support." Moving directly to meet Communist "armed invasion and war" in Asia, the President instructed the Seventh Fleet to "prevent any attack on Formosa," called on the Chinese Nationalists to halt all attacks on the mainland, ordered United States forces in the Philippines strengthened and moved to speed military assistance to those islands and to Indo-China. He instructed Ambassador Kirk in Moscow to urge the Soviet Union to help end hostilities. [1:8; map P. 2.]

Naval and air elements are "conducting combat missions south of the Thirty-eighth Parallel of Korea in support" of the Seoul Government, General MacArthur announced. An advance echelon of his General Headquarters has been set up in Korea, he added. Conflicting reports of the fighting showed positions little changed during the day. [1:5; maps P. 17.] In Washington it was said that General MacArthur had sufficient forces to give the South Koreans air and sea preponderance. [13:3.]

This country's new Far East policy was set at conferences during which the President's positive program and leadership convinced his top aides that his decisions "were both inevitable and right." [1:3-4.] He brought unity to an Administration that had been split on many vital policy issues. [4:6-7.]

Governor Dewey, speaking as head of the Republican party, pledged full support to the President [4:3] and Congress was almost unanimous in its endorsement. [1:7.] The House, 315 to 4, passed a one-year extension of the draft with broad new powers for the President; the Senate will vote today. [1:4.] Senate Republicans, however, blocked a vote today on the foreign arms-aid bill. [14:3.] The National Security Resources Board has ready for introduction a sweeping bill authorizing the President to freeze prices, wages, manpower and materials. [15:2.]

The United Nations Security Council, with Russia absent and Yugoslavia voting no, approved a United States motion to permit member nations to send armed forces to help repel the Korean invasion. [1:2.]

British parties united in supporting President Truman's program. The Labor Government won confidence votes on its refusal to join talks on pooling Europe's heavy industry. [19:4.]

John S. Service, a key figure in Senator McCarthy's charges of communism in the State Department, has been cleared by the department's Loyalty Security Board. [22:3.]

Index to other news appears on Page 28.

Statement on Korea

By The Associated Press.

WASHINGTON, June 27—The text of President Truman's statement today on Korea:

In Korea the Government forces, which were armed to prevent border raids and to preserve internal security, were attacked by invading forces from North Korea. The Security Council of the United Nations called upon the invading troops to cease hostilities and to withdraw to the Thirty-eighth Parallel. This they have not done, but on the contrary have pressed the attack. The Security Council called upon all members of the United Nations to render every assistance to the United Nations in the execution of this resolution.

In these circumstances I have ordered United States air and sea forces to give the Korean Government troops cover and support.

The attack upon Korea makes it plain beyond all doubt that communism has passed beyond the use of subversion to conquer independent nations and will now use armed invasion and war.

It has defied the orders of the Security Council of the United Nations issued to preserve international peace and security. In these circumstances the occupation of Formosa by Communist forces would be a direct threat to the security of the Pacific area and to United States forces performing their lawful and necessary functions in that area.

Accordingly I have ordered the Seventh Fleet to prevent any attack on Formosa. As a corollary of this action I am calling upon the Chinese Government on Formosa to cease all air and sea operations against the mainland. The Seventh Fleet will see that this is done. The determination of the future status of Formosa must await the restoration of security in the Pacific, a peace settlement with Japan, or consideration by the United Nations.

I have also directed that United States forces in the Philippines be strengthened and that military assistance to the Philippine Government be accelerated.

I have similarly directed acceleration in the furnishing of military assistance to the forces of France and the associated states in Indo-China and the dispatch of a military mission to provide close working relations with those forces.

I know that all members of the United Nations will consider carefully the consequences of this latest aggression in Korea in defiance of the Charter of the United Nations. A return to the rule of force in international affairs would have far-reaching effects. The United States will continue to uphold the rule of law.

I have instructed Ambassador Austin, as the representative of the United States to the Security Council, to report these steps to the Council.

NORTH KOREA CALLS U. N. ORDER ILLEGAL

Declares Security Council's 'Cease Fire' Invalid Without Assent of China and Russia

Special to THE NEW YORK TIMES

HONG KONG, June 27—The North Korean Government issued a statement today saying that it regarded the cease fire order of the United Nations Security Council illegal for two reasons. It said these were, one, because the Democratic Peoples Republic of North Korea was not represented when its affairs were discussed and, two, because the Soviet Union and (Communist) China did not participate.

On the latter point it cited the United Nations Charter, which requires unanimity of five permanent members of the Security Council on questions of substance. China and Russia are both permanent members. [But the Communist rulers of China have not been recognized by the United Nations as representing that country.]

Drastic measures were taken in North Korea yesterday to organize

Continued on Page 18, Column 5

LEGISLATORS HAIL ACTION BY TRUMAN

Almost Unanimous Approval Is Voiced in Congress by Both Sides—House Cheers

By HAROLD B. HINTON.
Special to THE NEW YORK TIMES.

WASHINGTON, June 27—President Truman's announcement today that United States air and sea power would be employed to expel the Communist invaders from South Korea evoked almost unanimous support in Congress. His statement was read by the majority floor leaders in both houses.

In the House of Representatives, the members rose to their feet and cheered as the reading was completed by Representative John W. McCormack, of Massachusetts. In the Senate, the reading by Senator Scott W. Lucas, of Illinois, brought immediate declarations of support from several Republican Senators.

Showing the same spirit of solidarity in the face of crisis, as the present situation was frequently described, Senate and House conferees agreed on legislation to ex-

Continued on Page 5, Column 1

Stocks Rally After Big New Losses In War Scare; Sales Near 5 Million

By ROBERT H. FETRIDGE

Securities markets the world over were subjected yesterday to wide fluctuations as the Korean situation approached a crisis of universal concern.

Calmer thinking emerged successful on the New York exchanges, but only after prices encountered terrific battering. Losses that at one time ranged to 5 points and even more in standard issues on the New York Stock Exchange were either trimmed or eliminated. Quotations were definitely on the recovery side at the close, with the final composite rate down only 0.75 point. As pictured by THE NEW YORK TIMES index, the market was midway between the highs and lows of the day at the final bell.

London was the worst sufferer among the major exchanges, while the Canadian markets followed the lead of New York.

It was a wild day on the trading floor of the Stock Exchange. Business almost reached the 5,000,000-share mark, the reporting ticker tape was constantly thrown behind actual transactions and at one time was twenty-seven minutes late. This necessitated "flash" prices on the ticker to keep brokerage offices at least abreast of the price changes in the key stocks.

The trend changed with such rapidity that selling orders were still being executed after the price direction changed for the better.

Continued on Page 41, Column 6

BID MADE TO RUSSIA

President Asks Moscow to Act to Terminate Fighting in Korea

CHIANG TOLD TO HALT

U.S. Directs Him to Stop Blows at Reds—Will Reinforce Manila

By ANTHONY LEVIERO
Special to THE NEW YORK TIMES.

WASHINGTON, June 27—President Truman announced today that he had ordered United States air and naval forces to fight with South Korea's Army. He said this country took the action, as a member of the United Nations, to enforce the cease-fire order issued by the Security Council Sunday night.

Then acting independently of the United Nations, in a move to assure this country's security, the Chief Executive ordered Vice Admiral Arthur D. Struble to form a protective cordon around Formosa to prevent its invasion by Communist Chinese forces.

Along with these fateful decisions, Mr. Truman also ordered an increase of our forces based in the Philippine Republic, as well as more speedy military assistance to that country and to the French and Vietnam forces that are fighting Communist armies in Indo-China.

After he had started these moves that might mean a decided turn toward peace or a general war, the President sent Ambassador Alan G. Kirk to the Russian Foreign Office in Moscow to request the Soviet Union to use its good offices to end the hostilities. This was an obvious proffer of an opportunity for Russia to end the crisis before her own forces might get involved.

Door Opened for Russia

In the capital this was regarded as being at once a possible face-saving device for Russia in a showdown crisis and a feeler to determine her intentions.

The decisions amounted to a showdown in the "cold war" with Russia, in which this country has at last decided to begin shooting in a limited area. Yet all the decisions followed a carefully worked out formula of action within the framework of the United Nations, as well as unilateral moves that avoided any direct provocation of the Soviet Union.

Mr. Truman based the decision to fight for the South Koreans entirely on the Security Council resolution which called upon all members of the United Nations to help carry it out. And at the Pentagon it was explained that our air and naval forces would fight only below the Thirty-eighth Parallel line that divides South Korea from the Russian-sponsored North Korea.

"The Security Council called upon all members of the United Nations to render every assistance to the United Nations in the execution of this resolution," Mr. Truman stated. "In these circumstances I have ordered United States air and sea forces to give the Korean Government troops cover and support."

Russia Is Not Mentioned

Mr. Truman carefully avoided mentioning Russia in his statement. He pivoted today's great shift in United States foreign policy on a conclusion that the "cold war" had passed from an uneasy passive stage to "armed invasion and war." He blamed "communism."

"The attack upon Korea makes it plain beyond all doubt that communism has passed beyond the use of subversion to conquer independent nations and will now use armed invasion and war," he said. "It has defied the orders of the Security Council of the United Nations issued to preserve international peace and security. In these circumstances the occupation of Formosa by Communist forces would be a direct threat to the security of the Pacific area and to United States forces performing

Continued on Page 2, Column 2

City, T.W.U. in 2-Year Peace Pact; Mayor Signs Fare Rise Resolution

Officials of the Transport Workers Union, C. I. O., the members of the Board of Transportation and Mayor O'Dwyer signed at City Hall yesterday a memorandum of understanding seeking to guarantee two years of peace in the city-owned rapid transit system.

The accord closely followed recommendations made on May 31 by the Mayor's Transit Fact-Finding Board, granting an 11-cent-an-hour increase to 35,929 operating employes, a third week of vacation after ten years and an additional holiday each year. The cost of the changes recommended by the fact-finders amounts to $13,188,515 a year.

The union bound itself not to engage in any strike or other interference with transit operations and not to seek any basic changes in the accord before July 1, 1952. It agreed to resolve all disputes in accordance with the grievance machinery set up in the pact. The union obligated itself also to recognize the board's managerial authority and to "cooperate in the attainment of efficient operations."

The Board of Transportation agreed to retain competent industrial engineers to report on a program for achieving a five-day, forty-hour week for all employes now having a scheduled work-week in excess of forty hours.

Mayor O'Dwyer also signed yesterday afternoon a resolution of the Board of Transportation, effective Saturday, increasing fares on the city-owned surface lines

Continued on Page 28, Column 4

"All the News
That's Fit to Print"

The New York Times.

LATE CITY EDITION
Sunny and warm today; fair to-
night, becoming cloudy tomorrow.
Temperatures Yesterday—Max., 83; Min., 63
Temperature Range Today—Max., 83; Min., 63
Full U. S. Weather Bureau Report, Page 27

Copyright, 1950, by The New York Times Company.

VOL. XCIX..No. 33,768.   Entered as Second-Class Matter,
Post Office, New York, N. Y.   NEW YORK, SATURDAY, JULY 8, 1950.   Times Square, New York 18, N. Y.
Telephone LAckawanna 4-1000   FIVE CENTS

TRUMAN ORDERS INCREASES IN ARMED SERVICES, DRAFT IF NEEDED; U. S. TANKS HEAD FOR FRONT; U. N. OPENS KOREAN COMMAND FOR M'ARTHUR

PAYMENTS UNION AS INTEGRATION AID VOTED BY EUROPE

17 Western Nations Accept Fiscal System as of July 1 —Sterling Area Included

CURRENCIES CONVERTIBLE

Effect of Plan Is to Make Debts Payable in Form That Will Unblock Trade Exchange

By HAROLD CALLENDER
Special to The New York Times.

PARIS, July 7—The European payments union, the major objective of the Economic Cooperation Administration for this year as a step toward European integration, became a reality today when the seventeen national governments represented in the Marshall Plan Council unanimously accepted it.

The payments union is to come into force as of July 1, although the formal convention will not be signed for two or three weeks.

The effect will be to make the currencies of the seventeen European member nations inter-convertible, thus removing the payments difficulties that have so far blocked intra-European trade. The newly acquired convertibility will extend to the entire sterling area by virtue of Britain's membership in the system.

With the passing of the payments difficulties, the Marshall Plan nations will be rid of the major cause or pretext for trade restrictions, although the protective grounds will remain. Consequently, a part of the agreement instituting the payments union provides for further removal of trade restrictions and of discriminatory practices. These provisions were strongly urged by the E. C. A.

Stikker Commends Unity

Dr. Dirk U. Stikker, Netherlands Foreign Minister and chairman of the Council, emphasized what he called the political aspect of the new monetary agreement. He said that the unanimity achieved today showed the ability of the democracies to unite in a time of "great international difficulties."

Milton Katz, who long has taken a leading part in the payments negotiations and who yesterday succeeded W. Averell Harriman as the Marshall Plan Ambassador in Europe, said that the agreement today "vindicates our faith that the community of interest among the Western nations which exists in fact will continue to be translated into a community of action."

E. C. A. officials recalled that after long hesitation the British had found a way to bring the sterling area into the payments union, and that in so doing they had modified their commercial policy, long based upon bilateral agreements and discriminatory practices to protect their balance of payments. The same officials expressed gratification that the union would include Switzerland, whose political neutrality and whose peculiarly strong financial position had caused her hitherto to remain only a kind of associate member of the Marshall Plan organization.

Decision Called Epochal

Robert Marjolin, French secretary general of the council, described today's decision as the most important in the monetary sphere since the Bretton Woods agreements establishing the International Monetary Fund and the International Bank for Reconstruction and Development. He declared that for the first time since the war Europe would have a "multilateral" monetary system; that is, one based upon general, instead of bilateral, trade arrangements.

Few persons understand the precise mechanism of the payments union, a plan for clearing current accounts among the member nations on a collective basis by offsetting their debits against their credits without regard to national currencies, so that in most cases they will be able to finance their imports in each other's currencies. The union is therefore a step

Continued on Page 5, Column 4

R.F.C. Spurs Output Of Synthetic Rubber

Special to The New York Times.

WASHINGTON, July 7—The Reconstruction Finance Corporation announced today that it will reactivate three Government-owned synthetic rubber plants which will increase the country's annual production of synthetic rubber by approximately 88,000 tons.

They are the Government-owned plant at Port Neches, Tex., with an annual capacity of 75,000 tons; the butadiene plant at Houston, and a facility for production of butyl rubber, a special purpose rubber, at Baton Rouge, La.

With their reactivation there will be a total of eighteen Government-owned synthetic rubber plants in operation and nine in standby status. Those operating will be capable of producing approximately 500,000 tons of general purpose rubber and 75,000 tons of special purpose butyl rubber annually.

EVACUATION IN WAR IS STUDIED BY CITY

Disaster Plans to Be Speeded —Wallander Is Invited to Head Civilian Defense

By PAUL CROWELL

The complex problem of civilian evacuation and maintenance in the event the city should be subjected to enemy bombing is being studied by Mayor O'Dwyer's Committee on Civilian Defense.

The Mayor said yesterday that orders had been given to prepare a "blueprint" for the coordination of all city departments and agencies that would be involved in personnel training and equipment, and transportation and maintenance facilities required to conduct a large-scale evacuation of civilians "in case of a serious emergency."

The evacuation, he said, might become vital before, during or after the impact of the emergency. He added that such an evacuation "doubtless would be conducted on a priority basis, with women, children and sick or disabled persons heading the list."

The Mayor announced that he had asked former Police Commissioner Arthur W. Wallander to become Director of Civilian Defense on a full-time basis. Mr. Wallander, who headed the city's civilian defense organization during World War II and is now an executive of the Consolidated Edison System, will give his answer at a meeting of the Mayor's committee at City Hall next Monday afternoon. A week ago he had been named the Mayor's personal adviser on defense matters.

The need for early action on a comprehensive emergency evacuation plan was emphasized yesterday at a meeting in the Mayor's office at City Hall, attended by members of a special committee representing agencies concerned with the city's transportation system and its bridges and tunnels.

Among those attending were

Continued on Page 11, Column 5

DEFENSE LINE IS SET

It Is Stabilized 10 Miles Behind Positions Left Under Red Pressure

FOE PUSHES SLOWLY

Moves On Despite Heavy Air Assault—South Koreans Regroup

By LINDESAY PARROTT
Special to The New York Times.

TOKYO, Saturday, July 8 — North Korean tank-led columns pushed slowly forward again today against the United States defense line temporarily stabilized roughly ten miles back from the advanced positions that the Americans evacuated Thursday under pressure of superior Communist forces equipped with heavy armor.

[The Associated Press quoted a MacArthur communique as saying that South Korean forces had regrouped and were battling the North Koreans southeast of Seoul, where, "in some cases," they had "gained ground."

[United States tanks and guns moved into position north of Taejon for a counter offensive.

[General MacArthur's latest communique, Saturday afternoon, Tokyo time, said United States combat forces in Korea had so far suffered 249 casualties; of these 192 were men missing in action who might yet get back to friendly lines.]

In clear weather, United States front-line activity was supported with heavy concentrations of fighter and jet-propelled rocket planes striking at North Korean tanks.

A Continuous Front Line

According to a communique from Gen. Douglas MacArthur early this morning, reporting the situation presumably as of yesterday afternoon, a fairly continuous front line has now been established. This runs from south of Pyongtaek twenty-five miles east to Magung, thence to Chunju and "generally east to the east coast."

This put the line almost directly east-west along the Thirty-seventh Parallel, just one degree south of the border between Communist North Korea and the Korean Republic, across which the North Koreans crashed a fortnight ago.

The two weeks of fighting, with enormous superiority of manpower and equipment, had won the Communists a general penetration of sixty miles.

The principal North Korean effort appeared to be made by the Third and Fourth Divisions, which, the communique said, were pressing forward with the threat of envelopment in the Magung area.

From east to west the invaders lined up their First, Third and Fourth Divisions in the front line. All these were using tank spearheads and included Koreans hardened in fighting with the Chinese

Continued on Page 2, Column 3

ACTION BY COUNCIL

Unit Gives Washington Authority to Designate Chief for Its Forces

STEP BACKED 7 TO 0

India Joins Yugoslavia and Egypt in Abstaining on the Resolution

By THOMAS J. HAMILTON
Special to The New York Times.

LAKE SUCCESS, July 7—The Security Council today authorized the United States to establish a unified command for the United Nations Armed Forces defending Southern Korea, paving the way for the appointment of Gen. Douglas MacArthur as Commander-in-Chief and the use of the United Nations flag.

The United States, Great Britain, France, Nationalist China, Cuba, Ecuador and Norway voted for the resolution.

The vote on the resolution, which was introduced by Britain and France, was 7 to 0. Seven is required for a majority. Egypt, India and Yugoslavia abstained, and the Soviet Union, which has boycotted meetings of the Council since January because of the Council's refusal to expel Nationalist China, was absent.

Warren R. Austin, the United States representative, who did not speak during the discussion of the resolution, told the Council afterward that he could not introduce it because of "the big and special responsibilities" that it placed upon the United States. He added that "the United States accepts the responsibility and makes the sacrifice that is involved in carrying out these principles of the United Nations."

"We have already accepted the responsibilities of this resolution," Mr. Austin said. "In spirit if not in word this resolution has been in effect since the very first resolution [the cease-fire resolution of June 25] adopted in response to the call for help from Korea."

In addition to armed forces supplied by the United States, Britain, Australia, Canada, the Netherlands and New Zealand have al-

Continued on Page 4, Column 2

Continued on Page 4, Column 2

THE U. N. SENDS ITS FLAG TO M'ARTHUR

Secretary General Trygve Lie handing the banner that flew over Palestine to Warren Austin. On the right is Arne Sunde of Norway, President of the Security Council.
The New York Times (by William C. Eckenberg)

M'ARTHUR DOUBLES JAPANESE POLICE

Directs That Coast Guard Also Be Increased in Actions to Insure Internal Security

Special to The New York Times.

TOKYO, Saturday, July 8—Gen. Douglas MacArthur, in a letter today to Premier Shigeru Yoshida, directed that the Japanese National Police and the sea-going Coast Guard be more than doubled to insure that the internal security of Japan "continue unchallenged by lawless minorities."

General MacArthur's directive came at a time when the Japanese police have been closely watching the activities of Korean and Japanese Communists who have been circulating anti-occupation propaganda condemning the United States and United Nations action in the Korean war. It followed a series of raids and arrests at establishments printing such propaganda and persons who have been distributing leaflets in trains, on street corners and in other public places.

General MacArthur authorized

Continued on Page 3, Column 8

President Asks 260 Millions To Expedite Hydrogen Bomb

By ANTHONY LEVIERO
Special to The New York Times.

WASHINGTON, July 7—President Truman asked Congress today to furnish $260,000,000 in cash for development of the hydrogen bomb. This action was taken in a day that was notable for a marked rise in White House activity bearing on national security in general and the Korean conflict in particular.

The request for funds, which was the first thus far made for the new weapon, was the only formally announced activity. The increased planning and actions to meet the problems arising from the Korean war were mostly shrouded in secrecy.

The Administration is making a studied effort to avoid sensationalism as part of a policy to avoid further complications in Korea and elsewhere. Reporters relied mainly on their observations of the comings and goings on national leaders to uncover some idea of what was going on.

The Cabinet figured in three important White House meetings. In the first, Mr. Truman told his official family of the hydrogen bomb request and of the decision, announced by defense officials in the afternoon, to seek more military manpower through volunteers.

In the second, seven Cabinet officers who are members of the National Security Resources Board held a meeting of that agency, with W. Stuart Symington, the chairman, presiding. The problem discussed was mobilization planning.

At the third meeting, the Cabinet members considered the impact on the economy and the Federal budget of United States combat operations in Korea. President Truman's mid-year economic report was to have gone to Congress on Monday, but it was held up to allow a restudy and a revision to take in the war repercussions.

Mr. Truman's appropriation re-

Continued on Page 5, Column 2

CHIANG BIDS NAVY SEARCH, SEIZE SHIPS

Resumption Applies to Craft Flying Red or Nationalist Flag—U. S. Scans Move

By BURTON CRANE
Special to The New York Times.

TAIPEI, Formosa, July 7—In a move described as self-protection the Chinese Nationalist Government has resumed the search and seizure of vessels flying either the Chinese Nationalist or the Chinese Communist flag.

Earlier this week the United States Government was informed of this exception to a broad interpretation of President Truman's request of June 27 that the Nationalists cease operations against the Communists on the mainland of China.

Thus far there has been no acknowledgment of this communication from Washington.

Nationalist war vessels have been instructed to halt and search but not to fire upon vessels covered by the order. Officials here explain that since Mr. Truman's order Hong Kong merchants have rushed eagerly to ship goods into ports formerly under effective blockade. Many of them are shipping goods on vessels chartered by trading companies owned by the Peiping Government. These fly either the five star flag of Com-

Continued on Page 4, Column 7

VOLUNTEERS SOUGHT

Truman Tells Services to Drop Peace Quotas and Build Forces

NO CALL TO RESERVE

Pentagon Plans Do Not Now Include Summons to Units of Guard

By AUSTIN STEVENS
Special to The New York Times.

WASHINGTON, July 7—President Truman today authorized the Army, Navy and Air Force to discard their "peacetime" manpower quotas and to build their forces, using Selective Service if necessary, to the limits needed to cope with the Korean situation.

The three armed services immediately issued a call for volunteers to fill out ground combat divisions, man ships and augment flight crews. Veterans and reservists with specialized skills are in the highest priority groups, but the Army said it would welcome all recruits. None of the services planned a compulsory call for Reservists, and present plans do not envisage the use of Organized Reservists or National Guardsmen as units.

The Chief Executive acted to round out the armed services combat elements and technical services on the advice of Secretary of Defense Louis Johnson and Gen. Omar N. Bradley, chairman of the Joint Chiefs of Staff, who this morning gave Mr. Truman and the Cabinet a picture of the Korean conflict and the drain it had already produced on this country's forces.

Budget Ceiling Off

Word of the emergency measure and abandonment of the projected $14,000,000,000 military budget, a fund ceiling set by Mr. Truman himself, was issued at the Pentagon this afternoon by Maj. Gen. Floyd L. Parks, chief of Army information.

A prepared statement, approved at the White House, was handed to reporters attending the regular 3 P. M. "briefing" held by the Army since the start of the Korean invasion. It read:

"To meet the situation in Korea, upon recommendation of the Joint Chiefs of Staff, concurred in by the Secretaries of the Army, Navy and Air Force and with the approval of the President, the Army, Navy and Air Force have been authorized to exceed the over-all budget ceilings for personnel.

"This action constitutes a first step to build up to full operating strength the units of the Army, Navy and Air Force to be used in the Korean operation, to provide further maintenance and support therefor, and to replace units to be moved to Korea.

"The use of Selective Service has been authorized. Voluntary enlistments will also be accepted."

General Parks declared at the outset that it was hoped that voluntary enlistments would produce the necessary manpower. He declared in answer to a question about an "immediate draft":

"With a situation like this confronting us a lot of men want to get back in harness. Some are itching to get in the scrap."

Silent on Number Needed

Neither General Parks nor representatives of the Navy or Air Force would say how many additional men they needed. But Rear Admiral Hugh Goodwin said the Navy's goal was to get its ships "up to operating strength"—they now operate at about two-thirds full complement—and Brig. Gen. Sory Smith announced that the Air Force's prime need was for skilled men, including navigators, bombardiers, weather and medical personnel. There might later be a call for pilots, the Air Force said.

Compared with this selective procedure of the Navy and Air Force, General Parks said to the reporters: "If you can tell the boys to go to the recruiting stations we'll be glad to see them." He added that experienced men

Continued on Page 3, Column 2

World News Summarized

SATURDAY, JULY 8, 1950

President Truman authorized the increase of the United States Army, Navy and Air Force to "full operating strength" yesterday, "to meet the situation in Korea." He said they were to be maintained on such a footing through voluntary enlistment and, if needed, by the use of a selective service draft. [1:8.] Induction in this city will begin as soon as orders have been received from Washington. [1:6-7.] Congress was asked by the President to earmark $260,000,000 for development of the hydrogen bomb. [1:6-7.] Senator Lodge urged the appropriation of an additional $2,000,000,000 to provide military assistance to countries opposed to communism. [5:5.]

United States tanks and big guns moved toward the Korean front as invading armored columns continued to push slowly forward against a defensive position stabilized roughly at the Thirty-seventh Parallel. The new tanks have not yet been in action. Clearing weather enabled heavy concentrations of fighter and jet-propelled rocket aircraft to attack Communist armor and infantry successfully. [1:3; map Page 2.]
The United Nations Security Council adopted an Anglo-French resolution empowering the United States to establish a unified command in Korea and to appoint a commander in chief, presumably General MacArthur; forces in the field may use their own national flag [1:4], as well as that of the United Nations. [4:3-4.]
The Lebanese Government has

broken the Arab neutrality bloc with a decision to support the United Nations appeal for aid to Korea. Syria and Iraq were expected to follow suit. [4:1.]

Japan's national police force and coast guard were doubled on General MacArthur's order, for internal security. [1:5.] Chinese Nationalist warships have resumed the search of vessels flying the Nationalist or Chinese Communist flags. Taipei justified this action as "self-protection." [1:7.]

Commissioner McCloy said he did not believe Russia would attack Western Germany but added that it was advisable, for political reasons, to increase Western military forces in Europe. [5:6-7.]

Seventeen countries represented in the Marshall Plan Council for Europe unanimously accepted a program for a European Payments Union, thereby removing major difficulties in easing trade between them. [1:1.]
René Pleven will try to form a new French government with compromise proposals designed to end the political crisis. [5:1.]
An appeal to the labor unions to gird themselves against communism was made by the Amalgamated Clothing Workers of America, C. I. O., in a statement supporting this country's action in Korea. [17:4.]
Evacuation of New Yorkers in the event of an emergency was being studied by Mayor O'Dwyer's Committee on Civilian Defense. The example of London in 1940 was examined. [1:2.]

Index to other news appears on Page 14.

Boy, 14, Admits Firing .45 Pistol At Time of Polo Grounds Killing

A 14-year-old boy confessed yesterday afternoon to the police that he had fired a .45-caliber pistol last Tuesday from the rooftop of his home at the time a man in the near-by Polo Grounds was killed by a bullet of that caliber.

The youth, Robert Mario Peebles, a junior high school student, was questioned by the police since the night of the accident. He was taken from his home at 515 Edgecombe Avenue after three .22-caliber weapons were found in an apartment.

The boy said he had the automatic pistol at a .45 degree elevation when he pulled the trigger. He denied he intended to fire into the Polo Grounds. From where he stood beside a shelter enclosing a stairway to the roof, the police said, he could not even see the ball park. A high parapet surrounds the roof, making it almost impossible for him to have fired down.

The boy placed the time at about

12:30 P. M. At that time, in the gradually filling ball park, Bernard Lawrence Doyle, a 54-year-old former fight manager of Fairview, N. J., sat in the upper tier grandstands behind left field, 1,120 feet from the roof. He had brought the 13-year-old son of a friend to see the Fourth of July double-header between the New York Giants and the Brooklyn Dodgers.

As Mr. Doyle turned to say something to the boy, he slumped forward, shot in the head. He was dead when an ambulance doctor reached him.

The Peebles boy told the police he was informed of the tragedy a half-hour later by a woman on Edgecombe Avenue and went to the basement of his home and took the weapon from its hiding place. The discharged shell he had discarded earlier down a toilet.

The lad said he took the weapon

Continued on Page 28, Column 6

Men of 25 Face Induction First, Then Those 24 Down Through 19

When and if a draft call is issued, inductions in this area and throughout the nation will be made by age groups, with the oldest going first, Selective Service officials reported here yesterday.

They said that, on an induction call from Washington, local draft boards first would go through their files of men who were 25 but who had not yet reached their 26th birthday. Those in that category who were classified 1-A would go into service first.

Men who had reached their 26th birthday, or who needed to attack Western Germany but added that it was advisable, for would be called, according to Selective Service officials.

The next inductions would be made from the 24-year-old group and so on down to the 19-year-olds. The 18-year-olds, who must register for the draft within five days of their birthday, would not be inducted until they became 19.

After a call for inductions was

made from Washington, it would take at least a month or two before anyone in this area put on a uniform, draft officials said.

Some of the preliminary work already has been done by the local draft boards. Each of the 600,000 or so registrants in the five boroughs has answered a questionnaire. These questionnaires are being processed, with those obviously not eligible for service being put in the exempt classifications—married men, World War II veterans, students, essential workers and others.

Those eligible for service will, when the time comes, be ordered to report for a physical examination. Then arrangements would be made for final physical examinations. This process, local Selective Service officials said, would take up to two months.

"We're ready," a spokesman for

Continued on Page 3, Column 2

Foreign films became popular with American audiences in the Fifties. This is a scene from Rashomon, a Japanese film.

Fred Astaire and Vera-Ellen were adorned in formal tails and top hats for this scene from Three Little Words.

"All the News That's Fit to Print"

The New York Times.

LATE CITY EDITION

Fair; scattered showers in afternoon. Fair, less humid tomorrow.

Temperature Range Today—Max.,89; Min., 72
Temperature Yesterday—Max.,90; Min., 74
Full U. S. Weather Bureau Report, Page 4.

Copyright, 1950, by The New York Times Company.

VOL. XCIX.—No. 33,792.

Entered as Second-Class Matter,
Post Office, New York, N. Y.

NEW YORK, TUESDAY, AUGUST 1, 1950.

Times Square, New York 18, N. Y.
Telephone LAckawanna 4-1000

FIVE CENTS

U.S. 2D DIVISION LANDS, RUSHES TO KOREAN LINE; 82,000 GUARDSMEN AND 32,000 MARINES CALLED; SOVIET TO ASK RED CHINA'S ENTRY IN U. N. TODAY

LEOPOLD AGREES TO DELEGATE RULE TO CROWN PRINCE

Tells Nation in a Broadcast He Will Abdicate When His Son Reaches 21

ACTS AS HIS FOES MARCH

Socialist Strikers Converging on Brussels From Walloon Centers Evade Roadblocks

By The United Press.

BRUSSELS, Belgium, Tuesday, Aug. 1—King Leopold III announced today that he would delegate his powers to his 19-year-old son, Crown Prince Baudouin, and would abdicate when the youth reached 21 years of age.

Leopold made the announcement in a radio broadcast to an anxious nation, brought to the brink of civil war, following a night of indecision and delay. Even as he spoke thousands of workers, many of them armed, marched on Brussels to demand his abdication.

"I have decided to ask the Government and Parliament to pass a law insuring attribution of my powers to my son, Prince Baudouin," Leopold broadcast.

Leopold said he would abdicate when Baudouin reached 21 on Sept. 7, 1951.

24 Hours of Negotiation

By MICHAEL CLARK

BRUSSELS, Tuesday, Aug. 1—After twenty-four hours of frantic negotiation, attempts to induce King Leopold III to relinquish the Belgian throne in favor of Crown Prince Baudouin apparently had come to naught early today.

By 8 P. M. Monday general agreement had been reached between the Social Christian (Catholic) Government and the Opposition parties on a solution to the royal question that had brought Belgium to the brink of civil war. Leopold had indicated his willingness to delegate the royal prerogative temporarily to his 19-year-old son with the understanding that the arrangement would subsequently become permanent. The parties had agreed that Prince Baudouin's twenty-first birthday should be the date for the King's final departure. The Prince will be 21 on Sept. 7, 1951.

[The Associated Press reported from Brussels that Leopold had attached two reservations to the agreement. The King refused to be bound to abdicate when Baudouin reached his majority. He also was reported to have decided that the party leaders on whether or not he should leave the country.]

Balks on Conditions

The agreement was drafted in the form of a proclamation to the Belgian people and required only the royal seal of approval before being broadcast to the nation. It had been scheduled for broadcast at 10 P. M.

The Belgian national radio, which normally goes off the air at midnight, was still transmitting recorded music at 3:30 A. M., but no proclamation had yet been read.

At midnight Premier Jean Duvieusart, accompanied by Viscount Albert de Berryer, the King's Chief of Cabinet, and Willy Weemaes, the King's private secretary, returned from an eleventh-hour consultation with Leopold at the Chateau de Laeken and immediately summoned the party leaders to his office.

The conference broke up at 1:50 A. M., when the former Socialist Premier, Paul Henri Spaak, emerged from M. Duvieusart's office. Asked whether a solution had been reached M. Spaak replied: "Ask Duvieusart. We don't want to aggravate the situation."

M. Spaak was followed by a Liberal delegation headed by Roger Motz, chairman of the party, who said: "This is beyond our comprehension. Negotiations are broken off. The stumbling block is the duration of the period of

Continued on Page 13, Column 3

HOUSE PAVING WAY FOR WIDE CONTROLS

Rules Group Clears Truman Bill, but Orders Debate on 'Tougher' Substitutes

By CLAYTON KNOWLES

WASHINGTON, July 31—The House Rules Committee left the door open today for passage of sweeping price, wage and rationing controls as it cleared the Administration's economic mobilization bill to the floor.

It approved a full day of debate for the measure, but under a carefully-worded rule, specifically authorized consideration of at least two substitutes. Each of these substitutes—one offered under Republican sponsorship and the other under Democratic—calls for blanket price and wage controls.

Administration forces, virtually conceding that the President's limited program would be expanded, hastily prepared to draft their own version of these controls. It will be offered as an amendment. Details were not available tonight.

Sentiment for all-out mobilization, sweeping through both houses of Congress with gathering force, was so great that the Senate Banking and Currency Committee, completing consideration of the President's proposals, decided to devote the whole of tomorrow to the question of expanding the controls.

The only action by the Security Council today was to adopt a resolution requesting Mr. Lie, the Economic and Social Council and other United Nations organs to cooperate in supplying relief for the civilian population of South Korea. The vote was 9 to 0, with Yugoslavia abstaining.

The Republican Policy Committee in the House will meet tomorrow morning to plot a party course. The Democratic Policy Committee in the Senate will meet in the afternoon, presumably to consider action on the same subject. The decision for both will be difficult because sentiment cuts across party lines.

Democratic Congressional leaders conferred this morning with President Truman. When they left the White House, the indication

Continued on Page 26, Column 4

Dewey Sees U. S. in Imminent Peril; No-Strike Pledge Offered by Meany

A warning by Governor Dewey that the United States was now in "imminent peril" and an official labor offer of a no-strike pledge to help meet that peril marked the opening yesterday of the four-day convention of the New York State Federation of Labor.

Mr. Dewey told 1,100 delegates at the Commodore Hotel, representing 1,300,000 members of organized labor, that this country's danger was "immediate, urgent, and perhaps desperate." Unless "fast and tough" action is taken immediately, he said, the free world is likely to be swallowed up by the Communist world.

Although not professing to know the "timetable of world communism," Mr. Dewey asserted that it obviously included "invasion in satellite nations from Bulgaria through Greece to the Mediterranean," an invasion of Yugoslavia, "which might come at any time," as well as the conquest of Tibet, Indo-China, and ultimately all Asia.

The grand goal of communism, short of absolute world domination, is winning the industrial capacity of Germany and Japan, which would free Russia from fear of American productive capacity, Mr. Dewey asserted.

He argued that Russia would be able to attack Alaska with an army of any magnitude that she chose, and that Soviet planes could easily bomb the great production centers and cities of the continental United States, with the Red pilots bailing out to become prisoners of war.

"It is believed that the Soviet could also easily conduct what is called 'Operation Hot Springs'—that is, sending planes to bomb the great production plants and cities of the entire country, then having the pilots bail out, and spend the rest of the war comfortably as prisoners of war at Hot Springs," the Governor explained. "Needless to say, we could not make similar plans with any confidence that our pilots would be similarly treated."

"It is reliably reported that mobilization of the nation's economic

Continued on Page 16, Column 1

U.S. OPPOSES MALIK

Will Demand Council Go Ahead With Korea, Condemn the North

SOVIET DEFEAT SEEN

Delegates Move to Get U. N. Relief Supplies for War Area Civilians

By THOMAS J. HAMILTON

LAKE SUCCESS, July 31—Jacob A. Malik, Soviet representative on the United Nations Security Council, who is president of the Council for August, proposed today that it take up the admission of Communist China as the first item on its agenda when it convenes at 3 o'clock tomorrow afternoon.

The United States delegation and other members of the majority made it clear today that, despite the agenda submitted by Mr. Malik, they would demand that the Council proceed with the Korean question tomorrow. To this end the United States delegation submitted a resolution this afternoon condemning North Korea authorities "for their continued defiance of the United Nations," and calling upon all nations to refrain from assisting them and "from action which might lead to the spread of the Korean conflict to other areas and thereby further endanger international peace and security."

Warren R. Austin, the United States representative, asked that the resolution be placed on the agenda of the next meeting, and it is understood that the resolution will be used by the United States to support its proposal that the Council reject Mr. Malik's version.

The agenda proposed by Mr. Malik, which reached Secretary General Trygve Lie by courier this afternoon, a few minutes after the Council had held its last meeting before the Soviet Union's return, listed the "peaceful settlement of the Korean question" as the second item.

The only action by the Security Council today was to adopt a resolution requesting Mr. Lie, the Economic and Social Council and other United Nations organs to cooperate in supplying relief for the civilian population of South Korea. The vote was 9 to 0, with Yugoslavia abstaining.

This resolution, it is believed, completes the measures needed immediately in the Korean situation. Proposals to amend the rules of procedure, so as to make doubly sure that Mr. Malik would not be able to prevent the Council from meeting to deal with another Communist aggression, were laid aside because a majority of the Council believed that it would be able to

Continued on Page 8, Column 3

4 DIVISIONS LISTED

Other Guard Units Set for Service by Sept. 1 Are 2 Combat Teams

FORCES GAIN 114,000

More Medium Bombers Sent to Help in Korea —Air Marine Expands

By AUSTIN STEVENS

WASHINGTON, July 31—President Truman today ordered to active duty in thirty days four of the nation's twenty-seven National Guard divisions, two Guard regimental combat teams, and other supporting units.

The President also authorized the expansion of two Marine Corps divisions to full wartime strength of about 23,000.

Today's steps will press into service in the armed forces some 114,000 men in addition to the 100,000 who will start to swell the Army's ranks through the Selective Service System. Of the 114,000, about 82,000 are Guardsmen who will go into the Army.

A National Guard division, at maximum strength, has about 18,000 men and a Guard regimental combat team some 5,000. The nature and size of the supporting units called today were not disclosed.

Expanding the two Marine divisions to war strength will mean an increase of 32,000 in the Corps. There are 14,000, about 7,000 each, in the two divisions now as compared with the 46,000 combined total they will have on a full combat footing. The Marines have already called 50,000 of their Organized Reserves.

The Chief Executive's action was announced at the Pentagon by General Tryve Lie and by letter from Louis Johnson, Secretary of Defense. The move had been recommended by the Joint Chiefs of Staff.

Names of the divisions involved were withheld pending their commanders' receipt of direct orders from the Defense Department.

Secretary Johnson announced

Continued on Page 17, Column 6

COVERING A KEY ROAD AT THE KOREAN FRONT

American soldiers manning a 75-mm. recoilless rifle
Associated Press Wirephoto

TRUMAN PLEA ADDS 4 BILLION ARMS AID

Congress Acts to Rush Extra Funds to Provide Weapons for Our Anti-Red Allies

By C. P. TRUSSELL

WASHINGTON, July 31—President Truman told Congressional key men today that he wanted to throw, as quickly as possible, an additional $4,000,000,000 into the arming of nations resisting communism. This would be on top of the $1,222,500,000 recently authorized by Congress to carry the Mutual Defense Assistance Program through its second year.

In another of the stepped-up developments today the Senate voted $2,450,000,000 to carry forward the Marshall Plan for the economic recovery of Western Europe. It warned the sixteen beneficiary na-

Continued on Page 15, Column 5

General at Chinju Reports Reds 'Beat Hell Out of Us'

By W. H. LAWRENCE

ON SOUTHERN FRONT, Korea, July 31—Northern Korean Communist troops "beat hell out of us" Monday morning, grabbed the town of Chinju and with it one of the best airfields in Korea.

That was the candid description of the battle given by a general officer of the United States Twenty-fourth Division, who directed the defense of the strategic rail-highway center during the final hours.

The Communist drive split the defending forces in two and sent them falling back in two different directions under heavy fire from the flanks.

Lost in the battle were three Sherman tanks, precious because they are scarce here. They were presumed destroyed by a tank company of fifteen men who stayed just outside fallen Chinju hours after American troops evacuated in the vain hope they would receive proper fanbelts, the lack of which had immobilized them, or that a railway train would come in the nick of time to haul them away.

Chinju itself fell between 5:30 and 6 A. M. Monday and by late afternoon United States troops had regrouped sufficiently to set up a new defense barrier on the main highway about six miles east of the town and only forty-six airline miles west of Pusan, United States main supply port and the obvious objective of this Red drive across the southern peninsula.

The semi-annual report of the Atomic Energy Commission said that the possibility of using radiological substances as war weapons was being investigated. It declared that the hydrogen bomb project was under way but could not be discussed. [1:6-7.]

The Soviet Union's delegate to the United Nations, Jacob A. Malik, who will assume the presidency of the Security Council for one month, recommended that the question of Communist China's admission to the United Nations be considered first when the Council meets today. Mr. Malik listed in second place on his proposed agenda the "peaceful settlement of the Korean question." [1:3.] The Council adopted a resolution calling for aid by United Nations agencies to South Korea's civilian population. [9:1.]

In London an official source disclosed that mediation of the Korean conflict by Asian nations might be proposed by Communist China. [5:1.]

King Leopold agreed to yield his powers to his son, the Crown Prince Baudouin, and to abdicate his throne when Baudouin reaches the age of 21. [1:1.]

NEW FORCES MOVED DIRECTLY FROM U. S.

Arrival of Fresh Troops in Pusan Stirs Optimism — Men Stand Voyage Well

By RICHARD J. H. JOHNSTON

PUSAN, South Korea, July 31—Heavily equipped and trained in peak efficiency, fresh combat troops of the United States Army poured from transports here today to add strength to hard-pressed American and South Korean forces against the battleline of North Korean Communist invaders.

Arrival of the fresh troops lifted much of the gloom of the Army command in this port over startling Communist successes in the south and west. Tonight there is an air of optimism that has not been observable for the last four days during which port units and engineers have been alerted for emergencies.

Arrival of the new forces gave heart to frontline elements who were informed within a few hours that reinforcements had come to

Continued on Page 6, Column 3

Weapons Using Radioactive Poison Pushed by Atomic Energy Board

By HAROLD B. HINTON

WASHINGTON, July 31—The Atomic Energy Commission reported to Congress today that it was continuing studies concerning the feasibility of using radiological substances as war weapons.

Such weapons would contain radioactive poisons in concentrations great enough to kill large populations if dropped on big cities.

Intimations that such work was under way were contained in the annual report Louis Johnson, Secretary of Defense, sent to President Truman last March 31.

The radiological warfare part of the commission's semi-annual report was a by-product of its discussion of protecting workers in atomic energy plants, as well as the populace living near such plants, from the hazards of intensive radiation. He said that no detector of the type of an ionization chamber would detect such a weapon, packaged for mass oceanic shipment, and that he knew of no other type of detector that would do it.

On the subject of the hydrogen

Continued on Page 18, Column 5

uid radioactive wastes through evaporation.

Such wastes may turn out to have industrial value, or may be used in the fabrication of weapons, according to Dr. Walter Claus, acting chief of the biophysics branch of the commission's Division of Biology and Medicine. He declined to conjecture whether such substances could be delivered on an enemy in a mist or dust.

Dr. Karl Z. Morgan, Director of Health Physics at the Oak Ridge installation, in discussing the report, minimized the possibility of detecting atomic weapons concealed on board incoming ships, as has been proposed in a bill passed by Congress. He said that no detector of the type of an ionization chamber would detect such a weapon, packaged for mass oceanic shipment, and that he knew of no other type of detector that would do it.

On the subject of the hydrogen

Continued on Page 18, Column 5

FOE SPURS ATTACK

Invaders in a Desperate Effort to Smash U. S. Defending Troops

AIM AT PUSAN, TAEGU

South Korean Workmen Digging Trenches and Gun Emplacements

By LINDESAY PARROTT

TOKYO, Tuesday, Aug. 1—Reinforcements from the United States landed in South Korea yesterday. Today the North Korean invaders drove against the whole western and southern section of the United States and South Korean defense line in a desperate effort to break through or at least smash the defending United States divisions.

Some additional United States reinforcements began arriving at a southern port last night. This morning the assembling of men and their weapons was in progress.

The new force, of an undisclosed number, together with those that had arrived yesterday lost no time in preparing to enter the battle against the hard-thrusting invaders along the defense perimeter in an attempt to win the race against time, bolstering the battle-weary defenders on the northern and western lines.

[News agencies identified the reinforcements as troops of the United States Second Infantry Division. The Associated Press reported that the United States troops that came ashore Tuesday moved up rapidly to bolster the front lines.]

Intelligence sources said that the Communists had launched their all-out push for a quick decision, using familiar, successful tactics. They were probing the outnumbered United States lines with infiltration around the flanks, then striking hard blows at weak points, firing on the defenders from the rear as they forced a retreat and hoarding their now scarce tanks for vital efforts.

Pusan and Taegu Objectives

Their objectives were the landing port of Pusan, key base of the bridgehead that is all that remains to the United Nations in the Korean peninsula, and the communications center of Taegu to the northward. Capture of either would cut off the United States troops in the north from the last good port in Korea.

The deepest point of penetration this morning was at Hyopchon, thirty-one air miles from Taegu. Hyopchon fell to a North Korean column that pushed due eastward from Kochang along country roads with a second force advanced northeastward from that road and rail center up the highway to Kumchon. It was halted south of Kumchon by the hurried formation of a new United States and South Korean line.

Hyopchon was taken almost without opposition until the last minute, the invaders penetrating through a hole punched in thinly held defenses. Two bridges blown out before the approaches to the town might have slowed but did not stop the advance.

The roads south and east of the town this morning was at Hyopchon, were dotted by thousands of white-clad South Korean laborers, working frantically in a blazing heat to dig trenches and gun emplacements as the defense prepared further stands until reinforcements could be built up behind them.

The heaviest concentrations still appeared to be along the south coast, where yesterday the invaders drove Americans of the Twenty-fourth Infantry Division from the blazing town of Chinju. They pushed ahead six miles east of the ruined city and, according to latest reports, were feeling United States positions forty-six miles from Pusan.

With the capture of Hyopchon and Chinju, the Communists definitely had crossed the mountain spine of Korea and had emerged into the fist river valley and paddy

Continued on Page 3, Column 1

World News Summarized

TUESDAY, AUGUST 1, 1950

Troops sent directly from the United States landed in Korea yesterday to help in the fight to hold the United States bridgehead. This area continued to shrink under the furious attacks of the North Korean armies on the entire western and southern sections of the front. The foe, advancing eastward from Kochang, seized Hyopchon, thirty-one miles from Taegu, and was threatening Kunchon. [1:8.]

The arrival of fresh troops had an electric effect in lifting the morale of the embattled American fighting forces. [1:7.] American troops at Chinju were forced to give up that key center and to fall back within forty-six airline miles of Pusan after a defeat. [1:6.]

General MacArthur rejected the offer of the Chinese Nationalists to send 33,000 troops from Formosa to aid in the defense of South Korea. [4:3.]

Four of the country's twenty-seven National Guard Divisions were ordered to active duty by President Truman, who also authorized that two under-strength Marine Corps divisions be built up to their full wartime power. [1:4.] The Chief Executive asked Congressional leaders for an additional $4,000,000,000 to be used for arming nations allied with the United States in combating communism. [1:5.] The Senate approved an appropriation of $2,450,000,000 for Marshall Plan assistance after having rejected attempts to reduce the allocation by $718,893,473. [17:4.]

The sentiment for full mobilization of the nation's economic

might was so great in Congress that it appeared likely that the lawmakers would provide for complete control of prices, wages and rationing. [1:2.]

The semi-annual report of the Atomic Energy Commission said that the possibility of using radiological substances as war weapons was being investigated. It declared that the hydrogen bomb project was under way but could not be discussed. [1:6-7.]

The Soviet Union's delegate to the United Nations, Jacob A. Malik, who will assume the presidency of the Security Council for one month, recommended that the question of Communist China's admission to the United Nations be considered first when the Council meets today. Mr. Malik listed in second place on his proposed agenda the "peaceful settlement of the Korean question." [1:3.] The Council adopted a resolution calling for aid by United Nations agencies to South Korea's civilian population. [9:1.]

In London an official source disclosed that mediation of the Korean conflict by Asian nations might be proposed by Communist China. [5:1.]

King Leopold agreed to yield his powers to his son, the Crown Prince Baudouin, and to abdicate his throne when Baudouin reaches the age of 21. [1:1.]

NEWS BULLETINS FROM THE TIMES

Every hour on the hour
7 A. M. through Midnight

WQXR AM 1560
WQXR FM 96.3

Index to other news appears on Page 24.

"All the News That's Fit to Print"

The New York Times.

Copyright, 1950, by The New York Times Company.

LATE CITY EDITION
Fair and pleasant today and tomorrow, but cool tonight.
Temperature Range Today-Max.,80; Min.,65
Temperatures Yesterday—Max.,69; Min.,65
Full U. S. Weather Bureau Report, Page 27

VOL. XCIX. No. 33,795. Entered as Second-Class Matter. Post Office, New York, N. Y. NEW YORK, FRIDAY, AUGUST 4, 1950. Times Square, New York 18, N. Y. Telephone LAckawanna 4-1000 FIVE CENTS

U. N. COUNCIL DEFEATS SOVIET BID FOR RED CHINA, VOTES U. S. AGENDA; HEAVY FIGHTING ON KOREAN FRONT

O'DWYER CRITICIZES 'POLITICAL' CONTROL OF M'DONALD POLICE

Mayor Charges Prosecutor Refused Officer Supervisor of Rookies in Inquiry

ACCEPTS GRAND JURY BID

District Attorney Terms Move 'Another Effort to Disrupt' Gambling Investigation

By MILTON HONIG

After having accepted an invitation to appear as a witness on Monday before the special grand jury in Brooklyn, Mayor O'Dwyer charged yesterday that District Attorney Miles F. McDonald's special staff of rookie patrolmen were being exposed to politicians.

The Mayor's critical remarks came after he had made public a report from Commissioner of Investigation James H. Sheils on an inquiry into charges of alleged misconduct by two of the young patrolmen who were assigned to the prosecutor's office for the gambling investigation.

The report said that according to the testimony at the hearings the two officers had "appeared to be under the influence of liquor" when they were involved in a fight with several youths on July 7.

It then asserted that last December, when patrolmen first were selected by Mr. McDonald for special assignment in connection with the inquiry, the Police Department offered the services of a superior police officer to supervise the "official" conduct of those chosen.

Says McDonald Refused Offer

Describing the offer as a "well-established" practice of the Police Department, the report said that Mr. McDonald received the opportunity of choosing any officer he wished.

"That offer was refused," it was said. "In connection with their special assignment, these policemen receive their assignments and instructions from civilian employes in the District Attorney's office, the Assistant District Attorneys, the chief investigator of the special investigating unit and investigators assigned. The policemen are not under the supervision of a superior police officer."

Mayor O'Dwyer was asked whether he felt a police officer, rather than a civilian, should be in charge of these men.

"In my five years as Mayor there never was one time when politicians were allowed to supervise policemen or have anything to do with them," he replied. "[William] Dahut comes from Frank Nolan's club and Frank Nolan is employed by Cashmore [Brooklyn Borough President John Cashmore]. I certainly do object to fifty-six policemen being exposed to that kind of political contact."

Mr. Dahut is chief investigator of the special investigating unit. Mr. Nolan is assistant Commissioner of Public Works in Brooklyn.

"I won the battle of keeping politics out of the Police Department until this time," the Mayor continued. "This time I lost because McDonald refused Chief Flath's [Chief Inspector August W. Flath] offer to have the men supervised by superior officers of the Police Department of his own choosing."

"Did Dahut have any particular qualifications for supervising the police?" he was asked.

"Dahut was appointed from Frank Nolan's club as a county detective in the District Attorney's office while I was in the Army. He's been there since."

Prosecutor Denounces Criticism

The Mayor's attack on Mr. Dahut was described by Mr. McDonald as "another effort by the Mayor to disrupt the investigation" and his remarks concerning political domination as "sheer hypocrisy."

"The Mayor, in attacking Mr. Dahut, has assumed the role of Goliath attacking David, and like David, Mr. Dahut is protected by the armor of truth and right," the prosecutor asserted. "The Mayor certainly should be able to find a more formidable adversary."

He pointed out that Mr. Dahut, who by statute has the equivalent of civil service status and cannot be removed except on charges by the District Attorney, was appointed a county detective by Mr. O'Dwyer's chief assistant, who acted as District Attorney while Mr. O'Dwyer was absent during the war.

Mr. McDonald said that he "believed" that Mr. Dahut had succeeded his father, who was "appointed by the Mayor himself."

"The Mayor's remarks concern-

Continued on Page 10, Column 5

Valuations in Nassau Rise by $108,739,480

Special to THE NEW YORK TIMES

MINEOLA, L. I., Aug. 3—Assessed valuations on which Nassau County's school tax rates are based have increased $108,739,480 over last year's figure.

Statistics released here today by Emil M. Podeyn, chairman of the Board of Assessors, showed the county's valuation for school purposes in 1950-51 is $1,366,928,954. This does not include the separate cities of Glen Cove and Long Beach.

Mr. Podeyn said the school tax rates would be established after local school board meetings to be held before Aug. 15. The rates are based on the sixty-two school district budgets voted locally.

Collection of school taxes in Nassau last year was above 99 per cent until the bankrupt Long Island Rail Road stopped its payments. This brought the figure down to 95.88 per cent, which, Mr. Podeyn said, was still the highest in the state.

POLICE TO QUESTION ALL SUGAR SELLERS

City Survey to Determine if Racketeers Are Active in Scare-Buying Market

By JOSEPH C. INGRAHAM

In the hope of determining if racketeers have moved into the sugar market here the city started yesterday to make a complete survey of the situation.

The police were assigned to question all retail tradesmen handling sugar about prices, quantities and sources of supply, while James H. Sheils, Commissioner of Investigation, said he had subpoened the records of refineries, wholesalers and brokers.

The main purpose of the investigation, Mayor O'Dwyer explained, "is to isolate persons who attempt unfair dealing." Eventually, he added, the city will look into price gouging and hoarding and check unsavory elements in other key industries where war-induced shortages may be felt by consumers.

The Mayor also made known that he had conferred for ninety minutes with Rudolph Halley, counsel to the Senate committee investigating organized crime. He described it as "a general discussion" and declined to say if it dealt with reports that a huge black market in sugar was flourishing here.

"The only comment I have," the Mayor said, is that "every help this Administration can give the Senate special investigators will be gladly given. We've been a long time waiting for this kind of help."

Sees New Brokers Active

Emphasizing that there was no shortage of sugar, the Mayor said that when a shortage in a basic commodity like sugar did occur there were complaints of under-the-table charges by new brokers who normally were not in that particular business.

"These brokers come out of the woods when there is a shortage," he added.

The Mayor also noted that shortages encouraged unfair dealings, and under-the-table practices affected retail prices. "The city intends to be on the job," he declared.

While Mr. Sheils acknowledged that the city could do nothing legally to curb hoarding or control prices, he said the sugar survey and the other food investigations to follow might be termed "a

Continued on Page 29, Column 4

AUTOMATIC CURBS IF PRICES RISE 5% PASSED BY HOUSE

Tentative Vote Is Taken in Hectic Session With Bill Being Redrafted on Floor

TRUMAN ASSAILS ACTION

He Argues Proposal Would Cause Price Increase, Leading to Higher Pay Demands

By CLAYTON KNOWLES

Special to THE NEW YORK TIMES.

WASHINGTON, Aug. 3—The House of Representatives approved on a tentative basis tonight an economic mobilization bill authorizing selective application of price and wage controls if retail prices go 5 per cent or more above the Government's Consumers' Price Index for June 15.

President Truman later vehemently assailed this approach for automatic controls as an invitation to a 5 per cent rise in prices.

A product of nearly eight hours of hectic and hurried legislating, the bill at this stage deviated in other substantial respects from what the President desires. At the day's end, Administration forces in the House were uncertain whether they wanted to pass it or kill it. Whichever way they turned, they were not certain they would have the votes to carry through on their decision.

The legislation in its present form was approved by the House, sitting as the committee of the whole, by a vote of 159 to 128. With the alternative before the House a Republican-sponsored substitute even more objectionable to the Administration, Speaker Sam Rayburn of Texas cracked the party whip for the measure at hand.

He swung about twenty-five Southern Democrats in line behind the measure with an unspoken understanding that they were free thereafter to vote their convictions.

The action taken today must, in effect, be reaffirmed again in committee, then be approved again, the House to prevail.

Major Changes Listed

As it stands, the bill departs from the Administration's wishes in the following aspects:

1. It mandates some form of price and wage controls when prices rise 5 per cent above the June 15 Consumers' Price Index of the Bureau of Labor Statistics.
2. The life of the legislation is limited to March 31, 1951, which would make it little more than a seven-month enactment.
3. Specific authority for the President to set up a War Labor Board to settle labor disputes was eliminated.
4. Provisions for regulation of commodity speculation. were dropped.

President Truman told his news conference this afternoon that he was completely opposed to any automatic price-wage controls. He said that he did not think much of the House action on this score.

If you set an automatic price rise, the President asserted, then you have got to meet an automatic wage rise, and the prices and wages will spiral as they did in World War II. He said that if the country was to have price control, it should have it and have it in the right way.

He said that it should be an authorization for a rollback on prices and wages to levels apply-

Continued on Page 30, Column 5

U. S. Cancels Robeson's Passport After He Refuses to Surrender It

By A. J. GORDON

The State Department has asked Paul Robeson, a native American, a noted singer and a leader in left-wing movements, to surrender his passport. He refused to give it up.

Local and national officials of the Immigration and Customs services and the Federal Bureau of Investigation have been ordered to stop Robeson if he tries to leave the country.

Any trip abroad that Robeson would make would not be in the interest of the United States, a spokesman for the State Department said last night. This official said the demand for the passport had been made a week ago.

Up to last night, the Passport Division of the State Department in Washington had not received compliance with the request for the passport. The State Department wants physical possession of the passport, and efforts will be made to obtain it, it was said.

Robeson's passport has been marked "null and void" on the records of the State Department. This notation, it was explained, will prevent Robeson leaving the country on any airplane, ship, bus, automobile or in any other manner at points at which Immigration or other Federal officials concerned with travel are stationed.

Although neither State Department nor Immigration officials would make extended comment, it was learned that Robeson's activities in left-wing movements and his outspoken criticism of this country's international dealings had much to do with the revocation of the passport. Government officials in Washington said it was an uncommon practice to "pick up" a passport, particularly if issued to a native-born person.

It was pointed out that Robeson,

Continued on Page 22, Column 3

REDS PUSHED BACK

Retreat After a Six-Hour Battle—25th Division Rushed to South

AMERICANS SET NEW LINE

Dig In Along Naktong River and Disperse Small Communist Patrols Getting Across

By LINDESAY PARROTT

Special to THE NEW YORK TIMES.

TOKYO, Friday, Aug. 4—Hard fighting raged last night and this morning on the southern Korean front as United States and South Korean defenders dug in new positions along the Naktong River line after yesterday's "planned" withdrawal.

The battle occurred east of Chinju, where the Communists attacked shortly after midnight and were driven back after a six-hour battle at 6 A. M. today. Gen. Douglas MacArthur's communiqué issued at 12:40 o'clock this afternoon called the engagement the only major conflict during the last twenty-four hours, as the Americans and South Koreans consolidated their lines behind the winding Naktong River and the Communists probed forward to find new weak spots.

The fighting on the south front, which has been held by the Twenty-fourth Division, was inaugurated when the invaders tried their familiar tactics of infiltrating behind the defense lines, then pushing their frontal assault to drive the defenders back upon roadblocks set up by infiltrators in their rear. This time, General MacArthur said, the tactic achieved "little success."

Official reports indicated that the invaders today rapidly were preparing a new assault before the United States reinforcements now landed in Korea could be brought to bear. Considerable rail and convoy movements are in progress behind the Communist lines, it was stated, the invaders apparently again daring daylight movements despite United States air superiority to reorganize and regroup their forces with the utmost rapidity regardless of loss.

The maximum pressure was in the south, where the Twenty-fourth Division, after a counter-attack toward Chinju and subsequent withdrawal, still apparently was holding bridgeheads across

Continued on Page 2, Column 2

MARINES IN KOREA ON WAY TO THE FRONT

Americans marching to a train to take them to the combat area after landing at a South Korean port.

Associated Press Wirephoto via Radio from Tokyo

DEFERMENT POLICY ON RESERVES IS SET

Also Covers the National Guard —Action Comes on Eve of Big Expected Call by Army

Statement of deferment policy on reservists, Page 11.

By AUSTIN STEVENS

Special to THE NEW YORK TIMES.

WASHINGTON, Aug. 3—The Department of Defense issued tonight, on the eve of an expected call to duty of a substantial number of Army Reservists, a strict policy governing deferments for Reserves of all armed services and the National Guard.

Affecting 2,555,000 members of the civilian components of the Army, Navy and Air Force, the policy stated that exemption from service would be granted only when the reservist was engaged in "a critical occupation necessary to a highly essential activity."

Deferments will be for maxi-

Continued on Page 11, Column 1

World News Summarized

FRIDAY, AUGUST 4, 1950

The United Nations Security Council in a bitter session yesterday rejected Soviet attempts to have it consider once more the admission of Communist China and scored another point over the Russians in deciding to discuss the "Complaint of Aggression" in Korea. Observers were disturbed over India's attitude and the prospect of propaganda gains by Moscow. [1:8.] Prime Minister Nehru in New Delhi defended his support of Communist China and denounced the Western powers for acting with "little awareness" of Far Eastern problems. [1:6.]

In the extreme south of Korea, a six-hour battle took place east of Chinju when the invading forces attempted to penetrate new defense lines. They were repulsed. Throughout the day artillery of both sides hammered communications. Small parties of the enemy crossed the Naktong River but were dispersed. American reserves were being rushed into position for the expected battle [1:4; map on page 2.] Enemy patrols reached the west bank of the Naktong. [1:6-7.] An American tank-led column patrolled successfully far into Communist territory. [3:1.]

President Truman announced that W. Averell Harriman would visit General MacArthur for a briefing on the political situation. [4:2.] The President signed and made final the authority to increase the armed forces to any level required by the present or future emergencies. [10:4.] The House has tentatively approved an economic mobilization bill providing for price and wage controls. [1:3.] A strict ruling on deferments, affecting about 2,500,000 reservists, was laid down by the Defense Department. [1:5.]

Britain has proposed an increase of 45 per cent in her defense budget, the details of which have been set forth in a memorandum to Washington. [1:7.] In Paris, the French have maintained that a maximum effort on their part must be paralleled by similar steps in London and Washington. They favor an over-all treatment of defense rather than a series of national programs. [4:5.]

The Senate refused to reconsider its approval of an E. C. A. loan to Spain, although the President had earlier strongly condemned it. [6:3.] Mr. Truman said the appointment of a regular Minister to the Vatican was being considered. [10:7.]

The State Department has ordered Paul Robeson, the singer and leader in left-wing movements, to surrender his passport. Mr. Robeson has refused. [1:2-3.]

Steps were taken by the city to act against possible racketeering in sugar. This will be the first of a series of investigations in key industries where shortages may be felt by the public. [1:2.]

NEWS BULLETINS FROM THE TIMES
Every hour on the hour
7 A. M. through Midnight
WQXR AM 1560
WQXR FM 96.3

Index to other news appears on Page 22.

Food Prices Jump 2 to 3% in a Month

By The Associated Press

WASHINGTON, Aug. 3—Led by meat, food prices rose an indicated 2 to 3 per cent in the month ended July 15 but other living costs held fairly steady, the Government reported today.

However, prices of many items besides food can be expected to climb later.

Ewan Clague, director of the Bureau of Labor Statistics, gave the information to the Senate Banking Committee, which wanted it in studying proposed price-control legislation.

NEHRU DENOUNCES WEST'S ASIA POLICY

Says Action Is Taken Without Knowledge of Orient, Although He Backs U. N. on Korea

By ROBERT TRUMBULL

Special to THE NEW YORK TIMES.

NEW DELHI, India, Aug. 3—Prime Minister Jawaharlal Nehru defended his support of the United Nations resolutions on Korea in a seventy-minute speech to Parliament today.

He digressed from the subject at considerable length to back the claim of Communist China to a seat in the United Nations Security Council and to castigate the Western powers for having adopted "decisions affecting vast areas of Asia without understanding the real needs and mind of the people."

There is no doubt that a resolution endorsing Pandit Nehru's actions in the Korean situation,

Continued on Page 7, Column 3

BRITISH TO ADD 45% TO DEFENSE OUTLAY

£3,400,000,000 Over 3 Years Hinges in Part on U. S. Aid—Truman Hails 'Example'

Text of British memorandum to U. S. on defense, Page 5.

By CLIFTON DANIEL

Special to THE NEW YORK TIMES

LONDON, Aug. 3—A 45 per cent increase in defense expenditure for the next three years was proposed by the British Cabinet tonight in a memorandum to the United States Government. The increase was, in part, conditional on American financial assistance.

The memorandum was prepared by the Cabinet in consultation with the chiefs of the military services in response to a request from Washington for information on the additional defense effort that Britain might undertake, including new arms production that might be started with United States assistance.

The information from Britain and the other European members of the North Atlantic Pact had been requested for use in planning the proposed $4,000,000,000 program of extra arms aid to the allies of the United States.

The British memorandum stated that the Government intended to increase defense expenditure to a total of £3,400,000,000 [$9,520,000,000] over the next three years, or an average of £1,100,000,000 a year, compared with the pre-Korean defense budget of £780,000,000.

This meant, the statement said, that the Government was prepared "in principle" to increase defense spending from nearly 8

Continued on Page 5, Column 1

Blasting of Bridges Impedes Foe In Push on Taegu From Northwest

By W. H. LAWRENCE

Special to THE NEW YORK TIMES

ON NAKTONG RIVER LINE, South Korea, Aug. 3—North Korean patrols reached the west bank of the Naktong river Thursday and the enemy's long-range artillery was shelling United States supply trucks moving on the main north-south road just a few miles southwest of Taegu.

There was one report that a small guerrilla force was loose in the mountains two miles southwest of Taegu on this side of the river and two truckloads of South Korean policemen were dispatched to wipe out this latest threat to the United States defensive positions.

All the United States forces north of the critical Chinju sector withdrew to the Naktong line late Wednesday, successfully disengaging themselves from the enemy without losses, avoiding pursuit and blowing up highway and rail bridges over which the enemy could move his heavy equipment.

The United States forces west of Pusan voluntarily gave up a possible mountain defense line that never had been tested in combat and took advantage of the terrain by blasting huge craters in the winding, hairpin mountain trail to delay the advance of the enemy's armor.

A single enemy plane harassed without damage the final United States convoy to leave the Koryong area about 4:45 A. M. Thursday. It attacked an empty truck convoy as it approached the town, putting a few bullet holes in one truck and it made one strafing attack upon a small troop concentration in the city later but no one was hit.

As the final forces moved east-

Continued on Page 2, Column 8

RUSSIA BEATEN, 8-1

Malik and Austin Bitter in Debate That Gives Moscow a Platform

PROCEDURE THE QUESTION

Aggression in Korea Will Be Discussed but Propaganda Victory for Reds Is Seen

Verbatim record of the U. N. meeting is on Pages 8 and 9.

By THOMAS J. HAMILTON

Special to THE NEW YORK TIMES

LAKE SUCCESS, Aug. 3—The United Nations Security Council, after bitter exchanges between the United States and the Soviet Union, tonight beat down Soviet attempts to have it take up once more the admission of Communist China, to be followed by consideration of the "Peaceful Settlement of the Korean Question."

Instead the Council voted to continue discussion of the Korean question under the same agenda heading, "Complaint of Aggression Upon the Republic of Korea," under which it has been dealing with the North Korean invasion since June 25.

As a result of the decisions tonight this is the only item before the Council, but the Soviet Union is expected to renew its campaign to have the Council take up again the admission of Communist China and review its decision to authorize the use of United Nations forces for the defense of South Korea.

Four Votes Are Taken

Four votes, taken in quick succession, finally extricated the Council from the procedural morass into which it had been plunged by the unexpected return of Jacob A. Malik, Soviet representative, who is president of the Council for August, from his walkout on the China question.

On Tuesday, at the first meeting called by Mr. Malik, the Council defeated his attempt to expel Dr. T. F. Tsiang, representative of Nationalist China, by the parliamentary maneuver of ruling that he was no longer a member of the Council.

Tonight the Council paved the way for the decisive votes by setting aside Mr. Malik's ruling that the Council vote in turn on the inclusion in the agenda of the admission of Communist China, the "Peaceful Settlement of the Korean Question," and the "Complaint of Aggression Upon the Republic of Korea."

British Motion Adopted

Instead the Council, by a vote of 7 to 2, adopted a British motion that it vote first on whether to continue discussing the Korean question under its previous heading. The vote was as follows:

For (7)—United States, Britain, France, Nationalist China, Cuba, Ecuador and Norway; against (2)—Soviet Union and India; abstain (2)—Egypt and Yugoslavia.

The votes on the inclusion of the three items on the agenda were as follows:

1. "Complaint of Aggression upon the Republic of Korea"; For (8)—United States, Britain, France, Nationalist China, Cuba, Ecuador, Egypt and Norway; against (1)—Soviet Union; abstain (2)—India and Yugoslavia.
2. "Recognition of the Representative of the Central People's Government of the People's Republic of China as the Representative of China": For (5)—Soviet Union, Britain, India, Norway and Yugoslavia; against (5)—United States, France, Nationalist China, Cuba and Ecuador; abstain (1)—Egypt. (Seven votes out of the eleven members is required for a majority in the Council.)
3. "Peaceful Settlement of the Korean Question": For (3)—Soviet Union, Egypt and India; against (7)—United States, Britain, France, Nationalist China, Cuba, Ecuador and Norway; abstain (1)—Yugoslavia.

But although views of the United States prevailed on every vote, a number of delegates that are its consistent supporters left Lake Success with a sense of foreboding over the possibility that the Soviet Union, from a propaganda point of

Continued on Page 9, Column 8

U.S. delegate Warren Austin was the cause of much excitement during the Korean debates at the U.N. in 1950, when he exhibited a Russian-made North Korean sub-machine gun to support charges of Soviet aid to North Korea.

General Douglas MacArthur, Allied Commander in Korea, shouts orders during the Inchon landing, 1950.

American soldiers charging past Communist dead in Korea.

"All the News That's Fit to Print"

The New York Times.

LATE CITY EDITION
Some cloudiness early today, fair and warmer later. Mild tomorrow.
Temperature Range Today—Max.,75°; Min.,60
Temperature Yesterday—Max.,65°; Min.,57
Full U. S. Weather Bureau Report, Page 31

Copyright, 1950, by The New York Times Company.

VOL. XCIX . No. 33,837.
Entered as Second-Class Matter,
Post Office, New York, N. Y.
NEW YORK, FRIDAY, SEPTEMBER 15, 1950.
Times Square, New York 18, N. Y.
Telephone LAckawanna 4-1000
FIVE CENTS

U. N. FORCES LAND BEHIND COMMUNISTS IN KOREA; SEIZE INCHON, PORT OF SEOUL; MOVE INLAND; U. S. WILL PRESS FOR A JAPANESE PEACE TREATY

2 GARMENT UNIONS ASK 15% WAGE RISE IN POLICY REVERSAL

Nation-Wide Demand Drafted by Big A.F.L. and C.I.O. Units to Match Costs of Living

KOREAN WAR EFFECT CITED

Long Reluctance on Economic Grounds Dropped—Mills in Northeast Grant 10%

The two largest garment unions in the United States announced yesterday that they would seek an immediate, country-wide general wage increase of 15 per cent for their thousands of members.

In this city the International Ladies Garment Workers Union, A. F. L., held a special meeting of its general executive board to formulate wage policy for 425,000 members. Locally, the union has received no pay rise since 1948, and its 80,000 dressmakers have been at the same wage level since 1947.

By a coincidence a subcommittee of the general executive board of the Amalgamated Clothing Workers of America, C. I. O., meeting in Asbury Park, N. J., drafted a similar plan to be presented to the full board today for ratification. This union will try to win higher wages for 150,000 men's clothing workers and 80,000 others engaged in the making of shirts and cotton garments.

Both organizations, which are among the most powerful and responsible in the country in wage matters, based their new demands on the rise in living costs since the start of the Korean war. Amalgamated members received their last rise, $5, in 1947.

Turnabout in Attitude

In recent years the two unions, facing poor conditions in their industries, have pursued a cautious pace in moving on the wage question. Now with nearly full employment, rising prices for textiles and mark-ups on finished products, they have come to the conclusion that pay rises are both necessary and justified.

The Amalgamated, which has a total membership of 490,000-50,000 of whom are in New York—had operated on the theory that wage rises would force up clothing prices in a period of slack demand and increase unemployment among the union's members. However, it won increases in pension and medical benefits, involving no rise in employer payroll contributions.

Amalgamated officials estimated yesterday that their full 15 per cent demand would raise the cost of making a suit by less than $1. Average clothing pay ranges from $1.50 to $1.62½ an hour. The new demand would add 22½ to 24½ cents to those rates. Cotton wages run from $1.02 to $1.10. These would be brought up by 15 to 16½ cents an hour.

Unlike the Amalgamated, which bargains on a national level with employer associations, the Ladies Garment Workers will try to win its demands on a local basis. Word has already gone out to the union's 400 locals over the country to press for increases in talks for new contracts, under wage-reopening clauses and through requests for voluntary adjustments.

Agreement for Conference

Officials of the Amalgamated said that the United States Clothing Manufacturers Association had agreed to confer with the union's bargaining committee, but that no date had been set for the first meeting. Wages within shirt manufacturers will begin next week in this city and other shirt centers.

The move by the Ladies Garment Workers, fifth largest affiliate of the American Federation of Labor, represented the first such attempt by a major A. F. L. union. In the C. I. O., of which the Amalgamated is the fourth largest unit, the United Automobile Workers

Continued on Page 19, Column 3

Excess Profits Tax Now Asked by House

By JOHN D. MORRIS
Special to The New York Times.

WASHINGTON, Sept. 14—The House went on record today, 331 to 2, as favoring action this session on an excess profits tax that would be retroactive to July 1, or Oct. 1.

The vote came on a motion by Representative Herman P. Eberharter, Democrat of Pennsylvania, to amend the pending general tax-increase bill in such a way as to require the House Ways and Means and Senate Finance Committees to bring out a separate excess profits measure before adjournment. The opposition votes were cast by Representative E. E. Cox, Democrat of Georgia, and D. W. Nicholson, Republican of Massachusetts.

The directive will not be binding however, unless it is contained in the final draft of the general tax bill, which now goes to a House-Senate conference committee for adjustment of differences between versions originally passed by the two chambers.

As passed by the Senate, the bill contained a provision direct-

Continued on Page 20, Column 2

TAFT AND WHERRY OPPOSE MARSHALL

Favoritism to Chinese Reds Is Charged—Senate Puts Off Action Until Today

Special to The New York Times.

WASHINGTON, Sept. 14—A small band of Republican Senators gathered today in opposition to the bill to waive existing law and permit General of the Army George C. Marshall, a professional soldier, to serve as Secretary of Defense.

The Republican leaders, however, made no attempt to declare it an all-party issue, and the Senate's passage of the measure, probably tomorrow, was thus assured.

It had been intended to open debate tonight, but unexpected difficulties intervened in other aspects of the Administration's final "must" list for this Congress.

At length, soon after 9 P. M., Senator Scott W. Lucas of Illinois, the Democratic Senate leader, not withstanding, "General of the Army Gen. George C. Marshall" is to be permitted to serve as Secretary of Defense.

The act forbids the office to a

Continued on Page 9, Column 2

SENATE UNANIMOUS FOR BIG ARMS FUND BUT VOTES AID CURB

Approval of 17 Billion Bars Economic Help if Ally Ships War Goods to Russia

MOVE IS AIMED AT BRITISH

Proposal Would Give Defense Secretary Authority Superior to That of E. C. A. Director

By WILLIAM S. WHITE
Special to The New York Times

WASHINGTON, Sept. 14—The Senate passed unanimously tonight an urgent and supplemental appropriation bill of $17,192,000,000. Nine dollars of every ten in it would go to strengthening the defense of the United States and the associates of the western world.

Added to this big measure was a rider intended to halt all Marshall Plan economic aid, but not military help, to any benefiting nation that shipped to the Soviet Union or any of its satellites any commodity or article deemed to be useful in the manufacture of "arms, armament, or military matériel."

This stipulation was offered mainly at the British, who long have been accused by the Republicans of sending to Russia or to Soviet friends articles that might be used in a war.

The effect was to put the Secretary of Defense in the great and delicate area of determining what would be useful to the Soviet war potential, far above the Marshall Plan agency, the Economic Cooperation Administration. Admittedly, it would give him a vast veto power over the trade practices of the European nations if he wanted to use it.

The prospective Secretary of Defense is the author of the Marshall Plan itself, General of the Army George C. Marshall.

The Senate's insistence upon this limitation over Mr. Hoffman as yet to meet the approval of the House of Representatives, as does the whole of the appropriations bill. That measure, which governs the legislative traffic in that chamber, will meet at 11 A. M. to give it a right of way for the floor.

The bill simply specifies that, the Military Unification Act notwithstanding, "General of the Army Gen. George C. Marshall" is to be permitted to serve as Secretary of Defense.

The act forbids the office to a

Continued on Page 4, Column 3

3 Robbers Shoot 2 Payroll Guards, Flee With $23,436 in Madison Ave.

Three robbers shot down two armed payroll messengers as the victims stepped into the lobby of 625 Madison Avenue early yesterday and fled with $23,436.

There were no outside witnesses to the crime and no worthwhile clues. Two small blood stains near the curb outside 35 East Fifty-eighth Street, the service entrance through which the thugs escaped, were reported as of little value but an alarm describing the getaway car with the notation that it might be blood-stained was broadcast. One robber might have been accidentally wounded by a companion, according to the police.

Fifty detectives were assigned to cover the East Side and to make a search through the city for the gunmen's car, and to check hospitals and offices of physicians for evidence of anyone treated for a gunshot wound. By last night detectives had questioned thirty per-

sons, including a number employed in the vicinity of the crime, in their search for clues.

The thugs fired five shots as they ambushed the couriers, Harold F. O'Connor, 43 years old, of 883 Columbus Avenue, and Joseph E. Gilgar, 54, of 34-59 Twenty-eighth Street, Long Island City, Queens. Although Mr. O'Connor managed to get his pistol from his holster as the last of the attackers sped out the side door he did not return the fire.

Herman Siegal, an employe of a laundry service, entered the building soon after the shooting and sounded the alarm. An elevator operator and a porter, the only two building service workers on duty at the time, also heard the shots but the first policemen were arriving when they came up from the cellar.

Mr. Gilgar, critically wounded

Continued on Page 22, Column 2

Backbone of Attack On Taegu 'Broken'

Special to The New York Times.

TAEGU, Korea, Sept. 14—Maj. Gen. Hobart Gay, commanding the United States First Cavalry Division, said today he believed "we have broken the backbone" of the North Korean attack on the key United Nations advance base at Taegu.

This, General Gay said, is the situation, at least, "at the moment," after four days of seesaw fighting north and west of the city. The Communists put an estimated three divisions in the attack, with a fourth behind the lines.

General Gay said he might have to change his mind but indications today were that the situation at Taegu had considerably bettered.

ATTLEE RISKS FATE ON STEEL QUESTION

Conservatives Offer Censure Motion on Labor's Decision to Implement Nationalization

Special to The New York Times.

LONDON, Sept. 14—The British Conservatives precipitated a Parliamentary crisis today by calling for a vote of censure after an announcement by the Labor Government that it intended to implement its authority to nationalize the country's steel industry.

The matter will be debated on Tuesday. If the Government, with its slim majority, is defeated it will resign and there will be a general election.

This is how the issue arose: There is on the statute books a law enabling the Government to take over the steel industry next January and appoint a board to do it by October. The Opposition asked today what the Government proposed to do about it. George Strauss, the Minister of Supply, said the Government intended to carry out the law, which Parliament had enacted when Labor had a bigger majority than it has now. Those were fighting words. They ended the political truce that Winston Churchill had proffered

Continued on Page 16, Column 5

ACTION BY TRUMAN

Right to Move Forces at Will in Islands Is Held U. S. Aim

MAY IGNORE SOVIET

Factors in Ending State of War With Germany Studied, He Says

By ANTHONY LEVIERO
Special to The New York Times.

WASHINGTON, Sept. 14—President Truman announced today that he had directed the State Department to begin a new effort to obtain a Japanese peace treaty. Behind the move was this country's resolve to produce a peace agreement, with or without Soviet participation.

[The Associated Press said Secretary of State Acheson had informed British Foreign Secretary Bevin and French Foreign Minister Schuman that the United States was ready to begin informal talks on development of a Japanese peace treaty.]

Our policy with respect to Japan, said the Chief Executive, was in harmony with our general aim to "end all war situations," including the deadlocks over Germany and Austria.

The President opened his news conference by reading a formal statement, announcing the new effort on the Japanese treaty, which would be made informally in discussions with members of the Far Eastern Commission. He said this would be done "in the first instance," leaving the implication that the U. S. would proceed further if the deadlock created by the Soviet Union in the commission persisted.

Informed sources said afterward that this country was determined to make some kind of peace settlement with Japan, without the Soviet Union if that country continues her obstructive tactics. The same sources said the United States would seek the right not

Continued on Page 15, Column 1

U. N. TROOPS MAKE LANDINGS IN KOREA

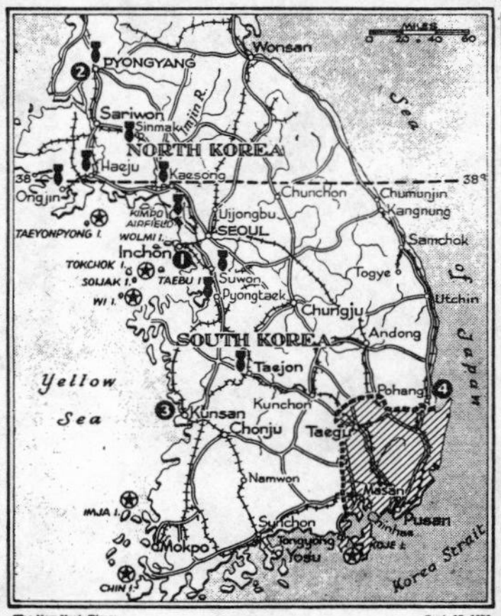

The New York Times
Sept. 15, 1950

United States and South Korean forces landed at Inchon (1) and drove inland, while other South Korean troops landed near Pohang (4) and at another point on the east coast about twenty-five miles north of Pohang. A fourth landing was reported made at Kunsan (3) on the west coast. Earlier, United Nations naval planes had battered targets from Pyongyang (2) and southward (points are indicated by bomb devices). South Koreans already hold islands marked by stars. The diagonally shaded area is the United Nations' southern beachhead.

'This Is Our Sunday Punch,' Task Force Observer Says

By ROBERT C. MILLER
United Press Correspondent

WITH UNITED STATES MARINES, at Sea, Friday, Sept. 15—This is the one we have been waiting for. Within a few hours ships of this blacked-out task force will begin a shore bombardment to pave the way for landing craft that will carry the Marines in for what we hope to be the final battle of the Korean war.

This is our Sunday punch. We will know by tonight whether it will knock out the North Koreans.

There are no excuses for this one—everything has been planned and worked out for weeks. The supplies are adequate, the men are trained and the plans drawn down to the merest detail. Everything that can be done to insure the success of this operation has been done.

This ship is like a highly trained boxer during those dreadful last hours before the bell, when the long weeks of training camp ordeal are finished and there is nothing to do but wait.

We are crammed with men who have been stacked into every corner of this assault ship. In the holds are the deadliest weapons we possess to arm them for the attack.

Every marine aboard is a combat veteran who came to a South Korean port directly from the front lines. They were loaded at the same port at which they arrived

Continued on Page 4, Column 3

Bevin and Schuman Agree to Seek Instructions on Arming of Germans

By THOMAS J. HAMILTON

Foreign Minister Robert Schuman of France and Foreign Secretary Ernest Bevin of Britain agreed yesterday to ask their governments for instructions regarding a Western Big Three discussion of the rearmament of Western Germany.

This decision was hedged with many conditions, but it is believed that it may open the door—if only partly—to acceptance of Secretary of State Dean Acheson's contention that Western Germans are absolutely essential for the defense of Western Europe against Soviet aggression.

According to well-informed sources, M. Schuman and Mr. Bevin agreed to send cablegrams to their Governments on the German rearmament with certain blanks. If these blanks were filled

satisfactorily, they would then be authorized to discuss the principle of Mr. Acheson's proposal on Monday, after the meeting today and tomorrow of the foreign ministers of the twelve countries that are parties to the North Atlantic Treaty.

It was understood that M. Schuman and Mr. Bevin were in effect suggesting that they be authorized to discuss Mr. Acheson's proposal if they obtained assurance regarding the three principal conditions fixed by M. Schuman and Mr. Bevin previously as a preliminary to any discussion of German rearmament:

1. The rearmament of the Western Allies must have priority.
2. Western German units must

Continued on Page 14, Column 3

Text of foreign ministers' interim communiqué appears, Page 14.

3 LANDINGS MADE

Allies Strike at Western Port and Two Points North of Pohang

4TH PUSH REPORTED

Units of U. S. Marines Join Blow Behind the Front Lines of Foe

By The Associated Press

TOKYO, Friday, Sept. 15—United Nations invasion forces landed today at Inchon, the port city for Seoul on Korea's west coast—150 miles behind the 130,000-man North Korean Army at the fighting front.

Covered by planes and warships, United States troops stormed ashore on the island of Wolmi, linked to Inchon by a causeway. South Korean Marines landed at Inchon.

In a simultaneous operation other United States forces landed immediately behind the Communist lines on the east coast. They made two landings—one two miles northeast of Communist-held Pohang, the other at Yongdok, more than twenty-five miles north of Pohang.

[Sources in Washington said the United States forces involved were units of the Second Marine Division.]

The west coast invasion, preceded by cruiser and destroyer bombardments and sweeping carrier plane strikes, paving the United Nations to the offensive for the first time since the Reds began the war last June 25.

Close to 38th Parallel

The invasion at Inchon, putting United Nations forces close to the Thirty-eighth Parallel which the North Koreans crossed June 25, was commanded by the South Korean Commander in Chief, Maj. Gen. Chung il Kwon.

He said that heavy pressure was quickly exerted by the invasion forces on the Communists near Kimpo airfield, Seoul's big air base. Kimpo is twelve miles northwest of Seoul and ten miles north of Inchon.

A report from Pusan said that still other United Nations forces had gone ashore at Kunsan, a west coast city 100 miles south of Seoul. The report came from Chin Soo, South Korean National Assembly-man, who said a warship bombardment had supported the landing.

One thousand South Korean commandos went ashore on the east coast near Pohang, striking at a coastal road that would bar the way to any retreat by the North Korean forces defending the port. The commandos quickly called for air support.

A big United States battleship was reported Thursday to be off Korea in the Pohang-Pyong-dok sector.

Invasion Follows Naval Attack

The North Koreans had been expecting an invasion at Inchon since Rear Adm. John M. Hoskins, commander of Task Force 77, sent British and United States cruisers and destroyers close in to bombard Inchon Wednesday. The targets included Wolmi Island.

While their shells hit the area, carrier planes for the second straight day ranged 210 miles from Kunsan to Pyongyang, capital city of the North Koreans, hitting at airfields.

B-29's coordinated these blows, blowing up an underground arsenal north of Pyongyang and severing rail lines from Pyongyang for 100 miles south to Seoul and for 200 miles southeast to Kumchon.

[Gen. Douglas MacArthur's headquarters announced at noon today, Friday, that United Nations forces were again in the walled city of Kasan, ten miles north of Taegu, from which they had been forced to retreat last weeks. The United Press reported.]

The Pyongyang radio broadcast claimed shore guns had sunk three destroyers and four landing craft Wednesday. United States officials in Washington quickly said the three destroyers had suffered

Continued on Page 5, Column 5

U. S. SHUNNED SIGNS ON KOREA, U. N. TOLD

Inquiry Report Says Republic Warned General an Invasion From North Was Near

By A. M. ROSENTHAL
Special to The New York Times

LAKE SUCCESS, Sept. 14—The United Nations Commission on Korea reported today that six weeks before the start of the war United Nations officers denied South Korean warnings that invasion from the north was imminent.

From January, 1950, to May 12, the commission reported, defense officials of the Korean Republic had warned that the Communist army was strong and getting stronger and that it was just a

Continued on Page 7, Column 3

Excerpts from findings of Commission are on Page 6.

World News Summarized

FRIDAY, SEPTEMBER 15, 1950

United Nations forces have struck in strength against the North Koreans with landings on both coasts behind the enemy's lines. A major amphibious blow was at Inchon, the port of Seoul, where United States and British warships had shelled the area Wednesday. At least two miles north of Pohang, Earlier, North Korean claims to have sunk landing craft were disputed. Along the United Nations defense perimeter in the south relatively light action was reported, except north of Taegu. [1:8; maps Pages 1 and 2.] Observers with United States Marines on the way to a landing looked to a quick knock-out effect on the North Koreans. [1:6-7.]

The Commission on Korea reported to the United Nations Security Council that six weeks before the invasion, American officers rejected South Korean warnings of an attack. The report blamed North Korea for an unprovoked aggression. [1:7.]

President Truman directed the State Department to try again to obtain a Japanese peace treaty and to seek some way to end the technical state of war with Germany. [1:5.] The State Department is studying a $250,-000,000 economic aid program for South Asia and the Middle East. [4:5.]

Foreign ministers of the United States, Britain and France discussed the "serious situation" affecting Europe and Asia. The British and French ministers agreed to seek new instructions on rearming Western Germany. Britain and France feel no military aid should go to the Germans until the North At-

lantic nations are armed. [1:6-7.] The North Atlantic Council will consider this subject at meetings opening today. [16:2.] Britain's Defense Minister predicted that a unified command would result from the talks. He disclosed that France planned to have ten divisions under arms next year and ten more later. [16:3-4.]

Britain's Labor government announced it would take over the steel industry in January. The Conservatives immediately demanded a no-confidence vote and the Commons will decide the issue next week. [1:4.]

The Senate unanimously passed a $17,192,000,000 money bill, mostly for defense, with a rider designed to end all Marshall Plan economic aid to nations shipping "arms, armament or military matériel" to the Soviet Union or its satellites. [1:3.]

The House sent the interim tax bill to conference, but voted 331 to 2 for Congress to stay in session until an excess profits tax was passed. [1:2.]

A Republican fight led by Senator Taft against enabling General Marshall to become Secretary of Defense delayed a Senate vote until today. [1:2.]

The A. F. L. and C. I. O. garment unions asked an immediate 15 per cent increase for their 655,000 members to meet higher living costs. [1:1.]

There will be no more dry days or water curbs in this city unless the situation again gets critical, but water must not be wasted, officials said. [27:8.]

NEWS BULLETINS FROM THE TIMES
Every hour on the hour
7 A. M. through Midnight
WQXR AM 1560
WQXR FM 96.3

Index to other news appears on Page 26.

Ted Williams, all-time batting great of the Boston Red Sox, is seen here at practice in 1950.

Thomson's home run culminated in a pennant-winning victory for the Giants in their playoff against the Dodgers. Durocher and Thomson obviously are elated.

New York Yanks' manager Casey Stengel guided the team to six world championships during the 50s. Stengel is shown here with Mickey Mantle, Yogi Berra and Hank Bauer, three of baseball's greats.

"All the News That's Fit to Print"

NEWS INDEX, PAGE 107, THIS SECTION

The New York Times.

LATE CITY EDITION
Fair and continued warm today and tomorrow.
Temperature Range Today—Max., 79; Min., 62
Temperatures Yesterday—Max., 77; Min., 60
U. S. Weather Bureau Report, Page 3; Sect. 1

Section 1

Copyright, 1950, by The New York Times Company.

VOL. C..No. 33,853. Entered as Second-Class Matter. Post Office, New York, N. Y. NEW YORK, SUNDAY, OCTOBER 1, 1950. Including Magazine and Book Review. FIFTEEN CENTS New York City / 50 Mile Zone | Elsewhere Twenty Cents

M'ARTHUR CALLS FOR NORTH KOREA SURRENDER; INDICATES CROSSING OF BORDER TO SUPERVISE IT; AUSTIN SAYS PRESENT DIVIDING LINE IS ILLEGAL

MURPHY CLEAN-UP SHIFTS DETECTIVES ON NUMBERS CASES

14 Working Out of Borough Commands Are Returned to Their Former Units

OFFICERS' ROLE STUDIED

Dewey Threatens to Supersede City Aides if Hunt Fails to 'Go All the Way Up'

By ALEXANDER FEINBERG

Police Commissioner Thomas F. Murphy made the first move against detectives yesterday in his continuing reorganization of the department. He relieved all fourteen detectives working out of borough commands on policy slip violations, sending them back to their original squads.

The step, Mr. Murphy said, was a follow-through on his decision to "start with a clean slate" in the enforcement of gambling laws.

Referring to the sweeping order of Friday in which he demoted and transferred to uniform the entire personnel of 336 men in the Plainclothes Division, the Commissioner pointed out: "I said then in substance that anybody who had anything to do with gambling had to be relieved."

It was recalled that in announcing the order at a gathering of police administrative heads, Mr. Murphy had said there was some evidence of corruption in the Detective Division to which attention would be given. With one or two exceptions, he had said, this evidence did not involve whole squads or appear widespread.

Policy on Numbers Awaited

Mr. Murphy left open the course he intended to pursue in the suppression of the "numbers racket." He said he could not indicate at this time whether the ousted detectives would be replaced by other detectives or by new details. In the case of the plainclothes men, he had declared that undercover methods and special squads were necessary to cope with the devious and involved operations of "skilled and crafty" gamblers.

Pointing out that the policy detectives were "relieved" rather than transferred, the Commissioner said: "Future plans are neither formulated nor ready to be announced."

In a television interview last night, Governor Dewey served notice that he expected to ferret out all the higher-ups that might be involved in the gambling-police tie-ups.

"I expect the authorities in the City of New York to go all the way up, whoever is involved, and if they don't, I will supersede whoever fails to do it," he declared in a statement on a television program during which he answered questions of passers-by in the Times Square and Rockefeller Plaza areas.

Mr. Murphy was asked what basis there was for the statement on Friday that "some commanding officers appear to be involved" in the corruption of police by bookmaking combinations.

"The general picture," he replied, "points to the fact that some commanding officers must of necessity have been involved. It just could not exist only on the lowest level."

Extent Still Undetermined

Here again, the Commissioner said, he as yet has been able to make no determination "as to how far up it [corruption] reached."

"I am trying to proceed slowly and justly to the men," he said. "I don't like to try cases in the newspapers. I want to be acquainted with the facts. I want to do an honest job and I want to do it intelligently."

Friday's mass ouster of the Plainclothes Division "was the result of intensive studying of a problem," Mr. Murphy said.

"Many people that I consulted in and out of the department had reached that same conclusion," he explained. "The move I made yesterday was just inevitable. It had to hurt some, but I just didn't have the time to find out exactly who everybody was. There was a sore

Continued on Page 86, Column 3

Dodgers Win, Can Tie Today; Other Major Sports Results

Brooklyn's pennant-hungry Dodgers slashed the stumbling Philadelphia Phillies' National League lead to one game, with one remaining, yesterday by capturing a thrilling 7-3 decision from the Phils before 23,879 wildly yelling Ebbets Field fans. The Dodgers thus carried the National League race into the final day of the season. The Phils now must take today's contest with the Brooks to win the flag. If the Dodgers come through again the two teams will wind up in a deadlock and a best-of-three play-off series starting in Brooklyn tomorrow will be necessary.

Football

Maryland toppled Navy, Michigan State upset Michigan, Southern Methodist beat Ohio State and Notre Dame defeated North Carolina in major collegiate contests. Army, Columbia, Yale and Princeton also won. Scores of leading games:

Alabama	26	Tulane	14	Notre Dame	14	N. Carolina	7
Army	28	Colgate	0	Oklahoma	28	Boston Coll.	0
California	28	Oregon	7	Penn State	34	Georgetown	14
Columbia	42	Hobart	12	Penn	21	Virginia	7
Cornell	27	Lafayette	0	Princeton	66	Williams	0
Dartmouth	21	Holy Cross	21	S. Carolina	7	Ga. Tech	0
Duke	28	Pittsburgh	14	S. M. U.	32	Ohio State	27
Indiana	20	Nebraska	20	Texas	34	Purdue	26
Maryland	35	Navy	21	U. C. L. A.	42	Wash. State	0
Mich. State	14	Michigan	7	Washington	28	Minnesota	13
Miss. St.	7	Tennessee	0	Yale	36	Brown	12

Horse Racing

George D. Widener's Battlefield finished with a rush to annex the $106,415 Futurity Stakes at Belmont Park in a photo finish with Big Stretch. Rough 'N Tumble was third.

(Complete details of these and other sports events in Section 5.)

Tammany District Chief Quits City Job to Back Impellitteri

By JAMES A. HAGERTY

Harry Brickman, a Tammany leader of the Second Assembly District, announced yesterday his support of Acting Mayor Impellitteri, mayoralty candidate of the independent Experience party. He said he was resigning his $8,850 position as First Deputy City Clerk to devote his entire time to the campaign.

Declaring that he refused to be a party to a deal that permitted a "splinter party," meaning the Liberal party, to dictate the Democratic nominee for Mayor, Mr. Brickman also announced that he would open this week headquarters of Democrats for Impellitteri. He called for the support of all candidates on the Democratic ticket other than Supreme Court Justice Ferdinand Pecora, nominee for Mayor.

Cheered by Mr. Brickman's announcement, supporters of Mr. Impellitteri declared that it marked the beginning of a revolt in Tammany against the leadership of Carmine G. DeSapio, whose support resulted in the nomination of Justice Pecora for Mayor. They asserted that other Tammany district leaders would follow Mr. Brickman's example and that there was an excellent chance that the revolt would extend to other boroughs of the city.

Mr. DeSapio had no comment on Mr. Brickman's defection. However, doubt was expressed at the Tammany headquarters in the Prudence building that many other district leaders would declare for the Acting Mayor.

It was said that, with the exception of Frank J. Sampson, a leader of the Third Assembly District, who previously had announced his support of Mr. Impellitteri, and Robert B. Blaikie, leader of the Seventh Assembly

Continued on Page 78, Column 3

10 STATES UNITING IN CIVILIAN DEFENSE

New England, Pennsylvania, New York, Jersey, Delaware to Map Joint Aid Program

Appointment of an interstate committee to draft a ten-state civil defense program providing mutual aid across state lines in a war emergency was announced yesterday.

The region embraces the six New England states, New York, Pennsylvania, Delaware and New Jersey. The announcement was made by the New York Joint Legislative Committee on Interstate Cooperation, 522 Fifth Avenue, through Assemblyman Harold C. Ostertag, its chairman. He said Congress would be urged to make consent to the plan a priority matter when it reconvened Nov. 27.

The Eastern Conference on Civil Defense, meeting here on Sept. 21 and 22 under the auspices of the Council of State Governments and New York's Joint Legislative Committee on Interstate Cooperation, had recommended that Congress approve a resolution consenting in advance to regional defense pacts. Congress adjourned without action on the recommendation. Mr. Ostertag declared that "the states have

Continued on Page 45, Column 3

Dewey, On Television, Answers Questions Posed in City Streets

By LEO EGAN

Governor Dewey employed television last night to answer a series of questions from persons picked at random from two busy sections of New York as part of his campaign for re-election. It was the first time television had been so used in a political campaign.

Eight questions in all were put to the Governor. They ranged in subject-matter all the way from queries of why he wore a mustache and what he thought of the Brooklyn Dodger baseball team's chances of winning the National League pennant to the New York City gambling inquiry, overcrowding in schools and discrimination in housing.

One question, put by Harvey Rothenberg of 25 West Eighty-first Street, a shirt manufacturer, was: "From a social and an etiquette point of view, do you think you were correct in criticizing the Russians for maintaining slave labor, in your recent talk at the Waldorf?"

Mr. Dewey's answer was: "It wasn't etiquette, but it was awfully good for the Russians." He added that he intended to continue his criticism of the Russians, because "so long as Soviet Russia has slave labor, and a totalitarian Government, none of the free people in the world are safe."

The telecast was an outgrowth of Mr. Dewey's statement in his acceptance speech at Saratoga that he intended to wage his campaign for re-election on every street corner in the state. The use of television to carry out this idea was developed in a series of conferences between Mr. Dewey's campaign advisers and radio technicians.

During last night's program, Mr.

Continued on Page 40, Column 2

U. S. PUTS VISA BAN ON TOTALITARIANS OF ALL DESCRIPTION

State Department Sends Order to Officials Abroad to Carry Out Internal Security Law

IS FACED WITH PROBLEMS

Trouble Is Seen in Applying Act So as Not to Alienate Argentina, Spain, Yugoslavia

By WALTER H. WAGGONER
Special to THE NEW YORK TIMES.

WASHINGTON, Sept. 30—The State Department has ordered its officials abroad to bar from entry into this country all Nazis, Fascists or totalitarians of any complexion.

The order went out in conformity with the terms of the recently enacted Internal Security Act of 1950, which prohibits the admission of present or former Communists, Nazis, Fascists or other varieties of doctrinaire totalitarians.

At the present time, visa officials will carry out these instructions under a "stop-gap" order, it was said, but detailed regulations are now in preparation and will probably be issued within a week.

Consular and other diplomatic authorities had been kept fully informed of the terms and progress of the anti-subversive measure passed by Congress by a generous margin over a Presidential veto on Sept. 23, and the "stop-gap" order went out immediately upon the bill's enactment, officials said.

The State Department took its action under those provisions of the new law that exclude several classes of aliens "from admission into the United States."

Communists were not specifically mentioned in the rulings just sent out because they were already barred from entry by the Immigration Act of Oct. 16, 1918, officials indicated.

The State Department had opposed the new law on several grounds relating to its new re-

Continued on Page 31, Column 3

U. N. ACTION URGED

U. S. Warns Reds Must Not Be Allowed to Flee and Pose New Threat

PRIORITY IS VOTED

Soviet Delaying Move Is Defeated in Noisy Committee Session

The text of Mr. Austin's U. N. address is printed on Page 3.

By A. M. ROSENTHAL
Special to THE NEW YORK TIMES.

LAKE SUCCESS, Sept. 30—The United States warned in the United Nations tonight that the North Korean Communists must not be allowed to retire behind the Thirty-eighth Parallel and pose a new threat to world peace.

Warren R. Austin, chief United States delegate, told the General Assembly's Political and Security Committee that the Thirty-eighth Parallel was an "imaginary line" that had no basis in law or logic.

Representatives of the sixty countries on the committee heard Mr. Austin say that the United Nations' goal of restoring peace to war-torn Korea demanded the taking of "appropriate steps" to eliminate the ability of the North Koreans to launch new attacks.

The Austin statement was delivered several hours before the release of Gen. Douglas MacArthur's message calling on the North Korean Communists to surrender. Diplomats here said Mr. Austin's warning could be taken as clear notice that the United States felt that General MacArthur had the right to order a crossing of the Parallel and that, with or without a surrender, United Nations forces would march across that line.

Mr. Austin's statement was delivered several hours after the committee had voted to give the Korea ase overriding priority. The

Continued on Page 4, Column 1

World News Summarized

SUNDAY, OCTOBER 1, 1950

General MacArthur called on the North Koreans to cease all further hostilities immediately. He told them that otherwise they would suffer "further useless shedding of blood and destruction of property." His terms for ending the war in Korea were made known to the North Korean Government in a broadcast from Tokyo and were also announced at Lake Success. [1:8.]

A few South Korean troops were, by unconfirmed reports, a short distance north of the Thirty-eighth Parallel in the course of normal military operations. The United Nations forces generally cleaned up pockets of the Communists. United States troops occupied the southwest port of Kunsan. [1:6-7.]

Some United States field officers in Seoul said that, with more time, much destruction in the city could have been avoided. [11:1.]

The nation's highest military honor, the Congressional Medal, was awarded by President Truman to Maj. Gen. William F. Dean, missing in action, for exceptional heroism in the defense of Korea. [10:3.]

United States delegate Warren R. Austin warned in the United Nations that the Thirty-eighth Parallel was an illogical "imaginary line" and the North Koreans should not be permitted to use it as a shield behind which they might prepare another threat to world peace. Enduring peace in Korea can be achieved only if "appropriate steps" are taken to do away with all potential North Korean threats to peace, he emphasized. [1:5.]

The United Nations Security Council rejected a Soviet demand that the international organization intercede to compel the United States to end "inhuman, barbarous bombings" in Korea. The vote was 9 to 1, with the Soviet Union casting the only ballot in favor; Yugoslavia abstained. [1:6-7.]

Communist China's Premier Chou En-lai, in a Peiping anniversary speech in which he called the United States Government "the enemy of the Chinese people," talked of "continued resistance" by the North Korean Reds. He predicted they would gain a "final victory." [48:1.]

Police and military forces were on guard against disturbances in Western Berlin and Western Germany that might occur this week-end in the Soviet-sponsored "peace drive." [47:1.]

The Canadian Government announced that it had decided to allow its dollar currency, now worth 91 cents in United States money, to float freely on the world's foreign exchanges for the first time in eleven years. [1:7.]

State Department officials abroad have been instructed to deny visas for entry into the United States to all Nazis, Fascists or Communists. The order was in conformity with the new subversive-control law. [1:4.]

In this city Police Commissioner Murphy continued his reorganization of the department by ordering back to their original units all of the fourteen detectives working out of borough commands on policy slip violations. [1:1.]

New York, New Jersey, Pennsylvania, Delaware and the six New England states will cooperate in drafting a civil defense program for mutual aid in a war emergency. [1:2.]

NEWS BULLETINS FROM THE TIMES
Every hour on the hour
8 A.M. through Midnight
Except at 12, 4 & 8 P.M. Today
WQXR AM 1560
WQXR FM 96.3

VISHINSKY MAKING A PROTEST

Soviet Foreign Minister demanding hearing for Czechoslovak delegate at Political and Security body session. At the left is Warren R. Austin. The New York Times (by Arthur Brower)

U. N. Force Reported Edging Over 38th Parallel on East

Special to THE NEW YORK TIMES.

TOKYO, Sunday, Oct. 1—Unofficial reports, unconfirmed here or at United States Eighth Army headquarters in Korea, said today that South Korean troops on the east coast had moved a few hundred yards across the border into North Korea.

[General MacArthur was reported to have authorized some South Koreans to cross the line in a necessary military move, said a Reuters dispatch from Korea.]

United Nations columns were closing in on the Thirty-eighth Parallel, the old boundary between the Republic of Korea and the Communist state to the north.

Some sources estimated that the enemy still had approximately 100,000 men in various states of equipment and training north of the Parallel, who were still in condition to offer considerable resistance.

The advance toward the Parallel was made in two sectors, north of the recaptured Republican capital at Seoul and on the east coast, where advance guards of the South Korean Third Division already had reached the border.

In the Seoul area, Marines of the First Division thrust forward from their positions north of Seoul. They moved behind the heaviest strike of war by Marine fighter bombers yesterday in which the City of Uijongbu, twelve miles north of Seoul and about an equal distance from the Parallel, was literally removed from the map.

After an hour-long attack in which thirty-five Corsairs and Tiger Cats from Kimpo Airfield took part, an Air Force announcement said that Uijongbu was "only a mass of blazing rubble."

The Marine pilots, in successive flights, used 500-pound demolition bombs, 265-pound demolition

Continued on Page 7, Column 1

CANADA ABOLISHES FIXED DOLLAR RATE

Finance Minister Announces Decision to Let Unit Find Its Own World Level

By P. J. PHILIP
Special to THE NEW YORK TIMES.

OTTAWA, Sept. 30—The Canadian dollar is to be allowed "for the time being" to find its own market level. This was announced this evening.

The fixed official rate of exchange which has been current for just over a year has been canceled and from the opening of trading on Monday the rate of exchange of the Canadian dollar will be determined by conditions of supply and demand for foreign currencies in Canada.

At the same time the general structure of exchange control, including control over security transactions between residents and nonresidents and control over payments of Canadian dollars to nonresidents will remain in force.

In a statement announcing the change, Finance Minister Douglas C. Abbott explained that a few amendments of the foreign exchange control regulations might be necessary. The objective, he

Continued on Page 58, Column 3

U. N. Council Again Rebuffs Soviet On Bid to End U. S. Korea Bombing

By GEORGE BARRETT
Special to THE NEW YORK TIMES.

LAKE SUCCESS, Sept. 30—A demand by the Soviet Union for intercession by the United Nations to make the United States end "inhuman, barbarous bombings" in Korea was flatly rejected today by the Security Council in a vote that found Russia standing alone in her protest.

The resolution, brought forward by Soviet Deputy Foreign Minister Jacob A. Malik, was substantially the same as one presented to the Council three weeks ago, and it was as thoroughly rejected in a 9 to 1 tally, with Yugoslavia abstaining.

It was Sir Gladwyn Jebb of Britain who set the tone of the majority's feelings by telling Mr. Malik that all the North Korean authorities had to do to end the bombings was to sue for peace at once, since even they must realize by now that their cause was "quite hopeless."

Mr. Malik had introduced his slightly revised resolution on the grounds that new evidence from the North Korean regime showed that United States Air Forces were "still" carrying on indiscriminate bombings of civilian centers and should be ordered by the Council without delay to "cease and henceforth forbid" bombardment of "peaceful towns and inhabited centers" as well as the "machine-gunning from the air of the peaceful population of Korea."

Speaking for the United States, Ernest A. Gross declared tartly that Mr. Malik was reintroducing a resolution that already had been

Continued on Page 25, Column 1

WHEN You Think of Writing Think of Whiting—Advt.

WAR'S END SOUGHT

General Demands Foes Lay Down Their Arms Throughout Country

SPEEDY REPLY ASKED

Message Is Broadcast, Leaflets Are Dropped by U. S. Air Forces

By LINDESAY PARROTT
Special to THE NEW YORK TIMES.

TOKYO, Sunday, Oct. 1—Gen. Douglas MacArthur called on the North Korean invaders today "to lay down your arms and cease hostilities" to avoid total defeat and destruction.

General MacArthur's call was made in a statement "to the Commander in Chief of the North Korean forces."

Recordings of a Korean translation were played repeatedly both from Tokyo and Seoul radio stations and at the same time Allied planes were dropping the ultimatum in leaflet form over North Korea.

General MacArthur offered the North Koreans no terms. He simply told the Communist army to lay down its weapons and accept "such military supervision as I may direct."

The general made it clear, however, that what he demanded was the surrender of all the North Korean armed forces, not simply the disintegrating Communist divisions trapped south of the Allied line across the Korean peninsula. He directed the surrender call to enemy forces "in whatever part of Korea situated" and "forthwith."

Warns Against Destruction

"The early and total defeat and complete destruction of your armed forces and warmaking potential is now inevitable," the message said.

Some sources here took the message as a clear intimation that failure of the North Koreans to comply would be an immediate signal to the United States and South Korean troops now moving up to battle positions to storm across the Thirty-eighth Parallel and continue their advance toward the Communist capital of Pyongyang and the North Korean frontiers with Manchuria and the Soviet Union across the Yalu River and just south of the Russian port of Vladivostok.

General MacArthur demanded the immediate liberation of all United Nations war prisoners and civilian internees with adequate provisions for their care, maintenance and "immediate transportation to such places as I indicate." He called for an "early decision" by the North Korean command to avoid further bloodshed and the destruction of property.

The United Nations commander's demand made no specific mention of the Thirty-eighth Parallel or of the repeated assertion of the South Korean Government that Communist violation of the line had wiped it out of existence and the country must now be unified only under an administration that the United Nations recognized.

He Avoids Political Issues

The document made no mention of the political considerations or the possible future status of the Communist regime.

General MacArthur pledged that the North Korean forces would receive the "care dictated by civilized custom and practices and be permitted to return to their homes as soon as practicable." The offer apparently included Communists who might yield to the demand to lay down their arms as well as the 15,000 prisoners of war already held in Allied stockades.

Though assessment of the MacArthur statement—since it omitted any references either to the future political status of Korea or

Continued on Page 5, Column 1

This section consists of 108 pages divided into three parts. The Index will be found on Page 107. Society news begins on Page 97 and obituaries on Page 104.

During the first three years of the Fifties, Harry S. Truman was President of the United States.

The assassination of President Truman was averted by alert guards at Blair House. The plot failed and the Puerto Rican gunmen were shot.

Truman decorates General MacArthur after their talk on the Korean War and peace. This historic meeting took place on Wake Island.

"All the News That's Fit to Print"

The New York Times.

LATE CITY EDITION
Partly cloudy, warm today; showers tonight. Much cooler tomorrow.
Temperature Range Today—Max., 77; Min., 56
Temperatures Yesterday—Max., 81; Min., 58.9
Full U. S. Weather Bureau Report, Page 63

Copyright, 1950, by The New York Times Company.

VOL. C..No. 33,885. Entered as Second-Class Matter, Post Office, New York, N. Y. NEW YORK, THURSDAY, NOVEMBER 2, 1950. Times Square, New York 18, N. Y. Telephone LAckawanna 4-1000 FIVE CENTS

ASSASSINATION OF TRUMAN FOILED IN GUN FIGHT OUTSIDE BLAIR HOUSE; PUERTO RICAN PLOTTER, GUARD DIE

KOREAN REDS HIT U. S. UNIT; NOW USE JETS

REGIMENT TRAPPED

Foe Employing Rockets Against First Cavalry Division at Unsan

U. N. TROOPS FORCED BACK

Only 24th Division Makes Gain and Then It Is Told to Halt Its Advance

By LINDESAY PARROTT
Special to The New York Times.

TOKYO, Thursday, Nov. 2—North Korean Communists, reinforced by troops of the Chinese Red Army, savagely attacked today advance guards of the United States First Cavalry Division thrown into action near the west coast of Korea to reinforce the weakening South Korean troops.

The attack made north and west of Unsan, where the Communists had concentrated their strength during the last few days and had driven back South Korean spearheads by as much as thirty miles in some sectors. Using tanks, artillery and heavy mortar fire, the North Koreans cut off one regiment of the United States Cavalry Division. Other units of the division were reported to be attempting to fight their way through to reach the isolated troops.

The fighting was in progress between Unsan and Taechon, but a spokesman for the United States First Corps said the situation was too vague and confused to locate the positions to which the United States troops had been forced to retreat.

Admits Chinese Are Fighting

For the first time a corps spokesman officially admitted that "Chinese troops" were launching an assault.

"We don't know whether they represent the Chinese Government," he said, and added that it also was unknown whether or not Chinese reinforcements made up the bulk of the new strength that had enabled the shattered North Korean Army to take the offensive again—at least locally—against the United Nations move toward the Manchurian border.

The Communists launched their attack in the morning. According to reports from Korea, they used heavy rocket bombardment for the first time in the war. The latest accounts said the enemy had overrun several First Cavalry positions, capturing weapons and turning them against Americans who had been hurriedly brought up to the combat line after all but one United States division—the Twenty-fourth Infantry, farther to the west—had been out of the contact with the enemy and behind the Korean Republican spearheads driven in by the enemy counter-attack.

This morning the North Koreans were reported to be within one half mile of Unsan.

Rockets Launched on Ground

The use of the rockets, fired from launchers on the ground, represented the second new weapon introduced on the North Korean side within the last two days. Yesterday for the first time the enemy flung jet-propelled fighter planes into combat.

Meanwhile, the ground advance of the Allied forces halted at Chongko, where the United States Twenty-fourth Infantry Division stood within eighteen miles of the border city of Sinuiju, reported to be the new capital of the North Korean Communist Government.

All along the rest of the front South Korean divisions were in retreat or on the defensive against enemy attacks strengthened by contingents of Chinese Communist soldiers trained in the Chinese Red Army.

Six enemy jet fighters made their appearance yesterday over Sonchon on the west coast, fought a brief dogfight with Mustangs of the United States Fifth Air Force and then flashed back toward the Manchurian border without casualties on either side. Observers said the jet-propelled planes resembled the Soviet model MIG-15, with swept back wings and a speed of 600 miles an hour. On the previous occasion jet planes were believed to have been seen over North Korea, but this was the

Continued on Page 3, Column 1

PLAYWRIGHT DIES

George Bernard Shaw
The New York Times

BERNARD SHAW, 94, DIES IN HIS HOME

Famous Irish Wit Had Been in Coma for Day—Broken Thigh Led to Final Illness

By The Associated Press.

AYOT ST. LAWRENCE, England, Thursday, Nov. 2—George Bernard Shaw, one of the modern age's greatest dramatists and its most caustic critic, died today at the age of 94. The white-bearded Irish-born sage, whose wit was renowned throughout the world for half a century, succumbed at 4:59 A. M. (11:59 P. M. Wednesday, Eastern standard time).

His death was announced to newsmen by his housekeeper, Mrs. Alice Laden. Wearing black, she appeared at the gates of the cottage, Shaw's Corner, and told the reporters: "Mr. Shaw is dead."

A few minutes after her announcement, Dr. Thomas Probyn, Shaw's physician, hurried into the house. Twenty minutes later, Shaw's longtime biographer, F. E. Loewenstein, told newsmen that the playwright died peacefully without regaining consciousness. Only two nurses were with him when death came.

The famed dramatist, who professed himself both a Communist and an atheist, was visited in his last hours by an Anglican clergyman, who said final prayers for the old sage's soul.

"It is wrong to say that he was an atheist," said the minister, the Rev. R. G. Davies. "He believed in God."

Shaw lapsed into his final coma yesterday morning at 3 o'clock (10 P. M. Tuesday, Eastern standard time) and never regained consciousness. Operated on seven weeks ago for a broken thigh suffered when he slipped and fell in his garden, he grew steadily weaker. A bladder ailment aggravated his condition.

Lights burned for two nights in Shaw's Corner, the red brick

Continued on Page 28, Column 2

LIE TERM EXTENDED AS U. N. SECRETARY FOR 3 YEARS, 46 TO 5

Assembly Vote Continues Him in Office Despite Bitter Attacks by Russians

ARAB BLOC, CHINA ABSTAIN

Australia Also Shuns Support—Final Move by Vishinsky to Block Step Fails

The text of Secretary Lie's address is printed on Page 3.

By THOMAS J. HAMILTON

Overriding last-ditch Soviet opposition, the General Assembly yesterday extended the term of Trygve Lie as Secretary General of the United Nations for another three years. The vote was 46 to 5, with only the five members of the Soviet bloc opposed.

However, Australia, Nationalist China and six members of the Arab bloc—Egypt, Iraq, Lebanon, Saudi Arabia, Syria and Yemen—abstained. Haiti was absent.

Mr. Lie, whose present five-year term will expire next Feb. 2, told the Assembly when it reconvened for the afternoon session that he interpreted the extension of his term as a vote of confidence and a reaffirmation of the independence and integrity of the position.

Mr. Lie did not refer to his stand in favor of United Nations action for the defense of South Korea, which had led the Soviet Union to veto his re-election. But he said that he had worked hard for the past five years to reconcile "the conflicting interests that divide the world" and that he would continue to do so.

Iraq Explains Abstention

Immediately after the vote Dr. Fadhil Jamali of Iraq explained that he had not been able to vote for the extension of Mr. Lie's term because he felt that, despite Mr. Lie's "many fine qualities," he had not been "entirely impartial" on the Palestine question. He added that "Mr. Lie did not react toward recent Jewish aggressions in Palestine with anything like the zeal which he displayed on the question of Korea."

"With due respect to Mr. Lie, we do not believe that he helped enough to make the United Nations bring about peace and justice to the Arabs of Palestine," Dr. Jamali said.

Nasrollah Entezam of Iran, President of the Assembly, who had given Dr. Jamali the floor to explain his vote, then pounded his gavel, declaring that this was not an explanation, and that Dr. Jamali could not "continue this way in attacking a person who is not present here and who has received the confidence of the General Assembly by forty-six votes in his favor."

Dr. Jamali then stepped down from the rostrum with the statement that "it would certainly have been a betrayal of Arab public opinion and sentiment if we had not abstained."

Sir Keith Officer, who then was recognized to explain Australia's abstention, said that Australia shared the view that Mr. Lie must not be punished for doing "his clear duty as regards the action of the United Nations in Korea," but that Australia had "genuine doubts" about the legality of the extension of Mr. Lie's term, which

Continued on Page 3, Column 5

CAPITAL STARTLED

Police Swiftly Cordon Blair House as Shots Attract Big Crowds

PHOTOGRAPHERS NEAR BY

Leap From Their Auto, Halted by Traffic Light, Into Action—Passers-by See Fight

By PAUL P. KENNEDY
Special to The New York Times.

WASHINGTON, Nov. 1—This city, which has heard the sound of assassins' guns before, reacted with electric suddenness today as shots exploded before the front door of President Truman's own residence.

Within a few moments after the firing had stopped in front of Blair House hundreds of spectators were straining at police cordons almost magically thrown up at the intersecting streets bounding the block in which the President's temporary residence is situated.

Street cars, which run along Pennsylvania Avenue in front of the White House and Blair House, were backed up three blocks from Jackson Place, which bounds the Blair House block on the east, and for as many blocks from Seventeenth Street, which bounds Blair House block on the west.

Automobile traffic snarls blocked the approach of a number of ambulances and police squad cars, and wailing sirens heightened the confusion.

Approaching the scene of the shooting from the outer fringe of the crowd, one picked up at least a dozen accounts of what had happened. The accounts grew less lurid toward the core of the trouble.

Rumors Fly Among Throngs

These reports were received from spectators, at least a half block from the Blair House, and from newspaper men scurrying from the scene to the nearest telephones. On the outer reaches of the crowd the rumor was that two or three persons had entered Blair House with submachine guns firing and that the President had been assassinated or wounded.

Even among the reporters and photographers directly in front of the Blair House, the early accounts were confusing. It was not until fully fifteen minutes after the firing that it was clearly estab-

Continued on Page 16, Column 6

WOULD-BE ASSASSIN OF PRESIDENT SHOT DOWN

Oscar Collazo lying at the bottom of the steps to the Blair-Lee House as White House guard is putting his revolver back in his holster. This picture was made by a photographer of The New York Times, who was waiting to accompany Mr. Truman to a dedication ceremony at Arlington Cemetery.
The New York Times (by Bruce Hoertel)

PRESIDENT RESTING

Awakened by Shots, He Sees Battle in Which Three Are Wounded

HE KEEPS APPOINTMENTS

Documents Link 2 Assassins, Who Lived Here, to Puerto Rican Extremist Leader

By ANTHONY LEVIERO
Special to The New York Times.

WASHINGTON, Nov. 1—Quick-shooting White House guards cut down two assassins this afternoon when they attempted to invade Blair House in a Puerto Rican Nationalist plot to assassinate President Truman.

Tonight one assassin and one policeman were dead, and two policemen were wounded, one critically. The other assassin, seriously wounded, told the United States Secret Service that he and his companion had come down from New York two days ago to kill Mr. Truman.

On the body of the dead assassin Secret Service agents found a letter and a "memorandum," both cryptic but indicative of conspiracy. The missives were in the same handwriting and on the same stationery. They bore in the form of a signature, the name of Pedro Albizu Campos, leader of the Puerto Rican Nationalist extremists who carried out the uprising in Puerto Rico Monday.

U. E. Baughman, chief of the Secret Service, cautioned reporters, however, that he had no proof that Albizu Campos was the author of the two documents.

THE DEAD

COFFELT, Pvt. Leslie, of Arlington, Va., White House guard.
TORRESOLA, Griselio, of 1259 Ward Avenue, New York, assassin.

THE INJURED

COLLAZO, Oscar, of 173 Brook Avenue, New York, assassin; shot in the chest.
DOWNS, Pvt. Joseph, of Silver Spring, Md., White House guard, in critical condition with multiple wounds.
BIRDZELL, Pvt. Donald T., of Washington, White House guard; in "fair" condition with knees shattered by bullets.

All three wounded are expected to recover.

Taking his usual afternoon nap and roused by a fury of shooting, Mr. Truman looked down from an upstairs bedroom of Blair House. In the bright sun of Pennsylvania Avenue was terror and confusion. At the foot of the stoop leading into Blair House lay one of the assassins, alive, blood flowing from the middle of his chest and staining his blue shirt.

"A President has to expect those things," Mr. Truman said, later.

Truman Keeps to Schedule

Serene, a man of good conscience, for he had told the people of Puerto Rico unequivocally that they were free to work out their own political destiny, Mr. Truman punctiliously kept his remaining appointments of the day.

The outrage, however, made the Federal police agencies increasingly alert, and new safeguards were put around the President and his family. Meanwhile, the Secret Service began to trace back the plot through New York, to its apparent source in the island possession in the Caribbean, which is

Continued on Page 16, Column 2

PUERTO RICO'S HEAD LINKS TWO ATTACKS

Governor Says Nationalist Forces Sparked by Reds Shot at Truman, Himself

By The United Press.

SAN JUAN, Puerto Rico, Nov. 1—Gov. Luis Muñoz Marin said tonight that Puerto Rican Nationalists were being used by the Communists both in the attempt to assassinate President Truman and in the abortive revolt here, in which he also was a target.

"This further crime—the Washington attempt—further confirms me in my conviction that the Nationalists are having their lunacy, fanaticism and irresponsibility manipulated for the benefit of Communist propaganda and strategy," the Governor said.

"We all feel deeply relieved that no tragic consequences resulted from this criminal action.

"The people are profoundly

Continued on Page 19, Column 2

Assassins' Kin and Friends Are Rounded Up in Bronx

By MEYER BERGER

Thirteen Puerto Ricans—six women and seven men—were taken to the offices of the United States Secret Service at 90 Church Street last night for questioning about the attempt yesterday on President Truman's life in Washington.

Policemen said they were the families and friends of the two assassins. Unofficially, Oscar Collazo of 173 Brook Avenue, the Bronx, one of the men who fired a gun at Blair House, was described as treasurer of the New York City branch of the Puerto Rican Nationalists, bitter enemies of the United States.

Collazo, wounded, is in the Emergency Hospital in Washington. The second gunman, tentatively identified by Secret Service men as Griselio Torresola of 1259 Ward Avenue in the East Bronx, was killed by police bullets.

Mrs. Rose Collazo, 42 years old, the wounded man's wife, was one of those taken into custody. She was arraigned at 2 o'clock this morning in Federal Court before United States Commissioner Edward M. McDonald on a charge of having conspired with the two assassins and two unnamed persons to harm a member of the Government. Commissioner McDonald held her in $50,000 bail for a hearing next Thursday.

Following the arraignment Secret Service men took her to the Federal House of Detention.

At the request of Assistant United States Attorney Irving H. Saypol, Commisisoner McDonald issued John Doe warrants for the two unidentified persons named in the conspiracy complaint.

Earlier Mrs. Collazo had told officials and newspaper men:

"I am Oscar Collazo's wife. He

Continued on Page 18, Column 3

PRESIDENT IS CALM AT DILL DEDICATION

Speaks, After Attempt to Kill Him, at Unveiling of Statue of British Field Marshal

By The Associated Press.

WASHINGTON, Nov. 1—Less than an hour after an attempt had been made to assassinate him, President Truman calmly dedicated a memorial to Britain's Field Marshal Sir John Dill at Arlington National Cemetery today.

"It is important to the peace of the world that peoples understand each other and have full faith in each other's sincerity," he said.

He made no reference to the gunfight in front of his Blair House residence. Many of the 600 dignitaries present at the unveiling wondered why Mr. Truman was surrounded by such an unusually heavy guard of Secret Service men.

The President in his address said that he welcomed "this opportunity to remind my countrymen that the maintenance of a perfect understanding between the people of Great Britain and the United States is of great impor-

Continued on Page 17, Column 2

Pope Affirms Dogma of Assumption Of Mary to Heaven 'Body and Soul'

By CAMILLE M. CIANFARRA
Special to The New York Times.

ROME, Nov. 1—Pope Pius proclaimed today the dogma of the Assumption into heaven of the Virgin Mary.

"We pronounce, declare and define to be a dogma revealed by God that the Immaculate Mother of God, Mary, ever virgin, when the course of her life on earth was finished was taken up body and soul into heaven," the Pope declared.

The Pontiff spoke ex cathedra as supreme pastor of the church and teacher of Roman Catholic doctrine during an open air ceremony of pomp and magnificence to an audience of thirty-six Cardinals and 480 Archbishops and Bishops in the grandiose setting of St. Peter's Square.

A throng of 200,000 faithful, including Holy Year pilgrims from so many countries that they could be said truly to represent the whole Catholic world, packed every inch of space of the oval-shaped square that had been transformed for the occasion into a vast Christian temple.

Beginning today 400,000,000 members of the Catholic religion must believe explicitly and without reservation—otherwise they will incur excommunication as heretics—the Catholic tradition of the Assumption now defined as a dogma or an article of faith. The Catholic Church holds that dogmas are truths revealed directly by God or through the apostles and contained in the two sole fonts of Catholic doctrine—the Bible and tradition.

As such they are irrevocably binding on all Catholics and may be defined by the Pope either alone as today or jointly with the Bishops in the Ecumenical Council repre-

Continued on Page 12, Column 1

Vatican texts on dogma and speech by Pope are on Page 12.

World News Summarized

THURSDAY, NOVEMBER 2, 1950

Two assassins, identified as Puerto Rican Nationalists, attempted to kill President Truman yesterday while he was taking an afternoon nap in Blair House. One assailant was killed and the other badly wounded in a gun fight outside the house with guards, one of whom died. Two policemen were seriously wounded. The President went to the window to see what had happened and was shooed to safety by alert agents. [1:8.] Later he dedicated a memorial in Arlington Cemetery honoring Sir John Dill, British Field Marshal. [1:7.]

Secret Service agents listed the two Puerto Ricans as Bronx residents, and last night six women and five men were taken to 90 Church Street for questioning. [1:6-7.] An hour before the Blair House attack an unidentified man threw two bottles of ignited gasoline into the Puerto Rican labor office in this city, but they did not explode. [17:7.] In Puerto Rico, which has been torn by Nationalist uprisings, the Government spurred its hunt for revolutionary leaders. [1:5.]

Washington, electrified by the attack, the sixth attempt on a President's life [16:8], crowded to the scene. Eyewitness reports were confusing and conflicting. [1:4]. An ironic twist to the assassination attempt was the fact that President Truman was a strong advocate of Puerto Rican independence. [16:1.]

Chinese and North Korean troops, using rockets and heavy guns, drove back United States troops in the Unsan area, trapping one regiment. Other United States forces were ordered to halt their advance 18 miles from the border. [1:1; map Page 2.]

India expressed "keen disappointment" in answering Communist China's rejection of her concern over the invasion of Tibet. [9:2.]

The United Nations General Assembly, 46 to 5, extended the term of Secretary General Lie for three years. Only the Soviet bloc voted no, while Australia, Nationalist China and the Arab states abstained. [1:3.]

France is ready to contribute half of forty divisions planned for Western Europe by 1953, Defense Minister Moch said. Secretary Acheson declared it was agreed there should be no German general staff, national army or war industries. [8:3.]

Pope Pius proclaimed as dogma the Assumption of the Virgin Mary into heaven. [1:2-3.]

George Bernard Shaw died at his home in England. He was 94 years old. [1:2.]

Theodore Roosevelt, Woodrow Wilson, Alexander Graham Bell, Dr. William C. Gorgas, Josiah Willard Gibbs and Susan B. Anthony were elected to the Hall of Fame. [34:3.]

The City Planning Commission approved a record $478,761,756 capital budget for 1951 and a $1,235,850,237 five-year program. [33:1.]

NEWS BULLETINS FROM THE TIMES
Every hour on the hour
7 A.M. through Midnight
WQXR AM 1560
WQXR FM 96.3

Index to other news appears on Page 32.

November Heat Record of 81° Set; Zoo and Parks Draw Big Crowds

By IRA HENRY FREEMAN

November came in like a lamb yesterday, a spring lamb.

On the fourth day of an unseasonably warm wave extending over the eastern third of the country, the temperature in this city climbed to 81 degrees at 1:15 P. M. It dropped one degree for an hour, but at 2:15 again reached 81, and the latter time was officially accepted as the record.

This was not only the warmest for any Nov. 1 but also higher than ever reached in November since the Weather Bureau began keeping records here in 1871. The previous record for Nov. 1 was 70 degrees in 1946, while the previous high for any November day was 80 on Nov. 6, 1948.

The coolest it got during the day was 59 degrees from 6 to 7 o'clock in the morning. That was two degrees above the normal maximum for Nov. 1, Col. James W. Osmun, chief assistant meteorologist in charge of the New York Weather Bureau, pointed out.

During the luncheon period when the mercury was rising 4 and 5 degrees an hour, throngs of office workers and shoppers on the mid-town streets were uncomfortably warm. In Bryant Park the benches were jammed with men in shirt sleeves and girls in summer blouses.

Some air-cooled restaurants and offices turned the refrigeration back on temporarily. Women shoppers in Fifth Avenue and Fifty-seventh Street strolled along with their suit jackets over their arms. The retail clothing business, incidentally, was slackened temporarily by the weather, Thomas A. Terry, executive vice president of the Fifth Avenue Association, reported.

The brass Prometheus bringing

Continued on Page 22, Column 1

Campos Captured In San Juan Home

By The United Press.

SAN JUAN, Puerto Rico, Thursday, Nov. 2—National policemen poured five heavy volleys of rifle and pistol fire into the home of Pedro Albizu Campos early today and captured the Nationalist party leader when he fled into the street.

The Puerto Rican Governor, Luis Muñoz Marin, earlier had accused the Nationalist extremist leader of responsibility for the assassination attempt made against President Truman yesterday. The would-be assassins were said to be members of the Nationalist party.

"All the News That's Fit to Print"

The New York Times.

LATE CITY EDITION
Partly cloudy and cold today.
Some cloudiness, cold tomorrow.
Temperature Range Today—Max.,43; Min.,29
Temperature Yesterday—Max.,40; Min.,31
Full U. S. Weather Bureau Report, Page 67

Copyright, 1950, by The New York Times Company.

VOL. C..No. 33,912. Entered as Second-Class Matter. Post Office, New York, N. Y. NEW YORK, WEDNESDAY, NOVEMBER 29, 1950. Times Square, New York 18, N. Y. Telephone Lackawanna 4-1000 FIVE CENTS

U. S. ACCUSES RED CHINA OF 'OPEN AGGRESSION'; 'NEW WAR,' SAYS M'ARTHUR; TRUMAN SEES AIDES; 200,000 OF FOE ADVANCE UP TO 23 MILES IN KOREA

CITY HALL PUSHES NEW DESAPIO FIGHT; TO CUT PATRONAGE

Leader's Supporters Will Be Replaced Without Reference to Organization Backing

SHAKE-UP BY LAW WEIGHED

Costello Never Influenced His Political Decisions, Tammany Chief Tells Grand Jury

By WARREN MOSCOW

The re-election of Carmine G. DeSapio as Tammany's representative on the Board of Elections on Monday night served to fan, rather than end, the conflict between Mr. DeSapio's leadership of Tammany Hall and Mayor Impellitteri's administration.

This was apparent yesterday as the DeSapio supporters sat back waiting for the Mayor to act and the Mayor's advisers, who had led the fight on Mr. DeSapio's continuation as Elections Commissioner, freely let it be known that a real war was about to start. Tammany men in the city administration who are supporters of Mr. DeSapio will be supplanted soon by Democrats without reference to organization endorsement and even some Republicans may be named, it was said.

While Mayor Impellitteri's forces were making their threats of patronage warfare, the Tammany leader appeared before a New York County grand jury that is studying reputed links between his organization and the underworld. Mr. DeSapio said he had told the panel that Frank Costello never had influenced his political decisions.

Might Let Tammany "Wither"

Several courses of action other than replacements in city jobs were being considered by the Mayor and his advisers, it was said. One was to let the Tammany organization "wither on the vine" by ignoring it as completely as if it did not exist.

A second course, and one that was outlined publicly yesterday for the first time by an Impellitteri chieftain—Robert B. Blaikie—was to reorganize Tammany by means of state legislation.

This course, considered privately for some time and mentioned by Mr. Blaikie at a luncheon of the New York Young Democratic Club at Oscar's Old Delmonico Restaurant on Beaver Street, would call for the passage of a bill requiring members of the Tammany executive committee to be members of their state committee as well.

As members of the state committee are elected directly at party primaries, only one of each sex to an assembly district, it would have the direct effect of cutting the number of Tammany district leaders from forty-two to sixteen and greatly increasing public participation in their selection.

The same thing could be accomplished by a change of party rules, but this would be asking the district leaders to abolish themselves and is not regarded as practical.

Dewey Aid Held Unlikely

There are, however, several obstacles to accomplishing the reform by legislation. One is that there would be arguments against doing it on other than a state-wide scale, affecting all parties, and the up-state Republicans might object to that.

A second is that even a bill affecting New York County alone would require the active support of Governor Dewey, who in the past has enjoyed considerable campaign success using Tammany as a whipping-boy, and who might not see the necessity for reforming it from the outside.

Mr. Blaikie, by his emphasis in his luncheon talk yesterday, seemed to see more chance for reform by legislation than from within the executive committee.

In his speech, and in answer to questions, he made a number of interesting revelations. While he made it clear he was speaking for himself alone, his position as a

Continued on Page 30, Column 3

U. S. Picks Site of Atom Plant To Help on Hydrogen Bomb

Tract of 250,000 Acres in South Carolina Chosen for Attempt to Make Components —Billion to Be Asked for Nuclear Work

By LEWIS WOOD
Special to The New York Times.

WASHINGTON, Nov. 28 — A 250,000-acre tract in South Carolina has been chosen for great new atomic energy production plants that will manufacture materials to be used in efforts to develop a hydrogen bomb.

The Atomic Energy Commission, announcing the project today, said that it would be situated in Aiken and Barnwell Counties near the Savannah River. The site lies about fifteen miles south of Aiken, S. C., and twenty miles southeast of Augusta, Ga.

An authoritative source said the South Carolina project would be the forerunner of a number of new or expanded atomic energy installations for which President Truman planned this week to ask Congress to appropriate possibly another $1,000,000,000. Much of this was expected to be sought for additional generating facilities and other plants in the general area of the Tennessee Valley Authority.

Congressional sources thought tonight that the expected $1,000,000,000 atomic weapons request from the President might get before the House of Representatives Appropriations subcommittee soon, perhaps at, or after, a special meeting tomorrow morning.

The group has been called to consider emergency defense requests, among which it had been predicted would be some for more atomic weapons facilities.

However, the huge figure disclosed tonight was far higher than most Congressmen had expected. A request for so much at this time, it was suggested, would indicate the Administration's feeling of urgency, and desire for a special consideration.

Production of hydrogen bombs will not be attempted at the Savannah River Plant, as the development will be known, the commission emphasized. The plant will produce "materials which can be used either for weapons or for fuels potentially useful for power purposes," the announcement said.

Continued on Page 26, Column 3

SIX SEIZED IN RAID ON BIG BOOKIE RING

Police Say Bronx Office Did Business of $250,000 a Day, Was City Headquarters

A bookmaking establishment described by the police as "general headquarters for New York City" was raided yesterday by seven detectives of Police Commissioner Thomas F. Murphy's confidential squad.

The place, on the ground floor of a six-story building at 263 East 150th Street, the Bronx, was said by Assistant Chief Inspector James R. Kennedy, who led the raiding party, to have been doing a business of more than $250,000 a day in bets. "It's the biggest I've ever seen," Mr. Kennedy said.

The detectives closed in on the place at 7:10 P. M. They were able to see six men inside through a barred side window. Five were operating adding machines and the other was at a telephone.

Although there were actually five means of exit from the complicated layout of the establishment, the men inside failed to avail themselves of any of them. Well-dressed and differing little from respectable business men in their demeanor, they surrendered quietly.

A clue to the efficiency with which the establishment was run was given by a memorandum for

Continued on Page 29, Column 1

60-DAY COMPROMISE ON RENT CURB SEEN

Senate Group Ready to Propose Shorter Period Than One Asked by President

By CLAYTON KNOWLES
Special to The New York Times.

WASHINGTON, Nov. 28—In a compromise with Administration wishes, the Senate Banking and Currency Committee is prepared to recommend a sixty-day extension of present Federal rent regulation.

The votes to report such a resolution are understood to be in hand if an array of Government officials, headed by W. Stuart Symington, Chairman of the National Security Resources Board, can justify an emergency extension at an executive session tomorrow afternoon.

A majority on the committee believes a limited extension, short of the ninety days asked by President Truman, will allow the incoming Eighty-second Congress sufficient time to decide whether a new rent control law should be drafted.

There is strong sentiment on the committee for a new law that would apply strictly to defense areas, possibly on a stand-by basis. With the Democrats in control of the new Congress, make-up of the committee will remain about the same.

Senator Burnet R. Maybank of

Continued on Page 37, Column 4

H. F. Sinclair Shorn of $500,000 In Miami Club, Senate Unit Hears

By HAROLD B. HINTON
Special to The New York Times.

WASHINGTON, Nov. 28 — The Senate Crime Investigating Committee was told today that Harry F. Sinclair, the oil man, lost $800,000 in two nights of gambling at the Golden Shores Club, north of Miami Beach, and that he settled the debt for $500,000. The big game took place last January or February, the witness said.

This testimony came from George Patton, a former deputy sheriff of Dade County, in which Miami and Miami Beach are situated. He said he learned about Mr. Sinclair's losses from Jack Friedlander, a Miami gambler who had an interest in the Golden Shores Club, along with Rudy Levitt and Artie Clark.

He said Mr. Sinclair had been steered to the place by a gambler named Ryan. Friedlander told of the occurrence, Patton said, because Artie Clark had not split up the profits in the pre-arranged ratio, and Friedlander wanted him run out of business in Dade County.

Patton told the committee he served with the Office of Strategic Services during World War II, specializing in commando warfare in Yugoslavia.

On another occasion last March, Patton said, Friedlander paid him and two other deputies $1,000 each to guarantee the Golden Shores Club would not be raided on a particular night when special clients from the North were to be entertained there. The highest fee Friedlander had previously paid for such purposes was $500, Patton said, and he never learned the identity of the clients whose uninterrupted custom was worth so much more money to the gamblers.

The witness told a long, detailed story of payoffs to himself and other deputy sheriffs by gamblers either to let their places alone or to give advance warning of raids.

Continued on Page 29, Column 4

U. N. LINE IN PERIL

Reds Drive Deep Wedge in West, Threaten to Turn Right Flank

ALLIES FORCED BACK

Enemy Reported in Rear of U. S. Forces in Push Through Republicans

By LINDESAY PARROTT
Special to The New York Times.

TOKYO, Wednesday, Nov. 29 — Chinese and Korean Communists with a total force of 200,000 thrust new, intensified attacks yesterday against the United Nations forces in Korea.

An Eighth Army spokesman said the United Nations withdrawals had been made at some points under heavy pressure and in others contact with the enemy had been broken as United States and South Korean forces took up better positions for defense.

On the right, the reorganization and regrouping of the hard-pressed South Korean Second Corps continued, Army headquarters said. The South Koreans still were under heavy pressure but the situation was somewhat stabilized on the dangerous right flank, the spokesman added.

[From recaptured Tokchon on the right flank, the Communists rolled twenty-three miles southwest to the town of Samso, behind the United States positions, The Associated Press reported. A battle was developing at Samso between United States First Cavalry units and the onrushing Communists. In this general area United States forces had been forced to give up Yongbyon and Won.]

In the northeast a counter-attack by what was said to be two Chinese

Continued on Page 3, Column 2

CAPITAL ANXIOUS

Chiefs of Security Meet President—Congress Units Hear Acheson

PLEDGE BY WHERRY

'Reiterates' the Desire to Cooperate—Factions Unite to Face Crisis

By WILLIAM S. WHITE
Special to The New York Times.

WASHINGTON, Nov. 28—President Truman, Congress and the diplomatic and military leaders of the United States drew together today in a new unity, quitting the harsh partisanship of only yesterday, to confront the crisis in the Orient.

This Government formally accused the Chinese Communist regime of open and deliberate aggression in Korea, and anxiously awaited the decision of the United Nations as to what was now to be done.

The President met in extraordinary session in the afternoon with the National Security Council, the highest strategic authority of this country, and the Joint Chiefs of Staff. This done, he held his regularly scheduled meeting with his Cabinet.

If any decisions were made by the Adminis ation, they were put in a wholly deferred status. Every responsible official in Washington looked, for the moment, only to the United Nations.

Secretary of State Dean Acheson went before the Senate Foreign Relations Committee and the House Foreign Affairs Committee for closed consultations, which were the gravest since the end of World War II.

A military informant of high responsibility told reporters that

Continued on Page 6, Column 3

World News Summarized

WEDNESDAY, NOVEMBER 29, 1950

Communist China was accused by the United States yesterday of "open and notorious" aggression in Korea as Peiping's representatives sat as invited guests in the United Nations Security Council. United States Representative Austin asked the Communists twenty questions aimed at throwing light on why they had intervened in the Korean fighting and what it was they wanted. The answer he got from Wu Hsiu-chuan was that the United States should end its "criminal acts of armed aggression" against Formosa and "intervention" in Korea. Mr. Austin pressed for passage of a resolution asking Peiping to quit Korea. The motion faced a certain Soviet veto and was scheduled to go before the General Assembly. [1:8.]

The harshness of the debate, coupled with news of United Nations reverses in Korea and General MacArthur's statement that "we face an entirely new war," spread gloom at Lake Success. [9:2.]

Chinese and Korean Communists continued to force back the United Nations troops and were pouring men and arms through a wide breach. The enemy sought to drive a wedge between the Eighth Army on the west and the Tenth Corps on the east coast. The Communists held a two-to-one advantage in manpower. [1:4; map P. 2.]

General MacArthur, in a special communiqué, said Peiping had sent more than 200,000 organized troops against the United Nations. He added that the solution of the problem thus raised lay "within the councils of the United Nations and the chancelleries of the world." He called his ground commanders to Tokyo. [1:6-7.] Criticism was voiced in Britain and France over General MacArthur's decision to take the offensive. [1:7.]

One Pentagon source held that our intelligence reports had been "very wrong." While disturbed, the defense officials were confident a new line could be held. [7:1.]

Partisanship was swept aside as Secretary Acheson detailed to Congressional committees the "grave dangers" now facing the free world. President Truman met with the National Security Council and the Cabinet. [1:5.] Prices on the New York Stock Exchange broke an average of 4.59 points, some issues losing as much as 9. [51:8.]

Other problems also plagued the West. The French Cabinet sought to resign when the Assembly, by a narrow margin, refused to order Defense Minister Moch to stand trial. [21:3.] Iraq followed Egypt in demanding an end to British military bases in the Middle East. [20:3.]

The Colombo Plan, a six-year, $5,040,000,000 project to develop Asia economically and counter Communist propaganda, was sent to the British Commonwealth Legislatures. [1:6-7.]

This country's new atomic energy production plant will be built on a 250,000-acre site in South Carolina. [1:2-3.]

New rules to permit the exclusion or deportation of politically undesirable aliens, including diplomatic and United Nations personnel, were issued by the Government. [28:2.] Abraham Brothman and Miriam Moskowitz received maximum jail terms and fines for conspiring to mislead a Federal grand jury investigating espionage. [25:1.]

In the Senate consideration of statehood for Alaska was blocked [37:1] and a committee favored a two-month extension of rent controls. [1:3.]

NEWS BULLETINS FROM THE TIMES
Every hour on the hour
7 A.M. through Midnight
WQXR AM 1560
WQXR FM 96.3

Index to other news appears on Page 34.

AFTER WHITE HOUSE CONFERENCE

Secretary of Defense George C. Marshall and Secretary of State Dean Acheson following a discussion on the Korean situation with President Truman and his top advisers.
Associated Press Wirephoto

M'Arthur Calls Aides, Hints He Needs New U. N. Orders

Special to The New York Times.

TOKYO, Nov. 28—The United Nations faces an "entirely new war" in Korea with enemy forces of more than 200,000 men, including a "major segment" of the Chinese Communist armies, now mustered there, Gen. Douglas MacArthur announced last night.

The general made the statement in a special communiqué over his own signature. Then, an hour later, he issued an additional final paragraph that some observers believed to be an appeal for permission to bomb the "protected bases" of the Communists in Manchuria, where the enemy has been able to concentrate men and supplies and pour them southward to Korea without fear of reprisal.

[*Text of the communiqué by General MacArthur, Page 4.*]

This new situation, with the Chinese taking a major role in the Korean war and United Nations forces again outnumbered by the enemy, General MacArthur said, calls for international action beyond the scope of his command.

"This situation, repugnant as it may be, poses issues beyond the authority of the United Nations military command — issues which must find their solution within the councils of the United Nations and the chancelleries of the world," he warned.

The communiqué was issued a few hours before the United Nations Commander in Chief had recalled his ground commanders from Korea for a secret conference here last night.

The subject of the conference

Continued on Page 4, Column 2

BRITISH SEE FORCES OF U. N. IMPERILED

Also Stress Gravity of U. S. Denunciation of Peiping—Korea Events Alarm Paris

By RAYMOND DANIELL
Special to The New York Times.

LONDON, Nov. 28—Officially the danger to United Nations Forces in Korea was regarded here tonight as "very great." And the diplomatic consequences of the United States denunciation of Communist China's "aggression" were regarded as "exceptionally grave."

[French opinion, alarmed by events in Korea and their repercussions in the United Nations, was inclined to blame Gen. Douglas MacArthur for taking the offensive. At the same time hope was expressed that a full-fledged clash with the Chinese Communist regime might be avoided by the creation of a neutralized strip of territory.]

There was no official guidance or reaction to indicate Britain's attitude in the event of the war's

Continued on Page 8, Column 3

$5 Billion Plan to Develop Asia Detailed by British Commonwealth

By CLIFTON DANIEL
Special to The New York Times.

LONDON, Nov. 28—A six-year £1,800,000,000 ($5,040,000,000) economic development program designed to counteract the appeal of communism in Asia was presented today to various Legislatures of the British Commonwealth.

"It is of great importance that the countries of South and Southeast Asia should succeed in this undertaking," said the document in which the program was outlined by experts and ministers of seven eastern and western countries of the Commonwealth.

"The political stability of the area and indeed of the world depends upon it," the report asserted, "and nothing could do more to strengthen the cause of freedom."

The program, called the Colombo plan, was evolved in a series of Commonwealth conferences that began last January in Colombo, Ceylon. It will apply to India, Pakistan, Ceylon, Malaya, Singapore, North Borneo, Sarawak and Brunei, and will take effect next July. By that time it is hoped that the non-Commonwealth countries of Burma, Thailand, Indo-China and Indonesia will have decided to participate.

When the program is completed, results on the following lines are expected by its authors:

Thirteen million acres or 3½ per cent more land will be under cultivation, 6,000,000 tons or 10 per cent more food grains will be produced, 13,000,000 acres or a 17 per cent increase in land will be under irrigation, and 1,100,000 kilowatts or 67 per cent more electricity generating capacity will be in operation.

Although such accomplishments would seem spectacular and the plan itself is more comprehensive than any ever undertaken in the backward areas of the world, the development program will be modest enough in relation to the magnitude of Asia's problem and the

Continued on Page 4, Column 5

U. N. HEARS AUSTIN

He Asks Peiping Whether It Wants Peace or War in the Far East

WU SHUNS QUESTION

Red Chinese Delegate Demands Withdrawal of U. S. Forces in Korea

Texts of the Austin and Wu addresses Pages 14, 15 and 16.

By THOMAS J. HAMILTON
Special to The New York Times.

LAKE SUCCESS, Nov. 28 — Warren R. Austin, United States representative on the United Nations Security Council, today accused Communist China of "open and notorious" aggression in Korea, and asked whether it wanted peace or war in the Far East.

Wu Hsiu-chuan, the Peiping representative, replied by announcing that he would not participate in any discussion of the "Complaint of Aggression Against the Republic of Korea," as submitted by the United States on June 25, under which Gen. Douglas MacArthur had reported three weeks ago the intervention of Communist China's forces.

In line with Soviet policy, he added that the "Chinese People's Republic" would not recognize any action by the Security Council, particularly regarding Asia, as long as the "Kuomintang reactionary remnant clique" held China's seat in the United Nations.

Sanctions Against U. S. Asked

However, the Peiping representative demanded that the Council "condemn, and take concrete steps to apply severe sanctions" against the United States for its "criminal acts of armed aggression against the territory of China, Taiwan (Formosa), and armed intervention in Korea."

Mr. Wu demanded also that the Council take "effective measures" for the withdrawal of United States forces from Formosa, and of those of the United States "and all other countries" from Korea, and "leave the people of North and South Korea to settle the domestic affairs of Korea themselves, so that a peaceful solution of the Korean question may be achieved."

The Council adjourned until 3 P. M. tomorrow without taking action. United States sources said that Mr. Austin would then ask for a night session if necessary to get a vote on a resolution, introduced by six Western powers on Nov. 10, which calls for the withdrawal of Communist China's forces from Korea.

Would Stay All Night

Mr. Austin, in fact, announced during the luncheon recess today that he was prepared to stay all night for a vote on the resolution, which also offers assurances that the Chinese frontier and China's "legitimate" interests in the frontier zone—mainly the hydro-electric plants that supply Manchurian factories—would be respected.

United States sources said that Mr. Austin had decided afterward not to ask for a night meeting to give delegates time to receive instructions from their Governments. Why additional instructions should be needed on a resolution introduced two and a half weeks ago was not clear. But it was understood that the United States now hoped that all members of the Council except Jacob A. Malik, Soviet representative, would vote for it. India and Egypt until now have been undecided.

Since Mr. Malik has already announced that he will veto the resolution, the only real advantage in taking a vote would be to prepare the way for action by the General Assembly, which earlier this session set up machinery whereby it can recommend the use of armed force against an aggressor if a veto prevents the Security Council from acting.

However, the failure of Mr. Aus-

Continued on Page 16, Column 6

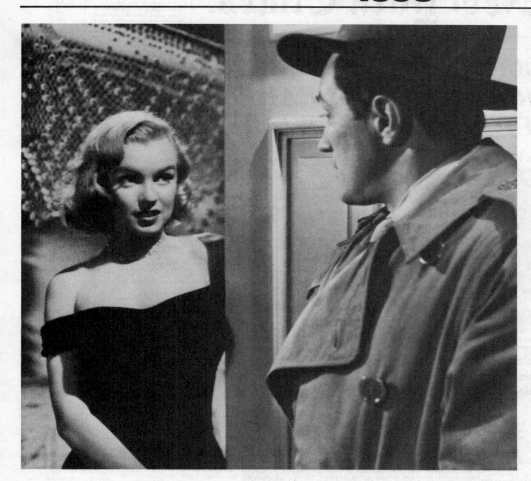

Marilyn Monroe appeared in The Asphalt Jungle, *a film that opened the door to her success and to a new era in crime films.*

Broderick Crawford and Judy Holliday in the marvelous gin rummy scene from Born Yesterday.

"All the News That's Fit to Print"

The New York Times.

LATE CITY EDITION
Mostly fair and cold today. Fair and continued cold tomorrow.

Temperature Range Today—Max., 35; Min., 27
Temperatures Yesterday—Max., 42; Min., 32
U. S. Weather Bureau Report, Page 7; Sect. 8

Section 1

NEWS INDEX, PAGE 87, THIS SECTION

VOL. C..No. 33,930.

Entered as Second-Class Matter,
Post Office, New York, N. Y.

NEW YORK, SUNDAY, DECEMBER 17, 1950.

Copyright, 1950, by The New York Times Company.

Including Magazine and Book Review.

FIFTEEN CENTS | New York City | Elsewhere | 25 Mile Zone | Twenty-five Cents

PRESIDENT PROCLAIMS A NATIONAL EMERGENCY; AUTO PRICES ROLLED BACK; RAIL STRIKE ENDS; ALLIES GIVE UP HAMHUNG; WU REJECTS TRUCE

U.N. 'TRAP' ALLEGED

Peiping Representative Says He Will Start Home Tuesday

BIDS U. S. QUIT KOREA

'Volunteers' to Withdraw if Formosa Also Is Yielded, He States

Text of press statement by Mr. Wu is printed on Page 12.

By A. M. ROSENTHAL

LAKE SUCCESS, Dec. 16—Communist China rejected today the United Nations plan for a cease-fire in Korea as a "trap," and Peiping's representatives here said they would leave for home on Tuesday.

The Chinese Communists warned that the great problems of the world could not be settled peacefully unless Peiping got a seat in the United Nations and a major voice in Asia. They made it clear that their conditions for peace in Korea remained United States withdrawal from the country and an end to American "aggression" in Formosa. On those conditions, they implied, Communist China would withdraw its "volunteer" troops from Korea.

Peiping's stand was outlined at a special press conference here called by its chief representative at the United Nations, the impassive Wu Hsiu-chuan. Before coming to the press conference Mr. Wu informed United Nations officials that he would leave for Peiping on Tuesday by air.

Wu Complains to Lie

Mr. Wu was reported to have told Secretary General Trygve Lie last night that his delegation had come to New York weeks ago to discuss Soviet charges of United States aggression against China and had not been invited to testify before the General Assembly's Political and Security Committee. The committee has opened debate on the item but recessed the discussion to take up the problem of Chinese intervention in Korea. Mr. Wu complained to Mr. Lie that there was no purpose in his staying if the committee did not discuss the Soviet charges, which are centered on Formosa and Korea.

The Secretary General immediately got in touch with the three-man cease-fire committee set up by the Assembly to sound out the United States and Communist China on the possibility of a cease-fire and efforts were said to have been made to persuade Mr. Wu to change his mind about leaving. But th e Chinese still were planning to leave Tuesday.

Delegation May Stay

Some diplomats said that developments Monday would decide whether the Chinese delegation would leave. The Political Committee is to map its remaining work on Monday and the Chinese Communists may attend in the visitors' section. If the committee votes to resume talk on Formosa immediately, it was believed, the Chinese may stay for a while.

For its part, the cease-fire committee announced that it would present an interim report to the Assembly on Monday, and stressed the word interim. The committee released a statement saying that it intended to go ahead with its efforts for a Korean cease-fire. It was reported that the three diplomats—Lester B. Pearson of Canada, Sir Benegal N. Rau of India and Nasrollah Entezam of Iran—would now try to make direct contact with Chinese Communist leaders in Peiping.

The committee met with Mr. Lie today twice before the Wu press conference. In another room, a little while later, Mr. Lie met with Mr. Wu and introduced him to Mr. Entezam, who is president of the Assembly. Sometime over the week-end, there will be another — and

Continued on Page 13, Column 5

TURNING DOWN CEASE-FIRE PLAN

Wu Hsiu-chuan, right, outlining Communist China's stand at special press conference he called at Lake Success. With him are Miss Kung Pu-sheng and Chiao Kuan-hua.

The New York Times (by Ernest Sisto)

Paris and London Void Pacts In Arming Bonn, Soviet Says

By HAROLD CALLENDER

PARIS, Dec. 16—The Soviet Government handed to the French and British Ambassadors in Moscow yesterday a note accusing France and Britain of violating their treaties with the Soviet Union by sponsoring rearmament of the Germans.

[Text of the Soviet note to France and Britain, Page 18.]

The step was considered an effort to hamstring defense discussions due to begin in Brussels Monday among the Foreign and Defense Ministers of the North Atlantic Treaty nations.

The new note was a sequel to that of Oct. 18 to France, Britain and the United States in which Moscow said it would not "tolerate" measures of the Western powers aimed at reviving the German Regular Army.

The treaties that Moscow now charges were violated are Britain's pact with the Soviet Union of May 26, 1942, and France's similar treaty signed Dec. 10, 1944. The principal content of both treaties was an agreement not to make a separate peace with Germany or to make any alliance against the signatories.

Both treaties were made when the Soviet Union was aligned with but not formally allied with the Western powers in the war against Germany, and when both France and Britain sought to insure against a revival of German power, which then seemed to them the greatest possible future menace.

A warning of yesterday's note was given to the French by Jacques Duclos, French Communist leader, who, in a speech at Brest last Sunday, said that in accepting rearmament of the Germans "the French Government repudiates the signature of France and deliberately violates" the treaties.

M. Duclos specified that the vio-

Continued on Page 19, Column 1

RED CHINA'S ASSETS IN U. S. ARE FROZEN

Washington Takes Unilateral Action—Tightens Ban on Shipping to Mainland

By WALTER H. WAGGONER

WASHINGTON, Dec. 16—The United States, in actions believed to have fallen just short of a war declaration, froze Chinese Communist funds in United States territory tonight and prohibited United States ships from calling at Chinese ports.

These steps, taken less than twelve hours after President Truman had proclaimed a national emergency, completed an economic embargo characteristic of a state of war.

The State, Treasury and Commerce Departments acted in concert on the moves.

The United States took this action alone. That the Government had consulted other friendly powers was not denied, and the fact that the United States acted unilaterally indicated disapproval by the other nations.

The State Department said the freezing of Communist China's assets and the barring of United States ships from her ports had been "forced upon us" by the in-

Continued on Page 16, Column 2

Nyack Area Fears the Thruway Means Razing of 250 Buildings

NYACK, N. Y., Dec. 16—Fear was widespread here today that the proposed Thruway crossing of the Tappan Zee would require the razing of 250 homes and other buildings and remove half the property in the village of South Nyack from local tax rolls.

Unpopular in this area from the time it was first contemplated, the Tappan Zee bridge project aroused fresh demonstrations of hostility as a relatively detailed map of the property needed for the bridge and approaches became available.

After examining the map, some residents asserted that the project would obliterate South Nyack al- most as if it had been the target of an atomic bomb.

The villages of Nyack, South Nyack and Grandview, which are in the path of the Thruway, are planning a joint suit to enjoin the

State Thruway Authority from proceeding with its plans. They are also arranging to send delegations to Governor Dewey and the Legislature to voice their demand for a change in plans.

Harold A. Williams, supervisor of the town of Orangetown, in which Grandview, South Nyack and Nyack are situated, received by messenger last night a copy of the new map from Bertram D. Tallamy, State Superintendent of Public Works and chairman of the Thruway Authority.

It showed the Rockland bridgehead of the Tappan Zee crossing in the northeast corner of Grandview. From that point the approach highway is sketched cutting diag-

Continued on Page 72, Column 3

BEACHHEAD IS CUT

U.N. Troops Forced Back to Narrowed Area as Foe Perils Lines

NAVY SHELLS REDS

MacArthur Aides Report Chinese Build-Up for Attack in West

By LINDESAY PARROTT

TOKYO, Sunday, Dec. 17—United Nations forces pulled back yesterday from the wrecked industrial city of Hamhung on the beleaguered northeast Korean beachhead to form a tight perimeter around the seaport of Hungnam. Off that port lay Allied warships to pour fire on advancing columns of Chinese Communists.

Hamhung was evacuated in mid-afternoon yesterday as Chinese troops began to pour into the city's northeastern suburbs. United States engineers blew bridges across the Tongsonchon River and smaller tributaries to delay the pursuit.

Reports this morning said the enemy occupied the city and in this area was about seven miles from the Hungnam beaches. Attacks from the northeast and northwest continued and at the deepest penetration the Reds were only three or four miles from the port.

The withdrawals came after heavy Chinese attacks on the northern and western faces of the United Nations area around the Hungnam beaches had made some penetrations south of Oro on a mountain highway down from the Changjin Reservoir and toward Chigyong where the Chinese were thrusting toward the important Yonpo airfield.

Indications were that the Communist invaders had massed ten to twelve divisions — more than 100,- 000 men — north and west of Hamhung in an attempt to drive

Continued on Page 5, Column 1

STRIKERS RETURN

Workers Heed Request of President—Freight Jam Is Melting

MAILS MOVING AGAIN

Pay Dispute Settlement Is Expected Quickly in Washington

By GEORGE ECKEL

CHICAGO, Dec. 16—Railroad transportation services were returning rapidly to normal today, as more than 10,000 switchmen ended their mushrooming three-day wildcat strike at the behest of President Truman.

The strikers were going back to work in fourteen of fifteen cities to which the walkout had spread. They did so without a settlement of the wage-hour dispute between the carriers and their union, the Brotherhood of Railroad Trainmen. The union, however, had not authorized the walkout.

[In Washington it was believed a quick settlement of the pay dispute underlying the strike would be effected, probably on terms long available to the union.

[In New York, mountains of mail and freight began to melt as virtually normal railroad service was restored.]

The last of the strikers to return were those at the Illinois Central yards in Birmingham, Ala. Strikers returned at the yards of the Southern Railroad in Birmingham a few hours earlier.

The Postoffice Department lifted its thirty-nine-hour embargo at 11:15 A. M., E. S. T., today, resuming "normal service" at once, and workers began the attack on mountains of backlogged Christmas parcels in the nation's key transport centers and transfer points as Chicago, St. Louis, Washington and Pittsburgh began to

Continued on Page 44, Column 1

Recent Auto Rises Canceled By First Price-Freeze Edict

'Ceiling Regulation No. 1' of Economic Stabilization Agency Holds Schedules to Dec. 1 Levels—Wage Study Set

By CHARLES E. EGAN

WASHINGTON, Dec. 16—The first price freeze and roll-back actions to result from the present national emergency were announced today by the Economic Stabilization Agency.

Under orders effective at once prices of passenger automobiles are frozen as of Dec. 1, and companies that have increased quotations for their 1951 lines are ordered to "roll them back" to that date or face Federal penalties.

Today's order, which came soon after President Truman's action, declaring a national emergency, was regarded here as a forerunner of a variety of similar edicts to issue from the agency beginning Monday.

[In Detroit, a Ford executive said the company would "conform promptly." The head of the automobile workers' union opposed "pin-prick" controls.]

The order was studied closely by representatives of business as they regarded it as setting a pattern for ensuing regulations. There was a general feeling that

Dec. 1 would be selected as the terminal date for price increase and that ceilings declared by the Economic Stabilization Agency over the coming month would use quotations of that date as determining factors in industries affected.

The price action in the auto industry is based upon the authority granted under the President's declaration of a national emergency. It is the first order also to affect the economy since the Office of Price Administration exercised its powers in World War II.

According to officials the order was issued to enable the Economic Stabilization Agency to make a comprehensive analysis of the effect of cost increases upon the profit position of the companies affected and to ascertain whether cost increases actually incurred justified the recent price increase. If the study justifies the price advances, it was added, the agency will make whatever changes in

Continued on Page 59, Column 3

U. S. Urges Defense Parley By All American Republics

WASHINGTON, Dec. 16—The United States proposed today an emergency meeting of the foreign ministers of the twenty-one American republics for tightening the defenses of this hemisphere against the threat of international communism.

Secretary of State Dean Acheson instructed the United States representative to the Council of the Organization of American States to request such a meeting, and he said he was acting under the direction of President Truman.

In making his request known today, Mr. Acheson declared:

"The United States, having embarked on urgent mobilization for the common defense, wishes to consult its fellow members in the inter - American community with respect to the situation which we all face and on the coordination of the common effort required to meet it."

He asserted that "the aggressive policy of international communism, carried out through its satellites, has brought about a situation in which the entire free world is threatened."

The Secretary added that the United States, after consultations with leaders of Congress and the other American Governments, would propose a time and place for the meeting and set forth an agenda for consideration.

Edward G. Miller Jr., Assistant Secretary of State for Inter-American Affairs, said it was the hope

Continued on Page 33, Column 3

DISASTER SERVICES PUT ON ALERT HERE

Wallander Orders Agencies to Be in Condition of Readiness on 24-Hour-a-Day Basis

By DOUGLAS DALES

City agencies that would have functions to perform in the event of an enemy attack were ordered yesterday to be maintained in a condition of readiness on a twenty-four-hour-a-day basis.

The order was issued by Arthur W. Wallander, Civil Defense Director, with the approval of Mayor Impellitteri after the declaration of a state of emergency by President Truman.

Twenty-two municipal divisions, including the five borough presidents' offices, were directed by Mr. Wallander to maintain at least skeleton staffs throughout the day and night. Some of the departments affected already operate on a twenty-four-hour schedule but

Continued on Page 39, Column 2

TRUMAN SETS DRIVE

Gives Wilson Sweeping Powers, Asks 'Mighty Production Effort'

U. S. RALLIES TO CALL

Congress Speeds Action —Stand of President Praised in Europe

Texts of proclamation and executive order are on Page 30.

By ANTHONY LEVIERO

WASHINGTON, Dec. 16—President Truman proclaimed a state of emergency this morning and delegated many of his own war powers to Charles E. Wilson, the new Mobilization Director. Soon afterward the defense program moved into higher gear.

Today was a day of action in the White House, in Congress and elsewhere in the Government as officials moved to implement the President's declaration to the nation and the world last night that the United States would meet the challenge of communism.

The Economic Stabilization Agency canceled the price increases made by Ford, General Motors and Chrysler in the last few days, and this was regarded as the harbinger of many new controls that eventually will encompass the entire economy.

Industry evinced its readiness to accept any war production goals, striking railroad men returned to work, and the general response from the public indicated an acceptance of the austerity program suggested by the President.

Proclamation Is Signed

Mr. Truman had pleaded for unity, like past Presidents coping with crises, and as in 1917 and 1941 the country was rallying with vigor.

In the free countries of Western Europe Mr. Truman was applauded for his no-appeasement speech in which he pledged to create an "arsenal of freedom" to strengthen all free countries. From Russia, which the President blamed directly for the postwar troubles of the world, came a typical blast that this country was warmongering.

Mr. Truman took two actions this morning to start a drastic increase of the mobilization program. He signed the proclamation of emergency, which unleashed scores of additional executive powers, and issued an executive order granting virtually blanket authority to Mr. Wilson to carry out all aspects of war production and economic control he deemed necessary. This authority received by Mr. Wilson will be subject in the Executive Branch of the Government only to the veto of President Truman.

Threat to Freedoms Cited

In his proclamation President Truman declared that conquest of the world was the objective of "Communist imperialism." He said this now constituted a threat to the freedoms guaranteed by the Bill of Rights, to the free enterprise system and to other rights, like collective bargaining, that free people had chosen for themselves.

These were the elements of a "full and rich life" that could be lost by the triumph of the Communist way of life, Mr. Truman said, calling for "a mighty production effort" for defense.

Mr. Truman called for sacrifices, for cooperation by state and local officials, for loyalty to the principles on which the nation was founded, and faith in our friends

Continued on Page 28, Column 3

In order to continue the complete presentation of the news THE NEW YORK TIMES was obliged to decline 192 columns of advertising for this issue.

World News Summarized

SUNDAY, DECEMBER 17, 1950

President Truman followed his Friday night message to the people that the nation was in grave danger by proclaiming yesterday a state of emergency. He delegated most of his own wartime powers to Charles E. Wilson, Director of the Office of Defense Mobilization, whose unparalleled controls over the country's economy will be subject only to Presidential veto. Shortly afterward, the Economic Stabilization Agency, in its first price-fixing action, ordered auto prices frozen at Dec. 1 levels. [1:6-7.]

In this city the declaration of emergency led to orders to twenty-two municipal departments that would have duties in the event of an attack to maintain around-the-clock duty. [1:7.]

In response to the President's appeal to end their wildcat strike, railroad switchmen returned to work. [1:5.]

Shortly before leaving for Brussels, Secretary of State Acheson, acting with Mr. Truman's approval, proposed an emergency meeting of the foreign ministers of the twenty-one American republics to consider the strengthening of hemispheric defenses. [1:6-7.]

The United Nations' plan for a cease-fire in Korea was rejected by the Chinese Communist delegation as a United Nations "trap." The Chinese accused this country of "aggression" in Korea and Formosa, but indicated that if this "aggression" were terminated Peiping would be willing to advise the Chinese "volunteers" in Korea to quit fighting. [1:1.]

Two drastic steps directed against the Peiping regime were taken by Washington: all Chinese Communist funds in United

States territory were frozen and all American ships were told to avoid Red China's ports. [1:2.]

Hamhung, in northeastern Korea, was abandoned to the enemy, as the defenders withdrew toward Hungnam. About 100,000 Chinese were reported pressing upon the shrinking beachhead. [1:4; maps, P. 2.]

Soviet Foreign Minister Vishinsky left Lake Success for home, expressing optimism and "wishes of peace, well-being and happiness" to the people of the United States. [5:1.] According to documents made public in Washington, Moscow's slave labor system has been a major factor in the economic organization of the Soviet Union. [20:1.] In new notes to France and Britain, the Soviet Government charged that London and Paris, by supporting the rearmament of Western Germany, were guilty of violating their agreements with Moscow not to participate in anti-Soviet alliances. [1:2-3.]

Prime Minister Attlee said there was no basis for the fear of wanton use of the atomic bomb by the United States. He warned Britons, however, that the future held disagreeable things in store for them, including a curb on improvements in their standard of living. [10:1.]

At the suggestion of Governor Dewey, Lieut. Gov. Joe R. Hanley has been named special counsel to the State Division of Veterans' Affairs. [1:6-7.]

NEWS BULLETINS FROM THE TIMES
Every hour on the hour
8 A. M. through Midnight
Except at Noon, 4 and 8 P. M. today
WQXR AM 1560
WQXR FM 96.3

Hanley to Get $16,000 State Job; Dewey Makes Good His Promise

By WARREN WEAVER Jr.

ALBANY, Dec. 16—The appointment of Lieut. Gov. Joe R. Hanley as special counsel to the State Division of Veterans' Affairs at an annual salary of $16,000 was announced today by Leo V. Lanning, director of the division. Mr. Hanley will take over the new post on Jan. 1.

Mr. Lanning said he had made the appointment "at the suggestion of Governor Dewey." Thus the Governor made good on a three-month-old pledge to give Mr. Hanley a state position, if the 74-year-old official should fail to win his Senatorial campaign against Senator Herbert H. Lehman.

The question of Mr. Hanley's future was one of the issues raised in the political storm that followed release Oct. 16 of the now-

famed Hanley letter, which was written Sept. 5. In the letter to representative W. Kingsland Macy, the Lieutenant Governor wrote:

"I have an iron-clad, unbreakable arrangement whereby I will be given a job with the state which I would like and enjoy (I have been told what it is) at sufficient compensation to make my net income more than I now have."

Subsequently both the Governor and Mr. Hanley denied that any specific post had been discussed between them. Both men reported, however, that Mr. Dewey had expressed reluctance to lose Mr. Han-

Continued on Page 68, Column 1

The George Burns and Gracie Allen Show *premiered in 1950 . Hal March and Bea Benaderet are seen here with Burns and Allen.*

Groucho Marx wisecracked on You Bet Your Life, *which began in 1950 and lasted ten seasons.*

Bert Parks, host of Break the Bank, *is seen here with elated contestants.*

The New York Times.

"All the News That's Fit to Print"

LATE CITY EDITION
Fair and cold; cloudy later today.
Fair and cold tomorrow.

Copyright, 1950, by The New York Times Company.

VOL. C...No. 33,933.

NEW YORK, WEDNESDAY, DECEMBER 20, 1950.

FIVE CENTS

EISENHOWER HEADS WEST'S ARMY; ALLIED PRODUCTION BOARD SET UP; NEW RED BLOWS IN KOREA PARRIED

DEWEY ORDERS CUT IN STATE'S EXPENSES NOT TIED TO DEFENSE

He Says No New Jobs Can Be Created Except in Health and Mobilization Agencies

NO DISMISSALS PLANNED

By WARREN WEAVER Jr.

Hutchins, C. C. Davis Join the Ford Fund

LOS ANGELES, Dec. 19—Paul G. Hoffman, president of the $258,000,000 Ford Foundation, announced today the appointment of Robert M. Hutchins.

GOVERNMENT SEEKS VOLUNTARY FREEZE AT PRICES OF DEC. 1

By CHARLES E. EGAN

AUTO EDICT STANDS, TRUMAN DECLARES

By LOUIS STARK

BEACHHEAD IS HELD

Regrouped Korean Foes Battered by Navy Fire —Airfield Yielded

CENTRAL SECTOR FLARES

By LINDESAY PARROTT

PRESIDENT REFUSES TO DISMISS ACHESON

AN ALLIED COMMANDER ONCE MORE

Gen. Dwight D. Eisenhower in St. Louis yesterday after his appointment as supreme commander of an international Army to defend Western Europe.

Truman Will Send More Men To Europe as Soon as He Can

By ANTHONY LEVIERO

WU FLIES FOR HOME AFTER ACCUSING U.N.

By WALTER SULLIVAN

ATLANTIC PLAN SET

Western Big 3 Will Ask Bonn Tomorrow to Join Nations in Defense

By C. L. SULZBERGER

World News Summarized

WEDNESDAY, DECEMBER 20, 1950

Fire Delays 55,000 on 2 Railroads As Truck Dives to Tracks in Bronx

Five Air Guard Groups Called Up For Active Duty Beginning Feb. 1

By AUSTIN STEVENS

1951

Katharine Hepburn and Humphrey Bogart made The African Queen a popular sensation.

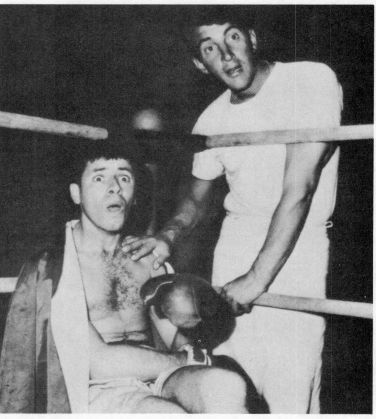

Martin and Lewis, the smash box-office comedy team of the early and mid-Fifties, in Sailor, Beware.

In Detective Story, a serious portrayal of police routine, Kirk Douglas played a tough cop.

100TH ANNIVERSARY
"All the News
That's Fit to Print"
1851 1951

The New York Times.

Copyright, 1951, by The New York Times Company.

LATE CITY EDITION
Cloudy, windy, with showers today, tonight. Cloudy, colder tomorrow.
Temperature Range Today—Max., 58; Min., 48
Temperature Yesterday—Max., 55; Min., 39
Full U. S. Weather Bureau Report, Page 39

VOL. C..No. 33,948. Entered as Second-Class Matter. Post Office, New York, N. Y. NEW YORK, THURSDAY, JANUARY 4, 1951. Times Square, New York 18, N. Y. Telephone Lackawanna 4-1000 FIVE CENTS

SEOUL ABANDONED TO RED ARMIES; CITY AFIRE; U. N. RETREAT ORDERLY; DEWEY ASKS STATE WAR FOOTING

LOFTUS RESTORED TO TOP FIRE POST IN WIDE SHAKE-UP

Monaghan Abolishes the Job O'Dwyer Created in 1946 for Murphy, Who Retires

OTHER 'STAFF' TITLES END

$1,000 Increase Will Be Asked for Chief—More Changes Are Predicted by Commissioner

By CHARLES G. BENNETT

In a sweeping reorganization of most of the top uniformed command of the Fire Department, Commissioner George P. Monaghan abolished yesterday the position of Chief of Staff and Operations, since 1946 the highest uniformed post of the department. Eighteen other "staff and operations" titles went into the discard.

The effect of the reorganization order was to restore Peter J. Loftus, Chief of the Department, to undisputed administrative command of the uniformed force under the Commissioner. The old arrangement left the Chief of Department little to do but take charge of actual fire fighting on the scene.

Frank Murphy, a close friend of former Mayor William O'Dwyer, who has held the Chief of Staff and Operations designation since the $12,000 post was created for him Dec. 19, 1946, filed for retirement effective last midnight. He is 65 years old and joined the department May 15, 1907.

Hennessy Also Retires

Elimination of the other "staff and operations" office titles resulted in one additional retirement, also effective last midnight, and a wholesale reshuffling of the holders of the remaining titles. The department's old borough commands were wiped out and the borough responsibilities were set up on a revised basis. All changes are effective at 9 A. M. today.

The second retirement was that of William J. Hennessy, Assistant Chief of Staff and Operations, who got $10,000 a year. Chief Hennessy, who is 60, entered the department Sept. 18, 1913.

The seventeen others who lost their titles were Deputy Chiefs of Staff and Operations. All of them revert to their Civil Service classifications of Deputy Chiefs of the Department, but some will have added responsibilities and most will receive higher pay.

In ordering the shifts, Mr. Monaghan said they were designed to bring about greater efficiency and centralized responsibility in the department. He said they would result in "slight budgetary savings" to the city, but would be worth while even if they caused a budget increase.

Other Changes in Offing

The Commissioner predicted there would be other changes before his reorganization was completed. He said also he expected to ask the city for more personnel, but could not say when the request would be made or how many additional men would be sought.

"In my judgment the reorganization will work for higher efficiency in fire extinguishment," he said. "Responsibility is clearly centered in the Chief of the Department and not diffused among a number of men. I can look to one man for responsibility under this system and the chief also can center responsibility."

Mr. Monaghan emphasized that in these times of "war scare" it was necessary to have senior fire officers in congested regions of the city. District Attorney Frank S. Hogan's current inquiry into the affairs of the Fire Department, the Commissioner said, had nothing to do with the shake-up.

Also, according to Mr. Monaghan, politics was not involved. But it was recalled by Fire Department aides that Chief Loftus had supported Mayor Impellitteri in the recent city campaign.

Through the reorganization the hand of Chief Loftus has been immeasurably strengthened in departmental affairs. As the top Civil Service official, he no longer must share his authority or be superseded by any other uniformed officer with a purely political or "office" designation.

Beginning last night Chief Loftus' name replaced that of Mr. Murphy on the departmental regular and special orders issued by the Commissioner. Yesterday, when he moved into an office close

Continued on Page 20, Column 6

CALIFORNIA Bound? Fly North American Airlines Douglas 4-Engine Liners only $88 + Tax Irregular Flights. Definite Reservations: call now. BRyant 9-6492. 508 5th, [illegible]

TOP FIRE FIGHTER

Chief Peter J. Loftus
The New York Times

HUGE STEEL MILL PLANNED IN JERSEY

Like U. S. Project, National's Million-Ton Paulsboro Plant Will Be on the Delaware

By THOMAS E. MULLANEY

The National Steel Corporation, the nation's fifth-largest steel-producing company, announced yesterday the purchase of a large tract of land in the Paulsboro, N. J., area on the Delaware River, about ten miles south of Camden, as the site for a new major mill. It would be the third large steel facility on the East Coast.

No date has been set for the start of construction, and the company did not disclose the contemplated size of the project, but it said plans were now under way to determine what types of steel would be produced at the mill. Steel authorities believe the plant's productive capacity may be around 1,000,000 tons of raw steel annually.

Ernest T. Weir, chairman of the board of National Steel, said the new plant "will provide a very substantial tonnage of steel products for an expansion of our domestic distribution and also for the company's export trade."

U. S. Steel Plans Mill Nearby

The report of National Steel's plans follows by about a week the announcement by the United States Steel Corporation that it would start construction in the spring of a $400,000,000 plant with an annual capacity of 1,800,000 ingot tons near Morrisville, Pa., also on the Delaware River. The two facilities will be about thirty-five miles apart.

At present, the only major steel operation on the East Coast is the Bethlehem Steel Corporation's big Sparrows Point plant near Baltimore. The New England Steel Development Corporation, however, has been attempting to obtain Federal tax concessions to allow it to build a big mill in the New England area.

These projects, together with other expansion programs by nearly all steel companies throughout the country, would bring the steel-producing capacity of the United States by the end of 1952 to around 115,000,000 tons annually, compared with the present capacity of approximately 103,000,000 tons. Achievement of that goal in the next two years would maintain this country's better than three-

Continued on Page 15, Column 2

FAIR DEALERS MEET DEFEAT AT OPENING OF 82D CONGRESS

House by 244-179 Restores to the Rules Body Powers It Voided in '49 for Truman

SOUTHERN COALITION WINS

Barkley Asks for Nonpartisan Action in Crisis—Rayburn Calls Isolation Ruinous

By C. P. TRUSSELL
Special to THE NEW YORK TIMES.

WASHINGTON, Jan. 3—The Eighty-second Congress convened at noon today and within four hours a coalition of Republicans and Southern Democrats dealt a resounding defeat to the Administration.

By a vote of 244-179, the House of Representatives restored to its Committee on Rules the powers the chamber took from it two years ago for blocking Fair Deal measures.

Under today's action, decisions by the rules body as to what legislation shall receive floor consideration may be over-ridden only by petition of a majority of the House membership or through special parliamentary tactics on special days.

Administration forces had asked the House to adopt for the new Congress the rules, including the restrictions on the Rules Committee, that were approved for the Eighty-first Congress, which ended yesterday. This request was rejected by a vote of 247—179.

Then the House restored the old powers to the rules body, which within itself has operated coalitions successfully.

Nonpartisanship Is Urged

This followed the opening of the new Congress amid calls by leaders for cooperative nonpartisan action on problems in the national emergency and a declaration in the House that isolationism meant disaster. The galleries were crowded with spectators.

Sam Rayburn of Texas, who had just been elected Speaker of the House for a sixth term, an experience attained previously only by Henry Clay, mentioned no names as he attacked isolationism. But it was taken generally at the Capitol that he was replying to former President Herbert Hoover's proposal that American troops and materials be withheld from Europe until the Europeans themselves made greater defense efforts. Mr. Rayburn said:

"There was a time when we boasted that we had two great friends, the Atlantic Ocean and the Pacific Ocean. During the last war they became hazardous things.

Rayburn Calls for Strength

"And let me say to you it matters not where other counsel comes from, I feel that I know the United States of America cannot wrap two oceans around it and stay secure, safe and free.

"We are a part of this world and we must remain in it. . . . My efforts shall be to join with all patriotic men and women in the House, and they are all patriotic and devoted to the high purposes and principles upon which this democracy was founded, to do the things that will make us so strong that international desperados and despots will fear to get in our path. This we must do if civilization itself is to survive."

In the Senate, Vice President

Continued on Page 22, Column 5

Senators See $150,000 Hanley Note But Fail to Verify Debt's Existence

Special to THE NEW YORK TIMES.

WASHINGTON, Jan. 3—Investigators for the Senate subcommittee on elections have failed to verify the existence of a debt of $150,000 reported to have been owed by former Lieut. Gov. Joe R. Hanley of New York, Senator Guy M. Gillette, Democrat of Iowa, its chairman, announced today.

The subcommittee has been looking into the circumstances of Mr. Hanley's decision to run for the United States Senate last November, after he had been promised a state job by Governor Dewey if he were defeated. Mr. Hanley had announced himself as a candidate for Governor of New York at the time when Mr. Dewey said he himself did not intend to run for re-election.

The promise of a State appointment first became known when a letter Mr. Hanley had written to Representative W. Kingsland Macy, Republican of New York, was made public during the recent campaign. In the letter Mr. Hanley also discussed debts he owed Mr. Macy and Frank Gannett, newspaper publisher.

The investigators have found, Mr. Gillette said, that Mr. Gannett and the Bank of Manhattan had advanced Mr. Hanley $28,500 in August, 1949, to make the last payment on the reported debt of $150,000. The Senator said Mr. Hanley was reported to have asserted he owed the money on a double-liability assessment against some bank stock left to him by his father.

After this advance Mr. Hanley, according to Senator Gillette, exhibited to a lawyer connected with the Gannett transaction what purported to be a canceled promissory note. The subcommittee's agents were able to obtain photostatic copies of the note.

The note was made to the order

Continued on Page 20, Column 4

Pravda Names Stalin 101 Times on a Page

By The Associated Press

LONDON, Jan. 3—A Yugoslav provincial newspaper took a wry glance today at a recent issue of the Soviet Communist party's paper, Pravda, and came up with these statistics:

In the Nov. 17 issue, Premier Stalin's name was mentioned 101 times on the front page alone in these forms:

Josef Vissarionovich Stalin, 35 times; Comrade Stalin, 33 times; great leader, 10 times; dear and beloved Stalin, 7 times, and great Stalin, 6 times.

The Zagreb daily, Naprijed, quoted here by the official Yugoslav news agency, Tanyug, also said:

"Other variations were 'Stalin the genius,' 'great leader of entire mankind,' 'great chief of all workers,' 'protagonist of our victories,' 'great fighter for peace,' 'Stalin the hope of fighting for peace,' 'faithful fighter for the cause of peace,' etc."

NEW ARMS AGENCY SET UP BY TRUMAN

Harrison Heads It With Full Charge of Defense Output—Board to Advise Wilson

By JOSEPH A. LOFTUS
Special to THE NEW YORK TIMES.

WASHINGTON Jan. 3—President Truman realigned the mobilization chain of command today to suit his new director, Charles E. Wilson.

He established the Defense Production Administration and appointed William H. Harrison to head it. Mr. Harrison will supervise the entire field of production, subject to the general supervision of Mr. Wilson. The President also established the Defense Mobilization Board with Mr. Wilson as chairman.

The Executive Order was largely a matter of internal organization. Certain production authority that had been delegated to the regular Government Departments was withdrawn and handed over to

Continued on Page 13, Column 1

GOVERNOR IS GRIM

Proposes Drastic Steps to Protect New York Against Any Attack

HOPES TO AVOID TAX RISE

Plans Pay-as-You-Go Policy and Urges Higher Pay for Teachers, State Workers

The text of the Governor's message appears on Page 16.

By LEO EGAN
Special to THE NEW YORK TIMES.

ALBANY, Jan. 3 — Governor Dewey urged the Legislature today, in his annual message, to put New York State on what would amount to a wartime footing.

He asked this to enable the state to resist any sudden hostile attack and make its full contribution toward rebuilding the nation's military might.

The Governor proposed immediate re-establishment of a State Defense Council and a vast enlargement of its powers. Further he requested clarification and strengthening of the powers of local defense agencies and the institution of a loyalty program for state employes.

Defense agencies, he declared, should receive the right to seize and use private property in the event of an emergency.

The Federal Government, he asserted, had "as yet revealed no adequate plans to provide civil defense," and New York State must act for its "own salvation."

The Governor called for sharp curtailment of state activities not related to defense and promised that the strictest of economy would be observed in the expenditure of state funds.

Mr. Dewey predicted that the state would end the current fiscal year with a small surplus and expressed a hope that next year's budget could be financed without any increase in tax rates. He said he would propose legislation to plug some tax loopholes and eliminate inequities but he would seek

Continued on Page 17, Column 1

World News Summarized

THURSDAY, JANUARY 4, 1951

Seoul was abandoned by the United Nations to Communist troops attacking the South Korean capital from two sides. Other enemy forces hit Allied lines elsewhere. [1:8; map P. 2.] The Communists, who found Seoul burning and largely in ruins, had been pushed back by United Nations counter-attacks before the city was given up. [1:6-7.]

This country is ready to hold talks with Communist China "at an appropriate time and in an appropriate forum," but "if hostilities continue our troops will fight on in Korea." Warren R. Austin said in the United Nations. The cease-fire committee received until tomorrow to consider further moves. [1:7.] A bitter Soviet attack on the United States was called more conducive to fighting than to peace. [6:1.] The British Commonwealth conference opening in London today will seek ways to improve relations with Peiping. [8:4.]

The Russians must clarify their stand on Big Four talks "before we can assume" they are "ready to accept our proposal to discuss the solution of outstanding problems," Secretary Acheson said. [1:6-7.] The French Cabinet decided to urge Washington and London not to close the door on talks. [9:1.]

The United States High Commissioner's Office for Germany is moving to Bonn, which will later house the Embassy. [11:1.]

Appeals for unity in the tense world situation marked the opening of the Eighty-second Congress. [1:3.] House Republicans and Southern Democrats joined forces to rebuff the Administration by restoring to the Rules Committee, controlled by the coalition, the power to bottle up legislation. [22:1.] Chairman Vinson of the Armed Services Committee introduced bills for an aircraft carrier of not more than 60,000 tons and for statutory reorganization of the Air Force. [15:1.]

"More and much heavier taxes" soon were forecast by President Truman when he signed the excess profits tax. [1:6-7.]

The President reorganized his mobilization command by creating a Defense Production Administration, headed by William H. Harrison, and a Defense Mobilization Board, with Charles E. Wilson as chairman. [1:4.] Plans for a second major steel mill on the Delaware River, a 1,000,000-ton plant for the National Steel Corp., were announced. [1:2.]

Criticizing the Truman Administration's "weakness and vacillation," Governor Dewey asked the Legislature to put New York State on a virtual wartime footing. [1:5.] In his annual message he made fourteen major recommendations. [16:6-7.] Nine bills to implement the message and six for increased safety on the Long Island Rail Road were among 197 introduced. [19:1.]

A law validating rules on freezing rents was agreed upon by the Rent Commission in Albany. [20:2.] In this city tenants of Stuyvesant Town and the Riverton project in Harlem received notice of proposed rent increases. [20:3.]

Drastic reorganization of the Fire Department wiped out two top offices created by former Mayor O'Dwyer. [1:1.]

NEWS BULLETINS FROM THE TIMES
Every hour on the hour
7 A.M. through Midnight
WQXR AM 1560
WQXR FM 96.3

Index to other news appears on last page of this section.

Seoul's Last Hours Chaotic But Evacuation Is Precise

Snipers' Guns Accent the Hysteria of Populace—Troops Show Heroism

By GREG MacGREGOR
Special to THE NEW YORK TIMES.

SEOUL, Korea, Thursday, Jan. 4—Machine gun and rifle fire clattered sporadically in the darkness here this morning as the doomed city, erupting into hundreds of fires, met a hideous dawn.

Swirling clouds of gray and black smoke rolled through the streets. Hurrying, hysterical civilians stumbled pathetically close to building walls trying to avoid interfering with the purposeful United Nations troops as the last hours of this South Korean capital drew swiftly to a close.

[The evacuation of the city was completed shortly after this dispatch was written.]

Jeeps, trucks, staff cars and other wheeled military vehicles,

Continued on Page 3, Column 5

Move Disappoints Units at Front After 2 Smashing Counter-Attacks

By MICHAEL JAMES
Special to THE NEW YORK TIMES.

OUTSIDE SEOUL, Korea, Thursday, Jan. 4—The United Nations evacuation of Seoul, completed this morning, was carried out with such precision as to indicate that elaborate planning had preceded its abandonment.

Following a day of sometimes heartening gains by United Nations forces in which they heavily counter-attacked the hard-driving Chinese Communists, the burning South Korean capital was left to the enemy as a smoke-shrouded blazing prize. Methodically destroying store installations that might be of value to the Communists, the withdrawing United Nations troops left in good order.

It was not clear whether all the

Continued on Page 8, Column 3

Acheson Deems Soviet Reply On Big 4 Parley Too Limited

By WALTER H. WAGGONER
Special to THE NEW YORK TIMES.

WASHINGTON, Jan. 3—The United States today turned away as too limited the Soviet Union's latest outline for a proposed Big Four conference. Secretary of State Dean Acheson said in a statement issued at his news conference that the Soviet recommendations for the conference were still unsatisfactory and did not constitute "an acceptance" of the proposals made jointly by this Government, Great Britain and France on Dec. 22.

"It is obvious that we must have further clarification of the Soviet position before we can assume that the U. S. S. R. is ready to accept our proposal to discuss the solution of outstanding problems, including Germany, to which the Soviet attitude has created a sense of insecurity in the minds of peace-loving nations," he declared.

Going beyond this in reply to a question, the Secretary termed the last Russian note a mere repetition of the Nov. 3 communication that suggested the Big Four meeting be limited to the German issue.

The Secretary added that the United States position taken with respect to that note still held. In effect, the United States declined to take part in a conference limited to Germany and proposed, with the two other Western Allies, that the talks embrace all the "causes of recent international tension throughout the world."

The Secretary's statement was moderate and his replies to questions were cautious. Asked whether yesterday's Soviet note had not provoked a difference of opinion between the United States and Britain and France, the Secretary said the differences were all in the press comments from the three capitals.

He said that the three Govern-

Continued on Page 9, Column 1

U. S. KEEPS AVENUE TO PEIPING PARLEY

Austin Says Talks With Red China Are Not Barred—U. N. Truce Body Reports Failure

The text of the cease-fire committee report is on Page 4.

By THOMAS J. HAMILTON
Special to THE NEW YORK TIMES.

LAKE SUCCESS, Jan. 3—The United States "remains ready to engage in discussions with the Chinese Communist regime at an appropriate time and in an appropriate forum," Warren R. Austin told the Political and Security Committee of the United Nations General Assembly this morning. Expressing opposition to appeasement, Mr. Austin said that "the people of the free world acting through the United Nations must decide how the Charter can best be upheld."

"If hostilities continue," he added, "our troops will fight on in Korea."

Mr. Austin spoke after Sir Benegal N. Rau of India, spokesman for the Assembly's Truce Committee, had reported the Peiping Government's refusal to agree to a cease-fire.

The committee report revealed

Continued on Page 4, Column 3

President Signs Profits-Tax Bill; Sees Much Heavier Levies Needed

By JOHN D. MORRIS
Special to THE NEW YORK TIMES.

WASHINGTON, Jan. 3—President Truman signed the Excess Profits Tax Act of 1950 today and notified the country anew that the defense program would require still "more and much heavier" levies.

The bill that became law by the President's action increases corporation taxes $3,300,000,000 a year, as compared with his original request for $4,000,000,000. It combines a $2,700,000,000 levy on profits defined as excessive with a $600,000,000 advance in regular rates.

Mr. Truman's forecast of the need for greater revenues was made in a statement announcing that he had signed the bill. Congressional tax leaders promptly pledged their cooperation. The outlook is for enactment this session of a measure raising taxes all along the line, with individuals as well as corporations paying a share.

The text of the President's statement was as follows:

"The Excess-Profits Tax Act of 1950, which I have signed today, is the second step the Congress has taken since the start of aggression in Korea to help meet the rapidly rising costs of national defense.

"The Congress and its committees have acted with commendable speed in completing this complex piece of legislation and thereby have provided evidence for all to see that we are determined to finance the defense program without jeopardy to the stability of our economic system or the soundness of the Government's finances.

"The 1950 tax legislation has increased Federal revenues very substantially. However, the task ahead

Continued on Page 24, Column 1

CHINESE IN CAPITAL

Big Guns of Fleet Off Inhon Protect Troops Withdrawing South

NEW BLOW IN CENTER SEEN

MacArthur Says Large Enemy Force Is Driving on Wonju, 55 Miles Below Seoul

By LINDESAY PARROTT
Special to THE NEW YORK TIMES.

TOKYO, Thursday, Jan. 4 — United Nations forces early this morning abandoned Seoul, and the capital of the South Korean Republic for the second time fell into the hands of invading Communist armies.

[The Associated Press reported Thursday morning that Chinese troops took Seoul after United Nations troops had blown the last bridge across the Han River and the last Allied plane had left Kimpo Airfield, ten miles northwest of the city.

[General MacArthur said that four, and possibly as many as seven Chinese armies (corps), numbering about 120,000 men, plus two North Korean Communist corps, were driving toward Wonju, fifty-five miles southeast of Seoul.]

The announcement of Seoul's evacuation was made by a spokesman for the United States Eighth Army. Earlier eyewitness reports said the city was blazing with more than 200 fires as some citizens destroyed their homes before fleeing to the south.

The Chinese, in the strength of at least two divisions with stronger forces echeloned behind them, flung final attacks against the barbed-wire entanglements the United Nations defenders had built in the outskirts of the city. Observers in Seoul last night could see trip flares go up in bursts of color as the Chinese forced their way through the wire.

Packed With Convoys

Roads leading south from Seoul were packed with heavy convoys while guns of the United Nations fleet off Inchon and United States and British rear guards covered the retreat. President Syngman Rhee and the remaining members of his Cabinet had left the city yesterday to establish again a provisional capital somewhere to the south, as they did last summer.

Official announcement identified the United States heavy cruiser Rochester and cruisers and destroyers of Britain, Canada, Australia and the Netherlands as standing by off the coast. The Rochester, the first ship to bring her 8-inch guns into play, opened fire on enemy positions last night.

Rear Admiral L. A. Thackery, commanding the United Nations naval forces in the Yellow Sea, said transports and chartered merchant ships were in position in case the ground forces should move by sea. The Navy said "thousands" of civilian refugees were being removed from the Communist-threatened area. Carrier-based planes armed with rockets and napalm were flying protective cover over the United Nations ground troops.

Refugees Mingle With Troops

Streams of refugees mingled with the retreat. Some of the refugees had previously moved out of the city, then returned, hoping the capital could be held.

Electric power and telephonic communication with Seoul were cut off last night and the last convoys moved through pitch-dark streets. Gunfire could be heard within three miles of the city's center, where the enemy apparently was laying down a mortar barrage on entanglements.

President Rhee and the Cabinet members left the city yesterday on a special plane. Last night, the last employes of the Republican Government, whose fate might be execution at Communist hands if they were left behind, were begging rides on trucks. Others were plodding down the roads on foot.

The Chinese attack on the city came from two directions: down the main coastal highway from Munsan and the inland road directly south from Uijongbu. Reports said the United States Twen-

Continued on Page 3, Column 1

The Goldbergs, *starring Gertrude Berg was a favorite in 1950. It went off the air in 1951 but was later revived briefly.*

The Kefauver Hearings continued to be broadcast live on television. Astonished TV viewers got an elucidating glimpse into the nature of crime.

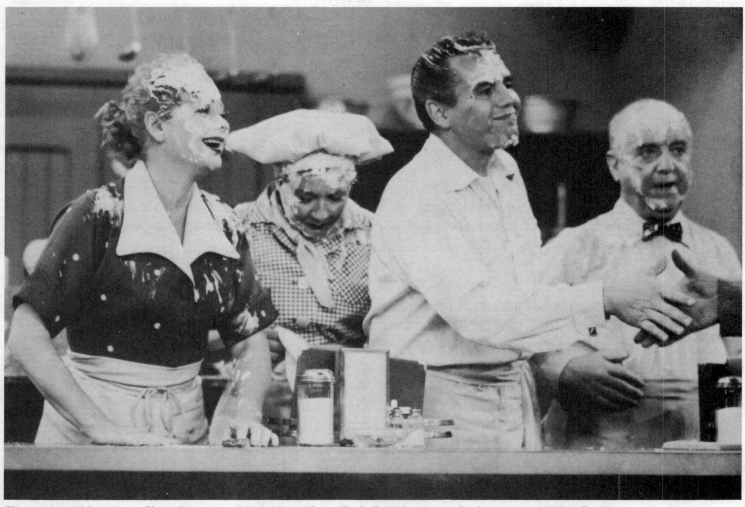

The renowned I Love Lucy Show *first appeared in 1951, with Lucille Ball, Vivian Vance, Desi Arnaz and William Frawley.*

100TH ANNIVERSARY
"All the News That's Fit to Print"
1851 1951

The New York Times.

Copyright, 1951, by The New York Times Company.

LATE CITY EDITION
Sunny, continued cold today. Fair tomorrow, becoming milder.
Temperature Range Today-Max., 32; Min., 18
Temperatures Yesterday—Max., 28; Min., 20
Full U. S. Weather Bureau Report, Page 33

VOL. C..No. 33,953. Entered as Second-Class Matter. Post Office, New York, N. Y. NEW YORK, TUESDAY, JANUARY 9, 1951. Times Square, New York 18, N. Y. Telephone LAckawanna 4-1000 FIVE CENTS

TRUMAN ASKS SWIFT STEPS TOWARD WAR BASIS; TELLS SOVIET 'WE WILL FIGHT TO KEEP FREEDOM'; ALLIES LOSE WONJU IN RETREAT, BUT PUNISH FOE

CHINESE ENTER CITY

In Some Areas Foe Has Pushed to 60 Miles Below Parallel

BATTLE LINES VAGUE

200 Sleeping Reds Killed —U. N. Unit Puts Off Action on Korea

By RICHARD J. H. JOHNSTON
Special to THE NEW YORK TIMES.

TOKYO, Tuesday, Jan. 9—The United Nations forces continued to pull back in battle-torn South Korea Tuesday morning. Rapid Chinese and North Korean advances into sectors abandoned by the United Nations troops placed the hard-pressing enemy in some sectors approximately sixty miles below the Thirty-eighth Parallel.

[At Lake Success, the Political and Security Committee of the United Nations General Assembly adopted a British proposal to adjourn until Thursday to give the truce committee a chance to make one more attempt to obtain a cease-fire in Korea.]

At noon yesterday the last troops of the defending forces pulled out of Wonju. Within half an hour the Communists entered the burning city, forty-five miles south of the Parallel, seizing control of the road network.

Sleeping Force Is Caught

The onrushing enemy troops two miles south of the town suffered a momentary setback, however, when a weary, confident Communist regiment lay down by a roadside to sleep. A United Nations battalion, probing northward after leaving Wonju, caught this force and slaughtered 200. The remainder of the surprised enemy fled back in the direction of Wonju.

Also taken yesterday by the Communists in their drive southward was Osan, twenty-eight miles south of Seoul. It was here that the first United States division clashed with the North Koreans last July and it was here that the first American died in the Korean war.

Eighth Army headquarters in Korea reported this morning that 7,000 Communist troops were now massed around Osan in the west and that thirteen divisions were massed in the Wonju area for what was expected to be a full-scale drive down the peninsula.

Withdrawal Is Orderly

Front-line reports said that no losses of territory thus far had been a direct result of clashes between the attackers and the defenders. United Nations withdrawals, they said, continued orderly, with skirmishes between Communist advanced groups and United Nations rear-guard contact elements.

At the present stage there is no battle line. When or where the bulk of the United Nations forces will close their ranks and turn and dig in in the face of the onrushing Communists is not yet revealed. However, the United Nations-held area in South Korea continues to shrink hourly as the hordes of Chinese Communist troops continue to spread out over the abandoned, burning, shattered areas.

Seemingly unmindful of the terrific toll taken by the United Nations air forces, the invaders pressed relentlessly into places given up by the United Nations forces.

Two South Korean soldiers, one released by the Reds and the other escaped, told United Nations officers that white-clad Chinese troops were moving on Yoju, eighteen miles west and southwest of Wonju, and that they had planned to take that city last Saturday night. United Nations patrols Sunday afternoon slipped into Yoju but found no enemy. However, it was regarded probable by front-line observers that the Reds had taken over the town by this time.

Gen. Douglas MacArthur's announcement of 4:40 P. M. yesterday placed the heaviest pressure of the Communists on the central

Continued on Page 4, Column 3

France Informs Eisenhower U. S. Must Quicken Arms Aid

Supreme Commander Is Reported Satisfied by Paris' Defense Contribution, Including Plans to Raise 20 Combat Divisions

By WELLES HANGEN
Special to THE NEW YORK TIMES.

PARIS, Jan. 8—The French Government told Gen. Dwight D. Eisenhower today that its ability to raise and equip twenty combat divisions by 1953 and to fulfill other military commitments in Europe and Indo-China depended on accelerated deliveries of United States war matériel, especially tanks and armored vehicles.

Here on the first leg of an inspection tour that will take him to the capitals of all ten European member countries of the North Atlantic Treaty organization, the new Supreme Commander of the Western defense forces heard a detailed exposition of the French military position by Defense Minister Jules Moch, after conferring briefly with Premier René Pleven and Foreign Minister Robert Schuman.

General Eisenhower arrived in Paris yesterday morning to begin the task of organizing a twelve-nation defense force to protect Western Europe against aggression.

Despite an admitted lag in French armaments production, the Supreme Commander was known to have expressed satisfaction with the preliminary accounting he received today of this country's present and potential contribution to European defense. Observers at the four-hour meeting in the Ministry of National Defense reported General Eisenhower had confined himself chiefly to listening.

He told M. Moch and the French

Continued on Page 18, Column 3

BONN ACCEPTS BID OF EAST WITH TERMS

Free Election Made Condition of Parley on Unification—Allied Talks Open Today

By JACK RAYMOND
Special to THE NEW YORK TIMES.

FRANKFORT, Germany, Jan. 8—Chancellor Konrad Adenauer and the Cabinet decided today to accept conditionally the East German proposal for bilateral talks on German unification, but the Chancellor made it clear immediately that he stood with the West on the program for defense against any military threat from the East.

On the eve of the first of the series of talks with the Allies on a West German military contribution to European defense, the Chancellor stressed with the Christian Democratic party members of the Bundestag, "we must be prepared to defend the West ourselves if we want to count on Americans to defend Germany."

At the same time Dr. Adenauer lashed out at Pastor Martin Niemoller, former Minister of the Interior Gustave Heinemann "and their henchmen" for attempting to "mislead the German people with dangerous sermons on imaginary German neutrality."

Dr. Adenauer said John J. McCloy, United States High Commissioner, had advised him the Germans must make a clear announcement of their determination to help defend the free world in view of the growing isolationism in the United States. The Chancellor also recalled Mr. McCloy's statement that in the event of Big Four talks

Continued on Page 19, Column 3

THEFTS OF SECRETS LAID TO REMINGTON

'Terrified,' He Still Gave Reds Plane and Synthetic Rubber Data, Miss Bentley Says

By KALMAN SEIGEL

Elizabeth T. Bentley, confessed former Soviet spy courier, testified yesterday that William W. Remington gave her what he called a "super-secret" formula for synthetic rubber and secret aircraft data in World War II.

She told Federal Judge Gregory F. Noonan and a jury of seven women and five men at Remington's perjury trial that the aircraft data — production figures, types and allocation—were copied because, she said, Remington had told her he was too "terrified" to give her original or carbon copies.

Miss Bentley, a major prosecution witness in the trial of the former Government economist, who is charged with lying when he denied under oath that he ever was a member of the Communist party, was the tenth Government witness as the trial entered its third week.

The self-possessed Miss Bentley in the main corroborated the testimony of Remington's divorced wife, Ann. She told of meetings in Washington with Remington, one of her alleged Communist party contacts, at which, Miss Bentley said, Remington "fed" her data for transmission to Soviet Russia.

She said that at one meeting in 1942 Remington told her he could get a formula for making synthetic rubber out of garbage. She said she then discussed it with

Continued on Page 17, Column 1

Princeton Buys an 800-Acre Tract For Forrestal Jet Research Center

Special to THE NEW YORK TIMES.

PRINCETON, N. J., Jan. 8—Princeton University has bought an 800-acre tract adjoining its campus to be used for a new research center on jet propulsion and related sciences, Dr. Harold W. Dodds, president of the university, announced today.

The center will be named for the late James Forrestal, the nation's first Secretary of Defense, who was a member of Princeton's class of '15.

This memorial to Mr. Forrestal will be established on property just acquired by the university from the Rockefeller Institute for Medical Research for "about $1,500,000," Dr. Dodds said.

The property already has two large laboratories and several smaller buildings, which were used by the institute's department of animal and plant pathology before its recent move to New York City.

Thus the new center will be able to start work within a few months, after various research equipment is transferred from the campus. With the installation of this equipment, the center will have a plant that could not be reproduced now for less than $3,000,000, it was said.

In a statement explaining the university trustees' decision to spend the $1,500,000, which they hope to get back through a special fund drive, Dr. Dodds said:

"Princeton possesses exceptional faculty assets for a major defense contribution, but we have felt that we could realize upon these assets only if major steps could be taken to integrate our scientific research and teaching and greatly expand the work space available for it."

With the acquisition of the new plant and property on the Brunswick Pike adjoining the university's campus on the east bank of Lake Carnegie, this integration and expansion become possible, he added.

The new James Forrestal Re-

Continued on Page 22, Column 5

G.O.P. IN CHALLENGE

Wherry Seeks Debate on Issue of No More Men for Europe

RESOLUTION OFFERED

Jenner Asks Ultimatum by Congress to the President on War

By WILLIAM S. WHITE
Special to THE NEW YORK TIMES.

WASHINGTON, Jan. 8—Republican objectors to the dispatch of more American troops to Europe challenged President Truman today within an hour of his opening message to the Eighty-second Congress.

Senator Kenneth S. Wherry of Nebraska, the Republican floor leader, moved to try to pitch the Senate's current debate on foreign policy as closely as possible to that single issue.

Mr. Wherry introduced a resolution that he requested be held on the table rather than referred to the Foreign Relations Committee so that it would be instantly and continuously available. The document declared:

"Resolved, that it is the sense of the Senate that no ground forces of the United States should be assigned to duty in the European area for the purposes of the North Atlantic Treaty pending the formulation of a policy with respect thereto by Congress."

Would Bar Other Forces, Too

The treaty binds this country and its eleven other signers to treat an attack upon one of them as an attack upon all, and to the principles of self-help and mutual aid in building a common military defense.

The Wherry resolution, in the unlikely event of its adoption in a Democratic-controlled Senate, would be at least a strong manifesto by the Senate. But it would not appear to be binding on the President.

Senator Wherry said tonight that while he had used only the term "ground forces," his intention also was to bar the use of naval and air forces without the express prior approval of both the

Continued on Page 14, Column 6

PRESIDENT DELIVERING STATE OF UNION MESSAGE

Mr. Truman before Congress yesterday. Behind him are Vice President Alben W. Barkley and House Speaker Sam Rayburn. On the left is House Parliamentarian Lewis Deschler.
The New York Times (by Bruce Hoertel)

14 BILLION IS ADDED TO DEFENSE BUDGET

Truman for 12 Billion in Arms and 2 Billion in Works—Bill Includes a Super-Carrier

By HAROLD B. HINTON
Special to THE NEW YORK TIMES.

WASHINGTON, Jan. 8—President Truman will send to the Capitol within a month a third supplemental bill for military appropriations carrying at least $12,000,000,000, Congressional leaders were told today.

Added to more than $42,000,000,000 voted for military expenditures at the last session of Congress, the new request, which it is taken for granted Congress will approve, will bring to a total of better than $54,000,000,000 the amount of money to be spent on the armed forces or obligated before June 30.

In addition, a military public works authorization bill amounting to about $2,000,000,000 is expected about March 1. This amount, if approved, will bring to a total of more than $4,000,000,000 the funds

Continued on Page 13, Column 4

World News Summarized

TUESDAY, JANUARY 9, 1951

"The only realistic road to peace" is to become so strong the "Soviet rulers may face the facts and lay aside their plans to take over the world," President Truman told Congress in his State of the Union message yesterday. We must be ready to fight for freedom if necessary, he said, and must realize that "the defense of Europe is part of our own defense." European nations are showing by "their actions" their willingness to defend themselves, he added. The address was solemn but frank in its discussion of the world crisis and its criticism of the Russians, who, he said, were fighting "an evil war by proxy" in Korea.

The country, the President reported, is in fine shape but we must all do our part and face "a major increase in taxes." Then he said: "I ask the Congress for unity in these crucial days. I do not ask, or expect, unanimity." He urged that every man "weigh his words and deeds" and put the country ahead of party and personal interest. Mr. Truman outlined in general terms a ten-point program that did not include any of his Fair Deal measures. [All the foregoing, 1:8.]

Industry, the President said, is being geared to turn out 50,000 military planes and 35,000 tanks a year "if we need them." [1:6-7.]

Within a month Congress will be asked to vote more than $14,000,000,000 more for military purposes. [1:5.] A Senate bill for stand-by universal military training was one of several moves to build a military manpower pool. [11:3.]

Senate Republicans gave little evidence that the President's message had softened their opposition. A resolution to halt further troop movements to Europe until Congress had set a policy was introduced. [1:4.]

Governor Dewey told the Legislature that the alternative to probable martial law in an emergency was to confer broad powers on him and a proposed state defense council. [1:7.]

The French Assembly gave final approval to a bill that will provide twenty army divisions by 1953. [19:1.] General Eisenhower was reported satisfied with the plans. [1:2-3.]

Western Germany, about to open talks with the Allies on its role in Europe's defense, has decided to accept conditionally the Soviet zone's proposal for talks on uniting Germany. [1:2.]

United Nations forces in Korea abandoned Wonju and Osan [1:1; map P. 2.] The Political Committee of the United Nations Assembly decided to give the Korea cease-fire group one more chance to act. [5:3.] Heads of the British Commonwealth have not yet found a formula to end the fighting. [7:2.]

NEWS BULLETINS FROM THE TIMES
Every hour on the hour
7 A.M. through Midnight
WQXR AM 1560
WQXR FM 96.3

Index to other news appears on last page of this section.

Potential of 50,000 Planes, 35,000 Tanks a Year Is Goal

By AUSTIN STEVENS
Special to THE NEW YORK TIMES.

WASHINGTON, Jan. 8—There was a historic ring to President Truman's statement today that the Nation's industrial structure was being geared to turn out 50,000 military aircraft and 35,000 tanks annually. Nothing like that production is envisioned under the present mobilization but, the President said: "We mean to be able to turn them out if we need them."

The goal of 50,000 aircraft was the same as the one President Roosevelt set on May 16, 1940. On Jan. 6, 1942, Mr. Roosevelt asked for 60,000 planes for that calendar year and 125,000 for 1943.

Mr. Truman announced no new actual size of the Air Force but John A. McCone, Under Secretary of the Air Force, declared at the Pentagon that under present plans the Nation's air arm was to become substantially larger than the eighty-four groups that last had been mentioned as the official target.

Much of the Air Force's expansion would be handled by full use of existing plants of the aircraft industry, Mr. McCone said, but requirements were scheduled to exceed their capacity and for that reason the automobile industry and other production would be used. The Air Force official said that planners expected to "tool up" to the point at which capacity could be doubled if necessary.

The immediate goal of eighty-four groups will be reached as soon as possible, perhaps within eighteen months, Mr. McCone declared.

Mr. McCone took issue with aircraft industry officials who had said that at the present rate of in-

Continued on Page 13, Column 2

DEWEY DISCLAIMS WAR DICTATOR AIM

Defense Provision Is Repulsive but Better Than Martial Law, He Says in Special Message

By LEO EGAN
Special to THE NEW YORK TIMES.

ALBANY, Jan. 8 — Governor Dewey disclaimed today any desire for dictatorial powers for himself and explained that the sweeping authority the proposed Civilian Defense Bill would confer on him and the State Defense Council was an alternative to martial law in the event of an emergency.

In a special message to the Legislature tonight, the Governor conceded that many of the provisions of the measure were repulsive and expressed a hope that they never would have to be used.

Explaining that it was impossible to know in advance, under present world conditions, when and where an attack would come, the message declared:

"It is better to be forehanded and ready and to have no attack than to find ourselves attacked and helpless."

Before the measure is put to a

Continued on Page 10, Column 4

Air Force Recruiting Halted Here For 10 Days by Rush of Volunteers

The Air Force, its training facilities swamped by a record rush of enlistments since New Year's Day, suspended recruiting yesterday in the Southern New York-New Jersey District for ten days.

The district recruited 2,009 men for the Air Force in the five days from last Tuesday to Saturday; shipped 1,223 of them to Lackland Air Force Indoctrination Center, San Antonio, Tex., and has 786 standing by for orders.

Col. William A. Haviland, district commander, at 39 Whitehall Street, said orders from Air Force Headquarters in Washington limited shipments from here to eighty men daily until further notice.

Accordingly, Colonel Haviland gave orders to recruiters to continue first processing of applicants but to accept no further enlistments until the current backlog of recruits was exhausted.

When enlistments are resumed, he indicated, they will be accepted in the order in which the applicants appear on waiting lists to be established at the New York, Camden and Newark recruiting stations during the suspension period.

Thereafter, he indicated, until additional training facilities are opened, Air Force applicants probably will continue to face a waiting period before shipment.

The Air Force has announced that the new indoctrination center under preparation at the former Sampson Naval Base near Geneva, N. Y., probably would be ready to receive its first recruits Feb. 15 and that it ultimately would accommodate 22,000 trainees.

The Air Force door was slammed shut, figuratively, at 3 P. M., to the disappointment of another of the large crowds of applicants that have jammed the corridors of recruiting stations since Jan. 2.

One of the last to slide through it was George Thansen, 21 years old, of Stony Point, N. Y., who had saved $400 in three years for an operation to correct a defect

Continued on Page 11, Column 4

WON'T QUIT EUROPE

President Says Its Fall Would Make U. S. Easy Prey for Russia

KOREA IS 'A SYMBOL'

Represents Stand of Free World, Congress Hears —10-Point Plan Set

The text of the President's message is printed on Page 12.

By W. H. LAWRENCE
Special to THE NEW YORK TIMES.

WASHINGTON, Jan. 8—President Truman told the Eighty-second Congress today that an "urgent and intense" defense production drive was being started to meet the threat of a Soviet Union bent on world conquest and already engaged in "evil war by proxy" in Korea.

And he called for preparation for the possibility of full wartime mobilization.

The President, delivering his annual State of the Union message, said the defense production program had two parts.

"The first," he said, "is to get our production program started as fast as possible.

"The second is to increase our capacity to produce and to keep our economy strong for the long pull. We do not know how long Communist aggression will threaten the world."

Asks Plants for Huge Output

Indicating the size of the production program ahead, Mr. Truman said that we must build up the productive capacity of the nation so that we could, if necessary, turn out 50,000 military airplanes and 35,000 tanks annually. But he added the hope that it never would be necessary to construct them.

There will be no appeasement, Mr. Truman declared.

"We are willing, as we always have been, to negotiate honorable settlements with the Soviet Union," he said.

But "we will fight, if fight we must, to keep our freedom and prevent justice from being destroyed," the President warned.

He appeared in person to deliver his message before the newly convened Congress, which he said would face in its two-year life "as grave a task as any Congress in the history of our Republic."

Mr. Truman called for national unity and refrained from specific mention of such controversial Fair Deal domestic measures as the repeal of the Taft-Hartley labor law or the enactment of the Brannan farm program. He devoted most of his message to the current dangers of the world situation and the need for the free nations to mobilize enough strength quickly to convince the Russian leaders that the Soviet Union could not conquer the world.

Calls for Appropriations

He outlined to the new Congress, in which Democratic majorities are sharply reduced, a ten-point legislative program as follows:

1. Appropriations for our military build-up.
2. Extension and revision of the Selective Service Act.
3. Military and economic aid to help build up the strength of the free world.
4. Revision and extension of the authority to expand production and to stabilize prices, wages and rents.
5. Improvement of our agricultural laws, to help obtain the kinds of farm products we need for the defense effort.
6. Improvement of our labor laws to help provide stable labor-management relations and to make sure that we have steady production in the emergency.
7. Provision for housing and training of defense workers, and the full use of all our manpower resources.
8. Means for increasing the supply of doctors, nurses and other trained medical personnel critically needed in defense.
9. Aid to the states to meet the

Continued on Page 12, Column 1

100TH ANNIVERSARY
"All the News
That's Fit to Print"
1851 1951

The New York Times.

Copyright, 1951, by The New York Times Company.

LATE CITY EDITION
Sunny and windy today; clear tonight. Fair tomorrow.
Temperature Range Today—Max., 39; Min., 32
Temperatures Yesterday—Max., 56; Min., 34
Full U. S. Weather Bureau Report, Page 59

VOL. C..No. 33,960. Entered as Second-Class Matter, Post Office, New York, N. Y. NEW YORK, TUESDAY, JANUARY 16, 1951. Times Square, New York 18, N. Y. Telephone LAckawanna 4-1000 FIVE CENTS

TRUMAN SUBMITS A 71½ BILLION CRISIS BUDGET; ASKS 16 BILLION TAX RISE, 61 BILLION FOR ARMS; ALLIES DRIVE IN WEST KOREA, QUIT WONJU AREA

M'GOLDRICK OFFERS PLAN ALLOWING RISE IN RENTS UP TO 15%

State Administrator Submits Changes Providing Seven Grounds for Advances

EASES CURB ON EVICTIONS

Increases Would Be Provided for Landlords Earning a Return of Less Than 4%

By LEO EGAN
Special to THE NEW YORK TIMES.

ALBANY, Jan. 15—Rent Administrator Joseph D. McGoldrick recommended state rent regulation changes today that would enable many landlords to get rent increases up to 15 per cent. In addition he proposed relaxing the restrictions on evictions.

Both the rent and eviction control changes become effective March 1 unless countermanded by the Legislature on or before Feb. 15. Some lawyers, however, question whether the new plan could be sustained in the courts unless the Legislature approved it by affirmative action. The Republican legislative leadership seeks to avoid an affirmative approval because of the possibility that it may split the majority ranks.

The new regulations would remain in effect until June 30, 1952.

Grounds for Increase Listed

Seven grounds for authorizing rent increases are provided in Mr. McGoldrick's plan. They are:

1. Proof by a landlord that he was earning a net annual return of less than 4 per cent on the equalized assessed valuation of the property. In such cases increases up to 15 per cent would be permitted. In most instances the landlord would be permitted to charge 2 per cent of the assessed value of the building alone to operating costs for depreciation. Interest on a mortgage or amortization payments would not be allowed as an operating charge.
2. Voluntary agreements between landlords and tenants for increases up to 15 per cent, provided a two-year lease is signed.
3. An increase in the value of the accommodations because of improvement or added service.
4. An increase in the number of subtenants or occupants, except where the increase is the result of children born to the tenants.
5. A disparity between the rents charged for a space and comparable space because of unusual circumstances, such as prior occupancy by the landlord's son.
6. An increase, since 1942-43, in operating costs of a building housing four families or less.
7. An increase, since 1942-43, in operating costs of hotels in New York City and Buffalo and of owners of cooperative apartments. This applies only to permanent tenants.

Except where a larger increase is needed to enable the landlord to avoid an out-of-pocket loss, no rent increase could exceed 15 per cent nor could there be more than one such increase in any one year.

Eviction Causes Widened

The present law permits evictions if the tenant is committing a nuisance or is putting the premises to illegal use or the landlord can show compelling necessity to obtain the space for himself or a member of his immediate family.

These grounds would be continued. In addition evictions would be permitted where possession was needed for alterations necessary to maintain the safety of the building; where remodeling was planned to increase the number of families that could be accommodated, and where the owner wanted to demolish the building to make way for a new structure.

Mr. McGoldrick recommended that legislation be enacted permitting evictions without a showing of "compelling necessity" in the case of the purchaser of a one- or two-family house who wanted to occupy the accommodations himself or in the case of an owner of

Continued on Page 25, Column 3

Taft Sees Constitution Crisis; Troop Concession Is Possible

Ohioan Calls on Congress to Reassert Rights to Pass on Foreign Policy

By RICHARD H. PARKE

Senator Robert A. Taft of Ohio declared here last night that the United States was facing a constitutional crisis, and called upon Congress to reassert its rights to pass upon fundamental principles of foreign policy.

[Salient parts of Senator Taft's speech are on Page 10.]

The Republican leader, continuing his debate with the Administration over the powers of the President, said he had been shocked at the speed with which "blind partisans" had rushed to the defense of the proposition that the President "can make war and war-like commitments."

"The basic liberties of the people of this country are imperiled," Mr. Taft asserted, "unless we can retain in Congress the right to pass on policies which involve the very life and being of the American people."

Speaking at a dinner of the Ohio

Continued on Page 11, Column 1

Connally Later May Offer Resolution to Give Senate Role in Sending Men

By WILLIAM S. WHITE
Special to THE NEW YORK TIMES.

WASHINGTON, Jan. 15 — The Administration's foreign policy leader, Senator Tom Connally, Democrat of Texas, may offer a concession later to those demanding that President Truman consult the Senate before sending troops to Europe.

Senator Connally, it may be stated, has no basic objection to the possible adoption of a resolution that would not seek to direct the President in any way but that would simply declare a belief by the Senate that the dispatch of troops would be desirable.

Such a procedure would give the Senate a sense of participation in the decision without giving it any assumed or real veto power. Mr. Connally has no intention of proposing such a resolution immediately but may do so as the Senate's foreign affairs debate goes on.

He will not move, however, until

Continued on Page 9, Column 3

BONN IS ADAMANT ON TERMS OF UNITY

Adenauer Asks Unconditional Acceptance of Its Standards for Talks With East Zone

By DREW MIDDLETON
Special to THE NEW YORK TIMES.

BONN, Germany, Jan. 15—Chancellor Konrad Adenauer today demanded unconditional acceptance by the East German Communists of Western standards of law, liberty and human rights as conditions for Western participation in any movement toward national unity.

Taking the offensive in the political struggle, the Chancellor declared that, although the West wanted unity, it could not deal with a nation in which liberties were suppressed and the People's Police was a tool of the Soviet Union.

Political liberties and the end of East German militarization through the People's Police emerged as iron-bound conditions for any further discussion of unity between the Federal Government and East Germany as a result of the Chancellor's statement.

The cleavage of Germany between the free West and the Communist East was deepened by the Chancellor's statement, which replied to the letter sent him last month by Otto Grotewohl, Premier of the East German Democratic Republic, asking for talks on German unity.

The Western Federal Government's rejection of Herr Grote-

Continued on Page 13, Column 1

BIG VIETMINH DRIVE FOUGHT BY FRENCH

Rebels Launch Attack on Wide Front North of Hanoi—Suffer Heavy Casualties

By TILLMAN DURDIN
Special to THE NEW YORK TIMES.

HANOI, Indo-China, Jan. 15—French-Vietnamese ground and air forces were today bitterly resisting the biggest Vietminh attack yet launched against the northern approaches to Hanoi. Together with reserves, the forces of the Vietminh, Communist-led insurgents against the French-supported Vietnamese state, are estimated at 20,000 to 30,000 men. The conflict began Friday night and has ranged at two extremities of the eighty-mile defense perimeter north of the Tongking capital.

The Vietminh has suffered heavy casualties and has been stopped without gains on the eastern flank. In the west, where the biggest Vietminh effort was made, the Vietminh has made gains in a day of savage fighting, but by nightfall tonight was weakening after having taken severe losses, especially from day-long air bombardment.

For the first time in the Indo-China warfare, the Vietminh today deployed in strength in open ground to challenge the French-Vietnamese troops. Gen. Jean de Lattre de Tassigny, French Commander in Chief, who arrived today from Saigon to direct operations, voiced satisfaction and confidence at the close of the day's fighting.

Continued on Page 6, Column 6

Germans Give Ilse Koch Life Term For Crimes Against Countrymen

Special to THE NEW YORK TIMES.

FRANKFORT, Germany, Jan. 15—A German court sentenced Ilse Koch today to life imprisonment at hard labor after having convicted her of inciting the murder of at least one inmate of the Nazi concentration camp at Buchenwald, where her husband had been commander. She is 44 years old.

The most notorious female war criminal was not at the Augsburg court in Bavaria to hear the verdict. She was in a padded cell at the Aichach women's prison, twenty miles away. Dr. Rudolf Englert, court physician, explained that she was unfit to appear because she voluntarily had brought on her hysterical state by simulating insanity.

Life imprisonment was the maximum penalty possible under the German Constitution, which forbids the death sentence. It was the same sentence that Frau Koch had received after her trial by a United States court in 1947. But Gen. Lucius D. Clay, then United States Military Governor, reduced it to four years on the recommendations of a review board.

Georg Maginot, president of the German court, rejected a defense contention of double jeopardy in the trial, which began Nov. 27. He said the United States tribunal had restricted itself to crimes against United Nations nationals, while the Germans were trying the defendant for crimes against Germans.

The sentence, which included also withdrawal of Frau Koch's civil rights, covered convictions on one count of incitement to murder, one of incitement to attempted murder, five of incitement to severe physical mistreatment of prisoners and two of physical mistreatment.

The severest proven charge

Continued on Page 5, Column 4

SEOUL APPROACHED

Reconnaissance in Force Comes as Invaders Mass for Drive

LINES STRAIGHTENED

U. N. Units Pull Back in Sector After Holding Salient 16 Days

By LINDESAY PARROTT
Special to THE NEW YORK TIMES.

TOKYO, Tuesday, Jan. 16—United Nations troops struck back hard yesterday at the Chinese and North Korean Communist invaders in the western sector of Korea, moving up to within twenty-five miles of enemy-occupied Seoul, old capital of the Korean Republic.

Columns of infantry and armor, backed by heavy airstrikes and artillery fire, recaptured Osan and Kumyangjang, and air observation said that the Communists were pouring northward out of Suwon, ancient walled city fifteen miles below Seoul on the main north-south highway. One flight of fighter-bombers of the Fifth Air Force cut down an estimated 800 to 1,000 of the enemy north of the blazing town.

[A later Associated Press report said that United Nations troops had driven beyond Osan to within five miles of Suwon. The United Nations unit that captured Kumyangjang withdrew to a defense position south of the town after having encountered heavily entrenched enemy troops in the hills to the north, The United Press reported.]

[In the central sector, according to The Associated Press, the United Nations forces pulled back from the area near Wonju after having held a salient there for sixteen days.]

The counter-attack came as the Communists were reported massing

Continued on Page 2, Column 2

DEFENSE PLAN VAST

41½ Billion Expenditure Is Estimated for the 1952 Fiscal Year

21 BILLION FOR 1951

Money to Provide Army of 3½ Million and Air and Sea Expansion

By AUSTIN STEVENS
Special to THE NEW YORK TIMES.

WASHINGTON, Jan. 15—President Truman in his budget message asked Congress today for an additional $60,971,000,000 to place the nation's armed forces and the military establishment as a whole in a state of war readiness.

He sought obligational authority for the expenditure, which would empower the Department of Defense to enter into contracts for goods or services that might not be delivered for several years.

At the same time the President estimated that actual expenditures for the military and related activities from the start of the Korean war to June 30, 1952, would total $62,415,000,000—$20,994,000,000 in cash to be paid out in the fiscal year ending June 30 and $41,421,000,000 in the twelve months thereafter. For military functions alone the above figures were given as $20,000,000,000 and $40,000,000,000.

The defense budget estimates—and the tentativeness of the figures was emphasized by both the President and Defense Department officials—are to provide for a 3,500,000-man armed force, a build-up of the Air Force to beyond eighty-four groups and the operation of some 500 combat Navy vessels.

It was the largest single military budget, in terms of obligational authority, since the wartime year of 1944 and raised to $115,000,000,000 the fund authority

Continued on Page 25, Column 4

World News Summarized

TUESDAY, JANUARY 16, 1951

A record peacetime budget of $71,594,000,000 and tax increases sufficient at least to meet a $16,456,000,000 deficit during the next fiscal year were recommended to Congress yesterday by President Truman. Expenses were estimated at 78 per cent higher than this year and receipts at an all-time high. To meet "the compelling demands" of security "in a period of grave danger," the President said, 69 per cent of the expenses were allotted to military and foreign aid. Although emphasizing the need of "strict economy" in nondefense spending, Mr. Truman urged several Fair Deal measures. [1:8.]

He asked authority to spend $60,971,000,000 more to put the armed forces in a state of readiness. Two-thirds of the total would be used in the next fiscal year. [1:5.] The President also asked Congress to authorize $10,956,000,000 for further military and economic aid to friendly nations and to increase the Export-Import Bank's lending power by $1,000,000,000 [1:6-7.]

Free, automatic life insurance of $10,000 for all service men, with benefits going to kin of Korean casualties, was urged by the President, who also asked a thorough overhaul of the veterans' program. [25:1.]

Congress seemed ready to grant the President's defense requests but there were protests against the Fair Deal aspect of domestic issues. [24:1.]

Men of draft age who wish to volunteer must enlist through their draft boards, the President ordered. All such volunteers will be assigned to the Army. [1:7.]

Washington barred new commercial construction without a special permit in a move to conserve materials. [1:6.]

During the debate on foreign policy, several Senators criticized the Korean cease-fire plan and the dispatch of more troops to Europe without prior Congressional consent. Senator Connally may move for some form of Senate expression. [1:3.] The issue, Senator Taft said, has raised a constitutional crisis. [1:2.] Harold E. Stassen urged other Republicans to abandon the "policy of despair" and unite behind "a sensible, practical internationalism." [12:4.]

United Nations troops in West Korea retook some ground in a "reconnaissance in force" but withdrew from the Wonju sector. [1:4; map P. 2.] In Indo-China, French and Vietnamese forces were resisting a heavy attack by the Communists. [1:3, map P. 6.]

Britain plans to double her troops in Europe in the next six months, General Eisenhower was told. William R. Herod was named coordinator of the North Atlantic Defense Production Board. [16.3.]

Chancellor Adenauer virtually rejected East Germany's bid for unity by demanding that political liberties be restored and militarization ended in the Soviet zone before talks start. [1:2.]

A German court sentenced Ilse Koch to life imprisonment as a war criminal. [1:2-3.]

Rent rises up to 15 per cent and easing curbs on evictions were recommended to the Legislature in Albany by Rent Administrator McGoldrick. [1:1.]

NEWS BULLETINS FROM THE TIMES
Every hour on the hour
7 A.M. through Midnight
WQXR AM 1560
WQXR FM 96.3

Index to other news appears on last page of this section.

11 Billion in Aid Proposed To Combat 'Peril' Abroad

President Would Use Most of $7,461,000,000 for Building Allied Defense Force—Extension of E. C. A. Is Projected

By FELIX BELAIR Jr.
Special to THE NEW YORK TIMES.

WASHINGTON, Jan. 15—President Truman submitted to Congress today in his budget message an estimate of nearly $10,956,000,000 for additional aid to peoples sharing the "common peril" of Communist aggression and for supporting activities.

Warning that "the entire free world is in grave peril" of the Kremlin's imperialist designs, the President forecast appropriations requests for $10,664,000,000 for direct military and economic assistance—$7,112,000,000 of the amount to be spent in the 1952 fiscal year—including another $1,000,000,000 of lending authority for the Export-Import Bank.

This "single package" foreign assistance program would include also requests of $115,000,000 for overseas information and education activities, $32,000,000 for United States participation in various international organizations and $145,000,000 for "other State Department activities."

The President gave only the broadest outlines of the combined military and economic aid program contemplated. He said the "great preponderance" of the $7,461,000,000 of proposed expenditures on all international programs in the 1952 fiscal year, starting next July 1, would go for the rapid build-up of "mutual defense forces." More than half the total would be for military equipment sent the allies, he said.

Some indication of the magnitude of the economic aid planned was given, however, by the President's statement during a press preview of his budget that it would be necessary to continue the Economic Cooperation Administration beyond its scheduled expiration date in July, 1952.

The President recognized that

Continued on Page 25, Column 7

U.S. ORDER FORBIDS BUSINESS BUILDING

Special Permission Required for 'Emergency' Cases—City Hit by Ban

Special to THE NEW YORK TIMES.

WASHINGTON, Jan. 15—The National Production Authority issued a ban today on virtually all new commercial building construction. Special permission for construction will be granted only in "emergency" cases. The order was made effective as of midnight last Saturday.

[In New York, builders expressed fear that the city would be hardest hit of all major communities by the order. Union leaders estimated that 20,000 skilled workers might be made idle in a few months. War plants were not expected to make up for the loss of commercial construction in the metropolitan area.]

The National Production Authority said its action was required to conserve critical materials for the defense mobilization program. It was issued in anticipation of a general licensing system for private cemmercial building construction to take effect Feb. 15.

Pending that date, the N. P. A. said, new commercial construction might be authorized on application when it could be shown to be in furtherance of the defense effort, essential to the public health, welfare or safety or necessary to alleviate or prevent a hardship to a

Continued on Page 32, Column 6

VOLUNTEER SERVICE IS MADE 21 MONTHS

Truman Order Will Let Men 18-26 Sign Up Before Draft for Tour of Army Duty

By HAROLD B. HINTON
Special to THE NEW YORK TIMES.

WASHINGTON, Jan. 15—President Truman instructed local draft boards today to permit men between 18 and 26 years old to volunteer for induction, instead of waiting to be called. They can now volunteer for twenty-one months of service, the same period they would be required to serve if they had waited for their involuntary induction.

It was explained at Selective Service headquarters that these volunteer inductees would be assigned to the Army; the only one of the armed services now utilizing inductees.

Voluntary inductions are distinct from voluntary enlistments. Voluntary enlistments, permitting the enlistee his choice of service, must still be for four years, and will be accepted only before the man has been ordered to take his physical examination for induction. inductees.

Under the procedure set forth in Mr. Truman's Executive order today, a man in the 18-26 age bracket, irrespective of whether he has registered with the Selective Service, may go to his local draft board and volunteer for immediate induction. If classified 1-A or 1-A-O (conscientious objector for noncombatant duty) he will be

Continued on Page 9, Column 1

High Court Voids City's Ordinance Requiring Street Preaching Permit

By JAY WALZ
Special to THE NEW YORK TIMES.

WASHINGTON, Jan. 15—The Supreme Court today struck down on the ground of free speech a New York City ordinance requiring police permits for preachers to conduct religious services in the streets.

The 8-to-1 decision was one of three bearing on freedom of expression and thought that the high court handed down on its opinion today. Chief Justice Fred M. Vinson wrote them all.

In a case similar to New York's, the court unanimously ruled that the City Council of Havre de Grace, Md., had wrongfully denied use of a city park for a religious service of Jehovah's Witnesses.

In a third case, however, the court decided, 6 to 3, that the Syracuse, N. Y., police had been within constitutional bounds when they arrested a student sidewalk speaker after he had said, among other things, "President Truman is a bum." The student had a right to say what he did, the court stated, but in the circumstances he was a threat to the peace.

The New York decision reversed the conviction of the Rev. Carl Jacob Kunz, a Baptist minister, of holding a street service without a permit. Mr. Kunz, who told officials he felt it his mission to "go out on the highways and byways and preach the word of God" held a permit to do so in New York at one time. In 1946, however, his permit was revoked after a hearing by the Police Commissioner, who found that the minister had "ridiculed" and "denounced" other religious beliefs in his meetings.

He was arrested for preaching without a permit in 1948, and on conviction was fined $10.

Chief Justice Vinson said lower courts that upheld this conviction

Continued on Page 33, Column 3

A PEACETIME HIGH

Arms and Foreign Aid Take 69% of Total—Fair Deal Included

IT IS TIED TO DEFENSE

Sentiment in Congress Accepts Military Cost, Is Cool to Others

Text of the budget message is on Pages 20 through 24.

By JOHN D. MORRIS
Special to THE NEW YORK TIMES.

WASHINGTON, Jan. 15—President Truman laid before Congress today a budget calling for $71,594,000,000 of expenditures in the fiscal year beginning next July 1 to meet what his accompanying message called "the compelling demands" of national security "in a period of grave danger."

He said that the budget, by far the largest in peacetime history, reflected this country's determination to achieve a twofold goal:

First, to strengthen itself and its allies sufficiently to deter further Communist aggression.

Second, to create reserves of trained manpower and industrial capacity to permit immediate mobilization of "all our power," if that should become necessary.

The President estimated receipts at $55,138,000,000 for a prospective deficit of $16,456,000,000 and indicated that he would soon request a tax increase of at least that amount.

Gives Revised 1951 Figures

"At this time," he asserted, "sound public finance and fiscal policy require that we balance the budget. I shall shortly submit to the Congress recommendations for new revenue legislation."

The new budget, setting forth in detail the Administration's program for the 1952 fiscal year and giving revised estimates of expenditures and receipts in the 1951 fiscal year, which ends next June 30, was presented to the House of Representatives and Senate by messenger shortly after they convened today.

Congressional comment indicated a general disposition to provide any funds necessary for the defense program, but there was widespread complaint that the President had failed to economize sufficiently in nondefense fields.

Bitter battles were predicted over Mr. Truman's renewal of many Fair Deal proposals, particularly one for the establishment of a Fair Employment Practices Commission, an issue that caused some Southern Democrats to bolt the party in last year's elections.

The President briefed reporters at a budget "seminar" on Saturday with the understanding that any information was to be withheld from publication until today.

Revenue Record Set in 1949

In reply to questions at that time, he said he might ask Congress for a tax increase of as much as $20,000,000,000, retroactive to Jan. 1; that the Marshall Plan would have to be continued beyond June 30 of 1952, and that he intended to continue pressing for his civil rights program.

On the expenditure side, the budget represented a 78 per cent increase over the 1951 total of $47,210,000,000, the previous peacetime record. Under the biggest wartime budget $98,703,000,000 was spent in 1945.

Prospective receipts were far above any other year, either in peace or war, even without allowing for further tax increases.

The $55,138,000,000 revenue estimated for the 1952 fiscal year compares with the current fiscal year's peacetime record, an estimated $44,512,000,000. The all-time record, established in 1945, was $44,762,000,000.

In his budget message, President Truman emphasized that military and international programs accounted directly for 69 per cent of the expenditures proposed for the 1952 fiscal year. Together, they

Continued on Page 24, Column 5

Vivien Leigh and Marlon Brando in A Streetcar Named Desire.

Gene Kelly, the great genius of the musical, in An American in Paris.

Eduard Franz (left) supervised the search for The Thing *in the movie of the same name.*

The New York Times.

LATE CITY EDITION
Becoming fair and windy today.
Partly cloudy, colder tomorrow.
Temperature Range Today—Max., 55; Min., 42
Temperature Yesterday—Max., 50; Min., 44
Full U. S. Weather Bureau Report, Page 26

Copyright, 1951, by The New York Times Company.

VOL. C No. 34,002.   Entered as Second-Class Matter, Post Office, New York, N. Y.   NEW YORK, TUESDAY, FEBRUARY 27, 1951.   Times Square, New York 18, N. Y.   FIVE CENTS

U.S. MARINES ENTER KOREAN OFFENSIVE; THAW HELPS ENEMY

Army's Third Infantry Joins Assault Also—Allies Plod Ahead as Much as 4 Miles

REDS RESISTING STRONGLY

Artillery-Backed Rear Guards Make Stand as Main Body of Foe Retires to Regroup

By LINDESAY PARROTT
Special to The New York Times.

TOKYO, Tuesday, Feb. 27.—United States Marines and the Army's Third Infantry Division have joined the United Nations offensive on a sixty-mile Korean front, Eighth Army headquarters announced today, as United Nations troops plodded forward through mud to register small gains against increasing Communist resistance following yesterday's lull in the fighting.

The Eighth Army's announcement revealed that seven United States divisions were now in the line—the Second, Third, First Cavalry, Seventh, Twenty-fourth and Twenty-fifth, and the Marines—plus the British Twenty-seventh Brigade and South Koreans. The Marines were fighting around Hoengsong in the Wonju valley in Central Korea, and the Third Division along the Han River on the west, headquarters said.

Front line reports said · the United Nations forces had made advances up to four miles today on the east flank near the crossroads of Pangnim, but in the west and center faced strong resistance from deeply dug-in enemy troops and artillery-supported rear guards screening what was believed to be a continued withdrawal by the Communists for regrouping before they launched an expected new attack of their own.

The Eighth Army announced the enemy's losses in killed and wounded in ground action Sunday as 1,361.

Reports Limited Gains

General of the Army Douglas MacArthur said in a communiqué reporting operations up to 6 A. M. (4 P. M. Monday, Eastern standard time) that United Nations troops had made "limited gains" in mud and rugged mountain country. General MacArthur said the action was centered west of Hoengsong, where the enemy resisted stubbornly.

Giving no details, the communiqué reported "substantial" gains for South Korean troops in the eastern sector north of Pyongchang.

Naval vessels maintained a "devastating ship - to - shore bombardment" along the east coast, headquarters said, while the 8-inch guns of the cruiser St. Paul and planes from the carrier Bataan silenced gun positions around Seoul.

Front line reports indicated the largest Communist masses were concentrating along the Han River northeast of the old South Korean capital of Seoul, and in the center near Yongdu and the crossroads village of Hoengsong.

United Nations patrols seeking to cross the Han near Seoul were turned back after having met heavy enemy fire. They observed new trenches along the north bank, where the Communists apparently were dug in solidly. Four enemy bunkers east of the former capital shelled yesterday and United Nations patrols met stiff resistance near Yangpyong, where the Allied line crosses the Han River at its big bend southward.

Reds Occupy Ridges

All ridges facing the river west and northwest of Yangpyong appeared to be occupied heavily by the enemy, tactical air observers reported. From 3,000 to 5,000 Communists were attacked from the air farther east toward Yongdu. United Nations troops four miles south of the town met stubborn resistance from enemy troops armed with automatic weapons and mortars.

Intelligence estimated the Communists had a whole division dug in in the general area northeast of Hoengsong.

Little contact was reported north of Chipyong on the central front, where British and United States troops thrusting along the Yangpyong-Hongchon road had been meeting strong resistance.

South Korean troops took heights one mile east of Hoengsong against resistance that was characterized as "moderate." Seesaw fighting in this area in the last three days left the positions almost unchanged, with the ruined village still a no

Continued on Page 2, Column 5

250,000 Men Now in Korea, Bradley Tells Draft Hearing

He Denies Call for Further Guard Units—Accepts Draft of Men 18½

By HAROLD B. HINTON
Special to The New York Times.

WASHINGTON, Feb. 26.—General of the Army Omar N. Bradley, Chairman of the Joint Chiefs of Staff, assured the Armed Services Committee of the House of Representatives today that the Department of Defense had no intention of calling further National Guard divisions to active duty.

Testifying on the pending draft bill, debate on which will start in the Senate tomorrow, General Bradley gave broad approval to the House version, which differs slightly from the version the Senate will discuss. In particular, he found no major objection to limiting to 18½ the age at which a man would be eligible for induction, instead of 18, as the Senate bill would provide.

Discussing the currently contemplated deployment of our armed forces, General Bradley said the plan was for three or four divisions in Europe and two in Japan.

General Omar N. Bradley
Associated Press Wirephoto

He indicated there were 250,000 men in Korea.

Their numbers are related to the total force of about 3,500,000 needed for the strategy formulated by the Joint Chiefs of Staff. General

Continued on Page 12, Column 4

Dulles Seeks to Sway Allies To Terms Accepted by Japan

By JAMES RESTON
Special to The New York Times.

WASHINGTON, Feb. 26.—The Truman Administration has received Ambassador at Large John Foster Dulles' report on his mission to Japan with extraordinary satisfaction and has authorized him to proceed with the completion of the Japanese peace treaty at the earliest possible date.

Mr. Dulles, who returned here yesterday from a trip to Japan, Australia, New Zealand and the Philippines, is understood to have made the following points in his report to the State Department today:

1. The Japanese Government agreed in detail to his suggestion that the United States retain broad military and naval rights within and around Japan after the signing of a peace treaty with the United States and other peace-loving states.

2. These military rights were accepted voluntarily by the Japanese Government. Mr. Dulles emphasized in Tokyo that the United States was not making any demands upon Japan and was not obligating itself at this time to defend the political independence or territorial integrity of the Japanese Islands.

3. The question of security guarantees could not arise until Japan was economically and politically in a position to demonstrate that she could carry out military policy or self-help and mutual aid. This fact was recognized by the Japanese Government. Moreover, the question of the future of the Ryukyu Islands, which Japan wants, was left for later discussion.

4. General of the Army Douglas MacArthur agreed upon the necessity of proceeding quickly to the negotiation of a peace treaty. He also agreed to work out and forward to Washington as soon as possible a list of items that Japan could manufacture to help at once in the rearmament programs of the Western nations. It was important to use Japanese manpower and manufacturing facilities in the production of such things as gun sights, binoculars and parachutes.

Continued on Page 5, Column 3

CLEMENTIS SEIZED AS SPY BY CZECHS

Ex-Foreign Chief Ousted From Party With 4 Other Leaders —Confession Reported

By The United Press.

PRAGUE, Czechoslovakia, Tuesday, Feb. 27.—Former Foreign Minister Vladimir Clementis has been arrested and has confessed to charges of espionage and conspiracy to overthrow the Government, it was announced today.

The Communist newspaper Rude Pravo said Dr. Clementis had "confessed be carried out continuous subversive activity * * * with the aim of hampering building socialism and aiding efforts of the class enemy to overthrow the People's Regime and restore capitalism."

Dr. Clementis was arrested and expelled from the Communist party with four other top Communist leaders, all of whom were accused of high treason in trying to turn Czechoslovakia into "another Yugoslavia" at the instigation of the Western powers. The arrests and expulsions were announced in a communiqué on last week's meeting of the Central Committee published today by the Government-controlled press.

[Reuters reported the Communist party announced that nearly 170,000 members and candidate-members had been expelled from the Czechoslovak party during a "screening" process that lasted six months.]

Dr. Clementis, who succeeded the late Jan Masaryk as Foreign Minister, had been denounced as a

Continued on Page 11, Column 5

Melish Loses Supreme Court Plea To Bar His Removal From Church

By The Associated Press.

WASHINGTON, Feb. 26 — The Federal Supreme Court denied today the Rev. Dr. John Howard Melish a review of his fight against removal as rector of the Protestant Episcopal Church of the Holy Trinity in Brooklyn.

The denial lets stand unchanged an injunction issued by a Kings County (Brooklyn) court. The injunction requires enforcement of a Bishop's order for removal of Dr. Melish. The latter appealed to the highest tribunal to set aside the state court injunction and to declare it violated the Constitutional principle of separation of church and state.

The Rt. Rev. James Pernette De Wolfe, Bishop of the Diocese of Long Island, ordered removal of Dr. Melish from the Brooklyn church forty-five years ago. The Bishop acted on a request by a majority of the vestrymen of the church.

Melish had refused to remove his son and assistant rector, the Rev. William Howard Melish. The complaint against the younger Melish was based on his "outside activities."

The son at the time was chairman of the National Council of American-Soviet Friendship. This organization later was included in the Federal Attorney General's subversive list. The younger Melish resigned the chairmanship, but remained a council director.

The appeal by Dr. Melish said that the state court action "constitutes an unwarranted intrusion of the civil power of the state in a religious controversy in violation of the Constitutional separation of church and state."

He said that the Brooklyn court's injunction had substituted an improper penalty (possible contempt action) for the exclusive one pre-

Continued on Page 14, Column 3

FORCE IN EUROPE TO 'DETER' RUSSIA OPPOSED BY TAFT

Ohioan Tells Senate Hearing Truman Is Misleading People on Size of U. S. Contribution

VETO BY CONGRESS URGED

Senator Would Bar Dispatch of Troops Until Allies Built Army to Hold Continent

By WILLIAM S. WHITE
Special to The New York Times.

WASHINGTON, Feb. 26.—Senator Robert A. Taft of Ohio demanded today a Congressional veto power over the dispatch of any American ground troops to help in Europe's defense. He proposed other Congressional restrictions as well.

Mr. Taft, Republican policy leader of the Senate, rejected, moreover, the basic concept of the North Atlantic Treaty arrangement for creating in Europe an international force sufficient to deter, if not necessarily actually to hurl back, any Russian invasion.

"I can't see that 'deter' business," he asserted.

Accordingly, he not only insisted that Congress have the privilege of approving the size of any troop commitment but also asked that Congress have the right to forbid any commitment until the Europeans had provided, with whatever American contribution was made, "an army sufficiently powerful to withstand an attack on Western Europe, including occupied Germany."

No American contribution should be made, he said, to a legion that was only a deterrent. It should be large enough actually to hold the continent, he added.

Mr. Taft testified before the Senate Foreign Relations and Armed Services Committees. Sitting jointly, they are considering the degree of voice that Congress should have in the Truman Administration's decision to assign American divisions to a European defensive army under the command of General of the Army Dwight D. Eisenhower.

The Senator accused the Administration of deliberately misleading the American people into supposing that the recently announced decision to send four more divisions, to join two already in Europe, would be the end.

"The refusal of the Administra-

Continued on Page 16, Column 3

DIRECTOR OF R.F.C. CALLS BOARD 'BAD' AT SENATE INQUIRY

Willett Admits He Was 'as Bad as Rest,' Agrees One Man Should Rule Agency

DISSENSION IS OUTLINED

Tobey Terms Stories 'Sordid,' Feels Best Thing Would Be 'Demise' of Lending Body

By C. P. TRUSSELL
Special to The New York Times.

WASHINGTON, Feb. 26.—William E. Willett, a member of the board of directors of the Reconstruction Finance Corporation, told the Senate Banking subcommittee investigating the loan agency today that it was "as bad a board" and that he was "as bad as the rest."

Mr. Willett was testifying in connection with "dissension" and "demoralization" at the R. F. C. loan branch at Dallas. Strife at that branch has figured largely in the subcommittee's investigation into alleged political influence and favoritism in R. F. C. operations.

Mr. Willett said he agreed with the subcommittee recommendation. As for himself, he added, he had wanted to discharge not only the two officials concerned but the agency manager, L. B. Glidden, as well.

This same time that and of five hours of testimony that a $10,100,000 R. F. C. loan to the Texmass Petroleum Corporation last year and insinuations that politics played a large role in the strife at the Dallas branch.

Mr. Glidden, as R. F. C. employe of almost nineteen years before his resignation last month, said he had tried for more than a year to bring about the dismissal of John B. Skiles, personnel manager for the branch, but that "power of some

Continued on Page 17, Column 2

World News Summarized

TUESDAY, FEBRUARY 27, 1951

No President after Truman will be able to hold that office more than two terms under the Twenty-Second Amendment to the Constitution, which became effective yesterday when Nevada, the thirty-sixth state, ratified it. [1:8.]

Directors and other officials of the R. F. C. denounced the agency and one another at a Senate hearing. [1:5.]

President Truman ordered a program drawn to curb inflationary bank loans in a way that would retain the Government's "easy money" policy on its own securities. [1:7.] Mayor Impellitteri and other local and state officials warned a United States committee that the proposed Federal tax on city and state bonds would cut local improvements. [18:4.] In Albany, the Mayor's plan to raise the city sales tax was attacked. [19:2.]

The Supreme Court held the Wisconsin utility anti-strike law illegal and in two other opinions extended the power of Federal courts to construe N. L. R. B. orders. [18:1.] It also upheld the right of the F. B. I. to withhold confidential data in open court but did not rule on its extent to which this was permissible. [18:2-3.] The Court refused to review the removal of the Rev. Dr. Melish as rector of Brooklyn's Holy Trinity Episcopal Church [1:2-3] or upset the contempt sentence imposed on a Communist for refusing to answer grand jury questions. [14:2.]

The American Bar Association's House of Delegates unanimously recommended that Communists be ousted from bar groups. [14:4.]

A jury was chosen in Washington to try Oscar Collazo, charged with killing a White House guard and wounding another in an attempt to assassinate Mr. Truman. [16:1.]

Senator Taft accused the Administration of deliberately mis-

leading the people into believing only six divisions would be sent to Europe. The Ohio Republican made his charge in insisting before two Senate committees that Congress limit the number of men to be sent abroad. [1:4.] "It would be useless to send a few troops" to be beaten, former Premier Speak of Belgium said in this city. If the United States does not help Europe "without limit" from the "very beginning" it will have to withdraw from the Continent, he declared. [11:1.] Britain's Home Fleet will remain under a British commander when a United States admiral heads the North Atlantic naval forces, Prime Minister Attlee told the Commons. [7:1.] France assured Yugoslavia she was closely watching the "menace" from her Soviet satellite neighbors. [8:5.] Palmiro Togliatti returned to Italy from Moscow to lead the Communist "peace" drive against rearmament. [8:2.] Czechoslovakia arrested former Foreign Minister Clementis as a spy. [1:2.]

Mud and rain showed the United Nations drive in Korea. Marines joined the fighting. [1:1; map P. 2] General Bradley disclosed that the Army alone had 250,000 men in Korea. [1:2-3.]

John Foster Dulles was authorized by the Administration to speed completion of a Japanese peace treaty. He is seeking to overcome trade, security and reparations demands presented by Allied nations. [1:2-3.]

Republican legislative leaders in Albany agreed on a $19,500,000 pay-rise program for state employes, ranging from $300 to $1,000 a year. [1:6.]

NEWS BULLETINS FROM THE TIMES

Every hour on the hour
7 A.M. through Midnight
WQXR AM 1560
WQXR FM 96.3

Index to other news appears on last page of this section.

2-TERM AMENDMENT IN FORCE AS THE 36TH STATE RATIFIES; TRUMAN EXEMPT FROM LIMIT

Text of the 22d Amendment

By the United Press.

WASHINGTON, Feb. 26—Following is the text of the Twenty-second Amendment limiting Presidents to two terms:

No person shall be elected to the office of the President more than twice, and no person who has held the office of President, or acted as President, for more than two years of a term to which some other person was elected President shall be elected to the office of the President more than once.

But this Article shall not apply to any person holding the office of President when this Article was proposed by the Congress, and shall not prevent any person who may be holding the office of President, or acting as President, during the term within which this Article becomes operative from holding the office of President or acting as President during the remainder of such term.

DEWEY FAVORS RISE FOR STATE'S AIDES

Albany Gets Bill to Increase Pay $300 to $1,000—Cost Is $19,500,000 Annually

By LEO EGAN
Special to The New York Times.

ALBANY, Feb. 26—Republican legislative leaders, in conference with Governor Dewey, decided tonight to recommend pay increases for employes of the state to range from $300 to $1,000 a year. The net cost to the state would be $19,500,000 annually.

At the same time it was announced that "substantial agreement" had been reached on the division of civilian defense cost between the state and municipalities. Exclusive of any outlays for the construction of shelters, the cost in the state would be $6,000,000 to $10,000,000, plus indeterminate contingent liabilities, and the cost to municipalities, $3,250,000.

The two decisions are expected to facilitate adjournment of the Legislature around March 15. The two subjects represented potential major controversies that could have upset adjournment plans.

The decision for pay increases for state employes was announced jointly by Senator Walter J. Mahoney of Buffalo and Assemblyman D. Mallory Stephens of Putnam, Republican chairmen, respectively, of the Senate Finance and the Assembly Ways and Means Committees.

The proposal provides for a 12½ per cent increase on the first $2,000 of compensation, 10 per cent on the next $2,000 and 7½ per cent on all pay of more than $4,000, with a provision that no increase shall be less than $300 nor more than $1,000.

Jesse B. McFarland, president of the State Civil Service Employes Association, with whom the schedule had been discussed before it was made public, announced immediately that the organization considered the increases as "inadequate." A meeting of the association's executive board has been called for Wednesday night to consider an official course.

The Civil Service employes had been pressing for 15 per cent on the first $3,000 of pay, 10 per cent

Continued on Page 19, Column 2

TRUMAN ASKS PLAN TO CUT BANK LOANS

But Wants Treasury's 'Easy Money' Policy Kept—Calls for 'Freeze' on U. S. Bonds

The text of the White House statement on credit on Page 34.

By FELIX BELAIR Jr.
Special to The New York Times.

WASHINGTON, Feb. 26—President Truman ordered his chief advisers on anti-inflation strategy today to develop ways and means of curbing excessive bank lending without interfering with the Treasury's "easy money" policy of public debt management or support of the Government bond market by the Federal Reserve.

Pending development of such a program in the next two weeks, the President asked for a "freezing" of the existing pattern of rates. He indicated that whatever was done about curbing inflationary bank credit there ought to be a "pegged" market for Government securities.

The President outlined his position in a lengthy memorandum that he read to the White House conference of economic, fiscal, monetary and defense mobilization chiefs. He left it to tour of them to work out a program that would "reconcile" the conflicting points of view of the Treasury and Federal Reserve Board but suggested a solution within the following framework:

1. Limit private lending by commercial banks and other institutions by:

   a. Voluntary action of the banking community, by industry-wide agreement.

   b. Government-sponsored voluntary action by banks as was done in a narrower field under the Capital Issues Committee of World War I when the effort was to limit borrowing to war-connected activity.

   c. Direct Government controls under the Emergency Banking Act of 1933 whereby Federal Reserve member banks may transact business only under regulations issued by the Secretary of the Treasury with approval of the President. Also extension of

Continued on Page 34, Column 1

NEVADA, UTAH VOTE

Proposal Becomes Law Automatically as Two Legislatures Approve

POLITICAL EFFECTS WIDE

President After 2d Election Would Have Less Control— 'Changing Horses' Possible

By ROBERT F. WHITNEY

WASHINGTON, Feb. 26 — The Constitution of the United States was amended tonight to forbid any President from being elected for more than two terms or from being elected more than once if he had served in excess of two years of his predecessor's term.

The amendment will not apply to President Truman. He may, again for his second elected term in the Presidential election of 1952 or in future campaigns, should his party wish to nominate him.

It was the Twenty - second Amendment to the Constitution and its ratification became complete with the approval of the Legislature of the State of Nevada providing the needed thirty-sixth states, or three-quarters' approval. Earlier in the day Utah's lawmakers had backed it as the thirty-fifth state.

It was eighteen years since the Constitution had been changed. Then the ratification was that of the Twenty-first Amendment repealing National Prohibition Dec. 5, 1933. The drive later that was initiated by President Roosevelt and completed in the first year of his first term.

Inspired by Roosevelt

It was President Roosevelt who "inspired" the Twenty-second Amendment by his election four times to the Presidency. The Eightieth Congress, in which the Republicans gained control for the first time since President Hoover's term, started the action on the opening day, the third of January, 1947.

This was the introduction of a joint resolution by Representative Joseph W. Martin Jr., of Massachusetts, then Speaker of the House of Representatives, and Senator Arthur H. Vandenberg of Michigan, then President pro tem of the Senate, both Republicans.

The amendment was prepared by former Representative Earl C. Michener, Republican of Michigan, then Chairman of the House Judiciary Committee.

It was passed in the House Feb. 6 and in the Senate March 12. The House agreed to a Senate amendment March 21. It was presented to the Secretary of State March 24.

The Twenty-second Amendment provides "no person shall be elected to the office of the President more than twice, and no person who has held the office of President, or acted as President, for more than two years of a term to which some other person was elected President shall be elected to the office of the President more than once.

Thus a Vice President or other person in the legal succession who became President on the death, resignation or impeachment of a President could be elected subsequently twice if that service were only two years but could otherwise only if it were more than two years.

Truman Is Exempt

The Amendment would not apply to the President holding office when it was first proposed to Congress (Mr. Truman).

The resolution on the proposed amendment required ratification within seven years of its introduction in Congress. The Twenty-second was well ahead of that time —March 24, 1954. But it was a flurry of action by the states that made it ratified.

Until late last month only twenty-four states had ratified. But in the last few weeks twelve "signed up" in a hurry. Before Utah and Nevada had come Indiana, Montana, Idaho, New Mexico, Wyoming, Arkansas, Georgia, Tennessee, Texas and North Carolina.

The twelve states that have not yet approved are: Alabama, Arizona, Florida, Kentucky, Maryland, Massachusetts, Minnesota, Oklahoma, Rhode Is-

Continued on Page 25, Column 7

L. I. U. Star of 2 Years Ago Seized After Night Questioning About 'Fix'

By ALEXANDER FEINBERG

Nathan (Natie) Miller, a Long Island University basketball player of two seasons ago, was arrested late last night on a charge of having accepted bribes to lose or limit the margin of victory on two games played in Madison Square Garden in December, 1948.

The announcement was made at the Criminal Courts Building at 11:35 P. M. after Miller had been questioned since shortly before 7 P. M.

Miller, 25 years old, lives at 150 Eastern Parkway, Brooklyn. After starting on the 1948-49 team, he was graduated from L. I. U. and is now attending New York University for his master's degree. He is married and a veteran of World War II.

His arrest, which indicated a widening of the scope of the inquiry into college basketball "fixes," was announced by Assistant District Attorney Morris Goldman shortly after Edward (Eddie) Gard, L.I.U.

a senior and a former teammate of Miller, had left the District Attorney's office.

Miller was booked at the Elizabeth Street station at 12:05 A. M. He was accused of accepting $1,000 to "throw" a game with Bowling Green University of Ohio on Dec. 4, 1948, and $500 for a game with Western Kentucky on Dec. 30, 1948. L. I. U. lost both games, Bowling Green winning 97—64 and Western Kentucky winning 53—58.

Gard had been questioned for twelve hours. Named as the intermediary in the "fixes" for Salvatore Tarto Sollazzo, 45-year-old jeweler and former convict, Gard had been held in protective custody as a material witness at his own request. There was no indication

Continued on Page 25, Column 2

Shelley Winters and Montgomery Clift as the ill-fated lovers in A Place in the Sun, *which also starred Elizabeth Taylor. The film was based on Theodore Dreiser's novel* An American Tragedy.

In this house trailer, 29-year-old ex-boxer James Jones wrote From Here To Eternity. In 1951, 240,000 copies were sold.

100TH ANNIVERSARY
"All the News
That's Fit to Print"
1851 1951

The New York Times.

LATE CITY EDITION
Fair today, increasing cloudiness tomorrow and mild both days.
Temperature Range Today—Max., 60; Min., 45
Temperatures Yesterday—Max., 65; Min., 48
Full U. S. Weather Bureau Report, Page 50

VOL. C..No. 34,045. Entered as Second-Class Matter, Post Office, New York, N. Y. NEW YORK, WEDNESDAY, APRIL 11, 1951. Times Square, New York 18, N. Y. Telephone LAckawanna 4-1000 RAG PAPER EDITION SEVENTY-FIVE CENTS

TRUMAN RELIEVES M'ARTHUR OF ALL HIS POSTS; FINDS HIM UNABLE TO BACK U. S.-U. N. POLICIES; RIDGWAY NAMED TO FAR EASTERN COMMANDS

HOUSE VOTES U. M. T. ONLY AS A PROGRAM; MARSHALL WORRIED

Chamber Accepts Compromise Setting Up Commission to Draft Details of Plan

FUTURE LAW IS REQUIRED

Congress' Approval Is Needed to Start Universal Training—General Sees Risk in This

By JOHN D. MORRIS
Special to THE NEW YORK TIMES.

WASHINGTON, April 10—Concessions offered by advocates of Universal Military Training to save the program from outright rejection were approved today by the House of Representatives, but it remained to be seen whether the aim had been achieved.

General of the Army George C. Marshall, Secretary of Defense, meanwhile voiced the fear that current maneuvering in the House might "largely emasculate" the training features of the pending draft and training bill.

It was not clear, however, whether he was concerned over the main fight, expected later this week, over a proposal to eliminate all Universal Military Training provisions from the bill.

It was to head this off that the bill's managers headed by Representative Carl Vinson, Democrat of Georgia, offered the concessions that were approved today. The House accepted them on a voice vote.

Further Action Necessary

Consequently, as the bill now stands, little more than the principle of Universal Military Training is retained. A commission to draw up a detailed U. M. T. plan would be created. A "National Security Training Corps" would also be established, at least on paper.

But before anyone could be drafted to serve in the proposed corps, there would have to be another formal act of Congress, subject to Presidential approval or veto like any other bill, authorizing details of the training program.

At the same time, however, the revised bill retains safeguards against future pigeon-holing of U. M. T. in the House Rules Committee or elsewhere. The planning commission, which also would administer the program once Congress had authorized its institution, would be required to submit a detailed training plan to Congress within six months. The House and Senate Armed Services Committees would be required to report out a bill or resolution within forty-five days of receiving the plan. The measure then could be called up at any time.

Opponents Withhold Attack

In the House, bills ordinarily must be cleared by the Rules Committee before they can be considered on the floor. The Rules Committee bottled up a Universal Military Training Bill in the Eightieth Congress.

Opponents of any form of U.M.T. legislation did not fight the concessions approved in the House today, explaining that the proposals would make the bill less obnoxious although still unacceptable to them.

They were still hoping for approval of a substitute sponsored by Representative Graham A. Barden, Democrat of North Carolina, that would retain only what they regard as the "emergency" features of the pending draft measure. These include a three-year extension of authority to draft men 19 through 26 years of age for actual military service.

The Barden bill would eliminate authority to lower the draft age to 18½ as well as all long-range training features of the pending measure.

The Senate has already passed a draft and training bill adhering closely to the Administration's recommendations. It would authorize the drafting of men at the age of 18 and permit the President to put Universal Military Training

Continued on Page 18, Column 4

Tobey Asserts He Recorded R. F. C. Talks With Truman

President Said to Withdraw Fee Accusation—Niles Held Attempting to Aid Dawson

By C. P. TRUSSELL
Special to THE NEW YORK TIMES.

WASHINGTON, April 10—Senator Charles W. Tobey, Republican of New Hampshire, was represented tonight as having told the Senate (Fulbright) subcommittee investigating the Reconstruction Finance Corporation that President Truman had charged in a telephone conversation with him that members of Congress had accepted fees for obtaining R. F. C. loans for constituents.

The Senator was said to have reported also that in a later telephonic communication the President had said that he had been mistaken.

Both telephonic conversations were said to have been recorded on disks in Mr. Tobey's possession. The date, or dates, were not made public. The Senator declined to discuss the matter and members of the investigating group also were silent.

In another development in the R. F. C. inquiry, former Senator Burton K. Wheeler, Democrat of

Burton K. Wheeler
Associated Press

Montana, said today that he had asked Senator Tobey to "go easy on" Donald S. Dawson, White House aide, during the Senate investigation of the agency. Mr. Wheeler asserted that he acted at

Continued on Page 25, Column 3

Sterling Hayden Was a Red; 'Stupidest Thing I Ever Did'

Special to THE NEW YORK TIMES.

WASHINGTON, April 10—Sterling Hayden, motion picture actor and decorated former United States Marine, told the House Committee on Un-American Activities today that he had been a member of the Communist party from June to December of 1946.

"It was the stupidest and most ignorant thing I ever had done in my life," he said. "I went into it with an emotional and very unsound approach, but I don't mean to imply that I was dragged into it. I went in voluntarily."

Mr. Hayden, a native of Montclair, N. J., said there were thousands of others like him, who should come in and tell their stories.

He added that shortly after the invasion of South Korea his attorney had written to J. Edgar Hoover, director of the Federal Bureau of Investigation, giving his Communist case history and seeking a means of eliminating any prejudice against his recall to the service.

Under questioning for more than three hours, the former husband of Madeleine Carroll, screen star, told of a restless life that started with his quitting high school at the age of fifteen and going to sea, and winding up in Hollywood. A Capt. Warwich Tompkins, described by him as an "open and avowed Communist," ran through his story.

He identified Captain Tompkins as an employe of Amtorg, the of-

Continued on Page 14, Column 5

PRICE AIDE RESIGNS, CONDEMNS DI SALLE

M. E. Thompson, Ex-Governor of Georgia, Hits 'Kansas City Crowd' in Administration

Special to THE NEW YORK TIMES.

WASHINGTON, April 10—With bitter words for Price Stabilizer Michael V. DiSalle, and for the "Kansas City crowd" he said was in the saddle in the national Administration, M. E. Thompson, former Governor of Georgia, resigned today as a consultant to the Office of Price Stabilization.

Mr. Thompson, once a power in Georgia politics, and who asserted that he battled successfully against the States Righters there who tried to keep President Truman's name off the ballot in 1948, declared that he would not support the Democratic party in 1952 if the "Kansas City crowd" still held control.

"If this be political treason,

Continued on Page 20, Column 1

Navy Suspends Explosives Expert; State Department Then Bars Wife

Special to THE NEW YORK TIMES.

WASHINGTON, April 10—The Navy Department suspended Dr. Stephen Brunauer today as a "security risk," giving the 47-year-old high explosives expert thirty days in which to answer the charges.

The State Department meanwhile, suspended Mrs. Esther Caukin Brunauer, wife of the Navy scientist, pending the outcome of the investigation of her husband. The State Department made it plain in a statement that the action against Mrs. Brunauer was based not on information about her, but only as a result of the Navy suspension.

Both of the Brunauers were named by Senator Joseph R. McCarthy, Republican of Wisconsin, in the course of his charges last year of Communist infiltration of the Government.

The announcement of Dr. Brunauer's suspension, effective immediately, was made while he was on a trip to New England for the Navy. Questioned by reporters at LaGuardia Field, on his way back to the capital, he said:

"I do not know for what reason I was suspended. I think some one made a mistake. I telephoned Washington and a Navy spokesman said he did not know the reason for the suspension. I do not want to comment further on anything."

Mrs. Brunauer issued a stout denial of the McCarthy charges on March 13, 1950, defending herself and her husband against the allegations they were Communists.

The Navy announcement of its suspension of Dr. Brunauer followed the disclosure by the State Department that the action had already taken place. The Navy gave no details of the charges, but said that Dr. Brunauer would have thirty days to answer the charges and request a hearing.

The decision of Francis P. Matthews, Secretary of the Navy will be final, it was said.

Asked whether the suspension of Mrs. Brunauer in response to charges against her husband was

Continued on Page 16, Column 3

RISE IN SALES TAX EXPECTED TO PASS CITY COUNCIL TODAY

Finance Committee Studies Bill at Length—Fight Against Measure Goes On

RUML A FISCAL ADVISER

Mayor Declines Challenge to Debate With Hoving—Joseph Suggests State-Wide Levy

The finance committee of the City Council spent an inconclusive three-hour executive session at City Hall yesterday afternoon weighing the merits of the proposed increase in the retail sales tax from 2 to 3 per cent, but when the meeting ended nothing had changed the prospect that the tax rise would be approved.

It was indicated that today the committee, after further behind-closed-doors deliberations, would favor the sales impost rise by a vote of 8 to 2, or possibly 7 to 3, and that later today the full City Council would adopt the measure by something like 19 to 6.

If the tax bill clears the Council hurdles today, as is indicated, it is expected that the Board of Estimate, whose members are committed to it, will give its approval at tomorrow's regular meeting.

Ruml to Advise Controller

Meanwhile, Controller Lazarus Joseph announced the appointment of Beardsley Ruml, business consultant, financier and economist, as a special deputy controller to advise Mr. Joseph on fiscal matters. Mr. Ruml, whose appointment was for an "indefinite" tenure, will serve without pay.

Mr. Ruml was at one time connected with the Federal Reserve Board and also with the New York Stock Exchange. He is a

Continued on Page 32, Column 4

U. S. PRODS NATIONS

Suggests U. N. Members Send More Troops to Fight in Korea

3 AVENUES ARE LISTED

Contributions Sought From Nations Not Yet Committed

By A. M. ROSENTHAL
Special to THE NEW YORK TIMES.

UNITED NATIONS, N. Y., April 10—The United States has been quietly suggesting that members of the United Nations increase, or at least maintain, their contributions of troops for the Korean war effort.

Informed sources here report that for some time the United States has been keeping in touch with members of the world organization to see if non-United States representation in the international army could be increased.

[Chinese Communist troops in Korea clung to their positions along the Hwachon Reservoir in the face of daylong United Nations attacks. Eighth Army headquarters clamped a stringent security blackout on news from the front as a major battle seemed to impend in the reservoir area.]

So far there has been no general appeal to the United Nations members to contribute more troops; it has all been on a country-to-country basis. Diplomats said that there was no indication that a new general request for troops in Korea was in the making for the time being.

But on a longer-range basis, the question of more troops may be considered by the committee set up by the General Assembly on Feb. 1 to plan possible sanctions

Continued on Page 5, Column 3

World News Summarized

WEDNESDAY, APRIL 11, 1951

President Truman relieved General of the Army MacArthur of his command in the Pacific because the United Nations commander had been unable to give his "wholehearted support" to United States and United Nations policies. The Presidential ouster has forced the general from all his commands, including his role in the occupation of Japan. Lieut. Gen. Matthew B. Ridgway has been designated to take over all the Far Eastern commands. [1:8.]

The United States has been asking other United Nations members to increase, or at least maintain, their forces fighting in Korea and asking for troops from countries that have sent none. [1:5.]

Enemy resistance increased in the Hwachon Reservoir area of Korea. The Communists still held the dam although Hwachon itself appeared deserted. [3:1; map P. 2.] Mao Tse-tung was said to have been officially reported ill and Liu Shao-chi was said to be acting in his place at the head of the Chinese Communist regime. [9:2.]

Britain has suggested that the United States invite Communist China to the discussions on a Japanese peace treaty and send Peiping a draft of the proposed pact. The treaty, Britain holds, should include the return of Formosa to China. [1:6-7.]

The days of "easy and automatic" relations between the United States and Canada are over, Canada's External Affairs Minister declared. "There will be frictions" that can be settled easily, he said, if the United States recognizes that Canada's acceptance of Washington leadership does not mean she is "willing to be merely an echo of somebody else's voice." [1:6-7.]

A "severe, but not crippling" budget was presented to Britain by the Labor Government, which chose to increase taxes, already heavy, rather than cut social welfare funds. [1:7.]

The bill giving West German labor equal rights with management in the operation of the steel and coal industries was passed by the lower house. [14:2.]

The House passed and sent to the Senate a supplemental defense money bill 43 per cent below Administration requests [29:1] and cut from the draft bill a provision for Universal Military Training in favor of a Presidential commission to draw detailed plans. [1:1.] Defense Secretary Marshall ordered all three armed services to share equitably draftees of superior standing. [19:3.]

Mobilization Director Wilson called for an end to complacency, selfishness and partisanship if we are to beat down the "dreadful shadow" of history's most "absolute and ruthless" dictatorship. [23:1.] M. E. Thompson resigned as consultant to the Price Stabilizer in protest against "political" control and general wastefulness. [1:2.]

Organized baseball was ordered not to raise players' salaries above a club's 1950 highest. [33:2-3.] The Army halted certain pay rises for nonoperating rail workers until a special panel ruled in the case. [33:1.]

Senator Tobey was said to have disclosed that he had recorded telephone talks with President Truman about the Senate R. F. C. inquiry. [1:2-3.]

The Navy suspended Dr. Stephen Brunauer, a scientist, as a "security risk" and the State Department dropped his wife, Esther, until the husband's case was settled. [1:2-3.]

Index to other news appears on last page of this section.

DISMISSED BY THE PRESIDENT

General of the Army Douglas MacArthur

Britain Asks That Red China Have Role in Japanese Pact

By WALTER H. WAGGONER
Special to THE NEW YORK TIMES.

WASHINGTON, April 10—Britain has suggested to the United States that Communist China be brought into the negotiations for a Japanese peace treaty. The British proposal also specifically asked that the United States send a copy of its treaty draft to the Peiping regime for its consideration, and, further, that the treaty provide for the ultimate if not immediate return of Formosa to "China."

By "China" the British mean the regime of Mao Tse-tung, since that is the China now recognized by London.

These suggestions have been made in the course of recent conversations between the two Governments. They represent another difference of opinion that has developed between London and Washington on both the procedure for negotiating a Japanese treaty and the form the settlement should have.

The basis for the British request that Peiping be given a look at the United States treaty draft is to enable the Chinese Communists to reject the proposal if they want to, as the Soviet Union is expected to do.

At the same time, it is vigorously denied here that Britain will refuse to sign any treaty draft that Communist China rejects. Reports that such an "or else" position has

Continued on Page 8, Column 5

BUDGET INCREASES BRITONS' TAX LOAD

Income, Profit, Purchase, Auto and Gasoline Imposts Rise —Social Services Uncut

By RAYMOND DANIELL
Special to THE NEW YORK TIMES.

LONDON, April 10—The already heavily burdened British people were called upon today to pay even higher taxes to preserve their welfare state. Hugh Gaitskell, Chancellor of the Exchequer, introducing his first budget, told the House of Commons that there were only two ways of meeting the extra cost of rearmament. One, which brought cheers from the Conservative Opposition, was by reducing expenditures for social welfare.

The alternative he offered was a sharp rise in both direct and indirect taxes. This brought cheers

Continued on Page 10, Column 3

Canada Bars a 'Yes' Role to U. S.; Pearson Sees Unity Despite Friction

By The United Press

TORONTO, April 10—Lester B. Pearson, Canadian Secretary for External Affairs, said today that "easy and automatic" relations between Canada and the United States were a thing of the past.

In a speech apparently aimed at United States consumption, Mr. Pearson said that Canada was not willing to be "merely an echo of somebody else's voice" and reserved the right to criticize "our great friend, the United States."

Mr. Pearson said that Canada intended to prevent the United Nations from becoming "too much the instrument of any one country" and that it was time for the United States to stop telling Canada "that until we do one-twelfth or one-sixteenth, or some other fraction as much as they are doing, we are defaulting."

He said that there might be "angry waves which may weaken the foundation of our friendship" but that Canada would march forward with the United States "in the pursuit of objectives which we share."

"Nevertheless, the days of relatively easy and automatic relations with our neighbor are, I think, over," he added.

Mr. Pearson indicated that one of the "angry waves" that could weaken relations between Canada and the United States was the controversy over General of the Army Douglas MacArthur's statement on the war in Korea.

Later, in a second speech, Mr. Pearson made an indirect reference to General MacArthur when he said that a successful foreign policy must work toward goals accepted by the majority of the people, and it would have a better chance of "reaching these goals if we abandon what has been called 'hoop-la diplomacy' at Lake Success, at Ottawa, or, I hasten to add, at Tokyo."

He said that the free nations stood in danger of "nothing less

Continued on Page 6, Column 3

PRESIDENT MOVES

Van Fleet Is Named to Command 8th Army in Drastic Shift

VIOLATIONS ARE CITED

White House Statement Quotes Directives and Implies Breaches

Texts of statements and orders in MacArthur dispute, Page 8.

By W. H. LAWRENCE
Special to THE NEW YORK TIMES.

WASHINGTON, Wednesday, April 11—President Truman early today relieved General of the Army Douglas MacArthur of all his commands in the Far East and appointed Lieut. Gen. Matthew B. Ridgway as his successor.

The President said he had relieved General MacArthur "with deep regret" because he had concluded that the Far Eastern Commander "is unable to give his wholehearted support to the policies of the United States Government and of the United Nations in matters pertaining to his official duties.

General MacArthur, in a message to House Minority Leader Joseph W. Martin Jr. of Massachusetts, made public by Mr. Martin last Thursday, had publicly challenged the President's foreign policy, urging that the United States concentrate on Asia instead of Europe and use Generalissimo Chiang Kai-shek's Formosa-based troops to open a second front on the mainland of China.

The change in command is effective at once. General Ridgway, who has been in command of the Eighth Army in Korea since the death in December of Gen. Walton H. Walker, assumes all of General MacArthur's titles—Supreme Commander, United Nations Forces in Korea, Supreme Commander for Allied Powers, Japan, Commander-in-Chief, Far East, and Commanding General U. S. Army, Far East.

Commanded in Greece

The Eighth Army command will pass to Lieut. Gen. James A. Van Fleet whose most recent important command was as head of the American military mission in Greece, when that country was repelling a Communist-directed guerrilla attack under the Truman doctrine.

In ousting General MacArthur for his public disagreement with American policy designed to localize the Asiatic war, the President said:

"Full and vigorous debate on matters of national policy is a vital element in the Constitutional system of our free democracy.

"It is fundamental, however, that military commanders must be governed by the policies and directives issued to them in the manner provided by our laws and Con-

Continued on Page 8, Column 1

News Stuns Tokyo; MacArthur Is Silent

By The Associated Press

TOKYO, Wednesday, April 11—A small brown envelope with "flash" printed on it in red carried to General MacArthur today the news that he had been discharged from his commands by President Truman.

It was delivered by a senior aide, Col. Sid Huff, who said that the General received the news without comment. Colonel Huff indicated that the General had no forewarning that he was being relieved.

The General announced that he would have no statement immediately.

The message came as a Signal Corps communication about the time and Army radio announced the news.

General MacArthur got the word while at lunch with his wife, Senator Warren G. Mag-

Continued on Page 8, Column 4

President Syngman Rhee inspired Koreans during war years and led in the rebuilding of his country.

Truman removed MacArthur from command in Korea on April 11, 1951. MacArthur is seen here addressing a joint session of Congress on April 19.

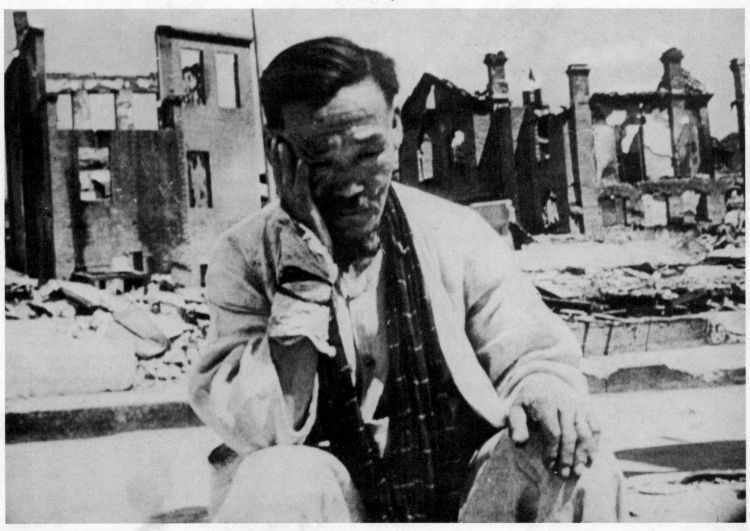

The devastation of Seoul.

MacArthur, still a hero to millions, received the most triumphant ovation ever given by New York City to a man who had just lost his job.

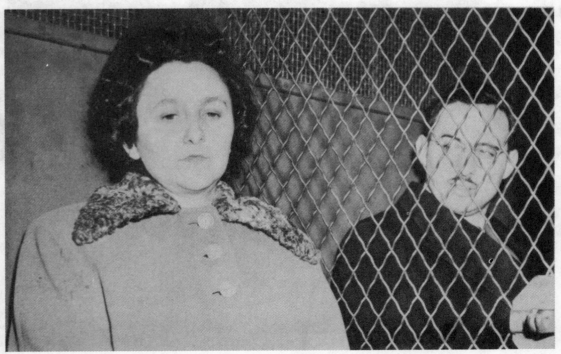

In March, 1951, Ethel and Julius Rosenberg were convicted of war-time espionage. They received the first death sentences ever imposed for this offense by U.S. civil court. They were executed in June, 1953, despite repeated appeals.

100TH ANNIVERSARY
"All the News
That's Fit to Print"
1851 1951

The New York Times.

LATE CITY EDITION
Fair and pleasant today
and tomorrow.
Temperature Range Today-Max., 81; Min., 63
Temperatures Yesterday—Max., 78; Min., 66
Full U. S. Weather Bureau Report, Page 33.

Copyright, 1951, by The New York Times Company.

VOL. C..No. 34,127. Entered as Second-Class Matter, Post Office, New York, N. Y. NEW YORK, MONDAY, JULY 2, 1951. Times Square, New York 18, N. Y. Telephone LAckawanna 4-1000 FIVE CENTS

CHINESE AND KOREA REDS AGREE TO TRUCE TALK; WANT IT NEAR KAESONG IN JULY 10-15 PERIOD; U. S. IS GRATIFIED; SPORADIC FIGHTING CONTINUES

DRIVE TO BOLSTER CONTROLS MEASURE IN HOUSE PLANNED

Holiday to Aid Administration Forces—President Spurns Bill Passed in Senate

O. P. S. CLARIFIES RULING

Explains Ceiling, Not Market, Prices Were Frozen—C.I.O. Assails 'Dixiegop Crime'

By CLAYTON KNOWLES
Special to THE NEW YORK TIMES.

WASHINGTON, July 1—The Truman Administration will set about regrouping its battered forces on Capitol Hill this week in an attempt to get through the House a stronger defense production bill than was approved in the Senate.

Operating under a temporary and restricted extension of the present law, the Administration was helped in its efforts by the fact that the midweek July 4 holiday would delay the start of voting in the House until July 9. The five hours of scheduled debate will begin on Thursday, immediately after the holiday, and probably will carry over to Friday.

In the interval, it is understood, President Truman will impress on Democratic leaders at their weekly conference tomorrow that the Senate version is entirely unacceptable to him. This measure, good for only eight months, knocks out rollbacks in prices below the levels of Jan. 25-Feb. 24, thereby keeping the cost-of-living at a near-peak.

Administration Aim Cited

The Administration had scheduled price cutbacks running to roughly $5,000,000,000. They were intended to eliminate inequities frozen into the price structure by the general ceilings applied Jan. 25. Excessively high prices would have been rolled back while prices kept low in response to earlier Administration appeals would have been rolled forward in many instances.

To eliminate these inequities, the Administration now contends it can obtain stabilization only by rolling prices forward. Such a step, it said, will result in forcing up the cost of living about 6 per cent.

In addition to the Congressional leaders, it is understood the President has invited the Chairmen of House and Senate Banking Committees to hear first hand the impelling reasons for improving upon the bill the Senate has passed.

The Office of Price Stabilization, meanwhile, announced that its order of Saturday, issued just before the effective date of the thirty-one day extension barring price rollbacks, froze existing ceiling prices rather than market prices.

In a clarifying statement, the agency said that Michael V. Di Salle, Director of Price Stabilization, "is of the opinion that pending further clarification and study manufacturers' ceiling prices should be kept at their existing level."

It said further that the effect "of this general overriding regulation is to eliminate all requirements for rollbacks after June 30, 1951, and to freeze ceiling provisions in effect on June 30, 1951."

Announcement Caused Concern

The original announcement had caused grave concern in quarters where products already under control were selling below ceiling prices. Today's statement by the price agency seemed to eliminate misgivings that the Administration might have pulled "a quick one" in the overriding order.

In a transcribed radio talk today, Senator Edward Martin, Republican of Pennsylvania, told constituents that the current fight against inflation became inevitable when President Truman failed "to freeze prices and wages immediately clear across the board."

The Congress of Industrial Organizations, attacking the Senate bill, said a "crime against American consumers" was being perpetrated by a Republican-Southern

Continued on Page 26, Column 1

Bob Feller Pitches His 3d No-Hit Game

Cleveland pitcher after yesterday's game.
Associated Press Wirephoto

Bob Feller, veteran right-hander of the Indians, pitched his third no-hit game yesterday to set a modern major league record. He beat the Tigers, 2 to 1, in the first contest of a double-header that Cleveland swept.

Detroit's run was the result of two errors, one by Feller, in the fourth inning.

Details on Page 18.

FORT DIX AIR CRASH KILLS 5, INJURES 16

C-47, Groping for Landing in Night Fog, Plows Into a Thicket Near Runway

Special to THE NEW YORK TIMES.

FORT DIX, N. J., July 1—A twin-engined Air Force C-47 transport plane, groping through heavy fog for a landing at Maguire Air Base here, crashed in a pine thicket at 3:30 A. M. today, killing five of the twenty-one persons aboard. The accident occurred a quarter of a mile from the runway the pilot was seeking.

The crew of three were among the dead. Four others were injured critically, and the remaining twelve were listed at the Fort Dix Army hospital today as in a "not critical" condition. Most of the passengers were on Fourth of July furloughs.

The plane was on a routine administrative passenger flight from Lackland Air Base, San Antonio, Tex., according to Lieut. John Boersig, Maguire Air Base Public Information Officer. En route it had dropped and picked up passengers at Kirtland and Sandia Air Bases, Albuquerque, N. M., and Scott Air Base, Belleville, Ill.

Air force officials said the plane's manifest listed twenty-three persons, but that it appeared

Continued on Page 14, Column 2

BRITISH AT ABADAN CUT BACK OIL 40% TO HALT SHUTDOWN

Company Acts to Keep Giant Iran Refinery Going—20 Days' Storage Seen

TEHERAN AIDES IN SPLIT

One Group Is Adamant, Other for Compromise—Regime Backs Seddon House Raid

By SYDNEY GRUSON
Special to THE NEW YORK TIMES.

ABADAN, Iran, July 1—A production cutback of more than 40 per cent was ordered at the Abadan refinery of the Anglo-Iranian Oil Company today in a move to postpone a complete shutdown of the giant plant as long as possible.

The cutback operation began at 9 o'clock this morning. By early evening the refinery was producing at the rate of 8,300,000 gallons a day, compared with 15,100,000 yesterday and a normal capacity of 18,000,000.

There is enough storage space ashore to keep going for about twenty days at the new rate of production, the refinery manager, B. K. Ross, said at a press conference at which the cutback was announced. But Mr. Ross made it clear that further reductions would be made to extend this period.

The move was in line with new British strategy in the dispute with the Iranian Government over the nationalization of the multi-million-dollar company. Last week it seemed as if the British would fill the storage tanks as quickly as possible and force the issue with the Iranians. Now, it is obvious, they will keep at least part of the refinery going until the very last minute in the hope that, as the British here put it, "sweet reason will prevail" among the Iranians.

Two Developments Noted

There have been two developments to support the British in their newly developed belief that the Iranians are beginning to realize that they have bitten off more than they can chew.

The first has been a sharpening split among the Iranian oil commissioners sent here from Teheran to take over the company. The opposing sides appear to be headed by Hussein Makki, firebrand Nationalist leader, and Dr. Matin Daftary, son-in-law of Premier Mohammed Mossadegh.

Mr. Makki has declared that "no compromise is possible," while Dr. Daftary, in an interview today, said that "there is a chance for a modus vivendi" with the British.

Some way or other must be found to per it the resumption of shipments to the nations of the

Continued on Page 5, Column 1

Tentative Contract Averts Wire Strike

Special to THE NEW YORK TIMES.

WASHINGTON, July 1—A threatened national walkout of Western Union telegraph employes was postponed indefinitely tonight after a tentative agreement had been reached between management and union representatives. The strike was to have started at 6 A. M. tomorrow.

The agreement was announced by J. R. Mandelbaum, Federal conciliator, who had persuaded both sides to join a series of conferences today. He was a witness to the agreement, which will be submitted to the membership of the Commercial Telegraphers Union, A. F. L., for ratification.

All adult employes, under the terms of the agreement, will receive a wage increase of 13 cents an hour effective today, and another 4 cents an hour effective

Continued on Page 12, Column 2

DEWEY OFF TO VISIT NATIONS OF PACIFIC

Reaches San Francisco After Being Forced Down by Plane Trouble at Kansas City

Governor Dewey flew to San Francisco yesterday on the first leg of a 25,000-mile trip to the Far East and Australasia to view at first hand an area he regards as of prime importance to the security of the free world.

As he took off from La Guardia Airport at 9:26 A. M. aboard a Trans World Airlines Constellation, Mr. Dewey was unaware of the latest Communist proposal for truce talks.

Informed of the development at Kansas City, Mo., where the plane made an unscheduled stop because of engine trouble, the Governor said he hoped the Chinese Communist acceptance of Gen. Matthew B. Ridgway's cease-fire proposal would "bring real peace" in Korea.

On his arrival at San Francisco at 10:25 P. M., Eastern standard time, Mr. Dewey said smilingly in

Continued on Page 7, Column 5

2 MAIN POINTS MET

No Political Questions Injected, 'Volunteer' Head to Participate

ACTION WILL SUBSIDE

U.N. Commander Told to Hold Military Activity to a Minimum

By JAMES RESTON
Special to THE NEW YORK TIMES.

WASHINGTON, July 1—The cease-fire phase of the Korean peace negotiations has gone better than officials here had hoped.

The place, and even the time, of the armistice talks were not regarded in official Washington quarters as vital. The two primary considerations here were that no political questions should be introduced into the armistice discussions and that the Chinese commander participate. Both of these points were satisfied by today's message from Peiping and Pyongyang.

Gen. Matthew B. Ridgway has been instructed to keep United Nations military activity to a minimum between now and the start of the talks. Aerial observation will be maintained over the entire country to ascertain whether the Communists are building up their supplies or moving troops in any large numbers.

Ground patrols will, of course, be keeping contact with the enemy, though it is generally realized here that the boys will be keeping their heads down until the fighting stops unless there is any evidence of a major enemy assault.

Both Commanders Sign

The answer to General Ridgway's offer of an armistice conference was signed by both Kim Il Sung, the commander of the Korean People's Army, and Peng Teh-huai, commander of the Chinese "volunteers."

It said "we" propose a meeting in the area of Kaesong, just south of the Thirty-eighth Parallel between July 10 and 15. Moreover it

Continued on Page 2, Column 7

Red Leaders and Their Answer

Gen. Kim Il Sung

Gen. Peng Teh-huai
Associated Press

Special to THE NEW YORK TIMES.

TOKYO, Monday, July 2—Following is the text, as broadcast by the Peiping and Pyongyang radios, of the Communists' acceptance of the United Nations' suggestion for a Korean truce conference:

General Ridgway,
Commander in Chief of the United Nations Forces:

Your statement of June 30 this year concerning peace talks has been received.

We are authorized to inform you that we agree to meet your representative for conducting talks concerning cessation of military action and establishment of peace.

We propose that the place of meeting be in the area of Kaesong on the Thirty-eighth Parallel. If you agree, our representatives are prepared to meet your representative between July 10 and July 15, 1951.

KIM IL SUNG,
Supreme Commander of the Korean People's Army.
PENG TEH-HUAI,
Commander of the Chinese Volunteer Forces.

U. N. ENCOURAGED BY REPLY OF REDS

Lie Says He Is 'Optimistic' but Some Diplomats Wonder at Request for 10-Day Delay

By KATHLEEN TELTSCH
Special to THE NEW YORK TIMES.

UNITED NATIONS, N. Y., July 1—United Nations leaders said today they regarded the Communist agreement to begin Korean peace talks as encouraging.

Secretary General Trygve Lie authorized a statement that United Nations officials were "optimistic" concerning the prospects for a cease-fire in Korea.

Mr. Lie's comment was the only official word from the world organization's top representatives. Privately, some officials and diplomats appeared surprised and somewhat concerned that the Communists had suggested that at least ten days elapse before the beginning of negotiations.

However, delegates in general were inclined to regard the Communist reply as both promising and reasonable. One dissenting opinion came from Col. Ben C.

Continued on Page 2, Column 8

PATROLS IN ACTION ON KOREA FRONTS

U.N. Troops Maintain Contact With Communist Forces as Warships Pound Coast

By GREG MacGREGOR
Special to THE NEW YORK TIMES.

TOKYO, Monday, July 2—War was still a definite reality yesterday to the fighting men in Korea, where sharp local action continued in all sectors.

The Air Force continued to pound away as usual at enemy positions, and one top-ranking officer explained, "We plan to continue operations until the whistle is officially blown."

The Communist forces showed no indications of altering their operational procedures. It was believed by well-informed United Nations personnel that many of the enemy were completely ignorant of the political maneuvers that may end the war. It is well known that Communist communications are poor and that military leaders tell their troops only what they want them to know.

Yesterday morning, light enemy

Continued on Page 2, Column 3

ANSWER BY RADIO

Foe Opposes a Meeting Aboard Hospital Ship in Wonsan Harbor

DATE PUZZLES ALLIES

Delay Believed Sought to Permit Consultation With the Kremlin

By LINDESAY PARROTT
Special to THE NEW YORK TIMES.

TOKYO, Monday, July 2—The Chinese and North Korean Communists accepted late last night the United Nations' proposal for a meeting to discuss a cease-fire in the Korean war, but named conditions differing from those broadcast to their high command by Gen. Matthew B. Ridgway, leader of the allied armed forces.

The Communists' answer came at 11 last night (9 A. M. Sunday, Eastern daylight time) over the Peiping radio, twenty-nine hours after more than 100 stations in Japan and Korea had begun broadcasting and rebroadcasting General Ridgway's proposal for a meeting aboard the Danish hospital ship Jutlandia in the harbor of Wonsan, deep in enemy territory in northeast Korea.

The official notification of acceptance bore the names of Kim Il Sung, Premier of North Korea and Commander in Chief of the Korean Comunist People's Army and Peng Teh-huai, leader of the Chinese "volunteers" in the Korean war.

Proposed Site Near Parallel

The Chinese and North Koreans, "after consultation," as it was announced by Peiping, ignored the proposal for a Wonsan meeting and named the area of Kaesong, just below the old Korean boundary on the Thirty-eighth Parallel, as their chosen place. They set the date for the armistice conferences to begin more than a week off—between July 10 and July 15.

The message was broadcast first in Chinese, then in English and two hours later in Korean by the radio station at the Korean Communist capital of Pyongyang.

No official reaction to the Communist counter-proposal was available immediately either here or at Eighth Army Headquarters, although informed quarters appeared to believe there was no reason why it should not be accepted promptly. Substitution of the Kaesong area south of the Thirty-eighth Parallel for Wonsan, in North Korean territory, was regarded as a device for saving "face," so important in the Orient.

The message reached General Ridgway as he was about to retire at his home in the United States Embassy here. The general had "no comment," an aide said.

Ridgway Awaits Orders

It was emphasized that, since General Ridgway broadcast his armistice proposal on instructions from the Joint Chiefs of Staff in Washington, he would make no further statement until additional orders were received on the attitude to be taken toward the enemy's answer.

Lieut. Gen. James A. Van Fleet, commander of the Eighth Army, who has been named as General Ridgway's probable representative at the truce negotiations, was asleep at his headquarters in Korea when the Peiping broadcast came in. He was not awakened, and learned of the proposal only this morning.

It was pointed out that the general had stated several times he was responsible only for the military campaign in Korea, where skirmishing continued along the front last night and the enemy launched light counter-attacks against United Nations patrols yesterday. General Van Fleet had pledged previously that there would be "no let-up" on the basis of cease-fire reports.

Immediate interest was attached here to several points in the Peiping message. First was the week's delay asked by the enemy before beginning the negotiations,

Continued on Page 3, Column 2

Peppery Briton's One-Man Revolt Restores Names to Countrymen

By CLIFTON DANIEL
Special to THE NEW YORK TIMES.

LONDON, July 1—Thanks to a fellow named Harry Willcock, Britons have partly regained one of the liberties they lost in 1939—the right to be known in ordinary circumstances by name instead of by number.

Mr. Willcock, a peppery little Yorkshireman with a ruddy face, sandy hair and a quick tongue, achieved this act of liberation by simply saying "No" to a policeman—something that a law-abiding Englishman rarely does.

By his defiance, said R. Hopkin Morris, a Liberal Member of Parliament, Harry Willcock "created anarchy in high places."

Nobody was more surprised than Mr. Willcock himself. His one-man revolution was entirely unpremeditated. It was the result of a reflex action that many free citizens feel when approached by a policeman.

Questioned a year ago about overtime parking in Truro, Mr. Willcock refused to produce the identity card that every adult Briton has been required to carry since 1939. He told the policeman who asked for the card to present his compliments to the police superintendent "and tell him to go to hell."

Nothing happened then but last December Mr. Willcock was stopped for speeding in Hornsey, a district of North London. Again he refused to show his card and continued to do so although he said he was "badgered" by the police for two months.

Finally, he was haled before the Hornsey magistrates, who ruled that he was obliged to show his card but imposed no punishment.

It was the first time since 1939 that anyone convicted of refusing to produce an identity card had received an absolute discharge. However, Mr. Willcock was not satisfied. He appealed.

Because of the importance of the case, seven High Court judges headed by the Lord Chief Justice were convened, for the first time

Continued on Page 5, Column 5

World News Summarized

MONDAY, JULY 2, 1951.

North Korea and Communist China have accepted General Ridgway's proposal for talks on a cease-fire in Korea. Twenty-nine hours after the United Nations commander had broadcast his offer, the Peiping radio issued the announcement signed by Premier Kim Il Sung, head of the North Korean Army, and Gen. Peng Teh-huai, leader of the Chinese "volunteers." They asked that the talks be held between July 10 and 15, in the "area of Kaesong." General Ridgway had proposed an immediate meeting on a Danish hospital ship off Wonsan. [1:8.] Kaesong, which was the sole area of contact between North and South Korea during the United States-Soviet occupation, is just south of the Thirty-eighth Parallel in western Korea. [3:6.]

Washington, minimizing the suggested change of time and place, seemed quite content with the fact that the Chinese commander would participate in the truce talks and that no demand to discuss political issues was made. Hope was expressed that the Communists would accept the authority of the United Nations over any agreement. [1:5.]

Although Secretary General Lie and most other United Nations leaders were encouraged by the latest developments, some were concerned over the motive behind the stipulation of a delay in the start of talks. [1:6.] The news reached Pusan, temporary South Korean capital, too late for official comment, but the day had been marked by popular demonstrations against a truce at the Parallel. [3:1.]

Governor Dewey, informed of the Communist reply while on the first leg of his trip to the Far East, said he hoped the move would "bring real peace" to Korea. [1:4.]

Against this background of steps to end the war, the fighting in Korea continued sporadic, with some sharp actions and air blows. [1:7; maps P. 2.]

The Anglo-Iranian Oil Company ordered production at Abadan cut 40 per cent and may reduce output even more in an effort to keep the refineries working as long as possible. There were indications that Iran might soften her position in the oil-nationalization dispute. [1:3.]

Saturday's stabilization order froze ceiling prices and not market prices, Stabilizer DiSalle explained. The Administration will seek a stronger control bill from the House than the one passed by the Senate. [1:1.] The inaction of the present Congress on reorganizing Federal agencies was in "striking contrast" to the record of the last Congress, the Citizens' Committee on the Hoover Report said. [26:1.]

A tentative agreement for a two-step 17-cent hourly pay rise removed the threat of a strike set for today against Western Union. [1:4.] Transit in Washington was paralyzed by a bus and trolley strike. [12:4.]

Ceremonies in Philadelphia opened a nation-wide observance of the 175th anniversary of the signing of the Declaration of Independence. [13:1.]

NEWS BULLETINS FROM THE TIMES
Every hour on the hour
7 A.M. through Midnight
WQXR AM 1560
WQXR FM 96.3

Index to other news appears on last page of this section.

Allies Plan Close Watch on Foe Till the Shooting Actually Stops

By GEORGE BARRETT
Special to THE NEW YORK TIMES.

EIGHTH ARMY HEADQUARTERS, in Korea, Monday, July 2—The request by the Communists for a front-line conference in the Kaesong area between July 10 and 15 presents many technical problems.

With the enemy now making it unmistakably clear that he wants an end of the war in Korea, there is some puzzlement over the time suggested by the Communists for the meeting, and the big question right now is: Are the soldiers to keep killing each other in the meantime?

In spite of the vast United Nations war machine of the armies, navies and air forces of sixteen nations, military leaders here were ready to spring into instant action for a cease-fire meeting when Gen. Matthew B. Ridgway sent his message to the Communists. In a matter of hours, the proposed meeting place, the Danish hospital ship Jutlandia, was cleared of wounded and made ready to sail north.

It is felt that the Communists should be able to meet with the United Nations without delay. This would seem particularly so now that the Communists have selected the Kaesong area, to which they can drive in a matter of several hours at most.

There is no question, of course, that the orders will be to keep fighting until cease-fire terms are agreed upon, and it is no secret that military plans call for maintaining direct contact with the enemy. This presumably will be true particularly in the critical time between now and the formal end of the war, since nobody on this side of the lines has any intention of being caught in a ruse.

At the same time, it is realized that orders to keep fighting—and dying—for another eight to thirteen days while plans are completed for cease-fire talks involve tremendous demands on the troops at the front, where there is a natural human reluctance already to

Continued on Page 3, Column 8

Jack Benny, seen here with Rochester, had a weekly series on CBS all through the Fifties.

Arthur Godfrey discovered Julius LaRosa and introduced him to TV viewers on his Talent Scouts show. By 1951 he was appearing regularly on Arthur Godfrey and his Friends.

Dean Martin and Jerry Lewis are shown here hosting the Colgate Comedy Hour.

100TH ANNIVERSARY
"All the News
That's Fit to Print"
1851 1951

The New York Times.

LATE CITY EDITION
Fair and cool with low humidity today, tonight and tomorrow.
Temperature Range Today-Max., 76; Min., 64
Temperatures Yesterday—Max., 77; Min., 63
Full U. S. Weather Bureau Report, Page 27

Copyright, 1951, by The New York Times Company.

VOL. C No. 34,160. Entered as Second-Class Matter. Post Office, New York, N. Y. NEW YORK, SATURDAY, AUGUST 4, 1951. Times Square, New York 18, N. Y. Telephone LAckawanna 4-1000 FIVE CENTS

DEADLOCK PERSISTS AS LINE FOR A TRUCE IS DEBATED 9TH DAY

Delegates Meet for Little More Than an Hour at Their 19th Session at Kaesong

RED VIOLATION IS NOTED

Admiral Joy Charges Armed Enemy Troops Passed Near U. N. Building in City

By LINDESAY PARROTT
Special to THE NEW YORK TIMES.

TOKYO, Saturday, Aug. 4—United Nations and Communist delegates debated for a little more than an hour today at their nineteenth session at Kaesong over a military demarcation line for an armistice in the Korean war. They adjourned until tomorrow with "no progress" toward ending their deadlock.

While there was still hope that a compromise could be reached eventually, today's brief session indicated that no new terms had been brought up, over which a lengthier discussion might have been expected.

[The Associated Press said Vice Admiral Charles Turner Joy, head of the United Nations delegation, had "noted for the record" a Communist violation of the conference site neutral zone, the passing of an estimated company of armed Chinese troops within a few hundred yards of the allied quarters near the conference building. A United Nations spokesman emphasized that the armistice talks had not been recessed because of the incident.]

Twentieth Session Set

The delegates sat down on schedule at 11 this morning (9 P. M. Friday, Eastern daylight time), after the allied party had arrived by helicopter. They adjourned at noon until 2 P. M., and quit for the day ten minutes later.

The twentieth meeting — the tenth on the question of an armistice line and buffer zone between the opposing armies—was set for 11 o'clock tomorrow morning.

Meanwhile, an allied spokesman here denied reports that the headquarters of Gen. Matthew B. Ridgway, United Nations commander, had demanded a demarcation line well north of the present combat area, as the Communist radio has been reporting. No headquarters policy to that effect has been announced, it was pointed out.

As far as is known, United Nations policy still is for a truce at the present battle positions, though perhaps with a neutralized zone to the northward inside North Korea.

A full complement of correspondents and service personnel was in the conference city today. The bridge across the Imjin River, washed out Wednesday, had been repaired, permitting passage of a jeep and truck convoy.

Argue for Viewpoints

As the allied communiqué again announced "no progress," it became clear that both sides had about exhausted what they had to propose. The enemy still insisted on a truce along the Thirty-eighth Parallel, in effect a re-establishment of the old political boundary of 1945, and the allies were holding out for an armistice on the present front line.

What both delegations are doing at the conference table is to present arguments to back up their viewpoints, some of which are definitely repetitious. The United Nations briefing officer said last night that the Communists' spokesman, General Nam Il, used

Continued on Page 2, Column 5

Elizabeth and Duke To Visit U. S. Oct. 24

By The Associated Press.

LONDON, Aug. 3—Princess Elizabeth and her husband, the Duke of Edinburgh, announced today that they would be guests of President and Mrs. Truman in Washington Oct. 24-26. They were expected to see New York in their brief visit.

The announcement said that they had accepted "with great pleasure" an invitation to visit the President. The Washington visit will follow a tour of Canada.

Whether the couple would stop at any other United States cities was not disclosed. Court circles noted, however, that Princess Elizabeth never had been on the American continent and that she had shown a lively interest in New York life.

Ridgway Sees Wedge Driven Between Chinese and Soviet

Headquarters Statement Says Red Losses in Korea May Bring On Tito-Like Break Splitting Mao and the Kremlin

Special to THE NEW YORK TIMES.

TOKYO, Saturday, Aug. 4—The headquarters of Gen. Matthew B. Ridgway has now adopted officially the theory that the Korean war and the heavy Chinese losses have driven a wide wedge between the regime of Mao Tse-tung and the Kremlin that might eventually result in a break similar to the split of Marshal Tito, the Yugoslav Premier, with the Cominform, it became known today.

Such a picture was drawn for the Japanese and foreign press this morning in a release by the Civil Information and Education Section of General Ridgway's headquarters. It was explained that the material given was usable in local or foreign newspapers as desired. The headquarters section is the agency that generally acts as liaison between Japanese information media and the Supreme Allied Command.

Entitled "The Significance of Korea," the headquarters announcement advanced the view that the Soviet Union expected the Korean fighting "to slash the strength of China, and this would be good because a strong China on Russia's southern frontier is the Kremlin's nightmare." The Information Section added:

"Russia's strategy has made the Chinese Reds less sure that the Kremlin is a friend. After all, China fought and bled while Russia looked on. To Mao Tse-tung this could hardly look like bosom comradeship."

The belief that the Chinese and the Soviet Union for some time have been rivals over the question which of the large Communist powers would have hegemony over North Korea has been held by some observers since the United Nations investigators moved into Pyongyang, the North Korean capital, after the collapse of the North Korean Communist armies last fall.

Already at that time, it was reported that the North Koreans, who had been under Soviet influ-

Continued on Page 2, Column 4

3 Western Powers Reject Bonn Bid for Saar Choice

Special to THE NEW YORK TIMES.

PARIS, Aug. 3—In a note reflecting their "complete accord" on the Saar, France, the United States and Britain rejected today a demand by Chancellor Konrad Adenauer of West Germany that the peoples of the Saar immediately receive the right to choose between France and Germany.

The note, drafted by representatives of the three Western powers meeting here this week, was delivered to Dr. Adenauer by John J. McCloy, United States High Commissioner in Germany. It reaffirmed the Allies' decision to support the present status of the Saar until conclusion of a peace treaty with the Bonn Republic, "or a treaty taking its place."

At present the Saar has its own government, and by an agreement of March 3, 1950, its steel and coal products will go to France for fifty years.

The note was issued in reply to a letter from Dr. Adenauer to the three Governments May 29. In it, Dr. Adenauer charged that France was attempting to make the Saar an independent, sovereign state. He asserted the region to be German, with the Saar people regarded as German nationals by the West German Government.

The Chancellor's protest arose from the Saar regime's banning of the Democratic party of the Saar for alleged Nazi tendencies. Dr. Adenauer criticized Robert Schuman, then French Foreign Minister, for having supported the ban. The party had favored return of the region to Germany.

Today's note virtually ignored this incident. French Government sources indicated that any statement on the matter would be regarded as "interference with a foreign country."

The note declared, however, that France, the United States and Britain strongly favored development in the Saar of "democratic institutions and respect for individual liberty," and expressed the hope that the area would not become the seat of a serious controversy.

The close and durable associa-

Continued on Page 3, Column 5

U. S. BARS DIRECT AID TO PAYMENTS UNION

Marshall Plan Council Agrees on Year's Halt to Dollar Flow, Help to Weaker Countries

By LANSING WARREN
Special to THE NEW YORK TIMES.

PARIS, Aug. 3—Direct United States dollar aid to the European Payments Union will be withdrawn for the coming year and in its place a system of indirect assistance to the weaker countries will be provided, in accordance with an agreement reached today in the Marshall Plan Council on the level of the ministers' deputies.

This is in conformity with the desire on the part of the Economic Cooperation Administration to keep the payments union from relying upon United States assistance and to build it up instead as a self-supporting organization. It was recognized, however, that at the present stage the payments union would require some assistance in an indirect form.

This is to be arranged in a way so as to bring the payments union a reduced supply of fresh dollars instead of the dollars the United States originally offered as the reserve dollar fund.

As explained today by experts working in the council here, the $350,000,000 reserve fund contributed by the United States last year will not be renewed. However, the United States Government has agreed to furnish aid to four of the member nations that have been formally recognized as structurally debtor countries. These are Greece,

Continued on Page 3, Column 7

4 Young Poles, One a Girl, Escape To Sweden in a Home-Made Plane

By GEORGE AXELSSON
Special to THE NEW YORK TIMES.

STOCKHOLM, Sweden, Aug. 3—Four Poles, one a woman 20 years old, made a successful get-away over night from their Communist-run country in the first trip of a home-built sports plane. They landed at 7:30 this morning at Malmoe Airport in southern Sweden.

This is the fourth incident in Sweden of its kind involving Poles within a month. Only yesterday mutinous Polish seamen brought a naval survey vessel into the port of Ystad, near here, after having overpowered their Communist officers.

The story told by the four who arrived by air was one of perseverance in building their plane out of spare parts and obtaining membership in an aviation club to have a license to fly and a field from which to take off.

They had to return the gunfire of police after their take-off was detected. They flew a zigzag course through clouds to shake off pursuers in a Polish military plane.

The fugitives' plane was apparently incapable of more than eighty miles an hour.

It had a Polish-make engine with an American carburetor, a nose-wheel from a German fighter and various mechanical details of Swiss make. The rudder was patched with a bit of leather, and the fuselage door shut so badly that it came open during flight and one of the young men was almost sucked out of the plane.

The plane was painted red and white and the rudder was inscribed "Wol Poznan," the name of the Polish aviation club of Poznan. The three men were all about 22 years old and one a skilled pilot. The girl was dark haired and slight. They started from the Wol Poznan

Continued on Page 4, Column 5

POINT FOUR GRANTS SOUGHT TO PROVIDE GIFTS OF MACHINERY

State Department Aide Gives Senators Plan for Adding to 'Know-How' Assistance

COMMUNISM CURB IS AIM

Opposition Is Indicated After Hearing—Turkey Safe From Attack, Connally Says

By C. P. TRUSSELL
Special to THE NEW YORK TIMES.

WASHINGTON, Aug. 3—A plan to broaden President Truman's "bold new program" for providing technical assistance to underdeveloped areas of the world beyond its original concept to include physical goods, such as farm machinery, is under consideration in a move to strengthen the resistance to communism.

This was told to the Senate Foreign Relations and Armed Services Committees today by George C. McGhee, Assistant Secretary of State for Near Eastern, South Asian and African Affairs. He appeared as the committees, holding joint hearings on the $8,500,000,000 foreign military and economic aid program, discussed the role to be played by the technical assistance project, known generally as Point Four.

The project was announced by President Truman when he was inaugurated in 1949.

Plan in Study Stage

Expansion of the program to provide farm machinery along with technical assistance was illustrative of the present planning, rather than a complete explanation of it. The extent to which material aid would accompany the teaching of know-how for economic advance had not been developed, it was stated.

In quarters away from the Capitol it was said that there probably would be some expansion of the program generally through liberalizations of policy relating to supplies. In some instances, it was added, the technical aid would be supplemented with "consumer goods," not identified.

It was emphasized, however, that no plans were "hard and fast" at this stage and that where "consumer goods" entered the picture it would be on a "relatively small scale."

Mr. McGhee apparently caught the joint group by surprise with his testimony. The extent to which he unveiled his proposals to the

Continued on Page 6, Column 6

NEW WAGE POLICY TIED TO LIVING COST DRAFTED BY BOARD

Plan Would Extend to Millions Negotiated Rises as Provided Under Escalator Clauses

JOHNSTON MUST APPROVE

Unanimous Action of 18 Labor, Industry and Public Members Called 'Major Achievement'

By LOUIS STARK
Special to THE NEW YORK TIMES.

WASHINGTON, Aug. 3—A major change in policy under which all wage earners in the jurisdiction of the Wage Stabilization Board would be allowed to obtain cost-of-living increases voluntarily negotiated was proposed by the board today.

Hitherto, cost-of-living increases tied to so-called escalator clauses for some 3,000,000 to 4,000,000 employes have been approved. That left millions of other wage earners at a disadvantage, because they did not have such contract provisions.

To make up for this inequity, the board has proposed the change to Eric Johnston, Director of Economic Stabilization. If he approves, a regulation will be adopted by the board to make the policy effective.

Mr. Johnston modified the Government's policy on March 1 to permit cost-of-living increases under escalator clauses signed before Jan. 25, the date of the wage freeze. The ceiling of 10 per cent on general wage increases, permitted without wage board approval, was not a bar. As a result, wage increases above 10 per cent were approved.

Price Index the Gauge

The usual type of escalator clause, such as that written into the General Motors contract with the United Automobile Workers, C. I. O., is geared to the consumers price index of the Bureau of Labor Statistics. Every three months, it is checked and wages are adjusted upward or downward one cent an hour for each 1.14 point change in the index.

The wage board, according to its chairman, Dr. George W. Taylor, discussed the situation created by escalator clauses and the lack of them, and finally arrived at a unanimous recommendation.

"We feel that this is a major achievement of the board," said Dr. Taylor. "It is an exceedingly important plank in the wage stabilization program. It illustrates

Continued on Page 6, Column 3

World News Summarized

SATURDAY, AUGUST 4, 1951

The United States Military Academy dismissed ninety cadets who had been found guilty of receiving improper outside help during examinations. The dismissed cadets, whose names were withheld, included many who had taken a leading part in Academy activities, including football. [1:8.] The surprise announcement caused great shock in the cadet corps at the Academy and elsewhere. [1:6-7.]

The United Nations and Communist conferees in Korea went on with the parleys in Kaesong, having still failed to break the deadlock over the issue of where the armistice demarcation line should be set. [1:1.]

Stiffening resistance by enemy forces slowed the pace of a limited United Nations push toward Kumsong on the east-central front. [2:8; with map.]

General Ridgway's headquarters depicted a widening split between Peiping and Moscow as a result of heavy Chinese losses in the Korean war. [1:2-3.]

India extended border security measures after intelligence reports had confirmed the presence in western Tibet of Chinese Communist troops. [2:2-3.]

Four Poles, one a woman, escaped to Sweden from their Communist-ruled homeland in a home-built plane. [1:2-3.]

A West German request that the Saar be allowed to choose for itself between union with Germany or with France was rejected in a note handed to Chancellor Adenauer in behalf of the United States, France and Britain. [1:2-3.]

An informal United States proposal put before a United Nations subcommittee suggests the use, against any future aggressor, of United Nations forces in coordination with General Eisenhower's military command of the North Atlantic Treaty Organization. [2:1.]

Under an agreement in the Marshall Plan Council, Washington will halt financial assistance to the European Payments Union for the coming year in favor of indirect aid to those countries needing it most. [1:2.]

The Senate hearings on the Administration's $8,500,000,000 program for foreign military and economic help heard a State Department spokesman outline a broadened White House plan for aiding the world's underdeveloped areas to resist communism by giving them physical goods such as farm machinery. [1:4.]

Following their tour of Canada, Princess Elizabeth and her husband will be guests of President Truman and Mrs. Truman in Washington late in October. They also may come to this city. [1:1.]

A new policy to allow workers voluntary cost-of-living wage increases was announced by the Wage Stabilization Board. [1:5.] The Ford Motor Company and the Chrysler Corporation formally requested the Office of Price Stabilization to authorize new passenger-car price increases of about 10 per cent to take care of increased costs of production. [6:8.] The Senate Finance Committee ended hearings on the tax-increase bill amid indications it would sharply revise downward the House measure calling for $7,000,000,000 in higher levies. [6:1.]

NEWS BULLETINS FROM THE TIMES
Every hour on the hour
7 A.M. through Midnight
WQXR AM 1560
WQXR FM 96.3

Index to other news appears on last page of this section.

WEST POINT OUSTS 90 CADETS FOR CHEATING IN CLASSROOM; FOOTBALL PLAYERS INVOLVED

Corps Is Bitter at Guilty Men And Blow to Academy Honor

News Stuns Students, but Attitude Is That Cheaters Deserve No Sympathy and School's Ideals Have Been Saved

By RICHARD H. PARKE
Special to THE NEW YORK TIMES.

WEST POINT, N. Y., Aug. 3—The cadet corps of the United States Military Academy here was stunned today to learn that ninety of its members had been discharged for cheating on examinations.

The news, announced prosaically in mimeographed releases that were stuffed in barracks mail bags for delivery throughout the vast post, did not come as a complete surprise. Rumors had circulated since the June Week that the corps had been touched by scandal and that inquiries were under way behind closed doors.

But no one knew—except those intimately associated with the investigation — the scope of the dereliction. Never in the academy's history have so many cadets been involved in similar charges.

The cadets took it hard. Cadet Regimental Commander William H. Geatches, 23 years old, of Linton, Ind., said he and his comrades felt no sympathy for the guilty men. Cadet Geatches asserted that the disclosure of the violation was not a sign of weakness in the honor code, but an indication of its strength.

"The code will continue in the future as it has for more than a century," he added.

Another cadet officer, Ralph W. Girdner, 24, of Amite, La., a company commander, said his own reaction was that "if the men violated the honor code, then I will be glad to see them go."

Proud of the Academy's honor traditions, the cadets also were

Continued on Page 5, Column 4

'CODE' IS VIOLATED

Answers Supplied Men in Advance of Tests, Charges Indicate

'MILD' DISCHARGES GIVEN

President Expresses Concern —Collins Says Infractions Stemmed From Varsity

Texts of statements by Army and Academy head, Page 5

By AUSTIN STEVENS
Special to THE NEW YORK TIMES.

WASHINGTON, Aug. 3—The Army today discharged ninety cadets of the United States Military Academy at West Point, many of them players on the Army's high-powered football team, for cheating during examinations.

All of the dismissed cadets are to receive a discharge that, while not "dishonorable," was described by an Army spokesman as "neither black nor white but gray in tone."

The scandal brought shocked reaction as Frank Pace Jr., Secretary of the Army, announced that the cadets had broken the sacrosanct "honor code" of the academy.

President Truman announced through a spokesman that he was very much concerned over the disclosures and some Senators criticized the Army for not having been more severe.

Started With Football Team

Gen. J. Lawton Collins, Chief of Staff of the Army, told a group of Senators a few minutes before the action was made public at the Pentagon, that the serious infractions of academy regulations and code had started with the football team and had spread to other groups in the cadet corps of about 2,500.

[General Collins told the Senators that the football team was "practically wiped out," the United Press reported.]

The ninety cadets, an Army spokesman said, were members of the present First (senior) Class, the one below it and possibly included students in their second year. The Army contended that none of the graduating class of two months ago had been involved.

A decision not to include as possible violators any of the most recent graduating class grew out of the fact that many of that class may at the moment have combat assignments and that some may even have been killed in Korea.

The Army, pressed on this point, took the stand that a man upon being commissioned from West Point was considered to have started with a "clean slate."

Army authorities said that the expelled cadets would be subject to the draft, but that their discharges would not necessarily prevent their advancement to commissions.

Ruling by Special Board

The discharges of the cadets, whose names were not made public, followed a unanimous recommendation by a special board headed by Judge Learned Hand, who recently retired as Judge of the United States Court of Appeals for the Second Circuit. The other members of the board were Lieut. Gen. Troy H. Middleton, Ret., president of Louisiana State University, and Maj. Gen. Robert M. Danford, Ret., a former commandant at West Point. The board's decision was unanimous, the Army said.

General Collins and Secretary Pace met with Judge Hand in New York recently and the reasons for the meeting at the time were guarded with extreme care. Even highly placed Army public information officers were denied access to the West Point investigation facts until a few hours before today's disclosures.

At West Point, Maj. Gen. Frederick A. Irving, Superintendent of the Academy, issued a statement declaring there had been a "serious breach" of the military school's code of ethics. He described the infractions as the "receiving of improper outside assistance in academic work."

General Irving's statement also said:

"In the group being discharged

Continued on Page 5, Column 5

ANTI-TYDINGS DRIVE HELD 'DESPICABLE'

Senate Group Censures Butler but Basis for Unseating Him Is Not Found

By JOHN D. MORRIS
Special to THE NEW YORK TIMES.

WASHINGTON, Aug. 3—A Senate subcommittee reported today that there was insufficient evidence to recommend the unseating of Senator John Marshall Butler, Republican of Maryland, but it denounced as "despicable" the campaign tactics used on his behalf against former Senator Millard E. Tydings, Democrat.

The subcommittee on privileges and elections called for the establishment of rules and standards to make "defamation, slander and libel" sufficient grounds for expelling a Senator. It cited four violations of State and Federal law by Butler campaign workers and recommended that the record of its long investigation be turned over to the Justice Department for "appropriate" action.

The thirty-nine page formal report on last fall's Butler-Tydings campaign was made to the Senate Committee on Rules and Administration, of which the subcommittee is a part.

It had the unanimous concurrence of the subcommittee's members, Senators Guy M. Gillette of Iowa, chairman, Mike Monroney of Oklahoma and Thomas C. Hennings of Missouri, Democrats, and Robert C. Hendrickson of New Jersey and Margaret Chase Smith of Maine, Republicans.

The investigation, which included nearly two months of public hearings last spring, was conduct-

Continued on Page 16, Column 4

NARCOTICS EMPIRE WAS GORDON'S AIM

Officials Say Ring, Competing Against Luciano and Mafia, Made Million a Year

Waxey Gordon and his narcotics syndicate were in the process of mushrooming their illicit drug traffic in the East when he and three henchmen were arrested here on Thursday evening.

Federal authorities reported yesterday that the beer baron of the prohibition era, competing with narcotics rings controlled by Charles (Lucky) Luciano and the Mafia had "taken over" territories of other rings broken up recently by arrests.

Gordon and his henchmen were seized at Sixty-eighth Street and York Avenue, a rendezvous set for the purchase by a Federal undercover agent of almost two pounds of heroin for $9,000. Gordon, whose real name is Irving Wexler, was said to have had seventeen and a half ounces of heroin in his possession.

Arraigned early yesterday before United States Commissioner Edward W. McDonald, Gordon was held in $250,000 bail. He said he lived at 1 St. Paul's Court, Brooklyn, and was 63 years old.

The other defendants were Samuel Kass, 39, of 161 West Seventy-fifth Street; Benjamin Katz, alias Ben Kassop, 35, of 68-37 108th Street, Forest Hills, Queens, held in $100,000 bail each, and Arthur Repola, 23, of 355 West 113th Street, $50,000 bond.

His captors described yesterday how the 63-year-old Gordon, a career-criminal whose million-dollar "junk pushing" capped a lifetime

Continued on Page 28, Column 3

Scientist a Suicide by Snake Venom After Ouster From U. of Michigan

By The Associated Press.

ANN ARBOR, Mich., Aug. 3—A world-renowned scientist killed himself with a hypodermic dose of snake venom late today because he could not bear the disgrace of being dismissed from the University of Michigan faculty for mishandling funds.

Dr. Malcolm H. Soule, 54 years old, was found dying by his wife, Alma, in the basement of their home here. The quick-acting venom, mixed with morphine, killed him in a matter of minutes.

The suicide occurred three hours after the university's Board of Regents informed him his resignation would not be accepted and he was dismissed and would be prosecuted.

On the record, apparently only $487.05 was involved. The board said Dr. Soule had made restitution for that amount. University officials declined tonight to amplify how funds were mishandled. He had been chairman of the Department of Bacteriology since 1935.

Dr. Soule was still conscious when his wife reached him. Apparently he had fallen prostrate at the foot of the stairs after injecting the poison into his bloodstream.

A bottle labeled "snake venom" and a hypodermic needle were found elsewhere in the basement.

Mrs. Soule went to the basement when he failed to respond to a call for dinner. Before lapsing into unconsciousness, he whispered to her:

"It won't do any good to call physicians. There is no known antidote for this snake venom."

Coroner Edwin C. Ganzhorn gave a finding of suicide. He said the snake venom apparently had been picked up by the scientist on one of his many trips into tropical countries.

Dr. Soule left a note addressed

Continued on Page 28, Column 7

100TH ANNIVERSARY
"All the News
That's Fit to Print"
1851 1951

The New York Times.

LATE CITY EDITION
Fair and pleasant today. Becoming cloudy late tomorrow.
Temperature Range Today-Max., 79; Min., 53
Temperatures Yesterday—Max., 71; Min., 53
U. S. Weather Bureau Report, Page 9, Sect. 5

Section 1

Copyright, 1951, by The New York Times Company.

VOL. C. No. 34,196. Entered as Second-Class Matter, Post Office, New York, N. Y. NEW YORK, SUNDAY, SEPTEMBER 9, 1951. Including Magazine and Book Review. FIFTEEN CENTS New York City / 50 Mile Zone } { Elsewhere Twenty-five Cents

PEACE TREATY WITH JAPAN SIGNED; GROMYKO WARNS STEP RISKS WAR; U. S. AND TOKYO IN SECURITY PACT

SENATE UNIT VOTES 11% RISE IN TAXES ON PRIVATE INCOME

House Increase of 12½% Is Cut by Finance Committee —An Alternative Given

PROFIT LEVY UNDISTURBED

Corporate Normal Payments in Bill Would Go Up From 25 to 27 Per Cent

By C. P. TRUSSELL
Special to The New York Times.

WASHINGTON, Sept. 8—An 11-per cent increase in the present income taxes of individuals was approved finally by the Senate Finance Committee today. It would become effective as of Nov. 1.

The House of Representatives in June approved a straight increase of 12½ per cent.

The Senate group would provide an alternative to the straight 11 per cent levy. A taxpayer instead could elect to pay 8 per cent on his surtax net income after deducting his present taxes. This alternative, however, would benefit only unmarried individuals with incomes of about $27,000 or married couples with about twice that much.

The day-long drive of the committee to complete the new tax bill failed.

Committee Recesses

Late today, after having been in closed session, with brief respite, since morning, the group recessed until Monday. Senator Walter F. George, Democrat of Georgia, the chairman, said the committee would hold a night session then, if necessary to finish the work.

The committee also voted finally to increase corporate normal taxes from the present 25 per cent to 27 per cent and surtaxes from 22 to [illegible] per cent. The House plan would raise normal taxes by 5 per cent.

The Senate group refused to increase excess profits taxes for most corporations, as had been proposed by the House, by reducing the credits before the application of this levy.

In affirming its previous decision on corporation normal and surtax rates, the Senate committee made changes to prevent any corporation from having to pay in taxes more than 69 per cent of its over-all earnings. Smaller corporations up to $300,000 of income would not go that high. It was in their interest that the change was made today.

Ceiling Rate Is Provided

The device would be to put a ceiling of 17 per cent on the excess profits tax and consolidated return tax and set no ceiling for income tax rates. This would be equivalent to providing a ceiling rate on income and excess profits levies that never would quite reach 69 per cent. A ceiling of 70 per cent, adopted previously, was canceled, so far as the Senate group was concerned.

The committee modified a previous decision to make the new corporate taxes effective as of Jan. 1, 1951, and made it April 1 of this year.

An estimated $1,293,000,000 of additional excise taxes won final approval of the Senate committee. They would include a 10 per cent gambling tax on wagers received by professional bookmakers and

Continued on Page 50, Column 1

Major Sports News

BASEBALL

The Yankees retained their lead in the American League by defeating the Senators, 4—0, on Mickey Mantle's three-run homer in the seventh inning before 35,314 fans yesterday. Preceding the regular Stadium contest, Joe McCarthy's Old-Timers downed Clark Griffith's team, 2—0. The Dodgers increased their first-place margin in the National League to six and a half games as Don Newcombe shut out the Giants on two hits, 9—0, at Ebbets Field. The Red Sox toppled the Athletics, 6 to 1, and the Indians beat the Browns, 6—3, in a night game.

HORSE RACING

Alerted, leading all the way, beat favored Battlefield by a head in the $20,000 added Discovery Handicap over a mile and an eighth at Aqueduct. Vulcania was third. The victor, timed in 1:50 2-5, paid $18.50 for $2 to win. Quiz Song scored a head victory in the Mermaid Handicap at Atlantic City and Palaja captured the Foxcatcher National Cup Steeplechase at Fair Hill, Md.

(Details in Section 5)

John Sloan, Artist, Dead at Age of 80

John Sloan
The New York Times, 1950

Special to The New York Times.

HANOVER, N. H., Sept. 8—John Sloan, dean of American artists died here today at the age of 80. The death of the noted painter, etcher and teacher occurred in Mary Hitchcock Hospital, where he had undergone an operation for cancer some days ago.

Mr. Sloan, whose home studio was in New York and who had spent the last thirty summers in Santa Fé, N. M., came here in June and since had decided to make his home near the Dartmouth campus. He was a distant cousin of Dartmouth's president, John Sloan Dickey. With him at the end was his artist wife, the former Helen Farr, whom he

Continued on Page 90, Column 2

AUTO POLICY RATES RAISED IN JERSEY

Insurance Up 11.4 to 21.7% Starting Tomorrow—Board Criticizes Design of Cars

By The Associated Press.

TRENTON, Sept. 8—The State Department of Banking and Insurance has approved a rise in automobile insurance rates. The increases, effective Monday, range from 11.4 per cent to 21.7 per cent. They will apply only to future policies, and not to ones in effect now.

The increases were broken down this way:

1. Passenger bodily injury and property damage rates were increased by approximately 21.7 per cent and 17.8 per cent, respectively.
2. Commercial bodily injury and property damage rates were increased by approximately 11.4 per cent and 18 per cent, respectively.

The department said the higher rates concerned policies written by companies affiliated with the National Bureau of Casualty Underwriters. These companies, the department said, write slightly more than half of the premium volume in New Jersey.

The increases were requested by the companies. The department said it approved the requests because the number of accidents had increased and claim costs had gone up.

Higher Verdicts Noted

"The current statistics," the announcement said, "merely confirm what has become common knowledge. Inflation has influenced courts and juries to render higher verdicts for injuries to persons and damage to property."

The department also criticized auto designers, traffic jams and irresponsibility.

"The extravagance of design of automobiles," the announcement said, "results in increased repair costs. The traffic congestion on our country roads and urban streets inevitably occasions more and more accidents. Finally, the stress and tension of the times apparently have resulted in a lowering of the normal sense of responsibility. The result of all these factors is converted into statistics and ultimately into insurance rates.

"Notwithstanding it is interesting to note that the new bodily injury rates for private passenger and commercial cars are still somewhat lower than those that were in effect prior to the second World War."

New York Rates Increased in June

New York State instituted a flat 20 per cent rise in automobile liability rates and a 10 per cent increase on property damage insurance last June 1. The rise, granted to insurers by the State Superintendent of Insurance, affected both passenger cars and commercial vehicles.

STILL AMERICA'S MOST COMPLETE LINE
Over 7,500 Different Brushes.
Solo-Barton Brush Co., New York 19—Advt.

ALLIES MAP STAND EAST OF THE RHINE AS STRENGTH RISES

Reinforcement of Continent Permits Planners to Scrap Fighting Withdrawal Idea

NEW DEFENSE IS DRAFTED

One Proposal Adapts Method Used to Defeat Germans in 'Battle of the Bulge'

By DREW MIDDLETON
Special to The New York Times.

BONN, Germany, Sept. 8—Allied strategic thinking about the best way to meet a Russian attack, long confined to the dismal prospect of a fighting withdrawal westward across the Rhine, is expanding with the reinforcement of the occupation armies in Germany and the general rearmament of Europe.

No Allied headquarters, from Supreme Headquarters Allied Powers in Europe, on down, discounts the capacities of the Soviet group of armies in East Germany, fighting with numerically superior air support.

But there is a general feeling that by the spring of 1952 the Allied forces in Germany and immediately available in France and the Low Countries will be strong enough to engage the Russian armies in strength east of the Rhine.

The Soviet threat that has terrorized Europe for half a decade no longer is considered a practical possibility. The Allies have taken on enough strength to plot how and where the Russian divisions pushing Westward could be trapped and [illegible].

First German Base Set Up

The first objective of Allied strategic thinking has been the establishment in Germany of a large firm base.

Until less than a year ago this base was neither large nor firm, since the forces available were too weak to hold the line of Rhine, which would have been its eastern perimeter.

Under those conditions the best the Allies could hope for was to jab at the oncoming Soviet armies before retreating over the river. But reinforcement has extended the eastern perimeter of the base well into area between the Rhine on the west and the Elbe and the Thuringian mountains on the east and given the Allies room for maneuver around the powerful Russian armies.

If the French Army in Europe, including five divisions raised this

Continued on Page 14, Column 1

A NEW SOVIET LINE

Gromyko Tells Signers They Invite Explosion in the Far East

SAYS JAPAN IS TO BE BASE

Insists That Russians Were Not Consulted on the Final Draft of Settlement

Text of Gromyko statement to press is on Pages 26 and 27.

By WALTER H. WAGGONER
Special to The New York Times.

SAN FRANCISCO, Sept. 8—Andrei A. Gromyko, Deputy Foreign Minister of the Soviet Union, warned the forty-eight nations that signed the peace treaty with Japan today that they must bear the responsibility for "the consequences of such a step," which he implied could be war in the Far East.

The head of the Soviet delegation to the conference here, having failed to obstruct the treaty settlement, appeared to have taken the new, more desperate course of holding over the signers the threat of widened conflict in the region where the settlement is designed to assure peace.

In both a long prepared statement and at a news conference, Mr. Gromyko pronounced his warning as his final response to a "peace of reconciliation" supported by all at the conference except the Soviet, Czechoslovakia and Poland.

His Warning to Signers

Devoting the first half-hour of the news conference to the now familiar charges against the Japanese treaty, Mr. Gromyko held his implied threat until he could play it as his last trump card.

"The Soviet Union," he declared, "would fail in performing its duty if it already at this moment had not publicly stated that it is not only disassociating itself from these plans for the preparation of a new war in the Far East, but that it is also warning that those who impose such a peace treaty with Japan take upon themselves all the responsibility before the

Continued on Page 25, Column 3

World News Summarized

SUNDAY, SEPTEMBER 9, 1951

The Japanese peace treaty was signed yesterday by Japan and forty-eight non-Communist nations attending the San Francisco conference. The Communist nations boycotted the signing ceremony [1:8], which required seventy-two minutes. [30:1.] Andrei A. Gromyko, chief Soviet delegate, implying that the treaty could be the prelude for a new Far Eastern war, warned that its sponsors must "take upon themselves all the responsibility before the peoples for the consequences of such a step." [1:4.]

The United States and Japan agreed on the terms of a bilateral security treaty that will allow the stationing of American troops on Japanese soil for an indefinite period. The treaty was signed by Secretary Acheson and Premier Yoshida five hours after the peace treaty. [1:6-7.]

Chinese Communist radio broadcasts renewed charges that the United States had tried to wreck the Kaesong negotiations for a Korean armistice. Reports said large enemy troop units and tank forces were sighted in and near Kaesong. [1:5.]

On the battlefront enemy counter-attacks slightly penetrated United Nations positions in the western sector as Allied patrols probed widely. [8:1.]

Allied strategists were veering toward the view that by the spring of next year Allied armies in Western Europe might be strong enough to hold any Soviet operation east of the Rhine in the event of the outbreak of hostilities. They no longer considered a virtually unhindered Communist "march to the Atlantic" a practical possibility. [1:3.]

About 2,000,000 Greeks are expected to elect a new Parliament today, with the main issue centering upon Field Marshal Papagos, who last spring broke with King Paul. [40:1.]

In India, Prime Minister Nehru won the presidency of the Congress party, replacing a consistent opponent, Purshottamdas Tandon, who had resigned. Mr. Nehru's victory was considered a defeat for the Hindu conservatives. Ousting of anti-Nehru elements was expected. [1.7.]

The Senate Finance Committee gave its final approval to an increase of 11 per cent in individual income taxes. The new rates, to become effective Nov. 1, are expected to produce additional revenue totaling $2,394,000,000 a year. The committee also reaffirmed earlier action increasing corporation taxes by $2,080,000,000 a year, but set April 1 as the effective date for the higher corporation levies. The committee's measure, which is expected to reach the Senate floor this week, is estimated to produce $5,765,000,000. [1:1.]

Continued cooperation between the American Federation of Labor and the Congress of Industrial Organizations in this state on problems of common concern was pledged. [45:3.]

The New Jersey Department of Banking approved a rise of 11.4 per cent to 21.7 per cent in automobile insurance rates. [1:2.]

NEWS BULLETINS FROM THE TIMES
Every hour on the hour
6 A.M. through Midnight
Except at 4 & 9 P.M. Today
WQXR AM 1560
WQXR FM 96.3

Index to other news may be found on Page 95.

A HISTORIC MOMENT AT THE PEACE CONFERENCE

Prime Minister Shigeru Yoshida signing the treaty. Looking on (left to right) Hisato Ichimada, Muneyoshi Tokugawa, Niro Hoshijima, Gizo Tomabechi, Hayato Ikeda, all members of the Japanese delegation, and John W. Foley Jr., treaty technician. Associated Press Wirephoto

ENEMY SAID TO MASS TANKS IN TRUCE CITY

Reports in Korea Put Division Near Kaesong—Ridgway Scorns Latest Red Notes

By LINDESAY PARROTT
Special to The New York Times.

TOKYO, Sunday, Sept. 9—The Communist radio renewed its barrage of accusations this morning that the United States had attempted to wreck the meetings at Kaesong for an armistice in the Korean war.

Meanwhile unconfirmed reports said enemy troops and tanks had rolled into the area around the city where the conferences were suspended last month by the Chinese and North Korean delegation.

One report from Korea, which was not verified by headquarters here, said one enemy division, plus one regiment with tanks, was in or around Kaesong. It is a standard Communist tactic to break up large armored units into sections.

[A later Associated Press dispatch from the western Korean front said three Red armored divisions were reported in the region, many Communist anti-aircraft batteries spotted around Kaesong and Red engineer units seen widening roads.

[General Ridgway's headquarters was quoted in a United Press dispatch as saying two Communist notes of Friday were "not worthy of further reply."]

U. N. Air Destroys Six Tanks

Fifth Air Force headquarters, in a report of the week's activities, said pilots flying over the enemy lines had seen more tanks near the front than any time since July, destroying six and damaging two. The allied fighters and fighter-bombers again spotted long columns of enemy vehicles moving in North Korea.

In the first seven days of September, it was announced, a total of 436 vehicles were destroyed, more than twice as many as during any similar period of the Korean war.

Reports of troops and armor in or near Kaesong came as the enemy apparently was shifting much of his weight westward.

Gen. Matthew B. Ridgway, United Nations commander, made public last week a report by his intelligence section estimating that forty refitted enemy divisions were aligned along the front now, with tanks, artillery and armored cars possibly operated by Caucasian specialist troops from Soviet satellite nations in Eastern Europe.

The possibility of a new offensive

Continued on Page 4, Column 1

2 Nations Sign Security Pact Keeping U. S. Units in Japan

Special to The New York Times.

SAN FRANCISCO, Sept. 8—The United States and Japan tonight signed a security pact under which Japan agreed to allow United States forces to remain indefinitely in Japan and to assist the United Nations in any action it may take in the Far East.

Signed at the headquarters of the United States Sixth Army at the San Francisco garrison, or Presidio, five hours after the treaty of peace was signed this noon at the San Francisco Opera House, the treaty forbids Japan to permit any other nation to have any bases or military authority within the Japanese islands without the prior consent of the United States.

[Texts of the security pact and notes with it, Page 3.]

The treaty was signed by Premier Shigeru Yoshida of Japan, and by Secretary of State Dean Acheson for the United States. Others who signed for the United States were: Ambassador at Large John Foster Dulles, Senator Styles Bridges, Republican of New Hampshire, and Senator Alexander Wiley, Republican of Wisconsin.

The Japanese Premier defined the origin and purpose of the treaty in remarkably blunt terms for the head of a state whose nation is still technically at war with the Soviet Union.

"It has always been my conviction that Japan, once she regains liberty and independence, must as-

Continued on Page 28, Column 1

INDIAN PARTY PICKS NEHRU AS ITS HEAD

Prime Minister Will Have Key Role in Naming Candidates for National Election

Special to The New York Times.

NEW DELHI, India, Sept. 8—Prime Minister Jawaharlal Nehru increased his power tonight with his election to the presidency of the governing Congress party.

At a meeting of the All-India Congress Committee, highest policy-making body of India's political governing organization, he was elected president with only four dissenting votes from among 295 members.

The action was a denouement of the political conflict between Mr. Nehru and Purshottamdas Tandon, who had resigned as Congress party president. The two represent in the public mind the Left and Right wings, respectively.

Mr. Nehru's victory was thought

Continued on Page 9, Column 3

2 Boys, Repentant, Confess Murder In Case Closed in 1950 as Accident

Special to The New York Times.

BORDENTOWN, N. J., Sept. 8—Their consciences bothered them, they said. So two teen-age boys, who had been serving time on burglary charges, confessed to the murder of a man whose death had been listed by the police as accidental and the case closed a year ago. Today the youthful prisoners arrived at the Bordentown Reformatory for possible homicide proceedings.

The youths are Bert Blaskow, 16 years old, of 91 Fourth Street, Passaic, and Fred Raue, 17, of Paterson. Until today they had been at the Annandale Reformatory, but they were transferred to the prison here for security reasons.

Their story started Aug. 9, 1950, in Paterson, where the two met at a movie on Van Houten Street. The younger boy decided he wanted to go to a dance and convinced his companion that they should take a bus to Passaic.

On the Monroe Street Bridge in Passaic, they told authorities, they recognized a loiterer and demanded money from him. He refused, and, the police said, the youths beat him with their fists and knees until he slumped to the sidewalk. When the boys saw a woman approach they threw the man into the Passaic River.

The body of William Krestner, 26, of 50 Market Street, Passaic, unemployed, was found floating in the river the next day. His eyes were blackened and there were bruises on the body. After an investigation the death was described as accidental and the files closed.

The youths separated immediately. The older one traveled south, worked as a circus laborer and was arrested several times. Finally, he headed north.

Last July the boys met acciden-

Continued on Page 72, Column 6

WHEN You Think of Writing
Think of Whiting.—Advt.

GOING TO BERMUDA?
Stop at the INVERURIE situated right at the water's edge.
For information call JUdson 6-1137.

REDS QUIT PARLEY

48 Other Nations Join With Tokyo in Ending State of Warfare

ACHESON HAILS ACCORD

Expresses Regret at Absence of Some Powers but Calls Pact 'Act of Greatness'

Texts of speeches by Morrison and Acheson, Pages 18 and 19

By JAMES RESTON
Special to The New York Times.

SAN FRANCISCO, Sept. 8—Twenty years almost to the day after the Manchurian incident started her people on a generation of aggression, Japan signed this morning a treaty of peace with forty-eight nations of the non-Communist world.

The treaty conference formally [illegible] at 11:54 A. M. [2:54 P. M., [illegible]rn daylight time.]

[illegible] Communist world, which [illegible]ike a great crescent around [illegible] remains of the once mighty [illegible]nese empire, boycotted the final ceremony in the big San Francisco Opera House.

Andrei A. Gromyko, Soviet Deputy Foreign Minister, who sought to impose a much more severe treaty on Japan, did, however, call a press conference to state his decision on the signature. This he did in the form of a warning that was almost a threat.

Stage Set for the Signing

By the time this ominous statement had been issued, the Japanese flag had been put in its place on the stage of the great hall, and the final details had been arranged for the signing of a bilateral security treaty giving Japan the protection of United States troops in the four main Japanese islands.

The peace treaty terms would do these things, among others:

1. Take away Japan's overseas empire, amounting to 45 per cent of all the territory she owned on Pearl Harbor Day, and reduce her to the four main islands of Honshu, Kokkaido, Kyushu and Shikoko. This would return her to the territorial status she held in 1854, when Commodore Matthew C. Perry of the United States introduced Japan to the modern world.
2. Obligate Japan to abide by the purposes and principles of the United Nations Charter in her intercourse with other nations.
3. Force Japan to pay limited reparations claims to the nations she damaged so badly in the war of 1941-45, particularly in Southeast Asia, and thus re-establish, under different circumstances the opportunity to resume commercial relations in her former "co-prosperity sphere."
4. Authorize Japan to sign separate treaties with those countries that did not attend this conference, and give her a choice of which China she wished to recognize—Nationalist China or Communist China.
5. Give her an opportunity to regain the Ryukyus and Bonin Islands, which include the major United States military base at Okinawa, provided she lives up to the terms of the treaty and proves to be a reliable partner in the defense of the Pacific.

Quick Ratification Seen

These terms will come into effect when they are ratified by the Untied States Senate and by a simple majority of the following states that signed the document: Australia, Canada, Ceylon, France, Indonesia, the Netherlands, New Zealand, Pakistan, the Philippines, and Britain.

Senator Ernest W. McFarland of Arizona, majority leader, said that an effort would be made to ratify the treaty before the Senate adjourns this autumn.

Though there was a sense of anxiety in the Opera House as a result of the Communist bloc's

Continued on Page 22, Column 1

This section consists of 112 pages divided into three parts. The Index will be found on Page 95. Society news begins on Page 98. Obituaries begin on Page 88.

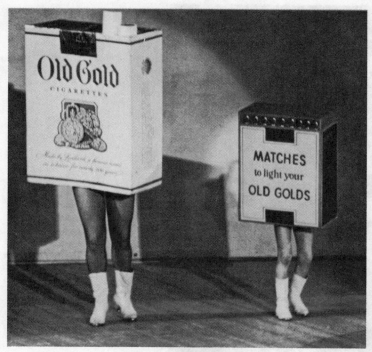

One of the early TV commercials—the dancing packs of cigarettes and matches.

Perry Como was the star of his own weekly show all through the Fifties.

When the President addressed the opening session of the Japanese Peace Treaty Conference in San Francisco (Sept 4, 1951), it was the first time that coast to coast audiences received live coverage. The four major networks joined resources to air the historic event.

1951

Yankee players Phil Rizzuto, Vic Raschi, Allie Reynolds and Yogi Berra are smiling after winning the fourth game of the 1951 World Series, 6-2.

Giants Bobby Thomson, Larry Jansen and Sal Maglie celebrate their team's victory against the Dodgers in the 1951 playoffs. The Giants later lost the World Series to the Yankees, four games to two.

100TH ANNIVERSARY
"All the News That's Fit to Print"
1851 1951

The New York Times.

LATE CITY EDITION
Foggy, becoming fair later today. Mostly fair tonight and tomorrow.
Temperature Range Today—Max., 68; Min., 56
Temperatures Yesterday—Max., 71; Min., 56
Full U. S. Weather Bureau Report, Page 63

Copyright, 1951, by The New York Times Company.

VOL. CI..No. 34,233. Entered as Second-Class Matter, Post Office, New York, N. Y. NEW YORK, TUESDAY, OCTOBER 16, 1951. Times Square, New York 18, N. Y. Telephone LAckawanna 4-1000 FIVE CENTS

EGYPT REJECTS 4-POWER BID; RATIFIES OUSTER OF BRITISH; IRAN KEEPS DOOR OPEN ON OIL

MORAN IS INDICTED AS 'GUIDING GENIUS' OF FUEL-OIL GRAFT

52 Counts Returned Against Former First Deputy Fire Commissioner Here

$500,000 A YEAR 'TAKE'

He Is Held in $25,000 Bail as Hogan Seeks His Successor as Head of Shakedown

By ALFRED E. CLARK

James J. Moran, former First Deputy Fire Commissioner, was indicted yesterday as the "guiding genius" of a $500,000-a-year shakedown of the city's 1,000 fuel-oil equipment installers. In announcing the fifty-two-count indictment for extortion and conspiracy District Attorney Frank S. Hogan revealed he is seeking Moran's successor as director of the lucrative racket.

Moran, the political protégé of former Mayor William O'Dwyer, was "eased out" little more than a week after last fall's elections but the shakedown continued in full operation until as late as the following Jan. 24, the prosecutor said.

Without naming the person who ordered Moran's ouster, Mr. Hogan declared:

"After the 1950 elections, Moran's place in the political sun was not so important. His collectors received new instructions as to the disposition of Moran's cut, which was an all-important 60 per cent of a 'take' that ranged between $5,000 to $10,000 weekly. Yearly, it probably ran to $250,000 to $300,000."

5 Sentenced to Prison

Already five former firemen have been convicted or admitted guilt to participating as collectors in the racket which, according to the District Attorney, was run as "a species of haphazard graft" before Moran reorganized it. The five, James F. Smith, James A. Keohane, James P. Digney, Harry C. Crew and Edward J. Donnelly, have been sentenced to prison terms ranging up to twenty-three years. However, execution of the sentences has been postponed and the men have been reported to have testified before the March, 1951, grand jury to their part in the shakedown.

This panel, last April 11, voted a fifty-eight count true bill against the five firemen. At that time, Mr. Hogan charged, the lion's share of $1,500,000 in graft they had collected had gone to a former high department official. Later in the firemen's trial, assistant District Attorney Alfred J. Scotti identified the official as the 50-year-old Moran.

Yesterday, Mr. Hogan compared the indictment naming Moran with the previous true bill. He stressed the importance of the dates of the alleged conspiracies, pointing out that both began on the same day, Dec. 1, 1947, but Moran's alleged part in the conspiracy ended Nov. 15, 1950, while the conspiracy involving the firemen ran on for ten weeks—until Jan. 24, 1951.

"Moran Was Eased Out"

"We know that Moran, even after he had been named to the Water Supply Board in July, 1950, continued for another four months to be the directing genius of the organized grafting operations," continued the prosecutor. "Our investigation also reveals that about Nov. 15, 1950, Moran was eased out."

A reporter asked, "His collectors fired him?"

"No," Mr. Hogan replied. Instead the collectors, who are named as co-conspirators, but not as defendants in the new indictment, received "new instructions" as to who would be the recipient of the major portion of the graft.

"These circumstances suggest several interesting questions," Mr. Hogan asserted and then posed three questions:

"Did someone succeed Moran as boss of the racket? Was that someone the same beneficiary in the same way that Moran was? Who got the money after Moran was out for the ten-week period from Nov. 15, 1950, to Jan. 24, 1951?"

The prosecutor supplied no answers to his questions, being content to say:

"This new line of investigation is being diligently pursued."

Mr. Hogan said that when Moran first took over the shakedown of installers of fuel equipment and storage tanks in the city the soliciting of graft was not systemized. "But after he took

Continued on Page 28, Column 3

MORAN IS BOOKED

The former First Deputy Fire Commissioner at Elizabeth Street police station yesterday. The New York Times

WILDCAT STRIKERS MAKE 15 PIERS IDLE

Longshore Walkout Ties Up 14 Ships, Including 5 Loading 'Vital' Cargo for Korea

By GEORGE CABLE WRIGHT

A wildcat strike of longshoremen began yesterday morning along the Hudson River waterfront in Manhattan and quickly spread to Brooklyn, from Montague Street to Bay Ridge. It threatened last night to tie up indefinitely a major segment of shipping in New York harbor.

More than 1,000 men were involved in the walkout and union officials gloomily indicated that they were powerless to halt it. Meanwhile, work ceased on at least fifteen piers and fourteen ships lay idle, two of these having been scheduled to sail during the day.

Most seriously affected was the Army Port of Embarkation at Fifty-eighth Street, Brooklyn, where three Navy transports and two cargo ships were being loaded with "vital" cargo. The vessels, which channel troops and arms to Korea and various United States military outposts, were reported by an Army spokesman to be taking on "pretty important cargo." He said officials at the base were "quite worried" about the walkout, which began there at noon.

Strike Protests New Pact

The strike, according to union leaders, was in protest against the ratification last week of a two-year contract between the International Longshoremen's Association, A. F. L., and employing stevedores from Portland, Me., to Hampton Roads, Va. The strikers all were members of dissident locals that had opposed ratification. They were Locals 791 and 1124 in the Chelsea area of Manhattan and Locals 808 and 968 in Brooklyn.

Joseph P. Ryan, international president of the union, visited the Chelsea docks during the day in a futile effort to persuade the men there to return to work.

"They won't listen," he said later. "They feel they have a

Continued on Page 26, Column 3

RIDGWAY IS ACTING TO AVERT INCIDENTS IN TRUCE TALK ZONE

Searchlight and Radio Beams Are Planned at Panmunjom to Warn Planes Away

ARMISTICE LINE DISCUSSED

General Declares Cease-Fire Must Be Set at Battle Front, Wherever It May Be

By LINDESAY PARROTT
Special to THE NEW YORK TIMES.

TOKYO, Tuesday, Oct. 16—The United Nations Command is planning concrete measures to prevent further Air Force violations of the neutral area set aside for negotiations for an armistice in the Korean war, Gen. Matthew B. Ridgway announced today. United States jet planes killed one Korean boy and wounded another in the demilitarized zone Friday.

Two of the measures being considered, the United Nations Command said, are establishment of a searchlight beacon and radio beam at Panmunjom, where liaison officers of both sides met again today to discuss resumption of full delegation meetings for a cease-fire. General Ridgway said he assumed that such action could be taken without further consent by the Communists.

With allied troops again grinding into North Korea, General Ridgway said the United Nations Command still intended to seek an armistice at or near the front-line positions, wherever these might be at the time when a truce was proclaimed.

[Meanwhile, United States troops surged forward again Tuesday in Central Korea, The United Press said, and captured two hills south of the Communist stronghold of Kumsong, breaking a temporary halt in the allied offensive.]

General Ridgway acknowledged that "full and timely information" had not been furnished by his headquarters to members of the United Nations through the allied press—which often is dependent on Communist sources for news of the truce talks.

Promises to Take Steps

He said some steps would be taken to correct the situation, although he contended it would be a matter of "bad faith" with the enemy to publish matters of substance in advance of their presentation to the conferences.

Such material as will be made available will be presented in a manner "best serving our interests," General Ridgway said.

Speaking at one of his rare press conferences, the general revealed for the first time that his promise of "prompt and appropriate disciplinary action" against the fliers who made the first admitted violation of the neutral zone Sept. 10 had been carried out.

This was a reprimand to the crew of a B-26 light bomber that had strafed near the quarters of the Communist truce delegates in Kaesong. But General Ridgway excused the incident and the second strafing, which took place last week.

In the first incident, "the "sole essential fact was faulty navigation," General Ridgway explained. In the second attack, by jet-propelled fighters flying at dusk and at low level, he asserted

Continued on Page 3, Column 2

34th St. Tie-Up Halts B. M. T. to Brooklyn

Express subway traffic to Brooklyn on the B. M. T. was interrupted yesterday for half an hour when a northbound West End express broke down at the Thirty-fourth Street Station at 4:55 P. M.

Coming at the start of the evening rush, the breakdown quickly caused a jam in the Times Square, Thirty-fourth Street, Fourteenth Street and Canal Street stations. Traffic was resumed at 5:25 P. M., after the disabled seven-car train had been towed to a "pocket" at the Times Square station.

Passengers on the stalled train were discharged at Thirty-fourth Street and, as soon as the cause of the tie-up had been ascertained, other northbound expresses were routed over the local tracks at Prince Street.

Extra policemen were rushed to the express stops in Manhattan to handle the crowds.

U. S. TAX UNIT OUSTS OFFICIAL IN NEWARK

Chief of Alcohol Inspection Suspended Pending Inquiry Into 'Serious Charges'

Special to THE NEW YORK TIMES.

WASHINGTON, Oct. 15 — The suspension of Dominic Vita, head of the Inspection Division of the Alcohol Tax Unit of Newark for sixteen years, was announced today by John B. Dunlap, Commissioner of Internal Revenue.

Mr. Dunlap said Mr. Vita, who is 55 years old, was suspended "pending full investigation of serious charges." His announcement contained no details of the charges and did not indicate whether other persons might be involved in this latest of a series of personnel changes in the Government's tax-collecting agency.

The suspended official has been with the Internal Revenue Bureau since 1920 when he began at a $1,600 annual salary. On Sept. 1, 1935, he was appointed to his present post. His salary was $6,800 annually at the time of his suspension.

Mr. Dunlap said the functions of Mr. Vita were "permissive, as distinguished from enforcement." Officials explained that as head of the inspection division, Mr. Vita directed some thirty inspectors in supervising the manufacture of liquor. He did not have such enforcement duties as tracking down "moonshiners" and other similar violators.

Today's suspension followed other personnel developments in the Internal Revenue Bureau arising from a series of charges and

Continued on Page 28, Column 2

PRESIDENT INVITES SOVIET TO DISCUSS PEACE, DISARMING

But Warns Free World Must Develop Strength if Russians Are to Keep Their Word

SPEAKS AT WAKE FOREST

Asserts War Is Not Inevitable —Decries Those Who Spread Suspicion and Fear

Text of the President's speech is printed on Page 22.

By W. H. LAWRENCE
Special to THE NEW YORK TIMES.

WINSTON-SALEM, N. C., Oct. 15—President Truman renewed today an invitation to the Soviet Union to talk peace and disarmament, but warned the free world that it must continue to develop its own strength if it expected the Russians to keep their pledged word and avoid the carnage of atomic warfare.

Speaking to an applauding crowd of 20,000 persons at ground-breaking exercises for a new $15,500,000 campus and plant for Wake Forest College, which is to be moved here from its site near Raleigh, Mr. Truman said that war was not inevitable if Americans dared to do what they thought was right and did not lapse into inaction because of fear that what they might do might be wrong.

While the speech had been billed in advance as nonpolitical, Mr. Truman scored opponents who spread "suspicion and fear," and those "who seem bent on persuading us that our country is on the wrong track and that there is no honor or loyalty left in the land, and that woe and ruin lie ahead."

First Trip to South Recently

It was his first speech-making excursion into the South in many months, during which there have been varying reports of his personal political popularity, chiefly because of his continued advocacy of a civil rights program.

In this community, however, he got a genuinely warm and noisy welcome from thousands of whites and Negroes who lined the streets to watch the motorcade. A big cheer resounded when he turned the first shovel of dirt on property donated by the R. J. and Z. Smith Reynolds Estates to make this new college possible.

This was not too surprising, however, because North Carolina's Democratic organization voted for the President's nomination at the

Continued on Page 22, Column 2

World News Summarized

TUESDAY, OCTOBER 16, 1951

Egypt rejected the four-power proposal for full partnership in a Middle East command and her Parliament unanimously voted to cancel treaties permitting Britain to keep troops in the Suez Canal area and share in administering the Sudan. [1:8.] Britain, Foreign Secretary Morrison said, will stand on her rights under the Suez pact and will not "sell" Sudan against the wish of her people as the "price" for agreement on defense. [11:1.]

Premier Mossadegh told the United Nations Security Council that Iran was willing to negotiate the oil dispute with Britain, but on Iran's terms. His statement and that of Sir Gladwin Jebb were temperate enough to encourage belief that new Anglo-Iranian talks were possible. [1:6-7.]

The Western occupation powers notified Chancellor Adenauer they would propose, as he had suggested, that the United Nations determine whether free elections could be held throughout Germany preliminary to unifying the country. [1:7.]

As Korean truce talks remained stalled, General Ridgway announced concrete steps would be taken to avoid new violations of the neutral zone. [1:3.]

United Nations troops drove to within six miles of Kumsong, Communist base in Central Korea, as U. S. troops opened new attacks to the west. [3:1; map P. 2.]

A Senate subcommittee will vote tomorrow on whether to recommend Dr. Philip C. Jessup as a United Nations delegate but there is doubt that the Senate can act before adjournment. [4:3.] The House, preparing for Universal Military Training, unanimously approved a new reserve set-up with limitations on the President's power to call reserves to active duty. [20:1.]

President Truman renewed his offer to talk peace and disarmament with the Russians. At Wake Forest College he denounced "sowers of suspicion" and "peddlers of fear" who cry the "country is on the wrong track" and "there is no loyalty left in the land." [1:5.] Senator Taft, who is expected to announce today his candidacy for the Republican Presidential nomination, told a Detroit audience the 1952 issues were corruption in Government, liberty at home and the Administration's "poor judgment" on foreign policy. [27:1.]

The Internal Revenue Bureau suspended Dominic Vita, inspection chief of the Alcohol Tax Unit at Newark, N. J., pending inquiry into "serious charges." [1:4.] In this city, former Deputy Fire Commissioner Moran was indicted on fifty-two extortion and conspiracy counts in connection with the "shakedown" of installers of fuel-oil equipment. [1:1.]

The Supreme Court agreed to hear this week the plea of twelve indicted Communist leaders for lower bail [23:1] and to rule whether commercial radio broadcasts in trolleys and buses made a captive audience of the passengers. [44:2.]

A wildcat dock strike tied up arms and troop shipments. [1:2.] A Left-wing union ordered a strike vote in protest against the C. I. O.'s acceptance of a General Electric pay rise. [25:4.]

NEWS BULLETINS FROM THE TIMES
Every hour on the hour
7 A.M. through Midnight
WQXR AM 1560
WQXR FM 96.3

Index to other news appears on last page of this section.

4 Quit School Jobs in Red Inquiry; 2 Others Deny Communist Links

Four public school teachers have resigned or retired in the last three weeks rather than answer questions regarding membership in the Communist party, it was learned yesterday.

Three other teachers were questioned recently by Dr. Frederic Ernst, Associate Superintendent of Schools, and a fourth was questioned yesterday by Saul Moskoff, an assistant corporation counsel. Mr. Moskoff has been assigned to the Board of Education to investigate Communist influence in the school system and has offices at 131 Livingston Street, Brooklyn, a block from the board's headquarters.

After protesting that their constitutional rights were being violated, two teachers told Dr. Ernst that they were not members of the Communist party. These were Max Gilgoff, a teacher of French for ten years, and Terry Rosenbaum, a social studies instructor for eleven years.

The other two refused to answer, charging they would not be party to a "witch-hunt" and "political inquisition." They were Samuel Wallach, a former president of the Teachers Union and a teacher for eighteen years, and Cyril Graze, a mathematics instructor and for ten years chairman of the union's committee on academic freedom, who appeared yesterday.

From a reliable source it was learned that three teachers resigned their school positions after being summoned to see Mr. Moskoff, and another teacher filed for retirement on being notified. Last year, Dr. William Jansen, Superintendent of Schools, announced that three teachers had resigned rather than face questioning.

On Feb. 8, eight teachers—all members of the Teachers Union of the United Public Workers—were dismissed after a series of departmental hearings for refusing to answer similar questions. An appeal on this case is now pending

Continued on Page 25, Column 2

RIVAL SPOKESMEN AT U. N.

Premier Mossadegh of Iran and Sir Gladwyn Jebb of the United Kingdom at end of yesterday's session. The New York Times

U. N. Body Hears Mossadegh Assail British 'Intimidation'

By WALTER SULLIVAN

Although bitter words were exchanged when Premier Mohammed Mossadegh of Iran made his appearance in the United Nations Security Council yesterday, the feeling among Council members when the meeting adjourned was that both sides still sought a negotiated settlement.

Dr. Mossadegh, disputing the Council's jurisdiction and answering Britain's charges in the oil dispute, was sharp at times, but left the door open for new talks. Sir Gladwyn Jebb of Britain was studied in his mildness.

He formally introduced the revised British resolution on the case that was made public last Saturday. The Council, which met at Flushing Meadow, is due to continue discussion there at 3 P. M. today.

[Jebb's statement and parts of Mossadegh's are on Page 6.]

Satisfaction with the day's developments was expressed by Warren R. Austin, United States representative on the Council. He said after the meeting that he was pleased with the "tone and color" of the statements by both sides. They showed, he added, that both sides were "interested in peace."

Mr. Austin added that he believed there was hope of getting Britain and Iran to reopen negotiations, a development that the United States has been working for ever since Dr. Mossadegh arrived here a week ago.

Observers felt that the long brief presented by Iran might have been more belligerent had it not been for United States efforts of

Continued on Page 7, Column 3

U.N. INQUIRY ASKED ON GERMAN UNITY

West Calls for Investigation to See if Conditions Are Right for Nation-Wide Election

Text of three-nation note to Dr. Adenauer is on Page 14.

By DREW MIDDLETON
Special to THE NEW YORK TIMES.

BONN, Germany, Oct. 15—The United States, Britain and France will propose that the United Nations investigate whether conditions in Eastern Germany are suitable for a general election, preliminary to reunification of the country.

Asserting their continued support for German unity, the Governments of the three Western powers told Chancellor Konrad Adenauer that they renewed their support for the "idea of elections" under conditions safeguarding liberties of the Germany people.

Thus, the Allies, in a letter to the Federal Chancellor, regained

Continued on Page 14, Column 4

3 PACTS ARE ENDED

Parliament in Cairo Is Unanimous—Crowd Jams Building

DEFENSE PLAN IS BARRED

Constitutional Change Placing the Sudan Under Farouk to Be Considered Tonight

By ALBION ROSS
Special to THE NEW YORK TIMES.

CAIRO, Oct. 15 — Egypt announced tonight she had decided to reject the four-power proposal to include her in a Middle Eastern defense command, and Parliament voted unanimously to abrogate the treaties giving Britain rights in the Suez Canal zone and joint rule with Cairo in the Sudan.

Announcement of the rejection of the proposals of the United States, Britain, France and Turkey was made to Parliament by Fuad Serag el Din Pasha, Minister of the Interior. The four powers had invited Egypt to become a full member of a Middle East defense command and to transform the Suez Canal base into a Middle East defense command base instead of a British base.

Both the Parliament building and the streets outside were crowded with a jubilant, restless throng as El Din Pasha, second in command of the governing Wafd party under Premier Mustafa Nahas Pasha, went to a microphone and stated:

Minister Announces Decision

"The British Government yesterday submitted to the Foreign Ministry through its Ambassador at Cairo new proposals and an invitation to Egypt to take part in a Middle East command. After having considered the proposals and the invitation, the Council of Ministers took a decision in the matter.

"You are certainly entitled to be informed of the Government's decision on the matter as you are studying the Government bills for abrogation of the treaty. The Government has decided to reject the proposals and to carry on the measures announced by the Premier."

This meant that the British plan for agreement on the Sudan and the institution in the Sudan of an international commission to watch over the constitutional development of Sudan's eventual status has been rejected.

The Chamber of Deputies and Senate voted the abolition of three laws passed in 1936 and 1941, that had ratified the 1936 treaty between Britain and Egypt, had confirmed the Anglo-Egyptian joint rule in the Sudan established in 1899, and had established the right of the British to certain facilities and privileges under the treaty and in connection with occupation of the Suez Canal base.

Parliament to Meet Tonight

Parliament was summoned to meet tomorrow night to amend the Constitution to provide for setting up a constitution for Sudan and proclaiming King Farouk as King of Egypt and Sudan. Parliament will meet again Wednesday night to approve formally a new Sudanese draft constitution.

The crisis has turned into an all-Middle Eastern affair. The Iraqi Minister to Egypt. Nagi Bal El Rawi, one of the principal foreign affairs advisers of the Iraq Government, has been summoned to Baghdad. Clamor for abrogation of the British-Iraqi treaty of alliance has increased following Premier Nuri es-Said's disclosure last week that he had asked in London recently for revision of the treaty.

The executive committee of the Premier's Constitutional Union party met in Baghdad today to discuss its revision, and other parties, notably the Iraqi United Popular Front, the National Democratic party and the Independence party, are preparing to take a decision on the issue. Prominent men in these parties have indicated that their groups will demand abrogation of the Anglo-Iraqi treaty, following the example of Egypt.

The Minister of Economy announced that the final text of an oil agreement between Iraq and the Iraq Petroleum Company had

Continued on Page 12, Column 3

Stratocruiser Feared Down at Sea; 11 Aboard Air Force Cargo Plane

By The United Press.

WESTOVER AIR FORCE BASE, Mass., Oct. 15—A double-decked Air Force Stratocruiser with eleven crewmen aboard was missing and presumed down in the Atlantic tonight and a vast search was mounted for it.

Air Force planes from both sides of the Atlantic were ordered into the search for the craft, a C-97 transport, which had enough fuel to stay aloft only until 5:42 P. M. It was flying here from Lages Field in the Azores on the last leg of a regularly scheduled flight from Rhein-Main Air Force Base in Germany.

Every available plane of the Military Air Transport Service on the East Coast was thrown into the search. Planes were ordered out from Iceland, Newfoundland, England, Bermuda, the Azores and Portugal. Washington estimated that at least fifty planes might be engaged in the search by tomorrow forenoon.

One of the B-29's in the search reported tonight that two of its engines had "conked out" and that it was returning to base at Kindley Field, Bermuda. The pilot radioed later that he had put one of the engines back into operation and was able to return to base safely.

The Stratocruiser carried three and a half tons of mail and four tons of miscellaneous cargo. There were no passengers. It took off from the Azores at 3:43 A. M. and was due to land here at 2:22 P. M. One hour after its take-off it radioed that it was proceeding on course. It was not heard from again.

[Kindley Air Force Base at Bermuda messaged it had picked up an S. O. S. from an unidentified source at 2:56 P. M., The Associated Press said, amid reports of a violent air turbulence west of the Azores.]

Nineteen Air Force planes, in-

Continued on Page 65, Column 5

I Was A Communist for the FBI, *starred Frank Lovejoy with Dorothy Hart. It was a patriotic film clearly calculated to convince the House Committee on Un-American activities that even if a few communists did turn up in Hollywood, the movie industry itself was certainly as patriotic as ever.*

Quo Vadis *was a box office smash.*

100TH ANNIVERSARY
"All the News
That's Fit to Print"
1851 1951

The New York Times.

Copyright, 1951, by The New York Times Company.

LATE CITY EDITION
Partly cloudy, mild today; cooler
tonight. Rain likely tomorrow.
Temperature Range Today—Max., 70; Min., 55
Temperatures Yesterday—Max., 70; Min., 47
Full U. S. Weather Bureau Report, Page 23

VOL. CI..No. 34,244.

Entered as Second-Class Matter,
Post Office, New York, N. Y.

NEW YORK, SATURDAY, OCTOBER 27, 1951.

Times Square, New York 18, N. Y.
Telephone LAckawanna 4-1000

RAG PAPER EDITION
SEVENTY-FIVE CENTS

TRUMAN PLEA TO PIER MEN IS UNHEEDED

TAFT LAW IGNORED

President Rejects Move by Industry After Talk With the Cabinet

BASES CALL ON DEFENSE

Insurgents Say No National Emergency Was Declared—Attack 'Unfair Verdict'

By GEORGE HORNE

President Truman appealed to New York waterfront strikers last night to return to work in behalf of the defense effort but the defiant strike committee immediately rejected the plea and called for widening of the costly stoppage.

The President, to whom Cyrus S. Ching, director of the Federal Mediation and Conciliation Service, had referred the dispute, discussed it with the Cabinet before making his decision not to accede to the demands of industrial leaders to invoke the procedure of the Taft-Hartley Act.

Mr. Truman said he had been informed that defense activity was being hampered and that "in the national interest" the employes ought to get back to their tasks.

The twelve-day strike started in a handful of locals on Oct. 15 and snowballed under pressure of roaming wildcat squads until it paralyzed the vast Port of New York, spread to Boston, halted work on military shipments and piled up cargoes estimated in value at nearly $300,000,000.

Demanded Pact Reopening

The intransigent strikers demanded reopening of a contract that had been negotiated through weeks of discussion with employers and was finally ratified by a 2-to-1 vote of the union's membership.

The new contract of the International Longshoremen's Association, A. F. L. and the New York Shipping Association, provided a 10-cent increase to make the basic hourly wage $2.10. It stipulated improvements in vacation terms, a single shape-up or work-call a day and other benefits which the majority of the union's 125-man wage committee approved and recommended.

Announcement of the plea from the White House was followed within ten or fifteen minutes by the insurgent rejection. John J. (Gene) Sampson, business agent of Local 791, spearhead local in the strike, said that the strikers would not accept the President's proposal since he had not seen fit to declare a national emergency.

The President could have invoked the Taft-Hartley Act despite the fact that the walkout involved an intra-union matter and not a labor-management dispute in which no contract existed. Moreover, he could have used a Wage Stabilization Board dispute procedure on a matter affecting national defense.

He had been urged by industrial and business associations and individuals in New York and New Jersey to apply the former procedure on the grounds that the stoppage was causing the loss of thousands of workers other than the 30,000 striking longshoremen and immobilizing ships, cargo and investments mounting into millions of dollars.

Two-Day Intercession Failed

Mr. Ching had sent the dispute to the White House following withdrawal of the Federal mediation agency after a boisterous and futile two-day intercession in New York.

Clyde M. Mills, No. 1 Ching aide and a trouble-shooter for the agency, had headed a commissioner's panel in New York in efforts to end the union's "family quarrel." The mediation men called it an "intolerable situation," a phrase that heightened the bitter feeling of recalcitrant strike leaders who described the Mills withdrawal announcement as unfair and tantamount to a verdict of guilt.

The text of Mr. Truman's statement follows:

"I have been informed by Mr. Charles E. Wilson, director of the Office of Defense Mobilization, that because of the work stoppage at the longshoremen the ports of New

Continued on Page 22, Column 7

Marciano Knocks Out Louis in 8th Round

Rocky Marciano, 27-year-old Brockton, Mass., boxer, became a leading contender for the world heavyweight championship when he knocked out Joe Louis, former holder of the title, in the eighth round of their scheduled ten-round bout in Madison Square Garden last night.

The defeat marked the end of the 37-year-old Louis' hopes of becoming the first ex-titleholder to regain the crown. Marciano dropped Louis for a count of eight before he sent him through the ropes with a right to the jaw at 2:36 of the eighth. Referee Ruby Goldstein disdained a count. It was Marciano's thirty-eight triumph in a row, thirty-three of them by knockouts.

Louis showed no signs of weakening until the seventh round. He weighed 212¾ pounds to Marciano's 187.

Details on Page 12.

FLATH'S VICE SQUAD UPSET BY MONAGHAN

Entire Personnel Transferred —Step May Foreshadow Clean Sweep of Plainclothes Men

By ALEXANDER FEINBERG

The entire personnel of the Chief Inspector's plainclothes squad, the top police unit assigned to the task of suppressing vice and gambling, was transferred yesterday by Police Commissioner George P. Monaghan.

Sixteen of the seventeen members of the squad were sent back to uniform a week after the retirement of August W. Flath as Chief Inspector and Mr. Monaghan's collateral declaration that all plainclothes squads would be reconstituted. The other member, formerly attached to the detective division, was reassigned there.

A year ago—on Sept. 29, 1950—Thomas F. Murphy, then Police Commissioner, on his fourth day in office ordered all of the 336 men in the plainclothes division back into uniform. He replaced them with selected patrolmen, "neither besmirched nor tainted," from the ranks of recruits and newly appointed policemen.

New Sweep Is Seen

Yesterday's action by Mr. Monaghan was believed to be the forerunner of a second clean sweep of all plainclothes personnel. In the shift, two acting lieutenants were reduced to sergeant, and an inspector, who headed the squad, a deputy inspector, an acting captain, two lieutenants and ten patrolmen were affected. Eight of the ten plainclothes men will take a loss of $240 a year in extra compensation.

Inspector Francis W. Flath and the squad under Chief Flath who last week was succeeded by Chief Inspector Conrad H. Rothengast.

Continued on Page 7. Column 3

Error in Race Placing at Jamaica Costs $15,655, Helps Cancer Fund

By JAMES ROACH

The Damon Runyon Fund for Cancer Research was the winner in the third race on the Empire City-at-Jamaica program yesterday—a horse race that the placing judges never will be able to forget.

The placing judges made a $15,655 mistake. Perhaps the fund will profit by as much as $10,000 from it.

A horse named Swing Cheer finished first, with Air Service second and by a nose over Sao Paulo. The mutuel-ticket numbers, in order, were 11, 13 and 5. But the numbers didn't go in the proper order or the result boards.

The three placing judges, in the unhappiest moment of their racing careers, reversed the place and show horses, and put up 11, 13 and 5.

They soon discovered their error, but not in time to prevent the flashing of the "official" sign, which set in motion the pay-offs. Apparently there were no complaints from any of the 10,359

Continued on Page 14, Column 1

KOREAN FOE DROPS DEMAND FOR TRUCE ON 38TH PARALLEL

But Enemy's Plan for 15-Mile U.N. Retreat From the Front Is Termed Unacceptable

REDS WOULD YIELD IN PART

Communists Propose to Move Out of Last Area They Hold South of Old Boundary

By LINDESAY PARROTT

Special to THE NEW YORK TIMES.

TOKYO, Saturday, Oct. 27—Although a Communist proposal for a fifteen-mile retreat by Allied forces in Korea was unacceptable to the United Nations Command, the negotiators for a truce were closer to geographical agreement on a cease-fire line today than at any time since the conferences started last July.

The enemy's proposal, providing for a United Nations withdrawal in the east and center, and for evacuation by the Communists of the last ground they hold in South Korea, was an abandonment of the Communist demand for a cease-fire based on the political boundary of the Thirty-eighth Parallel.

The plan was announced to Allied representatives at a ninety-minute meeting yesterday of subcommitteemen of both sides at their tent village near Panmunjom. There the United Nations on the day before had advanced its own proposal for a truce line and buffer zone close to the battle positions won by the Allied forces and grinding forward slowly into North Korea.

[The Associated Press said the third subcommittee session was held from 11 A. M. to 1 P. M. Saturday (9 to 11 P. M. Friday, Eastern standard time). The United Nations negotiators, Maj. Gen. Henry I. Hodes and Rear Admiral Arleigh A. Burke, failed to make any progress with the Communist representatives on the truce line issue. An afternoon session was scheduled for 3 o'clock.]

'Unilateral' Retreat Cited

Thus far, there has been no formal Allied rejection of the enemy proposal. But an official United Nations bulletin pointed out yesterday afternoon that the Chinese and North Korean plan required a "unilateral" withdrawal by United Nations forces from militarily important positions along virtually all of the present battle line.

Among these well-known ground at "Heartbreak Ridge" and the "Punchbowl" in the rugged mountains of the peninsula's eastern watershed, and the "Iron Triangle" in the center. It was estimated that the retreat would extend along a 100-mile front, ceding almost all of the territory gained by Gen. James A. Van Fleet's summer and autumn offensives, staged since the armistice talks began.

In exchange, the Communists offered to yield the Ongjin Peninsula and an area around Yonan. There, tongues of land thrust down into the Yellow Sea below the Thirty-eighth Parallel.

But this territory generally is considered indefensible, except by a force that also could hold an enclave to the north above the old boundary, and the United Nations in the present campaign never has made any serious attempt to challenge

Continued on Page 2. Column 5

MOSES SEEKS STEEL OF FOREIGN MAKERS

Would Meet Needs for Roads by Dealing Directly With Mills in Germany and Belgium

The quest of Robert Moses, City Construction Coordinator, for imported steel to fill the construction needs of traffic relief projects in the city has been frustrated thus far by soaring prices that far exceed the limitations of the public purse, he said yesterday.

Now he is seeking ways to get the essential metal directly from German and Belgian manufacturing bases without paying a middleman's profit to the importers in this country.

Mr. Moses pointed out that the Federal allocation system had seriously restricted domestic steel for city use.

The difficulties encountered in attempts to get foreign steel were

Continued on Page 34, Column 2

CHURCHILL IS RETURNED TO POWER WITH A MARGIN OF 26 OVER LABOR; WASHINGTON EXPECTS VISIT SOON

THE NEW PRIME MINISTER CONGRATULATED BY HIS WIFE

Winston Churchill as he appeared yesterday after late returns had assured his party of victory in the British elections
Associated Press Radiophoto

Gain for U. S.-British Ties Seen by Congress Members

By WILLIAM S. WHITE

WASHINGTON, Oct. 26—The return of the Conservatives to power in Britain will improve British-American relations as far as both parties in Congress are concerned. The success of the ticket headed by Winston Churchill likewise will tend to ease the way for any future programs in aid of Britain, be they economic or military, other things being equal.

Washington generally expected Mr. Churchill to come to this country soon for consultation with President Truman on the coordination of United States and British foreign policy. The Prime Minister and the President are old friends, their previous meetings having included the Potsdam conference of July, 1945.

There was much speculation here that Mr. Churchill would time his visit to coincide with the President's extended vacation at Key West, Fla., which starts Nov. 1.

Continued on Page 3, Column 7

World News Summarized

SATURDAY, OCTOBER 27, 1951

Winston Churchill, as the leader of the victorious Conservative party, was asked by King George VI to become the new British Prime Minister in place of Clement R. Attlee, who resigned. With four districts still unreported, the Conservatives had an overall majority of eighteen over Labor in the newly elected Parliament. [1:8.]

Mr. Churchill and his aides will face many heavy tasks, including the fulfillment of party pledge to "denationalize" the iron and steel industry and to decentralize the administration of the nationalized coal industry and of the rail and road transport system. [1:7.] Mr. Churchill, reflecting the sober mood in which the Conservative victory was accepted on all sides, said, "We shall do our very best." [3:1.]

The majority of the remnants of the once mighty Liberal party backed the Conservatives and this support was the major factor in the Conservative capture of twenty-one of the twenty-four seats won from Labor. [3:8.]

Congressional members of both parties foresaw an improvement in British-United States relations, particularly in the field of foreign policies. [1:5-6.] In Paris European observers also were optimistic of greater Allied unity as a result of the British election. [4:3.]

Yugoslavia will receive a larger amount of military aid from the United States under an agreement to be signed in Belgrade next week by representatives of the two countries. [1:6.]

In the Korean truce negotiations the Communists abandoned their demand that the demarcation line between the opposing armies be set along the Thirty-Eighth Parallel, but their newer proposal, calling for a fifteen-mile retreat by Allied forces, also was unacceptable to United Nations officials. [1:3.]

Allied fliers shot down two enemy jet planes and damaged three others in another air battle over Northwest Korea. [2:8; with map.]

The peace treaty signed at San Francisco was ratified by the lower house of the Japanese Diet, which also approved the security pact allowing the maintenance of a United States garrison in Japan. [2:1.]

President Truman, emphasizing the serious effect on the defense program of the walkout of New York dock workers, appealed to the strikers to return to work, but his plea was promptly rejected. [1:1.]

Thomas H. White, Cleveland industrialist, and his wife and daughter-in-law were killed when their private plane, piloted by Mr. White, crashed as it approached a landing at the Washington airport. [1:6-7.]

MANY CHANGES SET BY CONSERVATIVES

'Denationalization' of Steel, Tax Revision and Broad Housing Program Listed

By CLIFTON DANIEL

LONDON, Oct. 26 — Former Prime Minister Attlee said in his recent ill-starred election campaign that his Labor Government could not be expected to clear up in six years the mess of six centuries.

Next week the Conservatives will set about tidying up what they regard as the mess of Labor's six years. They have promised many changes, although not as many as the ideological differences between the two parties might indicate, and they have years of legislative work ahead of them.

Their program is not as ambitious as that of the 1945 Labor Government, which came to power with plans to remake the whole economic and social structure of Britain. Among the tasks that the Conservatives have set themselves are these:

1. To "denationalize" the iron and steel industry, the last enterprise taken under public ownership by the Labor Government last March.

2. To decentralize the administration of the Nationalized Coal Industry and of the state-owned railroad and road transport systems.

3. To build more houses, 300,000 a year being the stated target, and

Continued on Page 3, Column 4

U.S. WILL INCREASE ARMS TO YUGOSLAVS

Heavy Weapons Will Help Tito Resist Aggression—Pact to Be Signed Next Week

By WALTER H. WAGGONER

WASHINGTON, Oct. 26—The United States and Yugoslavia will sign a military aid agreement in Belgrade next week to assure new and larger shipments of American arms to Marshal Tito's anti-Soviet armed forces.

The agreement will bring to a close negotiations between the two Governments that formally got under way here last June, with the visit of Col. Gen. Kuca Popovic, Chief of Yugoslavia's General Staff, and concluded with the inspection trip to Yugoslavia earlier this month by Gen. J. Lawton Collins, United States Army Chief of Staff.

Arms that can then be expected to start flowing to the only Government holding out in Eastern Europe against Russian domina-

Continued on Page 5, Column 1

Industrialist Flying to See Marshall Killed as Plane Crashes in Potomac

Special to THE NEW YORK TIMES.

WASHINGTON, Oct. 26—Thomas H. White, Cleveland industrialist; his wife, the former Miss Kathleen York, and his daughter-in-law, Mrs. Robert White, were killed here this morning when a plane piloted by Mr. White fell into the Potomac River while approaching National Airport.

Mr. White, 57 years old, a grandson of the founder of the White Motor Company and White Sewing Machine Company, was piloting the plane, a single-engine Beechcraft Bonanza, from Hunting Valley Village, a Cleveland suburb, to Washington.

The plane had made a routine stop at Youngstown, Ohio, and was scheduled to arrive here at 10:15 A. M. The crash occurred at 10:12 A. M.

There was no immediate expla-

ATTLEE STEPS DOWN

King Then Calls on War Leader to Take Over at Time of Crisis

LABOR TOPS POPULAR VOTE

Party Polls 48.8% to Rival's 48.1 While Losing Out on Seats by 293 to 319

By RAYMOND DANIELL

Special to THE NEW YORK TIMES.

LONDON, Oct. 26—For the second time in both their lifetimes, George VI called upon Winston Churchill today to form a government at a time of national crisis.

A little earlier the King, who is convalescing from a serious operation, received Clement R. Attlee and accepted his resignation as Prime Minister because the verdict of the people of Britain had gone against the Labor party in yesterday's general election. Therefore, Mr. Churchill, leader of the Conservative party, now takes his place at the helm of the ship of state that Mr. Attlee has sailed according to Socialist navigation rules for the past six years, and with a depleted crew for nineteen months.

After the 1950 election Mr. Attlee's Labor Government never had a majority of more than seven. It seems now that Mr. Churchill in the skipper's role will not be much better off.

Over-all Margin Now 18

As matters stand now the Conservatives have a majority over all others of eighteen, and twenty-six more seats than the Labor party alone. The majority may increase or decrease but not enough to make any real difference.

There are only four constituencies remaining to be heard from in the present count. In addition there is a seat to be filled in a delayed election. If the Conservatives won all the remaining seats, which is unlikely, their over-all majority would be twenty-three. However, if these seats did not change the Conservative majority would be seventeen.

The present party standings follow:

Conservatives 319
Labor 293
Liberals 5
Independents 3

All of the Independents are Irish, two of them probably will not ever vote, and one of them leans toward Labor.

This accounts for 620 of the 625 seats in the House of Commons. Of the four constituencies remaining to be heard from, two have been held in the past by Conservatives, one by Labor and one by the Liberals.

Seat Held Safe for Labor

The fifth seat remains vacant because one of the candidates died during the campaign. It, however, is a safe seat for Labor and when the election is held it should add one more seat to Labor's strength in the House.

Mr. Attlee probably was right in ascribing his downfall to the way the Liberals voted. At party headquarters after he had taken leave of the King he said:

"I don't think there is any reason to dispute that our loss of seats has been due to the fact that when it came to the point more Liberals were Conservative than Labor."

How many more Liberals voted

Continued on Page 3, Column 2

Churchill in Office: A Wartime Study

The energy, versatility and qualities of mind that Mr. Churchill brings to the Prime Ministership are vividly illustrated in today's installment of his war memoirs. His ideas on diplomacy, his attitude toward Americans, his views on how to handle the Russians are set forth in a series of wartime minutes.

See Page 21

NEWS BULLETINS FROM THE TIMES
Every hour on the hour
7 A.M. through Midnight
WQXR AM 1560
WQXR FM 96.3

Index to other news appears on last page of this section.

49

100TH ANNIVERSARY
"All the News
That's Fit to Print"
1851 1951

The New York Times.

LATE CITY EDITION
Fair and cold today and tonight.
Cloudy tomorrow with snow later.
Temperature Range Today-Max., 29; Min., 22
Temperatures Yesterday-Max., 48.8; Min., 19.9
Full U. S. Weather Bureau Report, Page 61

Copyright, 1951, by The New York Times Company.

VOL. CI No. 34,297. Entered as Second-Class Matter, Post Office, New York, N. Y. NEW YORK, WEDNESDAY, DECEMBER 19, 1951. Times Square, New York 36, N. Y. Telephone LAckawanna 4-1000 FIVE CENTS

SNOW AND ICY RAIN DISRUPT ACTIVITIES THROUGH CITY AREA

Day-Long Storm Causes Many Road Accidents—389 Are Treated for Street Falls

TRAINS AND BUSES LATE

Forecast Is 'Cloudy, Cold and Windy' for Today With More Snow Tomorrow

A day-long storm marked by snow, sleet, drizzle and freezing rain plagued the city and suburbs yesterday. Ice-sheathed highways made motor travel hazardous. There were hundreds of minor accidents, thousands of suburbanites were marooned, and in hilly areas residents could not get milk or bread delivered as trucks were unable to negotiate the slippery grades.

Pedestrians had rough going, too. Between 8 A. M., when the light snow started falling, and 7 P. M., when the day's precipitation officially ended, 389 persons who had slipped on icy city streets required medical attention. The city's ambulance service was overloaded, according to Police Headquarters, and it was necessary to allocate calls. As a result some injured persons had to wait up to forty minutes for medical attention, the police said, but most found temporary shelter in doorways.

Morning Rush Hours Perilous

The worst perils of the storm came in the early morning rush hours and continued until about noon. During that period snow and drenching rain pelted the metropolitan area; all bus service in Richmond halted for two hours and service was suspended briefly on some routes in Brooklyn, Queens, the Bronx and Westchester. Surface transportation was on an "interrupted" basis but commuter railroad lines moved close to normal schedules.

Subways kept to schedules as long as they ran underground but in the Bronx and Brooklyn where they are elevated or move across open cuts service was slow and schedules snarled.

The storm here—a small brother of a raging mid-west blizzard—had repercussions all along the Atlantic Seaboard, and from Maine to Virginia a slick wet ice belt hampered highway travel. West of Albany railroad service was poor and while the New York Central System insisted that through trains from Chicago "averaged only two hours late" the Twentieth Century Limited pulled into Grand Central Terminal 2 hours 54 minutes behind schedule.

La Guardia Airport and New York International Airport at Idlewild, Queens, were shut down for a short period in the morning.

Late in the day, six further delays to international flights, both incoming and outgoing, were reported at Idlewild. Two of the flights were held at Boston for several hours awaiting better weather here.

Rising temperatures in mid-day took much of the sting out of the storm, but at night the mercury started toppling again and the few commuters who started home late suffered some delay.

Winds Up to 50 Miles an Hour

Sharp gusts of winds up to fifty miles an hour contributed to the day's discomfort and in outlying sections of the city power lines, heavy with a coating of ice, toppled into roadways. At 7 P. M. the police reported that twenty-nine lines had fallen, twenty-five of them in Queens.

In the Rockaways damage to overhead lines, attributed to wind and to trees blown against the wires, left an estimated 1,000 families, mostly in the vicinity of Neponsit and Belle Harbor, without lights during the afternoon. The Long Island Lighting Company said the trouble began at 2:30 P. M. and had been cleared up by 7:30 P. M.

A flash fire in a manhole at 207th Street and Jamaica Avenue, Hollis, damaged a feeder line and left 1,627 current users in that area without power from 9:48 P. M. to 10:23 P. M., when another feeder line was placed in service.

Queens also suffered from flooded cellars and wash-outs of secondary roads. This borough was the worst sufferer in the city limits but the damage was in no wise comparable to the blows dealt to suburban communities in Nassau, Suffolk, Westchester, northern New Jersey and Fairfield County, Conn.

One death in this area was at-

Continued on Page 34, Column 2

Soviet Tour by 18 Assailed; Passport Evasions Charged

McCarran Group Says 14 Had 'Communist' Records—Criticizes State Department for Letting Them Travel Abroad

Special to THE NEW YORK TIMES.

WASHINGTON, Dec. 18—A Senate Investigating subcommittee charged today that a party of eighteen United States labor union representatives, "at least fourteen" of whom had "notorious Communist records," were able easily to exceed their passport travel authorizations in April and May to make an all-expenses-paid visit to Russia and her satellite countries and contribute to anti-American propaganda.

Despite the records of most of them, the subcommittee stated, the members of the group had no difficulty in obtaining passports supposedly for visits only to France, England and Italy. From France, it was added, the party was flown first to Prague, Czechoslovakia, and then to Russia.

In Moscow, the subcommittee report stated, the group occupied a box close to Premier Stalin to witness the May Day parade. Before leaving Moscow, the report asserted, the group issued a statement to the Russian press critical of the United States and praising "peace efforts" of the Soviet Union and its satellites.

This statement, the reports declared, was subsequently reprinted in the Daily Worker, official organ of the Communist party in the United States.

In stressing its criticisms, the subcommittee noted that "the issuance of passports to citizens who are Communists facilitates the Cominform's courier system and the international control of the Communist apparatus."

The Senate unit, the Internal Security subcommittee of the Judiciary Committee, headed by Senator Pat McCarran, Democrat of Nevada, laid heavy blame upon the State Department for not having denied the passports. It contended that sufficient information was available at official quarters, and should have been at the State Department itself, to have prevented the party from leaving the country.

Transcripts of testimony taken

Continued on Page 3, Column 1

Dewey Fight on Tax Cut Seen As State's Expenses Increase

Special to THE NEW YORK TIMES.

ALBANY, Dec. 18—The Dewey Administration sounded a note of financial caution today against the growing chorus of demands for a substantial reduction in 1952 state taxes with the announcement that budget requests from just one group of state agencies were $30,000,000 above 1951-52 appropriations that totaled $167,000,000.

Without commenting directly on recent proposals for a $105,000,000 cut in personal income and business taxes, James C. Hagerty, secretary to Governor Dewey, said "inflation hits state costs the same as every family."

Mr. Hagerty said that if requests from just seven state agencies were granted, the Governor would have to recommend appropriations of $197,000,000, 18 per cent above the current figure. Appropriations for these agencies constituted less than a fifth of the state's 1951-52 general fund budget, he noted.

The agencies included are the Departments of Mental Hygiene, Correction, Health, Social Welfare and Labor, the Divisions of Parole and Veterans' Affairs, the Youth Commission and the Commission Against Discrimination. With the exception of the Veterans and Discrimination units, Mr. Hagerty said all the agencies in the group had asked for increases.

Although Administration fiscal leaders are reported to be "trimming to the bone" to keep the budget for the 1952-53 fiscal year that begins April 1 at the current budget level, present estimates indicate that it may exceed the $1,000,000,000 mark. The 1951-52 budget called for total appropriations of $999,000,000 and revenues of $959,000,000, with the difference accounted for by items appropriated by the 1951 Legislature but paid for before the current fiscal year.

None of the requests includes state aid to localities, which is to be dealt with in a later report. Some $27,000,000 of the $30,000,000 requested increase would go to

Continued on Page 36, Column 6

TAFT GAINING HERE IN SPITE OF DEWEY

Many Top Republicans Favor Senator and Are Expected to Defy Governor's Wishes

By WARREN MOSCOW

The contest between supporters of Senator Robert A. Taft and General of the Army Dwight D. Eisenhower for the Republican Presidential nomination has resulted in the developing of considerably more strength than had been expected for Senator Taft in New York State.

It exists among high-ranking Republican organization men, county chairmen and business men who have been delegates to past national conventions or are likely to be at the one in 1952. This is out of line with the announced policy of the Dewey state administration, which had been counted on to supply the largest block of delegates to the Eisenhower cause, and will still do so. But the state delegation of ninety-six will by no means be solid.

While no actual revolt is brewing against Mr. Dewey, either as Governor or political leader of his party in the state, the situation is shaping up in such a way that for the first time since 1940, Mr. Dewey will not be in complete control of a hand-picked, unanimous-voting delegation.

In 1940, the New York State delegation voted about two-thirds for Dewey on the first ballot, with scattering strength for other candidates, and switched to Wendell

Continued on Page 39, Column 2

5 Marines on Christmas Trip Home Die in Turnpike's First Fatal Crash

Special to THE NEW YORK TIMES.

BORDENTOWN, N. J., Dec. 18—Five young marines were killed and a sixth was injured critically early today in the first fatal traffic accident on the recently opened New Jersey Turnpike.

The sedan taking the marines home for Christmas from Camp Lejeune, N. C., crashed at high speed into the rear of a tractor trailer at 3:55 o'clock in near-by Mansfield Township, Burlington County.

The dead, all privates first class, are: Joseph Dupere, 21 years old, 62 Old Village, Plainfield, Conn.; Andrew M. Jacobs, 17, of 81 Holly Street, Carteret, N. J.; Joseph D. Harrop, 17, of 1604 North Main Street, Fall River, Mass.; John J. Rand, 17, of 95 Manthorne Road, West Roxbury, Mass., and Norman Violette, 18, of 19 Vernon Street, Hartford, Conn.

The only survivor in the wrecked sedan was Pfc. James L. Robertson, 17, of 121 Greenwood Street Springfield, Mass., who was transferred to the Philadelphia Naval Hospital after treatment at the Burlington County Hospital at Mount Holly.

Charles Cephas, 31, of Bridgeville, Del., driver of the fourteen-wheel tractor trailer, told the police that the accident occurred as the big van was moving slowly into the paved portion of the road from a shoulder. He was held on a technical charge of manslaughter.

As a result of the crash, Gov. Alfred E. Driscoll announced today that a study of law enforcement along the superhighway, "with particular reference to the number of troopers required to police the road," would be speeded up.

"The Turnpike Authority, the Department of Law and Public Safety, State Highway Commissioner Ransford Abbott and I are determined to make the turnpike the safest in the country," Governor Driscoll said.

"It must be remembered that nearly half a million vehicles have traveled millions of miles on the

Continued on Page 34, Column 6

STEEL TALK CALLED BY CHING IN EFFORT TO AVERT WALKOUT

Warning of Danger to Defense, He Summons Producers and Union to Capital Tomorrow

AGREEMENT IS DOUBTED

Industry's Parley With DiSalle on Prices Inconclusive—He Bars Any Peace 'Deal'

By JOSEPH A. LOFTUS
Special to THE NEW YORK TIMES.

WASHINGTON, Dec. 18—Facing a steel strike deadline set for New Year's Eve, Cyrus S. Ching, director of the Federal Mediation and Conciliation Service, today called the United Steelworkers of America, C. I. O., and ten representative employers to meet with him in Washington on Thursday.

"The possibility of an interruption of production in the steel industry is a matter of grave concern to the people of the United States," he telegraphed the parties.

"Any curtailment of operations in this key industry will seriously affect our national economy and have a direct and critical impact on our defense effort. The national welfare demands that I immediately place at the disposal of the parties all the facilities at my command to assist them in a speedy resolution of this dispute."

[In Pittsburgh steel producers and the union made no progress in contract negotiations, which were discontinued for the present. The union discouraged Federal hopes of averting a New Year's Eve strike. Rumors of a coming wage increase offer at Washington were discounted as involving an insufficient amount.]

Meeting Called Unprofitable

Meantime, the question of higher steel prices, believed to be the crux of the problem, were discussed at another inconclusive meeting of industry representatives and officials of the Office of Price Stabilization.

At the end of the meeting—the second in two days—Michael V. DiSalle, director of the price stabilization agency, said the steel industry would get what it was entitled to under the law, but not more.

"We are not going to buy labor peace in the steel industry with an unjustified price increase," Mr. DiSalle told reporters. He said he was not a party to any deal, nor would he become a party to any deal to use his price authority to avert a steel strike. He described

Continued on Page 28, Column 4

CHURCHILL PLEDGES CLOSER BRITISH TIE TO UNITY IN EUROPE

Approves Statement on Talks in Paris Endorsing 6-Nation Army and Schuman Plan

DEFENSE LINKS PROMISED

Eisenhower Believed to Have Influenced Briton's Decision During Luncheon Meeting

Text of communiqué on British-French talks, Page 24.

By LANSING WARREN
Special to THE NEW YORK TIMES.

PARIS, Dec. 18—Prime Minister Churchill approved tonight a statement pledging more positive British cooperation with the European army and the unity of Europe than has ever been officially expressed by a British Government before.

After a two-day conference that he and Foreign Secretary Anthony Eden had with Premier René Pleven and other French Cabinet Ministers the official French-British communiqué declared that:

1. The formation of a European army was "the right way" for the integrating of democratic Germany in Europe's defensive organization.
2. All steps leading to greater unity in Europe should be welcomed and encouraged.
3. Britain was resolved to maintain her armed forces on the European Continent, which will "be linked with those of the European Defense Community for training, supply and operations by land, sea and air."
4. Britain would "associate itself as closely as possible with the European Defense Community in all stages of its political and military development."

Major Step Toward Unity Seen

The statement added that the European army would be a major step toward the structure of a united Europe and would strengthen the defense of the North Atlantic area.

The joint statement also had words of praise for the Schuman plan for a coal-steel merger which, coming at this time and from Mr. Churchill, gave a more positive aspect to the British attitude toward a project for European unity that is a twin of the European army plan.

The statement said the British Ministers hoped the Schuman plan, which had just been ratified by the French National Assembly, would soon come into effect and

Continued on Page 24, Column 5

World News Summarized

WEDNESDAY, DECEMBER 19, 1951

The Allied Command in Korea began a close study of the prisoner list turned over by the Communists. One report said no discrepancies had been found with half of the United States list surveyed, while another was inclined to doubt the authenticity of the Reds' figures. The enemy said that of a total of 11,559 war prisoners, 3,198 were Americans and 7,142 Koreans. [1:8.] The next of kin were being notified [1:7] and the names of prisoners released for publication. [Pages 14 and 15.]

Maj. Gen. William F. Dean, missing since July 23, 1950, when his command, the Twenty-fourth Division, fought to protect Taejon, is a prisoner, according to the Communists, but his fate remains a mystery [1:6-7.] Allied prisoners are being held in eleven North Korean camps. [13:6, with map.] Captured South Koreans numbered at least ten times the total reported, officials in Pusan said. [9:1.]

The Communists claimed recapture of two small islands off West Korea; there was only scattered patrol action at the front [13:3, with map.]

Britain and France are in "complete accord" on "all" current international problems, said a joint communiqué on the talks by Prime Minister Churchill and Foreign Secretary Eden with French leaders. While the British showed a friendlier attitude toward a European army and Continental unity, they refused to join the projected army or participate in federating Europe. [1:5.] Mr. Churchill will meet his Cabinet today. [24:2.]

As a United Nations Assembly committee prepared to vote today on the West's disarmament plan, the Russians said they would attend meetings of a new commission. [23:1.]

The Moscow radio reported the execution of two alleged American-trained spies parachuted into Russia. [1:6-7.]

Eighteen American labor union representatives, "at least fourteen" of whom had "notorious Communist records," had no difficulty getting passports for a trip to Moscow, a Senate group charged in a critical report on the State Department. [1:2-3.] Senator McCarthy, the Justice Department said, never turned over "cases" or files of those he accused of being Communists. [3:1.]

Senate internationalists gained a new member when Senator Seaton of Nebraska, named to succeed the late Senator Wherry, rejected the latter's isolationism. [5:1.]

Federal Mediator Ching called union and industry leaders to confer with him tomorrow in an effort to avert a steel strike. National welfare, he said, demands a speedy resolution of the dispute. Price Stabilizer DiSalle said labor peace would not be bought with "an unjustified price increase." [1:4.] The industry may make its first pay offer in Washington. [28:1.]

A committee of the State Bar Association condemned television, radio, newsreel and camera reporting of executive and legislative hearings. [48:1.]

Greatly increased budget requests make reduction of state taxes in 1952 unlikely. [1:2-3.]

NEWS BULLETINS FROM THE TIMES
Every hour on the hour
7 A.M. through Midnight
WQXR AM 1560
WQXR FM 96.3

Index to other news appears on last page of this section.

REDS' CAPTIVE LIST REVEALED; U. N. STUDYING IT CLOSELY; U. S. NOTIFYING NEXT OF KIN

Listing of Dean as Prisoner Fails to Clear Doubt on Fate

Serial Number Not Given by Foe—General Reported Held at Pyongyang

By The United Press.

MUNSAN, Korea, Wednesday, Dec. 19—The name of Maj. Gen. William F. Dean appeared today on the list of war prisoners supplied by the Communists, but even this did not clear up completely the mystery of his fate.

The hero of Taejon, who won the Medal of Honor for his gallantry in the early, dark days of the Korean war, was reported held at Pyongyang.

The Communist listing did not give General Dean's serial number, and United Nations sources said they could not understand it. Only four other prisoners are listed without a serial number.

Allied spokesmen warned repeatedly that the Communist list had not been checked. And because the Reds have refused the Red Cross the right to visit the camps, it is not possible to check the lists accurately.

Men who last were with General Dean variously have reported him dead and alive. A curious sidelight on the case is the fact that until yesterday Communist correspondents have indicated they thought he was dead.

According to the Communist listing, Frank Noel, an Associated

Continued on Page 15, Column 2

Maj. Gen. William F. Dean
The New York Times

'NO DISCREPANCIES'

Aide of Ridgway Reports After Surveying First Half of the Names

SOUTH KOREANS SHOCKED

Figure Listed Is Only Tenth of Total Sought—No Gain in Truce Talks Reported

Communists' list of American prisoners, Pages 14 and 15.

By LINDESAY PARROTT
Special to THE NEW YORK TIMES.

TOKYO, Wednesday, Dec. 19—The United Nations command today studied the list of Allied prisoners captured in the Korean war that was handed over after long delay yesterday by the Communist truce delegation in the conference tent at Panmunjom.

The list was made public here this morning after it had been flown by a bomber from Korea. It included soldiers of eleven belligerent nations.

While it was conceded that the armistice talks had taken a step forward with final enemy agreement to turn over prisoner information as a preliminary to the discussion of an exchange of captives, the initial reaction of headquarters spokesmen was that much yet remained to be discussed before the Communist data could be accepted as final.

Brig. Gen. William P. Nuckols, briefing officer in Korea, told correspondents that the United Nations delegates, after a preliminary study, were "skeptical" as to the accuracy and detailed authenticity and completeness of the tabulation they had received.

[However, a spokesman for Gen. Matthew B. Ridgway's headquarters said later that approximately half the American Army names on the Communist list had been checked against records and "so far no discrepancy has been found," The United Press reported.]

Real Verification Impossible

It was said that no real verification of enemy statements was possible since the Communists had barred representatives of the International Red Cross from the prisoner of war stockades, as provided for under a Geneva convention.

The Army communiqué, issued last night after a stack of papers turned over by the enemy delegation had been brought back to advance headquarters near Munsan, said the Communist list included a total of 11,559 prisoners of all nations.

The United Nations, in exchange, gave the Communists the identities of 132,474 enemy prisoners taken up to Dec. 13.

Of the total Communist figure, the Army announcement said, 7,142 were Republic of Korea soldiers, 3,198 Americans, 919 British, 234 Turkish, forty Filipinos, ten French, six Australians, four South Africans, three Japanese—without rank and apparently houseboys who went to Korea in the early days of the war—and one each from Canada, Greece and the Netherlands.

First Data on Captives

The list constituted the first information regarding United Nations prisoners the Communists have given since August last year and a preliminary inspection indicated considerable discrepancies with what had been expected. There had been little hope, especially in view of the recent reports of the killing of prisoners by the enemy, that many more than 3,000 Americans survived behind the barbed wire of about 11,000 reported missing in action.

Of the total of 3,198 American prisoners, 2,994 were enlisted men, 201 were officers from first lieutenant to major general and five were warrant officers. They came from all the major units of the United States command—the Second, Third, Seventh, Twenty-fourth and Twenty-fifth Divisions, the First Cavalry Division, the First Marine Division and the 187th Regimental Combat Team. Included also were men of the Fifth Air Force and the Marine Air

Continued on Page 8, Column 3

$800,000,000 ASKED FOR ARAB REFUGEES

Church and Civic Leaders Offer Program to Resettle 876,000 Under U. N. Auspices

Special to THE NEW YORK TIMES.

UNITED NATIONS, N. Y., Dec. 18 — An ambitious $800,000,000 program for Palestine Arab refugees, to be financed by governments under the United Nations, was proposed here today by a group of church and civic leaders.

The two-fold program would allocate $300,000,000 to resettle the remaining 876,000 homeless Arabs in surrounding countries, and would devote the remaining $500,000,000 to development of the natural resources of the Arab states that would absorb the refugees.

Details of the proposed project, set forth in a 117-page report on the "Arab Refugee Problem: How It Can Be Solved," were dispatched today to Secretary General Trygve Lie in Paris and to delegates attending the overseas sessions of the sixth General Assembly.

The report was submitted to the world organization by Sumner Welles, former Under Secretary of State; Paul Porter, former United States member of the United Nations Palestine Conciliation Commission; Archibald MacLeish, former Assistant Secretary of State, and sixteen others.

The financing of the program

Continued on Page 20, Column 2

PENTAGON RUSHES MESSAGES TO KIN

Defense Department Stresses Tentativeness of List—Cautions on Optimism

By AUSTIN STEVENS
Special to THE NEW YORK TIMES.

WASHINGTON, Dec. 18—With more than 11,000 men carried as missing on their rolls, the armed services started tonight to notify the next of kin of 3,198 members of the armed forces listed as missing that there was hope their loved ones were held captive by the Chinese and North Korean Communists.

Minutes after the first names of the prisoners reported by the Communists started to be received early tonight at the Pentagon special staffs of the services prepared messages to the mothers, fathers, wives and other relatives listed as "emergency addresses." It will be the first word of any kind to be received since the men disappeared in the Korean fighting.

Late tonight, Defense Department spokesmen reported that approximately 1,000 names had been processed, and that in that number there were no blatant examples of false names or of the use of fictitious numbers. Except for some errors, described as "minor inaccuracies" the names and serial numbers provided by the Communists were said to be matching up

Continued on Page 12, Column 3

Tass Reports 2 Russians Executed As Spies Flown to Soviet by U. S.

By Reuters

LONDON, Wednesday, Dec. 19—Two United States-trained Russian spies, allegedly parachuted into southwest Russia on an espionage mission from a United States plane last summer, have been executed by a firing squad, the Moscow radio reported early today.

The radio, quoting Tass, the official Soviet news agency, said the two men had admitted having been recruited by the United States intelligence service in West Germany.

Tass gave the men's names as A. I. Osmanov and I. K. Sarancev. The agency said they were "American diversionists."

[In Washington, Michael J. McDermott, State Department press officer, said: "We know nothing of these men, and we know nothing of the incident."]

At the trial, the men were said to have been dropped on the Moldavian Soviet Republic last summer by a United States plane "under the cover of night," Tass reported.

The Moldavian Soviet Socialist Republic is in southwest Russia, between the Ukraine, Rumania and the Black Sea.

Soviet state security officers detained the men and found on them false documents, weapons and "other equipment for carrying out diversionist and terrorist activities," the Tass report continued.

It added that large sums of money had been found in their possession. Open parachutes were found near the spot where the men were arrested, Tass said.

Tass said Osmanov and Sarancev admitted they had been recruited by the United States intelligence service in West Germany, where they had been living in displaced persons camps.

They also were said to have admitted they had received special training from United States intelligence officers in topography, the use of weapons, parachute jumping and "organization of acts of

Continued on Page 14, Column 1

1952

"All the News That's Fit to Print"

The New York Times.

LATE CITY EDITION
Light snow this morning followed by clearing. Fair tomorrow.
Temperature Range Today-Max., 43; Min., 35
Temperatures Yesterday—Max., 45; Min., 33
Full U. S. Weather Bureau Report, Page 55

Copyright, 1952, by The New York Times Company.

VOL. CI..No. 34,347. Entered as Second-Class Matter, Post Office, New York, N. Y. NEW YORK, THURSDAY, FEBRUARY 7, 1952. Times Square, New York 36, N. Y. Telephone LAckawanna 4-1000 FIVE CENTS

KING GEORGE VI DIES IN SLEEP AT SANDRINGHAM; ELIZABETH, QUEEN AT 25, FLYING FROM AFRICA; PRESIDENT AMONG WORLD LEADERS IN TRIBUTE

2½% INTEREST RATE FOR SAVINGS BANKS APPROVED BY STATE

85% of Institutions Expected to Adopt 'Permissive' Rule Lifting 17-Year Ceiling

NEW U. S. TAXES A FACTOR

Board Adjusts Payments on Commercial Deposits, Acts to Clear Extra Dividends

By GEORGE A. MOONEY

New York's thrifty received a new incentive yesterday.

Terminating a policy that dates to 1935, the State Banking Board acted to raise its ceiling on interest-dividends paid on savings and thrift deposits from a 2 per cent maximum to 2½ per cent. Eighty-five per cent of the state's 130 savings banks are expected to put the increase in effect at an early date.

Last night the Dime Savings Bank of Brooklyn became the first in this area to announce it would pay 2½ per cent for the current quarter ending March 31.

Trustees of the Roosevelt Savings Bank announced they would meet today to increase the rate from 2 to 2½ per cent on account balances and deposits for the three-month period starting Jan. 1.

Other savings banks and competitive commercial banks, where possible, are likely to take similiar action soon.

Responding to the higher level of prevailing rates, and especially to Federal taxes imposed at the beginning of this year, several savings banks asked permission some weeks ago to pay larger dividends. Under the new tax law, savings institutions are made liable for income taxes at the regular corporate rate on all earnings after surplus and reserves total 12 per cent of deposits.

Regulation Is "Permissive"

William A. Lyon, Superintendent of Banks, in announcing the board's action yesterday said the new 2½ per cent rate was "permissive."

"Banks are permitted under the regulation to pay any rate up to that maximum which directors and trustees believe to be advisable in the light of the earning power and the capital or surplus position of their institutions," he explained.

Two other important amendments also were made in General Regulation No. 3, the dividend and interest rate regulation, Mr. Lyon said. In the first of these, relating to commercial banks' special interest and thrift deposits, the board approved a limit on interest payments at the maximum rate of 2½ per cent on the first $10,000 of any account and setting a ceiling rate of 1½ per cent on that portion of any special and thrift account in excess of $10,000.

The largest individual account that may be accepted by savings banks is $10,000, the maximum

Continued on Page 55, Column 6

Truman 'Shows Off' New White House

By W. H. LAWRENCE
Special to THE NEW YORK TIMES.

WASHINGTON, Feb. 6—Ducking nimbly around and under scaffolding, President Truman today took a few correspondents on a conducted tour of the White House, which is being reconstructed. He said it was still his hope that the First Family would be able to move into it early in April after three and one-half years in Blair House.

Mixing history and comment about the tribulations of a tenant who decides to get a house done over, Mr. Truman led the reporters through the building for forty minutes, answering questions and volunteering observations about nearly every room.

The hum of power saws as workmen went ahead with their jobs sometimes drowned his

Continued on Page 23, Column 1

1-Way Traffic Signs Due Soon in Times Sq.

By JOSEPH C. INGRAHAM

Conversion of Seventh and Eighth Avenues to one-way operation has been decided upon by Acting Traffic Commissioner T. T. Wiley despite objections of the New York City Omnibus Corporation.

Preparations for the new traffic pattern were well under way yesterday, with new guideposts rising in Times Square and the fittings all set to hold the one-way arrows. Work on the other sections of the one-way routes, which extend from Columbus Circle to below Canal Street, also was progressing. Seventh Avenue-Varick Street will handle southbound flow and Hudson Street-Abingdon Square-Eighth

Continued on Page 17, Column 5

CHARGES OF WASTE IN DEFENSE DENIED

Pentagon Aides Tell Senators of Savings—Admiral Calls Himself 'Oyster Fork Fox'

By HAROLD B. HINTON
Special to THE NEW YORK TIMES.

WASHINGTON, Feb. 6—Officials of the Department of Defense underwent a period of criticism before a Senate Appropriations subcommittee today and did not seem to like it. They were appearing in support of defense budget estimates of more than $52,000,000,000.

The principal witness was Vice Admiral Charles W. Fox, Chief of Naval Supplies, who told the Senators of the progress the Navy had made in simplifying the cataloguing of its supplies. When his presentation was interrupted by questions about allegations of waste and extravagance, the Pentagon contingent moved to the counter-offensive.

"I stand before you as Oyster Fork Fox," the admiral asserted, as the Senators and spectators laughed. "I am supposed to have bought 11,000,000 oyster forks for the Navy, and I had nothing more to do with it than you did."

He said that the Navy last

Continued on Page 4, Column 3

RED TRAPS FEARED IN FOE'S PROPOSAL FOR KOREA PARLEY

Communist Demand for Airing of Status of Formosa Viewed as Bar to U. N. Accord

TRUMAN CITED AS A GUIDE

Nam Il Argues Stand Taken by President on Blockading China Widens Issues

Text of Gen. Nam Il's statement is printed on Page 2.

By LINDESAY PARROTT
Special to THE NEW YORK TIMES.

TOKYO, Thursday, Feb. 7—The United Nations Command began today a detailed study of the Communist proposal for a top-level political conference three months after the armistice in the Korean war to deal with related issues in the Far East.

This morning no hint of Allied reaction had come from the advance camp at Munsan, where the United Nations representatives took the Communist program after it had been delivered to them at a plenary session of the truce delegations at Panmunjom, or at the headquarters of the United Nations Commander, Gen. Matthew B. Ridgway, in Tokyo.

The enemy proposal was made by North Korean Gen. Nam Il, head of the Chinese and North Korean delegation, who drove to the meeting place in a big American limousine with whitewall tires. He nodded coldly to the senior United Nations representative, Vice Admiral Charles Turner Joy, and then launched into his prepared introductory remarks — considerably more extensive, it turned out, than the brief formal proposal for a governmental conference for "peaceful settlement of the Korean question and other questions related to peace in Korea."

Before the session adjourned it was agreed that a new plenary sitting should be held by the delegates of both sides after the United Nations study had been com-

Continued on Page 2, Column 6

World News Summarized

THURSDAY, FEBRUARY 7, 1952

King George VI died in his sleep at Sandringham Palace yesterday morning; his daughter was proclaimed Queen Elizabeth II. The King, who seemingly had recovered from an operation for the removal of a growth on his lung, had felt so well he had been out shooting the day before. [1:8.] The British people were stunned by their sudden loss. [1:7.]

King George became the British ruler in 1936 when his brother, King Edward VIII and later Duke of Windsor, abdicated. He saw little peace during his reign. Threats of war, armed conflict and the "cold war" marked his tenure. [10:1.] During the bombing of London he refused to take special precautions or leave Buckingham Palace. [13:7-8.]

The new Queen started for London by plane when she learned of her father's death. She had been touring East Africa with her consort, the Duke of Edinburgh. [1:6-7.] She is the first Queen to ascend Britain's throne since 115 years ago, when Queen Victoria was crowned. [1:5-6.] The Duke of Windsor sails from New York tonight, alone, to attend his brother's funeral. [14:8.]

President Truman, Secretary Acheson and others expressed the sorrow of the United States [1:5] as did former President Hoover, Mayor Impellitteri and others in this city. [14:5.] United Nations flags were flown at half-staff. [15:1.]

The Soviet Union, for the fifth time, vetoed Italy's membership in the United Nations. [1:4.] The Russians did not join forty-seven other countries in pledging funds for expanded technical assistance this year. [3:4.]

Allied officers studied the Communist proposal for a political conference three months after a Korean armistice. [1:3.]

West German leaders were unmoved by American and British pleas to cool their anger over French moves in the Saar and not to endanger plans for West Europe's defense. [6:3.]

A masked witness told a House committee he had seen Russians kill hundreds of Polish officers in Katyn Forest in 1939. [4:3.]

Defense Department heads, testifying on the military budget before a Senate group, vigorously defended their spending. [1:2.] Mobilization heads also were under attack for plans to spread defense contracts to unemployment areas. [39:4.]

The slow-down in the military aircraft production rate will have little immediate effect on consumer goods but will avoid more stringent curbs later, a survey showed. [3:1.]

Governor Byrnes of South Carolina blamed "Negro politicians of the North" for the Democratic party's shift from a State's Rights program. [21:1.]

This state authorized banks to pay up to 2½ per cent on savings and thrift accounts. [1:1.]

Columbia University will increase tuition fees up to 25 per cent next fall and adjust faculty salaries upward. [29:1.]

NEWS BULLETINS FROM THE TIMES
Every hour on the hour
7 A.M. through Midnight
Except at 4 P.M. Today
WQXR AM 1560
WQXR FM 96.3

Index to other news appears on last page of this section.

THE NEW QUEEN AND THE LATE KING

ELIZABETH II — GEORGE VI — Associated Press

SOVIET AGAIN BALKS ITALY'S U. N. ENTRY

Russia for Fifth Time Vetoes Application—Is Beaten on En Bloc Admission Bid

By THOMAS J. HAMILTON
Special to THE NEW YORK TIMES.

PARIS, Feb. 6—Italy's application for membership in the United Nation's was vetoed by the Soviet Union tonight for the fifth time. Ten of the eleven members of the Security Council voted for a French resolution recommending the admission of Italy.

Jacob A. Malik, the Soviet representative, based his action on the refusal of the United States and other Western powers to accept a Soviet proposal for en bloc admission of fourteen applicants, including five Communist governments.

The Soviet resolution afterward was rejected by a vote of six to two. The United States, Brazil, Nationalist China, Greece, the Netherlands and Turkey voted against the resolution, while Pakistan joined the Soviet Union in supporting it. Britain, France and Chile abstained.

Mr. Malik accused the United States of blocking Italy's admission. He declared that "the Italian people will note that it is the United States, with the help of the United Kingdom" that had "provoked" the Soviet veto. He added that if the Western powers had wanted to get Italy admitted, they would have agreed to the Soviet proposal.

Gross Protests "Horsetrade"

Ernest A. Gross, the United States delegate, retorted that on the contrary the Italian people would hardly be grateful for being made a part of the proposed "horse-trade." He asked whether Mr. Malik really believed that Italy should be "put in the same basket" with such "a shadow state" as Outer Mongolia, one of the Communist candidates included in the Soviet resolution.

Mr. Gross also expressed regret that the new state of Libya, which came into existence on Christmas Day, 1951, had been included in the Soviet en bloc proposal—which presumably meant that it likewise would encounter a Soviet veto unless the Western powers agree to the Soviet mass entry proposal.

Mr. Malik replied that Outer Mongolia deserved to be admitted. He said that its participation in the war against Japan "along with that of the Soviet Union" saved 1,000,000 American lives. He said he based his statement on statements by the United States high command.

Reconsideration today of Italy's long-standing application was the result of a General Assembly resolution last fall requesting the Security Council to reconsider it in the light of Italy's responsibilities

Continued on Page 3, Column 5

Ruler Becomes Elizabeth II; Her Son, 3, Is Crown Prince

By CLIFTON DANIEL
Special to THE NEW YORK TIMES.

LONDON, Feb. 6—Britain entered a new Elizabethan era today. Upon the death of King George VI, Princess Elizabeth Alexandra Mary, his elder daughter, automatically became Queen of the United Kingdom and the Dominions Overseas at the age of 25.

Tonight at the first meeting of her Privy Council she was formally styled Queen Elizabeth II.

[Text of the Privy Council's proclamation is on Page 14.]

Thus, for the first time in 115 years, a woman ascended the world's most exalted and stable throne. At the Gloucester Assizes, as in other law courts of the land, the judges marshal closed the court with words not heard since the end of Queen Victoria's sixty-three-year reign in 1901: "God save the Queen and my lords the Queen's justices."

For the first time in British history the sovereign was abroad in the Empire at the moment of accession.

Already bearing the full responsibility of the crown, the new Queen will return here by air from Kenya in Africa tomorrow accompanied by her consort, the Duke of Edinburgh.

They were to have boarded the liner Gothic at Mombasa tomorrow to sail for Ceylon, Australia and New Zealand on a five-month ceremonial tour deputizing for the late King, whose illness prevented him from going.

With the accession of the Queen, her son Prince Charles, three years and two months old, became the Crown Prince and heir to the

Continued on Page 14, Column 3

TRUMAN EXPRESSES SORROW OF NATION

Voices Sympathy for British Over Loss of King—Acheson and Others Pay Tribute

Special to THE NEW YORK TIMES.

WASHINGTON, Feb. 6—President Truman and the nation paid tribute to King George VI today in extending this country's sympathy to the British people on his death.

"He played his part nobly and with full understanding of the responsibility which was his," the President said in a formal statement.

All official Washington responded in kind following the surprise and shock at the news of the monarch's passing early this morning. Highest officials in the Government and leaders of both House of Congress joined in expressions of sympathy and praise for the man who had been a steadfast friend of the United States, and, indeed, had been the first British King to visit the country.

Secretary of State Dean Acheson commented on the courage with which King George had borne his physical suffering and noted: "It is a characteristic English spirit and the King possessed it in abundance."

Envoy Calls on Acheson

Sir Oliver Franks, British Ambassador, accompanied by seven representatives of the British Commonwealth, called on Secretary Acheson shortly after noon to inform him formally of the King's death.

"A world personage who maintained the highest tradition of the English constitutional monarchy passes in the death of His Majesty King George VI," President Truman said in his statement.

"From his accession to the throne through all the ills which beset the world throughout the years of his reign—including the most disastrous war in history—he played his part nobly and with full responsibility which was his. His heroic endurance of pain and suffering during these past few years is a true reflection of the bravery of the British people in adversity.

"The King was ever conscious of his obligations as sovereign of a nation which through centuries has been the champion of personal liberty and those free institu-

Continued on Page 14, Column 5

LONDON IS STILLED AS BRITONS MOURN

All Amusements Closed, Lights Dimmed, Streets Nearly Empty After News Stuns People

By FARNSWORTH FOWLE
Special to THE NEW YORK TIMES.

LONDON, Feb. 6—This was a silent city tonight, with bright lights dimmed and all places of entertainment closed, as Londoners went home shocked by the death of their King.

The news reached most office workers at noon when they went out for lunch and found venders of early editions of afternoon papers shouting "The King is dead!"

"What King?" was a typical first reaction. It was hard to believe that it was indeed their own monarch, even though it had been generally realized since the King's operation last September that he might not have many years to live. Only a week ago tonight he attended a performance of "South Pacific" at the Drury Lane Theatre.

The suddenness of the news contrasted with the memory of how the public had been prepared during the final illness of the King's father, George V, with a broadcast communiqué saying, "The King's life is moving peacefully to its close."

Flags at half-staff appeared on public buildings and many private ones by noon. Theatres, cinemas and night clubs all shut down, as did the Stock Exchange and other markets.

The laughter of London's usually cheerful office girls was muted as

Continued on Page 13, Column 6

Elizabeth Weeps at News of Death, But Is Calm in African Take-Off

By The United Press.

NAIROBI, Kenya, Feb. 6—Young Queen Elizabeth II left hurriedly for home by plane tonight only a few hours after her husband had broken the news to her of her father's death.

The 25-year-old former Princess, after having broken down in tears, was composed when she departed early tonight on the long flight to London.

With Prince Philip she left the hunting lodge where the royal couple had been staying and drove in a closed automobile eight miles to a small airport near the East African town of Nunyuki. She took off in an East African Airways C-47 for Entebbe in Uganda, where the British Overseas Airways craft that had flown her to Africa waited to take her back to Britain.

The royal couple landed at Entebbe airport at 9:10 P. M. (1:10 P. M., Eastern standard time), but news of her arrival was kept from the local populace to spare the new Queen a further ordeal.

A tropical thunderstorm at Entebbe delayed the departure of the Queen's plane for more than two hours, but it finally took off at 11:47 P. M. for Libya as the weather cleared.

[The plane made a stop at the Royal Air Force base at El Adem, Libya, landing there at 1:15 A. M., Thursday, Eastern standard time, The United Press reported.]

At El Adem and Malta the Royal Air Force had planes standing by to escort the Queen's plane over the Mediterranean. It is scheduled to reach London at 4:30 P. M. Thursday, Greenwich time (11:30 A. M., E. S. T.)

Crowds of silent, sorrowful persons of all races lined the main street of Nunyuki as the Queen's party passed through. The Queen, her face showing the strain of the

Continued on Page 13, Column 8

15-YEAR REIGN ENDS

British Monarch's Death at 56 Follows a Lung Operation Last Fall

PARLIAMENT HALTED

Churchill Conveys News to Commons—Attlee Suspends Party Strife

By RAYMOND DANIELL
Special to THE NEW YORK TIMES.

LONDON, Feb. 6—In the early hours of this morning George VI died peacefully in his sleep at the royal estate at Sandringham. As night fell upon this mourning capital of a still great family of nations, his elder daughter was proclaimed Queen of this realm and its dependencies, head of the British Commonwealth and the Defender of the Faith, with the title of Elizabeth II.

She is flying home tonight from her tragically interrupted visit to East Africa with her consort, the Duke of Edinburgh, and is expected back tomorrow to assume her royal duties as the wearer of the crown that somewhat mystically binds the British Commonwealth together.

Like the Elizabeth of England's golden age, she takes the throne at the age of 25.

Operated On 4 Months Ago

The King's death occurred just a little more than four months after an operation for the removal of a growth in his right lung. This operation resulted in the loss of the lung. His recovery seemed assured and in recent days he had been seen publicly at the theatre and at London Airport when he bade good-by to his daughter, now the Queen, as she set out with Prince Philip, her husband, on a journey that was to take her to East Africa, Australia and New Zealand. Only yesterday he was out shooting, his favorite sport.

It was assumed that the King had died as a result of a heart attack, probably caused by coronary thrombosis.

Tributes to the late monarch poured into London from leading world figures and from persons of humbler station.

His death came in his 57th year. It was the beginning of the sixteenth year of an unhappy reign. He never wanted or expected the throne of Britain, but he ascended to it when his brother Edward VIII abdicated to marry "the woman I love," Wallis Simpson.

Six years of his reign were war years when he and Elizabeth, his Queen, who now becomes Queen Mother, endeared themselves to their people by their bravery and devotion to their predestined role.

When he was crowned King on May 12, 1937, he was King Emperor but the title of Emperor went with the granting of independence to India. His reign marked the end of an era of British power.

Parliament Is Suspended

His death also brought to an end this session of Parliament in the midst of a bitter and acrimonious debate on how far this country should go in aligning itself with United States policy in the Far East lest it be dragged into war. That debate, which began yesterday, was left in mid-air as Parliament put aside its controversies to swear allegiance to the new Queen and deterred its partisan arguments on controversial issues until a more seemly time.

At Sandringham when the King died there were his two grandchildren, whom he adored, Prince Charles and Princess Anne; Sir Alan Lascelles, his private secretary; Sir Harold Campbell, his Equerry, and Lady Hyde, Lady-in-Waiting to his Queen. Soon after his death had been discovered by a servant bringing early morning tea, Dr. James Ansell, "Surgeon Apothecary" to the royal household at Sandringham, was called. He said that the King had died in his sleep without pain.

The news of the King's death went out over the news tickers at 10:45 A. M. At 11:15 it was broad-

Continued on Page 13, Column 2

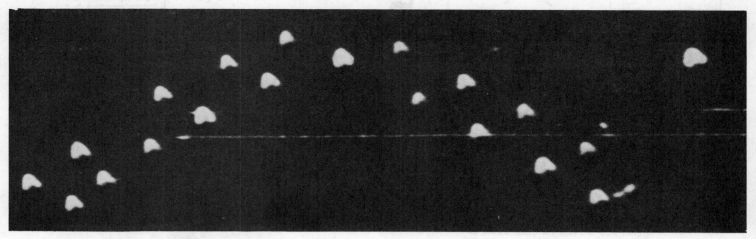

Flying saucers became a tantalizing controversy in 1952.

Alexander Calder became famous for his mobile sculptures made out of wire, wood, aluminum, paper and other odd materials.

Scrabble, first introduced in 1952, sent millions of people flying to dictionaries.

Parakeets became the rage in pets.

"All the News That's Fit to Print"

The New York Times.

LATE CITY EDITION
Mostly fair, mild in afternoon today. Partly cloudy tomorrow.
Temperature Range Today—Max., 51; Min., 37
Temperatures Yesterday—Max., 52; Min., 36
U. S. Weather Bureau Report, Page 8, Sect. 1

Section 1

NEWS SUMMARY AND INDEX, PAGE 95

VOL. CI No. 34,399. Entered as Second-Class Matter. Post Office, New York, N. Y. NEW YORK, SUNDAY, MARCH 30, 1952. Including Magazine and Book Review. FIFTEEN CENTS New York City 50 Mile Zone | Elsewhere Twenty-five Cents

TRUMAN ANNOUNCES HE WILL NOT RUN AGAIN; SAYS HE SERVED LONG, FEELS 'NO DUTY' TO STAY; NEWS STUNS DEMOCRATIC LEADERS AT DINNER

CATHOLIC SCHOOLS RAISE ENROLLMENT TO 4,000,000 PEAK

$250,000,000 Expansion Plan Is Under Way for Adding of 1,000,000 by 1960

PERSONNEL IS INADEQUATE

Survey Discloses High Cost for Lay Teachers to Fill Gap—Curriculums Improving

By BENJAMIN FINE

Growing at a rapid rate, the Roman Catholic schools and colleges in the United States have a record enrollment of 4,000,000 students, representing an increase of more than 35 per cent in the last ten years.

For the first time, the Catholic elementary schools have exceeded 3,000,000, while the secondary schools are above 600,000. The Catholic-supported institutions of higher learning have combined enrollments of 350,000. The increase is expected to continue, estimates by school officials placing the 1960 Catholic school and college enrollment at 5,000,000.

To meet the tremendous demands placed upon it, the Catholic school plant is in the midst of an expansion program that will cost $250,000,000. Under construction are facilities valued at $130,000,000, while $110,000,000 in construction is projected for next year. Only the shortage of steel or other critical supplies will slow this all-out expansion.

These findings are based on a nation-wide study of Catholic education by THE NEW YORK TIMES. Data were obtained from more than 75 per cent of the Catholic dioceses in the United States—ninety-four out of 126. Information also was supplied by representatives of the National Catholic Welfare Conference in Washington.

Teacher Shortage Acute

The teacher shortage in the Catholic schools is just as acute as it is in the public institutions. Many superintendents report they are unable to obtain the necessary teachers, either lay or religious. They say that because of this shortage the Catholic schools cannot expand as rapidly as they might.

Many Catholic officials report that they are turning more and more to lay teachers to fill the gap, though too often these teachers are not available because of the public schools' competition for their services. This year the Catholic schools employ a total of 109,118 teachers, of whom 97,068 are religious. Ten years ago the total number of teachers was 88,444.

In the United States today there are 11,519 Catholic schools, divided as follows: 8,845 elementary, 2,296 secondary and 378 unspecified.

The growth in Catholic school enrollment has been rapid on both the elementary and secondary levels. Each of the 126 dioceses conducts one or more schools. New York State leads with 900 elementary schools. Within the state the Archdiocese of New York (Bronx, Manhattan, Staten Island and Westchester County), with 284 elementary and ninety-nine secondary schools, and the Diocese of Brooklyn, with 227 elementary and fifty-two secondary schools, account for a majority of the Catholic-supported schools.

Facilities Dictate Rise

THE TIMES' survey indicates that about 60 per cent of Catholic children of school age (elementary and secondary) are attending parochial schools. The remaining 40 per cent attend public schools. In the 1951-52 school year the Catholic elementary schools have enrolled 3,035,033 children, the Catholic high schools 611,123. Approximately 350,000 students are attending Catholic-supported colleges, universities, teacher-training institutions and other post-secondary schools. In the 1950-51 school year 2,879,623 attended Catholic elementary schools and

Continued on Page 75, Column 1

Britain and Egypt Progress Toward Suez Compromise

London Said to Concede Troop Withdrawal and End of Sudan Condominium—Cairo Is Cautious on 'Exploratory' Talks

By ALBION ROSS
Special to THE NEW YORK TIMES.

CAIRO, March 29 — British-Egyptian talks, concerning unilateral concessions by London or mutual concessions that would start off favorably the new negotiations for settlement of the long-drawn-out and bitter British-Egyptian conflict, were moving fast today.

Sir Ralph Stevenson, the British Ambassador, saw the Egyptian Foreign Minister, Abdul Khalek Hassouna Pasha twice, once in the morning and once in the afternoon.

The general understanding was that Britain had agreed to declare her willingness to evacuate the British garrison from the Suez Canal Zone base but that the finding of a formula for settling Egypt's demands regarding the Sudan was proving difficult.

It was not known what, if anything, the Egyptians were prepared to concede in response to the British. What Britain and the West want, obviously, is a declaration that Egypt is prepared to enter some type of Middle East defense partnership with the West.

So far as the Sudan is concerned, it seemed that the British were prepared to recognize the end of the British-Egyptian condominium, which Egypt unilaterally abrogated last October at the same time that she abrogated the British-Egyptian alliance providing for the presence of a British garrison in the Suez Canal zone.

Britain would accept the proposition of a Sudan, sovereign and independent of the British crown, but whether she would be prepared formally to recognize the Egyptian claim of King Farouk as King of Sudan was not yet clear though it was believed that Britain would be willing to announce acceptance of King Farouk's sov-

Continued on Page 26, Column 5

Foe Says U. S. Would Intern Pro-Red U.N. Korea Captives

By LINDESAY PARROTT
Special to THE NEW YORK TIMES.

TOKYO, Sunday, March 30—The Peiping radio accused the White House today of "utter callousness and ill will" toward American prisoners captured by the Communists in the Korean war. The broadcast, monitored here, asserted that "the American warmongers do not want all their prisoners who are now in care of this side to be repatriated."

The Chinese radio made the statement in a long account of supposedly secret negotiations at Panmunjom on an exchange of prisoners in an armistice. The broadcast renewed charges that United Nations spokesmen had violated the agreement for secrecy, then itself went on to describe a "new proposal" it said had been advanced by Allied representatives in the conference tent.

No confirmation has been given here that such a proposal was made. A communiqué at Allied advance headquarters last night said only that the executive discussions had lasted three hours yesterday.

At Panmunjom today, staff officers sat through another unprofitable session, still debating the Communists' demand for inclusion of the Soviet Union as one of the "neutral" nations to police an armistice. The United Nations representative, Col. Don O. Darrow, told the Communists their persistence was simply delaying the armistice.

The Communist version of the United Nations stand broadcast by Peiping went back to Jan. 21, when, it was asserted, Rear Admiral Ruthven E. Libby, Allied delegate, told the Chinese and North Korean representatives that "only

Continued on Page 2, Column 3

'MET' MAY REVIVE REMODELING PLAN

Deferred Proposal to Revamp Theatre, Erected in 1883, Is Receiving Attention

A long-dormant proposal to rebuild the Metropolitan Opera House at a cost of $2,000,000 to $3,000,000 received renewed attention from officials and friends of the institution yesterday in the wake of news that the Columbus Circle site projected for a new home would not be available.

The deferred proposal, blueprinted some years ago, calls for extensive renovations inside and outside the theatre, which was built in 1883. The blueprints might have to be brought up to date, it was acknowledged yesterday, but any renovation of the old theatre would have these basic aims:

¶Modernization of production facilities. This would include better quarters backstage, enlargement of the pit and perhaps a more maneuverable stage.

¶Rearrangement of the aisles and the seating plan on the orchestra floor. It has been suggested that space for 300 or 400 more

Continued on Page 75, Column 5

Yugoslavs Stage Orderly Protest Against 3-Power Talks on Trieste

By M. S. HANDLER
Special to THE NEW YORK TIMES.

BELGRADE, Yugoslavia, March 29—Thousands of university and high school students paraded tonight through the streets of Belgrade in an orderly and disciplined manner in protest against the Western move to solve the question of Zone A of the Free Territory of Trieste without the consent or participation of Yugoslavia.

The columns of students appeared after nightfall and converged on the center of the city, carrying their national flags and big placards, the principal slogan of which read "No solution of the Trieste question without Yugoslavia." Many of the placards read "Down with the Italian Fascist warmongers," "Down with the Cominform - Fascist imperialists," "Togliatti-De Gasperi, the forerunners of fascism" (a reference to Premier Alcide De Gasperi and Palmiro Togliatti, leader of the Italian Communists). "We keep what is ours and don't want anything that belongs to anyone else."

The students chanted and sang as they marched. Some of their chants were "Trieste is ours," "No solution without Yugoslavia" and "Down with the Italian Fascists." But the more significant point was the resurrection of wartime Partisan songs and chants, such as "Tito and the army," "Long live the Yugoslav Army."

Deputy Minister of Foreign Affairs Leo Mattes told a joint session of the National Assembly tonight that the Yugoslav Government would refuse to recognize or be bound by any decision that might be reached at the forthcoming British - American - Italian conference in London on the administration of Zone A, now occu-

Continued on Page 25, Column 1

FRENCH KEEP RIGHT TO VOTE IN TUNISIA UNDER NEW PLANS

Schuman Outlines a Program to Transfer Internal Power to Area Within 5 Years

DEMONSTRATION IN TUNIS

New Premier Confers With Bey—Resident General Is Named Foreign Head in Cabinet

By ROBERT C. DOTY
Special to THE NEW YORK TIMES.

PARIS, March 29—France's new program of internal reforms for Tunisia envisages the transfer of most aspects of internal sovereignty to the North African protectorate within five years but clings to the old stumbling block of previous negotiations — voting rights for the French minority there.

The program outlined to the National Assembly's Foreign Affairs Committee today by Foreign Minister Robert Schuman is predicated on the election of municipal councils in Tunisia by popular suffrage—that is, with the protectorate's 150,000 French residents joining the 3,500,000 Tunisians at the polls. Resistance to this sharing of Tunisian sovereignty with non-Tunisians was a cardinal principle of the nationalist regime that was violently uprooted Wednesday by the French.

On the other hand, the mingling of Frenchmen and Tunisians in common institutions is an essential part of the long-term French aim.

[A late Paris dispatch of The Associated Press said telephone communication had been cut with Tunisia, possibly marking a clamping on of censorship as new violence was reported.]

The parts of M. Schuman's declaration to the Assembly committee that were made public made no mention of ultimate French Union membership for Tunisia, but this goal was defined by another authoritative official source.

In Tunis meanwhile the new pro-French Premier, Salah-Edine Ben Mohammed Baccouche, had his first interviews with Sidi Mohammed el Amin Pasha, the Bey of Tunis and the country's nominal ruler, and with the Resi-

Continued on Page 27, Column 1

RACE IS WIDE OPEN

Truman Decision Leaves Time for Intensive Party Contest

STEVENSON TO FORE

Barkley Also Mentioned in Addition to Those Already in Field

By ARTHUR KROCK
Special to THE NEW YORK TIMES.

WASHINGTON, March 29—President Truman's announcement at the Jefferson-Jackson Day dinner here tonight that he would not accept renomination threw wide open the contest for the Democratic party choice for the first time since 1932.

Though President Roosevelt in 1940 withheld announcement of his willingness to run again until just before the convention acted, and in 1944 kept the party leaders guessing until a few weeks before the hour of decision, the general belief never failed that he would accept renomination. Consequently nothing like an open contest occurred in either year.

Mr. Truman's withdrawal, however, occurs nearly four months before the Democratic national convention is to meet in Chicago, and this will afford ample time for those Democrats already in the field and others who will enter to make a positive and intensive campaign for the nomination.

Among the added starters the names most prominently mentioned tonight were those of Gov. Adlai E. Stevenson of Illinois and Vice President Alben W. Barkley.

Up to now Senators Kefauver of Tennessee, Russell of Georgia and Kerr of Oklahoma were running under the handicap of the President's silence. The fact that he could at any time cancel all their efforts by announcing that he was again a candidate, and the further fact that no one could be sure that he would not do so, had the effect of making their campaigns seem like shadow-boxing.

But now that the field is open, the more so because the President as yet has offered no public advice as to a successor, the Democratic battle has begun in earnest.

Continued on Page 66, Column 3

Kimball Says Navy Plans to Equip All Carriers for Atomic Warfare

Fleet to Be Able to Carry Bombs Wherever Needed, He Tells Congress—New U. S. Arms Surpass Russia's, Collins Asserts

By JOHN D. MORRIS
Special to THE NEW YORK TIMES.

WASHINGTON, March 29—Dan A. Kimball, Secretary of the Navy, has informed Congress of the Navy's intention "to develop the capability of delivering atomic bombs from all airplane carriers."

The Navy's plans for creating what would amount to a fleet of "tremendously effective" atomic carriers were sketched by the secretary to the Joint Congressional Committee on Atomic Energy in testimony made public today.

At the same time, the House Appropriations Committee published testimony by Gen. J. Lawton Collins, Army Chief of Staff, that the Army had increased its fire power by 50 per cent over World War II and was making "superior weapons to those of the Soviets."

The existing arsenal would be "tremendously effective" against any mass Russian attack in Europe, he said. The power of European defense forces will be greatly enhanced in the future, he added, by "atomic artillery and guided missiles with and without atomic warheads."

The Appropriations Committee also was told that Army draft calls would rise to about 50,000 a month after July as compared with 15,000 scheduled for May. Lieut. Gen. A. C. McAuliffe, Assistant Chief of Staff for Personnel, estimated that this would be necessary because 600,000 to 700,000 inductees, reservists and guardsmen, or almost half of the Army, would have to be released during the fiscal year beginning July 1.

Mr. Kimball, testifying behind closed doors Sept. 27, told the Joint Atomic Committee that the atomic bomb "is the most efficient weapon in our general arsenal and will have a multitude of uses in the execution of the Navy's mission."

"The role of the Air Force," he said, "is to handle the strategic [air] war, but we can and I am sure will be asked to take collateral missions and we are getting our carriers ready to deliver bombs wherever they want them delivered. And tactically I think the field has not been scratched."

The transcript of Mr. Kimball's testimony was edited for security reasons to such an extent that there were only brief and sometimes cryptic references to plans for converting the country's entire carrier force to atomic warfare. There was no indication of how long it would take.

But one implication was that the recently developed small atomic bomb could be carried by planes capable of landing and taking off from the smallest carriers. Also of possible significance was the ap-

Continued on Page 23, Column 1

'I SHALL NOT BE A CANDIDATE'

President Truman at the moment he announced his decision at Jefferson-Jackson Day dinner.

Political Circles Surprised; Some Hope 'No' Isn't Final

President Truman's announcement that he would not be a candidate for re-election was received with surprise in most political circles, and some Democrats expressed a hope that the decision was not final. Questioned by political leaders by THE NEW YORK TIMES, The Associated Press and The United Press last night, after the President had disclosed his decision, brought the following comment:

Gov. Adlai Stevenson of Illinois, who has been reported unofficially as the man Mr. Truman favors to succeed himself, told a reporter the decision "was all a surprise to me."

"I am still a candidate for the Governor of Illinois and nothing else," Mr. Stevenson said.

Asked if he would accept the Democratic nomination, he replied:

"I'll cross that bridge when I come to it."

Senator Richard B. Russell, Democrat of Georgia, an announced candidate for the Presidential nomination, said he had been convinced for a long time that the President would not run for re-election, and had been saying so at his own news conferences.

"I hope that it means a free convention," Mr. Russell commented.

In Hastings, Neb., Senator Estes Kefauver of Tennessee, an announced candidate for the Democratic Presidential nomination, said:

"President Truman has served the nation well during many years as Senator, Vice President and President. I think history will record as outstanding his great efforts to achieve world peace.

"I am sure the Democratic party will continue with its constructive platform both in the field of

Continued on Page 68, Column 3

BARKLEY ASSAILS M'ARTHUR CHARGE

Says General Perverts Truth—Denies Policy Will Lead to War or Socialism

Special to THE NEW YORK TIMES.

WASHINGTON, March 29—Vice President Alben W. Barkley tonight charged General of the Army Douglas MacArthur with grossly perverting the truth.

In a speech at the $100-a-plate Jefferson-Jackson Day dinner here the Vice President struck back sharply at the ousted Far Eastern Commander who recently indicated that he would accept a draft to become the Republican Presidential nominee.

The Vice President's speech was in response to General MacArthur's address to the Mississippi Legislature at Jackson last Saturday, in which he asserted that "wastrel" domestic policies of the Administration were leading the nation "toward a Communist state" and that its foreign policy was "preparing us for a war in Europe."

Mr. Barkley declared that "any assertion, or claim, or pretense that either our domestic program or our foreign policy is intended or calculated to foment war in

Continued on Page 65, Column 6

Crisis in Taft Race Seen Tuesday As Wisconsin and Nebraska Vote

By RICHARD J. H. JOHNSTON
Special to THE NEW YORK TIMES.

MILWAUKEE, March 29—The battle for Wisconsin's thirty Republican and twenty-eight Democratic convention delegates will go into its final round here tomorrow morning.

On Tuesday, from 6 A. M. to 6 P. M. in country areas and from 6 A. M. to 8 P. M. in the cities, an estimated 1,000,000 voters of this industrial, dairy and agricultural state, their ears still ringing with the echoes of campaign oratory, loud-speaker exhortations and political argument, will go to the polls and mark their Presidential preference primary ballots.

Five slates of delegates-at-large, listing ten names each, and ten of Congressional District delegates listing two names each will confront the voters.

At the top of the Republican

Continued on Page 46, Column 6

By WILLIAM M. BLAIR
Special to THE NEW YORK TIMES.

OMAHA, Neb., March 29—The big question in Nebraska today is whether the "grass roots" appeal of General of the Army Dwight D. Eisenhower, as manifested in Minnesota's write-in "miracle," can match and overcome the well-organized drive for write-in votes for Senator Robert A. Taft of Ohio in the state's Presidential preference primary on Tuesday.

Big money is being poured into the Nebraska campaigns. Every medium of mass communication is being employed. No holds are barred and the fight may go down to one of the bitterest finishes in this state's history.

The Eisenhower-Taft battle overshadows the important Demo-

Continued on Page 46, Column 4

HE BARS ANY DRAFT

President Also Maps the Party's Strategy, Says It Can Win Again

ASSAILS G.O.P. DRIVE

Lashes 'Dinosaurs' and 'Loud Talkers' Among the Republicans

Text of the President's speech is printed on Page 64.

By W. H. LAWRENCE
Special to THE NEW YORK TIMES.

WASHINGTON, March 29—President Truman dramatically announced tonight that he would not be a candidate for re-election and would not accept the nomination if he were drafted by the Democratic convention.

He made the announcement in almost dead-pan fashion toward the end of his speech before the 5,300 Democrats attending the party's traditional $100-a-plate Jefferson-Jackson Day dinner in the National Guard Armory here.

Following is the text of the statement interpolated into his prepared speech:

"I shall not be a candidate for re-election. I have served my country long and I think efficiently and honestly. I shall not accept a renomination. I do not feel that it is my duty to spend another four years in the White House."

The audience was taken completely by surprise by the announcement since there had been no indication anywhere in the earlier part of his speech nor in the advance word given to highest officials on his staff that he intended at this point to bow out of the 1952 political campaign.

"Oh no, oh no," shouted a few people on the floor.

Statement Total Surprise

But there was less demonstration than might have been expected because the huge crowd was taken totally by surprise.

Many of those in the audience appeared not to have heard or understood the import of Mr. Truman's statement. Others simply were stunned.

As soon as he had made his matter-of-fact disclaimer of any intentions to run again, Mr. Truman hurried on to finish the rest of the speech. The crowd applauded, not more vigorously than might have been expected, and the President hurriedly left the hall.

One man sitting near him said that the President's announcement, in long hand, rested on the speaker's rostrum alongside the typescript of his prepared speech.

The President inserted his statement just after he had declared that the record his administration had made would be the one on which the Democratic nominee would have to run "whoever the Democratic nominee * * * may be this year."

As the President left the armory he was stopped by reporters who asked, "Is this decision subject to any change at all?"

Any Change Ruled Out

"None whatsoever," Mr. Truman replied.

Mrs. Truman, who was with him, was asked whether she agreed with the decision.

"Of course," she said, "anything he says goes."

After the Trumans had returned to the White House Joseph Short, White House secretary, said that Mr. Truman had reached the decision to make his announcement tonight about a week ago while on vacation in Key West. Mr. Short underlined that the Key West decision was the timing of the announcement and not the basic decision itself. He would not say when Mr. Truman decided not to run again.

At his press conference Mr. Short was asked if he had any idea of Mr. Truman's plans for the time after he leaves the White House.

"I would suggest you ask him at

Continued on Page 65, Column 3

"The Honeymooners" were a regular part of The Jackie Gleason Show. Art Carney and Joyce Randolph are present at one of Gleason's confrontations with Audrey Meadows.

Dinah Shore was on TV from 1951-1957 with a 15-minute show. In the fall of 1957 she starred in the Dinah Shore Chevy Show. It ran, in color, for 5 years.

Kay Kyser's Kollege of Musical Knowledge had been a hit on radio for years. It switched to television in 1949 and ran till 1954. Seen here are Kay Kyser and Ish Kabibble.

1952

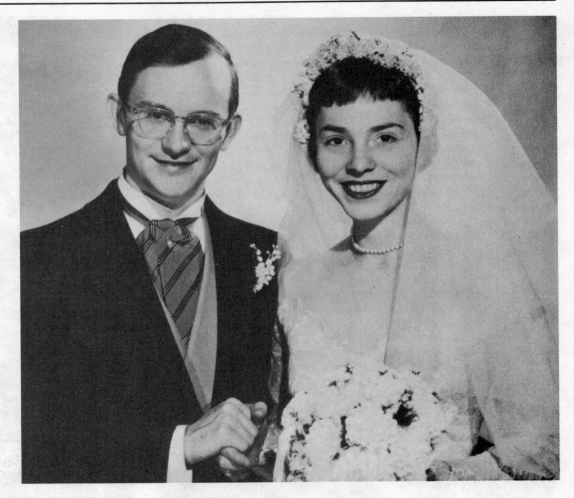

Mr. Peepers *made its debut in 1952. One of the biggest TV events of 1954 was Wally Cox's marriage to Pat Benoit.*

Dave Garroway *hosted* Today *when it first came to television.*

1952

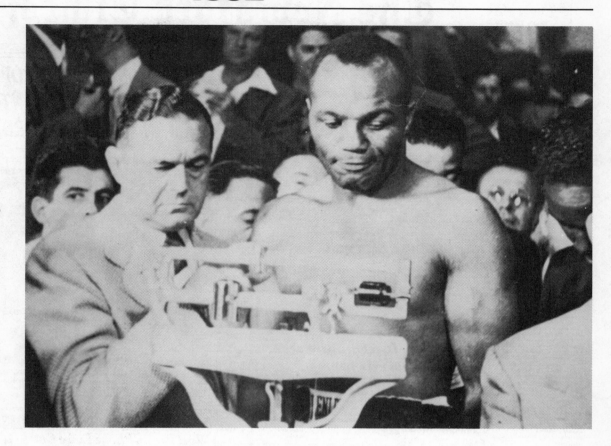

Jersey Joe Walcott seen here weighing in, lost the heavyweight title to Rocky Marciano.

Joe DiMaggio turned in his uniform to the Baseball Hall of Fame on Opening Day at Yankee Stadium in 1952.

"All the News That's Fit to Print"

The New York Times.

LATE CITY EDITION

Fair today; some showers tonight. Fair and not so warm tomorrow.

Temperature Range Today—Max., 72; Min., 58
Temperatures Yesterday—Max., 75; Min., 58
Full U. S. Weather Bureau Report, Page 39

Copyright, 1952, by The New York Times Company.

VOL. CI..No. 34,458.

Entered as Second-Class Matter,
Post Office, New York, N. Y.

NEW YORK, WEDNESDAY, MAY 28, 1952.

Times Square, New York 36, N. Y.
Telephone Lackawanna 4-1000

FIVE CENTS

JERSEY CITY MAYOR ON STAND 3 HOURS IN PIER CRIME STUDY

Kenny Questioned by New York Commission About Meeting of March 14 With Strollo

RYAN DENIES STRIKE PLAN

Proskauer Says Inquiry Has Provided Basis for Expose of Waterfront Conditions

By ALEXANDER FEINBERG

Mayor John V. Kenny of Jersey City was questioned for three hours yesterday by the State Crime Commission concerning his meeting in a New York hotel on March 14 with Anthony Strollo, alias Tony Bender. District Attorney Frank Hogan, who disclosed the meeting, had characterized Strollo as "a notorious underworld character whose gangster influence extends over northern New Jersey and lower Manhattan."

In another facet of the inquiry into waterfront conditions, Joseph P. Ryan, president of the International Longshoremen's Association, A. F. L., was called to the commission's offices at 270 Broadway for questioning on published reports that a strike threat on the Brooklyn piers had forced the withdrawal of subpoenas issued for longshoremen in the inquiry. Mr. Ryan disclaimed any such threat.

Overshadowing both appearances in long-range importance was official indication that after six months of intensive effort the groundwork has been laid for disclosing conditions existing on the 700 miles of New York-New Jersey waterfront.

Proskauer Discusses Plans

"We are collecting testimony and taking evidence which for the first time I think will disclose to what extent commerce is being diverted from New York by reason of abuses on the waterfront," former Supreme Court Justice Joseph M. Proskauer, chairman of the commission, said.

"We are particularly investigating," he added, "the relationship of union administration, and more particularly the administration of so-called locals, in connection with the difficulties that have arisen on the waterfront."

At hearings this fall, he said, the commission hopes to formulate "a report that will deal with these elements—crime on the waterfront" and what should be done with regard to the rehabilitation of the docks and piers of the whole port; and what procedure should be followed with respect to the methods of hiring, and also with respect to the relationship between the international and the local unions.

Mayor Kenny's appearance followed an exchange of letters with the commission. On April 18 the Court of General Sessions authorized Mr. Hogan to make available to the commission the prosecutor's affidavit reciting details of the Mayor's grand jury testimony. In his affidavit Mr. Hogan said that Strollo, an "associate" of Joe Adonis, Albert Anastasia, Frank Costello, Mike Coppola and Abner (Longie) Zwillman, among others, had "fixed" a strike called after Mayor Kenny had barred Dominick Strollo, Tony's brother, a

Continued on Page 32, Column 4

Musicians U. S. Bans Lose Toronto Posts

By HOWARD TAUBMAN
Special to The New York Times.

TORONTO, May 27—The rigid functioning of the United States Internal Security Act, known as the McCarran Act, has led the board of the Toronto Symphony Orchestra to dismiss six musicians, has stirred differences of opinion within the board on a matter of principle and has involved the Canadian Embassy in Washington in discussions with the State Department.

J. W. Elton, manager of the Toronto Symphony, said today that the orchestra did not wish to dismiss the musicians. As far as the management is concerned, they are good instrumentalists, they have violated no Canadian laws and there is no evidence that they are security risks.

A majority of the board members present at an emergency meeting held yesterday voted to support the management's decision not to renew the contracts of the six players, but they did so reluctantly. A minority, which indicated that the issue was not closed, apparently was opposed to knuckling

Continued on Page 35, Column 2

Taft and Eisenhower Forces Name Rival Slates in Texas

National Convention Must Rule on Claims —Backers of General Stage Walkout —He Gets 20 Connecticut Delegates

By W. H. LAWRENCE
Special to The New York Times.

MINERAL WELLS, Tex., May 27—Texas Republicans split into two conventions today and nominated rival slates of thirty-eight delegates to contest for recognition before the Chicago nominating convention.

One slate was predominantly for General of the Army Dwight D. Eisenhower, whose backers had piled up undisputed majorities in Republican precinct and county conventions, and the other was weighted in favor of Senator Robert A. Taft of Ohio, who had the backing of the "Old Guard" faction in this state.

The Eisenhower group was instructed to cast thirty-three votes for the general and five for Senator Taft. Technically, the other slate was "uninstructed" but Taft leaders said thirty to thirty-four members would vote for the Ohio Senator on the first ballot and General Eisenhower would have four to eight votes.

[The Republican state convention in Connecticut gave General Eisenhower twenty of its delegates to the national convention. The two others were uncommitted but had been privately indicated a preference for the general. William A. Purtell of West Hartford was nominated for the Senate by acclamation.]

Backers of General Eisenhower staged a noisy walkout from the regular Texas convention after the pro-Taft leaders had utilized their control of convention machinery to deny seats to Eisenhower men on the ground they had not been elected by "known Republicans."

Of 606 contested delegates from thirty-one of Texas' 254 counties, including all the large cities, only ten pro-Eisenhower delegates finally were seated. This followed hearings before the Republican State Executive Committee that lasted nearly twenty hours.

The action of the pro-Taft

Continued on Page 24, Column 1

Council Votes Taxi Fare Rise As Isaacs Demands Inquiry

By CHARLES G. BENNETT

The bill to raise taxi fares 27 per cent was passed yesterday by the City Council amid demands by two Councilmen that the entire taxicab industry in the city be investigated. The vote was 21 to 1, with one not voting.

In an atmosphere charged with the controversy that the taxi bill has generated at City Hall, Minority Leader Stanley M. Isaacs, Manhattan Republican-Liberal, demanded that any inquiry into the industry include "the relationship of the Police Department to the cab companies."

Mr. Isaacs charged that there was "something wrong about the way taxis are handled on the streets of New York. He wanted to know "why the police will not approve smaller taxicabs and why sharing of taxis by passengers is not permitted."

Voting on the Bill

Mr. Isaacs voted against the measure, while Mr. Quinn voted for it because, he said, friends among the independent cab operators had pleaded that they needed the increased fares "in order to keep from going under."

"But," Mr. Quinn shouted, "the industry stinks to high heaven and should be investigated. I told my friends that the fleet owners were making pawns and fools of them. I told them the fleets were using them for the fleets' own purposes."

On the roll-call, Councilman Samuel Davis, Manhattan Democrat, refrained from voting. Majority Leader Joseph T. Sharkey, Brooklyn Democrat, read a letter from Councilman Earl Brown, Manhattan Democrat, who was out of the city, saying he would have voted against the increase.

The bill must be passed by the Board of Estimate and signed by Mayor Impellitteri before it becomes law. It would raise taxi fares from the present 20 cents for the first quarter-mile and 5 cents for each additional quarter-mile to 25 cents for the first fifth-mile and 5 cents for each additional fifth.

The charge for waiting time

Continued on Page 41, Column 2

M'GRANERY SWORN, BARS 'WITCH-HUNT'

Perlman, at Ceremony, Scores 'Character Assassins' Among Justice Department Critics

By LEWIS WOOD
Special to The New York Times.

WASHINGTON, May 27—James Patrick McGranery was sworn in as Attorney General today after a vigorous defense of the Department of Justice by Solicitor General Philip B. Perlman. Mr. Perlman denounced "character assassins" among critics of the department and demanded that the "defamers be driven back into their holes."

The Solicitor General's remarks reflected the attitude of the Administration on what it deemed unjust criticism. Mr. Perlman drew hearty applause from about 3,000 persons in the Great Hall of the department.

Chief Justice Fred M. Vinson administered the oath. Mr. McGranery promised that violators of the law would be "apprehended, prosecuted and convicted," regardless of their position, in his pledged clean-up drive. This would be accomplished, he said, with due process of constitutional rights.

Will Avoid 'Terror-Harvest'

"This will be done," he added, "without the terror-harvest of the witch-hunt, and without the tumult and chaos that follows in the wake of scare headlines and in the wake of reckless charges and baseless accusations."

A few hours after Mr. McGranery's induction, it was disclosed that the Department of Justice had asked the Federal Bureau of Investigation to try to determine whether Representative Reva Beck Bosone, Democrat of Utah, had unlawfully accepted campaign contributions from two employes of her office.

A spokesman said the request for F. B. I. action preceded the swearing-in ceremony. The new Attorney General was asked about the case at his news conference, and replied he did not know anything about it.

Mrs. Bosone has confirmed that on her 1950 campaign contribution report she listed a gift of $400 from her secretary, Virginia Rishel, and another of $230 from her stenographer, Gayle Snow.

The Representative, an Administration supporter who is running for re-election, said she did not know that such contributions were made voluntarily, violated the Corrupt Practices Act. This law provides a maximum $500 fine and three years' imprisonment for any member of Congress who "directly or indirectly solicits, receives or is paid any money for any political purpose" from a Government employe.

Ovations were given to three former

Continued on Page 15, Column 1

SENATE STAVES OFF 2D BILLION AID CUT; NEW TEST UP TODAY

Taft Group, Defeated 35 to 27, to Ask Half-Billion Slash— Douglas, Carlson for It

DEMOCRATS DELAY VOTE

George Would Pare Domestic Military Budget for Saving —Harriman in Urgent Plea

By FELIX BELAIR Jr.
Special to The New York Times.

WASHINGTON, May 27—The Senate rejected by a vote of 35 to 27 today an attempt to slash a second $1,000,000,000 from the Mutual Security program. But the same group of adherents to Senator Robert A. Taft, Republican of Ohio and Presidential aspirant, who sponsored the proposal were preparing a second assault tomorrow that would cut the authorization by $500,000,000.

As it now stands, the measure would authorize $6,920,962,000 in the fiscal year 1953 to provide weapons, materials and equipment and technical assistance to free nations resisting Communist aggression and subversion. President Truman has asked for $7,900,000,000 and has denounced efforts to reduce the amount.

The vote sustaining the recommendation of the Foreign Relations Committee came after a warning from Senator Tom Connally, Democrat of Texas and chairman of the committee, that the proposal would "force a reconsideration of the whole defense set-up in Western Europe."

New Test Postponed

Administration leaders forced a postponement of voting on the $500,000,000 cut after it became apparent that some members on both sides of the aisle who had voted against the $1,000,000,000 reduction would accept the smaller slash. Among these were Senator Paul H. Douglas, Democrat of Illinois, and Senator Frank Carlson, Republican of Kansas and backer of General of the Army Dwight D. Eisenhower for the Republican Presidential nomination.

While the Senate Democratic Policy Committee was meeting to decide its strategy for turning back the second slashing amendment, W. Averell Harriman, Director for Mutual Security, appealed to the Senate in a statement issued by his office here to restore the cuts below the $6,900,000,000 level voted on the floor of the House of Representatives.

"But a further cut, such as that made on the floor of the House and such as is now being advocated by some Senators," he declared, "would seriously jeopardize North Atlantic Treaty Organization plans for building up forces to deter Soviet aggression or to meet it if it comes.

"I cannot believe that the American people want to barter their security for phony economy.

"It is phony economy to vote against funds which enable our Allies to raise forces and make their own weapons, when the re-

Continued on Page 6, Column 3

SIX NATIONS SIGN EUROPEAN ARMY PACT; U. S., BRITAIN GUARANTEE COMMUNITY; GERMAN REDS SET BORDER BUFFER ZONE

AT SIGNING OF EUROPEAN ARMY TREATY IN PARIS

Diplomats gathered at the Quai d'Orsay yesterday. Left to right, are Foreign Secretary Anthony Eden of Britain; Chancellor Konrad Adenauer of West Germany; Paul van Zeeland, Belgian Foreign Minister; Robert Schuman, Foreign Minister of France; Alcide De Gasperi, Premier of Italy; Joseph Bech, Foreign Minister of Luxembourg; Dirk U. Stikker, Foreign Minister of the Netherlands, and Secretary of State Dean Acheson.

Associated Press Radiophoto

Zonal Barrier 3 Miles Deep; West Berlin Phone Lines Cut

By WALTER SULLIVAN
Special to The New York Times.

BERLIN, May 27—The Soviet Union and the East German Government began today to build two walls—one around West Berlin and the other between East and West Germany. The East German Government decreed a prohibited zone three miles deep along its 600-mile border with West Germany. It also sliced Berlin's telephone system in two and cut most of the city's telephone lines to West Germany.

Soviet troops halted all Allied highway patrols that sought to enter the autobahn connecting Berlin with the West with one exception. A patrol jeep that was passed was backed up by three truckloads of troops from the United States Sixth Infantry Division, who were said to have been in full battle regalia.

No official explanation of this action was available from United States sources. It appeared, however, that its objective was to determine whether or not the Russians would let a military convoy, as opposed to routine highway patrols, use the autobahn.

Earlier this month Soviet authorities gave the Allies a preview of their present tactic. They halted routine highway patrols but allowed military police jeeps identical with those used in the patrols to pass if escorting a truck convoy. Thus the United States today apparently was not trying to make a show of force.

Other Traffic Is Unimpeded

Apart from the highway patrols, which are intended to aid Allied vehicles and personnel in difficulties, there was no unusual interference with traffic between Berlin and West Germany. Soviet jet planes swooped over the city during the day but there were no reports of trouble along the air corridors from the west. The activity of the Soviet fighters perhaps was slightly more than normal.

The question in every West Berliner's mind was how high the walls around the Western sectors of the city would be built. Berlin now is divided as New York would be if that portion below Forty-second Street were under Soviet control and the rest under Western administration.

During the night the telephone system was secretly divided so that in the morning when a West Berliner dialed any number in East Berlin he got a busy signal. The city's subway and elevated railway systems continued to operate on a city-wide basis.

Western officials, however, said the discharge by the East Berlin Railway Administration of 300 rail workers who resided in West Berlin might presage a further division.

Except for the stoppage of the highway patrols, which was done without explanation by the Russians, all the wall-building was

Continued on Page 15, Column 6

VAN FLEET CONFERS WITH RHEE ON ACTS

Arrest of Legislators Prompts Visit—Assembly Votes, 96-3, to End Pusan Martial Law

By MURRAY SCHUMACH

HEADQUARTERS, Eighth Army, in Korea, May 27—Gen. James A. Van Fleet, commander of the Eighth Army, conferred today with South Korean President Syngman Rhee about the bitter feud between the President and the Republic's National Assembly.

The chief reason behind the battle between President Rhee and his Assembly is the strong indication in recent weeks that the National Assembly is opposed to the re-election of Dr. Rhee. The President is chosen by the National Assembly and elections are slated for late next month.

[The Associated Press reported that the Assembly voted Tuesday, 96 to 3, to lift martial law in Pusan, overriding Dr. Rhee on this matter.]

After eight National Assemblymen had been thrown into jail on obscure charges, General Van Fleet and Alan E. Lightner, coun-

Continued on Page 3, Column 4

ALLIES TO LET BONN MAKE SOME ARMS

Artillery and Tanks Allowed —Planes and Atomic and Chemical Weapons Banned

Special to The New York Times.

PARIS, May 27—When the European Defense Community is finally established soon the ratification of the historic treaty signed here today, Western Germany will not be permitted to manufacture atomic, bacteriological and chemical weapons or magnetic mines. It furthermore has pledged itself to refrain from making any type of aircraft, civil or military.

However, the Bonn Republic will be allowed to fabricate tanks and artillery of all sizes as well as lighter arms. It will be permitted to conduct atomic research and experiments for civilian purposes.

Furthermore, in that region of Germany west of the Rhine river—which includes Cologne, Krefeld, Bonn, Coblenz, Bingen, Mainz and Ludwigshafen—it will manufacture explosives and propellants as well as shortrange (anti-aircraft) guided missiles.

West Germany stated in a unilateral letter from Chancellor Konrad Adenauer to the Western Big Three occupying powers that when the prevailing restrictive clauses prohibiting aircraft manufacture could be re-examined after differing conditions, it would do so in concordance with the United States, Britain and France.

The Bonn Government promised to limit its civilian atomic experimental installations to a production of 500 grams of fissionable material a year and to restrict its uranium production or importation annually to nine tons, or to a

Continued on Page 12, Column 3

BONN WILL BE ALLY

Tied to Atlantic Treaty —All Troops to Wear Same Uniform

ACHESON HAILS THE EVENT

Difficulties Seen in Gaining Approval of Parliaments and From Soviet Reaction

Summary of treaty and texts of two statements, Page 14.

By HAROLD CALLENDER
Special to The New York Times.

PARIS, May 27—The foreign ministers of eight Western countries and representatives of seven others gathered today in the famous Clock Room of the French Foreign Office a series of documents to create and guarantee a single unified European defense force and through it to bind Western Germany with the Atlantic defense system and with a gradually uniting Western Europe.

This ceremony was the sequel to that in Bonn yesterday when the foreign ministers of the United States, Britain, France and the West German Republic signed a virtual peace treaty with West Germany in the form of a Contractual Agreement giving that country a new and almost sovereign status on condition that it enter the six-nation European Defense Community, the charter of which was signed today.

The foundation of this community is to be a military alliance between France and West Germany which has no counterpart in modern times, unless it be the alliance between Napoleon and Prussia against Russia at the beginning of the nineteenth century.

One Uniform for Forces

The combined European defense force, or army, will be composed of conscripts as well as regular troops wearing a common uniform.

Into the alliance are to enter Italy, the Netherlands, Belgium and Luxembourg. But the indispensable core of it—as of its predecessor, the Schuman plan for merging the coal and steel resources of six European nations—could only be the alliance of the two major Continental nations of Western Europe that so long had been bitter foes.

The European Defense Community therefore represents a revolutionary project not only because it presupposes a defensive alliance of which France and Western Germany will form the nucleus, but also because the treaty to create it outlines steps to be taken to form a closer political union of European nations beginning with the six that signed the treaty today.

Supporting this community with guarantees of its security are to be the territory are the United States and Britain, personified at today's ceremony by Secretary of State Dean Acheson and Foreign Secretary Anthony Eden.

Mr. Acheson and Mr. Eden sat at opposite ends of the table at which sat the foreign ministers of the six uniting Continental countries, as if symbolizing the fact

Continued on Page 15, Column 1

Center Has Edge in Italian Election But Loses Heavily in Popular Vote

Special to The New York Times.

ROME, May 27—The latest returns tonight showed the Center parties, headed by the Christian Democrats, running ahead of their Left-Wing and Right-Wing rivals in the provincial and municipal elections that took place in Central and Southern Italy last Sunday and Monday, but the Center parties lost heavily in the popular vote compared with the general election of 1948.

The election results show that, as far as the main struggle between the Christian Democrats and Left-Wing parties is concerned, the political situation in Italy has relapsed to about what it was in 1947 and before—that is to say before the Marshall Plan and other forms of American aid that succeeded it were in effect.

Although the Center parties captured a majority of the Provincial and Municipal Councils their total force in votes is expected to be close to 1,000,000.

A part of the votes lost by Christian Democrats has gone to the Left-Wing parties, which have increased their strength over what it was four years ago, but by far a greater part went to the Right-

This applies. These emerge from the election as a powerful third force which, at least in Central and Southern Italy, is approximately as strong as the Christian Democrats and the Left-Wing parties.

This seems to indicate that the $1,300,000,000 that the United States has invested in Italian political stability through the Eco-

Continued on Page 6, Column 5

RED REPRISAL AGAINST WEST GERMAN PACT

A lone operator at work at the only switchboard in operation in Berlin Exchange after the Communists cut off telephone communications between East and West Berlin and 17 long-distance lines between West Berlin and West Germany.

Associated Press Radiophoto

1952

In 1952, The Roy Rogers Show, *which starred Rogers and his* *wife Dale Evans, was in its second season.*

Hopalong Cassidy *was an enormously popular early western* *series. "Hoppy" was played by William Boyd.*

Jack Webb starred as Dragnet's *Sergeant Joe Friday. He was also the* *director and wrote many of the scripts. He is seen here with Officer* *Frank Smith.*

"All the News That's Fit to Print"

The New York Times.

LATE CITY EDITION
Fair today; some cloudiness tonight. Becoming fair tomorrow.
Temperature Range—Max., 72; Min., 60
Temperature Yesterday—Max., 81; Min., 58
Full U. S. Weather Bureau Report, Page 39

Copyright, 1952, by The New York Times Company.

VOL. CI..No. 34,464.   Entered as Second-Class Matter, Post Office, New York, N. Y.   NEW YORK, TUESDAY, JUNE 3, 1952.   Times Square, New York 36, N. Y. Telephone LAckawanna 4-1000   FIVE CENTS

SUPREME COURT VOIDS STEEL SEIZURE, 6 TO 3; HOLDS TRUMAN USURPED POWERS OF CONGRESS; WORKERS AGAIN STRIKE AS MILLS ARE RETURNED

SWIFT SENATE VOTE ON BONN ACCORDS IS ASKED BY TRUMAN

Message Calls Defense Moves in Europe 'Great Forward Stride' Toward Peace

ACHESON REPORTS TO U. S.

Both President and Secretary Declare Soviet Measures Will Not Deter the West

Truman message and Acheson address are on Page 8.

By WALTER H. WAGGONER
Special to The New York Times.

WASHINGTON, June 2—President Truman urged the Senate today to approve two agreements putting West Germany on a footing of equality among nations and binding as enemy of World War II to the free world's defense alliance.

Asking for "early and favorable" action on the two pacts, signed by the diplomats of the Western Governments in Europe last week, the President said in a message to the Senate that the documents taken together "constitute a great forward stride toward strengthening peace and freedom in the world."

Accompanying his message were the so-called peace contract with West Germany, an arrangement just short of a formal treaty, and an amendment to the North Atlantic Treaty that would extend its defense guarantees to the Bonn Government in return for reciprocal pledges. Both require approval by the Senate to become effective.

European Pact Also Sent

For the Senate's information, Mr. Truman also attached a number of other documents signed in either Paris or Bonn, the major one being the treaty constituting the six-nation European Defense Community that would bring West German troops into a European army.

[In Bonn, Germany, Dr. Kurt Schumacher, Social Democratic leader, began the Opposition's campaign against ratification of the defense arrangements. He said that under the present terms the Germans would bear the brunt of the burdens involved in those accords while the Western Allies would enjoy the benefits.]

Even before the President's message arrived, Senator Tom Connally, the Texas Democrat who heads the Senate Foreign Relations Committee, predicted that the Senate would give Mr. Truman the approval he sought.

The Senator's forecast was made on the basis of two hours of discussion, at a joint session of the Senate Foreign Relations and House Foreign Affairs Committee, with Secretary of State Dean Acheson.

Mr. Acheson, meanwhile, went directly to the American people for understanding and support of the new agreements, addressing the nation by radio and television this evening on the nature and necessity of the new line-up of allies.

As President Truman had done, Mr. Acheson stressed the "very great stake" held by the United States in helping support and build the joint defenses of the free world as rapidly as possible, he said in a statement.

Secretary Acheson, meanwhile, went directly to the American people for understanding and support of the new agreements, addressing the nation by radio and television this evening on the nature and necessity of the new line-up of allies.

Mr. Acheson said that Mr. Acheson had assured the committees that "no secret or undisclosed commitments or guarantees" were made while he was on his European mission that produced the agreements.

Connally to Speed Action

The Senate's foreign policy spokesman said it was important that the treaties "go into effect as soon as possible" and he made it plain that he would do his part in speeding Senate action.

"In my view it is essential that Western Germany be accorded its proper place in the family of nations without delay so that we can proceed with the task of building the joint defenses of the free world as rapidly as possible," he said in a statement.

Continued on Page 8, Column 3

Red Leader Named Premier of Rumania

By The United Press.

BUCHAREST, Rumania, June 2—The National Assembly proclaimed Gheorghe Gheorghiu-Dej as new Premier of Rumania today to succeed Dr. Petru Groza, who was named President of the republic.

M. Gheorghiu-Dej was named Premier by a unanimous vote. Dr. Groza, who had been Premier since March 6, 1945, was elected President of the Assembly, a post tantamount to President of the republic.

The Government changes followed a request from the former President, Dr. Constantin Parhon, that he be relieved of his functions so he could dedicate himself entirely to his scientific work.

The Assembly took no action regarding Mme. Ana Pauker.

[The Bucharest radio revealed last week that Mme. Pauker, Rumanian Foreign Minister, had

Continued on Page 15, Column 2

ALLIES TERM TRUCE UP TO FOE IN KOREA

Reds Are Told World Opinion Will Judge Refusal to Agree to New Poll of Captives

By LINDESAY PARROTT
Special to The New York Times.

TOKYO, Tuesday, June 3—Maj. Gen. William K. Harrison Jr., senior United Nations truce delegate, told the Communists today: "The entire future of the armistice negotiations is now up to your side."

He warned the Chinese and North Koreans that the "court of world opinion" would judge their refusal to entertain the United Nations proposal that prisoners of war should be questioned by an impartial body in the presence of Communist representatives after a truce to determine how many wished to return to their former command.

General Harrison spoke during a thirty-minute session in the gravest warning given so far that the world would hold the Communists responsible for a delay in the truce and the failure of prisoners to return to their homes.

Outlining the proposal for "rescreening" of the prisoners, made after the enemy had challenged the result of an Allied poll that showed fewer than half the total wished to be freed to engage in such

Continued on Page 3, Column 3

Another Prisoner on Koje Is Killed; Clark Set to Use Force on Captives

By GEORGE BARRETT
Special to The New York Times.

KOJE ISLAND, Korea, Tuesday, June 3—The accidental firing by an Allied soldier of a heavy machine gun near a prison stockade on this island killed one North Korean captive and wounded another this morning.

This mishap followed a statement yesterday by the new Far East Commander, Gen. Mark W. Clark, that Allied camp authorities were prepared to use "maximum force" to restore uncontested control over Communist captives.

An Army spokesman said that the North Korean who was killed had been standing near the barbed wire of Compound 78 when the machine gun went off. Other prisoners dragged the body farther inside the enclosure and refused to surrender it to United Nations medical personnel. They also refused to yield the wounded man for hospitalization.

Gen. James A. Van Fleet, Eighth Army commander, who came with General Clark, compared the atmosphere in seventeen compounds with the captives' mood of only a few weeks ago and happily summed up the situation that way.

In a late development last night there was a sudden flare-up of resistances, in which the camp enclosures, to which the camp command had attempted to put an end. In Compound 76 captive North Koreans held a mock funeral, commemorating the five prisoners who were killed there last Friday. They hung black crepe

Continued on Page 3, Column 2

EISENHOWER YIELDS PAY IN RETIREMENT; FREE TO CAMPAIGN

He Leaves Army Duties Today —Waives $19,541 a Year to Avert Any Criticism

DECORATED BY PRESIDENT

Truman Hails Him as Symbol of Nation's Aim—General to Leave for Abilene

By JAMES RESTON
Special to The New York Times.

WASHINGTON, June 2—General of the Army Dwight D. Eisenhower has asked to be placed on the Army's retired list without pay, starting tomorrow. This request, which the Army said today had been approved by Secretary of Defense Robert A. Lovett, will release the general from the Army's regulations against political campaigning.

The current military appropriations legislation does not permit officers under the age of 62 to retire with pay unless the Department of Defense finds that this would cause personal hardship or be bad for the service.

[In South Dakota and California the final primaries will be held Tuesday, with the Dakota contest between General Eisenhower and Senator Robert A. Taft of Ohio attracting major attention. On the Democratic side, Senator Estes Kefauver is seeking delegates in both primaries. The Missouri Republican convention completed the formalities of naming a twenty-six-member delegation.]

General Eisenhower wrote to Mr. Lovett on May 28, asking that no special certification be made in his case, because his name was "directly involved in the national political campaign." The general, who is 61, would have been entitled to $19,541 a year in pay and allowances if, like General of the Army Douglas MacArthur, he had remained on the active list.

From his European headquarters, General Eisenhower wrote:

"There are a number of delegates already pledged to seek my nomination as the Republican Presidential candidate and, in the normal course of events, I will be talking to some of these delegates prior to the National Convention. As an officer on the retired list I would feel free to engage in such

Continued on Page 19, Column 1

TWO IMPORTANT STEPS YESTERDAY IN THE STEEL DISPUTE

Secretary of Commerce Charles Sawyer signing formal order returning nation's steel plants to owners.

Philip Murray, C. I. O. and steel union president, making call that sent 600,000 workers on strike.
Associated Press Wirephotos

REALTY TAX TO RISE 12 TO 15 POINTS HERE

Final Valuations Show Record City Rate of $3.08 Probably Will Soar to $3.21

By PETER KIHSS

A rise of twelve to fifteen points in the city's basic real estate tax rate of $3.08, already the highest in history, was forecast unofficially yesterday when the final valuations of taxable real estate and special franchises were set at $19,425,499,087 for the fiscal year beginning July 1.

The revised valuations were $58,392,794 less than the tentative valuations made public Feb. 1, but $648,742,541 above the final figure of $18,776,756,546 for the current tax year. The total was the second highest in the city's history, exceeded only by 1932's $19,616,-915,429.

While no city official would go on record with a tax forecast, pending a revised estimate of general fund revenues due from Controller Lazarus Joseph on June 20, the pencils flew at City Hall to make some approximations based on Mayor Impellitteri's budget message of April 1.

Mayor's Estimate of Need

The Mayor had estimated then that the new $1,469,265,102 expense budget would need a yield of $622,804,788 from real estate taxes. The Mayor reported that this was practically the maximum that could be levied on real estate within constitutional limitations.

Dividing this proposed yield by the final realty valuations would give a basic tax rate of nearly $3.21 for each $100 of assessed valuation, or thirteen points above the rate that has prevailed this year and last. Above this come borough rates, which this year have varied from 18 to 21 cents.

Municipal fiscal experts indicated this $3.21 basic tax rate approximation might still vary slightly, depending on revisions in the general fund. But they noted that the original general fund estimate had included $12,500,000 from an overnight parking tax, which the Mayor has been unable to get.

The main hopes in fiscal quarters appeared to be for rises in other general fund sources that might at least make up the loss from the parking tax estimate. In any event, each point in the real estate levy yields not quite $2,000,000.

The final realty valuations were transmitted to the Mayor by William E. Boyland, president of the seven-member Tax Commission. They consist of: ordinary real estate at $16,846,784,544, up $583,300,800 from last year; real estate of utility corporations at $1,738,-555,835, up $54,006,318, and special

Continued on Page 46, Column 7

600,000 Quit Steel Mills; Industry Offers to Bargain

By A. H. RASKIN

PITTSBURGH, June 2—The steel industry got its mills back today, but they were producing no steel. Six hundred thousand members of the United Steelworkers of America, C. I. O., quit work as soon as they learned that the Supreme Court had ruled against Government seizure of the steel plants.

Many did not wait even for formal strike orders from their union president, Philip Murray. They simply put aside their tools and streamed out of mills that normally produce 95 per cent of the country's steel. All who stayed were supervisors and maintenance men engaged in the orderly cooling of blast furnaces to prevent permanent damage to equipment.

CONGRESS HAILS END OF STEEL SEIZURE

Some Demand Constitutional Curb on President—Censure of Truman Is Hinted

By C. P. TRUSSELL
Special to The New York Times.

WASHINGTON, June 2—Congress generally hailed today the Supreme Court's 6-3 decision holding President Truman's seizure of the steel industry unconstitutional.

Many at the Capitol held to the view that Mr. Truman still had ample legal power to invoke the Taft-Hartley Act, which he has sought unsuccessfully to have repealed, and to let its injunctions against strikes settle the problem. There was much speculation as to whether the President now would invoke that law.

Prompt Congressional action to meet the problem of the steel walkout was in doubt, however. Demands were made that the court's verdict be clinched, either by giving the President the powers he thought he had, or by writing into the Constitution a prohibition against the use of seizure powers without specific backing in law.

Committee Meets Tomorrow

A House Judiciary subcommittee that has on its docket a dozen or so measures to impeach Mr. Truman, to censure him or to give him powers or deprive him of them was scheduled to meet Wednesday, it appeared tonight that it might recommend a censure on top of today's court defeat.

On the Senate calendar today was a bill that would amend the Constitution to bar the President from seizing any private property except under specific law.

This measure was "passed over." Its sponsor, Senator Pat McCarran, Democrat of Nevada and chairman of the Senate Judiciary Committee, was across the Plaza hearing the police of the East Thirty-fifth Street station and H. G. Brownson, vice president in charge of the Supreme Court's decisions.

Senator Homer E. Ferguson, Republican of Michigan, obtained the Senate's unanimous consent for the McCarran bill to remain on the calendar with no prejudice.

A single objection, under the rules of the calendar, could block a proposed Constitutional amendment under this procedure.

Another measure, sponsored by Senator Wayne Morse, Republican of Oregon, would provide Presidential

Continued on Page 22, Column 2

NEXT MOVE IN CRISIS IS CALLED TRUMAN'S

President Could Use Taft Act or Appeal to Congress—No Word From White House

By ANTHONY LEVIERO
Special to The New York Times.

WASHINGTON, June 2—With steel workers walking out of mills all over the country in the wake of the decision of the United States Supreme Court today nullifying the President's seizure of the industry, the next move was held to be up to Mr. Truman.

There was no indication from the White House tonight, however, as to what he might do. Meanwhile, Mr. Truman and his advisers were studying the seven opinions of the high tribunal.

Two obvious steps were presumably being considered by Mr. Truman.

The first would be to invoke the Taft-Hartley Act, which would require the union men to return to work for eighty days while a factfinding board prepared the wage dispute. The other move might be a renewal of the plea that Mr. Truman addressed to Congress soon after the seizure for specific statutory authority to deal with labor disputes in major industries in time of emergency.

In the courts and in Congress Mr. Truman has been severely criticized for not having used the Taft law that labor hates before he resorted to seizure. His answer has been that the steel workers had waited ninety-nine days while the Wage Stabilization Board studied the wage dispute.

Continued on Page 22, Column 7

Speedy Action by a Teller Foils Hold-Up in East 42d Street Bank

A would-be bank robber who escaped although three armed guards were near by was foiled yesterday in an attempt to hold up the Irving Trust Company at 100 East Forty-second Street by an alert 27-year-old teller, described by his superiors in the bank as a "guy with real guts."

This was the story as it was pieced together from accounts by the police of the East Thirty-fifth Street station and H. G. Brownson, vice president in charge of the bank's Forty-second Street office at Pershing Square:

At 2:50 P. M., an hour and ten minutes before the bank's closing time, a man about 45 years old, dressed in a gray suit and wearing a dark felt hat, approached a teller's cage about 100 feet from the Forty-second Street entrance to the bank.

There were 125 employes on duty, including the armed guards, and fifteen persons on the bank

floor, which is in the second story of the Continental Can Building.

The cage the man approached was occupied by Charles Lehanka of 460 Audubon Avenue, who has worked in the bank for a little more than a year.

Without a word, the man handed to Mr. Lehanka a two-page note. The writing was a combination of lettering and script and was done in pencil on unlined paper.

Mr. Lehanka read only the first couple of sentences of the 135-word message. They said: "Don't press the alarm button if you value your life. Give me all the folding money you have in that cage."

At this point, Mr. Lehanka made a swift and courageous action. He dropped to the floor and pressed the bank alarm, which sounded at Police Headquarters

Continued on Page 26, Column 4

BLACK GIVES RULING

President Cannot Make Law in Good or Bad Times, Majority Says

VINSON IS DISSENTER

Rejects Idea Executive Is 'Messenger Boy' in Crisis—Steel Curbed

The majority opinion, Page 22; others in part, Pages 22 and 23.

By JOSEPH A. LOFTUS
Special to The New York Times.

WASHINGTON, June 2—The Supreme Court of the United States ruled, 6 to 3, today that President Truman's seizure of the steel industry to avert a strike violated the Constitution by usurping the legislative powers reserved to Congress.

The President bowed promptly by directing Secretary of Commerce Charles Sawyer to release the properties to their private owners, and the United Steelworkers of America, C. I. O., went on strike.

As a result of the walkout the Government ordered a halt in deliveries of steel from steel warehouses to consumer goods producers in an effort to conserve steel for defense needs.

Authorities said the action was directed at preventing a drain on warehouses by buyers who usually got their steel at the mills. Manufacturers who ordinarily receive steel from warehouses will continue to do so, they added. No order was issued against steel exports.

The Supreme Court justices who voted to uphold District Judge David A. Pine's order dispossessing the Government were: Hugo L. Black, Felix Frankfurter, William O. Douglas, Robert H. Jackson, Harold H. Burton and Tom C. Clark.

Dissenting were: Chief Justice Fred M. Vinson and Justices Stanley F. Reed and Sherman Minton.

Founding Fathers' Action Cited

The court ruled in effect that when the President seized the steel mills he seized the lawmaking power, because only Congress could authorize the taking of private property for public use.

The Constitution did not subject this law-making power of Congress to Presidential or military supervision or control," said the opinion of the court, written by Justice Black.

The founders of this nation entrusted the lawmaking power to the Congress alone in both good and bad times," it added. "It would do no good to recall the historical events, the years of power and the struggle for freedom that lay behind their choice. Such a review would but confirm our holding that this seizure order cannot stand."

Chief Justice Vinson, writing a vigorous dissent, declared that the President's action to keep steel flowing was warranted by the world emergency.

"History bears out the genius of the founding fathers, who created a Government subject to law but not left subject to inertia when vigor and initiative are required," the Chief Justice wrote.

Vinson Criticizes Majority

"As the district judge stated this is no time for 'timorous' judicial action," he declared. "But neither is this a time for timorous executive action."

Chief Justice Vinson spoke for the majority of the court, not the minority, was seeking to amend the Constitution. He declared:

"The broad Executive power granted by Article II to an officer on duty 365 days a year cannot, it is said, be invoked to avert disaster.

"Instead, the President must confine himself to sending a message to Congress recommending action. Under this messenger-boy concept of the office, the President cannot even act to preserve legislative programs from destruction so that Congress will have something left to act upon.

The court, contrary to a widely

Continued on Page 22, Column 5

Kirk Douglas and Lana Turner in Vincente Minelli's film about film, The Bad and the Beautiful.

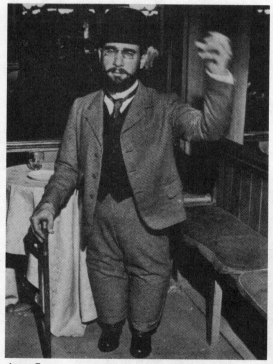

Jose Ferrer gave a stunning performance as Toulouse-Lautrec in Moulin Rouge.

Marilyn Monroe portrayed a mentally sick baby-sitter in Don't Bother to Knock.

One of Sid Caesar and Imogene Coca's most famous skits was a spoof of The Sheik, *Rudolf Valentino's famous love movie of the Twenties.*

The New York Times.

LATE CITY EDITION
Fair and warm today and tomorrow.
Temperature Range Today—Max., 85; Min., 64
Temperatures Yesterday—Max., 85; Min., 65
Full U. S. Weather Bureau Report, Page 29

Copyright, 1952, by The New York Times Company.

VOL. CI..No. 34,503.

Entered as Second-Class Matter,
Post Office, New York, N. Y.

NEW YORK, SATURDAY, JULY 12, 1952.

Times Square, New York 36, N. Y.
Telephone Lackawanna 4-1000

FIVE CENTS

EISENHOWER NOMINATED ON THE FIRST BALLOT; SENATOR NIXON CHOSEN AS HIS RUNNING MATE; GENERAL PLEDGES 'TOTAL VICTORY' CRUSADE

LONG U. N. AIR RAID POUNDS PYONGYANG AND REDS' BUILD-UP

Three-Wave Daylight Attack Is Followed by Smashing B-29 Blows at Night

NORTH'S CAPITAL AFLAME

Allied Land, Navy and Marine Fighter-Bombers Strike as Korea Truce Talks Drag On

By LINDESAY PARROTT
Special to The New York Times.

TOKYO, Saturday, July 12—Allied aircraft of many nations smashed yesterday at the North Korean capital at Pyongyang and the Communists' military build-up in western Korea in one of the largest and most devastating raids of the war.

Attacking in waves from 10 A. M. until late in the afternoon, the planes flew 1,200 sorties from ground bases and from the decks of United States and British carriers at sea.

Almost 600 tons of bombs fell on the daylight targets at Pyongyang and at Hwangju and Sariwon, on the rail line south of Pyongyang, where for months the Communist armies had stockpiled supplies of arms and munitions and placed military headquarters, communications centers and repair shops.

Meanwhile, the truce talks at Panmunjom continued, the secret sessions on the vexed prisoner question producing no indicated progress. A brief sitting was held this forenoon and another meeting was set for tomorrow.

Mass Night Strike

Last night, in what headquarters of the Far East Air Force here called the "largest night air strike of the Korean conflict," B-29 Superforts from Japanese and Okinawan bases returned to the Communist capital in a new blow. The medium bombers also fanned out over North Korea, hitting supply concentrations at Hamhung, on the east coast; Kyomipo, near Pyongyang, and Sinmak, to the north.

Fifty-four of the B-29's unloaded 540 tons of high explosives over Pyongyang, still blazing from the attack of it fighter-bombers during daylight. Industrial plants, vehicle parks and repair shops were reported hit, with "excellent" results.

Sixty-nine planes participated in the attacks throughout North Korea, with major concentration over selected targets at Pyongyang. The clouds that hung over the Pyongyang area during the afternoon had cleared at night and the bombardiers saw their projectiles fall in direct hits.

[Later, Far East Air Forces said one F-84 Thunderjet was lost in the day and night attacks, The Associated Press reported. All the Superforts returned safely to base. The F-84 was shot down by Communist ground fire. The report did not cover Navy or Marine or other Allied planes.]

Reds' Radio Makes Claim

The Reds' radio broadcast, on the air a few hours after the daylight strikes, claimed two Allied aircraft shot down.

No official estimate of the damage done in the day and night attacks had been made pending the study of aerial photographs taken from reconnaissance planes that followed close on the tails of the bombers.

Returning pilots spoke of huge secondary explosions that followed hits by bombs and rockets and big islands of fire raging last evening where hundreds of gallons of napalm—jellied gasoline—fell.

Pyongyang, the biggest railroad junction in North Korea, around which the enemy had built airfields, anti-aircraft positions and supply dumps and where some of the few remaining industrial targets north of the Thirty-eighth Parallel remained, was a mass of flames, observers said.

Pilots flying in the second wave of attack said smoke was rising thousands of feet from the

Continued on Page 2, Column 3

O'Dwyer Considers Staying in Mexico

By SYDNEY GRUSON
Special to The New York Times.

MEXICO CITY, July 11—Ambassador William O'Dwyer is seriously considering taking up permanent residence in Mexico when his job comes to an end.

All the Ambassador will say for public quotation at this time is that he has "made no definite plans" for the future. But he has recently told persons inquiring about his plans that settling down in Mexico is high among the possibilities.

The former New York Mayor celebrated his sixty-second birthday last Monday and in discussing the future, he has expressed concern for the financial security of his wife, the former Sloan Simpson, in the event of his death.

On his retirement from the mayoralty of New York to become Ambassador to Mexico, Mr.

Continued on Page 11, Column 5

STEEL LEADERS SEE UNION, THEN CONFER

Murray Awaits New Industry Offer in Pittsburgh—Talks Expected to Go On Today

By A. H. RASKIN
Special to The New York Times.

PITTSBURGH, July 11—Negotiations to end the crippling national steel strike waited on a new industry offer today.

After a ninety-minute meeting this morning with Philip Murray, president of the United Steelworkers of America, C. I. O., a committee representing the major steel and iron ore producers went to the headquarters of the United States Steel Corporation where they spent the afternoon in private conference with other steel company officials.

No report came from the closely guarded industry session, but there was hope that the committee would emerge with a new peace proposal to put before the union tomorrow.

Mr. Murray announced at 8:30 P. M. that no further joint meetings would be held today but that it was "reasonable" to expect there would be an industry-union meeting tomorrow.

"We did meet with the industry today, and that's that," the union leader said.

Leaders on both sides refrained

Continued on Page 23, Column 6

$445,560,000 SOUGHT FOR NEW SUBWAYS BY TRANSIT BOARD

Second Avenue Network and 2 Brooklyn Extensions Put Before Estimate Body

BENEFITS DESPITE DEFICIT

Traffic Relief Seen—Costs of Operation 17 to 20% Above Revenue Conceded

By PAUL CROWELL

The Board of Transportation authorized yesterday, subject to approval of the Board of Estimate, eight subway construction projects in Manhattan, Brooklyn, Queens and the Bronx with a total estimated cost of $445,650,000.

The projects listed were six routes of the Second Avenue trunk line, with connections with existing subway lines, and the proposed extensions of the Utica Avenue and Nostrand Avenue I. R. T. subway lines in Brooklyn. The cost of the Second Avenue project was estimated at $363,500,000, including $41,000,000 for equipment. The two Brooklyn extensions are estimated to cost $82,150,000, including $13,990,000 for equipment.

The proposals would include also a subway link-up in the form of a new line from Fifty-third Street and Avenue of the Americas to East Seventy-sixth Street and Second Avenue and thence running under the East River to Woodside Avenue and Thirty-eighth Avenue in Queens.

Not in Use Before 1957-58

In a report to the Board of Estimate the transit agency expressed the belief that ground for the eight projects could not be broken before next fall. It was indicated that the operation of the Second Avenue trunk line and its connections could not begin before 1958 and that of the two Brooklyn extensions before 1957.

The transit agency's report admitted that addition of the Second Avenue line and the two Brooklyn extensions to the existing rapid transit system would create an enlarged subway network unable to earn operating expenses under a 10-cent fare.

"The most desirable benefits to be derived from the proposed routes," the report said, "are those which will be realized by the mil-

Continued on Page 29, Column...

Freed American Tells of Drugging With 'Truth Medicine' in China

By HENRY R. LIEBERMAN
Special to The New York Times.

HONG KONG, July 11—Robert T. Bryan, China-born American lawyer who was held incommunicado for sixteen and a half months as a political prisoner in a Shanghai jail, said today that his Communist captors had drugged him with two injections of "truth medicine" to extract an acceptable "confession" and a separate statement denouncing the United States State Department.

Mr. Bryan, who served as municipal advocate for the Shanghai International Settlement from 1928 to 1941, was arrested Feb. 11, 1951.

He was subsequently accused of espionage and also charged with responsibility for extradition proceedings in which Communist political operatives had been turned over to the Nationalist Government during the days of extraterritoriality.

"They blindfolded me, put me on a table and stuck something in my spine," he said in describing the first drug injection. "After about ten or twenty minutes when they sat me down, I felt I was sitting in mid-air.

"I wrote something, but I do not remember what happened. It took my volition away. I awoke the next morning with a terrific hangover."

This was the first report by a released political prisoner that he had been drugged by the Chinese Communists to elicit a "confes-

sion." It raised immediate speculation about the "confessions" of Lieut. John Quinn and Lieut. Kenneth L. Enoch, the captured American fliers who were represented by the Peiping Government as having admitted the dropping of "germ bombs" in Korea.

In addition to the American prisoners captured by the Chinese Reds in Korea, thirty-seven American civilians are officially listed here as being imprisoned in China. Others are reported to be under house arrest.

Mr. Bryan, who has resided in China about forty-five of his fifty-nine years, and who was also interned during World War II, said he underwent his first drug injection last April, after two of his "confession" drafts had been pronounced unacceptable. He said the second was administered last month, when he again failed to satisfy his interrogators after having received the option of "establishing merit" either by denouncing his friends or criticizing the State Department.

Mr. Bryan said no, this could

Continued on Page 2, Column 3

THE 1952 STANDARD-BEARERS OF THE REPUBLICAN PARTY

Gen. Dwight D. Eisenhower, for President

Senator Richard M. Nixon, for Vice President

Associated Press Wirephotos

TAFT GIVES WINNER HIS PLEDGE OF AID

Pair Exchange Compliments in Cordial Chat but Supporters of Ohioan Are Bitter

By LEO EGAN
Special to The New York Times.

CHICAGO, July 11—General of the Army Dwight D. Eisenhower and Senator Robert A. Taft today had their first face-to-face meeting since the Republican convention opened and exchanged mutual professions of esteem and respect in an obvious effort to allay factional bitterness within the Republican party.

Senator Taft, his brother, Charles P. Taft, Republican candidate for Governor of Ohio, and David S. Ingalls, who managed the Senator's pre-convention campaign, all pledged themselves during the day to use their full influence to persuade the Senator's friends to give full support to the convention winner.

Usually it is the loser who calls upon the winner, but General Eisenhower reversed the custom to make a personal call on Senator Taft soon after the nomination and to bespeak the Ohioan's help in the campaign ahead.

Senator Taft, with three of his four sons standing beside him, received the general in his headquarters' suite at the Conrad Hilton Hotel and offered his congratulations. Later the two fought their way, with the help of a detail of Chicago police, into the entrance hall of the Taft headquarters where television and newsreel cameras had been set up and newspaper reporters and photographers were waiting.

General Praises Taft

As soon as he could make himself heard, Senator Taft stepped before the microphones and said:

"I want to congratulate General Eisenhower. I shall do everything possible in the campaign to secure his election and to help in his Administration."

General Eisenhower, flashing the grin he has made famous, then turned to the crowd, jammed shoulder-to-shoulder in the hall, and said:

"I came over to pay a call of friendship on a very great American. His willingness to cooperate is absolutely necessary to the success of the Republican party in the coming campaign and in the Administration to follow."

General Eisenhower's statement brought a chorus of cheers from Taft followers, who slightly outnumbered the reporters and television crew in the hall. Earlier, when the general first arrived, he had been greeted by a mixture of cheers and boos, followed by a "We want Taft" chant.

Obviously disturbed by the boo-

Continued on Page 6, Column 1

Nominee Asks Unity at Home And Just, Sure Peace Abroad

By JAMES RESTON

CONVENTION BUILDING in Chicago, July 11—General of the Army Dwight D. Eisenhower accepted the Republican presidential nomination tonight and summoned his party to a "great crusade" for "total victory" over the Democrats in November.

[Text of Eisenhower's speech of acceptance is on Page 4.]

Likening his new assignment to the historic "crusade" he led against Nazi Germany, the 61-year-old retired five-star general pledged himself to "a program of progressive politics" designed to produce unity at home and peace abroad.

To the obvious delight of a convention audience, many of whose members have feared that he would not conduct a fighting campaign against the Administration, General Eisenhower defined his first aim:

"To sweep from office an Administration which has fastened on every man of us the wastefulness, the arrogance and corruption in high places; the heavy burdens and anxieties which are the bitter fruit of a party too long in power."

Remembering at the same time the acrimonious arguments and sharp divisions that preceded his nomination on the first ballot this morning, General Eisenhower appealed for an end of squabbling at home and torment abroad in these terms:

"It is our aim to give to our country a program of progressive policies drawn from our ..nest Republican traditions, to unite us

Continued on Page 5, Column 1

VICTORS' STRATEGY OUTPACED RIVALS

Action on Doubtful Delegate Issue and on TV Ban Took Lead From Taft's Men

By JAMES A. HAGERTY
Special to The New York Times.

CHICAGO, July 11—General of the Army Dwight D. Eisenhower won the Republican nomination for President because the members of his board of strategy completely outmaneuvered the supposedly adroit group of politicians who managed the campaign of Senator Robert A. Taft of Ohio.

The initial break that started the chain of events that led to the nomination of General Eisenhower came even before the convention opened last Monday when the Taft-dominated Republican National Committee and its pro-Taft chairman, Guy George Gabrielson, refused to permit television, radio and motion picture coverage of the committee's hearing on delegate contests. The committee had even barred newspaper photographers from the hearings during previous Republican conventions.

Eisenhower Took Control

The result was that every television and radio chain in the country filled the air with protests against what they called an "Iron Curtain" on the committee's proceedings, demanded free access to the hearings and stressed that it was supporters of Senator Taft who had imposed the ban over the objection of supporters of General Eisenhower. This television and radio barrage proved very damaging to Senator Taft's candidacy.

With supporters of Senator Taft in control of the National Committee and its Committee of Arrangements for the convention, the Eisenhower campaign managers not only overcame this handicap but in test votes involving contests in Georgia, Louisiana and Texas, took control of the convention and went on to nominate General Eisenhower.

Heading the Eisenhower group and entitled to major credit for directing the Eisenhower campaign was Senator Henry Cabot Lodge Jr., campaign manager. Others who contributed largely to the convention victory were Herbert Brownell Jr. of New

Continued on Page 3, Column 4

Democrats Respond to Eisenhower By Urging Liberal as His Opponent

Democratic party leaders in various parts of the country reacted yesterday to the Presidential nomination of General of the Army Dwight D. Eisenhower on the Republican ticket by emphasizing the need for a liberal nominee to oppose the general.

Although many prominent Democrats, including Averell Harriman, Senator Estes Kefauver of Tennessee and Senator Richard B. Russell of Georgia, were outspoken in their views, President Truman, who stayed close to his television set in Washington watching the Republican proceedings in Chicago, maintained silence.

Mr. Truman had only one scheduled engagement yesterday forenoon, setting aside most of his time for studying the Republican situation.

Senator Robert S. Kerr of Oklahoma, a candidate for the Democratic Presidential nomination, had this to say about the nomination of General Eisenhower:

"General Eisenhower will find

Continued on Page 12, Column 2

NIXON, ACCEPTING, URGES G.O.P. SWEEP

Senator Was Selected Without Opposition—His Record and Youth Strong Factors

Text of acceptance speech by Senator Nixon, Page 4.

By WILLIAM S. WHITE
Special to The New York Times.

CONVENTION BUILDING in Chicago, July 11—Senator Richard Milhous Nixon of California was nominated without opposition today as the Republican candidate for Vice President of the United States. The whole proceeding required less than half an hour.

Senator Nixon, who is 39 years old, was the choice of all the leaders who supported his senior on the 1952 Republican ticket, General of the Army Dwight D. Eisenhower, and was, of course, acceptable to the general.

Accepting the nomination in a short speech to the Republican National Convention tonight, Senator Nixon put in a strong appeal for the election of a Republican Congress.

Control by the G. O. P. was vital, he said, and especially to put in places of power such men as Senator Robert A. Taft of Ohio, General Eisenhower's defeated antagonist for the Presidential designation.

It was only with a Republican Congress, Mr. Nixon declared, that the Republicans could consolidate

Continued on Page 6, Column 2

REVISED VOTE 845

Minnesota Leads Switch to Eisenhower and Others Join Rush

BUT SOME HOLD OUT

First Call of the States Gave General 595 to 500 for Taft

First ballot with revised vote is printed on Page 6.

By W. H. LAWRENCE
Special to The New York Times.

CONVENTION BUILDING in Chicago, July 11—General of the Army Dwight D. Eisenhower won a hard-fought first-ballot nomination today as the Republican candidate for President and Senator Richard M. Nixon of California was chosen by acclamation as his running mate for the Vice Presidency.

The former Supreme Allied Commander in Europe went before the 1,206 Republican delegates tonight to accept the nomination and pledge that he would lead "a great crusade" for "total victory" against a Democratic Administration he described as wasteful, arrogant and corrupt and too long in power. He said he would keep "nothing in reserve" in his drive to put a Republican in the White House for the first time since March 4, 1933.

The Republican convention adjourned finally at 8:21 P. M. Central daylight time (9:21 New York time) after it had heard Senator Nixon accept the Vice-Presidential nomination. He pledged a "fighting campaign" to insure election not only of a Republican President, but also a House and Senate controlled by his party.

Bitterly Divided Convention

General Eisenhower won in a bitterly divided Republican convention. In the last week the general had taken leadership in the contest from Senator Robert A. Taft of Ohio, the chief party spokesman in Congress, who was making his third unsuccessful bid for nomination to the office once held by his father, William Howard Taft.

Victory came for General Eisenhower on the first ballot. The official results were 845 for General Eisenhower, 280 for Senator Taft, 77 for Gov. Earl Warren of California, and 4 for General of the Army Douglas MacArthur.

But that figure did not represent truly the voting sentiments of those delegates as they faced the crucial and final showdown between General Eisenhower and Senator Taft.

When the first roll-call of the states was completed, General Eisenhower had 595 votes—nine short of the required majority of 604—and Senator Taft had 500. The balance of power rested with favorite-son candidates, such as Governor Warren, who had 81 votes, and Harold E. Stassen, former Minnesota Governor, with 20. General MacArthur had received only 10 votes.

Others Then Changed

And while Governor Warren's California delegation held firm for him in the hope of a deadlock, Mr. Stassen's Minnesota delegates, no longer bound because he had received less than 10 per cent of the votes, broke away and cast nineteen votes for General Eisenhower before a first ballot result could be announced.

The nineteen, added to the General's previous total, gave him 614, or ten more than a majority. Then other states began to change their votes in order to be recorded on the side of the winner.

Thus, while Governor Warren's nomination later was made unanimous on the motion of his principal backers of Senator Taft and Governor Warren, who pledged their support for their candidate to the nominee, it was made clear that General Eisenhower was the choice of a divided convention, and that one of his first tasks would be to restore party unity and heal the deep wounds inflicted during the

Continued on Page 7, Column 1

The most famous scene in This is Cinerama, *was the Coney Island roller coaster ride. Hollywood hoped to lure viewers from their television sets with this new process.*

Charlie Chaplin, as the "Little Tramp," and Claire Bloom in Limelight.

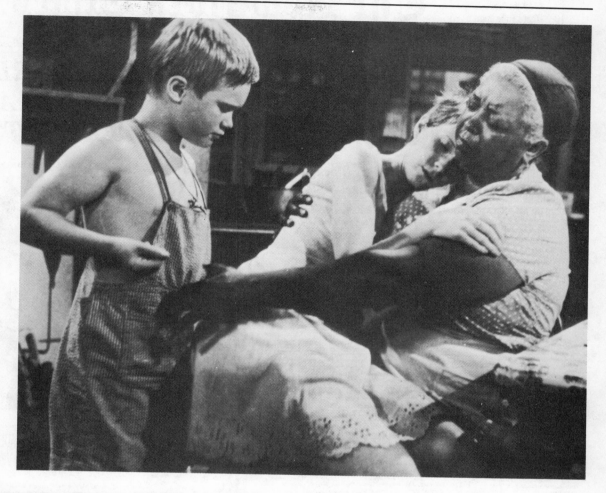

Brandon de Wilde, Julie
Harris and Ethel Waters
starred in the film version of
Carson McCullers' play, The
Member of the Wedding.

Cornel Wilde and Betty
Hutton in The Greatest Show
on Earth, which won an
Academy Award for Best
Picture.

"All the News That's Fit to Print"

The New York Times.

Copyright, 1952, by The New York Times Company.

VOL. CI..No. 34,517.

Entered as Second-Class Matter,
Post Office, New York, N. Y.

NEW YORK, SATURDAY, JULY 26, 1952.

Times Square, New York 36, N. Y.
Telephone Lackawanna 4-1000

LATE CITY EDITION
Fair and continued pleasant
today and tomorrow.
Temperature Range Today—Max., 84; Min., 66
Temperature Yesterday—Max., 82; Min., 66
Full U. S. Weather Bureau Report, Page 37

RAG PAPER EDITION
SEVENTY-FIVE CENTS

STEVENSON IS NOMINATED ON THE THIRD BALLOT; PLEDGES FIGHT 'WITH ALL MY HEART AND SOUL'; TRUMAN PROMISES TO 'TAKE OFF COAT' AND HELP

MOSSADEGH HINTS AT NEW ENDEAVOR TO SOLVE OIL ISSUE

Iranian Premier Tells Nation That 'Solution of Problem' Has Now Become 'Easier'

EARLY REFORMS PLEDGED

Government Leader Confers With Communists—Feeling Against U. S. Mounts

Special to The New York Times.

TEHERAN, Iran. July 25.—Premier Mohammed Mossadegh told the nation in a radio broadcast tonight that the tangled oil problem had taken a turn for the better and that therefore he was resolved to initiate and carry out reform measures and to take fundamental speedy steps he believed the country direly needed now.

[The Associated Press reported that the Premier made his statement in these words: "In view of the fact that a solution to the oil problem now is easier, I intend to institute reforms which the country needs. These reforms can take place only in a calm atmosphere. So long as there is disorder, there is no opportunity for any kind of improvements."]

Dr. Mossadegh summoned George Middleton, British Chargé d'Affaires, to his office. They conferred for more than two hours. The purpose of the visit has not been disclosed but Mr. Middleton said that a guess that it concerned oil would not be far wrong.

Dr. Mossadegh's internal authority is now unchallenged and the decision of the International Court of Justice that the Anglo-Iranian oil complaint was outside its jurisdiction improved considerably his international situation in approaching the oil issue. Speculation naturally is to the effect that, starting from this position, he may seek again some type of solution of the oil problem.

Mossadegh Sees Communists

Dr. Mossadegh received the leaders of the Tudeh Communist organization, which now calls itself the Association to Combat Imperialism. The subject obviously was the relation between the Government and the National Front on one hand and Communist leaders on the other after their opposition in last Monday's violent events, which drove Ahmad Ghavam from power.

In his radio address to the nation the Premier said:

"My dear compatriots, you will admit that no social reforms can be carried out without the existence of security forces. The maintenance of peace and security is the first condition of positive acts of the Government.

"The offenses and encroachments of some members of the security forces may have induced you to look askance on the entire security forces, but with the formation of a national government there is no reason why this suspicion should continue to exist.

Continued on Page 5, Column 3

U. S. Olympian Sets Steeplechase Mark

By ALLISON DANZIG
Special to The New York Times.

HELSINKI, Finland, July 25.—Horace Ashenfelter won today the fastest 3,000-meter steeplechase race ever run for the United States' twelfth gold medal in track and field and its first Olympic victory ever in this event.

In the remarkable time of 8 minutes 45.4 seconds, 18.4 seconds under the Olympic record that has stood in the books since 1936, the 29-year-old Penn State graduate from Glen Ridge, N. J., ran away from his world's best to win by thirty yards as the first eight to finish exceeded the old mark.

Vladimir Kazantsev of Russia, the favorite, who shadowed the special agent of the Federal Bureau of Investigation virtually all the way until he stumbled in

Continued on Page 16, Column 1

Snag on Iron Ore Pay Blocks Order to Reopen Steel Mills

600,000 Union Men Await Pact for Miners—Fairless and Murray Plan to Visit Plants to Promote Labor Harmony

By A. H. RASKIN
Special to The New York Times.

WASHINGTON, July 25.—The longest and most costly steel strike in the country's history was officially called off today, but an unexpected snag on wage rates for 23,000 iron ore miners blocked the sending of union back-to-work orders to 600,000 striking steel workers.

The last-minute difficulty, which both sides hoped would blow over in a few hours, cast a shadow over settlement arrangements that had indicated the steel dispute might provide a foundation for a new era of cooperative labor-management relations in the industry that represents the backbone of the American economy.

With only one dissenting vote, the 175-man Wage Policy Committee of the United Steelworkers of America, C. I. O., voted this afternoon to accept the settlement terms agreed upon at the White House yesterday by Philip Murray,

Continued on Page 30, Column 5

president of the union, and Benjamin F. Fairless, president and chairman of the United States Steel Corporation.

The agreement, which was personally announced by President Truman, provided a wage increase of 16 cents an hour, retroactive to last March 1; paid holidays, higher shift differentials and other "fringe" benefits that would cost 5.4 cent an hour more, and a modified union shop.

The agreement specified that iron-ore miners were to get all the same benefits, plus additional wage increases intended to bring their pay scales up to the steel level.

It was this provision that caused the difficulty today.

Under the agreement part of the difference in wage rates was to be made up at once and the rest at the end of the first year of the

Continued on Page 30, Column 5

U.N. Truce Team Walks Out Of Korea Talks for a Week

By LINDESAY PARROTT
Special to The New York Times.

TOKYO, Saturday, July 26.—The United Nations delegates walked out of the new plenary sessions at Panmunjom today and told the Communists they would return in a week for further discussion of an armistice in the Korean war.

The senior Allied delegate, Maj. Gen. William K. Harrison Jr., led the United Nations representatives out of the conference tent, after the enemy delegation had devoted much of the first of a new series of meetings to a violent repetition of charges against the United Nations Command. The two aides agreed, however, that during the week's adjournment staff officers would meet to see what could be done to draft new tentative armistice terms as a basis for further discussion.

Pooled dispatches from Korea said General Harrison was shaking with anger as he left the roadside tent, where the Chinese and North Koreans, after the breakdown of the last three weeks' attempt

Continued on Page 2, Column 3

6 AIDES OF FAROUK RESIGN AFTER COUP

5 High-Ranking Police Officials Jailed as Maher Cabinet Acts Speedily in Egypt

By The Associated Press.

CAIRO, July 25.—Gen. Mohammed Naguib Bey's Army-backed governmental house-cleaning reached to King Farouk's own palace today. Six of the monarch's top aides resigned.

At the same time Egypt's new strong man moved anew to crush opposition to the military coup by which he had installed the anti-corruption Government of Premier Aly Maher Pasha.

Maher Pasha's new Cabinet took over today, pledged to try to end the crisis that has swept this Middle East country for six months. The Cabinet hopes to end the corruption that, according to Maher Pasha, had brought the crisis about and to settle Egypt's dispute with Britain over the Suez Canal and the Sudan.

Police Officials Arrested

General Naguib Bey flew to Alexandria for a conference with Maher Pasha, leaving behind him a series of arrests. Among those held were five high-ranking political and police officials who were accused of conspiring against the public safety, an army communiqué said. Twelve generals of the Egyptian Army also were in custody.

The officials held included Maj. Gen. Mousif Mahmoud Pasha, Under Secretary of the Interior Ministry; the commandant of the Cairo police, the director of a special section of the Interior Ministry and two high officers of the political section of the police.

The communiqué said: "Although we have detained these few people * * * a much larger number of army men have been arrested." Maj. Gen. Sirry Amer Bey, commander of Egypt's frontier corps, was arrested at Salvin, on the Egyptian-Libyan border, and returned to Cairo.

General Naguib Bey received an ovation when he called on the new Premier. While they conferred for an hour, a crowd outside cheered and called the general "Protector of Egypt."

After the conference he told newsmen that their first aim was to assure the people of Alexandria

Continued on Page 2, Column 3

PRESIDENT IN FORM

Talks in 'Whistle Stop' Manner, Predicting Ticket's Victory

HITS AT EISENHOWER

Says 'People Will Not Choose Man Without Faith in People'

Text of the President's speech at the Convention, Page 4

By JAMES RESTON
Special to The New York Times.

CONVENTION BUILDING in Chicago, Saturday, July 26.—President Truman told a cheering Democratic National Convention early this morning that it had nominated a winner in Gov. Adlai E. Stevenson of Illinois.

The President promised that he would "take off my coat and go out to help him win."

In a direct attack on Gen. Dwight D. Eisenhower, the Republican Presidential nominee, Mr. Truman declared that the "people won't choose a leader who does not have faith in the people." He said he did not think the country would be turned over to "men who are more concerned with cutting the budget than with the security of the United States."

This was a reference to General Eisenhower's pre-nomination pledge to reduce the Federal budget by $40,000,000,000 under certain conditions.

How to Win Elections

Mr. Truman started to speak at 1:42 A. M., after a four minute ovation. He reminded the delegates that four years ago at about the same hour in the morning he had predicted victory for the ticket headed by himself and Senator Alben W. Barkley of Kentucky for Vice President.

"But you didn't believe me," said the President with a grin.

"I'm telling you now that Adlai Stevenson will win in 1952."

The President said that the real reason Democrats won elections "is perfectly simple—it is because they give the American people the kind of Government they want."

"The Republicans," he declared, "are going to throw millions of dollars into an attempt to confuse

Continued on Page 8, Column 8

GOVERNOR ACCEPTS

Humility Marks Speech by Nominee Before Cheering Delegates

HE HAILS PLATFORM

Illinoisan in Tribute to Losing Candidates— Bids for Unity

Text of the acceptance speech by Mr. Stevenson, Page 5.

By JAMES RESTON
Special to The New York Times.

CONVENTION BUILDING in Chicago, Saturday, July 26.—Gov. Adlai E. Stevenson of Illinois, in a speech marked both by humility in the face of the high honor and by a vigorous determination in the face of its challenge, early today accepted the Democratic nomination for President.

"I will fight to win that office with all my heart and soul." he told the cheering delegates. "With your help, I have no doubt that we will win."

Earlier, the "no" man from the Lincoln country, had for the first time said "yes."

"I did not seek it. I did not want it," he said a moment after he had been nominated by the Democratic National Convention.

"But to shirk it would be to repay honor with dishonor," he added.

The call, he continued, "asked of me nothing except that I give such talents as I have to the services of my country. That I will do."

"I feel no exaltation or sense of triumph whatever, nothing but humility. I shall go on my knees and I shall ask my God to give me strength and courage and to nourish my spirit for this great undertaking in this great hour of his history."

At the outset, he said, he had never been "more conscious of the appalling responsibility of office."

He went immediately to the convention hall from the home on Chicago's "Gold Coast" where he made his short statement.

The 52-year-old Governor developed this same solemn theme after he had been driven at breakneck speed through the late night traffic

Continued on Page 5, Column 4

THE DEMOCRATIC STANDARD-BEARER

Associated Press Wirephoto

ADLAI E. STEVENSON

300-VOTE SWITCH DECIDES CONTEST

Harriman's Withdrawal Swings Big State Blocs on Third Ballot to the Governor

Harriman statement, Kefauver and Russell talks, Page 4

By FELIX BELAIR Jr.
Special to The New York Times.

CONVENTION BUILDING in Chicago, Saturday, July 26.—A sudden switch of more than 300 votes gave Gov. Adlai E. Stevenson of Illinois a third-ballot victory and the Democratic Presidential nomination here early today after Averell Harriman had announced his withdrawal from the contest and New York, Pennsylvania, Massachusetts, Michigan and Arkansas had swung in behind the choice of President Truman.

The race came out just as predicted by the managers of Governor Stevenson's floor campaign. Paul E. Fitzpatrick, the New York State party chairman, took the speaker's platform during a dinner recess to announce Mr. Harriman's withdrawal. Averell Harriman's favorite son, Gov. Paul A. Dever, followed with the announcement to the convention that he, too, was withdrawing in favor of Governor Stevenson.

Mr. Fitzpatrick's statement in behalf of Mr. Harriman was followed much later in the session by speeches by Senator Estes Kefauver of Tennessee and Senator Richard B. Russell of Georgia, both conceding the nomination to the Illinoisan.

With the Harriman and Dever switches there were more than 100 votes right there to be added to Governor Stevenson's second ballot total of 423½. When Michigan switched its 40 votes from Senator Estes Kefauver it remained only for Pennsylvania to bring along the stragglers by giving the Governor all its 70 votes, a net gain of 30.

Texas held out with its big 52-vote bloc, as did other delegations favoring Senator Russell until the die was already cast.

Senator Kefauver came up the center aisle of the auditorium on the arm of Senator Paul H. Douglas of Illinois in an attempt to gain the platform to announce his plan to nominate Senator Douglas, who was not in nomination but who would then have withdrawn and urged all Kefauver delegates to vote for Governor Stevenson. But Speaker Sam Rayburn, the convention's permanent chairman, ruled that the balloting must proceed.

Governor Stevenson was within a few votes of the required 615½ majority when the roll-call of the states ended and Speaker Rayburn gave to Tennessee the first opportunity

Continued on Page 5, Column 1

LEADERS IN HUDDLE ON VICE PRESIDENCY

Balloting Is Postponed Until Noon Today as Kefauver Foes Present Objections

Special to The New York Times.

CONVENTION BUILDING in Chicago, Saturday, July 26.—Democratic party leaders went into a huddle early today immediately following the Presidential nomination of Gov. Adlai E. Stevenson for talks on the Vice Presidency.

The National Convention put off its choice until a noon session. The original program had called for selection of Governor Stevenson's running mate late this morning after his acceptance speech.

It was understood that the delay stemmed principally from some objections to Senator Estes Kefauver of Tennessee, who had night forged to the top of the "guess" list after he dramatically yielded in the Presidential race.

A late starter among the possibilities was Representative John W. McCormack of Massachusetts. Others mentioned were Vice President Alben W. Barkley, Senator John J. Sparkman of Alabama, Secretary of the Interior Oscar L. Chapman and Senator Richard B. Russell of Georgia.

Among those in the huddle at the near-by Stockyards Inn were Averell Harriman, who last night withdrew from the Presidential race, and Jake Arvey of Chicago, Governor Stevenson's principal backer in Illinois.

Regarding the possibility of taking the post, Senator Kefauver said:

"I haven't been offered the place and I really don't believe I would want to accept it. I haven't talked

Continued on Page 8, Column 7

RIVALS DROP OUT

Withdrawal of Harriman Starts States' Rush to the Governor

ILLINOISAN TRAILED

But Picked Up Strength From Larger States— Got C. I. O. Backing

The three ballots of Convention are printed on Page 6.

By WILLIAM S. WHITE
Special to The New York Times.

CONVENTION BUILDING in Chicago, Saturday, July 26.—Gov. Adlai E. Stevenson of Illinois was nominated early today on the third ballot for President of the United States by the thirty-first Democratic National Convention.

President Truman came here to salute him and to stand with him before the delegates.

Mr. Truman, cheerful and smiling, declared to the Convention:

"I'm telling you it is going to win in 1952 * * *. I am going to take my coat off and do everything I can to help him win."

Governor Stevenson told the delegates that he could never have sought such an honor, and adding:

"I have asked the merciful Father of us all to let this cup pass from me. But from such dread responsibility one does not shrink in fear, in self-interest, or in false humility."

"So," he went on, quoting from the Bible, "if this cup may not pass away from Me, except I drink it, Thy will be done."

Huge Demonstration

Mr. Truman walked, as an enormous demonstration beat the walls of this hall, the length of the platform to greet Mr. Stevenson and take him to face the crowd.

The convention adjourned at 2:35 A. M. (3:35 A. M., New York time), to meet again at 11 A. M.

Governor Stevenson's nomination—the first genuine draft since the Republicans demanded and got James A. Garfield in 1880—came after the withdrawal of Averell Harriman of New York who turned the great bulk of that delegation to the Stevenson standard.

A late starter among the possibilities was Representative John W. McCormack of Massachusetts. Tennessee put over the Stevenson selection. Tennessee cast its 28 votes for the Governor, who was then a handful short of the required 615½ needed for a majority in a total of 1,230.

'Did Best We Could'

Senator Richard B. Russell of Georgia, after Mr. Stevenson's nomination, pledged to join in efforts for a party victory in November.

Senator Kefauver told the convention that it had been "quite apparent" that someone here had to yield. His intention, he said, had been to nominate Senator Paul H. Douglas of Illinois and Senator Douglas had intended in turn to give his favor to Governor Stevenson.

But this had been made impracticable by the Stevenson rush, Mr. Kefauver said, in effect, so he was simply retiring. It had been a good fight, he observed, "and we did the best we could."

Senator Kefauver, it appeared, was heading instead for the Vice Presidential nomination. The selection of Vice President is scheduled to be made today.

Mr. Stevenson to the end had not been a candidate.

Four aggressive aspirants—Mr. Harriman, Senator Kefauver, Senator Russell and Senator Robert S. Kerr of Oklahoma—had struggled with the Stevenson draft movement until it became apparent that there was to be no stopping it. Senator Kerr had retired early—before dinner-time last night—when his own Oklahoma delegation had left him, obviously with his consent, though he did not make it formal until nearly midnight.

Mr. Harriman's announcement of retirement from the race came after Mr. Truman, a Stevenson backer, had arrived here. The

Continued on Page 5, Column 1

Two Coalitions Won Stevenson's Victory

By JAMES A. HAGERTY
Special to The New York Times.

CHICAGO, Saturday, July 26.—The strategy used by supporters of Gov. Adlai E. Stevenson to get him the Democratic nomination for President, like the horns of a dilemma, had two prongs.

First, by a coalition with supporters of Senators Richard B. Russell of Georgia and Robert S. Kerr of Oklahoma they brought about the seating of the Virginia, Louisiana and South Carolina delegations, members of which had declined to take the loyalty pledge imposed by the Credentials Committee as a condition of participation in the convention.

Having formed this temporary alliance with the conservative Southern delegates and leased

Continued on Page 6, Column 8

CONVENTION-BOUND PRESIDENT VOTES BY PROXY

At the precise moment Mr. Truman was waving farewell at the Washington Airport before starting for Chicago in his plane . . .

. . . Thomas J. Gavin was casting his vote as the President's alternate on the convention floor in support of Adlai E. Stevenson.

Associated Press Wirephotos

1952

Adlai Stevenson was President Truman's personal choice for the Democratic nomination in 1952. They are seen here at the convention.

The delegates to the 1952 Republican convention nominated Eisenhower and Nixon.

"All the News
That's Fit to Print"

The New York Times.

NEWS SUMMARY AND INDEX, PAGE 59

VOL. CI No. 34,518.

Entered as Second-Class Matter,
Post Office, New York, N. Y.

Copyright, 1952, by The New York Times Company.

NEW YORK, SUNDAY, JULY 27, 1952.

Including Magazine
and Book Review.

LATE CITY EDITION

Mostly fair and warm today.
Fair, continued warm tomorrow.
Temperature Range Today–Max.-90; Min.-70
Temperatures Yesterday–Max., 86; Min., 69
(Full U. S. Weather Bureau Report, Sect. 3, P. 7

Section
1

TWENTY CENTS
New York City | Elsewhere
56 Mile Zone | Twenty-five Cents

FAROUK OUT; QUITS EGYPT AFTER COUP

ARMY EXILES KING

He Sails With Queen and Infant Son, Who Is Named Fuad II

ITALY THEIR DESTINATION

Iran Premier Reported Ready to Negotiate With British on Nationalized Oil Concern

By The Associated Press

CAIRO, July 26—King Farouk I abdicated the ancient Egyptian throne today at the climax of a tank-supported Army clean-up campaign and sailed away in the Mediterranean aboard his Royal yacht, the Mahroussa. The Army said his family went with him for exile in Italy.

The Cabinet proclaimed Farouk's son, seven-month-old Crown Prince Ahmed Fuad, to be King Fuad II of Egypt and the Sudan.

[At Premier Mohammed Mossadegh of Iran presented his new Cabinet roster to the Shah, a National Front newspaper disclosed that the Premier had invited negotiations with Britain with a view to resolving the deadlock over the nationalized Anglo-Iranian Oil Company.]

Gen. Mohammed Naguib Bey, Egypt's new strong man and leader of the virtually bloodless Army coup, had surrounded the Royal palaces with armed forces. Soldiers arrested several officers of the Royal Guard in a showdown at Ras el Tin Palace in Alexandria, Egypt's summer capital.

In addition to 18-year-old Queen Narriman and the baby, Farouk's three daughters by former Queen Farida—Princesses Ferial, Fadia, and Fawzia—accompanied him into exile.

[The French Press Agency said it had learned authoritatively that Farouk intended eventually to go to the United States. He will sail first to Europe, it said, and will proceed to the United States when necessary formalities are completed.]

Naguib Salutes Monarch

General Naguib Bey, self-proclaimed Commander in Chief of the Army, shook hands with the ousted monarch and saluted him while the band played the Royal anthem. Farouk, wearing the uniform of an Egyptian admiral, waved good-by with his cap as a twenty-one-gun salute was fired.

The abdication of King Farouk, wealthy former playboy, marked the end of a reign of sixteen troubled years highlighted by World War II, during which his country occupied a vitally strategic position, and by a post-war dispute with a former mighty ally, Britain.

First reports quoted Queen Narriman as having said that she had wanted to accompany her husband but was prevented from doing so because she "must take care of the baby Crown Prince and help bring him up."

Late tonight King Farouk's

Continued on Page 3, Column 6

ABDICATES

Associated Press

King Farouk

STAFF TALKS GO ON AMID TRUCE RECESS

But U. N. Officers Are Doubtful That Review Asked by Foe Will Make Progress

By LINDESAY PARROTT
Special to The New York Times.

TOKYO, Sunday, July 27—Full-scale negotiations at Panmunjom for an armistice in the Korean war were in abeyance for a week today after an angry squabble yesterday when United Nations delegates walked from the conference tent, forcing a new adjournment.

Staff officers of both sides were to hold this morning the second of a new series of sessions called by the Communists to review the tentative truce agreement being used as a basis for 'ceccasion by the plenary delegations. United Nations spokesmen said they expected little progress toward settlement of the critical issue of prisoner exchange, which has blocked an armistice since December.

[The staff officers met for an hour and a half Sunday and agreed to meet again Monday forenoon, news agencies said.]

A senior United Nations staff officer, Col. Duncan S. Somerville, told correspondents after the thirty-nine-minute session yesterday that the Communist had given no indication that they placed particular emphasis on those paragraphs of the document dealing with the exchange of captives, but apparently wanted a review of the entire sixty-four-clause agreement, painfully hammered out at previous staff meetings and translated into official texts in three languages.

Somerville Is Pessimistic

Frankly pessimistic, Colonel Somerville told the enemy representative, Col. Chang Chun San, "Our main differences are issues that cannot be settled by editorial mumbo jumbo."

If differences are found to exist between the texts, he continued, they could be adjusted by translators without formal meetings at Panmunjom. However, the Communists apparently meant to keep the staff sessions open, possibly to communicate with the Allies if the main Chinese-North Korean delegation sought a new plenary meeting before Aug. 3.

The senior United Nations representative, Maj. Gen. William K. Harrison Jr., told his opposite number, North Korean Lieut. Gen. Nam Il, when he walked out of the session yesterday, "If you have anything to say, you can say it through our staff officers." But yesterday General Harrison indicated that only a "very important" development would bring the Allied negotiators back before the week was out.

Yesterday's walkout was the fourth by the United Nations since the discussion of prisoner exchange began, and a week's enforced adjournment was the longest pause thus caused in the truce talks. As on previous occasions, General Harrison led the delegation from the tent after the Communists, back in an open session after

Continued on Page 2, Column 6

600,000 STEEL MEN ORDERED TO MILLS; ORE ISSUE SETTLED

Murray's Bid to Union Follows Pay Increase Agreement for 23,000 Miners

WAGE BOARD IS RESTRICTED

Truman Puts It More Directly Under Economics Chief in Line With Congress' Plan

By A. H. RASKIN
Special to The New York Times.

WASHINGTON, July 26—The final obstacle to ending the steel strike was removed late this afternoon and union back-to-work telegrams started 600,000 strikers streaming into the steel mills after an absence of fifty-five days.

An all-day conference between industry and union leaders resulted in an agreement at 4:55 P. M. on a pay increase for 23,000 iron ore miners. This was the only issue that had stood in the way of terminating the walkout that had made 1,500,000 workers idle in steel and industries dependent on steel.

All other problems had been taken care of in a White House agreement signed on Thursday by Philip Murray, president of the United Steelworkers of America, C. I. O., and the "big six" steel companies. The agreement was ratified yesterday by the union's Wage Policy Committee.

The pact provided for a wage increase of 16 cents an hour, retroactive to March 1; paid holidays, higher shift differentials and other benefits that will cost 5.4 cents an hour more, and a modified union shop.

Pre-strike wages in the steel industry averaged $1.88 an hour.

Miners Get Other Gains

A companion agreement, also signed at the White House in President Truman's presence, specified that iron ore miners were to get all the same gains, plus additional wage increases intended to bring their pay scales up to the steel level.

The complication that delayed a full settlement for twenty-four hours was the timetable to be followed in equalizing the steel and the iron ore wages. Under the agreement part of the difference in pay rates was to be made up at once and the rest next July 1. The exact amount to be given each year was not set forth but was left for subsequent negotiation.

The average pay in ore mines is now 20 to 25 cents an hour below the steel average, but 8½ cents of this is offset by an agreement the employers made a year and one-half ago to put that amount into a fund to be used in equalizing iron ore wages.

Today's conference between union officials and heads of the major iron ore companies resulted in a decision to grant additional

Continued on Page 15, Column 1

TEAM TAKES SHAPE

Illinoisan Acts for Unity by Not Pressing Any Choice for Ticket

STARTS IN MIDDLE OF ROAD

Governor Takes Alabaman as Compromise and Introduces Him as a Real 'Prize'

By JAMES RESTON
Special to The New York Times.

CHICAGO, July 26—Gov. Adlai E. Stevenson took a position in the middle of the road today and started his journey in quest of the Presidency.

In agreeing to Senator John J. Sparkman of Alabama as the Vice Presidential nominee, the Democratic party's Presidential candidate approved the man who was least likely to upset either the North or South.

There was some feeling in the convention that Senator Estes Kefauver of Tennessee would have added more strength to the ticket or that a younger and more aggressive man would have countered the Republican Vice Presidential nominee, the 39-year-old Senator Richard M. Nixon of California, but Mr. Stevenson avoided an extreme position either way.

He did not oppose the Kefauver suggestion. He did not come out strongly for anybody. He saw that sentiment was moving toward Senator Sparkman, who is 52, as a compromise acceptable to the Old Guard in the South and the Young Turks of the North, so he pursued a policy of judicious leaving-alone.

Drives With Harriman to Hall

Likewise, he avoided any hasty action on the question of selecting a national chairman to see him through the campaign. He merely asked Frank E. McKinney of Indianapolis, the present chairman, to stay on for a while until he could study the situation, and Mr. McKinney agreed.

The Governor has had less physical strain on him in this convention than most other persons connected with it, but he was up until the middle of the night and then slept late this morning.

Averell Harriman of New York, who started the landslide for Mr. Stevenson last night by withdrawing from the race and urging his delegates to vote for the Illinoisan, had breakfast with the Governor late in the morning. Both then drove behind a police

Continued on Page 21, Column 1

SPARKMAN CHOSEN BY DEMOCRATS AS RUNNING MATE FOR STEVENSON; SENATOR HAILS PARTY SOLIDARITY

AT THE HEAD OF 1952 DEMOCRATIC NATIONAL TICKET

Associated Press Wirephoto

Gov. Adlai E. Stevenson, left, the nominee for President, holding up the hand of Senator John J. Sparkman, the candidate for Vice President, as the convention cheered.

TICKET ACCLAIMED

Nominees Pledge Strong Campaign—No Ballot Taken on 2d Place

TWO WOMEN ARE NAMED

India Edwards and Judge Sara Hughes Get Complimentary Mention, Then Withdraw

Text of Sparkman's acceptance speech is on Page 19.

By WILLIAM S. WHITE
Special to The New York Times.

CONVENTION BUILDING in Chicago, July 26—The thirty-first Democratic National Convention nominated Senator John J. Sparkman of Alabama for Vice President on the ticket headed by Gov. Adlai E. Stevenson of Illinois, and wound up its long, weary meeting in general party harmony.

The Senator accepted the nomination with a pledge to "te'e the message of democracy to the people of this country."

"I believe, I earnestly believe," he said, "that we will go out of this convention with greater solidarity, greater unity in all sections of the country and in all segments of our party than we have been able to achieve in a long, long time."

Mr. Sparkman, whose designation had been approved in advance by Governor Stevenson, was chosen on the motion of James A. Finley of New York that no ballot be taken. The designation of the Alabaman was described by the presiding officer, Representative Sam Rayburn of Texas, as one for acclamation on a voice vote.

At no point had there been any serious rival, though Mrs. India Edwards, vice chairman of the Democratic National Committee, and Judge Sarah Hughes of Dallas, Tex., had been put in nomination in a complimentary way.

Pledge Hard Campaign

Governor Stevenson came to the convention platform to stand with Senator Sparkman, their hands interlocked and raised high. They promised a hard campaign this autumn against the Republican nominees, Gen. Dwight D. Eisenhower and Senator Richard M. Nixon of California.

The convention was adjourned at 2:20 P. M., Central daylight time (3:20 New York time), on a note of North-South amity to which the selection of Senator Sparkman had contributed.

Some of the Northerners held misgivings, however, in spite of Mr. Sparkman's generally liberal political record, over what he would do in the campaign about the convention civil rights plank, which called for Federal legislation to help end racial discrimination.

Senator Herbert H. Lehman of New York called on Mr. Sparkman to embrace that plank wholeheartedly, saying that if he did not there was "no question" that the Democratic ticket would be imperiled in New York.

Mr. Sparkman, Senator Lehman said, is in every respect except possibly this one "a real fighting liberal."

Several Walk Out

Representative Adam Clayton Powell Jr. of New York and several other Negro delegates walked out of the hall in dissatisfaction before the nomination was achieved. The delegates on the whole accepted the designation in good part.

Mr. Sparkman, in his speech, reminded the delegates that he had been a member of the Resolutions Committee that drafted the platform. He said there had been some difficult problems involved, but "we sat and reasoned with one another until we came out with a platform on which we can all stand."

Mr. Sparkman had agreed upon before 6 o'clock this morning in consultations among President Truman, Governor Stevenson, Frank E. McKinney, and the Democratic National Committe

Continued on Page 15, Column 1

McKINNEY TO HOLD POST TEMPORARILY

National Committee Chairman Agrees to Stay on When Nominee Requests It

By WILLIAM M. BLAIR
Special to The New York Times.

CHICAGO, July 26—Frank E. McKinney of Indianapolis was retained as chairman of the reorganized Democratic National Committee today on a temporary basis at the request of Gov. Adlai E. Stevenson of Illinois, the party's Presidential nominee.

Governor Stevenson made a personal appearance before the committee to ask that Mr. McKinney stay on in his post because he had no organization of his own and was "utterly dependent on the National Committee."

Jacob M. Arvey, Illinois National Committeeman, who made the formal motion to retain Mr. McKinney and other officers temporarily, said later that Governor Stevenson "wouldn't talk about anything until last night."

"He hasn't made a choice because he hasn't considered it," Mr. Arvey added. "He has only met Mr. McKinney twice but considers him a fine and able man, but he just wouldn't say a word about anything."

Mr. McKinney told the committee prior to the Governor's appearance that he had "every intention to ask to be relieved." But when the Governor called him he agreed to stay on "in deference to Governor Stevenson, and until he, Senator John Sparkman and the executive committee have a chance to choose a new chairman."

There were reports that Mr. McKinney would carry on permanently after the Illinois Governor had surveyed the situation and decided on the kind of organization he wanted.

Sparkman Praises Chairman

Senator Sparkman, chosen by the party today as its candidate for Vice President, also appeared before the committee, which has a number of new members. He commended Mr. McKinney and also alluded to the convention fight over the seating of delegations from Virginia, South Carolina and Louisiana, which had refused to take a "loyalty pledge" to the party.

"The party has worked out of a very difficult situation from a national viewpoint," said the Alabaman.

The committee, he added, has labored hard to "the end that all wounds of the party could be healed." He earnestly hoped that "we all carry away from here the belief that what we have striven so hard to accomplish has been accomplished."

Among the changes on the committee was the selection of former Gov. Fielding L. Wright of Mississippi, who was the Vice Presiden-

Continued on Page 25, Column 1

Eisenhower Attacks Record And Platform of Democrats

By RUSSELL PORTER
Special to The New York Times.

DENVER, July 26—Commenting on the Democratic ticket nominated at Chicago, Gen. Dwight D. Eisenhower today struck the keynote of the Republican Presidential campaign. It combined a promise of lasting peace and expanding progress for the United States with an implied attack on the record of the Democratic Administration.

The general's statement follows:

"The Democrat party has named its candidates and offers them to the country on a one-plank platform: defense of the entire Administration record.

"I am confident that the American people will support the program that Senator Nixon [Richard M. Nixon of California, Republican Vice Presidential nominee] and I will outline during the campaign to retain and expand American progress and, in organizing for a lasting peace, make our country a healthier, stronger, happier and better America than anything we have yet known."

The general telephoned his statement from his fishing camp in the Colorado Rockies to James C. Hagerty, his press secretary, at summer campaign headquarters at the Brown Palace Hotel here.

In a message to the Republican state convention here, General Eisenhower also promised to make an "all-out" campaign for a "smashing" victory.

"In this crusade," he said, "I urge you to encourage the support of the young men and women of America, as well as the thousands of other citizens who are eager to rally to the Republican cause."

He said his election would mean

Continued on Page 25, Column 1

SPARKMAN WARNED ON RIGHTS PLANK

Lehman Says Full Backing Is Vital or the Ticket Will Be Weakened in New York

By LEO EGAN

CONVENTION BUILDING in Chicago, July 26—Senator Herbert H. Lehman of New York today urged Senator John J. Sparkman of Alabama, following his nomination for Vice President, to embrace without reservation the civil rights plank written into the Democratic platform earlier in the week.

"If he doesn't," Senator Lehman said, "there is no question but that it will weaken the ticket in New York."

Senator Sparkman's nomination for Vice President appeared to nullify the underlying strategy of New York's ninety-four-vote delegation yesterday in throwing the bulk of its support to Gov. Adlai E. Stevenson of Illinois for the Presidential nomination on the third ballot.

Although the change was made without any prior agreement with

Continued on Page 26, Column 1

Eva Peron Dies in Argentina; A Power as President's Wife

Buenos Aires Sets National Mourning—End Comes After Long Illness

Special to The New York Times.

BUENOS AIRES, July 26—Señora Doña Maria Eva Duarte de Perón, wife of President Juan D. Perón, who had made herself one of the most powerful women in the history of Argentina and of the New World, died tonight at 8:25 o'clock. She had long been ill.

According to the Argentine Who's Who, she was 30 years old. [Biographical material not currently published in Argentina gave Señora Perón's age as 33, her date birth May 17, 1919.]

The people of Argentina, who had been celebrating masses for the recovery of the First Lady, who was called "the spiritual chief of the nation," were well prepared for the event. During the course of the day the Sub-Secretariat of Information had issued three bulletins in rapid succession that clearly indicated the end was near.

President Peron, who was at her bedside when she died, had been staying nearly all week close to his wife in the Presidential Residence. Members of the Cabinet were there today.

At 9:42 P. M., all radio stations interrupted their programs to report:

"The Sub-Secretariat of Information fulfills the very sad duty of announcing that at 8:25 o'clock Señora Eva Perón, the spiritual

Continued on Page 5, Column 4

Associated Press, 1952

Señora Peron

chief of the nation, passed away."

The announcement was followed by religious music.

Señora Perón was operated upon last November for cancer. Her last public appearance was on June 4, when, looking extremely pale and worn, she attended the ceremony at which General Perón was inaugurated to succeed himself as President—largely through her help.

As news of the death was received throughout the country, each Province decided to send its own special delegations, presided over

Continued on Page 5, Column 6

Bank Robber Slays F. B. I. Agent In Gun Battle in W. 69th St. Hotel

By RICHARD H. PARKE

A Federal Bureau of Investigation agent was wounded fatally in the lobby of the Congress Hotel, 19 West Sixty-ninth Street, at 1:15 P. M. yesterday in a pistol battle that resulted in the capture of a Kansas bank robber sought as one of the nation's ten most-wanted criminals.

Joseph J. Brock, 44 years old, of 33-15 Eightieth Street, Jackson Heights, Queens, was shot by the robber, Gerhard A. Puff, 37, as the agent crouched behind a frosted-glass door waiting for his quarry to emerge from an elevator.

Puff, who slipped down a rear stairway and fired point-blank at the F. B. I. man, was himself brought down by a bullet in the left leg in an exchange of shots as he ran through the lobby past four other agents. He fell in the street outside.

Mr. Brock, who was married and the father of three children, was dead when an ambulance reached Roosevelt Hospital. Ed-

the bureau's New York office, said it was the first time in its memory that an agent in this city had met violent death in this area.

Puff, a bespectacled, mild-mannered man with a fondness for highly polished shoes, also was taken to Roosevelt Hospital, but later was transferred to the prison ward at Bellevue. He suffered a fractured leg. His condition was said to be good.

Last night, at the Federal Court House in Foley Square, James B. Kilsheimer 3d, an Assistant United States Attorney, filed a complaint signed by Arthur Duffy, an F. B. I. agent, before Federal Judge John F. X. McGohey charging Puff with murder in the first degree. The attorney's request that the prisoner be held without bail was granted.

Two young women seized in the Congress Hotel, an apartment hotel, told the agent that George Arthur

Continued on Page 19, Column 3

Major Sports News

OLYMPIC GAMES

Bob Mathias broke his own world record with 7,887 points as the United States swept the first three places in the decathlon yesterday. It was the Tulare (Calif.) star's second victory in that event. Milton Campbell of Plainfield, N. J., was second and Floyd Simmons of Los Angeles third. Joseph Barthel of Luxembourg defeated Bob McMillen of the United States in a close finish in the 1,500-meter final. Both were timed in 3:45.2, a new record.

BASEBALL

The Giants defeated the Reds, 7—2, and moved within four and a half games of first place as the Dodgers lost again to the Cards, 5—2. The Tigers beat the Yankees, 10—4, on Steve Souchock's homer in the eleventh.

HORSE RACING

To Market, 2-1 choice, easily won the $50,200 Arlington Handicap. Golden Gloves led the favored Next home in the feature at Jamaica.

(Details in Section 5).

THE PAPER of writing—Think of Wimn—
WINNING PAPER COMPANY—Advt.

The author of many bestselling detective stories, Mickey Spillane is best remembered for Kiss Me Deadly. The hero of his books is Mike Hammer, private investigator.

Moviegoers in their polaroid glasses, gaping at the new 3-dimensional films.

"All the News That's Fit to Print"

The New York Times.

LATE CITY EDITION
Mostly fair and continued cool today, tonight and tomorrow.
Temperature Range Today-Max., 68; Min., 54
Temperatures Yesterday—Max., 67; Min., 56
Full U. S. Weather Bureau Report, Page 47

VOL. CII..No. 34,577. Entered as Second-Class Matter, Post Office, New York, N. Y. NEW YORK, WEDNESDAY, SEPTEMBER 24, 1952. Times Square, New York 36, N. Y. Telephone LAckawanna 4-1000 FIVE CENTS

NIXON LEAVES FATE TO G.O.P. CHIEFS; EISENHOWER CALLS HIM TO A TALK; STEVENSON MAPS INFLATION CURBS

MARCIANO ANNEXES TITLE IN 13TH BY KO OVER JOE WALCOTT

Brockton Heavyweight Ends Reign of 38-Year-Old Rival With Right to Jaw

40,379 FANS WATCH BOUT

Hundreds Besiege Philadelphia Stadium in Wild Rush to Acclaim New Champion

By JAMES P. DAWSON
Special to THE NEW YORK TIMES.

PHILADELPHIA, Sept. 23 — Rocky Marciano, undefeated Brockton, Mass., fighter, knocked out Jersey Joe Walcott, 38-year-old ring warrior from Camden, N. J., tonight to become the world heavyweight champion.

With a devastating right to the jaw, Marciano ended the reign of the old champion after forty-three seconds of the thirteenth round. Until that moment it was a bruising battle that thrilled 40,379 fans from all over America in Philadelphia's Municipal Stadium. The receipts were $504,645.

Under the impact of that one terrific blow Walcott sank against the ropes, then slid head first to the canvas, while Referee Charley Daggert counted him out of the title he had won after much desperate effort slightly more than a year ago.

The knockout was the cue for a tremendous demonstration. Fans swarmed into the ring as the unbeaten Bay State boxer with the paralyzing punch stood in his corner, winner of the ring's richest prize after a battle that he could have lost as early as the first round. He was the first white heavyweight to hold the title since Jim Braddock was stopped by Joe Louis in Chicago in 1937. Here was the new champion and nothing could halt the crowd in its eagerness to acclaim him.

Many Trampled in Rush

From all sections of the vast arena, where Gene Tunney had lifted the title from Jack Dempsey just twenty-six long years ago, fans rushed on the ring to greet the conqueror.

Many were trampled in the rush, which started in the lower-priced seats in the permanent stands and, under increasing momentum, moved across and through the seats at the ringside.

For a time a wall of police about the working press rows checked the rush. Police climbed into the ring. A straggler broke through the cordon back of the press rows. Then another. Then it was a steady stream of humanity climbing and clambering over the backs of the writers.

Then the crush became too much for the police. They gave up and let the demonstration run its course. Several telegraph instruments and typewriters at the ringside were kicked under the ring. A movie camera was broken.

Most of the demonstrators were young fellows with the reckless abandon that only youth can boast. They risked broken and bruised limbs to get into the ring.

When Walcott had been counted out his stricken handlers leaped through the ropes to the side of their fallen idol and carried him to his corner. It was several minutes before he could be revived sufficiently to leave the ring, with the assistance of Trainer Dan Florio and his brother Nick, and his manager Felix Bocchicchio.

Marciano, on the other hand,

Continued on Page 41, Column 1

Frauds in U. S. Grain Are Put at 10 Million

By JOHN D. MORRIS
Special to THE NEW YORK TIMES.

WASHINGTON, Sept. 23 — The Senate Agriculture Committee blamed lax administration and poor enforcement policies today for the Federal grain storage scandals brought to light in public hearings earlier this year.

In a forty-one-page report of findings and recommendations, the committee estimated that 131 private warehouse men had embezzled about $10,000,000 of Government-owned grain over the last five years. Slightly more than $2,000,000 of the losses have been recovered, and some additional recoveries are possible.

The "conversions," as such embezzlement is called in the grain trade, were of crops stored for the Agriculture Department's Commodity Credit Corporation under the Federal farm price support program.

However, the report said, "no

Continued on Page 19, Column 1

Dodgers Take Flag By Defeating Phils

The Brooklyn Dodgers clinched the National League pennant last night with a 5-4 victory over the Philadelphia Phillies in the twilight opener of a double-header at Ebbets Field. The Dodgers lost the second game, 1—0, in twelve innings.

A two-run double by Duke Snider during a three-run fifth inning enabled Brooklyn to take the opener. The Brooks now lead the second-place Giants by six games. The Giants have only six to play and the Dodgers four. New York's double-header yesterday with Boston was rained out.

Gran Hamner accounted for the Phillies' runs with a third-inning home run against Johnny Rutherford, the winning pitcher, with the bases filled.

Details on Page 42.

U. N. IN NEW DRIVE ON BATTERED HILL

Reply to 'Harassing' Jabs Hits Enemy in West—Red Probes Repulsed on Wide Front

By LINDESAY PARROTT
Special to THE NEW YORK TIMES.

TOKYO, Wednesday, Sept. 24—United Nations troops struck back today at the Communists on the western front in Korea after the enemy, probing all along the 100-mile Allied line yesterday from Panmunjom in the west to the "Punchbowl" in the eastern Korean mountains, sought but failed to find weak spots.

Allied infantry jumped off this morning in an attack on "Kelly Hill," battered hillock in the west, which hard-fighting Chinese had captured last Thursday. Front reports said the combat still was in progress at 7:30 A. M.

For the second time United Nations infantry fought its way to the top, but resistance continued and the issue was in doubt. The Allies reached the summit Saturday, but were turned back later by an enemy counter-attack. Today's assault was the third effort to retake the hill, which is seven miles southwest of bitterly contested "Old Baldy," near Panmunjom, captured from the Chinese Sunday by a battalion from the United States Second Infantry Division.

Attacks at 20 Points

The enemy's series of local attacks yesterday were made in strength of no more than two platoons, but Eighth Army Headquarters said the jabs were delivered in twenty places along the outpost line. All were driven back.

A military spokesman said the Communist tactics probably were intended as "harassing actions" following the heavy local fighting of the last two weeks.

The enemy's apparent determination during the last fortnight to increase the scale of the ground fighting in a series of drives for outpost positions has cost the Chinese and North Koreans a considerable number of casualties, intelligence estimates said. Eighth Army Headquarters said 3,332 enemy were killed or wounded during the week of September 15-21, and 3,743 in the previous week. The total of more than 7,000 casualties is approximately the usual strength of an enemy division.

South Koreans Rewon Hill

The heaviest toll in the last few days was taken during the seesaw fighting for a hill north of the "Punchbowl," a strategic cup-shaped valley that controls the best lines of communication in the rugged eastern Korean watershed. Communist casualties there in fifteen hours of fighting Tuesday were estimated at 117 killed and 322 wounded.

The troops that stormed the hill in a tank-led attack after the heights had been seized by the enemy during darkness were identified as members of the Republic of Korea Eighth Division, one of the outfits of the retrained and re-equipped South Korean Army now holding much of the front. The R. O. K.'s recaptured the hill after Allied planes had made eighty-seven strikes against North Koreans dug in there.

Four new probes were made by the enemy yesterday on a four-mile front in the eastern sector, Eighth Army Headquarters said. In each case the Communists withdrew after engagements lasting up to a half-hour and the R. O. K.'s continued to hold the contested hill.

On the central front the enemy felt out Allied advance positions northwest of Yonchon, and in the west the Chinese Communists made five light attacks against scarred "Bunker Hill," won and lost several times in recent fighting. Contact was maintained during the night and up to 6 A. M.

Continued on Page 2, Column 6

WEST REJECTS BID FOR BIG 4 SESSION ON GERMAN TREATY

Reply to Moscow Insists That First Such Conference Deal Only With Free Elections

OCTOBER TALK SUGGESTED

Identical Notes Say Russians 'Shifted' Stand Since They First Urged Peace Moves

By WALTER H. WAGGONER
Special to THE NEW YORK TIMES

WASHINGTON, Sept. 23—The United States, Britain and France rejected today a proposal by the Soviet Union for a Big Four conference on a German peace treaty and insisted again that such a meeting be limited to making plans for free, all-German elections. The meeting "could take place in October," the Western powers said.

In identical notes delivered by their envoys in Moscow to the Soviet Ministry of Foreign Affairs, the Western Big Three restated their conviction and determination that first things come first — that machinery must be set up for carrying out free elections throughout divided Germany, that the elections must be held, and that a unified German government must be created before a German peace treaty could be discussed.

Today's note was the Western reply to the Soviet communication of Aug. 23, in which a three-point agenda for possible Big Four talks was proposed, with the "preparation of a peace, treaty with Germany" at the top of the list.

Eighth Item in Exchanges

The reply constituted the eighth item of correspondence between the three Western capitals and the Soviet Union, with four notes issuing from each side, since Moscow first formally suggested Big Four talks on Germany last March 10.

From the beginning, the Soviet Union has proposed talks on a broader basis than the Western powers, especially the United States, have been willing to accept. Countering, Washington, London and Paris have proposed an agenda, restricted to the question of free elections, that has not been acceptable to the Kremlin.

Western diplomats have shown no enthusiasm for getting into a propaganda battle with the Soviet Government on the question of Germany, which, they feel, would be a certainty if the Russians had all of Germany's difficulties, problems and grievances to work over in a forum as important as a Big Four conference.

Today's Western note, hinting at the prospects for Soviet propaganda blasts at a meeting on Germany, called attention to the "wholly unfounded attacks" on the Atlantic pact, the European Defense Community Treaty and the Bonn peace contract with the Western Allies in the Soviet communication of Aug. 23.

Describing all those develop-

Continued on Page 9, Column 1

PRAISE BY GENERAL

He Commends Senator for 'Magnificent' Talk on His Finances

STUMPS OHIO WITH TAFT

Then Discards Cleveland Text to Laud Running Mate as a Courageous Person

Text of the Eisenhower speech in Cleveland is on Page 24.

By JAMES RESTON
Special to THE NEW YORK TIMES.

CLEVELAND, Sept. 23—Gen. Dwight D. Eisenhower listened to Senator Richard M. Nixon's explanation of his defense fund tonight and immediately indicated that he would retain the Senator as his Vice Presidential running mate.

In an extraordinary evening that started with a defense of Senator Nixon's honesty and developed into a Hollywood-type story of the Senator's life, General Eisenhower told a roaring crowd of 15,000 in the Cleveland Public Auditorium that his personal admiration and affection for the Californian were "undiminished."

The Republican Presidential nominee, who watched the Nixon telecast while the audience in the Public Auditorium listened to it over a loudspeaker, withheld final judgment on the case, but he praised Senator Nixon's courage and left no doubt that, unless some wholly new element were introduced into the controversy, Senator Nixon would receive his endorsement. He also called the Senator to a personal meeting with him.

'Affection' Is Undiminished

General Eisenhower wired Mr. Nixon tonight as follows:

"Your presentation was magnificent. While technically no decision rests with me, yet you and I know that the realities of the situation will require a personal pronouncement, which so far as the public is concerned, will be considered decisive.

"In view of your comprehensive presentation, my personal decision is going to be based on a personal conclusion. To complete the formulation of that personal decision, I feel the need of talking to you and would be most appreciative if you could fly to see me at once. Tomorrow night I shall be at Wheeling, W. Va.

"I cannot close this telegram without saying that whatever personal admiration and affection

Continued on Page 25, Column 1

The New York Times

EXPLAINS SPECIAL EXPENSE FUND: Senator Richard M. Nixon, Republican Vice Presidential nominee, as seen on television screens here.

'I'M NOT A QUITTER'

Senator Says He'll Let Republican National Committee Decide

HE REVIEWS HIS FINANCES

Accepts Bid to Meet General—Cites Legal Opinions on Use of $18,235 Fund

Text of Nixon speech, Page 22; financial record, Page 23.

By GLADWIN HILL
Special to THE NEW YORK TIMES.

LOS ANGELES, Sept. 23—Senator Richard M. Nixon, in a nation-wide television and radio broadcast tonight, defended his $18,235 "supplementary expenditures" fund as legally and morally beyond reproach.

He laid before the Republican National Committee and the American people the question of whether he should remain on the Republican party's November election ticket as the candidate for Vice President.

Rising, near the end of his talk, from the desk at which he had sat, Senator Nixon urged his auditors to "wire and write" the Republican National Committee whether they thought his explanation of the circumstances surrounding the fund was adequate.

"I know that you wonder whether or not I am going to stay on the Republican ticket or resign," he said. "I don't believe that I ought to quit, because I'm not a quitter * * *.

Decision 'Not Mine'

"But the decision, my friends, is not mine. I would do nothing that would harm the possibilities of Dwight Eisenhower to become President of the United States; and for that reason I am submitting to the Republican National Committee tonight, through this television broadcast, the decision which it is theirs to make. * * *.

"Wire and write the Republican National Committee whether you think I should stay or whether I should get off; and whatever their decision is, I will abide by it."

Later he accepted an invitation from General Eisenhower for a conference.

In a half-hour talk that was partly personal, including a frank exposition of his finances, and partly an appeal for support of the Republican ticket such as he has been making in his current whistle-stop tour, the Senator declared of the Southern California supporters' fund disclosed last week:

"I say that it was morally wrong if any of that $18,000 went to Senator Nixon for my personal use.

"I say that it was morally wrong if it was secretly given and secretly handled.

"And I say that it was morally wrong if any of the contributors got special favors for the contributions that they made."

But he declared that, on all three points, the factual answer was negative.

Speaks With Assurance

The candidate, clad in a gray suit and a dark tie, delivered his address in a Hollywood radio-television studio—from which the public was excluded—with composure and assurance. His wife, Patricia, was seated close to him, and he made frequent references to her in detailing his career.

His talk also was peppered with barbed references to the Democratic opposition.

Referring to an Illinois political fund with which Gov. Adlai E. Stevenson, Democratic Presidential nominee, has been linked, Senator Nixon, while stipulating that he did not "condemn" this, suggested that both Mr. Stevenson and his running mate, Senator John J. Sparkman of Alabama, should "come before the American people" and report on their incomes.

"If they don't," he said, "it will be an admission that they have something to hide."

In support of his position, he cited two independent reports he had prepared, one on his finances and one on the legal aspects of the "supplementary expenditures" fund, for the information of Gov. Sherman Adams of New Hampshire, campaign executive of Gen-

Continued on Page 22, Column 1

OUSTER A MISTAKE, CAUDLE TESTIFIES

He Says He Was Told Truman Called It 'a Great Injustice'—White House Denies This

By LUTHER A. HUSTON
Special to THE NEW YORK TIMES.

WASHINGTON, Sept. 23—President Truman was quoted in testimony before a House of Representatives Judiciary subcommittee today as saying that he had done Theron Lamar Caudle "a great injustice" when he dismissed him as Assistant Attorney General in charge of the Tax Division of the department.

Mr. Caudle gave the testimony near the end of an emotional recital of his version of his dismissal. The President's statement, he said, had been made to Representative Frank W. Boykin, Democrat of Alabama, during a private interview at the White House last March. Mr. Boykin disclosed the conversation to Mr. Caudle and members of his family, the witness related.

When Mr. Boykin asked Mr. Truman what he was going to do to rectify the "injustice" the President answered, "What can I do?" Mr. Caudle testified.

Representative Boykin also said, according to Mr. Caudle, that Mr. Truman had told him that if Donald S. Dawson, one of the President's aides, had arrived at Key West two hours earlier "I never would have done it."

Dismissal Ordered From Florida

The President ordered Mr. Caudle's dismissal from Key West, Fla., where he was on vacation on Nov. 16 last. Mr. Dawson arrived soon after the action was taken.

The White House said that there was no truth in the statement that the President had told Representative Boykin he had done Mr. Caudle a great injustice.

At Mr. Boykin's office here it was said that he was in Alaska on a business trip and could not be reached immediately for comment.

Mr. Caudle was dismissed while a Congressional inquiry was under way into tax scandals in the Bureau of Internal Revenue and the Justice Department's handling of cases referred to it by the bureau. The only statement made at the time was that the President had acted because of "outside activities" incompatible with Mr. Caudle's responsibilities as a Government official.

Representative Frank L. Chelf, Democrat of Kentucky and chairman of the subcommittee, asked Mr. Caudle if he had ever heard "the basis upon which the President acted."

"No, sir," replied Mr. Caudle. "I never have found out."

Mr. Caudle said that Representative Boykin told him that during the White House interview "the

Continued on Page 12, Column 3

Stevenson Willing to Impose Tighter Controls if Needed

By W. H. LAWRENCE
Special to THE NEW YORK TIMES.

BALTIMORE, Sept. 23—Gov. Adlai E. Stevenson of Illinois told a cheering capacity audience of 9,000 Maryland Democrats tonight that he would not hesitate to impose tighter wage and price controls if necessary to halt inflation.

The Democratic nominee's speech was heard also by a nation-wide radio and television audience. It was made just after Senator Richard M. Nixon of California, the Republican Vice Presidential nominee, had concluded his report about his personal finances.

[The text of the Stevenson speech is printed on Page 26.]

But the Governor did not refer in any way to Senator Nixon's speech, of which he saw about two minutes on television before he left his hotel room, nor to the question of whether the Californian should be dropped from the Republican ticket.

As he was leaving the platform Mr. Stevenson was informed by a reporter of the gist of the address by Senator Nixon, in defense of his $18,235 expense fund. Asked to comment, he replied:

"I'll have nothing to say on that tonight."

[The American Federation of Labor convention in New York adopted a resolution on Tuesday giving unanimous support to Governor Stevenson. Similar action had been taken previously by the executive committee of the Congress of Industrial Organiations.]

The Baltimore speech, delivered in the Fifth Regiment Armory, was Governor Stevenson's set speech on the inflationary problem, for the solution of which he

Continued on Page 27, Column 5

U. S. WIDENS STUDY INTO NIXON'S FUND

Aide First Affirms Then Denies That Truman Asked Inquiry—Senator Tied to Tax Case

By ANTHONY LEVIERO
Special to THE NEW YORK TIMES.

WASHINGTON, Sept. 23 — The White House at first confirmed and later denied today that President Truman had directed James P. McGranery, Attorney General, to study the possibility of criminal prosecution of Senator Richard M. Nixon, Republican Vice Presidential candidate, and the seventy-six Californians who contributed $18,235 to his expense fund.

Before the White House had withdrawn its statement, however, a Justice Department spokesman confirmed that the study was being made. Moreover, the spokesman said that the study was wider in scope than at first indicated — wider in that he indicated an intent to assure the involvement of Senator Nixon if it was concluded that his seventy-six sponsors were liable to prosecution.

Meanwhile, The St. Louis Post-Dispatch reported that Dana C.

Continued on Page 17. Column 1

Teachers Union Witnesses Assail Senate Red Inquiry

By CHARLES GRUTZNER

Two officers of the Teachers Union testified under oath yesterday that they were not and never had been members of the Communist party, but they joined eight other witnesses who refused to tell a Senate Internal Security subcommittee whether they were Communists in denouncing the current investigation into communism in the schools as an attack upon the concept of the open mind in education.

Several of the witnesses in the Federal Court House on Foley Square charged that the "inquisition" of teachers had been inspired in church circles that were trying to "intrude" upon public education.

Charles J. Hendley, former president of the union, named George A. Timone, prominent Roman Catholic layman and chairman of the Board of Education's law committee, as a foe of the union because it "has defended the American principle of separation of church and state and has strenuously opposed clerical interference with public education."

Mr. Hendley, one of the eight who refused to say whether they were or ever had been Communists, denied that the Teachers Union was or ever had been controlled by Communists, as had been charged by Mr. Timone and Dr. Bella V. Dodd, former Communist functionary and former legislative representative of the union, in testimony two weeks ago.

Public hearings will continue today at 9 A. M. before Senator Homer Ferguson, Republican of Michigan, sitting as a one-man subcommittee, and Robert Morris, counsel to the subcommittee. After an hour of open testimony the committee will go into closed session to examine teachers in all four of the municipal colleges and several other local institutions, including Columbia, New York and Long Island Universities.

Additional officers of the Teachers Union will be questioned at the open hearings before and after the closed session. It is expected that members of the college and university faculties will be put on the stand at an open hearing tomorrow.

James Nack, the union treasurer, and Mrs. Mildred K. Garvin, vice president in charge of elementary schools, swore they never had been Communists. Mr. Nack is a mathematics teacher and director of the school honor society at Stuyvesant High School. Mrs. Garvin is a grade teacher at Public School 192, Manhattan.

Mr. Nack and Mrs. Garvin became the first, among twenty teachers or union officials questioned so far, to answer what have come to be known as the "$64

Continued on Page 4, Column 3

Truman Buys Painting for Wife, Trying His Art On First for Size

By PAUL P. KENNEDY
Special to THE NEW YORK TIMES.

WASHINGTON, Sept. 23—President Truman took a brief recess from the affairs of state and the political turmoil this afternoon for a bit of a esthetic shopping.

After a surprise visit to a Georgetown antique shop, the President came away with a Dutch castle scene, painter unidentified, which he will present to Mrs. Truman to be hung in their Independence, Mo., home.

In the course of seventeen minutes, Mr. Truman inspected about 150 paintings in a collection bought a year ago by Charles Kohen for his shop.

Quiet Georgetown was startled at 4 P. M. when a squad of Secret Service men set up a guard around Mr. Kohen's small shop. By the time the President's limousine rolled up thirty minutes later, followed by a Secret Service car, a handful of the curious had gathered in front of the shop.

Immediately on entrance, Mr. Truman was taken to the shop's second floor by Mr. Kohen. After one look at the large room, the walls of which were lined and the floors stacked with pictures, the President, according to Mr. Kohen, exclaimed:

"You've got too damn many pictures here."

The President, Mr. Kohen said, had no clear idea about the subject matter, the school or the painter, but he knew the exact size he wanted.

"I know exactly the place I want to hang it," the President explained.

He was finally torn between the Dutch painting and a landscape by Joseph Turner. The choice went to the Dutch picture, but the President was at first insistent on knowing the painter.

"Don't ask me that, Mr. Presi-

Continued on Page 13, Column 1

Thomas Mitchell (left), Gary Cooper and Grace Kelly in High Noon.

Shirley Booth and Burt Lancaster in Come Back, Little Sheba.

The New York Times.

LATE CITY EDITION
Mostly fair today and tomorrow, little change in temperature.
Temperature Range Today—Max., 70; Min., 58
Temperature Yesterday—Max., 70; Min., 58
Full U. S. Weather Bureau Report, Page 42

Copyright, 1952, by The New York Times Company.

VOL. CII..No. 34,578.   Entered as Second-Class Matter, Post Office, New York, N. Y.   NEW YORK, THURSDAY, SEPTEMBER 25, 1952.   Times Square, New York 36, N. Y. Telephone LAckawanna 4-1000   FIVE CENTS

---

800 NEW POLICEMEN WILL BE APPOINTED BY CITY WEDNESDAY

Funds for 200 Civilian Clerks to Be Asked to Release Men for Foot Patrol Duty

$5,500,000 NEW OUTLAY

Mayor's Move to Increase Force Prompted by Demands to Halt Crimes of Violence

By PAUL CROWELL

Mayor Impellitteri announced yesterday that 800 new policemen would be appointed next Wednesday. He announced also that the Board of Estimate would be asked at its meeting on Oct. 9 to provide funds for 200 civilian clerks to be assigned to the Police Department to make available for patrol duty an equal number of policemen now doing clerical work.

The Mayor's moves to place an additional 1,000 policemen on the streets to safeguard the city's residents from crimes of violence were made known after he had conferred at City Hall with Police Commissioner George P. Monaghan and Budget Director Abraham D. Beame.

"We have re-examined the pressing need for new patrolmen and have concluded that money must be provided even though appropriations for less essential services may have to suffer," the Mayor declared.

"These moves will give us an additional 1,000 policemen on the streets where they are needed. Police Commissioner Monaghan is in complete accord with me on the desirability of putting more men out on foot patrol."

Monaghan 'Personally Delighted'

Mr. Monaghan, when informed of the Mayor's announcement, said that he was "personally delighted" at the Mayor's decision to make more policemen available for patrol duty.

The 800 men to be appointed next Wednesday will be in addition to the 525 new policemen to be appointed between that date and July 1, 1953, in order to place the manpower of the Police Department on a forty-hour-a-week basis until Jan. 1 and a forty-two-hour week between Jan. 1 and next July 1.

The appointment of the 800 new policemen will represent an acceleration of the program announced by the Mayor several weeks ago, when he said that 400 new men would be named Oct. 1 and 400 more every three months thereafter until a total of 1,600 has been appointed by July 1. It was indicated at City Hall that there was a possibility that the total might be as high as 2,000.

Demands for Drastic Action

The moves announced by the Mayor plus the addition of 525 policemen to the force to allow for the shorter work-week program will cost the city about $5,500,000 more than is now provided in the Police Department's budget for 1952-53. The additional funds will be made available by the issuance of budget notes to be redeemed in the expense budget for 1953-54, by transfers of funds from other agency appropriations or by a combination of both methods.

The Mayor's moves to increase the police manpower available for foot-patrol duty were prompted by strong and insistent demands that drastic action be taken to prevent

Continued on Page 15, Column 4

---

28 in Police Case Identified By Gross, but Only 3 as Payees

Weary Gambler Names Bou, Regan and Scro in Pay-Offs—Repeats the Charge He Began Payments to O'Brien in 1943

By EMANUEL PERLMUTTER

Harry Gross, sallow-faced and hollow-eyed, walked through a courtroom in the Criminal Courts Building yesterday and picked out twenty-eight suspended plainclothes men whom he said he knew. Of the remaining three defendants in the departmental graft trial, two were absent and the third was excluded from identification because his lawyer was not present.

This perfect score by the former bookmaker seemed to cast a pall over the defendants and their lawyers. It didn't appear to brighten the countenance of the witness either. He walked sullenly and wearily back to the witness stand to begin the first day of his testimony against the policemen who allegedly had been on his payroll.

In the day's proceedings Gross specifically named three of the defendants who, he said, were involved in his graft payments. He also gave details of gambling bribes he allegedly made to former

Police Commissioner William P. O'Brien in 1944 when the latter was a deputy chief inspector in charge of the Thirteenth Division, Brooklyn.

The three defendants named by Gross in pay-offs were Capt. John Bou and Patrolmen Edward Scro and Daniel A. Regan. He mentioned five other defendants in testimony about his operations between 1942 and 1944, but did not say he made payments to them.

The former gambler, who has already served one year of a twelve-year sentence for bookmaking, said Captain Bou was the first of the defendants to whom he paid graft. He said he paid $100 a month to the captain in 1942 when the defendant was attached to the Police Commissioner's Squad.

Under questioning by Victor J. Herwitz, assistant corporation counsel, Gross testified that the payments to Bou were made for

Continued on Page 15, Column 1

Senate's Communist Inquiry Reaches Into Local Colleges

By CHARLES GRUTZNER

The Federal investigation into communism in the nation's schools reached yesterday into colleges in this area as faculty members of Columbia and Rutgers Universities and Hunter, Brooklyn and Queens Colleges testified at an open hearing of the Senate Internal Security Subcommittee in the Federal Court House on Foley Square.

Of ten witnesses heard yesterday, all but one refused to answer fully the twin questions whether they were or had ever been members of the Communist party. Lucille Spence, secretary of the Teachers Union and a biology teacher at Franklin K. Lane High School, Brooklyn, swore that she neither was nor had ever been a Communist.

All the witnesses denied, as had teachers from elementary and high schools at previous hearings, that they ever had seen any evidence of attempts by teachers in their schools to inculcate students with Communist ideology.

Evidence on Proposed Texts

The subcommittee put into its record, however, evidence that the Teachers Union suggested classroom use of material published by organizations which, according to Benjamin Mandel, research director for the Senate unit, had been listed by one or more Government agencies as subversive.

Mr. Mandel noted for the record that the union publication, The New York Teacher News, carried a regular column entitled "New Materials for Classroom Use," which frequently listed or reviewed publications of allegedly subversive groups. He said the paper also urged union members to attend meetings of such organizations.

Among the organizations listed by Mr. Mandel were the Committee for a Democratic Far Eastern Policy, the National Council of Soviet-American Friendship, the American Committee for Protection of the Foreign-Born, and the Council for African Affairs.

Three among the witnesses who refused to answer one or both of the "$64 questions" face automatic dismissal by the Board of Higher Education from their posts in municipal colleges under Section 903 of the City Charter, which provides that any city employe who refuses to testify before an authorized body on grounds of possible self-incrimination forfeits his job.

Teachers Are Named

They are Vera Shlakman, economics instructor at Queens College and union vice president in charge of colleges; Bernard Reiss, Professor of Psychology at Hunter, and Harry Slochower, associate professor in the Brooklyn College German Department, who has been teaching comparative and world literature.

Professor Slochower told Senator Homer Ferguson, Republican of Michigan, sitting as a one-man subcommittee, that he was not a Communist. He balked, however, at the companion question: "Have you ever been a member of the Communist party?"

A fourth employe of the Board of Higher Education, Frederic Ewen, assistant professor of English at Brooklyn College, forestalled dismissal by filing his retirement papers on Tuesday, as he was entitled to do, having put in thirty years of service. Professor Ewen announced his retirement from the witness chair. Neither

Continued on Page 11, Column 1

RED FORCE RETAKES WEST KOREAN HILL

Puerto Ricans Win Crest, but Shelling Beats Them Back —Clark Confers at Front

By LINDESAY PARROTT

TOKYO, Thursday, Sept. 25—Hard-fighting Chinese Red infantry threw United Nations forces back yesterday from "Kelly Hill" on the Western Korean front. But Allied troops scored in an eastern sector, smashing two enemy attacks on ridges south of Kosong near the Japan Sea.

Puerto Rican troops of the Sixty-fifth Regiment of the United States Third Infantry Division fought their way in the morning to the top of "Kelly Hill" in the Panmunjom sector, which was seized last week by the Chinese Communists. For a few hours, the Puerto Ricans held the crest, after savage hand-to-hand combat when two assault columns converged on an enemy's trenches and bunkers.

But heavy mortar and artillery fire pounded the hill from the enemy lines, and at noon the Puerto Ricans pulled back, leaving the slopes to the Communists. It was the third try that United Nations troops have made to recapture the much-battered hillock and the second time they have reached the crest, only to withdraw under the enemy guns.

The fighting flared up on the recently quiet East coast front when North Koreans, supported by 2,500 rounds of fire, attacked two hills south of Kosong.

One Red battalion struck shortly

Continued on Page 2, Column 2

'CLIQUE' IS BLAMED IN CAUDLE OUSTER; HE QUOTES M'GRATH

Former Official Says Superior Told Him White House Group Was 'After' Both of Them

HINTS AT A NEW SCANDAL

He Declares Ex-Justice Head Talked of Story That Would 'Blow White House High'

By LUTHER A. HUSTON
Special to THE NEW YORK TIMES.

WASHINGTON, Sept. 24—Theron Lamar Caudle testified today at a House of Representatives Judiciary subcommittee hearing that J. Howard McGrath, former Attorney General, had told him that a "clique in the White House" was "after him" and that the same "clique" was after Mr. McGrath.

Mr. Caudle also testified that Mr. McGrath had told him he had a story he could tell that would "blow the White House so high it would become another satellite and the force of gravity would never bring it back to earth."

The witness said Mr. McGrath did not tell him the story and he had no idea what it was. The White House said it would have no comment on Mr. Caudle's testimony.

Mr. Caudle was dismissed by President Truman last November from his post as assistant attorney general in charge of the tax division of the Department of Justice. Mr. McGrath's resignation was requested by the President in April.

Witness Names Three Men

The witness said Mr. McGrath did not name the members of the "clique." Asked if he knew who they were, he said he "had an idea." He then named Charles S. Murphy, David H. Stowe and the late Joseph Short.

Mr. Murphy is special counsel to the President, Mr. Stowe is an administrative assistant to the President and Mr. Short was White House press secretary until his death last week.

Mr. Caudle completed his testimony before the subcommittee, headed by Representative Frank L. Chelf, Democrat of Kentucky, that is investigating the Department of Justice.

Defends the Fund

Mr. Chelf and Representative Kenneth B. Keating of New York, the ranking Republican member of the group, issued a joint statement in which they said of Mr. Caudle that "we feel that he is an honest man who was indiscreet in his associations and a pliant conformer to the peculiar moral climate of Washington."

The conversation about the "clique in the White House" and the story that would blow the White House so high, took place, according to Mr. Caudle, in Mr. McGrath's home after Mr. Caudle was dismissed, but while Mr. McGrath was still Attorney General. Mr. Caudle had gone there, he

Continued on Page 24, Column 3

French Submarine Vanishes In Mediterranean; 48 Aboard

La Sibylle Fails to Surface After Dive Off Toulon— U. S. Sends Aid Team

By The United Press.

TOULON, France, Sept. 24 — The French submarine La Sibylle vanished off this naval base today and ships and planes were sweeping the Mediterranean Sea near here tonight for traces of the missing craft and her forty-eight-man crew.

The alarm was sounded when La Sibylle failed to surface on schedule after anti-submarine maneuvers at 10 A. M. Late tonight no sign of the submarine had been found and the French Navy expressed "serious anxiety" about her fate.

A veritable air-sea task force was ordered from Toulon to search the sea between the craggy isle of Porquerolles, about thirty miles offshore just east of Toulon, and the Riviera resort coast.

[One ship later saw a buoy bobbing about in the water fifty miles south of Porquerolles, according to Reuters.]

It was not clear how soon the TV equipment could be made available to the French search fleet in the Mediterranean.

The passing hours increased concern about La Sibylle's fate, and made it seem more and more certain that the missing submarine has added a burden to the

Continued on Page 9, Column 4

Scene of search (cross).

The New York Times Sept. 25, 1952

trace in 1948, carrying thirty-five men to their death.

A French naval spokesman in Paris warmly welcomed a British offer to lend France a special underwater detection camera developed during last year's search for the British submarine Affray. The camera found the hulk of the Affray on the bottom of the English Channel, but too late to save its seventy-five-man crew.

It was not clear how soon the TV equipment could be made available to the French search fleet in the Mediterranean.

Another French submarine, the 2326, was lost in approximately the same area late in 1946 with twenty-one men aboard. No trace ever was found of her or her crew.

The 2118, the only other submarine France has lost since World War II, also vanished without a

---

EISENHOWER CALLS NIXON VINDICATED; COMMITTEE VOTES TO RETAIN NOMINEE; STEVENSON BARS DATA ON ILLINOIS FUND

GIFT PLAN BACKED

Governor Says Program Lessened Sacrifice of Low-Paid Key Aides

RECIPIENTS' NAMES SECRET

Nominee Undecided on Listing the Identities of Donors, He Tells Baltimore Backers

Text of the Stevenson speech in Baltimore, Page 23.

By W. H. LAWRENCE
Special to THE NEW YORK TIMES.

SPRINGFIELD, Ill., Sept. 24—Gov. Adlai E. Stevenson of Illinois declared today that he had no intention of making public any details of the fund from which he gave secret extra compensation to some appointive Illinois state officials.

The Democratic Presidential nominee asserted he did not believe any useful purpose would be served by publicizing the names of the officials helped or the amounts they received. He also said that he did not know whether he would make public a list of the contributors who made possible these gifts "around Christmas time to a small number of key employes who were making sacrifices to stay in the state government."

The Illinois Governor gave this message to an audience of more than 500 leaders in the Volunteers for Stevenson movement at a $3-a-plate breakfast in the Sheraton Belvedere Hotel in Baltimore. He then flew back to his headquarters here for a thirty-four-hour respite before he hits the campaign trail again Friday morning. His next tour takes him to Evansville, Ind., and Indianapolis on Friday, and Paducah, Ky., and Louisville on Saturday. A big picnic will be held in midday Saturday at the farm home of Vice President Alben W. Barkley near Paducah.

Governor Stevenson, who has been extremely frank in discussing many of the issues of this campaign, has been reticent about telling the details of the Illinois fund, an issue raised against him by his opponents after disclosures had been made that Senator Richard M. Nixon of California, the Republican Vice Presidential nominee, had received more than $18,000 from a group of wealthy Californians to help meet heavy Senatorial and political expenses.

Continued on Page 22, Column 1

Associated Press Wirephoto
THEY "STAND TOGETHER": Gen. Dwight D. Eisenhower and his running mate, Senator Richard M. Nixon, left, respond to cheers of crowd that greeted them after they met last night in Senator Nixon's plane at airport in Wheeling, W. Va.

MESSAGES POUR IN BACKING NOMINEE

Wires at Rate of 4,000 an Hour Overwhelmingly in Favor of Retaining Californian

By CLAYTON KNOWLES
Special to THE NEW YORK TIMES.

WASHINGTON, Sept. 24—A flood of telegrams, pouring in on the Republican National Committee at the rate of 4,000 an hour, appeared tonight to have assured Senator Richard M. Nixon on the ticket, a survey by THE NEW YORK TIMES showed the committee overwhelmingly in favor of retaining the Californian.

With more than 75,000 messages tallied by 5 P. M., sentiment was running overwhelmingly in favor of the Californian's remaining as his party's Vice Presidential candidate.

Samplings both by the committee and by individual reporters who had free access to the great piles of telegrams showed that by a margin of about 200 to 1 voters wiring headquarters felt that Mr. Nixon's Los Angeles speech last night had put him in the clear on the controversial $18,235 "supplementary expenditures" fund put up by a group of wealthy California supporters.

Republican leaders said the reaction to the Nixon speech.

White House Is Silent

There was no comment at the Democratic National Committee or at the White House. Senator Clinton P. Anderson, Democrat of New Mexico, interviewed as he left the White House after a visit with the President, said that, as a Democrat, he felt any advantage arising from the incident would "be our way."

The impact of the Nixon talk also was apparent in editorial comment in the capital.

The Washington Post, supporting General Eisenhower, which last Saturday called upon the Senator to withdraw from the ticket, will say in an editorial to be printed in tomorrow morning's editions that Mr. Nixon's public report has "confirmed our belief that he has done nothing 'involving moral turpitude'—to quote the phrase he used in urging the resignations of William Boyle and Guy Gabrielson." The editorial continued:

"But we remain of the conviction that he has committed an error of judgment, however unwittingly * * *. Many people will continue to view the Nixon episode as typical of that the Eisenhower crusade is overtolerant of and within its own membership.

"For that reason, Senator Nixon

Continued on Page 24, Column 7

CANDIDATES MEET

Airport Greeting Warm— General Calls Senator a 'Man of Honor'

TICKET HARMONY ASSURED

Californian Now 'Stands Higher Than Ever,' Eisenhower Says of His Explanation

Texts of Eisenhower and Nixon speeches in Wheeling, Page 21.

By JAMES RESTON

WHEELING, W. Va., Sept. 24—Gen. Dwight D. Eisenhower said tonight that his Vice Presidential running mate, Senator Richard M. Nixon of California, had been "completely vindicated" of charges in connection with a privately raised expense fund.

Speaking before a cheering and enthusiastic crowd here, the Republican Presidential nominee announced that the 107 members of the Republican National Committee who could be reached had all voted for retaining Mr. Nixon on the ticket. There are 138 members on the full committee.

General Eisenhower declared he believed Senator Nixon "had been subjected to an unfair and vicious attack."

"He is not only completely vindicated as a man of honor but, as far as I am concerned, he stands higher than ever before," said the general.

Thus it was plain that, although there had been no official statement sealing the California Senator's place on the ticket, the general's statement taken with the report on the national committee, made it certain that Mr. Nixon would remain the Republican party's Vice Presidential nominee.

'A Man of Honor'

General Eisenhower's remarks were:

"Ladies and gentlemen, my colleague in this political campaign has been subject to a very unfair and vicious attack. So far as I am concerned, he has not only vindicated himself, but I feel that he has acted as a man of courage and honor and so far as I am concerned, stands higher than ever before.

"I am going to ask Senator Nixon to speak a few words to you this evening, but before he comes to this podium, let me read to you two messages. The first one is a tribute. This is a telegram to me:

"'Dear General: I am trusting that the absolute truth may come out concerning this attack on Richard and when it does I am sure you will be guided right in your decision to place implicit faith in his integrity and honesty. Best wishes from one who has known Richard longer than anyone else. His mother.'

"Now, as I waited on him at the plane this evening, I received a telegram from the Republican Na-

Continued on Page 26, Column 1

G. O. P. HEADS RALLY TO NIXON'S SUPPORT

Summerfield Asserts Attack Has 'Backfired'—Senator's Position Held Stronger

Before the announcement by Gen. Dwight D. Eisenhower last night that the Republican National Committee had voted 107 to 0 to retain Senator Robert M. Nixon on the ticket, a survey by THE NEW YORK TIMES showed the committee overwhelmingly in favor of the Senator.

The backers of the Republican Vice Presidential nominee included Arthur E. Summerfield, chairman of the committee.

On Tuesday night, at the end of Senator Nixon's half-hour broadcast explanation of the $18,235 expense fund donated to him by California supporters, he declared he was submitting the question whether he should stay in the race to the committee and would abide by its decision.

He made it clear that his own inclination was to remain, that his conduct was fully justified.

Mr. Summerfield declared in Cleveland that attacks on Senator Nixon because of the fund had "backfired." He predicted that Senator Nixon's speech would prove "the turning point of the campaign."

His views were echoed throughout the country by Republican officials as they attempted to dig

Continued on Page 27, Column 2

Iran Answers British-U. S. Oil Bid; Sets Time Limit on London's Reply

By ALBION ROSS
Special to THE NEW YORK TIMES.

TEHERAN, Iran, Sept. 24—The Iranian reply to the Churchill-Truman proposals for a settlement of the British-Iranian oil dispute was presented tonight to George Middleton, British Chargé d'Affaires, and Loy W. Henderson, United States Ambassador, by Premier Mohammed Mossadegh. The text will be published here tomorrow.

The note, which contains Dr. Mossadegh's counter-proposals, described as the final Iranian offer, was to have been handed over before noon today, but it was delayed by last-minute discussion of a covering note to Prime Minister Churchill and President Truman.

[In Washington the Iranian Ambassador informed President Truman that his country was confronted by a "very dangerous" economic condition. The envoy appealed to the United States to prevail upon Britain to drop the

blockade that prevents Iran from exporting oil.]

All reports indicate that the Iranian reply does not contain an ultimatum but sets a time limit for a British answer.

It contains a demand for an advance payment by the Anglo-Iranian Oil Company of £49,000,000 ($137,200,000) that is carried on the books of the company under an agreement of 1949 that Iran did not ratify. The demand is understood to have been put in such a form that the sum could be considered as an advance payment for oil deliveries that Iran is prepared to make if the International Court of Justice should find that the sum is not due Iran.

The way has also been left free for the Court to reject the adop-

Continued on Page 5, Column 2

Dewey, Blaming Truman for Korea, Says Eisenhower Is Hope of Peace

Charging that the United States is in a Korean war because the Democratic National Administration allowed the war by two acts of "supreme folly," Governor Dewey declared last night that the election of Gen. Dwight D. Eisenhower, Republican nominee for President, was essential to the survival of this country.

It was the Governor's first speech of the campaign and was carried by television and radio from the New York studios of the National Broadcasting Company.

Recalling that he had warned about Korea in 1947, Mr. Dewey said "the supreme folly was nevertheless committed of pulling our troops out of Korea because they [the Administration] let our Army run down, and then of announcing from the public platform that it was outside of our defense perimeter."

The Governor added that the National Administration might just as well have sent a telegram to

Stalin inviting him to conquer Korea, because we had thereby created "a vacuum of power."

Mr. Dewey said that we had had 117,000 American casualties to pay for Mr. Truman's "blunder." He asserted that we could not afford to continue to pay that kind of a price for "survival by a combination of the fumbling that brought us unprepared into World War II and bungled us into the Korean war."

In a caustic attack on the foreign policy of the Truman Administration, the Governor declared:

"The only solution I know for the survival of this country is that we've got to get rid of the traitors and the incompetent and the crooks in Washington, and get into the Government of this country the skill, the know-how and the vision to win the peace."

In discussing how we could pro-

Continued on Page 18, Column 1

Text of the Dewey address is on Page 18.

1952

Bob Mathias, shown here during the 1952 competition at Helsinki, was the only man to win the Olympic decathlon twice.

Nina Romaschkova won Russia's first Olympic gold medal at the Helsinki Olympics.

Jackie Robinson hit a home run for the Dodgers against the Yankees during the second inning of the first game of the World Series.

Cy Young, shown here at the Olympics in Helsinki, was the first American to ever win the javelin throw. He won it in the 1952 competition.

"All the News That's Fit to Print"

The New York Times.

LATE CITY EDITION
Fair, windy and cooler today.
Fair and cool tomorrow.
Temperature Range Today-Max., 60; Min., 45
Temperatures Yesterday—Max., 69; Min., 47
Full U. S. Weather Bureau Report, Page 33

VOL. CII. No. 34,608. Entered as Second-Class Matter. Post Office, New York, N. Y. NEW YORK, SATURDAY, OCTOBER 25, 1952. Times Square, New York 36, N. Y. Telephone LAckawanna 4-1000 FIVE CENTS

EISENHOWER WOULD 'GO TO KOREA'; STEVENSON ASSAILS 'SLICK' PLANS; ACHESON BARS PEACE OF DISHONOR

SUBWAYS STALLED BY SIGNAL FAILURE AT HEIGHT OF RUSH

Blast and Fire Halt I.R.T. and B.M.T. Trains, Then Force Them to Crawl for Hour

THOUSANDS ARE DELAYED

All of Brooklyn and Most of Manhattan Hit—Bingham Blames Old Equipment

By RALPH KATZ

A small explosion and fire in a manhole outside a powerhouse serving the B. M. T. and I. R. T. subway lines caused one of the city's worst delays in transportation last night at the height of the rush hour.

The fire affected the signal system on the I. R. T. throughout Brooklyn and most of Manhattan and on the B. M. T. from Times Square to the lower end of Manhattan. It caused a half-hour shutdown of service on the I. R. T. and a fifteen-minute shutdown on the B. M. T., after which there were slowdowns on most lines for nearly an hour.

When the trains resumed running they crawled through the tubes, halting intermittently between stations to make sure that all precautions were being observed.

Many thousands of homeward-bound riders and others converging into the Times Square area were caught in the tie-up and slowdown. More than 320 trains on both facilities were involved. The Times Square station became so crowded that the entrances were closed for an hour.

60,000 Stalled on I. R. T.

While the number of stalled trains was about equal on each line, an indication of the number of persons affected was contained in a report from the I. R. T. that between 100 and 125 of its trains held an estimated 60,000 persons.

Many left the trains and walked along subway catwalks to stations, where they sought alternate routes to their destinations.

The explosion and fire occurred at 6:03 P.M. in a manhole on Fifty-ninth Street between Eleventh and Twelfth Avenues. The fire itself was small and was easily put out, but its shorting of near-by circuits could not be handled by the circuit-breakers along the signal wires, which are designed to prevent burn-outs.

The result was a failure on the alternating current lines that feed thirteen sub-stations for the control of signal lights. The interruption of signal service advanced swiftly from breaker to breaker until it became necessary to shut down temporarily the running power in the affected areas.

Service Slow and Erratic

At the Times Square station, the tie-up was recorded as from 6:05 to 6:50 P. M. After that, the trains ran slowly and erratically. The shuttle service to Grand Central operated without interruption, but slowly because of the signal failure.

The seven entrances to the station were closed as soon as the halt developed as a move to prevent unusual crowding. Some of the station lights went out and others burned dimly. It was impossible to ascertain how many riders were in the station at the time, but at one entrance alone 480 accepted receipts for their fares.

A detail of police was sent to the subway station from the West Thirtieth Street police station to handle the crowds at the en-

Continued on Page 34, Column 2

Hurricane Injures 70 As It Pounds at Cuba

By The Associated Press.

MIAMI, Fla., Oct. 24—A hurricane packing 165-mile-per-hour winds slashed a broad path across Cuba today on a course that would take it near South Florida's Gold Coast.

The storm thundered inland over Cuba, with its center near Cienfuegos on the south coast, beating a sixty-mile-wide swath through rich sugar cane and ranch land. Gales lashed outward seventy-five miles from the center of the storm, described as one of the most violent to strike land in recent years.

Seventy persons were reported injured when their homes were blown down. These casualty figures covered only two areas in the path of the storm.

Heavy damage to roads, crops and fruit trees was reported in the Cayman Islands, 125 miles below Cuba. The commissioner

Continued on Page 33, Column 4

HARLEM TENEMENT CITED ON 91 COUNTS

First Week of Firetrap Survey Lays 84 Violations to Same Owner in 4 Other Buildings

By CHARLES G. BENNETT

The end of the first week of the city's firetrap survey in Harlem brought a crackdown yesterday by Frederick S. Weaver, Deputy Commissioner of Housing, on the Klahr Realty Corporation, owner of a five-story tenement building at 1 West 118th Street.

Notices that ninety-one violations of the multiple dwelling law had been found at the building, the first one searched by housing inspectors, were sent yesterday by Mr. Weaver to the Klahr Corporation at 1466 Fifth Avenue.

The owner was also notified of eighty-four violations found in four buildings it operates at 1462-66-68 Fifth Avenue, around the corner from the 118th Street address.

In all, the inspectors reported they had found 617 violations in the seventy-two apartment buildings in the block bounded by West 118th Street, West 119th Street, Lenox and Fifth Avenues. A team of eleven inspectors worked under the supervision of Patrick F. Kelly, chief of the Housing and Buildings Department's rodent control section.

Cases Going Directly to Court

Denouncing the Klahr corporation for its large number of violations, nine of them labeled "extremely hazardous," Commissioner Weaver said he would eliminate the usual departmental hearings and take the owner directly into the Magistrates' Courts.

"Because of the serious nature of many of these violations the owner corporation is not entitled to any consideration from this department," Mr. Weaver declared, adding that the notices served yesterday would be followed by court summonses within five days.

The Klahr Corporation and other Manhattan landlords subsequently brought into court in the continuing firetrap survey are scheduled to go before a special part of Municipal Term presided over by Chief Magistrate John M. Murtagh.

Mr. Murtagh, who has pledged the magistrates' cooperation with the housing campaign, accompanied the housing inspectors last Monday when they opened their drive. Aghast at the living conditions he saw in the crowded apartments in the 1 West 118th Street building, the Chief Magistrate ex-

Continued on Page 15, Column 5

COAL OWNERS ASK PUTNAM TO REVIEW W. S. B. WAGE CURB

Economic Stabilizer Gets Plea for Approval of the 40c Cut From Rise of $1.90 a Day

END OF STRIKE KEY AIM

Moses Says Operators Want to Reopen Pits—Anthracite Negotiations Recessed

By JOSEPH A. LOFTUS
Special to The New York Times.

WASHINGTON, Oct. 24—Northern soft coal operators asked the Government tonight to reconsider the Wage Stabilization Board's refusal to approve 40 cents of the wage increase of $1.90 a day they contracted to pay the miners. About 350,000 members of the United Mine Workers have been on strike since Monday in protest against the board's decision.

Harry M. Moses, president of the Bituminous Coal Operators Association, representing mainly northern tonnage, filed a petition with Roger L. Putnam, Economic Stabilization Administrator. Whether he also filed a petition with the Wage Stabilization Board could not be learned.

Mr. Moses would not indicate whether his appeal had any basis other than the willingnes of the operators to honor the contract he made and their desire to restore production.

The Wage Board majority of public and industry members held in their decision that an increase of more than $1.50 would give to the miners a larger increase than had been received by workers in any other major industry and might set a pattern for increases that would break anti-inflation controls.

Putnam Studying Petition

Mr. Putnam's office acknowledged this evening that the petition had arrived "a few minutes ago." A spokesman said that Mr. Putnam was "going to study it very carefully and in the meantime he is not going to say anything about it."

John L. Lewis, president of the United Mine Workers, had stated that the miners would go back to work when the operators paid them the full $1.90 increase. He had been reported willing to join the request for reconsideration of the W. S. B. cut in the wage increase, but whether he did could not be learned tonight.

[However, in New York a spokesman for Mr. Lewis said last night that the mine chief had joined Mr. Moses in the appeal to Mr. Putnam. He added that Mr. Lewis would not release information concerning the appeal until it was made public through other sources.]

Mr. Lewis did not join in the original petition to the board for approval of the wage increase.

He left late this afternoon for Morgantown, W. Va., where he will make a speech tomorrow night in behalf of the Democratic nominee for President, Gov. Adlai E. Stevenson.

Cole Working on Dispute

David L. Cole, director of the Federal Mediation and Conciliation Service, has been working on the dispute for the last two days. He conferred with Mr. Moses and Mr. Lewis again today, but declined to answer questions about the nature of their talks.

He refused to give any support to assumptions that private talks with Mr. Putnam and higher officials in the Administration preceded the filing of the Moses petition.

The Administration obviously is trying to end the coal strike before the election, but whether it is willing to do it with a straight-out reversal of the Wage Stabilization Board has not been indicated.

Mr. Lewis and Mr. Moses are eager to get the mines back into production, but both are reported averse to substituting "fringe" improvements—such as higher vacation pay or welfare fund payments—for the 40-cent cut ordered in the wage agreement.

The United Mine Workers and the anthracite operators continued their negotiations for a new contract. Talks were recessed late today until tomorrow.

Effects of Reversal Surmised

WASHINGTON, Oct. 24 (AP)—Any reversal of the Wage Stabilization Board decision on the coal wage would be bound to anger board members and might well lead to mass resignations, at least of the industry members, according to views expressed here tonight.

A reversal of the board, it was suggested, would furnish Republican party campaigners with pow-

Continued on Page 13, Column 5

Support of the U. N. Urged by Nominees

Gen. Dwight D. Eisenhower and Gov. Adlai E. Stevenson declared their support of the United Nations last night and called upon the people of the nation to back the world organization.

[Texts of messages by two candidates appear on Page 2.]

Commending the United Nations for its prompt action in Korea, General Eisenhower asked the American people "to reaffirm their devotion to the peaceful hopes of free men everywhere" and the United States "as a proud member of the United Nations pledge again our strength, our fortune and our sacred honor to the end that no free nation shall ever again be destroyed upon this earth."

In backing United Nation action in Korea, General Eisenhower supported the action taken

Continued on Page 2, Column 5

LONG FIGHT SURGES OVER KOREAN HILLS

U. S. and South Korean Forces Win and Lose Peaks as the Reds Pour In More Men

By LINDESAY PARROTT
Special to The New York Times.

TOKYO, Saturday, Oct. 25—United States and South Korean troops were locked today in a swaying battle with the Chinese Communists for "Triangle Hill" and "Sniper Ridge," outpost bastions of the enemy's main defenses on the central Korean front. The results were still in doubt at noon after thirty hours of continuous combat.

During the morning, weary infantrymen of the Republic of Korea's Second Division fought their way back to the crest of "Pinpoint Hill," dominating feature of "Sniper Ridge," north of Kumhwa. But the Chinese Reds were pouring a fresh regiment into the fight for the position, which had already cost the foe most of a division (12,000 men) in casualties.

Latest reports said the South Koreans held about half of "Pinpoint," the Reds the other half.

The South Koreans had gone forward through one of the heaviest barrages the Communists have fired in the current hill fighting. During the night, before the Chinese Reds' infantry drove the South Koreans off the summit, enemy guns had laid 17,000 rounds of mortar and artillery shells on the ridge.

Intermittent rain hampered close-

Continued on Page 3, Column 3

U. S. EXPLAINS VIEW

Secretary Tells U. N. Unit Washington Is Ready and Eager to End War

ASKS APPROVAL OF EFFORT

Again Rules Out Any Forcible Repatriation and Cites 17 Pacts Signed by Soviet

Excerpts from U. N. address by Mr. Acheson are on Page 4.

By A. M. ROSENTHAL
Special to The New York Times.

UNITED NATIONS, N. Y., Oct. 24—Secretary of State Dean Acheson told United Nations delegates today that the United States was ready and eager to end the Korean war but that peace could not be "purchased at the price of honor."

For almost three hours Mr. Acheson held the floor of the Political and Security Committee of the General Assembly, taking the sixty delegates on a carefully impassionate, calmly spoken and meticulously detailed review of the Korean war, all that led up to it and the long drawn-out attempts to end it. Several times in his speech he carefully underlined the charge that it was the Soviet Union that had trained and equipped the army of North Korea, sent it into a war of aggression and still was maintaining it in the field.

Mr. Acheson formally asked the General Assembly to give its approval to the United Nations conduct of the war through the United States, acting in its capacity as the Unified Command. Together with twenty other countries, the United States put before the committee a resolution calling on the enemy to accept the one principle that apparently has been holding up the signing of a truce, the principle that no prisoner of war should be sent back home against his will.

Soviet Signatures Cited

The Secretary of State, in a deliberately dry voice, read out seventeen treaties signed by the Soviet Union after World War I in which the principle of no forcible repatriation had been explicitly agreed to by the Soviet Government.

"Pretty good doctrine," Mr. Acheson said caustically.

Time and again Mr. Acheson, who spoke without a prepared text but relied on sheaves of notes, stressed the point that the United States had done everything honorable to reach a Korean peace. He revealed that not only had open

Continued on Page 4, Column 6

The New York Times (by Meyer Liebowitz)

ACHESON SPEAKS: The Secretary of State at United Nations Political and Security Committee of the General Assembly.

Stevenson Fears a 'Munich' In Rival's Asian Troop Plan

By W. H. LAWRENCE
Special to The New York Times.

ABOARD STEVENSON TRAIN, in New York, Oct. 24—Gov. Adlai E. Stevenson of Illinois told upstate New York audiences today that Gen. Dwight D. Eisenhower's "proposal of a quick and a slick way out of Korea" would risk a "Munich in the Far East, with the probability of a third World War not far behind."

The Democratic Presidential nominee worked hard, at fourteen stops, for New York's vitally important forty-five electoral votes. His day began with a trainside audience of almost 1,000 at Niagara Falls, at 7:15 A. M., and wound up with a formal speech, locally televised and broadcast, at the Rensselaer Polytechnic Institute at Troy at 9:30 P. M.

[Text of Stevenson talk in Rochester appears on Page 10.]

This was United Nations Day and Governor Stevenson hammered at the Republican Presidential candidate's proposal, first made in isolationist-minded Illinois, that South Korean troops should be trained and equipped to take over the Korean front lines by themselves so that American and other United Nations troops could be pulled back into reserve. In a speech at Champaign, Ill., early in October, General Eisenhower had said that if there must be a war in the Far East "let it be Asians against Asians."

"The war in Korea, my friends, is not Mr. Truman's war," Governor Stevenson told an enthusiastic audience at Rochester. "It is mankind's war. * * * The issues in this conflict are too grave and too great for partisan politics. And the proposal of a quick and a slick way out of Korea is false.

'Would Mean Surrender'

"My opponent has told us that we could leave the South Koreans to do the fighting alone against the Communists," Mr. Stevenson continued. "He has said that Asians should be left to fight Asians. If we were to follow the General's policy, we would risk a Munich in the Far East, with the probability of a third World War not far behind.

"Great as would be the increasing role bravely taken by the armies of the Republic of Korea, it is clear that the withdrawal of all American forces would mean ultimate surrender of South Korea to the larger, stronger forces of the Communists, and South Korea itself would become a base for further aggression and Communist pressure against Japan, Formosa and the Philippines. And, it would also release Communist forces for still greater adventures on the mainland of Asia."

Governor Stevenson asserted that Gen. James A. Van Fleet, Eighth Army commander in Korea, had declared that the South Korean army would not be strong enough to man the entire battle line by itself. Governor Stevenson went on to say that this "mistake" by General Eisenhower "could not be charged to ignorance." He said

Continued on Page 10, Column 6

U. N. EDITORIAL AIDE ADMITS RED LINKS

Confirms Chambers' Charges—Senator Criticizes Lie on Suspects' Paid Leaves

By RICHARD H. PARKE

A Democratic Senator acting as chairman of a Senate subcommittee strongly criticized Trygve Lie, United Nations Secretary General, yesterday for giving leaves of absence with pay to ten American United Nations employes suspected of Communist affiliations.

Senator James O. Eastland of Mississippi, who said Mr. Lie's action was "beyond my comprehension," asserted at the same time that his internal security subcommittee of the Senate Judiciary Committee had uncovered among American employes of the United Nations the "greatest concentration" of Communists in its hearings to date.

He made his statement as the committee wound up a session at the Federal Courthouse on Foley Square during which it wrung an admission from David Zablodowsky, a United Nations editorial official, that he had been a member of a Communist underground, al-

Continued on Page 5, Column 1

GENERAL IN PLEDGE

'First Task' Would Be 'Early and Honorable' End of the War

HE GIVES FOUR PROMISES

Bars Appeasement—Declares 'Record of Failure' Led to Far East Fighting

Text of the Eisenhower speech in Detroit is on Page 8.

By ELIE ABEL
Special to The New York Times.

DETROIT, Oct. 24—Gen. Dwight D. Eisenhower gave the nation his pledge tonight that if elected President he would go to Korea to seek an early and honorable end of the war there.

He promised to "forego the diversions of politics" and to concentrate on the task of closing the war—a conflict that was never inevitable or inescapable, he said, but one that resulted from the Truman Administration's repeated failures to heed the warnings of Republicans. The General's statement was cheered by an overflow crowd of 5,000 in the Masonic Auditorium here.

To pledge an end of the Korean fighting by any "imminent exact date" would be dishonest, the Republican candidate for President asserted, but it would be equally dishonest to tell the United States that it could only "wait—and wait—and wait" for peace.

The quest of an honorable end of the war requires a personal trip to Korea by the new President, General Eisenhower said, and added:

"Only in that way could I learn how best to serve the American people in the cause of peace.

"I shall go to Korea."

To 'Re-Examine Every Course'

He also outlined these four pledges to the American people:

1. That the first task of his Administration would be to "review and re-examine every course of action open to us with one goal in view: To bring the Korean war to an early and honorable end."
2. That he would go to Korea to see for himself how best to achieve this goal.
3. That the United Nations should step up the training and arming of the South Korean forces so that they might eventually defend their own frontiers. At the same time, the free nations should shape a program of psychological warfare capable of cracking "the Communist front" in the Far East.
4. That his Administration would always reject appeasement and vacillation, because appeasement was not the road to peace, but "surrender on the installment plan," he said, quoting the late Senator Arthur H. Vandenberg of Michigan.

Coming near the end of a half-hour radio and television address on the last night of his whistle-

Continued on Page 8, Column 2

Judge Hand Says U. S. Democracy Is Menaced by Suspicion and Fear

By MURRAY ILLSON
Special to The New York Times.

ALBANY, Oct. 24—Unfounded denunciations are spreading fears and suspicions that may lead to the destruction of the country's political institutions, Learned Hand, retired chief judge of the Second Federal Circuit Court of Appeals, asserted here tonight.

Making the principal address before a state-wide gathering of 600 education officials attending the eighty-sixth convocation of the Board of Regents of the University of the State of New York, Judge Hand said that the United States was threatened by internal as well as external perils and was facing "a test which it may fail to pass."

"Risk for risk, for myself I had rather take my chance that some traitors will escape detection than spread abroad a spirit of general suspicion and distrust, which accepts rumor and gossip in place of undismayed and unintimidated inquiry," the judge said, adding:

"I believe that that community is already in the process of dissolution where each man begins to eye his neighbor as a possible enemy, where nonconformity with the accepted creed, political as well as religious, is a mark of disaffection; where denunciation, without specification or backing, takes the place of evidence; where orthodoxy chokes freedom of dissent; where faith in the eventual supremacy of reason has become so timid that we dare not enter our convictions in the open lists to win or lose."

Judge Hand, who retired last year after forty-two years on the Federal bench, said that the fears he had cited were "a solvent which can eat out the cement that binds the stones together" and that they might in the end "subject us to a despotism as evil as any that we dread."

These fears, he added, "can be

Continued on Page 5, Column 3

Morse Resigns From G. O. P.; May Hold Key Vote in Senate

Oregonian Says He Acts for Good of Country—Will Be Independent

By LAWRENCE E. DAVIES
Special to The New York Times.

PORTLAND, Ore., Oct. 24—Senator Wayne Morse of Oregon announced tonight that he was resigning from the Republican party because the tenets of Abraham Lincoln no longer held in a party "dominated by reactionaries running a captive general for the Presidency of the United States." Henceforth, he said, he would be an independent.

His announcement, made on a recording played at a meeting and dance of Volunteers for Stevenson, followed by less than a week the Senator's word that he was supporting Gov. Adlai E. Stevenson of Illinois, the Democratic nominee, for President.

This was despite the fact, he said in his speech, that he was the first member of the Senate publicly to declare himself for Gen. Dwight D. Eisenhower as a potential Republican nominee.

Near the close of a seventeen-minute recording Senator Morse, who has been a controversial figure among Oregon Republicans almost since his election to his first term

Continued on Page 9, Column 2

Should Chamber Be Evenly Divided After Nov. 4, He Could Swing Control

By C. P. TRUSSELL
Special to The New York Times.

WASHINGTON, Oct. 24—Senator Wayne Morse of Oregon, who has bolted the Republican party as well as its Presidential nominee, Gen. Dwight D. Eisenhower, stepped tonight into a position where he might be able to dictate whether the United States Senate should be Republican or Democratic in the next Congress.

If the electoral battles in the various states where Senate seats are at stake this year should result in a Senate of forty-eight to forty-eight counting Mr. Morse as a Republican, under which party he was elected, the Oregon Senator could weight the scales by throwing his vote either way. The present division is forty-nine Democrats and forty-seven Republicans, counting Mr. Morse in the Republican total.

If he voted with the Democrats, they would control the Senate. If he elected to vote with his former colleagues, the Republicans, the resulting tie would have to be decided by the vote of the Vice President, and that Vice President

Continued on Page 9, Column 3

Retail Price Index Declines 0.2% After Steady Climb Since February

Special to The New York Times.

WASHINGTON, Oct. 24—The Government's retail price index dropped 0.2 per cent between mid-August and mid-September, the first decline since last February. The index had been rising steadily since then. A drop of 1 per cent in food prices was responsible for the decline. Prices for all other major groups went up.

The drop was about 0.5 per cent in the old index, which the Bureau of Labor Statistics still compiles as a convenience for unions and managements whose cost-of-living escalator contracts are geared to it.

The modernized index as of Sept. 15 was 190.8, as against 191.1 on Aug. 15. The drop of three-tenths of a percentage point amounted to about two-tenths of a per cent. This index carries a different weight for food than the old index and includes some new items, such as television sets and frozen foods.

The index rise since the Korean fighting began in June, 1950, has been 12.1 per cent. It is up 2.3 per cent above a year ago. The index base (100) is the price average from 1935 to 1939.

The old index on Sept. 15 stood at 191.4, as against 192.3 in mid-August.

The movement of the retail price index affects most wage rates sooner or later. Where escalator clauses are in operation, the effect is automatic, though most adjustments are made on a quarterly basis, rather than monthly. In the quarter ended Sept. 15, the rise in the old index was three-tenths of a percentage point, or about 0.2 per cent.

The price drop of 1 per cent put the food index at 233.2 per cent of the 1935-39 average. This is 2.6 per cent higher than a year ago and 14.8 per cent above June, 1950.

Chiefly responsible for the food

Continued on Page 14, Column 7

A Communist bomb explodes in Saigon. A new phase of the Indo-China struggle of the Viet Minh against the French began.

Gene Kelly in Singin' in the Rain.

"All the News That's Fit to Print"

The New York Times.

ELECTION EXTRA

Fair, warmer today. Some cloudiness and turning cooler tomorrow.
Temperature Range Today—Max., 62; Min., 38
Temperatures Yesterday—Max., 52; Min., 39
Full U. S. Weather Bureau Report, Page 55

Copyright, 1952, by The New York Times Company.

VOL. CII No. 34,619. Entered as Second-Class Matter, Post Office, New York, N. Y. NEW YORK, WEDNESDAY, NOVEMBER 5, 1952. Times Square, New York 36, N. Y. Telephone Lackawanna 4-1000 FIVE CENTS

EISENHOWER WINS IN A LANDSLIDE; TAKES NEW YORK; IVES ELECTED; REPUBLICANS GAIN IN CONGRESS

G.O.P. HOUSE LIKELY

But the Senate Margin Hangs in the Balance of Two Close Races

LODGE TRAILING RIVAL

President Eisenhower May Lack a Working Majority in Congress

By JAMES RESTON

It appeared at 4:30 this morning that control of the United States Senate could be determined by the outcome of the Senatorial races in Michigan and Massachusetts.

At that time the Republicans appeared to have picked up five new seats and lost three others, thus enabling them to wipe out the two-seat advantage held by the Democrats at the end of the Eighty-second Congress.

To assure the power to organize the Senate and place their Republicans at the head of its important committees, however, Senator Henry Cabot Lodge Jr., Republican of Massachusetts, would have to overcome an advantage of more than 75,000 held by Representative John F. Kennedy, his opponent.

And Representative Charles E. Potter, Republican of Michigan had to retain the 47,000 lead he held over the Democratic incumbent, Senator Blair Moody of Michigan.

Morse May Be Vital

So close was the Senate race that there was a possibility that control of the upper chamber could be determined by the decision of Senator Wayne Morse of Oregon, who was elected as a Republican, but who broke with his party during the campaign, and announced that hereafter he was an "independent."

Though it appeared that the Republicans had won control of the House, one thing was certain: that President Dwight D. Eisenhower would not have a comfortable working majority in either house and would require all his gifts of persuasion to win consent for his policies on Capitol Hill.

Several factors in the Senate race were noteworthy:

¶Of the ten so-called isolationist or extremist Republicans who went before the voters yesterday, seven seemed fairly sure of victory. These were Senators Joseph R. McCarthy of Wisconsin; John W. Bricker of Ohio; William E. Jenner of Indiana; Edward Martin of Pennsylvania; Arthur V. Watkins of Utah, George W. Malone of Nevada and Hugh Butler of Nebraska.

Three other Republicans in this same category, however, were in serious trouble if they had not actually been defeated. They were:

Continued on Page 15, Column 1

Electoral Vote by States

	Eisenhower	Stev'son		Eisenhower	Stev'son
Ala.	—	11	Neb.	6	—
Ariz.	4	—	Nev.	3	—
Ark.	—	8	N. H.	4	—
Calif.	32	—	N. J.	16	—
Colo.	6	—	N. M.	4	—
Conn.	8	—	N. Y.	45	—
Del.	3	—	N. C.	—	14
Fla.	10*	—	N. D.	4	—
Ga.	—	12	Ohio	25	—
Idaho	4	—	Okla.	8	—
Ill.	27	—	Ore.	6	—
Ind.	13	—	Pa.	32	—
Iowa	10	—	R. Isl.	4	—
Kan.	8	—	S. C.	—	8
Ky.	—	10	S. D.	4	—
La.	—	10	Tenn.	11	—
Me.	5	—	Texas	24	—
Md.	9	—	Utah	4	—
Mass.	16	—	Vt.	3	—
Mich.	20	—	Va.	12	—
Minn.	11	—	Wash.	9	—
Miss.	—	8	W. Va.	—	8
Mo.	13	—	Wisc.	12	—
Mont.	4	—	Wyo.	3	—
			Total	442	89

*Trend.

EISENHOWER TAKES JERSEY BY 300,000

Senator Smith Is Re-elected—Bond Issues Supported in Record Balloting

By RUSSELL PORTER

With more than three-quarters of New Jersey's vote counted early this morning, Gen. Dwight D. Eisenhower appeared headed toward a plurality of close to 300,000 in the state over Gov. Adlai E. Stevenson. This far exceeded Governor Dewey's 1948 plurality of 85,669 over President Truman.

United States Senator H. Alexander Smith, Republican candidate for re-election, won a sweeping victory over his Democratic opponent, Archibald S. Alexander, though Mr. Smith ran behind the head of his ticket. His indicated plurality was about 200,000.

The returns were:

PRESIDENT

3,461 precincts out of 3,840:

Eisenhower	1,203,120
Stevenson	921,375

UNITED STATES SENATOR

3,399 precincts out of 3,840:

Smith	1,089,883
Alexander	903,533

The Republicans appeared to have retained their majority of nine to five in New Jersey's delegation in the House of Representatives.

Both bond issues on the ballot

Continued on Page 23, Column 2

STATE LEAD 850,000

General's Upstate Edge Tops Million—He Loses City by Only 362,674

PROTEST VOTE SEEN

Albany County, Other Areas in Democratic Column Switch

State Presidential Vote

CITY SUMMARY

	Eisenhower (Rep.)	Stevenson (Dem.-Lib.)
Manhattan	300,234	447,877
Bronx	241,545	393,052
Brooklyn	447,148	656,278
Queens	449,505	331,633
Richmond	55,981	28,247
Total	1,494,413	1,857,087
Upstate	2,413,299	1,147,510
Grand total	3,907,712	3,104,597

4,394 election districts out of 4,394 in the city reporting and 5,222 out of 5,954 upstate.

By JAMES A. HAGERTY

Gen. Dwight D. Eisenhower, Republican nominee for President, carried New York State with its forty-five electoral votes with a plurality of landslide proportions that will reach nearly 850,000.

With 33 election districts missing, all outside this city, General Eisenhower led Gov. Adlai E. Stevenson, his Democratic opponent, by an actual plurality of 846,020 and an indicated plurality of 840,034.

To carry his adopted state by this astounding plurality, General Eisenhower held Governor Stevenson down to an actual plurality of 362,674 in this city, far less than the supporters of the Democratic candidate expected.

With the 33 election districts missing, General Eisenhower carried the state outside the city by an actual plurality of 1,265,789 and, assuming that his vote held up in the missing districts, by an indicated plurality of about 1,270,000.

Governor Stevenson carried Manhattan by 147,633, the Bronx by 151,597 and Brooklyn by 209,130, all far below Democratic expectations. General Eisenhower carried Queens by 117,872 and Richmond by 27,834, well above

Continued on Page 24, Column 3

New President and Vice President

DWIGHT D. EISENHOWER

RICHARD M. NIXON

The New York Times

IVES IS RE-ELECTED BY RECORD MARGIN

Defeats Cashmore by Biggest Plurality of Any Republican—Harding Mark Topped

Vote for Senator

CITY SUMMARY

	Ives (Rep.)	Cashmore (Dem.)	Counts (Lib.)
Manh'n	303,040	322,137	88,797
Bronx	233,548	277,506	101,014
B'klyn	398,498	522,751	147,370
Queens	429,225	265,812	62,558
Rich'd	51,939	28,742	2,044
Total	1,416,250	1,416,968	401,783
Up-state	2,399,770	1,099,842	5[illegible].259
Gr Totl	3,816,020	2,516,810	454,042

4,394 election districts out of 4,394 in the city reporting and 5,854 out of 5,954 up-state.

By LEO EGAN

Senator Irving M. Ives won re-election in a three-cornered race yesterday by the largest plurality ever obtained by a Republican candidate in New York State, topping President Warren G. Harding's record-setting margin of 1,089,929 in 1920 by more than 200,000 votes.

The former majority leader of the State Assembly and co-sponsor of New York's law against racial discrimination in employment thus became the first Republican Senator to win re-election in New York since the late James W. Wadsworth performed that feat in the Harding landslide of 1920.

Not only did Senator Ives carry the normally Republican upstate area by a plurality that may reach 1,297,972, but he came within 718 votes of capturing normally Democratic New York City as well.

The complete Senate vote in the city gave Senator Ives 1,416,250 to 1,416,968 for Borough President John Cashmore of Brooklyn, the Democratic candidate. Thus Mr. Cashmore's plurality within the city was held to 718 votes.

With 5,854 of the 5,954 districts outside the city totaled, Senator Ives had an actual plurality of 1,299,928. On this basis, his final up-state margin should reach 1,300,000.

Dr. George S. Counts, the Liberal party candidate, polled 454,042 votes in the same districts tabulated for Senator Ives and Mr. Cashmore. On this basis his final vote could reach 460,000. Corliss Lamont, the American Labor can-

Continued on Page 21, Column 2

NEW YORK TIMES news bulletins are broadcast over WQXR every hour.

Eisenhower Cracks South, Heads for Victory in Texas

By WILLIAM S. WHITE

Gen. Dwight D. Eisenhower, the Republican Presidential candidate, has smashed the traditionally Democratic Solid South in his national victory over Gov. Adlai E. Stevenson. He has carried outright Florida and Virginia, with their twenty-two electoral votes. This morning unofficial observers gave him the greatest Southern prize of all—Texas and its twenty-four electoral votes, the sixth biggest bloc in the United States.

Confirmation of this indicated loss would involve a Democratic disaster.

Apart from all this and from receiving the greatest popular ballot ever given a Republican in the South, General Eisenhower was first narrowly leading and then narrowly trailing this morning in Tennessee, which has eleven electoral votes. In Tennessee, the position was so close that the result probably will not be known until late this afternoon.

In Louisiana and South Carolina Governor Stevenson had slight leads after trailing often in the early returns.

Only the hardest of the hard core of the Old South has remained wholly faithful to the old Democratic tradition.

Mississippi, Arkansas, North

Continued on Page 22, Column 3

CONNECTICUT G. O. P. SEATS 2 IN SENATE

Benton and Ribicoff Concede to Purtell and Bush While Eisenhower Sweeps State

Special to THE NEW YORK TIMES.

HARTFORD, Conn., Wednesday, Nov. 5—Gen. Dwight D. Eisenhower swept to an amazing landslide victory in Connecticut yesterday, winning by a margin of nearly 130,000 votes over Gov. Adlai E. Stevenson in final returns from the 169 cities and towns in the state.

The victory astounded Republicans as well as Democrats. Prior to the election, Republican leaders had made cautious claims of victory by about 25,000 or 30,000 votes, while Democrats privately thought they had a chance to win the state.

The tremendous Eisenhower sweep carried two Republican United States Senators into office with him. Senator William A. Purtell of West Hartford defeated William Benton, Democrat, for the full six-year term by a margin of 90,286, and Prescott S. Bush, Greenwich banker, defeated Representative Abraham A. Ribicoff of Hartford, Democrat, by 30,373 votes. Mr. Ribicoff made a spectacular uphill run but was edged out by Mr. Bush's lead in the small towns that are traditionally Republican.

Final returns were:

PRESIDENT

169 precincts out of 169:

Eisenhower	610,989
Stevenson	481,482

UNITED STATES SENATOR

(For six-year Term)

169 precincts out of 169:

Purtell (R.)	575,445
Benton (D.)	485,159

(For Four-year Term)

Bush (R.)	559,586
Ribicoff (D)	529,213

The Eisenhower sweep enabled the Republicans to win five of the six seats from Connecticut in the House of Representatives, a gain

Continued on Page 28, Column 3

GENERAL APPEALS FOR UNITED PEOPLE

He Vows Not to Give 'Short Weight' as President—Thanks Rival for Pledge

By WILLIAM R. CONKLIN

A jubilant Gen. Dwight D. Eisenhower accepted his election as President early this morning with a pledge to the American people that he would not give "short weight" in the execution of his new responsibilities in Washington.

With his wife by his side, the Republican President-elect told 2,000 campaign supporters in the grand ballroom of the Commodore Hotel at 2:05 A. M. that it would take the support of a united people to carry his Administration to success in its efforts to build a "better future for America."

His remarks were carried by radio and television to all parts of the country.

He read a message he had sent a few minutes before to his defeated rival, Gov. Adlai E. Stevenson of Illinois, thanking him for his promise of assistance. General Eisenhower expressed hope that Americans of both parties would speedily forget campaign bitter-

Continued on Page 20, Column 2

RACE IS CONCEDED

Virginia and Florida Go to the General as Do Illinois and Ohio

SWEEP IS NATION-WIDE

Victor Calls for Unity and Thanks Governor for Pledging Support

By ARTHUR KROCK

Gen. Dwight D. Eisenhower was elected President of the United States yesterday in an electoral vote landslide and with an emphatic popular majority that probably will give his party a small margin of control in the House of Representatives but may leave the Senate as it is—forty-nine Democrats, forty-seven Republicans and one independent.

Senator Richard M. Nixon of California was elected Vice President.

The Democratic Presidential candidate, Gov. Adlai E. Stevenson of Illinois, shortly after midnight conceded his defeat by a record turnout of American voters.

At 4 A. M. today the Republican candidate had carried states with a total of 431 electors, or 165 more than the 266 required for the selection of a President. The Democratic candidate seemed sure of 69, with 31 doubtful in Kentucky, Louisiana and Tennessee.

General Eisenhower's landslide victory, both in electoral and popular votes, was nation-wide in its pattern, extending from New England—where Massachusetts and Rhode Island broke their Democratic voting habits of many years—down the Eastern seaboard to Maryland, Virginia and Florida and westward to almost every state between the coasts, including California.

General Wins Illinois

The Republican candidate took Illinois, Governor Stevenson's home state. In South Carolina, though he lost its electors on a technicality, he won a majority of the voters. And, completing the first successful Republican invasion of the States of the former Confederacy, the General carried Texas and broke the one-party system in the South.

The personal popularity that enabled him to defeat Senator Robert A. Taft of Ohio in the Republican primaries in Texas, and present him with the issue on which he defeated the Senator for the Republican nomination, crushed the regular Democratic organization of Texas that was led by Speaker Sam Rayburn of the House of Representatives and had the blessing of former Vice President John N. Garner.

The tide that bore General Eisenhower to the White House, though it did not give him a comfortable working majority in either the national House or the Senate (the Democrats may still nominally control the machinery of that branch), probably increased the number of Republican governors beyond the present twenty-five.

"My fellow citizens have made their choice and I gladly accept it," said Governor Stevenson at 1:46 A. M., Eastern standard time, and he asked all citizens to unite behind the President-elect. The defeated candidate said he had sent a telegram of congratulation to General Eisenhower.

At 2:05 A. M., from the Grand Ballroom of the Commodore Hotel, General Eisenhower said he recognized the weight of his new responsibilities and that he would not give "short weight" in their execution. He also urged "unity" and announced he had sent a telegram of thanks to the Democratic candidate for his promise of support.

The issues of the unusually vigorous campaign that was waged

Continued on Page 14, Column 3

Hill Battle Spurts in Korea; Allies Press 'Triangle' Fight

By LINDESAY PARROTT

Special to THE NEW YORK TIMES.

TOKYO, Wednesday, Nov. 5—The hard-fighting South Korean infantry, driving for the third time in three days up the slopes of the central Korean ridges, drove a penetration today into the Communist lines on the western flank of "Triangle Hill," a strategic position north of Kumhwa.

Early this afternoon, the Republic of Korea (R. O. K.) troops had captured one of the twin peaks that project from "Triangle"—named "Jane Russell Hill." The sharp, indecisive combat continued.

The attack on the twin peaks was tied in with a new drive against the central pyramid of "Triangle Hill." The South Koreans again thrust within yards of the crest.

The Chinese Reds struck again just to the east in a new attempt to capture the summit of "Sniper Ridge," flanking "Triangle" on the United Nations' right.

The crest of "Triangle" had been lost to the Chinese Communists after the United Nations limited objective offensive took it last month. The South Koreans pushed up southern slopes today to within fifty yards of the Reds' lines.

Some reports said the fighting again today was as furious as during the attacks Sunday and Monday, when the South Koreans desperately struggled to regain the positions.

Allied warplanes were out against the enemy guns. About fifty sorties had been flown by Fifth Air Force fighter-bombers before noon against Red artillery on high Papasan Mountain, the Communists' strongpoint just to the north of the central front.

At every opportunity, Allied guns pounded the Reds on the crest of "Triangle."

The Reds' guns dropped 5,000 rounds on the United Nations positions near "Heartbreak Ridge" and the "Punchbowl" in the mountainous eastern watershed, where the heaviest fighting of yesterday occurred. A North Korean battalion hit Allied defense positions on "Heartbreak" on the heels of the barrage, but the enemy failed to make a penetration.

On "Triangle Hill" and the twin peaks to the west of it, contact was light yesterday. At least temporarily, the South Koreans broke off attempts to storm two positions they had lost to the Chinese Reds' counter-attacks, after the United Nations limited objec-

Continued on Page 2, Column 3

M'Carthy Is Winner, But Is Last on Ticket

By RICHARD J. H. JOHNSTON

Special to THE NEW YORK TIMES.

MILWAUKEE, Wednesday, Nov. 5—Wisconsin went to the Republicans today for the third time in a national election since 1920.

The predicted Republican sweep of the state and capture of its twelve electoral votes became a certainty a few minutes after midnight.

Gen. Dwight D. Eisenhower, the Republican Presidential nominee ran second on the G. O. P. ticket with Gov. Walter J. Kohler Jr. leading the slate in his bid for re-election.

As the returns neared the final count, Gen. Dwight D. Eisenhower's vote indicated he would emerge as leader of the G. O. P. slate in Wisconsin. With 2,036 of the state's 3,224 vtoing precincts reported, his vote was 554,369 to Gov. Adlai E. Stevenson's 356,218.

Gov. Walter J. Kohler, seeking

Continued on Page 22, Column 6

Stevenson Concedes the Victory As Weeping Backers Cry 'No, No'

By WILLIAM M. BLAIR

Special to THE NEW YORK TIMES.

SPRINGFIELD, Ill., Wednesday, Nov. 5—Gov. Adlai E. Stevenson conceded defeat early today to his Republican opponent, Gen. Dwight D. Eisenhower, and pledged the support "he will need to carry out the great tasks that lie before him."

The Governor came from the Executive Mansion to the Democratic Headquarters in the Leland Hotel to make his announcement before a jammed ballroom of supporters, many of whom broke into tears and cried, "No, no."

Governor Stevenson said:

"General Eisenhower has been a great leader in war. He has been a vigorous and valiant opponent in the campaign. These qualities will now be dedicated to leading us all through the next four years.

"It is traditionally American to fight hard before an election.

"It is equally traditional to close ranks as soon as the people have spoken. From the depths of my heart I thank all of my party, and all of those independents and Republicans who supported Senator Sparkman and me."

The Governor said he had dispatched to General Eisenhower in New York a telegram which he read. It said:

"The people have made their choice and I congratulate you. That you may be the servant and guardian of peace and make the dale of trouble a door of hope is my earnest prayer. Best Wishes.

Adlai E. Stevenson."

Governor Stevenson did have a grin, however, for the crowd and displayed his ever-present humor to reporters. Asked how about 1956, the next presidential election year, he echoed in a loud voice and with mock surprise "56! Examine that man's head."

As for his immediate plans, he

Continued on Page 16, Column 3

"All the News
That's Fit to Print"

The New York Times.

LATE CITY EDITION
Cloudy, not so mild today. Rain, little
temperature change tomorrow.
Temperature Range Today—Max., 57; Min., 49
Temperatures Yesterday—Max., 63.6; Min., 49.4
Full U. S. Weather Bureau Report, Page 47

Copyright, 1952, by The New York Times Company.

VOL. CII...No. 34,631.   Entered as Second-Class Matter,
Post Office, New York, N. Y.   NEW YORK, MONDAY, NOVEMBER 17, 1952.   Times Square, New York 36, N. Y.
Telephone Lackawanna 4-1000   FIVE CENTS

PAPAGOS BLOC WINS ELECTION IN GREECE IN LANDSLIDE VOTE

Rally Group Appears to Have at Least 235 of 300 Seats in the New Parliament

PLASTIRAS IS DEFEATED

New Regime, Favored by U. S., Said to Have Good Chance to Bring Stability to Nation

By C. L. SULZBERGER
Special to The New York Times.

ATHENS, Monday, Nov. 17.—Field Marshal Alexander Papagos' Greek Rally won yesterday's national election in a landslide. His conservative party will almost assuredly have at least two-thirds of the membership of the next Parliament.

[With 85 per cent of the vote tabulated, said an Associated Press dispatch, the Papagos Rally had elected 235 members of the 300-seat Parliament, the biggest majority any group has won since World War II.]

As a result, under the new electoral law, which, among other innovations, provided for a choice by a majority vote, Marshal Papagos' Government should remain in office for the next four years, and has the greatest opportunity of any ministry since the war of assuring stability for Greece and accomplishing needed economic reforms.

The extent of the Papagos victory, which will be viewed with favor in Washington, became apparent early as results from all over the country proved the people wanted a change.

Former Premier Nicholas Plastiras, the Rally's main opponent, lost his parliamentary seat and will not stand in any by-elections.

Papagos Calls for Calm

Early today, Marshal Papagos issued a statement promising to "win the battle for peace" and asking the nation to observe calm and go to work immediately, rather than celebrate.

[Reuters quoted the statement as saying: "The new four-year era starting tonight shall be an era of constructive work. Greece will once more answer the call of other free nations who fought for democracy and freedom."]

Marshal Papagos, 70 years old, is a hero of Greece's campaign against the Axis invasion.

The Rally won large blocs of deputies in Athens and Salonika, and showed surprising strength in widely disparate areas. Under the majority system, this means that Papagos deputies will go to Parliament in solid blocs wherever the party wins.

The pro-Communist, anti-American EDA, or Union of the Democratic Left, seems to have held its recent strength of about 10 per cent. [The Associated Press said the Left had won only one seat however, with fifty-five seats for the Center and nine still unsettled.]

The United States, which has shown sympathy for the Papagos movement, obviously hopes he will be able to push through drastic economic and security reforms.

Three Coalitions in Race

It will take at least another day before the final results can be tabulated from the outlying islands and remote mountain fastnesses of this craggy and individualistic country, where the word "democracy" was invented.

Three party coalitions presented lists. In addition to the Rally, these were the bloc of General Plastiras' Progressive Union of the Center (EPEK) and Sophocles Venizelos' Liberals, led by the aged General Plastiras, and the EDA. Nicholas Zachariades, exiled leader of the Greek Communist party, ordered in broadcasts that his followers support the EDA.

The election was held under a somewhat complicated majority system established in the hope that, by doing away with proportional representation splinter parties would be eliminated and the next government would have more executive authority.

Right until the polling began rival leaders around dire rumors about each other. Both sides whispered that their opponent would stage a military coup if defeated. This is considered unlikely.

Nevertheless, it is assumed that Marshal Papagos will dismiss the principal army leaders of Greece from the rank of corps commander up as it is known that his supporters assembled near Athens to keep order are reported to be men loyal to General Plastiras.

Continued on Page 10, Column 3

VICTOR: Field Marshal Alexander Papagos, leader of the right-wing Greek Rally.
The New York Times

KOREA RAID RAZES RED POWER PLANT

Marine Fliers Bomb Facilities in East—Action on Ground Ebbs in Snow and Cold

By LINDESAY PARROTT
Special to The New York Times.

TOKYO, Monday, Nov. 17.—American planes destroyed yesterday a North Korean hydroelectric plant southwest of Tongchon on the Sea of Japan and north of the fighting front. Ground action dwindled to platoon engagements fought in snow and below freezing temperatures along most of the 155-mile battle line.

The raid on the Tongchon plant—smaller than the great Supung (Suiho) power installation on the Yalu River smashed by United Nations planes earlier this year—was made by Marine land-based fighter-bombers. The pilots said the power station was leveled.

The planes scored hits on a transformer yard and a power substation, which was reported to have been heavily damaged. A near-by pumping station was destroyed by bombs.

On the ground front, Chinese Communists made day-long harassing attacks yesterday on South Korean positions on ridges north of Kumhwa in the central sector. The Allied troops withdrew from an outpost at "Rocky Point," jutting eastward from embattled "Sniper Ridge."

They called down artillery fire on the enemy, then drove the Communists back in a brisk hand-grenade and small-arms fight and retook the position.

Throughout the day, the Chinese threw light attacks in strength up to about 100 men against a South Korean bastion on "Sniper Ridge," a rocky knob known as "Pinpoint Hill," which has been taken and retaken fifteen times during a

Continued on Page 3, Column 2

EISENHOWER SETS UP BUREAU TO HANDLE G. O. P. JOB APPEALS

Applications Are Pouring In —List of Federal Openings Not Yet Fully Compiled

LANE SLATED FOR OUSTER

General Is Coming Here After Seeing Truman—Talks With Congress Chiefs Scheduled

By LEO EGAN

Gen. Dwight D. Eisenhower has directed the establishment of a special personnel section at his temporary headquarters in the Commodore Hotel to handle the deluge of applications for jobs in the new Administration, now pouring in on him.

Temporarily, at least, the section will be headed by Herbert Brownell Jr., former Republican national chairman who served as a close adviser in both the General's pre-nomination and pre-election campaigns. In most instances the job applications will be referred to the Republican National Committee for investigation and recommendation.

After his inauguration as President in January, General Eisenhower plans to follow the same practice with respect to patronage, according to local Republican leaders. It is said that he plans to have a personnel officer in the White House to advise him on patronage, but will rely chiefly on the recommendations of the Republican National Committee, as transmitted by Arthur E. Summerfield, the national chairman.

In making his recommendations, Mr. Summerfield is expected to rely, in turn, on the advice of the various Republican state committees, as transmitted to him by the Republican national committeemen from each state. This is in accordance with understandings reached at Chicago last July when General Eisenhower was nominated and Mr. Summerfield elected as national chairman.

Coming Here Tomorrow

After his conference tomorrow afternoon with President Truman, General Eisenhower will return to New York City.

He has scheduled meetings Wednesday with Senator Robert A. Taft, Representative Joseph W. Martin Jr. and Senator Styles Bridges, who are all due to become Republican Congressional leaders in January.

He will also confer with H. Jack Porter, Republican national committeeman from Texas; Louis K. Gough, national commander of the American Legion; Senator Alexander Wiley, Republican of Wisconsin, and with Mr. Brownell.

Because of the huge volume of offices in New York that are expected to change hands after General Eisenhower's inauguration, a special top-level section committee may be set up here by the Republican National Committee.

Continued on Page 19, Column 3

British and French Annoyed By Rising Friction With G.I.'s

The presence of large United States military forces in Britain and France has given rise to many peacetime problems in the relations between the service men and civilians. The following dispatches describe these problems and how they are being met.

By CLIFTON DANIEL
Special to The New York Times

LONDON, Nov. 16.—A new problem in British-American relations has been created by the presence in Britain of a large United States military force. It is a problem that is not yet serious but one that is worrying both British and United States officials.

About three weeks ago attention again was focused on the issue when, after gangs in Manchester had attacked two United States Air Police patrols, the Air Force command at Burtonwood, the big United States supply base in the north of England, barred its men from entering the city for three days.

If United States airmen got into a brawl with civilians in Manchester, N. H., it is a minor breach of the peace. When the brawl occurs in Manchester, England, it may become an international incident, especially as there are many in this country who question the necessity and desirability of having the Americans here at all.

The Manchester incident and other recent ones have provided big black headlines for The Daily Worker, organ of the British Communists,

Continued on Page 10, Column 5

By ROBERT C. DOTY
Special to The New York Times

BORDEAUX, France, Nov. 16.—Relations between the United States military forces in France and their French hosts are officially "correct," but there is neither mutual sympathy nor any concerted effort by either side to create any such sympathy.

The prevailing mood—on the opposite sides of a language barrier—is one of indifference, with the Americans intent on accomplishing their military mission and the French preoccupied with swarming domestic political and economic problems.

In this situation only the Communists are active, exploiting the occasional barroom scuffle or highway accident involving Americans as evidence of intolerable aggression by the "imperialist occupants." Infrequently the Communists have resorted to direct action, as in the case of mob attacks on two United States installations last May, the diminishing wave of painted insults on walls and destructive mischief to unguarded American cars.

Various public relations techniques might be pushed with more vigor by both sides to ameliorate local patronage problems that

Continued on Page 9, Column 4

EXPERIMENTS FOR HYDROGEN BOMB HELD SUCCESSFULLY AT ENIWETOK; LEAKS ABOUT BLAST UNDER INQUIRY

Italians Sight End Of Overpopulation

By MICHAEL L. HOFFMAN
Special to The New York Times.

GENEVA, Nov. 16.—On the basis of new, although still preliminary, studies of the Italian population problem, Italian authorities believe that about 1965 the population growth in overcrowded Italy will come to an end.

This calculation, moreover, takes no account of possible emigration. If the present rate of net emigration of about 150,-000 individuals yearly continues (more than that leave but substantial numbers are unhappy outside their homeland and go back, even to poverty), in ten to twelve years, experts believe, the entire yearly growth of the population will be readily absorbed.

This glimmer of light ahead would be too distant to arouse any enthusiasm were it not for the corollary that a rate of emi-

Continued on Page 9, Column 6

GOVERNORS DOUBT 'TWO-PARTY' SOUTH

Eleven at Annual Area Parley Discount High G. O. P. Poll —McKeldin in Dissent

By JOHN N. POPHAM
Special to The New York Times.

NEW ORLEANS, Nov. 16.—Eleven Southern Governors, including three who turned from Democratic voting traditions this year and urged their followers to support the Republican Presidential candidacy of Gen. Dwight D. Eisenhower, discounted today a view that a two-party system had taken hold in the area.

A twelfth Southern Governor, Theodore R. McKeldin of Maryland, a Republican, took issue and declared that "Eisenhower's break-through in the South" definitely presaged a two-party development.

The expressions were in press interviews on the eve of the opening of the annual Southern Governors Conference. All the Governors appeared to be on friendly terms and there was much backslapping and exchanging of repartee at a buffet supper.

The political atmosphere was in marked contrast to that in the recent conferences of the last three years, when factional alignments were sharp and "loyal" and "dissident" Democrats expressed hostility or approval of the policies of the Truman Administration.

Some Retiring From Office

Virtually all of the Governors who had been outspoken in their support of the national administration in recent months arrived either as defeated candidates for re-election or as incumbents about to be succeeded Jan. 1 because of state laws that forbid successive terms.

These included Gov. Sidney S. McMath of Arkansas, close personal friend of President Truman, and Gov. Gordon Browning of Tennessee, also an Administration backer. These Governors were beaten in the primaries in bids for third terms. In the retiring group also are Gov. Fuller Warren of Florida and Gov. W. Kerr Scott of North Carolina, who were barred by law from seeking second successive terms.

The expressed beliefs that a two-party system had not yet started in the South despite the capture by General Eisenhower of the electoral votes of Tennessee, Texas Virginia and Florida had varying degrees of emphasis.

Gov. Hugh L. White of Mississippi declared that "it's no more likely than my flying to heaven."

Gov. Lawrence W. Wetherby of Kentucky commented that "it might develop if they handle it right in the months to come."

"Gov. Gordon Persons of Alabama, who was a strong supporter in the campaign of the Democratic Presidential nominee, Gov. Adlai E. Stevenson, said that "these Republicans are going to find it mighty different to run for office when their name isn't Eisenhower."

He asserted that Republicans in Alabama were already encountering local patronage problems that

Continued on Page 9, Column 4

FLASH IS DESCRIBED

Letter From Task Force Navigator Says Light Equaled 'Ten Suns'

3 ASSERT ATOLL VANISHED

Many at Scene Nov. 1 Believed That a Hydrogen Bomb Had Been Set Off

By The United Press.

WASHINGTON, Nov. 16.—The recent test explosion at Eniwetok was a devastating blast, according to composite eyewitness reports sent back by service men who evidently believed that a hydrogen bomb had been set off.

Service men's letters disclosed that "the bomb" had been transported to San Francisco under heavy guard, where it was loaded on a Navy vessel and placed in a special compartment. The door was welded shut and heavy chains were welded across the door.

Federal Bureau of Investigation agents accompanied "the bomb" aboard ship, and there were more civilian and security personnel aboard than sailors. There was a moment's anxiety when the ship's electronics gear picked up what was thought to be an unidentified submarine, but one letter writer said "nothing came of it."

The ship carried "the bomb" directly to the test island, apparently an atoll some thirty-five miles from Eniwetok in the Marshall group, where most United States atomic tests are held.

The test island apparently was about three miles long and somewhere between one-quarter of a mile and one mile wide, although the description of the island varied in the letters.

Vessels Scattered in Area

Vessels of the task force were scattered in an area around the island with the closest stationed about thirty miles from the center of the explosion, the letters said. Several ships apparently were thirty-five miles away. There was no indication whether land observers were closer to the scene.

But the letters clearly showed that the explosion took place on Nov. 1 with zero hour at 7:15 A. M., Eniwetok time.

Aboard the ships the men had donned protective clothing and had been instructed to turn their backs to the island ten seconds before the blast, close their eyes and cover their faces with their arms.

At 7:14 A. M. a voice over the loudspeaker of each ship started counting the seconds. During that time, one observer wrote home, everything was quiet. He said:

"In those last few minutes, especially when they were counting off the seconds, we all grew real tense and silence was so perfect you could hear a pin drop. In those last few seconds, I think everything I've been told ran through my mind. And in the last second, I said a silent prayer * * *."

For six seconds after zero there

Continued on Page 3, Column 1

TELLS OF NEW TESTS: Gordon Dean, chairman of the Atomic Energy Commission, making statement in Washington last night. Mr. Dean wears the commission's identification tag.
Associated Press Wirephoto

2 Boys Find Forgiveness at Home After Accidental Slaying of Sister

Two young brothers who fled their Bronx home in fear on Friday night after the older boy had accidentally killed his 11-year-old sister, Marion, with a .22-caliber rifle, were reunited with their tearful parents at 5:15 P. M. yesterday. The boys had boarded for two nights in a hotel in Spring Valley, N. Y., after signing false names on the register and giving a fictitious address.

Only minutes before the boys were brought to their home at 3862 Sedgwick Avenue, their parents, Mr. and Mrs. David M. Feiler, had returned from the funeral of their daughter.

This was the story of the boys' activities and the tragedy as it was pieced together by the authorities.

The boys, Daniel, 13, and Barry, 9, were left in their home on Friday about 7 P. M. when their parents went to a motion-picture theatre. Linda, a 5-year-old daughter, was in her room and Marion

Daniel went to the toy room and asked that Marion leave it so he could be alone to do his homework. When she refused to go Daniel decided he would frighten her into leaving. He went to the attic atop the two-story private home and found the rifle that his parents used on vacations for target practice. He loaded it, but Daniel found cartridges and loaded it.

The boy pointed the rifle at his sister and then it was accidentally discharged. The bullet struck Marion in the skull, killing her.

In panic and fear, Daniel announced to the younger boy and the younger sister that he was going to run away. He had several coins in his pocket and, going into his parents bedroom, he took $150 in three $50 bills from a drawer in his father's dresser.

Barry told his brother he wanted to run away, too. The boys took a bicycle belonging to Marion. Daniel pedaled and with Bar-

Continued on Page 18, Column 6

REPORT BY MURRAY ASKS PAY CURB END

Late C.I.O. President's Annual Resume Finds Price Controls Now Virtually Abandoned

By The Associated Press.

WASHINGTON, Nov. 16.—In his annual report to the Congress of Industrial Organizations, issued today, the late Philip Murray voiced a strong call for the end of all wage controls. Mr. Murray, who was president of the C. I. O., died a week ago.

The report declared the price control program had been virtually abandoned and cautioned that there was the danger of "a deflationary tendency" within the economy.

In an exhaustive resume of all C. I. O. activities during the last year, Mr. Murray said:

"The facts—a weak law, soft markets in some parts of the economy, and collapsing price and production controls—are clear. The basis for maintaining wage controls under these conditions at present no longer exists."

But Mr. Murray asked the new Congress, which will meet Jan. 3, to "arm the Government with authority to impose controls whenever necessary, without the legislative and administrative delays that occurred in 1950" and asked these controls should be imposed immediately if living costs moved up steadily. There have been sev-

Continued on Page 17, Column 2

DEAN BARES TESTS

Breaks Week's Silence on Unofficial Reports of Super-Explosion

HAILS 'REMARKABLE FEAT'

A.E.C. Head Says Eyewitnesses Who Wrote Letters About Blast May Be Disciplined

By JAY WALZ
Special to The New York Times.

WASHINGTON, Nov. 16.—The Atomic Energy Commission announced tonight "satisfactory" experiments in hydrogen weapon research amid informed speculation that this meant a super-atomic bomb had been exploded in recent United States tests.

In a three-paragraph announcement, the Commission did not go so far as to state that a full-scale hydrogen bomb had been detonated, but it did say "experiments contributing" to hydrogen bomb research had been completed recently during tests on Eniwetok atoll in the mid-Pacific.

Sources close to the commission said they interpreted the commission's announcement as meaning "something new has happened at Eniwetok." In Chicago, Dr. Harold C. Urey, Nobel Prize winner and a key figure in the wartime development of the atom bomb, said he believed the A. E. C. announcement meant that the United States had successfully exploded its first hydrogen bomb.

"It sounds like official language for a successful H-bomb," Dr Urey responded, when the announcement was read to him.

The Atomic Energy Commission, speaking cautiously for the record, said only that test officials had expressed "satisfaction" over the results as a whole.

Disciplinary Action Weighed

The announcement, issued at the unusual hour of 5:30 o'clock on a Sunday afternoon, broke the silence that the commission had maintained for a week over unofficial reports that the first hydrogen bomb in history — a super-atomic weapon—had been exploded in the recent Eniwetok tests.

The reports emanated from letters that began arriving in the United States from writers who said they had seen at first hand an explosion far more powerful than those resulting from previous atomic detonations.

Gordon Dean, chairman of the commission, said tonight his agency was looking into the question of whether the letters, presumably from Government personnel, had violated regulations or Federal law relating to security information.

Answering reporters' questions, Mr. Dean said the commission was investigating these letters to find out whether disciplinary action

Continued on Page 3, Column 4

CRIME STUDY SHIFTS TO POLITICAL REIGNS

Hearings Resuming Today Will Bare Means of Gaining Power and Perpetuating Regimes

By ALEXANDER FEINBERG

The State Crime Commission is prepared to embark today on the second phase of its four-point inquiry—the self-perpetuation of political machines through the operations of a "loaded" election law—at the third of its public hearings in the Supreme Court Building.

Sufficient testimony was developed at the sessions last Thursday and Friday, the commission feels, to demonstrate convincingly the thesis of its first point—that improper relationships exist between leaders of the underworld and entrenched political organizations and that these links constitute "a grave public abuse."

In outlining the pattern of the inquiry, former Supreme Court Justice Joseph M. Proskauer, commission chairman, said the hearings would concern themselves with these four matters:

1. Evidence of the existence of improper political tie-ups.
2. The methods by which those responsible for the tie-ups are chosen and remain in power.
3. The possible defects in the election machinery that enables them to remain in power.
4. The extent to which the exercise of that power has given influence to underworld characters and resulted in a deterioration of public service.

Minor Figures to Appear

At today's session eight or ten "minor participants in politics," whose names were not disclosed in advance, are expected to tell how they were chosen, who their bosses were and what considerations entered into the retention of their political posts.

Present or former district leaders are expected to testify publicly to what they have acknowledged in private examination—that seeming "small fry" in the political pot actually wielded fantastic powers that the electorate never intended them to exercise.

In his introductory statement at the opening of the hearings, Mr. Proskauer stressed the importance of the "powerful" county political committees, calling them "creatures of statute."

"They are public bodies," he said, "and they exercise a dominant influence in the formulation of public policies and in the selection and choice of public officials." An explanation of the commission's indecision on whether to pur-

Continued on Page 3, Column 4

West End Ave. to Get New Light Plan Today

By JOSEPH C. INGRAHAM

The oft-delayed plan to speed travel on West End Avenue by retiming signal lights for two-way progressive flow will go into effect at 10 A. M. today.

The new system primarily will benefit northbound traffic during the evening rush period from 4 to 7 P. M., when the lights will be set to provide progressive flow from Forty-first to 105th Street on West End and Eleventh Avenues. During that three-hour period, southbound traffic will be able to move only two blocks before being halted for a red light.

The old timing favored southbound traffic at all times, but now cars headed downtown will have progressive lights in their direction only during the morning rush. From 7 to 10 A. M. In the non-rush periods, from 10 A. M. today, a modified progressive plan, known as a group-alternating system, will be in force. Under that operation, vehicles in both directions should average up to six blocks before being halted for a red signal.

Originally slated for introduction last summer but repeatedly postponed because of short circuits on old interconnecting cables,

Continued on Page 34, Column 2

Dag Hammarskjold (left) succeeded the first Secretary General of the United Nations, Trygve Lie (right).

Thermonuclear progress was marked by the explosion of a "thermonuclear device"—a hydrogen or H-bomb.

Korean children were the hardest hit by the conflict. 100,000 orphans roamed the streets, scavenging or begging from soldiers.

The New York Times.

LATE CITY EDITION
Partly cloudy, slightly colder today. Cloudy, colder tomorrow.
Temperature Range Today—Max., 45; Min.,34
Temperatures Yesterday—Max., 53; Min. 37
Full U. S. Weather Bureau Report, Page 41

Copyright, 1952, by The New York Times Company.

VOL. CII...No. 34,669.   Entered as Second-Class Matter, Post Office, New York, N. Y.   **NEW YORK, THURSDAY, DECEMBER 25, 1952.**   Times Square, New York 36, N. Y. Telephone LAckawanna 4-1000   FIVE CENTS

M'CARRAN DEFENDS LAW AS U. S. BARS 271 OF LIBERTE'S CREW

Senator Says Nation's Security Is More Important Than Protests Against Act

ASSAILS TRUMAN'S GROUP

Screening on Voyage Excludes Aliens on Liner's Staff Who Refused Replies to Queries

Text of statement by Senator McCarran is on Page 4.

By JOSEPH J. RYAN

French seamen sailing in and out of New York for as many as twenty-five years were among 271 members of the crew of the French liner Liberté to whom shore leave was forbidden on arrival here yesterday as the controversial McCarran-Walter Immigration and Nationality Law went into effect.

The Liberté, the first vessel to arrive after the act went into force at midnight Tuesday, served as a "guinea pig" for a program under which aliens in the crews of passenger vessels entering the United States are to be screened during ocean crossings for possible subversive leanings.

Senator Pat McCarran, Democrat of Nevada and co-author of the law, returned yesterday with his wife on the Grace liner Santa Rosa after a six-week South American tour. He made a bristling comment on the protests that foreign Governments have made to the State Department on the screening procedure.

"My answer to all those attacks is A comes first in the alphabet with me, which means that America comes first at all times," Senator McCarran declared. "The security of the United States means more to me than any of the things I have heard against the bill."

Assails Truman Commission

The Senator also issued a prepared statement sharply criticizing the special commission appointed by President Truman, which, he said, will have only five working days to evaluate the operation of the act and report to the President. The statement also charged Harry Rosenfield, executive director of the commission, and Clarence Pickett, a member, had been associated with "Communist front" organizations and that Earl G. Harrison, another member and a former Commissioner of Immigration, had accepted an award from a "Communist front" organization.

In reply to a question, the Senator said that he foresaw no changes in the act and reminded interviewers that the measure had been worked on for five years and had met with the approval of all Government departments concerned with immigration.

He denied charges that there was racial prejudice in the law.

"Such statements," he declared, "are either intentionally put out with the purpose of arousing racial minorities or through ignorance or lack of knowledge of the act."

Asked about the opposition to the law expressed by President-elect Dwight D. Eisenhower, Mr. McCarran replied:

"I don't very much think that General Eisenhower has read the bill."

President Truman also has assailed the law, which was enacted over his veto.

The crew-screening program has elicited protests from the Governments of Great Britain, France,

Continued on Page 5, Column 1

Shake-Up in Police Shifts 19, Raises 99

Police Commissioner George P. Monaghan yesterday ordered the biggest shake-up he has made since taking office a year and a half ago. He transferred nineteen high officers "for the good of the service" and promoted ninety-nine others of all ranks, with warm praise for the department as a whole.

"The morale of the department is at an all-time high," he told the promoted men, together with 500 relatives and friends who attended the ceremony in the gymnasium at Police Headquarters. "It's beginning to get around that it isn't who you know but what you do that counts when it comes to promotions."

Mr. Monaghan said he was proud of the record the police made in the last year and was

Continued on Page 32, Column 5

Christmas Traffic Heavy but Smooth

Holiday travel to and from the city reached its peak yesterday and last night with a reported heavy but smooth flow on all major transportation facilities, and without major mishaps.

No reports were received to indicate that the burden of the flow—which was spread out between noon, the closing hour for many of the city's business houses, and 10 P. M.—had set any records, or that facilities were overtaxed.

Despite a four-day holiday for many persons and the prospect of good driving weather, no major congestion was reported on highways and tunnels and bridges.

The weather man had forecast some cloudiness for last night and today with continued mild temperatures for this season, reaching a high in the afternoon

Continued on Page 32, Column 2

KENNY 'PREPARED' FOR CRIME EXPOSE

Mayor Wants to Tell Jersey Law Group About Bergen Gaming as Well as Piers

By CHARLES GRUTZNER

Fireworks that may rock New Jersey's political structure were foreshadowed yesterday by an announcement from Mayor John V. Kenny of Jersey City that he would appear Monday before the state's Law Enforcement Council with a battery of lawyers and would "be prepared."

Mayor Kenny said he "trusted" that the council, which has subpoenaed him for questioning about his connection with waterfront racketeers and shipping interests, was "sincere" and would delve also into other matters, including gambling in Bergen County, outside his bailiwick.

A City Hall aide of Mr. Kenny, who gave out the Mayor's statement, was asked if he could explain the "be prepared" reference. The Mayor's spokesman replied:

"For the present we will allow to remain cryptic."

Mayor Kenny's announcement was made to deny rumors, circulated in northern New Jersey, that he would refuse to testify before the state agency.

Protection of Witnesses

New York City detectives, meanwhile, maintained protective guard over a witness who had given testimony unfavorable to Mayor Kenny at public hearings of the crime commission here last week.

They guarded the Bronx home of Riordan Roett, who had told of alleged "fixing" of criminal cases at the request of Mr. Kenny when he was a Democratic ward leader before his election as Mayor in 1949 and of his alleged dealings with Charles Yanowski, a gangster who was later murdered.

Mr. Roett's complaint to the crime commission that Jersey City police had tried to break into his Bronx home Monday night brought him the protection of New York City policemen who have been assigned to the commission.

New York City police are also

Continued on Page 41, Column 5

BOARD OF ESTIMATE MEETS TOMORROW ON THE BUS CRISIS

Mayor Phones for Emergency Session in Effort to Avert Strike Set for New Year's

NEW TALKS BROKEN OFF

Union Rejects 3d Ave. Plea for Delay — Impellitteri Home, to Talk to Aides Today

By A. H. RASKIN

The Board of Estimate was called yesterday to an emergency meeting tomorrow to grapple with the threat of a New Year's Day strike on bus lines that carry 3,500,000 riders a day in Manhattan, the Bronx, Queens and lower Westchester.

The call was telephoned to City Hall by Mayor Impellitteri a few hours before he left Miami to fly back to New York and assume personal direction of the city's sagging efforts to prevent a bus stoppage.

The Mayor arrived at La Guardia Airport at 10:15 P. M. and spoke briefly there of his plans for action in the bus situation.

"I intend to contact individual members of the Board of Estimate and of the Transit Advisory Commission tomorrow," he said. "I will then meet on Friday at 10 A. M. with the commission. Following this meeting the Board of Estimate will meet with the commission. I have not changed my mind in any way about a fare increase."

Asked whether he saw any hope of solving the bus deadlock, he replied: "I will exert every influence at my command to avert a strike."

Mayor Tanned and Fit

The Mayor looked tanned and fit as he disembarked from an Eastern Airlines plane. He wore a camel's hair coat against the chill at the field.

"I feel 100 per cent better," he said. "I feel completely rested and ready to get back on the job."

He declined to comment on the entry of the Federal Bureau of Investigation into the New York-New Jersey waterfront inquiry.

At the airport the Mayor was met by Mrs. Impellitteri, Dr. A. L. Garbat, his personal physician; John D. Tierney, his press secretary, and Arthur Halpern, a member of his staff. He went directly from the airport to Gracie Mansion in an official car.

At the time the Mayor's telephone message from Miami was received here, new contract talks between the Transport Workers Union, C. I. O., and the largest of the privately owned bus companies, the bankrupt Third Avenue Transit Corporation, were broken off. A company plea for a two-week postponement of the strike was rejected by the union.

The rupture came after Federal Judge Irving R. Kaufman had given public notice that he would order liquidation of the Third Avenue system unless the city authorized a higher fare as a means of providing the extra revenue required to finance a forty-hour

Continued on Page 32, Column 1

Chill Christmas at the Front: Silent G. I.'s Think of Home

Men in Bunkers in Korea Listen to Firing and Imagine What Families Are Doing— Reds' Yule Drive Fails to Develop

By ROBERT ALDEN
Special to THE NEW YORK TIMES.

AT THE KOREAN FRONT, Dec. 24—Christmas Eve is being observed here tonight in bunkers and on forward ridge lines in an atmosphere of melancholy that is almost heartbreaking.

For the most part the soldiers here, who have nothing between them and the enemy but a few hundred yards and a few strands of barbed wire, are sitting silent and alone with their thoughts.

From the few words they do say it is apparent they are thinking of three to a bunker. In one bunker one soldier sits looking through the machine-gun slit. Two others sit on improvised bunks next to the machine gun. The air is chill, though the edge of the cold is less sharp in the bunker because of an oilcan stove, whose dim flickering provides the only light.

No one seems to mention Christmas, but now and then someone says, "Damn, I wish I were home!" or "What a place to be!" and it is easy to tell what they are thinking about.

A lieutenant appears at the narrow entrance to the bunker.

Continued on Page 2, Column 8

FILIPINOS AFRAID OF '53 VOTE FRAUD

Quirino Opponents Fear Plot by Liberals to Seize Power May Result in Violence

By TILLMAN DURDIN
Special to THE NEW YORK TIMES.

MANILA, Dec. 24—Fear is growing among Filipinos that the 1953 national elections will be accompanied by fraud and violence that could wreck Philippine democracy, disrupt national unity and undermine suppression of the Communist-led Hukbalahap rebellion.

The Liberal party, now in power, used force and fraud in winning the 1949 national elections from the rival Nacionalista party. Opponents of the administration of President Elpidio Quirino, Liberal leader, who indicates he plans to run for re-election, charge that some key Liberals are laying plans for repeating the machinations of 1949 on a more extensive scale in 1953.

Liberal leaders deny the charges. President Quirino himself has said that he plans to see that honest elections are held in 1953.

[Other advices received in New

Continued on Page 6, Column 2

POPE BIDS MAN RISE ABOVE TECHNOLOGY

Christmas Message Criticizes U. S. Capitalism and Reds— 'Love for Poor' Urged

Excerpts from Pope's Christmas message are on Page 20.

By ARNALDO CORTESI
Special to THE NEW YORK TIMES.

ROME, Dec. 24—In a Christmas message to the world, in which he sharply criticized both capitalism, as exemplified by the United States, and communism, as exemplified by the Soviet Union, Pope Pius appealed today for greater solidarity and a more human conception of relations between man and man and between nation and nation. The Pope did not name the United States or Russia.

Pope Pius called for "a more intense and significant feeling for the poor" that should stir up "as it were, a flood of help heading in its holy impetuosity."

It was one of the most pessimistic speeches that the Pope has delivered. As he himself said, "no sense of confidence can brighten a panorama over which hovers the specter of that insoluble contradiction" represented by the fact that full employment requires constant expansion of business while at the same time it is a moot question "to what degree expansion is possible without provoking a catastrophe and above all without bringing mass unemployment in its wake."

Contrary to general expectation, the Pope's speech was almost exclusively nonpolitical and limited itself mainly to calling attention to "the mournful chorus of the poor

Continued on Page 20, Column 4

U. S. Irked by Menon, Bowles Tells India

Special to THE NEW YORK TIMES.

WASHINGTON, Dec. 24—The United States used a newspaper editorial to indicate to India its annoyance with the conduct here of V. K. Krishna Menon, an Indian delegate to the United Nations who recently sponsored a plan for a truce in Korea.

The text of an editorial in The Washington Post of Dec. 9 was cabled to United States Ambassador Chester Bowles in New Delhi. The State Department suggested that he use it at his discretion, not in conjunction with a formal protest, but as an illustration of public opinion in this country.

Ambassador Bowles showed the editorial to Indian officials and was told that Mr. Menon does not speak for the Indian Government on every occasion. The occasion criticized in the editorial was a

Continued on Page 2, Column 4

STALIN FOR EISENHOWER MEETING; TELLS THE TIMES THAT HE FAVORS NEW APPROACH TO END KOREA WAR

TRUMAN YULE PLEA

Calls On Nation to Pray for Troops in Korea— Grants Amnesties

PARDONS PARNELL THOMAS

Restores Rights to Veterans and to Deserters—Lights Tree at White House

WASHINGTON, Dec. 24—President Truman, in a Christmas message to the nation today, called on the people to pray for the troops in Korea, and to pray also that the spirit of God shall enter the lives of this country's enemies and "prevail in their lands."

In a series of holiday amnesties and pardons he also restored civil rights to deserters during the uneasy peace between the end of World War II and the beginning of the Korean war; restored those rights for veterans of the Korean war who have been convicted of crimes in the civil courts; and granted full pardons to two agents of the Central Intelligence Agency who had refused to testify against Henry A. Jarvinen, a Seattle travel agency executive accused of giving false information about Owen Lattimore.

Parnell Thomas Pardoned

The President signed a full pardon for J. Parnell Thomas, former Republican Representative from New Jersey, who served a prison term for padding his Congressional office payroll. There was no formal announcement, but a Justice Department spokesman tonight confirmed the President's action.

Mr. Thomas, who was once chairman of the House Committee on Un-American Activities, was freed on parole Sept. 10 from the Federal Correctional Institution at Danbury, Conn. He had served nine months of a six-to-eighteen-month sentence on his conviction.

He was convicted on charges of placing nonworking employes on his governmental payroll and collecting more than $8,000 in kickbacks. A $10,000 fine was part of his sentence.

Mr. Thomas, at the time of his release, expressed confidence that he would "in due time be judged innocent of any wrongdoing."

The effect of the President's Christmas Eve pardon was to restore full citizenship rights to the former legislator.

Asked for comment on the President's action, Mr. Thomas would only say:

"I've always differed politically with President Truman, but I thank him sincerely for his action on Christmas Eve."

Promotion on Staff

Then this morning Mr. Truman promoted Philleo Nash, a White House staff member handling problems of minorities and civil rights, to the position of administrative assistant. Mr. Nash got his commission while waiting in line in a reception that the Truman family held for the 350 persons who work in or are in some way attached to the White House.

The President voiced his Christmas message this evening when he switched on the colored lights of the National Community Christmas Tree in a carol-singing ceremony in the south grounds of the White House.

The men in Korea, said Mr. Truman, were "fighting and suffering and even dying that we may preserve the chance of peace in the world." While the struggle there was long and bitter, he declared, it had a hopeful meaning.

"It has a hopeful meaning because it is the common struggle of many free nations which have joined together to seek a just and lasting peace," he said. "We know, all of us, that this is the only way we can bring about peace in the conditions of our time on this earth. Whether we shall succeed depends upon our patience and fortitude. We all have a long road ahead of us before we reach our goal, We must remain steadfast."

Defense Department officials estimated that a total of 8,940 men convicted of desertion probably

Continued on Page 21, Column 1

Associated Press
Premier Stalin

TASS MAN IS SEIZED BY DUTCH AS A SPY

Arrested With Secret Papers in The Hague—Said to Have Wined and Bribed Officials

Special to THE NEW YORK TIMES.

THE HAGUE, the Netherlands, Dec. 24—The Foreign Ministry announced today the arrest on espionage charges of Lev Constantimovitch Pissarev, Russian correspondent in the Netherlands of Tass, Soviet official news agency.

Official sources said the police seized Pissarev last evening after having shadowed him to a rendezvous with a "contact man" on a bridge in an outlying part of The Hague. They said that papers were seen to change hands and that the correspondent had secret Dutch documents on his person when arrested a few moments later.

Dutch officials added that Pissarev, who is 37 years old, had been under surveillance for three months, since they had received reports that he was using bribes, champagne dinners and threats in efforts to extract military and political information from civil servants and army officers.

The rendezvous between Pissarev and the contact man was known in advance to the police. The police declined to reveal the identity of the contact man or what happened to him. However, it was believed he had been working with the police.

The Foreign Ministry said that Pissarev had no diplomatic immunity since, unlike his predecessor, he had never applied for diplomatic status. The ministry said he was being held pending investigation but declined to state whether he would be tried. It was

Continued on Page 3, Column 3

WOULD OPEN TALKS

Soviet Premier Willing to Start Negotiations to Ease Tension

CLASH 'NOT INEVITABLE'

In Reply to Questions, He Says 'U. S. S. R. Is Interested in Ending the War in Korea'

By JAMES RESTON
Special to THE NEW YORK TIMES.

WASHINGTON, Dec. 24—In reply to four questions submitted by this correspondent, Premier J. V. Stalin of the Union of Soviet Socialist Republics said in a message received tonight that he would favorably regard diplomatic conversations with representatives of the new Eisenhower Administration with the objective of holding a meeting between the President-elect and himself on easing world tensions.

Premier Stalin also said that he still believed that war between the United States of America and the Soviet Union could not be considered inevitable and that the two nations could continue to live in peace.

The Premier said further that he would cooperate in any new diplomatic approach designed to bring about an end of the Korean war "because the U. S. S. R. is interested in ending the war in Korea."

A White House spokesman, informed of the correspondence with Premier Stalin, said there would be no comment tonight.

[In New York a press assistant to General Eisenhower said that the President-elect had retired for the night and could not be reached for comment on Premier Stalin's statement. John Foster Dulles, the Secretary of State-designate, was reported to be out of town.]

The replies of Premier Stalin to the four questions were in response to a letter addressed to him by this correspondent Dec. 18, through Ambassador Georgi N. Zarubin, the envoy of the U. S. S. R. to the United States.

Embassy Gets Replies

His replies were received at the Soviet Embassy tonight under date of Dec. 24 and were translated by the embassy with the explanation that the translation necessarily had to be done in haste, that it was as close to the original as was possible in the time at hand. The letter of Ambassador Zarubin received by THE NEW YORK TIMES at 10:30 o'clock tonight is as follows:

Herewith are the replies of Premier J. V. Stalin to the questions you asked him in your letter Dec. 18, 1952, addressed to me:

Q.—At the beginning of a new year and a new Administration

Continued on Page 13, Column 1

C-124 Crash Is Laid to Failure To Unlock Controls Mechanisms

By The Associated Press.

WASHINGTON, Dec. 24—The Air Force reported today that the crash of a C-124 transport last Saturday at Moses Lake, Wash., with 86 dead, had resulted from failure to unlock control mechanisms before the take-off.

The men in Korea, said Mr. control surfaces. Every member of the ten-man crew is dead.

The controls normally are locked when the plane is on the ground. The purpose of the locking device is to prevent wind currents from slamming the movable portions of the wing and tail surfaces back and forth.

A special investigating board headed by Maj. Gen. Victor E. Bertrandias, Deputy Inspector General for the Air Force, made this report to Air Force headquarters.

"The C-124 has one mechanical control handle which locks the normal angle of climb after the three separate controls—the throttle, elevators, ailerons and rudder—when the plane is parked on the ground. All of these controls are unlocked by the control handle through its complete travel area.

"Indications are that in this case the control handle was moved partly but not completely through its full travel before the take-off and, as a result, the throttle was unlocked, permitting power to be applied, while surface control locks remained in a locked position. The investigation established that the

Continued on Page 32, Column 2

The New York Times
M'CARRAN ACT IN OPERATION: Senator Pat McCarran, right, a passenger on the Santa Rosa, which arrived yesterday, sits in on the screening of crew members with Assistant Purser Tom Hunt (seated, left) and Immigration Officer Edward Ferro (seated, second from right).

1953

1953

Ike's Cabinet and advisors through much of his Administration were: (Clockwise from lower left) Pres. Asst. Wilton Persons; Amb. to UN Henry Cabot Lodge; Interior Sec. Fred Seaton; Treasury Sec. George Humphrey (succeeded by Robert Anderson); Vice Pres. Nixon; Atty. Gen Herbert Brownell (succeeded by William Rogers); Commerce Sec. Sinclair Weeks (succeeded by Frederick Mueller); Welfare Sec. Marion Folsom (succeeded by Arthur Flemming); Civil Defense Administrator Val Peterson; Budget Director Percival Brundage (succeeded by Maurice Stans); Defense Mobilizer Gordon Gray; Labor Sec. James Mitchell; Postmaster Gen. Arthur Summerfield; Sec. of State John F. Dulles (succeeded by Christian Herter); the President; Defense Sec. Charles Wilson (succeeded by Neil McElroy, T. Gates); Agric. Sec. Ezra Benson; Sec. to Cabinet Maxwell Rabb; Asst. to the President Sherman Adams.

Dwight D. Eisenhower being sworn into office on January 20, 1953.

"All the News That's Fit to Print"

The New York Times.

Copyright, 1953, by The New York Times Company.

LATE CITY EDITION

Occasional rain today; rain ending tonight. Fair, mild tomorrow.
Temperature Range Today-Max., 42; Min., 37
Temperatures Yesterday—Max., 47; Min., 37
Full U. S. Weather Bureau Report, Page 55

VOL. CII..No. 34,696. Entered as Second-Class Matter, Post Office, New York, N. Y. NEW YORK, WEDNESDAY, JANUARY 21, 1953. Entered as Second-Class Matter, Post Office, New York, N. Y. FIVE CENTS

EISENHOWER SWORN, PLEDGES QUEST FOR PEACE; BACKS U. N., URGES WESTERN EUROPE TO UNITE; 750,000 SEE PARADE; MORSE BALKS CABINET VOTE

QUILL GETS READY TO END BUS STRIKE ON MAYOR'S TERMS

Gives Out Haywood Telegram Backing Arbitration and Has C. I. O. Council Approve It

BUT HE STILL CAN DITCH IT

Service Seen by Monday if All Goes Well—Two Companies Accept Impellitteri Plan

By A. H. RASKIN

Michael J. Quill, president of the Transport Workers Union, C. I. O., set machinery in motion yesterday for ending the twenty-day-old bus strike under Mayor Impellitteri's arbitration plan.

With the union, the bus companies and city officials jockeying over details of the plan, there was still a chance last night that the entire peace effort might collapse, but some observers expected that buses would be back in operation by Monday on routes that normally carry 3,500,000 daily riders.

Without surrendering his freedom to scuttle the Impellitteri formula if the details were not worked out to his satisfaction, Mr. Quill took two steps during the day that made it plain he was conditioning the 8,000 strikers to acceptance of the proposal in a secret-ballot vote later this week.

He made public a telegram from Allan S. Haywood, executive vice president of the Congress of Industrial Organizations, urging the union to go along with the Mayor's suggestion that the union and the struck companies pick their own three-man arbitration panel to decide the dispute over union demands for a forty-hour week with no loss in pre-strike take-home pay.

Haywood Comes to Quill's Aid

Mr. Haywood is always on tap when Mr. Quill needs someone to help him out of an embarrassing situation, and there was no doubt in the mind of anyone connected with the situation that the Haywood telegram was sent at Mr. Quill's instigation to combat rank-and-file resistance to arbitration of any kind.

The second development that indicated how Mr. Quill's mind was running was the decision of a delegation from the New York C. I. O. Council to recommend that the bus strikers accept the Impellitteri plan. Mr. Quill is president of the council, and the council's recommendation was in the nature of a man talking to himself.

The council committee, headed by Morris Iushewitz, secretary-treasurer, met with Mayor Impellitteri at noon to express its support of the Quill union's fight for a forty-hour week. The Mayor told the group he agreed that the bus workers were entitled to a forty-hour week, but that he opposed any settlement that would upset the 10-cent fare.

The unionists replied that they were equally concerned with keep-

Continued on Page 24, Column 7

12 Injured in Jersey As Bus Falls 25 Feet

Special to THE NEW YORK TIMES.

WEEHAWKEN, N. J., Jan. 20—One person was critically injured and eleven others cut and bruised this afternoon when the bus in which they were riding plunged twenty-five feet from Pershing Road into the New York Central West Shore Division freight yard at the waterfront here.

The bus, a Public Service system vehicle owned by the Interstate Transportation Company, was en route from the Hudson Place Terminal in Hoboken to the New York Central's West Forty-second Street ferry terminal when the accident happened at 2:20 P. M.

Descending the Palisades on the steep, cliffside road, the bus went into a skid on the wet cobblestone paving when the driver, Herman Ohm, 53 years old, of 321 Seventy-ninth Street, North Bergen, applied the brakes to go into an elbow bend that the road takes

Continued on Page 26, Column 5

Line 'Impregnable,' Korean Foe Boasts

By LINDESAY PARROTT
Special to THE NEW YORK TIMES.

TOKYO, Wednesday, Jan. 21—The Government-controlled Peiping radio boasted today that the Communists had built a fortified line across the Korean peninsula through which United Nations troops would be unable to break.

In a broadcast this morning, possibly timed to coincide with the inauguration of President Eisenhower, who promised to work for an early and honorable end of the Korean war, Peiping called its defenses "impregnable"—never before seen in the history of war. During a year of almost static fighting along the 155-mile front, the broadcast said, the "People's forces have built 'a great wall' across Korea."

Thousands of men, working day and night, have created an intricate system of tunnels,

Continued on Page 3, Column 5

CITY URGED TO FIGHT TO HOLD PORT RANK

Cavanagh Tells Crime Inquiry of Trade Shifts and Offers Plans for Expansion

By CHARLES GRUTZNER

This port is "just about keeping its head above water" in competition for the post-war increase in the nation's shipping, Edward F. Cavanagh Jr., City Commissioner of Marine and Aviation, told the State Crime Commission yesterday.

He expressed the belief that this port could gain a larger share of trade through legitimate political activity in Washington and by improving its physical facilities here. He is to make further recommendations at today's public hearing, starting at 10 A. M. in the County Court House on Foley Square.

Mr. Cavanagh supported in general the findings of Dennis J. Walsh Jr., consulting engineer, who testified that a survey of seven principal Atlantic and Gulf ports showed that New York had 53 per cent of today's "competitive" business, the same percentage as before World War II, and that New Orleans had increased its share from 13 to 17½ per cent, Baltimore had increased its percentage from 10 to 13, while other cities, Boston in particular, had suffered percentage losses.

Proskauer More Pessimistic

Mr. Walsh is a partner in the engineering concern of Sanderson & Porter, which made a $20,000 study for the State Crime Commission of shipping in the ports of New York, Philadelphia, Baltimore, Norfolk, Boston, New Orleans and Mobile. Joseph M. Proskauer, chairman of the Crime Commission, expressed disagreement several times with Mr. Walsh's interpretations of trade figures. Mr. Proskauer took a darker view of this port's competitive position than that indicated by Mr. Walsh's testimony.

After Mr. Proskauer had stressed one phase of the survey, which showed that New York had suffered relatively in coastwise shipping, although gaining in foreign trade, Mr. Walsh said the popular notion of rating a port's competitive status on a basis of gross tonnage was inaccurate. He said most coastwise shipping—petroleum, coal and some other bulk cargoes—was routed in accordance with rail differential rates and other factors that made such things as the port facilities and pier handling costs unimportant. Because of this, he said, the volume of such cargo has nothing to do with the competitive position of the individual ports.

Neither Mr. Walsh nor Commissioner Cavanagh made any mention of racketeering, labor trouble, pier violence or any of the other waterfront evils that the Crime Commission has been exposing since early last month.

Testimony of three other witnesses, however, touched directly on the more sensational aspects of the waterfront investigation.

A 69-year-old pier watchman for the Isthmian Steamship Line tes-

Continued on Page 38, Column 4

POSTS GO UNFILLED

Senate Approval of Eight Nominees Delayed by Morse's Objection

VOTE EXPECTED TODAY

Wilson Hearings Put Off Until Friday—Brownell May Offer a Solution

By C. P. TRUSSELL
Special to THE NEW YORK TIMES.

WASHINGTON, Jan. 20—Plans for President Eisenhower to carry eight of his nine Cabinet appointees into office with him today were blocked in the Senate within an hour after the inauguration ceremonies by Senator Wayne Morse of Oregon.

A few hours later it was announced that Senate hearings on the confirmation of the ninth appointee, Charles E. Wilson, the Secretary of Defense-designate, originally scheduled for tomorrow, had been put off until Friday.

Mr. Morse, who bolted the Republican party during the Eisenhower campaign and declared himself an independent, contended that he and perhaps others in the Senate had not had sufficient time to study the records that had prompted unanimous advance approval of appointments by Senate committees.

His single objection to immediate confirmation had the effect of delaying the votes for at least a day.

A mass Cabinet swearing-in ceremony, planned for late afternoon in the historic East Room of the White House, was called off, pending a settlement of the dilemma.

1933 Precedent Cited

Tonight the nine Government departments were without top officers. The Truman Cabinet left office at noon. The departments automatically went under the temporary management of officials of sub-Cabinet rank, most of them Democrats.

It had not been this way on March 4, 1933, when the late President Roosevelt took his first oath as President. His whole Cabinet was confirmed by the Senate and was sworn in that day. The Republicans, twenty years later, had cited this precedent and had tried to follow it.

The new President had given fast cooperation to carry out the Republican plan. He went directly from the inaugural stand into the Capitol and formalized the eight Cabinet nominations with his signature.

The Senate, too, planned fast work and went from the ceremonies to its chamber for action. As it re-

Continued on Page 19, Column 7

The New York Times Facsimile Transmission

"* * * I WILL FAITHFULLY EXECUTE THE OFFICE': Gen. Dwight D. Eisenhower, the thirty-fourth President of the United States, taking the oath of office, administered by Chief Justice Fred M. Vinson, on a platform in front of the Capitol. At the left are former Presidents Harry S. Truman and Herbert Hoover. At right is the new Vice President, Richard M. Nixon.

TRUMAN, TOO, GETS HIS BLAZE OF GLORY

'Old Has-Beens' Party Gives Roaring Ovation and 5,000 at Station Sing Farewell

By ANTHONY LEVIERO
Special to THE NEW YORK TIMES.

WASHINGTON, Jan. 20—Harry S. Truman headed tonight for Independence, Mo., a carefree man, leaving behind the New Deal-Fair Deal era and in a sense walking into the pages of history.

Yet he was walking off only a pace, for he expected to play a vigorous role as the Democratic party's elder statesman in the stirring times that were certain to follow the historic change of power today.

Mr. Truman has said that in about six months he would be ready for his new part.

Today, however, was somewhat symbolic of his Presidential career—he had risen to great popularity and had sunk, at times, to a low point in popular favor.

The day was symbolic of this because Mr. Truman made a backstage departure after the climactic moment on Capitol Hill.

But when he reached the home of Dean Acheson, his controversial Secretary of State, in old Georgetown, he received a tumultuous ovation that was as heart-warming as any he received during his

Continued on Page 16, Column 2

Croydon Hotel Hold-Up Frustrated By Policeman; 6 of 7 Thieves Seized

The alertness of a patrolman, combined with the wiles of a fast-thinking night watchman, frustrated a seven-man hold-up gang early yesterday at the Croydon Hotel, 12 East Eighty-sixth Street, off Madison Avenue, and resulted in the capture of six of the men.

One of the thugs later told the police that they were after what they believed was a large sum of money in safety deposit boxes in the hotel's safe. He said they were not out to hold up guests, none of whom were involved in the affray, during which a dozen shots were fired.

Flying bullets failed to find any marks and the only known injury was to one of the thugs who, trying to escape, leaped from a second-story window and broke an ankle. Another man fell to the sidewalk in front of the hotel as three shots were fired at him, but he got up and escaped into Central Park.

According to Deputy Inspector Francis J. M. Robb, in charge of the Sixth Detective Division, the affair began at 5 A. M. and ended about fifteen minutes later with the capture of the last three of the gang on the hotel's top floor. Detectives reconstructed the scene this way:

Patrolman Thomas Shore, 35 years old, of the East Sixty-seventh Street Precinct, who lives at 35-64 Eighty-fourth Street, Jackson Heights, Queens, and has been on the force six and a half years, was returning to the lobby from a washroom when he heard a man say: "Put your hands behind your back."

Stepping behind a pillar, he saw two men standing in front of the clerk's desk. Then he noticed five other men, apparently guests at first view, walk in the front door with three suitcases. As they joined the two men at the desk, however, the policeman stepped from behind the pillar with his pistol drawn.

One or more of the thugs immediately fired four shots at him and he emptied his own pistol at the group. As he backed out the front door to reload, one of the men darted out and fled west toward the park. Patrolman Shore fired three shots after him.

When he re-entered the hotel the six other men had disappeared and he put in a call for aid. A similar call was made from the

Continued on Page 13, Column 1

'Internationalist' Inaugural Acclaimed in Both Parties

By WILLIAM S. WHITE
Special to THE NEW YORK TIMES.

WASHINGTON, Jan. 20—Congress responded with general warmth and in many cases with profound bipartisan approval today to President Eisenhower's Inaugural Address. There was an all but visible gathering behind him of great blocs of members of both houses, Democrat and Republican alike, in his strong, somber pledge to carry this nation forward in full unity with the free world.

His speech, though lacking specifications, was interpreted by many as one of the most internationalist ever delivered to the country—not excluding the addresses of Franklin D. Roosevelt and Harry S. Truman.

President Eisenhower thus was heard with what almost amounted to joy by all those in both parties who for years had fought for foreign aid and foreign association and foreign alliance.

Some of the Democrats privately and jubilantly twitted some in the isolationist or near-isolationist wing of the Republican party to show where in world affairs General Eisenhower differed in any great principle from Mr. Truman and Mr. Roosevelt.

The Senate Democratic Leader, Senator Lyndon B. Johnson of Texas, carried this theme into a public statement. Senator Johnson first had commented only that the Inaugural Address as "a dignified statement of the dreams and aspirations that motivate millions of people."

But, on encountering a small group of reporters in the Senate dining room, he added:

"It was a statement, and a very good statement, of Democratic programs of the last twenty years."

Senator Robert A. Taft of Ohio, the Republican Senate leader, declared formally:

"It was a great and inspiring beginning, a great and inspiring speech."

Trouble Seen Later

A conservative pro-Eisenhower Senate Democrat of great influence made this observation as his summary of the attitude of the Taft group of Republicans, who always have differed with General Eisenhower to some extent on foreign policy:

"In the tone of this speech there is much that could cause trouble with the Taft people, if later President Eisenhower spells out, for example, what seems in some passages to be implied. Take the reciprocal trade program as an example. The General seems to be for it.

"But what is said in generalities, as in this Inaugural Speech, may differ much from what may come later on. I should say that no one thus far would be inclined to challenge General Eisenhower on anything he has said. That is likely to come later."

Many noted, too, that President

Continued on Page 19, Column 3

BRITISH SEEK HINTS OF NEW U. S. POLICY

Search for Inaugural 'Clues' on Tariff Cut—Tributes Flow From World Capitals

Special to THE NEW YORK TIMES.

LONDON, Jan. 20—Two phrases in President Eisenhower's inaugural address aroused special interest in Government circles here today. One was his hint that the new Administration might make trade a little easier, and the other was that the United States might expect a little more British cooperation toward European unity.

There was nothing very specific in the speech on either point, but there is enough sensitivity here to read meanings between the lines.

To many persons in the British Government, the most interesting passages in the General's speech were those in which he promised to help the proved friends of freedom to "achieve their own security and well-being."

Was this a pledge to lead a crusade for a lowering of tariff barriers against British goods?—that was the question that raised itself in the minds of British exporters,

Continued on Page 17, Column 3

Nixon, Though a Quaker, 'Swears' To Do His Duty as Vice President

By CLAYTON KNOWLES
Special to THE NEW YORK TIMES.

WASHINGTON, Jan. 20—Richard Milhous Nixon took a big forward stride in a meteoric political career today as he took the oath of office as the thirty-sixth Vice President of the United States.

Just 40 years old, Mr. Nixon, second youngest Vice President in history, has been in politics just six years. Elected to the House of Representatives in 1946 in his first political venture, he served there four years before moving up to the Senate.

A native of California, he is the first American from the Far West to assume the Vice Presidency. No one west of Texas had held the office.

Mr. Nixon took the oath of office at 12:23 P. M. It was administered by Senator William F. Knowland of California, with whom he had served as a member of Congress. Mr. Nixon, his right hand raised and his left hand resting on two old family Bibles, slowly and firmly repeated after Mr. Knowland the traditional oath of office.

This oath, which is twice as long as that which was administered to President Eisenhower, began: "I [Richard M. Nixon] do solemnly swear that I will support and defend the Constitution * * *."

It was noted that Mr. Nixon, though a Quaker, swore, rather than affirmed, as is Quaker custom, that he would faithfully perform his duties and defend the country and its institutions. He did not kiss the Bibles as Herbert Hoover, another Quaker, did on assuming the Presidency twenty-four years ago or as Alben W. Barkley did in taking the oath of office as Vice President in 1949.

The Nixon Bibles were open during the ceremony to that passage from the Sermon on the

Continued on Page 22, Column 4

LONG, GAY PARADE CHEERS PRESIDENT

He Takes Salute of All States as 750,000 Watch Frolic and Review of Might

By HAROLD B. HINTON
Special to THE NEW YORK TIMES.

WASHINGTON, Jan. 20—The nation's capital and its hundreds of thousands of visitors gave President Eisenhower a gay and colorful welcome today, with sunny skies bringing mild temperatures, jovial good humor and a carnival spirit to the city.

From shortly before two o'clock until long after darkness had fallen, it seemed that everybody in town was watching the parade. The police estimated that the spectacle drew 750,000 persons, probably more than any other procession of its kind in Washington's history. However some oldtimers thought otherwise and suggested that television was responsible.

Lasts Longer Than Planned

Although the parade lasted two and a half hours longer than planned, President Eisenhower and Vice President Richard M. Nixon held to their posts on the reviewing stand until the last two elephants wound up the procession at 6:58 P. M.

The new President saw samples of his country's military might, ranging from the eighty-five-ton cannon for atomic artillery shells to a California sheriff's posse riding palomino horses; from the Governor's Foot Guards of Connecticut and the Georgia Hussars of Savannah, in their Revolutionary uniforms, to the present-day

Continued on Page 21, Column 4

PRESIDENT'S PLAN

He Lists 9-Point Guide for Barring War but Bans Appeasement

ENDORSES AID ABROAD

Asserts Nation Is Ready to Join Move Seeking 'Drastic' Arms Cuts

Text of the inaugural address appears on Page 19.

By W. H. LAWRENCE
Special to THE NEW YORK TIMES.

WASHINGTON, Jan. 20—Dwight David Eisenhower was inaugurated today as the thirty-fourth President of the United States and he pledged that his Administration would "neither compromise, nor tire, nor ever cease" in its quest for an honorable world-wide peace.

While he expressed in his Inaugural Address abhorrence of war as "a chosen way" to end the threat of international communism and laid down a nine-point program to guide the nation's efforts for world peace, the new President also flatly banned appeasement of aggressor forces. He declared that "in the final choice a soldier's pack is not so heavy a burden as a prisoner's chains."

The former five-star General of the Army, who led Allied troops to victory in Western Europe in World War II, took the oath of office at 12:32 P. M. in solemn, moving ceremonies before the United States Capitol building. The term of office of Harry S. Truman, the retiring President, had expired constitutionally at noon, and the nation, for thirty-two minutes, technically was without a President.

Cabinet Confirmations Delayed

Richard Milhous Nixon, former California Senator, had been inaugurated as Vice President a few minutes earlier, succeeding Alben W. Barkley.

But these were the only two members of the new Administration team to take office today. A request of the new President that the Senate confirm at once eight members of his Cabinet, headed by John Foster Dulles as Secretary of State, was blocked by the single objection of Senator Wayne Morse, Oregon independent, who resigned from the Republican party last fall to give his support to Adlai E. Stevenson of Illinois, the Democratic Presidential nominee.

The controversial proposed appointment of Charles E. Wilson to be Secretary of Defense was not submitted to the Senate with the nominations of other Cabinet officers.

The biggest inaugural crowd in history, estimated by the police at 750,000, was on hand to celebrate the return of a Republican President to the White House for the first time since March 4, 1933. But President Eisenhower's sober appraisal of the world situation and of the steps this nation and the free world must take to meet the challenge of the forces of slavery gave his listeners few opportunities to applaud.

'Fixed Principles' for Peace

His comparatively short, 2,400-word Inaugural was devoted almost exclusively to foreign policy, with only passing reference to domestic concerns. He enunciated these "fixed principles" to direct the moves for world peace:

¶While the nation abhors war "as a chosen way to balk the purposes of those who threaten us, we hold it to be the first task of statesmanship to develop the strength that will deter the forces of aggression and promote the conditions of peace." The United States is willing to engage "in joint effort to remove the causes of mutual fear and distrust among nations, and so to make possible drastic reduction of armament" if methods can be provided "by which every participating nation will

Continued on Page 18, Column 4

"All the News
That's Fit to Print"

The New York Times.

LATE CITY EDITION
Cloudy, becoming fair this afternoon. Some cloudiness tomorrow.
Temperature Range Today—Max. 48; Min. 29
Temperature Yesterday Max. 39.6; Min. 14.5
Full U. S. Weather Bureau Report, Page 49

Copyright, 1953, by The New York Times Company.

VOL. CII...No. 34,709.

Entered as Second-Class Matter,
Post Office, New York, N. Y.

NEW YORK, TUESDAY, FEBRUARY 3, 1953.

Times Square, New York 36, N. Y.
Telephone LAckawanna 4-1000

FIVE CENTS

EISENHOWER FREES CHIANG TO RAID MAINLAND;
BIDS CONGRESS VOID ALL 'SECRET' PACTS ABROAD;
WOULD END CONTROLS; OPPOSES TAX CUTS NOW

EUROPE STORM TOLL EXCEEDS 1,400 DEAD AS FLOODS SUBSIDE

296 Die Along British Coast —Thousands Still Missing as Help Is Speeded

DUTCH COUNT 955 KILLED

Million in Netherlands Affected —Belgian Area Battered —Dunkirk Hard Hit

By TANIA LONG
Special to The New York Times.

LONDON, Tuesday, Feb. 3—As the gales abated and the raging waters of the North Sea began to recede, three nations counted their dead today and assessed the damage resulting from their worst flood disaster in recent history.

Hard hit were Britain, the Netherlands and Belgium, where huge waves swept across large sections of the coast Saturday night and early Sunday, breaking through dikes and seawalls and swallowing entire towns and villages.

[The Associated Press said the known dead in the storm area totaled more than 1,400 early Tuesday. In the Netherlands, 955 persons drowned. The toll in Britain stood at 443, including 296 killed in floods along the east coast, 132 who lost their lives in the sinking of the ferry Princess Victoria in the Irish Sea and fifteen lost on a missing trawler. Belgium had twenty-two dead.]

Several thousand persons were still missing, and it was feared that the death toll would mount heavily as rescue squads, made up of policemen, military personnel and civilian volunteers, completed their search of the devastated areas. On Canvey Island in the Thames Estuary, for example, where there were 100 dead, 500 men, women and children were still unaccounted for. Several thousand persons were evacuated from Canvey, which suffered by far the greatest damage of any British community.

Mobilize Full Resources

When the whole magnitude of the disaster that struck most heavily at Britain and the Netherlands was realized, the full resources of the two countries were quickly mobilized to give aid in the emergency. At the same time, assistance was sped to the Netherlands from France, Belgium and Denmark, and the United States forces in Europe, which also had their casualties.

The Swiss Red Cross Society announced it would begin an immediate collection of money to aid the British and Dutch flood victims, and there were offers of assistance, financial or material, from many other European countries and the United States.

In the meantime, the two nations worst affected put into action emergency plans to deal with the thousands rendered homeless by the floods. In Britain, civil defense plans prepared against a possible atomic attack were put into operation to shelter and feed the dispossessed.

Government Sends Help

The Government ordered its storehouses opened and sent thousands of blankets, mattresses and other items to the distressed areas, while the women's voluntary services brought out their trucks and set into motion the Flying Food Convoys, organized during World War II and kept in reserve against the possible outbreak of another conflict.

While evacuation of many thousands was being carried on, houses, telephone poles still tied together by wires, the gun barrels of an anti-aircraft battery, and, along the course of the Thames, reminders of industry and commerce—black oil tanks, stretches of raised railroad track, a long factory roof with a smokestack.

There was still danger that the combination of winds and high tides that caused the original disaster might bring a further influx from the sea.

Continued on Page 4, Column 5

Ships Arrive, Depart On Own in Tug Strike

Cargo and passenger vessels berthed and departed on their own power yesterday in New York, Philadelphia and Norfolk as the three-port strike of towboat crews continued without signs of a break.

Mild winds and calm waters here made it possible for most ships to dock or leave the harbor without the aid of tugs. A few inbound vessels, however, were held up at anchorage and several scheduled to leave were unable to do so.

Longshoremen shaped up and worked as usual. It had been feared that they might abstain from work in sympathy with the 3,500 strikers, who are members of Local 333 of the Marine Division of the International Longshoremen's Association, A. F. L.

One result of the strike was an interference with garbage collection.

Continued on Page 20, Column 4

A. F. L. ACTS TO END PIER UNION ABUSES

Breaking Traditional Policy, Its Council Orders Inquiry— Hogan Subpoenas Ryan

By A. H. RASKIN
Special to The New York Times.

MIAMI BEACH, Feb. 2—Acting to stamp out racketeering in its ranks, the American Federation of Labor made two sharp breaks today with its tradition of noninterference in the internal affairs of its affiliated unions.

Its executive council set up a committee of three federation vice presidents to consider means of cleaning up the gang-infested International Longshoremen's Association. The committee began its work at once and it was indicated that it would submit its report to the council within forty-eight hours.

[District Attorney Frank S. Hogan announced in New York Monday night that he had issued a grand jury subpoena for the appearance at 2 o'clock Tuesday afternoon of Joseph P. Ryan, president of the International Longshoremen's Association.]

The council also called on another affiliated union, the United Automobile Workers, to revoke the charter of a New York local headed by a convicted extortionist. If the automobile union refuses to comply, the council has the power to recommend that it be expelled from the federation at the next annual convention.

In a third action at the opening of its mid-winter meeting at the Monte Carlo Hotel here, the executive council set Feb. 24 as the date for resumption of formal peace talks between the A. F. L. and the

Continued on Page 20, Column 1

Southeast Britain's Coast Lifeless And Awash as Seen From Plane

By THOMAS F. BRADY
Special to The New York Times.

LONDON, Feb. 2—A vast coastal region of southeastern Britain lay submerged by salt water today, as the Romans found it 2,000 years ago. Seen from the air the land was awash and lifeless.

This report was written after a survey flight in a little Consul plane over Essex and Suffolk where the angry sea took several hundred lives Saturday night and Sunday. The scene from the air was a tragic disorder.

Miles of glistening gray water were broken by brown roofs of houses, telephone poles still tied together by wires, the gun barrels of an anti-aircraft battery, and, along the course of the Thames, reminders of industry and commerce—black oil tanks, stretches of raised railroad track, a long factory roof with a smokestack.

Above the Thames Estuary, thirty-five miles from London, the plane circled low over Canvey Island, where forty-eight hours earlier 13,000 persons had had their homes. Lower still a helicopter hovered, examining upper windows of houses for signs of life. The only other movement came

Continued on Page 4, Column 6

BRITAIN IS ANXIOUS

Makes Representations to U. S. on the Effects of Formosa Policy

PARLIAMENT AROUSED

Churchill Defers Debate Till Today, When Eden Will State Policy

By JAY WALZ
Special to The New York Times.

WASHINGTON, Feb. 2—Britain has made representations to the United States about President Eisenhower's decision to allow the Chinese Nationalists to raid the China mainland.

Anthony Eden, British Foreign Secretary, who is to make a statement on the subject before the House of Commons tomorrow, communicated with the State Department today.

It is understood that he advised diplomatic officials here that the British Government believed the new order to the Seventh Fleet would greatly complicate the political situation both in Europe and in the Far East.

In his communication, Mr. Eden is believed to have argued that the new order would intensify the Chinese civil war, raise the fears of a general war in the Far East and thus make any general settlement in the Far East even more difficult.

Bradley Discounts Risk

General of the Army Omar Bradley, chairman of the Joint Chiefs of Staff, said tonight that President Eisenhower's new policy on Formosa did not increase greatly the chances of the United States' becoming involved in a "big war" in the Far East.

The Eisenhower Administration contends that the United States, while intending no aggressive move, cannot permit its Navy, as the President put it, "to serve as a defensive arm of Communist China" by continuing its neutralizing function between the Nationalists and the Communists.

Some diplomatic sources feel that Britain's concern over developments may reflect general uneasiness among United States Allies in Europe over the direction of United States foreign policy.

Among these were British Embassy officials, who withheld comment pending Mr. Eden's statement in Parliament tomorrow.

However, F. S. Tomlinson, an Embassy counselor, called on Assistant Secretary of State John M. Allison last Saturday to express "concern" over reports of President Eisenhower's decision about

Continued on Page 11, Column 2

DELIVERS FIRST STATE OF UNION MESSAGE: President Eisenhower addressing a joint session of Congress yesterday. In background are Richard M. Nixon, Vice President, and Speaker of the House Joseph W. Martin Jr.

RED BLOW STOPPED BY SOUTH KOREANS

650-Man Attack on the Eastern Front Repulsed — Sabres Down Two Enemy Jets

By The Associated Press.

SEOUL, Korea, Tuesday, Feb. 3—North Koreans launched a 650-man attack on the eastern Korean front today, but stout South Korean defenders repulsed the assault and pursued the Communists across the craggy No Man's Land in below-zero cold.

The Korean Communists attacked at 12:45 A. M. across one mile of the mountainous front. They threw three companies into the attack and mounted two diversionary attacks of platoon size to the east.

Moving up under cover of a 680-round artillery and mortar barrage, the main force drove within forty yards of the main South Korean defenses.

"It is the height of impracticability," Mr. Capehart said, "to expect that the Congress can do a proper job of legislating a good control law into effect in a period of less than three months, and for such a law to begin properly functioning within seven months from the incidence of the request for the legislation."

The bitterly resisting South Koreans mounted a counter-attack at 2 A. M., drove off the Reds and chased them back across the snow-clad hills. An Eighth Army staff officer reported an estimated fifty-five of the enemy were killed.

Sabres Down Two MIG's

Special to The New York Times.

TOKYO, Tuesday, Feb. 3—Sabre jets of the United States Fifth Air Force shot down two Soviet-designed MIG jet fighters, probably destroyed another and damaged two more, while fighter-bombers and high-velocity tank-mounted guns hammered at the enemy-entrenched line across the peninsula.

Twelve Sabres clashed with eight MIG's in dogfights that ranged from 50,000 feet to 500 feet altitude, and from the Yalu River to Changchon on the west coast. The two kills were credited to Col. James K. Johnson and Maj. Foster I. Smith.

Meanwhile, more than 100 fighter-bombers, continuing the pattern of saturation raids on selected targets, plastered a big enemy troop concentration and storage area south of Chinnampo, seaport of the North Korean Communist capital at Pyongyang and important communications hub on the main route to the western front. The planes leveled thirty buildings, returning pilots said, and set off six large secondary explosions, indicating that ammunition storage areas had been hit.

Other fighter-bombers flying along the front lines knocked out

Continued on Page 3, Column 2

Capehart Moves to Retain Controls on Stand-By Basis

By CLAYTON KNOWLES
Special to The New York Times.

WASHINGTON, Feb. 2—Opposition cropped up today in an influential Republican quarter to President Eisenhower's proposal to let price and wage controls die on April 30 without maintaining them if needed.

Senator Homer E. Capehart of Indiana, chairman of the Senate Banking and Currency Committee, introduced a bill to set up such machinery within a few minutes after the President made his position known in his State of the Union Message.

He did not challenge the President's belief that price-wage controls had outlived their present usefulness but he did question the possibility of enacting a controls law quickly if one should be needed again.

He maintained that inaction during this enforced waiting period would promote hoarding, scare buying and indiscriminate spending, all of which contribute to inflation. He said this was precisely what happened after the outbreak of hostilities in Korea. Before a

Continued on Page 15, Column 4

Convicted Communists Snub Offer To Go to Russia Instead of Prison

By EDWARD RANZAL

Thirteen secondary Communist leaders got the chance yesterday to go to Russia as an alternative to going to prison for criminal conspiracy to teach and advocate the overthrow of the United States Government by force and violence. The offer was made by Federal Judge Edward J. Dimock.

Defense counsel and several of the defendants emphatically rejected the proposal, terming it "intolerable" and "unpalatable." Elizabeth Gurley Flynn, one of the thirteen, declared:

"We feel we belong here and have a political responsibility here. We feel we would be traitors to the American people if we turned our backs on them just to escape jail."

Judge Dimock also said he would not impose the maximum sentence of five years and $10,000 fine on the thirteen. However, United States Attorney Myles J. Lane recommended that the max-

imum sentence be imposed on each.

The actual sentencing was postponed until today by Judge Dimock after oral barrage by twelve of the thirteen defendants. At 4:40 P. M., after the court had been advised that in addition to the remaining defendant four defense attorneys would add to the voluminous record of the nine-and-a-half month trial, Judge Dimock adjourned court.

The first suggestion that Judge Dimock had an alternative plan came when the jurist asked Mr. Lane what he thought of the idea of permitting the defendants to go voluntarily to Russia rather than serve a prison sentence. Mr. Lane said he had no objection if the defendants first served their prison terms, then headed for the Soviet Union.

Then, after Miss Flynn had ad-

Continued on Page 5, Column 3

STATE OF THE UNION

President Sees No 'Logic or Sense' in Sea Patrol Helping Chinese Reds

HIS 'POSITIVE POLICY'

Reciprocal Trade Pacts, Aid to Europe Backed in Congress Message

Text of the State of the Union Message, Pages 14 and 15.

By ANTHONY LEVIERO
Special to The New York Times.

WASHINGTON, Feb. 2—President Eisenhower today ended the United States Seventh Fleet's protective screening of Red China, thus permitting the Nationalist forces of Generalissimo Chiang Kai-shek on Formosa to attack the Communist-held mainland.

The President also called upon Congress to repudiate any secret concessions made to the Russians at the World War II conferences at Teheran, Yalta and Potsdam.

Hours of applause greeted General Eisenhower's twin enunciations of a "new, positive foreign policy," made in his first State of the Union Message delivered before a joint session of Congress.

The new Republican President, to chart a course for the nation in two decades, General Eisenhower also dwelt on domestic affairs in his address, proposing a program that would turn the country toward a freer enterprise system and "natural" economic law.

His Program Detailed

In outlining his policies for the new Administration the President made these points:

¶There no longer was any "sense or logic" in the use of the Seventh Fleet to shield Red China.

¶The Government "recognizes no kind of commitment contained in secret understandings of the past with foreign governments which permit * * * enslavement."

¶The training and arming of South Korean troops would be accelerated.

However, as the new President made his exit, arms linked with Senator Robert A. Taft of Ohio, Senate Majority Leader, whom he defeated for the Republican presidential nomination, the speech appeared to leave in its wake a trail of issues that spelled Congressional controversy to come.

Although the new President's speech brought praise from Democrats as well as Republicans, President Eisenhower's decision to end the United States Seventh Fleet's role as a barrier against raids by the Chinese Nationalists on the Communist-held mainland seemed to bring much concern to many Congressmen. It was difficult to determine whether the Republican view that the action would end the stalemate in Korea outweighed fear, expressed largely by Democrats, that it might extend the Korean conflict and involve the United States more deeply in Asia.

¶Aid to Europe would be continued with the Allies required to be full partners matching United States contributions according to their capabilities.

¶The new foreign policy would be the true product of bipartisanship and cooperation between the President and Congress and it would be universal and global.

¶Incontrovertible evidence is at hand of Russian possession of atomic weapons and therefore civil defense preparedness is a "sheer necessity."

¶The reciprocal trade treaties should be continued, American investments abroad should be encouraged and customs procedures simplified.

¶The Secretary of Defense would take steps to obtain the maximum in national security at minimum cost.

¶The first order of domestic business should be to balance the budget, after which a reduction in taxation might be in order.

¶Wage-price controls would not

Continued on Page 15, Column 1

CONGRESS PRAISES EISENHOWER TALK

But 7th Fleet Decision Brings Fear of War Extension and Deeper U. S. Involvement

By C. P. TRUSSELL
Special to The New York Times.

WASHINGTON, Feb. 2—President Eisenhower's first message on the State of the Union, delivered personally today to a joint session of Congress in the packed House of Representatives chamber, got a rousing reception.

The Left Wing at some points and the Right Wing at other points were made far from happy, for varying reasons.

The prospect raised was that the President could count upon at least as much Democratic support as Republican support—and perhaps more—for his approach in these fields, which encompass some

Continued on Page 17, Column 1

CIVIL RIGHTS PLANS GET WIDE SUPPORT

Challenge to McCarthy Seen on Security Issues — Duel Over Immigration Looms

By WILLIAM S. WHITE
Special to The New York Times.

WASHINGTON, Feb. 2—President Eisenhower appeared to please nearly all the political Center in Congress today by the civil rights, loyalty and immigration policies laid down in his State of the Union Message.

He did not challenge the President's belief that price-wage controls had outlived their present usefulness but he did question the

Resentment Expressed

Senators and Representatives repeatedly asked whether releasing Generalissimo Chiang Kai-shek's Formosa forces to attack the Chinese mainland would imply that the United States would have to back up such actions with American men and planes. This, they contended, would mean deeper involvement and perhaps another world war.

Influential Democrats in Congress expressed resentment over the section of the President's address in which he contended, in effect, that the present assignment of the Seventh Fleet, made by former President Truman, constituted a protection for the Communist mainland while other Communists were fighting United Nations troops, mostly American, in Korea.

Representative John W. McCormack, Democrat of Massachusetts and House Whip, called it "hitting below the belt." He charged that President Eisenhower, in making for bipartisan foreign policy, was acting "to destroy it."

Opponents contended the Seventh Fleet decision would not

Continued on Page 17, Column 3

To Suburban Readers

The strike of newspaper deliverymen against suburban wholesalers has curtailed distribution of The New York Times outside New York City within a 50-mile radius. The Times may be obtained, however, at all newsstands within the New York City line. Suburbanites in New York during the evening are advised to get their copies before going home. Temporary mail subscriptions may be ordered for the duration of the emergency at the newsstand price by telephoning The Times. Information on how and where to get The Times is given at the end of The New York Times News Bulletins, which are broadcast every hour on the hour over WQXR, 1560 on the AM dial, and WQXR-FM, 96.3 on the dial.

Clark Gable and Grace Kelly are seen here in Mogambo, *which also starred Ava Gardner.*

Vincent Price tries to put out the fire in House of Wax, *which was filmed in 3-D and color.*

Eisenhower speaks to reporters at one of his regular press conferences which kept his name on the front pages.

The Supreme Allied Commander General Mark Clark signed the truce with Korea for the UN.

Josef Stalin, the Soviet Union's dictator, hated and feared, but obeyed by millions, dead at 73.

"All the News
That's Fit to Print"

The New York Times.

LATE CITY EDITION
Fair, little temperature change to-day. Mostly fair tomorrow.
Temperature Range Today—Max., 42; Min., 29
Temperatures Yesterday—Max., 44; Min., 33
Full U. S. Weather Bureau Report, Page 47

Copyright, 1953, by The New York Times Company.

VOL. CII..No. 34,740.
Entered as Second-Class Matter,
Post Office, New York, N. Y.

NEW YORK, FRIDAY, MARCH 6, 1953.

Times Square, New York 36, N. Y.
Telephone LAckawanna 4-1000

FIVE CENTS

STALIN DIES AFTER 29-YEAR RULE; HIS SUCCESSOR NOT ANNOUNCED; U.S. WATCHFUL, EISENHOWER SAYS

WORST CITY CRISIS SINCE 1933 IS SEEN IN STATE TAX PLAN

Moore and McGovern Demand Payroll Levy and Transit Unit Mandated to Raise Fares

MAYOR CALLS DEMOCRATS

Estimate Board to Get Report on Views of County Leaders —Bus Reduction Directed

By PAUL CROWELL

The city Government is facing the most serious financial and political crisis to confront any Administration since 1933, when leading banking houses rescued a Democratic regime from fiscal disaster.

This was the consensus last night of top city officials to whom Lieut. Gov. Frank C. Moore and State Controller J. Raymond McGovern had indicated earlier in the day that a sound fiscal program for 1953-54 and succeeding years should include both a city payroll tax and a transit authority with a duty to increase fares to meet operating deficits of the municipal lines.

That the city Administration realized the political dangers inherent in the adoption of the suggested fiscal program was indicated later in the day when Mayor Impellitteri, when consulting the Board of Estimate, asked the five Democratic county leaders to confer with him at noon today at City Hall. Among those invited was Tammany leader Carmine G. De-Sapio, the only member of the group who is at loggerheads with the Mayor on matters of patronage.

Leaders' Views Important

After a two-hour conference with Mr. Moore and Mr. McGovern at Mr. McGovern's office, 270 Broadway, the Mayor and Board of Estimate held an even fuller closed meeting at City Hall, which will be resumed at 3 o'clock this afternoon. At today's session an important factor will be the attitude of the five Democratic county leaders, as reported by the Mayor, toward the proposals upon which the two state officials apparently are insisting.

In another municipal development, the Mayor's Transit Advisory Commission demanded that the eight privately owned bus companies involved in the recent bus strike and Michael J. Quill's Transport Workers Union, C. I. O., take immediate steps to wipe out excess bus lines and to reduce the number of buses on lines that were needed. City tax relief was made dependent on such action.

The conference with Mr. Moore and Mr. McGovern was a continuation of last Monday's talks at Albany on the city's $218,700,000 fiscal program, which in effect already had been rejected by the two state officials in their joint memorandum of Feb. 22.

At the outset of the meeting the

Continued on Page 19, Column 1

Eisenhower Plans to Pare Policy-Level Civil Service

Directive Will Repeal 2 That Truman Issued Anchoring Some Democrats in Their Jobs —Organization of Administration Object

By PAUL P. KENNEDY
Special to The New York Times.

WASHINGTON, March 5—Several hundred persons face the possibility of losing Civil Service status and probably their Government jobs under an Executive Order to be issued by President Eisenhower next week.

In announcing the forthcoming order, James C. Hagerty, White House press secretary, said that all those affected would not necessarily lose their jobs. The announcement was generally interpreted, however, to mean that the Administration was preparing to clear out holdover Democrats in high policy-making and administrative positions in order to replace them with personnel of the Administration's own choosing.

President Eisenhower's order, which he directed to be drafted immediately, will repeal two Executive Orders of former President Truman in 1947 and 1948 in which certain persons on Schedule A of Civil Service rules would receive

Civil Service protection against separation from the Government.

The President's order will emphasize that the rights of veterans, as specified in the Veterans Preference Act of 1944 would be respected.

Schedule A is a list of positions to which appointments may be made without reference to Civil Service rules or regulations. The appointees may assume their positions without Civil Service examinations and their classifications are not subject to review by Civil Service Boards.

Mr. Hagerty said the "several hundred" persons to be affected by the order were employed in all departments and agencies of the Government. The order, he said, applied to people who had been put under Civil Service in the last twenty years.

The new order, effective, since coming into office Jan. 20, Mr.

Continued on Page 15, Column 2

President May Take a Hand If Inquiries Imperil Amity

By C. P. TRUSSELL
Special to The New York Times.

WASHINGTON, March 5—President Eisenhower indicated today that if the Senate investigation into the Voice of America, being conducted by Senator Joseph R. McCarthy, or other Congressional inquiries, reached a point of inviting international misunderstandings and difficulties he might intervene.

This, he emphasized at a news conference, would mean that he would have to desert his long-held conviction that the Congress had an inherent right to investigate as it pleased. He was still hoping, he said, to avoid a situation in which a spokesman for the Executive Branch of the Government would have to take issue with actions of the coordinate Legislative Branch.

The question that prompted these responses was based upon the hearings being conducted, largely before television, by the Judiciary subcommittee headed by Senator McCarthy, Republican of Wisconsin.

The group is inquiring into the management and personnel of the Voice, the Government's radio program for telling the story of America. Broadcasts are beamed to eighty-seven countries in nearly forty languages.

At yesterday's hearing Reed Harris, deputy director of the State

Continued on Page 14, Column 6

EISENHOWER PRAISES RESTRAINT IN PRICES

Asserts There Has Been Little Evidence of Gouging—More Controls Are Removed

By CHARLES E. EGAN
Special to The New York Times.

WASHINGTON, March 5—President Eisenhower today complimented business for what he termed the admirable restraint it had shown in pricing policies since the removal of most price controls.

General Eisenhower said at his news conference that since the program of removing major segments of the economy from price regulation got under way Feb. 6, there had been little discernible evidence of attempts to gouge consumers.

The President's observations came immediately before an announcement from the Office of Price Stabilization that it had removed price ceilings on another wide range of items, including bread and bakery products, new and used cars, major household appliances, dry cleaning and diaper services.

Hopes for a New Climate

Another development was a Senate committee hearing at which Charles R. Sligh Jr., president of the National Association of Manufacturers, attacked proposals to establish stand-by controls authority. With such authority, the President could declare a ninety-day "freeze" of all prices and wages in event of all-out war or other critical emergency.

About the only major price increase that has occurred since the Office of Price Stabilization began implementing its orders for relaxation of price ceilings, the President said, has been an expected rise of 6 to 7 cents a pound in copper.

The absence of price gouging, the President added, confirms his belief that the American people are ready to be considerate and moderate. He added that he hoped a climate might be established—a labor-management relations for instance—that would subminize harmful pressures on the economy

Continued on Page 14, Column 6

F.B.I. Agents Depict Rebuff by Monaghan

By LUTHER A. HUSTON
Special to The New York Times.

WASHINGTON, March 5—Leland V. Boardman, special agent in charge of the New York office of the Federal Bureau of Investigation, asserted today that Police Commissioner George P. Monaghan had notified him that he would not make New York City policemen available to any Federal law enforcement agency for questioning and that they would respond only to summonses from a Federal grand jury.

This policy, Mr. Boardman said, was founded upon a general agreement between the New York Police Department and the Criminal Division of the Department of Justice to "block out F. B. I. investigators from cases involving police brutality in civil rights cases."

Another agent quoted Commis-

Continued on Page 16, Column 2

VISHINSKY LEAVING

Foreign Minister Called to Moscow to Report —Will Sail Today

U. N. TO LOWER FLAG

Lie Praises Premier as Statesman — Pearson Hails Fight on Nazis

By THOMAS J. HAMILTON
Special to The New York Times.

UNITED NATIONS, N. Y., March 5—Soviet Foreign Minister Andrei Y. Vishinsky, who was reported to have been informed of the death of Premier Stalin before the public announcement by the Moscow radio, plans to leave for Moscow tomorrow.

Mr. Vishinsky and a party of Soviet officials are scheduled to sail aboard the French liner Liberté tomorrow at 4 P. M. Plans were disclosed at Police Headquarters. The police said they had been informed that the party would travel in seven automobiles from Glen Cove, L. I., where the Soviet delegation to the United Nations has headquarters, to Pier 88, Hudson River at Forty-eighth Street. The liner will sail at Plymouth and Le Havre.

Mr. Vishinsky has a heart condition and therefore avoids air travel whenever possible.

Valerian A. Zorin, Soviet representative to the United Nations, revealed this afternoon Mr. Vishinsky's decision to leave tomorrow. Mr. Vishinsky's decision was taken after he had received a telephone call from Moscow earlier in the day.

Disclosure by Consulate

There was no indication whether this telephone call had given any indication of Mr. Stalin's death. The news that Mr. Vishinsky had been informed prior to the public announcement came from a telephone inquiry at the Soviet Consulate at 680 Park Avenue.

Earlier inquiries at the headquarters of the Soviet delegation to the United Nations had brought repeated denials that Mr. Vishinsky was there. The consulate revealed, however, not only that Mr. Vishinsky was actually at the delegation headquarters but also that he had been informed of the news earlier.

According to United Nations protocol, the only flag that will fly at the United Nations flagpole tomorrow is the banner of the United Nations itself, and it will be at half-staff. The same procedure will be followed during the day of the funeral of Premier Stalin.

Informed of the death of Mr.

Continued on Page 13, Column 2

CONDOLENCES SENT

President Orders Terse Formal Note on Stalin Dispatched to Soviet

TRIBUTE IS OMITTED

Eisenhower Still Ready to Confer on Peace With the Kremlin

By JAMES RESTON
Special to The New York Times.

WASHINGTON, March 5—President Eisenhower authorized John Foster Dulles, Secretary of State, tonight to send the United States' "official condolences" to the Soviet Government on the death of Premier Stalin.

Earlier the President had told reporters at his press conference that he could not tell what effect the illness of the Premier would have on the "cold war." A definite watchfulness is our policy for the moment, the President added.

The President announced the statement of condolences less than an hour after he had been informed of Mr. Stalin's death by James C. Hagerty, press secretary, at 4:26 P. M. The statement was as follows:

The President authorized the Secretary of State to send the following message to the American Embassy in Moscow: The Government of the United States tenders its official condolences to the Government of the Union of Socialist Soviet Republics on the death of Generalissimo Joseph Stalin, Prime Minister of the Soviet Union.

Dulles Informed by Hagerty

Mr. Hagerty notified Mr. Dulles, who was a guest at the British Embassy, immediately after the President had been informed.

The press secretary said the President's message would be transmitted to the Soviet Government by Jacob D. Beam, Chargé d'Affaires in Moscow.

The terse wording of the message was noted here, especially the phrase "official condolences." Diplomatic circles suggested that the wording was about as brief and formal as possible under diplomatic protocol.

They recalled, however, that the President previously had expressed condolences. In the first White House statement issued after word had been received of the serious illness of Mr. Stalin, General Eisenhower directed his words to the Soviet people rather than the Premier or the Government.

Indications were that the President's official condolences would stand in so far as to publicly

Continued on Page 12, Column 5

PREMIER JOSEPH STALIN
A portrait released by Sovfoto, Soviet picture agency

Soviet Fear of an Eruption Discerned in Call for Unity

By HARRY SCHWARTZ

The fact that appeals for "monolithic unity" and "vigilance" have now become the main theme of Soviet domestic propaganda appears to be a clear indication that the present Soviet rulers fear that Mr. Stalin's death may result in an explosive resolution of the major tensions now repressed in the Soviet Union.

The unity theme dominates the official announcement of Stalin's death. It was first voiced in the initial communiqué regarding Stalin's illness issued by the highest Government and Communist party authorities. Unity and vigilance were the central ideas in the long leading editorials that appeared yesterday morning on the front pages of both Pravda and Izvestia.

Yesterday's Pravda editorial may also have given the first hint that Georgi M. Malenkov is leading in the succession race, but this hint seemed far from conclusive. The editorial mentioned by name only Lenin, Premier Stalin, and Mr. Malenkov, quoting the latter's speech last October when he said: "The prospects and ways of our progress are based on the laws of the national economy, on the science of the Communist social structure which have been evolved by Comrade Stalin."

The fact that Moscow has announced that Nikita S. Khrushchev will head the committee preparing

Continued on Page 12, Column 2

PREMIER ILL 4 DAYS

Announcement of Death Made by Top Soviet and Party Chiefs

STROKE PROVES FATAL

Leaders Issue an Appeal to People for Unity and Vigilance

Text of official announcement of Stalin's death, Page 6.

By HARRISON E. SALISBURY
Special to The New York Times.

MOSCOW, Friday, March 6—Premier Joseph Stalin died at 9:50 P. M. yesterday [1:50 P. M. Thursday, Eastern standard time] in the Kremlin at the age of 73, it was announced officially this morning. He had been in power twenty-nine years.

The announcement was made in the name of the Central Committee of the Communist party, the Council of Ministers and the Presidium of the Supreme Soviet.

Calling on the Soviet people to rally firmly around the party and the highest leadership, the announcement asked them to display unity and the highest political vigilance "in the struggle against internal and external foes." [No announcement was made of a successor to Premier Stalin.]

The Soviet leader's death from general circulatory and respiratory deficiency occurred just short of four days after he had been stricken with a brain hemorrhage in his Kremlin apartment.

Accompanying the death announcement was a final medical certificate issued by a group of ten physicians, headed by Health Minister A. F. Tretyakov, who cared for Mr. Stalin in his last illness under the direct and closest supervision of the Central Committee and the Council of Ministers.

Pulse Rate Was High

The medical certificate revealed that in the last hours Mr. Stalin's condition grew worse rapidly, with repeated heavy and sharp circulatory and heart collapses. His breathing grew superficial and sharply irregular. His pulse rate rose to 140 to 150 a minute and at 9:50 P. M., "because of a growing circulatory and respiratory insufficiency, J. V. Stalin died."

[The news of Mr. Stalin's death was withheld by Soviet officials for more than six hours.]

Pravda announced this morning with broad black borders around its front page, which was devoted entirely to Mr. Stalin. The layout included a large photograph of the Premier, the announcement by the Government, the medical bulletins and the announcement of the formation of a funeral comm.

Continued on Page 5, Column 5

AMMUNITION SHORT, VAN FLEET ASSERTS

He Affirms Scarcity in Korea and Byrd Writes to Wilson Demanding Explanation

By HAROLD B. HINTON
Special to The New York Times.

WASHINGTON, March 5—Gen. James A. Van Fleet, former Commander of United Nations ground forces in Korea, told the Senate Armed Services Committee today that he had been handicapped during the entire twenty-two months he had had the command by shortages of ammunition and manpower. He specified hand grenades, and mentioned "other types" of ammunition as having been severely short all the time and critically short on occasions.

The apparent contradiction of the General's testimony today with that of yesterday, in which he indicated there were no serious shortages of anything in Korea, was unexplained, except for the interpretation that yesterday he had been speaking for the present, whereas today he had been speaking for the past.

Praised by Symington

So much the general said before a public meeting of the committee. Senator Stuart Symington, Democrat of Missouri and former Secretary of the Air Force, praised General Van Fleet for his intelligence and courage in reporting these matters to the public. If other military figures would emulate the example, he declared, "we won't send our youth out to fight with these shortages, even if we have fewer television sets."

[In the Korean war action, Air Force Thunderjet fighter-bombers made a record 1,600-mile raid on a Communist industrial center on the northeast coast sixty miles from Siberia. Navy carrier bombers made heavy attacks in North Korea. Ground action was light.]

In a later closed session with the committee, General Van Fleet apparently amplified his discussion of the shortages. The amplification prompted Senator Harry F. Byrd, Democrat of Virginia, to write a letter to Charles E. Wil-

Continued on Page 3, Column 6

Treaties Manifesto Shelved in Congress

By WILLIAM S. WHITE
Special to The New York Times.

WASHINGTON, March 5—President Eisenhower's proposed United States declaration against "perversion" of the wartime Yalta and Potsdam agreements into instruments for enslaving peoples was put on the shelf in Congress today.

The announced Congressional reason was that the manifesto would be inopportune now in view of Premier Stalin's fatal illness, though the President himself indicated that he thought this need not delay action. The Congressional developments came before the announcement of Mr. Stalin's death.

The Republican leaders in Congress could not take the resolution to the floor of either house

Continued on Page 6, Column 4

Pole Flies to Denmark in First Intact Russian MIG-15 to Reach West

A young Polish pilot seeking political asylum flew this Soviet-made MIG-15 into a Danish airport at Bornholm yesterday, making it the first fighter plane of its type acquired undamaged by the West. Name of pilot (center figure) was withheld.

COPENHAGEN, Denmark, March 5—The first intact Russian-built MIG-15 jet fighter—the newest known type of Russian jet fighter—to land west of the Iron Curtain came down this morning at Roenne Airport on the Danish island of Bornholm. It came from a Polish Baltic base.

The 21-year-old Polish lieutenant who flew with the fighter gave himself up to Danish authorities as a political refugee and asked for asylum. Very little is known about his story. Danish authorities are keeping it secret for the time being.

The young Pole performed a fantastic maneuver in landing the jet fighter on the grass-cov-

ered airstrip at Roenne, only 1,200 meters (3,937 feet) long. Jet fighters normally require a 3,000-meter (9,843 feet) concrete runway to start and land.

At the farther end of the air-

Continued on Page 2, Column 3

Burt Lancaster and Deborah Kerr were both nominated for Oscars for their performaces in From Here to Eternity.

"All the News That's Fit to Print"

The New York Times.

LATE CITY EDITION
Mostly fair and cold today. Increasingly cloudy and cold tomorrow.
Temperature Range Today—Max., 38; Min., 30
Temperature Yesterday—Max., 41; Min., 32
Full U. S. Weather Bureau Report, Page 31

VOL. CII—No. 34,741.

Entered as Second-Class Matter,
Post Office, New York, N. Y.

NEW YORK, SATURDAY, MARCH 7, 1953.

Copyright, 1953, by The New York Times Company.

Times Square, New York 36, N. Y.
Telephone LAckawanna 4-1000

FIVE CENTS

MALENKOV IS NAMED NEW SOVIET PREMIER; WIDE CHANGES DISCLOSED TO AVOID 'PANIC'; THRONGS PASS STALIN BIER; RITES MONDAY

MAJORITY OF BOARD BARS STATE TERMS FOR CITY FISCAL AID

Stands on Mayor's Plan After Democratic Leaders Report Price Politically Ruinous

VOTE ON DECISION IS 5 TO 3

New York's Legislators Held Unwilling to Support Fare Rise or Payroll Impost

By PAUL CROWELL

A majority of the Board of Estimate decided yesterday to stand firm on Mayor Impellitteri's $318,700,000 fiscal program for 1953-54, refusing to purchase substantial financial aid from Governor Dewey's Republican Administration at price considered politically ruinous by the Democratic leaders of the city's five counties.

At an executive meeting of the board, five members holding a majority of its sixteen votes refused to modify the Mayor's program by including, at the virtual insistence of Lieut. Gov. Frank C. Moore and State Controller J. Raymond McGovern, a city payroll tax and a transit authority mandated to increase the fare on municipal subway and surface lines to meet operating deficits.

The Moore - McGovern position was outlined to the Mayor and the Board of Estimate on Thursday at a conference in Mr. McGovern's New York office. The Mayor and his colleagues were told that a number of major items in the city's program, including the Mayor's plan for a transit authority designed to preserve the 10-cent fare by subsidizing operating deficits with an income tax on business, were unacceptable to the state.

Tax Request Discounted

The city officials also were informed that their requested increase of power to tax real estate, estimated to yield an additional annual revenue of $100,000,000, had little chance of approval at Albany unless the payroll tax and the "higher-fare" transit authority were made part of the city program.

The state spokesmen asked for the city's decision by the end of the week. It was made known to Mr. McGovern by telephone late yesterday afternoon, but he declined comment, saying that he would discuss it with Mr. Moore over the week-end and possibly with Governor Dewey tonight.

Thursday's conference between city and state officials was followed by a long meeting of the Board of Estimate, at which no decision was reached. After the meeting, the Mayor invited State Democratic Chairman Richard H. Balch, the five Democratic county leaders and Assemblyman Eugene F. Bannigan, minority leader at Albany, to a luncheon meeting yesterday at the National Democratic Club, 233 Madison Avenue. The state's virtual ultimatum was discussed at this meeting.

Continued on Page 21, Column 4

Rowdy Pupils Cause A School Bus Strike

Special to The New York Times.

ATLANTIC CITY, March 6—Drivers of school buses serving this resort's north side went on "strike" today against high school students because they were "fed up" with the youths' rowdy, "almost savage" antics.

The drivers, who operate four special school buses for the Atlantic City Transportation Company in the morning and afternoon, reported to work but refused to make the school trips. They made regular passenger runs, however, during other parts of the day.

Roy L. Foley, president of Local 1358, Amalgamated Association of Street Electric Railway and Motor Coach Employes of America, said the union was supporting the "striking" drivers.

"We will not permit our men

Continued on Page 33, Column 5

Ammunition Ample to Repel Reds in Korea, Says Wilson

He Will Give 'Facts' to Senators Tuesday on Issue Raised by Van Fleet's Report —Clark Also Denies Shortage

By HAROLD B. HINTON
Special to The New York Times.

WASHINGTON, March 6 — Charles E. Wilson, the Secretary of Defense, assured the public today that "there is sufficient ammunition available in the Far East Command to counter any enemy attack in Korea."

The statement was contained in a letter to Senator Leverett Saltonstall, Republican of Massachusetts and chairman of the Senate Armed Services Committee. Most members of the committee had been aroused yesterday by testimony from Gen. James A. Van Fleet, former commander of the United Nations ground forces in Korea, that he had been handicapped during his entire twenty-two months of command by shortages of men and ammunition.

The Far East Command mentioned by Secretary Wilson includes Japan as well as Korea.

[In Korea, on an inspection, Gen. Mark W. Clark, the United Nations commander, said that "certain types" of artillery

shells had been rationed but that there was "ample" ammunition to repel any all-out Communist offensive.]

The Senate committee, after hearing General Van Fleet in two closed sessions, decided to invite Mr. Wilson, Robert T. Stevens, the Secretary of the Army, and Gen. J. Lawton Collins, the Army Chief of Staff, to give their views on the matter. Some members hoped that General Van Fleet could attend the closed hearing at which the other officials would appear next Tuesday morning.

Senator Saltonstall said he had also invited General of the Army Omar N. Bradley, Chairman of the Joint Chiefs of Staff, but that General Bradley would be in Europe on Tuesday.

The Pentagon officials, he said, will be asked "to place the rather confusing and conflicting views which have been laid before us in

Continued on Page 2, Column 6

HALLEY DEMANDS RENT LAW BE KEPT

He Proposes That Council Ask Legislature to Let City Control as Alternative

A demand that the Legislature extend the present State Rent Law or permit the city to enact its own controls was made yesterday by City Council President Rudolph Halley. At the same time he accused the State Administration of a "rent grab."

Acting jointly with Councilman Earl Brown, Manhattan Democrat, Mr. Halley placed in the City Council hopper for introduction next Tuesday a resolution setting forth his rent law proposals.

The proposed rent control now before the Legislature, as submitted by the Temporary State Commission on Rents and Rental Conditions, Mr. Halley charged, "permits a rent grab in that it authorizes blanket increases without regard to the nature or condition of the accommodations, without a showing of landlord need and without regard to the hardships of the tenants."

There is no proof that acute housing shortage in the city has been relieved, Mr. Halley asserted, and "no evidence to show that the low and middle-income families who make up the bulk of the tenants of the city can afford to pay increases."

Hardship Is Predicted

The Council President predicted that the proposed new state law would work a "serious hardship" on the majority of low and middle-income tenants here, "many of whom live in substandard dwellings and most of whom can ill afford to pay rent increases at this time."

"The clear evidence is," he declared, "that if a blanket increase either in rent or percentage of rent is authorized, the great majority of tenants in New York City will have no choice but to pay oppressive rents, because of the unavailability of apartments by reason of the housing shortage."

He added that the proposed state bill "ignores the problems and the needs of a great majority of the people of the city."

The resolution to be adopted by the City Council by Mr. Halley and Mr. Brown sets forth:

"That the Legislature of the State of New York either extend the existing rent control law without change for another two years or, in the alternative, that it authorize the City of New York to enact its own rent control laws so that those who know the facts and understand the problems of the people of the City of New

Continued on Page 21, Column 7

POLICE ALTER PLAN TO FIGHT GAMBLING

One Officer in Each Borough to Be in Charge—Brooklyn Clean-Up Discussed

The Police Department is planning to place the enforcement of gambling and vice laws in the hands of individual commanders for each of the five boroughs in a move to "concentrate responsibility."

This plan, and another to cope with assaults on the public in Brooklyn, were announced yesterday after Commissioner George P. Monaghan conferred for an hour with District Attorney Miles F. McDonald, County Judge Samuel S. Leibowitz, Raymond H. Chadeayne, foreman of the Brooklyn rackets grand jury, and Assistant District Attorney Julius Helfand.

The meeting took place in Judge Leibowitz' chambers in the Central Court Building at the request of Mr. Monaghan.

Judge Leibowitz explained that the meeting "so that we could sit down informally and see what we can do to correct, to clean up, the conditions that need cleaning up in the Borough of Brooklyn."

Judge Leibowitz, who acted as

Continued on Page 32, Column 2

Half-Staff Flags Here Stir Confusion

At City Hall for Mr. Hall
The New York Times

At U. N. for Premier Stalin
The New York Times

Most of Them Flown for the Late Head of Staten Island

Many flags flew at half staff here yesterday, but most were not a mark of respect for Premier Stalin of the Soviet Union. Only a few were.

Flags on public buildings, including the City Hall, were ordered flown at half staff by Mayor Impellitteri as a mark of respect for Cornelius A. Hall, retired Borough President of Richmond. Mr. Hall died Thursday, too.

At United Nations headquarters the United Nations flag was at half staff too, but this was out of respect for Stalin.

There were other tributes to the Premier. The national red ensign of Britain was at half staff on the Queen Elizabeth, and the tricolor of France was flown similarly on the Liberté.

Officers of the Queen Elizabeth said the red ensign had been lowered in respect to the Premier. But Mr. Mao, the Chinese Communist dictator, has French Line officials refused all explanation. However, Andrei Y.

Continued on Page 4, Column 4

VISHINSKY DEPARTS

Pays a Tearful Tribute to Stalin and Sails— Silent on Shake-Up

GROMYKO SENT HERE

U. N. Hears Indonesian Appeal for Eisenhower and Malenkov to Talk

By THOMAS J. HAMILTON
Special to The New York Times.

UNITED NATIONS, N. Y., March 6—Andrei Y. Vishinsky, in what turned out to be his last official act as Foreign Minister of the Soviet Union, delivered a tearful tribute here this morning to "the great Stalin," and sailed on the Liberté this afternoon for home and possibly an uncertain future.

He said just before the Liberté sailed that he had had no advance knowledge of the election of Georgi M. Malenkov as Premier, and declined to comment.

During the day's debate, Dr. L. N. Palar, chief Indonesian delegate, urged the United Nations to call for a direct meeting between President Eisenhower and Premier Malenkov as a move to ease world tensions and prepare the way for a settlement in Korea.

Andrei A. Gromyko, now Soviet Ambassador to London, who was permanent Soviet representative at the United Nations from 1946 until 1948, will come to New York to take over temporarily as representative to the United Nations. Mr. Gromyko left London hastily by air tonight. Headwinds forced his plane, a British Overseas Airways Stratocruiser, to stop at Shannon Airport in Ireland.

Speech Precedes Shake-Up

Mr. Vishinsky's statement in the Political and Security Committee of the General Assembly was made five hours before the Moscow radio announced the government changes, which included the appointment of Vyacheslav M. Molotov as Foreign Minister and the demotion of Mr. Vishinsky to Deputy Foreign Minister and permanent Soviet representative to the United Nations.

[Aboard the Liberté last night A. A. Soldatov, a member of the Soviet delegation to the United Nations, said that Mr. Vishinsky had been informed of his new job, but that he declined to comment for publication.]

Mr. Vishinsky showed so plainly his strain and grief during his United Nations appearance this morning that a delegate remarked, after Mr. Vishinsky had returned to the Soviet delegation's

Continued on Page 3, Column 6

HUGE FUNERAL SET

Body to Be Placed With Lenin's in Red Square After Ceremonies

MEMORIAL PLANNED

New Pantheon Is Due— Mourners in Moscow Offer Quiet Homage

Special to The New York Times.

MOSCOW, Saturday, March 7—Thousands of grieving Moscow citizens have filed past Stalin's bier in the Hall of Columns through the night. A Government announcement early today said that the body of the late Premier would be taken Monday to lie beside that of Lenin in the famous tomb in Red Square.

The funeral services will be held in Red Square at noon Monday. Hundreds and hundreds of thousands of Muscovites, possibly as many as 2,000,000, will have passed Stalin's bier before the funeral services.

Like that of Lenin, Stalin's body will be subjected to the embalming process developed by Soviet scientists to preserve it in unchanged condition indefinitely, the announcement added.

The Government also announced plans for the construction of what it described as "a monumental building—pantheon—memorial."

After this building has been completed, the bodies of Lenin and Stalin and those of other famous party figures and leaders, which now lie buried in the Kremlin wall, will be transferred, the Government said. Then the building will be opened for visitation by "wide masses of workers," the announcement said.

Meanwhile, the body of Stalin lay in state in the same chamber where his co-revolutionist lay in state on his death in January, 1924.

Throngs Fill City Streets

Mourners filled the streets for block after block around the Hall of Columns yesterday and lines stretched back as far as Moscow's Garden Circle Boulevard about a mile distant.

No man knew how many mourners would pass through the chandelier-hung funeral rooms during the period of lying-in-state. But it was evident that the total would be numbered in the millions—two or three.

In the hour of deep tragedy over Stalin's death, government functions operated with efficiency.

The death of Stalin was announced at 4 A. M. By 3 P. M. Stalin's body had been

Continued on Page 5, Column 2

NEW SOVIET LEADER: Georgi M. Malenkov, 51, who succeeded Joseph V. Stalin yesterday as Premier of Soviet Union.
Sovfoto

Britain Agrees to Step Up Economic War on Peiping

By JAMES RESTON
Special to The New York Times.

WASHINGTON, March 6—President Eisenhower declined to comment today on the selection of Georgi M. Malenkov as Premier of the Soviet Union. He concentrated instead on unifying British-American policies in the war against Communist aggression and apparently made some progress, particularly in the economic war against Communist China.

Secretary of State John Foster Dulles and the British Foreign Secretary, Anthony Eden, made a tour of the world political horizon this morning, while the President was discussing the Stalin crisis with his Cabinet. Mr. Eden then had a private talk with the President and stayed on at the White House for lunch.

Results of Conversations

The results of these and yesterday's political conversations with the British were understood to be as follows:

¶The British undertook to adopt new measures to reduce the flow of strategic materials to Communist China. These measures will include adding to the present list of goods on the "forbidden" list and supervising more closely the operations of British-owned and registered ships.

¶Agreement was reached on the advisability of disengaging United States, British and French armed forces in the Korean, Malayan and Indo-China wars and replacing them as fast as possible with dependable native troops. There was acceptance of the principle that these three wars were all part of a single campaign against the Communist aggressors and that strategy should be coordinated as much as possible.

¶Mr. Eden made clear that his Government had no intention of withdrawing recognition from the Chinese Communists. The United States also maintained its position on that subject; namely, that it would not recognize Mao Tse-tung, but continue to recognize Chiang Kai-shek.

¶However, it was reported that there was agreement on both sides that the death of Stalin and the selection of Mr. Malenkov as Soviet Premier increased the chances of a split between Moscow and Peiping, since Mr. Mao, the Chinese Communist dictator, has often regarded himself as the leading theoretician of the Communist world, next to Premier Stalin.

¶Both sides reached agreement on the policies the British were following in trying to reach a new understanding with Egypt, but found themselves far apart once more in their estimates of what would happen if the current negotiations collapsed in Iran. The United States position was that the British approach to the Iran-

Continued on Page 5, Column 3

EUROPE IS CAUTIOUS ON SOVIET FUTURE

London Shuns Predictions but Asks Vigilance—Paris, Rome Pay Stalin Formal Tribute

By RAYMOND DANIELL
Special to The New York Times.

LONDON, March 6—Persons here whose business it is to forecast the course of Soviet policy received little indication of its trend from the appointment of Georgi M. Malenkov as the successor to Premier Stalin.

The elevation of Mr. Malenkov was not entirely unexpected but British betting odds were about even between him and Vyacheslav M. Molotov who, at 63—twelve year's Mr. Malenkov's senior—again becomes Soviet Foreign Minister.

To that extent the death of Stalin is regarded here as something to regret, if not to mourn over, because in the course of years, this dictator with the power of final decision had followed a pattern of action that made intelligent prediction possible.

[Elsewhere in Europe the news of Stalin's death caused some apprehension regarding future developments in Soviet policy.]

Malenkov's Mind Unknown

Nobody here—not even those charged with the responsibility of knowing—knows how Mr. Malenkov's mind works, what are his ideas of foreign policy, nor, least of all, what real power lies behind his new title.

There had been some idea that Mr. Molotov might be Stalin's heir. It is believed now that his age ruled him out but there is a question about whether he is old enough to be ruled out for the future.

Will Lavrenti P. Beria, an aspirant for national leadership, be content to remain in what amounts to third place, in charge of home affairs?

The appointment of Marshal Nikolai A. Bulganin, who is 57, to the Ministry of War and of 72-year-old Marshal Kliment Y. Voroshilov to succeed Nicolai M. Shvernik as chairman of the Supreme Council of the Presidium, also attracted attention.

In any struggle for power, that

Continued on Page 6, Column 5

FOUR TO HELP RULE

Beria, Molotov, Bulganin and Kaganovich Are Deputy Premiers

TEN-MAN PRESIDIUM

Molotov Is Again Foreign Minister—Vishinsky Demoted to U. N.

Text of announcement of Soviet changes is on Page 3.

By HARRISON E. SALISBURY
Special to The New York Times.

MOSCOW, March 6 — Georgi Maximilianovich Malenkov was named head of the Soviet Government tonight in place of the late Joseph Stalin in a series of changes in the highest Soviet leadership.

Mr. Malenkov has assumed the post of Chairman of the Council of Ministers, which was held by Stalin.

At the same time he was named as first in the list of the Presidium of the Central Committee of the Communist party, which is composed of ten members and four alternates.

Standing beside him in the chief and most responsible posts of Government and party in this reorganized structure are four veteran Soviet leaders and co-workers of Stalin—Lavrenti P. Beria, Vyacheslav M. Molotov, Nikolai A. Bulganin and Lazar M. Kaganovich. These four became the First Deputy Chairmen of the Council of Ministers and with Mr. Malenkov constitute the Presidium.

The announcement over the Moscow radio at 11:30 o'clock tonight was made in the name of the Central Committee of the Communist party, the Council of Ministers and the Presidium of the Supreme Soviet.

Changes to Avoid 'Panic'

The changes in the directing bodies of the Government were made, it was announced, with the purpose of maintaining uninterrupted and correct leadership and avoiding "any kind of disarray and panic."

The announcement said the changes would secure the nation from any kind of interruption in directing the activity of state and party organs and "unconditionally secure" the successful carrying into effect of party and Government policies both internally and abroad.

The chief impression given by the Government both in tonight's announcement and in the proclamation of Stalin's death was one of firmness and the highest political vigilance, a sense of the tight together of party and Government forces to withstand any threats from within or from without.

The Government was acting with the greatest resolution and with marked vigor. Mr. Malenkov lost no time in demonstrating his will and determination to prove a worthy custodian of the policies of monolithic unity and steel resolu-

Continued on Page 3, Column 2

'Voice' Aide Charges Chief Parroted 'Reds'

By C. P. TRUSSELL
Special to The New York Times.

WASHINGTON, March 6—Howard Maier, a political specialist for the Voice of America, testified today that he had received a reprimand from the State Department group agreed with the denunciation.

It appeared from the reprinted, Mr. Maier told the Senate investigating subcommittee, headed by Senator Joseph R. McCarthy, Republican of Wisconsin, that is investigating the Voice, that a State Department group agreed with the denunciation.

Entered among the inquiry's exhibits was a column in The Daily Compass of New York, now out of

Continued on Page 16, Column 4

Alan Ladd and Brandon DeWilde in the western classic, Shane.

Marlon Brando and Mary Murphy in The Wild One.

Richard Burton in The Robe.

The New York Times.

Copyright, 1953, by The New York Times Company.

LATE CITY EDITION
Fair late today. Fair and cool
tonight and tomorrow.
Temperature Range Today–Max., 48; Min., 37
Temperature Yesterday–Max., 44; Min., 37
Full U. S. Weather Bureau Report, Page 42

VOL. CII.–No. 34,785.

NEW YORK, MONDAY, APRIL 20, 1953.

FIVE CENTS

PUBLISHERS REPORT PUBLIC IS SKEPTICAL OF RED 'PEACE' BIDS

Arriving for Newspaper Week, They Note Wide Support of Eisenhower's Address

BUSINESS OUTLOOK 'GOOD'

The Associated Press Will Hear Humphrey Today—A. N. P. A. Sessions Start Tomorrow

By PETER KIHSS

Reporting hopeful prospects for continued good business throughout the country, newspaper executives, here for their annual Newspaper Week, said yesterday that the American people appeared generally to be viewing Soviet "peace" moves with caution. They noted widespread support of President Eisenhower's call on the Soviet Union for deeds, and of the peace program that he set forth last Thursday.

Twelve hundred American and Canadian newspaper leaders are expected here for the week's program. Business sessions of The Associated Press, The United Press and The International News Service will be held today, with the annual Associated Press luncheon at the Waldorf-Astoria due to hear Secretary of the Treasury George M. Humphrey in his first address as a Cabinet member.

Tomorrow, the American Newspaper Publishers Association opens its sixty-seventh annual convention at the Waldorf-Astoria, winding up on Thursday with the annual dinner of its bureau of advertising, at which Vice President Richard M. Nixon is to speak.

Business 'Quite Good'

Typical of the executives' comments was that of J. E. Knowland of The Oakland (Calif.) Tribune. He reported business in his area was "quite good in most lines," with "a good deal of new industrial development." Even if a sudden end to the Korean War should throttle airplane and other defense industries, he said he believed "quite a little slack" could be taken up by commercial orders that had been sidetracked for Government contracts.

"There is a general public desire for peace," Mr. Knowland said. "We are right on the brink, the ocean side, and we see a great deal of it. The President's speech was very well received. The people have their fingers crossed because of our past experience, but they are hopeful of a little change in the new administration in Russia."

W. K. Blethen of The Seattle Times said that Seattle's business was "ahead of last year," and that he was "very optimistic about the rest of the year." The Boeing Airplane Company, he said, "is one of the mainstays of our economy, and doing the biggest job in the country on defense."

"People on the coast," Mr. Blethen said, "feel they are rather close to Russia. I think they are very suspicious of any move that the Russians or the Chinese Communists make. I might say they feel: 'Fish or cut bait.'"

St. Lou's 'Anxious and Hopeful'

Wilson W. Condict of The St. Louis Globe-Democrat said the outlook in his area was "pretty good, and a lot better than thirty days ago." Pre-Easter business had been good for a "dreary spring"—there hadn't been much sun, and St. Louis had a two-inch snowfall Saturday—but April has been "much better than March was," he said.

St. Louisans, Mr. Condict reported, are "100 per cent behind the Eisenhower plan and speech." They are "anxious and hopeful about Soviet peace moves," he added, but "we've all had our hopes brought up to the boiling point, and then gotten cold water thrown on them, so we're cautious."

John Cowles of The Minneapolis Star and Tribune, describing business as "fine," explained:

"We've got the Williston basin in North Dakota that is probably going to prove a big benefit to Minneapolis. Iron companies are spending about $1,000,000,000 on putting taconite plants in the Minnesota iron range to process lower-grade iron ore. Those two things, plus our normal agriculture, mean that things are very prosperous, and the forecast is very good."

Minnesotans, Mr. Cowles said, "hope the Russians are sincere, but they are under no illusions, and they want to see what the Russians will do."

John S. Knight, publisher of The Detroit Free Press, The Chicago Daily News, The Akron Beacon

Continued on Page 11, Column 3

Mayor Picks His 2 Members For City's Transit Authority

Their Names Will Be Made Public Today— Wagner Advises Against Appointments, Lest Court Fight Be Jeopardized

By PAUL CROWELL

Mayor Impellitteri, it became known yesterday, has decided upon the two men whom he will name today as members of the five-man New York City transit authority. This is the agency authorized by the 1953 Legislature at Governor Dewey's insistence to take over the municipal transit lines and run them at a fare sufficient to meet all operating charges.

Governor Dewey named two members of the new agency last Saturday. They are retired Maj. Gen. Hugh J. Casey, executive vice president of Melrose Distillery, Inc., and Henry K. Norton, trustee of the New York, Susquehanna and Western Railroad.

The Mayor has given no clue to the identity of his choices for six-year terms on the unsalaried authority board. It is known, however, that he picked his men from a long list that included John A. Coleman, financier; Thomas J. Shanahan, banker; Robert W. Dowling, investment expert; former Police Commissioner George V. McLaughlin; Harold Riegelman, lawyer; Walter Hoving, department store executive, and William G. Fullen, former chairman of the State Transit Commission, which was abolished in 1940.

The law creating the transit authority required the Governor and the Mayor to name two members each, with today as the deadline for appointments. The four members thus chosen have the power to name the fifth member and have until May 1 to do so. Should they fail to agree, the fifth member will be Howard S. Cullman, chairman of the Port of New York Authority, provided he accepts the post. If he declines, the fifth member will be a Port Authority member who is a resident of the city and chosen by the New York members of the bi-state agency.

Governor Dewey's appointments were praised by Sidney H. Bing-

Continued on Page 17, Column 3

N. A. M. Calls for Price Cuts Rather Than Pay Increases

By A. H. RASKIN

Organized industry struck yesterday at the principal prop supporting organized labor's demands for higher wages this year. The National Association of Manufacturers asserted that the benefits of increased industrial productivity should be distributed in the form of lower prices for all Americans rather than fatter pay envelopes for workers in unionized industries.

With the cost of living edging downward for the first time since the start of the Korean war, major unions have been transferring their emphasis from living costs to productivity in calling for a new round of wage increases in 1953.

The union contention is that the productive efficiency of the American economy has been going up at an average rate of 2 to 2½ per cent each year and that the purchasing power of workers must go up at least as fast if they are to buy the goods they make.

Automatic Annual Rises

This concept, first embodied in the long-term contract between the United Automobile Workers, C. I. O., and the General Motors Corporation in being used to provide automatic annual wage increases of 4 cents an hour to more than 2,500,000 workers. Most of these workers are in the automobile, aircraft and railroad industries.

The debate will go into its fourth week on Wednesday with opponents staging what Mr. Taft has called a filibuster as they denounce an asserted "$300,000,000,000 giveaway" to three states—Texas, California and Louisiana. Up to this point the opposition has rejected unanimous consent requests for a voting time.

Members of this group include, among others, such Fair Deal Democrats as Senators Herbert H.

Continued on Page 14, Column 6

RED TAINT CHARGED IN WELFARE UNION

McCarthy Warns 8,000 in City Jobs to Shun New Group With Teamster Charter

Welfare Commissioner Henry L. McCarthy warned his 8,000 department employes yesterday to be on guard against an active attempt by Communists to seize control of their activities through a new union sparked by some of the same persons who were thrown out of the Congress of Industrial Organizations as pro-Communist suspects.

Appearing before 750 members of the Ozanam Guild Communion Breakfast at the Commodore Hotel, in the annual gathering of the organization of Roman Catholic employes of the Department of Welfare, Mr. McCarthy said that officials of the City Employes Union, Local 237, had obtained a charter from the International Brotherhood of Teamsters, A. F. L., and had formally requested recognition as a welfare union.

The Welfare Commissioner said that he had noted the faces of some of those who had been in the United Public Workers, which has been gradually disintegrating since its ouster by the C. I. O. in 1948. These persons, Mr. McCarthy charged, are simply donning the "cloak of respectability of a new

Continued on Page 17, Column 1

TAFT URGES EFFORT TO SOLVE ALL ISSUES IN ASIA 'IN ONE BITE'

Senator Says Only by Accord Halting All Conflicts Can Permanent Peace Be Won

Special to The New York Times.

WASHINGTON, April 19—Senator Robert A. Taft of Ohio, Republican leader of the Senate, suggested today that every effort be made to "settle all the questions of the Far East in one bite."

Only by pursuing such a course, the Senator said, could the free world be assured of a peace that would be "really effective on a permanent basis." He contended mere agreement to stop the shooting in Korea would not even guarantee a united Korea.

The Ohioan's belief that the Communists must be induced to stop the fighting in such places as Malaya and Indo-China, as well as Korea, was one that others influential in Congress shared.

Some viewed with misgiving a seeming readiness on the part of President Eisenhower in his speech last Thursday to agree to a cease-fire order in Korea before any actual negotiations were begun.

President's Words Cited

This was the construction placed on the President's words when, in discussing an "honorable armistice" in Korea, he said:

"This means the immediate cessation of hostilities and the prompt initiation of political discussions leading to the holding of free elections in a united Korea."

Asserting that negotiations might be more productive before arms were laid down, Senator Taft added:

"Every effort should be put into attempts to settle the overriding issues of the Far East—to end the Communist threats against Indo-China and Malaya—as a part of the Korean truce agreement.

"Of course it would be better to have a cease-fire in Korea than to continue a stalemate war there, but I don't think we will ever get a united Korea by merely agreeing to stop the shooting."

The Senator's views on the Administration's new peace offensive, developed further last night by John Foster Dulles, the Secretary of State, at the annual banquet of the American Society of Newspaper Editors, were made known before the Ohio Senator left for Augusta, Ga., to visit the President and engage him on the golf links.

Speeding-Oil Vote a Problem

Mr. Taft's big problem as he returns to Washington will be to devise ways and means of speeding a vote on the bill before the Senate that would give the states title to submerged lands under the marginal seas that, in places, are rich with oil and gas.

Continued on Page 3, Column 2

PRISONER EXCHANGE STARTED IN KOREA; 30 AMERICANS AMONG 100 FREED BY FOE; ALLIES BEGIN RETURN OF 500 REDS DAILY

FINISHING TOUCHES: Pfc. Arthur Nowojcki of Buffalo painting sign reading "Welcome Gate to Freedom" forming archway under which U. N. prisoners will move into Freedom Village.

World Unions Ask U. N. Plan To Cushion Halt in Arming

By KATHLEEN McLAUGHLIN

Special to The New York Times.

UNITED NATIONS, N. Y., April 19—Through its official observer at the United Nations the International Confederation of Free Trade Unions is prepared to ask the Economic and Social Council tomorrow to take steps to avoid possible economic and financial dislocations that might arise from decreases in the tempo of rearmament. The confederation will urge the Council to place the problem on the agenda of its summer session.

With a world membership of 54,000,000, the confederation has been alert to the consequences, especially of an abrupt terminating of defense work, and has prepared an outline of remedies that it plans to present to the Council.

Even if the period of transition proves to be gradual, economic disturbances are bound to occur, officials of the confederation believe. They are accordingly advocating action on an international scale to supplement corrective devices employed by individual Governments.

"Although rearmament at the present scale does not automatically make a high proportion of the economic resources of the countries concerned as was the case during the war, it still appears necessary to draw on the lessons of history," Miss Toni Sender of the confederation said.

If tax reductions are utilized as one means of stimulating private consumption, they should be made supplementary to and part of governmental measures of a similar type, the confederation will argue. De-

Continued on Page 6, Column 6

YOSHIDA WINS LEAD IN JAPAN'S ELECTION

But Premier Lacks a Majority in New House as Socialists Gain—Reds Get a Seat

By The United Press.

TOKYO, Monday, April 20—Premier Shigeru Yoshida's pro-American Liberal party won 199 seats in yesterday's parliamentary elections, 35 short of the majority needed for control of the 466-seat House of Representatives (Diet).

The complete unofficial returns, compared with the party seating in the Parliament that ended March 14, showed:

Party	New	Old
Liberals	199	234
Progressives	76	62
Left Socialists	72	58
Right Socialists	66	60
Rebel Liberals	35	50
Farm-Labor party	5	3
Communists	1	0
Independents	12	2

Premier Yoshida dissolved the old Parliament after losing, 229-218, on a confidence vote in an effort to get the majority support of the electorate.

Premier Retains Hold

By WILLIAM J. JORDEN

TOKYO, Monday, April 20—Premier Shigeru Yoshida and his Liberal party to a commanding lead in returns today from yesterday's national election for a new House of Representatives.

It appeared likely that Mr. Yoshida, whose stand on the record of anti-communism and friendship with the West, would fail to win a clear-cut majority in the House, but would gain enough strength to undertake the forming of a new Government, his fifth post-war Cabinet.

Mr. Yoshida has recently said, according to his lieutenants, that his Liberals would be able to form a Government if they won at least 200 of the 466 seats.

Although Mr. Yoshida's party forged ahead of all other parties, observers noted that the Left-Wing and Right-Wing Socialist factions were doing better on the basis of more than half the vote counted.

Continued on Page 5, Column 2

CLARK GREETS G. I.'S

First Day's Repatriation Is Smooth—U. N. Men Tearful and Joyous

By ROBERT ALDEN

Special to The New York Times.

PANMUNJOM, Korea, Monday, April 20—One hundred United Nations soldiers, including thirty Americans, were freed from Communist captivity today as the exchange of sick and wounded prisoners under a recently negotiated agreement.

The 100th Allied prisoner was returned by the Communists shortly before noon [10 P. M., Sunday, Eastern standard time], fulfilling the Communist quota for the day. The United Nations at that hour was still in the process of returning the first of its daily quotas of 500 Chinese and North Korean prisoners.

The exchange of sick and wounded captives is expected to be completed April 30, when, if all goes according to plan, the Communists will have returned 600 Allied prisoners and the United Nations 5,100 North Koreans and 700 Chinese Communists.

Pleased by Smoothness

The first moments of the exchange were tense with drama as the United Nations captives stepped from Communist ambulances that had brought them from Kaesong, about five miles from this exchange point. [News agencies said Gen. Mark W. Clark was on hand to greet the liberated Allied captives.]

The first Americans were released at 9:04 A. M. [7:04 P. M. Sunday, Eastern standard time.]

Rear Admiral John C. Daniel, head of the Allied liaison group that negotiated the exchange, told correspondents he was pleased by the smoothness of the first day's transfer.

"It's been a tremendous emotional experience for us all," he said. "Not much was said between us here, but we are all very happy. In times of great emotional experience it is often like this."

The first moments were tense with drama as the men stepped from Communist ambulances. The first American soldier exchanged was Pvt. Carl W. Kirchenhausen of 214 Audubon Avenue, New York. He had suffered frostbite of the feet, and though he walked without a limp, his face was drawn and he was unsmiling. Another New Yorker freed was Pfc. Raymond H. Medina of 950 East 163d Street, the Bronx.

The first man of all Allied nationalities to come back was a South Korean, Sgt. Lee Chai Kook. [News agencies said he was exchanged at 8:55 A. M. (6:55 P. M. Sunday, Eastern standard time).]

Turkish Soldier Freed

Of the prisoners of other nationalities the first to return was a Turkish soldier, Cpl. Omar Ulu. The first of the British to be exchanged was Trooper E. O'Donnell of the Eighth Hussars, whose home is at St. Helen's, Lancashire, England.

The Communists had dressed the prisoners well for the exchange. They wore blue greatcoats and blue tennis shoes.

Just about the first thing the returned soldiers saw this morning was a big sign erected at the exchange site during the night. It read: "Welcome gate to freedom." They also saw twenty-five photographers and correspondents alongside the receiving tents where they were welcomed before starting their hose-and-a-half ambulance journey to Freedom Village.

There were tears of joy in some of the soldiers' eyes, and others wore thin smiles that spoke more eloquently than words. One soldier managed a grin and "Hi, fellows," to the few persons allowed in the exchange area. For the most part, however, the repatriated captives seemed nothing as they walked their first few feet in freedom.

No one was really sure until the last moment that the exchange really would take place.

The first sign that the exchange was really taking place was a smiling face of an American pressed against the glass of an ambulance window. The first voice was that of a Briton shouting from inside an ambulance:

"Lancashire. Tell them I am

Continued on Page 5, Column 6

CAPTIVE ISSUE STILL MAIN BAR TO TRUCE

Foe Gives No Hint of Relaxing Demand All Be Returned as Renewal of Talks Is Set

By LINDESAY PARROTT

Special to The New York Times.

TOKYO, Monday, April 20—The United Nations command prepared today to resume full-scale negotiations with the Communists for an armistice in the Korean war, with the vexed question of repatriation of prisoners still apparently the main obstacle in the path of an agreement.

Liaison officers of the two sides, meeting yesterday at Panmunjom, Korea, between the battle lines at 11 A. M. next Saturday [9 P. M. Friday, Eastern standard time] as the time and date for the renewal of the truce talks, in abeyance since last Oct. 8. But statements made by both sides at the twenty-minute session seemed to show that a considerable area of disagreement still existed. It will be the task of the full truce delegations to attempt to bridge that gap.

Rear Admiral John C. Daniel, head of the United Nations liaison group, told the Communists the Allied command agreed to resumption of the talks in expectation that the Chinese and North Koreans would present detailed suggestions for a prisoner exchange "as outlined by Lieut. Gen. William K. Harrison Jr., chief United Nations truce delegate, in

Continued on Page 5, Column 5

Joy Sweeps Freed Captives' Homes; Mother Hears News After Prayer

Joy and excitement swept last night through the homes of prisoners of war released from Communist camps in North Korea as their names were made public.

There were also fears about how badly wounded the soldiers were. And there was concern about some of the pro-Communist sentiments of the prisoners had expressed during their long captivity, and a general conviction that such sentiments had been a result of coercion.

But jubilation generally ruled last night.

Elation was evident in the apartment house at 214 Audubon Avenue as official reports arrived that Pvt. Carl W. Kirchenhausen had been the first American released in the captive exchange at Panmunjom, Korea.

There was joy, too, in the Bronx where neighbors rushed to the home of Mr. and Mrs. Anastacio Medina of 950 East 163d Street. Their son, Pfc. Raymond Medina, was the second New York area prisoner released. His mother had gone to the Rock of Salvation Evangelical Church at 799 Prospect Avenue last night to pray for the safe return of her son, and when she neared home afterward and she heard the shouts of joy announcing her son's liberation.

In Fieldsboro, N. J., Mrs. Margaret Porter, 28-year-old wife of M/Sgt. John P. Porter, wept with joy at the report of his repatriation after more than two years of imprisonment in North Korea. She has a surprise ready for her husband: their joint savings.

Continued on Page 5, Column 3

Elizabeth's Erasure of Son's Name on a Pub Sign Strikes Blow at Centuries-Old Tradition in Britain

Rebuff to an Intended Tribute Embarrasses Publicans Who Use Historic Designs

By THOMAS F. BRADY

Special to The New York Times.

LONDON, April 19—Queen Elizabeth II has put a stop to this kingdom's most popular form of Royal advertising, but her fiat cannot undo centuries of testimony to the loyal publicans of the realm to their affection for the monarchy.

The Queen has expressed her distaste for the naming of pubs after her children or, indeed, after any living members of the royal family.

The new regulation arose out of a contretemps at Great Missenden in Buckinghamshire, where the local folk had trouble sometimes remembering where they had spent the evening because there were two pubs named The Stag and Hounds.

The owner of one petitioned the Magistrates to change the title to the Prince Charles in honor of the 4-year-old heir apparent. The Magistrates approved, but last week the lawyer for the alehouse was back in court asking for authority to switch the name again, since the Queen's Secretary objected.

90 Inns in London Are Known as 'the Prince of Wales'— Many 'Queen's Heads'

we are sorry if it has offended the Queen.

A statement from the Home Office then established a prohibition for publicans: "Titles of living members of the Royal family may not be used without the express permission of the Sovereign who does not wish to give it in connection with the names of public houses. This is an instruction from the Palace."

Another incident involving alehouse lese-majeste came to light at the same time. A pub at Reading in Berkshire called The Duke of Edinburgh (after Queen Victoria's second son, who died in 1900) decided not long ago to bring its sign up to date with a picture of the present Duke, Prince Philip, the Queen's husband. The picture of the Duke in naval uniform—came down when observers noted that the naval headquarters objected, that should it be more than half the vote counted.

The office of Her Majesty's Secretary of State for Home Affairs—usually known as the Home Office—had represented to his client that the Queen objected to the use of her son's name in such a context.

Herbert Cross, the loyal licensee of what is now The Valiant Trooper, said sadly: "The name of Prince Charles had the whole village on its toes. We thought it would be appropriate as The Valiant Trooper.

Continued on Page 14, Column 5

1953

Steve Allen took over the late-night TV spot in 1953. He is seen here on a later show with Skitch Henderson, Eydie Gorme and Steve Lawrence.

Liberace, the pianist and entertainer who had a 15-minute TV show which ran from 1953-1955, achieved an intensely devoted following.

The four stars shown singing here on Your Hit Parade are Russell Arms, Giselle McKenzie, Dorothy Collins and Snooky Lanson.

"All the News That's Fit to Print"

The New York Times.

LATE CITY EDITION

Fair with little change in temperature today and tomorrow.

Temperature Range Today—Max., 72; Min., 52

Temperatures Yesterday—Max., 70; Min., 53

Full U. S. Weather Bureau Report, Page 59

Copyright, 1953, by The New York Times Company.

VOL. CII..No. 34,828. Entered as Second-Class Matter, Post Office, New York, N. Y. NEW YORK, TUESDAY, JUNE 2, 1953. Times Square, New York 36, N. Y. Telephone LAckawanna 4-1000 FIVE CENTS

2 OF BRITISH TEAM CONQUER EVEREST; QUEEN GETS NEWS AS CORONATION GIFT; THRONGS LINE HER PROCESSION ROUTE

AUTHORITY LEASES CITY TRANSIT LINES; FARE RISE IN SIGHT

Estimate Board Votes, 11-5, for 10-Year Pact Including Terms Asked by Joseph

EFFECTIVE DATE IS JUNE 15

New Agency Seeking Tokens From Mint, Indicating New Charge May Not Be 15c

Digest of lease signed by city and Transit Authority, Page 32.

By LEO EGAN

The Board of Estimate voted 11 to 5 yesterday to lease the city's $1,700,000,000 transit system to the newly created New York City Transit Authority for a period of ten years, during which the authority will be obligated to raise enough revenue from fares and incidental charges to meet operating costs.

By approving the lease, the board made it almost certain that the authority will raise transit fares by July 30 in an amount sufficient to overcome a prospective operating deficit of $47,000,000 for the fiscal year beginning July 1. A first step in this direction was taken by the authority within a few hours after the board acted when it decided to explore the possibility of obtaining from the United States Mint at Philadelphia an emergency supply of tokens, to be used on all three divisions of the rapid transit lines in the collection of a higher fare.

Casey Tells of Token Plans

The decision to request the Federal Government's help in obtaining enough tokens to put a fare change into effect by July 30, the statutory deadline, was announced by Maj. Gen. Hugh J. Casey, authority chairman, after a special authority meeting at the offices of the Board of Transportation, 370 Jay Street, Brooklyn.

Sidney H. Bingham, chairman of the Board of Transportation, will confer with the Director of the Mint at Philadelphia today on the possibility of obtaining 20,000,000 tokens, General Casey said. Subsequent additions to the supply would be obtained from private suppliers, he added.

To speed the negotiations with the Mint, the authority has requested Governor Dewey to intervene with the Secretary of the Treasury, General Casey said.

A design for the token was officially approved by the authority yesterday. It is a perforated coin, somewhat smaller than a dime.

By exploring the possibility of obtaining enough tokens for use on all three divisions, the authority indicated it might reject Mr. Bingham's recommendation for a 15-cent fare in favor of a smaller charge, perhaps 12 or 12½ cents a ride. The present fare is 10 cents.

A major justification for the Bingham recommendation was that it would involve use of tokens on only the I.R.T. division, which has electrically operated turnstiles. On the B.M.T. and IND divisions, which have mechanical turnstiles, two coins—a dime and a nickel—would be used to pay the fare.

General Casey emphasized in announcing the authority action that no decisions on a fare increase had been reached. It will not be possible to arrive at a conclusion, he said, until all pertinent facts are studied.

City Fiscal Problem Eased

The Board of Estimate's decision yesterday automatically relieved the city of the necessity of meeting the prospective operating deficit out of tax revenues in the new fiscal year that starts July 1. It likewise vested the city with power to collect $50,000,000 a year in additional taxes from real estate for general municipal purposes plus, for the next four years, enough to liquidate an accumulated deficit of $39,000,000 in the transit pension system.

Moreover, in accordance with special laws enacted by the Legislature earlier this year on the recommendation of Governor Dewey, transfer of the deficit-ridden transit system to the authority gives the city power at any time in the future to impose a one-half of 1 per cent payroll tax, payable in equal parts by employers and employes, estimated to raise $60,000,000 a year.

The city's budget for the new fiscal year, already approved by the Board of Estimate and City Council, contemplates full use of the additional real estate taxing powers, but no use of the payroll tax.

As had been forecast, Rudolph

Continued on Page 33, Column 2

Eisenhower Moves to Limit State Department to Policy

New Reorganization Plans Would Transfer Present Operating Functions to 2 Special Agencies, Information and Foreign Aid

By ANTHONY LEVIERO

Special to THE NEW YORK TIMES.

WASHINGTON, June 1—President Eisenhower proposed today to restore the State Department to its traditional pre-war policy-making role and to transfer virtually all its operating functions to new organizations—the United States Information Agency and the Foreign Operations Administration.

A far-reaching reorganization of the State Department was projected by the President in two plans submitted to Congress today, with a promise of further changes to be sought early next year.

Today he stressed two objectives:

1. To divest the department of the functional tasks that had involved it in political controversy during the post-war era.
2. To make the Secretary of State supreme, next to the President, in the policy supervision of all foreign information and aid programs.

The controversial Voice of America and other information programs would be swept out of the State Department, the Mutual Security Agency and other agencies and concentrated in the new Information Agency. The Mutual Security Agency itself would become the nucleus around which would be built the new Foreign Operations Administration to take over various other programs for technical, economic and military assistance.

Of operating programs, all that would be left in the State Department would be the programs for the educational exchange of persons.

The two new agencies would have administrative autonomy, just as the Mutual Security Agency has today. But a new idea in Government organization was introduced. The directors of the two agencies not only would be subject to close

Continued on Page 24, Column 4

Text of message on propaganda and aid plans, Page 24.

MRS. HOBBY WARNS DOCTORS ON TASKS

Social-Economic Problems in the Field Must Be Solved by A.M.A. or Others, She Says

Mrs. Oveta Culp Hobby, Secretary of Health, Education and Welfare, declared at the annual meeting of the American Medical Association, which opened yesterday, that organized medicine must find solutions to the social-economic problems facing medicine today or the solution would be taken out of its hands. She expressed confidence that the American Medical Association "will meet this challenge."

Addressing the House of Delegates, policy-making body of the association, at the Waldorf-Astoria Hotel, Mrs. Hobby said the social and economic demands on the medical profession "are only the continuing challenge in this long history of constant adaptation to a changing society, but never have these problems been more onerous and critical than today."

The association opened its 102d annual meeting yesterday. For five days progress in all branches of medicine will be reviewed in 400 reports by leaders in their fields.

The sessions are being held in seven hotels and in Town Hall while 635 scientific and technical exhibits are being displayed on four floors of Grand Central Palace. The exhibits are open only to doctors and their guests.

Mrs. Hobby in her speech to the delegates said she agreed fully

Continued on Page 26, Column 5

HUMPHREY OPPOSES REVENUE LOSS NOW

He Calls Cut Gamble With U.S. Security—Asks House Unit to Extend Excess Profit Tax

By JOHN D. MORRIS

Special to THE NEW YORK TIMES.

WASHINGTON, June 1—George M. Humphrey, Secretary of the Treasury, told Congress today that only "full mobilization" would justify tax increases to produce any more revenue than the Administration was now seeking.

The Government's chief fiscal officer so testified in opening the Administration's case before the House Ways and Means Committee for a six-month extension of the excess profits tax and the cancellation of automatic cuts in regular corporation and excise (sales) levies slated for next April 1.

The Administration, he said, wants those three phases of its tax program carried out in a single bill this year, though the committee has limited its present deliberations to extension of the excess profits law, which is due to expire June 30.

The Secretary asserted that losses in Federal revenue now would be an unsafe gamble with the country's security.

Mr. Humphrey also made the following points:

¶ That he was "very strongly opposed" to any change in the excess profits tax during the extension period.

¶ That he would fight any continuation of the levy beyond Dec. 31.

¶ That tax relief starting next

Continued on Page 47, Column 2

Harvard Elects Dr. N. M. Pusey, Midwest Educator, as President

Lawrence College Head, 46, Has 3 Degrees From University—Favors Humanities Study

By JOHN H. FENTON

Special to THE NEW YORK TIMES.

CAMBRIDGE, Mass., June 1—Dr. Nathan Marsh Pusey, president of Lawrence College in Appleton, Wis., was elected the twenty-fourth president of Harvard by the Harvard Corporation today.

Dr. Pusey, who is a native of Council Bluffs, Iowa, and 46 years old, is a scholar in Greek history, and holds three degrees from Harvard: Bachelor of Arts, magna cum laude, 1928; Master of Arts, 1932, and Doctor of Philosophy, 1937. He prepared for college at Abraham Lincoln High School in Council Bluffs.

The Iowa educator will succeed Dr. James Bryant Conant, who will become president-emeritus of Harvard University on Sept. 1. Dr. Conant, now on leave, is serving as United States High Commissioner for Germany.

Dr. Pusey's election by the Harvard Corporation is subject to the confirmation of the Board of Overseers. This confirmation, customarily a formality, is scheduled to be voted on June 10, the day before the Harvard commencement. On only one occasion, in 1868, have the overseers refused the corporation permission to elect a president.

Associated Press

Dr. Nathan M. Pusey

The occasion of the only refusal was in the election of Dr. Charles W. Eliot, the original choice of the corporation, as the twenty-first president. The corporation prevailed after a delay of six months, and Dr. Eliot became president in 1869.

Dr. Pusey, reached by telephone at Appleton, said that he considered the corporation's action "a tremendous honor." But he de-

Continued on Page 27, Column 5

RHEE BOWS TO U.S.; SAYS KOREA AGREES TO EISENHOWER AIMS

Statement on Message From Washington Hints Opposition to Truce Plans Is Easing

By The Associated Press.

SEOUL, Korea, June 2—President Syngman Rhee disclosed today he had received a three-point message from President Eisenhower, and added: "We must accept anything that the United States President wants."

"Common sense and wisdom require that we cooperate with the United States at any cost," Dr. Rhee said, without saying what President Eisenhower had told him.

The statement of the 78-year-old leader of the Republic of Korea indicated that South Korean opposition to the secret proposal by the United Nations Command for bringing an armistice in Korea was lessening.

Dr. Rhee also said he was looking for some one to take the place of Maj. Gen. Choi Duk Shin as the South Korean delegate on the United Nations armistice negotiation team.

Dr. Rhee declined to elaborate on his apparently conciliatory statement. He spoke to correspondents at a parade of the British Commonwealth Division honoring the Coronation of Elizabeth II.

Nor did he make it precisely clear whether he was ready now to accept the Allied truce proposal, to which he and his Government had expressed vigorous opposition.

South Korea's acting Premier, Pyun Yun Tae, threatened yesterday a break with the Allies and a go-it-alone policy for South Korea but deferred action until after next Thursday's critical truce session.

The Communists are expected to reply to the Allied proposal at Thursday's meeting.

Rhee Said to Seek Treaty

By JAY WALZ

Special to THE NEW YORK TIMES.

WASHINGTON, June 1—The Eisenhower Administration was reported today to have had a new request from President Syngman Rhee of South Korea for the pledge of a mutual defense pact and of military and economic help as a basis for the Seoul Government's support of present Allied truce proposals.

These conditions were said on good authority to be important features of a four-point program outlined in a letter forwarded to President Eisenhower through Ellis O. Briggs, United States Ambassador at Seoul.

The principal point in the still-secret United Nations proposal to the Communists for disposition of Korean war prisoners who refuse to return home was understood to be that final determination of the captives' fate would be up to the General Assembly of the United Nations.

Officially, the White House and State Department were silent on developments on Korea, and offered "no comment" even on reports that a letter from President Rhee might have been received.

Had Asked Pledge in Writing

The South Korean request for a mutual defense pact with the United States is not new. Dr. You Chan Yang, the Korean Ambassador here, has made repeated representations to the State Department for such a pledge of defense help in the event of future Communist aggression.

He has made the point that, while President Eisenhower has said publicly that the United States will never desert Korea, it would be more satisfying from the Korean standpoint to have "something down in black and white."

President Rhee's four points were reported to be (1) a pledge to sign a mutual defense pact with Korea; (2) a promise by the United States to provide military and financial help to Korea on a large scale; (3) withdrawal of all foreign troops on both sides as soon as a truce has started and prisoners have been exchanged, and (4) agreement that the United States would not stand in the way of South Korea in efforts to unite that country at some future time.

As far as the last point is concerned, sources felt South Korea did not have in mind the use of military force to bring together North and South Korea.

Meanwhile, some Capitol Hill leaders spoke out on recent Korean developments.

Senator William F. Knowland of California, who is chairman of the Senate Republican Policy Committee, said the United States should "risk" war with Russia to expand the fighting, if truce negotiations with the Communists collapsed at [illegible]

In anoth[illegible], Senator H. Alexand[illegible] Republican of New Je[illegible] he thought

Continued [illegible], Column 5

CROWDS DEFY RAIN

Face a Day of Showers After All-Night Vigil to Hail Their Sovereign

By RAYMOND DANIELL

Special to THE NEW YORK TIMES.

LONDON, Tuesday, June 2—This is the day that all London, all Britain, all the Commonwealth and half the world have been awaiting. It is the day on which the crown of her forefathers is placed upon the head of this old country's radiantly lovely young Queen Elizabeth II whose reign, it is hoped, will usher in another golden age.

The weather for the day was uncertain. By early morning the wind still blew, but rains that fell during the night had ceased, at least temporarily. The weather forecaster, however, was not optimistic about the prospects for the day, which was chosen originally because rain had not fallen on June 2 for many years. The forecast was for cool weather and showers, with sunny intervals.

Last night's gusts and rain discomfited the hundreds of thousands of persons who squatted the whole length of the royal way but if these hardships dislodged any it was unnoticeable because there were others waiting to take their places.

Some of these squatters, lacking reserved seats in the stands to accommodate 250,000 persons, began staking out their claims as early as midnight Sunday.

Squatters Sit on Curbs

By noon yesterday they were sitting on the curbs at Trafalgar Square and were packed two and three deep on the sidewalks along the Mall leading from Admiralty Arch to Buckingham Palace. By dinner time last night the East Carriage Drive in Hyde Park was filled with men, women and even young children with raincoats, blankets, lunch baskets and inflatable mattresses prepared to defend their little vantage points until the Queen's ornate gilded coach, with its eight gray horses, one named Eisenhower, had passed late in the afternoon.

During the day Queen Mother Elizabeth, accompanied by Princess Margaret, visited the palace to see the Queen on the eve of her coronation. By the time they left, an hour later, the crowd outside Buckingham Palace numbered nearly 50,000. The police, who had let the crowd swarm over the roadway, had to make strenuous efforts to clear a path for their car.

Later Princess Margaret made a visit to Westminster Abbey, where she was received by the Earl Marshal. Again the police had trouble clearing a way for her to return home.

Even Oxford Street, that busy shopping center, was taken over by sidewalk squatters almost as soon as the big stores closed. Trafalgar Square, through which the Queen will pass three times on her way from Buckingham Palace to Westminster Abbey, out again and back to the palace, was filled with curbstone sitters even at midday. Some of them had been there twelve hours then with an additional twenty-four in front of them.

The litter they made of sodden

Continued on Page 8, Column 1

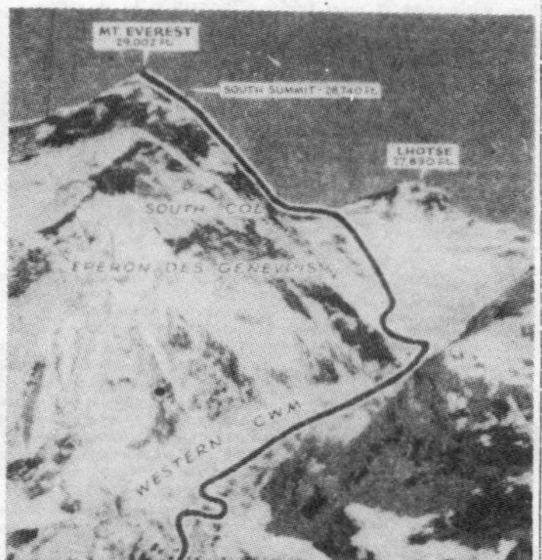

The New York Times June 2, 1953

AT THE TOP: Solid black line shows route of British expedition, the first to reach Mount Everest's summit.

Abbey, Bedecked and Aglow, Awaits the Coronation Hour

By TANIA LONG

Special to THE NEW YORK TIMES.

LONDON, Tuesday, June 2—As one enters Westminster Abbey, where Elizabeth II is to be crowned in a few hours, a magnificent scene greets the eye. The austere gray interior has been converted into a rich and glowing setting for the young Queen's coronation. Carpeting and hangings in warm tones of blue and gold, banners of white embroidered with the royal coats of arms, and the deep rose of the throne and the royal chairs blend into a splendid symphony of color.

In the pale light of early morning a hush lies over the Abbey. Only a few of the great assemblage of 7,000 guests have arrived, and there is little movement in the vast edifice.

From the great west door, where the Queen will enter, a thick carpet of deep azure blue reaches through the nave to the choir stalls. Hangings of blue silk with royal emblems embroidered in gold are draped over the edges of the stands and balconies, giving warmth to the gray fabric of the church.

From the choir to the altar in that area known as the Coronation Theatre the floor is covered in rich gold pile, against which the deep rose-covered throne and chairs, and the opulent blue hangings on the walls stand out in sharp contrast.

Under a huge chandelier in the center of the Coronation Theatre and raised on a dais stands the throne. Five steps lead up to it. It faces the altar, and because the Queen will be facing away from the majority of the guests, its back is low so that they too may see the Queen's crowned head during the latter part of the ceremony.

The throne chair is late seven-

Continued on Page 6, Column 3

Notables File Past Empty Thrones On Way to Offer Homage to Queen

By C. L. SULZBERGER

Special to THE NEW YORK TIMES.

LONDON, Tuesday, June 2—At 6 o'clock this morning the most distinguished men in Britain began filing past an empty throne. Within a few brief hours, seated upon it and wearing the heavy crown of St. Edward the Confessor, a young Queen will receive their homage.

For Britain and for her still vast empire, this is a significant moment. A new Elizabethan age of challenge and uncertainty has started.

Westminster Abbey, in its fullest splendor, with gold plate and regalia spread out on the altar, contains two thrones today. The first is that of King Edward I, a gnarled oaken chair having beneath it the Stone of Scone from the Scotland he had conquered.

Upon it the Queen is crowned. From it she will hear the acclaim of her subjects, the distant booming of her cannon and the solemn prayer of her primate, the Archbishop of Canterbury, exhorting:

"God crown you with a crown of glory and righteousness, that, having a right faith and manifold fruit of good works, you may obtain the crown of an everlasting kingdom by the gift of Him whose Kingdom endureth forever. Amen."

Only then, when she is fully consecrated and acclaimed, will the Queen, assisted by her lay and clerical peers, mount the royal throne on its dais.

Since the early dawn crept over the stirring city of London, pushing its light across gray Whitehall and through the soft rose and amber windows of this Holy Church of St. Peter, which is its rightful name, the Abbey has come to life for one of those great occasions when it nurtures monarchs.

Finely attired lords and ladies are sweeping to their places, bear-

Continued on Page 12, Column 3

DULLES SAYS U.S. AIM IS TO GAIN FRIENDS

Report on Near East-Asian Trip Urges 'Impartial' Approach to Arab-Israeli Dispute

Text of Secretary Dulles' talk about recent trip, Page 4.

Special to THE NEW YORK TIMES.

WASHINGTON, June 1—John Foster Dulles, Secretary of State, said tonight that it was the policy of the Eisenhower Administration to develop goodwill among the nations of the Near East and South Asia to thwart the Kremlin's desire to exploit their many differences.

To this end, he urged an "impartial" approach to Israeli-Arab disputes so as to win the support of both sides against the "common threat"—communism. He said the United States must make clear to all nations concerned with independence that the North Atlantic Treaty alliance was in no way related to a desire to help colonial powers keep or win back their colonies.

In a country-wide radio and television report on his twenty-day tour of the Middle East and South Asia, Mr. Dulles urged the strategic importance of that rich and populous area and said its problems could not be ignored without dangerous consequences.

'Primary Purpose' Stressed

The Secretary's half-hour address was carried over the radio and television networks of the American Broadcasting System and by the Du Mont television network, and the National Broadcasting Company radio network rebroadcast it. The Secretary gave a country-by-country account of the trip, on which he was accompanied by Harold E. Stassen, Director for Mutual Security. They made stops all the way from Egypt to Pakistan and India.

Mr. Dulles declared that the "primary purpose" of the trip "was to show friendliness and to develop understanding," and he added: "These people we visited are all proud peoples who have a great tradition and, I believe, a great future."

The Eisenhower Administration, he continued, plans to make "friendship—not fault-finding—the basis of its foreign policy."

Addressing himself to problems of the troubled Holy Land, Mr. Dulles said he had come back to Washington convinced that the Arabs were "more fearful of Zionism than of communism."

On the other hand, he added,

Continued on Page 5, Column 6

HIGHEST PEAK WON

New Zealander and a Guide Made the Final Climb to Top Friday

By Reuters.

KATMANDU, Nepal, Tuesday, June 2—The British expedition has conquered Mount Everest, a radio message flashed from Namche Bazar to the British Embassy here said today.

The message said Edmond Hillary, a New Zealand beekeeper and mountaineer, and Tensing Norkay, the famous Sherpa guide, had reached the hitherto unscaled summit from Camp Eight last Friday.

The news of this success had to be rushed by runner from the British expedition's base camp on Khumbu Glacier to the radio post at Namche Bazar.

It is understood here that this was the expedition's third attack on the last slopes leading to the summit, a first double attempt having failed.

Experts here said the success was largely due to the fine weather, combined with properly acclimatized climbers and the excellent organization and leadership of Col. H. C. J. Hunt.

Full details of the exploit are not expected to reach here for some days.

It is believed here that the news was transmitted specially to London by diplomatic channels so Queen Elizabeth could be told.

Queen Told at Palace

LONDON, Tuesday, June 2 (Reuters)—The Times of London reported the news of the scaling of Mount Everest in a copyrighted message today.

The news was published in a special edition of The Times on early sale among coronation crowds in London.

Queen Elizabeth, resting at Buckingham Palace, was told on the eve of her coronation that the British expedition had conquered the mountain. The news was brought to her as she spent a quiet evening "at home." The British climbers had succeeded in their plan to give her a world-shaking coronation present.

Mount Everest, the 29,002-foot giant, was the last main outpost of the world unknown to man.

The thirteen members of the expedition formed the eleventh team to try to conquer the mountain in the past thirty years. Many climbers have died in the high ice and snow of the Himalaya giant.

The Sherpa guide, Tensing Norkay, is a 42-year-old native veteran of more assaults on Mount Everest than any other man.

With 362 porters, twenty Sherpa guides and 10,000 pounds of baggage the expedition left the Nepalese base of Katmandu on March 10. Thus it took eighty days from start to finish.

The climbers carried three flags—the Union Jack, the United Nations flag and the Nepalese flag—to plant on the summit.

They made an approach to the "Goddess Mother of the Snows" from the south, or Nepalese, side.

It was the route reconnoitered by Sir Eric Shipton, who led a British

Continued on Page 14, Column 7

Tito Abolishes Rank Of Army Commissar

By JACK RAYMOND

Special to THE NEW YORK TIMES.

BELGRADE, Yugoslavia, June 1—President Tito abolished today the system of political commissars in the Yugoslav armed forces, asserting that present conditions no longer required them.

Not mentioned in Marshal Tito's order was the fact that this will undoubtedly make it easier for Yugoslavia to carry on with growing plans for integrating her military establishment with Western defense projects.

"It will be much easier to deal with Yugoslav military leaders now," said a Western military liaison expert here.

The political commissars, who wore uniforms and were equal in rank with military commanders in the Yugoslav Army, were introduced in imitation of Soviet military practice in the early days of partisan warfare against Germany.

Even after the break with the

Continued on Page 18, Column 3

The New York Times.

LATE CITY EDITION
Fair and mild today and tonight.
Increasing cloudiness tomorrow.
Temperature Range Today—Max., 78; Min., 58
Temperatures Yesterday—Max., 75; Min., 57
Full U. S. Weather Bureau Report, Page 52

Copyright, 1953, by The New York Times Company.

VOL. CII..No. 34,829.   Entered as Second-Class Matter,
Post Office, New York, N. Y.   NEW YORK, WEDNESDAY, JUNE 3, 1953.   Times Square, New York 36, N. Y.
Telephone Lackawanna 4-1000   FIVE CENTS

SERVICE SALES TAX DROPPED AS JOSEPH 'FINDS' $12,000,000

Mayor, Irked at Controller's Late Re-estimate of Cash Carryover, Dooms Bill

PLAN DISMAYED COUNCIL

Wide Opposition to Move in an Election Year Big Factor— $3,000,000 More in Sight

By CHARLES G. BENNETT

The proposed broadening of the city's sales tax was doomed yesterday after Controller Lazarus Joseph gave a re-estimate that the 1952-53 cash carryover of the city's general fund would be $12,000,000 higher than he had estimated previously. That led Mayor Impellitteri to announce last night that there was "no necessity" for the bill he had supported to extend the 3 per cent levy to more than thirty categories of services not now covered.

The Mayor killed the bill after a hectic day of City Hall maneuvering in which dismayed City Councilmen, unwilling to share responsibility for a new tax in a city election year, made it clear to Council leaders that they were considering voting against the bill, regardless of need.

It was no secret either that Mr. Impellitteri was resentful that the re-estimate of the general fund revenues had come only a week after the introduction of the sales tax measure at his request.

A memorandum containing the Mayor's view that there will be "no necessity" for the sales tax broadening will be delivered today to Majority Leader Joseph T. Sharkey, Brooklyn Democrat, and Charles E. Keegan, Bronx Democrat and chairman of the Council's Finance Committee.

The Mayor's memorandum is expected to lead to formal action by the Council next Tuesday to kill the tax bill.

Joseph Gives Revised Estimate

Early yesterday afternoon Controller Joseph met with the Council's Finance Committee at City Hall and told the members that the 1952-53 cash carryover—general fund revenues on hand at the end of a year available to be added to funds for the next year—would be $18,000,000. His earlier estimate had been $6,000,000.

The city's general fund consists of the yield from the sales tax, the nuisance taxes, fines, licenses and a variety of service fees.

With the $12,000,000 in sight and the possibility that $3,000,000 from other sources to offset the $15,000,000 estimated yearly return from the extension of the sales tax, the Councilmen were quick to seize the opportunity to turn against the new impost.

The proposed tax already had raised a clamor of opposition and threat of "all-out war" by civic and trade groups.

After the heated behind-doors finance committee session, Mr. Sharkey and Mr. Keegan told City Hall reporters there was "no possibility" that the finance committee would approve the tax extension. They said if it were possible for the bill to pass, they would have called a public hearing, but

Continued on Page 52, Column 6

Big Rise in Tax Is Due On Peak Realty Rolls

By LEE E. COOPER

New York property holders will pay taxes this year on the highest aggregate assessed valuations on record, and at a higher rate than ever before.

Final valuations fixed by the city for the coming fiscal year indicate that tax bills for the first six months in most boroughs will be based on a combined city-borough levy of more than $3.50 on each $100 worth of realty. In the second half of the year, under state authorization for additional municipal income, at least 25 points more will go on the bills, applicable over the entire year.

The mounting burden of levies, to be shared alike by the owners of small homes and of towering skyscrapers, was emphasized in a report on final assessed values for 1953-54 presented yesterday to Mayor Impellitteri by William

Continued on Page 36, Column 3

FARE RISE PROBLEM IS POSED BY TOKENS

The Mint Could Make Them by July 30, but Declines—Dewey May Be Asked to Intercede

By LEO EGAN

A serious question was raised yesterday as to whether the New York City Transit Authority could get enough tokens to increase fares by July 30 on the lines it is taking over from the city. The statutory deadline for fare action this year is July 30.

F. Leland Howard, Acting Director of the United States Mint reported in Washington that he had turned down a telephoned request from an authority representative to have an emergency supply of 20,000,000 tokens made at the Philadelphia Mint.

"We don't want the business; It belongs to private industry," he told the authority representative.

Nevertheless, Mr. Howard arranged for Sidney H. Bingham, chairman of the Board of Transportation, and a group of his associates to confer yesterday with Edwin H. Dressel, superintendent of the Philadelphia Mint.

Mint Could Do the Job

Mr. Dressel said after the conference that it would be possible for the mint to turn out the required number of tokens in time to meet the July 30 deadline if his superiors in Washington gave their approval.

Mr. Bingham was accompanied to the conference by William Lasgow, an assistant; J. P. Waring, superintendent of purchases for the Board of Transportation, and C. A. Reed, engineer in charge of line equipment.

Mr. Dressel reported after the meeting:

"We discussed what we could handle; that's the extent of it. We don't know if we'll do it or not—it's up to Washington.

"The only reason we could make them is that this is an emergency. But we want it clear that we are not interested in any way in competing with private industry."

Asked if there was any Federal law that would bar the mint from accepting the order, Mr. Dressel said he did not think so.

In view of Mr. Howard's attitude, several possibilities were open. Governor Dewey, whose help

Continued on Page 52, Column 3

G. O. P. CHIEFS YIELD TO PRESIDENT, SCRAP RIDER ON U. N. FUNDS

Agree After White House Talk on Milder Substitute Stating Opposition to Red China

By WILLIAM S. WHITE

WASHINGTON, June 2 — The Senate Republican leaders capitulated to President Eisenhower today and abandoned a Congressional rider that had been intended, in effect, to withdraw the United States from the United Nations if membership should be given to Communist China.

The victory was the President's first in a collision with Congress over foreign policy and marked the first time he had met such an issue head-on.

The result was to scrap the offending rider, which the Republicans had intended to attach to a pending appropriations bill, in favor of a noncontroversial substitute by which Congress simply would state the opinion that Communist China should not be admitted.

Such a declaration would not be binding, leaving ultimate decisions to the President.

The Republican leaders got in exchange what Senator William F. Knowland of California called a "most significant" commitment from the President.

Pledge 'For Foreseeable Future'

This, as Mr. Knowland related it, was that the Administration "not only was opposed to the admission of Red China but that we [the United States] will take an active part in the leadership in opposing admission."

Asked how long this Eisenhower pledge extended, Senator Knowland replied, "for the foreseeable future."

"Of course," he added, "if conditions should so change that everybody, including Congress, recognized that there had been a fundamental alteration, that would be a bridge to be crossed when it was reached."

Mr. Knowland disclosed that nothing was said by the President that would commit the United States to go so far as to use the veto in the United Nations against membership for the Communists.

The understanding reported seemed, moreover, to be in substance about what the President already had said in news conferences—that there was no intention to let the Chinese Communists in under present conditions and specifically not so long as they remained subservient to the Russians.

Democrats Jubilant

Senator Knowland, nevertheless, declared that the Senate Republicans were well satisfied.

"The President—to my knowledge for the first time—and the Executive Department of this Government for the first time have made it clear not only that they are opposed to Red China in the United Nations but that we will take an active part in the leadership in opposing admission," he observed.

The Democrats, who had stayed out of any open controversy though they were generally opposed to the rider, were jubilant at the outcome. Some of them had let the White House understand yesterday that they would take no position for the President and against the Republican rider unless the General came out publicly against it.

The President did that this morning. Urgently and on short notice, he summoned to the White House the Republican chieftains in both the Senate and House. The conference was announced only an hour and a quarter before it was begun.

Taft Unable to Attend

From the Senate went Vice President Richard M. Nixon, the body's presiding officer, and Senators Knowland, chairman of the Senate Republican Policy Committee and acting Republican floor leader; Styles Bridges of New Hampshire, the Republican dean of Colorado, chairman of the Republican party organization called the Conference, and Leverett Saltonstall of Massachusetts, party whip, or assistant floor leader.

From the House went Speaker Joseph W. Martin Jr. and Representatives Charles A. Halleck of Indiana, the Republican floor leader; Leslie C. Arends of Illinois, the Republican whip, and John Taber of upstate New York, chairman of the Appropriations Committee.

All those called to the White House were given to understand that their presence was imperative and that the matter would not permit delay. Mr. Martin had to take an airplane back from his home in

Continued on Page 26, Column 3

ELIZABETH II CROWNED IN ABBEY; MILLIONS CHEER PARADE IN RAIN; RULER BIDS SUBJECTS LOOK AHEAD

'GOD SAVE THE QUEEN!' The climactic moment of yesterday's coronation of Queen Elizabeth in Westminster Abbey, Archbishop of Canterbury is about to place St. Edward's Crown.   "at the sight whereof the people, with loud and repeated shouts, shall cry, 'God save the Queen!'" The Queen is flanked by the Bishop of Durham, left, and the Bishop of Bath and Wells.
The New York Times (by Jet Plane to North America)

TRUCE AIR UNCLEAR DESPITE RHEE SHIFT

South Korean Chief Eases Stand on U. N. Plan—Foe Yields Hill in Drive

By ROBERT ALDEN
Special to THE NEW YORK TIMES.

SEOUL, Korea, Wednesday, June 3 — The explosive Korean situation clouded today and will not be clarified until the release of a Republic of Korea Government statement now in the process of preparation.

The principal complicating factor was that for the first time there was at least a scrap of evidence that South Korean President Syngman Rhee might be yielding to the intense pressure being brought to bear on him from Washington. He indicated he might go along with whatever truce arrangement was made at Panmunjom, although a major condition would be an iron-clad defense agreement with the United States.

[The Communists asked for a meeting of truce liaison officers in Panmunjom at 4 P. M., Wednesday, Korea time—3 A.M., Eastern daylight time. Full negotiations were scheduled to resume Thursday morning, Korea time.

[South Korean troops in a fourth counter-attack within twenty-four hours threw back North Korean Reds from all the positions the foe had captured in heavy fighting. Allied bombers raked the enemy lines.]

The 78-year-old President, speaking after the coronation day parade conducted here by the British Commonwealth Division, declared to reporters:

"Out of gratitude to the United States, common sense and wisdom require that we cooperate with the United States at any cost. We must accept anything the United

Continued on Page 3, Column 2

People Voice Wild Acclaim As Royal Procession Passes

By CLIFTON DANIEL
Special to THE NEW YORK TIMES.

LONDON, June 2—Full throated and joyous, the people of Britain and their Commonwealth cousins poured out love, affection and loyalty for their newly crowned Queen in the rain-soaked streets of old London today.

A spectacle, breathtaking in its magnitude and brilliance, unfolded here as the Queen, surrounded by her loyal men at arms, passed among her adoring subjects, riding serenely in a golden coach.

In the tramp of ten thousand marching feet the oldest among the spectators heard an echo of the might and majesty of the greatest empire that the world has ever known. In the diversity of races and uniforms represented in the ranks the youngest saw a glimmer of the greatness of the British Commonwealth of Nations as it still is.

Only the British, among all the peoples of the earth, could have staged such a display and every moment of it seemed to be savored by an appreciative public drawn from the four quarters of the globe and from virtually every nation and people under the sun.

Every prospect was pleasing and only the weather was unkind. It rained and rained, and again it rained, and throughout the whole long day the sun deigned to show itself for only a few minutes at a time.

The British, who have almost come to believe that if their Queen smiles the sun will shine, were disappointed but dampened only in body, not in spirit. There was sunshine in their smiles and the warmth of summer in their cheers.

Some had waited forty-eight hours or more to do honor to the young Elizabeth; they slept in the parks or on the sidewalks until the hour when she appeared before them. Nearly all of the vast multitude that acclaimed her in the afternoon had assembled in their

Continued on Page 6, Column 1

COLLINS SEES PERIL IN ARMY REDUCTION

Refuses to Specify to Senators in Public the 'Risks' in Cuts Envisaged by Eisenhower

By HAROLD B. HINTON

WASHINGTON, June 2—Gen. J. Lawton Collins, outgoing Army Chief of Staff, testified to a Senate Appropriations subcommittee today that the manpower cuts in the ground forces envisaged by the revised defense budget President Eisenhower had presented to Congress carried "certain military risks and limitations" that he declined to specify in public.

He said that the "combat readiness of the units in the United States is not expected to reach a satisfactory state" until late in the fiscal year ending June 30, 1954, and that, to accomplish the reduction in personnel, "the Army will have to adjust the strengths of its commands overseas, as well as the strength of units in the United States."

While General Collins was on the stand, the Senate confirmed the nomination of his successor, Gen. Matthew B. Ridgway, now commander of the forces of the North Atlantic Treaty Organization, along with those of Admiral Arthur W. Radford to be Chairman of the Joint Chiefs of Staff, Admiral Robert B. Carney to be Chief of Naval Operations, and Gen. Nathan F. Twining to be Chief of Staff of the Air Force.

Calls for 117,000 Cut

General Collins was preceded by Robert T. Stevens, Secretary of the Army, who told the subcommittee, headed by Senator Homer Ferguson, Republican of Michigan, that the proposed cut of about $1,000,000,000 below the estimates presented by President Truman before leaving office would not affect adversely the current combat effectiveness of the Army.

He said the revised budget would call for a reduction of 117,000 men in the Army's strength below the Truman-projected level, the new level to be reached by June 30, 1954. If the Korean war should end before that time, he added, 50,000 more men would be released.

He explained that President Truman's request of $12,100,000,000 had been trimmed, on review by himself and the direction of Charles E. Wilson, Secretary of Defense, to about $11,100,000,000. To this was added, however, $2,-

Continued on Page 28, Column 5

OLD RITE, NEW HOPE

Queen's Husband Leads Peers in Swearing Oath of Fealty

Text of Queen's broadcast to the Commonwealth, Page 7.

By RAYMOND DANIELL
Special to THE NEW YORK TIMES.

LONDON, June 2—Elizabeth II was crowned today in Westminster Abbey and then received the homage of millions of her humble rain-drenched subjects as she rode in her gilded coach through five miles of this capital's royal route.

The crowds that lined the streets through which her procession passed were of this century. But the coach in which the Queen and her husband rode was not of this century or this world but out of the fantasies of the illustrators of children's books of fairy tales.

So, too, was the ceremony in Westminster Abbey. Out of the story books stepped the heralds of six centuries ago. Seated on her throne wearing her crown and holding the scepter and the rod with the dove, the fragile young girl, her head bowed under the weight of the crown upon it, might have been a character in a novel by Sir Walter Scott.

Yet once the Abbey ceremony was over the emphasis was on the future. Jet planes of the Royal Air Force roared across the Mall while the Queen, her husband the Duke of Edinburgh and their two rather bored and impatient children watched and waved at the massed crowds that stretched from Admiralty Arch to the palace yard.

Unity of Commonwealth

The Queen herself, who had gone through the ancient ritual of coronation in the Abbey with all the solemnity of a Bishop at his consecration spoke to her people at home and abroad in a radio address. She called upon them to look forward instead of backward, saying:

"I have when he not only the splendid traditions and the annals of more than a thousand years but the living strength and majesty of the Commonwealth and Empire, of societies old and new, of lands and races different in history but all by God's will united in spirit and in aim.

"Therefore, I am sure that this, my coronation, is not the symbol of a power and a splendor that are gone but a declaration of our hopes for the future and for the years I may by God's grace and mercy be given to reign and serve you as your Queen."

When the Queen spoke of the antiquity and variety of the realms over which she reigns but does not rule, she was merely putting into words what millions of persons all over the world saw for themselves either directly or through the twentieth century miracle of television.

There was also what the British call a "homely" touch in the Queen's speech. It was doubly

Continued on Page 7, Column 1

ABBEY RITE MARKED BY MEDIEVAL POMP

Religious Ceremony Witnessed by Country's Elite Garbed in Cloaks of Many Hues

By C. L. SULZBERGER
Special to THE NEW YORK TIMES.

IN WESTMINSTER ABBEY, London, June 2 — Amid ancient ceremony and medieval pomp in this abbey today, the Archbishop of Canterbury placed the heavy crown of Edward the Confessor upon the head of his radiant young sovereign, Elizabeth II.

For a brief moment a hush fell across the abbey. Then a fanfare of trumpets sounded. The peers and peeresses of the realm donned their coronets and a chorus broke forth "God Save Queen Elizabeth."

And through the tall Gothic windows, over the heads of those servants of the crown—the Queen's field and air marshals, generals, admirals and, most redoubtable of all, the Queen's Prime Minister, Sir Winston Churchill—came the dull boom of guns from the venerable Tower fortress down the Thames.

It was as if to signify that Britain, in a swiftly changing world, stood fast upon her own traditions, determined to maintain them in Britain's own way.

The curious mixture of religious, military and governing significance derives from those that Solomon King over Israel, from pre-Christian customs of the Saxon kings of Wessex, from the conquering

Continued on Page 19, Column 1

President Sets Up Loyalty Board To Check on U. S. Citizens in U. N.

Special to THE NEW YORK TIMES.

WASHINGTON, June 2—President Eisenhower ordered today the establishment of an International Organizations Employes Loyalty Board to evaluate as security risks United States citizens employed by, or applying for jobs with, the United Nations.

In effect, the Executive Order extended to Americans working for the world organization the same loyalty check and review procedure that the President put into effect for Federal Government employes by another Executive Order issued last April 27.

That order established a tighter security program for Federal employes and discarded the system set up by the Truman Administration that differentiated between loyalty and security.

The new board will be named by the Civil Service Commission from among its personnel and will have at least three members. The commission will provide the investigative and other services required by the board.

The President's order made "reasonable doubt as to the loyalty of the person involved to the Gov-ernment of the United States" the standard to be used by the board in evaluating information obtained regarding employes of the United Nations or persons being considered for employment who are Americans.

The order applies to United States citizens employed by or seeking employment with all international organizations of which this country is a member. The United Nations is primarily involved because questions of the loyalty of some Americans employed by it have been raised by the Senate Internal Security subcommittee and other legislative and administrative agencies.

The procedure established by the order is as follows:

The Civil Service Commission shall make a "full background investigation" of all such employes, which shall include reference to its own files as well as those of the Federal Bureau of Investigation, military and naval intelli-

Continued on Page 28, Column 3

Pier Union Moves to End Shape-Up And to Adopt Democratic Practices

By A. H. RASKIN

The New York district council of the racket-infested International Longshoremen's Association, A. F. L., took two major steps last night toward compliance with the clean-up mandate given the waterfront union by the American Federation of Labor several months ago.

The pier council voted to begin contract negotiations with the New York dock employers two months ahead of schedule, with a view to winning agreement on abolition of the shape-up system of hiring. The A. F. L. has insisted that steps toward elimination of the shape-up, long considered a principal source of waterfront crime, be completed by Aug. 10.

The council, which includes representatives of all sixty-two union locals in the Port of New York, also instructed its affiliates to take immediate action toward adoption of a code of democratic union practices, approved by the parent body.

Louis Waldman, counsel for the international union, said "only ten or twelve" of the locals in this area would have to revise their rules for conducting membership meetings, holding elections and making financial reports to comply with the new directive. He said the other locals already were conforming to the main precepts of the new code.

The council took no action on A. F. L. demands for the ouster of union officials who had taken bribes from employers or who had been convicted of crimes. Mr. Waldman said this was not a matter for consideration by the district council, but would be handled at a later date by the parent union and the locals.

The decision to ask the employers to enter into early negotiations for abolition of the shape-up represented a reversal of the action taken by the union's membership

Continued on Page 65, Column 2

A.F.L., C.I.O. in No-Raiding Pact; Accord Held First Step to Merger

By JOSEPH A. LOFTUS
Special to THE NEW YORK TIMES.

WASHINGTON, June 2—Leaders of the American Federation of Labor and the Congress of Industrial Organizations agreed today on a way to get rid of union raiding.

The compact was described as the first step toward organic unity of the two organizations. It will release staff energies for organizing the unorganized.

Subject to certain ratifications in the meantime, the agreement will go into effect Jan. 1 and run for two years. Ratifications are expected not only by the executive bodies and the conventions of the two federations but by each national and international union.

Disputes over interpreting and applying the agreement will go to an impartial umpire if they fail to yield to negotiation. The umpire's decision will be final. However, no formal disciplinary measures are provided for non-compliance.

The agreement deals only with raiding—that is, the transfer, or attempt to transfer, a recognized unit of employes from one federation to another. A unit of employes is considered to be the non-transferable property of a union if it has a contract with an employer or is certified by the National Labor Relations Board.

A union that receives a unit of employes from the other federation, even though it has made no overtures, will be guilty of raiding. Therefore, if a group of employes is dissatisfied with its representa-

Continued on Page 28, Column 5

Three queens mourn the death of King George VI—daughter Elizabeth II, mother Mary and widow Elizabeth.

Winston Churchill, in full regalia, at the coronation of Queen Elizabeth.

The newly crowned Queen Elizabeth, with her husband, Prince Philip.

"All the News That's Fit to Print"

The New York Times.

LATE CITY EDITION
Fair and quite warm today. Hot and humid tomorrow.
Temperature Range Today—Max., 89; Min., 66
Temperature Yesterday—Max., 85; Min., 63
Full U. S. Weather Bureau Report, Page 31

Copyright, 1953, by The New York Times Company.

VOL. CII . No. 34,846.

Entered as Second-Class Matter,
Post Office, New York, N. Y.

NEW YORK, SATURDAY, JUNE 20, 1953.

Times Square, New York 36, N. Y.
Telephone Lackawanna 4-1000

RAG PAPER EDITION
SEVENTY-FIVE CENTS

REDS INSIST U.N. RECAPTURE ALL RELEASED PRISONERS; TRUCE TALKS RECESS AGAIN

FOE WRITES CLARK

Questions if Allies Can Control South Korean Leaders and Army

Text of the Communist note to General Clark is on Page 3.

By LINDESAY PARROTT
Special to The New York Times.

TOKYO, Saturday, June 20—Communist armistice delegates at Panmunjom demanded today that the United Nations recapture all 25,000 anti-Communist prisoners of the Korean war released by the order of Dr. Syngman Rhee, South Korean President.

The demand was made in the course of a three-minute meeting of the full truce delegations called for this morning by the senior Communist truce representative, Lieut. Gen. Nam II of North Korea.

The Communist high command sent a strong protest to Gen. Mark W. Clark, United Nations commander, asserting that the Allies, equally with Dr. Rhee, must bear "serious responsibility" for the incident. The message was signed by the top enemy commanders, Marshal Kim Il Sung, North Korean Premier, and Chinese Gen. Peng Teh-huai.

The Communist protest was an angry one, and it was significant that it was made directly to the Allied commander, and not to the truce delegation. Yet it seemed to indicate that the enemy was not prepared to completely end the negotiations for an armistice.

The letter to General Clark repeated many of the old charges of American coercion and duplicity, but did not slam the door to further conversations.

The Associated Press said that Pyun Yun Tae, Acting South Korean Premier, demanded Saturday in a letter to General Clark that all anti-Communist North Korean prisoners remaining in Allied stockades be turned over to the Republic for immediate release.

[Soon afterward, in Tokyo General Clark's United Nations headquarters made public according letter to the South Korean President, saying General Clark could "not at this time estimate the ultimate consequences" of President Rhee's "precipitous and shocking" release of the 26,000 anti-Communist Korean war captives. General Clark accused Dr. Rhee of breaking a "personal commitment" not to take action.]

At the armistice conference, the Communists in effect, demanded that the Allied command promise that if the South Korean President from acting on his own. Pointedly, the Communists asked:

"Is the United Nations Command able to control the South Korean Government and Army? If not, does the armistice in Korea include the Syngman Rhee clique.

"If it is not included, what assurance is there for implementation of the armistice agreement on the part of South Korea?

"If it is included, then your side must be responsible for recovering immediately all the 25,952 prisoners—

Continued on Page 3, Column 4

U. S. SEES POSITION IN KOREA AS GRAVE

Dulles Meets With Both Parties and Envoys of U. N. Allies in Atmosphere of Urgency

By WILLIAM S. WHITE
Special to The New York Times.

WASHINGTON, June 19—The United States Government worked in haste today to save a Korean truce that some responsible men regarded as all but lost through South Korea's angry defiance of the United Nations.

The position was described authoritatively as the gravest since June 25, 1950—the day the Communists invaded the Republic of Korea.

There was hope, however, that if the Communists genuinely wanted peace they would not make capital of the defiance shown by Dr. Syngman Rhee, President of South Korea, to the United States and to its allies in the United Nations forces that went to the rescue of his country three years ago.

All the possibilities seemed in the end to narrow to this one, even though there was some speculation that it might be feasible to take some sort of action to replace Dr. Rhee. Senator Walter F. George of Georgia, the senior Democratic member of the Senate Foreign Re-

Continued on Page 2, Column 5

U. N. OFFICERS FELT RHEE WAS BLUFFING

Warnings Unheeded, Prisoner Command Took No Steps to Prevent Mass Escape

By ROBERT ALDEN
Special to The New York Times.

SEOUL, Korea, June 19—The United Nations Command was not prepared for the precipitate action taken by Dr. Syngman Rhee, President of South Korea, in freeing non-Communist prisoners of war.

According to an authoritative source in the Prisoner-of-War Command here, officials in Tokyo had been warned that such a measure might be taken by the Government of the Republic of Korea. However, the Prisoner-of-War Command was assured by higher headquarters that Dr. Rhee was "bluffing."

As a result, South Korean security guards were not replaced by American soldiers and other precautionary measures were insufficient.

However, the freeing of the prisoners came as no surprise to those who have been close to President Rhee these last few weeks. Nor was it a surprise to diplomatic circles in Pusan, the temporary South Korean capital.

They knew how defiant the President's attitude has been from the start, and they regard him as a rather unpredictable individual, apt to go off on a desperate tangent at almost any time.

Some Americans farther away from the scene, however, have had a tendency to underestimate what Dr. Rhee might do and to grasp at any straw that indicated that he was yielding ground in his fight. That was why the repeated threats to free the prisoners on the spot and the ample information available indicating that the South Korean Government was taking concrete steps along these lines were virtually ignored by those in a position to do something about it.

One reason for this reluctance to recognize the facts in the matter is that it is difficult for an American to understand Dr. Rhee's reasoning. The Korean leader feels that to accept a truce agreement, as drawn is tantamount to inviting self-destruction.

He is not only worried about the question of complete unification of his country, he has a great fear, for example, of allowing into the country Communist representatives and "pro-Communist" Indian guards.

President Rhee and those close

Continued on Page 3, Column 2

HIS ATTEMPT TO ESCAPE FAILS: A U. S. Marine, right, escorts a wounded prisoner in the prisoner-of-war camp at Ascom City, near Inchon, where about 500 anti-Communists escaped. Marines and other troops prevented a larger break-out.

West Asks Soviet to Bar Firearms In Keeping Order in East Berlin

By WALTER SULLIVAN
Special to The New York Times.

BERLIN, June 19—The three Western powers in Berlin urged the Soviet Union today to forbid the use of firearms by its troops and by the East German police in the Soviet sector of the city to prevent further bloodshed.

An announcement said Brig. Gen. Pierre Manceaux-Demiau, French Commandant in Berlin, and this month's chairman of the Allied Kommandatura, had made repeated vain attempts to see high Soviet authorities to discuss the problem. It added that finally he had gone to Soviet headquarters in East Berlin to deliver in person a note stating the point of view of the Western Commandants.

Meanwhile, as the eastern part of the city continued to appear quiet, United States authorities delivered Otto Nuschke, the East German Deputy Premier, was forced

Western powers in Berlin urged the Soviet Union today to forbid the use of firearms by its troops and by the East German police in the Soviet sector of the city to prevent further bloodshed.

Herr Nuschke, 70 years of age, was questioned thoroughly by both United States and West Berlin officials before being returned to the Soviet sector. According to an official announcement by the United States mission, he was asked whether he wanted political asylum in the West and said no.

The West Berlin police sought to determine whether he could be linked with a "kidnapping." Possibly this refused in the case of Dr. Walter Linse, anti-Communist leader, who was abducted from the United States sector last year.

East Germany's Communist newspaper, Neues Deutschland, conceded today that the work stoppages and disorders of the last few days had reached into the remote corners of that region. It expressed

AID BILL APPROVED AS DEMOCRATS SAVE MEASURE IN HOUSE

G.O.P. Split on Cutting Funds, but 280-108 Vote Prevails —4.9 Billion Authorized

By FELIX BELAIR Jr.
Special to The New York Times.

WASHINGTON, June 19—The House of Representatives authorized today an appropriation of $4,998,732,500 for military, economic and technical aid to fifty-six free governments and dependencies resisting communism. The vote sending the measure to the Senate was 280 to 108, with one Representative merely voting "present."

Throughout the afternoon, a smoothly functioning bipartisan majority shouted down repeated attempts to cut the authorization items below the recommendations of the Foreign Affairs Committee. But it was the Democrats under Representative Sam Rayburn of Texas, the minority leader, who provided the margin of victory.

Republicans by the score deserted the leadership of Speaker Joseph W. Martin Jr. to vote for economy amendments. There was no record vote on any of the attempts to slash the measure and, although the foreign policy prestige of President Eisenhower had been thrown into the debate by the Republican leadership, it was the Democrats who gave him his vote of confidence.

On the final vote, 160 Democrats joined with 119 Republicans and an Independent, Frazier Reams of Ohio, to provide the 280 majority for the bill. A total of eighty-one Republicans and twenty-seven Democrats voted against the measure. Representative Harold A. Patten, Democrat of Arizona, was the one who voted "present."

Members Rally to Vote

The high tide of opposition to the authorization—which is $476,000,000 less than the Administration had requested—came shortly before the final vote. Representative Hamer H. Budge, Republican of Idaho, offered an amendment to cut all the items by 10 per cent, but it was rejected by a standing vote of 152 to 101.

The same amendment had lost by a narrower margin a few minutes earlier when, on a count, the vote was put at 122 to 102. But when a vote by tellers was demanded, members burst from the cloakrooms on either side of the House to provide the extra voices.

An even harsher attempt to accomplish the same result and cut the authorization by $498,000,000 was made when Representative William M. Colmer, Democrat of Mississippi, sought to place a ceiling on the total authorization of $4,500,000,000. This move was rejected, 104 to 83.

The pattern of unrecorded voting on the amendments had been set shortly after the House met for business an hour before noon. Representative Lawrence Smith, Republican of Wisconsin, proposed to cut $329,186,000 from the section providing military aid to Western Europe. The amendment would have eliminated military aid totaling $216,906,000 for Yugo-

Continued on Page 18, Column 4

4-Day Seamen's Strike Ends As Wage Demands Are Met

By GEORGE HORNE

The four-day-old seamen's strike, which immobilized 128 vessels and threatened to paralyze one-half of the nation's fleet of 1,500 ships, came to an end at 12:45 A. M. today.

National Maritime Union seamen, who struck on Tuesday when the operators refused to accede to wage demands, signed with the dry-cargo shipping employers at the headquarters of the Federal Mediation and Conciliation Service, winning wage rises ranging from 2 to 6 per cent. The settlement terms constituted a complete capitulation by the operators.

A few minutes earlier, the striking American Radio Association, also an affiliate of the Congress for Industrial Organizations, signed for a 6 per cent wage increase with a group of tanker operators. Surrender of the employers on the basis of similar wage rises and other terms. After this agreement was reached, it was a foregone conclusion that the rest of the industry would follow.

The mediators brought the N. M. U. into contact again with the Committee of Companies and Agents, Atlantic and Gulf Coasts,

and it was apparent the costly hold-out of the companies was crumbling.

In its bargaining, the radio officer association also won its demands to gain full control over all radio telephones at sea, removing this equipment from the control of captains and other bridge officers. This was a major issue with the radio men.

The new contract for the dry-cargo men will run for only a year, with a wage reopening in the fall. Union leaders called the wage terms "the best increases won by any industry this year." They were preparing to send out telegrams releasing the immobilized ships throughout the nation, including the superliner United States, tied up in New York.

Continued on Page 22, Column 3

ROSENBERGS EXECUTED AS ATOM SPIES AFTER SUPREME COURT VACATES STAY; LAST-MINUTE PLEA TO PRESIDENT FAILS

SIX JUSTICES AGREE

President Says Couple Increased 'Chances of Atomic War'

Texts of related documents in case are printed on Page 7.

By LUTHER A. HUSTON
Special to The New York Times.

WASHINGTON, June 19—President Eisenhower and the Supreme Court refused today to save Julius and Ethel Rosenberg from death in the electric chair.

The high court vacated the stay granted to the atomic spies on Wednesday by Justice William O. Douglas. It upheld the legality of the death sentence imposed by Federal Judge Irving R. Kaufman. Less than an hour after the court had announced its verdict, President Eisenhower refused Executive clemency for the second time. He had denied a similar petition on Feb. 11.

"I can only say that, by increasing immeasurably the chances of atomic war, the Rosenbergs may have condemned to death tens of millions of innocent people all over the world," the President said. "The execution of two human beings is a grave matter. But even graver is the thought of the millions of dead whose deaths may be directly attributable to what these spies have done."

He was convinced, the President said, that the Rosenbergs had received "the fullest measure of justice and due process of law."

"When in their most solemn judgment the tribunals of the United States have adjudged them guilty and the sentence just, I will not intervene in this matter," the President declared.

Vinson Reads Court's Ruling

The prevailing opinion setting aside Justice Douglas' stay of execution was read by Chief Justice Fred M. Vinson and was concurred in by Associate Justices Stanley F. Reed, Robert H. Jackson, Harold H. Burton, Sherman Minton and Tom C. Clark.

Justices Douglas and Hugo L. Black dissented. Justice Felix Frankfurter announced neither a concurrence nor a dissent. In a brief separate opinion he said the questions raised were "complicated and novel" and that he felt the application of the Attorney General for revocation of the stay should not be disposed of until more time had been afforded for study and argument. He promised to set forth more specifically in due course the ground for this position.

Also read from the bench were a concurring opinion by Justice Clark, in which he was joined by Justices Vinson, Reed, Jackson, Burton and Minton, and a concurring opinion by Justice Jackson.

Continued on Page 8, Column 5

Their Death Penalty Carried Out

Julius Rosenberg   Ethel Rosenberg

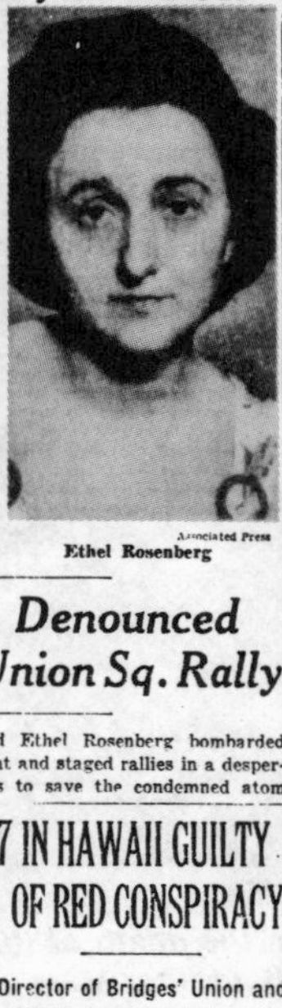

Associated Press

Eisenhower Is Denounced To 5,000 in Union Sq. Rally

Sympathizers of Julius and Ethel Rosenberg bombarded judges with new appeals last night and staged rallies in a desperate last-minute flurry of efforts to save the condemned atom spies from the electric chair.

As time ran out for the doomed couple, lawyers and sympathizers tried every avenue of appeal and protest in a feverish evening that included:

¶An order by Police Commissioner George P. Monaghan to all police commands to maintain a special city-wide vigil against any disorder or violence in connection with the execution.

¶Three separate appeals to Federal Judge Irving R. Kaufman, who sentenced the Rosenbergs, to stay their execution. He rejected all.

¶Two separate appeals to two Federal Circuit Court judges to grant a stay. These also were denied.

¶A rally by an estimated 5,000 persons in Seventeenth Street, west of the north end of Union Square, where members of the New York Clemency Committee of the National Committee to Secure Justice in the Rosenberg Case denounced President Eisenhower as "bloodthirsty."

Final Pleas to Kaufman

Judge Kaufman, for whom the police ordered a reinforced fifteen-man guard at his Park Avenue apartment, was importuned by attorneys making frantic new legal maneuvers to save the Rosenbergs. Daniel G. Marshall, a Los Angeles lawyer who had pleaded with the Supreme Court for a stay, begged Judge Kaufman to telephone the prison and delay the execution for one hour so that Mr. Marshall could elaborate his argument. But Judge Kaufman refused about twenty minutes before the executions began.

Milton H. Friedman, a lawyer representing the Rosenberg defense counsel, asked Judge Kaufman to stay the scheduled executions on the ground that they would constitute "an outrageous insult to world Jewry" if they were carried out on the Jewish Sabbath. Judge Kaufman rejected the plea, saying he had been assured the executions would not be within the Sabbath period.

Frank Scheiner, another lawyer representing the defense, asked Judge Kaufman to throw out the convictions of the couple on the same grounds argued yesterday before the Supreme Court. Judge Kaufman rejected this motion without any opinion.

Another defense lawyer, Arthur Kinoy, went to New Haven, Conn., in an unsuccessful effort to induce Judges Jerome N. Frank and Thomas W. Swan of the Federal Court of Appeals to block the executions.

'Prayer Meeting' Denunciations

In Seventeenth Street, more than 5,000 persons assembled for "a prayer meeting" for the Rosenbergs heard President Eisenhower denounced as "bloodthirsty."

He was linked with Attorney General Herbert Brownell, Jr. and Senator Joseph R. McCarthy, Republican of Wisconsin, and Senator William E. Jenner, Republican of Indiana, in "a plot" to destroy the rights and liberties of the American people.

A premature announcement at P. M. that the Rosenbergs had been put to death created such a wave of hysteria at the

Continued on Page 5, Column 5

IN HAWAII GUILTY OF RED CONSPIRACY

Director of Bridges' Union and Six Others Convicted of Violating the Smith Act

Special to The New York Times.

HONOLULU, June 19—A Federal jury today found Jack W. Hall, regional director in Hawaii for the International Longshoremen's and Warehousemen's Union and six other defendants guilty of a Communist conspiracy to teach and advocate the overthrow of the United States Government by force and violence.

Immediately after the verdict, stevedores halted work on all island docks in the possible forerunner of a general strike. The United Press reported Hall's verdict was announced. Hall's union suspended negotiations on a new contract and longshoremen began walking off the job at Castle and Cook Pier 32. By 5:30 P. M., Hawaii time, all Honolulu docks were abandoned and stevedores had walked off the only two ships in the port of Hilo on the island of Hawaii.]

The all-male, multi-racial jury returned its verdict shortly before (7 P. M., Eastern daylight time) after having deliberated for sixteen hours. Six men defendants clad in sports or aloha shirts and one woman heard the verdict read without any show of emotion as they stood behind the defense counsel's table.

A defense request for a poll of the jury revealed that the verdict was unanimous in each case.

The defense attorney, Richard

Continued on Page 6, Column 3

PAIR SILENT TO END

Husband Is First to Die —Both Composed on Going to Chair

By WILLIAM R. CONKLIN
Special to The New York Times.

OSSINING, N. Y., June 19—Stoic and tight-lipped to the end, Julius and Ethel Rosenberg paid the death penalty tonight in the electric chair at Sing Sing Prison for their war-time atomic espionage for Soviet Russia.

The pair, first husband and wife to pay the supreme penalty here, and the first in the United States to die for espionage, went to their deaths with a composure that astonished the witnesses.

Julius, 35 years old, was first to enter the glaringly lighted, white-walled death chamber. He walked slowly behind Rabbi Irving Koslowe, a chaplain at Sing Sing, who was intoning the Twenty-third Psalm, "The Lord is my shepherd, I shall not want." As Rosenberg neared the brown-stained oak chair he seemed to sway from side to side.

Guards quickly placed him in the chair. He was clean-shaven, no longer wearing his mustache, and wore a white T-shirt. At 8:04 o'clock the first shock of 2,000 volts, with its ten amperes, coursed through his body. After two subsequent shocks his life ended at 8:06½ P. M.

Dr. H. W. Kipp and Dr. George McCracken applied stethoscopes to his chest, and Dr. Kipp said: "I pronounce this man dead."

Wife Kisses Matron

Ethel Rosenberg, the 37-year-old wife, entered the death chamber a few minutes after the body of her husband had been removed. She wore a dark green print dress with white polka dots, and, like her husband, was shod in loafer-type cloth slippers. Her hair was closely cropped on top to permit contact of an electrode.

Just before she reached the chair the five-foot, 100-pound woman held out her hand to Mrs. Rosenberg drew her close and kissed her lightly on the cheek. Rabbi Koslowe, standing about ten feet from the chair, was intoning the Fifteenth and Thirty-first Psalms.

Mrs. Evans choked up at the final farewell and left the room quickly. Mrs. Lucy Many, a former matron who is now a prison telephone operator, also shook hands with the doomed woman.

Mrs. Rosenberg sat in the electric chair "with the most composed look you ever saw," one witness said.

She winced as the electrode came in contact with her head, but her arms remained relaxed under their binding straps. Silent, she waited while the guards dropped a leather mask over her face. To her right stood Joseph P. Francel, the state executioner, in an alcove.

The first of three successive shocks was applied at 8:11½ P. M. After the third shock the two doctors applied their stethoscopes and found she was still alive. After two more applications of the cur-

Continued on Page 5, Column 3

Professor Loses Fulbright Award After Wife Balks at Red Inquiry

By FREDERICK GRAHAM

A Fulbright award granted last April to Dr. Naphtali Lewis of Brooklyn College to study in Italy during the next academic year has been canceled by the State Department, Senator Joseph R. McCarthy, Republican of Wisconsin, said here yesterday.

"I think it [the cancellation] is an excellent idea," the Senator asserted at the end of a thirty-seven-minute hearing of the Senate Permanent subcommittee on Investigations into the background of litigations into the background of Dr. Lewis and his wife, Helen F. Lewis, who once held a teaching post at Brooklyn College.

The formal title of the Fulbright award is the United States Educational Exchange Award. The awards are granted to educators and students for study abroad under the Fulbright Act, which is sponsored by Senator J. William Fulbright, Democrat of Arkansas, who pioneered the program.

Senator McCarthy, who sat as a one-member subcommittee in the Federal Courthouse in Foley Square, said that the purpose of the inquiry was to learn whether Mrs. Lewis was now or ever had been a member of the Communist party.

Mrs. Lewis, "unable to elicit an answer on that score from Mrs. Lewis, Senator McCarthy asserted that her refusal to answer on the ground that it might tend to incriminate her was the same as saying that "I am a Communist."

Mrs. Lewis steadfastly refused to answer questions as to whether she had held Communist cell meet-

Continued on Page 5, Column 1

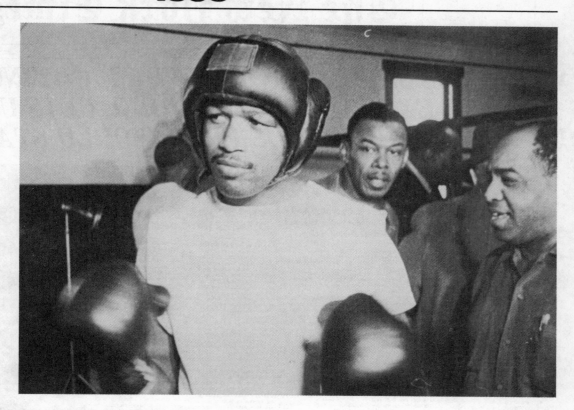

One of the boxing greats of the
Fifties, Sugar Ray Robinson.

Maureen Connolly of the United States winning
her grand slam. She was the first woman to win,
with victories in the French, Australian, English
and U.S. singles championships in the same year.

"All the News
That's Fit to Print"

The New York Times.

LATE CITY EDITION
Warm, humid, showers likely late today. Fair, not so warm tomorrow.
Temperature Range Today—Max., 88; Min., 68
Temperatures Yesterday—Max., 79; Min., 62
Full U. S. Weather Bureau Report, Page 16

Copyright, 1953, by The New York Times Company

VOL. CII..No. 34,883.   Entered as Second-Class Matter. Post Office, New York, N. Y.   NEW YORK, MONDAY, JULY 27, 1953.   Times Square, New York, N. Y. Telephone Lackawanna 4-1000   FIVE CENTS

TRUCE IS SIGNED, ENDING THE FIGHTING IN KOREA; P.O.W. EXCHANGE NEAR; RHEE GETS U. S. PLEDGE; EISENHOWER BIDS FREE WORLD STAY VIGILANT

GEROSA AND STARK PICKED BY WAGNER TO COMPLETE SLATE

Bronx Contractor to Run for Controller, Brooklyn Clothier for Council President

DESAPIO PRAISES CHOICE

Tammany Head Sees Approval This Week by Party Leaders Opposed to Impellitteri

By PAUL CROWELL

Lawrence E. Gerosa, a Bronx contractor, and Abe Stark, a Brooklyn merchant, were selected as running mates yesterday by Manhattan Borough President Robert F. Wagner Jr., who was chosen last week by the Democratic organizations of Bronx and New York Counties as their candidate for Mayor.

Mr. Gerosa was named as a candidate for Controller and Mr. Stark for President of the City Council. The slate headed by Mr. Wagner will wage a primary contest against the ticket headed by Mayor Impellitteri, whose running mates are City Councilman Charles E. Keegan of the Bronx for Controller and Julius Helfand, assistant district attorney of Kings County, for Council President.

The Impellitteri-Keegan-Helfand ticket has the backing of the Democratic organizations of Brooklyn, Queens and Staten Island.

At the Biltmore Hotel Mr. Wagner said that Mr. Gerosa and Mr. Stark were his personal choices but that he expected the Bronx and Tammany Hall executive committees to approve them without hesitation.

Wagner Voices Confidence

"I was given a free hand in picking my running mates," Mr. Wagner said. "I chose them after consulting with representatives of civic organizations, labor and business and the Bronx and Manhattan county leadership.

"I am confident that the Bronx and New York County executive committees will approve my choices. Speaking for myself and my running mates I am sure that we will win the primary contest next September and go on to win the November election."

Carmine G. DeSapio, the leader of Tammany Hall, expressed confidence that the executive committees of the Bronx and Manhattan organizations would approve Mr. Wagner's selections at a meeting to be held early this week. He described Mr. Gerosa and Mr. Stark as "outstanding representative business men who will make a great contribution to public service."

Mr. Gerosa, who was born in Milan, Italy, Aug. 10, 1894, lives at 615 West 252d Street in the Riverdale section. He is married and has three children.

He was designated in 1945 by four of the five Democratic county leaders as a candidate for Controller on a ticket headed by former Mayor William O'Dwyer, but withdrew in favor of Lazarus Jo-

Continued on Page 20, Column 4

Clark Ready to Start Release Of Red Captives in Few Days

But Allied Commander Says It May Be Two or Three Weeks Before Americans Freed by the Communists Arrive in U. S.

By JAMES RESTON
Special to The New York Times.

SOMEWHERE IN KOREA, July 26—Gen. Mark W. Clark said tonight he was prepared to start shipping Communist prisoners of war to North Korea and Communist China within a "few days," but he thought it would be two or three weeks before American prisoners would reach the United States.

The United Nations commander told several reporters aboard his plane en route to the signing of the truce agreement at Munsan, Korea, that while the Communists had comparatively few prisoners to send back, United Nations procedures for handling captives were undoubtedly faster.

The United Nations Command now holds 68,000 Communists and about 5,000 Chinese Communists who want to return to their native lands, and 8,000 North Koreans and about 15,000 Chinese Commu-

nists who have refused to return home.

In contrast, the Communists hold only 12,000 United Nations prisoners, of whom 3,000 are Americans.

Nevertheless, General Clark said, he thought it would be unwise for the Americans to expect that United States prisoners would be sent back as fast as the United Nations Command would return the Communists.

He said he expected the Communists to return the American captives at the rate of about fifty daily, while the Allies were in position to return as many as 2,500 Communists every day.

In accordance with plans that are now ready, General Clark asserted, the Communist captives would be put aboard small naval

Continued on Page 9, Column 2

Accord on plans for prisoners of war is on Page 7.

Eisenhower Accepts Aid Cut; Drive to Adjourn Advances

Special to The New York Times.

WASHINGTON, July 26—The drive for adjournment of Congress by Saturday appeared more certain of success today as the Eisenhower Administration privately indicated it could operate under the $4,562,664,000 foreign aid fund bill approved yesterday by the Senate Appropriations Committee.

The Administration decision, already conveyed to Senate leaders, was said to represent an understanding, reluctantly reached, that little improvement could be hoped for on the committee action, which restored half the $1,115,050,000 reduction made last week in the House of Representatives.

The Administration leaders in the Senate are being asked to do no more than "hold the line" when it comes to the floor for debate, and possibly a vote, on Wednesday.

For the record, the Administration still sought passage before adjournment of the postal rate increase bill, designed to produce an additional $240,500,000 in revenue, but the pressure for the proposal did not seem very great.

Summerfield Is Doubtful

Postmaster General Arthur E. Summerfield, guest on the National Broadcasting Company's "Meet the Press" television interview, said tonight he thought Congress should stay in session to pass the bill but conceded he did not know whether it would.

"I know they've had a busy six months," he said.

The House Post Office and Civil Service Committee, which has been conducting hearings for two weeks, has given no indication when a postal bill will be reported. The House leadership tentatively has scheduled the measure for midweek consideration on the floor. There have been no Senate hearings.

With debate beginning tomorrow, quick Senate approval was forecast for a compromise bill providing for the admission to this country over the next three years of 209,000 refugees, many of them from lands now behind the Iron Curtain. The Administration originally had proposed permitting the entry of 240,000 above-quota immigrants in two years.

The compromise figure, worked out with Senator Pat McCarran, Democrat of Nevada, who will continue to oppose the legislation but will not obstruct its passage, falls below the 220,000 admissions in three years approved by the Senate Judiciary Committee.

House Votes Wednesday

The House will vote Wednesday on its version of the bill in which 240,000 refugees would be admitted over a three-year period. Conferees later will agree to a median figure on entries.

Apart from conference reports, which will be coming up for votes daily, the refugee bill is the last major piece of legislation awaiting

Continued on Page 13, Column 2

55 REPORTED KILLED IN CUBAN REBELLION

Batista Voids Constitutional Guarantees, Hits Partisans of Ex-President Prio

By R. HART PHILLIPS
Special to The New York Times.

HAVANA, July 26—Fifty-five persons were reported killed and many more wounded in a rebellion today at Santiago de Cuba and near-by Bayamo. Martial law was imposed in Santiago following the uprising and military authorities began to round up members of revolutionary groups.

President Fulgencio Batista and his Cabinet in a special session tonight suspended constitutional guarantees for a period of ninety days, according to an official note from the Presidential Palace. The action was taken to enable the Government to cope with revolutionary activities following the revolt earlier in the day.

"Mercenaries in the service of those who became rich during the regime of Ex-President Prio," Carlos Prio Socarras], in conjunction with Communist elements" were accused of the attacks on the military posts at Santiago and Bayamo in a joint statement signed by the Ministers.

Continued on Page 11, Column 2

Arizona Raids Polygamous Cult; Seeks to Wipe Out Its Community

By GLADWIN HILL
Special to The New York Times.

SHORT CREEK, Ariz., July 26—A world by the towering cliffs and arid gorges of Arizona's wild and usual proclamation of insurrection, inaccessible "Strip" between the led the state's northern border at Grand Canyon and the Utah bordawn today and placed virtually der, members of the cult, organthe entire adult population under ized on a communal economic arrest in an effort to wipe out the basis, allegedly have been maintnation's last remaining center of taining as many as a half-dozen organized polygamy. wives and thirty children, and have fostered child marriages.

The defendants, thirty-six men and eighty-six women, constituted the principal membership of a professed Fundamentalist sect — disowned by the Church of Jesus Christ of Latter Day Saints (Mormon) in 1939—that has continued to practice the plural marriage renounced by the Mormon church in 1890.

In addition to 122 adults and child brides named in warrants held by a raiding force of 120 peace officers, the colony included some 263 children.

The state's avowed objective is to wipe out the community, imprison the adult ringleaders, and find new homes and lives for the children and for the numerous

Separated from the outside Continued on Page 36, Column 1

TALK CONDITION SET

U.S. to Boycott Political Parleys After 90 Days if It Finds Foe Stalls

By W. H. LAWRENCE

WASHINGTON, July 26—The United States has agreed to join South Korea in walking out of the projected Korean political conference ninety days after it begins if this Government is convinced that the Communists are not negotiating in good faith and that further sessions would be futile.

But this Government has not promised to resume hostilities in Korea at that time, nor has it promised to give South Korea any moral or material support if that Government carries out its threat to attempt to unify divided Korea by military force.

The conditional pledge to quit the Korean political conference after ninety days—if this Government believes it is futile — has been given to Dr. Syngman Rhee, South Korean President, who has already announced publicly that his agreement to cooperate in the armistice extends to only ninety days after the political conference convenes. Under the truce terms the conference will convene within ninety days after the signing of the armistice.

The Communists have not been told heretofore of this American intention to quit the political talks in any specified period if they seem to this Government to be fruitless. The United States continues to insist that the political talks would not violate the armistice.

U. S. to Make Decision

This Government is not committed to walk out of the peace talks simply if Dr. Rhee and the South Koreans walk out. The United States will make its own decisions as to whether the political negotiations are being carried on good faith.

There is not, so far as is known, any agreement by the other principal members of the United Nations to walk out at the same time that the United States might decide to leave the conference.

Observers here did not feel that the assurances given to Dr. Rhee were necessarily in conflict with the guarantee given the Communists by Lieut. Gen. William K. Harrison Jr., chief United Nations negotiator, that there would be no penalties attached to a walkout by either the United States or the Allies to continue negotiations if it

Continued on Page 3, Column 2

PRESIDENT IS HAPPY

But Warns in Broadcast That Global Peace Is Yet to Be Achieved

Special to The New York Times.

WASHINGTON, July 26—President Eisenhower greeted the news of the Korean armistice tonight with prayers of thanksgiving but warned the nation that the Allies had won an armistice only on a single battleground and had not achieved peace in the world.

The President spoke over radio and television networks about an hour after the official cease-fire documents had been signed.

General Eisenhower said the United States and all the free world must not relax its guard, or fail to be vigilant against "the possibility of untoward developments."

After the President had spoken, Charles E. Wilson, Secretary of Defense, issued a statement warning against any relaxation in the country's defense program because of the truce. He advised, too, that it would be a "long time" before American troops could be withdrawn from Korea "with safety."

"We must not be misled into the same demobilization which followed World Wars I and II," he said. "Such a demobilization would inevitably again tempt an aggressor."

Dulles Sees U. N. Victory

John Foster Dulles, Secretary of State, described the armistice as a great victory for the United Nations because "for the first time in history an international organization had stood against an aggressor and was marshaled force to meet force."

President Eisenhower spoke from the White House, across Pennsylvania Avenue and about a block east from Blair House, where President Truman decided thirty-seven months ago to commit United States forces to the defense of South Korea, then being overrun by the Communist armies from the north.

The President said he hoped that the coming of peace to Korea would at last convince all nations of the wisdom of composing their differences by negotiation before—rather than after "various resorts to brutal and futile battle."

He closed his brief speech by quoting from the final paragraph of Lincoln's Second Inaugural Address, which he said expressed the resolution and dedication of all Americans, now as in 1865.

These were Lincoln's words: "With malice toward none, with

Continued on Page 4, Column 2

REPORTS ON TRUCE: President Eisenhower making nationwide television broadcast from the White House last night.
The New York Times (by Fred J. Sass)

DEFENSE CHIEFS SEE BILLION CUT IN ARMS

Wilson Tells Quantico Parley Our Gain in Might Makes Any Attack on Us 'Foolhardy'

By AUSTIN STEVENS
Special to The New York Times.

QUANTICO, Va., July 26—Defense officials attending the high-level defense conference at the Marine Corps base here predicted today that with any kind of "decent" Korean truce defense spending could be trimmed by as much as $1,000,000,000 in the next twelve months.

Secretary of Defense Charles E. Wilson told the conference that "we have attained a strength which should make any attack upon us foolhardy in the extreme, and we are increasing our strength daily."

The previously stated defense spending figure for the fiscal year that started July 1 was $43,200,-000,000. Official announcement was made two days ago that W. J. McNeil, Assistant Secretary of Defense in charge of the budget, had told the conference, which included high military leaders, that the defense reductions would not be greater than $1,000,000,000 this year because so many fixed costs would continue.

The immediate economies would come in ammunition, trucks and other "consumption items" of war. Over-all military manpower gradually would be cut back from the present 3,500,000 by 200,000, perhaps more. One item mentioned today as an example was the full sight of fighting in the thirty-seven-month-old Korean war. Only a few hours before the armistice was signed at Panmunjom.

An estimated two enemy communist masses smashed into United Nations lines at the bend of the Kumsong River on the central front. South Korean forces fought the Reds hand-to-hand for more than an hour.

Allied troops all along the 155-mile line across the peninsula were ordered to hold casualties to a minimum and not to pick fights with the Reds.

The Allied orders were issued as Chinese Red shock troops just before dawn attacked United States Marines on a western front outpost for the fourth consecutive day. The Reds hit the hillpost positions northeast of Panmunjom in forces up to 200 men.

First Marine Division officers said the first wave of the attack was turned off without casualties among the Americans. The marine

Continued on Page 2, Column 1

MARINES STOP REDS IN LAST-HOUR FIGHT

Chinese Foe's Dawn Attacks Hit U. S. Units on West and South Koreans in Center

By The United Press

TOKYO, Monday, July 27—Chinese Communist troops threw "last hour propaganda" attacks at Allied forces on the central and western fronts of the rain-swept Korean battle line today, only a few hours before the armistice was signed at Panmunjom.

Continued on Page 2, Column 5

CEREMONY IS BRIEF

Halt in 3-Year Conflict for a Political Parley Due at 9 A. M. Today

Armistice text, on Pages 6, 7; Clark and Taylor statements, 9.

By LINDESAY PARROTT

TOKYO, Monday, July 27—Communist and United Nations delegates in Panmunjom signed an armistice at 10:01 A. M. today [9:01 P.M., Sunday, Eastern daylight time]. Under the truce terms, hostilities in the three-year-old Korean war are to cease at 10 o'clock tonight [9 A. M., Monday, Eastern daylight time].

[President Syngman Rhee of South Korea promised in a statement at Seoul Monday to observe the armistice "for a limited time" while a political conference tried to unify Korea by peaceful means, The United Press said.]

The historic document was signed in a roadside hall the Communists built specially for the occasion. The ceremony, attended by representatives of sixteen members of the United Nations, took precisely eleven minutes. Then the respective delegations walked from the meeting place without a word or handshake between them.

The matter-of-fact procedure underlined what spokesmen of both sides emphasized: That though the shooting would cease within twelve hours after the signing, only an uneasy armed truce and political difficulties, perhaps even greater than those of the armistice negotiations, lay ahead.

Signers Are Expressionless

The representatives of the two sides were expressionless as they put their names to a pile of documents, providing for an exchange of prisoners, establishment of a neutral zone for the cease-fire and later political conference that would attempt to settle the tragic Korean questions, unsolved by three years of fighting that caused hundreds of thousands of casualties.

According to the latest figures, revealed July 21 by the Department of Defense, the United States has suffered a total of 139,272 casualties. This included 24,965 dead, 101,368 wounded, 2,938 captured, 8,476 missing and 1,525 previously reported captured or missing, but since returned to military control.

Early this afternoon the Allied part in conclusion of the armistice agreement was completed at advance headquarters near Munsan, where Gen. Mark W. Clark, United Nations commander, put his name to the documents previously signed at Panmunjom.

General Clark signed in the presence of some of his high-ranking officers, Vice Admiral Robert P. Briscoe, commander of the naval forces in the Far East; Gen. Otto P. Weyland, head of the Far East Air Forces; Gen. Maxwell D. Taylor, Eighth Army commander; Lieut. Gen. Samuel Anderson of the Fifth Air Force, and Vice Admiral J. J. Clark, heading the Seventh Fleet.

Also present at Munsan was

Continued on Page 2, Column 5

U.N. Assembly Meets Aug. 17 To Plan Post-Truce Parley

Special to The New York Times.

UNITED NATIONS, N. Y., July 26—Promptly upon receiving formal notification of the signing of the Korean armistice, Lester B. Pearson of Canada, President of the General Assembly, issued a call tonight to member delegations for resumption on Aug. 17 of the suspended seventh Assembly session. The Assembly will consider details of the Far Eastern political conference scheduled to take place within ninety days of the signing of the truce agreement.

Official notification that the truce agreement had been signed was given orally to Secretary General Dag Hammarskjold and to Mr. Pearson by the permanent representative of the United States, former Senator Henry Cabot Lodge Jr., in the same committee room at headquarters here in which the Political and Security Committee held its lengthy debate on the Korean question some months ago.

Mr. Lodge then handed to the committee room, which, followed at 2200 hours [10 P. M.], July 27, 1953, Korean time. [The actual signing was at 10:01 A. M. Sunday, Eastern daylight time, or 9:01 P. M. Sunday, Eastern daylight time.]

"A report of the Unified Command transmitting the official text of the armistice agreement will be sent to you shortly."

Telegrams to the delegates, which had been prepared earlier, were dispatched to the delegations summoning them to report for the reconvened session in mid-August.

In a joint broadcast from the committee room, which, followed Washington, all three of the United Nations principals repeated for radio and television audiences statements issued earlier.

"The whole world is thankful that the negotiation at Panmunjom have brought the fighting in Korea to an end by the signature of an armistice agreement," Mr.

United Nations Command and the commanders of the Communist forces in Korea, i. e., the Korean People's Army and the Chinese People's Volunteers. The agreement was signed for the United Nations Command at 1000 hours [10 A. M.] July 27, 1953, Korean time, and becomes effective at 2200 hours [10 P. M.], July 27, 1953, Korean time. [The actual signing was at 10:01 A. M. Korean time, or 9:01 P. M. Sunday, Eastern daylight time.]

Official notification that the truce agreement had been signed was given orally to Secretary General Dag Hammarskjold and to Mr. Pearson by the permanent representative of the United States, former Senator Henry Cabot Lodge Jr., in the same committee room at headquarters here in which the Political and Security Committee held its lengthy debate on the Korean question some months ago.

"I have the honor to inform you that an armistice agreement has been entered into between the

Continued on Page 4, Column 5

Skeptical G. I.'s Finally Convinced; Most Take News With Little Elation

By GREG MacGREGOR

SEOUL, Korea, July 26 — Today, on the eve of the armistice, front-line G. I.'s faced their last full sight of fighting in the thirty-seven-month-old Korean war. Only a few minor clashes had taken place by early morning, and from all indications the war would be unofficially ended by dawn. No patrols were scheduled for tomorrow.

As news of the armistice filtered down to the men at the front, it left an atmosphere of mingled disbelief and temporary confusion in its wake. In many cases the soldiers flatly refused to accept the word of their own officers and noncommissioned officers. The men had so many disappointments over cease-fire reports in the past that they were slow to accept the truth.

"It will never happen," a Marine private manning the line on the central front said with a laugh when his sergeant told him the war would end tomorrow.

Not until the Armed Forces Radio broadcast was picked up at 6 P. M. tonight by portable receivers along the front were the men willing to believe the news. Then the announcer's words struck like a bolt of lightning.

Some G. I.'s stared dumbly at each other and others broke out in howls.

"Didja hear that—didja hear that?" one man kept shouting over and over as he ran from foxhole to foxhole.

"Wait'll they sign it—who knows what's going to happen?" a skeptic

Continued on Page 2, Column 7

1953

Milton Berle on The Texaco Star Theater. *He became known as "Mr. Television" since he had viewers glued to their sets every Tuesday at 8 P.M.*

Sid Caesar and Howard Morris watch as Carl Reiner destroys Caesar's bugle in their satire of From Here To Eternity, *on the Saturday night favorite,* Your Show of Shows.

Here are Howard Morris, Carl Reiner, and Sid Caesar in their take-off of Shane, "Strange."

The Lone Ranger, *starring Clayton Moore with Jay Silverheels as Tonto, was a favorite with youngsters.*

The stars of The Howdy Doody Show, *which ran from 1947 to 1960, were Howdy Doody himself, Clarabelle and Buffalo Bob Smith.*

TV's "Miss Frances," a Chicago teacher, made small children happy on Ding-Dong School.

Science Fiction, always a cult reading craze, was translated into TV programs like Captain Video, *featuring bizarre adventures.*

William Faulkner was the 4th U.S. author to win the Nobel Prize.

Senator John Kennedy's wedding to Jacqueline Bouvier. Robert Kennedy is at left.

Legendary writer Ernest Hemingway won a well-deserved Pulitzer Prize for his The Old Man and the Sea.

The New York Times.

LATE CITY EDITION
Scattered showers today; clearing
tonight. Fair, pleasant tomorrow.
Temperature Range Today—Max., 78; Min., 67
Temperature Yesterday—Max., 79; Min., 63
Full U. S. Weather Bureau Report, Page 78

Section
1

VOL. CII..No. 34,896.　Entered as Second-Class Matter, Post Office, New York, N. Y.　NEW YORK, SUNDAY, AUGUST 9, 1953.　Including Magazine and Book Review.　TWENTY CENTS New York City / Elsewhere In Mile Zone / Twenty-five Cents

Copyright, 1953, by The New York Times Company

'SHOCKING' WASTE IS FOUND IN UPKEEP OF CITY'S PROPERTY

Despite Vast Plant Valued at 12 Billion, No Inventory of Entire Assets Is Kept

DEBT SERVICE EXPENSIVE

Wide Survey Pieces Together Information to View the Municipality as a Whole

This is the first of six articles on the subject of this city's vast physical plant, its maintenance and plans for its future expansion.

By PETER KIHSS

New York City owns a physical plant worth more than $12,000,000,000 and perhaps as much as $14,500,000,000. It would cost at least that much to replace the schools, parks, transit, public housing, sewers, bridges and other properties built up over 300 years of history by the municipal corporation for the city's 8,130,000 inhabitants.

The municipal plant involves virtually every phase of the people's lives, even to a laboratory being added this fall to help purify the air they breathe. It covers hospitals in which one of every six babies here is born, shelter the city provides directly for one of every thirty residents, and graves in which it buries one of every eight who die each year, the 10,000 poor and alone.

Every year, the city spends about $340,000,000 to build new additions to that investment, beyond the sums it takes to run the city government. (This year's operating budget is $1,529,000,000, but $440,890,000 of it goes for debt service and pensions.) Taking their replacement value, the assets entrusted to the city administration exceed those of any of the nation's private corporations.

A Study of Important Questions

How well are those properties being kept up? Are they filling the people's needs? Is the city planning and building toward a better future? Over the last two months THE NEW YORK TIMES has assigned a team of nineteen reporters to attempt to answer some of these questions. This is the first of a series of reports on their findings.

One of the city's difficulties may be, as the Mayor's Committee on Management Survey said last March 30, that "perhaps the city is so big and so sprawling that the citizens never see it all or know what is happening to city property."

The committee reported after three years of study that the city was "shockingly wasteful" in systematically neglecting maintenance. It declared also that this neglect was not a recent development and "reaches back for at least a generation." World War II interrupted much maintenance and costs have risen since then, in part because of inflation.

The city has found it difficult to get all the revenues desirable both within available taxing powers and the political realities. Budget pressures have complicated the judging of priorities and management.

From the point of building new plant, the city each year invests $200,000,000 in capital improvements paid for by the taxpayers at large, plus $30,000,000 in improvements assessed on local benefit areas.

In addition, the self-supporting

Continued on Page 32, Column 1

Major Sports News

BASEBALL

The Yankees, behind the brilliant pitching of Whitey Ford and Bob Kuzava, shut out the White Sox twice yesterday, 1—0 and 2—0, to increase their American League lead to eight games. Kuzava had a no-hitter until one out in the ninth inning of the second game when Bob Boyd, Chicago rookie, slammed a double.

The Dodgers beat the Redlegs, 7—4, and the Giants lost to the Cards, 3—3, in night games.

HORSE RACING

Grecian Queen, 9 to 10, won the $39,300 Monmouth Oaks, while Tom Fool outraced Combat Boots in the two-horse Whitney at Saratoga, where Wise Pop took the United States Hotel Stakes.

TENNIS

Rex Hartwig defeated Hamilton Richardson and Lewis Hoad turned back Ken Rosewall in the Eastern grass court tourney to set up an all-Australian final.

(Details in Section 5)

U. S. to Return Some Islands To Japanese, Dulles Discloses

But Makes Clear in Tokyo That Major Strategic Ones Will Be Kept

By JAMES RESTON
Special to THE NEW YORK TIMES.

TOKYO, Aug. 8—John Foster Dulles, United States Secretary of State, arrived in Japan today bearing gifts for the increasingly restive people of this country.

He announced this evening, shortly after his arrival from Korea, that the United States had decided to return to Japan a small group of islands between Kyushu, the southernmost of the four main Japanese islands, and Okinawa.

These islands, which the United States held under Article 3 of the Japanese Peace Treaty, are known as the Amami group—about ten very small islands with a population of 213,650 persons who have been going on periodic hunger strikes against the American occupation ever since the end of the war.

Mr. Dulles, in making his announcement at the foot of the stairs of the United States Embassy this evening, made it clear, however, that the United States

Continued on Page 3, Column 1

SOUTH KOREA
JAPAN
KYUSHU
East China Sea
Pacific Ocean
AMAMI — KIKAI
TOKUNO — ERABU
YORON
OKINAWA
KITA-DAITO
MINAMI-DAITO

The New York Times Aug. 9, 1953
Cross indicates affected islands

and was generally regarded as an attempt to relieve the opposition in Japan to the American occupation.

Mr. Dulles is expected to hold out the prospect of further returns of territory to Japan as an inducement to a more cooperative attitude by the Japanese people. The Government here welcomed today's announcement, and it was generally expected to strengthen the hand of Premier Shigeru Yoshida in Japanese internal politics.

The United States decision to hand back the islands was welcomed here in official quarters.

Foe Sends 112 G.I.'s Back; Reds' Women Stage Scenes

By LINDESAY PARROTT
Special to THE NEW YORK TIMES.

TOKYO, Sunday, Aug. 9—Communist women prisoners of the Korean war staged scenes of hysteria today when the United Nations Command sent them with their children across the armistice line at Panmunjom to homes behind the Iron Curtain.

[List of Americans released in Korea appears on Page 2.]

The women, mostly in their twenties, were nurses, wives and camp followers rounded up by Allied troops when the North Korean perimeter in 1950. Many had been almost three years in United Nations stockades.

This morning as United Nations ambulances delivered the first installment of female captives—473 North Koreans and one Chinese—at the exchange point, they screamed insults at the guards, shouted, cheered and waved homemade North Korean flags.

Today's exchange included 112 Americans, the largest group yet to be returned, and 250 South Koreans, twenty-one Britons, thirteen Turks, two Australians, a Canadian and a Filipino.

The first Americans returned today were mostly Negroes, as was the case yesterday. In contrast to the first groups repatriated they appeared in good health and good spirits.

[The Associated Press reported that Frank Noel, press photographer, was freed in Sunday's exchange at Panmunjom. He was returned with the last group of prisoners at 11 A. M., or 10 P. M. Saturday, Eastern daylight time.]

Just before they reached the reception center most of the girls threw away their personal effects and the comfort packages given them by Red Cross representatives

Continued on Page 2, Column 7

THREATS TO DESAPIO AND 3 AIDES BARED

Leaders Warned to Quit Posts in Tammany—His Friends Blame a Big Gangster

By JAMES A. HAGERTY

Carmine G. DeSapio, who with Edward J. Flynn, Bronx leader and National Committeeman, is supporting Manhattan Borough President Robert F. Wagner Jr. for the Democratic nomination for Mayor, has received repeated threats of injury to himself and his family unless he resigns at once as leader of Tammany.

THE NEW YORK TIMES learned this yesterday on unquestioned authority. It also has been informed that Mr. DeSapio will not resign.

Three Tammany Assembly district leaders who stand with Mr. DeSapio in supporting Mr. Wagner for the Mayoralty nomination have received similar threats.

The threats to Mr. DeSapio have been received by telephone at his home and at his office and by letter addressed to his home. He also has been accosted at least twice on the street by well dressed men, unknown to him, who told him to quit as leader "or else."

No Active Politician Accused

There is no charge that any of the political figures known to be supporting Mayor Impellitteri against Mr. Wagner for the nomination for Mayor have any connection with the threats.

It is obvious, however, that any change in the Tammany leadership before the primary election on Sept. 15, either by Mr. DeSapio's resignation or his ouster by the Tammany executive committee, would increase the chance of Mayor Impellitteri's carrying Manhattan to such an extent that his nomination would seem probable. When questioned about the matter, Mr. DeSapio did not deny the receipt of threats but declined further comment.

Friends expressed the opinion that the threats did not come from a demented person or persons but from agents of the underworld, probably directed by a leading gangster who, unlike Frank Costello, Joe Adonis and Frank Erickson, has been able to escape a jail sentence as the result of recent crime investigations.

First Threat by Phone July 22

It is the firm conviction of Mr. DeSapio's supporters that the "mob" has moved in to attempt to oust him as the leader of Tammany. Members of the pro-Impellitteri group of Tammany district leaders made known on Friday that a petition was being circulated for a meeting of the Tammany executive committee in an effort to oust Mr. DeSapio as leader and that they agreed his removal this week. Mr. DeSapio's friends believe that the purpose of the threats to the three district leaders was to frighten them into "running out" on Mr. DeSapio and

Continued on Page 55, Column 3

Eisenhowers Fly to Colorado and Start Vacation

President and Mrs. Eisenhower just before boarding President's plane

Special to THE NEW YORK TIMES.

WASHINGTON, Aug. 8—President Eisenhower left Washington today at 12:13 P. M., Eastern daylight time, aboard his private plane the Columbine for a Colorado vacation expected to last three to four weeks. The

plane landed safely at Denver at 7 P.M. Accompanying the President were Mrs. Eisenhower and a small staff of military and civilian aides. The party landed at Lowry Air Force Base, outside of Denver, where the temporary White House will be

situated and the President will keep short office hours. The Eisenhowers will spend most of their vacation at the Denver home of Mrs. John S. Doud, Mrs. Eisenhower's mother. The President

Continued on Page 44, Column 1

U. S. WARNS ENEMY NOT TO RETAIN ANY OF KOREA CAPTIVES

Insists Jailed Men and Those Said to Refuse Repatriation Must Go to Neutral Body

Special to THE NEW YORK TIMES.

WASHINGTON, Aug. 8—The State Department warned Communist forces in Korea today that it would recognize no exceptions to the armistice rule that prisoners unwilling to be repatriated must be given into the custody of the Neutral Nations Repatriation Commission, where they can talk with United Nations officials. By "all" the department made it clear that it meant any prisoners who had received jail sentences while in custody.

The department, in a statement issued by Acting Secretary Walter Bedell Smith, expressed "great concern" over reports that the Communists did not intend to return all prisoners captured in the Korean fighting.

Appropriate steps to insure the enforcement of provisions of the armistice requiring that all prisoners reported as not desiring repatriation be turned over to the commission, which is made up of representatives from neutral nations, are to be taken "just as soon as definite facts are established," the department said.

Officials said that no accurate figures were available on the number of United Nations prisoners who did not wish to leave Red hands, or on the number of prisoners serving jail sentences behind the Communist lines.

Dulles and U. N. Aides Confer

Spokesmen for the State Department said that Secretary of State John Foster Dulles and United Nations officials in Seoul had discussed the possibility of the Communists' withholding some Allied prisoners.

At a news conference at the Pentagon Thursday, Gen. Mark W. Clark, United Nations Far East Commander, declared that he favored having this country use "any and every" weapon at its disposal, including the atomic bomb, should the Communists break the Korean truce.

General Clark emphasized that the Eighth Army would be kept in combat readiness, as would the Air Force and Navy units in Korea. He

Continued on Page 5, Column 3

MALENKOV CLAIMS THE HYDROGEN BOMB; DECLARES MONOPOLY OF U. S. IS BROKEN; LEADERS IN WASHINGTON ARE SKEPTICAL

EISENHOWER SILENT

But Aides Say Detonation of Weapon Would Have Been Detected Here

Special to THE NEW YORK TIMES.

WASHINGTON, Aug. 8—Premier Georgi M. Malenkov's announcement that the Soviet Union had mastered production of the hydrogen bomb was received calmly and with some skepticism here today.

Officially, there was neither confirmation nor denial of the Soviet leader's claim that the United States had "no monopoly" in production of the dread weapon. Its authenticity was strongly questioned, however, by persons in close touch with atomic energy matters.

Lewis L. Strauss, chairman of the Atomic Energy Commission, issued the following statement:

"We have never assumed that it was beyond the capabilities of the Russians to produce such a weapon, and that is the reason why more than three years ago it was decided to press forward with this development for ourselves."

Commission spokesmen refused to amplify the chairman's comment, and he was not available for questions.

Some See Exaggeration

President Eisenhower received word of Mr. Malenkov's speech before leaving for a Colorado vacation but had nothing to say.

Other well-equipped governmental sources voiced belief that the Soviet Premier, if not falsifying for propaganda purposes, was at least exaggerating the extent of progress made by Soviet scientists in the thermo-nuclear field.

The Soviet Union, it was said, could not possibly have detonated a hydrogen device without detection by United States experts, and no such explosion had been detected as far as these informants knew. Without a test explosion, there would be no way for the Russians themselves to tell whether they had mastered the production problem.

The greatest skepticism was expressed by several members of the Joint Congressional Committee on Atomic Energy, which is usually kept informed on major developments.

At the same time, the committee members stressed that it had always been merely a matter of time until the Soviet Union would end the hydrogen-bomb monopoly of the United States. The only surprising element in the Malenkov claim, if true, would be the achievement of the goal in less than four years after the first atomic explosion in the Soviet Union.

Regardless of the truth or fal-

Continued on page 24, Column 2

U. N. Sees Added Urgency For Atomic Energy Control

Hammarskjold Says Talk of Mass Weapons Stresses Need to Find Plan—Vishinsky Is Scheduled to Arrive Tuesday

By A. M. ROSENTHAL
Special to THE NEW YORK TIMES.

UNITED NATIONS, N. Y., Aug. 8—The United Nations official reaction to the hydrogen bomb statement from Moscow today was that new urgency had been given to the need for agreement on international atomic energy control.

Dag Hammarskjold, Secretary General of the organization, summed up his thoughts in one sentence: "New statements concerning the development and possible use of weapons of mass destruction only stress the need for achieving, through the United Nations, practical and effective means of international control of such weapons."

It seemed clear that Mr. Hammarskjold had in mind not only the statements from Moscow but also talk about using the atomic bomb in case of a new Communist aggression in Korea. On Thursday Gen. Mark W. Clark, United Nations commander, was asked if

Continued on Page 26, Column 1

Fuchs Gave Soviet the Secret Of Hydrogen Bomb in 1944

By WILLIAM L. LAURENCE
Special to THE NEW YORK TIMES.

OSLO, Norway, Aug. 8—The announcement by Premier Georgi M. Malenkov today that the Soviet Union had mastered the production of the hydrogen bomb will come as no surprise to the inner circle of atomic scientists closely associated with the United States hydrogen bomb project.

They knew as far back as January, 1950, when it was announced that the atomic spy Klaus Fuchs, who was sentenced to fourteen years in prison by the British, had confessed to betraying all major United States nuclear secrets to the Soviet Union, that Fuchs had known not only the secrets of the hydrogen fusion bomb as well as the details of the ordinary atomic fission bomb in 1944.

However, until there is actual evidence that the Russians have tested their first hydrogen bomb, the United States also must take into consideration the strong possibility, in view of the vast technical problems involved, that the Malenkov statement is largely a propaganda bomb.

Bomb's Developer in Group

Fuchs, a German-born physicist, who had served as a member of the British scientific team that went to Los Alamos, N. M., to help in the development of the atomic bomb, was one of those admitted to the circle of theoretical physicists that served as the intellectual high command of the fantastic atomic bomb laboratory hidden among the canyons of the New Mexico desert.

That elite group was headed by Prof. Hans A. Bethe of Cornell University, one of the world's top experts on the nucleus of the atom, and included Prof. Edward Teller, now at the University of California, under whose direction the first hydrogen bomb was developed and tested successfully last November at Eniwetok.

The possibilities of the hydrogen bomb, originally known as the "super-super" or just the "super," already had been discussed and outlined in some technical detail as early as the spring of 1945, when the scientists were putting the finishing touches on the first atomic fission bomb made up of uranium 235 or plutonium.

It was realized at the time that the successful explosion of a uranium or plutonium bomb would create a temperature of some hundred million degrees Fahrenheit, hot enough to promote the fusion of the nuclei of heavy hydrogen atoms, thus producing an explosion potentially 1,000 times that of the fission bomb. The atomic bomb, at that time expected to yield an explosive force equal to about 20,000 tons of TNT, was discussed, even before it was completed, as a potential fuse for a much more powerful weapon.

Fuchs was fully trusted with the

Continued on Page 27, Column 5

FRENCH STRIKERS RETURNING TO JOBS

Move Eases Paralysis Though Many Dissidents Hold Out— Regime Bars Compromise

By HENRY GINIGER
Special to THE NEW YORK TIMES.

PARIS, Aug. 8—While Premier Joseph Laniel and his ministers met in almost continuous session today the tide of protest against the financial and economic decrees they are about to issue slackened considerably, though it was still strong.

Most of the 2,000,000 workers who participated in yesterday's strike, which crippled France's public services and nationalized industries, returned to their jobs at least ended their strikes and were expected to be back on Monday. Others were continuing the strike until tonight. Still others, principally the postal unions, vowed to continue the stoppage until "complete success" was won, which presumably meant the abandonment by the Government of its projects.

This, the Government was not prepared to do, nor would it even talk to the unions about their

Continued on Page 13, Column 1

Steel Pool Nations Agree on Need For European Political Community

By M. S. HANDLER
Special to THE NEW YORK TIMES.

BADEN - BADEN, Germany, Aug. 8—The six foreign ministers of the nations of the European Coal and Steel Community terminated their conference today after having unanimously agreed on the necessity of creating a European political community.

A conference communiqué announced that the ministers' deputies would meet in Rome Sept. 22 "to elaborate proposals with a view to holding a new conference of foreign ministers" in The Hague on Oct. 20. The deputies will be instructed to facilitate rapid negotiations for the establishment of a European political community.

The conference, which met under the chairmanship of Paolo Taviani, Minister of Foreign Trade in the outgoing Italian Government and representative of Premier Alcide De Gasperi, held two sessions totaling eight hours. This morning's talks

were devoted to a discussion of the international situation in the light of the results of the recent Washington conference of United States, British and French foreign ministers, but a considerable time was spent in preparing a conference communiqué for the press.

The exchange of views on the international situation revealed anew, according to Signor Taviani, what he called the complete solidarity prevailing in Western Europe since the Washington conference.

Georges Bidault, the French Foreign Minister; Dr. Konrad Adenauer, West German Chancellor and Foreign Minister; Paul Van Zeeland, Belgian Foreign Minister; Johan W. Beyen, Netherlands Foreign Minister, and Joseph Bech, Luxembourg Foreign Minister, who spoke briefly after the com-

Continued on Page 13, Column 1

RUSSIAN CONFIDENT

Sees No Cause for War, but Says Soviet Can Crush Any Attack

Excerpts from Malenkov's speech are printed on Page 29.

By HARRISON E. SALISBURY
Special to THE NEW YORK TIMES.

MOSCOW, Aug. 8—Premier Georgi M. Malenkov told 1,300 cheering members of the Supreme Soviet in the Great Hall of the Kremlin today that the United States no longer had a monopoly of the hydrogen bomb.

Mr. Malenkov said that when the United States long ago lost its monopoly of the atomic bomb it began to comfort itself by talking about a monopoly of the hydrogen bomb.

"This is not so," said Mr. Malenkov speaking in solemn tones. "The Government deems it necessary to report to the Supreme Soviet that the United States has no monopoly in the production of the hydrogen bomb either."

Mr. Malenkov had hardly uttered the words when the joint assembly of the Council of the Union and the Council of Nationalities of the Supreme Soviet broke into vigorous and prolonged applause.

No Reason for War Seen

Mr. Malenkov declared "no objective grounds" existed for war between the United States and the Soviet Union and repeated with emphasis his declaration of last March that the Soviet Union was prepared to settle all disputed questions with other states including the United States by peaceful means. The policy of settling international controversies by peaceful means, Mr. Malenkov emphasized, is a basic Soviet policy, not a mere tactical device.

At the same time he declared the Soviet defenses were powerful and the Soviet was prepared to deal a crushing blow to any aggressor that attacked it.

Mr. Malenkov offered no elaboration of his statement and the delegates did not seem to think any elaboration was necessary.

The hydrogen bomb declaration was the high spot on one of the most detailed surveys of domestic and foreign affairs to be given by a Soviet leader in many years. For two solid hours Mr. Malenkov addressed the delegates at this concluding session of the Supreme Soviet. He spent one hour reviewing the domestic situation and outlining a program for greatly increasing the output of consumers goods and ameliorating the living conditions of Soviet citizens. The second half of the address was devoted to a detailed and confident review of the world situation.

The United States Ambassador, Charles E. Bohlen, and other members of the diplomatic corps listened from the galleries as Mr. Malenkov spoke. Several Western diplomats characterized Mr. Malenkov's address as "confident" and "self assured." They said they did not regard it as aggressive or blustering but rather the words of a leader who felt he was speaking

Continued on Page 31, Column 1

The outsider Dark Star beat the favorite, Native Dancer, in the 1953 Kentucky Derby.

Ben Hogan, shown here during the 1953 British Open at Carnoustie, Scotland, won two consecutive U.S. Open championships in 1950-1951.

Mickey Mantle (No. 7) hit the 4th grand-slam homer in World Series history.

"All the News
That's Fit to Print"

The New York Times.

LATE CITY EDITION

Rain, strong winds today; clearing tonight. Fair tomorrow.

Temperature Range Today-Max., 79; Min., 71
Temperatures Yesterday-Max., 81.2; Min., 67
Full U. S. Weather Bureau Report, Page 31

VOL. CII. No. 34,925. Entered as Second-Class Matter. Post Office, New York, N. Y. NEW YORK, MONDAY, SEPTEMBER 7, 1953. Times Square, New York 36, N. Y. Telephone Lackawanna 4-1000 FIVE CENTS

HOUSE UNIT HEARS OF NAVY DATA'S USE IN '4 PERCENTER' BID

Eisenhower Inaugural Official Is Said to Have Quoted Classified Information

INQUIRY REPORT AWAITED

Warren L. Stephenson Named as Seeker of Commission on Rocket Launcher Business

By CLAYTON KNOWLES

Special to THE NEW YORK TIMES.

WASHINGTON, Sept. 6—The story of how an official of President Eisenhower's Inaugural Committee quoted classified Navy information in an attempt to set himself up as a business representative is under final study by an investigating committee of the House of Representatives.

There was no official release of the story or comment tonight, but a full report is expected soon, possibly this week.

House hearings into the situation, carrying the first suggestion of influence peddling since the new Administration took office, ended in July but it was said that both the Navy and the Federal Bureau of Investigation still were seeking to discover how the secret information leaked out of the Navy Department.

A source close to the investigation disclosed that Warren L. Stephenson, executive secretary of the Eisenhower Inaugural Committee, sought $2,000 a month or 4 per cent of any extra business he could obtain for Century Industries Inc. of Burbank, Calif., makers of a special type of rocket launcher.

Disclosure of bid figures and other information on a Navy contract for 120,000 aerial rocket launchers, the Navy told the House Armed Services investigating subcommittee, not only involved military security but also made it more difficult to negotiate fair contracts.

Represented Several Concerns

Mr. Stephenson, a key witness at two of the nine days of secret hearings, admitted using the Navy information after first having denied he had done so, informants said. These sources stated that he finally said that, without knowing the information was classified, he had used it on May 19 in a telephone conversation with officials of the California concern.

Committee sources said Mr. Stephenson, who was not available today for comment, represented several companies in Washington, including the Drayer-Hanson Manufacturing Company of Los Angeles. Local newspaper stories identify him also as chairman of the Taft Committee for the District of Columbia last year when the Ohio Senator, who since has died, was seeking the Republican Presidential nomination.

An investigation of influence peddling, undertaken in the Senate several years ago, pointed up the fact that, while acting as a business representative on a percentage basis was perfectly legal, the influence peddling that attended some operations was in a borderline shadow.

Jail sentences arising out of the investigation, at which William P. Rogers, now deputy attorney general, was committee counsel resulted mainly, however, from conflicting stories told by some while under oath.

Representative William E. Hess, Republican of Ohio, who heads the House investigation, was not

Continued on Page 12, Column 3

Farm Income Dips 6% As Prices Drop 10%

By The Associated Press.

WASHINGTON, Sept. 6—Farmers got 6 per cent less for what they sold in the first eight months of this year than in the same period of 1952, the Agriculture Department reported today.

Their cash receipts from marketings amounted to about $17,700,000,000 in the January-August period. Average prices were down about 10 per cent, but the volume of marketings was a little larger than a year ago and this kept the cash backslide at the 6 per cent level.

Receipts from livestock and livestock products brought farmers $11,000,000,000 in the first eight months this year, a decline of 7 per cent from last year. The drop in the average prices of cattle sent the income from meat animals to 13 per cent below last year's total.

Dairy receipts, meanwhile, dropped 5 per cent—the volume

Continued on Page 14, Column 5

Rain, Wind Due Here Today As Hurricane Drives North

Beach Residents on Eastern Long Island Told to Go Inland — Clearing Skies Expected to Greet Peak Holiday Traffic Tonight

Rain and strong winds, joint side products of a hurricane that has been sweeping up the Atlantic Coast, will buffet the New York area today as the massive two-way parade of home-bound holiday travelers into and out of New York winds up the long Labor Day week-end.

Early this morning, the Weather Bureau said the center of the "still dangerous" Hurricane Carol, the third of the current season, was about 225 miles south of Nantucket, Mass., and was beating north from Bermuda toward Maine at about eighteen miles an hour.

The bureau advised "maximum precautions" along the New England coast, said New York city would suffer rain and winds below thirty-five miles an hour but that gale force wind and rain would hit the eastern half of Long Island.

Forecasters said that while the hurricane's course was unpredictable, it was expected to continue its present path or swing away from the coast as Hurricane Barbara did two weeks ago. At most, the Weather Bureau said, only the fringe of the hurricane was expected to hit this area with rain "probably ending this afternoon."

The Coast Guard took no chances. From Bellport to Montauk Point, Coast Guardsmen warned persons to leave shoreside homes for safer points inland and sent trucks along the beaches of eastern Long Island to spread the alarm. It also asked local police to advise residents of the possible danger.

Rough seas surged over beaches, dunes and on to roads in three places east of Shinnecock Inlet at Hampton Bays and covered dunes around East Moriches.

The Coast Guard reported "numerous" calls from small boats in distress. Two Coast Guard vessels rescued the forty-two-foot cabin cruiser Gypsy after it sent a call for help off Hither Hills, nine miles west of Montauk Point.

The yacht Wings, owned and

Continued on Page 11, Column 1

Riegelman Pledges Fairness In Reforming Civil Service

By JOSEPH C. INGRAHAM

A labor policy based on a partnership between the city administration and the leadership of civil service organizations was pledged to the electorate yesterday by Harold Riegelman, Republican candidate for Mayor.

Defining his position on labor, Mr. Riegelman said that he would not play fast and loose with the rights and property of working men and women and that his plan to reorganize and strengthen civil service would be accomplished without loss of pay or job by any employe of the city.

Mr. Riegelman charged that the Impellitteri administration had been hampered in preserving industrial peace by "unholy alliances" and had been "hobbled by indefensible lack of awareness of those tensions likely to produce disastrous and explosive war between labor and management."

As the largest of employers, the city in its relations with its workers should set a pattern here and across the country, the Republican designee for Mayor declared. He said he proposed to accomplish this by showing proper respect for the leaders of civil service groups and demanding in turn that they respect his administration.

Such a partnership is practicable because it worked well when he was acting as Postmaster, Mr. Riegelman noted.

Robert F. Wagner Jr. devoted most of his Labor Day message to a bitter attack on Republican "anti-labor" tactics and linked Mayor Impellitteri, Mr. Wagner's principal opponent for the Democratic Mayoral nomination, with the advocates of "creeping Republicanism."

The Manhattan Borough President characterized Mr. Impellitteri as "the dumb but willing accomplice" of Governor Dewey and asserted that the Mayor was "the mortal enemy of every member of the labor movement in this city."

Mr. Wagner declared that the Republicans were whittling away all of the labor reforms achieved in twenty years of Democratic rule

Continued on Page 14, Column 3

CALIFORNIA SEEKS MORE 'WETBACKS'

Labor Shortage Is Threatened, Nixon Asked to Help Ease Curbs, Newspaper Says

Special to THE NEW YORK TIMES.

LOS ANGELES, Sept. 6—The Los Angeles Times said today that Vice President Richard M. Nixon was expected to discuss with the Department of Justice soon the possible tempering of the stepped-up campaign against illegal immigration from Mexico, in the interests of assuring Southern California farmers of a supply of labor.

In a dispatch from its Washington bureau, the newspaper reported that Representative John Phillips, Republican, had conferred Thursday with his fellow Californian "about the need for making some special arrangements to offset a threatened labor shortage resulting from over-zealous law enforcement by Immigration Bureau agents hastily transferred to the southland [Southern California]."

[Mr. Nixon was spending the week-end at Governor Dewey's home in Pawling and could not be reached for comment. Mr. Phillips had left Washington and also could not be reached.]

The dispatch did not represent Mr. Nixon as taking any position on the question, but said "the Vice President is expected to discuss this situation with Attorney General [Herbert] Brownell [Jr.] in a few days."

Plan to Increase Force

Mr. Brownell visited the border three weeks ago and called the illegal influx of Mexicans—now proceeding at a rate of a million a year—"shocking." After conferring with President Eisenhower, he announced the Administration would take immediate steps to stop it.

Last Friday an official of the Immigration and Naturalization Service announced that it was planned to increase the present force of 300 border patrol officers in the east and central Texas zone to 500. There are about 750 patrol officers for the entire 1,600-mile border extending from Brownsville, Texas to San Diego, Calif.

The Los Angeles Times Washington correspondent, Warren Francis, said reports had reached the capital that border patrol officers "have been staging raids—sometimes several times in a single day—on farms in the San Diego area and herding large numbers of Mexicans over the border immediately."

The illegal aliens are known as "wetbacks" because many swim or wade the Rio Grande to sneak into the United States. Their services are in constant demand among some southwestern farmers because, as fugitives from justice, the "wetbacks" have to work for whatever they can get. Often their weekly wages are zero after deductions for food and housing.

Reported shortages of labor in

Continued on Page 14, Column 6

Furillo and Durocher Stage Battle; Dodger Player Fractures Left Hand

By LOUIS EFFRAT

It's getting so that fans who turn out to see the Giants and the Dodgers are not certain whether it's for a ball game or a fight. At the Polo Grounds yesterday, the spectators were treated to both. The Dodgers won the game, 6—3, but the jury is still deliberating over who won the fight between Leo Durocher and Carl Furillo, who wound up with a broken bone in his left hand. Furillo, the National League's leading batter, with a .345 average, will be sidelined for ten days.

In full view of 25,331 persons, the Brooklyn right fielder, enraged because he had been hit on the right wrist by a ball pitched by Ruben Gomez in the second inning, left first base, charged toward the New York dugout and was met by Durocher. The pair tore into each other, grappled on the ground and immediately members of both clubs joined in the melee, most of them in roles of peace-makers. Monty Irvin and Jim Hearn of the Giants and Gil Hodges of the Brooks appeared to be the most prominent among those trying to restore order.

When finally this was accomplished, Furillo and Durocher were banished by the umpires. Don Thompson ran for Carl and later replaced him in the outfield. Herman Franks took over Leo's coaching position at third base.

This outbreak had been a long time brewing. The bad feeling between Furillo and the manager of the Giants started in 1949, when Furillo was hospitalized after being hit by a pitched ball by Sheldon Jones, then a New York hurler. Ever since, Furillo has blamed Durocher for that and other beanings and brushbacks.

The outfielder continued to point his finger at Durocher yesterday. In the clubhouse, Furillo insisted that the order to hit him came from the club manager. "I will get him," Carl said. "The first time I see him—the first time we come face to face—I will get him. He has crossed me once too often." He was referring to Durocher, of course.

The dispute started shortly after a single by Jackie Robinson and Roy Campanella's thirty-eighth

Continued on Page 22, Column 1

U. N. WILL DEMAND REDS EXPLAIN FATE OF MISSING TROOPS

Prepares Roster of Men Known to Have Been Held but Not Returned at Panmunjom

Special to THE NEW YORK TIMES.

TOKYO, Monday, Sept. 7—United Nations Command authorities prepared today to demand that Communist officials on the joint Military Armistice Commission explain the fate of Allied soldiers held by the enemy and not returned in the prisoner exchange completed yesterday.

United Nations representatives will submit a list of names of men known to have been held captive. The number involved has not been disclosed, but is believed to be substantial.

The list has been compiled gradually since the beginning of the Korean war by the Intelligence Section of United Nations Command headquarters. Propaganda broadcasts in which the Communists listed names of Allied personnel taken prisoner were a basic source of information, and others were letters from the men themselves and information supplied by other prisoners released by the Communists.

Typical of those believed on the United Nations roster is Capt. Harold Fisher, jet pilot and double ace, whom the Reds asserted they shot down over Manchuria early this year and took prisoner. Captain Fisher had been expected to be among the final men sent back yesterday.

The Communists have admitted holding only "more than twenty" non-Koreans in addition to those returned during the exchange. That group was said by the Communists to have rejected the opportunity to be released under the voluntary repatriation clause of the armistice agreement.

Red Denial Expected

It was presumed that the Communists would deny they hold any other prisoners. If they explain at all the list to be presented by the United Nations at Panmunjom it was believed they would say the men had died of wounds or, as propaganda broadcasts have hinted, that the men had been killed by Allied air attacks on prisoner-of-war camps.

On the final day of the exchange the Communists returned twenty-five Allied airmen who the Reds asserted had confessed waging germ warfare in Korea. Most of these prisoners declined to talk with reporters and a few were withheld from interviews on medical grounds. Those who talked related tales of extreme torture by the Communists to extract false confessions.

Communist radio stations at Peiping and Pyongyang devoted much time today to an explanation of the release of "germ war criminals." The propaganda broadcasts named the men and summarized their "crimes," quoting from their alleged confessions.

They said the general political bureau of the North Korean Army had investigated the case and had concluded that "by taking part in this crime these twenty-five men have brought upon themselves a grave case and should have been given due punishment."

However, the broadcasts continued, in view of the fact that the men were "acting under orders of their superiors and were not them-

Continued on Page 2, Column 3

TITO ASKS TRIESTE BE MADE FREE CITY WITHIN YUGOSLAVIA

Proposes International Regime for Port in Policy Statement Before Crowd of 200,000

By JACK RAYMOND

Special to THE NEW YORK TIMES.

OKROGLICA, Yugoslavia, Sept. 6—Marshal Tito, President of Yugoslavia, proposed today internationalizing the city of Trieste and awarding to Yugoslavia all the Free Territory of Trieste around the port city.

Although the proposal appeared by far the strongest and broadest demand ever seriously put forward by Yugoslavia, it was delivered in terms and circumstances intended to emphasize this Government's readiness to settle the tempestuous dispute with Italy over the Free Territory of Trieste.

Rejection by Italy was expected by observers here and the new proposal was regarded as a Yugoslav effort to stake out the largest possible claims for future bargaining purposes.

At present the port city is in Zone A of the Free Territory established under the Italian Peace Treaty and occupied by United States and British troops. The other part of the territory, Zone B, is occupied by Yugoslavia.

The setting for the long-heralded policy statement was the anniversary celebration here of Yugoslavia's annexation during the war of the former Italian-held Istrian region, including for a while Trieste itself.

Marshal Tito addressed a crowd estimated at 200,000 persons in an open hillside field, five miles from the present Italian border, reported to be bristling with Italian troops, tanks and guns.

Ridicules Italian Concern

Resplendent in a creamy white uniform, Marshal Tito ridiculed the anxiety of the Italian Government, which said it took precautionary measures against possible overt annexation of Zone B.

"Why should we want to annex Zone B, when we are there already?" Marshal Tito said.

Yugoslavia, said Marshal Tito, is interested not only in Zone B, but in both zones. Italy, he asserted, wants to occupy Zone A, but "we will not give up Zone A."

The Yugoslav President accused Giuseppe Pella, Premier of Italy, of creating a "circus by sending troops to the border." Signor Pella, he said, was "striking the air with his saber" and the Marshal asked why Italy was using arms granted by the Allies against Yugoslavia, which he described as "a pillar of peace."

Diplomatic channels had been open to the Italians, said Marshal Tito. The danger of Signor Pella's action, he continued, was that the troop concentrations might result in incidents. Yugoslavia has troops and weapons, too, said the Marshal, but is keeping them back and will call upon them only in a "moment of danger."

The Yugoslav leader, with a touch of scorn, asserted that Yugoslavia was ready to stand up against anyone who sought to "take one centimeter of our land" and that in the last war Yugoslavia had had only a few weapons in fighting against Fascist Italy, "but what we needed we took from them."

Recalls Fascist Atrocities

Putting on spectacles and referring to notes in an otherwise extemporaneous address, Marshal Tito read off a long citation of atrocities allegedly committed by Italian Fascist troops against the Slovenes in the Trieste region and in Istria. He cited charges against the Italians dating from 1920 and laid emphasis on what he felt was the contrast between Italy's elimination of Slovene schools and the Yugoslavs' maintaining of Italian schools for their minority.

The President several times referred to the "good Italian people." Yugoslavia "esteems" the Italian people, he said. The trouble with the Italians, he added, is that they "always have bad governments."

Marshal Tito's proposal for internationalizing Trieste came at the end of a sixty-five-minute speech that was marked on the part of his audience by the relative absence of the usual activity by claque and shouting his name in hero worship. There were no placards on the field, but those on the roads that led to the field stressed Yugoslav claims on Trieste and Gorizia as well as the challenge that this area would never again be Italian.

Italy's claims on Trieste, he said, derived from the Roman Empire. By that token, he said, they might as well include claims on France, Britain and Africa. The peace treaty solution that created the Free Territory is no longer accept-

Continued on Page 7, Column 2

ADENAUER WINS DECISIVELY; BONN TIE TO WEST ENDORSED IN ROUT OF 'NEUTRAL' PARTIES

Associated Press Radiophoto

THE INCUMBENT VOTES: West German Chancellor Konrad Adenauer, the Christian Democrat leader, casting his ballot.

SOCIALISTS TRAIL

Extreme Left and Right Groups Suffer Heavily in Vote Returns

By CLIFTON DANIEL

Special to THE NEW YORK TIMES.

BONN, Germany, Monday, Sept. 7—Western Germany gave a resounding vote of confidence in yesterday's general election to Chancellor Adenauer and his policy of close cooperation with the United States and the Atlantic community in the defense of the West.

A record turnout of voters in the Federal Republic returned the 77-year-old "Iron Man" to power with an increased majority in Parliament vastly strengthening his hand in international and home affairs.

It seemed that the impassive Dr. Adenauer, already known in Sir Winston Churchill's phrase as the greatest German statesman since Bismarck, would become the strongest chief of government in Western Europe.

[The United Press said Monday that final unofficial returns showed that Chancellor Adenauer's coalition parties had received 15,813,000 votes compared with 7,893,000 for the opposition Social Democrats.]

In the early light of the morning after the election unofficial calculations were being made in Bonn that the Chancellor's Christian Democratic Union might go into the second Parliament of the post-war republic with a clear majority of its own. In 1949 Dr. Adenauer had to seek the aid of two minor parties to gain a majority in the Bundestag, the lower house.

Allied Groups Lose

His two allies, the Free Democratic and German parties, appeared to have lost strength yesterday, but the three together substantially increased their majority.

By contrast, the Social Democratic party led by Erich Ollenhauer, which has always deplored Dr. Adenauer's emphasis on integrating Germany with the West and demanded that the reunification of the country should come first, dropped far behind the Chancellor's party. Its policy was clearly repudiated.

Out of the 242 Bundestag seats filled by direct election in the constituencies, Christian Democrats won 172, the Free Democrats fourteen, the German party ten and the Center party one. All those could be counted for Dr. Adenauer.

The Socialists captured only forty-five seats.

There were still 242 more seats to be allocated on the basis of proportional representation.

Each elector yesterday had two votes to cast—one for a candidate and one for a party on the basis of proportional representation.

Vote Results Given

When the second vote had been calculated in 220 of the 242 constituencies, according to D. P. A., the West German news agency, the vote was as follows in round figures:

Christian Democrats, 11,300,000; Social Democrats, 7,100,000; Free Democrats, 2,300,000, and German party, 804,000.

The rest of the votes were divided among lesser parties, the chief one being the All-German bloc, with 1,300,000.

All those parties that advocated neutrality for the Federal Republic or collaboration with the Communist world were routed by the Chancellor's Government coalition. Some of the smaller ones attracted so little support that they will lose all their seats in Parliament. The extreme Right parties, the heirs of Hitlerism, suffered the same fate.

That was the picture this morning when nearly a third of the ballots soberly cast by a record turnout of West German voters had been unofficially tallied.

It had been predicted that the Chancellor would improve his position after four successful years in office, but none of the prophets had foreseen the real extent of his victory.

On the basis of direct votes in all 242 constituencies in the republic, D. P. A. announces at 5 A. M., the Christian Democrats had 172 seats of the 484 in the new Bundestag, the lower house of Parliament, the Free Democrats fourteen and the German party ten, for a total for the coalition of 196. The Social Democrats had forty-

Continued on Page 4, Column 4

Anti-Americanism in Japan Reported Gaining Sharply

Following is the first of two dispatches on the conditions contributing to the rise of anti-Americanism in Japan.

By WILLIAM J. JORDEN

Special to THE NEW YORK TIMES.

TOKYO, Aug. 30—Many Japanese officials and Americans here have become increasingly concerned over the growth of anti-United States sentiment among the Japanese people. These observers fear that if this attitude continues to develop, it could endanger, if not destroy, the bases of friendship patiently established between the two countries in the years since World War II.

That, of course, is the obvious goal of extremist elements, both Communist and ultranationalist, who are trying to take advantage of Japan's real and fancied grievances against the United States.

Evidence of the growth of anti-Americanism is not hard to come by today. Only rarely does the subject fail to come up in talks with informed Japanese. Excepted, for obvious reasons, are conversations with almost professional "pro-Americans," who either avoid the painful subject or pass it off as the sentiment of a small minority of "Communists and leftists."

A steady stream of articles dealing with the problem has occupied considerable space in Japanese newspapers and magazines in recent months. In addition to editorials and commentaries, the press also carries in its news columns frequent reports of rallies, petitions, demonstrations and other activities centered on the theme of anti-Americanism. Books and movies, usually throwing more heat than light on the problem, are being produced in increasing numbers.

Public opinion polls reflect this growing bias. One such poll, conducted recently by the influential and moderate newspaper Asahi,

Continued on Page 3, Column 2

TWO-PARTY TREND EMERGING IN BONN

Nine Groups Fail to Win One Constituency—Communist Hopes Are Smashed

By M. S. HANDLER

Special to THE NEW YORK TIMES.

BONN, Germany, Monday, Sept. 7—Chancellor Konrad Adenauer's sweeping victory in yesterday's general election established a trend toward a two-party system in Western Germany.

Nine of the fourteen parties that were in the running fell by the wayside. They failed to win a single constituency by direct election and failed to win the 5 per cent of the total national vote that would have entitled them to share in the distribution of seats under the system of proportional representation.

A tenth party, the Center party, survived the contest only because of a deal with Dr. Adenauer's Christian Democrats, who agreed to vote for its candidate in the Ruhr.

The next Bundestag therefore will be dominated by a very powerful Christian Democratic party and a stabilized Social Democratic Opposition. The third party of

Continued on Page 4, Column 1

Airliner Crash-Lands and Burns; 29 of 32 Aboard Hurt at Tacoma

By The Associated Press.

McCHORD AIR FORCE BASE, Wash., Sept. 6—A Northwest Airlines Constellation crash-landed and burned here early today, with twenty-nine of the thirty-two persons on board suffering burns and injuries as they leaped from the flaming craft.

With only one wheel down and two of its four engines dead, the plane rolled along the runway at this base, south of Tacoma, until it lost speed. Then the left wing dipped to the ground and gas in the wing tanks caught fire.

The craft swerved from the runway, skidded to a stop and burned as the twenty-six passengers, including three babies, and the six crewmen clambered to safety. Among those aboard were Mr. and Mrs. Lester Armour of Chicago, of the Armour packing family. They were not injured.

The Constellation was the same one in which Mrs. John Eisenhower, wife of Maj. John Eisenhower, the President's son, had arrived at Seattle at 12:25. Major Eisenhower arrived in Seattle yesterday on rotation from Korea. The plane had refueled and was on the return flight to Chicago when it was forced down.

Most of those burned and injured were released after receiving first aid treatment at the base hospital. The others, with the exception of Mrs. Doris Alfred, 29 years old, Covington, Ky., and her 22-month-old son, Terry, were released today. Mrs. Alfred and her son were described in serious condition from third degree burns.

The plane, running non-stop from Seattle to Chicago, had just taken off from the Seattle-Tacoma International Airport at 2:06 A. M. (Pacific Standard Time) when one engine failed.

The pilot, Capt. Russell Bird of

Continued on Page 33, Column 6

Mary Martin spoofed dress designs on the Ford Fiftieth Anniversary Show, *which also starred Ethel Merman.*

Eddie Fisher had a 15-minute TV show from 1953-1957. Later he had an hour long prime time show twice a month, which ran for two seasons.

The first national telecast of the Academy Awards in 1953 provided viewers with the opportunity to see Donald O'Connor congratulate Oscar winners William Holden and Donna Reed for their performances in Stalag 17 *and* From Here To Eternity.

Marilyn Monroe and Jane Russell are immortalized in cement.

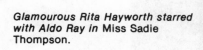
Glamourous Rita Hayworth starred with Aldo Ray in Miss Sadie Thompson.

U.S. highways began to groan under stupendous burdens in 1953. Without the cloverleaf intersections, traffic would have been even more hopelessly snarled.

Christine Jorgensen, an ex-G.I. who was a transvestite was transformed into a "woman" surgically by Danish doctors in Copenhagen.

A machine created by scientists smoked 60 cigarettes at once. The purpose was to investigate a possible link between nicotine and lung cancer.

The New York Times.

VOL. CIII...No. 34,949.   Entered as Second-Class Matter, Post Office, New York, N. Y.   NEW YORK, THURSDAY, OCTOBER 1, 1953.   Three Cents, New York City, Seven Cents Elsewhere   FIVE CENTS

Copyright, 1953, by The New York Times Company

EISENHOWER NAMES WARREN TO BE CHIEF JUSTICE OF U. S.; RULES OUT RETAIL SALES TAX

HAILS CALIFORNIAN

President Says Governor Will Preside Monday When Court Meets

Transcript of President's news conference is on Page 14.

By JAMES RESTON
Special to The New York Times.

WASHINGTON, Sept. 30—President Eisenhower said today that the fourteenth Chief Justice of the United States would be Gov. Earl Warren of California.

The President told his news conference he had looked for a man of honesty, integrity, experience, objectivity and moderate philosophy—and that the big, hearty, 62-year-old Californian was his man.

He will make "a great Chief Justice," the President predicted, adding that he expected Mr. Warren would preside over the Supreme Court when it convenes for the 1953-54 session next Monday.

Mr. Warren, the first Californian to preside over the court, and the first Chief Justice to be named by a Republican President since Charles Evans Hughes, replaces Fred M. Vinson of Kentucky, who died of a heart attack on Sept. 8. Mr. Hughes was appointed by President Hoover in 1930.

Other Conference Points

President Eisenhower also made these points in the course of the twenty-four-minute conference, his first in ten weeks:

¶On the reported Soviet hydrogen explosion: It was a fact of the utmost importance to the world and made the United States Government all the more interested in trying to reach some kind of negotiated settlement in which everybody could have confidence.

¶On the forced retirement of Stefan Cardinal Wyszynski in Poland: The heart of America resented things like this. Without freedom of religion and thought, without some evidence that the Communists were willing to honor these things, it was discouraging to try to reach real understanding in the world.

¶On the Government's legal debt limit: It probably wouldn't be necessary to bring Congress back to Washington before January to raise the statutory ceiling on the national debt. An increase in the debt limit would require a special session of Congress.

¶On a Federal sales tax—such as taxes were in the province of municipalities and states." did not rule out, however, the possibility of a manufacturers' excise tax.

¶On former Secretary of Labor Martin P. Durkin's statement that the President had broken his promise to propose revisions in the Taft-Hartley Act: He wasn't going to discuss personalities, but he would say this: To his knowledge he had never broken an agreement with any associate in his life. (There was a little bite in this remark.)

Few more important announcements have been made with so

Continued on Page 14, Column 3

Long-Distance Rates For Phones Rise 8%

By CHARLES E. EGAN
Special to The New York Times.

WASHINGTON, Sept. 30—In a split decision, the Federal Communications Commission authorized today a rate increase of 8 per cent for interstate long-distance telephone service of the Bell Telephone System, effective at midnight tonight. The increase is expected to bring the Bell System a gross increase of $65,000,000 and a net increase of $35,000,000 in annual revenues.

Commissioner Frieda B. Hennock, Democrat, was the lone dissenter. She based her objection on the fact that the commission had held no public hearings on the merits of the increase before approving it.

Effective tomorrow also will be an increase of 35 per cent in parcel post zone rates under an order approved last June by the Interstate Commerce Commission.

The parcel post increase will bring added $153,000,000 annually in revenue to the Post Office Department if the rates are allowed to remain in effect. This week

Continued on Page 51, Column 1

CONGRATULATIONS: Gov. Earl Warren, new Chief Justice, and his wife look over congratulatory telegrams at Sacramento.
Associated Press Wirephoto

President Leaves Door Open To a Tax on Manufacturers

By JOHN D. MORRIS
Special to The New York Times.

WASHINGTON, Sept. 30—President Eisenhower ruled out a national sales tax at the retail level today as a possible means of producing revenue needed by the Federal Government. He left the door open, however, for a general sales tax to be levied on manufacturers.

At the same time, he said the Government apparently would be able to get by until January without raising the statutory ceiling on the national debt. An increase in the debt limit would require a special session of Congress.

At his news conference, the President discussed taxes and the national debt. He volunteered the information on the decision against a general retail sales tax to set at rest continued speculation on the subject.

But one consequence was to intensify speculation over a possible general impost on manufacturers' sales of all products except food, as proposed by the National Association of Manufacturers. The N. A. M. would repeal existing excise taxes on everything except liquor, beer, wine and tobacco. Some of these are now levied at the retail level, others at the manufacturers' level.

The Treasury is considering about forty proposals, including various forms of sales taxes, in a study preparatory to making recommendations early in January for Congressional action. The problem is to offset, at least in part, automatic tax reductions that will cost the Government about $5,000,000,000 a year in revenues unless Congress acts.

Otherwise, according to present signs, the Administration will have to forgo its goal of a balanced budget in the 1955 fiscal year, which starts next July 1.

President Eisenhower gave indirect and inconclusive answers to questions on how much new revenue

Continued on Page 15, Column 2

PRESIDENT DENIES BREAKING PLEDGE

He Challenges Press Session to Contradict His Statement After Query on Durkin

By JOSEPH A. LOFTUS
Special to The New York Times.

WASHINGTON, Sept. 30—President Eisenhower declared emphatically today that he had never knowingly broken an agreement with any associate.

While avoiding direct mention of Martin P. Durkin, who said he quit as Secretary of Labor because the President had backed down on a promise to send certain Taft-Hartley Law recommendations to Congress, General Eisenhower faced squarely the question of conflicting agreements.

A reporter reminded him of Mr. Durkin's charge and of Vice President Richard M. Nixon's reported belief that it was all a misunderstanding, and asked the President for his version.

The President said he would not give the reporters a version on that conflict because he had consistently declined ever to speak of personalities publicly; that it was not his business as President.

Then, with a thrust of his jaw, he added that, to his knowledge, he had never broken an agreement with any associate in his life; that if he had ever broken an agreement it was something that he did not understand was made.

Emphasis Is Added

For emphasis, he added again that he had never broken one that he knew of. After a short pause, he continued, with even more emphasis. If there is anyone here who has contrary evidence, he said, that person could have the floor and make his speech. There were no further questions on that point.

That the President responded "at all to the question surprised many. He had already declined, with a no comment, to say what qualifications he was looking for in a new Secretary of Labor, or when he would appoint one.

Another resignation and an open clash between the Labor Department and the White House was barely averted this week.

Lloyd A. Mashburn, Under Secretary of Labor and Acting Secretary since the departure of Mr. Durkin, received a letter from Bernard M. Shanley, special counsel to the President, advising him to withhold the department's legislative recommendations pending the appointment of a new secretary.

The department's legislative recommendations normally go to the Bureau of the Budget at this time. Mr. Mashburn had decided to recommend, among other things,

Continued on Page 26, Column 2

U.S. and France Map Victory in Indo-China

By JAY WALZ
Special to The New York Times.

WASHINGTON, Sept. 30—The United States and France announced new plans today to destroy the Communist threat in Indo-China and speedily end the eight-year-old war there.

The plans call for more French and native troops and up to $385,000,000 of additional American aid. A joint communiqué issued here and in Paris expressed French determination to "break up and destroy the regular enemy forces in Indo-China."

"The additional United States aid," said the communiqué, "is designed to help make it possible to achieve these objectives with maximum speed and effectiveness."

The new American aid would be in addition to $400,000,000 approved by Congress before its adjournment last summer to buy planes, guns and ammunition for

Continued on Page 8, Column 2

69,374 SEE YANKS BEAT DODGERS, 9-5, IN SERIES OPENER

Collins' Homer in 7th Breaks Tie After Brooklyn Erases a 4-Run Deficit at Stadium

By JOHN DREBINGER

Baseball's golden anniversary world series opened at the Yankee Stadium yesterday and for more than three hours there followed some of the most violent cannonading a half century of inter-league warfare has seen.

But when finally the smoke had lifted and the dust had settled there unfolded before a gathering of 69,374 a spectacle that bore an old and familiar look. The Yankees were on top; the Dodgers were underneath, with the score reading 9 to 5.

Off to a four-run lead that routed Carl Erskine, the pride of Flatbush, in the first inning, Casey Stengel's Bombers were to see their own Allie Reynolds battered out of the arena amid a nerve-tingling counter-offensive that presently enabled Chuck Dressen's National League champions to draw even.

Then, with the score 5—all in the lower half of the seventh, Joe Collins, one of last October's two series "goats," who redeemed themselves on this warm and sunny afternoon, bashed a terrific homer into the right-field stand.

Three for Good Measure

It was the fifth circuit clout of the game and it was the pay-off shot, although in the next round the Bombers, always distrustful when the chips are down and the stakes high, lashed into their foe for three more tallies. Johnny Sain, mound winner of this maudlin struggle in a relief role, drove in two of those runs with a two-bagger. Collins, for good measure, belted home the third with a single.

Thus those mighty Yanks, to whom winning world series conflicts seems almost second nature, are once again on the move, and already one full stride toward their greatest goal of all, the bagging of a fifth straight title. The Dodgers, seeking their first after six futile tries, still are no nearer.

The crowd, which tossed a net sum of $387,574.74 into the series till for a single-game record, had barely settled back when the heavy firing began and it never stopped until a series mark of 46 total bases—23 for each side—had been equaled.

Two devastating triples had sent the Bombers off winging in that opening round to jar the Brooklyn horde right down to its heels. Hank Bauer hit the first one to drive in the first tally. The second, even more delivered by Billy Martin, the Yanks' peppery second sacker who presently was to pick up still more laurels and wind up sharing-hero honors with Collins and Sain.

For a time, that opening blast looked as if it had settled matters for the day as Reynolds, strong-armed Chief of Stengel's mound staff, held the straining Dodgers at bay for four innings. But in the fifth the first jarring note was struck as Junior Gilliam, the

Continued on Page 37, Column 2

PRESIDENT FAVORS STEPS TO SEEK OUT SOVIET'S INTENTION

Says Moscow's Gain in Nuclear Arms Forces West to Act, but Doubts Honoring of Pacts

By W. H. LAWRENCE
Special to The New York Times.

WASHINGTON, Sept. 30—President Eisenhower said today that the fact of Soviet possession of the hydrogen bomb was of the utmost significance and made it more important than ever to find out whether the Soviet Union and its satellites were interested in honestly attempting to reach some kind of a negotiated settlement in which the free world could have confidence.

At the same time, however, the President said at a news conference that those who hoped to reach real understanding in the world were discouraged by actions such as the Communists recently had taken in Poland in forcing the retirement of Stefan Cardinal Wyszynski.

He said in effect that it was difficult to believe that a nation that would not allow freedom of religion and of thought would honor understandings it might reach with other nations.

The President confirmed his intention to speak frankly to the nation and the world at some future date on the meaning of Soviet development of the atomic and hydrogen bombs and its relation to a changed international situation. Aides said that this meant a single speech, not a series of speeches of the sort urged by those who put forth the idea of "Operation Candor."

Difference With Churchill

The joking manner in which President Eisenhower opened the news conference, saying he guessed there was no news that would take interest from the world series, changed to one of deadly seriousness when he dealt with questions relating to foreign policy.

He left no doubt that he favored a new effort to reach an understanding with the Soviet Union and the general reduction of world tension, but he gave no indication that he agreed with Sir Winston Churchill, the British Prime Minister, that the present was the right time to do so.

Certainly we want to release and lower tensions, he said, but exactly how and when to do this is a difficult matter. We must avoid doing things in such a way as to make the situation worse instead of better, he emphasized.

The President offered no direct observation on Prime Minister Churchill's renewed effort this week to revive the proposal for top-level conferences between the United States, Britain, France and the Soviet Union in the immediate future. He said he had no knowledge of the latest report that Sir Winston was attempting to reach Bermuda, between himself, the Premier of France and President Eisenhower. That meeting had to be called off when Sir Winston fell ill.

Asked about the prospect of re-

Continued on Page 2, Column 4

EAST COAST PIER STRIKE IS ON; PRESIDENT EXPECTED TO ASK TAFT ACT INJUNCTION QUICKLY

Yonkers Track Ban Is Lifted; Races Start Tomorrow Night

955 Employees Cleared by Commission—Ownership Faces Study—City Police, Firemen Work at Nassau Raceway

By CHARLES GRUTZNER

The State Harness Racing Commission lifted its ban on Yonkers Raceway yesterday, but the cry of "the marshal calls for the trotters" won't bring out the horse-drawn sulkies in Westchester County until tomorrow night.

The track's license, the suspension of which had delayed since last Monday the start of the Yonkers fall trotting season, was removed after track officials had filed employment applications of 955 workers and a check of police and Federal fingerprint files had not upset the sworn statements that no one on the raceway's payroll had a criminal record.

To meet this requirement, the track had dismissed thirty-five employes whose police records were uncovered in the investigation that arose from the murder on Aug. 28 of Thomas F. Lewis, Bronx labor leader who had exercised influence over jobs at the track.

Neither the commission nor track officials disclosed how many other employes might have been dismissed. It was learned, however, that Harvey Rosen, the track's labor relations expert since 1951, had been taken off the payroll permanently. Mr. Rosen, a political aide of former Mayor William O'Dwyer, is a former secretary of the New York City Fire Department.

Although the restoration of the track's license was made effective as of today, which would have permitted racing tonight, track officials said they needed another day in which to notify employes, rearrange the schedule of entries and print their programs. William H. Cane, president of the raceway, said a full set of trotting and pacing races would be carded for tomorrow night.

John T. Cahill, special counsel to the racing commission, made the

Continued on Page 32, Column 2

U. N. Delays Debate on Korea Over Strong Soviet Protest

By THOMAS J. HAMILTON

UNITED NATIONS, N. Y., Sept. 30—The Political and Security Committee of the United Nations General Assembly decided today not to take up "the Korean question" until it had disposed of the six other items on its agenda.

The vote was 48 to 6, Yugoslavia joining the five members of the Soviet bloc in opposition. Afghanistan, Burma, India, Indonesia and Iran abstained, and France did not vote because the resolution affected the questions of Morocco and Tunisia.

The committee's action would prevent the Assembly from considering any change in the list of states that are to participate in the Korean peace conference on the United Nations side before Oct. 28, the deadline recommended in the armistice for the start of the conference."

However, the committee decided, over United States opposition, that if it wanted to do so later, it could move up the Korean item by a simple majority, instead of by the two-thirds vote required by the rules of procedure.

The vote on this question was 49 to 7, the United States and Nationalist China joining the Soviet bloc in opposition. Argentina, the Dominican Republic, El

Continued on Page 6, Column 3

BOTH SIDES HOLD UP TALKS TO P. O. W'S

Allies Willing to Wait and Let Freedom From Red Pressures Ease Men's Minds First

Text of rules with interviews with war prisoners is on Page 8.

By WILLIAM J. JORDEN
Special to The New York Times.

TOKYO, Thursday, Oct. 1—Both the United Nations Command and the Communists in Korea have decided not to begin today their efforts to convince their former personnel, prisoners of war now in neutral custody, that they should change their minds about returning to their homelands.

The Communist authorities expressed dissatisfaction with the facilities provided by the United Nations for the "explanation" sessions.

Allied officials said it would take several days to complete construction of the sites to meet the enemy's requirements. These include a new route around the prison camp area to replace a present path that leads between the compounds. The Communists have complained that the present route necessitates their representatives going too close for safety to compounds housing hostile anti-Red captives.

Allied Point of View

The United Nations Command said it was not beginning its approaches to the 23,000 Allied personnel, including twenty-three Americans, who have stated they wished to remain with the Communists. The United Nations gave no reason for the delay.

It appeared, however, that the United Nations officials did not consider it wise immediately to approach the prisoners who were released into neutral custody only less than a week ago after long periods of subjection to heavy doses of Communist pressures and propaganda. Allied circles had hoped that the very fact that these men were now free from direct control and surveillance by the North Korean and Chinese Communists and the Reds' indoctrination program might cause some of the Allied captives to soften their resistance to returning home.

United Nations officers also felt

Continued on Page 5, Column 2

50,000 CALLED OUT

Union Pledged to Obey Ban—A. F. L. Group to Respect Picket Lines

Text of Shipping Association's plea to Governors, Page 24.

By A. H. RASKIN

A strike of 50,000 longshoremen turned the sprawling water-fronts of New York and other North Atlantic cities into ghost ports at midnight last night, but there were strong indications that President Eisenhower would act, probably within twenty-four hours, to get the men back to work under an eighty-day Taft-Hartley injunction.

The strike was ordered by the crime-encrusted International Longshoremen's Association as the pivotal element in a fight for survival that pitted the pier union against the combined forces of the shipping employers, the American Federation of Labor, which expelled the union last week, and the Federal and state Governments, which had adopted special laws to break the union's grip on the New York-New Jersey docks.

Despite the underlike setting, the walkout went into effect with singular quiet. Dock workers, who had been laboring under arc lights to get ships ready for sailing before the zero hour, left the piers without demonstrations or clashes with A. F. L. partisans. The pressure to load ships had been so intense that few vessels were stranded by the tie-up.

President Eisenhower told his news conference in Washington yesterday morning that he was studying the advisability of asking for a no-strike order under the national emergency provisions of the Taft-Hartley Law. As the strike deadline passed, there was no official amplification of the statement.

Injunction Today Held Likely

However, persons in close touch with the situation reported that Governor Dewey and other high officials were lending strong support to pleas by the New York Shipping Association for speedy issuance of an injunction. They said it was probable that the President would act today, but this prediction could not be confirmed at the White House.

It was learned that an Executive Order creating a board of inquiry, the first step toward an injunction, had been prepared for the President's signature and that the necessary board members were under consideration. However, it was emphasized at the White House that this came under the head of preparing for every contingency and that no final decision had been reached on whether to proceed for an injunction. If violence erupts along the piers the President was reported likely to act at once.

The I. L. A., through its executive vice president, Patrick J. (Packey) Connolly, has promised that the dock workers would abide by an injunction, as they did in 1948, when President Harry S. Truman invoked the eighty-day Taft law provisions.

Some fear was expressed in shipping circles that issuance of

Continued on page 24, Column 3

State Group Offers City Executive Plan

By RUSSELL PORTER

A state commission recommended yesterday that New York City adopt a revised form of the city manager plan called the mayor-manager plan.

Under it there would be a $35,000-a-year appointive City Administrator to run all administrative agencies. He would be second in administrative command to the Mayor, who gets $40,000 a year. This was one of four commission proposals to improve the city government.

The others would:

¶Make the Deputy Mayor responsible for representing the Mayor in the Board of Estimate, in other official bodies and in certain public ceremonies.

¶Substitute a performance budget with a state-approved financial plan for the present line-item budget.

¶Establish a new Department of

Continued on Page 27, Column 2

Piccard Sets Mark in 10,330-Foot Sea Descent Off Italy

The fifty-two-foot diving craft Trieste, in which Prof. Auguste Piccard and his son, Jacques, descended yesterday a record 10,330 feet. This picture was made during a recent test.
Associated Press

Special to The New York Times.

ROME, Sept. 30—Prof. Auguste Piccard of Switzerland, who twenty-one years ago was the first man to rise high enough over the surface of the earth to enter the stratosphere, today became the man to have penetrated to the greatest depth under the surface of the sea. He

reached about 10,330 feet, easily beating the record of about 6,900 feet set by two French naval men last month. The 69-year-old scientist, who was accompanied by his 31-year-old son, Jacques, dived in a bathyscaphe, or depth craft, named Trieste and built on Professor Piccard's designs in Italian yards. The record was established some time between 8:18 o'clock this morning, when the bathyscaphe plunged under the sea, and 10:30, when it reappeared. The dive was made into what is known as the Tyrrhenian Trench, about fifty

Continued on Page 12, Column 4

The New York Times.

LATE CITY EDITION
Fair, seasonable temperatures today.
Fair and mild tomorrow.
Temperature Range Today—Max., 55; Min., 40
Temperatures Yesterday—Max., 55; Min., 44
Full U. S. Weather Bureau Report, Page 47

Copyright, 1953, by The New York Times Company.

VOL. CIII..No. 34,992.   Entered as Second-Class Matter, Post Office, New York, N. Y.   NEW YORK, FRIDAY, NOVEMBER 13, 1953.   Times Square, New York 36, N. Y. Telephone LAckawanna 4-1000   FIVE CENTS

IMMEDIATE PARLEY WITH JORDAN ASKED BY ISRAEL AT U. N.

Eban for Talks 'Without Delay' on Armistice Problems and Border Tensions

HE REGRETS KIBYA ATTACK

His Bid Denounced by Malik as Move to Curb Condemnation of Blow Fatal to 53 Arabs

Remarks in U. N. by delegates of Israel and Lebanon, Page 4.

By THOMAS J. HAMILTON
Special to The New York Times

UNITED NATIONS, N. Y., Nov. 12—Abba S. Eban, Israeli representative in the United Nations, proposed today that Israel and Jordan meet here "without delay" to discuss their differences.

He proposed that the meeting take up "armistice problems and especially the prevention of border incidents and the cooperation of the respective authorities in maintaining border security."

Mr. Eban's surprise proposal was made after he had told the Security Council "a campaign of organized murder" was being carried on across the central sector of the Israeli-Jordanian frontier and that this was being "allowed, if not encouraged" by the Jordanian Government.

He said Israel "deeply regrets and unreservedly deplores" the "loss of innocent life" in the raid on the Jordan village of Kibya, in which fifty-three persons were killed. However, he emphasized that such "counter-actions" were a result of "purposeful and deliberate" attacks on Israel's life, property and communications.

U. N. Suggested as Site

Mr. Eban said his Government had empowered him to represent it in talks with Jordan. He suggested United Nations Headquarters as the site because of the presence here of Dr. Yussef Heykal, Jordanian Minister in Washington, and Maj. Gen. Vagn Bennike, chief of the United Nations Truce Observation Organization.

Mr. Eban said his Government had repeatedly declared its willingness to find a solution "to the deteriorating security situation along the Israel-Jordan border." He added that Jordanian-Israeli talks here might result in the submission of "agreed conclusions to the Security Council for preventing violent incidents at the border."

After the meeting Dr. Heykal declined to comment on the Israeli proposal, declaring he had been authorized only to discuss the Kibya case in the Security Council. He added that any other action would have to be decided by his Government. General Bennike also declined to comment, as did United States and British spokesmen.

Dr. Charles A. Malik, Lebanese representative, accused Mr. Eban of having presented the Council with a "book" on "Israel, past, present and future," and of having attempted to drown the Kibya case, "the basic cause of our meeting together, in a flood of words."

Warns Against Repetition

Dr. Malik asserted the "indubitable facts" were that the Kibya raid had been carried out by Israeli military forces as culmination of an Israeli policy of violating the armistice agreements. He added that the repetition of "such acts of aggression" would certainly lead to "the breach of the peace in the Near East."

Dr. Malik declared that "the mildest form of action" by the Council would be to call on Israel to punish those responsible, pay compensation for loss of life and damage to property, and refrain from a repetition of the raid.

However, he suggested also that the Council ask other nations not to give military or economic aid to Israel without guarantees that Israel would refrain from such acts. Further, he said the Council would cause the Council to consider action under Chapter VII of the United Nations Charter—which authorizes the use of military force, as well as economic sanctions, to halt aggression.

Mr. Eban's two-and-a-half-hour speech, and that by Dr. Malik, which was half as long, required the Council to stay in session an hour longer than usual. In response to a British request for speed, the Council decided to take up the Kibya case again Monday, postponing until Wednesday consideration of another Palestine question—Syria's complaint against Israeli preparations to divert water from the Jordan River.

Mr. Eban's proposal for Jordan-

Continued on Page 4, Column 4

Iran Crushes Dissident Bid To Challenge New Regime

Troops and Police Use Tough Tactics to Halt Red-Led Demonstrators—Mossadegh, at Trial, Says He 'Shook' Colonialism

By ROBERT C. DOTY
Special to The New York Times

TEHERAN, Iran, Nov. 12—The Iranian security forces, with clubs, gun butts and scattered shots, today smashed a well planned major effort by the Communists and extreme nationalists to challenge the Government.

Forewarned of details of the plot, Maj. Gen. Farhat Dadestan, the tough and smart military Governor of Teheran, deployed the equivalent of two divisions of troops and police in and around the capital.

With rough, effective techniques, these forces swarmed all over the dissidents, denied them an opportunity to assemble and broke the first serious threat to the regime of Premier Fazlollah Zahedi before it could take shape.

The only success registered by the plotters was the closing of the hundreds of tiny shops in the bazaar area by a combination of threats and exploitation of the discontent of the merchants with Premier Zahedi's economic policies.

which have caused a decrease in the prices of their hoarded imported goods by the promise of a new and more liberal import policy. Late in the afternoon about 40 per cent of the shops had reopened.

By noon the menace was gone and by nightfall the results of the day were that three would-be demonstrators were wounded by gunfire, one policeman sustained a minor knife wound on the arm, about a hundred persons were arrested and scores of others were more or less seriously beaten up by the police and the troops. [According to Reuters, Iranian troops shot two demonstrators to death and arrested 140.]

At no time was anything that could be described as rioting permitted to break out.

Relaxed and confident, General Dadestan, in his headquarters tonight, said: "There's not much to it. The Tudeh (Communist party) wanted to make a demonstration

Continued on Page 8, Column 3

Basis to Start Trieste Talks Reported Accepted by Italy

Special to The New York Times

LONDON, Nov. 12—Manlio Brosio, Italian Ambassador, called on Foreign Secretary Anthony Eden today upon returning from consultations in Rome on the Trieste issue. The Foreign Office said it could neither confirm nor deny reports from Rome that Italy was favorably disposed toward the Yugoslav proposal for discussions to ascertain whether there was common ground for calling a conference on a higher level.

According to Yugoslav sources, the preliminary talks would be confined to technical experts from the United States, Britain, France, Italy and Yugoslavia. Belgrade has expressed belief that such a meeting should enable Yugoslavia and Italy to put aside any objections they might have to attending immediately a full-dress political conference.

However, information reaching here from Belgrade is that the Yugoslav statement as "hysterically untruthful." In the first place, he said the statement that Luciano had been pardoned was "wholly false." Luciano's fifty-year sentence was commuted after he had served ten years of his term, he explained.

Luciano was convicted in 1936 of compulsory prostitution. He was released on Jan. 3, 1946.

"No one in the State Government," Mr. O'Donnell's statement continued, "ever sought any aid of any kind from Luciano. The Armed Forces of the United States sought his aid in inducing others to supply information concerning possible enemy attack. When his sentence was commuted for deportation it was made clear that this was in the usual course and not on the basis of any information he supplied.

"There is no possible relationship between this proper official

Continued on Page 8, Column 4

LANIEL LIMITS GOAL IN INDO-CHINA WAR

Any Honorable Peace Solution Acceptable, He Tells French —Rebuff to Nixon Seen

Special to The New York Times

PARIS, Nov. 12—Premier Joseph Laniel told the Council of the Republic today that France was not seeking an unconditional surrender of the Communist-led enemy in Indo-China and would be happy to find "an honorable solution" to the conflict.

The Premier's statement, made during a debate in the upper house, aroused considerable comment here, since it contrasted with that made by Vice President Richard M. Nixon during his recent visit to Indo-China. Mr. Nixon told the Vietnamese and the French there that they could not lay down their arms "until victory is completely won" and warned that the United States would not approve any peace negotiation that would leave the Indo-Chinese in bondage.

M. Laniel, who is feeling heavy pressure from political forces who wish an end to the war, said his Government did not consider that the Indo-Chinese problem ought necessarily to receive a military solution.

"No more than the Americans in Korea will we require, if the case present itself, an unconditional surrender of the enemy to negotiate with him," he said. "Not any more than the United States is France making war for war's sake, and if an honorable solution was in sight locally or internationally France—I repeat, as the United

Continued on Page 3, Column 2

Eisenhower Leaves For Visit to Canada

By ANTHONY LEVIERO
Special to The New York Times

ABOARD THE PRESIDENT'S TRAIN, Nov. 12—President Eisenhower was en route tonight on a goodwill visit to Ottawa. Before leaving, he announced the formation of two joint agencies designed to strengthen the ties between the United States and Canada.

President and Mrs. Eisenhower and their party, including A. D. P. Heeney, the Canadian Ambassador, and Mrs. Heeney, left Washington at 5:35 P. M. They were scheduled to arrive in Ottawa at 11:30 A. M. tomorrow for two days of talks and ceremonies.

Several hours before the departure on the famous railroad train U. S. No. 1 the White House issued the announcement of the formation of the United States-Canadian Committee on Trade and Economic Affairs. Also announced was an agreement for the establishment of

Continued on Page 8, Column 4

G.O.P. ASKS OUSTER OF WICKS AS CHIEF; HE ACCUSES DEWEY

Senator Charges That Release of Luciano Was as Improper as His Visits to Fay

Texts of committee resolution and Wicks' reply, Page 18.

By LEO EGAN
Special to The New York Times

ALBANY, Nov. 12—The Republican State Executive Committee voted unanimously today to support Governor Dewey's demand for the ouster of Senator Arthur H. Wicks as Majority Leader and President Pro Tem of the State Senate. His office make him the Lieutenant Governor, in effect.

A formal resolution was adopted by the committee at a special meeting, with nine of its thirty members absent. It said that Mr. Wicks' visits to Joseph S. Fay, a labor union leader convicted of extortion, in Sing Sing prison had been improper and denoted a low standard of ethics.

Senator Wicks, fighting to win vindication from the Senate at a special session called for next Tuesday, countered immediately. In a statement, he declared his visits to Fay were no more improper than Governor Dewey's release of Charles Lucania, better known as Lucky Luciano, from prison for deportation in 1946. His statement carried an implication that he would have more to say on the Luciano case later.

Senator Wicks demanded that the Executive Committee, "in fairness, apply the same standard to the Governor" and call a special meeting before Tuesday. The Senator has steadily maintained that there was no wrongdoing in his visits to Fay. He has insisted they were made to seek Fay's help in preventing labor tie-ups in his Senate district.

[In New York, meanwhile, Democratic leaders decided to press for an investigation of the Luciano case.]

Dewey Ignores Charge

Governor Dewey was in New York tonight and ignored the Wicks charge. But Harry J. O'Donnell, his executive assistant, made a formal rejoinder in his own name. Presumably this was cleared with the Governor before it was issued.

Mr. O'Donnell described the Yugoslav Government still feels somewhat pessimistic about Italy's attitude and that the Yugoslavs are not yet aware that Rome has expressed approval of their proposal.

Basis of Negotiation Seen

But a dispatch from Rome to The Times of London tonight quoted authoritative political quarters there as saying that the Italian Government considered that the Yugoslav proposal provided a basis for opening discussions and had instructed Signor Brosio so to inform the British Government.

The proposal is understood to provide that neither Rome nor Belgrade would be asked to relinquish in advance any of the conditions they have already laid down as essential before they could meet at a conference table, and consequently neither would be exposed to a loss of prestige, The Times dispatch said.

The dispatch added that one administrative, but carrying it out will involve political considerations.

Continued on Page 18, Column 1

Hammarskjold's U. N. Staff Plan Calls for Dropping of 6 Top Aides

By A. M. ROSENTHAL
Special to The New York Times

UNITED NATIONS, N. Y., Nov. 12—Secretary General Dag Hammarskjold will propose a complete overhaul of the set-up of the United Nations staff, including elimination of the rank of Assistant Secretary General.

The six Assistant Secretaries General have been notified that their contracts will not be renewed when they expire next February. Some of them will be dropped from the payroll and others will be shifted to different ranks.

Mr. Hammarskjold's plan—some of it will be made public in a report tomorrow—is based on a belief that staff activities are too scattered. His idea is to cut through departmental lines and build new channels leading down from his own office in the hope of increased efficiency and economy. The administrative reins will be held by the Secretary General and four aides working directly under him.

Mr. Hammarskjold will put his reorganization proposals before the delegates to the United Nations General Assembly. It was reported that he was confident that he would receive the support of the Assembly to carry the plan through the sixty-nation Assembly and its Administrative and Budgetary Committee.

The new plan would also eliminate the rank of Principal Director, which is immediately below that of Assistant Secretary General. Some of the nine Principal Directors hold five-year or permanent contracts. But proposals have been submitted by Mr. Hammarskjold

powers and important areas of the world were represented in the United Nations' top echelon. The present Assistant Secretaries General are an American, a Russian, a Frenchman, a Chinese, an Indian and a Chilean.

In addition to heading their departments, they have often maintained an informal political liaison between their parts of the world and the Secretary General. In the future, the Secretary General will assign liaison work for specific problems to specific aides.

Mr. Hammarskjold's reorganization proposals before the delegates to the United Nations General Assembly. It was reported that he was confident that he would receive the support of the Assembly to carry the plan through the sixty-nation Assembly and its Administrative and Budgetary Committee.

The essence of the plan is administrative, but carrying it out will involve political considerations. The Assistant Secretaries General were originally handed out on a political and geographic basis to make sure that the major

Continued on Page 6, Column 5

WORD OF COUNSEL: Former President Truman leans forward for a confidential word with Samuel I. Rosenman, former White House adviser, during press conference here yesterday at which he announced his reply to subpoena of the House Committee on Un-American Activities.

BURKE TO GET POST AS CITY'S COUNSEL

Wagner's Campaign Manager to Succeed Hurley—Epstein May Be Deputy Mayor

Special to The New York Times

NASSAU, Bahamas, Nov. 12—Mayor-elect Robert F. Wagner Jr. announced today that he was appointing his long-time friend Adrian P. Burke, as Corporation Counsel.

Mr. Burke, who was manager for both the primary and the general election campaigns of Mr. Wagner, will receive $25,000 a year.

Mr. Wagner made no appointment of a Deputy Mayor, but he said that Henry Epstein, former State Solicitor General, was an able man and was being considered for the post.

The Mayor-elect said he wanted Mr. Epstein in a city post, but had not spoken with him yet and so could not say specifically what capacity Mr. Epstein would be invited to fill.

Mr. Wagner's press aide said tonight the Mayor-elect would not appoint a new Police Commissioner to replace George P. Monaghan until he returned to New York.

Mr. Wagner's stay here is expected to be extended. Members of his party said it was "unlikely" he would go back home to participate in the capital budget discussions next Monday and Tuesday as he had originally planned.

Mr. Epstein said last night he

Continued on Page 17, Column 2

Subway Round Trip Cut to 10c for Pupils

By LEONARD INGALLS

High school students will pay 10 cents instead of 15 for a round trip on the subway and elevated lines beginning Feb. 1.

The reduction was voted yesterday by the Transit Authority and a disparity in fares for high school students on city-owned rapid transit and on surface lines that has existed since fares were raised July 25. The authority's income will be cut an estimated $500,000 a year and 70,000 students are expected to benefit.

Maj. Gen. Hugh J. Casey, authority chairman, announced that he would attend a meeting Tuesday with Supreme Court Justice Walter R. Hart of Brooklyn, who has been acting as impartial adviser to the authority and the Transport Workers Union, C. I. O., in a dispute

*There's so much more to buy
in a City Stitched for FREE—"The Lure" booklet: Welfare Room 661, 511 Fifth Ave., N. Y. C.*

TRUMAN REJECTS SUBPOENA OF HOUSE AS HIS 'DUTY' UNDER THE CONSTITUTION; COMMITTEE WILL NOT ACT AGAINST HIM

CITES 16 PRESIDENTS

Separation of Powers Is Stressed by Truman in White Case Stand

Text of Mr. Truman's letter to Mr. Velde is on Page 14.

By MILTON BRACKER

Harry S. Truman declined yesterday to comply with the subpoena served on Tuesday on behalf of a House committee investigating the Harry Dexter White case.

At a terse and crowded news conference here, suggestive of his White House days, Mr. Truman said his position was based on "universally recognized constitutional doctrine."

"In spite of my personal willingness to cooperate with your committee," the former President said in a letter to the Committee on Un-American Activities, "I feel constrained by my duty to the people of the United States to decline to comply with the subpoena."

Mr. Truman cited sixteen other Presidents, including five Republicans since Lincoln, as having declined to respond to Congressional subpoenas or demands for information.

The former President made no reference to the late Mr. White, who has been called a spy for the Soviet Union, or to any of the political aspects of the case, which came before the public in Chicago last Friday.

At that time, Attorney General Herbert Brownell Jr. asserted that Mr. Truman had promoted Mr. White in 1946, despite a report by the Federal Bureau of Investigation that the expert on international finance was spying for Russia.

Would Be 'Happy' to Appear

Mr. White, who was an Assistant Secretary of the Treasury, was promoted to the higher-paying executive director in the International Monetary Fund.

Mr. Truman, who was President from April, 1945, through January, 1953, emphasized that in connection with his record as a private citizen, either before or after his career in the White House, he would be "happy" to appear before the committee.

But Mr. Truman insisted that if the doctrine of separation of powers—and the independence of the Presidency—was to have "any validity at all," it must apply equally to a President in office and to one who had left office—assuming the inquiry related to matters connected to his Administration.

The doctrine would fall, he continued, and the Presidency shrink to a mere arm of the Legislative Branch—"contrary to our fundamental theory of constitutional government"—if the President should feel during his term that his "every act might be subject to official inquiry and possible distortion for political purposes."

Later, before an audience of 1,000 persons last night at a dinner in the Waldorf-Astoria, Mr. Truman asserted that Americans must protect their freedom "against the onslaughts of fear and hysteria which are being manipulated in this country today purely for political purposes." The American Friends of the Hebrew University

Continued on Page 12, Column 4

Velde Unit 'Invites' Brownell And He Promises to Testify

By W. H. LAWRENCE
Special to The New York Times

WASHINGTON, Nov. 12—The Un-American Activities Committee of the House of Representatives bowed tonight to former President Truman's refusal to testify before it. No effort will be made to enforce the history-making subpoena the committee served on an ex-President and no motion will be made to cite him for contempt of Congress.

With this cause of Democratic versus Republican friction shelved temporarily, the committee voted unanimously to "invite" Herbert Brownell Jr., Attorney General, to appear before it at its convenience.

In this appearance he would offer evidence in support of his charge that the late Harry Dexter White "was known to be a Communist spy by the very people who appointed him to the most sensitive and important position he ever held in Government service."

Mr. Brownell accepted the invitation but said he would be "unavailable" tomorrow, according to Representative Harold Velde of Illinois, committee chairman. Mr. Velde said arrangements were being made for an early meeting to hear him.

Republicans beat down Democratic efforts to subpoena the Attorney General immediately. Thus far he has declined to hold a news conference or otherwise to offer substantive evidence in support of his charge.

Committee Holds Hearing

In a day packed with events, these were the other principal developments:

¶The House committee continued in effect its subpoena for Associate Justice Tom C. Clark to appear before it at 10:30 A. M. tomorrow, although no one expects the justice to appear. He has withheld all comment on this case, but several months ago he declined an invitation to testify before another House committee on constitutional ground.

¶The Senate Internal Security subcommittee held public and nationally televised hearings lasting little more than an hour in which no new facts were developed.

Its witnesses were Maj. Gen. Harry H. Vaughan, military aide to former President Truman, who received from the Federal Bureau of Investigation copies of its reports on Mr. White, and Theron Lamar Caudle, former Assistant Attorney General, summarily dismissed by Mr. Truman in 1951.

Mr. Caudle recalled that he had seen the F. B. I. report on Mr. White in February, 1946, and had taken it up with Justice Clark, then Attorney General.

¶High Administration sources forecast that Mr. Brownell would

Continued on Page 13, Column 5

G. O. P. LEADERS BAR CITING OF TRUMAN

National Committee Forestalls Contempt Action by House Group Over Subpoena

Gov. Byrnes' reply to questions of Senate committee, Page 12.

By CLAYTON KNOWLES
Special to The New York Times

WASHINGTON, Nov. 12—Behind-the-scenes efforts of the Republican National Committee succeeded today in forestalling any move in the House of Representatives Un-American Activities Committee to try to cite former President Truman for his refusal to respond to its subpoena.

So effective was the National Committee's work that the question of proceeding against Mr. Truman for contempt came up for only casual discussion in the House committee. The meeting lasted for nearly two hours.

The committee did not vacate its subpoena against Mr. Truman nor was an effort made to do so. The Democrats, beaten on two test votes, did not choose to make an issue on this point. So the subpoena, accepted by Mr. Truman,

Continued on Page 13, Column 4

Law Experts Say Truman Acted Beyond His Constitutional Right

By WILL LISSNER

Several of the country's leading authorities on constitutional law were unanimous in holding that former President Truman had no constitutional ground for declining to comply with a House of Representatives committee subpoena calling him as a witness in the Harry Dexter White inquiry.

The authorities differed on whether the former President had a right or duty to refuse to answer questions regarding matters relating to the Executive Council when he was in office.

Some held that the former President had the same right as any other citizen, has no personal immunity from the subpoena power of Congress. The courts have held it settled one. But the weight of judicial opinion on the power of Congress to inform itself is great.

On this account all the experts leaned to the idea that the former President, being now a private citizen, had no personal immunity from the subpoena power of Congress.

Some held that the former President had the same right as any other citizen. One held that he had no settled right, but would probably be sustained with respect to confidential communications as long as he personally was not charged with complicity in a crime.

There is no legal precedent governing the subpoena power of Congress with respect to a former President, so the point is not a settled one. But the weight of judicial opinion on the power of Congress to inform itself is great.

Whether he could have been compelled to testify, and whether he had an obligation to do so, are

Continued on Page 14, Column 5

1954

Judy Garland is seen singing in this scene from A Star Is Born.

A Hitchcock masterpiece of the mid-Fifties was Rear Window in which an immobilized James Stewart studied the goings-on in the apartment across the courtyard. Grace Kelly also starred.

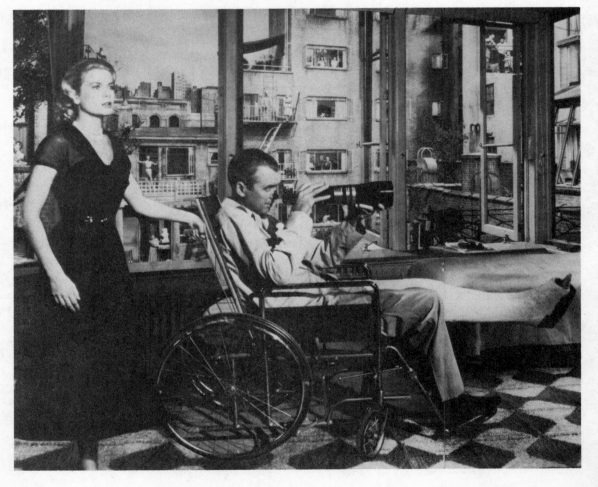

"All the News
That's Fit to Print"

The New York Times.

LATE CITY EDITION
Cloudy, windy and cold today.
Fair and cold tomorrow.
Temperature Range Today—Max., 25; Min., 21
Temperature Yesterday—Max., 55; Min., 30
Full U. S. Weather Bureau Report, Page 49

Copyright, 1954, by The New York Times Company.

VOL. CIII . No. 35,062.

Entered as Second-Class Matter,
Post Office, New York, N. Y.

NEW YORK, FRIDAY, JANUARY 22, 1954.

Times Square, New York 36, N. Y.
Telephone LAckawanna 4-1000

FIVE CENTS

ARAB LEADERS ASK SPANISH MOROCCO REPUDIATE SULTAN

Moorish Chiefs Deny Fealty to French-Appointed Ruler and Seek Separate Regime

PARIS POLICY CONDEMNED

Spain's Governor Attacks It — Coty Assures Sultan Rights Will Be Defended

Special to The New York Times.

TETUAN, Spanish Morocco, Jan. 21—Spain was asked by Spanish Moroccan notables today to separate her zone from the rest of Morocco, the largest part of which is governed by France.

This appeal would amount to a repudiation of the policy followed in the French protectorate and the "machinations that led to the dethronement of the legitimate Sultan."

[After the news that local Arab leaders in the Spanish zone had rejected the authority of the Sultan who had reached Paris the French Government told the Sultan it would defend his rights over all Morocco. The Sultan, Sidi Mohammed ben Moulay Arafa, was placed in power last August by the French after they had exiled the pro-nationalist Sultan, Sidi Mohammed ben Youssef.]

A green leather-bound gold-tooled copy of the petition, signed with 430 names, was presented to the Spanish Governor General, Gen. Rafael Garcia Valino. [The ceremony was held at a meeting of 30,000 Moroccans and 1,500 of their leaders, The United Press said.]

"We repudiate without reserve the policy followed in the French protectorate of Morocco and the machinations which led to the dethronement of the legitimate Sultan, Mohammed ben Youssef, as maneuvers of the French Residency and certain native elements which have turned their backs on the Moroccan people," the petition said.

Reject New Sultan's Authority

"We express our unconditional approval, together with our gratitude and that of the whole Moroccan people of the policy pursued in the Spanish zone by Your Excellency.

"As a consequence we declare we do not recognize the authority of [Sultan Sidi Mohammed ben] Moulay Arafa since he was imposed arbitrarily by France in contempt of the feelings of the Moroccan people. The only chief we recognize is the well-beloved Prince Moulay Hassan (the Caliph, Moulay el Hassan el Mehdi).

"Pursuing the fundamental concept always defended by Spain of Moroccan unity, we urge the separation of the Spanish zone so long as political conditions prevailing in the French zone remain unchanged."

In his reply, General Garcia Valino did not expressly accept these demands, though possibly he may do so tomorrow when he pays a formal visit to the Caliph, ending three days of festivities. He did say, however, that Spain and Morocco had gone through two grave crises together, in recent years.

"The first was in 1936 when Spain was threatened in its very existence by the occult forces of international communism," he said. "Again, in 1953, the existence of your nation was imperiled.

"France, co-protector with Spain

Continued on Page 2, Column 6

Big Vietminh Region Invaded by French

By TILLMAN DURDIN
Special to The New York Times.

TUYHOA, Vietnam, Jan. 20—French Union and Vietnamese troops landed at dawn today and took over this coastal town without a fight. The occupation of Tuyhoa was one phase of an operation designed to liberate 3,500,000 persons in this state of Indo-China from Vietminh rule.

Covered by aircraft and naval guns, the troops walked from American-built landing barges to find Tuyhoa empty of Vietminh forces. The main body of the Communist-led Vietminh troops had left, taking with them all able-bodied adult male inhabitants.

A few shots were fired by Vietminh snipers as the French and Vietnamese troops worked their way through Tuyhoa's maze of streets and pathways. Mines

Continued on Page 4, Column 5

Indians Send Notice to Reds To Take Back Their P.O.W's

Thimayya Tries Final Appeal to Get All, Including 21 Americans, Off His Hands —Neutral Guard Troops Leaving

By LINDESAY PARROTT
Special to The New York Times.

TOKYO, Friday, Jan. 22—Lieut. Gen. K. S. Thimayya of India asked the Communist Command again today to accept custody of the pro-Communist prisoners of the Korean war, including twenty-one Americans.

General Thimayya, chairman of the Neutral Nations Commission, sent a notice to the Red leaders that, if they refused, he would have to withdraw his guards anyway, at midnight tonight, from North Camp near the village of Songgong, where the pro-Red P. O. W.'s are housed.

"I shall be regretfully compelled to take the only course open to me," General Thimayya wrote the Communist commanders, "to withdraw custody of the

C. F. I. [Custodial Force, India] from the Songgong Camp."

General Thimayya had said earlier he was making this request "one more time."

Yesterday, the North Korean representative of the Communist Command, Lieut. Gen. Lee Sang Cho, had refused again to accept the prisoners. Red headquarters asked the Indians to keep custody of the twenty-one Americans, the Briton and the 325 or more South Koreans.

The Communists have insisted that no prisoners should have been turned back to the two Commands until an international conference decided their fate.

Continued on Page 5, Column 5

Quill Charges Against Klein Sifted by Kings Grand Jury

By LEONARD INGALLS

A grand jury investigation of an accusation against Harris J. Klein of the Transit Authority by Michael J. Quill was started yesterday by District Attorney Edward S. Silver of Kings County. Mr. Silver indicated that two possible violations of the law were involved —criminal libel or attempted bribery.

The investigation grew out of a statement made by Michael J. Quill, president of the Transport Workers Union, C. I. O., to reporters on Tuesday. He asserted that Mr. Klein had offered to support a $50,000,000 package of union demands on the authority if Mr. Quill would intervene with Mayor Wagner to obtain an appointment as Special Sessions justice for Mr. Klein.

Mr. Klein denied the allegation Wednesday and announced that he would sue Mr. Quill for slander in State Supreme Court and ask $100,000 in damages.

At its meeting yesterday the Transit Authority adopted unanimously a resolution expressing "continuing belief and confidence" in Mr. Klein's "honesty and integrity."

District Attorney Silver said the formal investigation of the Quill charge would get under way at 1 P. M. today with the questioning before the Kings County grand jury of four newspaper reporters to whom Mr. Quill made his statement about Mr. Klein.

Mr. Klein and Mr. Quill have been invited to appear before the grand jury Monday. Mr. Silver said Mr. Klein had agreed to be present, but that no answer had been received from Mr. Quill, who was in Chicago on business.

Also summoned to appear before the grand jury today was

Continued on Page 43, Column 5

COURT UPSETS BAN ON TRUCK PARKING

State's Highest Bench Finds Doubling Up Is Permissible if Travel Is Not Blocked

By PETER KIHSS

A new headache for the city's traffic planners developed yesterday. The Court of Appeals in Albany ruled that under present city regulations trucks could double-park while loading or unloading—provided they did not obstruct traffic.

The case, which the Traffic Police and Law Departments apparently did not even know had come before the state's highest court, grew out of an Ozone Park, Queens, incident. This incident had brought to a climax the irritation of the John H. Free, Inc., wholesale paper company of 330 Himrod Street, Brooklyn, over traffic summonses for parking and double-parking on deliveries.

Counting lost time, hire of substitute drivers during court appearances and overtime in delays, such cases may have cost the concern as much as $3,500 a year, according to Henry W. Schober of 1691 Putnam Avenue, Ridge-

Continued on Page 28, Column 7

ATOMIC SUBMARINE LAUNCHED BY U.S.; SUMMER TESTS SET

First Nuclear Ship Christened by Mrs. Eisenhower—Can Outrun Most Destroyers

By ELIE ABEL
Special to The New York Times.

GROTON, Conn., Jan. 21—The submarine Nautilus, man's first attempt to drive a ship by atomic power, splashed into the Thames River this morning.

It is expected that by midsummer the Nautilus will be ready for a grueling series of tests.

Seafaring men saw an auspicious omen in the sudden breakthrough of the winter sun, chasing the fog from the river, as Mrs. Dwight D. Eisenhower smashed a bottle of domestic champagne on the ship's blunted bow and christened her Nautilus.

It had been a dismal day for making history until that moment. Fog had blurred the 340-foot profile of the new submarine as a nine-car special train from Washington, carrying the President's wife and scores of Federal officials, pulled into the Groton shipyard of the Electric Boat Company, a division of the General Dynamics Corporation.

About 12,000 persons strained in the temporary bleachers at shipside to catch every detail of the ceremony. They had come to see the Navy open a new chapter in the history of transportation.

Though she was built for war, the $55,000,000 Nautilus also represents one of the first attempts to extract from uranium-235 sufficient power to light, in effect, a small city.

Sun Breaks Through

As the ceremony progressed, with speeches and prayer, the fog thinned and, an instant before the launching, the sun came out. Commander Eugene Parks Wilkinson, first skipper of the Nautilus, stood on the bow as Admiral Robert B. Carney, Chief of Naval Operations, described her potential for peace or war.

"Nautilus is a symbol of man's dreaming," the admiral said, "his bright dreams, certainly, and if man is not wise, his nightmares, too."

Capable of cruising around the world without once rising to the surface, because her atomic engine requires no air, the Nautilus has a fearsome potential for destruction. Her top speed is expected to be 30 knots, sufficient to outrun all but the swiftest destroyers.

If she lives up to expectations, however, the Nautilus may be more influential in pointing the way to such peaceful uses of atomic energy as power generation in areas with insufficient coal or water resources.

As Mrs. Eisenhower, in black jersey dress with surplice bodice, mink coat, pink gloves and flowered pinwheel bonnet of pink straw, made ready to splash

Continued on Page 3, Column 1

PRESIDENT ASKS 65.5-BILLION BUDGET; DEFICIT 2.9 DESPITE 5-BILLION CUT; 68% FOR DEFENSE; ARMY, NAVY PARED

ARMS FIGURE DOWN

37.5 Billion Requested —Top Reliance Put on Air-Atom Power

Special to The New York Times.

WASHINGTON, Jan. 21— President Eisenhower recommended today a $37,575,000,000 military spending program.

The military spending figure, added to the amounts requested for the Mutual Military Program, Atomic Energy Commission and stockpiling brought the total request for National Security purposes to 68 per cent of the entire budget.

In the military budget, the President placed first reliance on air-atomic power, rather than a large Army, to keep the peace.

His program for the 1955 fiscal year, starting July 1, represents a cut of almost $4,000,000,000 below the estimated military expenditure of $41,550,000,000 for the 1954 fiscal year.

This saving would account for three-quarters of the $5,300,000,000 reduction in the national budget that the President submitted to Congress.

The Army, in which President Eisenhower held five-star rank, will be cut from twenty to seventeen divisions in the next eighteen months if the proposed budget is adopted in its present form, a Defense Department spokesman said. Its spending will be reduced by exactly $4,000,000,000 from the current year's estimate of $14,200,000,000.

Air Force to Get More

While the Navy's spending also is to go down, from $11,300,000,000 in the current year to $10,500,000,000 in the 1955 fiscal year, the Air Force will go up by about the same amount, from $15,600,000,000 to $16,300,000,000.

On balance, therefore, the Army alone will provide the full amount of the defense budget reduction. It is the only one of the three services for which the President recommended no new obligational authority for major procurement and production.

These changes in emphasis, President Eisenhower said, are based on "a new concept for planning and financing our national security program."

Rather than aimed at building strength to peak at certain assumed dates of maximum danger, as in previous years, the new budget "is aimed instead at providing a strong military position which can be maintained over an

Continued on Page 19, Column 1

COME AND GO: Reducing the President's $65,570,000,000 budget to its simplest terms, Budget Director Joseph Dodge illustrates breakdown of the incoming and outgoing dollar.

Associated Press Wirephoto

BROWNELL BARS OUSTER DETAILS

Refuses to Separate 'Drunks' From 'Spies' in Security Program Dismissals

By W. H. LAWRENCE
Special to The New York Times.

WASHINGTON, Jan. 21—Attorney General Herbert Brownell Jr. refused today to separate the "drunks" from the "spies" among employes dismissed by the Government under the security program.

The Attorney General defended the right of the Eisenhower Administration to withhold from the public any detailed breakdown of the reasons for separating 2,200 employes from the Federal payroll.

Mr. Brownell held his first press conference since he charged last November that the late Harry Dexter White had been promoted by former President Truman despite reports by the Federal Bureau of Investigation that Mr. White was a Soviet spy.

The conference was held as the House Committee on Un-American Activities and Civil Service Committee, under Democratic

Continued on Page 12, Column 2

AIR ACADEMY WINS IN HOUSE, 329-36

Bill to Authorize 26 Million for Start of Third Service School Goes to Senate

Special to The New York Times.

WASHINGTON, Jan. 21—The House passed today by a roll-call vote of 329 to 36 the bill to authorize the creation of an Air Force academy.

The academy would be set up along the lines of the Army's academy at West Point and the Navy's at Annapolis. The bill calls for an appropriation of $26,000,000 to get it started. Estimates of the over-all cost range from $117,000,000 to $500,000,000. The measure was sent to the Senate.

Representative Dewey Short, Republican of Missouri, chairman of the Armed Services Committee, was House sponsor of the bill, which was the first piece of major legislation passed by the House at this session. An attempt by Representative Errett P. Scrivner, Republican of Kansas, to head off a vote through a recommittal motion was defeated, 131 to 25.

The bill provides that permanent location of the academy be decided by the Secretary of the Air Force. Secretary Harold E. Talbott has said that he would appoint a survey board as soon as the bill was passed by both houses.

The board would report to him within sixty days. Several sites have been recommended. The bill provides for the use of $1,000,000 for the establishment of a temporary academy at an Air Force base.

Until the permanent academy is well established, a period estimated in the legislation as six

Continued on Page 3, Column 7

TAX RELIEF URGED

Foreign Aid Estimates Unchanged—Disputes on Capitol Hill Seen

Text of Budget Message is on Pages 13 through 19.

By JOHN D. MORRIS
Special to The New York Times.

WASHINGTON, Jan. 21— President Eisenhower laid before Congress today a fiscal program dedicated to achieving, at least ultimately, what he called "the twin goals of a balanced budget and tax reductions."

In the first budget wholly prepared by the new Republican Administration, the President deferred until some future year the attainment of a balance between expenditures and receipts. But he made specific recommendations for immediate tax relief in the shape of selective reforms in various revenue laws. At the same time, he again asked Congress to cancel cuts in actual tax rates scheduled for next April 1.

The President's budget, based on the assumption that Congress would approve tax and other legislation he is proposing, blueprints expenditures of $65,570,000,000 in the fiscal year 1955, which will start July 1. It estimates receipts at $62,642,000,000.

This would produce a prospective deficit of $2,928,000,000.

Prospect Unspecified

President Eisenhower gave no indication when the budget might be balanced in fulfillment of what previously had been regarded as the chief fiscal aim of the year-old Administration. In separate news conferences, Joseph M. Dodge, Budget Director, and George M. Humphrey, Secretary of the Treasury, likewise declined to speculate on the outlook.

Instead, all three emphasized the desirability of gearing tax reductions to cuts in expenditures without making a prospective budget balance the primary condition.

The effect, whether intended or incidental, was to give hope and cheer to the many Congressional Republicans who have gained office on promises of tax relief under a Republican regime and who would again be seeking election next November.

On the score of slashing expenditures and reducing the annual deficit, the President could point at any rate to impressive progress.

"The trend," he said in his Budget Message, which was read to the Senate and the House of Representatives by clerks, "clearly is toward a balanced budget."

Deficit, Spending Reduced

His proposed spending figure of $65,570,000,000 for 1955 was $5,300,000,000 less than newly revised estimates of outlays in the present fiscal year, 1954. It was $12,300,000,000 below expenditures originally budgeted by the Truman Administration for 1954.

The prospective deficit of $2,928,000,000 was $345,000,000 below that of the present year and $6,461,000,000 less than the 1954 deficit projected by former President Truman last January in the budget that was later revised by the new Administration.

The Eisenhower budget would have shown a surplus of about $2,000,000,000 for 1955 without the automatic tax cuts that went into effect Jan. 1 and the proposed tax relief. On Jan. 1, the excess profits tax on corporations expired along with 1951 increases of about 10 per cent in individual income levies.

Actually, the so-called "cash" budget for 1955 shows a surplus of $115,000,000. It includes expenditures and receipts of the Social Security Old Age and Survivors Insurance program and several other accounts handled separately from the regular budget. The Social Security trust fund takes in about $2,000,000,000 more than it pays out. The cash budget measures the actual cash income and outgo of the whole Government.

While the Army and the Navy alone bore $4,800,000,000 of the $5,300,000,000 reductions from total estimated expenditures for the present year, the 1955 budget was still dominated by the requirements of national security in

Continued on Page 12, Column 6

City Water Post Goes To a Negro Engineer

By PAUL CROWELL

Arthur C. Ford was named yesterday as Commissioner of Water Supply, Gas and Electricity. He is the first Negro in New York history to be a commissioner.

Mayor Wagner, designating Mr. Ford as successor to Dominick F. Paduano, a holdover from the administration of former Mayor Vincent R. Impellitteri, announced also the appointment of Joseph P. Spagna, a lawyer, as Commissioner of Purchase. He succeeds John Spain, who held the office under former Mayors Impellitteri and William O'Dwyer.

Mr. Ford, who is 62 years old and lives at 176-03 Croydon Road, Jamaica Estates, Queens, has been a consulting engineer in the office of the Borough President of Manhattan since 1950. His appointment was described

Continued on Page 22, Column 3

The Words 'I Christen Thee Nautilus' Unfold a New Vista of U. S. Sea Power

With traditional champagne, Mrs. Dwight D. Eisenhower christens Nautilus. In rear is Comdr. E. L. Beach, President's naval aide.

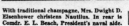

Slowly at first, but gaining momentum, the Nautilus, world's first nuclear-powered vessel, slides down ways into the Thames at Groton, Conn. Fog had lifted and the sun shone brightly as the 3,000-ton submarine was launched. She is third Navy submarine with name of Jules Verne's fictitious submersible.

The New York Times

113

The New York Times.

VOL. CIII..No. 35,101.

Entered as Second-Class Matter,
Post Office, New York, N. Y.

NEW YORK, TUESDAY, MARCH 2, 1954.

Times Square, New York 36, N. Y.
Telephone LAckawanna 4-1000

FIVE CENTS

Copyright, 1954, by The New York Times Company

LATE CITY EDITION
Considerable cloudiness today.
Partly cloudy, cold tomorrow.
Temperature Range Today—Max.: 40; Min.: 35
Temperature Yesterday—Max.: 56.4; Min.: 47.7
Full U. S. Weather Bureau Report, Page 49

HIDDEN OWNERSHIP OF RACEWAY STOCK BARED AT HEARING

Former Legislator, Intimate of O'Dwyer, Erickson Kin and Ex-Convict Are Identified

HOLDINGS PUT AT MILLION

Moreland Inquiry Opens Public Sessions, Gets Details of Yonkers Track Purchase

By EMANUEL PERLMUTTER

Politicians and persons with underworld backgrounds or friendships were found yesterday to have been the hidden owners of close to a million dollars' worth of stock in several New York harness racing tracks.

These disclosures were made as the Moreland Act Commission opened public hearings here on the scandal-ridden raceways. The proceedings are being held in the Criminal Court Building, 100 Centre Street.

Among those who were shown to have struck it rich secretly on the trotting tracks were former Assemblyman Elmer J. Kellam of Hancock, N. Y.; Irving Sherman, political intimate of former Mayor William O'Dwyer and admitted friend of gangsters; Frank J. Erickson, son of the convicted gambler, and Samuel J. Stirratt, an ex-convict with a long police record.

Additional testimony was introduced indicating that loans from racketeers had helped the original incorporators of the Algam Corporation to purchase the Yonkers Empire City Race Track —now Yonkers Raceway—for $2,400,000 in 1949.

Named a Racing Steward

Mr. Kellam, who served in the Assembly from Delaware County between 1943 and 1950, admitted on the witness stand that he had transferred 10,000 shares in Mid-State Raceway, near Syracuse, to a "dummy" owner after he had been appointed as a state racing steward last year.

The former Republican legislator said that he became the beneficiary of the stock, which was listed in the name of Marvin Wynkoop of Downsville, N. Y., and that he intended to sell it but had been unable to do so because of the pressure of his duties as a steward at Roosevelt Raceway, Westbury, L. I. He described the duties of a steward as "protecting the public, to see if the races are on the level."

"Did you think it was proper for a steward to own stock in a track?" Bruce Bromley, the commission chairman, asked him.

Mr. Kellam, a sandy-haired, florid-faced man, shook his head apologetically. "I don't think it's good judgment," he conceded. "But I never performed any duties at a track where I was a stockholder."

Still Owns Track Stock

The witness said he now owned 9,500 shares in the upstate track. He said he assumed he still held the job as racing steward.

At this point, Harness Racing Commissioner George P. Monaghan, sitting as a member of the Moreland Commission, interrupted to point out that stewards served for one year and that they had to be reappointed each racing season.

The testimony involving Irving Sherman, who was referred to as the contact man for Frank Costello during Mayor O'Dwyer's administration, was given by Sam Sherman, a raincoat manufacturer, of 30 West Fifty-fourth Street. He is not related to Irving Sherman.

Sam Sherman testified that although he was the listed owner of 22,500 shares of stock and $50,000 worth of bonds in the Algam Corporation, holding company for the Yonkers track, Irving Sherman actually owned 80 per cent of the investment.

In October, 1953, soon after the Moreland Commission was appointed, Algam purchased 30,-000 shares from him, Mr. Sherman said. He said the purchase price was $296,000, a total of $30 a share. Of this sum, he testified, he gave $145,000 to Irving Sherman, the remainder of the latter's share being tied up in litigation.

In addition, Mr. Sherman said, the 2,500 shares of voting stock that he and his secret partner owned were sold at the same time for $75,000 to M. Duke Manacher, a stockholder in Algam. He said he gave $60,000 of this sum to Irving Sherman. The $50,000 worth of bonds

Continued on Page 12, Column 3

Jarka, Big Stevedore, Quits Port Under Fire

By A. H. RASKIN

The Jarka Corporation, one of the world's largest stevedoring enterprises, decided yesterday to stop operating in the Port of New York.

The company and its president, Frank W. Nolan, are awaiting trial in Special Sessions on charges of having paid out $119,859 in bribes to shipping executives for steering contracts to Jarka. The Waterfront Commission has been conducting an investigation to determine whether the company should be barred from doing business here.

The Jarka decision to withdraw its application for a stevedoring license was the highlight of another hectic day on the strife-swept waterfront. Other developments included:

¶A controversy over the Continued on Page 11, Column 1

UNITY PLEA OPENS CARACAS MEETING

Hemisphere Accord Founded on Sovereignty and Equality Is Urged on Delegates

By SAM POPE BREWER
Special to The New York Times.

CARACAS, Venezuela, March 1—President Marcos Perez Jimenes of Venezuela opened the tenth Inter-American Conference today with a plea for closer unity among the American States on the basis of sovereignty and equality.

There is explosive material on the agenda in questions such as Communist infiltration in Latin America and the rules for granting political asylum. Yet all indications today were that most of the delegates were in a conciliatory mood and that means would be sought to avoid heated clashes.

The elaborate security precautions taken for the conference seemed to grow in importance when word of the shooting in the United States Congress was received.

[Guatemala lost her first test at the parley on a procedural question, while at home President Jacobo Arbenz Guzman denied any Soviet intervention in the country's internal affairs.]

Speaking at the first session in the great modernistic assembly hall of University City, President Perez emphasized that the idea of continental unity had existed from the day the American nations won their independence.

"The existence of basic factors of a type common to all the continent, and the desire to obtain and preserve independence are the fundamental reasons for which there appeared almost simultaneously in the greater part of the peoples of America, the idea of unity among them," he said.

He added, however, that "the unity of our peoples should be based on comprehension, the feeling of reciprocal assistance and mutual respect."

"We shall understand each Continued on Page 9, Column 1

Nehru Decries U. S. Policy On Asia and the 'Cold War'

By ROBERT TRUMBULL
Special to The New York Times.

NEW DELHI, India, March 1—Prime Minister Jawaharlal Nehru scathingly condemned virtually the entire United States policy in Asia and in the "cold war" today. His most outspoken speech among many on this subject, delivered to the House of the People, the lower chamber of Parliament, was repeatedly interrupted by thunderous applause. He was given a prolonged ovation at its end.

Mr. Nehru was commenting on President Eisenhower's personal letter last week informing the Indian leader of Washington's intention to furnish military aid to Pakistan and simultaneously offering the same assistance to India.

Mr. Nehru scorned General Eisenhower's tender with the statement that "in making this suggestion, the President has done less than justice to us or to himself."

"If we object to military aid being given to Pakistan, it would be hypocrisy and unprincipled opportunism to accept such aid ourselves," he added.

The Prime Minister told the cheering House that United States members of the United Nations cease-fire observer team—in Kashmir should be removed. He said that "these American observers can no longer be treated by us as neutrals" in India's dispute with Pakistan over possession of the strategic northern state.

[At United Nations Headquarters a spokesman said no action would be taken pending an official communication from India. In Washington a State Department spokesman said India would have to complain to the United Nations if she wanted the United States members withdrawn.]

In his tersely formal reply to General Eisenhower, which he read out, Mr. Nehru coldly thanked the President for his "assurances," but dismissed them with the curt statement: "You are, however, aware of the views of my Government and our people in regard to this matter. We shall continue to pursue that policy."

The Indian note ignored the offer of arms.

Mr. Nehru, in his speech, took especially heated exception to the version of United States policy in Asia as quoted from testimony by Walter S. Robertson, Assistant Secretary of State, before a Continued on Page 5, Column 2

31 KILLED IN SUDAN IN NATIVES' CLASH AS NAGUIB ARRIVES

117 Hurt in Battle at Khartum Palace Between Tribesmen and Pro-Egyptian Group

Dispatch of The Times, London.

KHARTUM, the Sudan, March 1—The arrival in the Sudan today of Maj. Gen. Mohammed Naguib, Egyptian President, revived factional passions of this nascent state in a clash in which at least twenty-two persons were killed. [The Associated Press placed the toll at thirty-one.]

Among the dead were eight of the police force, including the British police commandant of Khartum, H. S. McGuigan, and the superintendent, Mustapha el Mahdi. One hundred seventeen were wounded, of whom thirty-two were seriously injured.

The factional struggle was of a primitive nature. The dead and wounded were seen to bear the marks of clubs and spears, not gunshot wounds.

[Meanwhile, a spokesman for the ruling junta in Egypt said in Cairo Monday that General Naguib owed his reinstatement as President to agitation begun by eight Communist army officers.]

The tragedy here was enacted outside the Governor General's palace, which stands on the site of the residency where Gen. Charles G. Gordon, then Governor General, died from the thrusts of tribesmen's spears during the historic Khartum siege in 1885. Inside the residency, General Naguib, Sir Robert Howe, Governor General, and Selwyn Lloyd, Minister of State of the British Foreign Office, were at lunch during today's events.

Parliament Opening Put Off

In view of the passions aroused by the rioting, the Governor General postponed a meeting of the Sudanese Parliament, scheduled for this afternoon, until March 10.

It seemed today as though the army of Mohammed Ahmed, the Mahdi, or Moslem leader who defeated General Gordon, were on the march again. The rioters massed outside the Khartum airport, turbaned and robed in shining white, with their hundreds of banners waving above the throng. They were supporters of the patron of the Sudanese independence movement, Sir Abdel Rahman el Mahdi, mainly Baggara tribesmen from the provinces who gathered to greet General Naguib with chanted slogans demanding independence for the Sudan.

"No Egypt! No Britain!" they cried as they surged up to Sudanese Defense Force troops who barred their way to the airport.

This was no unkempt rabble; their banners were of trim red, green and black stripes, superimposed with a white spear cutting a white crescent.

General Naguib left his aircraft at Khartum airport at 10 A. M. He was accompanied by Maj. Salah Salem, Egyptian Minister of National Guidance and Minister of State for Sudanese Affairs. Sir Robert, Ismail el Azhary, Prime Minister of the Continued on Page 2, Column 2

FIVE CONGRESSMEN SHOT IN HOUSE BY 3 PUERTO RICAN NATIONALISTS; BULLETS SPRAY FROM GALLERY

SEIZED IN SHOOTING: Capitol police hold three Puerto Rican Nationalists after they fired from gallery seats into House chamber, wounding five Representatives. Prisoners, left to right, are Lolita Lebron, Rafael C. Miranda and Andres Cordero.

Associated Press Wirephoto

CAPITOL IN UPROAR

Woman, Accomplices Quickly Overpowered —High Bonds Set

By CLAYTON KNOWLES
Special to The New York Times.

WASHINGTON, March 1—Five members of the Congress of The United States were shot down on the floor of the House of Representatives today.

Their assailants, at least three Puerto Rican Nationalists, shouted for freedom of their homeland as they fired murderously although at random from a spectators' gallery just above the House floor. Possibly twenty-five shots were fired.

Bullets rained down from two German Lugers and other pistols of lesser caliber. They crashed through the table of the majority leader and chairs around it, and struck near the table of the Minority Leader beyond. The time was 2:32 P. M.

House members at first thought the sounds were those of firecrackers. But as their colleagues fell or took cover as they heard the slugs hit around them, all realized what was happening.

The wounded House members:
ALVIN M. BENTLEY, 35 years old, multimillionaire Michigan Republican, shot through lung, liver and intestine. Condition serious.

BEN F. JENSEN, 61, Republican of Iowa, shot in back. Condition serious.

CLIFFORD DAVIS, 56, Democrat of Tennessee, shot in the leg. Condition good.

GEORGE H. FALLON, 51, Democrat of Maryland, leg wound. Condition good.

KENNETH A. ROBERTS, 41, Democrat of Alabama, leg wound. Condition good.

Assailants Subdued

Within a matter of minutes, the episode, which threw the Capitol and most of official Washington into an uproar, was at an end. Gallery attendants, aided by spectators, Capitol police and even one House member, quickly overcame and disarmed the three gun wielders.

The three Puerto Ricans, all booked at police headquarters on charges of assault with intent to kill. They gave their names and addresses as:

LOLITA LEBRON, 34, 315 West Ninety-fourth Street.

RAFAEL C. MIRANDA, 25, 120 South First Street, Brooklyn.

ANDRES CORDERO, or FIGUEROA, 29, of 108 East 103d Street.

A fourth Puerto Rican, also resident in New York, was arrested at a downtown bus station and booked on the same charge. He was named as Irving Flores, 27, also of 108 East 103d Street, described by Police Chief Robert Murray as a fourth member of the shooting party who had fled the Capitol successfully. When arrested, Flores still had a .45 caliber pistol.

Later, United States Commissioner Cyril S. Lawrence ordered all four held under $100,000 bonds each. He put off a preliminary hearing until March 10 to give them time to get counsel. Five counts of assault with intent to Continued on Page 16, Column 1

M'LEOD AUTHORITY IS CUT BY DULLES

Friend of McCarthy Loses Personnel Duties, Keeps His Security Office

Special to The New York Times.

WASHINGTON, March 1—The Eisenhower Administration stripped Scott McLeod today of his authority over State Department personnel. It left him in charge of security matters.

This action, which was announced on the authority of John Foster Dulles, the Secretary of State, was widely interpreted as a thrust by the Administration at the McCarthy wing of the Republican party.

Mr. McLeod is a close friend of Senator Joseph R. McCarthy, Republican of Wisconsin. He went to the State Department last January from the office of Senator Styles Bridges, Republican of New Hampshire.

Mr. McLeod has served as administrative assistant to Senator Bridges and at one time was an agent of the Federal Bureau of Investigation.

Mr. McLeod made five speeches for the Republican party in the recent Lincoln Week series of partisan addresses, and there were Democratic protests that he was improperly using his office. A Republican member of the Civil Service Commission, George Moore, held informally that such political activity was forbidden by the Hatch Act, which limits the partisanship of certain Federal officials and employes.

Policies Criticized

On Jan. 16, five former United States Ambassadors charged in an open letter that State Department personnel and security policies might be "laying the foundations for a Foreign Service competent to serve a totalitarian government rather than the Government of the United States as we have heretofore known it."

They did not mention Mr. McLeod by name, but both the personnel and security policies were under his direction.

In a speech on Feb. 18 in Larchmont, N. Y., Mr. McLeod especially heated exception to the version of United States policy in Asia as quoted from testimony by Walter S. Robertson, Assistant Secretary of State, before a Continued on Page 15, Column 1

McCarthy, Dirksen Suggest Labor Camps for Army Reds

By W. H. LAWRENCE
Special to The New York Times.

WASHINGTON, March 1—Senators Joseph R. McCarthy and Everett M. Dirksen suggested today "disagreeable" labor camps for armed services personnel who were Communists or who invoked the Fifth Amendment when asked about Communist associations.

Their suggestion grew out of new disclosures by the Senate Permanent Subcommittee on Investigations of "contradictions" in the Army system of handling officers and enlisted men who were alleged Communists or admitted former Communists.

Senator McCarthy, Republican of Wisconsin, is chairman of the subcommittee, and Senator Dirksen, an Illinois Republican, is a member.

The subcommittee accepted an Army suggestion that it question Robert T. Stevens, Secretary of the Army, at a closed session on Thursday or next Monday. All advance indications on both sides were that it would be a "friendly" hearing and not a controversial showdown such as was threatened but called off last week.

With four Republicans and one Democrat present, the subcommittee today questioned in secret an Army private and a former private in considering a problem of fundamental importance to all the armed forces. Stated broadly, the subcommittee raised these questions:

¶Should admitted Communists, Continued on Page 14, Column 2

U. S. Dismissed 355 In Subversive Cases

Special to The New York Times.

WASHINGTON, March 1—The Civil Service Commission reported today that 355 Federal employes whose personnel files contained some allegations of subversive associations had been separated from the Government payroll between May 28 and Dec. 31, 1953.

The report was the first overall breakdown provided by the Administration to Congress since the controversy over the 2,200 persons said by President Eisenhower to have been separated as "security risks."

Philip Young, commission chairman, said the "security" separations totaled 2,224, of whom 963 were dismissed and 1,241 resigned. These figures included 211 dismissals and 231 resigna- Continued on Page 13, Column 2

WITNESS DESCRIBES SHOOTING, CAPTURE

Reporter Sees Firing in House —Struck on Cheek by Chip Torn Loose by Bullet

By C. P. TRUSSELL
Special to The New York Times.

WASHINGTON, March 1—Until the shooting in the House of Representatives today things were somewhat dull.

So dull, in fact, that a short time before members had been summoned by bells to the floor to listen to the issue at hand, whether they wanted to or not, as to the consideration of Mexican farm laborers.

The quorum bell was answered by 243 members, most of whom were still on the floor when the shooting started in what is called the Ladies' Gallery.

As a police reporter many years ago I was irked by eyewitnesses who had heard shots only as "backfiring automobiles," "blowouts" or "firecrackers." But this time I too thought that firecrackers were going off, and I thought it was a Latin demonstration.

But only for a moment. I saw two men and a woman, in the second row of the Ladies' Gallery, pumping at pistols. The two men appeared to be aiming at the desk of Representative Charles A. Halleck of Indiana, the Republican floor leader.

This statement from the head of the agency charged with protecting the President reflected the close watch that the Secret Service had kept on the Nationalist movement ever since two of its members tried to kill President Truman on Nov. 1, 1950.

A police guard was put around Continued on Page 17, Column 2

EISENHOWER TARGET FOR FANATICS ALSO

Secret Service Men Detected Puerto Rican Plot Against President in November

Special to The New York Times.

WASHINGTON, March 1—Puerto Rican extremists have been conspiring to harm President Eisenhower if they got the opportunity, according to the Federal Secret Service.

Henry Cabot Lodge Jr., chief of the United States delegation to the United Nations, was put under twenty-four-hour guard last November for the same reason.

U. E. Baughman, chief of the Secret Service, was asked tonight about the reports of a conspiracy against the President.

"Three or four months ago," he replied, "the Secret Service obtained information indicating the Puerto Rican Nationalists were still possibly interested in harming the President in their fight for independence."

Mr. Baughman said that the Secret Service had obtained information about designs on President Eisenhower last November. That coincided with the threat on Mr. Lodge. It was indicated that there was an apparent link between the threats to Mr. Lodge and the designs on the President.

Although one assassin was killed in the gun battle in front of Blair House and Oscar Collazo, his companion, is serving a life sentence, the Secret Service still carries the attempted assassination of Mr. Truman as an "open case." It does this because it has not given up the possibility of rounding up the conspirators who directed the assassins.

Continued on Page 16, Column 7

Atom Blast Opens Test in Pacific; No Hint of Hydrogen Plans Given

Special to The New York Times.

WASHINGTON, March 1—The Atomic Energy Commission today announced the first in a new series of test explosions at its Pacific proving ground in the Marshall Islands.

No further announcement on the tests was ended. A forty-two word statement told as much of the story as the commission wanted the public to know at this stage. It read:

"[Rear Admiral] Lewis L. Strauss, chairman of the United States Atomic Energy Commission, announced today that Joint Task Force Seven has detonated an atomic device at the A. E. C.'s Pacific proving ground in the Marshall Islands. This detonation was the first in a series of tests."

The language of Admiral Strauss' statement did not make clear whether the "atomic device" was of the fission or thermo-nuclear (hydrogen) type. There have been unofficial indications, however, that a variety of hydrogen weapons or devices will be tested during the next several weeks.

The most powerful of these is expected to be an actual hydrogen bomb with perhaps twice the explosive power of the experimental device that disintegrated an island of Eniwetok atoll on Nov. 1, 1952.

Representative W. Sterling Cole of upstate New York, the chairman of the Joint Congressional Committee on Atomic Energy, disclosed only two weeks ago that the first device had "completely obliterated" the island Continued on Page 6, Column 5

114

Representatives B.F. Jensen of Ia. (A); Kenneth Roberts, Ala. (B); George Fallon, Md. (C); Alvin Bentley, Mich. (D); Clifford Davis, Tenn. (E) were wounded in Congress by the gunfire of three Puerto Rican nationalists.

Albert Einstein, the great genius of the 20th Century, with close friend J. Robert Oppenheimer. The latter is the man who created the first atomic bomb. He was accused of being a security risk in a sensational "trial."

President Dwight Eisenhower and Secretary of State John Foster Dulles.

Television viewers across the nation watched the McCarthy Hearings in 1954 and listened as the Wisconsin Senator tried to repudiate Army charges that he sought to win special treatment for his aide, David Schine. Shown here is the moment when Senator Flanders (R-Vt.) handed McCarthy notice that he would speak against him in the Senate.

Edward R. Murrow became the first major commentator to attack Senator Joe McCarthy on his See It Now show of March 9.

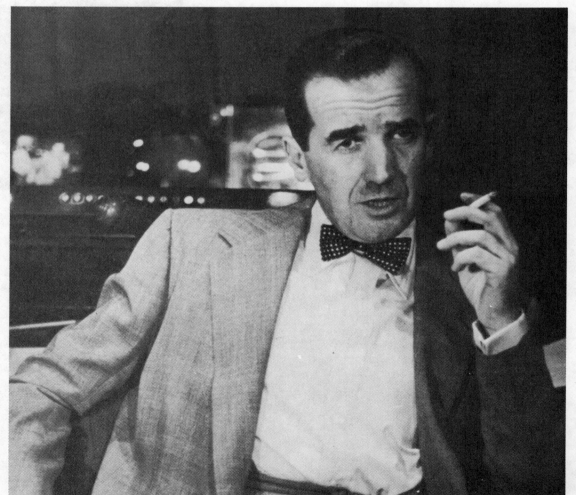

"All the News That's Fit to Print"

The New York Times.

LATE CITY EDITION
Increasingly cloudy today. Rain tonight and tomorrow.
Temperature Range Today—Max., 45; Min., 31
Temperatures Yesterday—Max., 46; Min., 31
Full U. S. Weather Bureau Report, Page 41

Copyright, 1954, by The New York Times Company.

VOL. CIII..No. 35,111. Entered as Second-Class Matter, Post Office, New York, N. Y. NEW YORK, FRIDAY, MARCH 12, 1954. Times Square, New York 36, N. Y. Telephone LAckawanna 4-1000 FIVE CENTS

ARMY CHARGES M'CARTHY AND COHN THREATENED IT IN TRYING TO OBTAIN PREFERRED TREATMENT FOR SCHINE

HALF OF DOCKMEN IN BROOKLYN JOIN OUTLAW WALKOUT

Huge Food Cargoes Reported in Danger of Spoiling—Trade Losses Mounting

COURT IS PICKETED AGAIN

Rally Backs a Tie-Up Until I. L. A. Is Certified—Jersey Strikers Pledge Return

By A. H. RASKIN

The outlaw dock strike got worse yesterday.

Half of the longshoremen in Brooklyn, the only section of the port that had been operating normally, joined the week-old walkout.

Importers notified the National Labor Relations Board that millions of dollars worth of fruit and vegetables were in danger of rotting on piers and in the holds of strike-stalled ships.

The tie-up turned into a blockade when Philadelphia locals of the old International Longshoremen's Association refused to unload passenger or cargo vessels diverted from New York. Rank-and-file leaders of the local stoppage sought to make the boycott coast-wide, but received no immediate assurances of help from other ports.

The Commerce and Industry Association reported that the turbulent dock labor situation was causing many large corporations to shunt their import and export schedules to other cities. The group predicted that 10 per cent of the lost trade never would be recovered.

The one bright spot in the waterfront picture was a promise by Jersey City strikers to go back to their jobs this morning. The promise was given by spokesmen for both of the warring dock unions—the I. L. A. and its American Federation of Labor rival—at a conference with Commissioner Lawrence A. Whipple in Jersey City.

Picket Line Is Crossed

The federation union, which has been opposing the walkout, mobilized 100 longshoremen to pierce an I. L. A. picket line at a Manhattan wharf of the United Fruit Company. Ignoring the jeers of several hundred members of the old union, five gangs of A. F. L. dock workers walked onto Pier 3, just north of the Battery, to unload coffee and miscellaneous cargo from Guatemala and Honduras. The cargo was aboard the freighter Lovland.

Two hundred and fifty I. L. A. strikers renewed the picketing of the United States Court House in Foley Square. It was the second time they had marched outside the building in protest against two anti-strike court orders.

One was an injunction forbidding the I. L. A. to strike or to interfere with waterfront truck movements. The other was a $100,000 contempt action against the union and three officers of its West Side locals.

The strike has been carried on in defiance of the two orders and in disregard of back-to-work appeals by Capt. William V. Bradley, president of the I. L. A. Strike leaders say the walkout will continue until the old union is certified as the sole bargaining agent for the port's 24,000 dock workers.

The threat to keep the port tied up for all the months that may

Continued on Page 43, Column 2

Wilson Aide Named Secretary of Navy

Associated Press Wirephoto

Charles S. Thomas, Assistant Secretary of Defense, after he was named the successor to Robert B. Anderson, right.

Special to THE NEW YORK TIMES.

WASHINGTON, March 11—Charles Sparks Thomas, Assistant Secretary of Defense, was nominated by President Eisenhower today to be Secretary of the Navy. Mr. Thomas, if confirmed by the Senate, will succeed Robert B. Anderson, who will become Under Secretary of Defense when Roger B. Kyes vacates the post on May 1. A successor to Mr. Thomas has not yet been chosen. The

Continued on Page 8, Column 4

'Direct' Warning to Reds Urged by U. S. at Caracas

By SYDNEY GRUSON
Special to THE NEW YORK TIMES.

CARACAS, Venezuela, March 11—The United States called on the Tenth Inter-American Conference today to issue a "simple, clear and direct" warning to the leaders of international communism to keep hands off the Americas.

The best way to do this, John Foster Dulles, United States Secretary of State, said, is to adopt the United States anti-Communist resolution without crippling amendments. These, he said, would "alter the heart" of the proposed denunciation of international communism as a threat to the hemisphere.

After a week of general debate the Communist issue was joined late today in the Political Committee when consideration of the resolution began. The Secretary made his third major speech on the question in an effort to block a series of crippling amendments submitted by Mexico.

Mr. Dulles sought to eliminate the fears of some delegates that the resolution could, in his own words, "be interpreted as intervention or justifying intervention in the genuinely domestic affairs of an American state."

'Natural Historical Fears'

"This concern is, we believe, due to natural historical fears rather than to any language in the United States proposal," the Secretary said.

Delegates of Argentina, Guatemala and Mexico, all of whom spoke in the wind-up of the general debate this morning, had expressed this fear. The spokesmen for Guatemala, where the Communists have won high positions in the Government, have charged that the United States was seeking to cloak interventionist ideas in the guise of collective action against Guatemala.

Mexico's delegate spoke twice today, in the general debate and in answer to Secretary Dulles' rejection of Mexico's amendments. On both occasions Roberto Cordova of Mexico emphasized that his country was not trying to defend international communism but only the right of any people to choose their own form of government and political institutions.

Mexico, he said, would willingly subscribe to the United States proposal if his delegation were convinced that it did not represent a backward step regarding intervention. But later he brushed aside Mr. Dulles' assurances on this point and in fact took no note of the Secretary's announcement that the United States was itself proposing an addition to the declarative portion of the resolution to declare:

"This declaration of foreign policy made by the American republics in relation to the dangers originating outside this hemisphere is designed to protect and not to impair the inalienable right of each American state freely to choose its own form of government and economic system and to live its own social and cultural life."

As the resolution stood before,

Continued on Page 6, Column 4

SCHWABLE TELLS OF P.O.W. ORDEAL

Tells How His Mental Torture by Reds Almost Made Him Believe Germ 'Confession'

By ELIE ABEL
Special to THE NEW YORK TIMES.

WASHINGTON, March 11—Col. Frank H. Schwable described today how a mature man could be conditioned to accept as real the fictions he had invented to appease the Communists.

Taking the witness chair for the first time, the lean, nervous Marine aviator talked for six hours before a court of inquiry. He tried to explain how it felt to have his brain washed, how reality became a blur in the mind, how the judgment could be fogged and the will destroyed.

He did not quite believe his own story that the United States had waged bacteriological warfare in Korea, Colonel Schwable told the court, which is investigating his false "confession."

"I was never convinced in my own mind that we in the First Marine Air Wing had used bug warfare," he testified. "I knew we hadn't. But the rest of it [the fraudulent confession] was real to me—the conferences, the planes and how they would go about their missions."

Rear Admiral Thomas J. Cooper, who was questioning the

Continued on Page 5, Column 5

264 Exposed to Atom Radiation After Nuclear Blast in Pacific

By The Associated Press.

WASHINGTON, March 11—The Atomic Energy Commission said tonight that twenty-eight Americans and 236 natives were "unexpectedly" subjected to "some radiation" during the recent atomic test in the Marshall Islands but all those exposed were "reported well."

The commission announced on March 1 that the first of a series of nuclear tests had started in the Pacific proving grounds.

The commission announcement today said:

"During the course of a routine atomic test in the Marshall Islands, twenty-eight United States personnel and 236 residents were transported from neighboring atolls to Kwajalein Island according to plans as a precautionary measure.

"The individuals were unexpectedly exposed to some radiation. There were no burns. All are reported well.

"After completion of the atomic tests, they will be returned to their homes."

The commission made no immediate amplification of this announcement. However, it seemed probably that a "fall-out" of radioactive waste and activated moisture from a cloud drifting from the explosion probably descended on the Americans and natives on the atoll to which they had been moved.

Atomic test officials try to make careful forecasts of wind directions but sometimes miscalculate.

Exposure to mild radiation is not necessarily dangerous. Reporters last spring were within two miles of an atomic explosion at the Nevada proving grounds and later walked to "Ground

Continued on Page 8, Column 4

SENATE COMBINES STATEHOOD PLANS BY VOTE OF 46-43

Ignores Eisenhower's Wishes for Action on Hawaii Alone—Democrats Score Victory

By CLAYTON KNOWLES
Special to THE NEW YORK TIMES.

WASHINGTON, March 11—The Senate disregarded Administration wishes in voting today to put Hawaiian and Alaskan statehood proposals into a single bill.

The decision to join the proposals carried by a vote of 46 to 43 and came a day after President Eisenhower had urged separate consideration of the statehood measures. He had asked for immediate statehood for Hawaii alone. This is the Republican party position.

The Senate's vote was mainly along party lines, with the Democrats winning. However, the plan to combine the bills prevailed by the margin of the votes of three Republicans who broke with their party on the question. They were Senators William Langer of North Dakota, John M. Butler of Maryland and George W. Malone of Nevada.

Forty-two Democrats and the Senate's one independent, Wayne Morse of Oregon, cast the other votes for a combined bill.

Forty-one Republicans and two Democrats, Spessard L. Holland of Florida and Russell B. Long of Louisiana, opposed the merger plan.

Knowland to Back Bill

The issue in the three-day debate preceding the vote was whether statehood aspirations of Hawaii and Alaska would be hurt or helped by putting them together. Senator William F. Knowland of California, Republican Senate leader, contended it would hurt. Senator Clinton P. Anderson, Democrat of New Mexico and sponsor of the one-package proposal, asserted it would help.

The vote along party lines stemmed largely from the fact that Hawaii is normally Republican and might be expected to send a Republican delegation to Congress, while Alaska is Democratic at the polls and probably would send Democrats to the Congress.

After the Senate action, Senator Knowland, conceding a chance to pass a combined bill, said he would vote for it. So did other Republicans in opposition on the vote today. Senator Hugh Butler of Nebraska, Interior Committee chairman who fought the Anderson amendment, said the Senate "might fool some people by passing the bill now before us."

The Nebraska Republican alluded to the fact that a group of Southern Democrats, numbering fifteen to twenty, had supported the Anderson amendment in the hope of defeating both statehood proposals. Senator George A. Smathers, Democrat of Florida, frankly conceded during debate

Continued on Page 13, Column 3

Lasting Prevention of Polio Reported in Vaccine Tests

Dr. Salk Says Discovery Fights Off All 3 Kinds of Crippling Disease

By WILLIAM L. LAURENCE
Special to THE NEW YORK TIMES.

NEW ORLEANS, March 11—The latest tests on children with the anti-polio vaccine have revealed that the vaccine provides the body with lasting defensive powers against the three types of viruses causing the disease, it was reported tonight.

This was described as the long-sought answer to a vital question, making it practically certain not only that the vaccine will produce effective immunity against all the three types of polio but also that the immunity will be of the lasting type, possibly for the individual's lifetime.

This could mean that within the next three to five years polio, crippler of young and old alike, will join diphtheria, smallpox, typhoid and other formerly dreaded infectious diseases as plagues finally tamed and conquered by man.

The newest findings were described here tonight before the New Orleans Graduate Medical Assembly by Dr. Jonas E. Salk, of the Virus Research Laboratory, University of Pittsburgh School of Medicine.

Associated Press

Dr. Jonas E. Salk

Dr. Salk developed the vaccine against the three types of polio-producing viruses, using viruses that had been rendered incapable of producing the disease while they still retained their power to produce immunity.

Replying to remarks made this morning in Detroit by Dr. Albert

Continued on Page 22, Column 3

SENATOR ATTACKS

Hits Back at Stevenson, Murrow and Flanders in Radio Broadcast

Special to THE NEW YORK TIMES.

WASHINGTON, March 11—Senator Joseph R. McCarthy struck back tonight at criticism of him by Adlai E. Stevenson, Edward R. Murrow and Senator Ralph E. Flanders.

The Wisconsin Republican said that Mr. Stevenson's assertion that only one alleged active Communist had been found in the Government in the last year was "absolutely false."

He called Mr. Murrow, Columbia Broadcasting System commentator, one of the "extreme Left Wing bleeding-heart elements of television and radio." He cited an article in The Pittsburgh Sun-Telegraph of Feb. 18, 1935, to charge that Mr. Murrow had been on the advisory council for a summer session of Moscow University, where overthrow of the existing social order was taught.

[Three and a half hours after Mr. McCarthy's broadcast, Mr. Murrow issued a statement in which he said that in 1935, in his capacity as assistant director of the Institute of International Education, he was a member of the advisory committee for a summer school in Moscow. He added, however, that "in actual fact the summer school was canceled by Russian authorities before it began."]

McCarthy Quotes Lincoln

Mr. McCarthy said he would rather stand with Abraham Lincoln, who said during Civil War times the danger to the United States was from within and not from without, rather than with Senator Flanders, a Republican of Vermont, who said the danger today is from without rather than from within.

Appearing on a question and answer radio broadcast with Fulton Lewis Jr., over the Mutual Broadcasting System, Senator McCarthy struck back at Messrs. Stevenson, Murrow and Flanders but made no mention of the implied criticism voiced by President Eisenhower at his news conference yesterday.

He also made no mention of his quarrel with the National Broadcasting Company and the Columbia Broadcasting System because they refused him free time for a reply to Mr. Stevenson and gave it instead to the Republican National Committee, which designated Vice President Nixon to make the official reply Saturday night.

Mr. Murrow had devoted a thir-

Continued on Page 11, Column 1

Cohn Scored When Woman Denies McCarthy's Charges

Mrs. Moss Counters Accusation as Red While Senators Decry 'Innuendo'—Crowd Applauds Hearing Scene

Special to THE NEW YORK TIMES.

WASHINGTON, March 11—Mrs. Annie Lee Moss, suspended Army Signal Corps employe, softly but flatly denied all Communist party activities or membership today.

The crowded caucus room of the Senate Office Building, where the Senate Permanent Subcommittee on Investigation was in session, rang with repeated applause as Democratic members struck at "convicting people by rumor and hearsay and innuendo."

The target of Democratic resentment was Roy Cohn, chief counsel for the subcommittee headed by Senator Joseph R. McCarthy, Wisconsin Republican. Mr. Cohn had countered Mrs. Moss' testimony by saying the subcommittee had still secret evidence that she was a Communist.

The Democrats, led by Senator John L. McClellan of Arkansas, demanded that he produce the evidence or refrain from public mention of it.

Senator McCarthy, in the original hearing at which the charges against Mrs. Moss were produced, had suggested she would "run the risk of indictment for perjury" when she appeared before the committee.

Senator McCarthy was absent from the committee room today when the scene over Mrs. Moss' testimony took place. He had gone to his office to prepare for his radio appearance later in which he answered criticism of him and the Republican party by Adlai E. Stevenson, the 1952 Democratic Presidential nominee.

No effort was made by the presiding officer, Senator Karl E. Mundt, South Dakota Republican, to check the crowd's applause or to interfere with the Democrats in their vigorous denunciation of Mr. Cohn's tactics.

Senator Mundt ordered Mr.

Continued on Page 10, Column 3

SENATE UNIT ASKS OUSTER OF CHAVEZ

Cites Election Irregularities in '52 but Does Not Accuse New Mexico Democrat

By WILLIAM S. WHITE
Special to THE NEW YORK TIMES.

WASHINGTON, March 11—A Senate showdown on a long-forecast Republican effort to unseat Senator Denis Chavez because of alleged election irregularities in 1952 drew near today. A Republican-controlled Senate subcommittee formally filed its expected report recommending that the New Mexico Democrat's seat be held vacant.

It also urged that the Senate find that "no member was elected from New Mexico in the 1952 general election."

The Republicans asserted that there had been no free expression of the will of the people, in part because of the alleged denial of the right of secret ballot. Senator Chavez nowhere was charged with fraud.

The Republican subcommittee chairman, Senator Frank A. Barrett of Wyoming, said there had been "no intention to cast aspersions" on Mr. Chavez. It simply had been impossible to determine whether Senator Chavez or his Republican opponent, Brig. Gen. Patrick J. Hurley, retired, actually had won, Mr. Barrett said.

Senator Chavez asserted the Republicans had delivered "a tremendous insult to the officials and people of New Mexico."

Democrats Are Confident

The Democrats, who had insisted on clearing the issue without further delay, plainly were confident he would be sustained. Disinterested observation seemed to support their confidence.

If Senator Chavez should be ousted and the Republican Governor of New Mexico, Edwin L. Mechem, should appoint a Republican as temporary successor, the Republican party would gain actual, as distinguished from its present nominal, control of the Senate.

The improbability of such an outcome, however, was reflected by the fact that there now were more Democrats in the Senate than Republicans and in the fact that it was the Democrats who were demanding decisive action.

The Democratic member of the subcommittee, Senator Thomas C. Hennings Jr. of Missouri, gave notice that he would file a dissenting report upholding Mr. Chavez' right to his seat.

The whole issue will go next week, probably on Tuesday, to the full Senate Rules Committee. The universal expectation in the Senate was that the full committee would sustain the Repub-

Continued on Page 14, Column 3

SHOWDOWN NEARS ON TAX EXEMPTION

Martin Admits Some Votes of Democrats Are Needed to Defeat Increase Plan

Special to THE NEW YORK TIMES.

WASHINGTON, March 11—The Administration will need the votes of some Democrats to win a showdown battle next week against higher personal income tax exemptions.

This was conceded by the Speaker of the House of Representatives, Joseph W. Martin Jr., Republican of Massachusetts. He said he realized some members of his party would break ranks on the issue but added:

"I am of the opinion that there will be enough responsible members of the Democratic party to more than offset what losses we may have."

His analysis was in response to a prediction by Representative Sam Rayburn of Texas, House minority leader, that the Democrats would win the fight for a $100 increase in present exemptions of $600 each for taxpayers and dependents.

Mr. Rayburn said after a caucus of House Democrats that he knew of none who would vote against the proposal. In that case, defection of half a dozen or so Republicans, depending on the absentee situation when the vote was taken, could bring victory for the Democrats.

Parliamentary preliminaries for the fight were completed this afternoon when the Rules Com-

Continued on Page 8, Column 6

STEVENS A TARGET

Report Quotes Counsel As Saying Secretary Would Be 'Through'

The text of the Army's report is printed on Page 9A.

By W. H. LAWRENCE
Special to THE NEW YORK TIMES.

WASHINGTON, March 11—The Army reported today it had been subjected to direct threats by Senator Joseph R. McCarthy and his chief counsel, Roy Cohn.

The threats, the Army said, had been made in an effort to obtain preferential treatment for G. David Schine, now a private in the Army but formerly an investigator for the McCarthy subcommittee.

In a thirty-four-page report sent to each member of Senator McCarthy's Permanent Subcommittee on Investigations and some members of the Armed Services Committee, the Army declared the Wisconsin Republican and Mr. Cohn first had sought a direct commission for Private Schine.

Failing in that, the report said, they had then demanded for him an assignment in the New York area so he could study alleged subversive material in West Point textbooks.

In the period between Oct. 18 and Nov. 3, before Senator McCarthy began his open fight with the Army, John G. Adams, Army Counsel, reported he had told Mr. Cohn that it would not be in the national interest to give preferential treatment to Private Schine.

"Mr. Cohn replied that if the national interest was what the Army wanted, he'd give it a little and then proceeded to outline how he would expose the Army in its worst light and show the country how shabbily it is being run," the report declared.

Threat to Stevens Cited

The report quoted Mr. Cohn as threatening on one occasion to "wreck the Army" and make certain that Robert T. Stevens was "through" as the Secretary of the Army. At another time, the report said, "Mr. Cohn stated to Mr. Adams that he would teach Mr. Adams what it meant to go over his head."

The report is expected to spur growing demands for Mr. Cohn's ouster.

Senator McCarthy made it clear in answer that he would accept battle with "one or two" in the Army high command on the Cohn-Schine case. He said he had instructed his own committee staff to pull out of its files everything bearing on the case and give them to him so they could be "made available to the American public."

"I don't like to do it," he told a New York Times correspondent. "The deeper I get into it, I'm convinced the Army as a whole is damn clean. What some people in the Army do doesn't mean the entire Army."

He said he had sought at a luncheon with Charles E. Wilson, Secretary of Defense, yesterday

Continued on Page 9-B, Col 2

White Meets Backers of Young; Denies Central Compromise Bid

By ROBERT E. BEDINGFIELD

William White, president of the New York Central Railroad Company, had two important visitors in his offices at 230 Park Avenue yesterday: Clint W. Murchison and Sid W. Richardson.

They are the Texas millionaires who bought 800,000 shares of Central stock—one-eighth of the outstanding shares—last month from the Chesapeake and Ohio Railway Company to help their friend Robert R. Young in his attempt to wrest control of the $2,600,000,000 New York Central System from its present management.

Versions of the events leading to the meeting differed sharply.

Mr. White said Mr. Murchison had arranged it on his own motion. But the Texans said it had been requested by John J. McCloy, chairman of the Chase National Bank, of which Percy J. Ebbott is president.

Mr. Ebbott is a Central director. The Chase National Bank was the trustee for the 800,000 shares of Central stock before they were sold by the C. & O.

Mr. McCloy, through a spokesman, said last night that the request for the meeting had originated with Mr. Murchison. But a spokesman for Mr. Young insisted yesterday that the visit had been in response to an appeal from the Central forces for a Young representative to discuss settlement of their differences.

Mr. White branded as a "plain lie" intimations that the Central management might be seeking a compromise with Mr. Young.

Mr. White summoned reporters late yesterday afternoon to deny the "compromise" rumors that had spread through Wall Street and the Grand Central Terminal area after it was dis-

Continued on Page 36, Column 3

The New York Times.

LATE CITY EDITION
Clearing and continued cold to-day; fair tonight and tomorrow.
Temperature Range Today—Max. 45; Min. 32
Temperature Yesterday—Max. 44; Min. 32
Full U. S. Weather Bureau Report, Page 43

Copyright, 1954, by The New York Times Company.

VOL. CIII.—No. 35,131.   Entered as Second-Class Matter, Post Office, New York, N. Y.   NEW YORK, THURSDAY, APRIL 1, 1954.   Times Square, New York 36, N. Y. Telephone Lackawanna 4-1000   FIVE CENTS

SOVIET IN BID TO JOIN NATO; U. S. SAYS 'NO'

OFFER BY MOLOTOV

He Urges West to Enter All-European Pact—Deplores 'Cold War'

Text of Soviet note to West on European security, Page 4.

By HARRISON E. SALISBURY
Special to The New York Times.

MOSCOW, March 31—The Soviet Union has proposed that the United States and West European states join a Soviet-sponsored general European security treaty. In return the Soviet Union is prepared to examine the question of assuming membership in the North Atlantic Treaty Organization.

The Soviet diplomatic move was contained in a note Vyacheslav M. Molotov, Soviet Foreign Minister, handed to Charles E. Bohlen, United States Ambassador, and his British and French diplomatic colleagues, Sir William Hayter and Louis Joxe.

There were qualifications and provisos, both written and implied, in Mr. Molotov's proposal, which was transmitted by the Western Ambassadors to Washington, London and Paris.

But the essence of what Mr. Molotov suggested was plain—that as soon as possible the "cold war," should be called off.

[The United States rejected the Soviet proposals. A State Department spokesman said the Soviet Government simply was continuing its effort to block the development of West European security. Paris sources called the Soviet note an attempt to spread confusion on the European Defense Community Treaty and to undermine the Atlantic alliance. British sources termed the Soviet suggestion of joining the alliance "just a Trojan horse."]

Defense Plan Main Target

The Soviet Foreign Minister made it plain that his immediate target was the European Defense Community.

But Mr. Molotov said the Atlantic alliance was another matter.

Mr. Molotov suggested that his proposed all-European organization and the Atlantic alliance be placed in balance. He proposed that all European powers, plus the United States, could join the Soviet - sponsored organization while the Soviet Union might become a member of the Atlantic alliance.

Mr. Molotov noted that the world was facing the peril of war in which atomic and hydrogen bombs threatened "incalculable disaster," including the annihilation of peaceful peoples, the wiping out of whole cities, of contemporary industry, culture and science, of "ancient centers of civilization" as well as "the great capitals of the states of the world."

Mr. Molotov asserted that in this moment all the world powers bore an especially great responsibility and said the Soviet Union

Continued on Page 5, Column 3

Reds in Mass Attack Against Dienbienphu

By TILLMAN DURDIN
Special to The New York Times.

SAIGON, Vietnam, March 31—Vietminh forces last night launched a new mass attack against the French defenses at Dienbienphu.

[The French High Command in Hanoi said three Vietminh divisions were assaulting Dienbienphu, The United Press reported.]

During a night of savage fighting the Communist-led Vietminh troops established a foothold within the French positions. However, they were pushed back this morning at some points by desperately resisting French Union contingents.

A late bulletin from French headquarters here said violent combat continued today. Bad weather yesterday facilitated the beginning of the Vietminh assault, but as the clouds cleared

Continued on Page 7, Column 1

France Ousts Juin For Anti-Pact Talk

Marshal Alphonse P. Juin

The New York Times

Special to The New York Times.

PARIS, Thursday, April 1—Marshal Alphonse-Pierre Juin was disciplined by the Pierre Cabinet at a special meeting early this morning for his speech against the European army treaty and for a snub to Premier Joseph Laniel.

Continued on Page 7, Column 3

PRESIDENT BACKS FIRM ASIA POLICY

Supports 'United Action' Plan of Dulles—Senator Douglas Urges Facing War Risk

By WILLIAM S. WHITE
Special to The New York Times.

WASHINGTON, March 31—President Eisenhower made it plain today that this Government was deeply committed to "united action" against any Communist effort to overrun Southeast Asia.

He underwrote every word uttered by his Secretary of State, John Foster Dulles, in proclaiming that policy in a speech two nights ago.

[The Soviet Foreign Ministry in Moscow denied Mr. Dulles' assertion that Foreign Minister Molotov had agreed the Geneva conference would not be a five-power meeting.]

The President defined "united action" as primarily the responsibility of the free peoples directly. He declared also that, speaking generally, the United States could put itself under no greater disadvantages than by spreading its ground forces and other forces about the

Continued on Page 13, Column 4

I.L.A. INSURGENTS REJECT PAY RISE, STALL PIER PEACE

Eisenhower, Putting Local Action First, Says U. S. is Prepared to Cooperate

By A. H. RASKIN

Insurgent elements in the old International Longshoremen's Association yesterday killed a union-inspired move to end their strike, the longest and costliest in the port's history.

The union's sixty-two-member wage-scale committee spurned an employer pay offer and demanded a contract that would make the I. L. A. sole bargaining agent for the 24,000 workers on New York and New Jersey piers.

The shipping industry retorted that it could not legally sign such an agreement until the National Labor Relations Board decided whether the old union or its American Federation of Labor rival was entitled to speak for the dock workers.

The only remaining hope for a quick end to the twenty-seven-day tie-up was the possibility that the union might order the strikers back to the piers after the labor board in Washington had ruled on a new election. A ruling is expected before the end of this week.

At a City Hall conference with Deputy Mayor Henry Epstein, I. L. A. leaders authorized a statement that the sooner the board handed down its ruling the sooner the men would be back on the job. However, they shied away from any clear-cut promise that the strike would be called off as soon as the board acted.

President Watching Strike

In Washington, President Eisenhower said the Government was alert to the strike situation and was prepared to take whatever action might be necessary to cope with it, in cooperation with state and city authorities. The President added that the White House would be guided by this rule: Everything is handled locally as long as it can be.

The collapse of the back-to-work effort here speeded Federal plans to obtain a blanket injunction banning pickets and "loiterers" from the waterfront. Charles T. Douds, regional director of the National Labor Relations Board, laid the groundwork for such an injunction by issuing a sweeping complaint against the I. L. A. last night.

The complaint, described by members of Mr. Douds' staff as the most drastic ever issued by the board, accused the old union and its locals of having intimidated dock workers through mass picketing, blocking pier entrances, physical assaults, overturning automobiles, slashing tires and congregating in large groups" to harass non-strikers.

Labor board attorneys are expected to go into Federal Court today to ask for an injunction based on the Douds complaint. Its purpose would be to halt all picketing and other interference

Continued on Page 47, Column 4

H-BOMB CAN WIPE OUT ANY CITY, STRAUSS REPORTS AFTER TESTS; U. S. RESTUDIES PLANT DISPERSAL

NEW PLANS NEEDED

Defense Experts to Go to Work at Once on Factory Shifts

Special to The New York Times.

WASHINGTON, March 31—Dispersal plans for defense production plants in major cities will have to be redrawn in the light of today's hydrogen bomb disclosures.

Plans for dispersing defense production plants to date have been based upon a ten-mile radius of "immediate danger," which officials conceded was outdated.

Reliable sources indicated the Administration's defense planners were scheduled to go to work at once to draw a new set of criteria for plant dispersal.

The aim of the plant dispersal program is to get new key production plants outside probable target areas. To make this attractive, the Government offers builders of such plants accelerated tax amortization certificates permitting them to write off the cost of the plants for tax purposes in five instead of the normal twenty or more years.

Another plan, effective tomorrow, to insure control of materials and production in event of atomic or hydrogen-bomb attack, was announced by the Government today. Nominal account will be kept of available materials and production facilities so that an orderly but rapid expansion for military atomic production and construction will be possible in an emergency.

Eighty-nine Surveys Undertaken

The industry dispersal program is under the supervision of the Office of Defense Mobilization but is handled by the Area Development Division of the Business and Defense Services Administration within the Department of Commerce.

The Area Development group so far has organized committees to make dispersal plans in many key communities. Of eighty-nine committees that have undertaken such surveys, thirty-five have reported and their plans have been approved by the Office of Defense Mobilization. Among these is the committee for the New York City metropolitan area, which completed its work last month.

Officials predicted that the New York City survey, as well as the others, probably would have to be redone in the light of the facts learned about the destructiveness of the hydrogen bomb.

In announcing the new Defense Materials System, the Business and Defense Services Administration explained it would

Continued on Page 23, Column 2

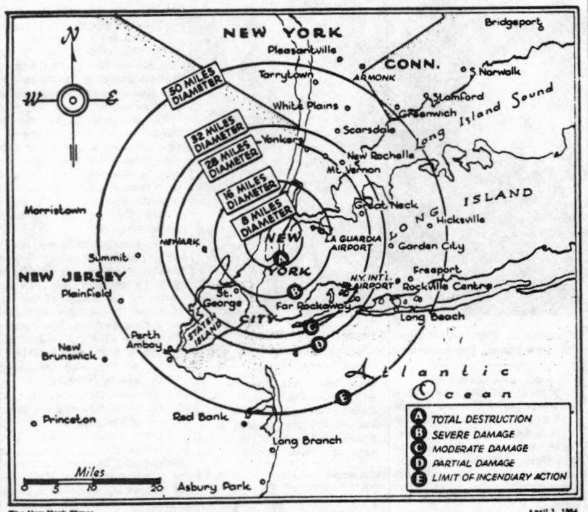

The New York Times   April 1, 1954

Extent to which a hydrogen bomb explosion could devastate New York and its environs

A	TOTAL DESTRUCTION
B	SEVERE DAMAGE
C	MODERATE DAMAGE
D	PARTIAL DAMAGE
E	LIMIT OF INCENDIARY ACTION

Senate Unit Votes Changes President Asked in Taft Act

By JOSEPH A. LOFTUS
Special to The New York Times.

WASHINGTON, March 31—The Senate Labor Committee approved a Taft-Hartley revision bill today with the Democrats crying "steamroller." The vote was 7 to 6 along party lines.

The bill deals only with President Eisenhower's recommendations, minus an Administration proposal to require Federally conducted elections among workers before a strike could be called.

Another Administration proposal, for standards to conserve union welfare funds, will be dealt with separately after an inquiry.

The House Labor Committee expects to report a bill on the same subject next week. It will contain many more revisions than the Senate bill.

Two provisions dealing with state powers were added to the Senate committee draft today just before the final vote to report a bill. They are certain to be fought vigorously.

One of these new sections deals with state emergencies. As finally approved, it reads:

"Nothing in this act shall be construed to interfere with the enactment and enforcement by the states of laws to deal in emergencies with labor disputes which, if permitted to occur or continue, will constitute a clear and present danger to the health or safety of the people of the state; provided, that no state shall be authorized by this subsection to take action in any labor dispute in which the Federal Government is acting pursuant to Sections 206 to 210, inclusive, of this act."

Sections 206 to 210 are the national emergency provisions of the Taft-Hartley Act. When these were invoked, state action would be superseded, but the

Continued on Page 24, Column 3

Calm in Middle East Urged by President

By The United Press.

WASHINGTON, March 31—President Eisenhower called on Israel and the Arab states today to restrain their extremists and permit other nations to help them settle their disputes.

He declined to answer a question at his news conference as to whether he believed the bitter Arab-Israeli feud, which recently erupted into new violence, should be referred to the United Nations Security Council. However, he said the United States had the full support of the United Nations in its plan to seek harmony in the Middle East.

General Eisenhower said the United States had been giving strong support to the plan to develop the resources of the area, including the water resources of the Jordan River, and hoped the plan would be accepted.

He said the Israeli-Arab issue was so charged with emotional

Continued on Page 2, Column 2

EISENHOWER SIGNS TAX CUT MEASURE

Excise Reductions Effective Today—President Voices Hope of Business Gain

By JOHN D. MORRIS
Special to The New York Times.

WASHINGTON, March 31—President Eisenhower signed the $999,000,000 excise tax reduction bill into law today. He voiced hope that the damage to Federal revenues would be offset to some degree by the resulting stimulation of business.

Federal sales taxes on a long list of items, from pocketbooks to household appliances, consequently will be reduced sharply as of 12:01 A. M. tomorrow. The savings are expected to be passed along to consumers, at least in part, by most of the industries affected. On a majority of the items covered, the tax cut amounts to 50 per cent.

Enactment of the bill adds an estimated $999,000,000 to the Federal deficit of $2,928,000,000 projected by President Eisenhower for the 1955 fiscal year, which starts next July 1.

On the ground that the Government could not afford such revenue losses in addition to those involved in other recent and pending tax cuts, the Administration is free to go ahead with plans for construction of 33,000 to 35,000 new low-rent public housing units.

The President told his news conference that, nevertheless, he was accepting the bill wholeheartedly. From the beginning, he explained, there was a difference of opinion on the revenue effects. One school of thought, he noted, believes that the reduction can stimulate business to

Continued on Page 16, Column 4

HOUSING BAN FOES CLAIM A 'VICTORY'

G.O.P. House Chiefs Foresee 33,000 Units in Fiscal '55 —Eisenhower 'Delighted'

Special to The New York Times.

WASHINGTON, March 31—What had been intended as a defeat for the Eisenhower Administration developed as a probable victory today as, a parliamentary tangle over public housing legislation began unraveling.

President Eisenhower himself said he was delighted at the outcome.

Republican leaders of the House of Representatives already had claimed a victory by interpreting the House yesterday, as meaning that the Public Housing Administration is free to go ahead with plans for construction of 33,000 to 35,000 new low-rent public housing units.

Today, the leaders moved to provide authority for an additional 35,000 units in the year starting July 1, 1955, by supporting an amendment to a general housing bill that comes before the House tomorrow.

Their aim is to give the President a legislative green light to carry out the first two years of his four-year program for 35,000 new units a year.

Action by Opposition

Yesterday's confusion in the House resulted from the attempt of public housing opponents, led by Representative Howard W. Smith, Democrat of Virginia, to kill the entire program by striking from a pending appropriations bill a "rider" allowing construction of 20,000 new units in the year starting next July 1.

The rider was eliminated from the bill on a point of order raised by Mr. Smith, who successfully challenged it as legislation on an appropriations bill in violation of House rules.

Killing the rider, according to Mr. Smith, would leave the Government without authority to start any new projects after next July 1. He based this position on existing law, enacted as a rider on the same appropriations bill last year, limiting new construction to 20,000 units in the present fiscal year and prohibiting any further commitments without Congressional authorization.

As soon as Mr. Smith had completed

Continued on Page 34, Column 4

VAST POWER BARED

March 1 Explosion Was Equivalent to Millions of Tons of TNT

Text of Strauss statement and conference transcript, Page 20.

By WILLIAM L. LAURENCE
Special to The New York Times.

WASHINGTON, March 31—The United States can now build a hydrogen bomb big enough to destroy any city.

In revealing this today, Rear Admiral Lewis L. Strauss, chairman of the United States Atomic Energy Commission, hinted that such a bomb could be delivered by plane.

The bomb tested at the Eniwetok proving grounds on March 1, Admiral Strauss announced, provided "a stupendous blast in the megaton range." He said it was "double that of the calculated estimate." A megaton is equivalent to 1,000,000 tons of TNT.

The explosive power attained in the test was reported by a member of the Joint Congressional Committee on Atomic Energy as twelve to fourteen megatons. This represents an explosive force 600 to 700 times greater than that of the bombs that destroyed Hiroshima and Nagasaki.

No Limit to Bomb Size

Admiral Strauss made his statement at the President's news conference. He declared that the hydrogen bomb could be made as large as desired—"large enough to take out a city, to destroy a city."

"How big a city?", he was asked.

"Any city?"

"New York?"

"The metropolitan area, yes," he replied.

Admiral Strauss explained later that by "metropolitan area" he meant the heart of Manhattan and not the actual metropolitan area, which covers 3,550 square miles.

[Prime Minister Churchill, yielding to Opposition pressure, agreed to debate the Government's policy on the hydrogen bomb in the House of Commons Monday.]

Despite the hydrogen bomb's enormous power, Admiral Strauss said, the test was "at no time out of control." Furthermore, he gave the nation and the world the assurance given to him by scientists that it was "impossible for any such test or series of tests to get out of control."

Admiral Strauss' appearance at the President's press conference was at President Eisenhower's request. He made available to the American people portions of the report he had made to President Eisenhower yesterday on the hydrogen bomb tests in the Pacific.

The tests of hydrogen weapons on March 1 and 26, he said, have "added enormous potential to our military posture." He later amplified this remark with a statement that "the results of these

Continued on Page 21, Column 4

Color Film of First H-Bomb Test Is Previewed by Press in Capital

Special to The New York Times.

WASHINGTON, March 31—The world's most fearsome weapon, the fusion bomb, was shown in action for the first time in public today before an audience of representatives of the press and other information media.

They saw a reproduction on color film of the phenomena that followed the explosion of the first full-scale hydrogen weapon on the Pacific proving grounds in the Marshall Islands in November, 1952.

The event marked the entry of mankind into the Hydrogen Age, taking the fateful step from the kiloton (thousands of tons) to the megaton (millions of tons) of explosive power in terms of TNT.

The film was released by the Atomic Energy Commission and the Department of Defense for public issuance by the Federal Civil Defense Administration. It was intended for general release at 6 P. M. April 7, and review

of it were to be embargoed until then.

However, a descriptive review by a syndicated columnist appeared in newspapers a few hours after the showing. Because of this The Times is publishing his review now.

The test in November, 1952, was known as Operation Ivy and the device tested was known as Mike. At the time it was made the explosion was the greatest in history. Since then, however, it has been greatly exceeded by the test explosions on March 1 and 26.

The film opens with an introduction by President Eisenhower, who recites an excerpt from his historic address before the United Nations on Dec. 8, 1953, relating to the need of the peaceful

Continued on Page 23, Column 2

---

10 Pupils Burned to Death in School Near Buffalo

Smoke and flames billow from frame annex of an elementary school in Cheektowaga, N. Y.

Associated Press Wirephoto

Special to The New York Times.

BUFFALO, March 31—Ten sixth grade pupils in the Cleveland Hill elementary school died today in a fire that trapped them in a room of the school's one-story frame annex

on Mapleview Drive in suburban Cheektowaga. Twenty-two other persons, nineteen of them children, were burned or injured and taken to hospitals. The school has an enrollment of more than 1,200. Hundreds

of pupils of the adjoining Cleveland Hill High School were sent home. The fire followed a blast that was described variously as an explosion and as "a

Continued on Page 34, Column 3

118

In Seven Brides for Seven Brothers, *Jane Powell gives a lesson on "goin' courtin'." Russ Tamblyn and Howard Keel also starred.*

Anthony Quinn in Fellini's La Strada.

Dorothy Dandridge and Harry Belafonte in an all-Black cast movie version of Carmen Jones.

This is how the Dodge of 1954 looked.

Marilyn Monroe with her husband, Joe DiMaggio, shortly after their marriage.

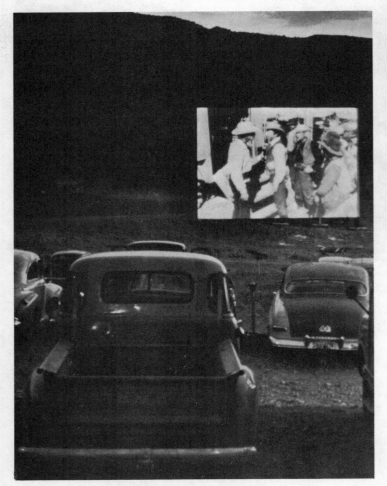

Drive-in movies became popular in the Fifties.

"All the News That's Fit to Print"

The New York Times.

LATE CITY EDITION

Fair today and tonight. Some cloudiness and warmer tomorrow.
Temperature Range Today-Max., 56; Min. 38
Temperatures Yesterday-Max., 57; Min., 45
Full U. S. Weather Bureau Report, Page 63

VOL. CIII . No. 35,143. Entered as Second-Class Matter. Post Office, New York, N. Y.

NEW YORK, TUESDAY, APRIL 13, 1954.

Times Square, New York 36, N. Y. Telephone LAckawanna 4-1000

FIVE CENTS

F. H. A. CHIEF OUT, FRAUDS CHARGED; U. S. OPENS STUDY

FILES TO BE SEIZED

Hollyday Is Said to Fail to Halt Wide Abuses —Cost in Millions

By ANTHONY LEVIERO
Special to The New York Times.

WASHINGTON, April 12—The White House today launched an inquiry into alleged nation-wide housing frauds that might have cost homeowners and the Government many millions of dollars.

White House action followed the disclosure by housing officials that many homeowners had been cheated through home-improvement loans and that many builders had obtained Government-insured construction loans far in excess of the costs of projects.

Associated Press Wirephoto
Guy T. O. Hollyday

Guy T. O. Hollyday, Commissioner of the Federal Housing Administration, submitted his resignation to President Eisenhower as the White House authorized Albert M. Cole, Administrator of the Housing and Home Finance Agency, to seize F. H. A. files.

The Federal Bureau of Investigation as well as the Housing and Home Finance Agency have already laid the groundwork for the inquiry.

James C. Hagerty, White House press secretary, said that Mr. Hollyday "is resigning to allow this investigation to be continued by someone else."

Mr. Cole said this evening at a news conference that Mr. Hollyday, who was appointed by President Eisenhower last year, had been aware of abuses and alleged frauds "but did not act."

He said that "Mr. Hollyday is in my opinion a good Christian gentleman."

Under Two Headings

Mr. Cole placed the alleged abuses, frauds or negligence under two headings:

1. He said that investigation had unearthed 251 cases, with more to come, that had their origins while the Truman Administration was in power. He asserted the 251 cases, in which builders got Federal loans far in excess of the cost of multiple-family projects under Section 608 of the Federal Housing Act, involved $75,000,000. Section 608 expired in 1950.
2. Mr. Cole charged that thousands of homeowners had been cheated out of millions. This was done by groups of high-pressure home improvement and repair salesmen who roved systematically from city to city and overcharged home owners on improvements or persuaded them to make unnecessary changes in their homes, he said. These alleged frauds were perpetrated under Title I of the Housing Act of 1950. Title I involves the program for insuring small loans for home improvements.

Mr. Cole predicted a shuffle of top officials of the F. H. A. and the dismissal of several. He said that he had ordered the F. H. A. to withdraw the resignation of Clyde L. Powell, assistant commissioner for multiple-family housing. Mr. Powell had submitted his resignation last week.

19 Indictments on Coast

"I'm directing F. H. A. to withdraw the resignation," Mr. Cole said, "until it can be determined if he (Mr. Powell) is personally responsible for what I deem very negligent operations in connection with the 608 program."

Mr. Cole said Mr. Powell had been with the Federal Housing Administration for several years.

Mr. Cole, the top Federal housing official, declined to specify cases or localities involved in the inquiry, except to acknowledge that nineteen indictments charging frauds under Title I were obtained last week in Los Angeles.

William F. McKenna, Los Angeles attorney, was appointed deputy administrator of the Housing and Home Finance Agency by Mr. Cole to direct the investigation.

Mr. McKenna, who has had broad experience in governmental investigations, according to Mr. Cole, will be assisted by Lester Condon, who was chief investigator of the House Government Operations Committee until last Friday.

Giving an example of one case

Continued on Page 38, Column 4

BENSON SEES VETO ON HIGH SUPPORTS

'Confident' President Will Kill Such a Farm Measure—House Lifts Research Fund

Special to The New York Times.

WASHINGTON, April 12—Secretary of Agriculture Ezra Taft Benson asserted today he was "confident" that President Eisenhower would veto any farm bill extending present high, rigid Federal farm price supports.

His statement came as the Administration won a minor test vote in the House of Representatives on its farm program.

On a standing vote of 59 to 38, the House tentatively increased funds for the Department of Agriculture's Research Service. The House Appropriations Committee, in a slap at Mr. Benson, had recommended that research funds be cut.

So surprising was the vote that bipartisan farm bloc leaders obtained a delay in further consideration of the agriculture appropriations bill until they could muster more support. As a result, the House put off until Wednesday further debate on the measure.

The vote came on an amendment to restore $2,198,635 to research funds. That would put the figure for research at $35,353,000, the amount asked by the Administration.

Representative H. Carl Andersen, Republican of Minnesota, and chairman of a House appropriations subcommittee that had criticized Mr. Benson on the ground that he had favored research and education over more direct financial aid to farmers, saw the Administration's victory as "temporary."

"It will be a different story on Wednesday," Mr. Andersen said. He pointed to the small number of members present for the vote

Continued on Page 53, Column 1

ANGRY CITY STAFFS DENOUNCE BUDGET, THREATEN STRIKE

Mass Picketing by Firemen, Teachers and Others Marks First Day of Hearings

By CHARLES G. BENNETT

City employes converged in droves on City Hall yesterday to tell the Board of Estimate one emphatic thing about the $1,639,388,325 city budget for 1954-55—they did not like it.

The employes' spokesmen told the board members in the first of three days of budget hearings that the $450 pay rises proposed for teachers and $150 to $250 for non-teaching employes were not enough. They insisted on increases ranging principally from $500 to $750 a year.

Speakers also variously demanded immediate installation of the forty-hour week, provision for overtime pay, a minimum wage of $3,000 and changes in pension ratio contributions from the 50-50 per cent contributions now in force to a 75-25 basis, under which the city would pay 75 per cent, the employes 25 per cent.

The board was told that employes are "angry" and "resentful" over city wage proposals. Several speakers suggested that city workers might go on strike for their demands.

Most of the teachers' arguments will be presented at today's hearing. But the teachers were strongly represented in demonstrations in City Hall Plaza. The rallies punctuated and pointed up the torrent of words being poured out before the board at the hearing inside City Hall.

1,000 Firemen Picket

In the morning 1,000 uniformed firemen picketed in the plaza. A thousand other employes, representing twenty-one city departments, milled about. Some were marching and shouting, carrying placards, others were storming at the rear door on City Hall's north side, awaiting admission to the hearing, which opened at 10:30 A. M.

After a midday outdoor lull, teachers began to assemble about 3:30 P. M. By 4 o'clock, 3,000 teachers were circling the plaza, carrying placards bearing such slogans as "Mr. Mayor, who gets the traffic money? Why not use it to pay teacher increases?"

After marching for an hour, the teachers assembled in Murray Street near City Hall for a rally that lasted from 5 to 5:30 P. M. The teachers participating in the demonstration represented mainly three different organizations, the Teachers Guild, A. F. L., the Teachers Union and the City-Wide Grass Roots Committee.

The committee is a temporary organization formed solely to seek salary increases in the 1954-55 budget. The Teachers Union was expelled from the Congress of Industrial Organizations for alleged Communist influences within its organization.

The strike threat, sometimes veiled, sometimes open, recurred several times both inside and outside City Hall. In a speech at the hearing in the early evening, Howard P. Barry, a member of Engine Company 44, speaking as president of the Uniformed Firemen's Association, A. F. L., asked:

"Are you serving notice that

Continued on Page 39, Column 5

Rumania Frees Boys Held as Spy Pawns

By DANA ADAMS SCHMIDT
Special to The New York Times.

WASHINGTON, April 12—Rumania has released two youths whom it used as hostages a year ago in an attempt to make their father, a naturalized United States citizen, spy for his former homeland.

Their release followed President Eisenhower's personal intervention in a letter to the Rumanian Government.

Today, after a seven-year separation, the two boys, Constantin and Peter Georgescu, aged 19 and 15, were reunited with their father, Valeriu C. Georgescu, at the airport at Munich, Germany. They telephoned from the airport to their mother at 45 East End Avenue, New York.

The State Department announced that "their departure from Rumania came about as a result of a long series of ap-

Continued on Page 10, Column 1

VIETNAM DRAFTING YOUTHS FOR ARMY

War Cabinet Invokes Policy to Spur Anti-Red Struggle—Bitter Fight at Dienbienphu

By TILLMAN DURDIN
Special to The New York Times.

SAIGON, Vietnam, April 12—The new Vietnamese war Cabinet, in its first meeting here today, adopted stringent measures for intensifying the struggle against the Communist-led Vietminh rebels.

It decided to mobilize all Vietnamese male citizens between the ages of 20 and 25 and to retain until further notice all persons now in the armed forces. It also decreed that laxity in making exemptions from military duty be ended and announced that the aim would be to make all social classes participate equally in the war effort.

The Cabinet decided to combat desertions by setting up military courts to try deserters and insubordinate service men. It ruled that all service men now absent without leave would be given until the end of this month to rejoin their units, after which they would be liable to court-martial.

Curb on Emigration Set

Another decision stated that "in principle" no Vietnamese citizen between 18 and 45 years would be permitted to leave the country.

In a bitter battle at besieged Dienbienphu, meanwhile, the French Union forces drove Vietminh troops from an important defense point the rebels had occupied on the east side of the main defense line.

The war Cabinet met under the chairmanship of the Premier, Prince Buu Loc. Others present included Le Thang, Acting Minister of National Defense, and Gen. Nguyen Van Hinh, Chief of Staff of the armed forces.

Today's decisions were described as "only the first in a series of measures designed to accentuate the effective mobilization of the country."

Gen. Nguyen Van Hinh is expected to leave today for important discussions in France regarding the Vietnamese Army. He had received a sudden summons from Bao Dai, Vietnamese

Continued on Page 3, Column 1

EDEN ASKS DULLES TO DEFER WARNING TO PEIPING ON ASIA

Suggests Allies Concentrate on Unity in Geneva Talks—Israel-Jordan Rift Weighed

By DREW MIDDLETON
Special to The New York Times.

LONDON, April 12—Britain urged Secretary of State Dulles today to accept Western unity of intention and action at the Geneva conference as an interim substitute for his proposal for an immediate warning to the Communist bloc against further aggression in Southeast Asia.

Diplomatic circles, both United States and British, believe that Mr. Dulles has modified his original suggestion of a Western declaration of "united action" in advance of the Western powers' meeting with the Soviet Union and Communist China in Geneva two weeks from today.

Anthony Eden, British Foreign Secretary, stressed his Government's view that priority in Western planning for the time being must go to the preparation of a united front for the coming conference. But the United States delegation has been told emphatically that Britain is just as aware of the dangers of Communist success against the French in Indo-China as is the Administration in Washington.

Should the Communists block progress toward a peaceful settlement in Geneva, Britain would be willing to join in a warning declaration and discuss the form and extent of a defensive alliance in Southeast Asia, official sources assert.

[In Paris, where Mr. Dulles will go Tuesday to continue his Far East talks, a Cabinet crisis arose. Without Cabinet approval Georges Bidault, French Foreign Minister, signed an agreement with Britain on the European army, and several Ministers threatened to resign.]

Talks Are Expanded

The United States-British talks, which appear to have expanded well beyond their original scope, opened in the morning with a discussion of the border disputes between Israel and Jordan.

Mr. Eden and Mr. Dulles considered how best to bring representatives of Israel and Jordan together at a conference where their differences could be discussed in a calmer atmosphere than would be possible in public proceedings.

Both Mr. Dulles and Mr. Eden favor the establishment of a small working party of the United Nations Security Council to consider the dispute between two Middle East nations, it was reported. The quarrel already has reached the Security Council, which has before it complaints from both sides. Israel has been sensitive about cooperation with the Mixed Armistice Commission, a Foreign Office official said, and Jordan has rejected an Israeli request to attend a conference under the armistice agreement.

Under the Israeli-Jordanian agreement, attendance at an armistice review conference called by either side is mandatory, as is the United Nations Secretary General's obligation to summon it.

In the afternoon the United States delegation of Mr. Dulles, Douglas MacArthur 2d, Coun-

Continued on Page 2, Column 4

DR. OPPENHEIMER SUSPENDED BY A.E.C. IN SECURITY REVIEW; SCIENTIST DEFENDS RECORD

The New York Times
Dr. J. Robert Oppenheimer

HEARINGS STARTED

Access to Secret Data Denied Nuclear Expert —Red Ties Alleged

Texts of charges and reply by Oppenheimer, Pages 16, 17, 18.

By JAMES RESTON
Special to The New York Times.

WASHINGTON, April 12—Dr. J. Robert Oppenheimer, the man who directed the making of the first atomic bomb, has been suspended by the Atomic Energy Commission pending a review of his security file.

A panel of the commission's Personnel Security Board, headed by Gordon Gray, president of the University of North Carolina and former Secretary of the Army, started hearings on the case today.

The other members of the three-man panel are Thomas Morgan, former chairman and president of the Sperry Corporation, and Ward V. Evans, Professor of Chemistry at Loyola University of Chicago.

Meanwhile Dr. Oppenheimer, who directed the Government's atomic bomb project at Los Alamos, N. M., in World War II, and now carries around in his head as much top secret information as any man alive, has been denied access to all Government security documents.

Charges Are Listed

The main charges against him—most of which had been reviewed by the A. E. C., the White House, and the Departments of Justice, State and Defense over a period of twelve years—were that he:

¶Associated frequently with Communists in the early Forties, including his brother Frank and Frank's wife; that he fell in love with one Communist and married another former Communist; and that he contributed regularly and generously to Communist causes from 1940 to April of 1942.

¶Hired Communists or former Communists at Los Alamos during the war.

¶Gave contradictory testimony to the Federal Bureau of Investigation about attendance at Communist meetings in the early Nineteen Forties.

¶Rejected as "traitorous" an attempt by an alleged Communist to get scientific information from him for the Soviet Union, but failed to report the incident to the Government's security officers for many months.

¶Strongly opposed the development of the hydrogen bomb in 1949, when he was chairman of the Atomic Energy Commission's General Advisory Committee, and lobbied against it even after President Truman ordered the A. E. C. to proceed with the project.

Dr. Oppenheimer, who has repeatedly admitted association with various Communists in the late Thirties and early Forties but flatly denied membership in

Continued on Page 15, Column 1

ARABS IN U. N. MAKE NEW DEBATE OFFER

Would Agree to General Talks if Council Denounced Israel Now for Nahhalin Attack

By A. M. ROSENTHAL
Special to The New York Times.

UNITED NATIONS, N. Y., April 12—The Arabs agreed conditionally today to take part in a wide debate on Arab-Israeli border clashes.

The condition was a major one: That the United Nations Security Council agree now to adopt a resolution on the March 28 attack on the Jordanian village of Nahhalin, which has been attributed to Israelis.

Dr. Charles Malik, Lebanese delegate and Arab spokesman in the Council, indicated after the Council meeting today that he was seeking a sort of "gentlemen's agreement" that the West would back a resolution condemning the Nahhalin attack. One of the Arabs' chief complaints against the general debate sought by Israel and the West has been that it would "drown" the Nahhalin incident.

The attack on Nahhalin, in which nine Jordanians lost their lives, has been condemned by the United Nations Israeli-Jordanian Mixed Armistice Commission, which Israel is boycotting. The Arabs have brought the case before the Council and have insisted on a separate debate on it.

Delegates of France, Britain and the United States have condemned the Nahhalin attack in speeches before the Council and have made it clear that they would support a resolution censuring Israel.

Israelis Denounce Malik

But there were no indications tonight whether the West would agree in advance to a resolution branding Israel. Israeli sources attacked Dr. Malik's suggestion as an attempt to get the Council to prejudge the incident before the body even looked into it.

Council delegates spent four hours at their second consecutive meeting discussing the issue of general or specific debate, and again came to no decision. The body will meet again Thursday. Much inter-delegation compromise-seeking probably will take place tomorrow and Wednesday.

This was the situation as Andrei Y. Vishinsky of the Soviet Union called the meeting to order:

Jordan had introduced an agenda item charging that the Nahhalin attack was an armistice violation. Israel later had introduced an item accusing Jordan of several attacks against Israelis. Israel also accused Jordan of hav-

Continued on Page 26, Column 5

BROWNELL SCORES RED-OUTLAW PLAN

Fears Driving Party Members Underground—Instead, He Asks for Stronger Laws

By C. P. TRUSSELL
Special to The New York Times.

WASHINGTON, April 12—Herbert Brownell Jr., Attorney General, urged Congress today to abandon its new concentration on legislation to outlaw the Communist party.

With more than a dozen such measures pending, Mr. Brownell followed up his report to the nation Friday night by recommending only a toughening of existing statutes, and enactment of an additional law or two.

Appearing before a Judiciary subcommittee of the House of Representatives, the Attorney General held that these measures would provide an effective program to destroy the Communist menace in this country.

The outlawing approach—making it a crime to belong to the party—he said, would weaken if not destroy the legal weapons at hand, which needed only more of the same power they had now.

The menace that was being fought here, he declared, was "the advance guard of the military power of Russia." It contained, he held, "a professional, skilled, highly organized and mobile cadre."

If such an outfit were permitted to go underground, rather than

Continued on Page 21, Column 3

3 on Hunter Faculty Suspended, First in Board's Own Red Inquiry

The Board of Higher Education last night suspended three associate professors at Hunter College on charges arising from a special investigation into Communist activities.

The board, meeting in regular session at its offices at 695 Park Avenue, ordered the suspensions into effect today at 9 A. M. for Dr. Louis Weisner, Department of Mathematics; Dr. Charles W. Hughes, Department of Music, and Dr. V. Jerauld McGill, Department of Psychology and Philosophy.

The veteran teachers, who have been on the faculty since 1927, in the cases of Professors Weisner and Hughes, and since 1929 in the case of Professor McGill, were suspended on the general charges of neglect of duty and conduct unbecoming members of the staff.

They all received ten days in which to answer the specific charges. At last night's meeting the board also set up a trial committee of three members to hear the charges against the suspended teachers. The committee consists of Dr. Charles H. Tuttle, as chairman; Mrs. Mary S. Ingraham and Dr. John E. Conboy.

The suspensions are the first made as a result of the board's own investigations into subversive activities, stemming from the establishment of a special committee in June, 1953. Thirteen other staff members of municipal colleges had been dismissed from their jobs prior to last night's action, but as a result of their refusal to testify before Congressional committees.

The charges made last night were signed by Gustave G. Rosenberg, chairman of the board's special committee. The three associate professors were suspended by Dr. John Meng, dean of administration at Hunter College, who is acting president in the absence of Dr. George Shuster.

Three specific charges filed

Continued on Page 23, Column 5

The New York Times (by Edward Hausner)
DEMAND SALARY INCREASE: Some of the 3,000 teachers who converged on City Hall to press for a $750 raise

On The Waterfront *won immediate recognition as one of the great American films. Marlon Brando's performance elevated him from a gifted newcomer to the most important actor in motion pictures at that time. Eva Marie Saint played Brando's girlfriend.*

Three Coins in the Fountain, *shot on location in Rome and Venice, entertained huge audiences. The three women who threw coins into the Trevi Fountain were Maggie McNamara, Jean Peters and Dorothy McGuire. They are shown here with Clifton Webb, Kathryn Givney and Howard St. John.*

The Creature from the Black Lagoon *featured the sad-eyed gill-man, one of the best-remembered monsters of the Fifties.*

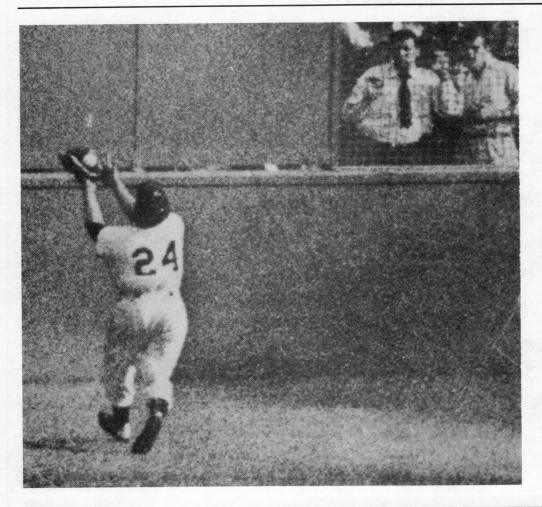

With the help of Willie Mays, the great outfielder, the Giants beat Cleveland in four straight games in the 1954 World Series. By this outstanding catch Mays saved the first game.

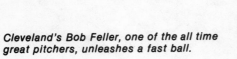
Cleveland's Bob Feller, one of the all time great pitchers, unleashes a fast ball.

"All the News That's Fit to Print"

The New York Times.

LATE CITY EDITION
Some cloudiness with showers today. Cloudy tomorrow.
Temperature Range Today—Max., 65; Min., 60
Temperature Yesterday—Max., 74.3; Min., 57.6
Full U. S. Weather Bureau Report, Page 40

Copyright, 1954, by The New York Times Company.

VOL. CIII..No. 35,153.
Entered as Second-Class Matter,
Post Office, New York, N. Y.

NEW YORK, FRIDAY, APRIL 23, 1954.

Times Square, New York 36, N. Y.
Telephone LAckawanna 4-1000

FIVE CENTS

EISENHOWER URGES PRESS TO LEAD WAY TO UNDERSTANDING

Ignorance Could Breed War, He Tells A.N.P.A. in Plea for Cooperative Peace

WARNS ON RULE BY REDS

1,000 Hail President Outside Hotel Here—A Big Police Detail Covers 5-Hour Visit

Text of the President's address is printed on Page 18.

By RUSSELL PORTER

President Eisenhower warned last night that if this is not to be an age of atomic hysteria and horror it must be made an age of international understanding and cooperative peace. And if the nations do not build a cooperative peace, he added, they will be forced one by one to accept an imposed peace, "now sought by the Communist powers as it was by Hitler."

The President spoke at a dinner of the Bureau of Advertising closing the sixty-eighth annual convention of the American Newspaper Publishers Association at the Waldorf-Astoria Hotel. His address was broadcast by radio and television. The Voice of America carried it overseas. More than 2,000 newspaper executives and their guests attended the dinner in the grand ballroom of the hotel. It was the first time a President of the United States had addressed the bureau while in office.

President Eisenhower was heavily guarded by more than 1,000 city policemen and a strong force of Secret Service agents during his short visit to New York. All cars, elevators and rooms he used while here were searched before his arrival and guarded during his visit.

Speaks in Washington

He flew here in his plane, the Columbine, from Augusta, Ga., where he has been having a golfing vacation. En route he stopped in Washington for another speech yesterday afternoon.

His plane landed at La Guardia Airport here at 4:55 P. M. Several hundred persons cheered and applauded and the President waved and smiled happily at them. He was sun-tanned and healthy-looking.

A motorcade and police escort took him and his party to the hotel, where he arrived at 5:20. A police helicopter hovered overhead. Crowds gathered in the street to watch him pass. More than 1,000 persons outside the hotel waved and some shouted "Hello, Ike!" He waved back and smiled.

The President was escorted to a suite in the Tower Apartments at the hotel. He remained there until 6:30, when he attended a reception in a room on the ballroom floor before taking his seat on the dais at 7 o'clock. He spoke from 9 to 9:30 o'clock and left at 9:35 for La Guardia Airport where he took off for Washington at 10 P. M. He reached the capital at 11:11 P. M.

The President said peace could not be assured without domestic unity and international understanding. He called upon newspapers, magazines, radio and television to take the lead in combating ignorance and misunderstanding which could breed war. Mankind hungers for peace and understanding.

Continued on Page 18, Column 2

U.S. for NATO Shifts Because of H-Bomb

By C. L. SULZBERGER
Special to The New York Times

PARIS, April 22—On the basis of reports on the capabilities of the hydrogen bomb, United States military leaders are preparing to recommend recasting of the size and organization of the North Atlantic Treaty ground forces.

On the eve of tomorrow's meeting of the North Atlantic council which will be attended by the foreign ministers of the fourteen member nations and devoted to political discussions, two significant military developments became known.

1. The alliance's commanders have decided in principle on a "new approach" to Continental defense problems in the light of the tactical and strategical implications of the hydrogen bomb.
2. The foreign ministers received a report from Supreme Headquarters.

Continued on Page 4, Column 4

Mayor Ready to Abandon His Sales Tax on Services

Threat of Businesses to Leave the City Impels Seeking Other Levies, Such as Charge for Overnight Parking

By CHARLES G. BENNETT

The Wagner administration, besieged by opposition, was about ready last night to abandon the highly controversial proposed 3 per cent retail sales tax on commercial services.

Mayor Wagner was represented as unwilling to run the risk of driving from the city advertising agencies, stock brokers, commercial airline services and many other businesses that have threatened to move away if the tax is enacted.

At City Hall yesterday the Board of Estimate, in executive session, made no secret of its distaste for the broadening of the sales impost. The chief problem appeared to be what revenue source could be used to replace the tax.

It appeared likely that serious consideration would be given to a proposal, put forward two years ago but abandoned in the face of opposition by automobile owners, to enact a $60-a-year

charge for overnight parking of cars in the streets.

Police estimates have put the potential yield of the overnight parking fee at $25,000,000 to $35,000,000. Should the levy adopt this levy, which it has the power to impose by previous legislative action, it probably also would approve one of several smaller-revenue measures open to it.

Such measures might be a juke-box tax, a tax on beer or an admissions tax. Revenue from the wider sales tax has been estimated at $30,000,000 a year. It, or its equivalent, is considered necessary to enable Mayor Wagner to include city employe pay rises in the $1,639,388,325 budget for 1954-55.

The Wagner administration emphatically slammed the door yesterday on any serious consideration of the proposal by Governor Dewey and State Controller

Continued on Page 28, Column 3

3 G.O.P. Senators Criticize Nehru for His Ban on Airlift

By WILLIAM S. WHITE
Special to The New York Times

WASHINGTON, April 22—The three top Republican leaders of the Senate denounced Prime Minister Jawaharlal Nehru today amid threats to halt or reduce United States economic aid to India. They rose in protest against Mr. Nehru's action in forbidding United States planes to cross India with French troops and supplies to help the defense of French Indo-China.

One of them, Senator Homer Ferguson of Michigan, accused the Prime Minister of "at least giving aid and comfort to the Communist world."

Senator William F. Knowland of California, the Republican Senate floor leader, led the demonstration. He was joined by Senator Styles Bridges of New Hampshire, the Republican dean of the Senate as its president pro tem, and Senator Ferguson, chairman of the Senate Republican Policy Committee.

Continued on Page 2, Column 6

WEST STILL SPLIT ON GENEVA POLICY

3 Powers Worried on How to Proceed—U. S. Warns of Walkout Over China

By BENJAMIN WELLES
Special to The New York Times

PARIS, April 22—The Western Big Three are baffled and worried by their inability so far to agree on procedure for the Geneva conference in the face of a rapidly deteriorating situation.

The United States has not yet won full agreement from Britain and France on keeping the Geneva talks, which open Monday, strictly a Big Four and not a Big Five conference.

It has had its allies and its other anti-Communist friends bluntly that it will walk out of the Geneva meeting if the Soviet Union is permitting to bring the Chinese Communists to the conference table as an equal "inviting" power along with the United States, Britain, France and the Soviet Union. These four powers set up the Geneva meeting at the recent Berlin parley.

Secretary of State Dulles, who conferred at length this afternoon at the French Foreign Office with the British Foreign Secretary, Anthony Eden, and the French Foreign Minister,

Continued on Page 2, Column 2

ANOTHER RUSSIAN DEFECTS TO WEST; BARS SLAYER ROLE

Secret Police Agent Quits Rather Than Kill an Official of Refugee Organization

By M. S. HANDLER

BONN, Germany, April 22—Another Soviet secret police agent has asked for refuge in the West.

His defection last February came to light today, when in an interview, he said he had surrendered to United States security agents rather than carry out a mission of assassination.

Today's disclosure of the Russian's plea for asylum came in the wake of recent defections by Soviet agents in Australia and Japan.

The latest defector, a captain of the Ninth Section of Soviet Ministry of Interior (M. V. D.) told his story before more than 200 reporters in Bonn.

The captain, Nikolai Evgenyevich Khokhlov, 32 years old, is a slight, scholarly-appearing blond young man. He was neatly dressed in a dark blue suit. He wore glasses.

He expressed himself well and firmly in Russian and handled himself adroitly in making his statement and in answering reporters' questions.

According to his story, which was supported by United States officials, who arranged and presided over the news conference in the main briefing room of the Office of the United States High Commissioner, Captain Khokhlov arrived in Frankfurt Feb. 17 to assassinate Georgi Sergeyevich Okolovich, an official of a Russian refugee organization named Natsionaly Trudovoi Soyuz, Dr. Alexander Truchnovich, a member of this organization, disappeared from West Berlin recently and was believed to have been kidnapped by Soviet agents.

German Accomplice Involved

Captain Khokhlov was preceded to Frankfurt by two German accomplices who had been recruited in Berlin. The day after his arrival in Frankfurt Captain Khokhlov visited Mr. Okolovich and informed him of the plot to assassinate him.

The intended victim got in contact with United States authorities. The next day, the 19th, Captain Khokhlov met his German accomplices and instructed them to meet courier No. 3 in Augsburg, where the murder weapons would be delivered.

Captain Khokhlov met United States agents Feb. 20 in the Opernplatz in a rendezvous arranged by Mr. Okolovich. Captain Khokhlov requested political asylum and stated his willingness to cooperate.

The Soviet captain then fixed a meeting with his German accomplices for the 20th. He persuaded the Germans to surrender to United States authorities. Later in the day, United States officials picked up ingenious murder weapons that had been deposited in the baggage room of the Frankfurt railroad station.

The murder weapons displayed to reporters by a United States official are supposed to represent new developments in the technique

Continued on Page 5, Column 4

STEVENS SWEARS M'CARTHY FALSIFIED, LAYS 'PERVERSION OF POWER' TO HIM; SENATOR IMPUGNS GENERAL'S MOTIVES

Principal Witnesses at the McCarthy-Army Inquiry

Secretary Robert T. Stevens   Maj. Gen. Miles Reber
Associated Press Wirephotos

HEARING IS STORMY

Gen. Reber Asserts Cohn Put Pressure on Him to Commission Schine

Transcript of hearing is printed on Pages 12 through 17.

By W. H. LAWRENCE
Special to The New York Times

WASHINGTON, April 22—The Secretary of the Army testified under oath today that Senator Joseph R. McCarthy had falsified in his charges against Army officials and about his efforts to get preferential treatment for Pvt. G. David Schine.

The appearance of Robert T. Stevens, Secretary of the Army, to back up his accusations of "perversion of power" against the Wisconsin Republican came near the end of the first day of public, televised and often stormy hearings before the Senate Permanent Subcommittee on Investigations.

New and special rules failed to restrain Senator McCarthy from interrupting witnesses and other Senators whenever he wished on what he called "points of order."

He suggested that one Army witness, Maj. Gen. Miles Reber, might have been motivated in his testimony by "the fact that your brother [Samuel Reber, former acting United States High Commissioner for Germany] was allowed to resign [from the State Department] under charges that he was a bad security risk were made against him as a result of the investigations of this committee."

Reber Insists on Answering

After a prolonged wrangle about the relevance of this question to the current inquiry, Senator McCarthy withdrew it. Then General Reber, pounding his hand in his fist as he talked to the Army's counsel, Joseph N. Welch, asked the subcommittee for special permission to answer it anyway.

"I do not know and have never heard that my brother retired as a result of any action of this committee," General Reber said. "The answer is positively no to that question."

Later, General Reber said that "as I understand my brother's case, he retired, as he is entitled to do by law upon reaching the age of 50."

"I know nothing about any security case involving him," he added.

A State Department spokesman in response to inquiries later said simply that "Mr. Reber retired voluntarily on July 31, 1953."

That clash with General Reber made it clear that Senator McCarthy will use every weapon at his command—and they are numerous—in this case in which he is one of the accused as well as accuser.

He clashed frequently with Ray H. Jenkins, special counsel for the inquiry, about argumentative questions and occasionally was overruled, but not before he had made his point to millions of television viewers across the land.

While all principals in the dis

Continued on Page 8, Column 2

FUTURE E. D. C. TIE HINTED AT BY TITO

But He Suggests the Project Will Fail Unless Nations Adjust Differences

By JACK RAYMOND
Special to The New York Times

BELGRADE, Yugoslavia, April 22—Marshal Tito said today Yugoslavia eventually might join the European Defense Community.

However, the European defense project must first develop beyond its present military framework and the differences of its members must be set aside, the Yugoslav President declared. He warned that otherwise the European Defense Community would be incapable of existing and fighting against aggression.

If members of the defense community reject "all egoistic matters and personal interests, we will support it and we will go so far as to join it when the time comes," Marshal Tito went on.

By differences among members it was believed, the Marshal meant French fears of West German remilitarization and Italian demands that the Trieste issue be settled before Italy ratified the European army treaty. Marshal Tito has endorsed West German rearmament within the European Defense Community. As for Trieste, both Italy and Yugoslavia have claims on the Free Territory of Trieste but have been unable to settle, despite the intervention of the Western powers.

Although delivered extemporaneously to a crowd that welcomed him here on his return from Tur

Continued on Page 4, Column 6

273 Housing Units Seized By U. S. Because of Defaults

By CLAYTON KNOWLES
Special to The New York Times

WASHINGTON, April 22—Defaults on Government-insured mortgages have forced the Federal Housing Administration to take over 273 apartment house projects at a cost of $119,339,991, according to official data. In another development in the housing scandals, Arthur H. Frentz was dismissed today as Assistant F. H. A. Commissioner in charge of home improvement loan insurance.

He had headed this section since 1947 and had been with the agency since 1934. This latest in a series of discharges within the F. H. A. was taken by Norman T. Mason, Acting Commissioner, on the recommendation of Albert M. Cole, Housing and Home Finance Administrator.

It is not known whether any of the 273 foreclosed projects were among the 1,149 on which it now can be said that there was almost $80,000,000 in "windfall profits" —that is an excess of F. H. A.-insured mortgage money over actual construction costs.

The Internal Revenue Service has reported to Congress that $65,557,000 of this windfall money has been distributed among stockholders of the building corporations involved. Most of it has been declared for tax purposes as capital gains, subject to a 26 per cent tax, rather than regular income, which would be taxable at far higher rates.

The Senate Banking Committee, which is investigating these windfalls and other abuses in the Federal housing programs, heard its chairman, Senator Homer E. Capehart, Republican of Indiana, describe today several instances from F. H. A. files in which builders had made large profits at little risk.

One case involved an unnamed New Yorker who got a $4,500,000 F. H. A. insured loan, which put

Continued on Page 7, Column 1

CONSUMER PRICES DROP 0.2% IN U.S.

Decline in Federal Index Is Led by Lower Costs for Food and Clothing

Special to The New York Times

WASHINGTON, April 22—The Consumers Price Index for the United States dropped 0.2 per cent between Feb. 15 and March 15, the Federal Bureau of Labor Statistics said today.

The decline was insufficient to make any significant change in the pay scales of those union members whose contracts included escalator clauses tied to consumer price indexes.

The bureau reported that food and apparel prices were 0.4 per cent lower on the average, rents were up 0.1 per cent and medical care rose by 0.2 per cent.

The March index stood at 114.8 per cent (using 1947-49 as 100), a drop of 0.5 per cent from the October, 1953, peak. It was 1.1 per cent higher than that for March, 1953, and 12.8 per cent above the level of June, 1950. On the former base of 1935-39 equaling 100, the March index stood at 191.9.

Officials said that the reduction in excise taxes and in the support price of butter, which became effective April 1, were too recent to be reflected in the present index.

Egg Prices Decrease 12%

The March food index stood at 112.1, which was 0.4 per cent above a year ago, but about 4 per cent below its August, 1952, peak. Egg prices dropped nearly 12 per cent, while dairy products declined 0.9 per cent.

Milk prices were reduced 1 to 5 per cent in many cities, and butter and cheese prices fell 1 per cent. Prices of all cuts of beef, veal and pork (except pork chops) decreased. Potato prices continued to decline, falling about 5 per cent over the month.

Coffee prices again rose, ranging up to 6 per cent above the preceding month and bringing the average price for the country to more than $1.05 a pound, or 15 per cent above the levels of last December.

After four months of steady decline, the bureau said, March apparel prices were down 1 per cent as against last October. Work clothes prices—on overalls, work trousers, shirts and dungarees—have been cut 20 to 50 cents in the last three months, it was said. Women's hosiery prices continued their decline.

Mrs. Aryness Joy Wickens, Deputy Commissioner of Labor

Continued on Page 35, Column 2

C.I.O. Ready to Speed Anti-Raiding Accord

By A. H. RASKIN

The no-raiding pact between the American Federation of Labor and the Congress of Industrial Organizations is likely to come alive next month. Implementation of the ban on inter-union warfare would reduce strikes and improve the outlook for labor unity.

The C. I. O., which has been refusing to exchange ratification signatures with the A. F. L., is expected to reverse its stand at a special meeting of its executive board, May 10, in Washington.

The pact technically went into effect last Jan. 1, but it has been in a state of suspended animation because of the C. I. O.'s refusal to deposit the signatures of any of its thirty-five international unions. The C. I. O. position was based on a boycott of the agreement by the 1,300,000-member International Brother

Continued on Page 49, Column 2

Inquiry's TV Rating Is Behind Kefauver's

By RICHARD T. BAKER

New Yorkers took the opening day of the televised Army-McCarthy controversy pretty much in their stride.

City-wide reports indicated that as yet the hearings before the Senate Permanent Subcommittee on Investigations had not captured the attention of the public in the way that Senator Kefauver's crime investigation did in 1951, and it appeared that the telecasting of some United Nations debates had reached a larger audience.

The C. F. Hooper organization, which devotes itself to measuring radio and television audiences, reported that the ratings for the afternoon session of the hearings in the argument between the Army and Senator Joseph R. McCarthy, Republican of Wisconsin, measured to a rating of 32 for the crime investigation telecasts of 1951.

When the testimony began at

Continued on Page 9, Column 4

Soviet Agent, Sent to West Germany for Political Killing, Sides With West

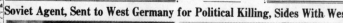

Capt. Nikolai Evgenyevich Khokhlov, right, greets Georgi S. Okolovich, the man he was assigned to kill, in Bonn.   Khokhlov's weapon. In false bottom is apparatus that fires poison-filled bullets with accuracy up to twenty-five feet.
Associated Press Radiophotos

1954

Roger Bannister of England won recognition at Oxford for breaking the four-minute mile record. On that historic day in 1954, he finished in 3:59.4.

Willie Mays, one of the great baseball players of the Fifties, was designated Rookie of the Year in 1951, the year the Giants won the pennant. He was later named Player of the Year when the Giants won the 1954 World Series.

"All the News That's Fit to Print"

The New York Times.

LATE CITY EDITION
Fair, moderate temperatures today. Partly cloudy tomorrow.
Temperature Range Today—Max. 63; Min., 45
Temperature Yesterday—Max., 59; Min., 47
Full U. S. Weather Bureau Report, Page 42

VOL. CIII..No. 35,167.

Entered as Second-Class Matter,
Post Office, New York, N. Y.

NEW YORK, FRIDAY, MAY 7, 1954.

Copyright, 1954, by The New York Times Company.

Times Square, New York 36, N. Y.
Telephone LAckawanna 4-1000

FIVE CENTS

WESTERN BIG THREE AGREE ON INDO-CHINA COMPROMISE FOR 'PROTECTED ARMISTICE'

U.S. FOR PARIS PLAN

Allies Will Suggest Reds Retire in Vietnam, Quit Laos and Cambodia

By JAMES RESTON
Special to The New York Times

WASHINGTON, May 6—The United States, Britain and France are now in substantial agreement on a compromise plan for a "protected armistice" in Indo-China.

It is understood that the Laniel Government in Paris has told Washington that it is prepared to fight on in Indo-China unless the Communists agree to evacuate Laos and Cambodia and withdraw to certain "fixed areas" in the third independent state of Vietnam.

The Eisenhower Administration, determined to block the Communist conquest of the whole peninsula, but unwilling to intervene at this time in the war with United States military power, is prepared to go along with Paris in its attempt to negotiate this compromise in Geneva.

The Secretary of State was reported tonight to have discussed this compromise arrangement with representatives of the Senate and the House of Representatives at the State Department last evening. He also outlined to them his own plans for the negotiation of an "extended" Southeast Asia security arrangement that would be designed to guarantee the terms of any honorable armistice that could be arranged.

Briefing by Dulles Reported

Washington tonight was full of gloomy reports that the Eisenhower Government had virtually abandoned hope of any "collective action" to save the major Indo-Chinese state of Vietnam, but as a matter of fact the Administration was actually a little more hopeful tonight that a "bearable compromise" could be negotiated.

President Eisenhower went over the Indo-China situation with the National Security Council today. John Foster Dulles, the Secretary of State, was represented by his associates in that body as having taken a solemn but not unhopeful view of the situation.

At the end of the meeting it was understood that the position of the United States was about as follows:

¶There was no question of direct United States intervention in the war in the foreseeable future, even though it was assumed that the French garrison at Dienbienphu would probably fall.

¶The United States should do what it could to negotiate a security pact for the defense of Southeast Asia, but there was no hope of doing so without a French promise of "unequivocal independence" to the three associated Indo-Chinese states of Vietnam, Laos, and Cambodia.

¶Meanwhile, the United States and Britain should go along with the French on trying to negotiate a "protected armistice" on the following terms: The Communists should withdraw from Southern Vietnam, Cambodia and Laos; there should be a "neutral zone"

Continued on Page 3, Column 2

Democrats Launch Attack On Dulles' Foreign Policy

Truman and Johnson Lead Assault — Latter Fears U.S. 'Naked and Alone'

By WILLIAM S. WHITE
Special to The New York Times

WASHINGTON, May 6 — An all-out Democratic attack on the Eisenhower Administration's foreign policy, the first such attack since the President took office, was opened tonight.

The effect was to put the Administration on dual notice (1) that the bipartisanship of the last sixteen months was breaking up and (2) that the Congressional Democrats could not be counted upon for unquestioning general support in the field of world affairs.

Senator Lyndon B. Johnson of Texas, Democratic leader of the Senate, and former President Harry S. Truman both took the occasion to declare that the Administration was alienating allies of the United States.

Senator Johnson said that the

Harris & Ewing
Senator Lyndon B. Johnson

Administration had put the United States "in clear danger of being left naked and alone in a hostile world."

The results thus far of a

Continued on Page 14, Column 3

SEAWAY IS VOTED BY HOUSE, 241-158; LONG BATTLE ENDS

Bill to Join Canada in Project Goes Back to the Senate for Approval of Minor Changes

By CLAYTON KNOWLES
Special to The New York Times

WASHINGTON, May 6—The House of Representatives voted today, 241 to 158, to authorize the United States to join Canada in constructing the St. Lawrence Seaway.

The vote gave President Eisenhower his biggest legislative victory in his seventeen months in office. Since World War I every President has urged passage of legislation to accomplish the Seaway project.

Approved Jan. 20 by the Senate in slightly different form, the measure now must go back to the upper chamber for concurrence in minor changes voted by the House. The Senate passed the bill by 51 to 33.

As was the case in the Senate, Democratic help was needed in the House to pass the Administration bill. On final passage, 144 Republicans, ninety-six Democrats and the one independent voted with the President. Ninety-four Democrats and sixty-four Republicans voted in opposition.

Strong Administration pressure was exerted for passage of the bill without change. The word was passed that the President "wanted the bill as it passed the Senate."

President Cites Satisfaction

Informed of the final vote, the President noted that it "marks the end of a long and historic effort." He said:

"It is a source of tremendous personal gratification to me that this Eighty-third Congress has made it possible for the United States to join hands with its close neighbor, Canada, in building this Seaway and by this means to contribute materially to the economic well-being and security of both our countries.

"The sponsors of the legislation are to be congratulated on their new approach to the St. Lawrence project which eliminated objectionable features responsible for the defeat of similar proposals in the past."

'Before final passage, Representative Charles A. Halleck of Indiana, the House Republican leader, led Administration forces in beating down a move that, it was contended, would "kill the bill."

The test came on an amend-

Continued on Page 18, Column 2

WIDER SALES TAX SEEMS INEVITABLE, MAYOR DECLARES

In Reply to Business Group's Protest, He Asks Its Help in Getting Action by State

Wagner and McGraw messages are printed on Page 34.

By PAUL CROWELL

Mayor Wagner declared yesterday that extension of the 3 per cent sales tax to commercial services was "seemingly" inevitable. Nothing else can be done, he said, unless a "practical" substitute source of revenue is made possible at a special session of the Legislature.

"We have an obligation to keep the government of the City of New York in first-class running order," the Mayor said. "To do this we need $30,000,000 more in funds than the state allows us to retain or collect except through the imposition of taxes like the 3 per cent service tax and others equally onerous. I regret to state that no practical substitute for that tax has yet appeared and that, barring an agreement on a special session and a program for that session, its imposition is seemingly our only present course of action."

Aid Asked for Special Session

The Mayor called upon business and financial interests opposing the extended sales tax to cooperate with the city in persuading Governor Dewey to call a special session.

The bill to impose the extended sales tax, estimated to yield an annual revenue of $30,000,000, is now in the hands of the Finance Committee of the City Council, which held a public hearing on the measure on April 20.

The Mayor's declaration of policy was made in a letter to Harold W. McGraw, chairman of the Joint Conference for Better Government, representing sixty-seven business, trade and taxpayer associations. The letter was in reply to a telegram sent to the Mayor by Mr. McGraw last Monday. The telegram urged the Mayor to drop the proposed extended sales tax and quit his "efforts to brush responsibility for this vicious tax to Albany."

A spokesman for the Dewey Administration, commenting in Albany on the Mayor's letter, hinted broadly that the special session sought by the city with the aid of pressure from business and financial groups affected by

Continued on Page 34, Column 5

M'CARTHY DEMANDS A TEST OF EXECUTIVE RIGHT TO BAR SECRET DATA TO CONGRESS

McClellan Suggests 'Crime' By McCarthy on Security

Says Receiver of Secret May Be Just as Guilty as Person Who Passed It

By ELIE ABEL
Special to The New York Times

WASHINGTON, May 6—A suggestion that Senator Joseph R. McCarthy may have violated the law in accepting material officially classified as confidential was put up to the Department of Justice today.

Mr. McCarthy has testified under oath that he had received an altered and abbreviated version of a confidential Federal Bureau of Investigation document from a young Army Intelligence officer whom he refused to identify.

Senator John L. McClellan called on Herbert Brownell Jr., the Attorney General, to determine whether "a crime was committed" by the receiver of the paper, as well as the man who passed it to him.

He said it was for this purpose that he had proposed that the Attorney General examine the record

Continued on Page 13, Column 4

CHALLENGES RULE

Asks Colleagues to Join After Brownell Rules Against Publicity

Excerpts from transcript of the hearing, Pages 12 and 13.

By W. H. LAWRENCE
Special to The New York Times

WASHINGTON, May 6—Senator Joseph R. McCarthy threw down the gauntlet today to President Eisenhower and the entire Executive Branch of Government.

The Wisconsin Republican served notice that he would not be bound by any secrecy decisions made by anyone in the Executive Department. He called on the Legislative Branch to join him in a clear-cut test of Presidential authority.

He demanded a closed session of the Senate Permanent Subcommittee on Investigations to decide "once and for all * * * this question of whether or not we are the lackeys who are obey and afraid to overrule a decision made by someone in the Executive Department."

The oratory of Senator McCarthy highlighted a day in which there were these developments:

¶Herbert Brownell Jr., Attorney General, ruled that the Senator was not authorized to have possession of information from a confidential report of the Federal Bureau of Investigation. The Attorney General said it would not be in the public interest to make this information public. The Senator threatened to make it public anyway.

¶Senator McCarthy testified under oath yesterday that he had received an altered, condensed version of a classified F. B. I. report from a young Army Intelligence officer who realized he was violating a Presidential directive. He refused to name the informer, and was not required to do so.

¶Senator McCarthy, on his side, suggested possible perjury charges against Robert T. Stevens, Secretary of the Army, and Maj. Gen. Ralph W. Zwicker, Commanding General of Camp Kilmer, N. J., but was rebuked by the committee for improperly suggesting legal conclusions in the guise of questions.

¶The Army presented a legal opinion by the Attorney General supporting its contention, challenged by Senator McCarthy, that it is not required to honor subpoenas for members of loyalty-security boards when it is aware the questions deal with activities kept secret by Presidential directive.

¶There was a long but indecisive wrangle about "Mr. X," a former member of the Army's loyalty-security "screening board." It was alleged by Senator McCarthy and his associates that Mr. X had a record of Communist-front activities. Secretary Stevens was succeeded on the stand by Mr. Adams, who developed testimony that the charges against Mr. X

Continued on Page 11, Column 1

The New York Times
Senator John L. McClellan

of the Army-McCarthy dispute "for such attention and consideration as it may merit."

It was not until after today's hearing that the Arkansas mem-

Continued on Page 13, Column 4

LANIEL IS UPHELD IN INDO-CHINA TEST

French Chamber, 311 to 262, Gives Him Confidence Vote —Deputies Avert Crisis

By LANSING WARREN
Special to The New York Times

PARIS, May 6—Premier Joseph Laniel won a vote of confidence today on his refusal to hold a debate on the Indo-China war. The vote was 311 to 262.

By reason of abstentions the vote fell short by three of a majority of the Assembly members and it gave an indication of a deep uneasiness in France about the Government policies in the Indo-China conference at Geneva.

Premier Laniel, nevertheless, avoided the necessity of giving information that might hamper Foreign Minister Georges Bidault in the Geneva negotiations and gained time for him to get some limited achievement through that conference before the Assembly's restiveness returns.

Discussions by the Deputies gave an indication that this might be soon in case of adverse events, such as the fall of Dienbienphu or of rebuffs to France by the delegations of Ho Chi Minh of Vietnam or the Chinese Communists.

Most of the speeches made in the debate today gave the impression of the strong desire of the French to get a cease-fire in the Indo-China war at once if only long enough to save the heroic garrison at Dienbienphu.

It was understood that one reason the Deputies avoided a crisis was the news that there was progress in the negotiations at Geneva and on the spot to get a truce at Dienbienphu for the evacuation of the wounded.

It was also obvious that the

Continued on Page 3, Column 5

PEACE PRESSURES ON BIDAULT MOUNT

Geneva Observers Consider French Vote as Move for Indo-China Settlement

By TILLMAN DURDIN
Special to The New York Times

GENEVA, May 6—Georges Bidault, French Foreign Minister, is believed in some quarters to be under increased pressure from Paris to agree to a settlement in Indo-China as a result of today's challenge to the French Government.

Although the Laniel Cabinet won today's Assembly confidence vote, informed French political sources here say that new moves against the Government can be expected shortly if M. Bidault does not achieve an early solution in Indo-China at the forthcoming Geneva conference sessions on the Indo-China problem.

Marc Jacquet, French Undersecretary of State for the Associated States, arrived here late today to report to M. Bidault on the result of the day's political activity in the French capital. It was reported that he brought new instructions on Indo-China for the Foreign Minister. He refused to give correspondents any indication of what they might be but the surmise in French quarters was that M. Bidault would be asked to reinforce his efforts to get an Indo-China settlement.

Start Remains Uncertain

However, the French Assembly vote at least gave M. Bidault assurance that he could look forward to continued participation in the Indo-China talks and plan accordingly. He dined tonight with M. Jacquet and representatives of the Associated States of Vietnam, Cambodia and Laos and there was a general discussion of prospects and policies for the talks.

Just when the Indo-China sessions will get under way remained uncertain tonight. Because a formal conference session on Korea has been arranged for tomorrow afternoon, and because the delegations for the Indo-China states are still incomplete, it was considered certain that there could be no Indo-China meeting tomorrow.

A French spokesman said it was possible that the Indo-China talks would start Saturday, but the Vietnamese representatives here doubt if the delegation will be ready by then. The chiefs for the Laotian and Cambodian delegations have not yet arrived in Geneva and these two delegations may also not be prepared to participate Saturday.

Nguyen Trung Vinh, chief of the Bao Dai delegation, arrived with a number of ranking delegation members this morning.

A Vietnamese spokesman said that Chief of State Bao Dai

Continued on Page 3, Column 1

NEW HAVEN DROPS COMMUTATION RISE

New President Wants Study of Railroad's Role—Dewey 'Discouraged' Over L.I.R.R.

The New York, New Haven and Hartford Railroad's new management withdrew yesterday a proposal its predecessor had made for a 24 to 30 per cent commutation fare increase.

Patrick B. McGinnis, newly elected president, said he first wished to study the various methods of travel used by commuters and to confer with governmental agencies on what part the railroad was to play in the future of mass transport.

Meanwhile, Governor Dewey in Albany termed "discouraging" the action by the Interstate Commerce Commission Wednesday which he said in effect sought to force a 25 per cent increase in Long Island Rail Road commutation fares in sixty days by the State Public Service Commission.

Governor Dewey summoned members of the Long Island Transit Authority to meet with him "at their earliest"—probably late next week—to discuss that line's problems. If some kind of plan for private rehabilitation of the bankrupt Long Island can be worked out, Mr. Dewey plans to call a special session of the Legislature in June.

New Haven Filed Dec. 30

The New Haven's former management had filed a Dec. 30 petition with the Interstate Commutation to raise commutation fares both interstate and within New York State. Plans were to ask the Connecticut, Rhode Island and Massachusetts Public Service Commissions for similar increases in their areas.

But Mr. McGinnis, who won control of the $500,000,000 New Haven in a management fight last April 16, asserted that "entirely new thinking must be introduced by railroad management to change the general trend from rails to rubber."

Asserting that rate increases "are attended by decreases in the number of commuters," Mr. McGinnis contended that the answer to problems of commutation trains rested in convincing more riders that it was as cheap and convenient to use trains as to use buses and automobiles.

The New Haven's new chief argued that the problem of mass transportation should be studied as a whole, rather than "merely as a railroad problem." He bid for conferences with the Port of New York Authority, the Triborough Bridge and Tunnel Authority and officials of New York State, New York City and Westchester County.

"Thus far," he said, "the tendency has been for these other agencies to avoid even discussing the problem with the rail-

Continued on Page 17, Column 2

AUTHORITY SPURNS TRANSIT PLANT BID

Terme Edison Offer So Low as to Make Modernizing of Power Facility Feasible

By LEONARD INGALLS

The Transit Authority rejected yesterday an offer by the Consolidated Edison Company to buy one of the three city-owned subway power plants.

Acting on a recommendation by Sidney H. Bingham, executive director and general manager of the transit system, the authority decided that it would be cheaper to rehabilitate the plant and continue to generate its own power rather than buy it from the utility.

The authority's decision was basic. Up to yesterday the question of whether to sell the power plants and buy electricity or to retain and modernize them had been unresolved.

By rejecting the Consolidated Edison proposal, the authority placed itself on record as favoring the latter course which would cost an estimated $176,500,000 in city capital funds.

Consolidated Edison, the authority reported, submitted a bid of $8,000,000 on Feb. 5 for the plant at Kent and Division Avenues, Brooklyn, which supplies power for the B. M. T. division. The land, structure and equipment are valued by the city's real estate assessors at $13,000,000.

Two power plants serving the I. R. T. are operated by the Transit Authority in Manhattan—one at West Fifty-ninth Street and the Hudson River and the other at East Seventy-fourth Street and the East River. Power for the IND subway division is

Continued on Page 17, Column 1

Junta Reported Ruling Paraguay After Army Ousting of President

By The United Press

ASUNCION, Paraguay, May 6—A junta took over the government today following an uprising by army cavalry forces that deposed President Federico Chaves yesterday.

In a statement signed by its leader, a civil engineer, Tomas Romero Pereira, the junta said the "present political situation in the country remains under the control of the Colorado party."

Dr. Chaves had been a leader of the Colorado party. There was no word on his fate.

The statement from the junta said order prevailed throughout the country.

The junta met here with all attention to consider steps toward full restoration of political normalcy. Gen. Alfredo Stroessner, Commander in Chief of the Paraguayan Army, broadcasting over a nation-wide hook-up, assured the people that "order has been

Continued on Page 8, Column 5

re-established in units of the First Cavalry Division, all garrisons are still obeying the orders of the Commander in Chief and of the Government Junta, and calm reigns in the republic."

The First Cavalry Division was the main factor in the rise against the Chaves Government and earlier reports indicated Dr. Chaves was a virtual prisoner of the armed forces.

[Buenos Aires reported indications of a severe censorship in effect in Paraguay. Communications were generally open, but subject to delays.]

Lieut. Col. Mario B. Ortega, new police chief in Asuncion, also assured the country that order had been restored and that the Army supported the Junta.

Colonel Ortega succeeded Police Chief Herbert L. Petit, who was killed yesterday when re-

---

4-Minute Mile Is Achieved By Bannister of England

Associated Press Radiophoto
Roger Bannister hits the tape in 3 minutes 59.4 seconds

By DREW MIDDLETON
Special to The New York Times

LONDON, May 6—Roger Gilbert Bannister ran a mile in 3 minutes 59.4 seconds tonight to reach one of man's hitherto unattainable goals.

The 4-minute time sought by every great miler for twenty years was beaten by the slim, sandy-haired medical student in a dual meet at Oxford University.

Running on the four-lap Iffley

Road track, Bannister swept through the final quarter in 57.5 seconds. The middle quarters of the race were run in 60:2 and 0:62.3. Then with a final explosive burst, Bannister raced to the record with 0:58.9 for the last quarter.

The 25-year-old miler ran under exceedingly unfavorable conditions. On a

Continued on Page 28, Column 1

Crippled Airliner With 62 Aboard Jettisons 'Gas,' Lands Safely Here

In a superb show of airmanship, a Pan American World Airways pilot brought a Boeing Stratocruiser—the world's largest and heaviest commercial transport—in to a safe landing here yesterday in spite of a damaged nosewheel.

None of the fifty-three passengers or crew of nine was even jarred.

The plane, bound for London, had taken off from the New York International Airport, Idlewild, at 4:23 P. M. Shortly after the takeoff the pilot, Capt. Cameron Walker of 115 Fox Boulevard, Massapequa, L. I., radioed back that the nosewheel was twisted to a 65-degree angle and would not retract.

Deciding to return, the former Marine Corps combat pilot took two-deck aircraft out over the Atlantic and dumped 25,500 gallons of the 4,000 gallons of gasoline aboard. Normally Stratocruisers carry nearly 8,000

gallons, but because of bad weather in the North Atlantic the plane had been routed via Bermuda and the Azores, and could have been refueled there.

When Idlewild learned of the plane's plight and Captain Walker's decision to return for an emergency landing, all measures were taken to handle what might well turn out to be a disaster. Five police cars, four ambulances, four Port of New York Authority fire trucks, two buses, a small derrick and two jeeps were called out to the end of Runway 31—a 9,500-foot strip.

Meanwhile, the passengers had been informed that the plane was returning because of mechanical difficulties. In the control cabin Captain Walker and his co-pilot, John H. Brink of Westbury, L. I., were confronted with a number of decisions.

The Stratocruiser, which weighs

Continued on Page 35, Column 7

Ho Chi Minh, Communist leader of the North Vietnamese who defeated the French at Dienbienphu.

A French soldier stands over an Algerian prisoner during France's attempt to quell the native rebellion for independence.

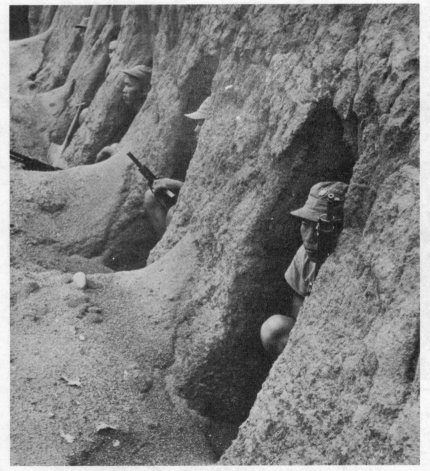

The Formosan crisis brought the United States closer to involvement in war. Chinese Nationalist troops on Quemoy Island, 10 miles off the Communist mainland, anticipate a possible assault.

"All the News
That's Fit to Print"

The New York Times.

LATE CITY EDITION
Cloudy, scattered showers today.
Partly cloudy, cool tomorrow.
Temperature Range Today—Max., 58; Min., 47
Temperature Yesterday—Max., 60; Min., 46
Full U. S. Weather Bureau Report, Page 27

Copyright, 1954, by The New York Times Company.

VOL. CIII.. No. 35,168.

Entered as Second-Class Matter,
Post Office, New York, N. Y.

NEW YORK, SATURDAY, MAY 8, 1954.

Times Square, New York 36, N. Y.
Telephone LAckawanna 4-1000

FIVE CENTS

PLEAS FOR SCHINE LACED BY THREATS, STEVENS TESTIFIES

Phone Calls Mingled Them, He Tells Jenkins, Who Brings Army Case to Sharp Focus

OFFICIAL DENIES 'BANTER'

Mundt Asserts Subcommittee Hit a 'Security Roadblock' on Monitored Conversations

Excerpts from transcript of the hearing are on Page 8.

By W. H. LAWRENCE
Special to The New York Times.

WASHINGTON, May 7—The Secretary of the Army testified today that Senator Joseph R. McCarthy and his key aides had mixed, in the same conversations, repeated requests for favored treatment for Pvt. G. David Schine with "threats" of continued exposure of alleged Communists in the Army.

Ray H. Jenkins, special counsel for the Senate subcommittee, propounded the queries to Army Secretary Robert T. Stevens that brought into sharp focus the heart of the Army case.

This was that the Senator and his staff had used the investigative power of the Senate to back up their demands for special favors for Private Schine, who, until he was drafted, was an unpaid subcommittee consultant.

As Mr. Stevens, on his twelfth day on the stand, neared the end of his testimony, Mr. Jenkins propounded a series of climactic questions.

"I'll ask you, he said, "whether or not • • • telephone calls were either transmitted to you or Mr. Adams (John G. Adams, Army Counselor) with reference to Mr. Schine."

"Yes sir," the answer came.

Subjects Intertwined

"I'll ask you," Mr. Jenkins continued, "whether or not in these telephone conversations there were discussions not only with reference to Schine but with reference to the McCarthy investigating committee's work at Fort Monmouth. Were those two subjects discussed in the same conversations, on numerous occasions, or on a few occasions, or on no occasions?"

"Yes, they were discussed on a number of occasions," Mr. Stevens declared.

"So that the conversations," Mr. Jenkins went on, "with reference to the investigation of Monmouth and with reference to Schine were intertwined, so to speak, in one telephone conversation. Is that right, Mr. Secretary?"

"Yes sir," the answer came.

"And did you not regard that," the counsel pursued, "as being a combination of a request for preferences for Schine, on the one hand, and correlated with a discussion or a threat of continued investigation of Fort Monmouth?"

"Yes, I couldn't separate the two," was Secretary Stevens' conclusion.

Mr. Stevens then coldly rejected suggestions by Senator Everett M. Dirksen, Illinois Republican, that the remarks taken as threatening might have been good-natured "banter." The Army Secretary said he regarded the threats as a "very serious matter."

Other major developments of

Continued on Page 8, Column 3

Seaway Bill Passed, Sent to Eisenhower

Special to The New York Times.

WASHINGTON, May 7—The Senate gave final Congressional approval today to the St. Lawrence Seaway bill.

It now goes to the White House where President Eisenhower has said he will sign the measure every President since Warren G. Harding has sought.

The Senate action was by voice vote. The Senate concurred in two minor changes made by the House of Representatives yesterday in giving approval of the bill by a vote of 241 to 158. The Senate had passed the measure, 51 to 33, on Jan. 20.

The bill, which authorizes the United States to join with Canada in constructing the project, calls for the establishment of a St. Lawrence Seaway Development Corporation to act for the United States subject to the supervision of the President. General Eisenhower will name

Continued on Page 18, Column 5

State to Get $113,000,000 Under New U.S. Road Law

Grants Will Be Allocated Over 2 Years— 4 Classes of Highways to Benefit— City Expected to Gain $5,000,000

Special to The New York Times.

ALBANY, May 7—The Public Works Department estimated today that New York would get $113,000,000 of the $1,932,000,000 in Federal highway grants authorized by President Eisenhower yesterday.

The figure in the new law represented an increase of $41,600,000 over New York's grants under the old Federal-aid highway measure. The new amounts will be spread over a period of two years, starting July 1, 1955.

The new Federal grants, as under the old law, will have to be matched by an equal amount of state funds. This represented no problem for the state since it already was planning a huge expansion in state highway construction funds.

At this year's legislative session alternative constitutional amendments to authorize state bond issues of either $500,000,000 or $750,000,000 for highway construction received initial approval. One of the two will be taken up for final legislative ap-

proval and submission to the voters next year.

The Public Works Department analysis put the state's share of the new Federal funds at roughly $56,500,000 a year for the fiscal years 1956 and 1957. The first of these starts July 1, 1955, and the second July 1, 1956.

Four classes of roads will share in this amount: primary highways, secondary highways, urban arterial highways and interstate highway routes. More than $14,700,000 a year is provided for primary highways. This is $3,200,000 a year more than New York has been getting.

For secondary roads the new annual allocation is $5,900,000, an increase of $1,300,000. For urban arterial highways the new allowance is more than $22,900,000, an increase of almost $5,000,000. For interstate routes the new allocation is $12,700,000, an increase of $11,600,000.

Since New York City usually

Continued on Page 36, Column 3

Steel Workers Set to Snub Union Anti-Raiding Accord

By A. H. RASKIN
Special to The New York Times.

PITTSBURGH, May 7 — The 1,250,000-member United Steelworkers of America, C. I. O., intends to boycott the no-raiding pact between the American Federation of Labor and the Congress of Industrial Organizations.

The decision of David J. McDonald, president of the giant steel union, to withhold his signature from the peace plan represents as crippling a blow to the pact's effectiveness as the refusal of Dave Beck, an A. F. L. vice president, to bring his 1,300,000-member International Brotherhood of Teamsters under the agreement.

Word of the steel union's plans leaked out here just one week after Mr. McDonald had forged an informal alliance with Mr. Beck and John L. Lewis, president of the United Mine Workers, independent, at a luncheon conference in Washington.

Close associates of the steel union head said he had "no evidence of it would make unnecessary the extension of the 3 per cent sales tax to commercial services, the civic group said.

It was expected that the Mayor, in line with his announced policy of discussing major city problems with all responsible organizations seeking conferences, would grant the request, although the meeting might take place later in the week if the Mayor's office commitments prevented a Wednesday conference.

The request for the meeting was made in a telegram sent the Mayor by Harold W. McGraw and John T. Clancy, co-chairmen of the Joint Conference for Better Government in New York City. This organization, claiming to represent sixty-seven business and taxpayers groups, is one of the leading opponents of the proposal to tax commercial services.

The telegram was in reply to the Mayor's letter of last Thursday in which he declared that extension of the sales tax to commercial services was "seemingly" inevitable unless a special session of the Legislature gave the city an acceptable substitute method of raising the $30,000,000 that the broadened sales tax would yield in 1954-55.

Continued on Page 23, Column 5

BUSINESS TO OFFER 3% TAX SUBSTITUTE

'Top Committee' Representing 67 Groups Seeks a Meeting With Mayor Wednesday

By PAUL CROWELL

Mayor Wagner was asked yesterday to discuss with a "top committee" of outstanding business men next Wednesday a "sound nonpartisan" proposal for added city revenue. The adoption of it would make unnecessary the extension of the 3 per cent sales tax to commercial services, the civic group said.

It was expected that the Mayor, in line with his announced policy of discussing major city problems with all responsible organizations seeking conferences, would grant the request, although the meeting might take place later in the week if the Mayor's office commitments prevented a Wednesday conference.

The request for the meeting was made in a telegram sent the Mayor by Harold W. McGraw and John T. Clancy, co-chairmen of the Joint Conference for Better Government in New York City. This organization, claiming to represent sixty-seven business and taxpayers groups, is one of the leading opponents of the proposal to tax commercial services.

The telegram was in reply to the Mayor's letter of last Thursday in which he declared that extension of the sales tax to commercial services was "seemingly" inevitable unless a special session of the Legislature gave the city an acceptable substitute method of raising the $30,000,000 that the broadened sales tax would yield in 1954-55.

In his letter the Mayor asked for the cooperation of the sixty-seven business and taxpayer groups in "a genuine non-partisan appeal to Albany." The McGraw-Clancy telegram assured the Mayor that the proposal to be presented for his consideration would represent the "high level non-partisan business thinking" of the "top committee," which would begin on Monday a series of executive meetings from which the plan would emerge.

The telegram expressed confidence that the plan would kill the "ruinous" sales tax proposal if the Mayor would "move sincerely" in cooperation with the business group.

The Mayor was informed that four members of the "top committee" had been chosen earlier in the day at a special meeting called to consider his letter.

They were Percy J. Ebbott, president of the Chase National Bank; Warren Lee Pierson, chairman of the board of Trans World Airlines, Inc.; Clinton W. Blume, president of the Real Es-

Continued on Page 23, Column 5

TAFT ACT CHANGES KILLED BY SENATE; DEMOCRATS SOLID

Party Prevails in 50-42 Vote to Return Bill — President Rebuffed on Program

Special to The New York Times.

WASHINGTON, May 7—The Senate today killed amendments to the Taft-Hartley Law for the 1954 session of Congress.

A vote of 50 to 42 sent the Administration bill to revise the labor act back to committee.

The Democrats engineered this with solidarity, something they had not achieved on a roll-call vote in the modern cycle of labor legislation going back to the Norris-LaGuardia Act of 1932. Three Republicans joined them, but their votes did not affect the result.

Forty-six of the Senate's forty-eight Democrats were for returning the bill and the two others were paired for recommittal.

Just before the tally, Senator William F. Knowland of California, the Republican leader, sternly told his colleagues that "A motion to recommit this bill is a motion to kill this bill as far as this session is concerned."

Nobody challenged this on or off the Senate floor.

Senator H. Alexander Smith, Republican of New Jersey, confirmed such a conclusion after the vote. As chairman of the Labor Committee, he was in charge of the bill on the floor, and though he lost he appeared happy that the fight was over.

Feels Sense of Relief

"I feel a sense of relief," he commented. "I'm just as cheerful as a dickey bird."

He said he did not think the issue of state's rights in labor matters should be opened again at this session by his committee, and he did not think the House of Representatives would produce a bill on the subject, either. The House Labor Committee has been writing a bill, but was deferring a final vote until the Senate acted.

The Republican Senators who voted to recommit were: William Langer and Milton R. Young of North Dakota and George W. Malone of Nevada. Senator Wayne Morse of Oregon, an Independent, also voted this way.

The stated reason for the Democrats' solid vote to recommit the bill was the fact that the Republican majority on the Labor Committee would not consider amendments outside the area of President Eisenhower's recommendations.

This was not considered the final reason, however, at least not the sole reason.

The Northern Democrats, most friendly to labor, had been persuaded that the Administration bill would make the Taft-Hartley Law more undesirable to them and that they might fare better by waiting until the next Congress was elected.

The Southern Democrats felt that some of the President's recommendations undesirably weakened some of the labor controls. Also, if the bill were not recommitted, they would face

Continued on Page 11, Column 2

DIENBIENPHU IS LOST AFTER 55 DAYS; NO WORD OF DE CASTRIES AND HIS MEN; DULLES SAYS UNITY CAN CHECK REDS

ASIA PACT PUSHED

Secretary Rules Out Armed Action Without Congress' Approval

Text of the Dulles address is printed on Page 4.

By WILLIAM S. WHITE
Special to The New York Times.

WASHINGTON, May 7—John Foster Dulles, Secretary of State predicted tonight that the current efforts toward collective defense in Southeast Asia ultimately would halt Communist aggression short of its aims.

Reporting in a broadcast on the Geneva conference on the Far East, Mr. Dulles made two points plain.

¶ 1. That the possibility of ultimate United States military intervention in Indo-China, in association with other free nations, was real.

¶ 2. That there was no intention, in any event, of committing United States forces without the sanction of Congress.

The French Union fortress of Dienbienphu in Indo-China fell only at the cost of "staggering losses" to the Communists, Mr. Dulles noted.

"An epic battle has ended but great causes have, before now, been won out of lost battles," he added.

Steps Proposed for U. S.

He declared that the Eisenhower Administration regarded as important the following steps for a solution of the Indo-China crisis:

¶The French should give greater reality to their intention to grant full independence to Vietnam, Laos and Cambodia, the three Associated States of the country. This would take away from the Communists their false claim to be leading the fight for independence.

¶There should be greater reliance upon the national armies which would be fighting in their own homeland. He believed this could be done if the peoples felt that they had a good cause for which to fight and if better facilities for training and equipment were provided for them.

¶There should be greater free-world assistance. France is carrying on a struggle that is overburdening her economic resources. "Much progress" has been made toward all those goals, the Secretary asserted.

As to the current negotiations for creating a free-world alliance in Asia, Mr. Dulles said that progress had been made and that "unity of purpose persists."

The fall of Dienbienphu will only "harden, not weaken, our purpose to stay unified," he added.

Geneva Hopes Stand

While "present conditions" in Indo-China do not "provide a suitable basis" for armed intervention by the United States, the possibility under other circumstances of "serious commitments" by the United States nevertheless exists, Mr. Dulles said.

The Geneva conference, he went on, may yet find a settlement by which an honorable armistice can be arranged, but the United States "would be gravely concerned" if the outcome should "provide a road to a Communist takeover and further aggression."

"If this occurs, or if hostilities continue, then the need will be even more urgent to create the conditions for united action in defense of the area," he said.

"In making commitments which might involve the use of armed force, the Congress is a full partner," Mr. Dulles continued. "Only the Congress can declare war. President Eisenhower has repeatedly emphasized that he would not take military action in Indo-China without the support of Congress.

"Furthermore, he has made clear that he does not seek that unless, in his opinion, there would be an adequate collective effort based upon genuine mutuality of purpose in defending vital interests."

This declaration took on added significance in light of the fact that earlier in the day Mr. Dulles had gone over with President Eisenhower for an hour and a

Continued on Page 4, Column 7

REVEALS MILITARY DEFEAT: Premier Joseph Laniel after he told French Cabinet of the fall of Dienbienphu.
Associated Press Radiophoto

WEST STILL PLANS ARMISTICE TALKS

Negotiations on Indo-China Set to Open in Geneva, Subject to Paris Action

By THOMAS J. HAMILTON

GENEVA, May 7—The United States, Britain and France decided tonight to go ahead with the opening of the Indo-China negotiations here tomorrow despite the capture of Dienbienphu. Their decision, however, was made subject to the action of the French Cabinet.

The three Western powers had previously agreed to submit to the conference on Far Eastern affairs a proposal for an armistice under which the Vietminh would withdraw from southern Vietnam and the Red River delta in northern Vietnam.

This is the program that Foreign Minister Georges Bidault has been fighting for, and if the Cabinet backs him up the Indo-China phase of the Far Eastern conference will start at 3 P. M. tomorrow.

However, if the Cabinet overrules M. Bidault and orders him to propose a simple cease-fire, the new-found unity of the Western powers will be destroyed and it will be necessary to postpone the opening of the conference while a new formula is negotiated.

Gen. Walter Bedell Smith, Under Secretary of State, busied himself

Continued on Page 3, Column 2

FRANCE IS SENDING MORE MEN TO WAR

No Protest Greets Laniel's Statement—Shock of Loss Seems to Unify Deputies

By LANSING WARREN
Special to The New York Times.

PARIS, May 7—The French Assembly heard Premier Joseph Laniel's statement on the fall of Dienbienphu in utter silence and adjourned for half an hour late this afternoon as a sign of mourning and respect for the valiant dead.

The shock was evidently great and most of the Deputies, as they discussed it, seemed to have been drawn together in a renewed determination that they would not now give up the fight. Even those members of the Assembly who had most strongly urged an end to the conflict were disposed to show that France would not capitulate.

No one protested when the Premier made the announcement that more troops were on the way to Indo-China so that the expeditionary corps would not be weakened.

The Cabinet, in unison, decided upon military steps to aid the troops in the other parts of Vietnam to hold out.

The Vietminh tactics of overwhelming Dienbienphu on the eve of the opening of the Geneva conference on Indo-China seemed in a fair way to result in bolstering French resistance and in

Continued on Page 6, Column 4

U. S. Rejects Soviet Note Seeking European Pact and Role in NATO

By DANA ADAMS SCHMIDT
Special to The New York Times.

WASHINGTON, May 7—The United States rejected today the Soviet Union's proposal of March 31 that the "cold war" be ended by formation of a new European security organization and its suggestion for Soviet admission

Text of United States reply to Soviet note is on Page 6.

to the North Atlantic Treaty Organization.

A State Department spokesman had rejected the Soviet proposal the day it was made as a transparent maneuver to upset Western plans to create a new formula in defending vital interests.

In the note delivered by United States Embassy in Moscow to the Soviet Foreign Ministry, John Foster Dulles, Secretary of State, spelled out the United States rejection and stressed that the Soviet Union demonstrate its good intentions in a

step by step elimination of the outstanding sources of international tension.

Possibly in response to criticism in Europe of the State Department's original out-of-hand rejection of the Soviet note of March 31, the new note emphasized that this reply had been worked out in consultation with the British and French Governments.

Mr. Dulles proposed that the Soviet Government join with France, Britain and the United States in a five-point program:

1. To find a speedy settlement of the Austrian question "that will restore to Austria its full sovereignty and independence."

He noted that in the Berlin conference, after the Western powers had offered to accept the Soviet text of every un-

Continued on Page 6, Column 4

ASSAULT SUCCEEDS

Fort Falls After 20-Hour Fight — Last Strong Point Is Silent

Special to The New York Times.

PARIS, May 7—The fall of Dienbienphu was announced today by Premier Joseph Laniel.

The news of the worst military defeat that the French have suffered since the Indo-China war began in December, 1946, came suddenly.

It was received with confused emotion. The heroic defense of Dienbienphu, besieged for fifty-five days, had been followed in screaming headlines since March 13, when the Vietminh launched its first attack — as if for the first time in more than seven years the public had fully realized that the country was fighting an enormously bloody and costly war.

M. Laniel told the Assembly that the heroic stronghold had been taken after twenty hours of fighting and continuous alertness for the last two months. He could not issue any information on the fate of the commander, Brig. Gen. Christian de Castries, or of the defenders or the wounded who have wasted underground for several weeks.

Final Concentration

All that he knew, the Premier said, was that the southern resistance point called Isabelle was still defended under the command of Col. André Lalande. French artillery with some tanks were concentrated at that center.

[Contact with the Isabelle outpost had been lost, according to an Associated Press dispatch from Saigon.]

"The Vietminh now are only a few meters away," were the last words heard from General de Castries over the radio-telephone, the French Cabinet was told. The last dispatch received from the battle was that the central strong point had been submerged.

For the defenders of Dienbienphu there was French pride in their heroism and sadness for their fate. There was also some grim anger against those who had engulfed them in defeat and, at least unkindly feelings for those responsible for French political and military policy.

Before last March the name of Dienbienphu, now solidly entrenched in French military annals, was unknown here, but not in Indo-China, where it had some importance.

The Vietminh had taken Dienbienphu, a peaceful community of 9,000 persons, who grew rice and poppy for opium, in February, 1953, and used it to help launch operations against Laos in the following April.

French Seizure Nov. 21

Last November when a Vietminh column was spotted heading northwest in the Thai country to the French base of Laichau, the French decided to evacuate Laichau and seize Dienbienphu, using parachutists from the Tonkin area.

A successful operation was launched Nov. 21 and after the Laichau garrison moved in the French began daily efforts to strengthen it by building underground fortifications, improving the airfield and setting up barbed wire.

The establishment of the Dienbienphu base had strategic and political reasons. Close to the Laotian border, it helped fend off the Vietminh attacks southward into Laos and against the capital of Luang Prabang by threatening the Vietminh rear and blocking supply lines.

The fact that the Vietminh withdrew from Laos and did not attack Luang Prabang was attributed to French control of Dienbienphu. The French also wished to remain in the Thai tribal country to encourage and help the Thai guerrillas hostile to the Vietminh.

Finally, Dienbienphu, because of its geographical position, was expected to require a large Vietminh force to attack it, thus relieving pressure on French defenses in the much more vital Tonkin delta area.

This is precisely what happened. The French garrison num-

Continued on Page 2, Column 4

Housing Unit Counsel Ordered To Answer Charges or Be Ousted

Acting Commissioner Directs Bovard, Now on Leave, to Act in 14 Days

By The United Press.

WASHINGTON, May 7—Norman P. Mason, acting Federal Housing Administrator, charged today that the agency's counsel, Burton C. Bovard, had failed to do his job "satisfactorily" and gave him fourteen days to answer the charges or be dismissed.

Mr. Mason, named to clean up alleged widespread housing scandals, said he had "no evidence of illegal activity" by Mr. Bovard. The charges involve his "failure to satisfactorily carry out the duties of general counsel of the F. H. A.," he explained.

While he gave Mr. Bovard fourteen days to show cause why he should not be removed, he said he might extend that time. If counsel fails to answer the charges, Mr. Mason added, he will be "removed from office" within thirty days.

Mr. Mason also offered to give Mr. Bovard a public hearing within twenty-one days if he agreed to testify under oath and be subject to cross-examination.

Burton C. Bovard
Associated Press

Meanwhile, Senator Harry F. Byrd, Democrat of Virginia, said he had sent to the Justice Department information that might be "helpful" in pinning down responsibility for Government hous-

Continued on Page 18, Column 7

1954

U.S. Supreme Court Justices are (seated left to right) William O. Douglas, Hugo L. Black, Chief Justice Earl Warren, Felix Frankfurter, Tom Clark. (standing) Charles Whittaker, John M. Harlan, William J. Brennan, Potter Stewart.

Attorney Thurgood Marshall (center) is congratulated on winning the Supreme Court case on March 17, 1954 in which the high court declared racial segregation in public schools unconstitutional.

130

"All the News That's Fit to Print"

The New York Times.

LATE CITY EDITION
Fair and cool today. Mostly sunny, continued cool tomorrow.
Temperature Range Today—Max., 68; Min., 52
Temperatures Yesterday—Max., 69; Min., 61
Full U. S. Weather Bureau Report, Page 31

Copyright, 1954, by The New York Times Company.

VOL. CIII... No. 35,178. Entered as Second-Class Matter. Post Office, New York, N. Y. NEW YORK, TUESDAY, MAY 18, 1954. Times Square, New York 36, N. Y. Telephone Lackawanna 4-1000 FIVE CENTS

HIGH COURT BANS SCHOOL SEGREGATION; 9-TO-0 DECISION GRANTS TIME TO COMPLY

McCarthy Hearing Off a Week as Eisenhower Bars Report

SENATOR IS IRATE

President Orders Aides Not to Disclose Details of Top-Level Meeting

President's letter and excerpts from transcript, Pages 24, 25, 26.

By W. H. LAWRENCE
Special to The New York Times.

WASHINGTON, May 17—A secrecy directive by President Eisenhower resulted today in an abrupt recess for at least a week of the Senate's Army-McCarthy hearings.

Democratic and Republican Senators, some publicly and some privately, predicted that the investigation might never resume in earnest. However, there were other Senators who insisted that the investigation would go on to completion.

The recess was voted after Herbert Brownell Jr., the Attorney General, disclosed formally that criminal prosecutions might be instituted against those involved in the "preparation and dissemination" of an altered, condensed but still confidential Federal Bureau of Investigation report. This was offered in evidence last week by Senator Joseph R. McCarthy, Republican of Wisconsin.

Republicans outvoted Democrats 4 to 3 on the Senate Permanent Subcommittee of Investigation to recess the hearings until 10 o'clock next Monday morning. They acted amid charges and denials that the way was being prepared for a "whitewash."

Constitutional Division Cited

President Eisenhower cited the constitutional separation of powers between the Executive and Legislative branches in directing that details and conversations at a "high level" Administration meeting on Jan. 21 must be withheld from the committee.

Testimony already has been given that top White House, Justice and Defense officials had made plans at that conference to deal with Senator McCarthy.

The Presidential order served effectively to seal the lips of John G. Adams, the Army's regular counselor, about what Sherman Adams, the chief Presidential assistant, said to him in advising that a written report be prepared on how Senator McCarthy and his chief counsel, Roy M. Cohn, persistenly sought preferential treatment for Pvt. G. David Schine.

Before his induction, Mr. Schine was an unpaid consultant to the McCarthy subcommittee, the same group that is now conducting the hearings under the temporary chairmanship of Senator Karl E. Mundt, Republican of South Dakota.

Senator McCarthy angrily denounced today's Eisenhower order as "an Iron Curtain." His ire was shared, but in more restrained terms, by all the Republican and Democratic members of the investigating committee.

The week's postponement of

Continued on Page 24, Column 1

Communist Arms Unloaded in Guatemala By Vessel From Polish Port, U. S. Learns

State Department Views News Gravely Because of Red Infiltration

Special to The New York Times.

WASHINGTON, May 17—The State Department said today that it had reliable information that "an important shipment of arms' had been sent from Communist-controlled territory to Guatemala.

It said the arms, now being unloaded at Puerto Barrios, Guatemala, had been shipped from Stettin, a former German Baltic seaport, which has been occupied by Communist Poland since World War II. The Guatemalan regime has been frequently accused of being influenced by Communists.

"Because of the origin of these arms, the point of their embarkation, their destination and the quantity of arms involved, the Department of State considers that this is a development of gravity," the announcement said.

A freighter arrived at Puerto

Gulf of Mexico
MEXICO
Caribbean Sea
BRITISH HONDURAS
GUATEMALA
Puerto Barrios
HONDURAS
Guatemala
EL SALVADOR
NICAR.

The New York Times May 18, 1954
Site of arms arrival (cross)

Embassy Says Nation of Central America May Buy Munitions Anywhere

Barrios last Saturday, the State Department reported, carrying a large shipment of armament consigned to the Guatemalan Government.

The State Department did not divulge the exact quantity of the arms, their nature or where they had been manufactured.

Reliable sources told The New York Times, however, that ten freight car loads of goods listed in the manifest as "hardware" had been unloaded from this ship and sent to the city of Guatemala since Sunday. Guatemala is 150 miles from Puerto Barrios. The

Continued on Page 19, Column 5

REACTION OF SOUTH

'Breathing Spell' for Adjustment Tempers Region's Feelings

By JOHN N. POPHAM
Special to The New York Times.

CHATTANOOGA, Tenn., May 17—The South's reaction to the Supreme Court's decision outlawing racial segregation in public schools appeared to be tempered considerably today.

The time lag allowed for carrying out the required transitions seemed to be the major factor in that reaction.

Southern leaders of both races in political, educational and community service fields expressed comment that covered a wide range. Some spoke bitter words that verged on defiance. Others ranged from sharp disagreement to predictions of peaceful and successful adjustment in accord with the ruling.

But underneath the surface of much of the comment, it was evident that many Southerners recognized that the decision had laid down the legal principle rejecting segregation in public education facilities.

They also noted that it had left open a challenge to the region to join in working out a program of necessary changes in the present bi-racial school systems.

Three of the most illustrative viewpoints were those expressed by Govs. James F. Byrnes of South Carolina and Herman Talmadge of Georgia, and Harold Fleming, a spokesman for the Southern Regional Council, the most effective interracial organization in the South.

Byrnes Sees Reversal

Governor Byrnes, who has vigorously defended the doctrine of separate but equal facilities in education, said that he was "shocked to learn that the court has reversed itself" with regard to past rulings on that doctrine.

However, Governor Byrnes, a former Associate Justice of the Supreme Court, noted that the tribunal had not yet delivered its final decree setting forth the time and terms for ending segregation in the schools.

Pointing out that South Carolina, a party in the litigation before the court, had until October to present arguments on how the Supreme Court should order the implementation of the decision, Governor Byrnes declared "I urge all of our people, white and colored, to exercise restraint and preserve order."

Governor Talmadge repeatedly has vowed there "will never be mixed schools while I am Governor" and has warned that school integration would lead to "blood-

Continued on Page 20, Column 1

Associated Press Wirephoto

LEADERS IN SEGREGATION FIGHT: Lawyers who led battle before U. S. Supreme Court for abolition of segregation in public schools congratulate one another ar they leave court after announcement of decision. Left to right: George E. C. Hayes, Thurgood Marshall and James M. Nabrit.

1896 RULING UPSET

'Separate but Equal' Doctrine Held Out of Place in Education

Text of Supreme Court decision is printed on Page 15.

By LUTHER A. HUSTON
Special to The New York Times.

WASHINGTON, May 17—The Supreme Court unanimously outlawed today racial segregation in public schools.

Chief Justice Earl Warren read two opinions that put the stamp of unconstitutionality on school systems in twenty-one states and the District of Columbia where segregation is permissive or mandatory.

The court, taking cognizance of the problems involved in the integration of the school systems concerned, put over until the next term, beginning in October, the formulation of decrees to effectuate its 9-to-0 decision.

The opinions set aside the "separate but equal" doctrine laid down by the Supreme Court in 1896.

"In the field of public education," Chief Justice Warren said, "the doctrine of 'separate but equal' has no place. Separate educational facilities are inherently unequal."

He stated the question and supplied the answer as follows:

"We come then to the question presented: Does segregation of children in public schools solely on the basis of race, even though physical facilities and other 'tangible' factors may be equal, deprive the children of the minority group of equal educational opportunities? We believe that it does."

States Stressed Rights

The court's opinion does not apply to private schools. It is directed entirely at public schools. It does not affect the "separate but equal doctrine" as applied on railroads and other public carriers entirely within states that have such restrictions.

The principal ruling of the court was in four cases involving state laws. The states' right to operate separated schools had been argued before the court on two occasions by representatives of South Carolina, Virginia, Kansas and Delaware.

In these cases, consolidated in one opinion, the high court held that school segregation deprived Negroes of "the equal protection of the laws guaranteed by the Fourteenth Amendment."

The other opinion involved the District of Columbia. Here schools have been segregated since Civil War days under laws passed by Congress.

"In view of our decision that the Constitution prohibits the states from maintaining racially segregated public schools," the Chief Justice said, "it would be unthinkable that the same Constitution would impose a lesser duty on the Federal Government.

"We hold that racial segregation in the public schools of the District of Columbia is a denial

Continued on Page 14, Column 6

SOVIET BIDS VIENNA CEASE 'INTRIGUES'

Envoy Warns Austrian Chief on Inciting East Zone—Raab Denies Charges

By JOHN MacCORMAC
Special to The New York Times.

VIENNA, May 17—The Soviet Union warned Austria today to put an end to "hostile and subversive intrigues" against the Soviet occupation forces, or Soviet authorities would do it themselves.

Ivan I. Ilyichev, Soviet High Commissioner, reverted to a practice of early post-war days by summoning Chancellor Julius Raab and Vice Chancellor Adolf Schaerf to give them this warning. The Chancellor denied the Soviet charges.

Mr. Ilyichev said the Austrian Government had been guilty of staging actions hostile to the Soviet while the Austrian press had published daily slanderous and inciting announcements about the Soviet Union and Soviet occupation troops.

The cessation of Soviet control over the movement of freight, said the High Commissioner, was abused to smuggle militarist literature and provocative incitements into the Soviet zone with the connivance of the Austrian Minister of Interior.

When Soviet authorities ordered the removal of anti-Soviet placards in their zone, the minister instructed his subordinotes to disregard the order and the Government approved his action, said Mr. Ilyichev.

He added that the Government, and particularly the Minister of Interior, had tolerated militarist propaganda by former soldiers' organizations and dissemination of propaganda for another Anschluss (union) with Germany.

The High Commissioner reminded the Government leaders that since Austria had not ob-

Continued on Page 9, Column 3

City Colleges' Board Can't Pick Chairman

The Board of Higher Education was unable to elect a chairman at its annual meeting last night at Hunter College.

A spokesman said it was the first time "within memory of board officials" that such a situation had occurred.

Nineteen of the twenty-one members of the board, which governs the four municipal colleges, attended.

Two members nominated for the one-year-term were unable to attain the required majority of eleven votes. They were Joseph B. Cavallaro, who was up for re-election as chairman, and Dr. Harry J. Carman, who was restored to the board on March 2 by Mayor Wagner.

The election was laid over until June 15.

INDO-CHINA PARLEY WEIGHS TWO PLANS

French and Rebel Peace Bids Will Be Studied Jointly as a Basis for Settlement

By THOMAS J. HAMILTON
Special to The New York Times.

GENEVA, May 17—The Far East conference decided today to take up French and Vietminh proposals jointly as a basis for settlement of the war in Indo-China.

The secret session, which lasted three and a half hours, was generally recognized as the opening round in what may turn out to be a long process of negotiation. Another secret meeting will be held tomorrow.

Western delegates felt that Vyacheslav M. Molotov, Soviet Foreign Minister, was continuing to give the impression that in the end he might throw Moscow's influence on the side of an agreed settlement.

However, the West failed to obtain answers to the two fundamental questions that are expected to determine whether the negotiations here will have any chance of success: Will the Communists agree to a separate settlement for Laos and Cambodia, and will they agree to an armistice in Vietnam without at the same time requiring a political settlement?

The conference will address itself tomorrow to the issue of Laos and Cambodia. The two Indo-Chinese states are relatively free from Communist infiltration, and their leaders contend, with the support of the French, that the only thing that needs to be done is the withdrawal of the Communists.

The Laos-Cambodia and Vietnam issues were discussed inconclusively today after the delegates had devoted the first part of their meeting to the intricate dispute over evacuation of French Union wounded from Dienbienphu, seized by the Communist-

Continued on Page 2, Column 2

2 TAX PROJECTS DIE IN ESTIMATE BOARD

Beer Levy and More Parking Collections Killed—Payroll Impost Still Weighed

By CHARLES G. BENNETT

Two possible new revenue sources were definitely eliminated yesterday by the Board of Estimate in executive session. They were the proposed 1-cent-a-glass tax on beer and the suggestion to extend metered parking into hours now "free."

In a three-hour City Hall parley the board failed once more to decide on a new impost or imposts to balance the 1954-55 budget of $1,639,438,325. Mayor Wagner said after the meeting that the highly controversial 3 per cent sales tax on commercial services was "still one of the taxes at the top of the list."

Saying he felt the Board of Estimate was close to a decision on the knotty tax question, the Mayor added that "there's no decision to discard any tax" except the two mentioned above, and that at the same time "no tax is inevitable."

The board will wrestle with the tax question again in executive session on Thursday at 2:30 P. M. The Mayor said the City Council, which is holding up a bill to impose the sales tax extension, would be invited to send a delegation to the Thursday session.

Mr. Wagner asserted that he would like to see the Board of Estimate decide the tax question

Continued on Page 32, Column 5

MORETTIS' LAWYER MUST BARE TALKS

Jersey Court Orders Counsel to Racketeers in Bergen to Divulge Data to Grand Jury

By GEORGE CABLE WRIGHT
Special to The New York Times.

TRENTON, May 17—The New Jersey Supreme Court today ordered a lawyer who once had represented top Bergen County racketeers to divulge to a grand jury the substance of confidential talks with those clients.

The four-to-three decision reversed the rulings of two lower courts. Involved was the refusal more than a year ago of John E. Selser, Hackensack attorney, to answer four questions put to him by the Bergen County grand jury.

Mr. Selser told the jury that one of his clients, Willie Moretti, slain gambler, had given him the names of persons connected with Walter G. Winne who had received protection money from syndicate gamblers. Mr. Winne, superseded prosecutor of Bergen County, was acquitted last week of nonfeasance in office.

But the attorney balked when asked to reveal these and the names of other persons who, his clients alleged, had been paid protection money or who had received political contributions on the state and county level. He pleaded that his lips were sealed by the duty of "nondisclosure of confidential communications between client and attorney."

Represented Morettis, Others

Mr. Selser had represented Moretti, who was murdered in Cliffside Park in October, 1951, and his brother, the late Salvatore Moretti, for many years. He also was the attorney of record for Joe Adonis, Arthur Longano and James (Piggy) Lynch. The last four were among five men convicted and sent to prison in May, 1952, as the leaders of the Bergen gambling syndicate.

Mr. Selser appeared before the grand jury in February, 1953. The present court action was brought by the state after his refusal to answer the above questions on that occasion and two other questions. The latter pertained to testimony by John J. Dickerson, former Republican state chairman, before the same grand jury.

Mr. Dickerson had testified that Adonis and the two Morettis visited his home in November, 1950, and that Willie told him then that $225,000 in protection money had been paid to Harold

Continued on Page 36, Column 2

RULING TO FIGURE IN '54 CAMPAIGN

Decision Tied to Eisenhower—Russell Leads Southerners in Criticism of Court

By WILLIAM S. WHITE
Special to The New York Times.

WASHINGTON, May 17—Congress as a whole grappled gingerly today with the profound political implications of the Supreme Court's anti-segregation decision.

It became clear at once—and by both parties was accepted in private as inevitable—that the court's action would figure importantly in the coming Congressional election campaigns.

Publicly, however, the Republicans and the non-Southern Democrats, on the whole maintained silence. The Southerners, all angry or sorrowing in one degree or another, were quickly articulate and split among themselves into at least three factions.

¶One Southern group, by all the indications not a large one, was openly defiant of the court, as typified by the comment of Senator James O. Eastland of Mississippi.

"The South," Mr. Eastland said, "will not abide by nor obey this legislative decision by a political court."

¶A second Southern group, while not openly challenging the court, began to threaten efforts to force an alteration of its view, as illustrated by the comment of

Continued on Page 20, Column 2

Churchill Asks Negotiated Peace With Guarantees for Indo-China

By DREW MIDDLETON
Special to The New York Times.

LONDON, May 17—Britain will seek effective international guarantees for any peace settlement in Indo-China, Prime Minister Churchill declared today.

Negotiation of an "acceptable" settlement at the Geneva conference remains the immediate task of the British Government, Sir Winston emphasized in a statement to the House of Commons.

Until the outcome of that conference is known, he added, "final decisions" cannot be taken by the Government about the establishment of a collective defense system in Southeast Asia and the Western Pacific.

Peace by negotiation emerged from Sir Winston's cautious statement as the only policy that the Cabinet was ready to apply to the problem of Indo-China. Observers were struck by the fact that, aside from the Prime Minister's reference to the necessity of backing a settlement there with guarantees, the British position was substantially the same as when the Geneva conference began.

[Indonesia is considering asking India and Burma to join her in a nonaggression treaty with Communist China as a means of offsetting United States plans for a Southeast Asian alliance.]

Sir Winston's adherence to negotiation is acceptable to both major parties in the Commons,

Continued on Page 4, Column 3

Costello Is Sentenced to 5 Years, Fined $30,000 in U. S. Tax Case

By EDWARD RANZAL

Frank Costello was sentenced yesterday by Federal Judge John F. X. McGohey to five years in jail and fined $30,000 for income tax evasion.

The dapper, 61-year-old gambler was remanded immediately. Later Judge Harold R. Medina in the United States Court of Appeals refused to set bail pending appeal. Costello, who listened to the sentencing in icy-calm manner, was taken to the Federal House of Detention, 427 West Street.

Besides the jail sentence and the fines, Judge McGohey also assessed Costello for court costs. Lloyd F. MacMahon, chief assistant United States Attorney, said the costs would be about $5,000, only a fraction of what it cost the Government in its investigation, which began in earnest in 1952.

Costello was convicted Thursday night by a Federal court jury of five women and seven men of three counts of a four-count indictment. They found the gambler guilty of evading a total of $51,095 in taxes from 1947 through 1949.

In 1947 Costello evaded $22,563; in 1948, $13,786, and in 1949, $14,746. He was acquitted of the charge of evading taxes in 1946. Costello's attorney, Leo C. Fennelly, told Judge McGohey that the acquittal on this count meant that the gambler was entitled to a refund for that year.

Before the sentencing Mr. MacMahon said that for years Costello had schemed to cheat the Government out of taxes. He added that the gambler had concealed at least $140,000 of his income from 1947 through 1949, more than half his income.

Mr. MacMahon contended that Costello, by devious means, had concealed the receipt of his income as well as the source by using cash in every transaction where it was possible.

Evidence at the six-week trial, the prosecutor said, showed that from 1937 through 1945 Costello deliberately underestimated his income by at least $202,000. The statute of limitations, he added, bars prosecution for the earlier tax evasions.

"Costello has spent a lifetime making money on the shady side

Continued on Page 36, Column 4

'Voice' Speaks in 34 Languages To Flash Court Ruling to World

Within an hour after the Supreme Court decision on school segregation yesterday afternoon, the Voice of America sent a news broadcast by shortwave to Eastern Europe.

The decision came in time for the regularly scheduled "Worldwide English Broadcast" at 2 o'clock. The broadcast was written in English on the Voice's central desk and was sent by teletype to the thirty-four language desks.

There it was translated and sent out in various foreign tongues all over the world as broadcast time arrived for each.

"The Supreme Court has ruled unanimously," the Voice said in its broadcast, "that racial segregation has no place in American public education. It held that separation of students on a racial basis denies equal educational opportunities.

"Chief Justice [Earl] Warren, reading the court's findings, said that the doctrine of providing separate but equal facilities has no place in public education. Separation of children solely because of race, he said, generates feelings in their hearts and minds which might never be undone. * * *

"The ruling in effect outlaws all segregation in public schools throughout the United States. The court held that to separate students is a denial of the due process of law guaranteed by the Fifth Amendment to the Constitution and equal opportunity

Continued on Page 15, Column 4

Tennessee William's Pulitzer-Prize winning play Cat on a Hot Tin Roof, *which exposed aspects of Southern life, starred Barbara Bel Geddes, Ben Gazzara and Burl Ives.*

In 1954 Bill Haley and the Comets' Shake, Rattle & Roll *was a smash hit. Another hit,* Rock Around The Clock, *which is considered the theme song of rock 'n' roll, followed in 1955.*

Everyone was learning the mambo.

"All the News That's Fit to Print"

The New York Times.

LATE CITY EDITION
Some cloudiness with a few showers today. Fair tomorrow.
Temperature Range Today—Max., 86; Min., 70
Temperatures Yesterday—Max., 88.3; Min., 68.8
Full U. S. Weather Bureau Report, Page 47

VOL. CIII No. 35,242.

Entered as Second-Class Matter.
Post Office, New York, N. Y.

NEW YORK, WEDNESDAY, JULY 21, 1954.

Times Square, New York 36, N. Y.
Telephone LAckawanna 4-1000

FIVE CENTS

Copyright, 1954, by The New York Times Company.

M'CARTHY ACCEPTS COHN RESIGNATION, TRANSFERS SURINE

Puts the Assistant Counsel on Own Payroll—Panel Defers Any Action on La Venia

CONFIRMS REST OF STAFF

Carr Among 22 Approved— Senator Calls Loss of Cohn 'Great Victory' for Reds

Texts of Cohn letter, McCarthy statement are on Page 10.

By ANTHONY LEVIERO
Special to The New York Times.

WASHINGTON, July 20—Senator Joseph R. McCarthy yielded today to the insistent demand for a staff housecleaning from a majority of the members of the Senate Permanent Subcommittee on Investigations.

The results, as the subcommittee met over a steak luncheon in the old Supreme Court chamber in the Capitol, were these:

¶Senator McCarthy reluctantly accepted the resignation of Roy M. Cohn, the subcommittee's chief counsel, denouncing those who had sought it and saying the result was a "great victory" for communism.

¶Mr. McCarthy transferred the controversial assistant counsel, Don Surine, from the subcommittee staff to his personal payroll, also with a vigorous defense of him.

Action on La Venia Deferred

Both these changes were personal actions of Senator McCarthy as chairman taken before the subcommittee met. In this way he headed off inevitable defeat on a staff housecleaning demanded by a majority of four of the seven members of the subcommittee led by Senator Charles E. Potter, Republican of Michigan.

The subcommittee itself then voted unanimously to withhold "without prejudice" confirmation of Thomas La Venia in his position as office manager and investigator until further consideration of his personal record.

The subcommittee then voted to confirm twenty-two other employes of the subcommittee in their present jobs. Among them were two others who had come under fire during the thirty-six days of the Army - McCarthy hearings that ended on June 17.

One was Francis P. Carr, staff director, who had been named as a principal in the controversy but was removed from that category before the hearings ended.

Juliana Approved

The other was James N. Juliana, a staff investigator, who assumed full responsibility during the hearings for cropping an Army colonel out of a photograph introduced in evidence. As produced by the McCarthy aide, this photograph showed only Robert P. Stevens, Secretary of the Army, and Pvt. G. David Schine.

There was no discussion by the subcommittee on whether to oust Mr. Carr, who said he was staying "unless I am voted out." Senator McCarthy said that all votes today were unanimous.

On Capitol Hill the staff changes were regarded as one of the few reversals ever suffered by Mr. McCarthy in his Senatorial career which began in 1946.

The action today was a direct

Continued on Page 10, Column 3

Miss Connolly Breaks Leg, Out of U.S. Play

By The Associated Press

SAN DIEGO, Calif., July 20—Maureen Connolly, the tennis queen, was so seriously injured when she was crushed against a big cement truck while riding her horse here today that she will be unable to defend her national title next month at Forest Hills, Queens.

Surgery and X-rays determined that the small bone in her lower right leg was broken and that muscles and tendons of the calf were damaged by a deep gash.

This definitely ends her hope of winning the United States championship for the fourth straight time.

She will hardly be able to get around, doctors said, by the start of the tournament on Aug. 28.

"Little Mo," who will be 20 on Sept. 17, was wheeled into surgery within an hour after reaching the hospital. She was conscious when she

Continued on Page 21, Column 2

House Inquiry Asked Into a House Inquiry

By C. P. TRUSSELL
Special to The New York Times.

WASHINGTON, July 20—The House of Representatives was urged today to investigate one of its investigations.

At issue was the inquiry into tax-free educational and philanthropic foundations that began in May.

Early this month the investigators decided to hold no more public hearings. At that point the witnesses, including two committee researchers, had been eleven to one in criticism of foundations. The foundations were given permission to file sworn statements in rebuttal.

A resolution was introduced in the House this afternoon by Representative Jacob K. Javits, Republican of Manhattan. It called on the Rules Committee,

Continued on Page 30, Column 7

SHOWDOWN TODAY ON T.V.A. CURB SET

Democrats Decide to Permit Vote on President's Order for Power Contract

By WILLIAM M. BLAIR
Special to The New York Times.

WASHINGTON, July 20—A band of Senate Democrats agreed tonight to a showdown vote tomorrow afternoon in their fight against President Eisenhower's order to the Atomic Energy Commission to carry out a private power contract.

They intimated, however, that if defeated they would renew what Senate Republican leaders have called a filibuster against the important atomic energy bill. The President's order directed the commission to negotiate a contract with a private utilities group to supply the Tennessee Valley Authority with power.

The Senate recessed at 9:31 P. M. after Senator William F. Knowland, the Republican Floor Leader, had said he hoped for a vote in the power fight tomorrow and completion of the bill by the same time tomorrow night.

He announced that he had instructed the Sergeant at Arms to set up cots in the Senate wing of the Capitol in the event it was necessary to work through the night to complete the entire atomic energy bill.

The Democrats' decision at a strategy meeting ended temporarily seven days of unlimited talking in the Senate that stalled the Administration's program.

Backed up behind the atomic

Continued on Page 8, Column 2

EISENHOWER LOSES ON PUBLIC HOUSING BY VOTE OF 234-156

House Rejects Plan to Build 140,000 Units in 4 Years —35,000 in One Voted

By CLAYTON KNOWLES
Special to The New York Times.

WASHINGTON, July 20—The House of Representatives killed the last real hope today to enact President Eisenhower's public housing program at this session of Congress.

By a vote of 234 to 156, it rejected a proposal sponsored by Democrats to write the President's request for 140,000 housing units over a four-year period into the compromise housing bill that emerged last week from Senate-House conference.

Arrayed against the proposal were 155 Republicans and 79 Democrats. Supporting the President's position in the vote were 105 Democrats, 50 Republicans and one Independent.

Soon after this test, the House approved, 358 to 30, terms of the omnibus compromise on housing. It contained provision for only 35,000 units in a one-year extension of the public housing program. Many asserted that this authorization was meaningless because of restrictions in the provision. Some said not 10,600 units could be built under it.

Action Regarded as Final

The House action, which promises to create a major political issue for the Congressional campaign, was as good as final even though the Senate still has to ratify the conference report. The original Senate bill carried the President's public housing program, but it was pared, almost beyond recognition, in conference.

The general belief was that the Senate would not even attempt to reinstate the President's program since today's vote was the second in which the House had rejected it. On April 2 the House, then considering the bill for the first time, turned down the 140,000-unit program, 211 to 176.

Representative Brent Spence, Democrat of Kentucky, made the motion to reinstate the President's program, on the ground that, without it, individuals of low income could only gravitate to the slums.

Representative Jesse P. Wolcott, Republican of Michigan, defending the proposition that a unit of slum housing must be razed before a unit of public housing could be built, declared: "With these limitations, we conferees believe we have done a masterful job on public housing.

Continued on Page 16, Column 4

Arrests Here Bare 'Sure Thing' Racing Fraud by Radio

AGREE ON TRUCE: Pierre Mendès-France, French Premier, as he appeared yesterday with Pham Van Dong, Vietminh Foreign Minister, left, at French headquarters in Geneva. Behind them are Guy de la Tournelle, wearing eyeglasses, and Georges Boris, aides to French leader.

Associated Press Radiophoto

Pocket transmitter at left sends race results to receiver near track, whence an agent phones data to an associate posted near a betting parlor. This man, using transmitter built into suitcase at right, relays result to a bettor, who gets electronic impulses through concealed dimes on receiver shown in left hand above. Agent then bets on horse that won.

The New York Times

The police cracked down yesterday on a gambling ring that has been using Dick Tracy techniques, complete with purse-size transmitters and skin-shock radio receivers, to flash race results far in advance of official returns. Twenty-eight persons were rounded up in fast-hitting raids in Manhattan, Brooklyn and Queens. Forty detectives and policemen under the command of Supervising Assistant Chief Inspector James Nidds, fanned out through the three boroughs at 8 A. M. After the half-hour round-up, when the twenty-eight captives were paraded before Queens Assistant District Attorney Lawrence Peraza, a crime-comics story on the use of ingenious electronic devices was unfolded. Race-track plotters were pictured tapping

Continued on Page 28, Column 3

INDOCHINA ARMISTICE IS SIGNED; VIETNAM SPLIT AT 17TH PARALLEL; U.S. FINDS IT CAN 'RESPECT' PACT

CAPITAL CAUTIOUS

Accepts in Principle— Bars Any Guarantee Except by Alliance

Special to The New York Times.

WASHINGTON, July 20—The United States Government will issue a unilateral statement tomorrow accepting in principle the terms of the Indochina cease-fire accord. It also will acknowledge its "ability to respect" such terms under the United Nations Charter, diplomatic officials disclosed tonight.

The decision to state the United States Government's position on the agreement—probably by President Eisenhower at his regular news conference tomorrow—was disclosed after diplomatic intelligence established the terms containing a clause permitting a free exchange of populations between northern and southern Vietnam.

For a period of one year, according to this understanding, no effort would be made to prevent movement between the two areas. Diplomatic officials attached the greatest importance to this clause, which they considered would avert the swallowing up of the anti-Communist and predominantly Catholic populations of parts of northern Vietnam by the Red regime.

Interruption Is Temporary

Of only slightly less importance is a provision in the agreement whereby the right of the free areas of the partitioned Indochina States to receive foreign military assistance would be interrupted only temporarily, so that no interference with their sovereignty would be entailed.

It was understood the temporary restriction on the receipt of military assistance from the United States and other free nations would end after a period of "disengagement" during which forces would be withdrawn from existing front-line areas.

Diplomatic officials conversant with the terms held that the cease-fire generally came within the terms of the seven principles that President Eisenhower and Prime Minister Churchill laid down three weeks ago.

These included division of the

Continued on Page 3, Column 5

SENATORS TO PUSH GERMAN REARMING

Leading Republicans Will Urge Action This Year in Addition to Granting Sovereignty

By WILLIAM S. WHITE
Special to The New York Times.

WASHINGTON, July 20—Powerful Senate Republicans will advise the Eisenhower Administration that West German rearmament and sovereignty should be pushed this year.

Diplomatic officials conversant with the terms held that the cease-fire generally came within the Administration that the United States-British plan to give sovereignty without the right to rearm, as an alternative to the faltering European Defense Community project, would not be realistic.

They will argue that implicit in sovereignty is the right of self-defense and that the two concepts cannot be separated validly, as John Foster Dulles, Secretary of State, has proposed to do.

Senator Homer Ferguson of Michigan, chairman of the Senate Republican Policy Committee, who is one of the leaders in this movement, expects some sort of Congressional resolution backing both German sovereignty and German rearmament to be offered before Congress adjourns this month or early next month.

Others, among them Senator William F. Knowland of California, Republican Senate floor leader, are taking a more reserved line pending a study by the State Department of the legal situation.

Mr. Dulles has adopted the position that the question of rearmament must be deferred un-

Continued on Page 5, Column 3

38 Jersey Forgeries Charged to Hoffman

Special to The New York Times.

TRENTON, July 20—The preliminary report of a handwriting expert released here today said that former Gov. Harold G. Hoffman apparently concealed his $300,000 defalcations by forging thirty-eight bank certifications in six years.

Attorney General Grover C. Richman made public the findings of Albert D. Osborne of Montclair, who for a month has been studying the signatures on the certifications from the South Amboy Trust Company.

The certifications of general state treasury funds deposited at the South Amboy bank cover a period from June 30, 1917, to Dec. 31, 1953. They all had the signature of George A. Kress, president of the bank. No breakdown of the defalcations by

Continued on Page 48, Column 1

French Call Pact No Victory But See Gains for Europe

By HAROLD CALLENDER
Special to The New York Times.

PARIS, July 20—The terms of agreement for the truce in Indochina were regarded here as presaging a peace without victory. Some called it a peace that would confirm a defeat for the West in Asia and would mark the most notable loss in battle of French territories since Louis XV lost Canada in the eighteenth century.

But it was expected that this ill wind in Asia might blow some good for France and the Atlantic alliance in Europe.

The truce seemed likely to give great prestige to Premier Pierre Mendès-France, and to enable him to stay in office to seek a decision on the European army treaty and to press for a program to stimulate the French economy.

It appeared probable tonight that the Premier would submit the treaty to the National Assembly early in August with suggested modifications that would not require further action by the parliaments of the other signatories. The West German Chancellor, Dr. Konrad Adenauer, has indicated that he would consider changes that could be made without resort to parliaments.

New Unity a By-Product

Removal of the uncertainty that has surrounded the treaty for two years would clear up the question of West Germany's sovereignty and rearmament and permit in this sphere a unity among the United States, Britain and France that has not yet existed. Such a gain in Europe might be considered as offsetting to some extent the failure of Western policy in Indochina.

A severe blow to French prestige in Asia and probably in North Africa was foreseen in the truce. In North Africa that prestige is far more important than in Asia because France's African territories are more important to her. But M. Mendès-France's argument was been that France must cut her losses in Asia in order to conserve her strength in Europe; and if she revamps her economy, as he desires, the net result may be to increase her influence and even her prestige in Europe and Africa.

M. Mendès-France has urged that the failure to reconcile Vietnam with the French Union by a prompt grant of independence should not be repeated in North Africa, where nationalist movements now are menacing.

The truce in Indochina will mark the frustration of a prolonged Western effort to resist the conquest of Vietnam, Laos and Cambodia by a nationalist movement that was anti-Western and Communist-led. Against it were employed unsuccessfully a French army, a native force and United States aid to the amount to $800,000,000 this year.

The truce will mark an advance of communism in the sense that

Continued on Page 3, Column 4

HANOI PREPARING FOR TRUCE PERIOD

French Study Plans Designed to Preserve Calm in Delta and Effect Evacuation

By HENRY R. LIEBERMAN
Special to The New York Times.

HANOI, Vietnam, July 20—Two kinds of preparations were being made here to cope with problems related to the surrender of North Vietnam to the Vietminh under a cease-fire. Hanoi will eventually be taken over by the Vietminh under a truce agreement.

French authorities were preparing security measures to "maintain calm" in this city of 340,000. Plans originally drawn up to evacuate French, foreign and a number of Vietnamese civilians under battle conditions were also being restudied in terms of a more leisurely evacuation.

It was being taken for granted today in this city, which is seven hours ahead of Geneva time, that the seven-and-a-half-year-old Indochinese war was drawing to a close.

Geneva reports aroused considerable interest in Hanoi but created no public excitement, in fact, despite a demonstration against partition yesterday by several thousand Vietnamese, there has been no major agitation

Continued on Page 2, Column 2

LONG WAR ENDING

2 Accords Completed —One on Cambodia Due Later Today

By THOMAS J. HAMILTON
Special to The New York Times

GENEVA, Wednesday, July 21 —Armistice agreements bringing the fighting in Vietnam and Laos to a halt were signed this morning by representatives of the French and Communist Vietminh forces.

A French spokesman said the armistice would take effect forty-eight hours later.

The signing ceremony, witnessed by representatives of the nine delegations participating in the Far Eastern conference here, began at 3:42 A. M. (9:42 P. M. Tuesday, Eastern daylight time). It brought to a close the eight-year struggle for Indochina.

The armistice in Cambodia will not be signed until later this morning. The Far Eastern conference will hold its final session this afternoon to complete work on the political settlement. Under it Laos and Cambodia will be neutralized and elections to create a unified government in Vietnam will be held within two years from the date of the armistice.

Pierre Mendès-France, French Premier, who had set July 20 as his deadline to obtain an armistice or resign, had missed it by a few hours. He canceled a radio speech to the French people and went to bed before the two agreements were signed at the Palais des Nations, former headquarters of the League of Nations, where conference sessions have been held since the Indochina negotiations began last May.

Rebels Get Northern Part

Under the Vietnamese agreement, Vietnam is to be divided into two parts, about equal in area and population, between the Communist-led Vietminh rebels who will hold northern Vietnam, north of a line along the Seventeenth Parallel, and the French-sponsored Government of Bao Dai.

The partition line thus is far enough north to preserve Hue, the ancient capital of Annam; Tourane, an important port and naval and air base, and the only major highway leading to Laos from the coast.

The French will not give up Hanoi and Haiphong, in the Red River delta area, in the north, for approximately a year, which will give them time to evacuate personnel of the French expeditionary force in the territory remaining to them in the delta plus civilians fearing persecution by the Communists.

Under the armistice agreements, the Communists recognize the Governments of Laos and Cambodia. However, regrouping areas for Communist troops were authorized in Laos. The forces of the Communist "resistance government" in Laos will be concentrated in two provinces near the frontier with Vietminh territory. [Some sources identified the two provinces as Samneua and Phongsaly.]

The Cambodian delegation held out against the provision, and prolonged sessions of the "drafting committee" of the Vietminh and Cambodian representatives

Continued on Page 2, Column 5

Reds Have Margin in Indochina Despite Even Split Under Truce

By TILLMAN DURDIN
Special to The New York Times.

GENEVA, July 20—In statistical terms, a balanced settlement on Indochina seems to have been reached.

The Communist Vietminh has gained the northern half of Vietnam, inhabited by about 12,000,000 persons. If the Vietminh forces evacuate other areas according to the terms, the southern half of Vietnam and the states of Laos and Cambodia will remain in non-Communist hands. Approximately 10,000,000 Vietnamese, 4,000,000 Cambodians and 1,100,000 Laotians live in the territories to remain outside Communist control. Northern Vietnam is somewhat smaller, both in population and area, than the sum of the parts of Indochina due to be non-Communist.

However, the Communists will have advantages not reflected by comparative figures. The Vietminh rebels will have under their control the more tough and vigorous northern Vietnamese, who are more tough and vigorous than the southern Vietnamese and the easygoing Buddhists of Laos and Cambodia. North Vietnam will envelop northern and eastern Laos and will be in a commanding strategic position with relation to Vietnam's western neighbor.

The Vietminh will have a disciplined, well-organized government and a powerful army.

Continued on Page 3, Column 2

133

George Gobel had an estimated following of twenty-five million viewers.

Carl Reiner, Sid Caesar and Howard Morris are seen here doing their routine as "The Haircuts" on Your Show of Shows.

Art Carney and Jackie Gleason, as the loudmouth, on The Jackie Gleason Show.

"Twelve Angry Men," a production of Studio One, featured an all-star cast.

Sid Caesar and Imogene Coca appeared together in Your Show of Shows from 1949 until 1954, when the show went off the air.

In 1954, the heartwarming Father Knows Best premiered. For years to come audiences would watch the interactions of Jim Anderson (Robert Young), his wife Margaret (Jane Wyatt) and their three children Betty, Bud and Kathy.

"All the News That's Fit to Print"

The New York Times.

LATE CITY EDITION
Fair and cold today and tonight.
Fair and milder tomorrow.
Temperature Range Today—Max.: 40; Min. 25
Temperature Yesterday—Max., 37.4; Min., 28.5
Full U. S. Weather Bureau Report, Page 51

Copyright, 1954, by The New York Times Company

VOL. CIV. No. 35,377

Entered as Second-Class Matter,
Post Office, New York, N. Y.

NEW YORK, FRIDAY, DECEMBER 3, 1954.

FIVE CENTS

POPE IN COLLAPSE, BUT REST FOLLOWS A DIFFICULT NIGHT

Morning Announcement Tells of the 78-Year-Old Pontiff's Battle Against Illness

KIN CALLED TO BEDSIDE

Trouble Laid to a Perforated Ulcer and Physicians Study Possibilities of Operation

By The Associated Press.
ROME, Friday, Dec. 3—The Vatican announced this morning that Pope Pius XII, gravely stricken, had survived the night. A spokesman said a more detailed bulletin would be issued later today.

The Pope suffered a severe collapse yesterday.

The first word this morning on his condition was given by Dr. Luciano Casimiri, spokesman for the Vatican press office, at 8:05 o'clock [2:05 A. M., Eastern standard time.]

"After a difficult night, the Holy Father is now resting," the spokesman said.

There were unconfirmed reports that the Pope had suffered a heart attack in the night, accompanied by more of the intense gastritis, nausea and hiccups for which he has been under treatment. There were indications also that the Pope's condition may be aggravated by a gastric ulcer.

His personal physician, Dr. Riccardo Galeazzi-Lisi, spent the entire night at his bedside, after making emergency X-rays yesterday and calling in a surgeon for consultation.

Grave Fears Felt

By ARNALDO CORTESI
Special to The New York Times.
ROME, Friday, Dec. 3—Pope Pius XII suffered a collapse at 3:30 o'clock yesterday afternoon due, it is believed, to a perforated ulcer.

The Pope fell into a coma and the gravest fears for his life were felt. He is 78 years old and has been weakened because for the last four days his feeding has been by artificial means.

Extreme unction was administered and Pius' nearest relatives—three nephews—were called to his bedside.

Five hours later, the Pope had overcome the crisis and his archiater, or chief physician, Prof. Riccardo Galeazzi-Lisi, said there was no immediate cause for alarm.

The Pope was stated to be resting as easily as could be expected under the circumstances, although breathing heavily and reduced to exhaustion.

It was learned that the possibility of an abdominal operation sometimes today or in the next few days was being considered. The exact nature of the operation under consideration was not stated but it is understood that a noticeable swelling of the Pope's abdomen developed yesterday, accompanied by cramps and excruciating pain. Radioscopic and clinical tests were made late in the evening to ascertain both the exact nature of the Pope's ailment and whether he is in condition to undergo surgery.

From the time he fell seriously ill in January of this year, Pope Pius had refused to take the barium meal necessary if full X-ray examination of his stomach.

Continued on Page 4, Column 1

Rio Conference Ends With Major Accords

By SAM POPE BREWER
Special to The New York Times.
PETROPOLIS, Brazil, Dec. 2—The twenty-one American republics ended tonight their first general economic conference with agreements on many major points and plans to hold another such meeting within two years.

Antonio Carrillo Flores, Minister of Finance of Mexico, said in the principal address at the closing session that public opinion of this hemisphere would find on studying results of the conference that its work "was not sterile."

Carlos Lleras Restrepo of Colombia introduced a dissenting note into the general air of agreement. He said at this final session that his country did not feel the conference had gone far enough toward increasing international banking facilities and stabilizing commodity prices. An

Continued on Page 10, Column 5

President Rejects Blockade Of China Now as Act of War

But He Pledges No Let-Up in Efforts to Free 13 Americans Jailed by Peiping— Holds Truce Obligates U. N. to Act

By JOSEPH A. LOFTUS
Special to The New York Times.
WASHINGTON, Dec. 2—President Eisenhower asserted today he was not going to be pushed emotionally into an act of war—such as a naval blockade of Communist China.

Neither, he said, is he going to let Peiping get away with the imprisonment of thirteen Americans on spy charges.

He insisted that the United Nations act for the release of at least eleven of the Americans because they were uniformed veterans of the Korean war and as such the United Nations was obligated to act in their behalf.

[At the United Nations, the United States said it wanted the world body to condemn the imprisonment by Red China of eleven American airmen shot down during the Korean war.]

"We are yet far from exhaustion of all of our resources" to liberate these men, the President said at his news conference: "I mention only one of those that is available to us."

He asserted that Red China deliberately timed its announcement of the imprisonment to divide the people of the United States as well as the United States from its allies. He added that the United States must be forever on its guard against this divide-and-conquer technique.

His personal feelings of anger, resentment and frustration were as great as any American's, he said, but he believed that restraint in public expression was the wiser course. To respond with patience rather than with truculence does not mean appeasement, he declared.

The President was clearly reading a lesson in the behavior of public officials to Senator Wil-

Continued on Page 2, Column 4

East Bloc Says Joint Army Will Counter Bonn in NATO

By CLIFTON DANIEL
Special to The New York Times.
MOSCOW, Dec. 2—In a declaration signed in the Kremlin tonight, eight European Communist regimes gave notice that if the Atlantic powers enlisted West Germany in their alliance, an East European defense organization would be created.

Representatives of eight governments concluding a four-day conference here said another meeting would be called to plan defense measures should the London and Paris agreements for West German armament and sovereignty be finally ratified.

The envisaged defense organization would have combined military forces under a joint command like that of the North Atlantic Treaty Organization. It would be in addition to the existing framework of treaties concluded long ago among the eight powers.

Communist China's complete approval of the declaration and the measures envisioned in it was signified at the final meeting of the representatives of the eight European powers today. China's endorsement was given by Chang Wen-tien, Peiping's Deputy Foreign Minister and Ambassador to Moscow.

Having in mind the combined strength of Communist China, the Soviet Union and seven other units in the East bloc conference, the delegates declared:

"Never before have the forces of peace and socialism been so mighty and so consolidated as now. Any attempts to attack, launch a war and interfere with the peaceful life of our peoples will meet with a shattering rebuff."

The declaration, bound in a red Morocco folder with ribbons

Continued on Page 5, Column 5

ATOM POWER SEEN AS COMMON IN 1976

Half of All Electric Plants Then Building Will Use It, G. E. Head Tells N.A.M.

By A. H. RASKIN
By 1976 atomic energy will be used to fuel half of all the electric generating plants then being built, it was predicted yesterday. This forecast was put before the National Association of Manufacturers by Ralph J. Cordiner, president of General Electric.

His estimate of the speed with which nuclear power would come into widespread use as a source of electric power was considerably more optimistic than most official calculations. Mr. Cordiner based his prediction as part of a plea to industrialists to shun "creeping conservatism" in their approach to business planning.

The head of the country's biggest electrical manufacturing company advised his fellow-executives to make their plans on a twenty-year basis, instead of limiting themselves to the ups and downs of the immediate sales market.

West Called Stronger

Other highlights at the second session of the association's fifty-ninth annual Congress of American Industry in the Waldorf-Astoria Hotel included:

¶An assertion by Gen. Walter Bedell Smith that the United States and its allies had built up a sufficient superiority over the Communist countries to "deter aggression and maintain peace." The former Under Secretary of State emphasized, however, that the balance of power was still "rather tenuous."

¶A report by a Dutch industrialist that five of his employes, who spent three months working in a Pennsylvania linoleum factory, had come home convinced that "America is a working man's world."

¶An attack by Charles R. Sligh Jr., N. A. M. board chairman, on union proposals for a guaranteed annual wage. He contended that wage guarantees would destroy business, rather than stabilize employment.

¶An assertion by Prof. Leo Wolman of Columbia University that the Taft-Hartley Act represented no substantial improvement over the old Wagner Act in curbing union power and preventing encroachment on management rights.

¶Election as N. A. M. president of Henry G. Riter 3d of Montclair, N. J., president of Thomas A. Edison, Inc., and chairman of the board of Copperweld Steel. Mr. Riter, who was an investment banker before he became an industrialist, succeeds H. C. McClellan of Los Angeles.

General Smith, who quit the State Department two months

Continued on Page 24, Column 2

EISENHOWER WARNS G. O. P. RIGHT WING; CHIDES KNOWLAND

Insists Party Must Follow a Progressive Course or Face Loss of Influence

Transcript and summary of the news conference, Page 18.

By WILLIAM S. WHITE
Special to The New York Times.
WASHINGTON, Dec. 2—President Eisenhower, reasserting leadership for his concept of a progressive Republican party, rebuked today the Senate Republican floor leader, William F. Knowland of California, and the party's right wing generally.

The President did not seek to disclaim the existence of a split in the party. He said instead that the party would not long be a force in American life unless it followed a course of progressivism.

As before, he defined this progressivism as a liberal attitude in the Government's relationship with the individual and a conservative attitude concerning the national pocketbook and the individual's pocketbook.

It was the first time since he entered the White House two years ago that General Eisenhower publicly and without apology had criticized a leading member of his party in Congress. Always before, he had avoided such criticism, relying frequently on the fact that the Constitution made Congress an independent branch of Government.

Even this time, the President somewhat softened his language toward the end, with the comments that while Senator Knowland sometimes made statements that certainly did not conform with the Administration's approach these normally affected method rather than principle.

China Blockade Urged

He made it clear, nevertheless, that distinctions in methods were important, suggesting that the methods of Senator Knowland might mean the difference between peace and war in Asia.

Senator Knowland, in the face of rejections from John Foster Dulles, Secretary of State, and the President himself, has been calling for a blockade of Communist China to force the liberation of United States citizens in Communist prisons.

Yesterday, moreover, Mr. Knowland broke with the Administration on another sensitive issue, coming out against a Senate censure of Senator Joseph R. McCarthy, Republican of Wisconsin.

The President said little about his differences with Senator Knowland over the McCarthy issue, observing only that it was up to the Senate to determine what was required for the preservation of its dignity.

On the point of the profound division within the Republican party over policy toward Red China, however, the President spoke extensively and voluntarily.

He took up Senator Knowland's

Continued on Page 18, Column 5

'Copter Saves 5 Plane Survivors Down 45 Hours on Mountainside

Two Perish in Crash of DC-3 in New Hampshire—Work of Stewardess Praised

By JOHN H. FENTON
Special to The New York Times.
BOSTON, Dec. 2—Five survivors of the crash of a Northeast Airlines plane were plucked by helicopter today from a bleak mountainside near the Maine-New Hampshire border. They had spent forty-five hours on the snow-covered spot in bitter cold.

The two others aboard the DC-3 died of injuries a few hours after the plane had fallen into a stretch of pine woods.

The dead were George McCormick, 37 years old, of Kingston, N. Y., co-pilot, and John McNulty, 39, of Boston, flight supervisor.

First to be rescued was the pilot, Capt. W. Peter Carey, 37, of Swampscott, Mass. He suffered severe head injuries. He and Miss Mary McEttrick, 23, of Boston, the stewardess, were flown here for medical treatment. Miss McEttrick suffered from shock and exposure.

The survivors praised Miss McEttrick for her coolness throughout the ordeal during which they huddled in the wrecked plane for nearly two days. Her cheerful attempts to make them com-

Associated Press Wirephoto
Stewardess Mary McEttrick in Berlin (N. H.) hospital.

fortable and her care of the injured prompted them to agree that "she's quite a girl."

Seventy-five Northeast employes, who were flown to Berlin,

Continued on Page 20, Column 4

FINAL VOTE CONDEMNS M'CARTHY, 67-22, FOR ABUSING SENATE AND COMMITTEE; ZWICKER COUNT ELIMINATED IN DEBATE

RANCOR CONTINUES

Welker Refuses to Let Flanders Apology Go Into the Record

By JAMES RESTON
Special to The New York Times.
WASHINGTON, Dec. 2—The McCarthy debate ended as it began in a spasm of rancor and vindictiveness that will divide the Senate and the country for a long time to come.

Though there were some light-hearted semantics at the close over whether Senator Joseph R. McCarthy was "censured" or "condemned," the underlying feeling among the principals ranged from uneasiness to sullen anger.

The junior Senator from Wisconsin himself produced almost the only hint of humor all day. Asked whether he thought the Senate had passed a resolution of "censure" or "condemnation," he replied:

"I wouldn't call it a vote of confidence."

He then announced that he was "very happy to get this circus over" and would get back to "the job of digging Communists out of the Government" on Monday.

Controversy Continues

Even after the vote was over, the controversy went on.

Senator Ralph E. Flanders, Republican of Vermont, arose and said he wanted to apologize to the Senate for some remarks he had made about Senator McCarthy some months ago. He added that he had told the Wisconsin Senator that he proposed to do so and had asked him to remain in the chamber, but Senator McCarthy had declined.

Then Senator Flanders asked for unanimous consent to have the Congressional Record amended to show that he had apologized for some of his remarks. This was blocked by Senator Herman Welker, Republican of Idaho, who angrily refused to give consent.

The usual lavish courtesy of the upper chamber gave way to biting sarcasm at the close. When Senator J. William Fulbright, Democrat of Arkansas, said he would try to answer a question by Senator Welker, the latter remarked that he would be "very surprised if a distinguished Rhodes scholar could not answer any question."

The End of a Phase

The main significance of the special session was that it ended that phase of the McCarthy controversy in which the Senate of the United States was hesitant to take action against the Wisconsin Senator.

For most of the five years since Senator McCarthy launched his anti-Communist crusade, the Senate of the United States has led a double life—critical of the Senator in private, and afraid of his political power in public.

During most of this period there has been a kind of political paralysis among the anti-McCarthy faction, and it was never entirely clear who was for him and who was against him. This doubt has now been removed.

The Senator from Wisconsin will remain for a month as chairman of the Government Operations Committee. He will lose none of his rights. He will have the power of subpoena and he will wield his gavel.

What has changed is not Mr. McCarthy but his opponents. They are now, for the first time, willing and in some cases eager to match his criticisms with their own. In short, the balance of criticism, dominated for so long by Senator McCarthy, has been reversed.

Behind this, too, is a decision by the Executive Branch of the Government to take a firmer position against his attempts to persuade Federal employes to give him documents they are not authorized to disclose.

So long as Congress hesitated to take action against Mr. McCarthy, the Executive itself was divided about how to defend its own classified files, but today's vote—regardless of what it is called—has stiffened the anti-McCarthy element in the Administration.

Thus, while he can exercise all

Continued on Page 16, Column 2

Associated Press Wirephoto
CONDEMNED ON TWO COUNTS: Senator McCarthy as he left the Senate floor last night after members adopted a resolution condemning his conduct. The vote was 67-22.

PRESIDENT ALERTS MAYORS ON ATTACK

Cities Are Front-Line Targets, He Warns—Asks Teamwork in Federal-Local Defense

By ELIE ABEL
Special to The New York Times.
WASHINGTON, Dec. 2—President Eisenhower warned today that United States cities were front-line targets for modern weapons "capable" of such destruction as to appall the imagination.

The President called for closer municipal-Federal cooperation in civil-defense planning as he welcomed about 240 mayors, city manager and other local officials to a two-day conference in the State Department auditorium.

Val Peterson, Federal Civil Defense Administrator, expanded on the President's warning in a guarded discussion of radioactive "fall-out," a phenomenon that adds a new dimension to the terror of thermonuclear (hydrogen) bombs.

The idea that only city dwellers need to worry about bombing is obsolete today, Mr. Peterson said. If a hydrogen bomb is detonated on or close to the ground, he explained, tremendous amounts of earth and debris are sucked up into the fireball and made radioactive.

Although the heavy particles will not travel far, he said, the lighter ones may be swept along by winds of the upper air, at alti-

Continued on Page 19, Column 1

SENATORS CLEARED ON M'CARTHY MAIL

Inquiry Indicates Request for Check Was Handled as Routine Matter

By WILLIAM M. BLAIR
Special to The New York Times.
WASHINGTON, Dec. 2—A special Senate committee apparently will report to the Senate that a check of Senator Joseph R. McCarthy's mail in 1952 was handled as a routine matter by a subcommittee's staff members.

Senator Walter F. George, Democrat of Georgia, indicated as much to Senator McCarthy this afternoon as the special five-member committee completed its overnight inquiry into how the mail check was authorized.

"There's nothing to be gained from pursuing the matter further," Senator McCarthy told Senator George, who replied, "I don't think so."

Senator George and Senator Homer Ferguson, Republican of Michigan, spent the day in closed session to hear testimony from persons on the staff of the Senate subcommittee on Privileges and Elections, which had inquired into Senator McCarthy's finances in 1952.

Mr. Ferguson said that a written report would be filed with the Senate. The report is expected to be filed with the secretary of the Senate tomorrow.

The two Senators were named by the Senate last night to in-

Continued on Page 15, Column 3

REPUBLICANS SPLIT

Democrats Act Solidly in Support of Motion Against Senator

Excerpts from transcript of Senate debate, Pages 12, 13

By ANTHONY LEVIERO
Special to The New York Times.
WASHINGTON, Dec. 2—The Senate voted 67 to 22 tonight to condemn Joseph R. McCarthy, Republican Senator from Wisconsin.

Every one of the forty-four Democrats present voted against Mr. McCarthy. The Republicans were evenly divided—twenty-two for condemnation and twenty-two against. The one independent, Senator Wayne Morse of Oregon, also voted against Mr. McCarthy.

In the ultimate action the Senate voted to condemn Senator McCarthy for contempt of a Senate Elections subcommittee that investigated his conduct and financial affairs, for abuse of its members, and for his insults to the Senate itself during the censure proceeding.

Lost in a day of complex and often confused parliamentary maneuvering was the proposal to censure McCarthy for his denunciation of Brig. Gen. Ralph W. Zwicker as unfit to wear his uniform.

This proposal was defeated by a parliamentary device that avoided a direct vote on the merits of the issue. Inquiry among influential Senators indicated they considered the Zwicker proposal a dilemma they wished to avoid.

Amendment Substituted

They said they wished to censure because the facts warranted it. If they failed to do so, they believed large elements of the public would feel the Senate took notice of offenses only against itself and not against ordinary citizens.

But also if they did censure for this, then Senator McCarthy could exploit the decision, contending he was being punished for his effort to expose former Maj. Irving Peress, the Army dentist who was promoted and honorably discharged, and who was denounced by Mr. McCarthy as a "Fifth Amendment Communist."

Mr. McCarthy's denunciation of General Zwicker, who was commanding officer at Camp Kilmer, N. J., when Dr. Peress was discharged, occurred when the Senator interrogated General Zwicker on the question of who had promoted Dr. Peress.

The direct test on the Zwicker issue was avoided by the substitution of the amendment to condemn Senator McCarthy for having insulted the Senate during his censure trial.

McCarthy Loses Three Tests

Thus in its final form the resolution of condemnation was in two parts, covering the offenses against the Elections subcommittee and its members in the first part, and against the Senate in the second. Three test votes were all lost by Mr. McCarthy before the final condemnation.

First was a motion to table the Zwicker proposal, made by Senator Styles Bridges, Republican of New Hampshire, the president pro tem of the Senate, who assumed the leadership of the effort to save Mr. McCarthy yesterday.

Such a motion, if it had succeeded, might have led to a situation that would have prolonged the debate.

But amid signs that the Zwicker issue would have tough sledding, Senator Wallace F. Bennett, Republican of Utah, served notice that if Mr. Bridges' move were defeated he would attempt to substitute for the Zwicker issue his amendment for abuse of the Senate. The significance of this was that an amendment by substitution would require no time out for debate.

Then the voting proceeded. The motion to table was defeated 55 to 33. Mr. Bennett's motion to substitute passed by 64 to 23 and in the next vote his amendment was adopted by the same tally.

The final vote placing Mr. Mc-

Continued on Page 14, Column 3

G.O.P. Weighs End of Rent Curb Outside of the Metropolitan Area

By LEO EGAN
Republican legislative leaders are giving serious consideration to relaxing state rent controls outside of the metropolitan area, leaving controls in effect only on apartments and tenements.

Both suggestions were formally advanced at a recent closed-door meeting of the Temporary State Commission on Rents and Rental Conditions, headed by Assemblyman Joseph F. Carlino of Long Beach, L. I.

As a result, Joseph D. McGoldrick, State Rent Administrator, was instructed by the commission to prepare a report and recommendations on both proposals covering the probable effect of such a relaxation of controls, the number of dwelling units involved, and the ratio of vacancies to dwelling units affected at present.

One proposal favored by some Republicans calls for decontrolling all rents outside of the New York metropolitan area.

Major up-state cities that would be affected by such a

all one and two-family houses outside of the metropolitan area, leaving controls in effect only on apartments and tenements.

Both suggestions were formally advanced at a recent closed-door meeting of the Temporary State Commission on Rents and Rental Conditions, headed by Assemblyman Joseph F. Carlino of Long Beach, L. I.

Such a proposal could set the stage for a major clash between Governor-elect Averell Harriman, Democrat-Liberal, and Republican majorities in the Senate and Assembly.

The Democratic platform on which Mr. Harriman was elected favors tightening rather than relaxing rent control. Moreover, Mr. Harriman affirmed his full support of this position on several occasions during the campaign.

So long as this is politically impossible or unacceptable they favor decontrolling

Continued on Page 24, Column 5

1955

Humphrey Bogart's only television appearance was in a play called The Petrified Forest. He is shown here in one of the scenes along with Jack Klugman and Richard Jaeckel.

Mama was a popular weekly television series about the Hansen family. Peggy Wood starred as Mama and Judson Laire played her husband. Also featured were Rosemary Rice as Katrin, Dick Van Patten as Nels and Robin Morgan as Dagmar.

Bob Keeshan as Captain Kangaroo.

"All the News That's Fit to Print"

The New York Times.

LATE CITY EDITION
Chance of snow and cold today.
Partly cloudy, cold tomorrow.
Temperature Range Today-Max., 34; Min., 26
Temperatures Yesterday—Max., 36; Min., 26
Full U. S. Weather Bureau Report, Page 33

VOL. CIV. No. 35,430. Entered as Second-Class Matter. Post Office, New York, N. Y. NEW YORK, TUESDAY, JANUARY 25, 1955. Times Square, New York 36, N. Y. Telephone LAckawanna 4-1000 FIVE CENTS

EISENHOWER ASKS FOR AUTHORITY TO DEFEND FORMOSA FROM REDS; CHOU WARNS U. S. MUST WITHDRAW

WAGNER PROMISES PAY RISE THIS YEAR TO 37,000 TEACHERS

It Will Take 'Goodly Portion' of $100,000,000 Sought for Budget, Mayor Says

MIXED REACTION TO PLAN

Reported Increase of $300 Is Held Inadequate by Groups That Have Asked $1,050

By CHARLES G. BENNETT

Mayor Wagner promised yesterday that salary increases for teachers would be included in the city's 1955-56 budget.

The exact amount of the rise in store for the city's 37,000 teachers was not indicated. However, the Mayor said the total would be a "goodly portion" of the $100,000,000 that officials of the city have estimated it will need in additional revenues in 1955-56.

Asked at the temporary City Hall, 63 Park Row, if the board planned pay rises for teachers in the fiscal year beginning July 1, Mr. Wagner said:

"That is in our program and we want to see that the salary increases are given."

Last year the Board of Estimate put $450 pay rises for teachers into the 1954-55 budget. The cost of the increase was about $18,000,000, of which the state provided $11,000,000.

2 Reports Circulate

Because several teacher groups last year were seeking a $750 rise—an amount privately favored by some members of the Board of Estimate—one report in city circles yesterday was that this year's increase might be $300 to make up the difference. Another report at the Board of Education was that the rise would be $350.

A $300 increase would cost the city more than $11,000,000 a year. The present salary range for the city's teachers is $3,450 to $6,750 a year, with $200 additional for those who hold masters' degrees.

Spokesmen for teachers' organizations, commenting on the Mayor's promise of a pay rise, asserted that few would be satisfied with $300 a year.

Both the Teachers Guild, A. F. L., and the Teachers Union, independent, asked $1,050 a year more. This and the 1954-55 $450 would add up to $1,500 additional a year, which they declared the Mayor had promised them in his 1953 campaign.

Both groups also demanded that the number of annual salary increment steps, currently sixteen, be cut to ten.

The High School Teachers Association asked for an immediate $550-a-year rise, with an even-

Continued on Page 23, Column 5

COSTA RICANS SET TO PURSUE REBELS

Figueres in Emergency Talks in Wake of Somoza Warning

By SYDNEY GRUSON
Special to The New York Times.

SAN JOSE, Costa Rica, Tuesday, Jan. 25—Costa Rican troops were poised early today to enter the neutral security zone along the Nicaraguan frontier in pursuit of an estimated 250 rebels on the Costa Rican side of the border.

But only a few hours before the 6 A. M. deadline set for the abrogation of the security zone, the Organization of American States investigating commission still was engaged in intensive discussions with President José Figueres on the deteriorating situation at the border.

The meeting between the President and the commission adjourned once to allow the President to preside over the second emergency meeting of his Cabinet within six hours.

The Cabinet meeting lasted half an hour. Then the Ministers left, and Señor Figueres and the commission resumed a session that had begun shortly after 9 o'clock last night.

There was an air of crisis over the proceedings, but exactly what was at stake was not disclosed. It seemed clear that the lengthy discussions were concerned with Nicaragua's threat of war if the frontier were violated in the

Continued on Page 13, Column 5

Jersey Asks N. Y. Ban Under-21 Drink Sales

By GEORGE CABLE WRIGHT
Special to The New York Times.

TRENTON, Jan. 24—The New Jersey Assembly called on New York today for legislation raising from 18 to 21 years the minimum age at which a person may buy liquor in that state.

A resolution embodying the request to Governor Averell Harriman and the New York Legislature was adopted by a vote of 52 to 0. Several members from North Jersey had taken the floor to stress the "growing problem" of keeping teenagers in that area from crossing into New York to drink.

The resolution adopted today did not require action by the State Senate. The minimum age for purchasing intoxicating beverages in New Jersey has remained at 21 years since 1933.

In introducing the measure,

Continued on Page 19, Column 5

HARRIMAN EASES BUILDING FREEZE

Permits Letting of Contracts for Mental Hygiene Projects and Grade Crossing Work

By WARREN WEAVER Jr.
Special to The New York Times

ALBANY, Jan. 24 — Governor Harriman's freeze on state construction projects appeared to have thawed somewhat today.

The Governor announced that he had authorized the State Public Works Department to proceed with letting contracts for work on mental hygiene projects and for grade crossing eliminations.

He said that these two classes of construction could be advanced because they were financed by special bond issues, rather than by money in the capital construction fund.

A Harriman aide said that there never had been any intention of halting projects that did not draw on the capital construction fund, since the ban had been based solely on doubt as to the amount of money in the fund.

Republicans See 'Retreat'

The Republican chairmen of the Senate Finance and Assembly Ways and Means Committees congratulated Mr. Harriman "for his partial compliance with our request of Jan. 5 to reconsider his capital construction freeze order."

They characterized his announcement as "a retreat from a hasty and ill-advised decision."

"Now that the Governor has begun to familiarize himself with the operation of the capital construction fund," they said, "we urge him to rescind completely the rest of his freeze order as soon as possible, so that other equally important parts of the state's construction program, for which appropriations have already been made, will not be jeopardized."

The Republican fiscal leaders, Senator Austin W. Erwin of Geneseo and Assemblyman William H. MacKenzie of Belmont, said that they assumed Mr. Harriman's advisers had found that the capital construction fund was not, in fact, overcommitted.

The Governor said that the authorization for construction of mental hygiene projects and grade crossing eliminations actually had been issued a week ago. He added that the State Budget Director, Dr. Paul H. Appleby, had been reviewing some individual projects and approving them for advancement.

Leaders Get Project List

Earlier in the day, the Republican leaders of the Legislature, Senator Walter J. Mahoney, Senate majority leader, and Oswald D. Heck, Speaker of the Assembly, made public a list of 260 projects pending in the State Public Works Department.

The list was prepared at their request by John W. Johnson, State Superintendent of Public Works, a Harriman appointee. The Republicans said that it would be necessary in "considering the Governor's budget proposals."

Senator Mahoney and Mr. Heck also requested Mr. Johnson to include a breakdown on all projects that would be affected by the freeze order as well as an estimate of the number of jobs that each would create if it were carried through.

The Republicans wrote Mr. Johnson again today, saying that he had failed to provide any information on the number of jobs

Continued on Page 19, Column 3

MAYOR BIDS STATE CLOSE LOOPHOLES ON GAMBLING, VICE

Proposes Bills to Permit New Curbs, Severer Penalties in Fight Against Crime

By RICHARD AMPER
Special to The New York Times.

ALBANY, Jan. 24 — Mayor Wagner urged the Legislature today to enact measures against bookmaking and vice "loopholes."

Through Victor F. Candello, New York City's legislative representative, the Mayor asked favorable committee action on bills that would:

¶Make mandatory a fine of at least $50 for a second conviction and imprisonment for at least ninety days for a third conviction for bookmaking or selling numbers or lottery tickets.

¶Prevent the operation of "outlaw" wire services from race tracks to bookmakers.

¶Give the police a new weapon against bookmakers who used a legitimate telephone in a private home to take bets.

¶Empower courts to deny bail to a person charged with living off the proceeds of prostitution or with illegal sale or possession of hypodermic syringes or needles whose criminal record indicated his freedom pending trial would be dangerous.

Inequality Is Noted

Three of the measures were introduced by Senator James J. Crisona and Assemblyman J. Lewis Fox, Democrats of Queens.

In a memorandum dealing with punishment for bookmaking, the Mayor noted that the present law provided no severer punishment for a habitual violator than for a first offender.

Under the new proposal, the present penalty of imprisonment for no more than a year and a fine of no more than $500 would be applicable only for a first conviction. For a second conviction, a fine of $50 to $500 and imprisonment up to a year would be required.

A third and subsequent conviction would be punishable by imprisonment for not less than ninety days or more than a year, and the court could impose a fine up to $500.

The bill on "outlaw" wire services would prohibit a person at a track from transmitting racing or gambling information within five minutes before or after the start of a race to any person outside the grounds except with permission of the State Racing Commission.

A violation would be a misdemeanor, punishable by a fine up to $500 and imprisonment up to a year, or both.

The memorandum noted that Francis W. H. Adams, New York City Police Commissioner, had recommended this measure as essential to fight the bookmaking racket.

"The bookmaker cannot operate his illegal business profitably unless he is able to obtain instantaneous racing information," the memorandum said.

The measure also would prohibit anyone outside the track from receiving or transmitting

Continued on Page 18, Column 3

BARS A CEASE-FIRE

Premier Charges U. S. Plans to Launch War Against Red China

Text of Chou En-lai's statement is printed on Page 4.

By ROBERT TRUMBULL
Special to The New York Times.

TOKYO, Tuesday, Jan. 25—Communist China has rejected the United States suggestion of a cease-fire in Formosa Strait.

Premier Chou En-lai of Red China, in a statement broadcast by the Peiping Government radio last night, called instead for the United States to "stop intervening in China's internal affairs and withdraw all its armed forces from Taiwan [Formosa] and the Taiwan Straits." The Formosa Strait is about 100 miles wide at its narrowest point.

Nationalist Government authorities also had indicated strong opposition to the cease-fire proposal now under informal consideration by various members of the United Nations. This move was given the approval of President Eisenhower last week as an alternative to continued armed action that might lead in the direction of extended hostilities, possibly involving the United States naval force guarding Formosa.

'Intervention' Charged

"The so-called cease-fire between the People's Republic and the traitorous Chiang Kai-shek clique that the United States Government and its followers are trying to engineer is in actuality intervention in China's internal affairs and alienation of China's territory," Premier Chou declared in a statement broadcast by the Peiping radio.

"They are using war threats and brandishing atomic weapons in an attempt to force the Chinese people into tolerating the occupation of Taiwan by the United States, giving recognition to the United States-Chiang Kai-shek mutual security treaty, and permitting the use of Taiwan by the United States as a military base for preparing a new war.

"The Chinese people absolutely cannot tolerate this. They firmly oppose it."

The Chinese Communist leader reiterated the determination of his Government to add the strategic Formosa bastion to Peiping's territories. He said this was in the interests of peace.

"To safeguard China's sovereignty and territorial integrity, to safeguard the security of China and peace in the Far East, the Chinese people must liberate Taiwan, and the United States must stop intervening in China's internal affairs and withdraw all its armed forces from Taiwan

Continued on Page 4, Column 2

Associated Press Wirephoto

DISCUSS FORMOSA SITUATION: Secretary of State John Foster Dulles pointing to map as he talked yesterday with Representative James P. Richards, chairman of the House Foreign Affairs Committee. On the map Formosa is called by Chinese name of Taiwan.

PLEA TO CONGRESS

President Hopeful, but Says We Must Show Readiness to Fight

Texts of Eisenhower message and resolution, Page 3.

By W. H. LAWRENCE
Special to The New York Times.

WASHINGTON, Jan. 24—President Eisenhower asked Congress today to authorize calculated risks of war aimed at averting Chinese Communist capture of Formosa and the Pescadores Islands.

He asked for a blank-check emergency authorization to use United States armed forces not only to defend these islands but also to permit attacks upon threatening Chinese Communist concentrations on near-by islands and on the China mainland.

Such action, he said, should reduce rather than increase the possibilities of armed conflict in the Far East.

Proclaiming his hope for peace, the President declared the United States "must remove any doubt regarding our readiness to fight, if necessary, to preserve the vital stake of the free world in a free Formosa, and to engage in whatever operations may be required to carry out that purpose."

The Administration policy was obviously based on a belief that the Communist world was not ready for World War III. It was based also on a belief that the Red Chinese Government would back down from its public threats to take Formosa in the face of United States determination and unity at the risk of war.

Quick Congress Action Likely

President Eisenhower's war-if-necessary message was sent to an approving Congress amid signs that a measure implementing it would be passed by both houses before the week is over.

The President again expressed his hope that the United Nations might arrange a cease-fire between the Chinese Nationalist and Communist Governments. However, he said the situation already was so critical that this Government could not wait for the United Nations to act.

"The actions that the United States must be ready to undertake are of various kinds," the President said. "For example, we must be ready to assist the Republic of China to redeploy and consolidate its forces if it should so desire. Some of these forces are scattered throughout the smaller offshore islands as a result of historical rather than military reasons directly related to defending Formosa. Because of the air situation in the area, withdrawals for the purpose of redeployment of Chinese Nationalist forces would be impractical with-

Continued on Page 2, Column 3

PRAVDA ATTACKS CONSUMER STRESS

Mikoyan Out as Trade Aide in Shift Linked to Return to Heavy Industry Line

By CLIFTON DANIEL
Special to The New York Times.

MOSCOW, Tuesday, Jan. 25—Advocates of increasing Soviet consumer goods production at the expense of heavy industry have been denounced by a high functionary of the Communist party.

The denunciation filled almost an entire page in yesterday's edition of Pravda, the party newspaper, and was signed by Dmitri T. Shepilov, Pravda's editor.

Today, the Presidium of the Supreme Soviet announced the resignation of Anastas I. Mikoyan, Minister of Domestic Trade. Mr. Mikoyan has been one of the most important advocates of increasing consumer goods output.

The announcement said Mr. Mikoyan, who still retains his Deputy Premiership and membership in the party's Central Committee, had asked to be relieved of his duties. Dmitri V. Pavlov was appointed in his place.

Security Held in Danger

In his article, the Pravda editor declared that giving consumer goods priority over the development of heavy industry would mean surrendering the initiative in modern industrial advancement to the capitalist countries. This, he added, would endanger the security of the Soviet Union.

"It would be difficult to imagine a more anti-scientific and rotten 'theory' and one that would more disarm our people," the Pravda editor declared.

He added that there was an "acute international situation that requires the Soviet people to exert the greatest vigilance."

"Forces of imperialist reaction armed to the teeth and arming themselves still further are preparing plans for a new world war," he continued.

"In these circumstances, the resulting decisive struggle for peace throughout the world and the continual strengthening of the Soviet motherland as well as its defensive capacity are the first sacred patriotic and international duty of the Soviet people."

Such a strong and categorical article probably would not have been written by an important journalist in the party's newspaper without the sanction of the presidium of the Central Committee of the Communist party. Premier Georgi M. Malenkov is chairman of the party presidium and Nikita S. Khrushchev is the first secretary of the party.

The thesis of the article presumably will find its expression in facts and figures and statements of policy when the mem-

Continued on Page 8, Column 3

Congress' Approval Likely; Resolution Wins First Test

By WILLIAM S. WHITE
Special to The New York Times.

WASHINGTON, Jan. 24—Congress appeared ready to grant quickly the wide authority President Eisenhower sought today to use military force to protect Formosa. The mood at the Capitol was not unquestioning, however, nor was it, on balance, eager. There was much private anxiety.

The prospect was that the House of Representatives would adopt by tomorrow night, and with only limited debate, a resolution to meet the President's request. But there was a good deal of largely private resistance in the Senate to any such early disposition of the grave issue there.

A resolution to carry out the President's request was introduced in both houses after his message had been read. Secretary of State John Foster Dulles then testified before the House Foreign Affairs Committee and before the Senate Foreign Relations and Armed Services Committees, sitting together.

One of the Senators who attended the session of the latter group said Mr. Dulles had agreed that the resolution conceivably was broad enough to permit the United States "to go to war" without further action by Congress. This view was, in fact, the generally accepted one on Capitol Hill.

Emerging from the House committee, Mr. Dulles told reporters: "In my opinion, if the resolution is passed, it will decrease the risk of general war in that area [the western Pacific]. If it is not passed it will increase the risk of war."

The resolution was approved by a vote of 28 to 0 late today

Continued on Page 3, Column 1

AIM IS TO PREVENT START OF BIG WAR

Administration Thinks This Can Be Done by Making U. S. Intentions Clear

By ELIE ABEL
Special to The New York Times

WASHINGTON, Jan. 24—The Administration's action today, though risking involvement in the shooting along Formosa Strait, was taken in the hope of snuffing out the possibility that a bigger war would flare up by miscalculation.

The risk is real, high Administration sources concede. They say President Eisenhower's request for Congressional authority to protect Formosa and the Pescadores from invasion could mean hitting at mainland airfields, troop staging areas and ships massed in Communist ports with United States air and sea power.

In its willingness to accept this risk, the Administration was influenced by its thinking about the origins of the Korean war. That point of view was expressed by Secretary of State John Foster Dulles in a speech before the American Legion convention at St. Louis on Sept. 2, 1953.

How Korean War Began

"The Korean war," he said, "began in a way in which wars often begin—a potential aggressor miscalculated. From that we learn a lesson which we expect to apply in the interests of future peace.

"The lesson is this: If events are likely which will in fact lead us to fight, let us make clear our intention in advance; then we shall probably not have to fight.

"Big wars usually come about by mistake, not by design. * * * It is * * * probable that the Korean war would not have occurred if the aggressor had known what the United States would do.

"The Communists thought, and had reason to think, that they would not be opposed, except by the then small and ill-equipped forces of the Republic of Korea. They did not expect what actually happened."

The parallel between Korea and Formosa is not exact, because Peiping has been on notice since 1950 that the Seventh Fleet would oppose any attempts to invade the main Nationalist base as well as the outlying Pesca-

Continued on Page 3, Column 6

Djilas and Dedijer Found Guilty; Yugoslav Court Suspends Terms

By JACK RAYMOND
Special to The New York Times.

BELGRADE, Yugoslavia, Tuesday, Jan. 25—Milovan Djilas and Vladimir Dedijer have been convicted of having waged hostile propaganda against Yugoslavia.

After a secret sixteen-hour trial they received suspended sentences and were permitted to return to their homes at 12:20 A. M. today.

M. Djilas, ousted former Vice President, was sentenced to one and one-half years and placed on probation for three years. M. Dedijer, biographer of President Tito, received a six-month term and was placed on probation for two years.

[Reuters reported that the official Yugoslav news agency, Tanjug, said M. Djilas and M. Dedijer had been heard during the morning proceedings Monday, but Tanjug did not report any of their evidence. There was no indication of the nature of their defense.]

They had been charged in Belgrade District Court under Article 118 of the Yugoslav Criminal Code, which provides possible imprisonment upon conviction. They had been accused of intent to "undermine the authority of the working people" of the Federal People's Republic of Yugoslavia.

Aleksander Atankovic, the prosecutor, said in his opening statement yesterday that the two men "gave slanderous statements to the correspondents of the foreign press." He said the statements had "wrongly interpreted the situation in the country"

In one interview M. Djilas had called for the creation of a new democratic Socialist party and asserted that the Communist party here was controlled by undemocratic elements. In another, M. Dedijer had confirmed that he had been called to account for his political attitude before a Communist control board in connection with M. Djilas' expulsion from the Central Committee last year.

M. Djilas, who had been regarded as a likely successor to Marshal Tito, was disgraced last January for having published articles appealing for "democratization" of the Communist League.

At first only members of the foreign press were barred from the trial on the ground that they were not trusted to report the

Continued on Page 7, Column 3

Defense Stocks Rise As Eisenhower Acts

The stock market reacted decisively yesterday to President Eisenhower's message asking Congress for permission to fight in defense of Formosa. Industries that would benefit directly from increased military spending recorded notable gains.

Aircraft issues in particular shot ahead. Steels, metals, machines and machine tools moved up. Other segments of the market, however, had a generally dull day.

Commodities also reacted to the news. Cocoa futures jumped the trading limit of 1 cent a pound. Rubber was up sharply. Hides, wool, zinc, lead, copper and cottonseed oil also rose.

Even before the President's message was released, stocks that would benefit from increased defense spending received buying support, owing to the deterioration of the Far Eastern situation over the

Continued on Page 33, Column 7

FLEET OFF CHINA NEAR READINESS

Admiral Sees His Forces Set in a 'Very Few Days'

By HENRY R. LIEBERMAN
Special to The New York Times.

TAIPEI, Formosa, Tuesday, Jan. 25 — The United States Seventh Fleet is ready to begin helping the Chinese Nationalists to evacuate the Tachen Islands off the Chekiang coast within "a very few days."

This was the assessment of the fleet's condition as described yesterday by its commander, Vice Admiral Alfred M. Pride.

He told correspondents that his ships and planes could "cope" with "any eventuality" if it were ordered to support a Nationalist withdrawal from the Communist-threatened Tachens.

Asked if he had the forces to deal with the Chinese Communists in the event that they tried to hamper a United States-supported evacuation there, Admiral Pride replied, "Yes, I certainly do."

In reply to another question on whether he expected opposition from the Communist armed forces, he said, "Only the Com-

Continued on Page 4, Column 7

Gordon MacRae and Shirley Jones in the movie version of the Broadway musical, Oklahoma.

James Dean, who appeared with Julie Harris in Elia Kazan's film, East of Eden, became a star preceding its release. He received enormous publicity and was soon named "the new Brando." Both the director and the star of the film, which was based on John Steinbeck's novel of the same title, received excellent reviews.

Betsy Blair and Ernest Borgnine as two shy, lonely people in the film version of Paddy Chayefsky's TV play, Marty.

"All the News That's Fit to Print"

The New York Times.

LATE CITY EDITION
Rain and mild today. Rain ending. turning colder tomorrow.
Temperature Range Today-Max., 43; Min., 32
Temperatures Yesterday-Max., 37.1; Min., 18.8
Full U. S. Weather Bureau Report, Sec. 5, Page 10

NEWS SUMMARY AND INDEX, PAGE 95

Copyright, 1955, by The New York Times Company.

SECTION ONE

VOL. CIV. No. 35,442. Entered as Second-Class Matter. Post Office, New York, N. Y. NEW YORK, SUNDAY, FEBRUARY 6, 1955. Including Magazine and Book Review. TWENTY-FIVE CENTS

SEVENTH FLEET ORDERED TO TACHENS, SAILS TO EVACUATE CHIANG'S TROOPS; U. S. PLANES DOWN 2 MIG'S OFF KOREA

$4,685,353 DEFICIT ON TRANSIT SHOWN IN 6-MONTH PERIOD

Agency Hopes to Keep Loss for Entire Fiscal Term, Ending in June, to $4,856,200

QUILL MAY UPSET PLANS

Demands of T.W.U. Head for 17c Pay Rise for 43,000 Could Cost $12,000,000

By STANLEY LEVEY

The half-yearly financial report of the Transit Authority is written in bright red ink.

Unpublished but official figures, independently obtained, show that for the first six months of the 1954-55 fiscal year the agency has run up an operating deficit of $4,685,353. For the entire year, ending next June 30, the authority hopes to hold the loss to $4,856,200.

But that is no more than a hope. Many factors could send the deficit figure spurting steeply upward, and the authority is uncomfortably aware of them. They include weather, a further loss of passengers and service cutbacks that — as one official phrases it—"have an adverse effect upon passenger revenue."

There is also one other factor—Michael J. Quill. The president of the Transport Workers Union, C. I. O., has made known that when he opens wage talks with the authority a week from tomorrow he will demand an average rise of 17 cents an hour for 43,000 employes. The cost of his proposal is put at $12,000,000 to $14,000,000 a year.

'Hidden Treasure' Sought

In preparation for the negotiations Mr. Quill asked for and received permission to have his accountants examine the authority's books. The union president insisted there was more to the financial picture than met the eye and spoke darkly of a "hidden treasure" of $38,000,000, which he intended to unearth.

Mr. Quill's accountants will begin their audit of the books tomorrow. Whether they will find the $38,000,000 in "hidden treasure" is doubtful, but they unquestionably will come across about $20,000,000 in unspent and unallocated deferred-maintenance funds, which the authority carries on its records as an expense item.

Mr. Quill can be expected to demand a slice of these funds for a wage rise. Maj. Gen. Hugh J. Casey, authority chairman, can be expected to remind him that any increase is dependent on three factors—the economic health of the agency, the success of its program to cut costs and the union's cooperation in eliminating abuses of the sick-leave system.

A year ago, at the end of its first six months of operation under the 15-cent fare, the authority reported an operating profit of $4,334,088. It ended the full fiscal year with a surplus of $4,406,466, even after granting wage increases costing $9,000,000.

Factors in Passenger Loss

The explanation for the present state of affairs where the authority is running steadily in the red ($9,019,442 behind the first half of the 1953-54 fiscal year) is as follows:

Passenger traffic has fallen off from last year by about 3.3 per cent instead of 2 per cent as originally estimated. In terms of an operating budget calling for more than $272,000,000 in revenues, the loss of more passengers than anticipated has been critical—and expensive.

In the fiscal year 1953-54 the passenger loss amounted to 11.1 per cent. This was attributed largely to the fare increase to 15 cents on July 25, 1953. But even so, in light of previous experience, it was expected that the passenger trend loss would be only 2 per cent for this fiscal year. A report submitted last week to the authority from its budget department had this to say on the subject:

"Exactly where and why the trend reversed its direction and

Continued on Page 88, Column 4

This section consists of 106 pages divided into three parts. The news summary and index will be found on Page 95. Society news begins on Page 90 and obituary articles will be found on Pages 88 and 89.

Associated Press Radiophoto

'I CANNOT CONCEAL MY EMOTION . . .': Pierre Mendès-France leaving the Elysée Palace after his defeat.

EISENHOWER BACKS HIS MODIFIED U.M.T.

Tells Officers Association It Is an Effective Way to Get Ready Reserve

By The United Press.

WASHINGTON, Feb. 5—President Eisenhower defended tonight the Administration's modified Universal Military Training plan.

He said it was an effective and economical way of producing "a Ready Reserve which is in fact ready, available and well-trained."

The President appealed for support of his controversial reserve program, now pending before Congress, in a message to the National Council of the Reserve Officers Association. Senator J. Strom Thurmond, Democrat of South Carolina and president of the association, read the presidential message at a council banquet.

President Eisenhower's reserve program was submitted to Congress in a special message on Jan. 13. He called for reorganizing the military reserves into two broad categories. One would be a Ready Reserve that would be available for "immediate mobilization" in case of war. The second would be a non-organized pool of men with previous service who could be called up on a selective basis in a general mobilization.

To maintain a steady flow of trained men into the Ready Reserve, the President proposed that youths 17 and 18 be allowed to volunteer for six months of basic training, followed by nine and one half years of compulsory reserve service. This would be in lieu of serving two years of active duty through Selective Service induction.

If an "adequate number" did not volunteer, the military would be given authority to draft youths 18½ and 19 to fill out the quota. The Defense Department has indicated that 100,000 volunteers a year would be adequate.

This modified version of Universal Military Training has run into considerable opposition in Congress, which several times has

Continued on Page 30, Column 1

Atka Finds Glaciers That Spill Icebergs

By WALTER SULLIVAN
Special to The New York Times.

ABOARD U. S. S. ATKA, off Antarctica, Feb. 4—A glacier that dumps its icebergs down a 2,000-foot cliff into the sea was sighted today.

This icebreaker pushed briefly off Peter I Island and found that ice blanketing the center of the island rose 4,000 feet above the sea. The peaks were hidden in clouds, but numerous icebergs that drain off the ice were golden in the sunshine as they cascaded into the ocean.

On the western shore of the fourteen-mile-long island was an awesome black precipice rising almost vertically from the sea. At its foot "bergy bits," shattered fragments of icebergs, floated in the water as if newly fallen.

Just below the clouds overhead an icecap 100 or 200 feet thick pushed out to the brink of the cliff and then cut off sharply

Continued on Page 22, Column 1

COSTA RICA TROOPS RETAKE AIRFIELD

Border Town Also Reported Cleared of Rebels—Somoza Protests Bombs at Line

By PAUL P. KENNEDY
Special to The New York Times.

SAN JOSE, Costa Rica, Feb. 5—Government forces recaptured the airstrip of Los Chilés this afternoon.

[The Government said its forces were in absolute control of the town as well as the airport, The Associated Press reported. President Anastasio Somoza of Nicaragua charged that Costa Rican planes had bombed Nicaraguan territory while taking action against the rebels in Los Chiles.]

Two C-47 transport planes with sixty-seven soldiers, all armed with submachine guns, landed on the airstrip shortly after 1 o'clock. The troops jumped from the planes before they had stopped moving and sprayed the area surrounding the airfield with machine gun fire.

It was not known whether rebel forces actually had intended to defend the airstrip. The planes took off as soon as the Government troops landed. One of the planes returned to San José and the other went to Puerto Limon on the Caribbean coast. Two more planes were scheduled to leave here late this afternoon with sixty more soldiers.

The DC-3 Lacsa airliner captured by the rebels yesterday

Continued on Page 10, Column 3

FRANCE'S POLICIES ARE LEFT UP IN AIR BY PREMIER'S FALL

Next Cabinet Must Deal Anew With Main Issues—Leaders Fear for National Unity

By LANSING WARREN
Special to The New York Times.

PARIS, Feb. 5—Not merely the North African policy but all the chief features of the Mendès-France program were called into question by the downfall of the French Cabinet early today.

The Paris agreements for arming West Germany, autonomy in North Africa, the peace in Indochina and the planned French social reforms will have to be tackled again by the next Premier.

Whatever may be the new approach, the coming Government will have to reckon with Pierre Mendès-France. For the former Premier has already made it plain that he will try to insure that his policies are carried out.

"I cannot conceal my emotion and regrets," he said on leaving the Elysée Palace after he resigned. "It is not for myself but for the country. I am sorry the work begun could not have been concluded. I hope the Government that succeeds mine will go on with the task and I hope for the sake of the nation that it will succeed."

French political leaders, after the tumultuous end of the all-night session when the retiring Premier was roughly hooted down, expressed fear that unity in France could not be easily restored. They also expressed fear that this largely personal crisis here would not be understood abroad.

President Consults Leaders

President René Coty started immediately to consult French leaders to end these uncertainties. It was thought his efforts might be aided by the recent changes in the French Constitution that simplified the selection of a Premier. It was the deep divergences and the turmoil in political parties caused by the overthrow of M. Mendès-France that mainly blocked the road.

Under the new procedure the Premier needs only a simple majority of the Deputies balloting in the 626-member National Assembly to win endorsement. Hitherto an absolute majority of the Assembly membership, or 314 votes, was required. The Premier had to seek endorsement and later present his Cabinet for another vote of approval. Under present procedure the Premier will form his Cabinet before he asks approval.

Premier Mendès-France was defeated by 319 votes, including ninety-eight Communists, to 273.

In the party disarray that followed the Cabinet downfall the chief problem for the victorious

Continued on Page 27, Column 1

Gov. Harriman Is Host to Shah of Iran and Stevenson

The New York Times

Governor Harriman, left, with Shah of Iran and Adlai E. Stevenson, right, before luncheon

Governor and Mrs. Harriman entertained the Shah of Iran and Queen Soroya at luncheon yesterday at their home, 16 East Eighty-first Street. Adlai E. Stevenson, Democratic candidate for President in 1952, and Margaret Truman, daughter of former President Harry S. Truman, were among the guests. The Shah and Mr. Harriman first met in Iran in 1942 when the Governor passed through Iran on his way to Moscow. They met again in 1951 when Mr. Harriman was President Truman's representative in the Anglo-Iranian oil dispute. Among the other luncheon guests were Nasrollah Entezam, Iranian Ambassador; Dr. Grayson L. Kirk, president of Columbia University; John J. McCloy, chairman of the Chase National Bank and former High Commissioner in Germany, and Mrs. McCloy; Admiral Alan G. Kirk, former Ambassador to Russia, and Mrs. Kirk; Richard C. Patterson Jr., former Minister to Switzerland, and Mrs. Patterson; Mr. and Mrs. William G. Lord, Mrs. Gardner Cowles, Mr. and Mrs. George Backer, and Ardeshir Zahedi, son of the Prime Minister of Iran.

8 RED JETS ATTACK

Survey Craft Escorted by Sabres Is Fired On Over Yellow Sea

By ROBERT TRUMBULL
Special to The New York Times.

TOKYO, Sunday, Feb. 6 — United States jet fighters shot down two of eight attacking Communist jet aircraft yesterday between Communist China and Korea.

The United States Far East Air Forces' headquarters identified the planes as Soviet-built MIG-15's. They were the same type as the fighter planes that United States F-86 Sabrejets outfought in the Korean war.

No further details were given, but it was assumed that the hostile fighters were manned by Chinese Communist pilots and that the survivors streaked for Red China bases. The incident occurred over the Yellow Sea.

The Air Force said four of the Communist fighters had attacked a United States RB-45, a four-engine jet bomber converted into a reconnaissance plane. The other four MIG's engaged the Saberjets that were flying "top cover" for the reconnaissance craft.

Routine Reconnaissance

The United States planes were said to have been on a routine reconnaissance mission.

[The United States Far East Air Forces Sunday placed the battle ten miles off the coast of North Korea and forty miles west of the North Korean capital of Pyongyang, The Associated Press reported.]

A brief Air Force communiqué said the Communist planes had attacked first and that the six surviving MIG's had "returned to Communist territory."

The United States personnel involved were from Osan air base, forty miles south of Seoul, the South Korean capital. It was not disclosed how many Sabrejets were involved. The pilots were under orders to shoot if fired upon. The Osan base is more than 600 miles from the Tachen Islands and 800 miles from Formosa.

The incident was the latest of eight involving United States and Communist planes in neutral areas since the end of the Korean war. A total of seven United States aircraft are reported to have been shot down.

The attack occurred while the

Continued on Page 3, Column 5

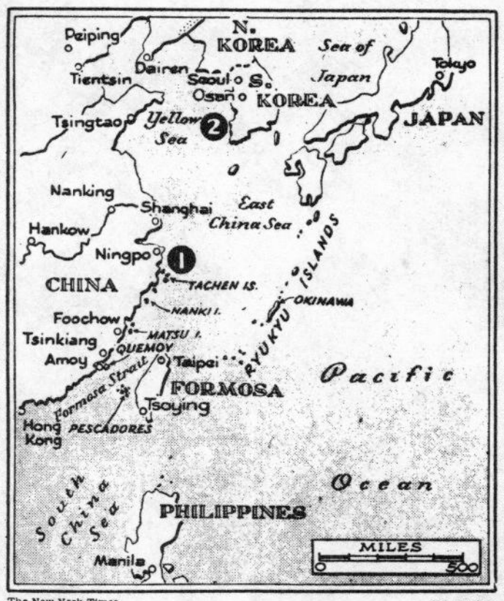

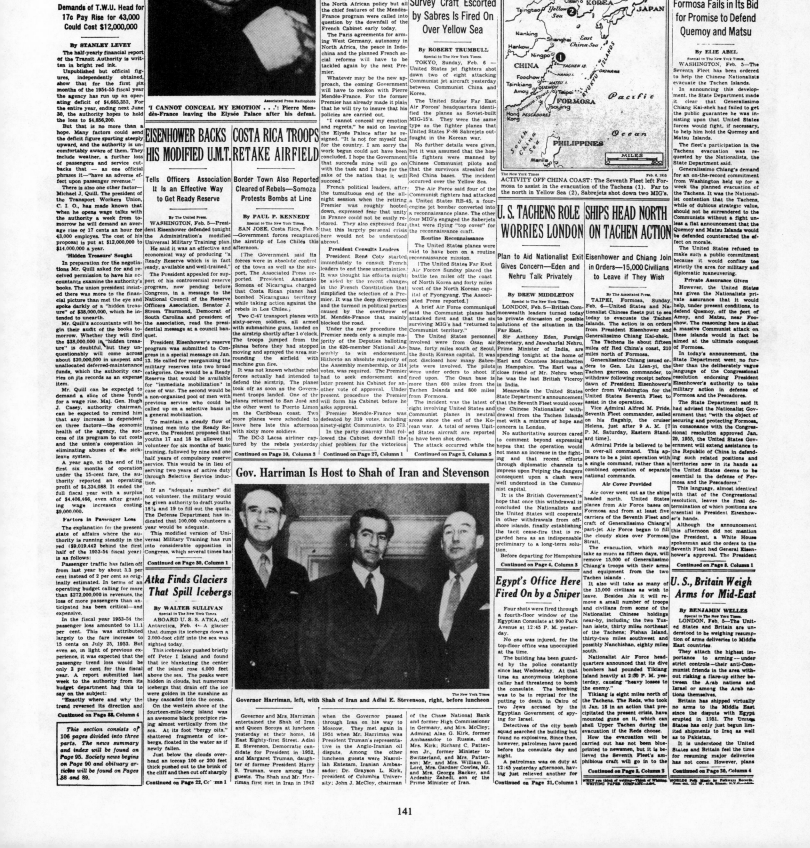

The New York Times Feb. 6, 1955

ACTIVITY OFF CHINA COAST: The Seventh Fleet left Formosa to assist in the evacuation of the Tachens (1). Far to the north in Yellow Sea (2), Sabrejets shot down two MIG's.

U. S. TACHENS ROLE WORRIES LONDON

Plan to Aid Nationalist Exit Gives Concern—Eden and Nehru Talk Privately

By DREW MIDDLETON
Special to The New York Times.

LONDON, Feb. 5—British Commonwealth leaders turned today to private discussion of possible solutions of the situation in the Far East.

Sir Anthony Eden, Foreign Secretary, and Jawaharlal Nehru, Prime Minister of India, are spending tonight at the home of Earl and Countess Mountbatten in Hampshire. The Earl was a close friend of Mr. Nehru when he was the last British Viceroy in India.

Meanwhile the United States State Department's announcement that the Seventh Fleet would cover the Chinese Nationalists' withdrawal from the Tachen Islands met with a mixture of hope and concern in London.

No authoritative sources cared to comment beyond expressing hopes that the operation would not mean an increase in the fighting and that recent efforts through diplomatic channels to impress upon Peiping the dangers consequent upon a clash were well understood in the Communist capital.

It is the British Government's hope that once this withdrawal is concluded the Nationalists and the United States will cooperate in other withdrawals from offshore islands, finally establishing the tacit cease-fire that is regarded here as an indispensable preliminary to a long-term solution.

Before departing for Hampshire

Continued on Page 4, Column 3

Egypt's Office Here Fired On by a Sniper

Four shots were fired through a fourth-floor window of the Egyptian Consulate at 900 Park Avenue at 12:45 P. M. yesterday.

No one was injured, for the top-floor office was unoccupied at the time.

The building has been guarded by the police constantly since last Wednesday. At that time an anonymous telephone caller had threatened to bomb the consulate. The bombing was to be in reprisal for the putting to death in Cairo of two Jews accused by the Egyptian Government of spying for Israel.

Detectives of the city bomb squad searched the building but found no explosives. Since then, however, patrolmen have paced before the consulate day and night.

A patrolman was on duty at 12:45 yesterday afternoon, having just relieved another for

Continued on Page 21, Column 1

SHIPS HEAD NORTH ON TACHEN ACTION

Eisenhower and Chiang Join in Orders—15,000 Civilians to Leave if They Wish

By The Associated Press.

TAIPEI, Formosa, Sunday, Feb. 6—United States and Nationalist Chinese fleets put to sea today to evacuate the Tachen Islands. The action is on orders from President Eisenhower and Generalissimo Chiang Kai-shek.

The Tachens lie about fifteen miles off Red China's coast, 210 miles north of Formosa.

Generalissimo Chiang issued orders to Gen. Liu Lien-yi, the Tachen garrison commander, to withdraw following receipt before dawn of President Eisenhower's order from Washington for the United States Seventh Fleet to assist in the operation.

Vice Admiral Alfred M. Pride, Seventh Fleet commander, sailed on his flagship, the cruiser Helena, just after 9 A. M. [7 P. M. Saturday, Eastern Standard time].

Admiral Pride is believed to be in over-all command. This appears to be a joint operation with a single command, rather than a combined operation of separate national commands.

Air Cover Provided

Air cover went out as the ships headed north. United States planes from Air Force bases on Formosa and from at least five carriers of the Seventh Fleet and craft of Generalissimo Chiang's part-jet Air Force began to fill the cloudy skies over Formosa Strait.

The evacuation, which may take as much as fifteen days, will remove 15,000 of Generalissimo Chiang's troops with their arms and equipment from the two Tachen islands.

It also will take as many of the 15,000 civilians as wish to leave. Besides this it will remove a small number of troops and civilians from some of the Nationalist Chinese holdings near-by, including the two Yushan islets, thirty miles northeast of the Tachens; Pishan Island, thirty-two miles southwest and possibly Nanchishan, eighty miles south.

Nationalist Air Force headquarters announced that its dive bombers had pounded Yikiang Island heavily at 2:50 P. M. yesterday, causing "heavy losses to the enemy."

Yikiang is eight miles north of the Tachens. The Reds, who took it Jan. 18 in an action that precipitated the present crisis, have mounted guns on it, which can shell Upper Tachen during the evacuation if the Reds choose.

How the evacuation will be carried out has not been blueprinted to newsmen, but it is believed the Seventh Fleet's amphibious craft will go in to the

Continued on Page 3, Column 2

WHEN you think of writing—Think of Whiting. WHITING PAPER COMPANY.—Advt.

U. S. BARS PLEDGE

Formosa Fails in Its Bid for Promise to Defend Quemoy and Matsu

By ELIE ABEL
Special to The New York Times.

WASHINGTON, Feb. 5—The Seventh Fleet has been ordered to help the Chinese Nationalists evacuate the Tachen Islands.

In announcing this development, the State Department made it clear that Generalissimo Chiang Kai-shek had failed to get the public guarantee he was insisting upon that United States forces would fight, if necessary, to help him hold the Quemoy and Matsu Islands.

The fleet's participation in the Tachens evacuation was requested by the Nationalists, the State Department said.

Generalissimo Chiang's demand for an on-the-record commitment from Washington held up for a week the planned evacuation of the Tachens. It was the Nationalist contention that the Tachens, while of dubious strategic value, should not be surrendered to the Communists without a fight unless a flat announcement that the Quemoy and Matsu Islands would be defended counteracted the effect on morale.

The United States refused to make such a public commitment because it would confine too strictly the area for military and diplomatic maneuvering.

Private Assurance Given

However, the United States has given the Nationalists private assurance that it would help, under present conditions, to defend Quemoy, off the port of Amoy, and Matsu, near Foochow. The reasoning here is that a massive Communist attack on these islands would in fact be aimed at the ultimate conquest of Formosa.

In today's announcement, the State Department went no further than the deliberately vague language of the Congressional resolution endorsing President Eisenhower's authority to take military action in defense of Formosa and the Pescadores.

The State Department said it had advised the Nationalist Government that "with the object of securing and protecting Formosa, in consonance with the Congressional resolution approved Jan. 29, 1955, the United States Government will extend assistance to the Republic of China in defending such related positions and territories now in its hands as the United States deems to be essential in the defense of Formosa and the Pescadores."

This language, almost identical with that of the Congressional resolution, leaves the final determination of which positions are essential in President Eisenhower's hands.

Although the announcement this afternoon did not mention the President, a White House spokesman said the orders to the Seventh Fleet had General Eisenhower's approval. The President

Continued on Page 3, Column 1

U. S., Britain Weigh Arms for Mid-East

By BENJAMIN WELLES
Special to The New York Times.

LONDON, Feb. 5—The United States and Britain are understood to be weighing resumption of arms deliveries to Middle East countries.

They attach the highest importance to arming—under strict controls—their anti-Communist friends in the area without risking a flare-up either between the Arab nations and Israel or among the Arab nations themselves.

Britain has shipped virtually no arms to the Middle East since the dispute with Egypt erupted in 1951. The United States has only just begun limited shipments to Iraq as well as to Pakistan.

It is understood the United States and Britain feel the time for resuming major deliveries has not come. However, plans

Continued on Page 20, Column 4

WORLDS Folk Music by Folkways Records. [illegible]

The Mickey Mouse Club, *which ran from 1955-1959, featured a cast of juvenile actors known as the "Mouseketeers."*

Queen for a Day *began as a radio show and shifted to television in 1955. Within months it became the No.1 daytime show. Jack Bailey is shown here crowning a new queen, a woman whose story was judged by the audience to be the most heartbreaking.*

Susan Strasberg portrayed Anne Frank, a young Jewish victim of Nazi persecution. She is shown here in a scene from the Broadway show The Diary of Anne Frank with Joseph Schildkraut who played her father.

Jack Kerouac, inspired by his travels around the United States, wrote the popular novel On The Road, in all of three weeks.

The New York Times.

VOL. CIV..No. 35,445.

Entered as Second-Class Matter,
Post Office, New York, N. Y.

Copyright, 1955, by The New York Times Company.

NEW YORK, WEDNESDAY, FEBRUARY 9, 1955.

Times Square, New York 36, N. Y.
Telephone LAckawanna 4-1000

FIVE CENTS

BULGANIN IS PREMIER AS MALENKOV RESIGNS, BUT KHRUSHCHEV IS VIEWED AS REAL LEADER; MOLOTOV, WARNING U. S., CLAIMS H-BOMB LEAD

EISENHOWER ASKS 7 BILLION PROGRAM TO BUILD SCHOOLS

Message to Congress Urges Federal-State-Local Plan for Grants and Loans

DEMOCRATS DECRY SCOPE

Leaders Denounce Proposal as 'Makeshift' — Demand Far Larger Expenditures

Text of the President's message is printed on Page 20.

By W. H. LAWRENCE
Special to The New York Times.

WASHINGTON, Feb. 8.—President Eisenhower proposed today a three-year $7,000,000,000 Federal-state-local school construction program.

He asked Congress to make available $220,000,000 in Federal grants and about $900,000,000 in loans to meet a current deficit of more than 300,000 school classrooms.

The message went to a Democratic-controlled Congress. Leaders in the education field in both the Senate and the House called it inadequate and "makeshift."

Some critics declared the Presidential program would be ineffective in about one-fourth of the states, which have constitutional limitations on incurring or increasing debts.

Indirectly, President Eisenhower also suggested higher pay for school teachers, but his message advanced no concrete proposals on this. He said low pay was a factor in the shortage of teachers, which he declared was "less obvious but ultimately more dangerous than the classroom shortage."

"Because of the magnitude of the job, but more fundamentally because of the undeniable importance of free education to a free way of life, the means we take to provide our children with proper classrooms must be weighed most carefully," the President said, continuing:

"The phrase 'free education' is a deliberate choice. For unless education continues to be free—free in its response to local com-

Continued on Page 20, Column 1

A. E. C. WON'T DROP DIXON-YATES PACT

2-1 Vote Disclosed by Board —Congress Plea Rejected

By WILLIAM M. BLAIR
Special to The New York Times.

WASHINGTON, Feb 8.—By a 2 to 1 vote, the Atomic Energy Commission has turned down a Democratic demand that the Dixon-Yates private power contract be canceled.

The split vote, taken on Saturday, followed the lead of President Eisenhower, who asserted three days before the vote that he would not withdraw the controversial contract to feed private power into the Tennessee Valley Authority.

Lewis L. Strauss, A. E. C. chairman, and Dr. Willard Frank Libby, a new member, voted to stick by the contract. Thomas E. Murray voted for cancellation.

As Mr. Strauss disclosed the decision today, Mr. Murray went before the Joint Congressional Committee on Atomic Energy to renew his charge that the Dixon-Yates controversy had interfered with the commission's primary job of developing atomic weapons and peacetime use of the atom.

His main concern, he testified, was "whether we will in the future maintain our present position of world leadership in the nuclear field." He concluded:

"The attention the commission today gives to making policy on the

Continued on Page 37, Column 6

President Appeals For Satellite People

Special to The New York Times.

WASHINGTON, Feb. 8.—President Eisenhower urged tonight a continuing effort to "intensify the will for freedom in the satellite countries behind the Iron Curtain."

He spoke from the White House on a closed-circuit television program in behalf of the Crusade for Freedom, which operates Radio Free Europe and the Free Europe Press. The crusade hopes to raise $10,000,-000 this year.

He took no cognizance of the resignation of Georgi M. Malenkov as Soviet Premier and his replacement by Marshal Nikolai A. Bulganin. His prepared text was left unchanged after the Moscow developments had become known.

The President emphasized that the masses imprisoned behind the Iron Curtain would remain potential deterrents to

Continued on Page 6, Column 6

HOUSE, 394-4, BACKS DRAFT EXTENSION

Four-Year Continuance Finds the Democrats Unanimous —New Features Added

By C. P. TRUSSELL
Special to The New York Times.

WASHINGTON, Feb. 8.—The House of Representatives voted 394 to 4 today to continue the draft for four years.

This extension, the fourth since 1940, was urged by President Eisenhower. The Administration concluded that the international situation generally required the maintenance of the United States armed forces of 2,850,000 officers and men. Such a force, experience had shown, could not be mobilized through voluntary enlistments.

The four who voted against draft extension were Republicans. Democrats supported the move unanimously. The four dissenters were Representatives Noah M. Mason of Illinois, Usher L. Burdick of North Dakota; Clare E. Hoffman of Michigan, and Wint Smith of Kansas.

The extension measure now goes to the Senate. There it is expected to win approval, with its opponents again on the Republican side. No one predicted that the extension would not be approved finally in Congress long before the present draft authorization expires June 30.

In granting the continuation of Selective Service the House added new features to the law. They included:

¶If the selective draft continued it should include all the benefits and allowance given to present draftees to aid their dependents. Also continued for four

Continued on Page 16, Column 4

Private Atom Reactor In This Area Planned

By PETER KIHSS

A plan for the nation's first nuclear reactor entirely owned and operated by private industry was announced here yesterday by the American Machine and Foundry Company. It would use radiations for confidential experiments for co-operating companies.

Gen. Walter Bedell Smith, retired, vice chairman of the foundry concern's board, said invitations to join the scheme had gone to companies in the fields of electronics, petroleum, food, pharmaceutical and chemical products, ceramics, rubber, metals, textiles, agriculture, machinery and others.

The project would occupy 250 acres somewhere in the New York area. A so-called swimming pool reactor would use uranium fuel surrounded by water serving as a moderator, cooler and shield.

The atomic furnace would

Continued on Page 19, Column 3

MIGHT IS STRESSED

Foreign Minister Says Soviet Force Is on Par With West

Excerpts from Molotov speech are printed on Page 6.

Special to The New York Times.

MOSCOW, Feb. 8.—Claiming superiority for the Soviet Union in hydrogen weapons, Foreign Minister Vyacheslav M. Molotov delivered to the United States today a warning of the strength of the world Communist forces.

His declaration reiterating the might of the Communist camp was made at a joint session of the Supreme Soviet, the national legislature of the Soviet Union. He spoke immediately following the change in Soviet Premiership that placed Marshal Nikolai A. Bulganin at the head of the Government.

[According to The Associated Press, the Soviet Parliament resumed its joint session at 2 A. M. Wednesday, New York time, and immediately began debating Mr. Molotov's speech.]

Laughter and applause greeted Mr. Molotov's taunts at, and defiance of, the United States, which he singled out as the leader of the "aggressive" Western coalition. He also called on the United States once again to evacuate Formosa.

Balance 'Quite Established'

In one of his most outspoken passages, Mr. Molotov declared that it must be understood that the balance of forces between the Soviet Union and the United States had been "quite established."

Comparing the two and taking into account the vast human and material resources of this country, the strength of its allies, and the justness of its cause, Mr. Molotov declared, "it will become clear that the Soviet Union is no weaker than the United States."

As for atomic strength, he said in an earlier passage that "the aggressive circles of the United States miscalculated again." They thought it would take ten or fifteen years for the Soviet Union to catch up with the United States, he asserted, but "the Soviet people have achieved such success that not the Soviet Union but the United States finds itself in the position of being behind."

In thus belittling and challeng-

Continued on Page 6, Column 4

CHANGE IN HIGH SOVIET COUNCILS: The scene yesterday in Supreme Soviet at Moscow after Marshal Nikolai A. Bulganin was elected to succeed Georgi M. Malenkov. Front row, from left, are Lazar M. Kaganovich, Marshal Bulganin, Nikita S. Khrushchev, Mr. Malenkov and Marshal Kliment E. Voroshilov. At far right in rear is Anastas I. Mikoyan.

Associated Press Radiophoto

SENATE UNIT VOTES FORMOSA TREATY

Committee Ballot Is 11 to 2 —Whole Chamber May Adopt Pact by Tomorrow Night

By WILLIAM S. WHITE
Special to The New York Times.

WASHINGTON, Feb. 8.—The Senate Foreign Relations Committee approved today the defense treaty with Nationalist China on Formosa. The vote was 11 to 2.

The committee's chairman, Senator Walter F. George, Democrat of Georgia, will take the pact to the Senate tomorrow in the hope that it can be cleared there by Thursday night.

Failing final action by then, he said he could be none before "the week after next.

Beginning Friday, the Senate, by old custom, will take an unofficial holiday from all important business for ten days while Republican speakers celebrate the birthday of Abraham Lincoln.

Mr. George recognized the possibility of delay, though he spoke out against it as undesirable in the light of the changing of com-

Continued on Page 14, Column 3

Khrushchev Comes to Fore In Compromise on Bulganin

The following article is by a member of The Times staff who is a specialist on Soviet affairs.

By HARRY SCHWARTZ

Nikita S. Khrushchev appeared to have emerged yesterday as the most powerful single person in the Soviet Union, the heir to Stalin's mantle.

Stalin ruled the Soviet Union during most of his reign without holding any Government post, content to be general secretary of the Communist party.

It was as first secretary, the new name for general secretary of the party that Mr. Khrushchev nominated Nikolai A. Bulganin to be Premier. But the largest ovation went to the first secretary, not to the new Premier.

Even before yesterday, Mr. Khrushchev had given abundant testimony that he, not some amorphous "collective leadership," is the leader.

It may be that his power is subject still to the majority of his colleagues in the Presidium of the Central Committee or to the will of the army leaders. But since last December the public image has been of a Mr. Khru-

Continued on Page 4, Column 5

This article is by a reporter of The Times who returned last fall after five years in Moscow.

By HARRISON E. SALISBURY

Marshal Nikolai A. Bulganin almost certainly is a compromise choice as Soviet Premier. He apparently represents a coalition of the party forces of Nikita S. Khrushchev and the army group headed by Marshal Georgi G. Zhukov.

The heralded showdown between Mr. Khrushchev and former Premier Georgi M. Malenkov has occurred more quickly than this observer had expected.

Apparently the army threw its backing to Mr. Khrushchev.

Regardless of the fire and vigor of Foreign Minister Vyacheslav M. Molotov's address yesterday, Soviet power in the international arena will remain weakened for a considerable time. The crisis that resulted in the execution of Deputy Premier Lavrenti P. Beria left little outward signs of cracks in the Kremlin wall. However, it seemed certain the Soviet Government would be a longer time in over-

Continued on Page 4, Column 7

MOSCOW SHAKE-UP

Malenkov Avows Guilt for Shortcomings in Agriculture

Texts of Malenkov statement and Khrushchev speech, Page 2.

By CLIFTON DANIEL
Special to The New York Times.

MOSCOW, Feb. 8.—On nomination by Nikita S. Khrushchev, first secretary of the Communist party, Marshal Nikolai A. Bulganin became head of the Soviet Government today. He replaced Georgi M. Malenkov, who had been Premier since the death of Stalin March 5, 1953.

Reproaching himself for inadequate leadership, Mr. Malenkov offered his resignation this afternoon to the Supreme Soviet, national legislature of the Soviet Union.

[News of the resignation was published in a Late City Extra of The New York Times on Tuesday.]

Mr. Malenkov said he would fulfill "with greatest conscientiousness" the duties that would now be assigned to him. Those duties were not stated at once.

In resigning Mr. Malenkov took on himself the "guilt and responsibility" for the present state of Soviet agriculture, which has been roundly criticized by Mr. Khrushchev.

To Support Party Line

Mr. Malenkov also proclaimed his understanding of the Communist party line that forced development of heavy industry must be the basis for increasing agricultural production and all other branches of the Soviet economy. That line has just been re-emphasized with new firmness by the Central Committee of the party and its propaganda organs.

The Central Committee's decision, taken in the last days of January on the initiative of Mr. Khrushchev, gave orders for still further efforts to increase Soviet agricultural output and Mr. Malenkov said today the decision had revealed to him his shortcomings as an administrator.

The change in the Premiership, accomplished in barely ten minutes of swift political action, left two major questions unanswered for the moment:

What will be Mr. Malenkov's future position and who will be Defense Minister of the Soviet

Continued on Page 2, Column 3

U. S. SEES STRUGGLE AS FAR FROM OVER

Experts on Moscow Conclude It Is Too Early to Decide About Effect of Change

By JAMES RESTON
Special to The New York Times.

WASHINGTON, Feb. 8.—The United States Government, concentrating on its plans for blocking Communist expansion, refused to comment today on the battle of the dictators in the Soviet Union.

The capital hummed with speculation all day. But after hours of cooperative guesswork the official experts on the Soviet Union decided to let events interpret the Moscow events.

Ambassador Charles E. Bohlen's first official cablegram on the news came in at 7:49 A. M. It was discussed briefly by Secretary of State Dulles at his 9:15 staff conference.

Thereafter the official advisers on the Soviet Union were instructed to analyze the published facts. Their conclusions—far less dogmatic than most opinion in the capital—were as follows:

¶There is trouble in the Soviet "paradise." Premier Georgi M. Malenkov was dismissed not because everything was going well; the dramatic news was a sign, not of Communist strength, but of weakness.

¶Nikita S. Khrushchev, the Communist party boss, is probably the most powerful figure for the moment. But the fierce struggle over succession, always a problem in Russia, even in the time of the czars, is far from over.

¶It is too early to reach any

Continued on Page 7, Column 1

TUNIS LEADER AIDS PINAY ON CABINET

U.S. Bipartisan Idea Adapted by Premier-Designate

By LANSING WARREN
Special to The New York Times.

PARIS, Feb. 8.—Premier-designate Antoine Pinay obtained some help today from the Tunisian Premier in his efforts to form a French Cabinet.

After their conference the Tunisian Premier, Tahar ben Ammar, said he had found that he and M. Pinay had similar ideas and that "I hope we shall continue the negotiations that were started with the Government of Mendès-France." M. ben Ammar declared that he was going full of optimism to Tunis to inform the Bey, Sidi Mohammed el Amin, about the consultations.

The statement will be used by M. Pinay in trying to convince the party groups that his Cabinet can handle the crisis in Tunisia.

In dealing with those groups today M. Pinay obtained support from M. Mendès-France's Radical group, but met a rebuff from the Socialists. The Radical executive body voted, 81 to 67, to participate in the Pinay Cabinet. This assures him of about two-thirds of the seventy-six Radical Deputies, who never vote in unison.

The Socialists, through Christian Pineau, former Minister of Finance, declined the invitation to join the Cabinet. M. Pinay had

Continued on Page 11, Column 2

All Civilians Off Upper Tachen; First U. S. Ship Returns to Formosa

American and Chinese military personnel, in the foreground, observe the evacuation operation on Upper Tachen Island.

Associated Press Wirephoto via Radio from Taipei

Special to The New York Times.

KEELUNG, Formosa, Wednesday, Feb. 9.—The first United States Navy ship with Chinese Nationalist civilians evacuated from the Tachen Islands docked here this morning. She was an 8,000-ton transport with 3,816 civilians on board. Vice Admiral Alfred M. Pride, Commander of the United States Seventh Fleet, announced last night that the evacuation of civilians from Upper Tachen Island was completed at 5:17 P. M. yesterday. [In Washington, the Navy announced early Wednesday that the Seventh Fleet had reported that the last "organized group" of civilians had been evacuated from South Tachen Island, The

Continued on Page 14, Column 5

U. S. Plane Downed By Reds in Tachens

By The Associated Press.

WITH UNITED STATES SEVENTH FLEET, in the Tachens, Wednesday, Feb. 9.— Red anti-aircraft batteries shot down a United States AD Skyraider plane twenty miles southwest of the Tachen Islands today, the Navy said.

The pilot and two crew members of the carrier-based plane were rescued by the destroyer Isbell, the Navy said.

WASHINGTON, Feb. 8 (UP)—The Navy said tonight that one of its patrol planes received three small holes in one wing. The small holes were caused by Chinese Communist anti-aircraft fire during the Tachens evacuation today, but returned safely from its mission.

The Navy released a terse message from Vice Admiral Alfred M. Pride:

"Vice Admiral Pride reported during the night that three small holes were inflicted in one wing during inspection after returning to base."

The Big Four conference that opened July 18, 1955, in Geneva, Switzerland, was ill-fated and dashed many high hopes.

Eisenhower and Bulganin met at the summit conference in Geneva. The results were not encouraging, but the two men kept up a fruitful personal contact.

Fess Parker, Buddy Ebsen and Hans Conreid in Davy Crockett, King of the Wild Frontier.

As a result of Disney's movie and his TV program that followed, youngsters everywhere were wearing Davy Crockett hats.

The New York Times.

LATE CITY EDITION
Becoming cloudy, warmer today.
Partly cloudy and cold tomorrow.
Temperature Range Today—Max., 46; Min., 34
Temperatures Yesterday—Max., 42; Min., 26
Full U. S. Weather Bureau Report, Page 35

Copyright, 1955, by The New York Times Company

VOL. CIV. No. 35,446. Entered as Second-Class Matter. Post Office, New York, N. Y. NEW YORK, THURSDAY, FEBRUARY 10, 1955. Times Square, New York 36, N. Y. Telephone Lackawanna 4-1000 FIVE CENTS

A.F.L. AND C.I.O. WILL MERGE, ENDING 20-YEAR LABOR SPLIT; MEANY WILL HEAD NEW BODY

15 MILLION UNITING

Formula Creates Place for Industrial Unions —Raiding Ban Set

Texts of the merger agreement and statement, Page 20.

By A. H. RASKIN
Special to The New York Times

MIAMI BEACH, Feb. 9.—A detailed formula for labor unity was approved today after twenty years of civil war.

The pact made it certain that the 15,000,000 members of the American Federation of Labor and the Congress of Industrial Organizations would come under one banner by the end of this year.

Every problem that could block a merger was overcome in the unity plan. Even the question of who would head the pooled organization was settled. He will be George Meany, now president of the A. F. L.

His opposite number in the C. I. O., Walter P. Reuther, announced that he would be happy to step aside in Mr. Meany's favor. William F. Schnitzler, secretary-treasurer of the 'A. F. L., will occupy the same post in the new group.

There was no formal name given as yet to the merged organizations. But the thirty-four unions now in the C. I. O. will go into it as a special department to be known as a Council of Industrial Organizations.

To Preserve Initials

This will enable the group to preserve the initials that were used in the unionisation of steel, automobile, rubber and other mass production industries in the early years of the split.

The ticklish issue of interunion raiding was settled through adoption of a joint declaration that the integrity of every A. F. L. and C. I. O. union would be preserved after the merger.

The new organization's constitution will contain a specific declaration that affiliated unions are to respect the established bargaining relationship of sister unions. It will call on all unions to avoid stealing members from one another.

The precise machinery for enforcing this anti-raiding provision was not specified. However, both sides agreed that "appropriate machinery" was to be established. Its nature was left to the committees charged with drafting a constitution.

In the meantime both groups will seek to get more unions to subscribe on a voluntary basis to the existing no-raid agreements between the A. F. L. and C. I. O. Seventy-seven of the 111 unions in the federation already have bound themselves to eschew poaching. On the C. I. O. side thirty out of thirty-four have signed.

These pacts are scheduled to expire at the end of this year. Part of the merger understanding is that the voluntary ban on

Continued on Page 20, Column 6

President Urges School Plan In Face of Congress Critics

Delivers 600-Word Defense of Program at Opening of His Press Conference —Hill Leads Opposition in Senate

By RUSSELL BAKER
Special to The New York Times

WASHINGTON, Feb. 9.—President Eisenhower used his news conference today as a sounding board to argue for passage of his $7,000,000,000 school construction program.

This program, he said, is vital if the nation's youth is not to be "robbed" of the kind of education needed to prepare it for responsible citizenship.

The President underscored his personal sense of urgency about the plan by making a 600-word announcement before questions were permitted. For a Presidential press conference, it was a long speech.

It came against a background of Congressional criticism of the program. The plan puts much of the burden for beginning new school building on state and local authorities. President Eisen-

hower defended this approach as consistent with constitutional principles.

Senator Lister Hill, Democrat of Alabama, is in the van of Capitol Hill critics. He is chairman of the Senate Labor and Public Welfare Committee, which will be the first to take up the legislation.

Last night Senator Hill said it offered only "interminable delay on the one hand or a meager dole on the other." Elaborating this criticism today, he said it would give only about $65,000,000 a year to file an appeal with the Federal Court of Appeals for the District of Columbia. Such an appeal is permitted by law within sixty days.

This he called "a very paltry sum." Senator Hill, supported by twenty-nine other Senators, has introduced his own bill. It would give the states a direct

Continued on Page 19, Column 1

BIG 'BONUSES' PAID FOR HOME LOANS

Queens Grand Jury to Study 'Funding Corporation' Plans That Cost 40 to 65%

By PHILIP BENJAMIN

A practice by which loan companies can legally extract from 40 to 65 per cent in "bonuses" and interest will come under the scrutiny of a Queens grand jury today.

District Attorney T. Vincent Quinn and Assistant District Attorney Lawrence Peirea described yesterday the "gimmick" that has enmeshed 8,000 home owners in high repayment rates and loss of certain Federal income tax deductions.

According to the two officials, "funding corporations" in the last year have sprung up with enticing advertisements. These promise home owners pressed for cash a quick loan secured by a second mortgage.

When the applicants sign up, they find that they have been incorporated. The loan company takes care of all the details, setting up a dummy corporation with three subscribers—usually employees of the company. In some cases, applicants receive impressive-looking stock certificates.

Because under state law there

Continued on Page 25, Column 3

WILSON ADAMANT ON MANPOWER CUT

Tells Senators Formosa Case Does Not Affect Program —Democrats Disagree

By ALLEN DRURY
Special to The New York Times

WASHINGTON, Feb. 9.—The Senate Armed Services Committee heard Secretary of Defense Charles E. Wilson defend the Administration's military manpower cuts today.

Democratic members made it clear they were not impressed. Their comments foreshadowed a possible attempt to force the Pentagon to modify plans to reduce the armed forces from approximately 3,000,000 men now to 2,850,000 by mid-1956.

The Secretary appeared at a day-long closed session of the Senate committee. At the same time, a House Armed Services subcommittee heard an outspoken opponent of the manpower cutback, Gen. Matthew B. Ridgway, The Army Chief of Staff testified on the Reserve program.

He described the Reserves as "in an unacceptable state of readiness, unable to reach combat effectiveness within any period of time likely to be available to us."

Senator Richard B. Russell, the committee chairman, quoted Sec-

Continued on Page 15, Column 5

DIXON-YATES WINS APPROVAL OF S.E.C.; COURT FIGHT LIKELY

Stock Proposal Is Backed by 4-1 Vote—No Injury to Public Interest Found

By WILLIAM M. BLAIR
Special to The New York Times

WASHINGTON, Feb. 9.—The Securities and Exchange Commission approved today 'he initial financing of the Dixon-Yates contract. The vote was 4 to 1.

This was another victory for the Administration and Dixon-Yates in the fight over the contract to pump private power into the Tennessee Valley Authority.

The commission found no basis for deciding that a proposed common stock issue by Dixon-Yates was contrary to the interest of the public, investors or power consumers. Opponents of the contract had argued that it was.

The agreement was negotiated by the Atomic Energy Commission at the direction of President Eisenhower. The foes viewed the S. E. C. ruling as expected. Their next step appeared to be a court appeal.

The State of Tennessee and a number of public power bodies in the T. V. A. area are expected to file an appeal with the Federal Court of Appeals for the District of Columbia. Such an appeal is permitted by law within sixty days.

Strauss to Answer Murray

A further airing of the friction within the Atomic Energy Commission on the contract will come tomorrow afternoon. Lewis L. Strauss, commission chairman, will testify then at his own request before the Joint Congressional Committee on Atomic Energy.

Mr. Strauss will reply to his fellow member, Thomas E. Murray, who charged again yesterday that Dixon-Yates was impeding the functioning of the commission. Mr. Strauss made the request in a letter to Senator Clinton P. Anderson, Democrat of New Mexico and joint committee chairman.

Mr. Murray's testimony "discloses a number of points on which I feel that your committee should be correctly informed," Mr. Strauss wrote.

The S. E. C. specifically authorized the sale by the Mississippi Valley Generating Company of $5,500,000 worth of common stock. The company was set up by Middle South Utilities, Inc., and the Southern Company to construct a private steam plant at West Memphis, Ark.

The plant would be built under the $107,250,000 twenty-five year contract with the Atomic Energy Commission. It would provide the T. V. A. with "replacement" power for about 600,000 kilowatts that the authority now supplies to the Paducah, Ky., atomic installation.

Middle South, headed by Edgar H. Dixon, will take about 79 per cent of the common stock. The Southern Company, whose chairman is Eugene A. Yates, will subscribe to the remaining 21 per cent.

Mr. Dixon and Mr. Yates noted

Continued on Page 19, Column 3

ZHUKOV IS SOVIET'S DEFENSE CHIEF; BULGANIN STRESSES RED CHINA TIE; EISENHOWER VIEWS SHIFTS CALMLY

IN 1945, COMRADES IN ARMS: General Eisenhower and Marshal Georgi K. Zhukov, new Soviet Minister of Defense, in Leningrad, which they visited at the end of the war.
Associated Press

SENATE APPROVES FORMOSA TREATY

Vote Is 64-6—Reservations by Morse to State Limit on Aid to Chiang Defeated

By WILLIAM S. WHITE
Special to The New York Times

WASHINGTON, Feb. 9.—The Senate approved tonight this country's defense treaty with Nationalist China on Formosa. The vote was 64 to 6.

The Senate acted after sharply rejecting two efforts to make reservations in the pact that would have required new negotiations with Generalissimo Chiang Kai-shek's regime.

Both proposed alterations were sponsored by Senator Wayne Morse, independent of Oregon.

The first was defeated 57 to 11. It would have stipulated that the treaty was not to give support to Nationalist claims to ultimate sovereignty over Formosa. The international legal status of which has not been fixed.

The second was defeated 60 to 10. It would have invalidated a section by which the United States could be pledged, subject to some subsequent treaty alteration, to help defend not only Formosa and the Pescadores islands but other Chinese National-ist territories.

The Senate chose to put in limitations on the United States commitment not in this manner but through "understandings" held by the State Department and by the backers of the treaty in the Senate to be morally binding on the Administration. These understandings were separate from the treaty text.

The decisive vote by which the Senate consented to ratification found these Senators standing

Continued on Page 14, Column 3

President Praises Zhukov, Recalling War Friendship

By JAMES RESTON
Special to The New York Times

WASHINGTON, Feb. 9.—President Eisenhower today discussed the Kremlin shake-up as calmly and objectively as a man speculating on some vaguely disturbing development on another planet. He attributed the Moscow change of command to internal dissatisfaction.

He said this country should be alert and continue building the free world's strength as a basis

Transcript and summary of the news conference, Page 18.

for a just and lasting peace. But he saw no reason for any basic change in the nation's policies.

In none of his previous fifty-nine Presidential news conferences had the President been more moderate or composed. He refused to prophesy what the struggle for personal power in Moscow would mean in the future, but for the time being he rejected almost all the ominous interpretations placed on yesterday's events.

Facing a capacity crowd of 230 reporters and a half-dozen television eyes, he told one questioner the rise of Nikita S. Khrushchev, Marshal Nikolai A. Bulganin and Marshal Georgi K. Zhukov did not necessarily mean a tougher policy toward the United States.

No Proof on Bomb Claim

Similarly, he told another questioner that there was certainly no proof that the Soviet Union had surpassed the United States in the production of hydrogen weapons—a claim made yesterday by the Soviet Foreign Minister, Vyacheslav M. Molotov.

And finally, he talked almost wistfully about his wartime "good friend," Marshal Zhukov, who was appointed today Defense Minister of the Soviet Union.

The President walked into his news conference on the fourth floor of the old State Department building at 10:31 A. M., wearing a gray suit, blue and white figured tie and white shirt. He began his conference by saying he was going to Georgia tomorrow with the Secretary of the Treasury, George M. Humphrey. He made some general statements on the Soviet changes and on his education bill, and then asked for questions.

The second one was on whether the President regarded the elevation of Marshal Zhukov as indicating a stronger defense policy toward this country.

He replied that he could not interpret what the Russians had in mind in elevating Marshal Zhukov, but that the wartime Zhukov was a competent soldier. No man, the President said, could have conducted the military campaigns Marshal Zhukov did, or explained them so lucidly in terms of his own strength and weakness, without being a "well-trained, splendid military leader."

"He and I," the President continued, "developed personally a practice of getting along and seeing eye to eye on a number of local problems in Berlin, and so

Continued on Page 2, Column 3

U. S. Won't Avenge Tachen Plane Loss

By HENRY R. LIEBERMAN
Special to The New York Times

TAIPEI, Formosa, Feb. 9.—The commander of the United States Seventh Fleet said today that the Navy would not retaliate for the shooting down of a plane along the East China coast.

The plane, a Douglas Skyraider from the carrier Wasp, crash-landed in the sea at 10:45 A. M. today four miles west of the Tachen Islands after having been hit by Communist anti-aircraft fire. Its three crew members, who escaped with minor cuts and bruises, were picked up by two Chinese Nationalist vessels.

Vice Admiral Alfred M. Pride made the statement in reply to a press question from Taipei asking him what the Navy proposed to do "in view of indications that the Communists will not be allowed to push Americans around." The

Continued on Page 10, Column 3

NEW PREMIER ACTS

Malenkov Made Deputy and Also Minister of Power Stations

Text of the Bulganin address is printed on Page 4.

By CLIFTON DANIEL
Special to The New York Times

MOSCOW, Feb. 9.—A professional soldier took command of the Soviet Union's defense establishment today. At the same time the nation's new Premier proclaimed defiance of United States "threats' and "aggression."

Marshal Georgi K. Zhukov, three times a Hero of the Soviet Union, a popular and influential personality in the Soviet Communist party and state, was appointed Minister of Defense in succession to Marshal Nikolai A. Bulganin, who became Premier yesterday.

Until today Marshal Zhukov, along with Marshal Alexander M. Vasilevsky, was a Deputy Minister of Defense.

With the appointment of Marshal Zhukov, Premier Bulganin named his predecessor, Georgi M. Malenkov, to the post of Deputy Premier and Minister of Electric Power Stations, a responsible but not a top-ranking position. Mr. Malenkov retained his seat in the Presidium of the Central Committee of the Communist party, the supreme leadership organization of the Soviet Union.

No Other Cabinet Change

In the ministerial post, Mr. Malenkov replaced Andrei S. Pavlenko, a professional engineer known for his work on major canals.

No other changes in the Government were made by the new Premier, who, still wearing his khaki Army uniform with gleaming golden shoulder boards, stood in the floodlighted Supreme Soviet chamber today and proclaimed his loyalty to the fixed policy of the Communist leadership and his intention to carry it through.

No part of the new Premier's inauguration address was applauded more enthusiastically or longer than his declaration of the Soviet Union's solidarity with Communist China in its dispute over Formosa.

China "can count upon the help of its faithful friend, the great Soviet people," Premier Bulganin declared.

That declaration was underscored by vigorous handclapping. When the gust of applause seemed to be dying down, it was picked up and renewed and went on for half a minute.

The Soviet Army, the Premier declared, has shown its superiority in skill and weapons and will hold its supremacy. Army, Navy and Air Force, he added, are ready to fulfill any task given to them by the party and state.

While the theme of defiance and confidence in the strength of the Communist powers welled

Continued on Page 5, Column 1

PINAY MEETS SNAG IN CABINET SEARCH

French Leader Unable to Get Support of 2 Key Factions —Decision Due Today

By LANSING WARREN
Special to The New York Times

PARIS, Feb. 9.—Former Premier Antoine Pinay seemed today to have little hope of forming a new French Cabinet. It was expected that tomorrow he would have to tell President René Coty he had found the task impossible.

Divergences between the parties appeared to have widened since the fall of Premier Pierre Mendès-France. It is the refusal of the Popular Republicans to join the Cabinet that is creating the greatest obstacle for M. Pinay, who is a member of the conservative Independent party.

Georges Bidault and Robert Schuman, leaders of the Popular Republican party, a Catholic group, favored M. Pinay but could not swing it to his support. The members would not assure M. Pinay they would give him outside support or even vote for his endorsement in the National Assembly.

Moreover, M. Pinay had not yet obtained backing from the Gaullist group, which was suspicious that he would revert to a

Continued on Page 6, Column 3

130 Negro Families Forced Out Of Johannesburg Under Guard

By LEONARD INGALLS
Special to The New York Times

JOHANNESBURG, South Africa, Feb. 9.—The forced removal of natives from their homes in Johannesburg began today.

The transfer of the first 130 Negro families from their slum dwellings to a new Government housing development beyond the city limits was carried out under close surveillance of 2,000 heavily armed policemen.

Although disturbances had been feared, there were no incidents and no arrests.

The resettlement of the natives to areas outside Johannesburg represents the application of the National Government's policy of apartheid, or separation of white and native communities.

The law under which the resettlement is taking place was introduced in Parliament last year by Dr. Hendrik F. Verwoerd, Minister of Native Affairs.

The first group of native fami-

lies had been scheduled to be relocated Saturday, but the operation was advanced three days in a surprise move to thwart demonstrations.

This step followed a ban yesterday on public gatherings in the Johannesburg area for the next twenty days because of apprehension over the possibility that violence might result.

Notices were served last night on 150 families in the native community of Sophiatown to be ready at 6 o'clock this morning to leave their homes and move to the new Government community at Meadowlands, eleven miles from the center of Johannesburg and four miles more distant than Sophiatown.

At 4 A. M. detachments of

Continued on Page 6, Column 5

Small Taxis Safer, Police Study Shows

By JOSEPH C. INGRAHAM

In its first evaluation of small taxicabs the Hack Bureau of the Police Department has reported that the stock models have had fewer accidents than jumbo-size cabs.

Since stock models were authorized last summer to compete with specially built taxicabs, they reportedly have rolled up an impressive safety record. The accident rate is 40 per cent lower than for the bigger cabs, and "short-stop" injuries, the bane of the jumbo cab operators, are the exception, it was said.

However, because the Hack Bureau report lacked statistical depth and, in Police Commissioner Francis W. H. Adams' opinion, drew unwarranted conclusions, he has refused to accept it. He has called for a more factual study.

The Commissioner's demand for more facts and less opinion

Continued on Page 39, Column 5

SEALING THE BARGAIN: George Meany, left, president of A. F. L., and Walter P. Reuther, head of C. I. O., after they announced yesterday that union groups had agreed on merger.
Associated Press Wirephoto

Mary Martin in her historic portrayal of Peter Pan, which also starred Cyril Ritchard as Captain Hook.

Lucille Ball was still getting into hilarious predicaments and viewers continued to tune in week after week.

"All the News That's Fit to Print"

The New York Times.

LATE CITY EDITION
Chance of some showers and mild today, tonight and tomorrow.
Temperature Range Today—Max., 65; Min., 47
Temperature Yesterday—Max., 66; Min., 43
Full U.S. Weather Bureau Report, Page 50

Copyright, 1955, by The New York Times Company.

VOL. CIV. No. 35,501.

Entered as Second-Class Matter.
Post Office, New York, N. Y.

NEW YORK, WEDNESDAY, APRIL 6, 1955.

Times Square, New York 36, N. Y.
Telephone LAckawanna 4-1000

FIVE CENTS

MANPOWER SLASH IN MARINES, NAVY BACKED WITH 'IFS'

Carney and Shepherd Call Reduced Budget Adequate if No Emergency Occurs

DEMOCRATS CONCERNED

But They Are Assured Corps' Ability to Strike Quickly in an Attack Won't Suffer

By C. P. TRUSSELL
Special to The New York Times.

WASHINGTON, April 5—Top uniformed officers of the Navy and Marine Corps supported the President's reduced armed services budget today. At points, they appeared to be salting loyalty to the Commander in Chief with reservations.

The $34,000,000,000 budget for the fiscal year starting July 1, it seemed, was all right as of now. It was evident, however, that if the "international situation worsened, more money would be requested in a hurry.

Those testifying before a Senate Appropriations subcommittee were Gen. Lemuel C. Shepherd Jr., Commandant of the Marine Corps, and Admiral Robert B. Carney, Chief of Naval Operations.

Meanwhile, more civilian heads of the armed services continued to support the reduced budget. They included Charles E. Thomas, Secretary of the Navy, and Harold E. Talbott, Secretary of the Air Force.

A spokesman for Robert T. Stevens, Secretary of the Army, is expected to back the other civilian leaders tomorrow. Mr. Stevens is out of the country.

Frank Answers Sought

Democrats of the subcommittee, which is headed by Senator Dennis Chavez, Democrat of New Mexico, continued to search for blunt answers from the uniformed officers as to how they felt about the military cuts.

The Democrats do not like proposed cuts in Marine Corps forces. General Shepherd was asked how he squared his support of a reduction in the armed forces with the mission of the Marine Corps to be the first to fight in case of an attack.

"It is manifest," he replied, "that reductions of the magnitude with which we are confronted [a cut from 215,000 to 193,000] involve some sacrifice.

"However, we are determined that the sacrifice will not be made in readiness of our basic striking forces. The reduction will be absorbed primarily by disbanding certain reinforcing combat and logistic units and by reducing the manning levels of other supporting units.

"Operationally, the effect of these actions will be to diminish somewhat the staying power of

Continued on Page 14, Column 7

JERSEY SEIZES 62 IN HOT-ROD TRAP

Racers Caught on Unlighted Road Used as Speedway

Special to The New York Times.

CHATSWORTH, N. J., April 5—It's a rare man who can lay hands on a will-o'-the-wisp, especially if it's motor-powered. Yet that's what State Trooper Leonard Miller did under a bright moon last night.

For weeks now, nocturnal travelers through the lonely pine lands of Burlington County have been frightened almost off the highway by dabs of light whooshing past them at breakneck speed.

The police, who had their suspicions about the souped-up will-o'-the-wisps, were hard put to track them down. One night the reports came from here, the next from there. Always the apparitions appeared from unlighted stretches along Route 72, which runs from the center of the state to the coast. Among other attractions for hot-rodders it has a fourteen-mile stretch that is almost ruler-straight.

Last night the state troopers set a trap along a section that was without highway lamps but bright in the moonlight.

Trooper Miller, on watch near the Pennsylvania Railroad overpass, heard, at about 10:30 P.M., a buzz and then a roar. Out of the west came four blobs of light, spanning the two-lane roadway.

Trooper Miller stepped onto the

Continued on Page 33, Column 5

Harriman and Wagner Plan Own City-State Fiscal Study

Financing by a Private Foundation May Be Sought for Project Ignored by the Legislature, Mayor Announces

By CHARLES G. BENNETT

Governor Harriman and Mayor Wagner will go ahead soon with the appointment of a committee to make a long-range study of state-city relationships. It is possible that funds will be sought from a private foundation for the study.

Mayor Wagner announced this yesterday as he discussed the city's fiscal situation in an interview in his office, 63 Park Row, and later before 300 members of the Bond Club at a luncheon at 120 Broadway. He forecast that Republicans as well as Democrats would be invited to serve on the fiscal study committee.

The Mayor expressed hope that the committee would find a formula for taking the whole city-state financial problem "entirely out of politics." He predicted that the prestige of the study committee members would be so great that the state Legislature could not afford to ignore its suggestions.

At this session just ended, the Legislature failed to take any action creating a legislative commission to make the statecity financial study. Mayor Wagner, backed by the Governor, had called for such a survey in an effort to end the recurring crises that send the Mayor and his aides to Albany each year seeking state aid and authorization for new taxes.

At his interview yesterday Mayor Wagner commented that the city had had more cooperation than usual from the Legislature in approval of city bills.

At the same time he noted that the Legislature had helped to solve city fiscal woes for "this year only" and that the city financial measures did "not call

Continued on Page 21, Column 3

Canada Cuts Income Taxes In a Bid to Spur Prosperity

By RAYMOND DANIELL
Special to The New York Times.

OTTAWA, April 5—The Canadian Government decided tonight to cut taxes. The national debt will be increased in the interest of national prosperity. Indirect and direct personal and corporate income taxes were cut to increase purchasing power and investment capital, with the advance knowledge that the Government would be collecting less than it plans to spend.

This is in accord with the expressed Liberal policy of taxing for surpluses in good and prosperous times and accepting a deficit when business, agriculture and industry run into trouble. The Canadian economy is not in serious trouble, but unemployment, a slowing down of industry and a drop in farm income have raised danger signals.

Tonight, in presenting his first budget as Minister of Finance, Walter Harris, in spite of an unexpected deficit of nearly $150,000,000 last year, proposed new tax cuts that will reduce the Government's revenues by about $207,000,000 in a full year based on normal expectations of increased prosperity.

Mr. Harris proposed a new schedule of taxes to reduce the personal income tax by 12 to 13 per cent for 85 per cent of the country's taxpayers. There are 2,800,000 persons in this category in this country of 15,000,000 inhabitants.

This, of course, will add to the country's national debt. This Mr. Harris asserted, should be no cause for alarm. He was taking into account an expected rise in the country's gross national product of about 5 per cent, Mr. Harris said, in reducing the scale of taxes. With more wealth being produced, he said, it was possible to reduce

Continued on Page 12, Column 5

RED CROSS EASES FUND DRIVE RULES

Permits Chapters to Join in Community Campaigns Under Some Conditions

By The Associated Press.

WASHINGTON, April 5—The American National Red Cross announced today that it had relaxed its rules so that under certain conditions local chapters could participate in Community or United Fund raising drives.

Most Red Cross chapters have refused to become a part of fund-raising campaigns such as Community Chest and United Fund Drives. In these, welfare agencies are grouped. Each receives a percentage of the funds raised.

E. Roland Harriman, national Red Cross chairman, said the board of governors had adopted the policy yesterday.

With the changes, he said, "Red Cross chapters will be able to plan in a more direct and helpful manner with other agencies and community leaders in matters of united or federated fund raising."

The board said the United States Government had established the American National Red Cross as this nation's official volunteer agency under the Geneva conventions. It added that this "unique and official" status made certain conditions of fund-raising necessary.

Units Control Own Budgets

The board said each local Red Cross chapter would keep its rights:

¶To determine and control its budget and goal.

¶To conduct a roll-call for members and funds in the month designated by the board of governors.

¶To conduct emergency campaigns in disaster, war or other unforeseen need when authorized by the board of governors.

¶To issue a membership card to each person from whose contribution the Red Cross received $1 or more.

The Councilmen—there were three—decided "there ought to be a law." So now there probably will be.

The amended policy keeps the provision that all chapters will "participate in annual campaigns for members and funds for the purpose of enrolling members and obtaining adequate voluntary contributions to finance the budgetary requirements of the chapters and the national organization."

Red Cross headquarters here said it would be possible for a local chapter to participate in a United Fund Drive and also conduct its own campaign later if needed to reach its goal.

Local chapters may work out their own programs, headquarters said. They may get all their funds from the United Drive, merely retaining the "right" to their own drive.

Since most United Fund Drives

Continued on Page 24, Column 6

WEST BIG 3 BAR AUSTRIAN ACCORD WITH SOVIET ONLY

Joint Declaration Advises Both Vienna and Moscow Big 4 Approval Is Needed

Special to The New York Times.

WASHINGTON, April 5—The Western Big Three cautioned Austria and the Soviet Union today against making bilateral commitments on the terms of an Austrian state treaty.

The United States, Britain and France issued a joint declaration noting that conclusion of the long-pending past was of concern to all of the Big Four powers as well as Austria.

If the Soviet Union should offer "proposals which hold clear promise of the restoration of freedom and independence to Austria, these would appropriately be discussed by the four Ambassadors in Vienna with the participation of the Austrian Government," the joint declaration said. It was made public simultaneously here and in London and Paris.

While it was not specifically directed to either the Moscow or Vienna Government, the statement was interpreted here as advice to both of the Western Big Three's attitude toward the Soviet-Austrian meeting scheduled for next week in Moscow.

West Wary on Concessions

The Western Big Three were understood to be particularly concerned lest Julius Raab, the Austrian Chancellor, make concessions to the Soviet Union that would be unacceptable to them.

Chancellor Raab and a delegation of Austrian officials will fly to Moscow Monday to discuss new ways of arriving at a treaty. The mission is being undertaken at the March 24 invitation of Vyacheslav M. Molotov, Soviet Foreign Minister.

The West has never opposed military neutrality for Austria and never has planned to include Austria in the North Atlantic alliance. The concern is more over a possible attempt by the Soviet Union to insist on unacceptable guarantee terms with respect to either or both of Mr. Molotov's points.

In the past, one of the main barriers to a pact restoring Austria's freedom and ending the four-power occupation has been the Soviet Union's insistence on the maintenance of occupation troops until a German treaty has been completed.

The text of today's three-power declaration follows:

"For many years the Governments of the United Kingdom, the United States and France have sought to conclude an Austrian state treaty. They have made ceaseless efforts thus to bring about the restoration of

Continued on Page 12, Column 3

3 Hefty Councilmen in Small Cab Say Rule on Front Seat Must Go

Six hundred and thirty-five pounds of City Councilmen found themselves uncomfortably squeezed recently into the back seat of one of the new small taxicabs. In front, the seat next to the driver beckoned, empty and inviting. Under the law nothing could be done about it. The Councilmen had to stay put.

Mr. Cunningham, who weighs 225 pounds, was one of the three Councilmen who took the back seat ride in discomfort. The others were James J. Murphy, Staten Island Democrat, weighing in at 316 pounds, and James J. Boland, Manhattan Democrat, a mere 200-pounder.

There was no ready explanation as to why Mr. Merli, who tips the beam at substantially less than 200 pounds, was a co-sponsor of the amendment. Other Councilmen guessed that he was "just going along for the ride."

Councilman Cunningham noted, in explaining his bill after yesterday's Council session, that the proposed amendment would be of aid not only to overweight passengers but also to three passengers who want to ride in the full complement of three in the back. The law says nothing about the sizes and weights of these back-seat riders.

Yesterday, "Fat Man's Amendment" was introduced into the City Council to distribute the small-taxi fare weight more evenly.

The amendment, referred to the Council's General Welfare Committee, would permit a passenger to ride in front with either two or three passengers on the back seat. The sponsors of the amendment were Edward A. Cunningham, Bronx Democrat, and John J. Merli, Manhattan Democrat.

CHURCHILL QUITS AS PRIME MINISTER; DECLINES DUKEDOM TO STAY AN M. P.; EDEN TAKES OVER LEADERSHIP TODAY

ON WAY TO RETIREMENT: Sir Winston Churchill moist-eyed as he arrived in auto yesterday at Buckingham Palace to tender resignation as Prime Minister to Queen Elizabeth.
Associated Press Radiophoto

BRITISH ERA ENDS

Aged Statesman Tells Queen of Decision— Cabinet Shifts Due

By DREW MIDDLETON
Special to The New York Times.

LONDON, April 5—Sir Winston Churchill resigned as Prime Minister today. Age has done what Britain's enemies and his political rivals could not accomplish.

Tomorrow Queen Elizabeth II will summon Sir Anthony Eden to Buckingham Palace and ask him to form a new Government. Sir Anthony's accession as Prime Minister will mark the passing of the Churchill era.

While shadows lengthened on the palace lawns, Sir Winston stood talking with the Queen at her study window. Their business was his resignation. When the audience ended he passed out of the palace, through cheering ranks of his countrymen.

The most important change in British political life since the end of World War II was announced from Buckingham Palace in a single sentence:

"The Right Honorable Sir Winston Churchill had an audience of the Queen this evening and tendered his resignation as Prime Minister and First Lord of the Treasury, which Her Majesty was graciously pleased to accept."

Transition to Eden Era

Thus Sir Winston, Knight of the Garter, Privy Councilor, Order of Merit and Companion of Honor, left the office he has held at two different times for a total of eight years, seven months and twenty-five days.

While Sir Winston, who is 80 years old, moved homeward to crowds shouting "Good old Winnie!" in Downing Street tonight, political London bubbled with anticipation.

When Sir Anthony is asked by the Queen tomorrow to form a Government, all the Ministers will place their offices at his disposal. This will open the way to changes that, immediately or after the election, will change the Churchill Government into the Eden Government.

The decision on the date of a general parliamentary election is Sir Anthony's. Polls conducted by newspaper men in the House of Commons indicate that a great majority of the Members of Parliament expect the election will take place May 26.

If this date is chosen, the new

Continued on Page 11, Column 2

DULLES SAYS U. S. WON'T START WAR

Holds Any Conflict in Formosa Area Would be Reds' Doing —Restates Quemoy Stand

By DANA ADAMS SCHMIDT
Special to The New York Times.

WASHINGTON, April 5—Secretary of State Dulles said today that if there was war in the Formosa Strait it would be the Communist Chinese who started it.

The United States, he asserted, has made "perfectly clear" its desire for a cease-fire and peace in the strait. But the Chinese Communists, he declared, unfortunately do not seem to be much under the influence of the peace propaganda they disseminate.

The Secretary made his observations in reply to a request for an assessment of the prospects for war or peace in the Formosa Strait at the first news conference he has held since March 15.

"To answer that question would require me to read the minds of people to whom I have no access, that is, the Communist leaders in Peiping," Mr. Dulles replied.

The Secretary was asked about continuing demands in Congress that the United States make known now whether it will defend Quemoy and Matsu Islands against Communist attack. Mr. Dulles said he knew the answer to that one by heart. There was no commitment of any kind, overt or description, expressed or implied, he declared, binding the United States to the defense of anything except Formosa and the Pescadores.

'Very Difficult Ground'

The suggestion that the United States should announce how it proposed to fulfill its treaty commitments entered onto "very difficult ground," he said. He did not see how it could be done.

The Secretary observed that the United States also had a commitment to defend the United States of America but no one had yet asked for a commitment as to how that would be done.

Asked whether that meant the United States would not fight for the defense of Quemoy and Matsu for the sake of the morale of Chinese Nationalist troops in Formosa, he replied that it would not, "unless that was vital for the defense of Formosa and the Pescadores. It all comes back to that."

President Eisenhower has told Congress that he and he alone would make the decision whether the United States should defend Quemoy and Matsu. He said his decision would depend on whether the invasion of the offshore islands was recognizable as a preliminary to invasion of Formosa or the Pescadores.

While Mr. Dulles was speaking to the press, Secretary of

Continued on Page 7, Column 5

President Declares Allies Still Will Heed Churchill

By W. H. LAWRENCE
Special to The New York Times.

WASHINGTON, April 5—President Eisenhower declared today that leaders of the free world were bound to ask Sir Winston Churchill's counsel and advice, even in retirement. Democrats and Republicans joined the President in personal tributes to the retiring British Prime Minister.

There were formal statements from John Foster Dulles, Secretary of State; Vice President Richard M. Nixon, and from a host of Senate and House members.

The President went into the White House Rose Garden to record for newsreels and television cameras his personal tribute to his long-time associate in war and peace.

It is not usual for the head of the United States Government to express himself so feelingly when the head of another government resigns from office. But Sir Winston's departure changed all the rules. The President spoke into the cameras in the obvious hope that the British statesman himself would see the pictures and hear the words.

"We have just had official word that my old and very dear friend, Sir Winston Churchill, has retired from his position as head of Her Majesty's Government in the United Kingdom," he said.

"Naturally, an event such as this recalls to my mind many stirring incidents both of war and peace. I have greatly respected and valued my association with a man so great as Winston Churchill.

"And now, if I dare, I should like to adress a word directly to Sir Winston.

"All of us in the free world

Continued on Page 11, Column 7

Vietnam Dissidents Give Warning to U.S.

By ROBERT ALDEN
Special to The New York Times.

SAIGON, Vietnam, April 5—The groups fighting Vietnam's Government warned tonight that continued United States support of Premier Ngo Dinh Diem might lead to civil war.

They said that as far as they were concerned the truce was ended and that "all responsibility for bloodshed—Vietnamese and foreign—would rest on Ngo Dinh Diem."

It was further charged that the United States had turned over four tanks to the Government. As far as can be determined, the United States does not have any tanks in Vietnam.

The Ngo Dinh Diem Cabinet voted today to stand firm in the face of the Opposition's threat. As the situation in Saigon grew more tense by the hour, officials made it known that the Government had

Continued on Page 12, Column 3

CHURCHILL BARS OFFER OF PEERAGE

Prefers to Stay Commoner. He Replies to Queen's Bid —Britons Acclaim Him

By BENJAMIN WELLES
Special to The New York Times.

LONDON, April 5—Sir Winston Churchill declined a dukedom today to remain in the House of Commons.

In an audience with Queen Elizabeth II in her study in Buckingham Palace, he tendered his resignation to his sovereign. The Queen accepted it and then offered him the highest titular dignity in the land. But Sir Winston, a grandson of the seventh Duke of Marlborough, humbly yet firmly declined it.

He had been a "House of Commons man" for almost fifty years, he recalled, and he preferred to remain one rather than accept a peerage and enter the House of Lords.

The decision showed that Sir Winston, after laying down the cares and responsibilities of high office, would continue as an elder statesman in the Commons, which he has loved—and which he has intermittently loved him—during that half century.

Had Declined Earldom

It was not the first time Sir Winston, had turned down the offer of a peerage to remain in the lower but more powerful legislative chamber. In the aftermath of victory in 1945 he was offered an earldom, but he refused it.

The 28-year-old Queen and the 80-year-old statesman each knew what was in the other's mind when they met today. He knew in advance what she would offer and she knew what his reply would be. But Elizabeth and Sir Winston, both exemplars of tradition in a tradition-loving land, observed the forms and courtesies due between the sovereign and a retiring counselor and friend.

The last non-royal dukedom was given to the Marquess of Westminster in 1874, the year of Sir Winston's birth. There are now twenty-six dukes in the United Kingdom peerage, in addition to the royal dukes—Edinburgh, Cornwall, Gloucester, Kent and Windsor.

Sir Winston's refusal of the proffered peerage means that his name will remain as it is. His knighthood, acquired in 1953

Continued on Page 11, Column 2

SOUTH AFRICA OUT OF UNESCO RANKS

Quits United Nations Agency Over Racial Issue

By LEONARD INGALLS

JOHANNESBURG, South Africa, April 5—South Africa has withdrawn from the United Nations Educational, Scientific and Cultural Organization.

Eric H. Louw, Minister of External Affairs, said today in Capetown that it had been decided to terminate his country's participation in the United Nations agency of the United States. The decision to withdraw, Mr. Louw said, was made recently.

The Minister announced also that South Africa would not participate in deliberations in May before the International Court of Justice on its administration of the territory of South-West Africa under the League of Nations mandate. The territory was incorporated by South Africa in 1949

The first step of incorporation was resented by the United Nations, which sought to have South Africa accept trusteeship of South-West Africa under United Nations supervision. South Africa ignored the United

Continued on Page 5, Column 2

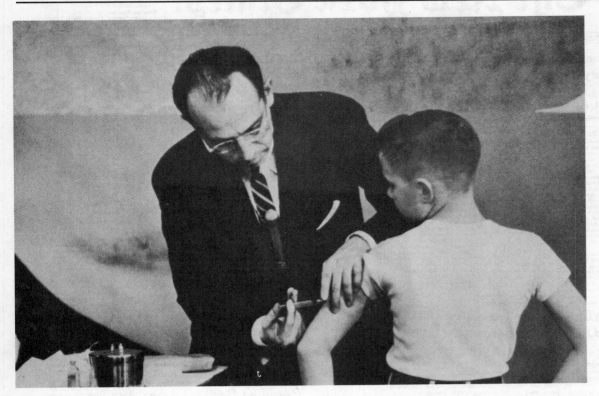

Dr. Jonas E. Salk innoculates a schoolboy with his polio vaccine.

Nobody since Billy Sunday had ever drawn such large and enthusiastic audiences as Billy Graham.

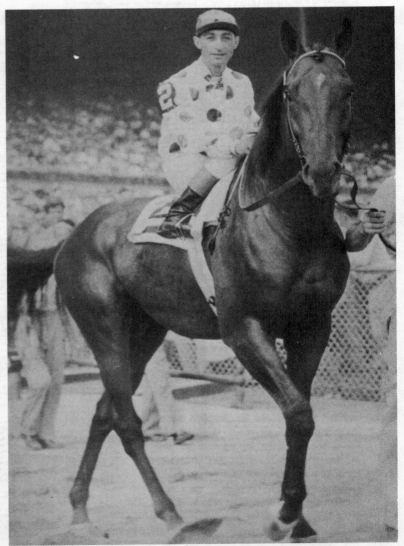

Eddie Arcaro was one of only two men to have won five Kentucky Derbys. He is shown here on Nashua, the winner of two of the three Triple Crown races in 1955.

"All the News That's Fit to Print"

The New York Times.

LATE CITY EDITION
Cloudy with some rain today.
Chance of showers tomorrow.
Temperature Range Today—Max., 56; Min., 42
Temperature Yesterday—Max., 63; Min., 41
Full U. S. Weather Bureau Report, Page 59

VOL. CIV. No. 35,508.

Entered as Second-Class Matter,
Post Office, New York, N. Y.

Copyright, 1955, by The New York Times Company.

NEW YORK, WEDNESDAY, APRIL 13, 1955.

Times Square, New York 36, N. Y.
Telephone Lackawanna 4-1000

FIVE CENTS

STEVENSON COPIED PLAN ON FORMOSA, DULLES CHARGES

He Says Democrat Proposed as His 'Original' Ideas the Administration's Policy

SOME DIPLOMATS DIFFER

Know of No U.S. Moves in U.N. or With Allies Paralleling Views of 1952 Candidate

Special to The New York Times.

WASHINGTON, April 12 — Secretary of State Dulles said today that Adlai E. Stevenson advocated "as original ideas" the same steps toward peace in the Formosa Strait that the Administration was exploring.

The only major point of difference between the proposals made by the 1952 Democratic Presidential candidate in a Chicago speech last night and his own idea, Mr. Dulles said, lay in the degree of solicitude the United States should show toward Nationalist China.

"Mr. Stevenson speaks feelingly about our 'allies'," the Secretary of State said at his news conference this morning. "However, he forgets one ally, namely, the Republic of China.

"It is upon the loyalty and resources of that ally that the free world must primarily depend for the defense of Formosa. Yet Mr. Stevenson seems to assume that that ally can be ignored and rebuffed.

"Aside from this, Mr. Stevenson has in fact endorsed the main features of this Administration's program in relation to Formosa."

News to Some Diplomats

Mr. Stevenson's speech was on the whole more warmly received in the embassies of the major powers allied with the United States in Europe and Asia.

In these quarters, however, there was some puzzlement among some diplomats over Mr. Dulles' statement that the ideas advanced by Mr. Stevenson in his Chicago speech were "the very approaches which the Government has been and is actively exploring."

If the State Department was exploring with its allies a joint pledge for the united defense of Formosa combined with an effort to extricate the Chinese Nationalists from the Matsu and Quemoy Island groups, that was news to several senior diplomats today. Mr. Stevenson had urged such steps.

These diplomats did not know either, of any active move by the United States and its allies calling on the United Nations General Assembly to "condemn any effort to alter the present status

Continued on Page 4, Column 3

CENSORSHIP MOVE DENIED BY WILSON

Secretary Defends His Curb on Giving Information

By ANTHONY LEVIERO
Special to The New York Times.

WASHINGTON, April 12 — Charles E. Wilson, Secretary of Defense, defended today his directive for control of defense information, denying that it was "censorship."

He said in a news conference that the widespread publication of technical information in the hydrogen bomb age made national security a "greater problem than ever before in history."

He declared he would be willing to pay hundreds of millions of dollars to get the same kind of information about the Soviet Union as that country gets about the United States in its newspapers and periodicals.

The Secretary outlined a dilemma created by the great outpouring of technical information in a free and highly industrialized society. He said "our top folks" felt too much was being published as a result of rivalries between corporations with defense contracts and between the armed forces, and of the enterprise of a free press and the historical tendency of scientists to report all the latest developments.

Mr. Wilson said the Administration was grappling with a complex problem the solution

Continued on Page 11, Column 1

Dulles Doubts Corsi Ability; Ex-Aide Charges Untruths

Edward Corsi at his Arlington, Va., home yesterday as he replied to charges made by Secretary of State Dulles.

Special to The New York Times.

WASHINGTON, April 12 — It was open war today between John Foster Dulles, Secretary of State, and his former "old friend," Edward Corsi.

Mr. Dulles accused the New Yorker of making reckless charges, of trying to circumvent the law and of not being qualified to run the refugee relief program. Mr. Corsi charged the

Secretary of State with "a whole string of falsehoods," adding that he was "terribly shocked and astounded that a man like Dulles for whom I had such respect could stoop so low."

Only four months ago Mr. Dulles had appointed Mr. Corsi his special assistant on refugee

Continued on Page 16, Column 6

SOVIET ARMED AID OFFERED AFGHANS

Moscow Said to Back Kabul in Dispute With Pakistan on North-West Frontier

By JOHN P. CALLAHAN
Special to The New York Times.

KABUL, Afghanistan (via Peshawar, Pakistan), April 11 — The Soviet Ambassador was reported today to have offered help to Afghanistan's Premier. The aid was to be military support if Pakistan or her Western allies "threaten aggressive interference" in Afghanistan's demand for a plebiscite in the adjoining North-West Frontier Province. The Soviet Union borders on Afghanistan.

The report of the Soviet offer was made by an Afghan Government officer who has been observing the almost daily meetings since March 30 between Soviet Ambassador Mikhail V. Degtyar and Premier Sardar Mohammed Daud of Afghanistan.

It followed by a few hours a report, confirmed by foreign envoys, that King Mohammed Zahir Shah had informed the Ambassadors of the United States, Britain and Turkey that he was prepared to replace Premier Daud with his predecessor, Mahmood Zahir if their Governments would assure Afghanistan of "full" support in event of attacks by "unfriendly powers."

Embassy spokesmen said Washington and London had been informed of the King's request and that they were awaiting replies. The Ambassadors of

Continued on Page 2, Column 3

Austro-Soviet Talk Toasted by Bohlen

By CLIFTON DANIEL

MOSCOW, April 12 — In the presence of senior leaders of the Soviet state, Charles E. Bohlen, United States Ambassador, offered a toast this evening to the speedy restoration of Austria's independence and freedom.

Vyacheslav M. Molotov, Soviet Foreign Minister, said it was a good toast and raised his glass. So did Premier Nikolai A. Bulganin and Deputy Premiers Lazar M. Kaganovich, Anastas I. Mikoyan and Mikhail G. Pervukhin.

Drinking with them were Julius Raab, Chancellor of Austria, and other members of the Austrian delegation that arrived here yesterday. The Austrians opened negotiations with Mr. Molotov during the afternoon on the terms of a treaty intended to achieve

Continued on Page 8, Column 3

HIGH COURT HEARS SOUTH WILL DEFY QUICK END TO BIAS

Gradual Approaches Urged for Integration of Schools— Negro Lawyers Opposed

By LUTHER A. HUSTON
Special to The New York Times.

WASHINGTON, April 12 — Spokesmen for South Carolina and Virginia told the Supreme Court today that their people would not obey a decree ordering an immediate end to racial segregation in the public schools.

When Chief Justice Earl Warren asked S. E. Rogers, representing Clarendon County, S. C., if he were willing to say that an "honest attempt" would be made to conform to whatever decree the court might issue, Mr. Rogers said:

"Let's get that word 'honest' out of there. It would depend upon the kind of decree. The white people would not send their children to school with Negroes."

Archibald O. Robertson, who represented Virginia, said that Virginia would not defy the court; but that there were "subtle ways" of not complying with an order for an abrupt end to segregation. One would be for the voters to refuse to approve funds for an immediate integration of a school system.

Time Asked for South

J. Lindsay Almond Jr., Attorney General of Virginia, said that "forthwith enforcement of integration would be pre-emptive of the rights of a sovereign people." He asserted that the schools of his state "might have to close" if an abrupt end to segregation were ordered.

Throughout the second day of arguments on the type of decree the court should issue to carry out its decision of last May 17 that public school segregation was unconstitutional, the Southern states pleaded for time to adjust their educational systems to the new order.

The states were not specific, however, as to the length of time they would need. Estimates ranged from a tentative one year to as high as the year 2045.

The lawyers for the Negro side, however, were specific. Thurgood Marshall, counsel for the National Association for the Advancement of the Colored People, submitted two proposed decrees. One would end all school segregation everywhere next September.

An alternate decree, which Mr. Marshall said was the least the Negroes should be asked to accept, would terminate separate schools for white and Negro pupils by September, 1956.

Mr. Marshall asserted that there could not be a "moratorium on the Fourteenth Amendment or local option" to enforce a constitutional decision of the court. The Fourteenth Amendment to the Constitution prohibits a state from denying to

Continued on Page 18, Column 5

YONKERS IS FACING LOSS OF STATE AID

Albany Threatens to Cut Off Grants Unless Schools Are Improved by Jan. 1

By LEONARD BUDER

The State Education Commissioner warned the City of Yonkers yesterday that it would lose its state grants to aid education unless it improved its public school system.

The Commissioner, Dr. Lewis A. Wilson, acted in response to charges, of trying to circumvent an appeal made last year by a group of Yonkers residents who charged that the city's "starvation" budgetary allowances had produced "shocking" school conditions. He set Jan. 1 as the deadline for the Yonkers Board of Education to submit "sufficient evidence of an adequate program, both in respect to its educational offerings and its building needs for the ensuing year."

Commenting upon his action, Dr. Wilson said that his threat to withhold state aid to Yonkers was an "uncommon" but not an unprecedented move.

Yonkers this year is receiving $2,046,000 in regular state aid

Continued on Page 32, Column 5

281,853 ELIGIBLE FOR VACCINE HERE

City to Vote Fund Quickly for Equipment — Experts to Set Number of Shots

Mayor Wagner announced yesterday that a special appropriation of $100,000 would be made to speed the city's polio vaccination program.

Elated by the success of the Salk vaccine, city officials said they were ready to begin vaccination on April 25. Those eligible to receive free inoculations from the city are 281,853 school children. These include all first and second graders and those third and fourth graders who received dummy shots in last year's field trials.

In New York State, 725,000 children between 5 and 14 years of age will be vaccinated by June 1. In making this announcement, Dr. Herman E. Hilleboe, State Health Commissioner, said that if the dosage was reduced from three shots to two, the number of children immunized could be increased to 1,100,000.

In New Jersey, a procedure would make it possible to give 13,500,000 children primary inoculations immediately upon approval of the vaccine by the National Institutes of Health. When the seven-month period had elapsed, additional vaccine would have been produced.

Dr. Salk also urged that all children who received inoculations during the 1954 field trials be given an additional booster dose in 1955. This is necessary, he said, because the three doses

Continued on Page 22, Column 6

T. V. A. Detractors Scored by Lilienthal

By JOHN N. POPHAM
Special to The New York Times.

CHATTANOOGA, Tenn., April 12 — David E. Lilienthal made a blistering attack tonight on the economic and political detractors of the Tennessee Valley Authority, "from the White House down."

The former chairman of the authority said that as a one-time neighbor he felt impelled to return to the valley region to help warn its residents concerning the tactics of the enemies currently waging a "cold war" against the famous river resources agency.

Mr. Lilienthal traced the development of T. V. A. through a succession of national controversies from 1933 to 1946. Then he spoke for public power philosophies espoused by the Federal Government, in contrast with this Administration of accusing the present Administration of accusing the

Continued on Page 15, Column 3

SALK POLIO VACCINE PROVES SUCCESS; MILLIONS WILL BE IMMUNIZED SOON; CITY SCHOOLS BEGIN SHOTS APRIL 25

WORDS OF HOPE: Dr. Thomas Francis Jr., left, and Dr. Jonas E. Salk on speakers' platform at Ann Arbor, Mich., where they addressed scientists on effects of polio vaccine.

Supply to Be Low for Time, But Output Will Be Rushed

By DAMON STETSON
Special to The New York Times.

ANN ARBOR, Mich., April 12 — The Salk vaccine for poliomyelitis will be made available for the immunization of children as rapidly as possible, but it is expected to be in short supply temporarily. The National Foundation for Infantile Paralysis announced today that vaccine already purchased for 9,000,000 immunizations (three inoculations a child) would be turned over to state and territorial health officers.

This amount will be offered to all children who participated in last year's field trials but who did not actually receive vaccine. Children enrolled in the first and second grades of all public, private and parochial schools in the United States, Hawaii and Alaska also will be offered the vaccine.

Dr. Jonas E. Salk, who originated the vaccine, reported his belief that the maximum effect of the third (booster) inoculation could be achieved only if administered at least seven months after the primary inoculation of two shots.

Such a procedure would make it possible to give 13,500,000 children primary inoculations immediately upon approval of the vaccine by the National Institutes of Health. When the seven-month period had elapsed, additional vaccine would have been produced.

"It's a great day. It's a wonderful day for the whole world. It's a history-making day."

Continued on Page 22, Column 6

6 VACCINE MAKERS GET U. S. LICENSES

Government Clears the Way for Quantity Production of Salk Preventive

By BESS FURMAN
Special to The New York Times.

WASHINGTON, April 12 — The Federal Government today quickly gave a clear track to Salk polio vaccine.

It licensed six concerns to manufacture and distribute throughout the country the protective substance developed by Dr. Jonas E. Salk of the University of Pittsburgh.

The key action in the licensing was the signature of Oveta Culp Hobby, the Secretary of Health, Education and Welfare. Federal approval is required by the National Biologics Control Act. As she signed Mrs. Hobby said:

"It's a great day. It's a wonderful day for the whole world. It's a history-making day."

Licensed Concerns Named

The concerns approved to make and sell the product are: Cutter Laboratories, Berkeley, Calif.; Eli Lilly Company, Indianapolis; Parke, Davis & Co., Detroit; Pittman-Moore Company, Zionville, Ind.; Sharp & Dohme, Philadelphia, and Wyeth Laboratories, Inc., Marietta, Pa.

Mrs. Hobby affixed her signature at 5:15 P. M. Had it been possible for her to sign at 4 P. M., the signing would have been what Washington calls a "full dress" ceremony for photographers and the press.

This press meeting was canceled because Mrs. Hobby had to wait for the final judgment of the Public Health Service on the vaccine evaluation study made public today by Dr. Thomas Francis Jr.

Thus it happened that although Surgeon General Leonard A. Scheele of the Public Health Service and a few other members of the departmental staff were present when Mrs. Hobby signed.

Earlier Dr. Scheele had said the delay had been because of "things running late out in Ann Arbor." He reminded that before licensing a new drug the Public Health Service must approve both safety and potency.

"The data on safety had all

Continued on Page 24, Column 4

TRIAL DATA GIVEN

Efficacy of 80 to 90% Shown—Salk Sees Further Advance

Abstract of report, summary of data on tests, Page 22.

By WILLIAM L. LAURENCE
Special to The New York Times.

ANN ARBOR, Mich., April 12 — The world learned today that its hopes for finding an effective weapon against paralytic polio had been realized.

The triple anti-polio vaccine originated by Dr. Jonas E. Salk works. This was revealed in the long-awaited report on the mass field trials of 1954, largest of their kind in medical history.

In these tests the vaccine, designed to protect against the crippling effects of all the three types of virus known to produce paralytic polio, was administered to 440,000 children in forty-four states.

The report, a medical classic, was presented at a special scientific meeting at the University of Michigan by Dr. Thomas Francis Jr. It was he who had directed the evaluation of the vast mass of data provided by the tests, involving the correlation of 144,000,000 separate items of information.

Half Got Dummy Shot

Dr. Francis reported the vaccinations had been 80 to 90 per cent effective on the basis of results in eleven states.

In these states, which included New York, half of the children vaccinated got the Salk vaccine. The other half received a placebo, or dummy shot.

These results, Dr. Francis reported, were looked upon with "greater confidence" than the figures in other areas. In these results the results indicated an effectiveness of 60 to 80 per cent against paralysis by any polio virus.

Dr. Salk reported at the meeting that new and more potent vaccines and more effective methods of administering them, were ready for the 1955 vaccinations.

Dr. Salk, who is a member of the faculty at the University of Pittsburgh's School of Medicine, said:

"Theoretically, the new 1955 vaccines and vaccination procedures may lead to 100 per cent protection from paralysis of all those vaccinated."

The new procedures he had outlined

Continued on Page 20, Column 2

FANFARE USHERS VERDICT ON TESTS

Medical History Is Written in Hollywood Atmosphere

Special to The New York Times.

ANN ARBOR, Mich., April 12 — The formal verdict on the Salk vaccine was disclosed today amid fanfare and drama far more typical of a Hollywood premiere than a medical meeting.

The event that made medical history took place in one of the University of Michigan's most glamorous structures—Rackham Building. Television cameras and radio microphones were set up outside the huge lecture hall. Inside the salmon-colored hall a battery of sixteen television and newsreel cameras were lined up across a long wooden platform especially built at the rear.

At 10:20 A. M. Dr. Thomas Francis Jr., director of the Poliomyelitis Vaccine Evaluation Center and the man of the hour, was introduced. A short, chunky man with a close-cropped mustache, he was wearing a black suit, white shirt and striped gray tie.

He stepped up to a lectern decorated with a blue and gold banner bearing the seal of the university. He appeared neat, hidden up to his breast pocket by the lectern, as he looked out toward his audience of 500 scientists and physicians. Cameras ground and spotlights played

Continued on Page 20, Column 6

Eisenhower Gets Degree From Clark at The Citadel

President Eisenhower and Gen. Mark W. Clark, retired, review honor guard at The Citadel

By W. H. LAWRENCE
Special to The New York Times.

AUGUSTA, Ga., April 12 — President Eisenhower declared today that military men of the present and future must be "apostles of peace" working to understand what makes humans and nations "tick." This was his advice to the corps of cadets at The Citadel, the military college of South Carolina, in Charleston. He received an honorary Doctor of Laws degree from retired Gen. Mark W. Clark, president

of The Citadel, and reviewed the cadets en route here for an eight-day golfing vacation. Greeting the cadets and applauding thousands who lined Charleston's streets, the Presi-

Continued on Page 12, Column 4

1955

Gunsmoke was the first of many "adult Westerns" to appear on television. For the following 20 years James Arness starred as Marshal Matt Dillon. Dennis Weaver played the role of his deputy.

The Ernie Kovacs Show ran on NBC from the end of 1955 through July 1956. In this short time, the show established Kovacs' reputation for zany originality.

"All the News
That's Fit to Print"

The New York Times.

LATE CITY EDITION
Some cloudiness today; cooler
tonight. Fair, mild tomorrow.
Temperature Range Today—Max., 71; Min., 58
Temperature Yesterday—Max., 68.5; Min., 50.2
Full U. S. Weather Bureau Report. Page 66

VOL. CIV...No. 35,557.

Entered as Second-Class Matter,
Post Office, New York, N. Y.

Copyright, 1955, by The New York Times Company.

NEW YORK, WEDNESDAY, JUNE 1, 1955.

Times Square, New York 36, N. Y.
Telephone LAckawanna 4-1000

FIVE CENTS

PRESIDENT WARY ON PEIPING MOTIVE IN FREEING FLIERS

Cautions Against Guessing, Though Conceding Easing of Tension Is Implied

HE ASKS FURTHER STUDY

U. N. Head Urges Red China to Release 11 More—'Ice Cracking,' George Says

Transcript and summary of the news conference, Page 18.

By ELIE ABEL
Special to The New York Times

WASHINGTON, May 31—President Eisenhower cautioned today against "hit or miss" guesses on Peiping's motives in releasing four imprisoned United States airmen.

Asked whether he regarded the Chinese Communist action as "a sincere effort" to relieve international tensions the President replied:

"Our messages from various sources imply that that is their stated thought; that it was a token on their part to do something in helping release tensions."

He added that the Communist move would have to be "studied" and "examined" before a conclusion was reached. The President said that he had no information about the prospects for release of fifty-two other Americans still imprisoned or detained in Communist China.

Plane Awaits Airmen

Senator Walter F. George, Georgia Democrat and chairman of the Senate Foreign Relations Committee, gave it as his opinion that the release of the four fliers "indicates a cracking of the ice." He predicted that the United States citizens remaining in China would be loosed eventually. "I don't think it will happen quickly," Senator George said.

A Constellation, with Col. James K. Dowling in charge representing the Air Force Secretary, Harold E. Talbott, will remain in Hawaii to carry the released airmen home with their families.

President Eisenhower was neither optimistic nor pessimistic in discussing the news from Hong Kong, where the four pilots were set free. His attitude was calm and matter-of-fact.

The State Department, likewise, was careful not to raise the hopes of the country about the possible release of the United States citizens still in Chinese prisons. Henry Suydam, the department spokesman, said nothing was known here about the chances that all the Americans might be released.

His silence was in keeping with the policy laid down last winter by Secretary of State Dulles that United States officials should say nothing that might complicate the task of Secretary General Hammarskjold of the United Nations in pressing

Continued on Page 2, Column 3

Fliers Freed by Chinese Reds Speed Home as V. I. P.'s

LOWU

Associated Press Radiophoto from Hong Kong via Tokyo

Four U. S. airmen released by Chinese Reds are shown leaving Lowu border bridge with Lieut. Col. J. A. Norcross, right, Air Force doctor. Left to right: Capt. Harold E. Fischer Jr., Lieut. Roland W. Parks, Lieut. Lyle W. Cameron and Lieut. Col. Edwin L. Heller.

By HENRY R. LIEBERMAN
Special to The New York Times

HONG KONG, May 31—Four happy and perky United States fliers headed home with great big smiles today, less than three hours after their "deportation" from Red China.

The fliers, captured during the Korean war, had been imprisoned for more than two years. They left Hong Kong for Honolulu in a four-engine United States Air Force plane at 5:20 P. M. [4:20 A. M. Eastern daylight time]. In their luggage were four new pairs of silk pajamas and reserved for them aboard the C-54 transport were lots of filet steaks as well as four V. I. P. bunks. The released fliers are: Lieut.

Continued on Page 3, Column 4

Eisenhower Will Address Meeting of U. N. on Coast

By W. H. LAWRENCE
Special to The New York Times

WASHINGTON, May 31—President Eisenhower announced today he would welcome United Nations delegates to their tenth anniversary session, opening in San Francisco June 20. Earlier the White House had turned down an invitation for the President to speak at the closing session June 25, the actual tenth anniversary of the signing of the charter.

The latter date conflicted with that for a New England trip planned by the President to Vermont, New Hampshire, and Maine. A San Francisco visit June 25 also carried with it the possibility that he might be asked to intervene in the discussions of the Big Four foreign ministers about arrangements for the meeting of the heads of government of the four major powers. The consultations of the foreign ministers will be held simultaneously with the United Nations meetings.

President for U. N. Review

"I should like very much to extend to this group a welcome on behalf of the people of the United States on the tenth anniversary," the President said at his news conference today. "I think it is well that the whole country review the record of accomplishment and failure, and we kind of fix in our own minds again what are our hopes and expectations for such a body.

"So I would hope to do my little part by going out there to bring us all to thinking about it a little more seriously."

Diplomatic circles were elated by the change in arrangements so that President Eisenhower would be on hand for at least a part of the United Nations meeting in San Francisco. They had feared that his absence from such a session would be interpreted as a lack of interest and support for the United Nations at a time when the Big Four was approaching a conference again.

The President plans to make a quick trip to San Francisco, probably avoiding even an overnight stop in that city.

The President is scheduled to make what the White House considers important speeches in Rutland, Vt., Concord, N. H. and Augusta, Me., between June 22 to June 27.

At his news conference, the President emphasized anew his concept of the top-level conference as one where areas for later discussion by the foreign ministers would be mapped. Once again, he expressed doubt that the Big Four heads of government would reach any final decisions at a brief session.

He repeated an earlier statement that he did not think members of Congress should attend the small, brief heads-of-government meeting, but should be included in the conference delegations when decisions were being made.

The President was asked specifically about a proposal by Representative Joe L. Evins,

Continued on Page 10, Column 3

QUEEN PROCLAIMS CRISIS IN STRIKE

Grants Extra Powers to Deal With Rail Walkout Snarls —Parliament Advanced

By THOMAS P. RONAN
Special to The New York Times

LONDON, May 31—Queen Elizabeth II proclaimed a state of emergency today because of the nation-wide railway strike.

Under the Emergency Powers Act of 1920, the Queen signed a series of directives enabling the Government to insure the continuance of essential supplies and services.

They were not designed to break the strike, which has cut railroad service to about 20 per cent of normal. They were intended to relax or waive the usual legal restrictions so that needed supplies can be moved again what are our hopes and spectations for such a body.

One regulation provides penalties for acts of sabotage against essential services. But Maj. Gwilym Lloyd-George, Home Secretary, said this and similar provisions simply gave the Government reserve powers in case of breaches of public order.

"The regulations represent the minimum required to enable the

Continued on Page 10, Column 3

TITO, KHRUSHCHEV CONCUR ON AIMS

Leaders Agree in Principle on International Relations and Own Coexistence

By M. S. HANDLER
Special to The New York Times

BLED, Yugoslavia, May 31—Nikita S. Khrushchev, Soviet Communist party secretary, and Premier Nikolai A. Bulganin tonight after having concluded an agreement in principle with President Tito.

The accord ranged the field of international relations and co-existence between the Soviet Union and Yugoslavia. The agreement was reached on Brioni Island in the Adriatic Sea.

The Soviet and Yugoslav negotiators failed, however, to reach agreements concerning East-West relations. Marshal Tito advocated the dissolution of the two opposing power blocs as the indispensable precondition for the establishment of peace. The Russians refused to consider abandonment of a system of power blocs as a basis of their foreign policy.

"This morning the Yugoslav President left for Belgrade, accompanied by Andrei A. Gromyko, a Soviet Deputy Foreign Minister, and Dmitri T. Shepilov, chairman of the Foreign Affairs Committee of the Soviet of Nationalities, to draft a final communiqué on the talks. That text will be issued in the Yugoslav capital Thursday evening or Friday morning.

Mr. Khrushchev and Marshal

Continued on Page 14, Column 4

VACCINE PROGRAM IN PART OF JERSEY DELAYED TO FALL

65.9 Turnout a New Low Here —President Finds Supply Situation Improved

Text of President's statement appears on Page 24.

By PETER KIHSS

Continuing delays in clearing vaccine led yesterday to the removal of nearly 20,000 New Jersey children from the polio vaccination program until the fall.

Newark, Hackensack, Ridgefield Park, Bogota and Somerville all preferred to avoid giving the inoculations during the approaching polio season and noted that school closings were drawing near.

In Washington, President Eisenhower said the vaccine supply situation now was such that all first and second grade pupils would be inoculated before the peak polio season in mid-August.

He said the polio program "seems to be losing some of its difficulties and inescapable snarls."

In other developments on the polio-fighting front:

¶New York City set another low turnout—65.9 per cent—on the eighth day of its inoculations, falling below last Friday's revised 66.5 per cent, The Health Department corrected an originally announced turnout of 64.5 per cent for Friday. The over-all response here has been 161,538 children vaccinated out of 230,037 originally scheduled, or 70.2 per cent.

¶In Albany the State Advisory Committee on Poliomyelitis acted to provide booster shots for nearly 120,000 children vaccinated last year—including 21,500 here—before second injections are given to those just inoculated in the 1955 program. State Health Commissioner Herman E. Hilleboe said the booster program could use about 92,500 doses likely to be left over from 676,980 units delivered for the first round.

¶The National Foundation for Infantile Paralysis, through Dr. G. Foard McGinnes, medical consultant, said it would make available free vaccine for youngsters who have received their first shots, even if this required going beyond an original June 30 deadline. But in response to a question, Dr. McGinnes said a new policy decision would have to be made on supplying communities dropping out until the fall.

New Jersey is one of five states that have received foundation vaccine, but have been unable to start vaccinations pending reapproval of their supply by the United States Public Health Service.

The New Jersey shipment came from the Wyeth Laboratories of Marietta, Pa.

The other states — Maine, Montana, North Dakota and South Dakota — had been supplied by the Pitman-Moore Company of Zionsville, Ind.

Newark's program was under-

Continued on Page 22, Column 3

City Surplus Fund Set Up For Financial Rainy Days

By CHARLES G. BENNETT

The City Council voted yesterday to create a city stabilization fund. The Charter amendment would provide a fiscal umbrella to protect New York on financial rainy days. In effect, the measure would give New York a limited surplus that could be used in any year when the city's revenues failed to come up to the amount anticipated. Its passage by the Board of Estimate and signature by Mayor Wagner are expected.

The law would require the stabilization fund to be built up to a minimum of $80,000,000, or about 10 per cent of the city's tax levy. The maximum would be $240,000,000, or about 30 per cent of the tax levy.

At present the city has $22,-000,000 in a restricted tax appropriation reserve fund which, under the proposed Charter amendment, would become the starting amount for the new stabilization fund.

Creation of the stabilization plan was urged by Controller Lawrence E. Gerosa, who held that the fiscal cushion would enable future city Controllers to be more realistic in their periodic estimates of general fund revenues.

Mr. Gerosa noted that at present, without any such cushion, the Controller is inclined to

Continued on Page 39, Column 3

HIGH COURT TELLS STATES TO END PUPIL SEGREGATION WITHIN 'REASONABLE' TIME

Southerners React Quietly, Although Some Are Defiant

Court Ruling Brings Feelings of Relief— Tensions Reduced by the Absence of Desegregation Time Limit

By PETER KIHSS

Southerners generally reacted quietly to yesterday's Supreme Court decision calling for public-school desegregation as soon as feasible.

Except for some mutterings in the Deep South there was evident a general feeling of relief. Tension appeared to have been reduced by the absence of any deadline for changing long-established local customs.

Referring the problem of timing to local Federal courts that will take into account local conditions was expected to ease tightly-drawn emotions.

The more moderate advocates of continued segregation seemed pleased that the Supreme Court had sided with them against fixing any deadline and for stressing local conditions. Many had feared a much harsher ruling from Washington.

Some thought the decision

Continued on Page 30, Column 3

NO DEADLINE SET

Federal District Courts Get Job of Checking on Compliance

Text of Supreme Court ruling is printed on Page 26.

By LUTHER A. HUSTON
Special to The New York Times

WASHINGTON, May 31—The Supreme Court directed the states today to end racial segregation in the public schools within a "reasonable" time.

Regional Federal courts were entrusted with the responsibility for determining whether local authorities made a prompt start, whether their plans were effective, and whether they were carried out in good faith.

No deadlines were fixed in the unanimous opinion written by Chief Justice Earl Warren. The court devised a flexible formula to effectuate the court's ruling of May 17 last year that separation of school pupils because of color was unconstitutional.

Full consideration was accorded the "complexities" involved and the wide variety of local conditions that must be dealt with by the authorities.

In the court's opinion, however, plainly warned those who disagreed with the ruling not to attempt to frustrate today's judgment by unreasonable or unnecessary delays. The jurisdiction of the Federal courts to act against those who "drag their feet" was retained.

Prompt Compliance Ordered

Compliance with the ruling, the court said, must begin promptly. It must be carried out in a "systematic and effective" manner and in good faith.

Officials of the Eisenhower Administration generally were gratified by the court's ruling. President Eisenhower said last November that he understood the high court did not intend to be arbitrary in establishing procedures.

The Department of Justice, in briefs and arguments submitted to the court, advocated a "middle-of-the-road" approach to the problem. Officials of the department noted with satisfaction that today's ruling included most of the basic proposals they had put forward.

Congressional reaction, for the most part, indicated relief that the court had not ordered a summary end to segregation under a rigid mandate. By permitting a gradual transition from segregated to integrated school systems, many felt, serious repercussions probably had been avoided.

Most Senators and Representatives from southern states appeared to believe, however, that complete integration of their public schools was many years away.

Negro lawyers had asked the high court to order segregation

Continued on Page 28, Column 3

EISENHOWER HINTS DELAY IN TAX CUT

Puts Balanced Budget First, Says Combination of Both Would Be 'Wonderful'

By CHARLES E. EGAN
Special to The New York Times

WASHINGTON, May 31—A balanced Federal budget takes priority over any possible cuts in taxes next year, President Eisenhower told his news conference today.

He said a combination of a balanced budget and a cut in taxes "would be a wonderful thing," but he added that the first thing to do must be to balance the budget.

The President's comments arose from questions based on reports that George M. Humphrey, Secretary of the Treasury, and other advisers had told him recently that the expanding national economy would make both the budget and tax objectives possible in the fiscal year 1957, which begins on July 1, 1956.

General Eisenhower said that none of his advisers had given him emphatic assurances on either taxes or the budget.

Against Stand-by Controls

Asked if the recent revelations about a build-up of Soviet air strength might force an increase in the budget allocations for defense, the President said he was not sure.

General Eisenhower said that he had not yet received any recommendation from the Air Force for including additional funds in the budget because of progress made in aircraft by the Soviet Union. He declared that the Government had "a very good plane" in the interim B-36 bomber, which is now equipped with jet as well as auxiliary engines, and had authorized factories producing heavy B-52 jet bombers to step up production.

On the question of economic controls the President said his Administration would not ask Congress for stand-by authority on wages and prices in event of a national emergency.

Congress must act before the end of June if the existing Defense Production Act is to continue. Unless renewed the act expires at midnight June 30.

There has been considerable discussion within the Administration on the advisability of

Continued on Page 18, Column 2

Psychiatrist for Court Here Held In Rockland as Antiques Burglar

Special to The New York Times

PIERMONT, N. Y., May 31—Dr. Price Adams Kirkpatrick, a New York City court psychiatrist, was arrested here today as a burglar.

Accused of stealing antiques valued at $1,000, he was seized at 2 A. M. when he returned to recover his own valuable camera and tripod, which he had left on the porch of the house he had robbed.

Police Chief Wallace Kile, who charged Dr. Kirkpatrick with burglary in the third degree and grand larceny, said the psychiatrist readily admitted the crimes. His only explanation of motive, the chief said, was that he liked antiques and wanted to outfit his office with them before his marriage June 10.

The loot, recovered from Dr. Kirkpatrick's Manhattan office at 120 East Seventy-second Street, consisted of a ship model valued at $500, two antique guns, six decorative copper pans, six books with rare bindings, a

hooked rug and an ancient three-foot Asian figure of carved wood.

Dr. Kirkpatrick is 33 years old and has been director of the New York City Domestic Relations Court's Bureau of Mental Health Services since Oct. 1, 1954. When arraigned before Police Judge John Gallucci here he waived examination and was held in $2,500 bail to await action by the Rockland County Grand Jury. He was lodged in the County Jail in New City pending the posting of bond.

The robbed dwelling, which was unoccupied, is on Ferndon Avenue and is owned by Charles Sparhawk, chemist and manufacturer. Mr. Sparhawk played a leading role in the psychiatrist's arrest.

Neighbors heard unfamiliar noises from the Sparhawk property about 11 o'clock last night. They telephoned the police, Chief

Continued on Page 39, Column 2

Associated Press Radiophoto

TITO ENTERTAINS SOVIET LEADERS: President Tito of Yugoslavia, smoking a cigarette in a long holder, displays model airplane to Nikita S. Khrushchev, center, Secretary of the Soviet Communist party, and Premier Nikolai A. Bulganin at Brioni Island.

President's Liking For Office Growing

By JAMES RESTON
Special to The New York Times

WASHINGTON, May 31—President Eisenhower spoke about the office of the Presidency today in more laudatory terms than at any time since he entered the White House.

In fact, he not only had a few good words to say for the Presidency as a "very fascinating experience," but he also handed down a significant personal opinion about the Vice Presidency—namely, that a Presidential nominee should get an "acceptable" Vice Presidential running mate or immediately resign.

Summarizing his political experience three years after he returned from Paris to seek the Republican Presidential nomination, the President told reporters at his seventieth news conference that he "still didn't like politics"—in the derogatory sense of that term—but

Continued on Page 19, Column 4

153

Rebel Without A Cause *was released after James Dean's death at the age of 24, in 1955.*

1955

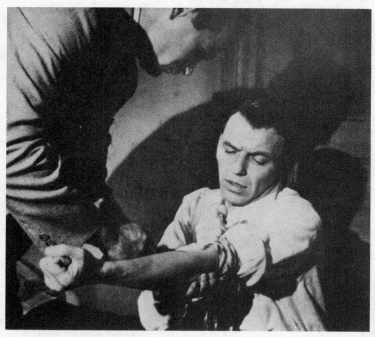

Frank Sinatra played a heroin addict in The Man With the Golden Arm.

Anna Magnani and Burt Lancaster in The Rose Tattoo.

Kirk Douglas in Ulysses, a lusty costume extravaganza.

The New York Times.

VOL. CIV. No. 35,572.   Entered as Second-Class Matter, Post Office, New York, N. Y.   NEW YORK, THURSDAY, JUNE 16, 1955.   Copyright, 1955, by The New York Times Company   Times Square, New York 36, N. Y. Telephone LAckawanna 4-1000   FIVE CENTS

STRIKE OF SEAMEN ON COAST TANKERS CALLED FOR TODAY

Spread of Walkout to Dry Cargo and Passenger Lines Appears to Be Imminent

600 SHIPS ARE INVOLVED

Conferences Continued in Hope of Avoiding General Tie-Up of Vessels

By GEORGE HORNE

A strike of seamen against the major oil tanker operators of the Atlantic and Gulf Coasts was called early this morning after all-night negotiations collapsed.

It appeared likely that in addition to the 200 oil vessels involved, the strike would spread by morning to the dry cargo and passenger fleets representing a major segment of the merchant marine.

About 600 ships were involved in the negotiations that have dragged on for weeks. Federal mediators intervened in the dispute around midnight last night, but the talks bogged down on the employer refusal to meet what was termed excessive money demands from the unions.

A total strike would affect about seventy-five United States flag vessels in the Port of New York and at least forty others along the Atlantic and Gulf.

Four unions had been holding caucuses and joint talks with the employers all day yesterday as the midnight termination of their contracts neared.

Unions Insist on Pact

The unions held to their threat, reiterated the day before yesterday, that they would cleave to their traditional policy of refusing to work in the absence of a contract.

The unions are the National Maritime Union, the Marine Engineers Beneficial Association and the American Radio Association, all affiliates of the Congress of Industrial Organizations, and the International Organization of Masters, Mates and Pilots, of the American Federation of Labor.

Joseph Curran, president of the National Maritime Union, sent out the strike call to eighteen ports, notifying its men that the tanker companies had rejected union proposals; that "we have no contracts as of June 15" and that the vessels of the struck companies should not be sailed "under any circumstances."

The twenty-two tanker companies include Gulf Oil, Texas, Sinclair Refining, Keystone Tankship Corporation, National Bulk Carriers and American Oil Company.

Their spokesman said the talks were suspended on the major question of the union's unemployment insurance benefits, patterned after the suc-

Continued on Page 63, Column 2

U.S. WEIGHT LIFTER AMAZES RUSSIANS

Anderson Hero in Moscow as He Sets 2 World Records

By CLIFTON DANIEL

MOSCOW, June 15—Muscovites had a new sports hero tonight—an American. In the presence of 15,000 of them, Paul Anderson of Toccoa, Ga., a lad of 22, weighing 340 pounds, set two world weight-lifting records.

The crowd, sitting in a drizzle in the Green Theatre of the Gorki Park of Rest and Culture, was delighted with Anderson and the new records.

"Chudo prirody" (a wonder of nature), one spectator called him.

The Georgia youth was one of a team of six weight lifters from the United States who met a Russian team in the first athletic competition held solely between the two countries since World War II.

The arrival of the Americans was hailed by friendly articles in the Soviet press, and tonight every seat in the arena was occupied, although it was raining when the match started. A large contingent from the United States diplomatic colony was present to hear the Star-Spangled Banner played—a bit awkwardly—by a police band. It

Continued on Page 45, Column 5

Argentina Deports Prelates To Rome as Riot Leaders

Six-Car Caravan of Policemen Carrying Tommyguns Escorts 2 Monsignors, Citizens, to Italy-Bound Plane

By EDWARD A. MORROW
Special to The New York Times.

BUENOS AIRES, June 15—The Argentine Government today deported two Roman Catholic monsignors accused as ringleaders of demonstrations against the regime last weekend.

After having spent twelve hours at police headquarters, Msgr. Manuel Tato, Auxiliary Bishop of Buenos Aires, and Msgr. Ramon Pablo Novoa, Canon Deacon of the diocese, were driven to Ezeiza Airport early in the morning and placed on an Aerolineas Argentinas plane bound for Rome.

Both prelates were born in Argentina and it was not ascertained under what laws they were being expelled.

[The United Press reported that Santiago Luis Cardinal Copello had conferred with four other prelates and Jeronimo Remorino, Minister of

Foreign Affairs and Worship. The Cardinal told reporters the Catholic hierarchy had demanded an official explanation of what had happened to Msgr. Tato and Msgr. Novoa.]

Eyewitnesses at the airport said the prelates had arrived in a caravan of six cars filled with plainclothesmen and policemen. As the prelates were escorted from the cars to the terminal they were guarded by policemen carrying tommyguns.

The airport was fogbound at the time and the plane, whose departure was scheduled at 8 A. M., left forty-eight minutes late. The plane received priority over other international flights. It was understood that special passports had been issued to the prelates and that these had been put in custody of the pilot.

Continued on Page 10, Column 3

U. S. and Bonn Adopt Plans For Talk With Soviet Union

By JAMES RESTON
Special to The New York Times.

WASHINGTON, June 15—The United States and West Germany have agreed on the procedures to be followed in the forthcoming conversations with the Russians. It is understood that Chancellor Konrad Adenauer and President Eisenhower reached full understanding on the following points:

¶Neither side would enter into any agreement with the Russians on any question affecting the rights of the other without prior consultation.

¶Neither side would open the highly controversial question of Germany's eastern frontiers except to reaffirm that this question was to be determined at some future date in a definitive German peace treaty.

¶Chancellor Adenauer would go to Moscow to confer with the Russians about "normalizing" relations between Bonn and Moscow, but his mission to Moscow would follow the Big Four conference in Geneva starting July 18, and it would take place only if there was prior agreement on two points.

The first point on which agreement was required was that it should be made clear in advance that the Chancellor's acceptance of the Moscow invitation did not in any way indicate the recognition by the Adenauer Government of the Communist East German Government.

[In London, Mr. Adenauer said Wednesday the West must avoid appeasement and cynicism in its conference with the Soviet Union.]

The second point was that Chancellor Adenauer must have some indication in advance that the Soviet Union would agree in Moscow to the principle of releasing German prisoners of war.

Continued on Page 2, Column 3

WEST'S MINISTERS MEET HERE TODAY

Dulles, Macmillan and Pinay to Confer 2 Days on Plans for Big Four Parley

By THOMAS J. HAMILTON

The foreign ministers of the United States, Britain and France meet here today to consider the subjects their chiefs wish to discuss with Premier Nikolai A. Bulganin next month.

The Western heads of government will confer with the Soviet Premier in Geneva starting July 18.

The Western ministers will meet at luncheon to start the two days of conferences. Secretary of State Dulles flew here from Washington yesterday. Harold Macmillan, British Foreign Secretary, and Antoine Pinay, French Foreign Minister, will arrive this morning. Mr. Dulles will join them in the Riverdale home of Sir Pierson Dixon, British representative at the United Nations.

The three Western ministers, with their advisers, will hold their first formal session this afternoon, either in Sir Pierson's home or in the Waldorf-Astoria Hotel. Tomorrow morning they will meet in the Waldorf-Astoria, where Dr. Konrad Adenauer, Chancellor of the German Federal Republic, will join them for luncheon.

San Francisco Sessions

The Western ministers, with Dr. Adenauer, will hold a final meeting in the afternoon, and Mr. Dulles will return to Washington in the evening.

Sunday morning the Western ministers will take separate planes to San Francisco, where they will attend the tenth anniversary meetings of the United Nations and hold talks preliminary to the Geneva conference with Vyacheslav M. Molotov, Soviet Foreign Minister.

Dr. Adenauer, after being the guest of M. Pinay at luncheon here Saturday, will fly to London for talks with Prime Minister Eden.

Since the Soviet Union has agreed to the Western proposal for the time and place of the meeting of the heads of governments, the principal issues that remain to be discussed, and if possible settled, with Mr. Molotov in San Francisco are:

¶The length of the meeting. The Western powers proposed three or four days, and the Soviet Union complained that this would not be long enough.

¶Whether the four heads of government should try to reach definitive settlements of East-West issues or merely fix the methods by which their subor-

Continued on Page 2, Column 5

A. M. A. QUESTIONS 'RUSH' IN RELEASE OF SALK VACCINE

But O'Connor Tells Senate Hearing No Other Shots Had Better Testing

By WILLIAM M. BLAIR
Special to The New York Times.

WASHINGTON, June 15—The American Medical Association questioned today the justification for "rushing" Salk poliomyelitis vaccine into wide use.

Basil O'Connor, president of the National Foundation for Infantile Paralysis, fired back a denial.

"No vaccine in the history of the world has had the preparation, testing, and evaluation that the Salk vaccine did," he asserted.

"There was no rush whatsoever in this thing," he told the Senate Labor and Public Welfare Committee. Representatives of the A. M. A. also were heard.

The vaccine, Mr. O'Connor said, resulted from eighteen and more years of "intensive scientific research" and there was a "moral obligation" to get it out of the laboratory research stage.

Mr. O'Connor also told the committee that "surely in July" the foundation should complete second shots for 9,000,000 first and second grade school children. First shots, he said, should be finished this week in scattered communities where the halt in the mass immunization program had delayed inoculations.

Two Viewpoints Offered

He said the foundation had indications that no more vaccine would be cleared by the Public Health Service "until the end of the month."

A foundation spokesman reported that no complete state had decided to postpone first shots until the fall school term so far as was known. However, scattered counties and communities in a few states have decided against summer-time vaccinations. He described the situation as fluid, with many areas still undecided or holding off until more news was offered on the availability of vaccine.

The A. M. A. and National Foundation viewpoints on the vaccine presented to the public evidence of the contention between the groups. Their views were elicited by questions from committee members although they had been called to testify on Democratic and Administration bills to provide free vaccine.

Dr. Julian P. Price of Florence, S. C., a trustee of the A. M. A., made clear that the Chancellor's acceptance of the Democratic plan for free vaccine to all children was "completely unnecessary." He said if it were enacted it would result in an unreasonable expenditure of Federal funds.

Furthermore, Dr. Price said, it possibly may impair state, local and voluntary programs that already are established or that now are being formulated. He also condemned indirectly

Continued on Page 34, Column 1

Molotov Visits Museum and U. N.

Vyacheslav M. Molotov is welcomed by Dag Hammarskjold. In rear are Arkady A. Sobolev, left, Soviet U. N. delegate, and Alexander Troyanovsky, Mr. Molotov's interpreter.

The New York Times.

By HARRISON E. SALISBURY

Vyacheslav M. Molotov got his first look at modern American abstract art during an impromptu tour of the Metropolitan Museum of Art yesterday. Like many other tourists, the Soviet Foreign Minister had a puzzled look and asked his guide: "What

does it mean?" Mr. Molotov's visit to the Metropolitan was the high spot of his day in New York, which began at 6:52 A. M., when he debarked from the Queen Elizabeth. As he left the Cunard pier he spoke a few words of greeting to

Continued on Page 3, Column 2

'H-BOMBS' TEST U. S. CIVIL DEFENSE; GOVERNMENT IS MOVED TO HIDE-OUTS; CITY RAID ALERT TERMED A SUCCESS

GOVERNMENT LEADERS AT SECRET BASE: President Eisenhower with Cabinet members and other aides in tent during alert. Seated from left: Postmaster General Arthur Summerfield; the President; Val Peterson, Civil Defense Director; Lewis L. Strauss, chairman of Atomic Energy Commission; Arthur Flemming, across from President, Defense Mobilizer; Treasury Secretary George M. Humphrey; Attorney General Herbert Brownell Jr.

Associated Press Wirephoto

City Clears Streets Quickly As Big Zone Is 'Wiped Out'

By PETER KIHSS

The city's millions faced up to a simulated hydrogen bomb attack yesterday for the first time. On a gloriously warm and sunny day traffic was stilled and citizens generally moved indoors for ten minutes. For their disciplined cooperation they won the praise of civil defense leaders.

There were shadows on the test. A premature all-clear siren blast sent citizens in the Times Square area swarming back into the streets four minutes before the scheduled end of the public drill at 2:15 P. M. Downtown, a siren went off at the Elizabeth Street police station two minutes before time.

Thirty-one persons were arrested for non - cooperation. Twenty-eight were pacifists in a joint sit-down demonstration in City Hall Park, and another was a lone picket there. Still another was a pedestrian who refused to take shelter in Harlem. The other was a driver who wouldn't get out of his truck in the Bedford-Stuyvesant section of Brooklyn.

State law makes non-compliance with Civil Defense orders in such exercises a misdemeanor, punishable by up to a year in prison, $500 fine or both.

But behind the relatively placid and short-lived street phases of the test, in which a big zone of the city was theoretically wiped out, 22,000 civil defense workers — mostly volunteers — were starting a twenty-six-hour drill, wrestling with problems that would be posed by a bomb literally wiping out the heart of the city.

The imagined missile—equivalent to 5,000,000 tons of TNT—supposedly slammed down at

Continued on Page 17, Column 3

TRADE BILL SENT TO WHITE HOUSE

Senate Approves Extension Measure — Byrd Cites 'Reasonable' Protection

By ALLEN DRURY
Special to The New York Times.

WASHINGTON, June 15—The Senate approved and sent to the President today a bill extending the reciprocal trade program to June 30, 1958.

Passage was by voice vote. The House of Representatives passed the bill yesterday by a roll-call vote of 347 to 54.

The measure continues the President's authority to cut tariffs without previous approval of Congress in return for trade concessions from other nations. He would be empowered to cut most tariffs 5 per cent below the levels of last Jan. 1 in each of the next three years.

Opposition Collapses

The bill also contains several "protectionist" amendments approved by a joint Senate-House conference committee over protests of some House Democrats. Their general effect is to make it easier for domestic industries to appeal for higher tariffs on imports when they can show they are being injured by competition.

Some Democrats had said the amendments would cripple the program by making it easier to bring pressure on the President. But the White House said they were acceptable, and the opposition collapsed.

Before the vote, Senator Harry F. Byrd, chairman of the Finance Committee that wrote the limiting amendments asserted that conference bill "offer the best approach that could be devised to continue our foreign trade on a basis of reciprocity and, at the same time, protect in reasonable fashion the proper interests of American industry."

The Virginia Democrat said his committee favored changes in the bill, which was passed by the House without amendment at White House insistence, for two reasons.

Since the program began in 1934, he said, the nation's wage scale has risen much faster than in other countries. At the same time, he continued, thanks to the foreign-aid program, "the industrial plants of importing nations, especially of textiles and chemicals, have been rebuilt and modernized without cost to such nations."

Continued on Page 24, Column 6

---

3 Steal 18 Weapons In 5th Ave. Gunshop

Three robbers acquired a choice arms collection yesterday.

They even took their own ammunition to a hold-up of the Stoeger Arms Corporation, 507 Fifth Avenue, near Forty-second Street, and used it to load one of the company's finer shotguns, then they held up Val Nisbeth, 32-year-old manager, who was alone in the second-floor shop, and escaped with sixteen pistols and two shotguns.

The value of the loot was $1,160. The police of the East Thirty-fifth Street station, however, were more concerned with the probability that the crime was the prelude to a series of major hold-ups.

For Mr. Nisbeth, who lives in Chappaqua, N. Y., told detectives the three apparently had "cased" the shop on Tuesday,

Continued on Page 16, Column 6

---

61 CITIES 'RUINED'

President and Cabinet 'Flee' Capital With His Key Aides

By ANTHONY LEVIERO
Special to The New York Times.

EMERGENCY PRESS HEADQUARTERS, Operation Alert, June 15—The nation's ability to cope with a hydrogen-bomb attack was tested today for the first time.

Millions of Americans were assumed to be killed and scores of cities left in flaming, radioactive ruins by the simulated attack.

The upper echelons of the Executive branch of the Government were actually dispersed in about thirty hide-outs, with President Eisenhower directing national affairs from a secret headquarters.

Late this afternoon the East Coast, including New York and New Jersey, the West Coast and the twin cities Minneapolis and St. Paul in the Midwest, were reported struck by simulated atomic and hydrogen bombs.

Vital centers of the nation were under the assumed blight of radioactive fall-out from hydrogen bombs that could paralyze them for some time.

In a recapitulation tonight, the Federal Civil Defense Administration estimated assumed casualties at 5,000,000 killed and almost 5,000,000 injured. It also estimated that 10,000,000 persons had been made homeless, creating serious welfare problems.

New England Hard Hit

The heaviest casualties were assumed to be in New England, with 3,000,000 supposedly dead and 2,579,000 injured. The number of persons estimated displaced in New England was 6,733,000.

The agency also said that fifty - five cities in the continental United States and six in the territories had been struck by assumed weapons ranging from 600 kilotons in atomic bombs and from one to five megatons in the hydrogen bomb category.

The results of the test ranged from indifference and confusion in some cities to well-disciplined drills and even evacuations in others. The nation's biggest centers "counted" casualties in the hundreds of thousands—760,- 340 presumed killed and 383,860 injured in Philadelphia; 513,225 dead and 422,270 injured in Chicago, 57,600 killed and 94,800 hurt in Detroit, 584,000 killed and 502,000 hurt in Los Angeles

Continued on Page 16, Column 2

EISENHOWER GOES TO SECRET CENTER

Takes Command, Broadcasts Declaration of Emergency in Simulated Bombings

By W. H. LAWRENCE
Special to The New York Times.

EMERGENCY WHITE HOUSE, June 15—President Eisenhower took personal command tonight of a nation supposedly devastated by a mock surprise atomic attack that smashed more than fifty of its cities.

He declared a simulated state of national emergency, calling into play his vast reservoir of powers as President and Commander in Chief of the Armed Forces. He reported to the nation by radio and television on the exercise designed to test the ability of the Government to recover and operate in a sudden attack.

Tonight he established his headquarters at a temporary White House relocation center in a mountainous wooded area within 300 miles of Washington.

He left Washington by automobile after noon as the sirens wailed their warning. It was three hours and twenty minutes before enemy planes supposedly dropped a hydrogen bomb with the explosive power of 5,000,000 tons of dynamite.

Cabinet Precedes Him

In his speeding Cadillac, he signed the declaration of emergency as he headed toward the relocation center to which his Cabinet and other key officials had moved by automobile and helicopter.

It was from this center that he reported to the nation by television and radio and then held a ninety-minute emergency session with key Government leaders.

Major television and radio networks were less than an hour's notice that the President would utilize the closed circuit network the Government had constructed and held in readiness for just such an emergency.

The broadcast was carried "live" by the National Broadcasting Company and DuMont television networks, and on radio by the National Broadcasting Company, the Columbia Broadcasting System and the American Broadcasting Company.

"We are here," the President told the nation, "to determine whether or not the Government is prepared in time of emergency to continue the function of government so that there will be no interruption in the business that must be carried on."

His press secretary, James C. Hagerty, said that if this test were the real thing the President would have used the radio and TV networks to report personally "to every citizen on the

Continued on Page 16, Column 6

WARNING FLASHED TO CONTROL POINTS

Operation Room Integrates Reports of 'Damages'

By DAMON STETSON
Special to The New York Times.

BATTLE CREEK, Mich., June 15—Shortly after 11 A. M., Eastern standard time today, the commanding general of the Thirtieth Air Division, United States Air Force, warned of an impending but hypothetical attack in the Michigan area.

The air warning officer of the Federal Civil Defense Administration at the division's headquarters picked up his telephone and flashed the word to Civil Defense headquarters here.

At the same time, the warning went by connecting lines to key centers throughout Michigan, Wisconsin, Indiana, Ohio, Kentucky and portions of other states within the Thirtieth Air Division's jurisdiction.

The warning, which set condition Lemon Juice—nickname for today's alert—was received in the operations center of National Civil Defense headquarters at 11:05 A. M. (12:05 P. M., Eastern daylight time).

Elsewhere in the nation similar warnings were flashed as hypothetical enemy bombers were reported over central Can-

Continued on Page 15, Column 2

Vic Morrow, Sidney Poitier and Glenn Ford in Blackboard Jungle.

Spencer Tracy and Ernest Borgnine in
Bad Day at Black Rock.

1955

Gary Grant and Grace Kelly
on the Riviera in To Catch A
Thief.

James Cagney and Henry
Fonda in Mister Roberts.

"All the News
That's Fit to Print"

The New York Times.

LATE CITY EDITION
Fair and seasonably warm today.
Fair, quite warm tomorrow.
Temperature Range Today—Max., 80; Min., 67
Temperatures Yesterday—Max., 77.5; Min., 66.5
Full U. S. Weather Bureau Report, Page 26

Copyright, 1955, by The New York Times Company.

VOL. CIV. No. 35,616.

Entered as Second-Class Matter,
Post Office, New York, N. Y.

NEW YORK, SATURDAY, JULY 30, 1955.

Times Square, New York 36, N. Y.
Telephone LAckawanna 4-1000

FIVE CENTS

TALBOTT QUITTING, PERHAPS AT ONCE, G. O. P. SOURCES SAY

But the White House Asserts 'There's Nothing Before Us' —Secretary 'Sits Tight'

ANOTHER INQUIRY LOOMS

Democrats Charge He Misled Them on Chrysler Stock by Giving It to Children

By ALLEN DRURY
Special to The New York Times.

WASHINGTON, July 29—Republican Senators high in Administration councils said tonight that the resignation of Harold E. Talbott as Secretary of the Air Force was "imminent."

The Senators, who declined to be quoted by name, said the resignation might be announced over the weekend. At the White House, the Presidential press secretary, James C. Hagerty, would say only, "There is nothing before us."

Mr. Talbott said he was "sitting tight" and "has no more idea than a jackrabbit" that he was resigning.

He said he would be at his office in the morning and that he was "going ahead and try and run the Air Force if I have tried to do through all of this."

[A possibility, at least, that the Secretary would resign was discerned by The Associated Press, which quoted him as having said later, "I will do nothing at any time to embarrass President Eisenhower, and I will do whatever the President wishes me to do."]

The embattled Cabinet officer, already under investigation with business for a management consultant corporation in which he was a partner, appeared to be headed for still another inquiry.

Senators Differ With Him

This one would revolve around a promise he made at the time of his appointment in 1953 to divest himself of 2,000 shares of Chrysler stock.

The new investigation, it was indicated, might be instigated by Democratic members of the Senate Armed Services Committee, which handled the Talbott nomination two years ago. They charged today that he had "improperly misled" them at that time concerning his plans for the stock.

Mr. Talbott testified Wednesday before the Senate Permanent Subcommittee on Investigations that he had given the stock to his four children, two of them minors. The Secretary said he had made it clear to the Armed Services Committee that he might give the stock away instead of selling it outright. But members of that committee said today they had had no such understanding.

A report that Carmine G. De-Sapio, head of Tammany Hall, was a guest at the Islip home, presumably to discuss the appointment of a new Police Commissioner, was spiked by the Mayor. Mr. DeSapio, he said, was not there and was not expected.

"I'll name the new Police Commissioner myself without consultation with anybody," the Mayor declared.

The Mayor did receive visits

Continued on Page 6, Column 7

Court Rejects Plea To Deport Bridges

Special to The New York Times.

SAN FRANCISCO, July 29—Federal Judge Louis E. Goodman today refused to strip Harry Renton Bridges, Pacific Coast labor leader, of his United States citizenship.

Judge Goodman, in the Government's fourth attempt to deport Mr. Bridges to his native Australia, ruled the prosecution had not proved its charges that the longshore leader had been a member of the Communist party before he was naturalized Sept. 17, 1945.

United States Attorney Lloyd H. Burke and Lynn J. Gillard and Robert H. Schnacke, assistant Federal attorneys, prosecuted the case. They said a decision to appeal would depend on the outcome of consultation with Department of Justice officials in Washington.

Continued on Page 10, Column 6

J. E. HOOVER SHUNS CITY POLICE POST

Declines Mayor's Bid to Be Commissioner—Wagner Is Said to Seek Outsider

By PAUL CROWELL

J. Edgar Hoover, director of the Federal Bureau of Investigation, has declined an invitation by Mayor Wagner to become the city's next Police Commissioner.

The offer of appointment to the $25,000 post now held by Francis W. H. Adams was made by the Mayor early this week through an unidentified emissary described at City Hall as a close friend of the F. B. I. chief.

Mr. Adams announced his resignation last Sunday but is remaining at his post until the Mayor appoints a successor.

The first announcement of Mr. Hoover's rejection of the Mayor's offer came from Washington. It was made by Louis B. Nichols, an assistant director of the F. B. I., after he had talked on the telephone with his chief. Mr. Nichols said Mr. Hoover was traveling "somewhere on the West Coast."

"Mr. Hoover has no plans to leave the F. B. I. and has declined Mayor Wagner's kind offer," Mr. Nichols said. He then telephoned the same announcement to William R. Peer, the Mayor's executive secretary. Mr. Peer passed the word along to the Mayor, who is spending the week-end at his summer home in Islip, L. I. The Mayor had no comment.

CONGRESS CHIEFS ABANDON PLANS TO ADJOURN TODAY

House to Meet on Monday —Fuel Gas Bill Sidetracked —Public Housing Set Back

Special to The New York Times.

WASHINGTON, July 29—Congress was caught tonight in the traditional minor frenzy of the eleventh hour as the controlling Democrats labored urgently toward bringing this session to an end.

All hope for an adjournment by tomorrow night, as had long been planned, was abandoned.

The Senate was in position to finish its work by then but the House of Representatives had a solid docket of work still ahead. Late in the day the House Democratic floor leader, Representative John W. McCormack of Massachusetts, officially announced that there would be a House meeting on Monday.

He prepared a calendar of business that will result in carrying Congress into next week.

The House quit for the night at 6:17 P. M. and will reassemble at 10:30 tomorrow morning.

Pressing to meet the original quitting date as nearly as they could, the Senate leaders officially cast aside until next year the most controversial single measure remaining on that side.

Defeat for President

This was a bill, passed 209 to 203 last night by the House, to exempt natural gas producers from Federal price control.

The decision was in a modified sense a blow to the President, who had expressed support in principle for the bill.

It was a much heavier blow. It enabled the leading Democrats of Congress, including Sam Rayburn of Texas, Speaker of the House of Representatives, and the ailing Senate Democratic chieftain, Senator Lyndon B. Johnson of Texas.

While many Republicans had gone along with the bill, its essential backers were the leaders and other Southern and Southwestern Democratic members of Congress from the gas-producing states.

Adamantly against the project was the great bulk of the Northern wing of the Democratic party in Congress, especially the members from urban consumer areas.

The President, too, was suffering setbacks, however provisional some might turn out to be. For the White House was understood to be appealing privately for some aspects of his program.

The House, with the encouragement of the Republican administration leadership, by 217 to 188 knocked all public housing out of an omnibus housing bill.

The President had requested authority for the construction of 35,000 public housing units a year for two years.

One hundred fifty-one House Republicans voted with sixty-six Democrats to deny even this much public housing, though for complicated reasons not necessarily

Continued on Page 6, Column 4

U.S. TO LAUNCH EARTH SATELLITE 200-300 MILES INTO OUTER SPACE; WORLD WILL GET SCIENTIFIC DATA

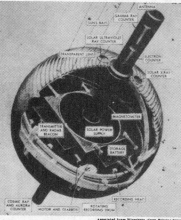

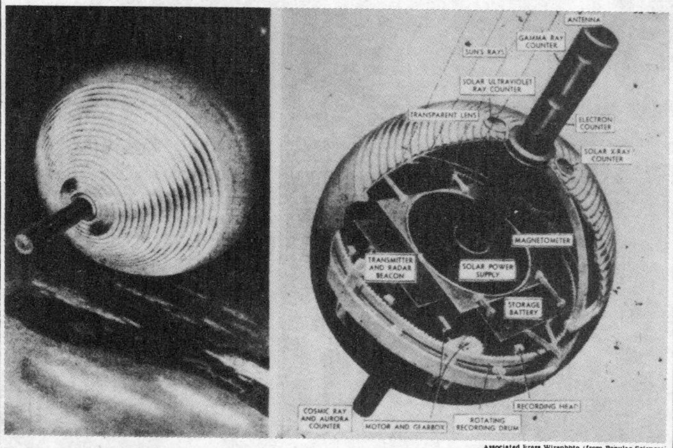

MAN-MADE SATELLITE: Artist's renditions of the earth-circling satellite, based on a concept of Prof. S. F. Singer of the University of Maryland. Professor Singer's specifications—diameter of about two feet, weight 100 pounds and speed 17,280 miles an hour—conform closely with those of the announcement from the White House.

Associated Press Wirephoto (from Popular Science)

PACE 18,000 M.P.H.

Rocket to Start Object Size of a Basketball in 1957 or 1958

Texts of press conference and documents, Pages 8 and 9.

By RUSSELL BAKER
Special to The New York Times.

WASHINGTON, July 29—This country plans to launch history's first man-made, earth-circling satellite into space during 1957 or 1958.

Tentative plans envision an unmanned globular object about the size of a basketball. The satellite will flash around the earth about once every ninety minutes at a speed of 18,000 miles an hour in a fixed path 200 to 300 miles above the ground.

These plans were announced this afternoon at an extraordinary White House news conference attended by a battery of prominent scientists.

James C. Hagerty, White House press secretary, joined the scientists in stressing the satellite's immense scientific value to all nations and minimizing its threat as a potential instrument of war.

All nations, including the Communist countries, will have complete access to all scientific data gathered beyond the earth's known frontier, Mr. Hagerty said.

American scientists also will give the world the plot of the satellite's orbit, or course through space, so that scholars of all countries may study it.

Data Available to All

If the object carries radio equipment for transmitting scientific data to the earth, other nations will receive the broadcasting frequencies so they can tune in.

The satellite will girdle the earth "entirely for scientific purposes," Mr. Hagerty said.

"Do you mean as distinct from war-making purposes?" he was asked.

"If you wish, yes," he replied.

Scientists said they were convinced that the satellite was now "feasible" with available technological methods and materials.

Once aloft, they said, it is expected to produce new information about the unexplored outer atmosphere that is necessary before human travel in space can be undertaken.

As the scientists depicted it, the satellite would be hurled into space under rocket power. The rocket, in several stages, would fall away piece by piece as each stage burnt out its fuel load.

At a point somewhere between 200 and 300 miles above earth, the satellite—or "the bird," as the scientists call it—would get one final mighty blast from the rocket's last stage.

This would send it hurtling into its orbit at a speed of 18,000 miles an hour. A man standing on earth could perhaps barely

Continued on Page 7, Column 1

R.A.F. IS RETURNING 400 U.S. SABRE JETS

Set to Replace Fighters With British-Made Aircraft, to Be Paid For in Aid Funds

Special to The New York Times.

LONDON, July 29—Britain announced today she was returning 400 Sabre Jet fighters to the United States and replacing them with British-made Hawker Hunters.

The British jets will be paid for by the United States under the Mutual Defense Assistance Program. The contract for the planes totals $140,000,000. It was signed more than a year ago, but the Hunter has been haunted by production delays.

Today's announcement indicates both the United States and Royal Air Forces are confident that the Hunter's time of trial is over, and that the planes are being produced in satisfactory numbers.

"Several" Royal Air Force squadrons are already equipped with them, an Air Ministry spokesman said.

The Hunter, which is comparable in performance with the Sabre Jet, or North American F-86F, flies about 650 miles an hour in operational trim.

The 400 Sabre Jets are being replaced not because they are

Continued on Page 3, Column 3

Russians Already Striving To Set Up Space Satellite

By HARRY SCHWARTZ

The United States and the Soviet Union now appear to be in a race for the glory of making the first major step toward interplanetary flight—the launching of an earth satellite in space. Soviet determination to achieve this objective was announced last April 15 in the newspaper Vechernaya Moskva (Evening Moscow).

The newspaper revealed then that a committee of top Soviet scientists, including the renowned physicist Prof. Peter Kapitsa, had been set up to devise a satellite in space somewhat similar to that outlined in Washington.

Research scientists in the Pentagon said the man-made satellite, whizzing around the earth with a tumbling motion, would give them valuable information. This could be applied to flight studies for the intercontinental ballistics missile, a dread atomic weapon now being developed for wars between the continents.

There are two important things that the satellite will not be able to do:

1. It will have no utility for gaining terrestrial data that might be used as part of President Eisenhower's Geneva plan for inspecting the military establishments of the United States and Russia.

2. It will not be able to drop nuclear weapons, or anything else for that matter, back on tile country.

The first satellite may have a mouse aboard, but scientists said they could not foresee the time when human beings would be able to go into outer space as passengers.

The Return Expected

The greatest return the scientists expect from the first satellite will be knowledge of conditions in the outer atmosphere —for instance, the density of it at different altitudes, a field of knowledge with large gaps in it.

The first satellite also is expected to provide new information about:

¶The nature of the sun.
¶Solar radio noise.
¶Cosmic radiation.
¶Magnetic noises and their causes.
¶The aurora, or luminous, static - producing phenomenon that radiates from the north and south magnetic poles.

Defense Department research scientists pleaded with reporters to repress any tendency to exploit speculations that have been popularized in recent years by fiction writers. They said the possibility of human passengers in a man-made satellite and its use for military purposes were so remotely in the future that speculations about it were practically useless.

In stressing that all the data they will gain will be in abstract and basic science, the military

Continued on Page 7, Column 6

NO MILITARY ROLE FOR GLOBAL BALL

Device Cannot Survey Land Nor Can It Drop Bomb— Its Goal Is Defined

By ANTHONY LEVIERO
Special to The New York Times.

WASHINGTON, July 29—The earth satellite will have no practicable military application in the foreseeable future. However, it will help man come to a better understanding of the natural laws of the universe.

A. E. C. CITES GAINS IN H-BOMB FIELD

Designs of New Arms Based on '54 Tests—Reactors for Plane Engines Advanced

Special to The New York Times.

WASHINGTON, July 29—Hydrogen weapons, apparently of several types, have been produced for the United States atomic arsenal in the first six months of this year.

The atomic energy commission disclosed this today in its eighteenth semiannual report. The design of the new weapons was based on the results of the spectacular 1954 hydrogen bomb tests in the Pacific.

The weapons advance was one of several major developments reported by the commission. Others were:

¶The commission's program for developing reactors for industrial and military electric power and for naval and aircraft propulsion "made greater strides during the first six months of 1955 than in any earlier half-year."

On the aircraft problem the

Continued on Page 15, Column 4

Three Ex-G. I. Turncoats Land in San Francisco and Are Jailed by Army

Capt. Walter R. Leahy, right, reads a summary of court-martial charges against the turncoats before formally taking them into custody. The prisoners are, from left, Otho G. Bell, William C. Cowart and Lewis W. Griggs.

Associated Press Wirephoto

President Sees Party In Control 'Forever'

Special to The New York Times.

WASHINGTON, July 29—President Eisenhower said today that a properly unified Republican party could retain control of the national Administration "forever."

Addressing a Republican pre-adjournment breakfast rally, the President urged Republican legislators to get behind the principles he advocates.

He gave no sign whether he intended to lead the party again next year, but Republicans who have been urging him to run for re-election appeared encouraged.

Reporters were not invited to the meeting this morning. It was attended by all but a few of the Republicans in the Senate and House of Representatives, and members of the Cabinet and several members of the White House staff. James C. Hagerty, White House press secretary, gave a summary of

Continued on Page 6, Column 6

By LAWRENCE E. DAVIES
Special to The New York Times.

SAN FRANCISCO, July 29—Three dishonorably discharged soldiers who renounced America two years ago for life in Communist China came home today to an emotional greeting from relatives and to an Army stockade. They promised to "gladly accept whatever punishment is coming to us."

When the American President liner President Cleveland docked this afternoon after a trip from the Orient military policemen promptly arrested William C. Cowart, 22 years old, of Dalton, Ga.; Lewis W. Griggs, 22, of Jacksonville, Tex., and Otho G. Bell, 24, formerly of Hillsboro, Miss. They listened intently and soberly while Capt. Walter R. Leahy of the provost marshal's office at the San Francisco Presidio read a 400-word summary of court-martial charges based on their alleged

Continued on Page 10, Column 8

U. S.-Peiping Trade Of Shows Proposed

By THOMAS F. BRADY
Special to The New York Times.

PARIS, July 29—A Chinese Communist theatrical company and an American theatrical company have exchanged invitations to appear in each other's country.

The reciprocal invitations are subject to Government approval on both sides, but it is known that both Governments are aware of the project.

The participants, whose cultural olive branches may add another bit of greenery to the signs of post - "cold - war" spring, are the Peiping Opera, which is now touring Europe, and the Everyman Opera, which has presented George Gershwin's "Porgy and Bess" in most major European cities west of the Iron Curtain.

On the Chinese side the project has at least semi-official approval already. The invitation was extended by

Continued on Page 15, Column 5

Sofia Offers Israel Air Crash Damages

Special to The New York Times.

TEL AVIV, Israel, July 29—The Bulgarian Government has agreed to pay at least part compensation for the shooting down of an Israeli airliner Wednesday. Fifty-eight persons, including twelve New Yorkers, died in the crash.

A Foreign Office spokesman said today the Bulgarian promise was made yesterday in a note to Baruch Nir, Israeli chargé d'affaires in Sofia.

Bulgaria will permit three Israeli aircraft investigators, who have been waiting in Greece, to go to the scene of the crash, Athens reported Friday.

The Bulgarian note expressed the Sofia Government's "profound regret" and notified Israel of the appointment of a special Government commission to inquire into the circumstances of what it called "the deplorable accident." The Bul-

Continued on Page 2, Column 8

Marilyn Monroe and Tom Ewell in the world-famous scene from The Seven Year Itch.

Kay Starr's #1 hit was Rock and Roll Waltz.

Dungaree Doll, On the Street Where You Live and Cindy, Oh Cindy kept Eddie Fisher in the public eye in the Fifties.

Among Little Richard's greatest hits were Tutti Fruitti, Long Tall Sally, Slippin' and Slidin' and Good Golly Miss Molly.

Chuck Berry rocketed to fame with Sweet Little Sixteen, Maybelline and Roll Over Beethoven.

"All the News That's Fit to Print"

The New York Times.

LATE CITY EDITION
Heavy rain and high winds today; clearing tonight. Fair tomorrow.
Temperature Range Today-Max., 79; Min., 71
Temperatures Yesterday-Max., 78.6; Min., 67
Full U. S. Weather Bureau Report, Page 61

VOL. CV..No. 35,668. Entered as Second-Class Matter, Post Office, New York, N. Y. NEW YORK, TUESDAY, SEPTEMBER 20, 1955. Times Square, New York 36, N. Y. Telephone LAckawanna 4-1000 FIVE CENTS

PERON'S REGIME IS OVERTHROWN; JUNTA WILL MEET WITH REBELS; CROWDS HAIL FALL OF DICTATOR

GALES MOVE ON THE CITY; SOUTH IS HIT

DAMAGE IS SEVERE

New York Area Due to Feel the Effects of Hurricane Today

By PETER KIHSS

Hurricane Ione tore wide destruction in coastal North Carolina when it roared in from the Atlantic Ocean yesterday morning.

Then it slowed down and became a tricky problem that kept the entire Eastern Seaboard worried.

In Washington the United States Weather Bureau said at 3 o'clock this morning that the tropical twister was centered about twenty miles southeast of Norfolk, Va., with winds of over thirty-five miles an hour swirling outward 200 miles to the north and east.

Swirling northeastward at eight to ten miles an hour, it is expected to pick up speed and intensity as it swings out to sea. It was expected to be off the Delaware coast this morning and southeast of Long Island in the afternoon.

Ernest J. Christie, in charge of the Weather Bureau here, said at 3 o'clock this morning that New York City would feel the worst effects of the storm later today.

The center of the storm, he said, would pass southeast of the city during the day. New York City, on the northern fringe of the storm, would have heavy rain at times with wind velocities of forty to fifty miles an hour and gusts possibly up to sixty miles an hour. Clearing weather was forecast for tonight.

Forecasts Are Qualified

Hurricane force is seventy-five miles an hour or more, according to the Weather Bureau scale.

But meteorologists were qualifying all their forecasts, warning that Ione—whose name comes from the Greek word meaning "go"—was an erratic personality.

Ione, hatched last Wednesday east of Puerto Rico, did millions of dollars worth of damage as it roared overland across the coastal areas of North Carolina with winds up to 107 miles an hour.

Communications lines were down, roads and bridges washed out, crops destroyed, large areas of cities flooded and hundreds made homeless.

Reports of the damage were fragmentary, but mounting rapidly as communications were restored. Four persons were reported dead at New Bern, N. C., and three at Beaufort, N. C. The Red Cross said it was providing shelter for 1,800 persons in the state.

New Bern, a city of 15,000 persons, was jammed before the hurricane with hundreds of refugees from tidal river lowlands. Forty blocks of the city were flooded and for fifteen hours the community was without power, communications and drinking

Continued on Page 24, Column 1

Hilda Rips Tampico In 'Worst Disaster'

By The United Press.

MEXICO CITY, Sept. 19—President Adolfo Ruiz Cortines tonight ordered unlimited Government aid for storm-lashed Tampico as Hurricane Hilda sent a flood of "catastrophic proportions" over three-quarters of the port city.

The President said Tampico, cut off by winds and water from the outside world, was confronted with "the worst disaster in its history."

[The Associated Press said Monday that Gov. Horacio Teran reported the hurricane had killed twelve persons and injured 350 in Tampico. The Governor of Tamaulipas State said 90 per cent of the buildings in the city had been damaged and 15,000 were homeless. A state of emergency was ordered.]

A medical brigade of 200

Continued on Page 24, Column 7

CITY IS PREPARED FOR STORM'S FURY

Lines Kept Open From Center at Police Headquarters to Waiting Emergency Men

Residents of the metropolitan area battened down for Hurricane Ione yesterday while Government and welfare agencies made elaborate plans to mitigate the fury of wind, rain and high tides.

New York and surrounding communities, long forewarned, appeared to be prepared as never before to weather a big storm.

The focal point of relief, rescue and damage control activities was Mayor Wagner's board of planning and operations sitting at Police Headquarters.

A communications center in the line-up room, staffed by 114 policemen, maintained open lines to all city departments and welfare agencies. Representatives of each organization were posted there at nightfall ready to flash orders to emergency crews on stand-by throughout the city.

Police Commissioner Stephen P. Kennedy urged the public, in event of emergency, to telephone available information to the Police Department.

The Civil Defense Administration, on alert since Sunday night, had its 149 fire and rescue units ready for instant action. At 5 P. M. Robert E. Condon, City Director of Civil Defense, ordered his top personnel to remain on duty until further notice.

Two thousand Red Cross workers were standing by in the city and neighboring communities. The city's Department of Welfare was similarly prepared to staff 100 relief centers in the five boroughs.

In Albany three units of the New York National Guard, including the Forty-second Division station here, were alerted.

Continued on Page 24, Column 8

HARRIMAN READY TO COMPETE IN '56, ADVISER DECLARES

Prendergast Says Governor Would Oppose Stevenson if Party Wanted Him

By WARREN WEAVER Jr.
Special to The New York Times.

ALBANY, Sept. 19—Governor Harriman will seek the Presidential nomination next year if "convinced the convention wanted him," the Democratic State Chairman said today.

The chairman asserted the Governor would do this even in the event of a floor fight with Adlai E. Stevenson.

Michael H. Prendergast, the Governor's chief political lieutenant, declared that under such conditions Mr. Harriman would take the nomination "regardless of whether Stevenson stepped aside or not."

This was the first public indication from within his official political family that Mr Harriman's repeated expressions of support for Mr. Stevenson might be weakening in the face of insistence that he seek the nomination.

Charles Van Devander, the Governor's press secretary, said tonight there would be no comment from his office on the Prendergast statement. He said the Governor was in New York City. The Governor's aides in New York likewise said there would be no comment.

For the last year whenever Presidential politics were discussed, Mr. Harriman has said "I'm for Stevenson." smiled broadly and declined to discuss any other possibilities.

Says Democrats Can Win

Mr. Prendergast is the Governor's personal choice to succeed Richard H. Balch as head of the Democratic State Committee last July.

The Democratic chairman characterized as "a lot of nonsense" Republican assertions that no opponent could beat President Eisenhower.

"I don't give a damn who they run," Mr. Prendergast declared. "We can win next year with the right man, and I think Harriman is the right man. Regardless of who he says he's for, I'm representing the Democratic party—the rank and file of it—when I say I'm for Harriman."

Although Mr. Prendergast said he could not speak for the Governor, he described Mr. Harriman indirectly as a man who was thinking now in terms of his own candidacy, rather than Mr. Stevenson's or anyone else's.

"I know Mr. Harriman well enough to know that he is so definitely interested in a Democratic victory in 1956 that if he felt someone else, other than himself, were stronger and had a better chance of winning, he would be for him regardless," the state chairman declared.

Mr. Prendergast's analysis of the situation was made at a press conference. He called the session to announce that former President Harry S. Truman would speak at the state-wide Democratic candidate's rally here on Oct. 7.

The state chairman was generally deprecatory of Mr. Stevenson's chances. He said that the former Illinois Governor's announcement of his plans in November "isn't going to stampede anybody." He predicted that getting the nomination would be "no walkover for Stevenson."

Sees Swing to Harriman

On the contrary, Mr. Prendergast said, prospects that the national convention might look favorably on Mr. Harriman appear to be increasing daily.

"I think we're going into the convention with a lot of sentiment in our favor," he asserted. "Unless something unforeseen happens, I don't see how we can miss."

He later amended this to say he believed that the Governor has "a better than even chance of getting the nomination."

Mr. Prendergast was asked if the Governor had requested him to "soft-pedal" his Harriman-for-President campaign, inasmuch as Mr. Harriman was on record for Mr. Stevenson.

"No, he's said nothing about that," the chairman replied.

Mr. Prendergast also announced that he would open an upstate office for the State Committee in the Sheraton Ten Eyck Hotel here on Oct. 1. It will include offices for Miss Mary Louise Nice of Tonawanda, state committee vice chairman, and Carmine G. DeSapio, the party's national committeeman.

The Democratic leader said he was particularly glad to have

Continued on Page 22, Column 5

U. S. TIES HINTED

Will Grant Recognition to Insurgents as They Take Over Nation

By DANA ADAMS SCHMIDT
Special to The New York Times.

WASHINGTON, Sept. 19—Administration officials said tonight that the United States would undoubtedly recognize any new Argentine Government that showed it was in control of the country.

The State Department, insisting that any comment at this time would be a form of interference, declined to discuss the attitude the United States might take toward a new Argentine Government.

However, other officials of the Administration pointed out that the United States had followed the practice of recognizing Latin-American revolutionary governments as soon as they exercised full authority. In some cases there has been preliminary discussion with other Latin-American governments.

But the fact that relations between the United States and President Juan D. Perón were frequently strained during his nine years as President made it unlikely the United States would hesitate, these officials said.

Hostile Attitude Cited

For several years after President Perón had taken power his attitude toward the United States was hostile, thus playing upon popular antipathies toward the "Yankee imperialists." However, in recent years relations between Washington and Buenos Aires have been correct, although "hardly warm," in the view of one diplomatic student of Latin-American affairs.

President Perón has sought and obtained from the United States a number of loans that have helped his Government through the difficulties that followed the application of "Perónist economics." This consisted of building up industry at the expense of agriculture.

As to whether the United States has ever "supported" the Peronist regime, there are strong differences of opinion among officials. The prevailing view is that the United States Government's attitude has been carefully "objective."

While avoiding anything that would look like official interference, State Department officials told a Congressional committee after the unsuccessful June 16 rising in Argentina that they were seeking to use United States influence quietly to prevent persecution of the Roman Catholic Church.

Catholic groups in the United States at that time demanded that the United States openly

Continued on Page 2, Column 6

COMMAND VAGUE

Rebels Believed to Be in 3 Groups, With No Over-All Chief

By TAD SZULC
Special to The New York Times.

SANTIAGO, Chile, Sept. 19—Broadcasts from Argentina indicated today that the rebel forces were operating with at least three separate commands and that no over-all chief of the movement had yet emerged.

Admiral Issac Rojas was in charge of the naval operation along the Argentine coast and of the marine units ashore. There were contradictory reports as to the identity of the leaders of the insurgent army forces operating inland.

In a telephone interview from the headquarters of the rebel-directed Second Army in Mendoza, in the foothills of the Andes, a general who identified himself as the chief of staff of the revolutionary command said that Gen. Eduardo Leonardi was the top military leader of the movement.

He said that General Leonardi was in Cordoba, where attacks of the Government forces had been fought off for several days.

General About 52 Years Old

He described General Leonardi as a "respected" officer who had served at one time as an Argentine military attaché abroad. He said General Leonardi was about 52 years old. No other data about General Leonardi were available here.

A virtually independent command in Mendoza, embracing the provinces of Mendoza, San Juan and San Luis, was held by Gen. Julio Alberto Lagos.

In an earlier telephone interview General Lagos identified himself as the chief of the revolution. But his chief of staff said later that General Lagos meant he was merely in charge of the three western provinces.

The chief of staff said that the coordination among the various commands was still deficient and he refused to say what plans the rebels had to take over the Government of Argentina. He declined to say what form of revolutionary government was being contemplated.

He declared that communication among the various commanders was by radio and ourier planes.

Broadcasts picked up in Santiago told the series of dramatic events that culminated today in the virtual surrender of the man who for twelve years had ruled Argentina as a dictator.

It came on the fourth day of the bloody rebellion against President Juan D. Perón by the Navy and sections of the Army as the insurgent fleet stood off

Continued on Page 2, Column 3

GEN. JUAN D. PERON

PEACE IS SOUGHT

Government Orders Its Forces to End Fight —Port Is Shelled

Texts of the Government and Perón statements, Page 3.

By EDWARD A. MORROW
Special to The New York Times.

BUENOS AIRES, Tuesday, Sept. 20.—The Government of President Juan D. Perón fell last night.

A four-man junta of army generals assumed command of the forces that had fought unsuccessfully to keep General Perón in power. He had been master of Argentina since Oct. 17, 1945, and its President for nine years.

[A loyalist military junta told the rebels that General Perón had officially resigned the Presidency, The Associated Press reported.]

The junta quickly entered into negotiations to end the four-day civil war. Army and Navy units had joined in the rebellion and forced the resignation of the President, the Cabinet and other authorities.

Among those who tendered their "irrevocable" resignations was the Minister of the Army, Gen. Franklin Lucero. On June 16 he had quelled a navy-led revolt.

There was no news about the whereabouts of President Perón tonight. Some reports had him in asylum at the Paraguayan Embassy in Buenos Aires. The reports were denied.

Perón Statement Read

The low ceiling prevented any planes from leaving the city's army airport and seemed to cast doubt on other reports that the President had fled to Paraguay.

General Perón offered his resignation yesterday afternoon in a statement read for him over the state radio. He suggested that the Army take charge. He had made a somewhat similar offer to resign Aug. 31 but withdrew it after "protests" from his followers.

It was widely rumored that General Perón had committed suicide. There was no official announcement to this effect, and well-informed diplomats doubted the report.

[A rebel radio broadcast from Bahia Blanca said the Argentine Confederation of Labor was planning a general strike for dawn Tuesday in an effort to restore General Perón to power, The Associated Press reported.]

The Government ordered troops that still remained loyal to it to cease fighting. It asked the rebels to do likewise to prevent further bloodshed after the Navy had shelled the seaside city of Mar del Plata and the rebels had shown other signs of strength throughout the country.

Large sections of the Buenos Aires population braved a light rain this afternoon to stage joyful demonstrations in the city's streets. The Plaza de Mayo, scene of many mass Peronist demonstrations in the past, had a small number of the Presi-

Continued on Page 3, Column 5

MOSCOW TO INSIST ON BONN-RED TALK

Soviet Will Shun Any Voice in German Domestic Rifts in Treaty Due Today

By CLIFTON DANIEL
Special to The New York Times.

MOSCOW, Sept. 19—Measures to force West Germany to deal directly with the East German Communist Government were being planned today in Moscow.

Walter Ulbricht, East German Deputy Premier and Communist party chief, declared that in the future there would be no other way of settling questions in dispute between the two parts of Germany.

He said that under the treaty to be concluded with the Soviet Union here tomorrow the East German Government would control the border with West Germany and communications between West Germany and West Berlin.

"The sooner the politicians of Bonn and West Berlin realize that they cannot undermine the East German regime, the better it will be for the populace of West Berlin," Herr Ulbricht said ominously.

His implication seemed to be that the East German Government would be in a position to impose a new blockade on Berlin and that on such matters the Bonn Government would have to negotiate not with mere officials but technicians but with the East German Government itself.

Sovereign Status Due

Herr Ulbricht spoke during the negotiations with Soviet leaders on a treaty that will give to the East German regime the same sovereign status the Western Allies gave West Germany.

Upon conclusion of the treaty the Soviet Government will abolish the office of High Commissioner in Germany, Marshal Nikolai A. Bulganin, Soviet Premier, disclosed in a speech.

Henceforth, the Soviet Ambassador to East Germany will deal with the United States, British and French representatives in West Germany on questions concerning Germany as a whole and on questions arising from four-power agreements, the Soviet Premier declared.

In addition, Marshal Bulganin said all laws, decrees and directives promulgated by the four-power Allied Control Council for Germany would be annulled on the territory of East Germany. Those regulations were enacted between 1945 and 1948, when the Soviet representative, Marshal Vassily D. Sokolovsky, withdrew and the Allied Control Council ceased to function.

The treaty between the Soviet Union and East Germany will provide that East Germany is free in all internal and foreign affairs, including relations with West Germany, Herr Ulbricht

Continued on Page 8, Column 3

FINNS AND SOVIET RENEW ALLIANCE

Moscow Agrees to Withdraw Its Military and Naval Forces Within 3 Months

Special to The New York Times.

MOSCOW, Sept. 19—Finland and the Soviet Union renewed their mutual defense alliance today for a period of twenty years.

At the same time the Soviet Government formally agreed to withdraw its military and naval forces from their base on Finnish territory within three months.

Those were the results of the Soviet-Finnish negotiations concluded here today and they gave "great joy" to the witty and lively old man who is President of Finland, Juho K. Paasikivi.

"I am here in Moscow for the seventh time for negotiations on affairs of state concerning Finland and the Soviet Union," the President said this evening at a party held in the Kremlin to celebrate the signing of the two agreements.

"But this is the first time that I return to our capital satisfied," he said. "Usually I have returned unsatisfied."

His audience laughed and applauded.

Exactly eight years ago today President Paasikivi was here on one of those unsatisfying missions. He signed a fifty-year lease that gave to the Soviet Union a naval and military base on the Porkkala Peninsula as provided by the truce agreement that ended the war between the two countries in 1944.

Tonight President Paasikivi observed that the Porkkala base now to be handed back to Finland was situated only twelve

Continued on Page 6, Column 3

Governor Calls for Federal Aid To Save Nation's Ailing Schools

But Royall Tells Conference That the Education System Should Be Contracted

By BENJAMIN FINE

A sweeping program of Federal aid to education, on both school and college levels, was advocated yesterday by Governor Harriman.

Speaking before 800 community, labor, business and school leaders at the New York State Conference on Education, the Governor said that nothing but Federal support could solve the critical problem in American education.

The two-day meeting at the Biltmore Hotel is a preliminary to the White House Conference on Education in Washington from Nov. 28 to Dec. 1. Major school issues are on the agenda, for both the New York and the Washington sessions.

Unexpectedly, the conference opened on a controversial note. The chairman of the New York State committee, Kenneth C. Royall, who was the keynote speaker, told the delegates they should be thinking of ways to contract, not expand, the educational system. Mr. Royall, who was Secretary of War under President Truman, said that too many young people were attending college who should not be there.

He deplored the "widespread feeling" among educators that every high school boy and girl should go to college. He said

Kenneth C. Royall

Continued on Page 25, Column 6

Democratic Farm Experts Call Republicans' Program Ruinous

By RICHARD J. H. JOHNSTON
Special to The New York Times.

CHICAGO, Sept. 19—The nation's farmers face a grim future unless action is taken immediately to relieve them of economic stress, a Democratic agricultural advisory committee said today.

Under the chairmanship of Claude R. Wickard, former Secretary of Agriculture, the fourteen-man committee met here in the Conrad Hilton Hotel to "explore all aspects of our agricultural problems."

This was the first meeting of the group that was formed to guide the Democratic farm policy fight. It was created on Aug. 31 at the behest of Paul M. Butler, chairman of the Democratic National Committee.

[Meanwhile, Democrats in Washington opened a drive to goad the Administration into unveiling its farm plans before Congress reconvenes in January. This was part of a Democratic effort to keep the offensive in building sagging farm prices and income into a major issue of the 1956 Presidential election.]

The advisory committee, which included another former Agriculture Secretary, Charles F. Brannan, as well as former Agriculture Department aides and five farmers, according to Mr. Wickard, had reached the conclusion that the Eisenhower Administration was neglecting the farmers' plight and ignoring distress.

While the committee went into executive session, Mr. Butler issued a statement on its aims and purposes. The statement bore down hard on the Republican Administration, which, he said, was both "ill-tempered and

Continued on Page 23, Column 4

U.N. Opening in Harmony Today; Chilean Next Head of Assembly

By THOMAS J. HAMILTON
Special to The New York Times.

UNITED NATIONS, N. Y., Sept. 19—A noncontroversial start is assured for the 1955 session of the United Nations General Assembly, which will convene tomorrow afternoon.

The only important business scheduled for tomorrow is the election of José Maza, a veteran Chilean diplomat, as President of the Assembly.

Some delegates believe that Vyacheslav M. Molotov, the Soviet Foreign Minister, will immediately put forward the standard Soviet demand for the seating of Chinese Communist representatives.

If he should do so, it would not cause more than a short flurry, since the United States is ready with its equally standard counter-proposal that the question of Chinese representation should not be taken up at the current session. The United States is known to have enough votes to assure the adoption of its resolution.

Dr. Joseph M. A. H. Luns, co-Foreign Minister of the Netherlands, will call the Assembly to order in the absence of the President of the 1954 session, Dr. Eelco N. van Kleffens, Dutch Minister to Portugal. The election of vice presidents and committee chairmen will take place Wednesday and the opening debate will begin Thursday.

Secretary of State Dulles will speak Thursday morning and Mr. Molotov on Friday. The two other Big Four Foreign Ministers, Harold Macmillan of Britain and Antoine Pinay of France, will not speak until next week.

In any event, the speeches by Mr. Dulles and Mr. Molotov are expected to set the keynote for

Continued on Page 12, Column 1

All Americans were cheered when Ike recovered from his illness promptly, and was again able to take up his responsibilities.

Dr. Martin Luther King, believer in equality and nonviolence, gave the civil rights movement a new leader.

"All the News That's Fit to Print"

The New York Times.

LATE CITY EDITION
Fair and pleasant today. Fair and cool tomorrow.
Temperature Range Today—Max., 70; Min., 59
Temperature Yesterday—Max., 70.9; Min., 61
Full U. S. Weather Bureau Report, Page 91

NEWS SUMMARY AND INDEX, PAGE 95

Copyright, 1955, by The New York Times Company.

SECTION ONE

VOL. CV...No. 35,673.   Entered as Second-Class Matter, Post Office New York, N. Y.   NEW YORK, SUNDAY, SEPTEMBER 25, 1955.   Including Magazine and Book Review.   TWENTY-FIVE CENTS

PERON IS GRANTED PARAGUAY REFUGE BY REBEL REGIME

Lonardi Government Asserts It Respects Right of Asylum and Pledges Guarantees

NEW MINISTERS SWORN

10 Cabinet Officials and Vice President in Office—Troops Fight Peronists in Rosario

By TAD SZULC
Special to The New York Times.

BUENOS AIRES, Sept. 24.—Former President Juan D. Perón was authorized tonight by the revolutionary Government to leave Argentina for asylum in Paraguay.

He is expected to sail soon for Asuncion, the Paraguayan capital, aboard a Paraguayan gunboat.

Meanwhile, the Lonardi Government swore in ten Cabinet Ministers and the Vice President. It was engaged in Rosario, the second largest city, in putting down the last die-hard Peronist resistance. Fifteen were reported killed and more than fifty hurt in fighting with troops.

A communiqué broadcast by the state radio at 6 P. M. said the provisional Government of President Eduardo Lonardi, "respectful of the right of asylum, pledges itself to grant General Perón "every form of guarantees."

The Paraguayan Ambassador, Juan R. Chavez, said tonight the Argentine Government announcement meant "naturally" that safe-conduct was being given to General Perón, who was ousted by the armed forces' insurrection Monday.

Señor Chavez said "the actual safe-conduct is just a piece of paper and I expect to receive it any time."

Gunboat at Wharf

He declined to say precisely when General Perón would leave, but it was understood it might be during the night.

The 900-mile trip north up the Parana and Paraguay Rivers is estimated to take three and one-half days.

The gunboat Paraguay, aboard which General Perón and his aide de camp, Maj. José Ignacio Cialceta, went at noon Tuesday, is tied at a wharf on the Rio de la Plata (River Plate), a mile from the Casa Rosada (Government House).

The Government announcement said: "The provisional Government, respectful of the right of asylum, asserts that the former President of the Republic, General Perón, is aboard a military vessel belonging to a friendly country, where he sought voluntary refuge. The provisional Government declares in a final form that it will grant him every form of guarantee."

This appeared to be the end of the mystery of General Perón's whereabouts. Although it has been reported for days that the Paraguayan Embassy had confirmed it—that he was aboard the gunboat, many had expressed doubt.

It has been generally expected that the safe conduct requested for General Perón by Ambassador Chavez would be given, as General Lonardi did not seem inclined to make a martyr out of the former President and obvi-

Continued on Page 2, Column 3

France Recalls Foe Of Morocco Reform

By HENRY GINIGER
Special to The New York Times.

PARIS, Sept. 24.—The mission to Morocco of Pierre Montel, head of the National Assembly's Defense Committee, has been withdrawn. M. Montel returned to Lyons today.

The official mission to inspect the military set-up in the protectorate had been used by M. Montel to agitate against a Government plan to end the political crisis there. The mission was withdrawn yesterday by the Ministry of National Defense. Because of this official slap, M. Montel flew from Rabat, Morocco's political capital, to Lyons, which he represents as a member of the conservative Independent party in the Assembly.

M. Montel specifically campaigned against a plan to replace the present Sultan, Sidi Mohammed ben Moulay Arafa, by a regency council. He had

Continued on Page 9, Column 1

Mr. Truman's Memoirs:
He Becomes President

Life Magazine
The former President working on his memoirs in Kansas City

Herewith The New York Times begins publishing the Memoirs of Harry S. Truman. The memoirs are written in two volumes. The present installments are excerpts from the first volume, which is entitled "Year of Decisions." After today the installments are to appear daily except Sunday.

BY HARRY S. TRUMAN

Dedication
To The People of All Nations

Preface

I HAVE often thought in reading the history of our country how much is lost to us because so few of our Presidents have told their own stories. It would have been helpful for us to know more of what was in their minds and what impelled them to do what they did.

The Presidency of the United States carries with it a responsibility so personal as to be without parallel.

Very few are ever authorized to speak for the President. No one can make decisions for him. No one can know all the processes and stages of his thinking in making important decisions. Even those closest to him, even members of his immediate family, never know all the reasons why he does certain things and why he comes to certain conclusions. To be President of the United States is to be lonely, very lonely at times of great decisions.

Unfortunately, some of our Presidents were prevented from telling all the facts of their Administrations because they died in office. Some were physically spent on leaving the White House and could not have undertaken to write even if they had wanted to. Some were embittered by the experience and did not care about living it again in telling about it.

As for myself, I should like to record, before it is too late, as much of the story of my occupancy of the White House as I am able to tell. The events, as I saw them and as I put them down here, I hope may prove helpful in informing some people and in setting others straight on the facts.

No one who has lived through more than seven and a half years as President of the United States in the midst of one world crisis after another can possibly remember every detail of all that happened. For the last two and a half years I have checked my memory against my personal papers, memoranda and letters and with some of the persons who were present when certain decisions were made, seeking to recapture and record accurately the significant events of my Administration.

I HAVE tried to refrain from hindsight and afterthoughts. Any schoolboy's afterthought is worth more than the forethought of the greatest statesman. What I have written here is based upon the circumstances and the facts and my thinking at the time I made the decisions, and not what they might have been as a result of later developments.

That part of the manuscript which could not be physically included in the two volumes of the "Memoirs," I shall turn over to the library in Independence, Mo., where it will be made available to scholars and students of history.

For reasons of national security and out of consideration for some people still alive I have omitted certain material. Some of this material cannot be made available for many years, perhaps for many generations.

In spite of the turmoil and pressure of critical events during the years I was President, the one purpose that dominated me in everything I thought and did was to prevent a third world war. One of the events that has cast a shadow over our lives and the lives of peoples everywhere has been termed, inaccurately, the "cold war."

What we have been living through is, in fact, a period of nationalistic, social and economic tensions. These tensions were in part brought about by shattered nations trying to recover from the war and by peoples in many places awakening to their right to freedom. More than half of the world's population was subject for centuries to foreign domination and economic slavery. The repercussions of the American and French revolutions are just now being felt all around the world.

This was a natural development of events, and the United States did all it could to help and encourage nations and peoples to recovery and to independence.

Unhappily, one imperialistic nation, Soviet Russia, sought to take advantage of this world situation. It was for this reason, only, that we had to make sure of our military strength. We are not a militaristic nation, but we had to meet the world situation with which we were faced.

We knew that there could be no lasting peace so long as there were large populations in the world living under

Continued on Page 64 Column 1

ANZUS DECLARES PACIFIC DEFENSES MUST BE KEPT UP

U.S., Australia, New Zealand Stress Need Till Geneva Promise Is Fulfilled

By ELIE ABEL
Special to The New York Times.

WASHINGTON, Sept. 24.—Australia, New Zealand and the United States agreed today that it would be folly for the free nations to drop their guard in the Pacific so long as the promise of Geneva had not been fulfilled.

The foreign ministers of the Anzus powers met for three hours in the State Department to survey the military, economic and political situation in the Far East and Southeast Asia.

In a joint statement, issued as the foreign ministers adjourned to Blair House for luncheon, the partners in the Anzus alliance declared that they "noted with satisfaction the efforts made at the Geneva meeting of heads of government" last July to reduce the causes of international tension.

"They expressed the hope," the communiqué added, "that these preliminary steps would be followed by positive action.

"They were in firm agreement that world developments do not so far justify any relaxation of the efforts of the free world to maintain a posture of defensive strength."

Richard G. Casey of Australia, Minister for External Affairs, and Thomas L. Macdonald, who holds the same portfolio in the New Zealand Cabinet, said at the end of their meeting with Secretary of State Dulles that they were completely satisfied with the morning's discussion.

'Ripped Through' Agenda

"We accomplished more in three hours than I believed possible," Mr. Casey said to reporters. "We ripped through all the subjects on the agenda and got all the answers we sought."

The meetings of the Anzus Defense Council, held in Washington for the last several years while the Australian and New Zealand foreign ministers were in the United States for the United Nations General Assembly, have developed an informal pattern of their own.

There are no set speeches. The agenda is never made public. The foreign ministers range quickly over the whole Pacific horizon, discussing frankly the troubled situations that need correcting or shoring up.

When pressed by reporters to say what topics had come up in the meeting, Mr. Casey replied: "You know what the trouble spots are as well as I do. We took them all up, country by country."

Communist subversion, long regarded as the major threat in Southeast Asia, was discussed at some length, Mr. Casey said, adding that "it comes up in a lot of places."

Each of the foreign ministers was accompanied by high-level political and military advisers. Admiral Felix B. Stump, Commander in Chief of the Pacific Fleet, and Herbert Hoover Jr., Under Secretary of State, assisted Mr. Dulles, along with Walter S. Robertson, Assistant Secretary for Far Eastern Affairs; Livingston T. Merchant, Assistant Secretary for European Affairs, and Douglas MacArthur 2d, counselor of the State Department.

Mr. Casey was accompanied

Continued on Page 13, Column 5

Soviet in U. N. Woos Newly Freed Lands

By LINDESAY PARROTT
Special to The New York Times.

UNITED NATIONS, N. Y., Sept. 24.—The Soviet Union has intensified its courtship of newly independent lands in Africa and Asia and of national groups now seeking independence.

This emerged from the first week of sessions of the United Nations' tenth General Assembly here. The situation was underlined both in the major policy address of Foreign Minister Vyacheslav M. Molotov yesterday and in the proceedings on the Assembly floor and in debate in the powerful Steering Committee.

The development, according to some official observers here, apparently is linked with the Soviet campaign for the elimination of United States military bases on foreign soil. United States air power and strategic reserves are widely

Continued on Page 15, Column 1

NEW SOVIET BLAST OF NUCLEAR TYPE DETECTED BY U.S.

Atomic Energy Agency Says It Indicates Continuation of Weapon Tests

Special to The New York Times.

WASHINGTON, Sept. 24.—The Soviet Union set off another nuclear explosion in the last few days.

This was announced late today by the Atomic Energy Commission, which said the latest explosion indicates a "continuation of Soviet tests of nuclear weapons."

In keeping with past practice, the commission said it would not report the discovery of any further explosions in the new test series unless "information of particular interest develops."

[No announcement of any atomic test was made in the Soviet press or over the Soviet radio, The United Press reported from Moscow.]

Lewis L. Strauss, chairman of the Atomic Energy Commission, last announced a new series of atomic tests by the Russians Aug. 4, nearly two weeks after the Geneva conference of the Big Four heads of government.

That announcement was the first since Oct. 26, 1954, when the commission reported its detection system had picked up the start of a test series that had begun in mid-September.

The A. E. C. Statement

The brief announcement today follows:

"Lewis L. Strauss, chairman of the United States Atomic Energy Commission, stated today that another Soviet nuclear explosion had occurred in recent days, indicating a continuation of their tests of nuclear weapons.

"Further announcements concerning the Soviet tests series will be made only if some information of particular interest develops."

Officials of the agency refused to elaborate on the announcement, but the use of "nuclear weapons" could mean either atomic or thermonuclear (hydrogen) explosions.

While the commission has never disclosed any details of how it detects the Soviet nuclear tests, the agency presumably uses delicate instruments that pick up radioactivity in the air. Radioactive particles of nuclear explosions are carried great distances by the winds and it is possible by collecting fall-out samples to estimate the type and power of the weapons.

Accordingly, there is usually a lag of a few days between the actual explosion in the Soviet Union and an Atomic Energy Commission announcement here that it had occurred.

The announcement today came as the United States and the Soviet Union were trying to find some common ground for agreement on disarmament.

Bulganin Cited Objections

President Eisenhower has proposed an exchange of military blueprints and aerial reconnaissance. In a letter to the President made public yesterday, Soviet Premier Nikolai A. Bulganin avoided acceptance of the proposals by suggesting certain conditions.

Marshal Bulganin said the President's blueprint proposal did not include military establishments outside the United States and the Soviet Union. He also objected on the ground that proposals for reducing armaments and banning nuclear weapons were not included.

The White House was disappointed. Administration officials noted, however, that the Bulganin message at least was not an outright rejection of the President's plan.

The Soviet Union previously had called for a ban on nuclear weapons and abolition of nuclear weapons, but the United States has maintained that this would be meaningless without strict enforcement and inspection procedures.

The President and other high Administration officials have taken the position since the Geneva conference that the new Soviet nuclear tests do not necessarily mean a change in the conciliatory attitude shown by the Russians in recent months.

At a news conference after the Atomic Energy Commission's announcement last August, the President said that the tests could mean simply that the Russians had come to that point in the scientific development of nuclear weapons where "they could go no place further" without test explosions.

The first Soviet "atomic explosion" was announced by President Truman Sept. 23, 1949.

EISENHOWER IS IN HOSPITAL WITH 'MILD' HEART ATTACK; HIS CONDITION CALLED 'GOOD'

Profound Effect on 1956 Is Expected in the Capital

Friends Reported to Believe President Will Decide Against Running Again —Family's Opposition Noted

By JAMES RESTON
Special to The New York Times.

WASHINGTON, Sept. 24.—President Eisenhower's illness was expected in Washington tonight to have a profound and perhaps decisive effect on the 1956 Presidential campaign.

Even on the most optimistic assumption of his rapid recovery, his intimate friends were inclined to believe that the "mild coronary thrombosis" he suffered last night would lead him to decide against seeking re-election in 1956.

Thus, even on the basis of the cryptic medical reports released at the Summer White House in Denver this evening, the President's illness was regarded here, not only as a great personal misfortune to one of the most popular military and political figures in American history, but also as a political event of world significance.

Continued on Page 46, Column 1

TWO PARTIES PUSH FARM PRICE FIGHT

Democrats Blame G. O. P.'s 'Unkept Pledges'—Truman Is Scored by Hall

Special to The New York Times.

WASHINGTON, Sept. 24.—Falling farm prices continued to supply ammunition today for Democratic and Republican verbal brickbats.

In a "fact sheet" destined to be mailed to 2,000 Democratic public officials and party leaders as well as to agricultural leaders throughout the country, the Democratic National Committee blamed the Eisenhower Administration and its "unkept promises" for the decline in agricultural income.

Leonard W. Hall, chairman of the Republican National Committee, countered with a statement saying the "Truman mess" inherited by President Eisenhower had caused the farm problem. The Republican spokesman added that he had "every confidence" that President Eisenhower's Administration would meet and solve the problem.

Mr. Hall also took the opportunity of denouncing Senator Paul H. Douglas, Democrat of Illinois, for "dangerous talk" about the drop in farm prices.

"It appears," Mr. Hall said, "that the somber Senator from Illinois is set on going down in

Continued on Page 31, Column 3

NIXON GETS NEWS AHEAD OF PUBLIC

White House Phones Him— 3 in Cabinet to Go Ahead With Trip to Canada

Special to The New York Times.

WASHINGTON, Sept. 24.—The exact whereabouts of Vice President Richard M. Nixon remained a mystery tonight. His aides reported he was in town, but would not say where.

They said, however, that Mr. Nixon was told by telephone of President Eisenhower's heart attack before the formal announcement was made at Denver this afternoon.

The Vice President is still scheduled to go to Denver Monday. He had planned to preside Tuesday at a Conference on Physical Fitness of American Youth called by the President.

Mr. Nixon's aides said he had no plans to go to Denver before then. Murray Snyder, Assistant White House Press Secretary, indicated at Denver late tonight that Mr. Nixon would make the trip as scheduled.

Mr. Nixon's aides reported that the Vice President and members of the Cabinet were being kept informed of the President's condition. They said he was told of the heart attack in a telephone call from the temporary White House at Denver.

Continued on Page 49, Column 1

STRICKEN IN SLEEP

President Is Placed in an Oxygen Tent but Only as Precaution

By RUSSELL BAKER
Special to The New York Times.

DENVER, Sunday, Sept. 25.—President Eisenhower suffered a heart attack early yesterday morning and has entered Fitzsimons Army Hospital near Denver.

At 10:20 last night (1:20 A. M. Sunday, New York time) the White House reported that the President had been under an oxygen tent since being admitted to the hospital at 2:30 P. M.

James C. Hagerty, the White House press secretary, said at 1:30 A. M. today that three physicians who had examined the President had given an optimistic report on his condition.

Their bulletin, Mr. Hagerty said, stated that: "from the original onset, at 2:45 A. M. Saturday, the President has withstood the attack well. At this time there are no complications. His blood pressure and pulse have remained stable. The President has been resting comfortably."

Mr. Hagerty added that there was no special significance to the President's being in an oxygen tent. The three physicians, he reported, said "that was routine—to permit the President to secure complete rest."

Three See President

The three physicians saw the President about ten minutes at 12:30 A. M. The White House physician, Col. Thomas W. Mattingly, chief of cardiology at Walter Reed Hospital in Washington, and Col. Bryan E. Pollock, chief of heart services at Fitzsimons.

Dr. Mattingly, who examines the President on his regular physical check-ups in Washington, had arrived by plane in Denver only some forty-five minutes before seeing General Eisenhower.

He consulted with General Snyder and Dr. Pollock at the hospital, then the three saw the President. General Eisenhower had been sleeping but awoke when they entered, Mr. Hagerty said.

Mr. Hagerty stressed that at no time in any of the President's routine check-ups at Walter Reed had Dr. Mattingly previously detected signs of heart trouble.

In his first report Dr. Snyder said that the attack was mild and the outlook for his recovery good.

General Snyder at the time described the attack as "a mild coronary thrombosis" and said it had affected the anterior, or front, portion of the heart.

In his statement issued shortly after the President entered the hospital, however, it was noted that Dr. Snyder had dropped the qualifying word "mild."

Murray Snyder, the acting White House press secretary, declined to say whether this change in the wording of the doctor's report meant that the President's condition was more serious than indicated by the first diagnosis.

Specialist Arrives in Denver

In his fifth bulletin of the day on the President's condition, the press secretary said there had been no change from the doctor's earlier report that General Eisenhower's condition was good.

At 11:48 o'clock last night, a military plane bearing Colonel Mattingly landed in a driving rain at Stapleton airport. Dr. Mattingly went directly to the hospital. The plane landed at Stapleton rather than Lowry Air Force Base because rain and fog closed in the runways there.

Mr. Hagerty arrived with Dr. Mattingly. He had nothing to say before speeding off to Fitzsimons.

At 6 P. M. yesterday, three and a half hours after the President had entered the hospital, General Snyder reported that he was "resting well" and that his condition was good.

Ninety minutes later, Mrs. Eisenhower went to the hospital to join her husband.

Continued on Page 41, Column 1

Durocher Resigns as Manager; Rigney Is Named to Lead Giants

Leo Durocher

Associated Press
Bill Rigney

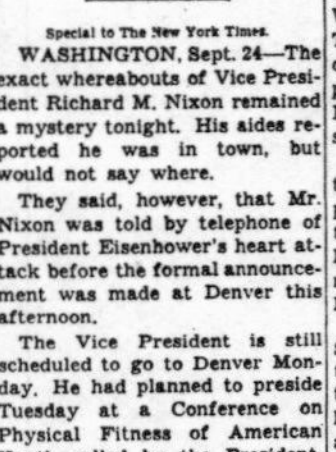

Leo Durocher resigned as manager of the New York Giants yesterday. Bill Rigney, manager of the Minneapolis club, was named to succeed him, effective next season.

FOOTBALL

Columbia, Maryland, Pitt and Colgate won major games in the East. Results of leading contests:

Colgate ....21 Dartmouth .20
Columbia ....14 Brown 12
Cornell ....1 Lehigh 0
Maryland ....7 U. C. L. A....0

Navy ....7 Wm. & Mary..0
Notre Dame.17 S. M. U. 0
Pitt ....22 Syracuse ...12
Princeton ....41 Rutgers 7

HORSE RACING

High Gun, 9—2, took the $106,700 Sysonby Stakes at Belmont Park. Jet Action was second and Nashua third. Blue Choir won the United Nations Handicap at Atlantic City.

Details in Section 5

1956

1956

In The Ten Commandments, *one of the classic films of the Fifties,* Charlton Heston starred in the role of Moses.

Robert Newton, Shirley MacLaine, Cantinflas and David Niven are shown here in a scene from Around The World in Eighty Days, *based on the novel by Jules Verne.*

William Holden and Kim Novak embrace in a scene from Picnic.

Marilyn Monroe as Cherie in Joshua Logan's Bus Stop.

"All the News That's Fit to Print"

The New York Times.

LATE CITY EDITION
Condensation of U. S. Weather Bureau forecast: Mostly fair and somewhat milder today. Partly cloudy tomorrow.
Temp. range today: 43-25; yesterday: 35-23
Full U. S. Weather Bureau Report, Page 66

VOL. CV..No. 35,831. Entered as Second-Class Matter, Post Office, New York, N. Y. NEW YORK, THURSDAY, MARCH 1, 1956. Times Square, New York 36, N. Y. Telephone LAckawanna 4-1000 FIVE CENTS

EISENHOWER SAYS HE WILL SEEK A 2D TERM; CONFIDENT OF HEALTH; BARS 'BARNSTORMING'; PRAISES NIXON BUT DOES NOT ENDORSE HIM

U.S. JUDGE ORDERS ALABAMA CO-ED TO BE REINSTATED

Bids School Admit Miss Lucy by Monday—Bars Contempt Action Against Trustees

CITES THEIR 'GOOD FAITH'

He Finds That Reaction Was Underestimated—Negro Says She Will Return

By WAYNE PHILLIPS
Special to The New York Times.

BIRMINGHAM, Ala., Feb. 29—The University of Alabama was ordered today to reinstate Autherine J. Lucy, its first Negro student, by Monday morning.

Miss Lucy, 26 years old, of Birmingham, was enrolled at the university Feb. 1 after a three-year court fight. She was suspended five days later after a series of campus disorders protesting her presence.

Federal Judge Hobart H. Grooms also vacated a contempt motion, sought by Miss Lucy, against the board of trustees and officials of the university. He said the trustees had acted in good faith in suspending Miss Lucy. If they had not done so, he ruled, "she might have suffered great bodily harm."

Miss Lucy sat tense and nervous today in the Federal District Court here as a succession of witnesses recounted the events leading to her suspension. Some said that if she returned to the campus she might be killed.

Feared for Life, She Says

She said on the witness stand that while she was a virtual prisoner in a classroom building held in a state of siege by a howling mob outside, she feared that she might be killed. She said she had prayed.

With deliberation and occasional flashes of dry wit she answered the questions of the university's attorney, Andrew J. Thomas. Beside her, when she sat at the counsel table, was a well-worn copy of the Bible.

After she heard the decision of Judge Grooms readmitting her, she said again that she would return to the campus.

"That girl sure has guts," her attorney, Thurgood Marshall, chief counsel for the National

Continued on Page 28, Column 1

TEAMSTERS UNION FACES SUSPENSION

Meany Weighs Tie to I. L. A. —Internal Strife Rises

By A. H. RASKIN

The International Brotherhood of Teamsters, most powerful unit in the merged labor movement, is facing possible suspension over its alliance with the exiled International Longshoremen's Association.

The possibility of punitive action by the parent federation arose yesterday amid fresh outcroppings of internal strife within the 1,300,000-member truck union. The uprisings were designed to prevent domination of the union by James R. Hoffa, international vice president and chairman of the Central States Conference of Teamsters.

The Detroit unionist announced Monday that the teamsters would deposit $400,000 to the credit of the I. L. A. to enable it to pay its debts and to participate in a joint organizing drive. The pier union was expelled from the American Federation of Labor in 1953 on charges of gang domination.

In Washington, George Meany, president of the united labor movement, announced that he had begun an investigation into the teamster-longshore pact. He pledged that he would take

Continued on Page 23, Column 3

Testimony Clashes At Gas Gift Inquiry

By RUSSELL BAKER
Special to The New York Times.

WASHINGTON, Feb. 29—Senate investigators were told today that John M. Neff had offered a $2,500 campaign contribution in Iowa for the chance to talk with Senator Bourke B. Hickenlooper about the natural gas bill.

However, Mr. Neff, an attorney for the Superior Oil Company of California, denied the story under oath. The conflicting testimony will be sent to the Department of Justice for possible perjury action.

The witness who testified that the offer had been made was Robert K. Goodwin, a Des Moines manufacturer and banker and Republican Committeeman for Iowa.

The two men, smiling wanly, confronted each other under the great glass chandeliers in the Senate caucus room, then

Continued on Page 13, Column 3

G.O.P. TAX CUT BILL VOTED AT ALBANY

Legislature Acts in Face of Veto Threat—Committees Propose Budget Slash

By LEO EGAN
Special to The New York Times.

ALBANY, Feb. 29—Republican majorities rammed their $50,000,000 income tax cut bill through both Senate and Assembly this afternoon. They did this despite warnings the bill would be vetoed by Governor Harriman, a Democrat.

In the Senate the vote was 35 to 23. In the Assembly it was 84 to 58. All the Democrats voted against the measure in both houses.

The Senate deliberately voted down the Governor's plan today. The vote was 36 to 22, one Democrat, Joseph Zaretski of Manhattan, voting with the Republicans in opposition. He explained he was opposed to any tax cut this year.

While the bill was under discussion, the Republican controlled Senate Finance and Assembly Ways and Means Committees proposed reductions totaling $25,528,072 in Governor Harriman's record high $1,494,700,000 state-spending program for next year.

Democrat Hits Action

Among the suggested cuts were the elimination of a $9,900,000 appropriation to give New York City a share in motor vehicle license fees and the elimination of a $2,400,000 item for state subsidies for child daycare centers, most of which would have gone to New York City.

Passage of the Republican income tax cut bill today represented an abrupt termination of negotiations between the Governor and legislative leaders for a compromise on this subject.

Assemblyman Eugene F. Bannigan, the Democratic minority leader, charged on the floor that Republicans were courting a veto of the tax-cut bill to justify a refusal to increase gasoline and Diesel fuel taxes. Such increases have been recommended by the Temporary Highway Finance Commission to support a $500,000,000 highway bond issue and an expanded highway construction program.

Lacking the two-thirds majorities needed in each House to repass a bill over the Governor's veto, the Republicans are expected to abandon their efforts for an income tax cut after today.

Mr. Harriman announced that he was still willing to resume compromise tax-reduction negotiations. But his offer is unlikely to be accepted.

The Republican bill as passed today would give all taxpayers a credit of 20 per cent on the first $100 of taxes due on April 15 and a 10 per cent credit on the next $400, with a limit of $60 to any one taxpayer. Governor Harriman had proposed a sub-

Continued on Page 25, Column 4

DULLES SUGGESTS SOVIET MAY FAVOR CUT IN ARMS COST

Tells Senate Unit, However, U. S. Will Not Be Misled Into Weakening Defenses

By ELIE ABEL
Special to The New York Times.

WASHINGTON, Feb. 29—Secretary of State Dulles suggested today that the Soviet Union might welcome some reduction in the present burden of armaments.

Testifying before a special Senate Foreign Relations subcommittee on disarmament, Mr. Dulles qualified this statement with assurances that the Administration would not jeopardize the nation's security by accepting at face value Soviet promises to disarm.

"We do not minimize the difficulties of dealing in these matters with a potential enemy who is untrustworthy and who in manifold ways has demonstrated that he is a past master of the art of evasion and secretiveness," the Secretary of State said.

"However, there is some reason to believe that the Soviet Union itself would welcome relief from the present burden of armament," he added.

Russians Called Dissatisfied

Mr. Dulles said this assessment was based on the "logic" of the present situation within the Soviet Union. He depicted the Russian people as being "in a state of very considerable dissatisfaction" with their low standard of living.

It would be logical for the Soviet leaders to agree to spend less on armaments so they could apply an increased share of their production to raising the living standards of their own people, Mr. Dulles said. In addition, the Soviet Union would thus have more to spend on its new program of economic aid to underdeveloped countries in South Asia and the Middle East, he added.

The Secretary of State, who leaves for Pakistan Friday afternoon to attend the council meeting of the Southeast Asian Collective Defense Treaty in Karachi March 6 to 8, appeared before a subcommittee headed by Senator Hubert H. Humphrey, Democrat of Minnesota, which is surveying the whole disarmament problem.

Senator Leverett Saltonstall, Republican of Massachusetts, asked Mr. Dulles whether "face-to-face" meetings with the Soviet leaders offered the best hope of achieving a disarmament accord.

"I don't know any other way," Mr. Dulles replied. "I don't get

Continued on Page 6, Column 3

Gronchi in Congress Discounts Arms Tie

By DANA ADAMS SCHMIDT
Special to The New York Times.

WASHINGTON, Feb. 29—President Giovanni Gronchi of Italy urged Congress today to lead the Western world away from military alliances and toward economic cooperation to counter Communist expansionism.

"The reorganization of the Western world is the central problem of the day," he declared in an address before a joint session of the Senate and the House of Representatives.

As an early step he proposed that the North Atlantic Treaty Organization be "brought into line" with today's realities, in which "military imbalance has been reduced," but in which, none the less, "the world is no more secure than it was one or two years ago."

The North Atlantic alliance,

Continued on Page 5, Column 3

PARIS ARMY CHIEF QUITS ON ALGERIA

Guillaume Out After Policy Dispute—Special Powers Asked by Government

By ROBERT C. DOTY
Special to The New York Times.

PARIS, Feb. 29—The French Government reorganized its high military command today and asked for special powers to deal with the Algerian revolt.

Gen. Augustin Guillaume was replaced as Chief of the General Staff following disagreement with his civilian chiefs over military policy in North Africa. He was succeeded by Gen. Paul Ely, a member of the high council of the armed forces.

Late today, Premier Guy Mollet submitted to Parliament a request for extensive powers in the fields of administration, economic and social affairs, and security for Robert Lacoste, Minister Residing in Algeria.

Details were not revealed, but the special powers were reported to include authority to reinstate the "state of urgency" in Algeria or even, if events should warrant it, full martial law.

Debate on this measure, probably early next week, was expected to present the left-of-center Republican Front Cabinet with its first serious political test. Some observers doubted that the National Assembly would grant the Government's request.

Neither here nor in Algeria has M. Mollet's appeal to the rebels to lay down their arms and accept the arbitration of new elections aroused any enthusiasm.

Conservatives, including most

Continued on Page 3, Column 2

9,000 Jam Court as Scofflaws Rush to Beat Amnesty Deadline

By JACK ROTH

The last day of the amnesty period for scofflaws found 9,000 persons in the Criminal Courts Building at 100 Centre Street yesterday. The worst jam in Manhattan Traffic Court history ensued.

About 6,000 persons waited in long lines in the lobby to pay their fines at the court clerk's windows. Three thousand of these were scofflaws. At one point the lines backed up a stairway leading to the second floor.

In addition, another 3,000 repentant drivers crowded about the Traffic Summons Control Bureau on the third floor. Tables were supplied in the corridors for the scofflaws to fill out forms.

Chief Magistrate John M. Murtagh called the amnesty a "great success" and estimated that of the 20,000 persons categorized as scofflaws all but about 6,000 had appeared.

He predicted that when all the scofflaw tickets of the amnesty period had been processed, the accounting would show that the city had collected nearly $750,000 in fines on long-ignored traffic summonses.

"Because of the last-minute influx of scofflaws," Mr. Murtagh said, "there will be a delay of perhaps a week before we can turn over the warrants to the police for the arrest of the remainder. We must make certain that none of the warrants apply to people who appeared at the last minute.

"But early next month the police will swing into action. Our goal is 100 per cent compliance with every summons issued since 1950."

He reiterated an earlier statement that this amnesty for scofflaws would be the last such grace period, because "motorists must be taught to answer summonses on time." There were two previous amnesties.

Concerning the last-minute rush, which was marked by confusion and grumbling, Mr. Murtagh admitted such great numbers had not been anticipated.

The confusion was caused by the fact that five patrolman, suddenly called to keep the lines

Continued on Page 25, Column 3

2D SPOT IN DOUBT

Foes of Vice President Now May Push Drive to Block Him

By W. H. LAWRENCE
Special to The New York Times.

WASHINGTON, Feb. 29—President Eisenhower passed up today two opportunities to give an automatic immediate endorsement to renomination of Vice President Richard M. Nixon.

General Eisenhower said he properly could not speak out on the choice of a running mate until after the Republican National Convention itself had picked its Presidential nominee.

He mixed repetition of previous high praise for Mr. Nixon with what sounded at least like indirect criticism of the Vice President for his recent effort to continue a Republican party label on Chief Justice Earl Warren. The President said he personally would never admit that any Supreme Court justice continued to have a political designation while on the high court.

President Eisenhower's failure to call at once for Vice President Nixon's renomination undoubtedly will put new steam behind an effort already under way by some influential Republicans to select another running mate. These anti-Nixon men argue that the 1956 campaign involving a President who has suffered a heart attack will place new emphasis with voters on the Vice Presidential nominee.

Silent on Running Mate

In his radio-television address to the nation, the President made no mention at all of Mr. Nixon or any other possible running mate.

The omission by the President may not be meaningful, however. General Eisenhower is assured of renomination by acclamation, and the convention unquestionably will nominate any man he favors for Vice President. So he could speak up for Mr. Nixon even at the last minute and insure his renomination.

The Nixon question was raised in two ways immediately after the President had disclosed he would be available for renomination and re-election if the Republican party and a majority of the people wanted him.

He was asked directly whether he would again want Mr. Nixon as his running mate.

"As a matter of fact," President Eisenhower responded, "I wouldn't mention the Vice Presidency, in spite of my tremendous admiration for Mr. Nixon, for this reason: I believe it is traditional that the Vice President is not nominated until after a * * * Presidential candidate is nominated; so I think that we will have to wait and see whom the Republican convention nominates, and then it will be proper to give an expression on that point."

Respect 'Unbounded'

Asked whether, if nominated, he would have a personal preference for Mr. Nixon's renomination, the President responded:

"I will say nothing more about it. I have said that my admiration and my respect for Vice President Nixon is unbounded. He has been for me a loyal and dedicated associate, and a successful one.

"I am very fond of him, but I am going to say no more about it."

The indirect criticism came when President Eisenhower was asked his own reaction to the Vice President's characterization of Mr. Warren as a Republican Chief Justice.

The President said he would not comment, and never had, on a comment by someone else. He added:

"But I will say this: Once a man has passed into the Supreme Court he is an American citizen and nothing else in my book until he comes out of that court, and I believe that it would be—I would never admit that he was—longer had a political designation."

There has been sharp political controversy over the Vice President's recent contention in a New York speech that the Su-

Continued on Page 16, Column 5

Associated Press Wirephoto

EXPLAINS DECISION: President and Mrs. Eisenhower at the White House last night, before his TV-radio speech.

Butler Questions Fitness; Republicans Hail Decision

By JOHN D. MORRIS
Special to The New York Times.

WASHINGTON, Feb. 29—The physical fitness of President Eisenhower to serve another term was challenged sharply today within minutes of his announcement that he was willing to run. "The American people will never elect a President who, at 65, has had a serious heart attack and who is unable to be a full-time Chief Executive," Paul M. Butler, the Democratic National Chairman, declared.

While Mr. Butler raised the issue of health, other leaders of

The texts of Butler and Hall statements are on Page 17.

both parties publicly hailed the President's decision.

The prevailing Democratic line was one of gratification that General Eisenhower considered his recovery sufficient to permit him to stand the rigors and pressures of four more years in the White House. But warnings of a hard campaign "on the issues," requiring vigorous activity by both candidates and ending in a Democratic victory, also came from leading party spokesmen.

Republicans responded to the announcement with enthusiasm that promised the President's renomination without a dissent by the national convention at San Francisco next August.

Predictions that the delegates would choose him by acclamation came from Vice President Richard M. Nixon and Senator Wil-

Continued on Page 17, Column 1

Two Senators Ask Inquiry on Benson

By WILLIAM M. BLAIR
Special to The New York Times.

WASHINGTON, Feb. 29 Two Senate Democrats suggested today that the special lobby investigating committee explore what they charged were efforts by the Secretary of Agriculture to influence Southern Senators to vote against rigid farm-price supports.

Senator Hubert H. Humphrey of Minnesota said that Ezra Taft Benson, the Secretary, appeared to have violated a law prohibiting lobbying with Federal appropriations. The situation is "close enough to make it appear necessary for our new committee on lobbying to look into it most carefully," he declared.

Senator Allen J. Ellender of Louisiana accused Mr. Benson of "trying to buy votes of

Continued on Page 12, Column 3

STEVENSON CALLS DECISION PROPER

Bids President 'Set Terms of Debate' on His Health —Sees 'Vigorous' Drive

By CLAYTON KNOWLES

Adlai E. Stevenson called upon President Eisenhower yesterday to "set the terms of the debate" on the issue of his health, now that he has declared his availability for a second term.

Most active of the Democratic candidates for the Presidency, the former Illinois Governor stressed that it was General Eisenhower who had "drawn the distinction between the private matter of his personal health and the public question of how the office of President shall be conducted."

In Washington, it was felt that President Eisenhower's decision would help Mr. Stevenson's chances for the Democratic nomination.

Mr. Stevenson said it was fitting that President Eisenhower, before whom he went to defeat in 1952, should be the candidate and thus defend the policies and record of his Administration.

This view, given in a brief statement, was echoed by other Democrats across the country and by leading Republicans, too, if with a noticeable change in inflection. And Mr. Stevenson noted also that the President must look forward to carrying the "burden of what will be a very vigorous campaign."

This was a point that other Democratic candidates, announced and unannounced, stressed as well.

In Albany, Governor Harriman asserted that the President "can no longer shift responsibility to associates and subordinates." Mr. Harriman asserted that the President murt now answer for "surrender to the domination of one group in our country—the big interests"—and for policies abroad that have "undermined our prestige and shaken the confidence in us of the people of the free world."

And at Milwaukee, Senator Estes Kefauver, like Mr. Steven-

Continued on Page 19, Column 2

CAN 'LAST 5 YEARS'

President Finds 'Not Slightest Doubt' of Fitness for Duty

Conference transcript, Page 14; text of speech, Page 15.

By JAMES RESTON
Special to The New York Times.

WASHINGTON, Feb. 29—He said "yes."

Dwight David Eisenhower, the thirty-third President of the United States, agreed this morning to a second-term nomination. He explained why in a television-radio report to the nation tonight.

Speaking slowly and in a slightly hoarse voice, General Eisenhower said tonight: "After the most careful and devoutly prayerful consideration * * * I have decided that if the Republican party chooses to renominate me, I shall accept."

The 65-year-old President frankly told his party tonight, however, that because of his heart attack last Sept. 24, he must restrict his activities in the conduct of his office and in the Presidential campaign.

The President had raised personally the problems created by his heart attack at a crowded news conference this morning at which he said: "I assure you of this: My answer would not be in the affirmative unless I thought I could last out the five years."

Can Perform His Duties

And he told the nation tonight:

"As of this moment, there is not the slightest doubt that I can perform as well as I ever have all the important duties of the Presidency. This I say because I am actually doing so and have been doing so for many weeks."

Speaking of the Presidential campaign, General Eisenhower warned that "neither for renomination nor re-election would I engage in extensive traveling and in whistle-stop speaking—normally referred to as 'barnstorming.'" He added:

"I had long ago made up my mind, before I ever dreamed of a personal heart attack, that I could never, as President of all the people, conduct the kind of political campaign where I was personally a candidate. The first duty of a President is to discharge to the limit of his ability the responsibilities of his office."

General Eisenhower did not mention the Vice-Presidency in his radio address. He was cautious about committing himself

Continued on Page 15, Column 6

MARKET SURGES, THEN FALLS BACK

News Sets Off Buying Wave, but Stocks End Lower

By BURTON CRANE

Wall Street had its day of anticlimax yesterday. The President's announcement that he would seek re-election brought a boiling market of 3,900,000 shares, a ticker tape that ran nineteen minutes behind the floor for a time, an uprush of prices for a single hour—and a net loss on the day.

More stocks fell than rose. Seven of the ten most heavily traded issues closed lower. The New York Times combined average of fifty stocks fell 2.62 points to 322.88, a drop of more than 4/5 of 1 per cent.

Expectations that the President would announce his decision jammed the two galleries of the New York Stock Exchange well before its opening at 10 A. M. The east gallery was largely reserved for reporters, photographers and newsreel and television cameramen. The general public thronged the west gallery.

At the opening, the market was active and strongly higher, starting with gains of 1 and 2 points on good-sized blocks. United States Steel, for example, was up ⅞ on 10,000 shares. Volume continued heavy and

Continued on Page 47, Column 8

The New York Times.

"All the News That's Fit to Print"

LATE CITY EDITION

VOL. CV..No. 35,881.

NEW YORK, FRIDAY, APRIL 20, 1956.

FIVE CENTS

HOUSE UNIT VOTES A 1.2 BILLION FUND FOR '56 SOIL BANK

Committee Bases Its Action on '36 Act—Benson Sees Cart Put Before Horse

PLAN HELD UNWORKABLE

Secretary Insists New Law Is Needed to Operate His Proposal to Cut Acreage

By WILLIAM M. BLAIR

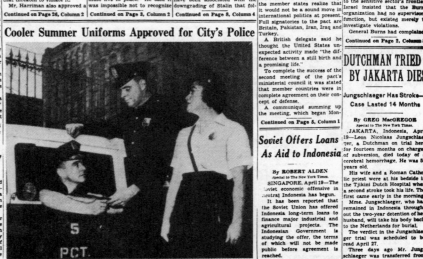

WANTS SOIL BANK LEGISLATION: Secretary of Agriculture Ezra Taft Benson, testifying before the Senate Agriculture Committee, calls for additional legislation to put the Administration's soil bank plan into operation.

U. S. Court Acquits Icardi; Defines Limits on Inquiries

By ANTHONY LEWIS

TEAMSTER JAILED IN JURY CONTEMPT

Official of One of New Locals Gets 6 Months in Failing to Produce Records

By EDWARD RANZAL

MEDINA CRITICAL OF STATE COURTS

Tie-Up Between Politics and System Is 'Blight,' He Says

By RUSSELL PORTER

High School Teachers Withdraw From Joint Negotiations on Pay

By BENJAMIN FINE

BILL TO CONTROL WELFARE FUNDS OF UNIONS SIGNED

Only Accounts Administered With Employers Covered—Harriman Sees Slight

KHRUSHCHEV ASKS BRITAIN TO AVOID PRESSURE IN TALK

Sees Failure if Hosts Demand 'the Impossible' of Soviet—Avows 'Open Heart'

By DREW MIDDLETON

ISRAEL AND EGYPT ENFORCE TRUCE NEGOTIATED BY U. N.; BORDER WATCH IS WIDENED

Turn of Events in Mideast Lifts Hopes in Washington

But the Outlook Is Tempered by Caution —Cease-Fire, Baghdad Pact Links, Soviet Attitude Held Encouraging

By DANA ADAMS SCHMIDT

Malenkov Influence Is Reported Rising As Molotov's Wanes

By HARRISON E. SALISBURY

BEN-GURION BOWS

Hammarskjold Gains Greater Freedom for Observers

By HOMER BIGART

U. S. EXTENDS TIES TO BAGHDAD PACT

Agrees to Set Up a Military Liaison Group and to Join Counter-Subversion Unit

By SAM POPE BREWER

DUTCHMAN TRIED BY JAKARTA DIES

Jungschlaeger Has Stroke—Case Lasted 14 Months

By GREG MacGREGOR

Cooler Summer Uniforms Approved for City's Police

New lightweight summer uniforms, optional alternatives to regular ones, are modeled by Patrolmen Thomas Conley, in car; Donald McWeeney, and Policewoman Virginia Dunne.

Soviet Offers Loans As Aid to Indonesia

By ROBERT ALDEN

168

1956

This was the Oldsmobile of 1956.

Grace Kelly gave up her Hollywood stardom to marry Prince Rainier of Monaco. They are seen here being received by President Eisenhower.

The Beat Generation of the Fifties was an avant-garde, anti-materialist group. Two of the spokesmen for the group were Jack Kerouac and Allen Ginsberg who is seen here reading his poetry in Washington Square Park in New York City.

The Four Lads were popular for No, Not Much.

Elvis Presley had four #1 songs in 1956: Heartbreak Hotel, Don't Be Cruel, Hounddog, *and* Love Me Tender.

Marty Robbins' Singing The Blues *was a favorite.*

"All the News That's Fit to Print"

The New York Times.

© 1956, by The New York Times Company.

LATE CITY EDITION
Condensation of U. S. Weather Bureau forecast:
Mostly fair and cool today and tonight.
Cloudy and cool tomorrow.
Temperature range today: 71-60.
Temperature range yesterday: 81.7-62.7.
Full U. S. Weather Bureau Report, Page 40.

VOL. CV. No. 35,931. Entered as Second-Class Matter, Post Office, New York, N. Y. NEW YORK, SATURDAY, JUNE 9, 1956. Times Square, New York 36, N. Y. Telephone LAckawanna 4-1000 FIVE CENTS

PRESIDENT UNDERGOES SURGERY ON INTESTINE BLOCK AT 2:59 A. M.; DOCTORS PRONOUNCE IT SUCCESS

CONDITION IS GOOD

Operation Lasts Hour and 53 Minutes—13 Attend Him

Text of news conferences and medical bulletins, Pages 8, 9, 10.

By ANTHONY LEVIERO
Special to The New York Times.

WASHINGTON, Saturday, June 9—President Eisenhower was operated on at 2:59 A. M. today for relief of an intestinal obstruction. At 4:55 A. M., the operation was pronounced a success by the surgeons.

James C. Hagerty, White House Press Secretary, telephoned the good news to temporary press headquarters from a point outside the operating room in the Walter Reed Army Hospital. He said:

"The operation was concluded at 4:52 A. M. The operation was successful. The President's post-operative condition was very satisfactory. He left the operating table in excellent condition."

The operation lasted one hour and fitfy-three minutes.

Mr. Hagerty's brief announcement gave no clue to the exact nature of what the thirteen doctors had described as a partial obstruction of the small intestine.

The Operation Starts

The tense drama began at 2:59 A. M. Mr. Hagerty had announced at 2:14 A. M. that the President's doctors had reached the decision to operate immediately. He said he expected them to place General Eisenhower under the knife in about fifteen minutes.

Mr. Hagerty came back to press headquarters in the Army's Walter Reed Hospital at 3:04 A. M., however, to announce the operation had not started until 2:59 A. M. The President had been wheeled into the hospital's big operating room number six in the main building.

A general anesthetic was administered and the surgical effort began "to find the cause of the obstruction and to relieve that cause."

Earlier Mr. Hagerty had refused to characterized the seriousness of the operation except to quote the doctors as saying the President's condition was not "critical."

He was also asked if a malignancy might be involved and replied::

"I have not heard that considered by the doctors at any time."

Obviously, however, the 65-year-old President was undergoing major surgery, and the necessity for that surgery under a general anasthetic had created a crisis comparable to the one he surmounted in his heart attack in Denver last September.

More than an hour after the operation began, it was possible to get a veiled impression of the drama as the team of six surgeons and physicians hovered over the President. The front of the operating room on the third floor, with its face of glass, looks

Continued on Page 9, Column 2

Associated Press Wirephoto

ARRIVE AT HOSPITAL: Maj. John S. Eisenhower assisting his mother from car yesterday afternoon at Walter Reed Army Hospital, to which President had been taken.

HOUSE TURNS BACK MOVES TO CUT AID TO TITO AND NEHRU

Bipartisan Majority Defeats Curbs—Foes Sought End to Funds to Yugoslavs

EISENHOWER IS UPHELD

Bid to Obtain U. S. Trials for Troops Stationed Abroad Is Also Voted Down

By WILLIAM S. WHITE
Special to The New York Times.

WASHINGTON, June 8—The House of Representatives rejected today attempts to deprive Communist Yugoslavia of all United States aid. It also voted down an attempt to limit neutral India to a small technical assistance fund.

These substantial victories for the Eisenhower Administration and the Democratic and Republican House leadership came as debate went forward on the bill, which extends and expands the foreign-aid program.

Another major restriction was proposed by Representative Frank T. Bow, Republican of Ohio. It would have directed the Administration to cancel agreements by which American troops on duty overseas can be tried in foreign courts for off-duty crimes. It failed by a vote of 93 to 30.

The measure, from which the House earlier voted to cut $1,000,000,000 of the $3,000,000,000 military assistance program sought by the President, was thus brought well along toward final passage Monday.

The House carried its second day of debate on the bill into the evening, adjourning at 7:24 P. M.

The Administration is urgently turning to tne Senate, which has yet to act on the issue, to restore at least some of this reduction.

Alternate Measure Backed

Today's most critical struggle came on a proposal to put an absolute prohibition on aid to Yugoslavia because of Marshal Tito's recent reconciliation with the Kremlin.

The proposal was defeated, not on a frontal test but by so diluting it as to leave future aid to Yugoslavia within the discretion of the President—where, in fact, it lies now.

An amendment by Representative Edna F. Kelly, Democrat of Brooklyn, flatly directed the Administration to extend no more assistance. Specifically at issue was $15,000,000 for economic purposes and an undisclosed sum for military aid.

Apparently fearing failure in an effort simply to defeat the rider, the bipartisan leaders for the bill threw their support behind an alternative version by Representative Harrison A. Williams, Democrat of New Jersey.

This amendment stipulated that aid to Tito could continue upon a determination by the President that Yugoslavia was not under Soviet domination and had not taken up policies hostile to the United States.

The Williams version prevailed by an unrecorded voice vote of 123 to 95 to vindicate Speaker Sam Rayburn of Texas and his senior Democratic associates and the Republican floor leader, Rep-

Continued on Page 3, Column 5

Adenauer Arrives Today for Parleys

By M. S. HANDLER
Special to The New York Times.

BONN, Germany, June 8—Chancellor Konrad Adenauer left by plane tonight for the United States. He hopes to ascertain there whether the time is ripe for the Western powers to revive with the Soviet Government the question of Germany's reunification.

He was scheduled to devote next Tuesday and Wednesday to an exchange of views with President Eisenhower and Secretary of State Dulles, but the President's illness may make it difficult for the Chancellor fully to carry out his mission.

The problems Dr. Adenauer intended to discuss with the President and Mr. Dulles were:

¶The attitude of the United States Government toward the Soviet Union's campaign to bring about a relaxation of East-West tensions without

Continued on Page 6, Column 1

MOROCCAN SEEKS TALK ON U.S. BASES

Foreign Minister Denounces Report Rabat Will Seek Rental for Airfields

By THOMAS F. BRADY
Special to The New York Times.

RABAT, Morocco, June 8—Foreign Minister Ahmed Balafrej said today that the United States should negotiate directly with Morocco as soon as possible on the future of American air bases here.

Reports that the Moroccan Government would ask $430,000,000 a year as rental for the bases is without foundation, Mr. Balafrej said. His Government has not even decided that "rental" of Moroccan territory would be a suitable arrangement for the future of the bases, he added.

The rental figure of $430,000,000 has been widely circulated here and in Paris and has been attributed to a member of the Moroccan Government. The annual rental figure is roughly equivalent to the total United States investment in the bases.

Mr. Balafrej said that if a member of the Government had suggested such a figure it was purely a personal idea and had no validity or backing from the Government.

His comment that no decision has been taken on the principle of "rent" is significant because the United States is opposed by policy to paying rent for overseas bases. Economic aid agreements have frequently paralleled base agreements in such a way as to provide the equivalent of rent, but the United States theory of a mutually valuable defense arrangement between

Continued on Page 3, Column 8

BULGANIN LETTER BIDS WEST REDUCE FORCE IN GERMANY

Soviet Leader Asks Direct Action to Bypass U. N. Disarmament Talks

Text of Bulganin letter to the President, Page 2.

By ELIE ABEL
Special to The New York Times.

WASHINGTON, June 8—Marshal Nikolai A. Bulganin has called on the United States, Britain and France to cut their armed forces in Germany without waiting for an over-all disarmament agreement.

The Soviet Premier's letter, delivered yesterday afternoon by Ambassador George N. Zaroubin, was made public at the White House this evening. It was dismissed by diplomats here as barren of new ideas and an obvious attempt to exploit the Soviet military manpower cut anounced May 14 for its propaganda value.

Writing off the recent London talks of the United Nations Subcommittee on Disarmament as "extremely complicated" and a drag on progress, Marshal Bulganin said the time had come for a new approach.

That approach, as was reported in The New York Times today, was that the Western powers should follow the example of the Soviet Union and cut their armaments as well as armed forces without bothering about international control and inspection.

'Concrete' Action Asked

The Russians, who appear to regard the Bulganin letter as an important diplomatic initiative, sent copies not only to President Eisenhower but also to Chancellor Konrad Adenauer of West Germany, Prime Minister Eden of Britain and Premier Guy Mollet of France.

Marshal Bulganin said the Soviet Union found it difficult to expect that the United Nations talks, scheduled for resumption in July, would "lead to concrete results in the area of disarmament in the very near future."

The Soviet leadership is "deeply convinced," he said, that in the present state of the world "the efforts of states should be directed toward each one's taking concrete measures for reducing armaments, which measures could be carried out without waiting for the conclusion of an international agreement on disarmament."

Such measures, modeled on the announced Soviet cut of 1,200,000 men, "would undoubtedly contribute to further lessening of international tension and to strengthening of mutual trust among the nations," Marshal Bulganin contended.

He pressed President Eisen-

Continued on Page 2, Column 6

Roosevelt Assured Of Convention Role

By LEO EGAN

Franklin D. Roosevelt Jr. received assurances yesterday that he would be named as one of twenty-four New York State delegates at large to the Democratic national convention.

The assurances are reported to have been given by both Governor Harriman and Carmine G. De Sapio, leader of Tammany and national committeeman for New York.

At the same time it became known that both Democrats and Republicans are being beset with delicate political problems in the choice of delegates at large. Neither party has enough places to accommodate all the important figures who want the posts and who have a serious po-

Continued on Page 12, Column 4

HARRIMAN URGED TO QUIT '56 RACE

Dubinsky Calls on Governor to Support Stevenson and Seek Liberal Platform

By RALPH KATZ

David Dubinsky, president of the International Ladies Garment Workers Union, urged Governor Harriman yesterday to give up his aspirations for the Democratic Presidential nomination.

Mr. Dubinsky, a vice chairman of the State Liberal party, said it was now clear that Adlai E. Stevenson would be the nominee and would be selected "if not on the first or second ballot, by the third ballot."

The union leader spoke before 200 delegates at the ninth triennial convention of the Hat, Cap and Millinery Workers Union in the Statler Hotel. Alex Rose, president of the Hatters Union, also is a state vice chairman of the Liberal party.

Mr. Dubinsky declared that the New York Governor should go to the convention as a favorite son, but should not campaign against the selection of Mr. Stevenson. Mr. Harriman should be ready to withdraw his candidacy and support Mr. Stevenson, the union president asserted.

Charles Van Devander, Governor Harriman's press secretary.

Continued on Page 12, Column 6

NEW ISSUE RAISED

A Wider Race Foreseen Whether His Illness Is Short or Long

By W. H. LAWRENCE
Special to The New York Times.

WASHINGTON, June 8—President Eisenhower's sudden new illness shook the political world today.

Politicians believed it would be bound to have an effect on the 1956 Presidential election whether the illness turned out to be serious and long, or minor and brief.

It is certain to bring the health question into sharper focus, thus making the race more wide open than it had seemed.

Having recovered from his coronary thrombosis of Sept. 24, the President had gone into this campaign backed by the opinion of medical specialists. They said his chances were good to survive five to ten years of heavy responsibilities.

The new illness raised again the possibility that the President might decide not to run. The President has not excluded the possibility that he would resign if his health did not permit him to carry out fully the duties of his office.

President's Stand Recalled

On March 7, at a news conference, President Eisenhower was asked what he would do if he found out before the Republican National Convention on Aug. 20 that his physical condition was below the par he had expected.

The President made this reply:

"I have said, unless I felt absolutely up to the performance of the duties of the President, the second that I didn't, I would no longer be there in the job or I wouldn't be available for the job."

The President later amplified that answer by asking reporters not to hold him to any suggestion of withdrawal "if I get a week's case of the flu or something else."

"But I am talking about my general, let's say, organic fitness for the job, as I see it, and that means carrying a burden of hard work right on through the year and through the months," He added.

"Now, any time that I believe that has failed to the point of

Continued on Page 10, Column 2

Queen Elizabeth Greeted by Swedish King on Arrival for State Visit

Associated Press Radiophoto

King Gustaf Adolf welcoming Queen Elizabeth as she and the Duke of Edinburgh came ashore. At right is Queen Louise.

By FELIX BELAIR Jr.
Special to The New York Times.

STOCKHOLM, Sweden, June 8—The first state visit of a reigning British sovereign in fifty years put this capital in high excitement today. Half an hour after Queen Elizabeth II stepped ashore from a royal barge to be greeted, along with the Duke of Edinburgh, her husband, at least 300,000 residents of Stockholm, who lined the route of their drive around the city, had put aside their accustomed reserve to cheer and shout their welcome of the smiling couple. It was in the same open horse-drawn carriages and over much the same streets that King Edward VII of Britain in 1907 began the only other visit of state from a reigning British monarch. As the royal couple stepped ashore to be greeted by King Gustaf Adolf and Queen Louise, sister of Admiral Earl Mountbatten, Britain's First Sea Lord, a twenty-

Continued on Page 13, Column 7

Soviet Foreign Chief To Visit Cairo Soon

By JACK RAYMOND
Special to The New York Times.

MOSCOW, June 8—Dmitri T. Shepilov, the Soviet Union's new Foreign Minister, will go to Cairo "within a few days," it was announced this evening.

Tass, Soviet news agency, said the Foreign Minister would participate in Egypt's Evacuation Day celebration, June 18, a national holiday celebrating the departure of the last British soldier from the Suez Canal zone.

Mr. Shepilov's visit to Egypt will be his first abroad since he succeeded Vyacheslav M. Molotov as head of the Foreign Ministry June 1.

In this connection it was noted that Premier Gamal Abdel Nasser of Egypt was due to pay a state visit here this summer.

It also was announced today that the Soviet Government had invited Crown Prince Aayf al-

Continued on Page 3, Column 2

Country's Concern For the President Voiced by Leaders

President Eisenhower's illness produced throughout the country yesterday mingled feelings of concern, regret and hope for his swift recovery.

Overseas, former President Harry S. Truman, who is vacationing in Paris, declared: "I sure hope it's not serious. I sure hope not."

The same wish was echoed in varied forms by leaders in politics, business, industry and labor. Expressions of regret and wishes for the President's recovery came from Republicans and Democrats alike and transcended comment on any political implications of his illness. Some Republicans sought to minimize the seriousness of the illness.

Senator Styles Bridges of New Hampshire, chairman of the Senate Republican Policy Committee, said he was "sorry to hear the President is indisposed" but added that he felt there was "nothing serious" about the illness.

William F. Knowland of California, Senate Republican leader, reserved comment pending further details. Mr. Knowland, who withdrew as a Republican Presidential candidate after the President announced Feb. 29 that he would seek re-election, had disclaimed knowledge of a California movement to boom him for the nomination if the Presi-

Continued on Page 10, Column 4

Reds in Italy Plan A 'Democratic' Line

By HERBERT L. MATTHEWS
Special to The New York Times.

ROME, June 8—The Italian Communist party is preparing for a major change in its strategy.

The party's leaders are in a fever of discussion and analysis intended to prepare Italian communism for adopting methods of Western-style democracy. It is insisted that this new line is not merely tactical but a strategic development imposed by changes in the Soviet Union and in world affairs.

What the Italian Communists have in mind is a change of methods, not of ideological doctrines or Socialist goals.

They say they want to use democratic methods because they have become convinced that in today's world these methods are the best and are what the people want.

The Italian Communist party

Continued on Page 4, Column 6

MARKET HARD HIT; SELLING IS HEAVY

Stocks Dip $2 to $7 a Share on News About President, but Rally Toward End

By ROBERT E. BEDINGFIELD

The stock market reacted sharply yesterday to the President's illness. Prices broke $2 to $7 a share under heavy selling, but a late rally erased one-third to one-half of the losses.

At the close, stock prices as measured by The New York Times average of fifty issues stood at 316.38. This represented a net loss of 5.32 points, but was 4.69 points above the day's low of 311.69, reached about 2:30 P. M.

The volume of trading on the New York Stock Exchange reached 3,628,000 shares, second largest of the year and 2,000,000 shares more than on Thursday. The ticker tape was unable to keep up with floor transactions four times—three times while prices were falling and once while they were rising at the close.

Despite the big volume, few really large blocks changed hands. Some observers interpreted the selling as coming from small investors who had decided they didn't want to see their bull market profits dwindle any farther.

Reaction Is International

There were several other explanations for the lack of large individual trades. For one thing, many prominent Wall Streeters were far from the financial district for a long week-end. Others were at the New York Bond Club's annual outing at the Sleepy Hollow Country Club, Scarborough, N. Y.

By the time the opening gong sounded on the Stock Exchange at 10 A. M., securities markets in other countries already had reacted to the news from the White House. London stock prices turned downward, while in Paris the "black market" rate for the United States dollar dropped 10 per cent.

The Montreal and Toronto Stock Exchanges weakened during the day along with the New York market. The Toronto board saw 5,310,000 shares change hands, with leading industrial stocks marked down as much as 6½ points. On the less active Montreal exchange, steel, mining and Western oil shares all were offered in volume.

Domestic grain futures, on the other hand, rose, as they did last

Continued on Page 27, Column 1

House Group Votes Rise in Veteran Aid

By JOHN D. MORRIS
Special to The New York Times.

WASHINGTON, June 8—The House Veterans Affairs Committee approved today an omnibus bill to liberalize Federal benefits to war veterans and their widows. The cost was estimated at $1,240,657,000 in the first year.

The election-year measure includes provisions for pensions of at least $105 a month at the age of 65 to all low-income veterans of World War I and II and the Korean conflict. This was the American Legion's No. 1 legislative goal for 1956.

Other benefits would be increased under the catch-all bill, which other veterans' organizations also had backed. The cumulative cost in the next forty-four years was unofficially estimated at more than $100,000,000,000.

The measure was reported to

Continued on Page 41, Column 8

Chet Huntley and David Brinkley were selected to anchor the evening news shortly after they had joined Bill Henry for TV coverage of the 1956 Republican convention.

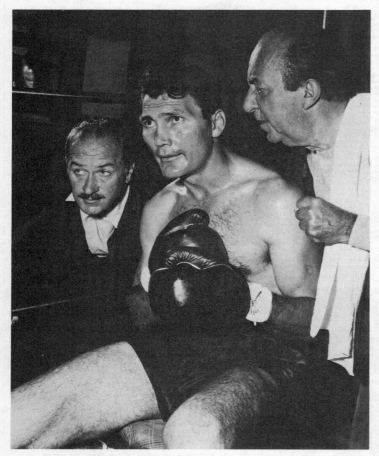

Keenan Wynn, Jack Palance and Ed Wynn starred in the tense television drama Requiem for a Heavyweight which was shown on Playhouse 90 during its first season. The program won an Emmy for 1956's Best Program and Rod Serling won for Best Original Teleplay.

Jack Benny and Bob Hope appeared regularly on television throughout the Fifties.

"All the News That's Fit to Print"

The New York Times.

7:30 A. M. EXTRA
Condensation of U. S. Weather Bureau forecast:
Mostly sunny and warm today.
Mostly fair and warm tomorrow.
Temperature range today: 84—69.
Temperature range yesterday: 85.2—67.
Full U. S. Weather Bureau Report, Page 16

VOL. CV No. 35,978.   Entered as Second-Class Matter, Post Office, New York, N. Y.   © 1956, by The New York Times Company.   NEW YORK, THURSDAY, JULY 26, 1956.   Times Square, New York 36, N. Y. Telephone LAckawanna 4-1000   FIVE CENTS

ANDREA DORIA AND STOCKHOLM COLLIDE; 1,134 PASSENGERS ABANDON ITALIAN SHIP IN FOG AT SEA; ALL SAVED, MANY INJURED

STASSEN SUGGESTS EISENHOWER STATE IF HE IS FOR NIXON

Aide to End Pro-Herter Drive If the President Gives Nod to the Vice President

GETS NO G.O.P. BACKING

Says Hall Tries to Foreclose Choice of Delegates in Advance of Convention

By JAMES RESTON
Special to The New York Times.

WASHINGTON, July 25 — Harold E. Stassen, the loneliest man in Washington, said today he would abandon his anti-Nixon campaign if President Eisenhower personally expressed a preference for Vice President Richard M. Nixon on the 1956 election ticket.

In the absence of such a statement from the President, the White House disarmament aide made it clear that he would continue to advocate the Vice-Presidential nomination of Gov. Christian A. Herter of Massachusetts.

The President has let it be known he was "delighted" that Mr. Nixon was available for the Vice - Presidential nomination. But he has not expressed a clear preference for him over other possible candidates.

Takes Aim at Hall

However, a reliable source informed The New York Times today that Governor Herter agreed to nominate Mr. Nixon for the Vice Presidency yesterday after a telephoned message from the White House saying that it was the President's wish that he do so.

Mr. Stassen was left today without the cooperation of Governor Herter or the public support of a single influential Republican politician.

Nevertheless, he took dead aim both at Mr. Nixon and the chairman of the Republican National Committee, Leonard W. Hall.

The 49-year-old ex-Governor, Mr. Stassen said, ran last in a private poll he conducted on eight potential Republican Vice - Presidential candidates. He did not say who was polled, or who did the polling, or what questions were asked—only that Mr. Nixon, Governor Herter and Mr. Stassen himself were among the eight.

He also wrote a letter in the middle of last night to Representative

Continued on Page 8, Column 5

Jordanian Group Attacks U. N. Palestine Truce Unit

Villagers' Fire Wounds One Observer —Burns Scores Incident — Amman Puts the Blame on Israelis

By HOMER BIGART
Special to The New York Times.

JERUSALEM, July 25—Jordanian villagers attacked a team of United Nations military observers today near Jerusalem. Lieut. Col. E. H. Thalin of Sweden was seriously wounded by the Jordanian fire, United Nations sources said.

They reported that the villagers "went berserk" after an exchange of fire with Israelis in which several Jordanians were wounded. During the engagement the Israelis employed mortar fire. There were no Israeli casualties.

[Jordanian sources in Amman said Israeli fire had been responsible. The Amman reports said ten Jordanians were wounded.]

Colonel Thalin was the third United Nations casualty in two days. Yesterday two Canadian officers were seriously wounded

In a mine explosion on Mount Scopus.

Maj. Gen. E. L. M. Burns of Canada, United Nations truce supervisor, said tonight that he was "astonished and deeply concerned by the attack by the Jordanian villagers."

He had already made arrangements to confer tomorrow with Maj. Gen. Ali Abu Nuwar, Chief of Staff of the Jordanian Army, on measures to be taken by Jordan to reduce the number of provocative incidents along the Israeli frontier. Israel's Premier, David Ben-Gurion, has threatened punitive action unless the provocations cease.

The current trouble spot on the frontier is in the Judean hills only five miles from Jerusalem where raw, new houses

Continued on Page 2, Column 3

DOWNTOWN TO GET 4TH NEW BUILDING

25-Story Structure Is Slated on Broad Street Site of R. C. A. Communications

By GLENN FOWLER

Another large office building is soon to rise in the downtown Manhattan financial district.

The building, the fourth large structure to be planned in the area within the last two years, will be twenty-five stories high. It will cover the block front on Beaver Street between Broad and New Streets, near Bowling Green.

It will stand on a plot of 48,000 square feet, running back 215 feet along Broad Street and 200 feet along New Street.

To be known as 60 Broad Street, the building will have an aluminum facade and a beacon light atop the roof. It will be fully air-conditioned, will have acoustic ceilings and will be equipped with operatorless elevators. Garage space will be provided in the basement. There will be 650,000 square feet of floor space above the ground floor.

The property on which the structure will be built is owned by R. C. A. Communications.

Continued on Page 41, Column 2

CONFEREES VOTE 3.7 BILLION IN AID

Reappropriated Fund Lifts Total to $4,006,570,000— Curb on Tito Supported

Special to The New York Times.

WASHINGTON, July 25— Conferees from the Senate and House of Representatives agreed today on a compromise foreign aid appropriation of $3,766,570,000.

This sum to carry the Mutual Security Program for another year would be increased by $240,000,000 of reappropriated money to a total of $4,006,570,000.

The bargain struck by the conferees amounted to a substantially even split between the $4,110,920,000 in new money originally allocated by the Senate and the $3,425,120,000 provided originally by the House.

President Eisenhower initially had asked for $4,900,000,000 for the fiscal year that opened July 1, although the appropriation for the fiscal year just ended was only $2,700,000,000.

Retained by the conferees was a rider in the Senate bill directing President Eisenhower not to give new military assistance funds to Communist Yugoslavia except for spare parts and replacements.

This stipulation was primarily the work of the Senate Republican leader, William F. Knowland of California. It did not affect $100,000,000 in military aid to Yugoslavia that already is "in the pipeline," nor did it

Continued on Page 12, Column 1

Eisenhower's Four Years

An Analysis of Agriculture Policy And Steps Taken to Meet Problems

This is the fifth of a series of articles analyzing the record of the Eisenhower Administration at the start of the Presidential election campaign.

By WILLIAM M. BLAIR
Special to The New York Times.

WASHINGTON, July 25— President Eisenhower has faced a number of stubborn dilemmas in the last four years but no other problem on the home front has been comparable to the one on farms.

Like the Communist problem overseas, it has absorbed his attention. From time to time it has been mitigated by his policies. Always, however, it has returned to plague him in one form or another.

In his home town of Abilene, Kan., in mid-1952 the President began formulating his program to reconcile freedom and prosperity for the American farmer. As he put it later, "full parity in the market place" and a minimum of Government regulation were his aims.

It has been a long, perplexing struggle for the President. But despite a notable effort, success has eluded him. The farmer still is tied up in Government con-

Continued on Page 12, Column 1

CRAFT RUSH TO AID

Terse Radio Messages of the Rescue Vessels Depict Operations

Help for the stricken liners Andrea Doria and Stockholm flowed almost instantly from all points of the compass to the spot at which they collided last night.

Ships large and small, Coast Guard vessels, luxury liners, Gloucester fishing boats, coastal steamers, all headed for the spot off Nantucket Lightship where the lives of some 2,500 persons were in danger.

It was 11:22 last night when the ships collided in a dense fog. The Andrea Doria, luxury liner of the Italian Line, shaken dangerously despite a double hull and other special safety features, sent out the first SOS less than a minute later.

The Coast Guard, with stations at Cape Ann, Cape Cod, Boston and other near-by points, sent out every available craft as soon as the position of the crash had been determined. Then came reassuring promises of help from the Ile de France and other craft within quick reach of the spot.

The Search and Rescue Division of the Coast Guard in New York received its first alert at 11:25 last night. It was then that the Coast Guard radio station at East Moriches, L. I. notified New York headquarters.

Coast Guard Cutters Aid

The East Moriches radio had picked up simultaneous SOS messages from the ships a minute or two before. The next hour was spent verifying positions and notifying all Coast Guard and merchant ships of the disaster and calling on them for help. The Coast Guard sent out ten cutters from New York, Boston and New London, Conn. and diverted three other ships cruising in that area.

The stark drama being played on the open ocean in darkness and fog was pictured in tense, taut radio messages recorded by the wireless room of The New York Times. They read:

12:21 A. M.—S. S. Stockholm says: Badly damaged. The whole bow crushed and No. 1 hold filled with water. Have to stay in our position. If you [Andrea Doria] can lower your lifeboats we can pick them up.

12:21 A. M.—S. S. Andrea Doria replied: You have to row to us

12:38 A. M.—S. S. Cape Ann reports: Now between the two ships and her boats are ready. Has two lifeboats.

12:45 A. M. Coast Guard boat says: Ten miles away; have eighteen boats.

1:12 A. M. Andrea Doria says: Needs more lifeboats still.

1:13 A. M. Unidentified ship, when queried, says: We have twelve lifeboats.

Stricken Ship's Boats Useless

1:21 A. M. Cape Ann asks Doria: How close do you want our ship to come to you?

1:24 A. M. Cape Ann reports: We have two boats for Andrea. Now proceeding to get close to her.

1:26 A. M. Andrea Doria reports: Danger immediate, need lifeboats, as many as possible. Can't use our lifeboats.

1:30 A. M. Stockholm gives position: Lat. 40:34 N; Long. 69:45 W.

1:33 A. M. Cape Ann asks Andrea: Want Cape Ann to move in any closer than Cape Ann is now?

1:34 A. M. Ile de France says: We are nine miles from you. Will launch as many boats as possible.

1:43 A. M. Doria repeats earlier message: Here danger immediate. Need lifeboats, as many as possible. Can't use our lifeboats.

1:46 A. M. Unidentified ship radios Andrea: Two lifeboats on way over to you.

1:53 A. M. S. S. Manaqui radios both ships: Will arrive yours. 0800 G. M. T. 15 A. M., E. D. T.) Have two lifeboats.

1:54 A. M. Andrea replies: O. K. Thanks.

1:56 A. M. Unidentified Nor-

Continued on Page 15, Column 1

The 29,000-ton Italian Line vessel, the Andrea Doria, which carried 1,134 passengers

The 12,644-ton Swedish American liner Stockholm, largest liner ever built in Sweden

SHIPS' PIERS QUIET IN NEW YORK PORT

Crowds Expected at Andrea Doria's Docks—Relatives Begin Calling Lines

The sea disaster had not early today awakened the pier at West Forty-fourth Street where the Andrea Doria had been scheduled to dock later in the morning.

This pier, as well as the terminal at West Fifty-seventh Street, where the Stockholm had left just before noon yesterday in a gala sailing, remained dark and quiet.

However, unaccustomed night lights began blinking on at the Italian Line's office at 24 State Street before 4 o'clock after began arriving.

They had been rounded up from their scattered homes around the Metropolitan area by officials of the line under Fosmino Pernigotti, assistant general manager of the company here.

The company officials were making plans to handle expected crowds at West Forty-fourth Street during the morning. Several thousand visitors were expected to begin gathering there by 8 o'clock, some not knowing about the collision.

It is an axiom in the harbor that every arriving passenger attracts five or more relatives and friends as welcomers, and the Italian Line officials were preparing to give them the tragic news and to forestall a rush by worried relatives on the line's downtown office.

Many of the relatives already knew of the crash at sea, and the office and pier of the com-

Continued on Page 14, Column 3

Many Notables Are Listed Aboard the Andrea Doria

Persons prominent in business, the theatre, politics, journalism and government were among the passengers aboard the Andrea Doria when she collided last night with the Stockholm. Two directors of the Standard Oil Company (New Jersey) were on the passenger list. They were Stewart Coleman, traveling with his family, and Marion W. Boyer, accompanied by his wife. Mr. Coleman, 57 years old, lives at 365 Barrett Road. Mr. Boyer, 54, lives in Greenwich, Conn.

Another passenger was Richardson Dilworth, Mayor of Philadelphia, and his wife. Mr. Dilworth, a lawyer by profession is 57. He served as a Marine in both World Wars, and received the Purple Heart in World War I and the Silver Star in World War II.

Ruth Roman, Hollywood motion picture star, and her son, Richard Hall, were on the Andrea Doria. Miss Roman recently divorced Mortimer Hall, owner of a Los Angeles radio station.

Two refugees from behind the Iron Curtain, the dancers Istvan Rabovsky and his wife Nora Kovach, also were passengers. In May, 1953, they fled to the West from East Berlin, where they had gone for a dancing engagement. In 1954, they came to this country.

Also on board were Camille M. Cianfarra, Madrid correspondent of The New York Times. A native of New York, Mr. Cianfarra joined The Times in 1935 in Rome. He became a specialist in Vatican affairs, and has written two books about the Vatican. He became Madrid correspondent in 1951.

Others on board included Ferdinand M. Thieriot, circulation manager of The San Francisco

Continued on Page 15, Column 3

SHIP BUILT TO TAKE COLLISION SAFELY

Andrea Doria Hull Divided to Give Stability—Lifeboats Could Carry 2,000

The Andrea Doria was specially built to give her more stability in case of just such a collision as she had last night with the Stockholm.

The hull was subdivided into eleven watertight compartments extending the entire length of the ship. Bulkheads parallel with her engine rooms were designed to lessen the effect of a collision.

The ship carried lifeboats with a capacity of 2,000 persons. Some of these boats were made of light metal alloy and were hung from davits operated by motor-driven winches. Two of the boats were motor-driven and fitted with radios.

Luxurious to the last detail, the ship was completely fireproofed and radar-equipped.

The ship has two groups of turbines capable of generating 50,000 horsepower to turn its three blade propellers, each weighing sixteen tons. They are nineteen feet in diameter and turn 143 revolutions a minute.

The Andrea Doria and the Stockholm had been the pride of the Italian and Swedish merchant marines.

The Stockholm, when launched in 1948, was the largest passenger vessel ever to have been built in Swedish yards. The Andrea Doria, when launched in 1951, was the last word in modern design and comfort. Each was flagship of its line until supplanted by new vessels a few years later.

When she went into service as flagship of the Swedish American Line, the Stockholm had a capacity of 364 passengers and 150 officers and crew. Alterations in 1953 increased the capacity to nearly 600 because of a proportionate increase with a proportionate increase in the size of the crew.

The Stockholm had an over-all length of 510 feet and a beam of

Continued on Page 15, Column 6

Cause of the Crash Puzzles Radar Men

Experts on radar said today they could not explain how the collision between the Andrea Doria and the Stockholm could have taken place because both vessels were equipped with radar equipment.

"They all said that even with the "visibility nil" conditions reported in the vicinity each ship should have been able to observe the other for distances up to fifty miles.

The experts declared that, even without knowing precisely what systems the vessels had, they almost certainly were standard on large passenger vessels. They should have been capable of two types of operation — generalized scanning all about the vessel, and a narrow restricted sector of the horizon. They should also have been

Continued on Page 14, Column 4

2D VESSEL IS SAFE

Ile de France In Today With Survivors From Crash Off Nantucket

By MAX FRANKEL

The trans-Atlantic liners Andrea Doria and Stockholm collided in a heavy Atlantic fog at 11:22 o'clock last night, forty-five miles south of Nantucket Island.

The Andrea Doria ordered her 1,134 passengers aboard to abandon ship. All were reported to have been rescued at 4:58 A. M. There was no immediate word, however, on the fate of her crew of 575.

At 5:15 A. M. today, however, the Ile de France reported from the scene that no more help was needed.

The French Liner estimated at 7 A. M. that she would arrive in New York shortly after 4 o'clock this afternoon with 1,000 survivors from the Andrea Doria. It was not clear to which ports the other survivors would be taken.

The Stockholm, although it had taken water through a crushed bow, was able to keep her 550 passengers and crew of 200 aboard. She was waiting for an escort to attempt to return to New York at a slow speed.

Many survivors of the Italian ship were said to have been seriously injured. The Stockholm said she had five "critical" cases aboard. Desperate and repeated calls for medical assistance were radioed from the score of rescue vessels in the area.

Deck Dips in Water

The Andrea Doria lay helpless in the thick fog. The black-and-white ship reported she was listing "very badly." She gave no other indication of the extent or nature of her damage nor was there word whether she could remain afloat.

The Stockholm reported at 6 A. M. that the Andrea Doria's main deck was dipping to the surface of the water.

The 29,000-ton Italian Line vessel apparently was listing so severely that she could launch no more than two of her lifeboats. Her lifeboats can carry 2,000 persons.

The French Ile de France, largest of the rescue vessels on hand, and the Stockholm apparently recovered the bulk of the Andrea Doria's passengers. At one time as many as 100 lifeboats probably were in the area. It was not clear how the passengers were loaded into the lifeboats.

At 4:58, the master of the Ile de France told the Stockholm: "All passengers rescued."

Bulkheads parallel "Proceeding to New York full speed."

The Ile de France left New York yesterday bound for Le Havre.

Just shortly after the collision, the Andrea Doria had run her lights and radio on emergency power and said she did not know much longer she could keep in touch with rescue craft. Her radio was so weak the Stock-

Continued on Page 14, Column 5

Continued on Page 8, Column 3
Continued on Page 41, Column 2
Continued on Page 12, Column 1
Continued on Page 10, Column 3
Continued on Page 15, Column 1
Continued on Page 14, Column 3
Continued on Page 15, Column 3
Continued on Page 15, Column 6
Continued on Page 14, Column 4
Continued on Page 14, Column 5

Ailing Millikin Plans To Leave the Senate

By WILLIAM S. WHITE

WASHINGTON, July 25— Senator Eugene D. Millikin of Colorado, a powerful member of the Republican leadership, said a farewell today in the Senate.

He was compelled by long and agonizing illness to announce that he would not seek re-election in the fall.

The decision was a heavy blow to the Republican party generally, and to its conservative wing in particular.

Mr. Millikin as a well campaigner would have been a formidable favorite to keep his seat safe for the Republicans. Even as an ailing prospective campaigner he had been greatly feared by the Democrats.

His retirement seemed plainly to forward Democratic prospects for retaining control

Continued on Page 10, Column 3

SCENE OF THE COLLISION: The liners Andrea Doria and the Stockholm stricken off Nantucket Island (cross).

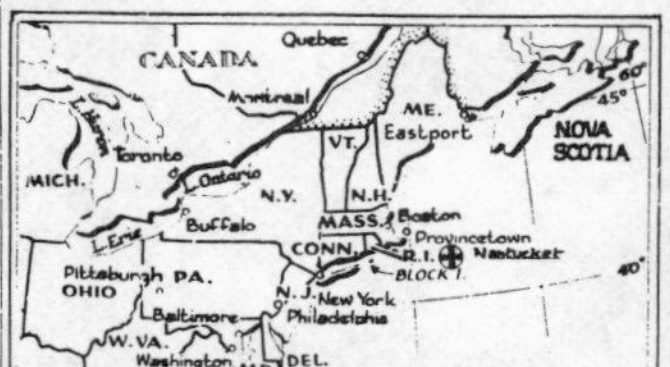

The New York Times   July 26, 1956

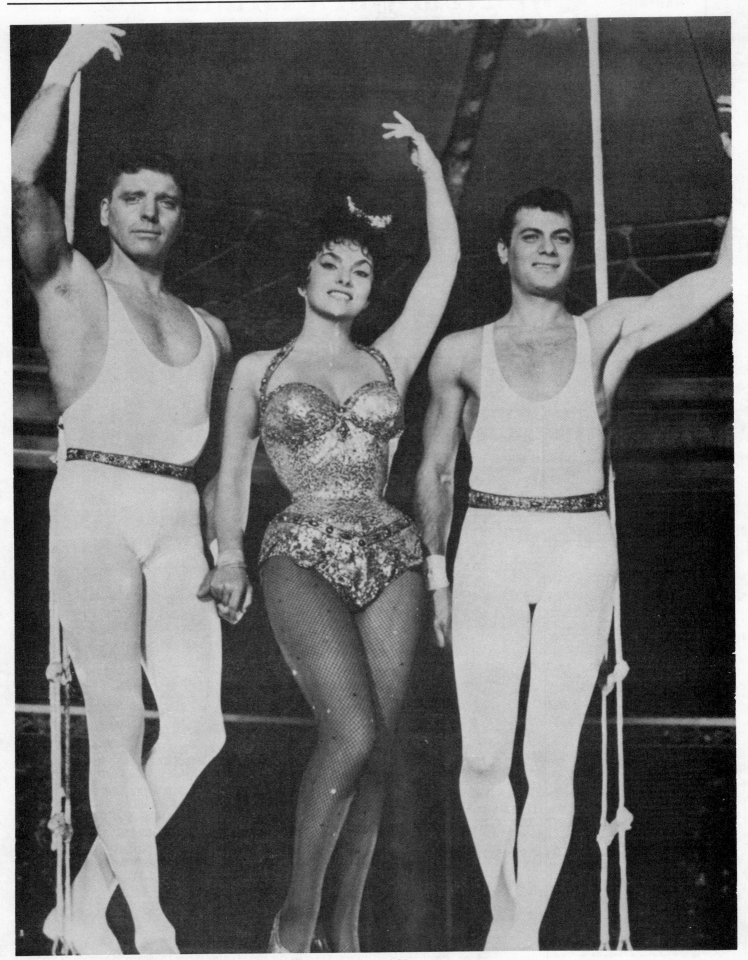

Audiences loved Trapeze, which starred Tony Curtis, Burt Lancaster and Gina Lollobrigida.

"All the News That's Fit to Print"

The New York Times.

© 1956, by The New York Times Company.

LATE CITY EDITION
Condensation of U. S. Weather Bureau forecast: Warm, humid, chance of afternoon or evening showers today and tomorrow.
Temperature range today: 85—72
Temperature range yesterday: 87.1—72.5
Full U. S. Weather Bureau Report, Page 42.

VOL. CV..No. 36,000. Entered as Second-Class Matter, Post Office, New York, N. Y. NEW YORK, FRIDAY, AUGUST 17, 1956. Times Square, New York 36, N. Y. Telephone Lackawanna 4-1000 FIVE CENTS

STEVENSON NOMINATED ON THE FIRST BALLOT; OVERWHELMS HARRIMAN BY 905½ VOTES TO 210; PUTS RUNNING MATE UP TO THE CONVENTION

DULLES PROPOSES A BOARD FOR SUEZ WITH LINK TO U. N.

Agency Would Include Egypt —Shepilov Conciliatory As Meeting Opens

Texts of Dulles and Shepilov statements on Page 3.

By HAROLD CALLENDER
Special to The New York Times.

LONDON, Aug. 16—Secretary of State Dulles presented to the Suez Canal conference today what was, in effect, a United States-British-French plan for the future of the waterway.

His proposal, made on the first day of the conference of twenty-two nations, was that the operation of the canal should be entrusted to an international board established by treaty and "associated" with the United Nations. Egypt would be represented on the board.

From the Soviet Union, represented by its Foreign Minister, Dmitri T. Shepilov, came a long comment, not on the three-power plan but on the conference. Mr. Shepilov's speech reiterated the criticisms and reservations lengthily expressed in the Soviet note of Aug. 9 questioning the composition and competence of the conference. But it ended in an ostensible offer to cooperate to make the conference a "first step" in a negotiation on the Suez problem.

Nasser Aide Is Firm

But negotiation seemed to be rejected by an apparent spokesman for President Gamal Abdel Nasser of Egypt, who arrived here tonight by plane from Cairo. He was Wing Comdr. Ali Sabry, political adviser to the President.

To reporters who met him at London Airport he said President Nasser would not acknowledge any independent authority over the canal, which must be under Egypt's sole control. He said: "There will be no compromise that interferes with the independence and sovereignty of Egypt."

It was assumed here that Wing Commander Sabry would speak for President Nasser in the informal talks that will take place outside the conference, which decided today to meet only in the afternoons.

In a short speech welcoming the conference to London, Prime Minister Eden said the occasion

Continued on Page 3, Column 5

POLAND TO WIDEN PRIVATE BUSINESS

To Encourage Limited Group of Service Industries

By SYDNEY GRUSON
Special to The New York Times.

WARSAW, Aug. 16—The Polish Communist party has started to encourage limited private enterprise. Thus it is reversing one of the basic tenets of its economic philosophy.

The Government has decreed a number of inducements to rebuild small service industries where a minimum of materials is required and the main value is in the labor. Included under the decree are bakers, tailors, cobblers, plumbers, blacksmiths, mechanics and producers in the traditional cottage industries such as embroidery and woodworking.

It is not likely that this will lead to an immediate increase in retail shopkeeping because manufactured goods still will have to be bought by shopkeepers from Government stores at retail prices.

All other East European Communist countries have a small number of private shops. These are the remains of the campaign against private enterprise. But no other satellite has permitted the opening of new shops or small industries as Poland is now going to.

The Polish moves to encourage

Continued on Page 5, Column 3

AP Correspondent Freed by Hungary

By JOHN MacCORMAC
Special to The New York Times.

VIENNA, Aug. 16—Dr. Endre Marton, Hungarian correspondent of The Associated Press imprisoned since February, 1955, on charges of spying, was released from prison today. Word of his release came from Budapest.

His wife, Ilona Nylas Marton, who was arrested on similar charges four months later, was set free last April when accusations against her were said to have been found baseless. She had worked as United Press correspondent in Budapest.

The arrest of the Martons came shortly after the return of Matyas Rakosi to complete power in Hungary as Com-

Continued on Page 4, Column 4

WIDE ARAB STRIKE PROTESTS PARLEY

Egypt Virtually at Standstill but Canal Is Unaffected— Violence in Libyan City

By OSGOOD CARUTHERS
Special to The New York Times.

CAIRO, Aug. 16—Cairo, the greatest metropolis in Africa and the Middle East, was virtually a dead city today.

A Government-sponsored twenty-four hour strike throughout Egypt brought the nation almost to a standstill. The strike was in protest against the opening today of the London conference on the status of the Suez Canal.

Reports from the rest of the Arab world said similar protest demonstrations in various forms had been staged in support of Egypt's opposition to the conference.

Among the few operations unaffected by the Egyptian strike was the passage of the daily convoys of ships through Suez Canal. The state authority that has taken over control of the canal since President Abdel Gamal Nasser nationalized the Suez Canal Company ordered that work go on there as usual.

Public utilities also were kept in operation.

Cairo Airport Is Closed

The international airport at Cairo was closed. All airlines using it had canceled their flights for the day.

Shops in Cairo, Port Said, Ismailia, Suez and Alexandria were shuttered. The streets of these usually teeming cities were virtually deserted.

No incidents were reported throughout the country. The Government had issued orders against either rallies or street demonstrations. Security measures imposed by Colonel Nasser's police force were totally effective.

Streets approaching foreign embassies were heavily guarded by policemen on foot, on horseback and in radio cruise cars.

Ordinary Government offices were closed. However, top officials stayed at their posts and continued intensive diplomatic and political activities in connection with the Suez Canal crisis. They studied reports from London on the progress of the Suez conference.

The Soviet Union's Cairo Embassy was reported to have kept open direct telephone and telegraph lines to London throughout the day. Western embassies worked at full pace, although some of their Egyptian employes stayed away for the day.

Tear Gas Used in Tripoli

CAIRO, Aug. 16 (Reuters)—Among the incidents reported today in the Moslem world was the arrest of several Libyan demonstrators in Tripoli.

Policemen there broke up a pro-Egyptian demonstration with tear gas. Also in Tripoli, a small boy threw a stone through a window of a United States cultural affairs center.

In Casablanca, Morocco, crowds thronged the streets shouting anti-British and anti-French slogans and "Vive Nas-

Continued on Page 2, Column 4

TRUCE IN CYPRUS URGED ON BRITISH BY UNDERGROUND

Leaflet by Pro-Greek Force Proposes Negotiations— London Awaits Word

By The United Press.

NICOSIA, Cyprus, Aug. 16—The Greek Cypriote underground organization, blamed for much of the terrorism that has swept this Mediterranean island in the last year and a half, offered Britain a military truce today.

The appeal for the truce by the National Organization of Cypriote Fighters, known as E. O. K. A., was made in leaflets distributed on the streets of Nicosia.

The leaflets said that E. O. K. A. was asking for a cease-fire to test the British Government's good faith. If the truce call was ignored, "operations will be resumed on a fiercer and more intensive scale."

Observers said the proposed truce might indicate the first sign of a take-over of underground activities by Anargyros Karadimas, who has been reported as successor of the long-hunted Col. George Grivas.

The Underground Leadership

The truce leaflets were signed by "Dighenis," the traditional name for a Cypriote nationalist, ethnic Greek outlaw leader. Since E. O. K. A. began its anti-British terrorism April 1, 1955, Dighenis is believed to have been Colonel Grivas, a 58-year-old former Greek Army officer.

The truce offer came shortly after Field Marshal Sir John Harding, the British Governor of Cyprus, outlined his terms in an interview with the English-language Times of Cyprus:

"Let the murderers make the first move if there is to be a stopping of violence and its consequences on this island," Governor Harding said.

The "consequences" to which he referred were a British crackdown on terrorism with added military and police force, as well as the recent hanging of at least five convicted extremists.

Governor Harding said the pro-Greek terrorists had committed more than forty murders before the first hanging took place. In July, he said, the illegal underground group committed seventeen murders.

"If we have to look for responsibility for the deaths of these men [the executed extremists], we must look back to the people who started the terrorist movement and persuaded them to take up murder," the Governor added.

The E. O. K. A. leaflets said that, awaiting a reply by the British, the underground had halted its operations. "But," the leaflets added, "E. O. K. A. is

Continued on Page 4, Column 5

Russians Exporting New Bible to U. S.

By HARRISON E. SALISBURY

Godless Russia is now exporting Bibles to God-fearing America.

In the newest twist of Communist policy the Soviet state book monopoly is shipping Bibles, in the Russian language, to the United States. They are now on sale in New York at $10 a copy.

The Russian Bibles are published in excellent type on good quality paper by the Moscow Patriarchy of the Russian Orthodox Church. They are distributed abroad, however, by Mezhdunarodnaya Kniga, the Soviet state book monopoly.

An initial shipment of fifty copies of the new Bible was received by the Four Continent Book Corporation, 821 Broadway. It was said to be selling well.

The American shipment is part of a first printing of 25,000 Bibles. A second printing, numbering 75,000, is expected soon. In view of the

Continued on Page 11, Column 1

GEROSA REBUFFED IN ECONOMY PLEA

City Units Ask $408,335,704 More in New Capital Than His Report Had Advised

By PAUL CROWELL

City departments and agencies have asked the City Planning Commission to allocate in its 1957 capital budget $589,035,704 of new funds chargeable against the municipal debt limit. The over-all total of capital budget requests is $1,064,452,161.

The $589,035,704 in requests for new funds is $408,335,704 more than Controller Lawrence E. Gerosa believes the city can borrow for public works projects without having to impose new nuisance taxes to help balance its expense budget for 1957-58.

On Wednesday Mr. Gerosa warned the Board of Estimate and other city agencies that borrowing for public works projects must be curtailed if new nuisance taxes were to be avoided. He estimated that it would be unsafe for the city to borrow more than $180,300,000 within the debt limit for such projects in 1957.

In Chicago, where he is attending the Democratic national convention, Mayor Wagner said he was confident that the city would be able to produce a balanced budget for 1957-58 without recourse to any new nuisance taxes.

The Mayor took issue with

Continued on Page 12, Column 1

4 Israelis on Bus Killed, 7 Hurt In an Ambush in Southern Negev

Attackers Said to Have Come From Jordan—Land Mine Blast Injures Five

Special to The New York Times.

ELATH, Israel, Aug. 16—Gunmen who were believed to have infiltrated from Jordan killed four Israelis today in an ambush of a bus and its military escort in the Negev. Seven others were wounded in the attack on the road to this frontier town on the shore of the Red Sea.

Elsewhere in the bleak Negev today five civilians were hurt when the truck in which they were riding north of Sde Boker was blown up by a land mine.

A Government spokesman said the Foreign Ministry had apprised Maj. Gen. E. L. M. Burns of Canada, chief of the United Nations truce team in Palestine, "of the particular gravity of the situation."

Today's dead were three soldiers who had traveled in a jeep as a vanguard, and one bus pas-

Continued on Page 4, Column 4

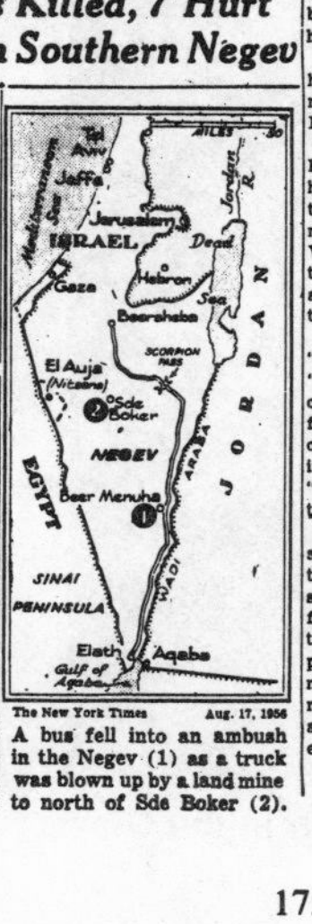

The New York Times Aug. 17, 1956

A bus fell into an ambush in the Negev (1) as a truck was blown up by a land mine to north of Sde Boker (2).

RACE IS LEFT OPEN

Humphrey, Kefauver Leading in Contest for Vice President

Text of Stevenson talk after nomination is on Page 7.

By JAMES RESTON
Special to The New York Times

CHICAGO, Aug. 16—Adlai E. Stevenson, the Democratic party's Presidential nominee, made a dramatic personal appeal to the convention tonight to make a free and solemn choice of his Vice-Presidential running-mate.

In a move designed to point up the controversy in the Republican party over the nomination in San Francisco next week of a running-mate for President Eisenhower, Mr. Stevenson told the convention that he would not try to hand-pick the Democratic Vice-Presidential nominee.

President Eisenhower has been challenged by Harold E. Stassen, his special assistant on disarmament, to give the Republican convention a similar free choice. The President has indicated that he would be "perfectly satisfied" with Vice President Richard M. Nixon on the Republican ticket this year, but has also said he wants an open convention.

"The choice will be yours," Mr. Stevenson told the delegates shortly after 11 o'clock. "The profit will be the nation's."

Great Care Urged

Mr. Stevenson emphasized that seven of the thirty-four Presidents in the history of the United States had reached the White House as a result of the death of the President.

This, he said, placed an especially heavy obligation on the convention to choose the Vice-Presidential nominee tomorrow with great care.

There was a prolonged backstage dispute this afternoon and night over whether Mr. Stevenson would make his acceptance speech tonight immediately after he was nominated for the second time by acclamation.

Mr. Stevenson wanted to accept tonight rather than tomorrow, when he was scheduled to come before the convention and share the platform with former President Harry S. Truman, who waged an open campaign to defeat him here this week.

The chairman of the convention, Speaker Sam Rayburn, and the chairman of the Democratic National Committee, Paul M. Butler, insisted, however, that the original program be followed even if it was distasteful to the nominee.

Mr. Stevenson then asked and was granted permission to make his appeal on the Vice Presidential question.

No Mention of Truman

Unlike most of the speakers before the convention, Mr. Stevenson did not address Mr. Truman as he opened his remarks before the jammed convention hall.

Mr. Truman sat in a box on his right, but Mr. Stevenson merely addressed the chairman, Mr. Rayburn, and the delegates.

"The responsibility of the Presidency has grown so great," he said, "that the nation's attention has become focused as never before on the office of the Vice Presidency. The choice for that office has become almost as important as the choice for the Presidency."

Mr. Stevenson then added that "each political party" had the "solemn obligation" to offer the country a person fully equipped first to assist in the discharge of the duties of the most exacting job in the world, and second, "to himself assume, if need be, this highest responsibility."

"I have decided," Mr. Stevenson said, "that the selection of the Vice-Presidential nominee should be made through the free processes of this convention so that the Democratic party's candidate for this office may join me before the nation not as one man's selection but as one chosen by our great party even as I have been chosen."

He said there were several

Continued on Page 9, Column 1

Associated Press Wirephoto

THE WINNER: Adlai E. Stevenson as he appeared last night at the convention hall, after he had been nominated.

Stevenson Pledges to Fight 'All the Way' in Campaign

By WILLIAM M. BLAIR
Special to The New York Times.

CHICAGO, Aug. 16—Adlai E. Stevenson, the Democratic nomination in his pocket, lost no time tonight in starting the long hard race against President Eisenhower. "This is the end of a long journey," he told his cheering campaign workers, "but it is also the beginning of a long journey. And I'm going to fight all of the way."

The Democratic candidate addressed his supporters at the Conrad Hilton Hotel less than an hour after he told the Democratic National Convention that it would have a free choice of the Vice-Presidential candidate.

This action, together with his other activities throughout the day, was a clear indication that he had been thinking ahead and planning his campaign against the Republican President who is considered certain of renomination at San Francisco next week.

In a number of statements earlier in the day, Mr. Stevenson had shown solicitude for the big-city voters, with their concern over civil rights, and the traditionally Democratic states of the South.

First of all, he had said that he would have preferred a "specific endorsement" of the Supreme Court's decision against school segregation in the platform.

But he had balanced this with friendly words for the South. He called the Democratic party the "only North-South party." And

Continued on Page 7, Column 3

High Police Press Delinquency Drive

By CLAYTON KNOWLES

An unusual meeting at Police Headquarters, called to intensify the city's war against juvenile delinquency, last night produced demands for funds for 5,000 more patrolmen.

The department's entire approach to the juvenile problem was reviewed in the light of a 41.3 per cent rise in crimes by youths for the first six months of the year over the comparable period of 1955.

Commissioner Stephen P. Kennedy, conceding that the police "cannot do this job alone," appealed to leaders of the Youth Councils to step up their efforts as the new school year started. The councils are citizen groups that work with the police at the precinct level. All precinct captains and the youth officers who work with them were present.

Notably absent were represen-

Continued on Page 44, Column 1

HARRIMAN PLANS '58 ALBANY RACE

Governor Also Pledges Aid to Stevenson in Drive to 'Put Him Over'

By LEO EGAN
Special to The New York Times.

CHICAGO, Aug. 16—Governor Harriman of New York pledged his help to Adlai E. Stevenson tonight less than half an hour after the former Illinois Governor had defeated him for the Democratic nomination for President.

Earlier, in a television appearance on the Columbia Broadcasting System, Mr. Harriman made it unmistakably clear that he intended to seek in 1958 a second term as Governor.

In the broadcast Mr. Harriman said he expected to remain as Governor of New York "for many, many years" if he failed to win the Presidential nomination. He remarked that "you know there's another election in 1958." That is the year in which the next state election of a Governor takes place.

The Governor said he intended to call on Mr. Stevenson following his television concession of defeat to congratulate the winner in person. "We are old friends, you know," he observed.

The Governor said he would campaign from one end of the state to the other because he regarded Democratic victories in the national election and in Congressional and legislative races as important.

The Governor kept score on the balloting in an air-conditioned room off the main convention hall. With him as the roll was called and his fate sealed were George Backer, a personal associate; Charles Van Devander, his press secretary; Walter Mordaunt, an assistant press secretary; Theodor Tannenwald, a friend; Daniel E. Gutman, his counsel, and Mrs. India Edwards, chairman of the women's division of his campaign committee.

Mrs. Harriman and the Governor's two daughters, Mrs. Stanley Mortimer and Mrs. Shirley

Continued on Page 7, Column 7

VICTOR IS CHEERED

Wins by Acclamation Upon Motion of the Harriman Camp

Texts of Kennedy and Gary speeches are on Page 8.

By W. H. LAWRENCE
Special to The New York Times.

CHICAGO, Aug. 16—Adlai E. Stevenson won renomination for President on the first ballot at the Democratic National Convention tonight.

The roll-call gave Mr. Stevenson 905½ votes, with only 686½ required for victory. Governor Harriman of New York ran a poor second with only 210 votes despite all the help that former President Harry S. Truman could give him.

Gov. Raymond Gary of Oklahoma, who had placed Governor Harriman in nomination, moved to give Mr. Stevenson the unanimous support of the convention.

Speaker Sam Rayburn, the Permanent Chairman, put the question as one of choosing the nominee by acclamation. There was an ear-splitting roar of "ayes."

"There are no 'noes,'" announced Speaker Rayburn without asking whether there was any opposition.

Mr. Stevenson announced at once that he wanted the convention to have a free-and-open choice of his Vice-Presidential running mate without his indicating in advance any preference. That vote will be taken tomorrow afternoon.

Cheered by Delegates

The Presidential nominee received a tremendous ovation when he appeared before the convention to express his thanks and to make his suggestion that the delegates themselves choose the Vice-Presidential nominee.

He did not say so, but it was obvious that the purpose of his move was to contrast the Democratic method choosing a Vice-Presidential nominee with that of the Republican party. The top G. O. P. leadership has joined in slating renomination of Vice President Richard M. Nixon as President Eisenhower's running mate.

Upon receiving news of the nomination, Mr. Stevenson said: "I feel relieved and happy." Later he told the delegates:

"My heart is full and I am deeply grateful but I did not come here to speak of the action you have just taken. That I shall

Continued on Page 6, Column 3

DE SAPIO SUFFERS LOSS OF PRESTIGE

But Wagner Gains Stature as Backer of Stevenson

Special to The New York Times.

CHICAGO, Aug. 16—Adlai E. Stevenson's nomination for President raised tonight the possibility of major power shifts in the Democratic party in New York State.

Carmine G. De Sapio's prestige as a state and national political leader has suffered a setback because of Governor Harriman's failure to make a better showing, in the opinion of many New York delegates.

As the leader of Tammany Hall, national committeemen for New York and unofficial manager of Mr. Harriman's campaign, Mr. De Sapio came to the convention as a prospective kingmaker. He will leave as a local politician.

Mayor Wagner, on the other hand, will leave with more prestige and, possibly, political power than when he entered it. From the start, Mr. Wagner was outspoken in his preference for Mr. Stevenson over Governor Harriman. His one concession to party "unity" was an agreement to waive this preference for one ballot to give Mr. Harriman a courtesy vote.

Should Mr. Stevenson be elected, it is the view of most

Continued on Page 9, Column 1

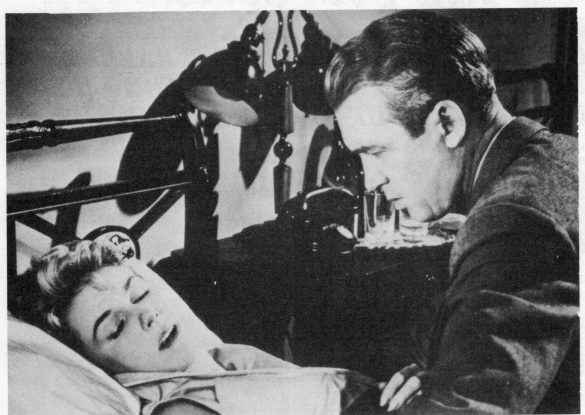

James Stewart consoles Doris Day, distressed because their son has been kidnapped, in Alfred Hitchcock's The Man Who Knew Too Much.

Deborah Kerr as Anna in the spectacular movie, The King And I.

Lee. J. Cobb, Jennifer Jones and Gregory Peck in a scene from The Man in the Gray Flannel Suit.

"All the News That's Fit to Print"

The New York Times.

LATE CITY EDITION
Condensation of U. S. Weather Bureau forecast: Hot and humid today and tonight. Hot tomorrow, thunderstorms later.
Temperature range today: 90—76.
Temperature range yesterday: 88.7—71.8.
Full U. S. Weather Bureau Report, Page 38.

© 1956, by The New York Times Company.

VOL. CV..No. 36,001. Entered as Second-Class Matter, Post Office, New York, N. Y. NEW YORK, SATURDAY, AUGUST 18, 1956. Times Square, New York 36, N. Y. Telephone LAckawanna 4-1000 FIVE CENTS

KEFAUVER NOMINATED FOR VICE PRESIDENT; BEATS KENNEDY, 755½-589, ON SECOND BALLOT; STEVENSON VOWS DRIVE FOR A 'NEW AMERICA'

SHEPILOV REJECTS WEST'S SUEZ PLAN; ASKS WIDER TALK

But Russian Stresses World Interest in Canal While Backing Egypt's Claims

Excerpts from Shepilov and Pineau speeches, Page 3.

By HAROLD CALLENDER
Special to The New York Times.

LONDON, Aug. 17—The Soviet Union rejected today the British-French-United States plan for international operation of the Suez Canal.

At the same time Moscow called for another and wider conference on the canal. It emphasized the international interest in the waterway as well as Egypt's rights. And it asserted that the Soviet Union, like the West, was concerned to assure free navigation through the canal. Egypt nationalized the Suez Canal Company July 26.

The Soviet view—expressed in an hour-long speech delivered to the Suez Canal conference here by Dmitri T. Shepilov, Soviet Foreign Minister—was that Egypt should assume obligations to guarantee free transit, to maintain and improve the canal and to fix tolls only after international consultation.

Russian to See Dulles Today

After this speech, whose negative aspects were conspicuous, it was learned that Mr. Shepilov had made an appointment to visit Secretary of State Dulles at the United States Embassy tomorrow morning. Mr. Shepilov made a similar visit Wednesday.

The United States view was that Mr. Shepilov's speech today was a moderate restatement of the Soviet Union's declaration of Aug. 9 in which it agreed to come to the present conference. Nothing very new was seen in what Mr. Shepilov said except the proposal for a committee to prepare a second conference.

French officials, however, suggested that the speech might "open a door" and that it merited close study. They stressed what they called Soviet recognition that the Suez situation could not remain in its present state and that some new kind of guarantee of freedom for shipping through the canal was necessary.

Others also saw more in Mr. Shepilov's speech than in the earlier Soviet declaration. While insisting upon respect for Egypt's rights, Mr. Shepilov spoke of international cooperation, in forms acceptable to Egypt, for the application of the convention on free navigation. His words, while not crystal clear in the English text, appeared to suggest some international supervision of Egypt's administration of the canal.

Mr. Shepilov proposed that the present conference formulate general principles for a settlement to be negotiated at a later

Continued on Page 3, Column 3

F. B. I. Solves Riesel Case; Reports Acid-Hurler Slain

Hoodlum Scarred in Attack Was Killed Here July 28—2 Ex-Convicts Held—Attempt to Silence Writer Charged

By STANLEY LEVEY

The Federal Bureau of Investigation untangled yesterday the mystery of the acid attack that cost the sight of Victor Riesel, labor columnist.

Two men, ex-convicts who were linked to labor rackets in the garment industry, were arrested and held in $100,000 bail each. They were accused of trying to prevent Mr. Riesel from testifying before a Federal grand jury investigating industrial rackets here.

The hired acid thrower, according to the F. B. I., was a 22-year-old petty hoodlum named Abraham Telvi of 2506 Avenue X, Brooklyn. He was murdered July 28 on the lower East Side, where he grew up. His killing may have been part of a triple gangland slaying with broad ramifications, it was indicated.

By an ironic twist, Telvi's acid attack on Mr. Riesel, which took place in the early morning hours of April 5, may have marked him for death. Some of the sulphuric acid that he dashed into the columnist's eyes splashed his own face, leaving him with scars.

Acting United States Attorney Thomas B. Gilchrist Jr. said yesterday that the underworld felt the facial burns made Telvi "too hot" and that his assassination was ordered. In fact, he added, there was an earlier attempt to take Telvi for "a ride." This failed when the thug became suspicious.

The two ex-convicts were

Continued on Page 30, Column 2

PLATFORM HAILED

Acceptance Talk Also Welcomes Truman Aid in Campaign

The text of Stevenson's speech appears on Page 8.

By WILLIAM M. BLAIR
Special to The New York Times.

CHICAGO, Aug. 17—Adlai E. Stevenson called tonight for a rebirth of leadership to "give us a glimpse of the nobility and vision without which peoples and nations perish."

In a fighting speech he accepted renomination as the Democratic candidate for President with a pledge to work with all the resources at his command to carry out the Democratic platform. He called the platform "a signpost" toward a "new America."

Mr. Stevenson said:

"I mean a new America where poverty is abolished and our abundance is used to enrich the lives of every family.

"I mean a new America where freedom is made real for all without regard to race or belief or economic condition.

"I mean a New America which everlastingly attacks the ancient idea that men can solve their differences by killing each other."

Mr. Stevenson, pledging to work for these objectives, declared:

"These are the terms on which I accept your nomination."

Scores 'Personality Cult'

He blasted the Republicans with a charge that the Administration had not told the truth to the country.

"I say that what this country needs is not propaganda and a personality cult," he said. "What this country needs is leadership and truth, and that's what we mean to give it."

He saluted former President Harry S. Truman, who fought to block his nomination.

"I am glad to have you on my side again, sir!" he said.

He called Mr. Truman the "distinguished American who has been more than equal to the hard test of disagreement and has now reaffirmed our common cause so graciously."

He also told the cheering delegates to the national convention that their free choice of Senator Estes Kefauver of Tennessee as his running mate had "renewed and reaffirmed our faith in free Democratic processes."

The office of Vice President, he said, has been "dignified by the manner of your selection as well as by the distinction of your choice."

Before speaking Mr. Steven-

Continued on Page 7, Column 1

Associated Press Wirephoto

THE DELEGATES' CHOICE: Adlai E. Stevenson and Senator Estes Kefauver on the rostrum last night at the convention in Chicago. At the right is former President Truman.

FINISH DRAMATIC

Bay Stater Nearly In When Stampede to Rival Is Set Off

By W. H. LAWRENCE
Special to The New York Times.

CHICAGO, Aug. 17—Senator Estes Kefauver seized the Democratic Vice-Presidential nomination by an eyelash today.

The Tennessean edged out Senator John F. Kennedy of Massachusetts on the second ballot in an open floor fight to become the running mate of Adlai E. Stevenson of Illinois. Mr. Stevenson was renominated for the Presidency last night.

The Democrats picked two men who fought each other bitterly in the primaries to oppose the Republican slate in November. President Eisenhower and Vice President Richard M. Nixon are expected to be renominated at San Francisco next week.

The Stevenson-Kefauver team shared the spotlight at the final session tonight of the Democratic National Convention with former President Harry S. Truman, who had opposed the selection of both.

Tonight they came to accept their nominations. Mr. Truman came to bid for party unity and to take back some of the harsh things he had said against Mr. Stevenson this week. Besides saying that Mr. Stevenson was "too defeatist to win," Mr. Truman in his private conversations has mispronounced the Tennessean's name as if it were spelled "Cowfever." Tonight he pronounced it correctly.

States Switch Votes

After Mr. Stevenson's speech and the singing of "The Lord's Prayer" the thirty-second convention ended at 10:52 P. M., Central daylight time [11:52 P. M. Eastern daylight time].

The final ballot was as dramatic as any Democratic convention has witnessed.

Senator Kefauver's nomination was made by acclamation upon the motion of Senator Kennedy. When the second roll-call was completed, but before the result had been announced, Senator Kennedy had 648 votes, 38½ votes short of the required majority. He was far ahead of the Tennessee Senator.

Then the states began to wave their standards to switch their votes. The lead seesawed. At that point, Senator Albert Gore of Tennessee, who was running third, withdrew in favor of his colleague and released the delegates pledged to him.

That started a stampede to the 53-year-old Mr. Kefauver. The Senator went over the top on the basis of new votes that Missouri had cast for Senator Hubert H. Humphrey of Minnesota.

The final official tabulation as reported by The Associated Press gave Senator Kefauver 755½ votes and Senator Kennedy 589. This Convention had 1,372 delegates, with 686½ votes comprising a majority.

Earlier figures on the final

Continued on Page 6, Column 1

INDONESIA URGES WARNING TO WEST

Sukarno Proposes All Newly Free Lands Join in Saying: 'Hands Off Egypt!'

By ROBERT ALDEN
Special to The New York Times.

JAKARTA, Indonesia, Aug. 17—President Sukarno called today upon the newly independent nations, especially those in Asia and Africa, to unite in warning: "Hands off Egypt!"

"If I were to decide, I would immediately convoke a second Asian-African conference to discuss this call," the Indonesian President declared in a major speech marking the eleventh anniversary of his country's independence. The first Asian-African conference was held in Bandung, Indonesia, in 1955.

The President said Indonesia placed complete confidence in Egypt's guarantee that the Suez Canal would always be open to international traffic. Indonesia's attendance at the London conference on the status of the Canal is in "defense of Egypt's sovereign rights and in defense of peace," he added.

The Indonesian President said that his country's stand was plain, that Egypt was acting within her inalienable rights as a sovereign state in nationaliz-

Continued on Page 2, Column 5

Bonn's High Court Outlaws Red Party And Front Groups

By M. S. HANDLER
Special to The New York Times.

BONN, Germany, Aug. 17—The Federal Constitutional Court outlawed the West German Communist party and its numerous front organizations today.

Alerted early in the morning in anticipation of the court's decision, the state police occupied the party's headquarters in Duesseldorf. The party's central newspaper, Freies Volk, published in Duesseldorf, also was closed but only after the staff had succeeded in getting out the day's issue.

The state police in other parts of the country moved in and occupied local party headquarters and publishing offices. However, according to reports reaching Bonn, the police managed to seize only propaganda material.

Party records, membership lists and confidential documents had long since been moved to undisclosed destinations, presumably in East Germany. Several truckloads of material were intercepted at Helmstedt on the border of East Germany, but the contents have not yet been examined.

The court's decision was given in answer to a charge filed by the Bonn Government in November, 1951, that the Communist party was committed to the overthrow of the constitutional

Continued on Page 4, Column 3

KEFAUVER SCORES NIXON FOR 'SMEAR'

Tells Convention That He'll Never 'Demean' Office of Vice President

Text of the Kefauver speech is printed on Page 8.

By ANTHONY LEWIS
Special to The New York Times.

CHICAGO, Aug. 17—Senator Estes Kefauver accepted the Democratic nomination for Vice President tonight with a jab at his prospective Republican opponent, Vice President Richard M. Nixon.

"The chief function of the Vice President should not be that of a political sharpshooter for his party," Senator Kefauver told the Democratic National Convention. "It should not be that of providing the smear under the protection of the President's smile ***.

"As your Vice-Presidential candidate, I promise you that I will never demean that high office to traduce fellow-Americans. I will never use it to sow division and distrust."

This was a reference to Democratic charges that throughout his political career, and notably in the election of 1954, Mr. Nixon used half-truths and insinuations to smear the Democrats as pro-Communist.

Senator Kefauver began his speech by saying he was proud to have been selected as the Vice-Presidential candidate by the new device of an open convention.

"It will be very interesting to

Continued on Page 7, Column 5

Truman Terms Stevenson 'A Fighter' Who Can Win

By ANTHONY LEVIERO
Special to The New York Times.

CHICAGO, Aug. 17—Harry S. Truman declared tonight that Adlai E. Stevenson was "a real fighter." The former President came out battling for the Democratic party. He told the convention delegates that the Democratic standard-bearer had given him "a pretty good licking, and he's going to give Eisenhower a better one."

Mr. Truman reversed his bitter attitude toward Mr. Stevenson in making the opening speech at

Text of the Truman address will be found on Page 8.

the night session of the convention. Only two days ago he had branded the Democratic Presidential candidate as a political weakling who would deliver his party into a conservative-reactionary caretakership for the next four years.

Last night in nominating Mr. Stevenson the convention delivered a trouncing to Mr. Truman, who had headed a faltering cause in behalf of Governor Harriman. Today the convention rebuffed Mr. Truman again in nominating Senator Estes Kefauver as the Vice-Presidential candidate. The former President has a pronounced antipathy for the Tennessean.

But in returning to party regularity the former President called on every Democrat to throw "the Republicans out of office." He attacked the Eisenhower Administration on seven major issues.

Calls Kefauver 'Able'

Mr. Truman's speech was written before the nomination of Mr. Kefauver. After the convention had acted he applied this political benediction to Mr. Stevenson's running mate:

"The convention has given Governor Stevenson an able and efficient running mate in Estes Kefauver. He will add great strength to the ticket."

Speaker Sam Rayburn, the convention chairman, introduced the former President and said "we should not remember the shots he made from the hip—and he made many of them."

Mr. Rayburn added that Mr. Truman had made some of the most far-reaching decisions in history.

The vast audience was more than willing to forget the shots from the hip. They gave the old party warhorse a roaring ovation that echoed to the rafters until Mr. Truman himself gaveled for silence so that the program could be kept on schedule.

In no time at all he had the audience completely with him, cheering and laughing.

Mr. Truman ad libbed to make even more gracious his formal admission that he had taken a

Continued on Page 9, Column 2

NEW YORK IS COOL TO TENNESSEAN

Leaders Wanted Catholic on Ticket to Help Carry State in November

By LEO EGAN
Special to The New York Times.

CHICAGO, Aug. 17—A deep conviction that Adlai E. Stevenson will need help to carry New York was behind the battle waged by New York leaders today to obtain the Vice-Presidential nomination for either Mayor Wagner or Senator John F. Kennedy of Massachusetts.

Representative Charles A. Buckley said that Mr. Stevenson could not carry New York without help. He made the statement in urging the delegation to switch from Mayor Wagner to Senator Kennedy between the first and second ballots.

Mr. Buckley is the Democratic leader of the Bronx, which usually casts the highest percentage of Democratic votes of any county in the state.

"Anyone who would vote for Kefauver would vote for Stevenson," he told Carmine G. De Sapio, chairman of the New

Continued on Page 9, Column 4

L. I. Boy Calls Nasser 'Nice Man' After Visiting Him

Associated Press Radiophoto

President Gamal Abdel Nasser, left, with Dennis Briody and his father, Charles Briody

By The United Press.

CAIRO, Aug. 17—Dennis Briody, 13 years old, of Massapequa, L. I., met Lieut. Col. Gamal Abdel Nasser, President of Egypt, today and thought he was "a real nice man." The boy came to Egypt as Colonel Nasser's personal guest Aug. 8. Today the President received the young visitor and his father, Charles, in the Presidential office. Dennis wrote Colonel Nasser that "some people in the United States have misconceptions about Egypt." Dennis told Colonel Nasser he had enjoyed his visit to points of interest. While in Cairo, and before he awaited the Nasser interview, Dennis went sight-seeing.

9 Egyptians Killed In Gaza Zone Fights

By JOSEPH O. HAFF
Special to The New York Times.

JERUSALEM, Aug. 17—Nine Egyptian soldiers were killed in two incidents near the Israeli border in the Gaza Strip last night, the United Nations Truce Supervision organization said here tonight.

Maj. Gen. E. L. M. Burns of Canada, the United Nations Chief of Staff here, was examining all the data. He will send a report to Secretary General Dag Hammarskjold.

Following a day-long investigation into the incidents, the United Nations Truce Supervision Headquarters reported that an exchange of fire between Egyptian and Israeli patrols in the Egyptian-controlled territory south of the city of Gaza at 6:30 P. M. had resulted in the death of three Egyptian soldiers. United Na-

Continued on Page 29, Column 2

Soviet Will Reverse Two Arctic Rivers

By HARRISON E. SALISBURY

Georgi M. Malenkov, former Soviet Premier, recently outlined to a visiting American publisher a plan for increasing the power output of the Volga River by reversing the flow of two Arctic rivers.

The previously undisclosed Soviet plan was discussed by Mr. Malenkov in an interview with Shelton Fisher, publisher of Power magazine, a McGraw-Hill publication. Mr. Fisher recently returned from the Soviet Union.

Mr. Malenkov, now Minister of Electric Power Stations, disclosed that the great Volga project was already on the engineering drafting boards. It is designed to stabilize the year-around waterflow in the Volga. Mr. Malenkov estimated that power production would be increased by 11,000,000,000 kilo-

Continued on Page 2, Column 4

Republicans Hail 'Good News,' Chide Foes on 'Picking a Loser'

By LAWRENCE E. DAVIES
Special to The New York Times.

SAN FRANCISCO, Aug. 17—Republican spokesmen exuded optimism today over prospects not only of retaining the Presidency but also of obtaining control of the Senate. They did this on the basis of what they called "the good news" from Chicago.

Almost on the eve of the opening Monday of their own national convention here in the Cow Palace, party leaders chided the Democrats for "picking a loser"—Adlai E. Stevenson—to run against President Eisenhower.

Then, with Senator Andrew F. Schoeppel of Kansas, chairman of the Senate Republican Campaign Committee, in the lead, they analyzed prospective Senate battles and predicted a net gain of "four or five seats."

Senator Schoeppel was reminded that this claim was much more optimistic than a picture drawn twenty-four hours earlier by Senator William F. Knowland of California, the minority leader. Mr. Knowland had told a Western Republican conference that with work the Republicans could capture the House, but that the Senate was "going to be more difficult."

"I am more optimistic," Senator Schoeppel declared, "after seeing what the Democrats have done at Chicago. They have nominated a loser. We beat him once and we'll beat him again. He can't win. Former President Truman said that and so did John L. Lewis [president of the United Mine Workers of America]. On top of that the Democratic platform set forth the most glib

Continued on Page 10, Column 4

1956

The running mates for the 1956 Presidential election, Adlai Stevenson and Estes Kefauver, are seen here at the Democratic convention.

Victorious for a second time, "Ike and Mamie" and "Dick and Pat" respond to cheers on election night.

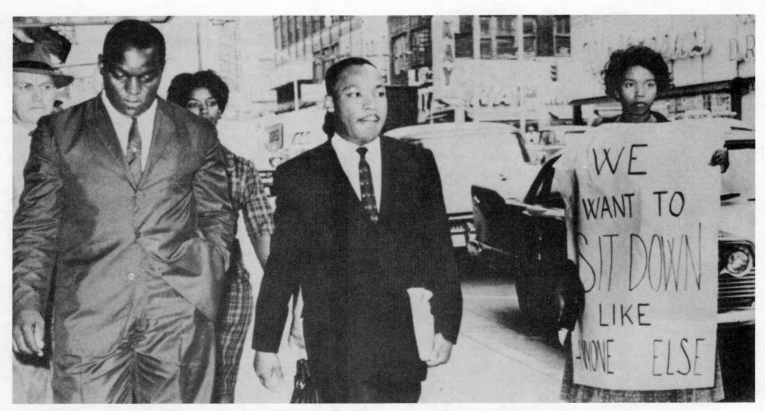

Atlanta Police Captain R.E. Little arrests Dr. Martin Luther King during the boycott of the bus company there.

"All the News That's Fit to Print"

The New York Times.

LATE CITY EDITION
Condensation of U. S. Weather Bureau forecast: Mostly fair today; showers possible tonight. Clearing tomorrow. Temperature range today: 72—62. Temperature range yesterday: 69.3—61.6. Full U. S. Weather Bureau Report, Page 52.

VOL. CV. No. 36,006. Entered as Second-Class Matter, Post Office, New York, N. Y. NEW YORK, THURSDAY, AUGUST 23, 1956. Times Square, New York 36, N. Y. Telephone LAckawanna 4-1000 FIVE CENTS

EISENHOWER AND NIXON ARE RENOMINATED; G. O. P. CONVENTION IS UNANIMOUS ON BOTH; STASSEN GIVES UP, SECONDS VICE PRESIDENT

SOVIET AND INDIA BAR BID TO EGYPT TO DISCUSS SUEZ

Block Proposal for Talk on Canal's Regime—Action Prolongs London Parley

The text of Selwyn Lloyd's address is on Page 2.

By HAROLD CALLENDER
Special to The New York Times.

LONDON, Aug. 22—The Soviet Union and India joined today to block a proposal to ask Egypt to negotiate with other nations for an international regime for the Suez Canal:

They thus prolonged the Suez Canal conference of twenty-two nations, which was to have finised today. It will meet again tomorrow to try to decide how negotiations with Egypt are to begin. Egypt, which refused to attend the conference, nationalized, on July 26, the company operating the canal.

The nations supporting the United States proposal for such negotiations now number eighteen. France and Spain withdrew today the reservations they had made yesterday.

[Some diplomats in London from the smaller European countries are predicting a Western defeat in the Suez crisis. As a result, they have begun talking of a whole new European approach to the nations of the East. One diplomat said a "new way of living" would have to be worked out "without special Western spheres of influence."]

Held Essential to Solution

Informally declaring Britain's adherence to the United States proposal, as amended yesterday to win the backing of Eastern nations, Selwyn Lloyd, British Foreign Secretary, seemed to insist that an international operating agency for the canal was beyond negotiation. He said such an agency was "an essential part of any settlement."

British officials contended today that the United States proposal, even in its amended form, still expressed sufficiently clearly the determination of the Western powers to refuse any compromise on the principle of international operation of the canal.

The French back the same principle. They were not too pleased when the term "international board" was dropped from the United States text in favor of "a Suez Canal board" representing Egypt and other states.

Nor were they content with the terms of the New Zealand proposal put to the conference today. This suggested that negotiations be offered to Egypt "on the basis of" the United States proposal, or "statement," as it is called in the terminology of this conference. The French had urged in private talks that

Continued on Page 3, Column 5

Cairo Issues Threat Of Canal Priorities

By OSGOOD CARUTHERS
Special to The New York Times.

CAIRO, Aug. 22—Egypt threatened today to give priority in the Suez Canal to ships other than those of Britain and France if British and French canal pilots quit their jobs.

The threat was made by Nabih Yunis, Under Secretary of the Ministry of Finance and a member of the twelve-man managing board of the Egyptian Government's new Suez Canal Authority.

[In London, the chief spokesman of the Foreign Office said the Egyptian threat "appears to be a clear case of discrimination." Selwyn Lord, Foreign Secretary, disputed Soviet contentions that the canal was being run smoothly.]

Mr. Yunis charged bitterly that "some British and French pilots resort to the trick of

Continued on Page 3, Column 1

CYPRUS BAND GETS 3 WEEKS TO YIELD

Terrorists Given a Deadline by British to Surrender Under Amnesty Offer

By BENJAMIN WELLES
Special to The New York Times.

LONDON, Aug. 22—The British Government has offered the Cypriote terrorists three weeks in which to surrender with their arms.

Those who take advantage of the offer, which is effective at midnight tonight, can choose either to go freely to Greece, if Greece will have them, or to remain in Cyprus under detention. Any among those who stay who are implicated in crimes of violence against persons will be tried, the Government announced.

The British offer, made today by the British Governor, Field Marshal Sir John Harding, in Nicosia, was announced by the Colonial Office. It was described officially as a move to test the value of the pamphlets recently distributed in the island crown colony by the National Organization of Cypriote Fighters, oth-

Continued on Page 9, Column 3

Associated Press Radiophoto

PROLONGS SUEZ TALKS: V. K. Krishna Menon of India. He is shown leaving Foreign Office yesterday after session with Selwyn Lloyd, British Foreign Secretary.

U. S. NAVAL PLANE MISSING IN ATTACK OFF CHINA'S COAST

16 Men Aboard Patrol Craft—Fighter Cover Is Sent With the Search Party

Special to The New York Times.

WASHINGTON, Aug. 22—A Navy patrol plane is missing after having been attacked by aircraft off the coast of Communist China.

In reporting the incident tonight the Navy said an air and surface search with an "air cover" of fighting planes was under way. A brief statement by the Navy said:

"The Navy reported that one of its planes is missing and unaccounted for after having been under attack by aircraft. The identity of the attacking air craft has not yet been determined.

"The commander of the United States Seventh Fleet, Vice Admiral Stuart Ingersoll, has initiated an air and surface search for the plane or survivors and has provided air cover for the planes and ships taking part in the search.

"The plane's reported position at the time of the attack was approximately 160 miles north of Formosa [Taiwan] and about thirty-two miles off the China coast over international waters.

"The plane, a P4M Martin Mercator, is powered by two jet and two reciprocating engines. It is designed for long overwater patrols and photographic reconnaissance. It normally carries a crew of nine. The missing plane was on a routine patrol flight at the time of attack."

Attacked at Night

Later the Navy reported that the attack took place at 12:25 A. M. Thursday, Taiwan time (12:25 P. M. Wednesday, Eastern standard time).

[A spokesman at headquarters of the Far East Air Forces in Tokyo said Thursday the missing plane was carrying sixteen men, The Associated Press reported. Chinese Nationalist authorities on Taiwan said no plane of theirs had been involved in the attack, Reuters reported.]

Admiral Arleigh A. Burke, Chief of Naval Operations, has notified all Government authorities of the incident. It was assumed that word had been sent to President Eisenhower and Charles E. Wilson, Secretary of Defense, who are at the Republican National Convention in San Francisco, and Secretary of State Dulles, who is taking part in the London conference on the Suez Canal.

Although there had been many instances in which United States planes were shot down or attacked by planes belonging to Soviet satellite nations over the last few years, this type of incident had appeared to be occurring less frequently.

The last Navy plane to suffer

Continued on Page 5, Column 3

NIXON FLIES TO HIS FATHER: Vice President Richard M. Nixon and Mrs. Nixon leave San Francisco for bedside of Mr. Nixon's father, critically ill at La Habra, Calif.

Associated Press Wirephotos

THE PRESIDENT MEETS STASSEN: President Eisenhower confers with Harold E. Stassen, who said he was ending campaign to replace Vice President Nixon on the ticket.

NIXON AT BEDSIDE OF AILING FATHER

Flies to His Home on Word of Critical Illness—Return to Convention Uncertain

By The Associated Press.

WHITTIER, Calif., Aug. 22—Vice President Richard M. Nixon flew here from the Republican National Convention today to take up a vigil at the bedside of his father, who is critically ill.

Little hope was held for the recovery of 77-year-old Francis A. Nixon. He was stricken with bleeding of the major artery leading to the abdomen in his home at La Habra, near here, at 4 A. M. today. He was intermittently unconscious during the day.

The Vice President whose home is in Whittier, canceled all engagements and sped to his father. He was accompanied by his wife and brother, F. Donald Nixon of Whittier, and sister-in-law, Mrs. Clara Jane Nixon.

On learning of the convention results, Mr. Nixon said:

"We've just heard the proceedings and were very gratified by the results in the renomination of President Eisenhower and appreciative too for the support of the delegates for the nomination of Vice President.

"I'll work harder than in previous campaigns to see that leadership is available to the United States and the world for four more years."

After being with his father several hours, Mr. Nixon said his return to San Francisco depended on his father's condition

Continued on Page 13, Column 5

Stassen Reverses Position After Visiting Eisenhower

By WILLIAM S. WHITE
Special to The New York Times.

SAN FRANCISCO, Aug. 22—Harold E. Stassen capped an unconditional surrender in his campaign to "stop" Richard M. Nixon tonight by seconding the Vice President's renomination at the Republican National Convention. Earlier, after a short talk with President Eisenhower, Mr. Stassen had phlegmatically reversed himself. He had promised to support and work for the re-election of Mr. Nixon as well as of President Eisenhower. He also had announced his intention of staying in his job as disarmament adviser to the President—and had firmly closed the door on the recent past.

At all events, Mr. Stassen came to the convention hall tonight to salute the man he had attacked as recently as yesterday as harmful to the Republican ticket this fall—Vice President Nixon.

He thus came full circle—not only now accepting Mr. Nixon but also praising him. His brief act of rebellion had represented the only breach in the picture of total unity that the Republicans had presented here.

[In La Habra, Calif., Mr. Nixon said he was "deeply appreciative" of Mr. Stassen's changed position. He said this would help the party "present a united front" for the election campaign.]

Mr. Stassen was well received—there were no boos—as a prodigal who had come home. He called Mr. Nixon "able" and "experienced," and appealed to independents, dissident Democrats and minority voters over the country to support the Vice President in the fall.

He asked to be allowed "respectfully to plead" with the party leadership not to forget these groups in their campaign plans.

He said that his own act of retreat did not foreclose others from voting for some person other than Mr. Nixon, if they chose, but he added that Mr. Nixon would "give very ounce of his intelligence and devoted efforts" toward the re-election of President Eisenhower.

He pledged his own "wholehearted and all-out efforts" for the Eisenhower-Nixon ticket, saying that when "points of decision" arose in the party he would always be "a team player."

He asserted that a continuation of the Eisenhower-Nixon leadership, with the cooperation of members of Congress of both parties, offered "the best prospect" for reaching a sound system of world disarmament in hydrogen and other weapons.

He spoke eleven minutes to a convention that seemed basically friendly but unstartled. What he would do here tonight had for hours been known.

He had an eleven-minute conference, from 10:53 A. M. to 11:04 A. M., with President

Continued on Page 15, Column 7

DEWEY SAYS G. O. P. WILL GUARD PEACE

Cites President's Record—Calls His Re-election Best for Nation's Prosperity

The text of speech by Dewey will be found on Page 16.

By LEO EGAN
Special to The New York Times.

SAN FRANCISCO, Aug. 22—Thomas E. Dewey told the Republican National Convention tonight that America's best hope of continued peace and prosperity depended on President Eisenhower's re-election.

In a speech that frequently brought outbursts of applause and cheers from the delegates, Mr. Dewey assailed Democrats for inconsistencies, past misdeeds and ineptness.

It was the kind of speech the delegates seemed to have been waiting for since the convention opened. They took full advantage of it to voice their confidence in winning this year's election.

As proof that the nation could not depend on Adlai E. Stevenson, the candidate for President named by the Democrats last week, Mr. Dewey cited opinions expressed by two outstanding Democrats at Chicago.

Averell Harriman, who succeeded him as Governor of New York, asserted, Mr. Dewey recalled, that he was the only Democrat able to deal with Communists. Harry S. Truman, who defeated Mr. Dewey for President in 1948, was quoted as having warned Democrats that the nation would face a trial-and-error period in foreign relations if Mr. Stevenson were elected.

The former Governor asserted that the nation was indebted to Mr. Truman for this "involuntary lapse into objectivity."

Mr. Dewey's gibes at the former Democratic President evoked both laughter and applause. So did later references to Mr. Truman's "squirrel head" remark to describe some military men during his recent European trip and his allusions to some letters Mr. Truman had written as President.

The speech, even more than

Continued on Page 17, Column 4

HALLECK, HERTER NOMINATE TICKET

President Is Hailed as Man 'Equal to the Times'—Nixon Called Dedicated

Texts of Halleck, Herter and Stassen speeches, Page 14.

By ALLEN DRURY
Special to The New York Times.

SAN FRANCISCO, Aug. 22—Representative Charles A. Halleck of Indiana placed President Eisenhower's name in nomination today for a second term.

He told a cheering Republican National Convention that General Eisenhower was "the most universally respected, the most profoundly dedicated man of our times."

Later, Gov. Christian A. Herter of Massachusetts nominated Vice President Richard M. Nixon for a second term. He called him "a great Vice President" who had made his office "more significant, more influential, more useful than ever before in our history."

Mr. Halleck told the enthusiastic delegates that now, as in Abraham Lincoln's time, "a Divine Providence has again given us a man equal to the times."

Referring to Democratic charges that General Eisenhower had been "a part-time President," Mr. Halleck shouted:

"Are peace and military might—balanced budget and stable dollar—Federal payroll and tax cuts—farming at peace instead of war—huge highway program—expanded housing, Social

Continued on Page 13, Column 3

TWO ACCEPT TODAY

Eisenhower Says That No Rival to Nixon Came Forward

Transcript of the Eisenhower news conference, Page 15.

By W. H. LAWRENCE
Special to The New York Times.

SAN FRANCISCO, Aug. 22—Roaring Republicans unanimously renominated President Eisenhower and Vice President Richard M. Nixon tonight.

A "dump Nixon" movement collapsed completely with the unconditional surrender of its leader, Harold E. Stassen. Mr. Stassen had tried in vain to get Gov. Christian A. Herter of Massachusetts to oppose Mr. Nixon.

General Eisenhower summoned a special, nationally televised press conference to announce that Mr. Stassen's campaign had ended and that all barriers to Mr. Nixon's renomination had been removed. Mr. Stassen later seconded Mr. Nixon's nomination.

Mr. Nixon's victory was made unanimous and complete when a Nebraska delegate, Terry Carpenter, capitulated. On the first roll-call Mr. Carpenter had passed because the convention chairman, Representative Joseph W. Martin Jr. of Massachusetts, had ignored his joking attempt to place in nomination the name of "Joe Smith." Just before the vote was announced, Mr. Carpenter gave in, and the Nixon total climbed to 1,323 votes.

Convention Is Jubilant

It was a moment of triumph and tragedy for the Vice President. He was at the bedside of his critically ill father, Francis A. Nixon, at La Habra, near Los Angeles, when the convention made him its choice for a second term. The elder Nixon is 77.

The nominating processes gave the confident delegates something to cheer and demonstrate about as they sent the victorious team of 1952 back into battle against a Democratic slate again headed by Adlai E. Stevenson of Illinois. Mr. Stevenson's new running mate, picked in an open floor fight at Chicago last week, is Senator Estes Kefauver.

Both the President and Vice President are scheduled to make their acceptance speeches at the final session of this convention tomorrow afternoon. But there was doubt tonight Mr. Nixon could leave his father's bedside. And there was talk of a special television broadcast by him from Los Angeles to the delegates in this hall.

The convention recessed tonight at 9:05 P. M. (12:05 A. M. Eastern daylight time), until 4 P. M. tomorrow when it will hear the acceptance speech of President Eisenhower at least. An organizational meeting of the new national committee was called for 11:30 A. M. tomorrow by Perry W. Howard, Mississippi

Continued on Page 12, Column 1

3d Ave. to Be Zoned For a Model Street

By CHARLES G. BENNETT

General rezoning of Third Avenue from East Fifteenth to East Ninety-sixth Street was approved yesterday by the City Planning Commission.

Essentially, the thoroughfare is to be more restricted than at present. The rezoning proposal now goes to the Board of Estimate, where prompt approval is expected.

It is proposed to make certain that stores and other commercial establishments moving to Third Avenue will conform to plans for making it one of the city's model thoroughfares.

The new zoning will introduce a "retail" classification to Third Avenue, a designation that has been written into the zoning law since the statute was adopted in 1916.

Retail designations permit residential and commercial uses while providing tighter restric-

Continued on Page 53, Column 2

Drive to Draft Wagner Gaining Among Delegates of State C.I.O.

By STANLEY LEVEY
Special to The New York Times.

ALBANY, Aug. 22—A labor drive to draft Mayor Wagner of New York as the Democratic candidate for United States Senator was developing here today.

Leaders of the State Congress of Industrial Organizations, which will open its sixteenth annual convention tomorrow, reported strong sentiment for the Mayor among the group's 1,000,000 members throughout the state.

Mr. Wagner, who took himself out of contention for the nomination earlier this week, will speak tomorrow afternoon. His appearance is expected to inspire a demonstration among the delegates urging him to change his mind.

Sharing the platform with him will be Senator Herbert H. Lehman. Senator Lehman announced yesterday that he would not seek re-election. At the same time he said he would support Mr. Wagner with "satisfaction, pleasure and full confidence" if the Mayor were the choice of the Democratic State Convention next month.

The feeling among union delegates gathering here was that Mr. Wagner was a "natural" for the nomination. They cited his labor record as Mayor and that of his father, the late Senator Robert F. Wagner, author of the Wagner Labor Relations Act.

The State C. I. O. has indicated that its political activity in the coming campaign will be vigorous. Louis Hollander, president of the organization, said committees would be formed throughout the state to work with groups representing

Continued on Page 13, Column 6

Character by Name of Joe Smith Nearly Opens Up the No. 2 Race

Special to The New York Times.

SAN FRANCISCO, Aug. 22—A "Democrat" bored by the unanimity of the proceedings, infiltrated the Republican National Convention tonight and nominated "Joe Smith" for Vice President.

The one lonely "no-man" in the whole convention was Terry Carpenter, a bona fide delegate from Nebraska, who served as a Democrat in Congress from 1933 to 1935.

His first effort was to put Secretary of Interior Fred A. Seaton of Nebraska in nomination as Vice President, but Joseph W. Martin Jr. of Massachusetts, convention chairman, refused on the ground that this was against Mr. Seaton's wishes.

But that did not stop Mr. Carpenter, a large, bespectacled white-haired man, who insisted on substituting the name of "Joe Smith."

"Joe who?" inquired Mr. Martin. "Joe Smith," firmly replied Mrs. George P. Abel of Lincoln, chairman of the Nebraska delegation.

Reporters and television operators immediately converged on the lone dissenter, from all over the Cow Palace, as Gov. Christian A. Herter of Massachusetts was starting to nominate Richard M. Nixon.

The commotion was too much for Chairman Martin.

Banging his gavel and leaning over the rostrum he said:

"Take your Joe Smith and get out of here."

The reporters, together with Mr. Carpenter, were pushed from the hall by the sergeants-at-arms. Once outside, Mr. Carpenter was pinned against a wall. In that uncomfortable position

Continued on Page 17, Column 2

"All the News That's Fit to Print"

The New York Times.

LATE CITY EDITION
Condensation of U. S. Weather Bureau forecast: Mostly fair today and tomorrow.
Temperature range today: 65—48.
Temperature range yesterday: 62.2—48.1.
Full U. S. Weather Bureau Report, Page 74.

VOL. CVI—No. 36,074. Entered as Second-Class Matter, Post Office, New York, N. Y. NEW YORK, TUESDAY, OCTOBER 30, 1956. Times Square, New York 36, N. Y. Telephone LAckawanna 4-1000 FIVE CENTS

ISRAELIS THRUST INTO EGYPT AND NEAR SUEZ; U.S. GOES TO U.N. UNDER ANTI-AGGRESSION PACT

Budapest Rebels Refuse to Yield Until Soviet Troops Leave

EISENHOWER BIDS SOUTH FIGHT BIAS ON A 'LOCAL BASIS'

In Miami He Stresses Roles of States—Hails Byrd in Speech in Virginia

Texts of Eisenhower speeches are on Pages 24 and 25.

By RUSSELL BAKER
Special to The New York Times.

RICHMOND, Va., Oct. 29—President Eisenhower, campaigning in the South today, urged that the problem of achieving racial equality be handled largely "on a local and state basis."

He told a Miami Airport audience he was convinced that progress today in equality of opportunity and equality before the law had "to be achieved finally in the hearts of men rather than in legislative halls."

The President was applauded lightly when he said that "there must be intelligent understanding of the human factors and emotions involved if we are to make steady progress in the matter rather than simply to make political promises never intended to be kept."

In the field of civil rights, he added, he had tried to bring "reason, good sense and good judgment to the performance of clear duty."

Makes 1,800-Mile Trip

Though he delivered three airport speeches in an 1,800-mile aerial campaign in Florida and Virginia, he touched on the civil rights issue only once.

That was in Miami, in the President's first speech today.

In Jacksonville, Fla., and Richmond, Va., where the southern tradition is stronger than in Miami, he did not discuss the racial theme. Nor did he refer directly in any of his speeches to the controversial school integration issue or the Supreme Court decision.

He concentrated instead on three matters: peace, prosperity and attacks on the Democratic ticket.

And at Miami General Eisenhower tried for the first time the handshaking style of campaigning developed to a high art by Senator Estes Kefauver.

Surrounded by several hundred rabid admirers on his way to his plane after speaking, he shook hands by the score with a zest rarely matched by Senator Kefauver and a folksiness as impressive as the Senator's own.

"Hi ya, folks," he said, and

Continued on Page 24, Column 4

PRESIDENT GIVEN MINNESOTA LEAD

Resurvey Finds Him Moving Ahead in a Close Contest

A Times Team Report

Teams of New York Times reporters have recently surveyed political trends in twenty-seven closely contested states. They are now rechecking the most doubtful states. Following is a resurvey report from Leonard Buder, Donald Janson and W. H. Lawrence.

By DONALD JANSON
Special to The New York Times.

MINNEAPOLIS, Oct. 28—President Eisenhower appears to hold a tenuous lead in the race for Minnesota's eleven electoral votes.

A month ago New York Times reporters found the President and Adlai E. Stevenson running neck and neck in this state. The Eisenhower victory margin of four years ago—155,000 out of 1,379,000 votes cast — had buckled under the impact of defections by farmers who were caught in a cost-price vise.

The farm revolt remains strong today in some areas.

Continued on Page 26, Column 2

Stevenson Says U. S. Gets 'Less Than Truth' on Strife

Charges President Endangered the Nation by 'Good News' From the Mideast—Boston Crowds Hail Candidate

By HARRISON E. SALISBURY
Special to The New York Times.

BOSTON, Oct. 29—Adlai E. Stevenson charged tonight that President Eisenhower had given the nation reassurances about the Middle East that had been "tragically less than the truth."

"The Government has not been telling us the whole truth," Mr. Stevenson said.

Texts of Stevenson statement and speech, Page 28.

The Presidential nominee addressed an overflow Democratic throng of more than 8,000 in Mechanics Hall in the climax of his drive for Massachusetts' sixteen electoral votes.

Mr. Stevenson's address was televised nationally by the American Broadcasting Company. After the telecast was completed, Mr. Stevenson appended one of his sharpest challenges to President Eisenhower's leadership. The Democrat declared:

"I deeply believe that we cannot afford another four years under a part-time leader of a party which will not plan, which will not create, which will not dare to see the vision of a new America and make that vision come true.

"As a campaigning politician there is none better. It is as a performing politician, as a President who knows how to control his own party, who knows how to grasp the reins of Government that he fails."

Several times Mr. Stevenson's partisan audience booed references to the President. The chorus of boos every time he mentioned Vice President Richard M. Nixon started the moment the crowd sensed that Mr.

Continued on Page 29, Column 3

POLAND'S LEADERS BACK HUNGARIANS

Support Demands for Exit of Soviet Troops—Call for End of Strife

By SYDNEY GRUSON
Special to The New York Times.

WARSAW, Oct. 29—The Polish Communist party, differing sharply once again with the Soviet Union, came out formally today in support of Hungarian demands for the withdrawal of Soviet troops from Hungary.

Yesterday the new leadership of the Polish United Workers (Communist) party rejected the Soviet allegation that foreign agents and counter-revolutionaries were responsible for the Hungarian tragedy. Today the Poles stood up again on the side of the Hungarians.

An appeal to those on both sides of the barricades in Hungary to halt fratricidal strife was issued by Wladyslaw Gomulka, the Polish party's First Secretary, and by Premier Jozef Cyrankiewicz.

Emphasizing the growing insistence here for independence in foreign as well as internal affairs, the party statement ignored the Soviet charges of Western interference in Hungary.

For the Poles the statement of solidarity was a means of publicly expressing their appreciation for Hungarian help when Poland was threatened by the Soviet leaders a week ago. Poland escaped Hungary's fate

Continued on Page 22, Column 1

Russians Befriend One Hungarian City

By HOMER BIGART
Special to The New York Times.

GYOR, Hungary, Oct. 29—The small Soviet garrison of this industrial city has retired to a near-by wood, giving the townspeople free rein to rally and shout against the Nagy Government and demand democratic national elections.

The Russians here must be credited with sensible behavior. They abandoned their barracks a few days ago under no pressure and took to the wood.

There the Soviet officers are living with their wives and children in tents. They have not shot anyone. The townspeople show their gratitude by taking the Russians eggs and milk.

And although Gyor has

Continued on Page 13, Column 1

FIGHTING PERSISTS

Russians Still Pulling Out, With Hungarian Units Taking Over

Text of editorial in Communist newspaper on Page 10.

By ELIE ABEL
Special to The New York Times.

VIENNA, Tuesday, Oct. 30—Soviet troops remained in control of Budapest this morning while the Government of Imre Nagy pleaded with the stubborn revolutionaries to lay down their arms.

But the rebels refused to give up the fight until Mr. Nagy had made good on his promise that the Soviet forces would evacuate the battered city, monitored reports from the Hungarian capital said.

This morning the Budapest radio broadcast the following communiqué:

"While Soviet forces are being withdrawn from Budapest, Hungarian police and armed youth units are maintaining order. Such armed groups as are still resisting will lay down their arms at 9 A. M. [3 A. M. New York time] and will then take part in maintaining order."

[Up to 5 A. M. New York time there had been no further reports on the situation in Hungary.]

Appeal Is Pressed

Earlier this morning the Budapest radio broadcast an appeal by Karoly Janda, Defense Minister, to the rebels to lay down their arms before 9 A. M.

In spite of the gradual Soviet withdrawal, fighting in Budapest flared up again last night. Soviet tank forces engaged in heavy combat in several parts of the city. Latest reports said artillery fire was heard in Budapest all night.

Rebels from eastern Hungary and from the region of Gyor in the west were understood to have joined the insurgents in the capital.

The rebel-held Miskolc radio in northeast Hungary, in a broadcast monitored here, urged anti-Communists in Budapest not to lay down their arms before the last Soviet soldier had left the country.

A general strike called by the rebel leaders appeared to be continuing in many parts of Hungary for the fifth day. Most factory workers, railroad men and miners stayed away from their jobs again this morning despite pressing appeals from Mr. Nagy's Government to resume work.

Nearly complete was an unofficial school strike. Instead of attending classes many teenagers in Budapest did courier work for the rebels and even

Continued on Page 10, Column 4

Patrols in Budapest Are Trigger-Happy From Propaganda

By JOHN MacCORMAC
Special to The New York Times.

BUDAPEST, Hungary, Oct. 29—The seventh day of the Hungarian revolution has dawned with Soviet soldiers still patrolling the Budapest streets despite a promise by Hungary's new Government that they would be withdrawn. The Government had qualified its announcement yesterday with the condition "as soon as order has been completely restored."

As far as could be learned, armed resistance in Budapest has ceased, even in the Maria Theresa barracks in Ulloi Ut, which was holding out late yesterday. But that order can ever be completely restored in Budapest as long as the Russians are here seems unlikely because of the fears and propaganda with which the Soviet troops seem to be filled.

At 10 o'clock last night, for instance, a Soviet soldier guarding an area known as Szent Istvan Ut shot and seriously wounded Noel Barber, London Daily Mail correspondent. Mr. Barber had been making a tour of inspection to get the public's reaction to Premier Imre Nagy's announcement that there would be no further firing and that the insurrection had been recognized by his Government as

Continued on Page 15, Column 1

1950 PLEDGE CITED

White House Recalls Promise to Assist Victim of Attack

By DANA ADAMS SCHMIDT
Special to The New York Times.

WASHINGTON, Oct. 29—The United States will take the movement of Israeli forces into Egypt to the United Nations Security Council tomorrow morning.

The planned appeal to the United Nations was announced by the White House tonight after President Eisenhower had held an emergency meeting there with Secretary of State Dulles and six other high officials.

[An emergency meeting of the Security Council was set for 11 A. M. Tuesday.]

The White House statement follows:

"At the meeting, the President recalled that the United States under this and prior Administrations has pledged itself to assist the victim of any aggression in the Middle East. We shall honor our pledge.

"The United States is in consultation with the British and French Governments, parties with us to the tripartite declaration of 1950, and the United States plans as contemplated by that declaration that the situation shall be taken to the United Nations Security Council tomorrow morning.

Special Session in Abeyance

"The question of whether and when the President will call a special session of the Congress will be decided in the light of the unfolding situation."

The statement was read by James C. Hagerty, Presidential press secretary. He said it had the full authority of the President and the other conferees.

Others at the meeting, in addition to Mr. Dulles, were Charles E. Wilson, Secretary of Defense; Admiral Arthur W. Radford, Chairman of the Joint Chiefs of Staff; Sherman Adams, Assistant to the President; Herbert Hoover Jr., Under Secretary of State; Allen W. Dulles, director of the Central Intelligence Agency, and Wilton B. Persons, deputy assistant to the President.

The one-and-a-half-hour meeting at the White House took place immediately after the President's return by air from a campaign trip in Florida and Virginia.

The State Department said Americans "not performing essential services" would be asked to leave the Middle East. Among the first to leave was a group that flew from Israel to Athens.

Earlier, Secretary of State Dulles had initiated the joint steps with Britain and France.

The State Department an-

Continued on Page 3, Column 1

The New York Times Oct. 30, 1956

ISRAELIS OPEN DRIVE: The advance into Egypt was reported made at and below Kuntilla, with a thrust near the Suez Canal. There was a flare-up in Gaza area (cross).

Cairo Says Egyptian Units Have Engaged the Israelis

By The United Press.

CAIRO, Tuesday, Oct. 30—The Egyptian Army said today it had begun "liquidating" an Israeli force that had thrust deep into Egyptian territory toward the Suez Canal. Egyptian army headquarters announced that the Israeli force had suffered "heavy casualties" in the night-long fighting. It gave no precise figures.

"The enemy's plan to penetrate deep inside Egyptian territory failed," the Egyptian communiqué said. "Egyptian armed forces early this morning started liquidating the enemy forces."

[Iraq informed Egypt early Tuesday that Iraqi troops were ready to offer immediate assistance against the Israeli thrust, The Associated Press said. The offer was announced after an urgent morning meeting of Premier Nuri as-Said's Cabinet in Baghdad.]

Leaves Are Canceled

The high command of the Egyptian armed forces recalled all officers and enlisted men on leave to meet the Israeli threat. Orders broadcast by the Cairo radio said all must "report immediately to their units." Reservists were not affected.

The Egyptian communiqué identified the three frontier checkpoints where it said the Israeli raiders had been halted at Kuntilla, Nekhet and El Mimet. All are on the eastern side of the rocky Sinai Peninsula. [No additional details on the fighting were received up to 5 A. M.]

Suez Canal authorities in Cairo said the situation along the waterway was normal. They said no blackout has been imposed and no emergency alert sounded.

Continued on Page 6, Column 2

FRANCE ACCUSES FIVE OF TREASON

Files Formal Charges Against Algerians Seized in Plane —Sends Aide to Tunisia

By ROBERT C. DOTY
Special to The New York Times.

PARIS, Oct. 29—Five leaders of the Algerian rebellion, seized a week ago, were formally charged today with treason against France. The offense is punishable by death.

The five are Mohammed ben Bella, Mohammed Khider, Mustafa Lachraf, Mohammed Boudiaf and Hossein Ait Ahmed, all members of the Algerian National Liberation Front, which has directed the two-year rebellion against France from headquarters in Cairo.

Their arrest Oct. 22, while aboard a Moroccan plane flying to a conference of North African leaders in Tunis, set off a wave of anti-French protest and violence. Arab anger was based on the theory that the five men were under the protection of Sultan Mohammed V of Morocco, with tacit French consent, at the time of their arrest.

[In the United Nations Security Council, France formally charged Egypt with gunrunning for the Algerian rebels.]

As Algerians, the five seized rebel leaders are French citizens, hence subject to a treason

Continued on Page 10, Column 2

Maria Callas Bows At Opening of 'Met'

By ROSS PARMENTER

Bellini's "Norma" has never been notably popular in this country. But last night, when it opened the Metropolitan Opera's seventy-second season, it established a compound record. Never have so many Americans tried to pay so much money to hear an opera.

The actual sum paid by those who managed to crowd into the opera house was $75,510.50. This exceeded by more than $10,000 the previous box-office record of $65,336, which was set with the opening night "Faust" in 1953. The larger sum, though, was not paid by a larger number of persons. After all, sell-outs have been customary on first nights, and fire regulations re-

Continued on Page 43, Column 4

DEEP DRIVE MADE

Tel Aviv Declares Aim Is to Smash Egyptian Commando Bases

Text of Israeli statement will be found on Page 4.

By MOSHE BRILLIANT
Special to The New York Times.

TEL AVIV, Israel, Oct. 29—An Israeli military force thrust into the Sinai Peninsula of Egypt today. It was reported to have reached within twenty miles of the Suez Canal.

Army sources said the Israelis were west of the crossroads where the road to Kuntilla branches off from the Suez-Quseima highway.

The Israelis were said to have halted there and to have dug in.

A Foreign Ministry statement said the operation had been started "to eliminate the Egyptian fedayeen [commando squad] bases in the Sinai Peninsula."

Army sources said the Israelis had smashed the Egyptian position at Kuntilla and Ras el Naqb at the southern end of the international border. The forces then advanced more than seventy-five miles.

No fighting was reported on the northern end of the border or in the Gaza Strip, which is heavily populated.

'Too Big for a Reprisal'

Reports from the Sinai area described the fighting as "too big for a reprisal and too small for a war." Details of the fighting were not available tonight, but reliable sources said there had been no aerial bombardment of Egyptian positions.

It was not clear tonight whether the Israelis proposed to push on to the Suez Canal or withdraw to Israeli territory, as they have done after reprisal raids. A high official said: "I do not know. It depends on developments."

Yesterday the Israeli Government attributed its decision to call up reserves to what it said was a renewal of commando activities, to the Egyptian-Jordanian-Syrian military alliance negotiated last Wednesday, to Arab declarations that "their principal concern is a war of destruction against Israel" and to the movement of Iraqi forces to Jordan's border.

According to information here, the Egyptians have a considerable part of their Army in the Sinai Peninsula. Their land forces are reported equipped with the

Continued on Page 5, Column 5

CITY SCHOOL AIDES SPUR INTEGRATION

District Lines Are Shifted in Some Brooklyn Areas

By BENJAMIN FINE

Without any public announcement, the Board of Education has quietly begun a program to integrate white and Negro pupils in areas where a segregation pattern has existed in the past.

A score of schools in the Bedford-Stuyvesant area of Brooklyn have become interracial since the fall term opened. Children are taken from the all-Negro schools and put into the formerly all-white schools.

At the same time, fairly large groups of children—ranging from fifty to 200—have been taken from a number of all-white schools and placed in the all-Negro schools. In doing this, the board has amended or discarded the old district and school zoning regulations.

This step is part of a "positive program" on integration, Charles H. Silver, Board of Education president, said yesterday. The board has asked its forty assistant superintendents to do everything possible to place Negro and white children in the same schools.

The superintendents are doing

Continued on Page 30, Column 3

Associated Press Radiophoto

AMERICANS LEAVE ISRAEL: Wives and children of State Department personnel boarding Air Force transport plane last night at Lydda Airport near Jerusalem. They were flown to Athens. More dependents are to follow today.

Three Penny Opera, *a revival of a German play of the Twenties was an off-Broadway hit in the Fifties. For some time, it starred Lotte Lenya.*

My Fair Lady *opened in 1956 and was an instant success. The only way to get a ticket was to join the long line at the box office. Rex Harrison and Julie Andrews made this adaptation of Shaw's* Pygmalion *into one of the best musicals of the decade.*

"All the News That's Fit to Print"

The New York Times.

LATE CITY EDITION
Condensation of U. S. Weather Bureau forecast: Partly cloudy, little temperature change today and tomorrow.
Temperature range today: 66—51.
Temperature range yesterday: 66.3—53.
Full U.S. Weather Bureau Report, Page 48.

VOL. CVI—No. 36,078. Entered as Second-Class Matter, Post Office, New York, N. Y. NEW YORK, SATURDAY, NOVEMBER 3, 1956. Times Square, New York 36, N. Y. Telephone Lackawanna 4-1000 FIVE CENTS

BRITISH AND FRENCH PUSH TOWARD LANDING; ISRAELIS CAPTURE GAZA AND CONTROL SINAI

Hungary Protests to Soviet Against New Troop Moves; West Urges Action by U.N.; Tension Is Rising in Poland

STEVENSON OFFERS A PROGRAM TO END STRIFE IN MIDEAST

Calls for a Cease-Fire and Israel's Security—Detroit Crowd Boos President

Speech at Detroit and remarks at Cleveland, Page 20.

By HARRISON E. SALISBURY
Special to The New York Times.

DETROIT, Nov. 2—Adlai E. Stevenson offered tonight a program to restore peace in the Middle East, based on the security of Israel and restoration of the Western Alliance.

Mr. Stevenson submitted his program to an enthusiastic overflow audience at the Fox Theatre.

He charged that President Eisenhower did not know what had been happening in the Middle East and that "someone had misled him."

Mr. Stevenson's program called for these steps:

¶A cease-fire in the Middle East.

¶Restoration of the Western grand alliance of the United States, France and Britain.

¶Security for Israel against Arab attack.

¶Establishment of the principle of international concern for the Suez Canal and an end of one-man or one-country control.

¶An all-out attack on resettlement of 900,000 Arab refugees in Middle Eastern lands.

¶A joint program for improvement of economic conditions in the Middle East.

Mr. Stevenson's address was carried on a state TV network. Several thousand persons were unable to gain admission to the theatre.

Earlier today, Mr. Stevenson spoke in Cleveland's Public Square. A huge throng heard him demand United Nations action in behalf of the new Hungarian regime.

Democratic officials put the crowd at 65,000. Newspaper reporters estimated it at closer to 30,000. There was agreement, however, that it was larger than General Eisenhower drew in the same place and time three weeks ago.

Tonight Mr. Stevenson asserted that the first task in the

Continued on Page 20, Column 3

HUNGARIAN PREMIER Imre Nagy, Communist who took office during national anti-Soviet uprising, addressing nation by radio. Date when photograph was taken was not given.
Associated Press Radiophoto

NEW PLEA BY NAGY

Premier Asks That U.N. Defend Neutrality of Hungary

By JOHN MacCORMAC
Special to The New York Times.

BUDAPEST, Hungary, Saturday, Nov. 3—The Hungarian Government made three oral protests yesterday to the Soviet Ambassador in Budapest, complaining that Russian reinforcements were still pouring across the frontier.

[Soviet tanks sealed the main crossings of the Austrian-Hungarian border Friday. This was regarded as a preliminary to dealing sternly with the insurgents.]

Premier Imre Nagy also sent a new appeal to the Secretary General of the United Nations to guarantee Hungary's neutrality and to bring her case before the General Assembly.

Similarly Joseph Cardinal Mindszenty, primate of Hungary, appealed to the West for political support of the revolutionaries and relief for the needy.

Soviet Forces Approaching

Early today, forces at the command of the Revolutionary Council of the Hungarian Army occupied the Foreign Ministry. Other Army units cordoned off the Parliament Building and took up posts on and near all bridges spanning the Danube.

These measures were prompted by information that Soviet forces were approaching the capital.

In his plea to the Secretary General of the United Nations, Premier Nagy said that Hungary's first demand for the withdrawal of Soviet troops had been received favorably by Moscow. In spite of this, he went on, fresh Soviet troops were brought in to Hungary on Tuesday and Wednesday.

The Hungarian Government then denounced the Warsaw Pact, proclaimed Hungary a neutral state and demanded the withdrawal of all Soviet troops. Budapest also proposed the appointment of two joint Hungarian-Soviet committees, one political and one military, to discuss the terms and set the timetable for this withdrawal.

The Premier said that he had protested against any further influx of Soviet soldiers, pointing out to the United Nations that new Soviet units had entered

Continued on Page 15, Column 1

Israelis Are Mopping Up; Egypt Braces for Landing

12,000 Prisoners Taken

By HOMER BIGART
Special to The New York Times.

TEL AVIV, Israel, Saturday, Nov. 3—Israel's lightning conquest of Egypt's Sinai Peninsula and the Gaza Strip is complete except for minor mopping-up operations. The ancient Philistine capital of Gaza was the last town to fall.

In its drive, Maj. Gen. Moshe Dayan's tough Army had killed, captured or put to flight 30,000 Egyptian troops east of the Suez Canal.

With Israel's southern flank secure after only four days of operations, the Government faced with calm confidence reports that Jordan was being reinforced by Syrian troops and that the Syrian-Jordanian-Egyptian defense pact was about to become operative.

Gaza collapsed after a three-hour fight yesterday morning. A United Nations truce aide,

Continued on Page 3, Column 5

Cairo Defense Held Ready

By The United Press.

CAIRO, Nov. 2—Waves of British and French bombers and fighters blasted Cairo and outlying villages today. An Egyptian communiqué said 100 persons had been killed in one town alone.

Simultaneously, President Gamal Abdel Nasser announced that Egyptian forces in the Sinai desert had "completed their withdrawal safely."

"Now we are waiting for the British and French in the delta," he said. Only "suicide commandos" had been left in Sinai to harass the advancing Israeli forces, he added.

The communiqué asserted that fourteen British and French planes had been shot down in today's raids. An earlier communiqué had claimed three kills in the last twenty-four hours in addition to six reported downed yesterday morning. This would

Continued on Page 3, Column 2

BOMBING PRESSED

Planes Center Attacks on Army After Cairo Loses Airpower

By DREW MIDDLETON
Special to The New York Times.

LONDON, Nov. 2—The neutralization of the Egyptian Air Force, a primary condition to successful landing operations, was claimed tonight by British and French airpower.

More than a hundred Egyptian planes have been destroyed or damaged at airfields by bombers and fighters of Royal Air Force and French Air Force. A high proportion of these were Soviet-built MIG-15 jet fighter planes and Ilyushin-28 twin-jet bombers, R. A. F. sources said.

At the outset of the operations the Egyptian Air Force had ninety MIG's and fifty Ilyushins. Since not all of these were airworthy Wednesday when the attack began, the allies' claim to have neutralized Egypt's air-power appears valid.

Transit Camp Bombed

The British-French air attack is shifting away from air bases onto the Egyptian Army's central forces, now known to be moving slowly northward and northeastward away from the Cairo area.

British air reconnaissance reported the movement of tanks and infantry into the area around Port Said, one of the three sites chosen by the allies for occupation.

One target successfully attacked was a military transit camp, around which tanks and guns were concentrated, about fifteen miles northeast of Cairo in the El Khanka area.

[The British reported that the Egyptians had sunk seven ships in an effort to block the Suez Canal. It was not known in London whether the Egyptian effort had succeeded. No word of an allied landing in Egypt had been received up to 4 A. M., New York time.]

Information that the Syrian Government was placing its armed forces under the commander in chief of the Egyptian forces has not altered British or French planning for forthcoming operations.

As part of the psychological preparation for the allied landing operations the Cairo Radio, the Voice of Arabia, was silenced

Continued on Page 2, Column 3

Eisenhower Sees Victory, Leaves Campaign to Nixon

By RUSSELL BAKER
Special to The New York Times.

WASHINGTON, Nov. 2—President Eisenhower now is so confident of re-election Tuesday that he is treating Adlai E. Stevenson's driving campaign finish with a show of indifference. This was emphasized last night in Philadelphia when he indicated that, from his point of view, the campaign was over and that henceforth he would address the nation only in the nonpartisan role of President.

It was pointedly driven home today when the White House noted that Vice President Richard M. Nixon, rather than the President, had been selected to reply tonight to the Democratic nominee's attack on foreign policy.

James C. Hagerty, White House press secretary, said the President's discussion of the Middle Eastern and Central European crises Wednesday had been "nonpolitical." Mr. Stevenson's reply last night, he added, "was strictly political."

Mr. Hagerty's implication was that the President no longer intended to trouble with replies to Mr. Stevenson's "political" charges and that this chore now could be handled adequately by Mr. Nixon.

The President, he added, knew in advance the substance of the Vice President's speech. The White House staff had helped Mr. Nixon get "the facts to refute a lot of misstatements that Mr. Stevenson made last night," Mr. Hagerty said.

The White House also an-

Continued on Page 19, Column 6

PRESIDENT LEADS IN PENNSYLVANIA

Slim Edge Not Widened Yet by Crises Abroad—Clark's Margin for Senate Cut

A Times Team Report

Teams of New York Times reporters have now completed a survey of political trends in twenty-seven closely contested states. They have rechecked eight of those states—the most doubtful ones. Following is a final resurvey report by Leonard Buder, Donald Janson and Wayne Phillips.

By WAYNE PHILLIPS
Special to The New York Times.

PHILADELPHIA, Nov. 2—President Eisenhower is clinging to a lead in this state so insubstantial that it could be washed away by a heavy rain on election day.

Depending upon developments in the Middle East crisis, he may be able to increase that lead in the four days remaining before the election. But at the moment the world crisis has served only to create doubts in the minds of voters on both sides of the fence. Those doubts have not yet crystallized in favor of either candidate.

Two weeks ago a New York Times team found the Pennsylvania Democrats well organized and confident. They were fighting an uphill battle against the popularity of the President's personality, but the odds were on their side in a state that once was a bastion of Republicanism.

They appeared to have won the public—and some Republican newspapers, too—to their Senatorial candidate, Joseph S. Clark Jr. They had created a substantial indecision among the 1952 supporters of President Eisenhower, and had won over enough of them to give some hope of carrying the state for Adlai E. Stevenson.

For Mr. Stevenson this state is the keystone in any arch of triumph he may hope to build. Its thirty-two electoral votes, with various combinations of states, could carry him to a

Continued on Page 18, Column 3

TROOPS REPORTED CROSSING POLAND

Soviet Movement Is Said to Be to East Germany—Panic Buying in Warsaw

By SYDNEY GRUSON
Special to The New York Times.

WARSAW, Nov. 2—Reports reached Warsaw tonight of large-scale Soviet troop movements across Poland from Russia to East Germany. No details were available.

The purpose and the meaning of the troop movements were not disclosed. But even before they had been reported the situation in Poland had reached a point of extreme tension.

All through the day the Polish radio repeated its broadcast of an appeal by the Communist party's new leadership for "calm, discipline and a sense of responsibility" within the nation.

In Warsaw panic buying began. People bought up all the foodstuffs in the stores and then after withdrawing their money from the banks began to buy jewelry and valuables.

Word came from various parts

Continued on Page 14, Column 4

Nixon Hails Break With Allies' Policies

By WILLIAM M. BLAIR
Special to The New York Times.

HERSHEY, Pa., Nov. 2—Vice President Richard M. Nixon hailed tonight this country's break with Anglo-French policies as a "declaration of independence that has had an electrifying effect throughout the world."

Speaking with the full backing of President Eisenhower, he assailed Adlai E. Stevenson for charging that the Administration's foreign policy was a failure and that the President should have averted the Middle East crisis.

He said that the United Nations General Assembly vote gave "the lie to [Mr. Stevenson's] preposterous charge" that the United States stood alone "in an unfriendly world."

The General Assembly early

Continued on Page 19, Column 1

U.N. SPEAKERS ASK HELP FOR HUNGARY

Override Soviet Objections as Security Council Argues International Action

Excerpts from Security Council debate are on Page 16.

By LINDESAY PARROTT
Special to The New York Times.

UNITED NATIONS, N. Y., Nov. 2—The Western powers overrode Soviet objections today and called on the United Nations to take measures against Soviet military action in Hungary.

An emergency meeting of the Security Council heard all nations that spoke, except the Soviet Union, appeal for international action against the reinforcement of Soviet troops in Hungary, where rebel nationalists appear to have taken control. Imre Nagy, Hungarian Premier, asked the United Nations yesterday to guarantee the country's neutralism.

No decision was reached at the two-hour session of the Council tonight. The members will meet again tomorrow afternoon in an attempt to decide on a course of action.

The meeting was sparked by a new message from Mr. Nagy distributed to Council members tonight.

The letter, couched in terms similar to the one Mr. Nagy sent to the United Nations yesterday, charged that "large" Soviet military units had crossed the Hungarian border. Moving toward

Continued on Page 16, Column 5

PARIS ACTS TO BAR CEASE-FIRE NOW

Fears That Immediate Halt In Military Operations Would Save Nasser

By HAROLD CALLENDER
Special to The New York Times.

PARIS, Nov. 2—The French Government moved fast today to prevent a United Nations cease-fire in the Suez Canal Zone.

It feared a halt in military operation now would save Gamal Abdel Nasser, President of Egypt, whose regime the French and British seek to liquidate. In that case the French would feel deprived of a victory they regard as already within their grasp.

This was the explanation of the hurried trip to London during the day by Christian Pineau, French Foreign Minister, that was given by high political authorities here tonight.

In London, M. Pineau, Prime Minister Eden and Selwyn Lloyd, British Foreign Secretary, were reported to have agreed they would not accept a cease-fire at least until British-French troops had landed. They were expected to land tomorrow.

Action by U. N. Noted

The United Nations General Assembly voted early today for a cease-fire in the Middle East but the question was how it could be carried out.

[Prime Minister Eden rejected a Laborite demand that he order an immediate end to British attacks on Egypt. This was in response to Laborite pressure that he comply with the resolution of the United Nations General Assembly calling for a cease-fire.]

The fear that took possession of French officials was that Prime Minister Eden might agree to a premature cease-fire. If so, he would do it, according to these officials, because he is harried by the British Labor party to call off the French-British military expedition to Egypt, and because he is pressed by Secretary of State Dulles, who is credited here with desiring a cease-fire before the United States election Tuesday.

It was even suggested that the United States Sixth Fleet, now in the Mediterranean, might be assigned by the General Assembly to occupy the Suez Canal zone, instead of the French-British forces now preparing to occupy it.

This fear arose because Lester B. Pearson, Canadian Secretary of State for External Affairs, proposed yesterday in New York that the General Assembly should authorize the immediate

Continued on Page 6, Column 4

U. S. Protests Refusal by Soviet To Let Americans Quit Hungary

Special to The New York Times.

WASHINGTON, Nov. 2—The United States protested tonight to the Soviet Union against the action of Soviet troops who prevented a convoy of Americans from leaving Hungary.

A report of the incident from the United States Legation in Budapest reached the State Department in early evening. Deputy Under Secretary of State Robert Murphy called in Georgi N. Zaroubin, the Soviet Ambassador, at once.

Mr. Zaroubin told Mr. Murphy he would get in touch with his Government in Moscow about the matter.

A State Department spokesman said Mr. Murphy spoke "energetically" to the Soviet Ambassador against the "interference with American official personnel."

According to the official report, the convoy consisted of dependents—wives and children—of diplomatic personnel at the American Legation. Lincoln White, State Department press officer, said the convoy returned safely to Budapest and would attempt to leave the city again tomorrow.

"We had a report from Budapest that a convoy of our legation dependents was turned back near the Austrian border this afternoon by Soviet tank blocks," said Mr. White. "They returned to Budapest safely."

According to Mr. White, Mr. Murphy told the Soviet envoy he "assumed the incident must be due to an error on the part of the Soviet military commander, although he could not imagine why Soviet forces were in that area."

"The Ambassador said he had no information on this, Mr. White told reporters, but added "he would immediately communicate with his Government and that he assumed the matter would be straightened out."

Special to The New York Times.

BUDAPEST, Hungary, Nov. 2—A diplomatic convoy carrying out the wives and children of a United State legation staff in Budapest as well as French, British and American correspondents was turned back from the Austrian border by Soviet troops at 4:30 P. M. today.

"Polemics are useless," a Soviet officer told them. "It is requested that you turn around

Continued on Page 16, Column 3

Eisenhower Offers Relief to Hungary

Special to The New York Times.

WASHINGTON, Nov. 2—President Eisenhower late today offered $20,000,000 worth of food and medical supplies to relieve the suffering in Hungary resulting from the revolt against Soviet domination.

The White House announcement of this offer followed a conference between the President, Secretary of State Dulles, and Under Secretary of State Herbert Hoover Jr.

The aid would consist of $15,000,000 in surplus foodstuffs and $5,000,000 in specially purchased meats, oils, fats, and medical supplies.

The President urged the American people to continue their contributions to the American Red Cross, which is pouring relief supplies into

Continued on Page 16, Column 7

COUNCIL HEARING ON QUINN SLATED

Mayor Backs Tenney Report on Official's Carting Job

By CHARLES G. BENNETT

The City Council will hold hearings soon to consider charges against Councilman Hugh Quinn, Queens Democrat.

In a report to Mayor Wagner on Thursday, Investigation Commissioner Charles H. Tenney found that Mr. Quinn had committed an "apparent" violation of the City Charter and had given grounds for his removal from office.

Yesterday Mayor Wagner said he agreed with the Investigation Commissioner's conclusions.

Council Majority Leader Joseph T. Sharkey, Brooklyn Democrat, said he would call the Councilmen together next week, probably Wednesday, to arrange for hearings in the Quinn case. A question for the Councilmen to determine, Mr. Sharkey said, is whether the hearings will be public or private.

The Council, under the Charter, is the judge of the qualifications of its members. It may expel a member by a two-thirds vote.

Mr. Sharkey said he thought

Continued on Page 45, Column 3

ARABS SAID TO PUT TROOPS IN JORDAN

Syrian and Iraqi Forces Are Reported on March

By DANA ADAMS SCHMIDT
Special to The New York Times.

WASHINGTON, Nov. 2—Syrian and Iraqi troops are marching into Jordan, according to information telephoned from Cairo, the Egyptian Embassy press counselor announced tonight.

The official, Mohammed Habib, reported also that Lebanese workers had cut one of the pipelines that carry Arabian oil to the Mediterranean.

The report of the troop movements followed announcement by Syria, in a formal note to the State Department, that she had placed her armed forces under Egyptian command. This was done under terms of the Syrian-Egyptian defense pact, the Syrian Chargé d'Affaires, Mamoun Jamui, informed the State Department.

"The Syrian armed forces are now taking orders from the Egyptian Commander in Chief, Gen. Abdel Hakim Amer," Mr. Jamui said, continuing, "Syria

Continued on Page 2, Column 3

General Moshe Dayan with his Israeli troops who took complete control of the Gaza Strip in 1956.

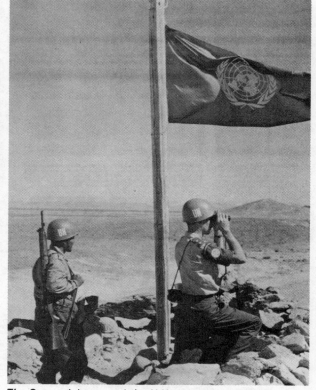

The Suez crisis caused the U.N. to send an Emergency Force to the Suez Canal area to maintain the truce.

Rebels wave the Hungarian flag over a Soviet tank, which was captured in the streets of Budapest, during an unsuccessful revolt.

The New York Times.

LATE CITY EDITION
Condensation of U. S. Weather Bureau forecast:
Considerable cloudiness, seasonably cool today and tomorrow.
Temperature range today: 58—49.
Temperature range yesterday: 53.6—48.2.
Full U. S. Weather Bureau Report, Page 85.

NEWS SUMMARY AND INDEX, PAGE 95

VOL. CVI.. No. 36,079.   Entered as Second-Class Matter, Post Office, New York, N. Y.   © 1956, by The New York Times Company.   NEW YORK, SUNDAY, NOVEMBER 4, 1956.   Including Magazine and Book Review.   SECTION ONE   TWENTY-FIVE CENTS

SOVIET ATTACKS HUNGARY, SEIZES NAGY; U. S. LEGATION IN BUDAPEST UNDER FIRE; MINDSZENTY IN REFUGE WITH AMERICANS

U. N. Assembly Backs Call to Set Up Mideast Truce Force

STEVENSON HOLDS PRESIDENT LACKS 'ENERGY' FOR JOB

In Last Big Address, He Asks if Nation Is Prepared to Accept Nixon as Leader

Stevenson statement, Page 72; text of speech, Page 73.

By HARRISON E. SALISBURY
Special to The New York Times.
CHICAGO, Nov. 3—Adlai E. Stevenson charged tonight that President Eisenhower "now lacks the energy" to cope with world problems such as the present crisis in the Middle East.

He asked the nation whether it was prepared to accept Richard M. Nixon "as Commander in Chief to exercise power over peace and war."

"Every consideration," Mr. Stevenson said, "the President's age, his health and the fact that he cannot succeed himself make it inevitable that the dominant figure in the second Eisenhower term would be Richard Nixon."

This was the first time that Mr. Stevenson in direct fashion had raised the question of General Eisenhower's health, his physical strength and his ability to survive his full term if re-elected.

It placed—on the eve of the election—the question of General Eisenhower's age and his health directly in the forefront of the campaign.

Nixon Draws Boos

Mr. Stevenson's every reference to Mr. Nixon brought forth a hurricane of boos that was equaled only by several waves of boos for General Eisenhower's foreign policy and references to the asserted errors of John Foster Dulles, Secretary of State.

Mr. Stevenson's remarks, which were carried to the nation by television, were cut off the air on a chorus of boos for Mr. Nixon. The conclusion of his address ran over the allotted air time.

General Eisenhower is 66 years old. Mr. Stevenson had foresworn any discussion of the President's health, insisting that this was a matter for each individual voter.

However, in charging tonight that the crisis in world affairs had stemmed directly from the President's "part-time conduct" of his office, Mr. Stevenson took a look into the future.

The fact is, he asserted, General Eisenhower "in the next years would inevitably recede more and more from the picture."

The President, Mr. Stevenson.

Continued on Page 73, Column 2

Major Sports News

FOOTBALL

Yale, Navy, Syracuse, Columbia and Army won major Eastern contests yesterday. Scores of leading games:

Amherst ....6 Tufts 0
Army ....55 Colgate 46
Columbia ...25 Cornell 19
Georgia Tech 7 Duke 0
Illinois ....7 Purdue 7
Michigan ...17 Iowa 14
Michigan St..33 Wisconsin ...0
Minnesota ...9 Pitt 6
Navy ....33 Notre Dame. 7
Ohio State.. 6 Northwest'n.2
Oklahoma ...27 Colorado ...19
Penn ....28 Harvard 7
Princeton ...21 Brown 7
Rutgers ....20 Lafayette ...19
Syracuse ...13 Penn State..9
Tennessee ..20 N. Carolina. 0
T. C. U. ....7 Baylor 6
U. C. L. A...14 Stanford ...13
W. Virginia .14 Wash'gton .0
Yale ....19 Dartmouth ..0

HORSE RACING

Summer Tan took the Gallant Fox Handicap in a track record time at Jamaica.

Details in Section 5.

London, Paris Bar Truce; Eden Pledges Israeli Exit

U. N. Occupation Offered

By HAROLD CALLENDER
Special to The New York Times.
PARIS, Nov. 3—Britain and France rejected today the United Nations call for a cease-fire in the Suez area.

At the same time they made a counter-proposal designed to bring their independent military action under the authority of the United Nations. They thus sought to heal the breach between the two powers on the one hand and the United Nations and the United States on the other.

The United Nations General Assembly recommended the cease-fire Thursday by adopting a resolution introduced by the United States.

The two European powers de-

Continued on Page 18, Column 1

Prime Minister Speaks

By DREW MIDDLETON
Special to The New York Times.
LONDON, Nov. 3—The British Government will insure the withdrawal of Israeli forces from Egyptian territory once British and French troops have occupied

key points on the Suez Canal. Sir Anthony Eden declared tonight.

The objective of his policy of intervention in the Middle East is a lasting settlement in the area, and a stronger United Nations, able "to act as well as to talk," the Prime Minister told

Eden's text and Gaitskell excerpts are on Page 28.

Continued on Page 28, Column 6

EISENHOWER PLANS TALKS TOMORROW

To Make 2 Short Speeches on TV—Mitchell Reports Advances by Labor

By CHARLES E. EGAN
Special to The New York Times.
WASHINGTON, Nov. 3—Politics held an active, if subordinate, role in White House operations on this Saturday before election.

While the President was closeted with advisers in discussions of events in the Middle East and Europe, his top aides found time:

¶To consult with Leonard W. Hall, chairman of the Republican National Committee, on campaign strategy.

¶To issue a special report by James P. Mitchell, Secretary of Labor, detailing gains given to workers by his department under the present Administration.

¶To give a preliminary outline of the President's two Election Eve television appearances on Monday.

Mr. Hall arrived at the White House at 11:30 this morning. He spent more than an hour there first with Sherman Adams, the Assistant to the President, and later with James C. Hagerty, White House press secretary.

Continued on Page 78, Column 4

DULLES IS GAINING AFTER OPERATION

Part of His Large Intestine Is Removed—He Will Stay in Hospital 2 Weeks

By EDWIN L. DALE Jr.
Special to The New York Times.
WASHINGTON, Nov. 3—John Foster Dulles, Secretary of State, underwent successful surgery today for removal of a perforated portion of his large intestine.

It was announced after the two-and-one-half-hour operation that Mr. Dulles had "left the operating table in good condition" and that he was "resting comfortably."

The announcement was made by a State Department spokesman, Lincoln White, at Walter Reed Army Hospital. It said Mr. Dulles, 68 years old, probably would be in the hospital for two to three weeks and that he "should be able to return to his desk in approximately six weeks." Mr. Dulles' pulse was reported to be 76, his blood pressure 128/75.

The surgery was performed by Maj. Gen. Leonard D. Heaton, commanding officer of Walter Reed, who had operated on President Eisenhower in June for ileitis. He was assisted today by

Continued on Page 78, Column 3

President Expected to Win; Democratic Congress Seen

New York Times Team Reports

Following are summaries of the apparent voting trends for President and the United States Senate and House of Representatives. They are based on the reports of the New York Times teams that have surveyed twenty-seven closely contested states and of correspondents in twenty-one other states.

Presidential Race

By W. H. LAWRENCE
Surveys indicate that President Eisenhower and Vice-President Richard M. Nixon will be re-elected on Tuesday by comfortable majorities of both the popular and electoral votes.

Reports from New York Times correspondents who have investigated political sentiment in the forty-eight states indicate these probable results:

For President Eisenhower—A minimum of twenty-seven states with 285 electoral votes, or nineteen votes more than required for a majority of the 531-member Electoral College.

For Adlai E. Stevenson—A landslide toward President Eisenhower would, of course, alter every present prospect. The weight of all current evidence suggests clearly, however, these approximate results:

¶The Democrats should at least retain their present thin margin of control in the House

Continued on Page 60, Column 5

Congressional Race

By WILLIAM S. WHITE
The Democrats appear likely to hold Congress in Tuesday's national elections in spite of the prospect that President Eisenhower will retain the White House for the Republicans.

The outlook thus is for a continuation of the divided form of government that has guided the country since 1954.

A landslide for President Eisenhower would, of course, alter every present prospect. The weight of all current evidence suggests clearly, however, these approximate results:

¶The Democrats should at least retain their present thin margin of control in the House leaning toward President Eisenhower—Eight states with seventy-six electoral votes.

¶There should be a Democratic House of Representatives again with no less than the

—49 Democrats to 47 Republicans.

¶There should be a Democratic House of Representatives again with no less than the

Continued on Page 60, Column 2

BID TO U. N. CHIEF

Canada's Motion That He Plan Suez Unit Adopted, 59 to 0

Texts of draft resolutions and debate excerpts, Page 29.

By KATHLEEN TELTSCH
Special to The New York Times.
UNITED NATIONS, N. Y., Sunday, Nov. 4—The General Assembly voted early today to ask the Secretary General to submit a plan for creation of a United Nations police force to obtain and supervise a cease-fire in the Middle East.

The policing proposal, sponsored by Canada, was adopted 57 to 0, at 2:17 A. M. at an emergency session of the Assembly.

Nineteen states abstained, among them Israel, France and Britain. The latter two earlier had rejected an Assembly call for a cease-fire and said they would keep on with their "police action" in Egypt to safeguard the Suez Canal.

The proposal, made by Lester B. Pearson, Canada's Secretary for External Affairs, calls on Secretary General Dag Hammarskjold to submit blueprints within forty-eight hours for an "emergency international United Nations force."

New Truce Plan Adopted

No details were suggested by Mr. Pearson, but such a police force presumably would have to include several thousand men. The Canadian spokesman has said he would recommend Canada's participation. His proposal, however, left all arrangements to the Secretary General.

Within minutes, the emergency session adopted a second resolution, co-sponsored by nineteen Asian and African countries. This renewed the cease-fire appeal made two days ago and asked Mr. Hammarskjold to report within twelve hours on whether the states had complied.

The second resolution was approved, 59 to 5, with twelve abstentions. Among the abstainers were France, Britain, Israel, Australia and New Zealand.

[In Moscow, Marshal Kliment Y. Voroshilov, Soviet chief of state, told President Shukry al-Kuwatly of Syria at a farewell reception that the Soviet Union was prepared to give Syria the "necessary assistance" to reinforce her independence against foreign threats.]

2-Nation Plan Criticized

The Government spokesman offered no reason why the Israelis had entered the proscribed zone. But the Israelis are increasingly disturbed over the slowness of British and French forces in occupying the canal.

In warmly supporting the Ca-

Continued on Page 29, Column 8

Mideast Oil Lines Reported Blown Up

By SAM POPE BREWER
Special to The New York Times.
BEIRUT, Lebanon, Nov. 3—Pipelines carrying more than half a million barrels of oil daily from Iraq to the Mediterranean coast have stopped operating as a result of the fighting in Egypt.

Reports circulating here were that the Iraq Petroleum Company's three pumping stations in Syria known as T-2, T-3 and T-4 had been blown up and burned.

[At the United Nations an Egyptian spokesman was quoted by The United Press as having said all oil pipelines in every Middle East country except Saudi Arabia had been blown up or shut down.]

No oil installations in Lebanon were damaged up to tonight. Reports abroad to that effect are incorrect, according to

Continued on Page 30, Column 4

SOVIET ROAD BLOCK IN HUNGARY: Soviet tank obstructs road near Magyarovar.

Associated Press Radiophoto

ISRAELI PATROLS REACH SUEZ BANK

Penetrate Zone at 3 Points as Delay in British-French Landings Irks Regime

By HOMER BIGART
Special to The New York Times.
TEL AVIV, Israel, Sunday, Nov. 4—Israeli patrols reached the east bank of the Suez Canal yesterday.

A Government spokesman said Israeli columns had penetrated at three places the ten-mile buffer zone east of the canal that Britain and France wanted kept clear of warring Israeli and Egyptian forces.

Meanwhile, the Cabinet of Premier David Ben-Gurion studied reports that Syrian and Iraqi troops had entered Jordan. The developments in Jordan were followed with "concern and alertness," according to a Foreign Ministry source.

The announcement that Israelis were within ten miles of the canal at three points—opposite El Qantara in the north, Ismailia in the center and Suez at the southern terminus—may have been timed to coincide with reports here that the British-French invasion had been put off because of United States pressure.

The British-French proposals for an international police force to occupy the canal zone were regarded here as "unrealistic."

Until its announcement, the Israeli Government had indicated compliance with the British-French ultimatum.

But Israel has insisted that no firm deal was made with the French on where the advance would be halted.

Lieut. Col. Moshe Pearlman, Government and Army spokesman, said that the whole area was "relatively quiet" and that the "entire peninsula in very short time will be in Israeli hands."

British Embassy sources said

Continued on Page 30, Column 6

British Bomb Raids On Egypt Continued In Landing Prelude

Texts of the communiqués are printed on Page 26.

By LEONARD INGALLS
Special to The New York Times.
LONDON, Nov. 3—British bombers turned their heaviest attack today from airfields in Egypt to ammunition dumps, barracks and armored weapons depots of the Egyptian Army.

There were indications that the landing by British and French forces in the Suez Canal Zone would be made by paratroopers and seaborne troops units within the next forty-eight hours.

The Beirut radio, quoting an Egyptian communiqué, reported that a British-French force attempted to land at the southern entrance to the canal, but was driven off with heavy losses.

The Egyptians said they had sunk four British naval vessels and captured three troop landing craft at Suez with fire from shore batteries and torpedo boats. One British ship was said by the Egyptians to have been sunk by gunfire, and a British destroyer, a troop carrier and another British naval unit were said to have been sunk by torpedoes.

The Egyptians also reported they had shot down seventeen British-French planes over the Suez Canal area.

[There was little additional information on the military situation in announcements or dispatches from Cairo.]

An Admiralty spokesman said "there is no information in London to support the Egyptian

Continued on Page 17, Column 1

Nutting Quits Post; Churchill For Eden

The text of Churchill letter will be found on Page 24.

Special to The New York Times.
LONDON, Nov. 3—Anthony Nutting, Minister of State in the Foreign Office, resigned from the Government tonight because he strongly disagreed with its policy of armed intervention in Egypt.

The blow to the Government represented by the defection of one of its best-known and most effective young ministers at a critical juncture was balanced by a resounding declaration of support from Sir Winston Churchill.

Writing from his lair at Chartwell, the old lion of British politics blamed Egypt for provoking war with Israel, criticized the United States for failing to cooperate fully and

Continued on Page 24, Column 3

SOVIET VETO BARS ACTION IN COUNCIL

Censure Move in U. N. Over New Attack on Hungary Carried to Assembly

Excerpts from statements in Security Council, Page 35.

By LINDESAY PARROTT
Special to The New York Times.
UNITED NATIONS, N. Y., Sunday, Nov. 4—The Soviet Union early today vetoed a United States resolution proposing Security Council censure of the Russian military attack on Hungary.

Nine nations favored the United States proposal and one abstained, Yugoslavia.

The veto was at 5:15 A. M. Henry Cabot Lodge Jr., United States representative, immediately moved for an emergency session of the General Assembly to take up the Hungarian crisis.

The Assembly already was in permanent special session over the French-British intervention in the Suez Canal area.

Council's Will 'Thwarted'

Angrily, Mr. Lodge told the Council that the will of the world organization had been "thwarted" by the Soviet veto and that the eleven-nation body had been prevented from fulfilling its responsibilities. In this "grave situation," he said, Assembly action was required.

The Council adopted the United States resolution for reference to the Assembly by a vote of 10 to 1. This ballot came at 5:21 A. M.

The Assembly meeting was set for 8 o'clock tonight.

The Council adjourned at 5:24 A. M.

The Council's action, marking the Soviet Union's seventy-ninth veto, was taken after the United States had called the group together at 3 A. M. to protest against the reoccupation of Budapest by Soviet troops. According to the latest reports early today, the Hungarian capital was in the hands of Soviet troops after Russian tanks earlier had ringed the city.

The United States legation was understood to have been under fire. Mr. Lodge also reported that Joseph Cardinal Mindszenty and his staff had taken refuge in the legation.

The Security Council had adjourned shortly after midnight.

Continued on Page 35, Column 6

This section consists of 140 pages divided into three parts. The news summary and index will be found on Page 95. Society news begins on Page 90 and obituary articles will be found on Pages 86 and 87.

CAPITAL STORMED

Freedom Radios Fade From Air as Russians Shell Key Centers

By PAUL HOFMANN
Special to The New York Times.
VIENNA, Sunday, Nov. 4—Soviet troops started attacking Budapest and other Hungarian cities, towns and key military installations at dawn today.

At 9 A. M., local time (3 A. M. Eastern standard time) four hours after Budapest had been awakened by Russian artillery fire, overpowering Soviet tanks and infantry forces had stormed the Parliament Building and made Premier Imre Nagy and most members of his government prisoners.

Fighting in Budapest and many other parts of the country was continuing, but the prospects for the free Hungarian Government forces were nearly hopeless in the face of crushing Soviet superiority.

The Budapest radio and other Hungarian freedom stations went off the air one after another.

Before going silent, they directed desperate pleas to the West, especially to the United States, and to the United Nations for help to save the Hungarian people from "annihilation."

Mindszenty in U. S. Legation

Joseph Cardinal Mindszenty, Roman Catholic primate of Hungary, who had been freed from detention last week, and his secretary had taken refuge in the building of the United States Legation.

The United States legation, near the Parliament Building, was under fire at 9:30 A. M.

At 7 A. M., "several hundred" Soviet heavy tanks were reported attacking key Hungarian Army positions on the outskirts of Budapest and attempting to penetrate the city. The main thrust of the Soviet forces came apparently from the southeast.

Shortly before 7 A. M. the Budapest radio repeated Premier Nagy's announcement of the Soviet attack. It directed an appeal to Dag Hammarskjold, Secretary General of the United Nations. At the same time the M. T. I., Hungarian news agency reported:

"Russian troops have suddenly attacked Budapest and the entire country. They have opened fire everywhere in Hungary. It is a general attack.

"Janos Kadar [since Oct. 24 secretary of the Hungarian Communist party], Gyorgy Marosan and Sandor Ronai have formed a new Government and started crushing the counter-

Continued on Page 34, Column 6

Pravda Denounces Nagy for 'Reaction'

By Reuters.
LONDON, Sunday, Nov. 4—The Soviet Communist party newspaper Pravda attacked early today, the Hungarian capital was in the hands of Soviet troops after Russian tanks earlier had ringed the city Hungary today "in strong terms," according to the Moscow radio.

Pravda said: "The task of barring the way to reaction in Hungary has to be carried out without the slightest delay—such is the course dictated by events."

The broadcast quoted Pravda as saying: "Imre Nagy turned out to be, objectively speaking, an accomplice of the reactionary forces. Imre Nagy cannot and does not want to fight the dark forces of reaction."

Continued on Page 15, Column 1

184

One of Nat "King" Cole's classic songs was Too Young To Go Steady.

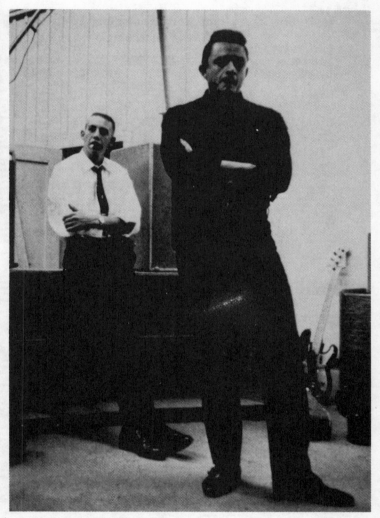

Johnny Cash's famous song, I Walk The Line, was a hit in 1956.

Andy Williams' big hit was Canadian Sunset.

"All the News That's Fit to Print"

The New York Times.

LATE CITY EDITION
Condensation of U. S. Weather Bureau forecast: Some cloudiness today; cloudy to-night. Clearing, cooler tomorrow.
Temperature range today: 66—50.
Temperature range yesterday: 65.4—52.2.
Full U. S. Weather Bureau Report, Page 69.

VOL. CVI. No. 36,082. Entered as Second-Class Matter, Post Office, New York, N. Y. NEW YORK, WEDNESDAY, NOVEMBER 7, 1956. Times Square, New York 36, N. Y. Telephone LAckawanna 4-1000 FIVE CENTS

EISENHOWER BY A LANDSLIDE; BATTLE FOR CONGRESS CLOSE; JAVITS VICTOR OVER WAGNER

Suez Warfare Stopped Under British-French Cease-Fire

MAYOR CONCEDES

Javits, Swept In With the Eisenhower Tide, Wins Stiff Contest

Vote for Senator
CITY SUMMARY

	Javits (Rep.)	Wagner (Dem.-Lib.)
Manhattan ...	270,146	393,462
Bronx	218,895	374,810
Brooklyn	398,088	605,002
Queens	400,832	372,505
Richmond ...	49,694	32,881
Total	1,337,655	1,778,660
Upstate	2,362,618	1,478,238
Grand total	3,700,273	3,256,898

All E. D.'s of 4,607 in city and 6,522 of 6,525 upstate.

By DOUGLAS DALES

Attorney General Jacob K. Javits was swept to victory yesterday in the Eisenhower Republican landslide in his race against Mayor Wagner for the United States Senate.

Mayor Wagner conceded defeat in a statement at 1:22 A. M. after the trend to Javits' victory became unmistakable.

Mr. Wagner carried three boroughs in the city—Manhattan, Brooklyn and the Bronx—but lost in Queens and Richmond.

The city-wide complete totals gave Mr. Javits 1,337,655 votes to 1,778,660 for Mayor Wagner. The Mayor's total included 233,560 on the Liberal party line. The Liberal line attracted 404,769 votes in the city four years ago, when the party ran its own candidate for the Senate, George S. Counts.

The victor's margin was expected to reach 444,000 with the final results. With all city districts and 6,522 of 6,525 districts upstate reported, Mr. Javits had an edge of 443,375.

Mayor Wagner carried two of the fifty-seven upstate counties, Erie and Albany. Eisenhower carried both.

Everywhere outside the city, Mr. Javits ran substantially behind the President's vote. On the other hand, Mayor Wagner ran well ahead of Adlai E. Stevenson, the Democratic candidate for President.

In view of the size of the

Continued on Page 26, Column 2

PRESIDENT SCORES NEW HIGH IN STATE

Plurality Tops 1,500,000 as He Cuts Rival's City Edge

State Presidential Vote
CITY SUMMARY

	Eisenhower (Rep.)	Stevenson (Dem.-Lib.)
Manhattan ..	299,929	378,018
Bronx	256,909	343,656
Brooklyn ...	459,703	558,187
Queens	471,144	313,311
Richmond ..	64,236	196,653
Total	1,551,921	1,614,825
Upstate	2,766,183	1,127,403
Grand total	4,318,104	2,742,228

All E. D.'s of 4,607 in city and 6,522 of 6,525 upstate.

By LEO EGAN

President Eisenhower swept New York yesterday by a plurality that dwarfed all previous records.

With sixty-one of the state's 11,132 election districts still to report this morning, General Eisenhower's margin exceeded 1,500,000.

The previous record for a Presidential plurality in New York was established in 1920, when the late Warren G. Harding, Republican, defeated James M. Cox, Democrat, by 1,139,927.

All the missing districts are in Republican territory upstate.

Continued on Page 22, Column 1

An International Summary: The Mideast and Hungary

Following are summaries of the leading developments in the Middle East and Europe. The full foreign news report begins on the first page of the second part.

Cease-Fire Is On

Britain and France put a cease-fire into effect and halted their advance in Egypt. Prime Minister Eden told Commons that conditions had been established for an international police force under the United Nations to promote settlement of Middle Eastern issues.

Invaders Hold Canal

The invasion forces claimed control of the Suez Canal Zone. They took Port Said and drove south before the cease-fire became effective.

Egyptians Halt Fight

The Egyptians decided to hold their fire at the deadline in the hope that the United Nations resolution of Nov. 2, providing for withdrawal of all forces behind armistice lines, would be carried out.

Soviet May Send 'Volunteers'

Indications in Moscow were that Soviet "volunteers" who began applying for service with Egyptian forces might go to the Middle East despite the cease-fire. Moscow broadcast a Cairo appeal for aid.

Troop Withdrawal Asked

Asian and Arab states drafted a United Nations resolution calling on Britain, France and Israel to withdraw their troops from Egypt immediately. A special session of the General Assembly called for last night was postponed until this morning.

Hungarian Battle Persists

Stubborn Hungarian revolutionary forces are continuing to fight the Soviet army in Budapest, according to diplomatic reports received in Vienna. Women and children were said to be fighting alongside the men in a house-to-house struggle. The General Assembly scheduled a special session this afternoon to consider Soviet intervention in Hungary.

EISENHOWER SETS RECORD IN JERSEY

Margin of 700,000 Carries All 21 Counties—G. O. P. Wins 2 Hudson Seats

By GEORGE CABLE WRIGHT

President Eisenhower yesterday scored the greatest victory in New Jersey political history.

With most of the state's ballots tallied early this morning, his margin over Adlai E. Stevenson had soared above 700,000, almost double that of 1952. He became the first candidate in modern times to carry all twenty-one counties.

The returns were:

PRESIDENT
4,017 districts out of 4,155.

Eisenhower	1,522,971
Stevenson	821,067

The most startling aspect of his victory was the complete turnabout of Hudson County, for half a century a Democratic stronghold.

This county gave the President a majority of 76,554. In 1952 Mr. Stevenson had carried Hudson by 7,886 votes.

In fact, Republicans swept every county contest. When residents of Hudson awake this morning it is certain that many will find it hard to believe that for the next two years they will be represented in Congress by not one, but two, Republicans. There was no precedent there for that.

A third Democratic incumbent, Representative Harrison A. Williams Jr., went down to defeat in Union County.

Thus, the Democratic representation of six in the House was cut in half. All eight Republican incumbents were re-elected.

President Eisenhower became the first Presidential candidate to carry the solidly Democratic bailiwick of Jersey City since Warren G. Harding did it in 1920. Long the citadel of the late Frank Hague and now of John Kenny, it gave General Eisenhower a majority of 31,527 over Mr. Stevenson. In 1952 the Democratic candidate had carried the city by 8,251.

But the trouncing of the former Illinois Governor was by no means restricted to Hudson. Camden and Mercer Counties, which also went to Mr. Stevenson in 1952, likewise turned their backs to him this year.

Continued on Page 28, Column 5

BUSH RE-ELECTED IN CONNECTICUT

Plurality for Eisenhower of 303,036 Biggest in State in a Presidential Race

By RICHARD H. PARKE
Special to The New York Times.

HARTFORD, Nov 6—President Eisenhower scored an easy victory in Connecticut today. He carried to victory with him Senator Prescott S. Bush, the Republican incumbent.

The President's plurality of 303,036 votes over Adlai E. Stevenson, Democratic candidate, was the greatest margin the State ever has given a Presidential contender. The previous high figure was 136,138 votes, achieved by Prseident Coolidge in 1924.

The President, whose 1952 plurality of 129,363 was considered of landslide proportions, defeated Mr. Stevenson today by 708,995 votes to 405,959, according to complete but unofficial returns.

The Republican sweep was general throughout the state. It carried in Senator Bush by a plurality of 129,544 votes. He defeated his Democratic opponent, Representative Thomas J. Dodd, by 607,330 to 477,876.

The Republicans also retained

Continued on Page 28, Column 5

SENATE IN DOUBT

Democrats Lag in East on War Issue but Gain in the West

By WILLIAM S. WHITE

The Democrats and Republicans fought along a swaying electoral battle line early today for control of the oncoming Eighty-fifth Congress.

Not all the power of President Eisenhower's landslide victory had been enough to put his Republican Congressional colleagues in front.

The Senate race, in which the Republicans were attempting to overturn a present 49-to-47 Democratic margin of control, was an affair of hairbreadth drama.

Small net Republican gains for the House of Representatives were indicated. But whether these would continue or would be enough remained wholly in doubt.

The Republicans needed a net gain of 15 House seats, and the capture of 2 additional and now vacant seats that had been Republican.

The pattern of the Congressional contest was this: The East, more sensitive than other sections to the last-minute issue involved in the Middle Eastern and Central European war crises, on the whole was hitting the Democrats hard. The appeal of "don't change horses in midstream" was strong in this area. In the interior, however, Democratic organizational strength, farm discontent and other factors were turning up great Democratic strength.

Cooper Wins in Kentucky

The position on the Senate in some critical states was this:

KENTUCKY—A gain of one Republican seat in former Senator John Sherman Cooper's defeat of his Democratic challenger, Lawrence Wetherby, for the seat made vacant by the death of Senator Alben W. Barkley. The possibility of another gain for the Republicans in the fact that the assistant Democratic leader of the Senate, Earle C. Clements, was running behind Thruston B. Morton, a former assistant Secretary of State in the Eisenhower Administration.

NEW YORK—A Republican gain in the victory of Jacob K. Javits over Mayor Wagner for the seat being vacated by Senator Herbert H. Lehman, Democrat-Liberal.

OHIO—A Democratic gain in the defeat by Gov. Frank J. Lausche of Senator George H. Bender.

ILLINOIS—Senator Everett M. Dirksen, Republican, ran ahead of his Democratic opponent, Richard Stengel.

PENNSYLVANIA—Joseph S.

Continued on Page 3, Column 1

Coudert Wins in Close Contest; Vote in Queens 7th Rechecked

By CLAYTON KNOWLES

The Republicans emerged from a hard-fought Congressional campaign early today with a possible net gain of one in the state delegation to the House of Representatives.

At 4:20 A. M. a final decision rested on the outcome of the race in the Seventh district of Queens. Here Representative James J. Delaney, Democratic incumbent, claimed victory at 4:15 A. M. by forty votes, but a final tally was unavailable.

An hour and a half earlier, Delaney supporters were conceding the election of Joseph Stockinger, a Republican, but the contest was so close that all 217 districts were being rechecked.

The announced vote for 202 districts was 72,186 for Mr. Stockinger to 72,112 for Mr. Delaney, who ran with Liberal party backing.

The prospect that the Republicans would pick up a House seat in the state, giving them twenty-seven of a total of forty-three, arose when Representative Frederic R. Coudert Jr. staged an eleventh-hour triumph in the Manhattan Seventeenth District.

He prevailed once more over Anthony B. Akers, Democrat-Liberal who had come within 314 votes of defeating him in 1954. This time Mr. Coudert won, 68,862 votes to 66,207.

If Mr. Delaney should go to defeat, the Republicans will have seven of the twenty-two House seats filled in the city.

President Eisenhower's land-

Continued on Page 30, Column 6

PRESIDENT EISENHOWER

VICE PRESIDENT NIXON

G. O. P. MAKES BID TO CAPTURE HOUSE

Picks Up 9 Seats in East, but Drive Eases in West —Midwest to Decide

By JOHN D. MORRIS

Republicans got off to a fast start in their bid to recapture control of the House of Representatives, but appeared to lose steam early today as returns trickled in from the West.

As of 3 A. M., results from yesterday's Congressional races indicated a decided Republican trend, with some major upsets for the Democrats. However, with control of nearly two-thirds of the 435 seats still in doubt, victory for either party was far from certain.

The undecided contests were almost entirely in the Midwest, where the issue of declining farm income was a factor favoring the Democrats, and in the the Far West.

G. O. P. Gains in East

Such returns as were available from those areas indicated possible Democratic gains in Iowa, California and South Dakota.

Eastward, where the only decisive tallies were available, Republicans had picked up nine seats held by Democrats in the Eighty-fourth Congress while holding their own in all other contests where returns were conclusive. One, in New York City, was subpect to a recount. Democrats had failed to capture any Republican seat except one that they took in the Maine election on Sept. 10.

Republican incumbents were easy victors in a number of contests that had promised to be close.

The most outstanding upsets were in New Jersey, where the Hudson county Democratic stronghold of the late Mayor Frank Hague of Jersey City unseated its two Democratic Representatives, T. James Tumulty and Alfred D. Sieminski, in the Thirteenth and Fourteenth Congressional Districts.

Mr. Sieminski lost to Norman H. Roth, Republican. Mr. Tumulty, a 300-pound legislator, was defeated by Vincent J. Dellay, Republican.

A third Democratic incumbent in New Jersey, Harrison A. Williams, lost to Florence P. Dwyer, Republican.

Republicans also picked up one Democratic seat in Connecticut, one in Deleware, one in Pennsylvania, one in Indiana and

Continued on Page 3, Column 2

Stevenson Concedes Defeat and Wishes President Success

Stevenson and Kefauver talks appear on Page 13.

By HARRISON E. SALISBURY
Special to The New York Times.

CHICAGO, Wednesday, Nov. 7—Adlai E. Stevenson conceded the election of President Eisenhower in a statement made public at 12:25 A. M. Central standard time today (1:25 Eastern standard time).

In a telegram to President Eisenhower, the Democratic candidate expressed his understanding of "grave difficulties" that the Administration faced and wished all success to General Eisenhower in the years ahead.

Mr. Stevenson coupled his telegram of congratulations to the President with an appeal to his followers to carry forward in the crusade for what he called a "New America."

He called on America's leaders to recognize that the nation "wants to face up squarely to the facts of today's world."

"We don't want to draw back from them," Mr. Stevenson said. "We can't. We are ready for the test that we know history has set for us."

Mr. Stevenson in his statement took note of the troubled conditions of the world.

"Beyond the seas, in much of the world, in Russia, in China, in Hungary, in all the trembling satellites, partisan controversy is forbidden and dissent suppressed," Mr. Stevenson said.

Mr. Stevenson also took note

Continued on Page 13, Column 5

Electoral Vote by States

	Eisenhower	Stevenson		Eisenhower	Stevenson
Ala.	—	11	Nev.	3	—
Ariz.	4	—	N. H.	4	—
Ark.	—	8	N. J.	16	—
Calif.	32	—	N. M.	4	—
Colo.	6	—	N. Y.	45	—
Conn.	8	—	N. C.	—	14
Del.	3	—	N. D.	4	—
Fla.	10	—	Ohio	25	—
Ga.	—	12	Okla.	8	—
Idaho	4	—	Ore.	6	—
Ill.	27	—	Pa.	32	—
Ind.	13	—	R. Isl.	4	—
Iowa	10	—	S. C.	—	8
Kan.	8	—	S. D.	4	—
Ky.	10	—	Tenn.	11	—
La.	10	—	Texas	24	—
Me.	5	—	Utah	4	—
Md.	9	—	Vt.	3	—
Mass.	16	—	Va.	12	—
Mich.	20	—	Wash.	9	—
Minn.	11	—	W. Va.	8	—
Miss.	—	8	Wisc.	12	—
Mo.	—	13	Wyo.	3	—
Mont.	4	—			
Neb.	6	—	Total	457	74

EISENHOWER VOWS TO TOIL FOR PEACE

Hails Landslide Re-election as Proof Nation Wants 'Modern Republicanism'

Texts of the Eisenhower and Nixon talks on Page 12.

By RUSSELL BAKER
Special to The New York Times.

WASHINGTON, Wednesday, Nov. 7—President Eisenhower hailed his landslide re-election victory today as proof that his "modern Republicanism has now proved itself and America has approved of modern Republicanism."

He pledged in a victory statement early this morning to work with "whatever talents the good God has given me for 168,000,000 Americans here at home and for peace in the world."

Addressing a jubilant crowd of party workers at Republican election headquarters here and the nation, over television, the President declared that so long as the G.O.P. pursued the "ideals, the hopes and aspirations" of the people, it would continue to flourish.

"If it is anything less," he said, " it is only a conspiracy to seize power. And the Republican party is not that."

'Looks to the Future'

Thus, in his moment of triumph, General Eisenhower claimed a sweeping triumph for what his Administration's philosophers had styled the "new Republicanism" and what he himself termed this morning "modern Republicanism."

"Modern Republicanism," he said, "looks to the future and this means it will gain constantly new recruits." So long as it continued to remain "modern," he added, it would "continue to increase in power and influence for decades to come."

So long as it clings to its "modern" ideals, the President declared, it would "point the way to peace among nations and prosperity, advancing standards here at home in which everyone will share."

The President delivered his victory statement at 1:45 A. M., about fifteen minutes after this restive crowd gathered in the mammoth ballroom of the Sheraton-Park Hotel had heard Adlai E. Stevenson concede defeat in Chicago.

General Eisenhower had been waiting upstairs in a third-floor suite for three and a half hours,

Continued on Page 12, Column 1

41 STATES TO G.O.P.

President Sweeps All the North and West, Scores in South

By JAMES RESTON

Dwight David Eisenhower won yesterday the most spectacular Presidential election victory since Franklin D. Roosevelt submerged Alfred M. Landon in 1936.

The smiling 66-year-old hero of the Normandy invasion, who was in a Denver hospital recuperating from a heart attack just a year ago today, thus became the first Republican in this century to win two successive Presidential elections. William McKinley did it in 1896 and 1900.

Adlai E. Stevenson of Illinois, who lost to Mr. Eisenhower four years ago, thirty-nine states to nine, conceded defeat at 1:25 this morning.

At 4:45 A. M. President Eisenhower had won forty-one states to seven for Mr. Stevenson. His electoral lead at that time was 457 to 74 for Stevenson, and his popular vote was 25,071,331 to 18,337,434—up 2 per cent over 1952. Two hundred and sixty-six electoral votes are needed for election.

Victory in All Areas

This was a national victory in every conceivable way. It started in Connecticut. It swept every state in New England. It took New York by a plurality of more than 1,500,000. It carried all the Middle Atlantic states, all the Midwest, all the Rocky Mountain states and everything beyond the Rockies.

More than that, the Republican tide swept along the border states and to the South, carried all the states won by the G.O.P. there in 1952—Virginia, Texas, Tennessee and Florida—and even took Louisiana for the first time since the Hayes-Tilden election of 1876.

For the President and his 43-year old Vice Presidential running mate, Richard M. Nixon of California, who carried much of the Republican campaign, it was a more impressive victory than for the Republican party.

So close were many races for

Continued on Page 2, Column 3

CLARK LEADS DUFF IN PENNSYLVANIA

Democrat's Edge Dropping —President Takes State

By WILLIAM G. WEART
Special to The New York Times.

PHILADELPHIA, Wednesday, Nov. 7—Joseph S. Clark Jr., former Mayor of Philadelphia, was running ahead of Senator James H. Duff early today.

But his margin was ebbing as returns from rural areas and small towns began to offset the lead he piled up in large cities.

President Eisenhower won the state's thirty-two electoral votes by a plurality that was steadily mounting.

Mr. Clark expressed disappointment at the defeat of his party's standard-bearer. He attributed General Eisenhower's victory to his "personal popularity." Mr. Clark's campaign manager, Mayor Richardson Dilworth of Philadelphia, said the President's re-election was due to the "emotion caused by the war situation."

In the event the final tally in the Senatorial race is close, an estimated 50,000 absentee votes cast by servicemen and hospitalized veterans may decide the outcome. Under the law, absentee ballots are mailed to county

Continued on Page 13, Column 6

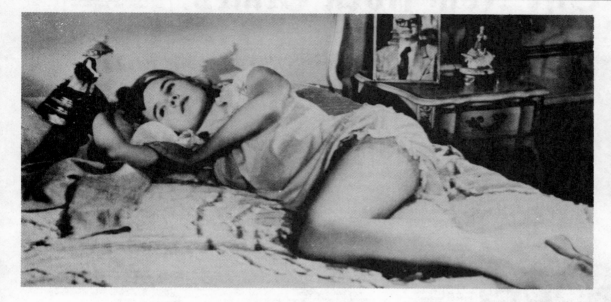

Sex goddesses of the mid-Fifties were suddenly permitted to pose on the screen in positions that were previously prohibited by the Production Code. Carroll Baker caused a sensation in Baby Doll.

Elvis Presley's first film was Love Me Tender which co-starred Richard Egan and Debra Paget.

James Dean and Elizabeth Taylor starred in Giant, which was released in 1956.

"All the News That's Fit to Print"

The New York Times.

LATE CITY EDITION
Condensation of U. S. Weather Bureau forecast: Cloudy and cooler today; clearing and colder tonight. Fair, cold tomorrow.
Temperature range today: 50—42.
Temperature range yesterday: 57—50.
Full U. S. Weather Bureau Report, Page 36.

VOL. CVI—No. 36,084. Entered as Second-Class Matter, Post Office, New York, N. Y. NEW YORK, FRIDAY, NOVEMBER 9, 1956. Times Square, New York 36, N. Y. Telephone LAckawanna 4-1000 FIVE CENTS

ISRAEL AGREES TO LEAVE EGYPT WHEN U.N. SENDS PATROL FORCE; U. S. TO ADMIT 5,000 HUNGARIANS

5 KILLED AS PLANE HITS VIDEO TOWER AND APARTMENTS

North Bergen Crash in Fog Sets Building on Fire and Strews Debris—16 Hurt

2,500 ARE EVACUATED

Mast Struck by Private Craft Was Unused—Its Removal Long Sought by Town

By PETER KIHSS
Special to The New York Times.

NORTH BERGEN, N. J., Nov. 8—Five persons were killed today when a private plane struck an 810-foot television tower and crashed into a five-story apartment house.

Mayor Angelo Sarubbi, bitterly recalling a long effort to get rid of the unused tower, said five bodies had been found. It was still uncertain whether there might be another fatality.

After striking the tower in a fog, the plane stayed aloft for a distance of five blocks before plunging into the building and setting it on fire.

Sixteen men were injured in rescue efforts, including four hospitalized.

Town authorities started evacuating 2,500 persons from their homes in a fifteen-block area around the tower tonight as a precaution against its having been damaged so much that it might topple.

Woman Killed in Jump

Mrs. Harriet Phelps, 58 years old, who was in the top-floor apartment into which the plane plunged, jumped out a window to her death to escape the flames from the crash.

Three persons were reported aboard the Beechcraft plane, according to the Civil Aeronautics Administration. Presumably all were killed. They were Russell S. Williams, president of the Bonded Gasoline and Oil Company of Indianapolis; William Cromley of Trafalgar, Ind., the pilot; and a passenger thus far unidentified.

Another top-floor tenant, Mrs. Florence Pyne, was listed by the police as missing. Mayor Sarubbi said two bodies, perhaps those of Mr. Williams and Mr. Cromley, had been discovered next to the piled-up plane in the Phelps apartment. Also in the house, he said, were the body of a woman and a "small body."

Wreckage Imperils Area

The accident toll could easily have been higher, for parts of the disintegrating plane hurtled down on an area of small homes and businesses.

One engine buried itself in a garage behind the Immaculate Heart of Mary Chapel, beside a parochial school in which 250 children are enrolled. Twenty-five kindergarten children had been lined up outside in the street when the accident occurred at 12:45 P. M.

The circumstances recalled a similar accident July 28, 1945, in which a twin-engine B-25 Mitchell bomber struck the 1,250-foot-high Empire State Building in Manhattan. In that crash, 915 feet above street level, thirteen persons died and twenty-five were injured.

The tower in today's accident is believed to be the tallest structure in New Jersey. It has a fifty-foot mast atop a 760-foot

Continued on Page 31, Column 4

The New York Times (by Carl T. Gossett Jr.)
SCENE OF PLANE DISASTER: A twin-engine private plane crashed into this apartment house in North Bergen, N. J., yesterday after clipping the unused television tower in rear. Fog and rain had caused poor visibility.

Bulganin, Voroshilov Hail President as Great Leader

Special to The New York Times.

MOSCOW, Nov. 8—Two Soviet leaders have hailed President Eisenhower as "a great American statesman and leader" and have congratulated him upon his re-election as President of the United States.

Separate telegrams were sent to General Eisenhower by Nikolai A. Bulganin, chairman of the Council of Ministers, and by Kliment Y. Voroshilov, chairman of the Presidium of the Supreme Soviet. Their messages were the only notable reaction to the American election seen here.

Marshal Bulganin said the Soviet Union knew that President Eisenhower favored relaxation of international tension. He said that the American leader had sought to establish "peaceful and fruitful relations with all states and peoples," including the Soviet Union.

The Soviet leaders wished General Eisenhower "greatest success" in his activities as well as "strength and good health."

Soviet Leaders' Message

LONDON, Nov. 8 (Reuters)—Following is the message sent by Marshal Bulganin to President Eisenhower:

"Esteemed Mr. President, we send you our hearty congratulations and best wishes in connection with your election to the office of President. You are known to us as a great statesman and leader of the U. S. A. who is striving for the relaxation of international tension and the establishment of peaceful and fruitful relations between all states and nations, as well as the establishment of such relations between our countries.

"We were and are supporters of the most fruitful and friendly relations between our nations and our states.

"We sincerely wish you, Mr. President, the greatest success in your activities. We wish you strength and good health."

The message of Mr. Voroshilov follows:

"Esteemed Mr. President, in connection with your re-election to the office of President of the U. S. A. I beg you to accept my sincere congratulations and best wishes in your highly responsible activities for the benefit of the great American people.

"I would allow myself to express the assurance that your activities in the office of President will assist in strengthening friendly relations between our peoples and in attaining the great aim: the creation of a lasting and durable peace."

Israelis Ask About Dulles
Special to The New York Times.

TEL AVIV, Nov. 8—Israelis showed more interest today in a possible successor to John Foster Dulles as United States Secretary of State than they did in the re-election of President Eisenhower.

The Republican Administration, in the view of Israelis, has been less friendly to Israel than was the Democratic regime of former President Harry S. Truman. However, the feeling today in the cloakroom of the Knesset

Continued on Page 22, Column 1

DEMOCRATS CLING TO SENATE EDGE

49-47 Count Likely to Stand —Lausche Move Dims Republicans' Hopes

By ALLEN DRURY
Special to The New York Times.

WASHINGTON, Nov. 8—The Republican acquisition of a second Senate seat in Kentucky today brought Senate party alignments for the Eighty-fifth Congress in January to just where they had been for the last two years: forty-nine Democrats and forty-seven Republicans.

At the same time, a statement issued by Gov. Frank J. Lausche of Ohio, Democratic Senator-elect, apparently scotched rumors that he might vote with the Republicans to permit them to organize the Senate and take control of its committees.

In Kentucky, Thruston B. Morton, former assistant Secretary of State took a final and commanding lead early today over Senator Earle C. Clements, the assistant Democratic floor leader in the Eighty-fourth Congress, to decide the last remaining Senate race.

In the House, latest returns indicated that the Democrats had won 232 seats and were leading in three races, for a probable total of 235. Republicans had won 199 and were leading in one race for a total of 200. A margin

Continued on Page 22, Column 2

City Transit Regaining Riders After Drop That Began in '48

By STANLEY LEVEY

The Transit Authority said yesterday it had stopped losing riders for the first time since 1948.

In fact, the agency said, it is regaining customers on subway and surface lines at a slow—but steady and heartening—rate.

The trend started last March, but spasmodically. One month there would be a gain of passengers, the next a loss. But, beginning with July, the increase in riders and passenger revenue has been uninterrupted.

In the four-month period ended Oct. 31, the number of passengers increased by 7,003,459 (or 1.25 per cent) over the same period in 1955. Passenger revenue was up $884,728, or 1.7 per cent.

Charles L. Patterson, chairman of the authority, said he was baffled by the reason for the improvement.

Joseph E. O'Grady, who handles labor relations for the agency, said:

"We'd like to think it's our good management. But we honestly don't know."

The passenger and revenue figures for the last four months do not include data for the new line to the Rockaways, which was opened on June 28. That line is the one major trouble spot in the authority's financial picture.

Originally, the agency had estimated that revenues on the new line would total $3,500,000 for the 1956-57 fiscal year and would result in an operating deficit of $750,000. But experience indicates that revenues will be only about $1,500,000 and that the deficit will be $2,000,000.

Even so, the authority expects to end the fiscal year with a substantial operating surplus

Continued on Page 28, Column 7

EISENHOWER ACTS

Plans Special Steps to Speed Machinery of Refugee Law

By RUSSELL BAKER
Special to The New York Times.

WASHINGTON, Nov. 8—President Eisenhower ordered "extraordinary measures" today to get 5,000 Hungarian refugees into the United States through the barrier of the Refugee Relief Act.

The President gave the act's administrators an enormous task to help Hungarian victims of what he called "the brutal purge of liberty" conducted by "imperialist communism."

To complete the job in the limited time allowed, the tough restrictive Refugee Relief Act may have to be bent, if not broken, the White House said.

The President was reported so determined to get the job done that he was prepared to take "extraordinary" action and go to Congress later for legal backing.

Pierce J. Gerety, deputy administrator of the act, said that he was prepared to relax the strict security check required for all refugees and to ease assurance requirements.

Appeal to the Nation

The problem confronting the administrators is to compress into seven weeks visa-processing work that normally takes months and sometimes a year or longer.

The act expires Dec. 31 of this year, and with it all legal authority for issuing United States visas to refugees from behind the Iron Curtain.

To help ease the job, President Eisenhower appealed to the nation today for "all Americans who are willing to give assurances of employment, housing or financial assistance" to refugees to wire Mr. Gerety, Deputy Administrator of the Refugee Relief Act, Washington 25, D. C.

"Few events of recent times have so stirred the American people as the tragic effort of Hungarian men and women to gain freedom for themselves and their children," he said. "The brutal purge of liberty which followed their heroic struggle will be long and sorrowfully remembered, not only by those

Continued on Page 12, Column 8

NOTE TO HUNGARY

Hammarskjold Asks Regime to Let In U. N. Observers

Texts of resolutions proposed in U. N. Assembly, Page 12.

By LINDESAY PARROTT
Special to The New York Times.

UNITED NATIONS, N. Y. Nov. 8—Secretary General Dag Hammarskjold asked Hungary today to admit United Nations observers to report on Soviet intervention there.

The Secretary General's message was sent this afternoon while the General Assembly, in special session, again debated the Hungarian question. The seventy-six-nation body heard a challenge to the right of the new Government of Premier Janos Kadar to be represented in the coming regular session.

The Credentials Committee, after sharp debate this afternoon, declined to approve or disapprove the Hungarian representative, Dr. Janos Szabo.

[Premier Nikolai A. Bulganin of the Soviet Union told President Eisenhower that a Soviet withdrawal from Hungary was the business of the Hungarian and Soviet Governments. Meanwhile, the Budapest regime tackled a huge task of recovery.]

Adjourned Until Today

The special session of the Assembly adjourned until 10:30 tomorrow morning. Late this afternoon, Dr. Leonardo Vitetti of Italy made known that he might introduce a resolution tomorrow, calling for action by an international police force in Hungary or along her borders.

The United States, meanwhile, accused the Soviet military authorities in Hungary of interferred with the shipment of relief goods into Hungary. A United States draft resolution asked that the Soviet Union "cease immediately" such action. It urged member nations to make contributions for refugees from Hungary, as many nations already have done.

Cuba, Ireland, Pakistan and Peru backed the proposed joint resolution. José Felix de Lequerica of Spain had previously

Continued on Page 12, Column 4

Balloonists Soar to 76,000 Feet, Then Survive Out-of-Control Fall

Plastic Navy Craft Breaks Record in Flight From South Dakota Hills

By The Associated Press.

BROWNLEE, Neb., Nov. 8—Two Navy balloonists soared to a record altitude of more than fourteen miles today. When trouble developed they plummeted unexpectedly, but safely, to earth in Nebraska's sparsely settled sandhills.

The balloon, taking off at the Stratobowl, in the Black Hills, near Rapid City, S. D., carried Lieut. Comdrs. Malcolm D. Ross, 36 years old, and Morton L. Lewis, 43, both of Washington, D. C., to 76,000 feet.

They reached that height at 10:09 A. M., Central standard time (11:09 A. M. Eastern standard time) two hours and fifty minutes after the cast-off. Outside their seven-foot pressurized aluminum globe, they saw a "dark blue-black" sky. The earth looked black, too.

They began to descend at 1,000 feet a minute. At 56,000 feet Commander Lewis radioed that they were sipping coffee and "we invite you in."

Then something went wrong. The airmen said later "we had no idea what."

The rate of descent increased to 1,400 feet a minute.

"We are cool, calm and collected," they reported. "We think we will stay with the balloon as long as we can."

They began pitching out their oxygen and radio gear trying vainly to reduce their rate of

Continued on Page 58, Column 3

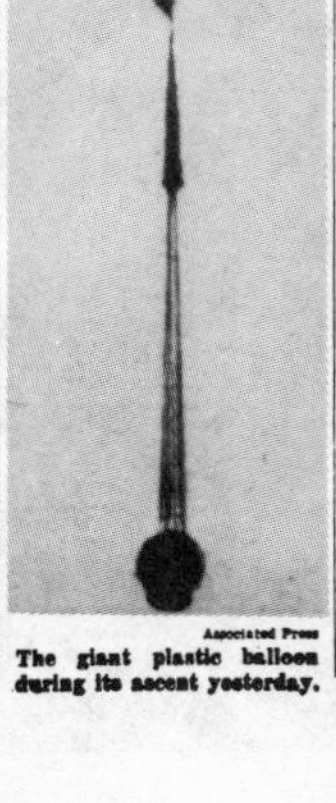

Associated Press
The giant plastic balloon during its ascent yesterday.

More Russians Volunteer For Service With Egypt

Students, Farmers and Factory Workers Apply at Cairo's Embassy—Peiping Sets Up Committee on Assistance

By WELLES HANGEN
Special to The New York Times.

MOSCOW, Nov. 8—The flood of Soviet "volunteers" for service with the Egyptian armed forces is continuing to rise.

Applications are arriving at Egyptian Embassy here from universities, institutes, youth organizations, farms and factories throughout the Soviet Union but particularly from the Moslem republics of Soviet Central Asia.

[The Peiping radio reported Communist China had formed a committee to aid Egypt.]

An Egyptian Embassy spokesman said today that "several hundred" telegrams had been received. Some are from individuals but most are collective applications by the entire personnel of a particular institution or enterprise to serve beside the Egyptian troops.

Most "volunteers" are reserve officers or enlisted men of the Soviet armed forces.

Although the number of applicants is constantly increasing, apparently the Soviet Union is prepared to hold the "volunteer" program in abeyance until the situation in Egypt has been clarified. For this reason no arrangements have been made yet between Cairo and Moscow for the actual incorporation of Soviet "volunteers" into the Egyptian forces, according to the Egyptian Embassy spokesman.

The spokesman said negotiations for Soviet material assistance to Egypt, including medical supplies, were being conducted in Cairo between Yevgeny D. Kiselev, Soviet Ambassador to Egypt, and representatives of

Continued on Page 6, Column 5

SOVIET PRESSURE ON POLAND RISING

Moscow Seeks to Forestall Sweeping Change Planned for Warsaw Government

By FLORA LEWIS
Special to The New York Times.

WARSAW, Nov. 8—Poland is again being subjected to considerable Soviet political pressure, this time to forestall sweeping changes that had been planned in the Government, according to Polish Communist sources.

The newly elected Politburo was meeting late tonight to decide what to do. The Politburo and the new First Secretary of the United Workers (Communist) party, Wladyslaw Gomulka, were chosen just over three weeks ago in defiance of Soviet demands that the old leaders be retained. At that time there were menacing troop movements to back up the Soviet demands, but since then the Russians have gone much further in Hungary.

Troop Movements Continue

So far as is known no open military threat has been made to prevent the expected drastic reorganization of the Polish Government.

But the significance of events in Hungary, of Soviet troop concentrations on Poland's eastern border, and of the continued transport of Soviet Army units across Poland to East Germany has been keenly appreciated here. Reliable Polish sources said the westward movement of Soviet troops had now gone on without interruption for six days.

The Government changes were to have been announced at the opening of the current session of Parliament Wednesday. And it was said that they would be disclosed Friday. Now a new decision from the Politburo is being awaited.

Pressure More Subtle

A wide variety of reports about the new Government have been circulating among usually well-informed Warsaw officials for the last two days. There were different versions but all of them indicated that scarcely a single minister would be left in his present job and that many new names would appear on the Cabinet and ministerial lists.

The forms of Soviet pressure have been more subtle than during the crisis of Oct. 19-20, but this time the Polish leaders are more sensitive to the power that lies behind the pressure.

Soviet dipomats are reported to have told Polish leaders during the celebration of the Russian Revolution yesterday that Government changes should be made very gradually and that only distressing consequences could result from the radical changes that were planned.

The Poles were told, in effect,

Continued on Page 18, Column 3

EGYPT TO PERMIT U.N. TEAM'S ENTRY

Observers Will Watch Suez Cease-Fire — Israeli Step on Sinai Transit Awaited

By OSGOOD CARUTHERS
Special to The New York Times.

CAIRO, Nov. 8—Egypt has agreed to permit a team of ten United Nations observers into the country to watch over the shaky cease-fire in the Suez Canal area, Maj. Gen. E. L. M. Burns said today.

General Burns, who heads the United Nations Palestine Truce Supervision Organization, said he was still awaiting Israeli approval of the plan to have observers drive across the Sinai desert—now occupied by Israel—to take up new posts in Egypt.

The observers, apparently, would supervise the cease-fire until a United Nations police force could be brought in to enforce peace.

General Burns flew to Cairo this afternoon in a United Nations white twin-engined plane from Lydda Airport near Tel Aviv. He plans to return to Jerusalem tomorrow.

His plane was the first to land in Egypt from abroad since last Tuesday. The Canadian general said he probably would be relieved of his truce supervision post when he takes over command of the United Nations police force, now being formed.

Shortly after his arrival General Burns had a short meeting with Dr. Mahmoud Fawzi, Egyptian Foreign Minister.

He said at a press conference

Continued on Page 5, Column 4

GAZA IS INCLUDED

U. S., Soviet Pressure Upon Israel Evident in the Decision

By THOMAS J. HAMILTON
Special to The New York Times.

UNITED NATIONS, N. Y., Nov. 8—Israel agreed tonight to withdraw her troops from Egypt as soon as "satisfactory arrangements" were made about the proposed United Nations police force.

Britain and France already had agreed to pull their troops out of the Suez Canal area as soon as the United Nations force could take over.

The Israeli message, therefore, brought renewed efforts to establish United Nations forces in Egypt within a week—before the danger of Soviet intervention with "volunteers" might become greater.

Based on Arrangements

The Israeli communication, delivered to the United Nations Secretary General, Dag Hammarskjold, said that "the Government of Israel will willingly withdraw its forces from Egypt immediately upon the conclusion of satisfactory arrangements with the United Nations in connection with the emergency international force."

A dispatch from Tel Aviv said that Premier David Ben-Gurion, in a late night broadcast to the Israeli people, announced that the program of withdrawal, as the United Nations force took over, would include pulling Israel's troops out of the Gaza Strip.

The report of Mr. Ben-Gurion's announcement said that the United States' and the Soviet Union's diplomatic pressures upon Israel had influenced the decision to agree to the United Nations plan.

Aqaba Isles in Doubt

It was not clear whether Israel would agree to withdraw her forces from the two small islands in the Gulf of Aqaba that she captured. They are regarded as belonging to Saudi Arabia and administered by Egypt with Saudi Arabia's consent.

The islands, merely dots on a map, are Jez Tiran and Sinafir. Their importance derives from the fact that the channel to the Israeli port of Elath passes through the island territory waters. Israel charges Egypt has been using them to interfere with shipping bound to or from Elath.

Dr. Omar Loutfi, Egyptian delegate to the United Nations, said tonight that the Israeli message was not entirely specific and that "it would have been better to comply with the resolution of the United Nations calling for their withdrawal to the armistice line."

Under the basic resolution, introduced by the United States on the evening of Nov. 1 and approved early the next morning, the emergency session of the General Assembly called for an immediate cease-fire and with-

Continued on Page 4, Column 7

Port Said Is Quiet Under Truce; British-French Build-Up Goes On

By HANSON W. BALDWIN
Special to The New York Times.

PORT SAID, Egypt, Nov. 8—This crossroads city, battered and scarred from its two days of war, was quiet today as all military operations marked time.

The unofficial but tacit truce that started at 2 A. M. yesterday was continuing, broken only by intermittent sniper fire, clean-up operations in Port Said, detonations from burning ammunition stores and one brief patrol clash on the Suez Canal road.

The British-French troop build-up in Port Said went on. But the spearhead on the canal road was still halted at Kilometer 38, a point about twenty-four miles south of here. This point is three miles north of Qantara and about twenty miles north of Ismailia.

No attempt was being made to push southward, even though a small Egyptian build-up in the Bund area north of Qantara had been reported.

A parachute regiment is on the canal road. Israeli forces have been reported on the east bank of the canal, but French troops assigned to the parachute command are expected to cover this flank.

Egyptian forces opposite the parachute command on the 100-yard front are estimated at about one company in strength, supported by a few tanks.

Meanwhile, British-French patrols with tanks probed through the rubble in Port Said. Some of it was ten to fifteen feet high in the old part of town.

Water and electricity were restored to much of the city last night and this morning. The city was without them yesterday.

The main problem now appeared to be caring for the large numbers of Egyptian wounded,

Continued on Page 4, Column 6

1957

"All the News That's Fit to Print"

The New York Times.

LATE CITY EDITION
Condensation of U. S. Weather Bureau forecast:
Sunny and cold today. Partly cloudy and milder tomorrow.
Temperature range today: 32—15.
Temperature range yesterday: 39.2—20.9
Full U. S. Weather Bureau Report, Page 46.

© 1957, by The New York Times Company.

VOL. CVI...No. 36,147. Entered as Second-Class Matter, Post Office, New York, N. Y. NEW YORK, FRIDAY, JANUARY 11, 1957. Times Square, New York 36, N. Y. Telephone LAckawanna 4-1000 FIVE CENTS

MACMILLAN SUCCEEDS EDEN AND BARS ELECTIONS NOW; MAY GET A BID TO VISIT U. S.

CHOSEN BY QUEEN

Butler Is Passed Over as Churchill Helps Sway Sovereign

By DREW MIDDLETON
Special to The New York Times.

LONDON, Jan. 10—Queen Elizabeth II chose Harold Macmillan today as Prime Minister of the United Kingdom.

The 62-year-old former Chancellor of the Exchequer and former Foreign Minister at once began the formation of a new Conservative Government to meet the pressing internal and foreign problems facing Britain.

There will be no general election, he declared. But, he added defiantly, when one occurs the Conservatives will win.

Mr. Macmillan was named Sir Anthony Eden's successor by the Queen after powerful intervention on his behalf by Sir Winston Churchill, who favored the new Prime Minister's candidacy over that of R. A. Butler, Lord Privy Seal and leader of the House of Commons.

Sir Winston and the Marquess of Salisbury, Lord President of the Council, advised the sovereign on her choice and then Mr. Macmillan was summoned to Buckingham Palace for an interview with Queen Elizabeth.

Palace Issues Announcement

After his departure the following announcement was issued from the Palace:

"The Queen received the Right Honorable Harold Macmillan, M. P., in audience this afternoon and offered him the post of Prime Minister and First Lord of the Treasury. Mr. Macmillan accepted Her Majesty's offer and kissed hands upon his appointment."

Mr. Macmillan intends to change the composition of the Conservative Government drastically, it was learned on the highest authority. His first move in foreign affairs will be to seek restoration of the old intimacy between Downing Street and the White House.

The Prime Minister is expected to use his position as an old, valued and outspoken friend of General Eisenhower to urge upon the President a more sympathetic attitude toward Britain's international problems, especially in the Middle East, and a realistic appraisal of the present state of the trans-Atlantic alliance.

Although Mr. Macmillan represents the right wing of the Conservative party, Mr. Butler,

Continued on Page 2, Column 3

Associated Press Radiophoto

QUEEN'S CHOICE: Harold Macmillan outside his home in London after Queen Elizabeth had named him Prime Minister.

Invitation by White House To Macmillan Is Expected

By DANA ADAMS SCHMIDT
Special to The New York Times.

WASHINGTON, Jan. 10—Administration officials said today they expected an invitation soon from President Eisenhower to Britain's new Prime Minister, Harold Macmillan, to visit him here. This was Washington's way of welcoming Mr. Macmillan's appointment.

Although Mr. Macmillan fully backed his predecessor, Sir Anthony Eden, in the invasion of Egypt, Administration officials thought the change in leadership would make it easier to bridge differences between the United States and Britain on the Middle East and to refresh their traditional cooperation on world issues.

This is just what Sir Anthony, before his resignation, hinted he would have liked to do. But President Eisenhower rebuffed his overtures. Presumably the President resented Sir Anthony's concealment from him of Britain's plan to attack Egypt.

Friendship to U. S. Stressed

In most comments today, Mr. Macmillan's reputation as a good friend of the United States and his long personal association with President Eisenhower and Secretary of State Dulles outweighed the preference of many officials for R. A. Butler.

Mr. Butler, in contrast to Mr. Macmillan, was known to have opposed the Suez venture.

Mr. Dulles, in many meetings before and after he became Secretary of State, established a close, first-name relationship with Mr. Macmillan. When Mr. Macmillan was appointed Foreign Secretary in 1955, Mr. Dulles sent him a telegram of congratulation.

"You well know my conviction," Mr. Macmillan replied, "that the fundamental interests and ideals of our two countries are the same and that if there

Continued on Page 2, Column 6

HUNGARY INQUIRY VOTED BY U. N., 59-8

5-Nation Committee to Hear Refugees—Soviet Group Opposes It—10 Abstain

By KATHLEEN TELTSCH
Special to The New York Times.

UNITED NATIONS, N. Y., Jan. 10—The General Assembly voted today to establish a five-nation committee to watch the situation in Hungary.

The committee will take testimony from refugees who have fled from Hungary since the revolt against Soviet control broke out in Budapest last October.

Establishment of the committee was approved, 59 to 8, with ten abstentions. The resolution was co-sponsored by the United States and twenty-three other states. The text of the resolution was printed in The New York Times Wednesday.

The eight opposing votes came from the Soviet Union and its allies, indicating that Moscow would not heed a provision in the resolution that it help the committee enter Hungary for an investigation.

[In a broadcast, Hungary declared that no United Nations inquiry group would be allowed within her borders.]

Hungarians Stay Away

Most of the resolution's supporters, in fact, have acknowledged that they do not think the present resolution, the eleventh on Hungary, will persuade either Moscow or Budapest to alter the refusal to admit United Nations observers.

Hungary's delegation stayed away from the Assembly meeting, in keeping with its policy of boycotting all sessions on this issue.

The five nations named in the resolution to serve on the inquiry panel are Australia, Tunisia, Ceylon, Denmark and Uruguay. A Uruguayan spokesman said tonight it was hoped that the five could hold a preliminary meeting tomorrow afternoon and get a quick start on the fact-finding mission.

The vote on the twenty-four-power resolution showed much the same line-up as on the Assembly resolution adopted Dec. 12, which condemned the Soviet Union's military intervention in Hungary and called for the with-

Continued on Page 3, Column 3

NOW AT KNABE. Trade-in Piano Sale. Save on grands, spinets & consoles. KNABE, 10 E. 48 St. PL 3-3300—Advt.

U. N. CHIEF STUDIES 3-STAGE SUEZ PLAN

Weighs Negotiations to Find Definitive Settlement

By THOMAS J. HAMILTON
Special to The New York Times.

UNITED NATIONS, N. Y., Jan. 10—Dag Hammarskjold, Secretary General of the United Nations, has under consideration a three-stage plan for negotiating a definitive Suez settlement.

The three phases would be the following:

1. Since Egypt refuses to sit in the same room with British and French representatives, the Secretary General would act as an intermediary to relay suggestions between the two sides.
2. Assuming that sufficient progress was made by this method, there would be exchanges of views in Mr. Hammarskjold's office between British, French and Egyptian representatives. This was the method used in the discussions here last October, before the outbreak of hostilities.
3. Assuming that the second stage also proceeded satisfactorily, three or four additional nations would join the final stage of negotiations, which thus would be a round-table conference.

Mr. Hammarskjold, according to reliable sources, has mentioned the possibility of including Norway, Italy and Ceylon. Norway is a principal user of

Continued on Page 5, Column 3

Chou May Caution Poles to Slow Revolt

By M. S. HANDLER
Special to The New York Times

WARSAW, Jan. 10—Premier Chou En-lai of Communist China is scheduled to arrive tomorrow from Moscow.

The small group of Polish Communists who forced through the liberalizing October revolution are no longer awaiting the Chinese Premier's five-day visit in cheerful expectation.

They expect that Mr. Chou may urge Wladyslaw Gomulka, First Secretary of the United Workers (Communist) party, and his associates to slow down the revolution to a walking pace and minimize differences with the Soviet Union because the world situation requires the solidarity of Communist countries.

At the time the Premier's visit was first announced, the Poles were hopeful of obtain-

Continued on Page 3, Column 5

ACHESON ASSAILS PLAN FOR MIDEAST AS A WAR 'THREAT'

'Reckless' Idea Not a Policy but a Plea to Congress to Devise One, Inquiry Told

Text of Acheson statement will be found on Page 4.

By RUSSELL BAKER
Special to The New York Times.

WASHINGTON, Jan. 10—Dean Acheson took a critical look today at the Administration's new Middle East proposal and pronounced it vague, meaningless, hackneyed and dangerous.

In presenting the plan to the public and Congress, the former Secretary of State said, the Administration used "reckless talk" and "vague phrases" freighted with the "catastrophic threat" of nuclear war.

In fact, Mr. Acheson argued before the House Foreign Affairs Committee, the so-called Eisenhower doctrine is not a policy at all, but merely an "invitation" for Congress to devise one.

He strongly advised against granting the President legislative stand-by authority to fight "overt" Communist aggression in the Middle East. As interpreted by John Foster Dulles, Secretary of State, this authority apparently would give the White House a blank check to resort to nuclear war, Mr. Acheson said.

Resolution Suggested

He urged, instead, that Congress confine itself to framing a resolution that would express the "sense" of the Congress about United States interests and responsibilities in the Middle East.

In this way, he suggested, the Congress effectively can declare American intentions in the area while advising the President as to the course he should follow in the formulation and conduct of Middle East policy.

Mr. Acheson spent four and a half hours in the witness chair before the committee, which has been conducting hearings on the Middle East proposal since Monday.

The hearings arose from President Eisenhower's request for Congressional authority to use United States force against overt aggression in the Middle East by any Communist-dominated power. The President also proposed a two-year, $400,000,000 program of economic aid for the Middle East. The money would be spent in ways unspecified.

Most Seem Unsure

The long questioning of Mr. Acheson today by the Representatives indicated that they, for the most part, were baffled by and unsure about the complicated Middle East problem and the meaning of the action they were being asked to take.

The session was enlivened by an exchange between Mr. Acheson and Representative John M. Vorys, Republican of Ohio, about foreign policy under the Truman Administration. This was highlighted by an inconclusive debate over whether Mr. Acheson, Mr. Vorys or General

Continued on Page 4, Column 6

BUS RUNS HALTED IN ALABAMA CITY AFTER 6 BOMBINGS

4 Negro Churches and Homes of 2 Ministers Attacked in Montgomery Outbreak

By The Associated Press.

MONTGOMERY, Ala., Jan. 10—The worst outbreak of violence in the fight over bus segregation left Montgomery without public transportation today.

City authorities halted bus service indefinitely after nighttime bombing attacks on four Negro churches and the homes of two anti-segregation ministers. One of the ministers is white. No one was reported injured.

The City Commission order suspending busline operations "until further notice" forced thousands of bus riders, white and Negro, to find other means of transportation to and from work.

[In Atlanta, five Negro ministers were arrested for refusing to observe the state law on segregated seating on a city bus. The group sought a court test of the law.]

Extra Police Called Out

Police Commissioner Clyde Sellers ordered all auxiliary policemen on duty, and the commission suggested a midnight curfew for teen-agers.

There was the possibility of a Federal investigation of the violence. The Justice Department in Washington said the Federal Bureau of Investigation was looking into it to see if a Federal law had been violated.

Meanwhile in Mobile, 200 miles to the southwest, an explosion slightly damaged a Negro's home. Attempts were made, the police said, to bomb the homes of two others.

In Montgomery the Rev. Robert Graetz, a white clergyman who has fought against segregation, escaped unhurt with members of his family when one of the bombs tore down a door at his home.

11 Sticks of Dynamite

But the police said another bomb tossed in Mr. Graetz' front yard might have caused death or serious injury except for a faulty fuse. Officers found eleven sticks of dynamite tied to a metal tube.

Detective Capt. E. P. Brown said police experts hoped to get fingerprints from a rack attached to the bomb, but that the dynamite itself had been thrown in the river.

Officers removed the two-foot fuse. But Captain Brown said the department had no demolition specialists and the bomb was "too dangerous to fool with."

The bomb throwers also shattered the home of another integration leader, the Rev. Ralph D. Abernathy, a Negro minister, and four churches, including the First Baptist, where Mr. Abernathy is pastor.

Part of the basement and roof were damaged at the first church. Across town other bombs ripped large holes in the Bell St. Baptist Church and the Mount Olive Church. The Hutchinson Baptist Church near Mr. Abernathy's home was also hit. Part

Continued on Page 13, Column 2

One-Way Traffic Approved For 3 Arteries in Midtown

Broadway, Sixth and Seventh Avenues Are Affected in Shift Due Feb. 17

By CHARLES G. BENNETT

Traffic Commissioner T. T. Wiley's plan for extending one-way traffic operation in midtown sections of Broadway, Seventh Avenue and the Avenue of the Americas was unanimously approved yesterday by the Board of Estimate.

In accepting Mr. Wiley's plan, the board overrode opposition voiced by Fifth Avenue Coach Lines, Inc., and Local 100 of the Transport Workers Union. The coach company operates buses over the three avenue segments.

The board's action constituted one more step in effectuating Mr. Wiley's traffic control plan for Manhattan. The plan is designed to reduce congestion and accidents, shorten travel time and increase the traffic-carrying capacity of crosstown streets.

The over-all plan calls for ultimate one-way operation on all of the north-south arteries, except Park Avenue. It also calls

Continued on Page 46, Column 2

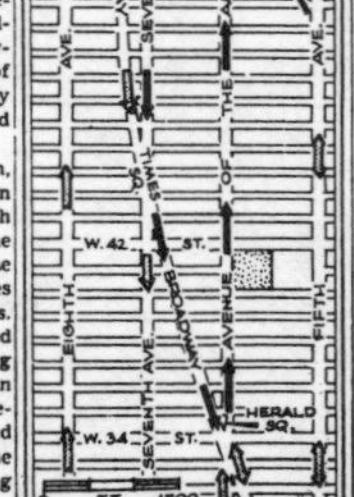

The New York Times Jan. 11, 1957

New one-way patterns approved by city board are shown by heavy arrows, existing ones by light arrows.

PRESIDENT'S MESSAGE PUTS STRESS ON INFLATION PERIL; RENEWS PLEA ON MIDEAST

RESTRAINT URGED

State of Union Report Bids Business and Labor Cooperate

Text of President's message is printed on Page 10.

By W. H. LAWRENCE
Special to The New York Times.

WASHINGTON, Jan. 10—President Eisenhower warned Congress today against the dangers of inflation from excessive price increases, wage rises or Government spending.

His preoccupation with inflation and its threat to the United States economy stood out in a generalized Message on the State of the Union delivered in person before a joint session.

Republicans and Democrats listened without enthusiasm. They interrupted with applause only five times as compared with fifty-seven interruptions in the 1953 message, forty-five in the 1954 message, and twenty in 1955.

The 1956 message was not delivered in person because the President still was convalescing from the heart attack he suffered in September, 1955.

This address differed from previous messages on the State of the Union in that it did not contain many specific legislative recommendations. These were reserved for the Budget Message, which will be submitted Jan. 16, and some special messages later.

Repeats Mideast Appeal

The President discussed in general terms the state of the nation's economy and the role of the United States in world affairs. He restated basic Administration aims at home and abroad, but offered no major new proposals.

He reiterated his appeal of last Saturday for swift action on a resolution pledging armed resistance by this country to any effort by international communism to take over any countries of the Middle East.

He argued anew the need for cooperation with the rest of the free world to counter the continuing threat of "a strongly armed imperialistic dictatorship." The nation, he said, must remain strong, militarily and economically.

While he reported "an unprecedented peak in our economic prosperity," General Eisenhower devoted a considerable section of his speech to the con-

Continued on Page 10, Column 3

Associated Press Wirephoto

RESPONDS TO APPLAUSE: President Eisenhower just after he had completed delivery of his address to Congress.

Eisenhower Asks Controls For 'Outer Space' Missiles

By JACK RAYMOND
Special to The New York Times.

WASHINGTON, Jan. 10—President Eisenhower proposed today international control of "outer space" missile and satellite development as a disarmament measure. It was the first time that any world statesman had brought up the subject of controls against military use of the projectiles designed to be fired beyond the earth-enveloping air.

The President's offer to enter a "reliable agreement" in this field was made in his State of the Union message. Presumably it covers intercontinental ballistics missiles and types of artificial earth satellites.

It will be presented to the United Nations by Ambassador Henry Cabot Lodge Jr. next week as one of the elements in a new approach to disarmament. The United States hopes its pending program will break the stalemate in negotiations with the Soviet Union.

A Primary 'Truth'

Though President Eisenhower referred to coming disarmament negotiations as "a major part of our quest for a confident peace in this atomic age," he related these negotiations to a broad foreign policy program.

He stated it as a primary "truth," that "America alone and isolated cannot assure even its own security."

He asked Congress to authorize this country's membership in the Organization for Trade Cooperation as a contribution to improving conditions of free world trade.

He said he would also ask Congress to authorize participation in the new International Atomic Energy Agency. He endorsed West European efforts to cooperate in the field of atomic energy and to establish a common market. He repeatedly

Continued on Page 6, Column 5

CONGRESS REACTS CALMLY TO SPEECH

President's Report, Setting a Moderate Course, Is Viewed as Constructive

By JOHN D. MORRIS
Special to The New York Times.

WASHINGTON, Jan. 10—Congress found little to cheer or criticize in President Eisenhower's Message on the State of the Union today, but that seemed to be the way the President wanted it.

By a deliberately restrained speech devoted mainly to enunciating broad principles accepted by all Americans, the President achieved what perhaps was his chief purpose.

That, by all signs, was to set a tone of moderation and understanding for relations between the Republican Administration and the Democratic Congress.

Republicans and Democrats alike found no fuel for major new partisan fires in the few specific legislative recommendations.

With two or three exceptions, such as monetary and public power policies, all issues raised by President Eisenhower promised to stir controversy of factional rather than party nature. Chief among these was his civil rights program, which brought the customary dissent from Southern Democrats.

Johnson Praises Message

The broad outlook, as indicated by Congressional reaction to the President's message, was for a continuation of the generally satisfactorily working relations that have characterized a politically divided Government in the last two years of the Republican President's tenure.

Such a prospect was particularly evident in the comments of Senator Lyndon B. Johnson of Texas, the leader of the narrow Democratic majority in the Senate. As in the last two years, Mr. Johnson must depend on a coalition of conservative-to-middle-of-the-road Senators for action on much legislation.

The majority leader said the President had given "a comprehensive and thoughtful analysis of the problems which confront our people today and the broad policies which he believes suitable to the resolution of such problems," Senator Johnson added.

"The Senate, together with the House, will study carefully these problems and policies. In a cooperative and constructive spirit, I am confident that we will legislate the best judgment of our

Continued on Page 11, Column 4

Fund Voted to Start 2 Bridge Projects

By JOSEPH C. INGRAHAM

The Port of New York Authority allotted $13,000,000 yesterday to start construction of the often-delayed $600,000,000 arterial highway relief program.

The authorization was contained in the agency's 1957 budget, which anticipates a record expenditure of $223,614,500. It is the first budget in the authority's thirty-six years to exceed $200,000,000. It includes capital expenditures of $148,561,900, mainly for airport expansion.

In adopting the budget, the commissioners authorized $10,386,400 to start work on the second lower deck of the George Washington Bridge and $2,778,600 for the proposed Narrows Bridge.

The commissioners of the bi-state agency also approved

Continued on Page 12, Column 4

ALBANY MAY KEY JOB AID TO PRICES

Both Parties Favor Raising Benefits as Costs Rise

By A. H. RASKIN

The state may for the first time gear its insurance programs for unemployed, sick and injured workers to changes in the cost of living.

Ranking members of the Harriman Administration and the Republican-controlled Legislature indicated yesterday that they favored providing an inflation hedge along the line of the escalator clauses now contained in many major union contracts.

Under these labor-management agreements, wages go up when the consumer price index rises. A floor is usually provided to limit wage cuts when prices decline.

In his message to the Legislature Wednesday, the Governor confined himself to a recommendation that the ceiling on unemployment insurance, workmen's compensation and sickness disability benefits be raised to $45 a week. The present top is $40 for sickness and $36 for job and compensation payments.

The Republican legislative program suggested that there be no fixed maximum benefit. Instead, the majority party proposed that workers qualifying for state insurance get a peak payment equal to one-half the average weekly wage of production workers. This figure would

Continued on Page 47, Column 3

"All the News That's Fit to Print"

The New York Times.

LATE CITY EDITION
Condensation of U.S. Weather Bureau forecast: Partly cloudy today; snow or rain likely late tonight or tomorrow.
Temperature range today: 38—25.
Temperature range yesterday: 39.4—23.
Full U. S. Weather Bureau Report, Page 62.

VOL. CVI..No. 36,200. Entered as Second-Class Matter. Post Office, New York, N. Y. NEW YORK, TUESDAY, MARCH 5, 1957. Times Square, New York 36, N. Y. Telephone LAckawanna 4-1000 FIVE CENTS

BEN-GURION ORDERS WITHDRAWAL; GEN. BURNS AND ISRAELIS ARRANGE GAZA AND AQABA TAKE-OVER BY U.N.

Associated Press Radiophoto

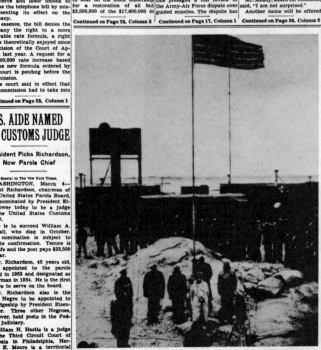

U. N. FORCE IS READY: Maj. Gen. E. L. M. Burns, left, U. N. Emergency Force commander, and Maj. Gen. Moshe Dayan, Israeli Chief of Staff, complete plans for Israeli withdrawal from Gaza Strip and Gulf of Aqaba coastal area in favor of troops of United Nations. The officers conferred for seventy minutes at Lydda Airport, near Tel Aviv.

ASSEMBLY VOTES BILL TO PREVENT PHONE RATE RISE

Sends Measure to the Senate On a 120-to-24 Ballot—No Debate Is Held

HARRIMAN BACKS CURB

But Asserts Company Has Right to Spend $500,000 to Tell Public Its Side

Special to The New York Times.

ALBANY, March 4—The Assembly passed and sent to the Senate tonight a bill designed to block approval of a $55,400,000 rate increase sought by the New York Telephone Company.

The vote was 120 to 24. There was no debate. All the negative votes were cast by Republican members. Approval of the measure in the Assembly had been forecast since it was reported by committee last week at the behest of Speaker Oswald D. Heck.

In the Senate there is no present assurance that the measure will be approved. Opposition there is reported to center on the majority leader, Senator Walter J. Mahoney, who so far has not signaled the emergence of the bill from committee.

'Outrageous,' Says Harriman

Governor Harriman earlier branded as "an outrageous piece of business" the company's attempt to obtain a rate increase on a standard different from that applied to other utilities.

He said in a radio interview that he did not feel it was "proper" for the company to try to justify higher rates on the basis of a formula not available to gas and electric companies and other quasi-public industries under government regulation.

Mr. Harriman asserted that he had "no basic objection" to the company spending $500,000 in the last three months in an attempt to defeat a bill that would return it to the same status as other utilities.

"They've got a right to put their case before the public," he said, "even if the utility does collect back from the consumer the money it spends on this kind of campaign. I believe in free discussion of these things."

'Propaganda' Charged

The Public Service Commission charged yesterday that the company had spent that much money in a "propaganda campaign" and had succeeded in persuading some chambers of commerce and labor unions to oppose the telephone bill by misrepresenting its effect on the company.

In essence, the bill denies the company the right to a more favorable rate formula, a right it has theoretically enjoyed since a decision of the Court of Appeals last year. A request for a $55,400,000 rate increase based on the new formula ordered by the court is pending before the commission.

The court said in effect that the commission had to take into

Continued on Page 23, Column 1

U. S. AIDE NAMED A CUSTOMS JUDGE

President Picks Richardson, Now Parole Chief

Special to The New York Times.

WASHINGTON, March 4—Scovel Richardson, chairman of the United States Parole Board, was nominated by President Eisenhower today to be a judge of the United States Customs Court.

He is to succeed William A. Ekwall, who died in October. The nomination is subject to Senate confirmation. Tenure is for life and the post pays $22,500 a year.

Mr. Richardson, 45 years old, was appointed to the parole board in 1953 and designated as chairman in 1954. He is the first Negro to serve on the board.

Mr. Richardson also is the first Negro to be appointed to a judgeship by President Eisenhower. Three other Negroes, however, hold posts in the Federal judiciary.

William H. Hastie is a judge of the Third Circuit Court of Appeals in Philadelphia, Herman E. Moore is a territorial

Continued on Page 20, Column 5

State Road Plans Snarled By Political Tugs of War

Study of Long-Range Program Linked to National System Finds a Financial Muddle and Lack of Initiative

By JOSEPH C. INGRAHAM

New York State's highway program is as snarled as the traffic it is supposed to relieve.

Virtually every highway expert in and out of public office agrees that the state's millions of motor-vehicle users face long delays in getting new and better roads. Moreover, there is growing concern that some hoped-for construction may be curtailed owing to rising costs and specific restrictions of highway allotments.

For obvious reasons, mainly fear of political reprisals, most of the experts asked to remain unidentified. But a consensus showed that the prime reason for the confused highway picture was the jockeying for political advantage between the Harriman administration and Republican legislative leaders.

A general lack of initiative at the top level of highway administration, coupled with a conservative budgeting attitude, also was mentioned for the lag and for a lack of clarity in meeting road problems.

There is no clear idea of how much money is required to meet the demands for better roads and new routes. The cost varies with the source with estimates ranging from a total program of $3,810,000,000 to one of more than $5,000,000,000. In some instances different units in the same agency are working with different figures.

One thing has become distressingly clear, the experts agree. In spite of Governor Harriman's emphasis on highway improvements it is apparent that his administration expects to be aided more heavily than most states by the Federal $33,800,000,000 road program.

In essence, the critics hold that the state's program will be

Continued on Page 24, Column 1

G. O. P. WON'T ACT ON 'LUXURY' RENTS

State Chiefs Bow to Demand in City and Leave Ruling on Curbs to Weaver

Special to The New York Times.

ALBANY, March 4—Republicans agreed at a top policy conference today to leave the decontrol of luxury apartments to Robert C. Weaver, State Rent administrator.

They had been debating among themselves the desirability of exempting such accommodations from rent controls in a bill to extend state curbs for two more years.

Abandonment of the idea resulted from strong pressure brought on the Republican legislative leadership by Thomas J. Curran, New York County Republican chairman.

Most of the luxury apartments that would be affected are in New York County. Moreover, they are concentrated in areas where the Republican party has its greatest strength in New York.

Mr. Curran and other New York City Republican leaders were likewise bringing pressure to bear on the state leadership for a restoration of all but $2,500,000 of the $17,600,000 in

Continued on Page 23, Column 3

Colonel Will Face Open Army Trial On Missiles Leak

Special to The New York Times.

WASHINGTON, March 4—A public general court-martial was ordered today for Col. John Nickerson Jr., senior officer at Redstone Arsenal in Huntsville, Ala., the Army's major ballistic missile agency.

One of the charges is that Colonel Nickerson divulged secret documents "relating to the national defense of the United States and containing information which he had reason to believe could be used to the injury of the United States or to the advantage of a foreign nation."

He is alleged to have turned over to representatives of industrial concerns and newspaper men copies of official documents and his own memorandum disputing Defense Department policies on the development and utilization of guided missiles.

Lieut. Gen. Thomas F. Hickey, Third Army commander, directed that "only if true national security is in jeopardy of compromise will the court enter into executive sessions in the course of the court-martial." The directive was issued from headquarters at Fort McPherson in Georgia.

According to some sources, this presaged a full review of the Army-Air Force dispute over guided missiles. The dispute has

Continued on Page 17, Column 1

MITCHELL REJECTS BECK AS DELEGATE TO I. L. O. SESSIONS

Acts After Seeing McClellan —Notes Teamster Chief's Failure to Testify

By JOSEPH A. LOFTUS

Special to The New York Times.

WASHINGTON, March 4—The Government shortened Dave Beck's European itinerary today.

James P. Mitchell, Secretary of Labor, announced he would not appoint the labor leader as a United States representative to an International Labor Organization meeting as Mr. Beck had expected. The meeting is set for March 11 through March 23 in Hamburg, Germany.

Secretary Mitchell acted after conferring with Senator John L. McClellan, Democrat of Arkansas and chairman of the Select Senate Committee on Labor and Management Practices.

The committee wants Mr. Beck, who is president of the International Brotherhood of Teamsters, to testify at hearings. Mr. Beck had advised Senator McClellan he would be back in this country about March 26, after the I. L. O. meetings.

Two Were Recommended

The Hamburg meeting was called by the Inland Transport Committee of the I. L. O. The I. L. O. is a United Nations agency and is made up of government, employer, and employe representatives.

In January, George Meany, president of the American Federation of Labor and Congress of Industrial Organizations, according to custom, recommended two unionists to be the labor representatives from the United States. One was Mr. Beck, the other Howard Ulrich of the Brotherhood of Railway and Steamship Clerks.

Secretary Mitchell, in a statement tonight, said that after Mr. Beck's name had been recommended to him the Senate committee invited the labor official to testify on teamster union affairs.

Name To Be Offered

"He has thus far failed to do so," said Mr. Mitchell, "giving as one reason among others that he expected to be out of the country attending the Inland Transport Committee meetings in Hamburg.

"Therefore, I have decided not to nominate Mr. Beck as a member of the United States delegation to the Hamburg conference." The secretary said he would ask Mr. Meany for a substitute recommendation.

Mr. Meany, asked for comment, said, "I am not surprised."

Another name will be offered

Continued on Page 26, Column 2

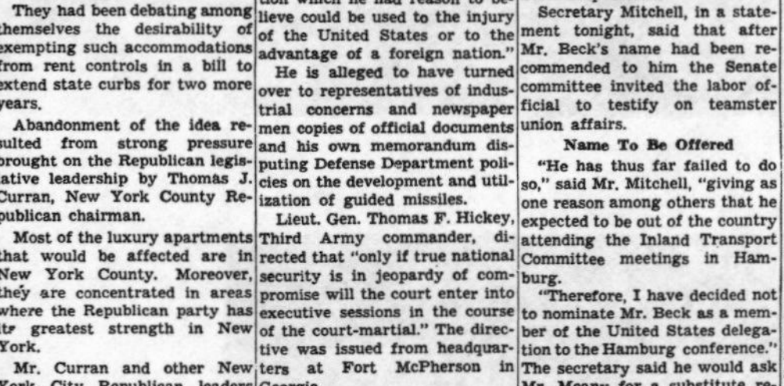

The New York Times (by Walter Sullivan)

HISTORIC OCCASION IN ANTARCTICA: On Feb. 16 the American flag was flown for first time over an outpost in Wilkes Land at commissioning ceremony for Wilkes Station.

(A full page of photographs of Antarctic expedition is on Page 15)

SENATE MAY VOTE ON MIDEAST TODAY

Leaders Expect a Sweeping Victory for the President —Aid Projects Ready

By WILLIAM S. WHITE

Special to The New York Times.

WASHINGTON, March 4—The Senate opened today its third week of debate on President Eisenhower's Middle East proposals.

The Democratic leader, Lyndon B. Johnson of Texas, said he hoped that a final vote could be reached tomorrow.

The resolution would commit the United States, at the President's discretion, to use military force against any Communist aggression in the Middle East wherever a victim asked for help.

It would permit the President to spend free of present restrictions up to $200,000,000 of already appropriated foreign aid funds for special projects in the Middle East.

John B. Hollister, director of the International Cooperation Administration, announced at a news conference that these projects could be put into motion rapidly once Congress had finally acted.

Mr. Hollister said James P. Richards, who will head a special mission to the Middle East,

Continued on Page 5, Column 1

DUES CHECK-OFF BY CITY BLOCKED

U. S. Bars Housing Authority Move on Union Deductions

By A. H. RASKIN

Federal officials have prohibited the City Housing Authority from instituting a check-off of union dues.

The city agency had voted to deduct the dues from the salaries of any of its 6,000 employes who authorized such action. The decision was in line with a policy approved by the Board of Estimate last year for most city departments.

Under the policy, the unions pay all the administrative costs of the check-off program. Individual employes are free to cancel their authorization any time they wish to stop paying union dues. The program is open to all unions of Civil Service workers.

Herman D. Hillman, regional director of the Federal Public Housing Administration, notified the city last week that the proposed check-off was "objectionable and contrary to the long-standing policy of the P. H. A."

Even though the veto applied only to projects built with Federal subsidies, the City Housing

Continued on Page 26, Column 5

Russia and India, in U. N., Score Israel 'Assumptions'

By THOMAS J. HAMILTON

Special to The New York Times.

UNITED NATIONS, N. Y., March 4—The Soviet Union and India launched an attack today on the "assumptions" under which Israel has agreed to withdraw from the Gaza Strip and the Gulf of Aqaba area.

Arkady A. Sobolev, the Soviet delegate, told the General Assembly that the "assumptions" would lead to the indefinite occupation of both areas by the United Nations Emergency Force.

Israel's statement and excerpts from debate, Page 4.

He charged that Israel would not be using such "delaying tactics" if she did not have the support of the United States and of Israel's "partners in aggression," France and Britain.

Right of Control Stressed

Mr. Sobolev added that it should be remembered that when "the sword of war" hung over Egypt, Egypt did not find herself alone. He emphasized that "dozens" of powerful "peace-loving states" had sufficient means to put an end to aggression "from whatever quarter and wherever it occurred," including the Middle East.

Arthur S. Lall of India insisted that Egypt had a right to control the Strait of Tiran, at the mouth of the Gulf of Aqaba, and that Egypt also had the right to resume full control of the Gaza Strip, which she has administered under the Israeli-Egyptian armistice of 1949.

Mrs. Golda Meir, Israeli Foreign Minister, announced at the start of the meeting that Maj. Gen. Moshe Dayan, Israeli Chief of Staff, and Maj. Gen. E. L. M. Burns, commander of the United Nations Emergency Force, had "come to full agreement as to the technical details for the withdrawal and take over."

Hammarskjold Confirms

At the close of the meeting Dag Hammarskjold, United Nations Secretary General, confirmed the agreement. He gave no details, but said that he had instructed General Burns "to arrange for full and unconditional withdrawal of Israel's military and civilian units with initial take-over exclusively by the United Nations Emergency Force."

The Assembly adjourned tonight without fixing the date of its next meeting. It is expected to resume the debate Thursday. Arab delegates insist that by that time Israel should have completed the withdrawal. It was understood, however, that the final withdrawal will take about a week.

Dr. Mahmoud Fawzi, Egyptian Foreign Minister, told the Assembly that Israel's withdrawal should take place "in a day or two at most." He warned that Israel would be held accountable by the Assembly if the withdrawing forces committed atrocities and destructions" like those that, he said, were commit-

Continued on Page 4, Column 2

CAPITAL RELIEVED BY ISRAEL ACTION

State Department Now Aims at Removing Arab Fears of U. S. Concessions

By DANA ADAMS SCHMIDT

Special to The New York Times.

WASHINGTON, March 4—United States officials generally welcomed somewhat wryly today the order by Premier Ben-Gurion of Israel for a withdrawal from the Gaza Strip and the Gulf of Aqaba area.

The attitude of these officials was that any further delay in carrying out the pledge made by Mrs. Golda Meir, Israeli Foreign Minister, at the United Nations last Friday would have been difficult to understand.

Lyndon B. Johnson, leader of the Democratic majority in the Senate, issued one of the few formal statements on the subject in the capital today. He said Premier Ben-Gurion was "to be congratulated."

It is now "the obligation of the responsible nations of the world to move as rapidly as possible to bring the difficult problems of the Middle East to a solution," the Senator said.

He asserted that this effort must be made in spite of "obstructionist efforts by the Soviet Union." Although Soviet trouble-making was "not exactly news," he observed it was "somewhat unusual that the

Continued on Page 6, Column 5

STUDENTS PROTEST

Military Agreement to Be Referred to Hammarskjold

By SETH S. KING

Special to The New York Times.

JERUSALEM, March 4—Premier David Ben-Gurion ordered the Israeli Army today to withdraw from the Gaza Strip and the Gulf of Aqaba region.

The Premier's abrupt action came after he apparently had persuaded his coalition Government to hold together against a move to call off the withdrawal.

Soon after the Premier's decision, the first step toward the withdrawal of Israeli troops was taken at a meeting at Lydda Airport, in central Israel, by Maj. Gen. E. L. M. Burns of Canada, commander of the United Nations Emergency Force, and Maj. Gen. Moshe Dayan, Israeli Chief of Staff.

The two generals reached full agreement on the replacing of the Israeli units in the Gaza Strip and the Gulf of Aqaba area with troops from the United Nations force.

Cabinet Meeting Canceled

Details of the arrangements for the withdrawal were withheld pending a report by General Burns to Dag Hammarskjold, United Nations Secretary General.

The Burns-Dayan meeting was the climax of a series of events that began early this morning.

After a night-long conference with his party leaders, Premier Ben-Gurion suddenly canceled a Cabinet meeting that had been scheduled for this afternoon. He also called off an appearance before the Knesset (Parliament).

General Dayan was ordered to make contact with General Burns as soon as possible to arrange for a "prompt and complete withdrawal" from the Gaza Strip and from Sharm el Sheikh, at the mouth of the Gulf of Aqaba.

Mr. Ben-Gurion will still face a restless Knesset tomorrow afternoon. But he now has a majority behind him.

Regime Said to Be Secure

"Nothing can stop the withdrawal now," a Foreign Ministry official said tonight. "Nor is it likely that the Government will fall, although Mr. Ben-Gurion's prestige may be badly dented."

This afternoon Jerusalem's streets were filled with groups of students protesting the withdrawal. The police were called out to break up several demonstrations. Twelve persons were arrested at the height of one meeting.

Sound trucks roamed through the city tonight as representatives of the right-wing Herut (Freedom) party called for more protest meetings tomorrow. Herut members have demanded a vote of no confidence in Mr. Ben-Gurion when the Knesset meets.

The Israeli Premier is risking his political future because of his "faith in the international community," a Government spokesman said.

"The basic question now is whether world opinion will be brought to bear on Egypt to abandon her policy of belliger-

Continued on Page 4, Column 7

Nasser Vexed by Nixon's Tour Of Nations at Odds With Egypt

By HOMER BIGART

Special to The New York Times.

CAIRO, March 4—Egypt continues to take a cynical view of President Eisenhower's Middle East policies despite a grudging admission that the United States was the compelling force in the Israeli decision to withdraw.

President Gamal Abdel Nasser is reported to be disturbed at signs that the United States is attempting to isolate him. Washington's "playing up" to King Saud of Saudi Arabia was annoying enough.

More vexing was Vice President Richard M. Nixon's itinerary. For next week Mr. Nixon will visit three neighboring countries whose relations with Cairo are strained.

Two of these countries, Ethiopa and the Sudan, are seeking economic and military aid from the United States. Libya, the third country, tends toward acceptance of the Eisenhower Doctrine.

President Nasser's dream of hegemony over these countries is jarred by any suspected intrusion of foreign influence. Thus the Cairo press is putting the most sinister interpretations on the Nixon tour.

[Prime Minister Kwame Nkrumoh of the Gold Coast, which becomes Ghana Wednesday, told Vice President Nixon in Accra Monday that the new nation "could never be neutral" in the "cold war."]

Today's Rose el Youssef had a cartoon depicting the Vice Pres-

Continued on Page 5, Column 4

Spencer Tracy is seen here in the classic The Old Man and the Sea.

Mildred Natwick helps Tammy (Debbie Reynolds) with her make-up in a scene from Tammy and the Bachelor.

"All the News That's Fit to Print"

The New York Times.

© 1957, by The New York Times Company.

LATE CITY EDITION
Condensation of U.S. Weather Bureau forecast:
Mostly fair today; rather cloudy tonight and tomorrow.
Temperature range today: 43—28.
Temperature range yesterday: 41.9—23.
Full U. S. Weather Bureau Report, Page 62.

VOL. CVI..No. 36,201. Entered as Second-Class Matter, Post Office, New York, N. Y. NEW YORK, WEDNESDAY, MARCH 6, 1957. Times Square, New York 36, N. Y. Telephone LAckawanna 4-1000 FIVE CENTS

SENATE APPROVES EISENHOWER PLAN FOR MIDEAST, 72-19

HOUSE MUST ACT

Two Versions Differ—President May Get Bill This Week

Text of the Senate's version of the resolution, Page 8.

By WILLIAM S. WHITE
Special to The New York Times.

WASHINGTON, March 5—The Senate approved tonight a solemn warning by the United States against Communist aggression in the Middle East.

It adopted by a vote of 72 to 19 the Eisenhower Administration resolution pledging this country to use military force to keep the peace and to supply immediate economic-military aid to Middle Eastern countries in need.

The substance of the policy now approved by the Senate had been voted by the House of Representatives on Jan. 30 by vote of 255 to 67.

President Eisenhower in a special message on Jan. 5 had asked the Democratic - controlled Congress to join him in this proclamation of United States determination.

Thus the Senate's action came just two months from the day he had requested it.

Resolution Goes to House

The Senate version of the resolution involved a revision of what the President first had asked and what the House itself had approved.

The Senate's text now will be sent to the House, which may adopt it without argument or may insist on conferences between the two chambers to reconcile the differences.

If the House adopts the first and more probable course—that of quick concurrence with the Senate version—the resolution will reach the President for his signature before the end of the week.

$200,000,000 in Aid

A principal point in the text passed by the Senate was a declaration of high policy that the United States, if the President should deem it necessary, would commit its military forces against Communist aggression in the Middle East wherever a victim requested help.

The second main point was an authorization to the President to spend free of restrictions up to $200,000,000 in already appropriated foreign aid funds for special projects to strengthen the Mid-

Continued on Page 8, Column 3

STATE TO REPEAT INCOME TAX CUTS; BUDGET REDUCED

Legislature Votes Maximum Credit of $35 for Persons and Small Concerns

1.5 BILLION TO BE SPENT

G. O. P. Trims Harriman's Program by 30 Million—Asks 'Gas' Levy Rise

By LEO EGAN
Special to The New York Times.

ALBANY, March 5—The Legislature voted today to continue for this year the $40,000,000 personal income tax reduction it approved last year.

At the same time it approved another Republican bill to cut taxes due this year from unincorporated businesses and small corporations by $1,690,000.

The personal income tax reduction will allow the taxpayer to deduct 15 per cent from the first $100 of tax owed and 10 per cent from the next $200. The Governor has said that he will sign the measure.

The two measures were sent to Governor Harriman along with a state budget providing for expenditures estimated at $1,586,585,518. The budget total is $30,810,482 less than the one recommended by Governor Harriman.

Bill to Raise 'Gas' Tax

While the budget and tax cuts were under debate, the Legislature received a bill to increase gasoline and Diesel fuel taxes by 1 cent and 1½ cents a gallon, respectively, effective next Jan. 1.

The revenue from these increases would be used to finance the $4,536,800,000, ten-year highway construction program recommended by the Temporary Highway Finance Commission.

Two other bills to implement commission recommendations were also submitted. One would set up a special highway construction account in the budget bureau. The other would allocate 15 per cent of the collections from the motor fuel tax increase to counties for highway building.

Battle in Prospect

The three measures were introduced by the Senate and Assembly Rules Committees at the request of Senator Earl W. Brydges, Republican of Niagara Falls, and Assemblyman Ray S. Ashbery, Republican of Trumansburg, near Ithaca. Both were members of the commission.

Indications are that the gasoline tax increase faces heavy going in the Legislature. Many upstate Republicans have committed themselves against it. Assemblyman Eugene F. Bannigan of Brooklyn, the Democratic minority leader, promised that

Continued on Page 24, Column 4

CAUDLE, CONNELLY GET 2 YEARS EACH

Former Truman Aides Fined $2,500 in Tax Conspiracy

Special to The New York Times.

ST. LOUIS, March 5—T. Lamar Caudle and Matthew J. Connelly, former officials in the Truman Administration, were sentenced to two years in prison and fined $2,500 each today on charges of conspiring to defraud the Government in an income tax case.

Before pronouncing sentence, United States District Judge Gunnar H. Nordbye overruled a motion for a new trial. The defense contended that the late United States Judge Rubey M. Hulen had not been "in a proper mental and physical condition" to conduct their trial.

Judge Nordbye, who took over the case after Judge Hulen was found shot dead three weeks after the trial ended, permitted the defendants to remain at liberty on $5,000 bonds pending an appeal.

Judge Hulen had been scheduled to enter a hospital on the day he was found shot in the rear yard of his home. A revolver was near by. A coroner's jury returned an open verdict, saying it could not determine whether death was accidental.

Caudle, former head of the Justice Department's Tax Division, and Connelly, former appointments secretary to President Truman, were convicted by a jury here last June 14. They

Continued on Page 21, Column 5

Negro Nation of Ghana Is Born in Africa

Associated Press Radiophoto

Vice President Richard M. Nixon meets a tribal chieftain on campus of Accra University

Gold Coast Becomes Ninth Member of Commonwealth

By THOMAS F. BRADY
Special to The New York Times.

ACCRA, Ghana, Wednesday, March 6—A new Negro nation was born at midnight.

As the British flag was lowered from the staff of the Legislative Assembly here and the new red, green and gold flag bearing a star rose in its place, the British colony known as the Gold Coast ceased to exist and the sovereign state of Ghana became the ninth member of the Commonwealth.

Prime Minister Kwame Nkrumah had told the final session of the colony's Legislative Assembly a few minutes earlier that the "chains of imperialism and colonialism which have hitherto bound us to Britain" were left behind as Ghana redeemed "her lost freedom."

Ghana is the name of the ancient West African empire that flourished about a thousand years ago. After it disintegrated, it remained a legend of Negro power and magnificence.

Attending the celebrations of the rebirth of Ghana are representatives of more than fifty nations, including the Soviet Union and Communist China. Vice President Richard M. Nixon heads the United States delega-

Continued on Page 12, Column 3

PRESIDENT GIVES DROUGHT AID PLAN

Wants the States to Assume at Least 25% of Certain Disaster Operations

By W. H. LAWRENCE
Special to The New York Times.

WASHINGTON, March 5—President Eisenhower proposed to Congress today that the states pay 25 per cent of certain farm disaster relief operations.

The Administration's future drought relief program was submitted to Congress in a special message by the President. It was explained in more detail in an accompanying letter from Ezra Taft Benson, Secretary of Agriculture.

Agricultural Department officials estimate the states now pay less than 1 per cent of agricultural disaster relief operations, which in the last three and one-half years cost $658,000,000.

They would not estimate the chances of getting Congressional approval for forcing the states to pay more, nor would they specify in detail the precise programs for which they want state governments to put up one-fourth of the cost.

Based on Drought Tour

The President's message was based on his drought tour in mid-January and conferences with state and local officials that followed it.

With the President's backing, Secretary Benson also proposed in the most general terms an expanded program of "deferred grazing," meaning payments to farmers who leave drought-stricken grass lands to grow and hold moisture by removing their herds.

But there was no official estimate as to how large in acreage this program would be, nor what it would cost. The issue, officials said, still was under study in the Administration.

But it was made clear that the Administration program was less ambitious than the measure sponsored by Representative W. R. Poage, Texas Democrat, which already has passed the House. This measure, fought by the Administration, would cost about $25,000,000 annually, according to Mr. Poage.

Program Deals with Floods

Agriculture aides said the programs presented today dealt not alone with droughts, but also with floods, the effects of hurricanes and other natural disasters that deal a heavy blow to agriculture.

Basically, the program offered was a continuance of the ones in effect, with some modifications.

The most notable change proposed was that the states be required to pay a minimum of 25 per cent "in certain future emergency agricultural programs for disaster relief."

But officials were unwilling to say which programs, or how much this might cost the states.

"Most state legislatures are now in session," Secretary Ben-

Continued on Page 22, Column 6

Oregon Officials Linked To Union in 'Whitewash'

By JOSEPH A. LOFTUS
Special to The New York Times.

WASHINGTON, March 5—Senators heard today that a link between certain union officials and a Governor of Oregon and a District Attorney led to the "whitewash" of the State Liquor Commission. The witness before the Select Committee on Labor and Management Practices again was James B. Elkins, confessed racket operator who is cooperating with the committee. The Governor, now dead, was Paul Patterson. The other official was William M. Langley, District Attorney of Multnomah (Portland) County, who is now under indictment. Mr. Langley is scheduled to testify before the committee this week.

The committee also heard:

¶That two women opened a house of prostitution on assurances that the District Attorney would not molest them.

¶That a teamster union official plotted with Elkins to use inside information on a city building project to make a big profit on real estate.

¶That a union official's air travel card was used for a gambler's trip to see a prize fight.

Ousted Aide Reinstated

Elkins related that when a liquor commission official was discharged for accepting gratuities, a teamster official said it was time to "run a test to see whether we have bought a pig in a poke or whether he can perform." This was an allusion to the Governor.

The discharged official was reinstated and lost only a month's pay.

Elkins also told how the Attorney General tried to get an order from the Governor to conduct the liquor commission investigation and was refused; how Mr. Langley, after conferences with the Governor, undertook the "whitewash."

The witness said there had been actually two indictments

Continued on Page 26, Column 3

Fluoridation Faces Public Clash Today

By CLARENCE DEAN

A prolonged and stormy hearing on fluoridating the city's water to cut tooth decay is expected today.

By yesterday afternoon, more than 200 persons had notified the Board of Estimate that they wished to be heard. Arrangements were made to accommodate 600 by using both the board's chamber and the City Council chamber, linked by a public address system.

The Mayor had announced earlier that everyone who wished to speak would be heard. This made it inevitable that the hearing would last at least all day.

The emotion that has marked the controversy, as well as the intensiveness of the preparations being made by both sides, also indicated that the session would be dramatic.

It will present, among other

Continued on Page 36, Column 6

AUTO UNION PLANS 'COURT' OF APPEAL

Rank and File Could Turn to Outside Panel for Review of Disciplinary Cases

By A. H. RASKIN

The United Automobile Workers plans to set up an outside appeals "court" to which its 1,385,000 members can turn if they feel they have not received justice from the union's own disciplinary machinery.

A specific review program is being worked out by Walter P. Reuther, president of the union, and its international executive board for action by 3,000 delegates at the union's biennial convention in Atlantic City next month.

Approval of the plan would make the auto union the first major union to establish an impartial tribunal to protect the democratic rights of its rank and file. However, one smaller organization — the 60,000-member Upholsterers International Union—has had such a program in operation for three years

To Insure Fair Treatment

The upholsterers have a nine-man panel of jurists, educators and public officials, with authority to act on complaints that members have not had a fair trial or have been punished arbitrarily within the union. Only one member has appealed since the panel was appointed in 1954, and the union's executive board was upheld in that case.

Sal B. Hoffmann, president of the union, said last night that the upholsterers felt the experiment in union democracy had proved a success.

"It has given the union's members confidence that they will receive fair treatment," Mr. Hoffmann said, "and it has kept the executive boards of the international union and of all its locals on their toes to make certain that there will be no injustices to submit to the review board."

A spokesman for the United Auto Workers said that no decision had yet been made on the precise form of appeals machinery to be set up in that union, but that the aim was to make it wholly independent of direct union control. Special attention has been given to the upholsterers' program as a possible model.

No protests against the conduct of union trials have prompted Mr. Reuther and his

Continued on Page 26, Column 6

BRITAIN TO TRIPLE NUCLEAR ENERGY

Revised Program Will Cost $2,573,200,000 When It Is Completed in 1965

By DREW MIDDLETON
Special to The New York Times.

LONDON, March 5—The British Government has adopted a bold program to triple production of nuclear energy for industry by 1965. It will cost $2,573,200,000.

The dawn of "a new power revolution" was announced by Lord Mills, Minister of Power, in the House of Lords today. The goal of the program is a capacity of between 5,000 and 6,000 megawatts (a megawatt equals 1,000,000 watts) of electricity by nuclear power stations eight years hence.

Twenty of these stations are to be built, one of them in Northern Ireland. A full year's operation of these stations at capacity would save the nation 18,000,000 tons of coal, which Lord Mills called "our main, practically our only natural resource."

Tripling nuclear power also will help to counteract the British economy's dependence on oil imports. These have been drastically reduced since Egypt blocked the Suez Canal. The Soviet infiltration into the Middle East, in the opinion of the Cabinet, makes the future availability of oil supplies doubtful.

The boldness of the Government's approach to the solution of the nation's power problems is demonstrated by a comparison

Continued on Page 15, Column 3

AID STUDY BACKS OUTLAYS ABROAD AT PRESENT PACE

President's Advisory Group Doubts the Program Can Come to an End Soon

Text of major findings in the report is on Pages 16-17.

By EDWIN L. DALE Jr.
Special to The New York Times.

WASHINGTON, March 5—A special advisory committee reported to President Eisenhower today that the nation's foreign aid and collective security programs "are proving their worth, and we should hold firmly to them."

The committee of seven private citizens was appointed last year to survey the whole subject of foreign aid.

Their report today said outlays abroad "need not exceed" present levels. Such levels, they said, "should under present conditions be adequate to provide a reasonable expectation of achievement of the goals of United States foreign policy without undue strain on the domestic economy."

The group expressed "hope" that foreign aid spending might decline in time, but added:

"The United States must resolve to stay the course and must abandon the false hope that collective security costs are temporary."

Fifty Recommendations

The report put the current annual level of foreign assistance at $8,000,000,000. This included not only the regular military and economic aid program but also farm surplus sales for local currencies, spending of dollars by American military forces abroad and gross new loans by the Export-Import Bank.

The report contained about fifty recommendations for changes or shifts in emphasis in the program. But few were specific and some appeared contradictory. There was no detailed analysis either of individual country's programs or of the various categories of foreign aid.

But the major conclusion was stated without qualification: that both military and economic aid programs had successfully countered Soviet expansion and should be continued.

Some Took World Tour

The committee was headed by Benjamin F. Fairless, former chairman of the board of the United States Steel Corporation. Some of its members undertook a world tour in which they visited many of the countries now being aided.

The major new specific recommendation in the report was that each Congress, rather than each session of Congress, vote a foreign aid program. This would mean that each foreign aid bill would cover two years, making possible "more efficient planning and utilization of funds."

The report was equivocal on perhaps the most controversial question about foreign aid: whether the United States should undertake an enlarged program of aid to the underdeveloped countries. Most of the largest

Continued on Page 18, Column 5

Israel Pins Her Economic Hope On Oil Line and Aqaba Transit

Looks to Negev Fuel Conduit as an Alternative Route From Mideast to Europe

By KATHLEEN TELTSCH
Special to The New York Times.

UNITED NATIONS, N. Y., March 5—A stretch of oil pipeline and free transit for Israeli shipping in the Gulf of Aqaba could open a new economic future for Israel.

This prospect evidently weighed significantly in Israel's decision this week to evacuate her troops from Egyptian territory on the assumption that Israeli vessels would move unmolested to Elath through the Strait of Tiran into the gulf.

Elath is now a small coastal port at the head of the 100-mile-long gulf. But Israeli planners see the day when trade through the gulf will open Pacific and Indian Ocean ports to Israeli commerce.

As they see it, Israel's chemical industry will be able to supply Far East countries with needed fertilizers. Potash from the Dead Sea would go as far as Japan and a new prosperous era would begin for Israel, which

The New York Times March 6, 1957

Route of projected pipeline

has been struggling for years to sustain her economy.

The first link of the planned

Continued on Page 3, Column 5

U. N. Rule in Gaza Is Seen in 2 Days

By THOMAS J. HAMILTON
Special to The New York Times.

UNITED NATIONS, N.Y., March 5—Dag Hammarskjold informed his advisory committee tonight that the United Nations was ready to take over the provisional administration of the Gaza Strip within forty-eight hours.

The administration would be under Maj. Gen. E. L. M. Burns, commander of the United Nations Emergency Force, with the assistance of United Nations civilian officials. The Secretary General told the committee that the officials were already stationed in nearby areas, awaiting the Israeli withdrawal.

One reliable source said tonight that he understood that Israel planned to begin the withdrawal from the Gaza Strip tonight. Arrangements were completed yesterday between General Burns and Maj.

Continued on Page 5, Column 4

ISRAEL'S PREMIER DEFENDS DECISION

Ben-Gurion Urges His Nation to Accept 'Settlement' in Return for Withdrawal

Excerpts from Ben-Gurion's speech are on Page 6.

By SETH S. KING
Special to The New York Times.

JERUSALEM, March 5—Premier David Ben-Gurion called on his people tonight to accept the "settlement" offered to Israel in return for the withdrawal of her troops.

Facing one of his gravest hours as Israel's leader, Mr. Ben-Gurion told the Knesset (Parliament) that he was keenly aware of the dangers involved in pulling Israeli units out of the Gaza Strip and the Gulf of Aqaba area.

But Israel's immediate need to absorb thousands of immigrants and to expand the foundations of her economy made it essential for her to risk these dangers, the Premier declared.

[Mr. Ben-Gurion was expected to win Wednesday when he would be faced by a motion of no confidence offered by Opposition parties, The Associated Press said.]

He Stresses Security Need

In defending his decision to withdraw behind the 1949 armistice lines, Mr. Ben-Gurion said the struggle for Gaza and Sharm el Sheikh, at the mouth of the Aqaba Gulf, must be regarded as having been "staged in a prolonged process" of consolidating Israel's security.

The problem of maintaining this security had, as a result of the Sinai campaign, now become "a question of conscience for many states," the Israeli leader declared.

The United States and other nations have "approved" Israel's assumption that the United Nations will administer the Gaza Strip until a peace settlement has been reached, he said.

"In spite of all this, I must state that there is no certainty that the Egyptians will not return as a civilian administration, or through military occupation," Mr. Ben-Gurion said.

Gaza Is Called Trouble Spot

"But I must shatter an illusion that has taken root among many of us," he continued. "The Gaza Strip under any regime and any administration is a source of trouble so long as the refugees have not been resettled elsewhere. Anyone who speaks of the Gaza Strip without understanding all the complications and dangers arising out of the composition of its population is living in a fool's paradise."

There was no guarantee that the United Nations Emergency Force would be kept at Sharm el Sheikh, Mr. Ben-Gurion said, but Israel's occupation of this area had not been in vain.

"It has aroused the public opinion of the world, especially the great maritime countries,"

Continued on Page 6, Column 2

DULLES REPROVES EGYPT OVER SUEZ

Says Cairo 'Drags Its Feet' in Clearance Operations

The transcript of Dulles news conference is on Page 4.

By DANA ADAMS SCHMIDT
Special to The New York Times.

WASHINGTON, March 5 — Secretary of State Dulles said today that Egypt had shown "a tendency to drag its feet" in the matter of clearing the Suez Canal.

He expressed hope at his news conference for a change on Egypt's part when evidence reaches Cairo that Israeli troops are evacuating the Gaza Strip and the Gulf of Aqaba area.

He added that the Canal, which has been obstructed since the Israeli and British-French invasions of Egypt last fall, probably could be reopened in about ten days "if the work goes ahead vigorously."

Other State Department officials said that although no direct word had come from the Egyptians, "we do have good reason to believe that final clearance will now go ahead."

Lieut. Gen. Raymond A. Wheeler, chief of the United Nations Suez project, has been waiting for Egyptian permission to remove two sunken craft. A twenty-five-foot-deep channel could then be opened and 75 per cent of normal traffic resumed,

Continued on Page 4, Column 4

Eddie Albert, Errol Flynn, Tyrone Power and Ava Gardner starred in the film version of Hemingway's novel, The Sun Also Rises.

The Bridge on the River Kwai was a huge success, both critically and financially. Alec Guinness won an Academy Award for Best Actor and the film was named Best Picture. William Holden and Jack Hawkins also starred.

The Girl Can't Help It established Jayne Mansfield as the most popular of all Marilyn Monroe imitators.

"All the News That's Fit to Print"

The New York Times.

LATE CITY EDITION
U. S. Weather Bureau report (Page 49) forecasts: Rain, drizzle early today; brightening later. Fair and warm tomorrow.
Temp. range: 64—54. (Yesterday's: 58.6—50.6)

VOL. CVI..No. 36,252. NEW YORK, FRIDAY, APRIL 26, 1957. Times Square, New York 36, N. Y. Telephone LAckawanna 4-1000 FIVE CENTS

U.S. ORDERS 6TH FLEET TO MIDEAST, SAYS COMMUNISTS MENACE JORDAN; HUSSEIN PROCLAIMS MARTIAL LAW

EISENHOWER ASKS FULL DISCLOSURE OF LABOR FUNDS

Administration Calls for Laws to Wipe Out 'Abomination' of Union Racketeering

RANK AND FILE PRAISED

President and Mitchell Put Stress on Moves to Block 'Punitive' Legislation

Text of Eisenhower statement appears on Page 14.

By W. H. LAWRENCE
Special to The New York Times.

AUGUSTA, Ga., April 25—The Eisenhower Administration decided today to ask Congress for full public disclosure of union receipts and expenditures.

James P. Mitchell, Secretary of Labor, reported the interim legislative program for labor after a ninety-minute conference with President Eisenhower at the President's temporary office at the Augusta National Golf Club.

Mr. Mitchell said the legislative proposals had grown out of evidence of improper practices already developed by the Senate Select Committee on Improper Activities in the Labor or Management Field. The committee is headed by Senator John L. McClellan, Democrat of Arkansas.

Secretary Mitchell warned against a "headlong" rush "impelled by the hysteria of the moment to secure punitive legislation aimed at undermining or weakening the general body of organized labor."

A Request Renewed

He said the Administration proposals were designed to strengthen the rights of the union rank and file and to "help the American labor movement to clean house in those areas where they need help."

Specifically, the President and the Secretary of Labor renewed their three-year-old request to Congress that it pass laws providing for the registration, reporting and disclosure of funds deposited under welfare and pension plans.

In addition, Secretary Mitchell said the President also had approved a proposal that Congress authorize the Labor Department to make public the reports now filed with it concerning union funds in general under the Taft-Hartley Act. Those reports now are not made public.

Secretary Mitchell indicated that the Administration later might ask Congress for Federal review and audits of the union financial statements. These are

Continued on Page 14, Column 3

Associated Press Wirephoto
CONFER IN GEORGIA: President Eisenhower with James P. Mitchell, Secretary of Labor, in Augusta yesterday. They drew plans for laws dealing with labor unions.

M'CLELLAN WARNS OF 'GANGSTERISM'

Tells Publishers Momentum of Rackets Perils U. S.—Mrs. Luce Chides Press

Text of McClellan's speech will be found on Page 16.

The chairman of the Senate committee investigating union rackets said last night that it intended to continue its exposures of wrongdoing until Congress had enough information to "clean up the mess."

Senator John L. McClellan, Democrat of Arkansas, made his statement at a dinner of the Bureau of Advertising of the American Newspaper Publishers Association. He predicted that the investigation, which he said was still in its early stages, would produce legislation to protect union members, management and the public.

The committee chairman, speaking at the Waldorf-Astoria Hotel, warned that racketeering now had enough momentum to bring about a "gangsterism economy" and threaten liberty in the United States if it were not stopped.

'Shock Troops' of Diplomacy

Mrs. Clare Boothe Luce, former Ambassador to Italy, urged the press and public to support the American Foreign Service. Mrs. Luce spoke of the "shock troops of our diplomatic front lines" and termed them a vital instrument for the preservation of world peace.

The occasion, the Bureau of Advertising's forty-fourth annual dinner, marked the end of the seventy-first annual convention of the bureau's parent organization, the American Newspaper Publishers Association. It also marked the end of New York's annual Press Week.

As Senator McClellan spoke, preparations were made for a closed hearing on labor-management abuses in the New York area at the United States Court House today. Three officials of one of the union locals under investigation were indicted by a New York County grand jury yesterday on charges of steal-

Continued on Page 16, Column 2

De Sapio Leadership Extolled by Wagner Before Party Chiefs

By CLAYTON KNOWLES

Ringing praise for Carmine G. De Sapio and predictions of a great victory for Mayor Wagner this fall marked speeches at the annual dinner of the New York County Democratic Committee last night.

The Mayor, a candidate for re-election, was lavish in proclaiming the "forceful, dynamic, political brilliance" of Mr. De Sapio, leader of the Tammany organization for the last eight years.

About 2,200 persons attended the $50-a-plate dinner, which was held at the Commodore Hotel.

In his text Mr. Wagner said also that Mr. De Sapio had set "an example of undivided allegiance to the principles of good government—of government devoted exclusively to the needs and the welfare of the people."

Called Friend of Decency

Extemporizing in delivery, he added that Mr. De Sapio had been the "stalwart friend of decency, honesty and integrity in government." He said he was "proud to call him my friend."

The extent of the accolade took on significance in view of the start next Monday of public hearings by the Republican-dominated legislative committee into the Joseph (Socks) Lanza parole case.

Lanz has Tammany connections. And there has been reference to aid sought from "the man with the glasses." Mr. De Sapio, who wears dark tinted glasses, has scoffed at the suggestion that the reference might have been to him.

In his own speech last night, Mr. De Sapio said that he still felt, as he had when he as-

Continued on Page 12, Column 4

PRESIDENT PLANS OIL IMPORT STUDY; SEES PERIL TO U.S.

Gets O.D.M. Report Warning of Rise in Foreign Fuel —Quotas May Result

By RICHARD E. MOONEY
Special to The New York Times.

WASHINGTON, April 25—President Eisenhower announced today he would order an investigation to determine whether imports of crude oil threatened national security. He asserted "there is reason for the belief" that such a threat exists.

The President, in Augusta, Ga., acted after receiving advice from Gordon Gray, Director of the Office of Defense Mobilization. Mr. Gray said that the trend of imports and forecasts for coming months had given reason to believe there was a threat. Mr. Gray released his and the President's memoranda at a news conference here.

If the President finds a threat to national security, he is required by law to take action that will reduce imports. This presumably would be done by placing them under quota limitations or by raising the tariff.

Independents Skeptical

General Eisenhower asked Mr. Gray to explore the possibility of limiting imports by voluntary action. This would be done while the Presidential investigation was under way.

Major importers might prefer voluntary restrictions, rather than legal quota limitations or higher tariff charges. But the independent producers in this country, with no overseas operations, feel efforts for voluntary curtailment are futile.

The question of import limitation has been introduced by the appeal of a number of independent companies, They contend that national security is being threatened because increased oil imports discourage exploration for new oil resources in this country—resources on which the United States would depend in time of war.

Voluntary Pact Sought

The Office of Defense Mobilization has tried for two years to get voluntary agreement among importers. Mr. Gray's certification to the President that a threat exists is the most forceful step that has been taken so far. In fact, it is the first such action under the law—Section 7 of the Trade Agreements Extension (Reciprocal Trade) Act of 1955.

The actual Presidential order for an investigation awaits the selection of a group to make the study, and the preparation of necessary papers.

The United States produced more than 2,600,000,000 barrels (forty-two gallons a barrel) of crude oil last year, or an average of more than 7,100,000 barrels a day. Refineries consumed a little more than 2,900,000,000 barrels.

On the basis of pure physical capacity, the nation's wells

Continued on Page 5, Column 4

KING SCORES CAIRO

Installs a New Cabinet —Vows Fight to the Finish on Reds

By OSGOOD CARUTHERS
Special to The New York Times.

AMMAN, Jordan, April 25—King Hussein proclaimed today a fight to the finish against a conspiracy to overthrow him. He imposed martial law and formed a new Government.

The 21-year-old monarch charged openly for the first time that the conspiracy was getting its support from Egypt.

Moving swiftly, the King placed the principal cities of Amman, Jerusalem, Ramallah, Nablus and Irbid under a total curfew. He also placed the Jordanian police force under direct command of the Army.

[The Associated Press reported from Amman that King Hussein had abolished Jordan's ten political parties.]

The monarch appeared to have emerged as a mature and grimly determined fighter, defending his throne against efforts by Egypt and Syria to turn Jordan into their anti-Western satellite.

His imposition of an armored fist on the Palestinian part of Jordan and his warning, in a pre-dawn broadcast, that "conspiracies might take away the remaining part of Arab Palestine" made clear that he would fight to prevent cession of the west bank and would be ready against possible Israeli attack.

Plans Carefully Laid

Events moved swiftly last night, but it was evident that the King's plans had been carefully laid. During the early evening the Government of Premier Hussein Fakhri Khalidi finally carried out an earlier decision to quit.

The Khalidi Government had been formed on the basis of support of all parties, including the National Socialists, the left-wing Baath (Resurrection) party and their pro-Communist supporters. That support was withdrawn the day before yesterday and these parties, encouraged by the Cairo radio, called the people out on a general strike and ineffective riots.

King Hussein was ready for these developments. He kept the rioters tightly confined and there was no bloodshed. In addition the monarch had a new Cabinet at his palace, ready and waiting to take over as soon as the Khalidi Government resigned.

The new Government is headed by Ibrahim Hashem, 69 years

Continued on Page 3, Column 3

The New York Times April 26, 1957
NAVAL MOVEMENT: Ships of the United States Sixth Fleet left Cannes (1) and Naples (2) to deploy in the eastern Mediterranean, perhaps from Egypt to Turkey (3), in a measure to help Jordan (4) remain independent.

Nasser Sees Syria's Leader On Mounting Jordan Crisis

By HOMER BIGART
Special to The New York Times.

CAIRO, April 25—In an atmosphere of deepening crisis, President Gamal Abdel Nasser conferred again tonight with President Shukri al-Kuwatly of Syria on what to do about Jordan. The Egyptian President is reported eager to avoid any break with King Hussein of Jordan.

But the formation of an avowedly pro-Western government in Amman has sharpened Egyptian suspicions of some grand strategic design by the Western powers to bring Jordan into the Baghdad Pact.

In an apparent effort to patch up relations with King Saud of Saudi Arabia, who has been backing Hussein, President Nasser will send a three-man mission to Riyadh tomorrow. Mr. al-Kuwatly will accompany the Egyptian team and it was reported that he would later go to Amman for a talk with King Hussein.

President Nasser's decision to send a special mission to Saudi Arabia came after he had received a message from King Saud, the contents of which were not disclosed. The Egyptian mission will consist of President Nasser's political adviser, Col. Ali Sabry, Sheikh Hassan el Bakouri, Minister of Works, and Anwar el Sadat, head of the Islamic Congress and publisher of the newspaper Al Gomhouria.

Chief Aides at Talks

Mr. al-Kuwatly arrived unexpectedly this morning from Damascus and for several hours Egypt tried to keep his arrival secret. The Cairo radio finally broke the news at 2:30 P. M. after Damascus had announced Mr. al-Kuwatly's departure for Egypt.

President Nasser and President al-Kuwatly conferred for three hours and met again tonight in another emergency session. The Egyptian Commander in Chief, Gen. Abdel Hakim Amer, and the Syrian Chief of Staff, Gen. Tewfik Nizam el-Din, attended both meetings.

Also present were Colonel Sabry, the Syrian Foreign Minister, Salah Bitar, and the Syrian Minister of Public Works, Fakhir Kayyali.

No communiqué was issued. Diplomatic sources speculated that neither President Nasser

Continued on Page 4, Column 1

MOSCOW ACCUSES U. S. OF MEDDLING

Broadcast Attacks 'Blatant Interference' in Jordan— Hussein Also Scored

By The Associated Press.

LONDON, April 25—Moscow accused the United States tonight of "blatant interference" in the internal affairs of Jordan.

An anonymous commentator on the Moscow radio's home service said the Jordanian situation remained tense amid an "atmosphere of deep internal political crisis."

The Moscow radio said the United States, "by means of behind-the-scenes machinations, is trying to set up a Jordanian Government that would adopt the aggressive Eisenhower Doctrine and give up the policy of protecting the national interests and [Jordan's] unity with other free Arab countries."

Later tonight, an Arabic-language broadcast from Moscow said, "One is surprised, to say the least, at what King Hussein said about international communism seeking to destroy Jordan." King Hussein, in interviews yesterday, attributed Jordan's troubles to international Communist propaganda and subversion.

U. S. Agitation Alleged

The commentator went on:

"We cannot but see in this statement an unsuccessful attempt to stir up suspicions against the Soviet Union. It is well known that the Soviet Union has never interfered in the internal affairs of Jordan. On the contrary, the Soviet Union has always firmly supported the struggle of the Jordanian people against all imperialists to build up their free and independent country.

"We must also point out that this statement is but a repetition of the false allegations that are being used by American propaganda to lay responsibility and consequences on others."

The broadcast said "the intervention of United States diplomacy in the internal affairs [of Jordan] is getting more open and brazen."

Dulles' Speech Criticized

By WILLIAM J. JORDEN
Special to The New York Times.

MOSCOW, April 25—The Soviet Union's leaders insisted tonight they were not trying to export the Communist revolution. They said they could not understand why Secretary of State Dulles insisted on advocating a policy of "liberation" from communism for the countries of Eastern Europe.

The Kremlin roundly castigated Mr. Dulles for the speech he made before a gathering of American editors three days ago. A statement criticizing his speech and attributed to "leading circles of the Soviet Union" was

Continued on Page 3, Column 2

A SHOW OF FORCE

British Also Say a Free Jordan Is Essential to Mideast Peace

By DANA ADAMS SCHMIDT
Special to The New York Times.

WASHINGTON, April 25—The United States deployed its military and political power today to assure the survival of an independent Jordan.

It sent the Sixth Fleet, with the aircraft carrier Forrestal, hurrying back from the western to the eastern Mediterranean so suddenly that 150 sailors were left stranded on leave in Paris.

[A British Foreign Office spokesman said that Jordan's independence and integrity were "essential elements" in maintaining Middle East peace.]

The United States also began to set out the political justification for any future intervention. This justification is, in the Administration's view, that Jordan is menaced by the forces of international communism.

A State Department declaration to this effect, following a similar statement by King Hussein of Jordan yesterday, seemed designed to make the Eisenhower Doctrine applicable in the struggle over Jordan.

Statement Expanded

The declaration expanded President Eisenhower's statement yesterday in Augusta, Ga., that preservation of Jordan's independence was "vital to the national interest."

Lincoln White, press officer of the State Department, read this statement:

"The statement issued in Augusta, Ga., represented a reminder to the world by the President that a finding had been made in the Joint Resolution of the Congress on the Middle East [the Eisenhower Doctrine] that the preservation of the independence and integrity of the nations of the Middle East was vital to the national interest of the United States and to world peace.

"This reminder was appropriate because of the threat to the independence and integrity of Jordan by international communism as King Hussein himself stated."

Generally, according to Administration experts, international communism works indirectly in Jordan through the left-wing and extremist nation-

Continued on Page 2, Column 4

CITY BARS HOUSING AT CANCER CENTER

Relocation Problems Cited —Bridge Routes Filed

By CHARLES G. BENNETT

After months of hearings, the Board of Estimate yesterday rejected a proposal to build a $6,500,000 middle-income housing project in Yorkville.

The proposal had been made by the Memorial Center for Cancer and Allied Diseases, the Sloan Kettering Institute and the Rockefeller Institute for Medical Research.

The board acted on two other major items of city business.

It received and referred to city agencies the plans for Brooklyn and Staten Island approach routes to the Narrows Bridge and for the Queens and Bronx approaches to the Throgs Neck Bridge. Robert Moses, chairman of the Triborough Bridge and Tunnel Authority, submitted the plans.

The board approved $25,000 to put under way initial studies of the rehabilitation of the downtown area of Brooklyn, including the feasibility of a sports center that would serve as a home for the Brooklyn Dodgers baseball team.

In the case of the rejected Yorkville project, the sponsoring institutions had sought permission for nearly two years to construct two buildings. One would be for nurses and would contain 287 apartments. The other was for technical, research and professional personnel. It was to have 189 apartments.

The site for the proposed im-

Continued on Page 17, Column 5

Recording by Lanza Is Reported Missing

By LEO EGAN

A tape recording of one conversation between Joseph (Socks) Lanza and his wife and others at the Westchester County jail was reported missing yesterday.

The disclosure was made by Arthur L. Reuter, Acting State Commissioner of Investigation. The Commissioner is conducting one of two investigations into the dismissal of parole violation charges against Lanza, a convicted extortionist.

The missing recording was made a half-hour before Lanza's release on Feb. 20. He had been arrested as a parole violator on Feb. 5. His release followed the dismissal of the charges against him by Parole Commissioner James R. Stone.

Commissioner Stone subsequently resigned from the Parole Board while being questioned about his decision by

Continued on Page 15, Column 2

N. Y. U. Hospital Is Planned, With Research Chief Goal

This is a drawing of the new nineteen-story hospital building that will rise at New York University-Bellevue Medical Center. The architects are Skidmore, Owings & Merrill.

By ROBERT K. PLUMB

Plans for a new hospital to make the New York University-Bellevue Medical Center a pioneering scientific research institution were announced yesterday. The plans call for a nineteen-story building of white brick and glass just south of Thirty-fourth Street and east of First Avenue. But the plans tell only part of the story. For it is the intention of New York University medical men to use the new $20,000,000 institution to find out how to reduce the time lag between laboratory science and bedside medical practice. Other possible improvements in medicine may in part be "built into" the new hospital,

Continued on Page 18, Column 3

A. E. C. Aide Says Dr. Schweitzer Errs

By EDWARD L. DALE Jr.
Special to The New York Times.

WASHINGTON, April 25—The scientist member of the Atomic Energy Commission sharply disputed today the contention of Dr. Albert Schweitzer that nuclear weapons tests were creating "a danger for the human race."

Dr. Willard F. Libby, the commission member, wrote to Dr. Schweitzer "as a scientist, to present data bearing on a scientific fact." He made his letter public two days after a broadcast from Oslo of Dr. Schweitzer's warning.

After paying tribute to Dr. Schweitzer, humanitarian and winner of the Nobel Peace Prize, Dr. Libby said he feared Dr. Schweitzer's appeal was not based on the latest information on radioactive fall-out. Dr. Libby added: "I know you have the intellectual strength

Continued on Page 6, Column 4

U. N. CHIEF LOOKS TO COURT ON SUEZ

Hammarskjold Says It Could Settle Israeli Ship Issue

By THOMAS J. HAMILTON
Special to The New York Times.

UNITED NATIONS, N. Y., April 25—Dag Hammarskjold suggested today that the question whether Israeli ships had the right to use the Suez Canal be decided by the International Court of Justice.

The Secretary General of the United Nations asserted at a news conference that the "Governments concerned" could decide. He added, however, that "as a reasonably well-informed observer," he saw a possibility that the issue could be resolved under procedures set forth in the Egyptian declaration yesterday on operation of the canal.

The declaration provided that any unresolved differences among the signatories over the meaning of the Constantinople Convention of 1888, guaranteeing freedom of navigation, would be referred to the International Court.

Egypt apparently promised to accept compulsory jurisdiction. However, Israel and the United States, which were not parties to the convention, could not take the issue to the Court.

Further questions brought out the contradictory language of the convention, which provides that while the canal should be open to the shipping of all nations, both in war and peace, Egypt is entitled to take action to guard her security. Reminded that this right was qualified by

Continued on Page 4, Column 5

Dick Clark's American Bandstand made its network debut in 1957 and was immediately popular with teenagers.

Kukla, Fran and Ollie went on the air in 1947 and remained on for ten years. Seen here are Kukla, Burr Tillstrom, Fran Allison and Ollie.

"All the News That's Fit to Print"

The New York Times.

LATE CITY EDITION
U. S. Weather Bureau Report (Page 70) forecasts:
Partly cloudy today; fair tonight.
Variable cloudiness tomorrow.
Temp. range: 75—60. Yesterday: 71—56.8

VOL. CVI..No. 36,292.   © 1957, by The New York Times Company.   NEW YORK, WEDNESDAY, JUNE 5, 1957.   Times Square, New York 36, N. Y.   Telephone LAckawanna 4-1000   FIVE CENTS

U.S. AGREES TO LET JAPANESE TRY G.I. IN WOMAN'S DEATH

Wilson and Dulles Decide Firing of Empty Shell Was Not Authorized

PRESIDENT BACKS STAND

But Congress Members and Veterans' Leaders Assail Government's Action

Text of statement on Girard case is on Page 4.

By E. W. KENWORTHY
Special to The New York Times.

WASHINGTON, June 4—The United States agreed today that a Japanese court should try an American soldier charged with having killed a Japanese woman.

The soldier is Army Specialist 3/c William S. Girard, 21 years old, of Ottawa, Ill.

Last Jan. 30 Girard fired an empty cartridge case from a grenade launcher to frighten away several Japanese scavenging for metal on the firing range at Sagahara. Mme. Naka Sakai, 46 years old, was hit in the back by the shell case and killed.

In a joint statement issued at the Pentagon today Secretary of Defense Charles E. Wilson and Secretary of State John Foster Dulles said that Girard's action "was not authorized" and therefore was not done in the performance of duty.

Consequently, the two officials said that they had concluded that the trial of Girard in Japanese courts was "in full accord" with an agreement between Japan and the United States governing the status of American forces in Japan.

A Heated Issue in Japan

The question of jurisdiction in the Girard case has become a heated issue in the Japanese press and has inflamed public opinion.

The Government's decision in the Girard case came less than two weeks after the destructive anti-American rioting in Taipei, Taiwan. The rioters, who sacked the United States Embassy and the United States Information Agency building, were angered by a United States Army court-martial's acquittal of a sergeant accused of having killed a Chinese Peeping Tom.

Americans in Taiwan in official capacities are outside the jurisdiction of the Chinese Nationalist courts.

High Japanese officials hailed the Wilson-Dulles decision. On leaving the White House after he had presented his credentials, the new Japanese Ambassador, Koichiro Asakai, said he had not discussed the Girard case with the President. But he said he was pleased that "this matter had been settled" before the arrival of Premier Nobusuke Kishi.

Continued on Page 4, Column 3

EGYPT AND SOVIET IN RIFT ON TRADE

Moscow Envoy's Sudden Trip Home Is Linked to Tension

By OSGOOD CARUTHERS
Special to The New York Times.

CAIRO, June 4—The Soviet Ambassador flew to Moscow today. Diplomatic circles believed he would take part in urgent talks on the mounting differences between Egypt and the Soviet Union on economic affairs.

The Ambassador, Yevgeni D. Kiselev, left on a Moscow-bound plane early this morning only a few hours after he had held a long conference with the Egyptian Minister of Finance, Abdel Moneim el-Kaissouni.

Despite the close ties between the two countries in the foreign policy field, economic relations have hit rough weather during recent months.

There is a growing impression among Western and neutral diplomatic, as well as in Egyptian circles, that President Gamal Abdel Nasser now would like to reduce his country's heavy involvement in trade commitments to the Eastern bloc and swing back toward Egypt's more traditional trade with the West. The current efforts on the part of the Nasser regime to reach a rapprochement with Britain are

Continued on Page 6, Column 5

TO GO OR NOT TO GO was still the question yesterday for Giants and Dodgers. At City Hall news conference on move to California were, in foreground from left: Walter F. O'Malley of the Dodgers, Mayor Wagner, Horace C. Stoneham of Giants, John Cashmore, Borough President of Brooklyn, and William R. Peer, executive secretary to Mayor Wagner.

The New York Times

Eisenhower Not to Match Khrushchev TV Interview

By DANA ADAMS SCHMIDT
Special to The New York Times.

WASHINGTON, June 4—President Eisenhower will not try to match on Soviet television screens Nikita S. Khrushchev's interview on a United States network. "It has been decided that the President has no intention of answering Mr. Khrushchev," James C. Hagerty, White House press secretary, said today.

He made it clear that the President did not want to reply directly in any form to the First Secretary of the Soviet Communist party, who was interviewed on a Columbia Broadcasting System program Sunday. But Mr. Hagerty observed that questions on Mr. Khrushchev's appearance might come up tomorrow at President Eisenhower's weekly news conference.

Whether to have someone other than the President make a formal reply to Mr. Khrushchev, or whether to let the matter drop, has not yet been decided, Mr. Hagerty said.

Troop Offer Recalled

In the hour-long interview the Soviet leader made a sweeping offer to withdraw Soviet troops from Europe if the United States and its allies would do likewise. He also predicted that questions on Mr. Khrushchev's appearance include a new stadium for the Dodgers. The project would involve, the grandchildren of Americans living today would live under a Socialist system.

[Soviet propaganda agencies have deleted a key passage in the interview of Mr. Khrushchev in which the party secretary denied there were any "contradictions" between the Soviet leaders and the masses of the people.]

Generally, United States Governmental circles, dismissed what Mr. Khrushchev said as empty propaganda. For instance, they are quite sure that the Soviet Union has no intention of evacuating East Germany. They presume Mr. Khrushchev felt safe in offering to do so because he was sure the West would reject a balancing withdrawal on its side.

But Administration officials still have not made up their minds whether the United States Government should seek reciprocity for the fact that Mr. Khrushchev appeared on television screens in the United States.

The staff of the State Department

Continued on Page 14, Column 5

95 REBELS KILLED IN ALGERIA BATTLE

10 Frenchmen Die in Hill Clash—Pro-Paris Moslem and Nephew Are Slain

By The United Press.

ALGIERS, Algeria, Wednesday, June 5—French troops and nationalist rebels clashed early today in a fierce battle in mountains about sixty miles east of Algiers.

First reports said ninety-five rebels and ten French soldiers were killed. At least fifteen Frenchmen were said to have been wounded.

A French helicopter was reported to have crashed on to the battlefield. The battle was under way in the Great Kabylia Mountains northeast of Fort-National, a city of 15,000 built around an army camp.

[Meanwhile, France's governmental crisis, brought on partly by the rebellion in Algeria, seemed to be deepening into one of the gravest of the Fourth Republic. Pierre Pflimlin appeared near failure in his efforts to form a Cabinet.]

The mountain fighting marked the latest clash in a continuing eruption of violence. Yesterday, a rebel stole up to the training center of the French Foreign Legion at Sidi bel Abbes and shot a sentry dead at point-blank range. The rebel wounded a policeman as he fled, but was cornered and slain by French patrols in a wheat field.

Assassinations in West

By THOMAS F. BRADY
Special to The New York Times.

ALGIERS, June 4—A 71-year-old Moslem notable was assassinated with his nephew in western Algeria today.

Adda Bazane, the slain leader, was a member of the administrative commission of Mostaganem, a seaport city of 50,000, forty-five miles northeast of Oran.

He was the third member of the commission to be killed by terrorists. Ali Chekkal, who was shot last week in a Paris suburb, also belonged to the commission.

Mr. Koussa, a former member of the now-defunct Algerian Assembly, was en rout• with his nephew from Mostaganem to Ain Tedeles when rebels shot them. A French patrol found their bodies this morning in their automobile, which had been burned, two miles from Ain Tedeles. It was established that they had been killed by gunfire.

Near the Moroccan frontier tonight, a rebel commando raid caused havoc and bloodshed in the Algerian city of Tlemcen. First reports gave the casualties as three Moslem dead and

Continued on Page 2, Column 3

BASEBALL PARLEY A SCORELESS TIE

Giants and Dodgers Have No Commitments to Move or Stay, They Tell Mayor

By WAYNE PHILLIPS

The presidents of the Dodgers and the Giants met with Mayor Wagner yesterday and told him they were willing to remain in New York if suitable new homes were found for them.

What had been billed as a showdown meeting on the possible move of the two baseball clubs to the West Coast ended only in more suspense.

Both Walter F. O'Malley of the Dodgers and Horace C. Stoneham of the Giants assured the Mayor that they had no commitments to move out of New York—and none to remain.

The Mayor agreed to lend the city's help to the Giants in trying to find a suitable site in Manhattan for a new stadium to replace the aging Polo Grounds, but he promised no financial aid.

Reports to Be Speeded

The Mayor also promised to expedite reports on the engineering and financial aspects of a project to develop downtown Brooklyn. The project would include a new stadium for the Dodgers. Mr. Wagner said he hoped these reports could be ready in about six weeks, and that the city then would be ready to sit down with Mr. O'Malley to see what could be worked out.

After the conference—it lasted an hour and fifteen minutes—none of the participants was willing to express more than a "hope" that the two National League clubs would decide to remain in New York.

However, Mr. O'Malley, in his press comments about the meeting, made it clear that he was preparing to transfer the Dodgers to Los Angeles in short order unless the city came up with what he wanted in the way of a stadium.

Parking a Major Problem

Mr. Stoneham, who appeared considerably less unhappy with New York than Mr. O'Malley, gave no indication of how serious he was in his threat to move to San Francisco.

Both owners have received permission from the National League to move to the West Coast, but only if they go together and make their decision before Oct. 1.

Mr. O'Malley arrived at City Hall at 10:30 A. M., followed a few minutes later by Mr. Stoneham. The conference began at 10:55 o'clock and ended at 12:10 P. M.

John Cashmore, Brooklyn Borough President, and Louis A. Cioffi, Manhattan Commissioner of Borough Works, representing Borough President Hulan E. Jack, also participated. Mr. Jack is vacationing in the Virgin Islands.

"Mr. Stoneham advised us that one of his major problems is the parking facilities at the Polo Grounds," the Mayor said afterward.

"We agreed that the office of the Borough President will work with the Giant organization to look over other sites. There was no talk of the city building a stadium, but we will assist in reviewing other sites.

"This will be at no cost to

Continued on Page 28, Column 1

Truman's Daughter Has 6½-Pound Boy

A son was born to Mr. and Mrs. Clifton Daniel at 12:11 o'clock this morning in Doctors Hospital. Mrs. Daniel is the former Margaret Truman, daughter of former President and Mrs. Harry S. Truman.

Mrs. Daniel and the child were reported to be "doing fine." Mr. Daniel, a member of the staff of The New York Times, said the 6½-pound baby had not been named yet.

When the Trumans were notified at their home in Independence, Mo., Mrs. Truman said: "We're very happy." She added: "We are leaving by train in the morning for New York."

The baby was delivered by Dr. Louise M. Dantuono, assistant professor of obstetrics and gynecology at New York University Medical School and Bellevue Hospital.

BECK JR. INVOKES THE 5TH 100 TIMES; FACES A CITATION

Cousin Also Balks Senators on Union Pay—McClellan Sees 'Flagrant Abuse'

By JOSEPH A. LOFTUS
Special to The New York Times.

WASHINGTON, June 4—Dave Beck Jr. echoed his father's Fifth Amendment plea before Senate racket hunters more than a hundred times today.

He and a cousin by marriage, Joseph McEvoy, refused to say whether they had drawn a total of nearly $100,000 in salaries and expenses from the International Brotherhood of Teamsters for doing nothing.

The Senate Select Committee on Improper Activities in the Labor or Management Field put into the record documents showing that young Beck had drawn about $69,000 in the 1954-56 period and that Mr. McEvoy had drawn more than $29,000 in a two-year period.

Committee questions implied that there was no evidence that Mr. Beck, 36 years old, and Mr. McEvoy, also in his thirties, had contributed anything to the union for this money.

Contempt Citation Likely

After the two witnesses had invoked constitutional protection against possible self-incrimination more than 200 times, Chairman John L. McClellan declared he would seek a contempt citation for "flagrant abuse" of the Fifth Amendment.

The Arkansas Democrat said the Fifth Amendment had a "noble purpose" but he doubted that the founding fathers "ever conceived the time would come when such flagrant abuse would be made of it * * * and particularly such abuse as has been made of it here today."

Senator McClellan said he did not believe a witness could invoke the Fifth Amendment "unless he honestly believes a truthful answer would tend to incriminate him."

He said "I think we have got to find out in this country." And he added, "I know of no way to find out except to place this record before the court, even if it has to go to the highest court in the land."

Senator McClellan asserted: "If you are right and the court sustains you, then America faces a grave danger. The law can break down all over the country. It can break down every investigative process, every judicial process. This committee would be derelict in its duty, the Senate would be derelict, if it did not vote contempt proceedings."

Mundt Supports View

Senator Karl E. Mundt, Republican of South Dakota, "speaking for the Republican side," said he wished to associate himself with the chairman's remarks.

Senator McClellan's purpose is not to test the Fifth Amendment as such, but rather how it may be used. When he asks a witness, for example, whether he received money from the Teamsters Union and the witness refuses to answer on different grounds, he raises no legal challenge.

However, when the chairman follows that by asking, as he often does, "do you honestly be-

Continued on Page 27, Column 3

Cigarette Smoking Linked To Cancer in High Degree

American Society Makes Final Report on Study of 187,783 Men—Industry Disputes Statistical Studies

By HAROLD M. SCHMECK Jr.

A report to the American Medical Association yesterday showed a high degree of association between cigarette smoking and total death rates. It added that there was an "extremely high" association between cigarette smoking and death from lung cancer.

It was a final major report on the American Cancer Society's massive statistical study of

Texts of report and industry statement are on Page 24.

smoking and death rates. It confirmed earlier interim reports from the same study.

In addition to noting a high degree of association between cigarette smoking and total death rates, the report said "extremely high" associations were found between cigarette smoking and deaths from cancer of

the lung, larynx and esophagus. A similarly high association was noted between cigarette smoking and death attributed to gastric ulcers.

A far lower degree of association was found between total death rates and cigar smoking and a "small degree" of association between total death rates and pipe smoking.

Shortly after the report was presented the Tobacco Industry Research Committee issued a statement reasserting its view that "the causes of cancer and heart disease are not yet known to medical science." The statement said the current report does nothing to change this fact and added that statistical studies do not prove cause and effect relationships.

The cancer report was based

Continued on Page 25, Column 1

4 Geneticists Say Fall-Out Perils Future Generations

By JOHN W. FINNEY
Special to The New York Times.

WASHINGTON, June 4—Four prominent geneticists told Congress today that radiation from atomic weapon tests would harm tens of thousands and perhaps millions of children in future generations.

They agreed that immediate damage would be small in relation with the world population or the total figures on death and sickness.

However, they emphasized that the hazard could not be ignored in deciding whether to continue weapons testing.

The scientists testified before a special Atomic Energy subcommittee that is studying the danger of fall-out from explosions.

They were Drs. James F. Crow of the University of Wisconsin; A. H. Sturtevant of the California Institute of Technology; Hermann J. Muller of Indiana University, a Nobel Prize winner for research in genetics, and H. Bentley Glass of Johns Hopkins University.

Doubtful on Effects

All are members of the National Academy of Sciences and served last year on an academy committee that reported on the genetic effects of atomic radiation.

Their general conclusion was that any amount of radiation could damage reproductive cells, thus causing mutations in the hereditary pattern.

In genetics, they warned, there is no such thing as a "safe dose" of radiation. They suggested that they might have underestimated previously the genetic damage caused by radiation.

According to them, the damage to reproductive cells would be passed on to future generations in the form of harmful mutations, which would persist for hundreds of years.

These mutations, or changes, in the hereditary cells would have such effects in future generations as physical impairment,

Continued on Page 16, Column 3

EISENHOWER TOLD HIS BUDGET STAND CUTS GIFTS TO G.O.P.

Alcorn Says Big Contributors Balk in Protest, but That Party Won't Be Hurt

COMPLAINTS ARE CITED

Report on Republican Views Notes Opposition to Low Tariffs and School Aid

By W. H. LAWRENCE
Special to The New York Times.

WASHINGTON, June 4—Republican campaign strategists advised President Eisenhower today that his big budget proposals had slowed campaign contributions, particularly from those who formerly were big givers.

The President acknowledged he had heard previously about this drop in campaign funds as a result of complaints in the business community over proposed Administration spending.

Meade Alcorn, Republican national chairman, and other party leaders talked to the President about the complaints they had heard against his program from Republicans at a series of six regional conferences just concluded.

They brought him a fifty-eight-page, typewritten, leather-bound confidential report of the deliberations. A national party conference is scheduled here for Thursday and Friday.

Vice President Richard M. Nixon will speak Thursday. The President will fly back from a cruise off the Florida coast on the aircraft carrier Saratoga to speak on Friday afternoon.

Complaints on School Aid

Mr. Alcorn indicated there had been other complaints from Republican leaders about proposed Federal aid for school construction and low tariff policies—programs close to the President's heart.

The Republican chairman would not indicate how deeply campaign contributions had been cut in protest against the budget. But he forecast that the party would not "be hurt in the long run."

"The business leaders are beginning to realize what their alternatives are," he said.

The Republican leaders took a reasonably optimistic outlook about the 1958 elections. The President has pledged his help to try to restore Republican control of Congress.

Mr. Alcorn said the party's district-by-district analysis of Republican and opposition strength and weakness indicated "reasonable gains" for the Republicans in the House of Representatives, and a net gain of enough seats to win control. Democrats control the House with 234 members to 200 Republicans. There is one vacancy.

Mr. Alcorn said the battle for control of the Senate appeared

Continued on Page 18, Column 4

28 JUDGES ACCEPT PAY WITH PROTEST

Failure of City to Equalize Increases Is Questioned

By DOUGLAS DALES

Most of the Supreme Court justices of the First and Second Judicial Districts are signing their pay checks under protest. Their purpose is to lay the basis for possible future claims against the city for back pay.

The legal question involved is whether the Board of Estimate had the authority to vote a $2,500 pay increase last Feb. 28 for the Appellate Division justices in the First and Second Districts without according identical treatment for the Supreme Court justices.

Members of the Appellate Division bench are Supreme Court justices serving on the intermediate appeals court by appointment of the Governor. While there always has been a differential in the salaries for the two courts, the differential heretofore has been provided by the State Legislature.

The First Judicial District is comprised of New York and Bronx Counties. The Second District is made up of Brooklyn and Richmond.

The City Treasurer's office confirmed that nineteen of the twenty-nine justices in the First

Continued on Page 29, Column 1

PRESIDENT PUSHES IMMIGRATION RISE

Held 'Anxious' Over Lag in Congress—New House Bill Would Reunite Refugees

By C. P. TRUSSELL
Special to The New York Times.

WASHINGTON, June 4—President Eisenhower was pictured by Republican Congressional leaders today as being concerned over delays of consideration of his proposals to liberalize immigration laws.

The President made his formal proposals Jan. 31. They have not yet undergone committee hearings. At a meeting today with the minority leaders, General Eisenhower was described as being "very anxious" for early Congressional activity. At this point it is doubtful whether he will get it.

The program seems to remain in an atmosphere of indifference or hostility.

Democratic-controlled committees continued today consideration of other matters. On the House side, the Judiciary Immigration subcommittee is headed by Representative Francis E. Walter of Pennsylvania, co-author of the existing Immigration and Naturalization Law.

Walter for Hearings

The law is under attack as being discriminatory and lacking provisions for the admittance of new citizens who would give credit to the country.

Mr. Walter has said he wants to hold hearings on the President's proposals. Particularly he wants critics of the Walter-McCarran Act to attempt to prove their complaints against it.

The Senate Judiciary Committee is headed by James O. Eastland, Democrat of Mississippi. This panel has been concentrating upon the civil rights legislation.

Representative Kenneth B. Keating, Republican of upstate New York, tried to break the ice this afternoon. He introduced a bill to reunite families of refugees who had fled Iron Curtain countries.

Would Aid Refugees' Families

There have been about 58,600 members of families of refugees admitted to this country who were caught in the "pipeline" of a relief bill that expired last Dec. 31. Mr. Keating's bill would let them in if they met the stringent requirements for admittance.

Nonquota visas would be issued to those stranded from their families on condition that assurances of American sponsorship for their livelihood and future were promised and verified.

The present total quota is 154,847 a year. The President would raise the total immigration to 190,000 a year and pool unused 90,000 visas not used by persons from those countries that had exhausted their quotas.

Continued on Page 29, Column 1

WITHHOLDS ANSWERS: Dave Beck Jr. on witness stand at Senate hearing yesterday. He invoked Fifth Amendment.
Associated Press Wirephoto

"All the News That's Fit to Print"

The New York Times.

LATE CITY EDITION
U. S. Weather Bureau Report (Page 36) forecasts
Some cloudiness, warm today.
Partly cloudy, humid tomorrow.
Temp. range: 88—70. Yesterday: 86.4—61.4.

VOL. CVI..No. 36,321. © 1957, by The New York Times Company, Times Square, New York 36, N. Y. NEW YORK, THURSDAY, JULY 4, 1957. 10c beyond 100-mile zone from New York City FIVE CENTS

PRESIDENT BARS BALLOT ON RIGHTS; WOULD HEAR FOES

Rejects Proposal by Russell to Hold Referendum, but Plans to Study Bill

CITES COURT'S DECISIONS

'Ready to Listen' to South's Arguments — Senator Welcomes the Offer

News conference transcript and summary, Page 13.

By WILLIAM S. WHITE
Special to The New York Times

WASHINGTON, July 3—President Eisenhower made it plain today that he was taking another and a closer look at the implications of the Administration's civil rights bill in the wake of vehement Southern attacks on it.

At the same time, he rejected a proposal from the Southern opposition that the bill be submitted directly to the people in a national referendum.

He declared at his news conference, however, that he was "ready to listen" to any presentation of their side from the embattled Southerners.

Their chief spokesman, Senator Richard B. Russell, Democrat of Georgia, denounced the bill yesterday as so "cunningly contrived" that it could be questioned whether the President himself understood its full scope.

Opponents Map Strategy

Senator Russell was holding a strategy meeting at the Capitol with fellow Senators while the President was speaking. By coincidence, they themselves about that time were discussing the possibility of going to him in a group to offer their views.

Some were at first disposed not to attempt this course, lest be interpreted as a sign of weakness.

Told later of the President's remarks, however, Senator Russell said:

"If the President wishes to talk to us on this matter, his wish—as would be the wish of any President of the United States—will be to us a command. I should be glad to meet with him in any circumstance; he might prefer—alone or with others as he might wish."

From the Senate floor, Senator Russell charged yesterday that the Attorney General, Herbert Brownell Jr., had prepared a "deceptive piece of legislation" that would amount to "an unlimited grant of powers to the Attorney General to govern by injunction and Federal bayonet."

Bill Passed by House

As passed by the House of Representatives, the bill would:

¶Permit the Justice Department to intervene in behalf of any individual, with or without his consent, whose civil rights had been denied or were under threat of denial. This would be done by obtaining a Federal court injunction against the violator or imminent violator. If he refused to obey this writ, he could be held in contempt by a judge, sitting without a jury, and fined or imprisoned.

¶Set up a special civil rights division within the Justice Department.

¶Create a Federal civil rights commission to investigate and attempt to rectify cases of racial discrimination.

The civil rights advocates, Mr. Russell contended, are pretending that their main concern is to protect the right to vote, but in fact are seeking means to force racial integration in the South, in the schools and elsewhere, even to the point of possible use of Federal troops.

Russell Sees Pretense

The President at his news conference today showed that he had been disturbed by the comments of Senator Russell, with whom he had had many agreeable relationships.

During his military career, General Eisenhower often appeared before the Senate Armed Services Committee, of which Mr. Russell is chairman.

On Senator Russell's suggestion of a referendum, the President said he doubted that there was any constitutional basis for such a step; that Congress itself had the responsibility to enact legislation, and that in any case the issue would not make a very good subject for a referendum, even if you could have one.

On Mr. Russell's general denunciation of the bill, however, President Eisenhower did

Continued on Page 20, Column 7

Eisenhower Raises Atomic Fuel Quota

By JOHN W. FINNEY
Special to The New York Times

WASHINGTON, July 3—The White House more than doubled today the amount of nuclear fuel the United States would make available for atomic power plants at home and abroad.

President Eisenhower announced that he was allocating an additional 59,800 kilograms—or 131,560 pounds—of uranium 235 for peaceful purposes in domestic and foreign nuclear power projects.

Including its previous allocations, the United States has now pledged to make 100,000 kilograms—or 220,000 pounds—of uranium fuel available for peaceful purposes. At current atomic energy commission prices, the value of this fuel is $1,100,000,000.

The 100,000 kilograms will be

Continued on Page 12, Column 2

DEMOCRATS BACK EASING OF CURBS ON ALIEN QUOTAS

Key Legislators in Agreement on Compromise to Bring in 140,000 More in 2 Years

By JOHN D. MORRIS
Special to The New York Times

WASHINGTON, July 3—Key Democrats in Congress have quietly reached substantial agreement on a compromise plan for easing restrictions on immigration.

The compromise, described as acceptable in nearly all major respects to legislators most interested in the problem, is embodied in a bill introduced last Thursday by Senator John F. Kennedy, Democrat of Massachusetts.

The measure has the backing of Lyndon B. Johnson of Texas, the Senate Democratic leader, Representative Francis E. Walter, Democrat of Pennsylvania, who holds the key to action by the House of Representatives, also participated in the unpublished negotiations that preceded its introduction. Sponsors look for his cooperation.

The bill would permit the entry over a two-year period of 140,000 to 150,000 regular immigrants and refugees who otherwise would be excluded.

Eisenhower Plan Included

While it includes features of President Eisenhower's immigration program, it stops short of making some basic changes that he had proposed in the McCarran-Walter Immigration and Nationality Act.

The President's recommendations, outlined Jan. 31 in a special message to Congress, asked authority to bring in 190,000 more persons a year.

The annual quota under present law is 154,857, of which 60,000 quota numbers expire unused each year. Total entrances, including unrestricted immigration from Western Hemisphere countries, amounted to 321,625 in 1956.

Democratic strategists hope to obtain Republican help in steering the Kennedy bill through Congress toward the end of the session without public hearings.

The tentative plan, similar to one that failed in the last hours of the 1956 session, is to attach the measure to a minor immigration bill passed by the House and now pending on the Senate calendar.

Tactic Failed Last Year

Senate passage of the combined bill would send it to a Senate-House conference committee for agreement on the final version.

The tactic failed last year when Representative Walter, chairman of the House Judiciary Subcommittee on Immigration, invoked a parliamentary technicality to keep a similar bill from going to conference.

This time, according to Senator Kennedy, Mr. Walter "has

Continued on Page 11, Column 1

CITY BUILDING UNIT STUDIED BY STATE

Heck Announces Watchdog Inquiry—Step Welcomed by Mayor and Aides

By EMANUEL PERLMUTTER

The Republican-controlled legislative watchdog committee has begun an investigation of the New York City Department of Buildings.

This was disclosed yesterday by Assemblyman Oswald D. Heck, Republican Speaker of the Assembly. He said the committee was checking reports of "graft, corruption and extortion" in the department.

Confirmation was given by Senator William F. Horan, Republican of Tuckahoe, chairman of the Joint Legislative Committee on Government Operations, the official name of the watchdog unit.

Mr. Horan said the committee's staff was making "preliminary investigations into those and other matters."

Mayor Gives His Views

Mayor Wagner said his Administration welcomed the watchdog committee's investigation.

"I have said time and again that we would welcome any investigation of any city department," he declared. "We have nothing to hide. If there is wrongdoing no one is more important than I to root it out and take swift, decisive action.

"I have already asked those with complaints against the Department of Buildings to come in and state their complaints. I have promised full protection to all who cooperate in this fashion."

Charles H. Tenney, the City Investigation Commissioner who has begun his own inquiry into rumors that building inspectors were shaking down property owners guilty of violations and those seeking building permits,

Continued on Page 37, Column 3

G.O.P. Picks 3-War Marine To Oppose Jack in Borough

By RUSSELL PORTER

Melvin L. Krulewitch, 61-year-old lawyer and twice-wounded Marine Corps Reserve veteran of three wars, was designated yesterday as the Republican candidate for Borough President of Manhattan. He will oppose Hulan E. Jack, the Democratic incumbent in the November election.

Mr. Krulewitch, who is a major general in the Reserve, was the only Republican named for Borough President or the District Attorney at meetings of the executive committees of the New York and Kings County Republican Committees.

The following three Democrats, who already had their own party designations, were endorsed by the Republicans for re-election as Borough President or District Attorney:

Borough President John Cashmore of Brooklyn.

District Attorney Frank S. Hogan of New York County (Manhattan).

District Attorney Edward S. Silver of Kings County (Brooklyn).

Both executive committees formally approved the recent designation of three Republican city-wide candidates by the five county leaders. These candidates are Robert K. Christenberry for Mayor, Mrs. Caroline K. Simon for President of the City Council and State Senator Walter

Continued on Page 20, Column 7

G. McGahan of Queens for Comptroller.

Mr. Krulewitch's designation marked a departure from the Republican practice in the 1953 municipal campaign. At that time the Republicans picked a Negro, Elmer A. Carter, who lost to Mr. Jack, who is also a Negro.

Thomas J. Curran, the Republicans' New York County leader, said after yesterday's meeting that Mr. Carter, a member of the State Committee Against Discrimination, did not want to run for Borough President this year. According to Mr. Curran, Mr. Krulewitch was the only person mentioned for the post.

Mr. Krulewitch told Negro reporters yesterday that he had served with Negro troops at Iwo in the Pacific in World War II. "They were fine troops," he said.

The candidate is a tall, husky, clean-shaven man of military bearing. He wears dark horn-rimmed glasses and his hair is getting thin and gray. He has been a member of the Republican County Committee for eight years but has never run for public office. He has a law office on Madison Avenue and lives at 45 Gramercy Park North, in Mr. Curran's home district.

"Are you an Eisenhower Re-

Continued on Page 20, Column 7

WIDE SHAKE-UP IN KREMLIN OUSTS MOLOTOV, MALENKOV, KAGANOVICH AS KHRUSHCHEV TIGHTENS REINS

U. S. IS GRATIFIED

State Department Says Ousters Show Strain in Soviet System

By JAMES RESTON
Special to The New York Times

WASHINGTON, July 3—Official Washington tried hard to conceal its pleasure over the latest shake-up in the Soviet Union today but didn't quite succeed.

"No comment," said James C. Hagerty, White House press secretary, grinning broadly, and the grin was the most tangible and significant act in a day devoted mainly to gleeful speculation.

News of the official Soviet announcement of the dismissal of Vyacheslav M. Molotov, Lazar M. Kaganovich, Georgi M. Malenkov and Dmitri T. Shepilov was brought to President Eisenhower during a meeting of the National Security Council in the afternoon. Reports of developments were rushed to the White House from the State Department and the Central Intelligence Agency throughout the day.

Mr. Hagerty told the press in midafternoon that the Administration had advance indication of the ouster. He noted that Nikita S. Khrushchev, First Secretary of the Soviet Communist party, and Marshal Nikolai A. Bulganin, Soviet Premier, had recently postponed a visit to Czechoslovakia, and that an aerial demonstration over Moscow, to which Communist bloc leaders had been invited, had suddenly been canceled.

Beyond that, however, he would not comment.

White Reads Statement

The State Department was more explicit. In answer to reporters' questions, Lincoln White, press officer, read the following statement:

"It has long been known that the Soviet system operates under stresses and strains. Arbitrary and abrupt dismissals without public discussion of the issues are also characteristic of the system.

"The official Soviet press has at various times suggested there have been disagreements over basic policies in such fields as Government organizations, agriculture, heavy industry, consumer goods and satellite affairs.

"The serious nature of the divergence of views is clearly shown by the number and importance of the persons dismissed or shifted. We are naturally following these developments closely for the effect they may have on Soviet basic policy."

Effect on U. S. Policy Seen

The Soviet changes have come at a critical time in the development of United States foreign policy and is expected to have some influence on that policy, particularly as it affects Communist China and the Soviet

Both the Executive and Legislative branches of the United States Government have been divided about how to deal with Moscow and Peiping. Some legislators and officials have favored making a major effort to reach a disarmament agreement with the Soviet Union and acquiescing in an accommodation with the Chinese Communists.

Others have been opposing this on the ground that the whole Communist world was in ferment. They have been going along reluctantly with the current United States policy in the disarmament talks in London, but insisting that the way to break up the Communist alliance between Moscow and Peiping was to maintain the economic pressure.

Secretary of State Dulles, who left for his Great Lakes retreat on Duck Island today, said only yesterday that he was opposed to making concessions to the Chinese Communists, and regarded dictatorial communism in both Peiping and Moscow as "a passing phase."

Today's developments in Moscow, coming on top of a noisy debate in Peiping over ideological questions, are expected to strengthen those who have contended that the thing to do was to keep the pressure on, not to grow weary of the long struggle, not to make risky concessions.

Continued on Page 3, Column 4

Vyacheslav M. Molotov

Georgi M. Malenkov

Lazar M. Kaganovich

The New York Times / Associated Press / Soviofo

U. S. MAY SPREAD 'CLEAN' BOMB DATA

President Weighs Proposal to Give Others Knowledge on Eliminating Fall-Out

By JACK RAYMOND
Special to The New York Times

WASHINGTON, July 3—President Eisenhower said today he was thinking of sharing with the Soviet Union and other countries the knowledge of how to produce "clean" hydrogen bombs.

Such a step would require legislation, he said. But he disclosed that he had asked his scientific advisers about the possibility of sharing, and they had suggested such a course might be adopted as soon as they had proved they could produce a bomb totally free of dangerous radioactive fall-out.

The President said that in the meantime he intended to invite foreign countries to make their own measurements of the percentage of radioactivity on the site of the next United States hydrogen bomb detonation.

This should serve as an appropriate test by doubters of the contention that even now only 4 per cent radioactivity results from the explosion of United States hydrogen bombs, the President declared.

U-235 Given to Others

President Eisenhower opened his news conference with an announcement that the United States was making more uranium-235 available in the peaceful uses of atomic power.

In response to questions about United States policy on disarmament and the effects on that policy of reduced radioactive fall-out in bomb explosions, the President emphasized:

¶The United States stands firm on its position at the London disarmament conference, agreeing to a temporary suspension of nuclear arms tests if it will lead to an end of bomb-making.

¶The United States disarm-

Continued on Page 12, Column 2

Moscow Ousters Termed Victory for 'Liberal' Policy

By HARRISON E. SALISBURY

Nikita S. Khrushchev, First Secretary of the Soviet Communist party, appears to have won a smashing victory for his "New Look" policies of easing tensions at home and abroad. This was the initial reaction of competent specialists in Soviet affairs to the dramatic decisions of the latest meeting in Moscow of the party's Central Committee.

With the firm support of the Soviet Army, the Communist party apparatus and the Government bureaucracy, Mr. Khrushchev has ousted from the Soviet ruling group a powerful bloc of Stalinist oppositionists.

Mr. Khrushchev's ability to remove from the party's Presidium and Central Committee such veteran party chieftains as Vyacheslav M. Molotov, Lazar M. Kaganovich and Georgi M. Malenkov was testimony to the power he had now mustered behind his leadership.

Indictment Is Stressed

Of great importance in international relations was the nature of the indictment placed against them. Mr. Khrushchev and his victorious Central Committee majority charged Mr. Molotov, Mr. Kaganovich, Mr. Malenkov and their supporters with persistent and deliberate efforts to sabotage every effort to ease international tensions, improve the life of Soviet citizens at home and destroy the vestiges of Stalinist oppression.

The communiqué announcing the expulsions contained a platform of the Khrushchev faction, which promised to continue striving for better international relations.

While the main force of the Khrushchev indictment was directed against Mr. Molotov, Mr. Kaganovich and Mr. Malenkov, they were not the only targets. In effect Mr. Khrushchev made a clean sweep.

He also ousted Dmitri T. Shepilov, the former Pravda editor and Foreign Minister who was identified with the "Young Turk" faction of the party. Mr.

Continued on Page 3, Column 2

---

3 STALINISTS OUT

Shepilov Also Dropped for Opposing Current Policies of Soviet

Texts of communiqué, Pravda editorial, Pages 2 and 4.

By WILLIAM J. JORDEN
Special to The New York Times

MOSCOW, Thursday, July 4—The Soviet Communist party has accused Vyacheslav M. Molotov, Georgi M. Malenkov and Lazar M. Kaganovich of anti-party activities and has ousted them from the country's leadership.

They were removed both from the Presidium of the party's Central Committee and from the Central Committee itself. However, they remained as members of the party.

Dmitri T. Shepilov, who was said to have joined them in opposing the party majority, was also ousted from alternate membership in the Presidium, from the Central Committee and from his job as one of the party secretaries.

Three Linked With Stalin

The three Communist leaders, all known for their connections with Stalin, were accused of having tried to restore "methods of leadership that were condemned by the Twentieth Party Congress," an allusion to the system prevailing in Stalin's time. They were said to have tried to form an anti-party faction to achieve their aims.

The action against them was taken during an eight-day meeting of the Central Committee from June 22 through 29. The text of the committee's resolution was released by Tass, Soviet news agency, last night.

Of the former eleven members of the party Presidium only six remained. They are Nikita S. Khrushchev, Nikolai A. Bulganin, Kliment Y. Voroshilov, Anastas I. Mikoyan, Mikhail A. Suslov and Alexei I. Kirichenko.

Zhukov Is Elevated

Marshal Georgi K. Zhukov, and Miss Yekaterina A. Furtseva, the only woman on the Presidium, were among five alternate members who were raised to full rank. Four other regular members were newly added to the Presidium.

In addition to the four leading figures who were ousted for severe criticism and ousted from the Presidium, Mikhail G. Pervukhin and Maxim Z. Saburov also were dropped from the group.

Mr. Pervukhin was demoted to the position of alternate member of the Presidium, but nothing was known of Mr. Saburov's present position. He was not mentioned as having been dropped from the Central Committee itself.

Messrs. Molotov, Malenkov and Kaganovich were said to have opposed all the major policy moves of recent years that have come to be associated with the name of Mr. Khrushchev. The section of the Pravda editorial concerning the failure of "sectarians and dogmatists" [Stalinists] to understand the necessity of consolidating the Socialist camp was read here as aimed against Mr. Molotov.

Continued on Page 2, Column 3

Italy Holds TV Aide In Give-Away Fraud

By PAUL HOFMANN

ROME, July 3—One of Italy's best-known television personalities is in prison today, charged with rigging give-away shows.

Giuseppe Ruggiero, 42, never spoke a line before television cameras and never was introduced to watchers. But he sternly benevolent face is familiar to millions because it used to appear on the screen whenever something was to be won.

In his wordless way Signor Ruggiero was quite a performer. To the unseen audience he was fair play personified. As chief of the promotion department of the state broadcasting and television system Signor Ruggiero presided over the distribution of thousands of television sets, automobiles, refrigerators and record players, etc.

Now he is accused of having

Continued on Page 37, Column 3

SOVIET EXPECTED TO EASE BLOC TIE

Shift in Leadership Viewed as Move to Consolidate the Communist Orbit

By SYDNEY GRUSON
Special to The New York Times

PRAGUE, Czechoslovakia, July 3—The changes in the Soviet Communist party's leadership, announced in Moscow tonight, may have ushered in a significant period of readjustment in relations between the Soviet Union and other Communist countries.

The changes, and the Pravda editorial accompanying them, were considered of such basic importance that people here and in Warsaw hesitated to comment until a more thorough study became possible. But among their first impressions were that:

¶Nikita S. Khrushchev had consolidated his position as the first among equals in the new Presidium of the Soviet party.

¶Mr. Khrushchev was bent on a determined effort to narrow the steadily widening gap between the Soviet party and some of the other Communist parties, particularly that of Communist China.

To Lessen Antagonism

The dismissal of Vyacheslav M. Molotov would be bound to lessen the sharp antagonism between Moscow and Belgrade, Yugoslavia, and the differences between Moscow and Warsaw as well. In both Belgrade and Warsaw Mr. Molotov had been considered the prime architect of a tough policy toward parties straying from the Soviet line.

Continued on Page 3, Column 7

Holiday Traffic Exodus Begins; 952 Police Cars Will Patrol City

Police Commissioner Stephen P. Kennedy yesterday declared "all-out war" on reckless drivers in a move to help law-abiding citizens survive the Fourth of July holiday week-end.

Fifty-two unmarked cars and 900 regular radio patrol cars were assigned to watch traffic from 4 P. M. yesterday until 8 A. M. Monday.

The holiday exodus began yesterday afternoon. It was estimated that 1,000,000 cars would carry 3,500,000 persons out of the city during the four-day week-end.

Most of the nation was promised generally fair and warm weather today with which to celebrate the 181st anniversary of the adoption of the Declaration of Independence by the Continental Congress.

The Weather Bureau said temperatures here — which climbed to 86.4 degrees at 4:40 P. M. yesterday — might reach 85 to 90 degrees today. Yesterday was the first day to exceed 80 degrees since last Friday. The outlook for tomorrow and Saturday is partly cloudy, warm and humid.

The National Safety Council

estimated that 45,000,000 motor vehicles would be on the roads. It feared a possible record Independence Day toll of 535 highway deaths between 6 P. M. yesterday and midnight Sunday.

The council warned that eight of every ten fatal accidents occur in rural areas; speed is involved in seven out of ten, and drinking is a factor in almost half. Indiana and Iowa detailed National Guardsmen to aid road patrols; Kentucky and Georgia planned road blocks to check drivers, and New Mexico ordered jail for reckless drivers until their records could be checked.

In the city, 120 police cars will operate in a safety-chain plan, each patrolling back and forth on a single mile of the major parkways and highways. Six cars of the accident investigation unit will be on around-the-clock duty. Tow police helicopters will help unsnarl traffic tie-ups.

The major delays yesterday affected traffic leaving the city for the George Washington Bridge. Between 5 and 6:40 P. M., cars on the West Side

Continued on Page 36, Column 2

Pat Boone was the recording industry's answer to the establishment's objections to rock 'n' roll. He starred in Bernardine, *playing the typical American boy.*

Fred Astaire and Audrey Hepburn danced their way through Funny Face.

"All the News That's Fit to Print"

The New York Times.

LATE CITY EDITION
U. S. Weather Bureau Report (Page 46) forecast:
Fair, warmer today. Fair, little change in temperature tomorrow.
Temp. range: 85—64. Yesterday: 80.7—62.3.

VOL. CVI..No. 36,356.

© 1957, by The New York Times Company.
Times Square, New York 36, N. Y.

NEW YORK, THURSDAY, AUGUST 8, 1957.

10c beyond 100-mile zone from New York City

FIVE CENTS

SENATE APPROVES RIGHTS BILL, 72-18, WITH JURY CLAUSE

HOUSE MUST ACT

Its Acceptance Likely— President Expected to Sign Measure

By WILLIAM S. WHITE
Special to The New York Times

WASHINGTON, Aug. 7—The Senate approved tonight the first major civil rights legislation to clear that body since the Reconstruction period after the Civil War.

A bill providing Federal steps to enforce the right to vote in the South was adopted by a vote of 72 to 18.

Forty-three Republicans and twenty-nine Democrats voted for the bill and eighteen Democrats against it. Seventeen of the opposition were from the Deep South. They were joined by Wayne Morse, Democrat of Oregon, who was dissatisfied with the "softness" of the bill.

Five Southern Democrats broke with tradition and voted for the bill. They were Senators Lyndon B. Johnson of Texas, the Senate Democratic leader; Ralph Yarborough of Texas; Estes Kefauver and Albert Gore of Tennessee, and George A. Smathers of Florida.

Measure Rewritten

It was a measure rewritten from what President Eisenhower had sought and what the House of Representatives had voted. It largely bore the imprint of Senator Johnson.

At its heart was a guarantee to the right of jury trial in criminal contempt, but not civil contempt, cases arising from violations of Federal injunctions to protect the voting right.

It strongly appeared that the House, in the process of reconciliation between the two differing texts, ultimately would go along basically with the Senate's approach. It also was expected that President Eisenhower would sign the final bill.

Earlier today, the Justice Department sent a memorandum to the Senate pointing out that the jury trial provision might hamper the procedures of the Supreme Court and the Federal Appellate Courts.

President Eisenhower at his news conference this morning had repeated in general terms his objection to the Senate's version of the bill. He had reaffirmed a statement of Friday, attacking some of its aspects, but had refused to go into any detail. And, pointing out that the completed bill was not before him—

Continued on Page 12, Column 4

EISENHOWER PICKS FOREIGN AID CHIEF

Selects James H. Smith Jr. to Succeed Hollister

By ALLEN DRURY
Special to The New York Times

WASHINGTON, Aug. 7—James H. Smith Jr. of Aspen, Colo., has been selected by President Eisenhower to head the International Cooperation Administration.

Mr. Smith is a former Assistant Secretary of the Navy for Air. He will succeed John B. Hollister of Ohio as head of the agency that administers the Mutual Security Program.

Mr. Smith's selection was disclosed today as the President warmly supported foreign aid at his news conference and as a Senate-House conference started work on a compromise bill authorizing reduced funds for the program for the fiscal year.

Mr. Smith held his Navy post from July 23, 1953, to June 20, 1956. He is 46 years old, a graduate of Harvard University in 1931 and of the Columbia University Law School in 1936.

He served as a Navy pilot in World War II and was on the staff of Admiral Arthur W. Radford, recently Chairman of the Joint Chiefs of Staff.

He was a vice president of Pan American Airways from 1946 until 1949, and in recent years has been an official of Slick Airways.

The Congressional conference that began meeting today has

Continued on Page 2, Column 4

MEYNER APPOINTS WEINTRAUB HEAD OF JERSEY COURTS

Picks Francis and Proctor as Associates on Supreme Bench and 4 Other Judges

Special to The New York Times

TRENTON, Aug. 7—Gov. Robert B. Meyner named Associate Justice Joseph Weintraub of West Orange today to be Chief Justice of the State Supreme Court. As such, he will head New Jersey's entire state court system.

The appointment of Justice Weintraub was one of seven announced by the Governor. The six others were:

Superior Court Judge John J. Francis of South Orange to be an Associate Justice of the Supreme Court.

Superior Court Judge Haydn Proctor of Interlaken to be an Associate Justice of the Supreme Court.

Samuel P. Orlando of Haddonfield to be a Superior Court Judge.

W. Orvyl Schalick of Salem to be a Superior Court Judge.

John B. Wick of Woodbury to be a Superior Court Judge.

Alvin R. Featherer of Penn's Grove to be county judge in Salem County.

Governor Meyner announced the appointments at a news conference. He will send the nominations to the State Senate on Aug. 19, when it meets in special session.

Favored by G. O. P. Leader

Senator Richard R. Stout, Republican of Monmouth County, chairman of the Senate Judiciary Committee and majority leader, said he knew of no opposition to the appointments by the Democratic Governor. He said he would seek quick confirmation of Judge Proctor, who is from his own county.

The appointments will give the Democrats a majority (4 to 3) of the Supreme Court for the first time since New Jersey's court system was reorganized in 1947.

Justice Weintraub, a Democrat, will succeed the late Chief Justice Arthur T. Vanderbilt, Republican. Until his death last June, Justice Vanderbilt had headed the Supreme Court since its establishment under the new State Constitution of 1947.

Under Chief Justice Vanderbilt, the Supreme Court consisted of four Republicans and three Democrats.

Essex Gets Four Justices

Judge Francis is a Democrat and Judge Proctor is a Republican. Justice Weintraub and Judge Francis come from Essex County, which will now have four of the seven Supreme Court justices.

Justice Weintraub is an adherent of the Jewish faith, Judge Francis is a Roman Catholic and Judge Proctor a Protestant.

Judge Francis will succeed Justice Weintraub as an Associate Justice. Judge Proctor will succeed Associate Justice A. Dayton Oliphant, a Republican, who will reach the retirement age of 70 on Oct. 28.

Justices Weintraub, Francis

Continued on Page 11, Column 4

M'ELROY IS NAMED TO WILSON'S POST

Eisenhower Calls President of Procter & Gamble 'One of Most Capable' Men

By JACK RAYMOND
Special to The New York Times

WASHINGTON, Aug. 7—President Eisenhower today nominated Neil H. McElroy, president of the Procter & Gamble Company to succeed Charles E. Wilson, as Secretary of Defense.

The President sent the nomination to the Senate this afternoon, after describing Mr. McElroy at his morning news conference as "one of the most capable and the highest type of people that I know in the country."

The Cabinet nominee is 52 years old, six feet four inches tall and weighs 210 pounds. The Harvard graduate, he rose in the soap company as an advertising and promotion man. He served as chairman of the White House Conference on Education in 1956 and won the President's high praise for his work.

Congressmen Favorable

Mr. Wilson's letter of resignation was received at the White House today. However, it was not made public, as the resignation is not expected to take effect for at least one month.

At the Capitol, reaction among legislators appeared favorable to Mr. McElroy. However, questions of conflict of interest were expected to be raised. Barring a special meeting, the Senate Armed Services Committee is expected to hold a formal hearing on Aug. 19.

The Cincinnati soap executive is reputed to own substantial securities in major defense concerns as well as in his own company. His salary is $285,000 a year. The Cabinet post pays $25,000.

It was recalled that when Secretary of General Motors, joined the Cabinet in 1953 he was required

Continued on Page 9, Column 1

TO BE DEFENSE CHIEF:
Neil H. McElroy at office in Cincinnati yesterday.
Associated Press Wirephoto

U. S. Will Share Cost Of 53 Cargo Vessels

By RICHARD E. MOONEY
Special to The New York Times

WASHINGTON, Aug. 7—The Government and Lykes Brothers Steamship Company signed a subsidy contract today for the construction of fifty-three cargo ships to replace the company's present fleet.

The contract was the largest since the program for replacing obsolete vessels was authorized by Congress in 1936.

The cost of the project was estimated at $500,000,000. The ships will be built in American yards and the Government will pay the difference between this cost and the smaller cost of building them abroad. This difference in costs would amount to about $50,000,000.

The contract also provides for Government subsidization of Lykes shipping operations over

Continued on Page 44, Column 2

President Bars Extending Arms Check to All Bases

Says Inclusion in a First-Step Accord Would Create Problems, Especially if Red China Area Were Involved

By RUSSELL BAKER
Special to The New York Times

WASHINGTON, Aug. 7—President Eisenhower appeared to rule out today any possibility that all Western and Communist military bases would be

News conference transcript and summary, Page 6.

opened to inspection under a first-step disarmament agreement.

In his news conference he suggested these reasons why all bases should not be included:

¶It would be extremely difficult to arrange permission with the "dozens and dozens of countries" in which the United States has overseas bases.

¶It would be "complicating" to the course of the disarmament negotiations to try to bring in Communist bases in "the Red China area." This was an oblique reference to United States refusal to bring Communist China

into the disarmament talks at this stage.

¶The desired goal of an aerial and ground inspection program at this point was the creation of mutual "confidence" and for this purpose the omission of some bases would not be "critical."

Thus the President answered a question that has also been raised by the Soviet delegation to the United Nations Disarmament Subcommittee about the new Western inspection proposal.

United States spokesmen thus far have been emphasizing that the chief value of the proposal, which would create aerial and ground inspection of much of the Northern Hemisphere's land area, would be a guarantee against large-scale surprise attack.

Moscow, however, has shown

Continued on Page 7, Column 4

BRITISH ADVANCE ON OMAN REBELS

Desert Force Enters Village Unopposed in Support of Sultan Against Imam

By SAM POPE BREWER
Special to The New York Times

IZZ, Oman, Thursday, Aug. 8—British troops advancing across the desert in support of the Sultan of Muscat and Oman have entered this village in a drive against the rebellious Imam of Oman.

It capitulated without resistance yesterday morning. Local sheikhs assured a representative of the Sultan, Said bin Taimur, that there had been no support for the Imam in Izz.

This desert village is situated twelve miles southeast of Nizwa, which is the headquarters of the Imam, Ghalib bin Ali, and the objective of the expedition.

Advance From Fahud

Forces of the Sultan and British troops assembled here last night after a day's unopposed advance over rough tracks from the desert base of Fahud.

They were poised early this morning to take over Firq, a major outpost of Nizwa. Local sources said that the track to Firq was mined and that resistance could be expected from the Imam's forces entrenched there.

If Firq holds out, the attack will be led by a squadron of Trucial-Oman Scouts and British officers. A heavy weapons company of Cameronians, a Scottish infantry unit, will give mortar and machine-gun support if needed.

Special to The New York Times

FAHUD, Oman, Aug. 6—British-led troops at this base prepared tonight to advance to

Continued on Page 4, Column 6

AUSTERITY BUDGET APPROVED IN PARIS

Cabinet Backs Finance Chief on Spending Cuts—Wage Demands Pose New Fight

By ROBERT C. DOTY
Special to The New York Times

PARIS, Aug. 7—The French Cabinet approved today an "austerity" budget, the first step in a general belt-tightening designed to restore France's sagging finances and economic prospects.

Félix Gaillard, dynamic young Radical Finance Minister, backed by Premier Maurice Bourgès-Maunoury, won a personal victory by cutting 600,000,000,000 francs ($1,710,000,000) from the original spending requests of his Cabinet colleagues for 1958.

With France's gold and dollar reserves nearing exhaustion, internal prices mounting and the franc dropping to new lows on international markets, M. Gaillard called governmental economy a fundamental step toward redressing the situation.

Price, Wage Battle Looms

With the budget battle out of the way, the Premier and the Finance Minister girded for the next engagement—a struggle to keep price and wage rises from wiping out the beneficial effects of the limitations on Government spending.

This promises to be even more difficult because labor, backed by important political forces in the National Assembly, has served notice that it will exert maximum pressure to obtain wage increases to offset recent price rises.

"The severity shown by the state must be emulated by all," said the Cabinet communiqué today. "The defense of the money could not be assured if

Continued on Page 2, Column 6

KHRUSHCHEV SAYS SOVIET SUPPORTS GERMAN RED AIMS

Promises Full Backing for Unity and Other Plans on Reaching East Berlin

By HARRY GILROY
Special to The New York Times

BERLIN, Aug. 7—Nikita S. Khrushchev, First Secretary of the Soviet Communist party, began today a week-long visit in East Germany. It was evident purpose was to back the East German Communist leaders.

Mr. Khrushchev at once disposed of rumors that Walter Ulbricht, East German Communist party leader and Deputy Premier, might be out of favor because of too persistent loyalty to Stalin.

The Soviet party leader gave Herr Ulbricht a warm embrace when they met in the main East Berlin railroad station. The two political leaders exchanged cordial greetings in speeches that followed.

Mr. Khrushchev brought along a delegation of ten officials, including Anastas I. Mikoyan, a Deputy Premier, and Andrei A. Gromyko, Soviet Foreign Minister.

New Soviet Jet Plane Used

The Soviet party flew from Moscow to Schoenefeld airfield in East Berlin, apparently in one of the new Soviet planes. D. P. A., the West German news agency, said the plane was a TU-104 jetliner.

The Soviet and East German official parties proceeded to East Berlin by train. Outside the railroad station Mr. Khrushchev addressed a crowd assembled by Herr Ulbricht's Communist party organization. One estimate was that 25,000 East Germans were in the assemblage.

Felix Gaillard, dynamic young speaking in Russian, which was translated into German. He underscored Soviet support for the East German state. He said that in a decisive sense peace and European security depended on German-Soviet friendship.

"That is why the Soviet people value so highly the efforts of the Government and all the progressive forces of the [East] German Democratic Republic to maintain and strengthen German-Soviet friendship," Mr. Khrushchev asserted.

Khrushchev Waves to Crowds

At the end of the speeches the official groups rode away, with Mr. Khrushchev standing in an open car and waving to the public. The Soviet delegation will be housed in an old residence of the German royal family.

The drive through East Berlin was the last part of the day's program that Western reporters were permitted to observe. However, the East German radio announced tonight that Soviet and East German party leaders had begun discussions.

It also announced that the Soviet leaders would pay a call this evening on President Wilhelm Pieck. The 81-year-old President, who is ill, is at a va-

Continued on Page 3, Column 2

RUSSIAN COLONEL IS INDICTED HERE AS TOP SPY IN U.S.

A NINE-YEAR PLOT

Suspect Said to Have Used Brooklyn Studio to Direct Network

By MILDRED MURPHY

An ordinary looking little man who operated a photographic studio in Brooklyn was indicted yesterday as the most important Soviet spy ever caught in the United States.

A Federal grand jury said the unobtrusive tenant of the studio on the top floor of 252 Fulton Street was a colonel in Soviet intelligence, with headquarters in Moscow.

He is Rudolf Ivanovich Abel, a 55-year-old, Moscow-born citizen of the Soviet Union who entered the United States illegally in 1948.

He had been arrested here June 21 on a charge of illegal entry and was placed in an alien detention camp in McAllen, Tex. Yesterday he was moved to a jail in Edinburg, Tex., to await a court order authorizing his return to Brooklyn on the three-count espionage indictment.

If convicted, he faces a possible death sentence, which would be the third in this country for espionage on behalf of the Soviet Union. Julius and Ethel Rosenberg were executed June 19, 1953, for spying for the Russians.

Intricate Plot Charged

Abel's illegal entry into this country in 1948 was, according to the charges set forth in the indictment, the beginning of a nine-year spy plot more devious and intricate than the nightly procession of conspiracies flashed across TV screens.

A script writer might hesitate to put his spy in a building within yards of a Federal courthouse, but Abel had his studio just across the street from the courthouse in which he was indicted.

It was in that shabby, one-room studio, according to the indictment, that he acted as the mastermind of an espionage network that sent United States defense secrets to Moscow.

Abel, described as a man of medium height with faded blue eyes and thinning hair, was taken into custody in the single room he had been occupying at the Latham Hotel, 4 East Twenty-eighth Street. Federal agents said that when they inspected his room they realized they had a bigger fish than simply a violator of the immigration laws.

They found a short-wave radio

Continued on Page 10, Column 4

CHARGED WITH SPYING:
Rudolf Ivanovich Abel at the court in Edinburg, Tex.
Associated Press Wirephoto

SENATOR SCORES INQUIRY LAWYERS

Kennedy Says They Do More Than Advise Labor Clients —Dio Linked to Payoffs

By JOSEPH A. LOFTUS
Special to The New York Times

WASHINGTON, Aug. 6—A Senator investigating labor-management misdeeds said today that the bar associations should check some of the lawyers who had appeared in the Senate racket hearings.

Senator John F. Kennedy, Democrat, of Massachusetts, named names as he spoke at a hearing of the Select Committee on Improper Activities in the Labor or Management Field.

"We have seen lawyers doing more than advising clients of their legal rights," he said.

Senator Kennedy referred by name to Herman E. Cooper of New York of the Bakery and Confectionery Workers International Union, Joseph Jacobs of Atlanta and Sam Bassett of Seattle of the International Brotherhood of Teamsters and Alfons Landa of Washington, who was a director of Fruehauf Trailer Company.

Endorsed Teamster Loan

Mr. Landa endorsed a $1,500,000 loan from the teamsters to the Fruehauf Foundation for the purchase of Fruehauf stock.

"I hope," Senator Kennedy said, "that the respective bar associations are getting the transcripts of these hearings and will see if these lawyers are meeting their responsibilities to the bar.

The Ethical Practices Committee of the American Federation of Labor and Congress of Industrial Organizations is attempting to meet its responsibilities."

Mr. Bassett, reached in Seattle, said that the committee, through its chief counsel, Robert F. Kennedy, had subpoenaed him two months ago.

"My appearance was post-

Continued on Page 45, Column 2

CITY MAPS ATTACK ON RACKET UNIONS

Wagner Opens 4-Step Drive to Aid Exploited Workers

By STANLEY LEVEY

Mayor Wagner yesterday threw the city's power and prestige behind a drive to end the exploitation of Puerto Rican and Negro workers by union racketeers and unscrupulous employers.

After a two-hour meeting at City Hall with representatives of labor and industry, the district attorneys of all five boroughs, no police officials and the heads of key city departments, Mr. Wagner announced the following program of action:

¶An appeal to all victims of such exploitation to get in touch with a legitimate labor union or any city department and make known their grievances.

¶A designation of the city Labor Department, headed by Harold A. Felix, to handle such complaints and to relay them to the proper department for investigation and action. The Mayor said all departments would assist in the program.

¶The establishment of a citywide committee composed of representatives of labor and industry, city officials and members of the Puerto Rican Labor Department here. This group will meet continually to review progress in the drive to plan strategy.

¶The appointment at a later date of a committee to study

Continued on Page 34, Column 2

President Says Washington, Too, Had Critics

Calls Attacks 'Weak' in View of the Abuse Predecessor Took

By JAMES RESTON
Special to The New York Times

WASHINGTON, Aug. 7—President Eisenhower took a philosophical attitude today toward political critics who have recently been accusing him of flabby leadership and "self-righteous moralizing."

Go and look up what the papers said about Gen. George Washington in his second term, the President advised reporters at his news conference this morning.

"When I compare the weak, inconsequential things they say about me," he said, "compared to what they said about the man who I think is the greatest human the English-speaking race has produced, then I can be quite philosophical about it."

Among the charges recently leveled at President Eisenhower are that he pronounces principles he does not follow in action, that he accepts gifts he should not accept, that he defends legislation without knowing what is in it, that he introduces policies that he later abandons, that he nominates unqualified men he

President Eisenhower
The New York Times

President Washington
Portrait by Wertmueller

does not know, that he "has no brains" in economic matters, that he does not read and that sometimes he does not tell the truth.

A study of this catalogue compared with what was said about President Washington between

Hails Nation's First Leader as 'Greatest Human' of Race

"liar" when he said the defeat of the school construction bill was not his (the President's) fault.

For in the brass-knuckles days of early American journalism "liar" was almost a term of endearment, and President Washington was accused of everything from treason to royalty.

Benjamin F. Bache and William Duane of The [Philadelphia] Aurora, James T. Callender of The Richmond Inquirer, and Thomas Paine, the pamphleteer heaped one calumny after another on the first President.

Bache described him as "treacherous," "mischievous" and "inefficient." He accused Washington of "stately journeying through the American continent in search of personal incense," of "ostentatious professions of ingratitude," of "littleness of passions" and of "insignificance."

James E. Pollard of Ohio State University, who is the chief chronicler of Presidential misery in the press, recalls in his book, "The Presidents and the Press," that General Eisenhower was a

1789 and 1797 supports the Eisenhower assertion that this is "weak, inconsequential" stuff indeed. And that still goes if the Eisenhower catalogue is padded to include Representative Cleveland M. Bailey's recent charge

Continued on Page 6, Column 2

Juvenile Gangs Quiet As Patrol Goes On

More than 500 student policemen completed their second tour of duty on youth crime beats in the city last night. With minor exceptions, they maintained Tuesday night's record of peace and quiet.

Early today, an officer at Police Headquarters said: "There have been no arrests of gang activity and unlawful assembly during the night."

The police reported that Tuesday night was the quietest in almost two months. The rookie policemen, after only a month's training at the Police Academy, were assigned in pairs to patrol twenty-five so-called hazardous precincts between 6 P. M. and midnight.

But Acting Police Commissioner James R. Kennedy warned: "It is too early and too soon to evaluate the effectiveness of the assignment of the rookie policemen to patrol duty."

Shortly after the rookies began

Continued on Page 21, Column 3

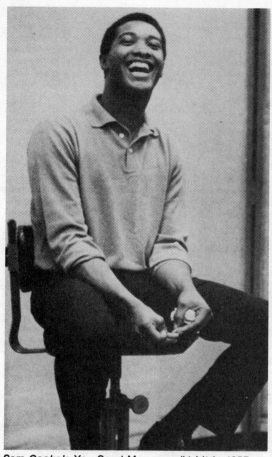

Sam Cooke's You Send Me *was a #1 hit in 1957.*

The Coasters made Searchin' *famous. Their #1 song the following year was* Yakety Yak.

Diana *was a smash hit for Paul Anka in 1957. In the years that followed his success increased.* You Are My Destiny *was popular in '58 and* Lonely Boy *was a #1 hit in '59.*

Johnny Mathis hits flooded 1957 with songs like It's Not for Me to Say; Chances Are; Wonderful, Wonderful; No Love *and* Wild is the Wind.

Jack Paar replaced Steve Allen on the Tonight *show in 1957. Jack is seen here with his guests Buddy Hackett and Alexander King.*

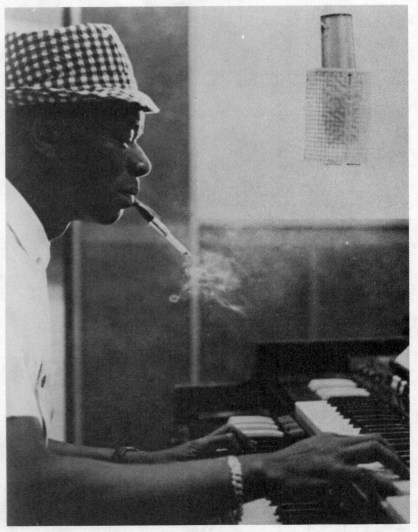

Joyce Brothers' immense knowledge of boxing helped her to win $64,000 on the $64,000 Question, the show that shook up the industry when it became apparent that some contestants had been given the answers beforehand. Another winner of the top prize was Bronx shoemaker Geno Prato, who answered questions on opera.

Nat King Cole, in 1957, was the first Black to have his own network variety series.

"All the News That's Fit to Print"

The New York Times.

LATE CITY EDITION
U. S. Weather Bureau Report (Page 59) forecasts:
Mostly fair and seasonable today and tomorrow.
Temp. range: 70—57. Yesterday: 67.7—55.9.

VOL. CVII—No. 36,404   © 1957, by The New York Times Company. Times Square, New York 36, N. Y.   NEW YORK, WEDNESDAY, SEPTEMBER 25, 1957.   10c beyond 100-mile zone from New York City   FIVE CENTS

PRESIDENT SENDS TROOPS TO LITTLE ROCK, FEDERALIZES ARKANSAS NATIONAL GUARD; TELLS NATION HE ACTED TO AVOID ANARCHY

WEST AGAIN BARS SOVIET PROPOSAL ON MIDEAST TALK

U. S. Says Latest Moscow Note 'Cynically Distorts' American Actions

Text of U. S. note to Soviet will be found on Page 5.

By DANA ADAMS SCHMIDT
Special to The New York Times.

WASHINGTON, Sept. 24—The United States, Britain and France rejected today the latest in a series of Soviet bids for recognition of the Soviet Union's role in the Middle East.

A brief United States reply delivered in Moscow said that a Soviet note of Sept. 3 was "offensive in tone and cynically distorts United States objectives and actions in the Middle East."

It accused the Soviet Union of setting in motion "a chain of events leading to the present dangerous situation" by shipping large quantities of arms into the area.

U. S. Affirms Doctrine

The note also warned the Soviet Union that the United States Government intended to carry out the national policy laid down in the Eisenhower Doctrine, which "regards the preservation of the independence and integrity of the nations of that region as vital to world peace and as vital, therefore, to its own national interests."

The doctrine, proclaimed in a Joint Resolution of the House of Representatives and the Senate on March 9, 1957, also affirmed the President's authority to use United States forces to aid any Middle East state that asked for help against aggression by a power controlled by international communism.

The Soviet Union's note had accused the United States of seeking to overthrow the Syrian Government and of generally fomenting trouble in the Middle East.

3d Rejection of Soviet Bid

It had proposed, for the third time, a four-power declaration renouncing the use of force in the area. Earlier Soviet proposals for such a declaration, also rejected by the West, were made Feb. 11 and April 19.

As interpreted by United States sources on the Middle East, these notes were meant to convey the idea that the four powers should meet to negotiate a settlement of their rivalries in the Middle East. The first of the notes even went into detail with a proposal for an embargo on shipment of arms to the area.

Because the Soviet Union has asserted its presence in Syria, and because there seems to be little the Western powers can do to reverse developments in the area,

Continued on Page 5, Column 3

Rebel Chief Seized In Algiers Gunfight

By THOMAS F. BRADY
Special to The New York Times.

ALGIERS, Algeria, Sept. 24—The chief of the nationalist terrorist organization in Algiers was in the hands of French parachute troops today. The rebel leader, Saadi Yacef, 29 years old, had eluded capture in the crowded Casbah for more than two years.

With him was 24-year-old Miss Zorah Drif, an Algerian revolutionary, who was condemned to death in absentia by a French military tribunal.

A parachute colonel told reporters this evening that Mr. Yacef and Miss Drif had surrendered at 5:30 A. M. after the terrorist chief had wounded a lieutenant colonel and a master sergeant of a Foreign Legion parachute regiment. The colonel then took reporters to a hideout high in the Casbah where he described how the

Continued on Page 4, Column 3

London and Bonn Rule Out Any Currency Revaluation

Britain Tells Monetary Fund Session She Will Draw $500,000,000 in Stand-By Credit From Export-Import Bank

By EDWIN L. DALE JR.
Special to The New York Times.

WASHINGTON, Sept. 24—British and West German spokesmen and the Managing Director of the International Monetary Fund said today that the question of exchange rates for the pound and the mark was "definitely settled." There will be no change.

At the same time, Britain, through Peter Thorneycroft, Chancellor of the Exchequer, announced she would draw "over the coming weeks" the $500,000,000 stand-by credit she arranged last winter with the United States Export-Import Bank.

In his speech at the annual meeting of the fund, Mr. Thor-neycroft indicated that Britain was drawing the money to demonstrate to speculators that she had the resources to defend the pound.

Both the British and the West Germans emphasized that the recent huge flow of gold and dollars out of Britain and into West Germany had been based solely on speculation, not on basic factors in their foreign trading accounts.

Per Jacobsson, the Fund's Managing Director, said: "The growing knowledge that there will be no alteration in the value of either the Deutsche

Continued on Page 8, Column 3

SOVIET ASSAILED BY LLOYD AT U. N.

Briton Suggests Arms Sent Arabs May Be Stocks for Future Bases

Excerpts from Lloyd's speech are printed on Page 4.

By THOMAS J. HAMILTON
Special to The New York Times.

UNITED NATIONS, N. Y., Sept. 24—Britain denounced today Soviet arms shipments to Arab countries. Selwyn Lloyd, British Foreign Secretary, suggested that the purpose might be to "pre-stock forward bases" for the Soviet Union itself."

Mr. Lloyd told the General Assembly that Soviet arms had been delivered "on such a scale as to give some color to this suggestion." He added that Britain viewed the Syrian situation "with grave concern." In addition, he criticized Soviet policy throughout the area.

Mr. Lloyd devoted most of his speech to the Middle East and to disarmament. He did not say what action the Assembly should take on either subject.

However, he declared that Secretary of State Dulles, in

Continued on Page 4, Column 3

City Approves Plan By Wiley to Build Midtown Garages

By JOSEPH C. INGRAHAM

The Board of Estimate has approved in principle the program of Traffic Commissioner T. T. Wiley for garage construction in the heart of lower and mid-Manhattan.

The decision clears the way for a start on $24,000,000 of garages. It also settles a three-year dispute between Mr. Wiley and other city executives that has stymied off-street parking relief.

As a result, the first of the projects—a garage in the Herald Square area—will be on the board's calendar on Oct. 9. Eight other garages are to be centrally located in Manhattan and two in the busiest parts of the Bronx.

The Herald Square garage will be east of the Avenue of the Americas between West Thirty-fifth and Thirty-sixth Streets with entrances and exits on both streets. There will be space for 610 cars on eight levels accessible by ramps. Rates will be geared to "meet the heavy unsatisfied demand for short-time parking," Mr. Wiley said.

Rates proposed by the Commissioner would be 25 cents a

Continued on Page 25, Column 1

SOLDIERS FLY IN

1,000 Go to Little Rock —9,936 in Guard Told to Report

The texts of Executive orders on troops are on Page 16.

By JACK RAYMOND
Special to The New York Times.

WASHINGTON, Sept. 24—The Army ordered all Arkansas National Guardsmen to report for Federal duty tonight and rushed 1,000 airborne troops of the Regular Army into Little Rock to preserve order.

The Regulars were members of the 101st Airborne Division, which won fame in World War II under the command of Gen. Maxwell D. Taylor, now Chief of Staff of the Army.

Maj. Gen. Edwin A. Walker, a much-decorated combat commander with a reputation for toughness, was put in command of the Regular Army contingent and the federalized Guardsmen in Arkansas. He is the commander of the Arkansas Military District.

General Walker's mission is to make sure that no one frustrates Federal court order that nine Negro pupils be admitted to Central High School.

Wilson Carries Out Order

Charles E. Wilson, Secretary of Defense, carrying out President Eisenhower's mandate, earlier had called the entire Arkansas Army and Air National Guard, totaling 9,936 men, into Federal service.

At the same time, an Army spokesman said that it was planned to make "the absolute minimum demonstration of force necessary."

Immediately after Secretary Wilson signed the federalization call to the Arkansas Guard at 2:25 P. M., Secretary Brucker telephoned the office of Gov. Orval E. Faubus in Little Rock.

At the same time he sent a telegram to the Governor, explaining that President Eisenhower "desires" the personnel of the Arkansas Army and Air National Guard organizations

Continued on Page 14, Column 2

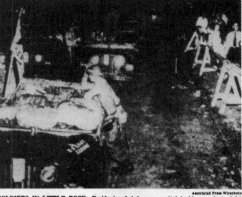

SOLDIERS IN LITTLE ROCK: Residents of Arkansas capital looking on last night as men of the 101st Airborne Division took positions outside the Central High School.

Associated Press Wirephoto

GOVERNORS URGE WHITE HOUSE TALK

Southerners Move to Set Up Mediation Machinery in Use of Federal Troops

By JOHN N. POPHAM
Special to The New York Times.

SEA ISLAND, Ga., Sept. 24—Southern Governors moved tonight to establish mediation machinery that would remove Federal troops from the South. The Governors acted a few hours after the President had federalized the Arkansas National Guard.

Gov. Luther Hodges of North Carolina, chairman of the Southern Governors Conference in session here, announced that two proposals would be submitted to the resolutions committee of the conference for formal consideration tomorrow.

One is a proposal of Gov. Frank G. Clement of Tennessee to establish an informal committee of Southern Governors to seek a meeting with President Eisenhower in a search for a solution to the Little Rock school integration crisis.

The other is a request to the President to hold off the use of Federal troops and to agree

Continued on Page 16, Column 4

Price Index Up .2%; Sets Another High

By RICHARD E. MOONEY
Special to The New York Times.

WASHINGTON, Sept. 24—The United States Consumers' Price Index rose two-tenths of a per cent in August, setting another record. It was the twelfth consecutive monthly increase, but among the smallest of the twelve.

The Labor Department's Bureau of Labor Statistics reported today that the index rose in August to 121, using the price average in the 1947-49 period as a comparison base of 100. All the major categories of prices increased, but food and housing were the strongest factors.

The August index was 3.6 per cent higher than that of a year earlier. This meant that a typical city family paid $1.03 3/5 in August 1957 for the goods and services that cost $1 in August 1956.

The Commerce Department

Continued on Page 24, Column 3

Troops on Guard at School; Negroes Ready to Return

By BENJAMIN FINE
Special to The New York Times.

LITTLE ROCK, Ark., Sept. 24—Troops from the Army's crack 101st Airborne Division, carrying carbines and billy clubs, took posts around Central High School tonight. They were here to see that court-ordered integration is carried out.

With police sirens wailing and headlights flashing, Army trucks loaded with soldiers roared into position. The soldiers represented about a quarter of the contingent of 1,000 crack troops of the division that was ordered to Little Rock by President Eisenhower to prevent mob riots and violence.

The first group of 500 airborne soldiers came to the city this afternoon from Fort Campbell, Ky., and a second group of 500 arrived by plane this evening. The bulk of the two groups bivouacked for the night in areas away from the school.

With the arrival of Federal troops, including some Negro soldiers who were not expected to be on duty at the school, Negro students were ready to try again to enter the high school.

A mob of 1,000 persons yesterday forced the city and school authorities to withdraw nine Negro students who had attended integrated classes for 3 hours and 13 minutes. The students did not try to enter the school today.

Mrs. L. C. Bates, president

Continued on Page 15, Column 1

Aiken Defends Move

Senator John L. McClellan, Democrat of Arkansas, said he believed such use of military force by the Federal Government was "without authority of law."

He said he was "very apprehensive that such action may precipitate more trouble than it will prevent."

The Labor Department's Bureau

Senator Richard B. Russell, Democrat of Georgia and leader of Southern opposition to the Civil Rights Bill in the last session, said that President Eisenhower's use of troops might "put Negro children in the white schools," but that it would "have a calamitous effect on race relations and on the cause of national unity."

On the other side of the issue, Senator George D. Aiken, Republican of Vermont, said the President "is undoubtedly with-

Continued on Page 17, Column 3

EISENHOWER ON AIR

Says School Defiance Has Gravely Harmed Prestige of U. S.

Text of President's address appears on Page 14.

By ANTHONY LEWIS
Special to The New York Times.

WASHINGTON, Sept. 24—President Eisenhower sent Federal troops to Little Rock, Ark., today to open the way for the admission of nine Negro pupils into Central High School.

Earlier, the President federalized the Arkansas National Guard and authorized calling the Guard and regular Federal forces to remove obstructions to justice in Little Rock school integration.

His history - making action was based on a formal finding that his "cease and desist" proclamation, issued last night, had not been obeyed. Mobs of pro-segregationists still gathered in the vicinity of Central High School this morning.

Tonight, from the White House, President Eisenhower told the nation in a speech for radio and television that he had acted to prevent "mob rule" and "anarchy."

Historic Decision

The President's decision to send troops to Little Rock was reached at his vacation headquarters in Newport, R. I. It was one of historic importance politically, socially, constitutionally. For the first time since the Reconstruction days that followed the Civil War, the Federal Government was using its ultimate power to compel equal treatment of the Negro in the South.

He said violent defiance of Federal Court orders in Little Rock had done grave harm to "the prestige and influence, and indeed to the safety, of our nation and the world." He called on the people of Arkansas and the South to "preserve and respect the law even when they disagree with it."

Guardsmen Withdrawn

Action quickly followed the President's orders. During the day and night 1,000 members of the 101st Airborne Division were flown to Little Rock. Charles E. Wilson, Secretary of the Defense, ordered into Federal service all 10,000 members of the Arkansas National Guard.

Today's events were the climax of three weeks of skirmishing between the Federal Government and Gov. Orval E. Faubus of Arkansas. It was three weeks ago this morning that the Governor first ordered National Guard troops to Central High School to preserve order. The nine Negro students were prevented from entering the school.

The Guardsmen were gone yesterday, withdrawn by Governor Faubus as the result of a

Continued on Page 14, Column 6

CONGRESS IS SPLIT ON USE OF TROOPS

Johnston Calls for Faubus to Resist President but Others Hail His Move

By JOHN W. FINNEY
Special to The New York Times.

WASHINGTON, Sept. 24—Congressional reaction to President Eisenhower's decision to use troops in the Little Rock integration crisis ranged from angry denunciation to outright praise today.

Southern Senators sharply criticized the President and suggested he had exceeded his legal authority. Northern Senators supported the President, but some of them expressed reservations that the action was rather belated.

Expects Faubus to Act

Maj. Gen. Edwin A. Walker, commander of the Arkansas Military District, issued a formal order to the people of Little Rock not to collect in crowds and to let Central High School be integrated peaceably.

Senator Olin D. Johnston, Democrat of South Carolina, suggested that Gov. Orval E. Faubus of Arkansas "stand up for states' rights" and force a showdown with the President by calling out the Arkansas National Guard on his own.

Senator Johnston, a former Governor of South Carolina, said if he were Governor Faubus, "I'd proclaim a state of insurrection down there, and I'd call out the National Guard, and I'd then find out who's going to run things in my state."

Asked by reporters whether he believed Governor Faubus would take such steps, Senator Johnston said, "I think he will and I hope he will."

Continued on Page 14, Column 3

Textile Union Gets 30 Days to Reform

By A. H. RASKIN

A scandal-tainted textile union was ordered yesterday to oust its two chief officers within thirty days or face possible suspension from the merged labor federation.

The ultimatum was given to the 40,000-member United Textile Workers by the executive council of the American Federation of Labor and Congress of Industrial Organizations.

It foreshadowed the fixing of a similar clean-up deadline today for the 1,400,000-member International Brotherhood of Teamsters and the 140,000-member Bakery and Confectionery Workers International Union.

The federation's Ethical Practices Committee has found all three unions guilty of violating the anti-racketeering provisions of the A. F. L.-C. I. O. constitution. The findings are based

Continued on Page 13, Column 8

U. S. Cutters Conquer Northwest Passage

3 Coast Guard Craft First of the Nation to Make Transit

By JOHN H. FENTON
Special to The New York Times.

BOSTON, Sept. 24 — Two Coast Guard cutters were saluted in Boston Harbor today at the end of a successful mission to find a practical Northwest Passage—a route around the top of the North American Continent.

A third cutter, the Spar, proceeded directly to her home port at Bristol, R. I., to be welcomed there as the first United States vessel to circumnavigate the continent.

The cutters Storis, from Juneau, Alaska, and the Bramble, from Miami, Fla., put in here for their welcoming. They will continue their homeward voyages later in the week.

The three cutters were the first United States vessels to make the passage.

The shrill sirens of waterspouting fireboats and the deeper - throated whistles of other craft sounded a "well done" as the two bulky cutters made their way up the harbor.

Ranking Coast Guard officers and civil officials joined with members of families of the crews in a dockside welcome as the cutters tied up at

Continued on Page 10, Column 1

Coast Guardsmen on the stern of the Spar view her sister cutters, Bramble, left, and Storis, during the transit of Simpson Strait. This was a difficult part of the voyage.

U. S. Coast Guard

1957

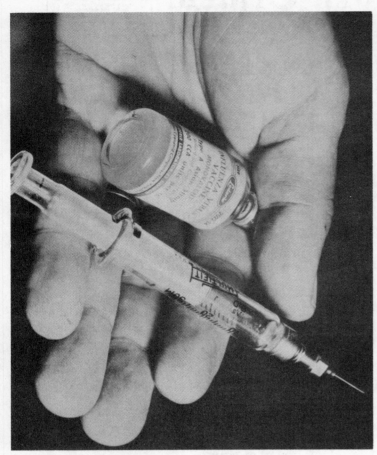

The Asian flu epidemic in 1957-58 caused 20 million deaths in the United States. A vaccine was prepared to combat the new virus.

The United States would send monkeys into space, as opposed to the dogs used by Russia, to determine the extent of the hazards space would present to man.

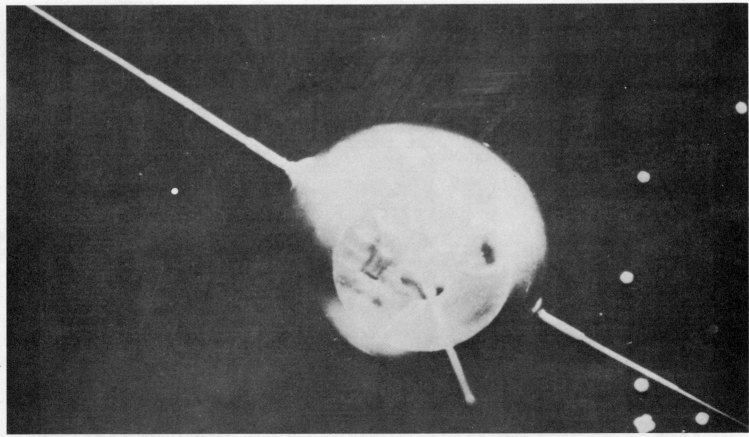

The U.S.S.R. launched Sputnik, their space satellite, in 1957. Before the U.S. had fired one, the Russians had fired three, including one carrying a dog named Laika, who later died from the effects of a lack of oxygen.

"All the News That's Fit to Print"

The New York Times.

LATE CITY EDITION
U. S. Weather Bureau Report (Page 35) forecast:
Cloudy and cool today and tonight.
Mostly fair tomorrow.
Temp. range: 65—53. Yesterday: 62.4—49.2.

VOL. CVII..No. 36,414.

© 1957. by The New York Times Company.
Times Square, New York 36, N. Y.

NEW YORK, SATURDAY, OCTOBER 5, 1957.

10c beyond 100-mile zone
from New York City

FIVE CENTS

SOVIET FIRES EARTH SATELLITE INTO SPACE; IT IS CIRCLING THE GLOBE AT 18,000 M. P. H.; SPHERE TRACKED IN 4 CROSSINGS OVER U. S.

HOFFA IS ELECTED TEAMSTERS' HEAD; WARNS OF BATTLE

Defeats Two Foes 3 to 1 —Says Union Will Fight 'With Every Ounce'

Text of the Hoffa address is printed on Page 6.

By A. H. RASKIN
Special to The New York Times.

MIAMI BEACH, Oct. 4—The scandal-scarred International Brotherhood of Teamsters elected James R. Hoffa as its president today.

He won by a margin of nearly 3 to 1 over the combined vote of two rivals who campaigned on pledges to clean up the nation's biggest union.

Senate rackets investigators and Hoffa critics in the union rank-and-file immediately opened actions to strip the 44-year-old former warehouseman from Detroit of his election victory.

A jubilant Hoffa exhibited, however, greater concern over the possibility that his union might be ousted from the American Federation of Labor and Congress of Industrial Organizations. He appealed for time to prove that he could make the teamsters "a model of trade unionism."

The parent organization has ordered the 1,400,000-member Teamsters Union to get rid of corrupt leadership by Oct. 24 or face suspension. Hoffa said he felt actions by the union at its week-long convention here should satisfy the federation.

Warns Union Will Fight

He made it plain to the 1,700 cheering delegates that he did not intend to go before the convention in the role of suppliant. He said expulsion would not destroy the teamsters. He warned that the union would fight "with every ounce of strength we possess" if it found itself outside.

In such a civil war the teamsters would start with a war-chest of $38,000,000 in the hands of the international union and much more at the disposal of its locals. The teamsters also count on their strategic power over other unions through their control of trucks and warehouses.

The Hoffa victory brought warnings of repressive legislation from James P. Mitchell, Secretary of Labor, and Senator John L. McClellan, Democrat of Arkansas. The Senator heads the Select Committee on Improper Activities in the Labor or Management Field, which has accused Hoffa of gangster associations and questionable financial practices.

Winner on First Ballot

A three-hour roll-call gave Hoffa the $50,000-a-year union presidency on the first ballot. His machine, in full command of the convention since it opened Monday, registered 1,208 votes for Hoffa.

William A. Lee of Chicago, the union's seventh vice president, was second with 313 votes. Thomas J. Haggerty of Chicago, secretary-treasurer of the Milk Wagon Drivers Union, Local 753, trailed with 140 votes.

The Hoffa forces then began providing the new leader with a rubber stamp board. It elected five of thirteen vice presidents and would have elected the rest today if time had permitted completion of the cumbersome balloting procedure.

Hoffa repeatedly indicated his irritation that some of the old vice presidents marked for elimination had refused to give up without the formality of a roll-call.

Even before the voting, the McClellan committee subpoenaed the full records of the convention's credential committee. A United States marshal served the subpoena this morning on Joseph Konowe of New York, the committee secretary. He was directed to turn over all

Continued on Page 6, Column 7

IN TOKEN OF VICTORY: Dave Beck, retiring head of the Teamsters Union, raises hand of James R. Hoffa upon his election as union's president. At right is Mrs. Hoffa.
Associated Press Wirephoto

FAUBUS COMPARES HIS STAND TO LEE'S

Says He Will Remain Loyal to People of Arkansas— All Is Quiet at School

By HOMER BIGART
Special to The New York Times.

LITTLE ROCK, Ark., Oct. 4 —Gov. Orval E. Faubus said today that he had made a decision as painfully difficult as the one that had confronted Robert E. Lee at the outset of the Civil War.

"Lee was offered command of the Federal Army in 1861," Governor Faubus recalled. "Lee decided to remain loyal to the people of his state.

"The Democratic party of the North wants me to go along with them on the integration issue. I will remain with the People of Arkansas."

Governor Faubus said he had come under no local pressure to change his stand on integration at Little Rock Central High School. It was a stand that forced President Eisenhower to send Federal troops into this city to uphold Federal Court decisions and to safeguard the nine Negro students registered at Central High.

Winthrop Rockefeller, chairman of the Arkansas Industrial Development Commission, broke silence today on the Little Rock integration crisis, declaring it had "damaged" the state's prospects for economic progress. He called events of the past month "tragic."

It was a quiet day in Little Rock. The nine Negro boys and girls attended school without incident. But no early solution to the crisis seemed likely.

There was no break in the impasse reached Tuesday night when a compromise plan for the

Continued on Page 18, Column 2

Flu Widens in City; 10% Rate Predicted; 200,000 Pupils Out

By ROBERT ALDEN

Asian influenza continued to spread through the city yesterday.

Commissioner of Hospitals Morris A. Jacobs reported that there were ten times more respiratory infections than during the comparable period a year ago.

Attendance in the city's schools fell again. The Board of Education said that close to 200,000 of the city's 941,000 pupils were not in their classrooms yesterday. On Thursday 160,000 pupils were absent.

The attendance estimates were based on a sampling of the schools by the board. The sampling showed that in some schools in the Harlem area—the section hardest hit by the epidemic—more than 50 per cent of the pupils were absent. The board estimated that the over-all city absence rate was 20 per cent.

3,000 Teachers Absent

About 3,000 teachers out of about 39,000 were not in their classrooms yesterday, compared with 2,700 absent on Thursday.

The city's acting Health Commissioner, Dr. Roscoe P. Kandle, said he expected that the total number of people affected by the highly infectious disease would run closer to 800,000 rather than 1,600,000 as predicted in some quarters.

It was estimated Thursday that 200,000 persons in New York had contracted the respiratory infection, and the total yesterday was believed to be somewhat higher.

Commissioner Kandle explained that any attempt to project the ultimate number of cases would involve conjecture.

Continued on Page 8, Column 1

ARGENTINA TAKES EMERGENCY STEPS

State of Siege Proclaimed in Buenos Aires Region —Arrests Reported

By Reuters

BUENOS AIRES, Oct. 4 —A state of siege, suspending constitutional guarantees, was proclaimed tonight in Buenos Aires city and Province.

The Under Secretary of the Ministry of Interior, Garcia Puente, announced the state of siege at a news conference.

He said the emergency move suspended for thirty days the constitutional guarantees in the capital and the Province of Buenos Aires, but not in the remainder of the nation.

He said the measure was aimed exclusively "at defending the normal development of the Government's political plan, jeopardized through sabotage and social unrest."

The proclamation of the state of siege followed the arrest of scores of labor leaders during the day. The number arrested was estimated by observers as 100 to 300.

Bankers, telephone workers, oil workers, seamstresses and other unions reported tonight that their leaders had been detained and were taken aboard

Continued on Page 4, Column 5

COURSE RECORDED

Navy Picks Up Radio Signals—4 Report Sighting Device

By WALTER SULLIVAN
Special to The New York Times

WASHINGTON, Saturday, Oct. 5—The Naval Research Laboratory announced early today that it had recorded four crossings of the Soviet earth satellite over the United States.

It said that one had passed near Washington. Two crossings were farther to the west. The location of the fourth was not made available immediately.

It added that tracking would be continued in an attempt to pin down the orbit sufficiently to obtain scientific information of the type sought in the International Geophysical Year.

[Four visual sightings, one of which was in conjunction with a radio contact, were reported by early Saturday morning. Two sightings were made at Columbus, Ohio, and one each from Terre Haute, Ind., and Whittier, Calif.]

Press Reports Noted

Soviet newspapers reported several weeks ago that the Soviet satellites would broadcast on frequencies in the neighborhood of twenty and forty megacycles. More exact frequencies were given by Soviet scientists at a conference on rockets and satellites that took place here this week.

Presumably the Naval Research Laboratory, which is responsible for the United States satellite program under the National Academy of Sciences, immediately set up receivers on those frequencies.

The tracking system established in this country to monitor its own satellites uses 108 megacycles, since much more accurate positions can be obtained with the higher frequencies. The Russians at first agreed to use equipment "compatible" with that of the United States, but then announced the lower frequencies.

Deception Ruled Out

American scientists believe this was because of a shortage of Soviet receivers capable of handling the higher frequency. It was not thought to be an attempt to hide the satellite since the Soviet signals are within easy reach of American listeners.

This was demonstrated last night as amateur and commercial radio stations, as well as the Naval Research Laboratory, reported hearing them.

Teams of visual observers at 150 stations in the United States and other Western nations were alerted during the

Continued on Page 3, Column 6

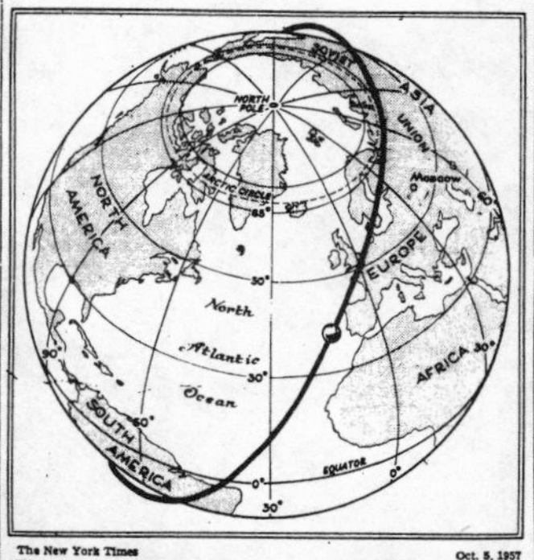

The New York Times   Oct. 5, 1957
The approximate orbit of the Russian earth satellite is shown by black line. The rotation of the earth will bring the United States under the orbit of Soviet-made moon.

Device Is 8 Times Heavier Than One Planned by U.S.

Special to The New York Times.

WASHINGTON, Oct. 4—Leaders of the United States earth satellite program were astonished tonight to learn that the Soviet Union had launched a satellite eight times heavier than one that contemplated by this country.

Dr. Joseph Kaplan, chairman of the United States program for the International Geophysical Year, described the 184-pound weight as "fantastic." The heaviest American satellites are to weigh twenty-one and a half pounds.

The actual launching, nevertheless, did not take the American scientists by surprise. At the end of working sessions on the International Conference on Rockets and Satellites, which has been taking place here, some said they thought the pitching of a Soviet satellite into the sky was imminent.

The satellite must fly at a speed of about 18,000 miles an hour to counteract the force of gravity at an altitude of 560 miles. The initial announcement in Moscow did not make it clear whether or not the rocket that placed it in orbit was aimed north or south.

Its Direction in Doubt

This would determine whether or not the satellite's initial crossing of the United States was northbound or southbound. Since the earth rotates within the orbit the satellite should in one day traverse almost all nations of the world.

With an orbit inclined 65 degrees to the equator, its sweep would cover virtually the entire region between the Arctic circle and the Antarctic circle.

William A. Holaday, special assistant to the Secretary of Defense for guided missiles, said the launching was not evidence of Soviet technological superiority in missile and rocket developments.

Mr. Holaday noted that Project Vanguard, the United States satellite program, had been an "open" project as part of the International Geophysical year and there has been no

Continued on Page 3, Column 7

560 MILES HIGH

Visible With Simple Binoculars, Moscow Statement Says

Text of Tass announcement appears on Page 3.

By WILLIAM J. JORDEN
Special to The New York Times.

MOSCOW, Saturday, Oct. 5—The Soviet Union announced this morning that it successfully launched a man-made earth satellite into space yesterday.

The Russians calculated the satellite's orbit at a maximum of 560 miles above the earth and its speed at 18,000 miles an hour.

The official Soviet news agency Tass said the artificial moon, with a diameter of twenty-two inches and a weight of 184 pounds, was circling the earth once every hour and thirty-five minutes. This means more than fifteen times a day.

Two radio transmitters, Tass said, are sending signals continuously on frequencies of 20.005 and 40.002 megacycles. These signals were said to be strong enough to be picked up by amateur radio operators. The trajectory of the satellite is being tracked by numerous scientific stations.

Due Over Moscow Today

Tass said the satellite was moving at an angle of 65 degrees to the equatorial plane and would pass over the Moscow area twice today.

"Its flight," the announcement added, "will be observed in the rays of the rising and setting sun with the aid of the simplest optical instruments, such as binoculars and spyglasses."

The Soviet Union said the world's first satellite was "successfully launched" yesterday. Thus it asserted that it had put a scientific instrument into space before the United States. Washington has disclosed plans to launch a satellite next spring, Oct. 4.

The Moscow announcement said the Soviet Union planned to send up more and bigger and heavier artificial satellites during the current International Geophysical Year, an eighteen-month period of study of the earth, its crust and the space surrounding it.

Five Miles a Second

The rocket that carried the satellite into space left the earth at a rate of five miles a second, the Tass announcement said. Nothing was revealed, however, concerning the material of which the man-made moon was constructed or the site in the Soviet Union where the sphere was launched.

The Soviet Union said its sphere circling the earth had opened the way to interplanetary travel.

It did not pass up the opportunity to use the launching for propaganda purposes. It said in its announcement that people now could see how "the new socialist society" had turned the boldest dreams of mankind into reality.

Moscow said the satellite was the result of years of study and research on the part of Soviet scientists.

Several Years of Study

Tass said:

"For several years the research and experimental designing work has been under way in the Soviet Union to create artificial satellites of the earth. It has already been reported in the press that the launching of the earth satellites in the U. S. S. R. had been planned in accordance with the program of International Geophysical Year research.

"As a result of intensive work by the research institutes and design bureaus, the first artificial earth satellite in the world has now been created. This first 'satellite was successfully launched in the U. S. S. R. October four.'

The Soviet announcement said that as a result of the tremendous speed at which the satellite was moving it would

Continued on Page 3, Column 8

SATELLITE SIGNAL BROADCAST HERE

Impulse Carried on Radio and TV—First Reported by Long Island Station

By ROY SILVER

Radio signals from the first satellite launched yesterday by the Russians were broadcast to radio and television audiences here last night.

The first word that the signals had been received in this country was reported by RCA Communication, Inc. It said that its receiving station at Riverhead, L. I., had picked up what it believed to be impulse signals from the Soviet satellite.

The National Broadcasting Company and the Columbia Broadcasting System broke into their radio and television programs to enable their audiences to hear the pinging sound of the "moon's" signal. The British Broadcasting Corporation in London said it had tuned powerful receivers to the Soviet earth satellite frequencies. Reuter's radio station north of London reported hearing the signals.

RCA Communications, a subsidiary of Radio Corporation of America, said the first signal had been received at 8:07 P. M. on a frequency of 20.005 megacycles on the 15-meter wave length.

One hour and twenty-nine minutes later, at 9:36 P. M., Project Vanguard, the United States satellite program, had been an "open" project, about eighty miles from the city, reported that the satellite was making another round of the earth. Other approaches to

Continued on Page 2, Column 4

Ex-Premier Mollet Accepts Bid To Form a New French Cabinet

Socialist Leader Agrees With Reluctance and Without Giving Much Hope

By ROBERT C. DOTY
Special to The New York Times.

PARIS, Oct. 4—Former Premier Guy Mollet agreed reluctantly and without much hope today to try to form a new French Cabinet.

M. Mollet's pessimism, shared by many observers here, was based on the fact that both he and his party, the Socialists, still hold strongly to the policies that caused the defeat of the last two Cabinets, M. Mollet's own and that of Premier Maurice Bourgès-Maunoury, a Radical.

Thus the Socialists still support the views on economic and social questions, including the demand for extensive governmental decree powers in those domains, that brought M. Mollet's Government down last May after a record-breaking sixty-age Cabinet's life span has been twenty-one weeks.

At the same time the Socialists regard as a minimum of

Continued on Page 6, Column 6

Guy Mollet
Associated Press

City Sifts Charge That Schupler, Brooklyn Councilman, Sold a Job

By PAUL CROWELL

The city is investigating a complaint that Councilman Philip J. Schupler accepted a $500 fee last year in exchange for a promise to get a job for a Brooklyn business man.

William R. Peer, executive secretary to Mayor Wagner, said yesterday that the inquiry was started several weeks ago after the complaint had been made by Sol L. Hoffman of 1934 Sixty-third Street, Brooklyn.

At the office of Investigation Commissioner Charles H. Tenney, who is making the investigation, it was said that no findings or conclusions had been reached.

The charge was denied by Mr. Schupler, a Democrat-Liberal, in a telephone interview.

He said that he had received a $500 check from Mr. Hoffman in May, 1956, but that it was given to him as a campaign contribution. Mr. Schupler was then a candidate for re-election as a Democratic district leader. He was defeated in the primary election a month later.

Disclosure of the investigation brought from Robert K. Christenberry, the Republican candidate for Mayor, the charge that "corruption and scandal in our City Council is symptomatic of the Wagner administration."

In a formal statement commenting on the Schupler case Mr. Christenberry called upon the city's voters to support him

Continued on Page 16, Column 3

Warsaw Crushes New Protest; Clubs, Tear Gas Rout Students

By SYDNEY GRUSON
Special to The New York Times.

WARSAW, Oct. 4—Policemen and students clashed again in the streets of Warsaw tonight.

Security chiefs, seemingly nervous, threw a guard of several hundred workers' militia around the downtown headquarters of the ruling United Workers (Communist) party.

For the second successive night the police broke up demonstrations by firing tear gas and beating students and others with rubber truncheons.

What began last night as a protest against the closing of one newspaper was turning tonight into a general clamor against police brutality and the suppression of free speech. By midnight the city had quieted

down and the people had left the streets.

Among those clubbed tonight was Franco Fabiani, permanent correspondent here of the Italian Communist paper L'Unita. He suffered two minor head wounds.

Signor Fabiani was caught in crowds charged by the police after about 3,000 students had met in the Polytechnic and adopted a resolution protesting both the closing of the newspaper Po Prostu and the "brutal interference" of the police at last night's meeting.

Tonight's trouble centered on the Polytechnic, the huge advanced technical school near the heart of Warsaw. It was

Continued on Page 5, Column 2

Algerian home rule outlined in the framework law that was defeated in the Assembly Monday. In both cases, opposition from the Right-wing Independents constituted the margin of defeat.

If M. Mollet should find it impossible to muster a new majority

Continued on Page 6, Column 6

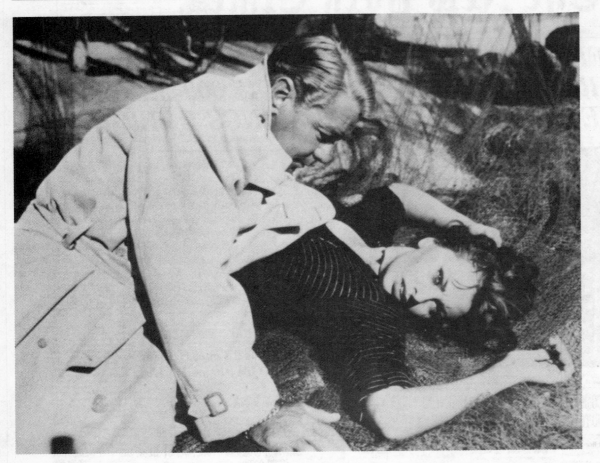

Boy on a Dolphin *was turned into one of 1957's major money-making films by importing Sophia Loren, the screen's latest Italian siren, to star with Alan Ladd.*

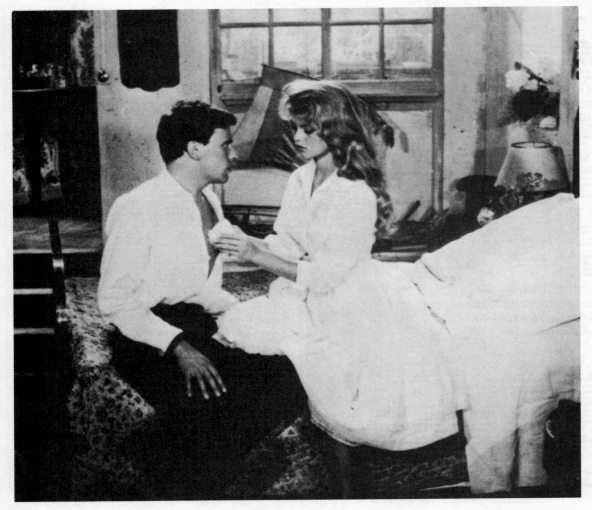

Brigitte Bardot cares for wounded Jean-Louis Trintignant in a scene from And God Created Woman. *The movie and its star shocked American audiences and established Bardot's reputation as a box-office draw.*

"All the News That's Fit to Print"

NEWS SUMMARY AND INDEX, PAGE 95

The New York Times.

LATE CITY EDITION

U.S. Weather Bureau Report (Page 96) forecasts: Rain early today; cloudy later; rain late tonight and tomorrow. Temp. range: 65—55. Yesterday: 62.0—55.2.

SECTION ONE

VOL. CVII—No. 36,443. © 1957, by The New York Times Company. Times Square, New York 36, N. Y. NEW YORK, SUNDAY NOVEMBER 3, 1957. 35c beyond 100-mile zone from New York City TWENTY-FIVE CENTS

SOVIET FIRES NEW SATELLITE, CARRYING DOG; HALF-TON SPHERE IS REPORTED 900 MILES UP

Zhukov Ousted From Party Jobs; Konev Condemns Him

MEYNER'S VICTORY IS SEEN IN SURVEY OF JERSEY VOTERS

Democratic Governor Likely to Win Re-election Over Senator Forbes Tuesday

A Times Team Report

A team of New York Times reporters has just completed a survey of political trends and issues in New Jersey. Reports on the election campaign there come from George Cable Wright, Milton Honig, Alfred E. Clark, Leonard Buder, John W. Slocum and Layhmond Robinson.

By GEORGE CABLE WRIGHT

The curtain will descend tomorrow night on the New Jersey Governorship campaign. The contest—on the surface, at least — appears to have been enacted before a relatively bored audience.

Neither Gov. Robert B. Meyner, the Democratic incumbent, nor State Senator Malcolm S. Forbes, the Republican candidate, has exhibited the ability to rouse the voting public markedly from its apparent apathy.

Beyond the Hudson and the Delaware, however, far greater interest is being manifested in the contest.

The Eisenhower Administration has staked its prestige on the results of the balloting as never before in a state-wide race. Republicans and Democrats alike at the national level are eagerly awaiting the vote tally. Each party hopes to gain from it a trend in its favor.

Surprise Possible

The apparent lack of interest locally may well be misleading. It is not an uncommon trait of the state's electorate, as witness 1953, 1954 and 1956. In those years, the pre-election temper turned out to be a "sleeper." The voters, from Cape May to High Point, set their alarms for election morn and flocked to the polls.

As the present campaign progressed, it became increasingly evident that, in all probability, it would be decided on the basis of personality rather than on issues. This was verified by a team of New York Times reporters in the field.

On the basis of findings of The Times' survey team, victory for Mr. Meyner is definitely in-

Continued on Page 60, Column 6

Major Sports News

FOOTBALL

Navy beat Notre Dame in the nation's top college contest yesterday. Scores of leading games:

Alabama	14	Georgia	13
Amherst	19	Tufts	6
Army	53	Colgate	7
Auburn	13	Florida	0
Cornell	8	Columbia	0
Dartmouth	14	Yale	14
Delaware	23	Rutgers	19
Georgia T.	13	Duke	0
Harvard	13	Penn	6
Iowa	21	Michigan	21
Michigan St.	21	Wisconsin	7
Minnesota	34	Indiana	0
Missouri	9	Colorado	6
Navy	20	Notre Dame	6
N. C. State	19	Wake Forest	0
Ohio State	47	Northwestern	6
Oklahoma	13	Kansas St.	0
Oregon	27	Stanford	26
Oregon St.	39	Wash. St.	25
Penn St.	27	W. Virginia	6
Princeton	7	Brown	0
Purdue	21	Illinois	6
Syracuse	24	Pittsburgh	21
T. C. U.	19	Baylor	6
Tennessee	35	N. Carolina	0
Texas A.&M.	7	Arkansas	6
Vanderbilt	7	L. S. U.	0

HORSE RACING

Eddie Schmidt won the $86,900 Gallant Fox Handicap at Jamaica by half a length. Bold Ruler was first in the Benjamin Franklin Handicap.

HOCKEY

The Rangers routed the Boston Bruins, 5—0.

Details in Section 5.

President and Class Honor Academy

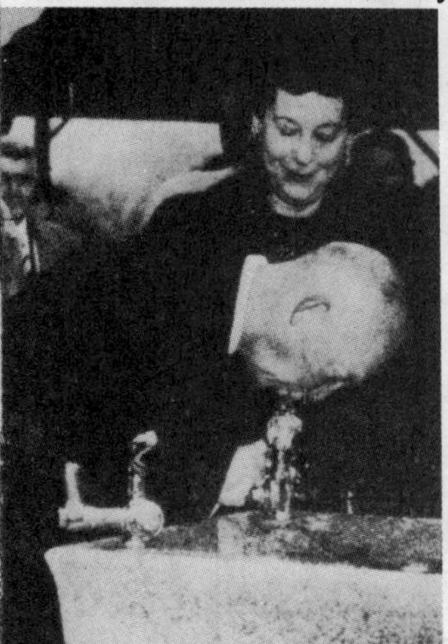

The New York Times (by Arthur Brower)

The President drinks from fountain he and other members of 1915 class gave to academy. Mrs. Eisenhower watches.

By W. H. LAWRENCE
Special to The New York Times.

WEST POINT, N. Y., Nov. 2 — President Eisenhower watched Army defeat Colgate today as the climax to a nostalgic reunion with his 1915 Military Academy classmates. Like any other old grad, the President leaped to his feet and cheered whenever Army threatened or scored—and he had many opportunities this afternoon as the West Point

Continued on Page 45, Column 1

DEMOCRATS COUNT ON PARTY VICTORY

Believe Wagner Can Win Without Liberal Votes in Mayoral Race

By LEO EGAN

Democratic leaders were counting confidently yesterday on obtaining enough votes on their party's line alone to insure the re-election of Mayor Wagner and his running mates next Tuesday. If they can do so it will be the first time since 1932 that a Democrat has received a majority of all the votes in a New York City Mayoral election.

Four years ago Mr. Wagner won by virtue of a split in the opposition between Harold Riegelman, Republican, and Rudolph Halley, Liberal and independent. Mr. Wagner received just over 45 per cent of the total vote cast.

This year the Liberal party is backing Mayor Wagner and his two city-wide running mates, Controller Lawrence E. Gerosa and City Council President Abe Stark. But Democratic leaders would like to be able to say they could have won without the Liberal endorsement.

Alex Rose, state vice chairman and spokesman for the Liberal party, referred to this Democratic attitude yesterday in appealing for a large Wagner-Gerosa-Stark vote on the Liberal party line.

"A large vote on the Liberal line is a vote with a special message to the city administration to be independent and is the best guarantee for a clean and effective administration on all levels of city government," he said.

"A large vote on the Liberal line will continue the Liberal party as the political conscience

Continued on Page 53, Column 3

This section consists of 136 pages divided into three parts. The news summary and the index will be found on Page 95. Society news begins on Page 90 and obituary articles will be found on Pages 88 and 89.

Voters Will Settle 7 State Questions; Issues Are Listed

Special to The New York Times.

ALBANY, Nov. 2—Voters who go to the polls on Tuesday will have a chance to pass on six proposed amendments to the State Constitution and whether a constitutional convention should be held.

If performance runs true, only about half those voting will bother to answer the seven questions across the top of every ballot.

The type on the ballot is small and the questions do not always express in the limited space the impact of the proposition.

Following is a description of each proposal, what it would do and the arguments for and against it:

The ballot asks:

"Shall there be a convention to revise the Constitution and amend the same?"

Approval would mean the voters would elect delegates on a party basis in 1958 and those elected would hold a convention the following year, probably in the summer. The convention

Continued on Page 62, Column 4

A.F.L.-C.I.O. TARGET RESIGNS AS CHIEF OF TEXTILE UNION

Valente Voices Hope Group Will Stay in Federation —2 More Actions Taken

Special to The New York Times.

WASHINGTON, Nov. 2—The president of the United Textile Workers, Anthony Valente, resigned today. He said he was acting to help his union retain its membership in the American Federation of Labor and Congress of Industrial Organizations.

The 44,000-member union was one of three cited for corruption last month by the executive council of the parent labor organization. Mr. Valente was declared ineligible to hold office.

Tonight, the leadership of the union accepted the resignation of Mr. Valente and announced other steps to conform with demands by the A. F. L.-C. I. O. to "clean up" the textile workers operations.

Francis Schaufenbil, secretary-treasurer of the union, told reporters at the end of an all-day meeting of the organization's executive board that "we certainly hope" the actions taken would keep the textile workers in the parent body.

Other Measures

The board meeting was called today to answer charges brought by the A. F. L.-C. I. O. council.

In addition to accepting Mr. Valente's resignation, the board took these two actions to comply with the council's demands:

1. It agreed to call a special convention "as soon as possible" to elect new officers. The session will be in Washington, New York or Philadelphia.
2. The board "rescinded" a $104,000 severance pay deal for Lloyd Klenert, resigned secretary-treasurer, and "has not obligated" the union on any financial arrangement with any other resigned officers. This was, presumably, a reference to Mr. Valente.

Senate investigators have accused Mr. Valente and Mr. Klenert of buying their homes with union funds and using devious bookkeeping to cover their tracks.

Criticizes Members of Council

Mr. Valente resigned at a meeting of the Textile Workers Executive Board, called to answer the council's charges. Talking with reporters during a recess, he loosed bitter criticism against twelve of the twenty-nine members of the A. F. L.-C. I. O. council.

He said the twelve had pledged him their support, but "they reneged on their commitments." He did not name the twelve.

This development in the labor

Continued on Page 44, Column 3

British and French, a Year After, Say Suez Invasion Was Justified

London Reconciled

By DREW MIDDLETON
Special to The New York Times.

LONDON, Nov. 2—In the view of some of those who planned the British-French invasion of Egypt, the situation obtaining in the Middle East a year later justifies that attempt to halt the march of Arab nationalism and its ally, Soviet communism, in the area.

A year ago the Soviet Union had one client and ally in the Middle East, Egypt. Today it has two, Egypt and Syria. The withdrawal of the British and French forces from Suez at the behest of the United Nations has been interpreted by Arab nationalism as a victory and has created a power vacuum into which Soviet imperialism has moved, it is noted.

The view that the invasion

Continued on Page 33, Column 3

Paris Still Bitter

By ROBERT C. DOTY
Special to The New York Times.

PARIS, Nov. 2—The weekend of the first anniversary of the British-French invasion of Egypt finds most Frenchmen, including those who planned the action, convinced that it was a good idea.

There is no tendency here to push such an idea aggressively. On the contrary, French high officialdom seeks to liquidate as speedily and unobtrusively as possible the remaining economic, political and diplomatic consequences of last fall's events. This is regarded as the logical prerequisite to a restoration of complete interallied confidence and effective action to repair the Western position in the Middle East.

Furthermore, the French-

Continued on Page 33, Column [illegible]

ZHUKOV HUMBLED

He Admits 'Mistakes' —Accused of 'Cult' in Armed Forces

Text of Soviet communiqué is printed on Page 4.

By WILLIAM J. JORDEN
Special to The New York Times.

MOSCOW, Sunday, Nov. 3—Marshal Georgi K. Zhukov, dismissed a week ago as Defense Minister of the Soviet Union, has been removed from all his top posts in the Soviet Communist party.

The party's Central Committee announced last night that Marshal Zhukov had lost his place on the party's central policy-making group, the Presidium, as well as on the Central Committee itself. The principal charge against the hero of World War II was that he had tried to eliminate the Communist party's direction and control of the Soviet armed forces.

The Communist party newspaper Pravda reported this morning that Marshal Zhukov had admitted his "mistakes" during the Central Committee meeting at which he was expelled from the party leadership.

Anti-Stalin Phrase Used

He tempered that acceptance somewhat by telling his party comrades that he accepted their criticism of him as being "in the main correct." He also was said to have accepted the attack on his leadership of the armed forces as being of "comradely party assistance to me personally and to other military workers."

The barrel-chested, square-jawed soldier was charged with promoting his own "cult of personality" in the army. This is the phrase used here in reference to Stalin's one-man rule, which was vigorously condemned by the Twentieth Congress of the Communist party last year.

"With the help of sycophants and flatterers," the Central Committee said, "he was praised to the sky in lectures and reports, in articles, films and pamphlets, and his person and role in the Great Patriotic War [World War II] were overglorified."

The result, the Central Committee charged, was that the whole history of the war had been "distorted." It said that by building himself up Marshal Zhukov had belittled the efforts of the Soviet people, of the

Continued on Page 3, Column 1

Marshal Is Linked to Stalin In Blame for '41 Reverses

Konev Charges Ex-Chief Distorted History to Create Hero's Role

Special to The New York Times.

MOSCOW, Sunday, Nov. 3—Marshal Ivan S. Konev, long companion and subordinate of Marshal Georgi K. Zhukov, condemned the former Defense Minister today for "errors in military science."

Marshal Konev's attack was the first derogatory statement leveled against Marshal Zhukov on military grounds.

Soviet commander of the Warsaw Pact forces, Marshal Konev issued his condemnation in an article in today's Pravda, the Communist party organ.

The Konev article said that Marshal Zhukov was responsible along with Stalin for lack of preparedness in the Soviet Union to meet the imminent German attack in June, 1941. It belittled Marshal Zhukov's role in the victories at Stalingrad and Berlin and accused Marshal Zhukov of undue pride and of twisting historical fact.

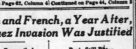

Associated Press

Marshal Ivan S. Konev

Marshal Konev's attack on Marshal Zhukov was bitter and extensive. Marshal Konev noted that his former comrade in

Continued on Page 3, Column 4

SOVIET 'STRESSES' SEEN BY THE U.S.

Washington Expects Strain Behind the Iron Curtain From Zhukov Disgrace

State Department statement will be found on Page 6.

By RUSSELL BAKER
Special to The New York Times.

WASHINGTON, Nov. 2—The State Department said tonight that the downgrading of Marshal Georgi K. Zhukov showed the "strains and stresses" present in the Soviet Union and the countries dominated by the Soviet Communists.

In a brief formal statement, the department noted that Marshal Zhukov's "disgrace" followed only by a short time the expressed desire of Nikita S. Khrushchev, First Secretary of the Soviet Communist party, to send the military leader on a special mission to the United States.

The department said this, following so closely "similar action against" other one-time Soviet leaders, demonstrated the polit-

Continued on Page 7, Column 1

SATELLITE SIGNAL RECEIVED AT M.I.T.

Scientists Believe That Orbit Repeats First Sphere—Trackers Are Alerted

By The United Press.

CAMBRIDGE, Mass., Sunday, Nov. 3—The first American pick-up of the new Soviet satellite's radio signal was reported early today to the Smithsonian Astrophysical Observatory.

Leon Campbell at the observatory said that the report was received from William S. Cooper of the Massachusetts Institute of Technology. Mr. Cooper said that he heard the signal at 2:02 A. M., between 20 and 20.5 megacycles.

Dr. J. Allen Hynek of the observatory staff said that the satellite apparently was in roughly the same path of 65 degrees as the first Soviet satellite.

The perigee (minimum altitude) probably is about 140 miles, the same as the first satellite, Dr. Hynek said. "It seems like a repetition of the orbit of the first satellite," he added.

The Soviet launching of the

Continued on Page 26, Column 4

Associated Press Radiophoto

CHINESE COMMUNIST LEADER GREETED IN MOSCOW: Mao Tse-tung, left, the chief of state and Communist party chief, as he arrived yesterday at the capital airport. [illegible] were Nikita S. Khrushchev, center, Soviet Communist chief, and Premier [illegible]. Mr. Mao will [illegible] the Bolshevik Revolution.

ORBIT COMPLETED

Animal Still Is Alive, Sealed in Satellite, Moscow Thinks

By The Associated Press.

LONDON, Sunday, Nov. 3—The Soviet Union announced today it had launched a second space satellite—this one carrying a dog. Radio signals indicated that the animal was living, the Russians said.

A satellite six times as heavy as the one sent up Oct. 4 now is circling the earth every hour and forty-two minutes at a height of 937 miles, Moscow said. This means that the speed is nearly 18,000 miles an hour for the 1,110-pound satellite.

The dog was reported hermetically sealed in a container equipped with an air-conditioning system.

Moscow Radio said data received from the second satellite indicated the "functioning of scientific instruments and control of the living activities of the animal are taking place normally."

First Trip Reported

The new satellite carries transmitting equipment and apparatus for measuring cosmic rays, temperature and pressure. It also carries equipment for reporting the condition of the dog.

It first passed over the Soviet capital at 11:20 P. M. Eastern Standard Time last night and then completed its first trip around the earth over Moscow at 1:05 A. M. today, the Soviet Union reported.

The announcement said the second satellite was "dedicated to the fortieth anniversary of the great October revolution," which the Communist world will celebrate in Moscow beginning next Thursday.

The new earth satellite is completing its orbit in about seven minutes more than the original Sputnik, still circling the earth.

Japan Receives Signals

Moscow said the second sphere was sending out two radio signals.

One, like the "beep" signal transmitted by the first satellite, is on a frequency of 20.005 megacycles. The other signal, at 40.002 megacycles, is a continuous note.

In Tokyo the Japan Broadcasting Corporation announced that radio signals from the second satellite were being heard.

The corporation picked up the signals twenty-three minutes after Moscow's announcement. The "beep" was at intervals of three-tenths of a second.

A three-stage rocket shoved the original satellite into its orbit. The first Moscow announcement of the second sphere did not explain how it had been sent up.

Although the announcement of the satellite's passing over Moscow indicated an interval of one hour and forty-five min-

Continued on Page 26, Column 3

Mao Is in Moscow; He Hails Soviet Tie

By MAX FRANKEL
Special to The New York Times.

MOSCOW, Nov. 2—Mao Tse-tung, leader of Communist China, arrived in Moscow today. He is probably the most important of the gathering here to show the unity and might of international communism.

Virtually all the reigning heads of Communist nations and parties, with the notable exception of President Tito of Yugoslavia, will make the pilgrimage here to join in next week's celebrations of the fortieth anniversary of the Bolshevik Revolution.

Expected in addition to Mr. Mao, who is the Chinese Communist chief of state and party chairman, are Poland's party leader, Wladyslaw Gomulka, and Premier Jozef Cyrankiewicz, Premier Janos Kadar of Hun-

[illegible] Page 27, Column 3

"All the News
That's Fit to Print"

The New York Times.

LATE CITY EDITION
U. S. Weather Bureau Report (Page 54) forecasts:
Mostly fair today. Considerable
cloudiness and mild tomorrow.
Temp. range: 45—29. Yesterday: 43.9—33.7

VOL. CVII...No. 36,467.   © 1957, by The New York Times Company, Times Square, New York 36, N. Y.   NEW YORK, WEDNESDAY, NOVEMBER 27, 1957.   10c beyond 100-mile zone from New York City   FIVE CENTS

LINCOLN SQ. PLAN WINS FINAL VOTE FOR EARLY START

Estimate Board Unanimous in Approving Project for Huge Cultural Center

$205,000,000 COST SET

Condemnation to Begin in 2 Weeks, but Litigation Will Delay Demolition Work

By PAUL CROWELL

The $205,000,000 Lincoln Square slum clearance and redevelopment project was unanimously approved by the Board of Estimate yesterday.

The board authorized the condemnation and resale of a sixty-eight-acre tract north and west of Columbus Circle. It thus took a long step toward the establishment of a cultural and collegiate center and modern housing facilities in an area of thirteen city blocks now considered substandard.

Some minor details of the project will be ironed out at a meeting of the board on Jan. 23. However, condemnation proceedings are expected to start within two weeks, but actual demolition of buildings now on the site may be delayed by litigation to be started soon by opponents of one phase of the project.

Fordham Project Opposed

The litigation will seek to enjoin the demolition pending a court ruling on a contention that a new campus for Fordham University in the project would be a violation of the state and Federal constitutions. This protest charges the alleged expenditure of public funds in aid of a sectarian institution.

The Lincoln Square development is a Title I project under the National Housing Act. The statute enables the city to acquire slum sites and sell them to private developers. Any loss incurred in the resale, together with the cost of community facilities in connection with redevelopment, will be shared two-thirds by the Federal Government and one-third by the city.

The most recent estimates of project cost are $163,000,000 for the private developers, $28,000,000 for the Federal Government and $14,000,000 for the city. The project involves the relocation of 6,500 families now living in the site area and several hundred businesses.

The city's Committee on Slum Clearance, which negotiated the contracts with the Federal Home and Loan Administration

Continued on Page 20, Column 6

JANSEN OPPOSES POLICE IN SCHOOLS

Calls Proposal 'Unthinkable' —Leibowitz Backs Idea

By LAWRENCE FELLOWS

Superintendent of Schools William Jansen yesterday condemned as unthinkable a grand jury recommendation that a uniformed city policeman be assigned to every public school in the city.

The proposal was made Monday by a special grand jury investigating lawlessness in public schools in Brooklyn. It had asked that police "patrol the corridors, the stairways and the recreation yards" of schools throughout the city to help prevent outbreaks of violence.

"To me," Dr. Jansen said, "the proposal to have an armed policeman regularly stationed in every school is unthinkable.

"We do not want a Little Rock in New York City," he added.

Dr. Jansen's statement followed the third charge to the jury, made yesterday by Kings County Judge Samuel S. Leibowitz, who is presiding over the investigation. He said:

"The court feels certain that this grand jury would not have made this unusual request were it not for the fact that the grand jury has evidence before it to establish that conditions are alarming and that the school authorities have been utterly incapable of coping with the situation."

The jury has been meeting three times weekly since Nov. 6.

Continued on Page 20, Column 3

Jupiter Fails Test; Congressmen Watch

By The United Press.

CAPE CANAVERAL, Fla., Nov. 26—A test of the Jupiter missile failed tonight in the presence of members of Congress who are studying the nation's missile program.

To dozens of observers on near-by beaches the Jupiter firing seemed successful. However, a Defense Department statement immediately after the launching at 9:12 P. M. said that "the missile failed to complete its programmed flight because of technical difficulties."

The announcement did not say if the missile was intentionally detonated by remote control from the ground, but observers said it seemed to explode in a distant ball of flame just before it disappeared from sight.

The Defense Department announcement also said that

Continued on Page 17, Column 4

WHITE HOUSE ASKS SACRIFICE FOR AID

Talking Here for President, Mitchell Stresses Need to Help Free World

By A. H. RASKIN

President Eisenhower's chief labor officer served as spokesman for his ailing chief last night in urging the country to accept the "austerity and privations" needed to extend military and economic aid 'to the free world.

Secretary of Labor James P. Mitchell departed from a prepared speech of his own to deliver the gist of a talk the President had planned to broadcast from Cleveland on the importance of international cooperation in halting Soviet imperialism.

Mr. Mitchell said the Administration believed "no investment we can make pays greater dividends than reasonable economic aid to friendly nations." He listed specific points the President had intended to make before times forced him to cancel his broadcast.

Program Outlined

The points he listed were:

¶A plea for fullest public support of the mutual security program in both its military and economic aspects.

¶A recommendation that Congress act in January to provide broader authority for the negotiation of reciprocal trade pacts and to prolong the expiring Trade Agreements Act for more than the present three-year term.

¶A call for United States participation in the Organization for Trade Cooperation, which Mr. Mitchell described as "a businesslike unit," to guarantee maximum benefits from the negotiation of trade agreements.

The Cabinet officer spoke at a dinner of the Manufacturing Chemists Association at the Statler Hotel. Five hours before he began his speech at 8:45 P. M., he talked with White House officials from his Washington office. It was decided that he would use the occasion to give the essence of the message the President had prepared.

Had President's Text

At 4 P. M. a Presidential courier put a copy of the Eisenhower draft text on Secretary Mitchell's desk in the Labor Department. He made extensive notes before boarding a Military Air Transport Service plane for New York a half hour later. The notes were the mainstay of Mr. Mitchell's talk to the 950 chemical manufacturers at the dinner. His remarks were not broadcast.

He urged all citizens to put aside "partisanship and short-sighted narrowness" in evaluating the accomplishments of technical assistance and loans to underdeveloped countries in Asia and Africa.

"We can't have peace in this world without working for it and without paying for it," Mr. Mitchell declared. "One of the principal programs for peace is our mutual aid program."

He said the $700,000,000 being spent this year on economic aid

Continued on Page 17, Column 1

DOOLITTLE BACKS A GENERAL STAFF TO RULE SERVICES

But Sees It Far in Future —Satellite Project Lacked Priority, Senators Told

Excerpts from testimony are printed on Page 16.

By JACK RAYMOND
Special to The New York Times.

WASHINGTON, Nov. 26— Lieut. Gen. James H. Doolittle advocated today a reorganization of the Pentagon that would lead ultimately to the creation of a single general staff for the three armed services.

In testimony at the Senate defense inquiry, General Doolittle also repeated the warnings given yesterday by scientists. They had said that the Soviet Union led the United States in long-range ballistic missile development.

Because of the heavy bombers of the Strategic Air Command, General Doolittle said, the United States still has an over-all military advantage. But the Russians are increasing their strength at a greater rate of speed, he added.

Unless the United States spends more money on the military and the people make greater sacrifices and work harder, the general said, the Soviet will assume a commanding military lead.

Heads Three Committees

General Doolittle, who has retired from the Air Force, told the Senate Preparedness subcommittee that he was serving on a number of Government committees and was chairman of three.

A second witness, Dr. John P. Hagen, director of the Vanguard satellite program, told the Senators that the United States could have put up an earth satellite ahead of the Russians if an all-out effort had been made.

However, the Vanguard project suffered from money limitations while priority was given to military ballistic missiles, Dr. Hagen testified.

Dr. Hagen said that the United States had suffered psychological and political damage when the Russians were first to launch a satellite. He revealed that he had sought top priority for the project in 1955, but that it had been turned down by a high official whose identity he did not know.

Dr. Hagen agreed that "we took a calculated risk and lost."

On the status of United States plans to launch an earth satellite, he said little more than that tests "have exceeded our expectations."

The committee later heard

Continued on Page 16, Column 2

NIXON IN SESSIONS

Calls President 'Fully Capable' of Making Needed Decisions

By RUSSELL BAKER
Special to The New York Times.

WASHINGTON, Nov. 26— Vice President Richard M. Nixon spent almost eight hours today at the White House conferring with the Administration's leading strategists on problems arising from the President's illness.

Before he left late this afternoon announcing that he would be back again tomorrow, one influential Republican Senator already had urged that he take over some of the President's duties.

Senator Styles Bridges of New Hampshire said that scheduled White House conferences with Congressional leaders should go ahead as planned next Tuesday and Wednesday.

No Delegation of Powers

"Vice President Nixon should head up those conferences in the place of the President to show the country that the business of the Government is going on in spite of the unfortunate illness of the President," Mr. Bridges said.

Mr. Nixon, however, told reporters that the President was "fully capable" of making necessary decisions. He said that he and other members of the Cabinet had been informed by William P. Rogers, the Attorney General, that no delegation of Presidential authority was necessary at present.

In reply to questions the Vice President said that Mr. Rogers had reached this decision after noting the President's condition and what was required. The Vice President said that he had not seen General Eisenhower during the seven hours and forty minutes he spent in the White House today.

With extraordinary pressures for planning and decision-taking building under the Government, Mr. Nixon nevertheless seems assured of a major leadership assignment in the weeks ahead.

The Administration must brief Congress on its plans for the coming session, get its budget into final shape and arrive at major decisions on defense and foreign policy during the time the President will be inactive.

Many Critics Won Over

Much of the responsibility appears certain to devolve upon Mr. Nixon. He seems the only figure among the White House aides and advisers who commands political respect in Congress and he is universally regarded as the heir-apparent to the Presidency.

Curiously, the prospect of Mr. Nixon's operating so close to the seat of power worries Washington today less than it would have a few years ago when he was widely known as "Tricky Dick."

Even among his once most-violent critics, hardly anyone calls him by the old epithet these days. He has disarmed many of his critics, abandoned the old razor-sharp campaign style that made Democrats despise him and applied himself so assiduously to studying for the Presidency that even his old enemies concede he has "matured."

Tireless Campaigner

The consensus, in short, is that he has grown in the Vice Presidency.

The Nixon that went to the White House today made his debut on the national political stage with the opening of last year's Presidential campaign. The "old Nixon" with his "instinct for the jugular" and his slashing attacks on the Democratic party for "softness" toward communism never showed up for the 1956 race.

Instead, what the nation saw was a tireless campaigner who stressed the positive side of the Republican record and did his utmost to convince the electorate that he was a responsible

Continued on Page 2, Column 2

AT MISSILE INQUIRY: Dr. John P. Hagen, director of Project Vanguard, displays model of three-stage rocket to be used to launch U. S. satellite.

Associated Press Wirephoto

NIXON TALKS TO NEWSMEN: Vice President Nixon (hatless, in center of group) as he left White House yesterday after long visit. He discussed the President's condition.

Associated Press Wirephoto

EISENHOWER HAS A MILD STROKE; SPEECH IMPAIRED, BUT IMPROVES; RECOVERY OUTLOOK 'EXCELLENT'

REST IS ORDERED

Physicians Prescribe Decreased Activity for a Few Weeks

White House statements and medical bulletins, Page 10.

By JAMES RESTON
Special to The New York Times.

WASHINGTON, Nov. 26— President Eisenhower has suffered a small blood clot or blood vessel spasm of the brain, but is making good progress toward complete recovery, the White House announced tonight.

The President will not attend the North Atlantic Treaty heads of government meeting in Paris on Dec. 16, the White House said. He "will require a period of rest and substantially decreased activity estimated at several weeks," it added.

This was the President's physical situation tonight, as reported by a special panel of physicians who examined the President:

¶"An occlusion [closing] of a small branch of a cerebral vessel" has "produced a slight difficulty in speaking," but this has improved in the last twenty-four hours.

¶The President's reading, writing and reasoning powers have not been affected.

¶His physical strength is normal, and he is allowed to be up and around the White House.

¶His temperature, blood pressure, and pulse are normal, and "there is no evidence of a cerebral hemorrhage, or any serious lesion of the cerebral vessels."

¶"He is alert, his spirits are good, and he discussed with interest and clarity recent events."

Hagerty Back From Paris

James C. Hagerty, White House press secretary, arrived here late tonight from Paris. He told reporters the President had a light supper and watched TV for two hours before going to sleep.

Mr. Hagerty said there would be no further medical bulletins until tomorrow.

The first bulletin, issued this afternoon, described the attack as "mild and transitory in nature." It added:

"The outlook for complete recovery within a reasonable period of time is excellent."

The bulletin asserted that hospitalization would not be necessary.

The second bulletin, issued tonight by a separate panel of physicians, concurred in the "mild and transitory" diagnosis.

At the White House, optimism and hopefulness were the mood. Officials there said they would not characterize the President's illness as a stroke, but outside physicians did not hesitate to do so. In general, they tended to withhold judgment pending developments in the next eight or ten days.

All political movements here today seemed to confirm the optimistic nature of the official bulletins. This illness occurred at a more difficult time than in September of 1955 when the

Continued on Page 11, Column 1

DULLES AND KING CONFER ON BASES

Secretary Is Substitute for President in Conference With Moroccan Leader

By DANA ADAMS SCHMIDT
Special to The New York Times.

WASHINGTON, Nov. 26— Secretary of State Dulles substituted for President Eisenhower today at a two-hour White House conference with King Mohammed V of Morocco.

Mr. Dulles said later that the talks were "preliminary" and had gone "very well." It was understood that they reviewed the problems of United States bases in Morocco, Algerian hopes for independence and Morocco's prospects for more United States aid.

The meeting took place in the Cabinet room of the White House after the King, with his son Prince Moulay Abdullah, had posed for pictures in the President's empty office.

Although King Mohammed likes to conduct official conversations in Arabic, through an interpreter, he carried on part of today's meeting with Mr. Dulles in French.

Mr. Dulles was understood to have expressed to the King the hope that before his three-week visit to the United States was over the President would be well enough to see him.

President Eisenhower suffered the closure of a cerebral vessel a few hours after meet-

Continued on Page 3, Column 2

President's Trip to Paris For NATO Talk Canceled

By E. W. KENWORTHY
Special to The New York Times.

WASHINGTON, Nov. 26—The White House announced this afternoon that President Eisenhower would be unable to attend the scheduled Paris meeting of the heads of government of the Atlantic alliance.

The decision to cancel the President's trip, made as a result of his current illness, has produced some confusion among those planning the mid-December session of the North Atlantic Council.

The State Department said it had asked Paul-Henri Spaak, Secretary General of the alliance, to determine how other members wished to proceed.

[Reports from Paris said the Permanent Council of the alliance would discuss the matter Thursday.]

In Washington, these three alternatives were suggested:

1. To go ahead with the planned meeting of the heads of government and have Vice President Richard M. Nixon deputize for President Eisenhower.
2. To have the normal meeting of foreign, defense and finance ministers who make up the Council.
3. To postpone the Council meeting altogether until President Eisenhower had recovered and was able to attend.

Vice President Nixon said that the North Atlantic Council meeting definitely had not been called off. The only question is whether the other heads

Continued on Page 12, Column 3

STEVENSON SAYS HE WILL STAY ON

Accedes to Dulles' Request —It Now Seems Probable He Will Go to Paris

By JOHN W. FINNEY
Special to The New York Times.

WASHINGTON, Nov. 26— Adlai E. Stevenson said today that he had agreed to stay on as a consultant to the State Department.

Echoing the feelings expressed by many of his fellow Democrats, the Presidential candidate in the 1952 and 1956 campaigns said he was distressed at the President's illness and prayed he would make a quick recovery.

Asked by reporters at the State Department how the President's illness would affect his own plans, Mr. Stevenson replied:

"The Secretary of State has asked me to continue to assist in the preparations of the NATO meeting next month and I will do so."

NATO Attendance Seen

President Eisenhower's inability to attend the meeting of the North Atlantic Council scheduled to open Dec. 15 in Paris increased the probability that Mr. Stevenson would go to it. It has been the assumption of Administration leaders that Mr. Stevenson will attend, but he has not committed himself.

Mr. Stevenson's presence at the meeting, observers believed, would demonstrate both at home and abroad this nation's solidarity at a critical time with the free world's policy under reappraisal and the President removed from active leadership.

General Eisenhower's illness, observers would seem to have increased unexpectedly Mr. Stevenson's importance in foreign policy planning. Similarly, the President's incapacitation may have the effect of forcing the Administration and the Democrats in Congress into closer collaboration on foreign policy questions.

Mr. Stevenson took up his duties only a week ago, at the

Continued on Page 12, Column 4

France Offers to Admit 10,000 To Observe an Algeria Election

By THOMAS J. HAMILTON
Special to The New York Times.

UNITED NATIONS, N. Y., Nov. 26—France has told United Nations delegates that she will be willing to admit as many as 10,000 observers for proposed Algerian elections.

The French have not revealed their position on how the observers should be chosen. However, they are understood to have said they come only from countries that have free elections. This would bar the Soviet bloc and some Arab countries.

This offer is the principal new element in the French position as revealed in the last few days to delegates from Latin America, the British Commonwealth and Western Europe. M. Pineau will be the first speaker tomorrow afternoon when the General Assembly's Political Committee opens

its debate on the Algerian question.

The Dominican Republic, Colombia and Bolivia, however, are discussing a move to postpone the debate until later in this Assembly session, or until next year. If they obtain sufficient support, they are expected to ask the Latin-American bloc, which will meet tomorrow morning on another matter, to give the move its endorsement.

[In Paris talks with British leaders, France won formal recognition of her "leadership" in North Africa.]

Reliable sources disclosed today that the Asian-African group would not offer a resolution calling for Algerian independence.

Supporters of the Algerian

Continued on Page 4, Column 6

Stock Market Dips On News of Illness

The stock market reacted yesterday to news of President Eisenhower's latest illness much as it did after his heart attack in September, 1955. On both occasions prices dived sharply and something almost like "panic" was in the air.

This time, however, the break was confined to the twenty-minute period between the news flash and the close of trading.

The market reaction following other illnesses of the President was far less sharp.

Yesterday The New York Times combined average closed off 7.63 points as leading stocks suffered losses of $1 to $7 a share. Volume was 3,650,000 shares.

Among some major losses: Gulf Oil by $7; Amerada Oil, $6.75; Douglas Aircraft, $6.12; Zenith Radio, $6; Lukens Steel,

Continued on Page 15, Column 2

Jailhouse Rock *cast Elvis Presley as an angry young man and gave him the opportunity to sulk volcanically. The title song became an instant hit.*

"All the News That's Fit to Print"

The New York Times.

LATE CITY EDITION
U. S. Weather Bureau Report (Page 66) forecasts: Occasional rain today. Mostly fair and colder tomorrow.
Temp. range: 52—42. Yesterday: 40.7—27.0

VOL. CVII . . . No. 36,477.

NEW YORK, SATURDAY, DECEMBER 7, 1957.

10c beyond 100-mile zone from New York City — FIVE CENTS

A.F.L.-C.I.O. OUSTS TEAMSTERS UNION BY VOTE OF 5 TO 1

DRAMA AT SESSION

A Last-Minute Peace Move Collapses—Hoffa Defiant

By A. H. RASKIN
Special to The New York Times.

ATLANTIC CITY, Dec. 6—The giant International Brotherhood of Teamsters was expelled from the merged labor federation today on charges of domination by corrupt elements.

The victory for George Meany and other leaders of the clean-union forces in the American Federation of Labor and Congress of Industrial Organizations came by a margin of nearly five to one at the federation's second biennial convention.

It followed the collapse last midnight of cloak-and-dagger moves to arrange a peace meeting at which James R. Hoffa, the chief target of the federation's charges, was to have stepped down as president-elect of the 1,333,000-member truck union. The federation refused to hold off the ouster vote until Monday to give Hoffa a final chance to abdicate.

Lewis Fight Recalled

The convention session was the most dramatic held by a labor organization since John L. Lewis punched William L. Hutcheson of the Carpenters Union in the nose at the start of the split between the old A. F. L. and C. I. O. twenty-two years ago.

Both the teamsters and the federation pledged themselves to seek to avoid a new civil war as an aftermath of the ouster. However, the bitterness of the debate made an increase in interunion raids, strikes and economic conflict appear inescapable.

The actual vote to eliminate the scandal-stained teamsters from the mainstream of organized labor was 10,458,598 to 2,266,497. It was based on the membership strength of the unions that voted for and against the ouster.

Roll-Call Vote Taken

The teamsters were drummed out through a roll-call vote. Fewer than 1,000 delegates were able to cast the total of 12,275,095 votes, because the due-paying strength of their union determined how many ballots each group was entitled to. Thus, in the case of the huge auto union, each delegate was recorded as having 35,275 votes. In smaller organizations, delegates cast as few as twenty-five votes each.

The teamsters mustered the support of twenty-one international unions, four others split their votes and eight indicated their lack of sympathy for the orphaning of the country's largest and most powerful union by staying away from the meeting.

Ninety-five unions voted to expel the teamsters. Included were the only two others in the million-member class—Walter P. Reuther's United Automobile Workers and David J. McDonald's United Steel-

Continued on Page 14, Column 2

1,600 Garbage Men Go on Strike Here

A strike of 1,600 privately employed garbage collectors in the metropolitan area began suddenly last night in the midst of negotiations on a new contract.

The walkout, against 550 private carting firms, will halt all refuse removal at about 122,000 establishments in the city's five boroughs and parts of Westchester County and Nassau County.

Of these, the most severely affected will be hotels, hospitals and restaurants, as well as numerous business and industrial buildings.

Anticipating the walkout, the city prepared emergency stand-by procedures for removing any waste deemed a health or safety hazard by the Health Department and Fire Department. The strike was

Continued on Page 13, Column 3

FRANCE SEIZES 30% OF BANKS' DOLLARS

Imposes 3% Loan of Assets Abroad to Help Bolster Vanishing Reserves

By ROBERT C. DOTY
Special to The New York Times.

PARIS, Dec. 6—French banks have been ordered to surrender 30 per cent of all their dollar holdings abroad as a forced loan to bolster France's vanishing foreign currency reserves.

This means that all Frenchmen holding legally declared and authorized dollar accounts abroad must lend the Government nearly one-third of their dollar credits at 3 per cent interest.

According to one informed but unofficial estimate, the measure is likely to bring between $60,000,000 and $70,000,000 into the Bank of France. This is expected to serve as a timely stop-gap to meet trade deficits, now running at about $30,000,000 a month, or to pay off Government debts to private foreign creditors falling due at the end of the year.

This effort to tap the last available French dollar resources, and the Government's current attempt to reduce the budget deficit and put public finances in order, are both part of preparations to negotiate foreign loans to tide the nation

Continued on Page 3, Column 3

ITALY URGES U. S. JOIN WEST EUROPE IN A MIDEAST FUND

Suggests Development Plan With Contributions Based on Marshall Plan Loans

Text of Italian memorandum is printed on Page 2.

Special to The New York Times.

WASHINGTON, Dec. 6—Italy has proposed that the United States and Western Europe pool financial resources in a program of economic development for the Middle East.

Under the proposal, a new Middle Eastern development fund would be set up with contributions based on a "Marshall Plan formula."

The United States would contribute the European repayments on its Marshall Plan loans, made under the post-war economic aid program announced in 1947 by General of the Army George C. Marshall, then Secretary of State.

The repayments are scheduled to begin next year.

System of Contributions

Each European country with a Marshall Plan obligation would contribute to the proposed Middle Eastern fund an amount equal to 20 per cent of its annual repayment to Washington.

European countries without Marshall Plan loans—West Germany, Switzerland, Greece and Austria, for example—would make contributions within the maximum and minimum limits of the other European allocations.

Precise figures were not available tonight, but a tentative estimate was that the first year's contributions would give the fund a starting capital of about $100,000,000. In addition, American and European private industry would be encouraged to participate.

As set forth in an Italian memorandum put before the United States Government, the fund "could provide loans, mainly of a soft character, at terms and conditions to be determined" with each project.

Industry's Share Detailed

The private groups could "intervene with participation in the equity capital of the enterprises operating—or to be set up—in the underdeveloped countries," the memorandum said.

In substance, the Italian memorandum proposed that the West cooperate in a bold economic initiative for the Middle East. The Western approach should be so diffused as to remove any possible Middle Eastern suspicion of military motivation or colonial" design, the Italians asserted.

This proposal was discussed today by Secretary of State Dulles and Giuseppe Pella, Italian Foreign Minister, who is here to canvass plans for the forthcoming Paris meeting of

Continued on Page 2, Column 4

NIXON ADVOCATES TRADE OFFENSIVE TO COMBAT SOVIET

Tells N.A.M. Foreign Aid Is Urgent—Voices View That Budget Can Be Balanced

Text of Nixon speech will be found on Page 16.

By PETER KIHSS

Vice President Richard M. Nixon declared last night that increased foreign aid, trade and information programs were necessary to counter a nonmilitary "offensive" being conducted by the Soviet Union for world domination.

But, despite substantial increases in United States defense spending, he said, "the prospects are good that the Administration will be able to submit its fourth balanced budget in a row next January."

Mr. Nixon's expression of hope for a balanced budget won applause from 1,800 persons attending a dinner of the National Association of Manufacturers at the Waldorf-Astoria Hotel. But much of the rest of his intensely delivered message was received in perhaps glum silence.

He Puts Security First

The budget balance, he said, might be effected by cuts in domestic programs without a tax increase—but "obviously" with no tax cut. And if security required, he added, budget balancing would give way.

Mr. Nixon spoke to the conservative industrialists as a frank salesman for the plans of the Eisenhower Administration as laid before Congressional leaders in Washington earlier this week.

He was applauded three times in his introductory remarks, and once when, apropos of yesterday's misfiring of the United States space satellite, he said that the United States was behind but "will not stay that way." Thereafter, his speech had but five interruptions for applause—three of them for praise of the private enterprise system.

As he has since the Russians launched their first space satellite Oct. 4, the Vice President reaffirmed that militarily the United States and the free world "over-all are stronger than any potential aggressor, including the Soviet Union."

The Means to Catch Up

"We have the will, ability and resources," he said, "to catch up in those areas where we are behind and to retain our over-all position of superiority."

Asserting that "the strain on the Soviet economy will be greater than on ours," Mr. Nixon added:

"The strongest military establishment in the world will not save American freedom if we fail to meet the threat which the Communists present in the nonmilitary areas.

"And if we in the United States take a worm's eye view of the world conflict and cut foreign aid, hamstring reciprocal trade and emasculate our information program, I can tell you that the billions we spend for missiles and submarines and aircraft will be going right down a rathole."

If the Communists gain control of the 1,000,000,000 people and resources in "the uncommitted countries of Asia, the Near East and Africa," Mr. Nixon said, "they will hold the

Continued on Page 16, Column 5

VANGUARD ROCKET BURNS ON BEACH; FAILURE TO LAUNCH TEST SATELLITE ASSAILED AS BLOW TO U.S. PRESTIGE

Associated Press Wirephoto (U. S. Navy)

MISFIRE: Nose cone starts to fall to right as the rocket burns. Stand is at the left.

SPHERE SURVIVES

But Carrier Rises Only 2 to 4 Feet Before Flames Wreck It

Excerpts from transcript of news conference, Page 8.

By MILTON BRACKER
Special to The New York Times.

COCOA BEACH, Fla., Dec. 6—The rocket bearing the United States test satellite burst into flame and was almost consumed on Cape Canaveral beach this morning two seconds after firing. It had risen two to four feet.

The seventy-two-foot Vanguard vehicle—only forty-five inches in diameter at its widest point—was wrecked by a great fiery billow of flames nearly twice as high as the rocket itself.

Surprisingly, the satellite-bearing third stage, embedded in the nose of the second stage, survived the crash of the rocket. It was thrown clear.

However, it will not be usable, said J. Paul Walsh, deputy director of Project Vanguard.

Satellite Undamaged

Even more remarkably, the satellite itself—weighing barely four pounds, and about the size of a grapefruit or softball—was undamaged.

[In Washington, Dr. John P. Hagen, chief of Project Vanguard, said that the failure of the rocket was "undoubtedly a failure of some individual part" rather than one of design.]

Mr. Walsh said that the satellite had continued to send out its radio signals by its two transmitters. Technicians would have to open the satellite to turn off the transmitters, he explained.

The Department of Defense, in a brief statement, said that the launching was "not successful and the rocket burned on the pad." The statement used the verb "exploded," noting that all fires had been extinguished and all personnel was safe.

Although it was "up" barely two seconds, the rocket's telemetering system in its second stage functioned for that period. The data it transmitted, Mr. Walsh said, were "stuff worth its weight in gold."

Data to Be Studied

These data—amounting to hundreds of items—will take several days to evaluate, according to Mr. Walsh and Elliott Felt, operations manager for the Martin Company of Baltimore, primary contractor on the Vanguard rocket.

Mr. Felt, whose demeanor indicated he felt the disaster keenly, interposed that "what we know is the end of a chain of events and we are trying to find out what happened—what caused it."

Although Mr. Walsh and associates repeatedly mentioned loss of thrust in describing the rocket disaster, they also said several times that the cause could not necessarily be attributed to any phase of the

Continued on Page 8, Column 3

4 MISSILES BASES IN BRITAIN MAPPED

Pact With U. S. Revealed as McElroy Flies to London for Parleys on NATO

By JACK RAYMOND
Special to The New York Times.

WASHINGTON, Dec. 6—The United States and Britain have agreed to establish four squadrons of intermediate-range ballistic missiles in the British Isles.

The cost of building the sites is estimated at $84,000,000, to be borne largely by Britain. Three of the squadrons will be British and the fourth will be under the United States Air Force.

This became known today as Neil H. McElroy, Secretary of Defense, left by plane for talks in London and a visit to United States troops in West Germany. He is due in Paris Thursday to be on hand for the conference of the North Atlantic Treaty Organization, Dec. 16-18.

Secretary of State Dulles is expected to leave Wednesday or Thursday. No decision has been announced whether President Eisenhower will attend the meeting as had been planned before he suffered a slight stroke.

In London, Mr. McElroy will confer with Prime Minister Harold Macmillan and Defense Minister Duncan Sandys. The two British leaders have been directly involved in the program for missile bases in their country since the Eisenhower-

Continued on Page 10, Column 8

Khrushchev Says Rocket Of 1st Satellite Fell in U.S.

By WILLIAM J. JORDEN
Special to The New York Times.

MOSCOW, Dec. 6—Nikita S. Khrushchev asserted tonight that part of the carrier rocket that launched the first Soviet earth satellite had landed in the United States. The Communist party chief said the carrier rocket descended from the upper atmosphere last Sunday.

He said the Soviet Government would make an official announcement about the rocket "soon" and that it would ask the United States authorities to return it.

"We know it fell on the United States," he said. "But they do not want to give it back to us."

[In Gettysburg, Pa., James C. Hagerty, White House press secretary, denied any knowledge of the landing of the Soviet rocket. In Washington, three governmental agencies issued a similar disclaimer.]

Insists Rocket Did Not Burn

Mr. Khrushchev did not say how the Kremlin knew that the rocket or parts of it had fallen on United States territory. He insisted that it was not a case of the carrier's burning out over American territory but that part of the rocket itself had landed.

"Apparently part of it fell on the United States," he said, when asked whether he did not mean that it had perhaps disintegrated in flames over the United States. He also said, in answer to a clarifying question, that when he used the word "America" he meant the United States and not part of the American Continent.

When this correspondent asked whether he was really serious or merely joking, Mr. Khrushchev replied: "I was absolutely serious."

"We relied on them," Mr. Khrushchev said of the United States, "trusting in their decency, but they did not live up to it."

Talks at Reception

Mr. Khrushchev made his assertion concerning the Soviet rocket in a talk with foreign correspondents at a reception in the Finnish Embassy. The Finns were celebrating their National Day.

Mr. Khrushchev was asked about the American satellite.

"We have been waiting for the American sputnik to be launched," he replied. "I am sure it will be launched sooner or later."

Even as Mr. Khrushchev spoke, a spokesman for the Defense Department in Washington was announcing that the Vanguard rocket that was to carry the small United States satellite into its orbit had gone

Continued on Page 10, Column 5

CAPITAL DISMAYED AT TEST'S FAILURE

Johnson, Russell, Rayburn Appalled—Some in G.O.P. Voice Sharp Criticism

Special to The New York Times.

WASHINGTON, Dec. 6—The failure of the Vanguard satellite rocket saddened and humiliated the nation's capital today.

From Dr. John P. Hagen, the Vanguard chief, who in his disgust said "Nuts!" to Washington's ordinary citizens the feeling was one of great shock.

In Congress angry Democrats and some Republicans charged that the highly publicized Vanguard failure had been a severe blow to the political prestige of the United States abroad and the Eisenhower Administration at home.

The Democrats, who control Congress and its investigating committees, were the most critical. They promised the fullest inquiries.

Senator Lyndon B. Johnson of Texas, Senate Democratic leader, called it "one of the best publicized and most humiliating

Continued on Page 9, Column 3

Associated Press Wirephoto

TEAMSTERS LEAVE AFTER EXPULSION: John F. English, right, secretary-treasurer of the International Brotherhood of Teamsters, leaving convention of A. F. L.-C. I. O. yesterday in Atlantic City. He had made a speech before ouster. At left is Tom C. Healey, Boston delegate.

U. S. to Let Families Visit China Captives

By RUSSELL BAKER
Special to The New York Times.

WASHINGTON, Dec. 6—The State Department abandoned a long-standing policy today and agreed to let relatives visit American prisoners in Communist China.

The department attributed its decision on humanitarian motives and emphasized that the general policy against permitting travel to the Chinese mainland remained unchanged.

Although the State Department said visitors would have to pay their own expenses, relatives of some of the six captives said they would go as soon as they could.

It is not known whether Peiping will permit prisoners' relatives to enter the country. At various times in the past, the Communists have said they

Continued on Page 6, Column 3

Dutch to Seek Support of Allies On Jakarta Rift at NATO Talk

By WALTER H. WAGGONER
Special to The New York Times.

THE HAGUE, the Netherlands, Dec. 6—The Netherlands appealed tonight for a show of solidarity by her Western allies on behalf of Dutch interests in Indonesia.

A Government statement issued after a day-long Cabinet meeting said the Netherlands' representative in the North Atlantic Treaty Organization had been instructed to call for an emergency session of the organization's permanent council to hear the Hague's explanation of its dispute with the Jakarta Government.

The Dutch representative will at this session "request all measures of solidarity that are required by the present situation," the Cabinet decided. The Foreign Ministry later said that the NATO unit had agreed to hear the Dutch case tomorrow.

The Government statement noted a growing number of measures "led, encouraged or allowed" by the Indonesian Government that are being directed "against Dutch nationals and Dutch economic activities in Indonesia, measures in conflict with the elementary principles of international law and human dignity."

[In Indonesia the continued take-over of Dutch enterprises by workers' groups provoked a strong official warning. Information Minister Sudibyo said "the masses are not obeying Government orders" against such actions.]

The actions under protest have included premature cancellation of landing rights in Jakarta by KLM, the Royal Dutch Airline; a strike against

Continued on Page 4, Column 3

Rocket Disappoints President; He Calls for Report on Failure

By RICHARD E. MOONEY
Special to The New York Times.

GETTYSBURG, Pa., Dec. 6—President Eisenhower asked the Defense Department today for a full report on what happened when the Vanguard rocket did not blast off into space. He was naturally disappointed.

As the time for firing approached, shortly before noon, the White House in Washington cleared telephone lines to the Cape Canaveral launching pad and to James C. Hagerty, the President's press secretary, in his Gettysburg hotel room.

Mr. Hagerty listened as word of the final countdown was relayed by staff officers in the capital. When the word of failure came through, he had the White House call transferred to the President at his farm on the edge of town.

General Eisenhower came here yesterday for a few days of rest to speed recovery from his mild cerebral attack of last week. He had spent part of the morning on an enclosed porch of the big farmhouse, painting a portrait of his oldest granddaughter from a snapshot.

He also talked several times by telephone with members of his staff in Washington, about Vanguard and other things, and once with John Foster Dulles, Secretary of State.

When newsmen asked Mr. Hagerty whether the President had expressed any disappointment over Vanguard to him, Mr. Hagerty replied, "certainly."

Mr. Hagerty said the Defense Department report would probably take more than a day to prepare.

Mr. Hagerty would not com-

Continued on Page 12, Column 3

1958

First prize in the International Tchaikovsky Piano Concert competition in Moscow went to Van Cliburn, a 23-year-old pianist from Texas. When he returned to the U.S. he received the first ticker tape parade ever given to a musician.

On January 31, 1958, the blast-off of Explorer I catapulted the U.S. into the space race. In its first satellite-boosting task, the Army's Jupiter IRBM rocket performed flawlessly.

Sherman Adams was considered one of the most important officials of the Eisenhower administration. In 1958 he resigned after charges were raised alleging that he intervened with federal agencies for the benefit of a friend, Boston industrialist Bernard Goldfine.

The New York Philharmonic gained popularity with Leonard Bernstein conducting. In 1958 CBS broadcast the first of Bernstein's Young People's Concerts.

"All the News That's Fit to Print"

The New York Times.

LATE CITY EDITION
U. S. Weather Bureau Report (Page 38) forecasts:
Snow ending late today.
Clearing and cooler tomorrow.
Temp. range: 35—30. Yesterday: 44.4—32.2.

VOL. CVII..No. 36,533.   © 1958, by The New York Times Company. Times Square, New York 36, N. Y.   NEW YORK, SATURDAY, FEBRUARY 1, 1958.   10c beyond 100-mile zone from New York City   FIVE CENTS

ARMY LAUNCHES U.S. SATELLITE INTO ORBIT; PRESIDENT PROMISES WORLD WILL GET DATA; 30-POUND DEVICE IS HURLED UP 2,000 MILES

KHRUSHCHEV SAYS HE WOULD AGREE TO DELAY PARLEY

But Wants Summit Meeting at Earliest Possible Date —For Gradual Steps

Special to The New York Times.

LONDON, Jan. 31—Nikita S. Khrushchev said today that he was willing to agree to some delay in convening a summit meeting, but that the conference should not be postponed into the indefinite future.

The First Secretary of the Soviet Communist party made the statement in an interview in Moscow with Iverach McDonald, correspondent of The Times of London. The two-hour talk was conducted in Mr. Khrushchev's offices in the headquarters of the Central Committee of the Communist party.

If the West regards a conference within the next two or three months as too soon, Mr. Khrushchev said, he is ready to agree to whatever is considered the earliest possible date.

Experience as Miner Cited

But, he added, the Soviet Union does not want a repetition of the sort of experience he had in the days when he was a mechanic in the coal mines.

Pay day, he recalled, used to be put off and off in spite of a notice that said: "Pay day at the end of the month." The trouble was, he remarked, that the notice did not specify which month or even which year.

Mr. Khrushchev reiterated his distaste for a preliminary meeting of foreign ministers because, he said, some foreign ministers are like midwives who are not interested in insuring the birth of the child.

He agreed that the foreign ministers would have to meet after a conference of heads of government in any event. But he said the top-level meeting was necessary to break the present inertia in international affairs and provide an "impetus toward agreement." The force of public opinion, he said, would then be behind the foreign ministers because the people are tired of the "cold war."

Mr. Khrushchev insisted that his views on disarmament were flexible and that he believed the question should be tackled by

Continued on Page 8, Column 4

MAYOR SETS STUDY ON SCHOOL CRIME

He and Bar to Examine Feud on Brooklyn Delinquency

By EDITH EVANS ASBURY

Mayor Wagner and the City Bar Association moved yesterday to inquire into the acrimonious dispute over Brooklyn school delinquency. The Mayor announced that he would meet with members of the Board of Education and other school officials Monday at 4:30 P. M. in Gracie Mansion.

The bar group's Committee on Municipal Affairs was asked by Louis M. Loeb, president, to investigate the actions of Judge Samuel S. Leibowitz and the Kings County grand jury in relation to the Board of Education.

The special grand jury has been investigating juvenile violence in Brooklyn schools. It and Judge Leibowitz have been sharply critical of the Board of Education.

The board's resentment of that criticism culminated Thursday evening in a formal statement accusing the grand jury of "gross abuse and personal attack" on board members.

The board also charged that George Goldfarb, a high school principal who committed suicide Tuesday at a time when he was scheduled to appear before the jury for the third time

Continued on Page 10, Column 3

UNITY: President Gamal Abdel Nasser of Egypt, left, welcomes President Shukri al-Kuwatly of Syria at Cairo airport. They met to announce merger of their countries.
Associated Press Radiophoto

Syrian President in Cairo To Join Nation With Egypt

By FOSTER HAILEY

CAIRO, Jan. 31—President Shukri al-Kuwatly of Syria arrived here today to join in a proclamation uniting his country with Egypt. The announcement of the merging of the two Arab states will be made simultaneously before the National Assemblies in Cairo and Damascus tomorrow or Sunday, it was predicted in both capitals.

President Gamal Abdel Nasser of Egypt and the Syrian President were in conference most of the day at the Presidential palace, Al 'Qoubba. It was assumed they were working out the final details of the proclamation.

Plebiscite in February

Syria's 4,000,000 citizens and Egypt's 24,000,000 will be asked to approve the union in a plebiscite next month. Feb. 20 was reported to have been tentatively selected as the date.

It is accepted that the Egyptian leader will be the first head of the new state, which is being called here the United Arab State.

There has been no official announcement in either country of exact details of the union. But informed sources here and in Damascus say there have been agreed on:

¶Cairo is to be the capital.

¶A united government is to be formed after the plebiscite, with President Nasser heading a Cabinet of twenty members of whom at least five would be Syrians.

¶The Syrian Army is to be

Continued on Page 3, Column 3

OIL INCOME POOL IN MIDEAST URGED

Iranian Views Combination of Resources as Way to End Need for Aid

By DANA ADAMS SCHMIDT
Special to The New York Times.

WASHINGTON, Jan. 31—Dr. Ali Amini, Ambassador of Iran, advocated today pooling the oil incomes of Middle Eastern nations.

By thus combining their resources, he declared, "I am confident many of the present-day political tensions, which tax so much of the attention and of the effort of the Western world, will be automatically eliminated."

Ambassador Amini did not detail just how the pool would operate.

Middle Eastern oil income is about $1,000,000,000 a year, almost all of it produced by Kuwait, Saudi Arabia and Iran, in that order.

Further Rise Envisaged

In all these countries it is rising steadily. In the case of Iran, according to Dr. A. J. Meyer of the Center of Middle Eastern Studies at Harvard University, recent discoveries give promise of increasing the annual income $1,000,000,000 in fifteen years.

Ambassador Amini and Dr. Meyer spoke at the annual conference on Middle Eastern affairs of the Middle East Institute.

Addressing a luncheon meeting, the Iranian Ambassador observed that United States aid had helped overcome the capital shortage of some countries of the Middle East.

But United States aid "is certainly not sufficient," he said. Furthermore, some Middle Eastern countries "earn more than they can use," the envoy declared.

The pooling program, Ambassador Amini said, would "do away with the existing poverty in the midst of plenty in the area" and release the money now spent in the Middle East by the United States and international agencies "for use in other parts of the world which are not as fortunate as the oil-

Continued on Page 3, Column 5

EISENHOWER SPURS G.O.P. VOTE DRIVE TO WIN CONGRESS

Sees 'Good Start' to Victory —Assures Committee of Pre-Election Upturn

Excerpts from the President's speech are on Page 8.

By WILLIAM S. WHITE
Special to The New York Times.

WASHINGTON, Jan. 31—President Eisenhower exhorted the Republicans today to work hard, with "faith in a good cause," for a party victory in the Congressional elections in November.

He made no prediction that the Republicans would regain control of Congress from the Democrats, but said that they were "off to a good start."

He gave assurance, too, that business would be on the upswing before the election.

Speaking to a meeting here of the Republican National Committee, called to help propel the Republican campaign, the President acknowledged that "the political prophets" had predicted hard times for his party this year.

Cites 'Decisive Element'

"But," he went on, "these calculations overlook the decisive element: What counts is not the size of the dog in the fight—it's the size of the fight in the dog."

Vice President Richard M. Nixon, in an informal talk to the committee, likewise offered no explicit prediction that the Republicans would win.

Mr. Nixon conceded, moreover, according to an authorized summary of his remarks given out from the national committee's closed sessions, that the Republicans could not win without favorable economic conditions.

The Vice President went on to predict that such favorable conditions would exist.

The President reiterated his earlier forecasts that, although "business in general has been falling off in late months," the economy would turn upward "late in the year."

He struck at a "few political Cassandras," who, he said, were suggesting that "deep depression is just around the corner."

Continued on Page 8, Column 3

Stevenson Calls for World Panel Of Citizens to Sift Arms Plans

THE LAUNCHING: The Jupiter-C as it rose last night from Cape Canaveral, Fla., with the satellite at its top.
Associated Press Wirephoto from U. S. Air Force.

Mrs. Franklin D. Roosevelt and Adlai E. Stevenson at the National Roosevelt Day Dinner at Waldorf-Astoria Hotel.
The New York Times

By RICHARD AMPER

Adlai E. Stevenson proposed last night a new kind of United Nations effort to end the East-West deadlock over disarmament.

He suggested that the Secretary General select a group of

Text of Stevenson's address is printed on Page 2.

private citizens from over the world to evaluate the present disarmament recommendations so as "to clear the air of all the bunk and phony proposals."

"This committee would be composed of private citizens, top men of affairs and of science, chosen by the Secretary General from anywhere and everywhere and acceptable to the nuclear powers," he said. "It would work in private. It would render an advisory report."

Mr. Stevenson also called on the United States to compete with the Soviet Union in

Continued on Page 2, Column 3

Meyner Is Critical Of Administration

By GEORGE CABLE WRIGHT
Special to The New York Times.

WASHINGTON, Jan. 31—Gov. Robert B. Meyner asserted today that much of the leadership of the nation had been transferred from "amateurs" in the White House and the Administration to practical and effective politicians in Congress.

He maintained that these politicians were now giving the defense program the "forward push that it needed" and that they were refusing to "treat our defense lag in any petty partisan way."

The New Jersey Democrat placed the responsibility for many of the United States difficulties in the last few years on what he called the lack of effective political leadership in the Eisenhower Administration.

Mr. Meyner made his remarks at a luncheon meeting of the

Continued on Page 9, Column 2

JUPITER-C IS USED

Roars Up in Florida Tense 15¾ Seconds After It Is Fired

By MILTON BRACKER

CAPE CANAVERAL, Fla., Jan. 31—The United States' first earth satellite was borne spaceward tonight on a tremendous golden jet that roared its way across the sky from the base of the Army's Jupiter-C rocket.

At 10:48 P. M., after an agonizing fifteen and three-quarter seconds between the actual firing command and the lift-off, the giant rocket lit up the night with a seething burst of flame and gradually accelerated directly upward from the pad.

As the Jupiter-C gained speed, it emitted a violent roar that filled the entire area.

Never wavering on its course, the rocket rose faster and faster, cut through a layer of overcast and reappeared as a steadily diminishing spark burning its way out of sight.

Tracking Stations in Action

From the vicinity of the Cape, the launching appeared perfect. Radio-tracking stations went into action at once.

Searchlights picked out the Jupiter-C before launching so as to reveal clearly its unusual conformation.

As soon as the rocket got off the ground, the Air Force, which is in charge of Missile Testing Center here, distributed information on it to newsmen.

This data said the Jupiter-C was about 68.6 feet long, and the pointed cylindrical satellite case containing the scientific instruments was 80 inches long and 6 inches in diameter.

The weight of the satellite proper was 18.13 pounds, and the final stage of rocket after burn-out weighed 12.67 pounds, giving a total weight of the satellite of 30.8 pounds.

The "payload" instruments weigh about 11 pounds exclusive of the protecting steel case, which weighed 7½ pounds, the Air Force said.

"The satellite and final stage rocket were designed to remain together and circle the earth as one unit," the Air Force said. "The satellite is not designed to be recovered."

One of the most dramatic

Continued on Page 7A, Column 1

Nation Hails News; Nixon Sees Victory For Peace Policy

The nation rejoiced early this morning as the news spread that the United States now had its own satellite, "The Explorer," circling the earth.

The weight of the satellite proper was 18.13 pounds, and Vice President Richard M. Nixon, handed the news while at a party in his home, said that the launching of the satellite "demonstrates to the world that there's no monopoly on scientific capability." The Vice President continued:

"The achievement with the Jupiter-C emphasizes the wisdom of President Eisenhower's proposal for the development of space exploration in the cause of peace rather than in the wastage of war."

In Huntsville, Ala., where the Jupiter-C was born, thousands of residents poured into the streets within minutes of the rocket's launching in Florida.

It was like New Year's Eve. Fire engines and police cars raced through the streets, their sirens shrieking. Motorists all over the city sounded their horns.

The people waved placards saying, "Move over, 'Sputnik' Space Is Ours" and "Our Missiles Never Miss."

The Mayor, who joined in the celebration, estimated the crowd at 10,000.

In Washington Lieut. Gen. James M. Gavin, retiring Chief

Continued on Page 7A, Column 5

Blue Cross Rate Rise Is Rejected by State

The state's insurance superintendent yesterday turned down a request by New York Blue Cross for an average increase of 40 per cent in its hospitalization insurance rates.

An increase would have meant higher premium payments for nearly 7,000,000 subscribers to the hospital insurance plan in the city and near-by counties. Opponents of the rise had argued that it would have cost these subscribers as much as $50,000,000 a year in additional payments.

In a six-page decision Leffert Holz, the superintendent, noted that New York Blue Cross had a free surplus of $14,000,000 that could be exhausted "no earlier" than June 30.

He said that though the application was being rejected at this time, he would give immediate attention to a new request

Continued on Page 22 Column 8

SUCCESS ATTAINED

At His Georgia Retreat Eisenhower Gives News of Ascent

By FELIX BELAIR Jr.
Special to The New York Times.

AUGUSTA, Ga., Saturday, Feb. 1—President Eisenhower announced early today the successful launching of an earth satellite into orbit by the United States.

The statement by President Eisenhower said:

"Dr. J. Wallace Joyce, head of the International Geophysical Year office of the National Science Foundation has just informed me that the United States has successfully placed a scientific earth satellite in orbit around the earth."

"The satellite was orbited by a modified Jupiter-C rocket."

"This launching is part of our country's participation in the International Geophysical Year. All information received from this satellite promptly will be made available to the scientific community of the world."

Capital to Give Data

In releasing the President's statement, James C. Hagerty, White House press secretary, said that all further information on the satellite would come from the National Academy of Sciences in Washington.

According to Mr. Hagerty, the President's first words on being informed of the successful ascent of the satellite were: "That's wonderful."

Mr. Hagerty met with the White House press here shortly after 1 A. M. today. An hour earlier he had told how the President had interrupted an evening of bridge, as well as his usual dinner hour, to receive military intelligence reports on the progress of the satellite launching.

President Eisenhower arrived here yesterday for the first golfing vacation he has had since suffering his slight stroke on Nov. 26.

Gets Report From Capital

Mr. Hagerty told reporters here how the President was kept abreast of the launching by a special communication set-up from Washington to his vacation headquarters here.

The President received word of the launching over a phone line from Washington that was kept open beginning at 10:40 P. M.

The President received his first report from Mr. Hagerty at his cottage here after a 5:30 P. M. telephone call from Gen. Andrew J. Goodpaster, White House staff secretary for Pentagon information, in Washington.

At that stage, the main concern was whether the weather would permit the scheduled 10:30 P. M. firing. Mr. Hagerty informed the President, who had just finished a round of golf, that the weather was improving and that it was expected that

Continued on Page 7B, Column 2

SATELLITE TAKES 114-MINUTE ORBIT

Scientists Estimate Speed at 18,000 Miles an Hour —'Exotic' Fuel Used

Text of Defense Department fact sheet is on Page 7A.

By JOHN W. FINNEY
Special to The New York Times.

WASHINGTON, Saturday, Feb. 1—The earth satellite launched by the Army last night is circling the earth at a peak altitude of 2,000 miles.

The 30.8-pound satellite is following an elongated elliptical orbit. At its closest point it is 230 miles from the earth's surface.

With this orbit, it was estimated that the satellite would have a life span of several months.

However, other Army estimates put its minimum life at two and one-half years.

The satellite is traveling at a speed of about 18,000 miles an hour and completed its first orbit around the earth in 114 minutes.

Special Fuel Employed

The Army said it had used a special "rather exotic" fuel in the first stage of the rocket.

The satellite is equipped to measure the cosmic radiation encountered in space. On its first trip around the earth the satellite was reported to be sending back usable information detected by its miniature scientific instruments.

It was a proud moment for the Army missile team, which had succeeded, with a late start, in launching the United States' first earth satellite.

Congratulatory statements flooded in from Army, Defense Department and International Geophysical Year officials.

Present for the crowded news conference were the three officials primarily responsible for designing and launching the 30.8-pound satellite.

They were Dr. Werner von Braun, technical director of the Army's Ballistic Missile Agency; Dr. William H. Pickering, director of the Jet Propulsion Laboratory at the California Institute of Technology, and Dr. James A. Van Allen of the State University of Iowa, who is chairman of the instrumenta-

Continued on Page 7B, Column 1

U.S. Satellite Heard Here and on Coast

By ROBERT ALDEN

The radio signal from the United States satellite "Explorer," now in orbit, was picked up over California early this morning.

The rising and falling tone of this radio could be heard clearly at the RCA receiving station at Point Reyes Station, just north of San Francisco. It was also heard at the Press Wireless receiving station in Napa, Calif., thirty-five miles north of Oakland.

The signal was picked up at 12:41 A. M. New York time, just one hour and fifty-three minutes after the Jupiter-C rocket carrying the satellite had been blasted from its launching pad at Cape Canaveral, Fla.

The signal was monitored at 108.3 megacycles, one of the announced frequencies for the

Continued on Page 7A, Column 7

"All the News That's Fit to Print"

The New York Times.

LATE CITY EDITION
U.S. Weather Bureau Report (Page 56) forecast:
Partly cloudy today; fair tonight and tomorrow.
Temp. range: 43.—31. Yesterday: 46.3—33.1.

VOL. CVII..No. 36,578.

© 1958 by The New York Times Company.
Times Square, New York 36, N. Y.

NEW YORK, TUESDAY, MARCH 18, 1958.

10c beyond 100-mile zone from New York City

FIVE CENTS

FEBRUARY OUTPUT DOWN BY 3 POINTS; 6-MONTH DROP 10%

Decline Matches January's —Dip Now as Great as That of 1953-54 Slump

PRESIDENT SETS PARLEY

Asks Governors to Confer at White House on Plan to Prolong Jobless Aid

By EDWIN L. DALE Jr.
Special to The New York Times.

WASHINGTON, March 17—Industrial production dropped 3 points in February, the Federal Reserve Board reported today. This matched the 3-point decline in January.

The production index, using average output in the 1947-49 period as 100, was 130 in February after seasonal adjustment. The peak was 147 in December of 1956. It was 146 in February a year ago and 145 in August, when the index began its sharp decline.

The drop since August has been 15 points or 10.3 per cent —as much as the entire declines in the 1953-54 and the 1948-49 recessions. Because this index is the best measure of the broad industrial sector of the economy, any further decline in it would make this the worst of the post-war recessions. It already is the worst in terms of unemployment.

Decline Grows Steeper

The February figures also confirmed that the decline in output has been steeper in this recession than in 1953-54.

President Eisenhower, meanwhile, invited the nine members of the executive committee of the Conference of State Governors to a White House meeting on his plan for extending the duration of unemployment compensation benefits.

The President said he wanted the Governors' comments on his "tentative plan."

At the Capitol, Congress continued its consideration of moves to stem the recession.

Senator Lyndon B. Johnson of Texas, the Democratic leader, threw his backing behind a $2,000,000,000 program of Federal loans to states and local governments for public works. He indicated a bill carrying out the program would have priority and also suggested that any tax-cutting bill should include provisions improving social security benefits.

Meany Makes Appeal

George Meany, president of the American Federation of Labor and Congress of Industrial Organizations, took to Senator Johnson and House Speaker Sam Rayburn, Democrat of Texas, his plea for immediate further action, including a tax cut.

Mr. Meany, a spokesman said, gave the two Congressional leaders the same economic assessment that he gave President Eisenhower last week — that March was showing no improvement.

The Administration view was reiterated by the Secretary of the Treasury, Robert B. Anderson, who told a meeting of Republican women that a "steady as you go" attitude toward the recession was called for.

He again said a decision on tax cuts would await clarification of "the impact of current developments on the economy."

Continued on Page 15, Column 2

Felt Takes Charge Of City Realty Unit

By CHARLES G. BENNETT

James Felt took over the city's scandal-ridden Bureau of Real Estate yesterday, fortified by Mayor Wagner's promise of a free hand "to clean up the situation."

At the Municipal Building offices of the Real Estate Bureau, Mr. Felt said he would "make an examination of what we have here and reorganize the bureau if that is warranted."

Meanwhile, it was reported that "thousands of documents" with sufficient evidence to warrant indictments against persons involved in the affairs of the Nassau Management Company, Inc., had been sent to District Attorney Frank S. Hogan.

Carl Madonick, Assistant Attorney General in charge

Continued on Page 49, Column 4

COL. MOORE DENIES INFLUENCING F.C.C.

Testifies at House Inquiry He Had No Role in Award of Miami TV Channel

By JAY WALZ
Special to The New York Times.

WASHINGTON, March 17—Col. George Gordon Moore talked today of sugar, ships and factor fees. Colonel Moore, the brother-in-law of Mrs. Dwight D. Eisenhower, swore that none of these had anything to do with the Federal Communications Commission's award of a Miami television channel to a National Airlines subsidiary.

Colonel Moore's testimony took the House Subcommittee on Legislative Oversight on a brief trip from Miami to the Dominican Republic. The colonel, a Washington business man, said he went to the Caribbean island in the late summer of 1955 to buy sugar.

Managed Shipyard

He came back a few months later, he said, with $8,000 for managing a new shipyard built for the Government of Generalissimo Raphael Trujillo, the republic's strong man.

All this constituted an attention of the subcommittee because two National Airlines directors, George W. Gibbs Jr. and John W. Cross, were closely identified with the shipyard venture.

The subcommittee earlier heard testimony that Colonel Moore, as a friend of George T. Baker, president of National, had "engineered" the award of Miami's Channel 10 to the air-

Continued on Page 22, Column 3

TUNISIA SOFTENS STAND ON FRANCE; AGREEMENT SEEN

Ex-Protectorate Is Ready to Negotiate on Future of Bizerte Naval Base

By THOMAS F. BRADY
Special to The New York Times.

TUNIS, March 17—A compromise settlement of the French-Tunisian crisis was predicted in well-informed quarters here today.

Robert Murphy, United States Deputy Under Secretary of State, and Harold Beeley of the British Foreign Office flew to Paris with a series of Tunisian proposals far more moderate than any expected last week.

The conciliators lunched with President Habib Bourguiba at his house in Sayda just before they boarded their plane.

The minimum Tunisian position is understood to include a demand for a clear declaration of Tunisian sovereignty over the naval base and port of Bizerte. Following that, bilateral negotiations would determine the future status of Bizerte.

Tunisian Concession Seen

This constitutes a Tunisian concession because it does not include an outright demand for the evacuation of Bizerte or even for a declaration of French intention to evacuate.

Tunisia also is said to seek establishment of a schedule of evacuation of French posts and military facilities elsewhere in the country; to be completed in a relatively brief period.

The "neutralization" of four air bases slated for evacuation is another reported Tunisian objective. Tunis has proposed an inspection of the bases by the British and United States Ambassadors or their representatives. The proposed inspection is intended to assure that the Algerian nationalist rebels cannot use the bases against the French Army. The problem is not regarded as significant here.

Consulates Raise Problem

Another Tunisian proposal provides for individual examination of the status of about 150 French families evacuated from the frontier region for "security reasons." Well-informed Tunisian circles concede privately that the political activity of some of the persons evacuated was a reason for their removal.

The Tunisians also are said to seek discussion with the French Government of problems raised by the closing of four French consulates and one vice consulate.

Behind these proposals is the basic Tunisian concession of accepting direct negotiation with the

Continued on Page 9, Column 3

NAVY PUTS VANGUARD IN ORBIT; 2D U.S. SATELLITE UP 2,513 MILES; EXPECTED TO LAST 5 TO 10 YEARS

NEW TESTS AHEAD

Project Plans to Fire Large Satellites in Space Study

By JOHN W. FINNEY
Special to The New York Times.

WASHINGTON, March 17—The Navy's tiny test satellite—a humming symbol of success after months of frustration—seemed destined today for a life of up to ten years in space.

The first indications were that the three-and-a-quarter-pound sphere not only had gone farther out into space than preceding satellites but also would circle the earth much longer.

Two hours after the Navy finally launched a satellite a beaming Dr. John P. Hagen, director of the Navy's Project Vanguard, predicted that Vanguard I would be "a very long-lived satellite."

Dr. Hagen said preliminary estimates showed that the satellite, with its humming radio voice, was following an egg-shaped path, reaching a peak altitude of 2,513 miles and coming as close as 407 miles to the earth.

A Day of Exultation

If these estimates are borne out by further tracking, Dr. Hagen said, the silvery sphere could have a life of five to ten years in space.

After months of internationally publicized setbacks and failures, the exultation of Project Vanguard officials soared with the satellite as they finally got the complex three-stage rocket off the ground.

The first announcement that the 6.4-inch sphere had gone into orbit came from President Eisenhower at the White House at 9:40 A. M.—some two and one-half hours after the bullet-shaped, seventy-two-foot-long rocket was fired from its launching pad at Cape Canaveral, Fla.

Dr. Hagen, meanwhile, was announcing initial success for his Project Vanguard to reporters at the Naval Research Laboratory on the outskirts of the District of Columbia.

Dr. Hagen wore a broad smile that lifted his prominent double chin.

"I can't keep from smiling," he confessed as he introduced

Continued on Page 15, Column 3

Associated Press Wirephoto (from U. S. Navy)
SUCCESS: The Navy's Vanguard rocket rises above servicing tower at Cape Canaveral

MEDAN RETAKEN, JAKARTA ASSERTS

Airport and Port Also Said To Be Recaptured in Day— Rebels Dispute Claims

By BERNARD KALB
Special to The New York Times.

JAKARTA, Indonesia, March 17—The Indonesian Army claimed victory tonight in a one-day struggle with the rebels for Medan, biggest city on Sumatra.

The announcement said control of the North Sumatran city, its airport and its near-by harbor of Belawan on the Strait of Malacca was regained in the morning. The insurgents "retreated" from the city, it added. No mention was made of casualties.

[The rebel radio at Padang denied the central Government's announcement. However, a Medan broadcast supported the Government statement that Medan had been recaptured.]

The Medan area had been regarded as pro-Jakarta in the Central Government's military campaign to crush the Central Sumatran rebels. The area is surrounded by territory that is either sympathetic to the rebels or neutral. The city was the scene in December, 1956, of a short-lived anti-Jakarta coup

Continued on Page 6, Column 3

Castro Proclaims All-Out Cuban War Starting on April 1

Special to The New York Times.

HAVANA, March 17—Fidel Castro, Cuban rebel leader, has declared "total war" on the Government and has set April 1 as the date for the start of the final struggle.

In a manifesto to the public, Señor Castro said the overthrow of the Government would be accomplished by a general strike backed by armed action. No date was fixed for the strike.

"Revolutionary action will be carried out progressively from this instant until it ends in the strike that will be ordered at the proper moment," Señor Castro said. He warned the public against "false orders" to strike.

Manifesto Distributed

The manifesto was being clandestinely distributed tonight throughout Cuba. It is not believed that the rebel leader has sufficient armed strength to defeat the forces that President Fulgencio Batista is throwing against the rebels in Oriente Province.

While the general public believes that the present situation cannot continue, Cubans are somewhat skeptical as to the "total war" declared by Señor Castro.

The rebel leader, who has led insurgents against Government troops since December, 1956, told members of the armed

Continued on Page 10, Column 3

EISENHOWER PLANS REPLY TO CRITICS

Will Defend Foreign Policy in Speech Before Editors in Capital April 17

By FELIX BELAIR Jr.
Special to The New York Times.

WASHINGTON, March 17—President Eisenhower has decided to answer mounting criticism of his foreign policy in an address here April 17.

The White House announced today that the President would speak on his foreign policy at a joint luncheon meeting of the American Society of Newspaper Editors and the International Press Institute.

In the past annual meetings of the American Society of Newspaper Editors have been the occasion of major policy pronouncements by General Eisenhower.

With the two editorial organizations meeting together for the first time and with about eighty European and Asian editors attending, the President is expected to redefine United States policy aims abroad.

To Review Arms Impasse

Besides replying to his critics he is expected to bring the country up to date on the impasse with the Soviet Union on disarmament and a heads-of-government conference.

[Another Soviet note on the proposed top-level talks has been sent to Harold Macmillan, Prime Minister of Britain.]

Announcement of the President's decision to address the editors' meeting followed a scathing attack on the Administration by Senate Democratic leaders for having permitted the Soviet Union to achieve a propaganda victory with its recent proposal for international control of outer space.

Senator Mike Mansfield of Montana, the Democratic whip, charged on the floor that in advancing the international control plan the Soviet Union had stolen an idea first advanced last January by Lyndon B. Johnson, Democrat of Texas, Senate majority leader.

The Soviet proposal for a United Nations agency to space the peaceful use of space was described by the Montana

Continued on Page 2, Column 3

SIGNALS RECEIVED

Sphere Carries Solar Batteries—Part of Rocket Trails It

By RICHARD WITKIN
Special to The New York Times.

CAPE CANAVERAL, Fla., March 17—Scientists of Project Vanguard fired a 6.4-inch satellite sphere into orbit around the earth today.

The firing ended months of frustration on the project conducted by the Navy.

The three-stage test rocket, shaped like an elongated rifle shell, kicked from its launching pad at 7:15½ A. M.

It climbed into a lovely blue sky, its fragile seventy-two-foot frame gradually disappearing into the diamond-like brilliance of its trailing flame. It headed southeast down the Caribbean island tracking range, aimed to cross the Equator at an angle of about 32 degrees.

Washington Informed

At 9:36 A. M. a Navy minitrack station at San Diego, Calif., picked up signals transmitted from the grapefruit-sized sphere as it entered the last portion of its first round-the-world trip.

The word was relayed to Washington. Vanguard I was in orbit.

[According to the Smithsonian Astrophysical Observatory at Cambridge, Mass., the satellite will not be visible. However, the fifty-pound casing of the last stage of the Vanguard, which is orbiting just behind the tiny sphere, may be seen with instruments.]

It was the nation's second artificial satellite and the world's fourth. Estimates put the apogee (highest point) and perigee (lowest point) of its elliptical path at 2,513 and 407 miles above the earth.

The figures far exceed those of any of the other satellites.

Carries Two Transmitters

However, their particular significance was dimmed somewhat by the small weight of Vanguard I, only 3¼ pounds compared with 30.8 for Explorer II, 184 for Sputnik I and 1,120 for Sputnik II.

Vanguard I is simply a test sphere. It has minimum instrumentation—two radio transmitters, one powered by conventional batteries, the other by solar batteries, which draw their power from the sun. The fully instrumented satellite package to be launched eventually will weigh 21½ pounds and can be expected to orbit at considerably lower altitudes than Vanguard I.

Yet, there was no dimming

Continued on Page 14, Column 1

JACK BENNY LOSES IN SUPREME COURT

TV Parody of 'Gaslight' Held to Infringe Copyright

By ANTHONY LEWIS
Special to The New York Times.

WASHINGTON, March 17—An evenly divided Supreme Court affirmed today a lower court ruling that Jack Benny violated the copyright laws when he parodied the movie "Gaslight" on television.

The ruling was regarded as a blow to the ancient art of parody. It apparently means that you can't take substantial quotes from a copyrighted work even if you spoof it unless you have the copyright holder's permission.

The exact scope of the decision is uncertain because there were no opinions. By tradition, the court does not write opinions when it is equally divided, nor does it announce how Justices voted. An equal division has the effect of affirming the judgment below.

The vote was 4 to 4. The tie was made possible because Justice William O. Douglas did not participate in the decision.

The Justices customarily do

Continued on Page 58, Column 3

Harriman Vetoes G. O. P. Crime Bill

By LEO EGAN
Special to The New York Times.

ALBANY, March 17—Governor Harriman vetoed tonight a Republican bill to broaden the power of Attorney General Louis Lefkowitz to investigate crime.

The veto gave rise immediately to a Republican charge that the Governor, a Democrat, was putting "considerations in partisan politics" above the public welfare. Mr. Lefkowitz is a Republican.

The Republican comment on the veto was made by Walter J. Mahoney of Buffalo, majority leader of the Senate, and Oswald D. Heck, Speaker of the Assembly.

The bill would have em-

Continued on Page 25, Column 2

Pipes Skirl, Skirts Swirl as 122,000 Salute the Green

The New York Times (by Patrick A. Burns)
On reviewing stand Governor Harriman shows a passing marcher his blackthorn stick. It's the same old shillelagh given to him by Robert Briscoe, former Lord Mayor of Dublin. Others in the front row are, from the left, John J. Sheahan, chairman of the parade committee; former Mayor William O'Dwyer, and James Carroll, Lord Mayor of Dublin.

By BILL BECKER

The Emerald Isle's traditional phalanx toed the green line up Fifth Avenue yesterday in one of the city's more colorful St. Patrick's Day parades. Skirts a-swirling and pipes a-skirling, an Irish and Irish - at - heart brigade, estimated at 122,000 marchers, moved for a pulsating six hours from Forty-fourth to Ninety - sixth Street. Not only the vaunted green, but virtually every color in the spectrum dazzled

Continued on Page 31, Column 2

more than 750,000 by the police. Additional thousands looked down from office buildings, department stores and hotels. The crowd of watchers along the route—a dozen deep in many places — was estimated at

Westchester to Help Railroads; Tax Cut, County Agency Urged

By MERRILL FOLSOM
Special to The New York Times.

WHITE PLAINS, March 17—After thirty years of vainly fighting railroad fare increases and service reductions, Westchester County decided today on a new course. It plans to deal with the railroads as sick industries in need of help. These proposals were made officially:

¶The setting up of a county authority to operate passenger trains and buses on coordinated schedules.

¶The expansion of such an authority to embrace Putnam County in this state and Fairfield County in adjacent Connecticut, to operate coordinated trains and buses in similar manner.

¶The granting of tax conces-

sions to the New York Central Railroad on the $1,324,000 a year it pays in Westchester and the $559,000 similarly paid by the New York, New Haven and Hartford Railroad.

As a start, the Westchester Board of Supervisors unanimously authorized the establishment of the first comprehensive Westchester County Committee on Commutation.

It is to survey "as expeditiously as possible" the entire bus and rail problem, seek agreements with officials of the lines and draft a procedure to perpetuate public transportation.

The committee is to comprise the County Executive, the Coun-

Continued on Page 24, Column 1

Sidney Poitier and Tony Curtis portrayed two escaped convicts in *The Defiant Ones, a significant film which had a theme of racial brotherhood.*

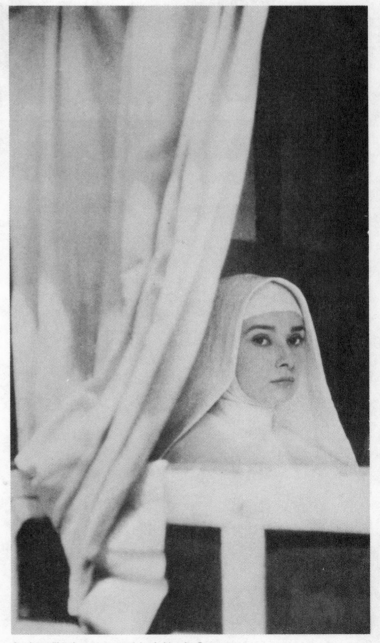

Audrey Hepburn starred in A Nun's Story.

1958

The hit Born Too Late *belonged to the Poni-Tails.*

Peggy Lee recorded Fever in 1958. It became one of the giant hits of her career.

The Shirelles sang I Met Him On A Sunday.

The New York Times.

LATE CITY EDITION
U.S. Weather Bureau Report (Page 50) forecasts:
Partly cloudy today; mostly fair tonight and tomorrow.
Temp. range: 49.—36. Yesterday: 46.8—37.9.

VOL. CVII..No. 36,588. © 1958, by The New York Times Company. Times Square, New York 36, N.Y. NEW YORK, FRIDAY, MARCH 28, 1958. 10c beyond 100-mile zone from New York City FIVE CENTS

STEVENSON JOINS PRESIDENT IN PLEA FOR WORLD TRADE

They Back Reciprocal Tariff Act as Vital for Nation and Call for Extension

RALLY HEARS WARNINGS

Peace and Prosperity Linked — Measure Is Attacked at a Rival Conference

Speeches by Eisenhower and Stevenson on Page 12.

By JOHN D. MORRIS
Special to The New York Times.

WASHINGTON, March 27—President Eisenhower and Adlai E. Stevenson appealed today for Congressional support of a liberal foreign trade policy as vital to domestic prosperity and world peace.

The President and his Democratic opponent in 1952 and 1956 addressed separate sessions of a day-long rally to demonstrate wide bipartisan backing for the Reciprocal Trade Program. The rally was sponsored by the National Conference of Organizations on International Trade Policy.

Vice President Richard M. Nixon, four Cabinet officers, several members of Congress and leaders of business, industry and labor were among the speakers.

President Eisenhower, in a speech to the dinner session tonight, declared that "both job security and national security demand an enlightened trade policy."

'Good for America'

He said the program, now before Congress for renewal, was "good for America on straight pocketbook grounds" because it would protect "millions of jobs" that depend on foreign markets. He estimated that 4,500,000 were employed in such jobs.

It will also help to build the road to peace, he continued, and is "vital to national security."

"So compelling and justifiable are these individual and collective reasons," the President asserted, "that even those who previously opposed reciprocal trade should see the need for changing from their former position and so measure up to this inescapable duty of our day."

Mr. Stevenson told a luncheon session that any retreat on United States trade policy would have "forbidding and unalterable consequences."

Sponsors of Conference

"It will further weaken our alliances, further enfeeble confidence in our leadership, push the great undeveloped areas into Communist arms and in the long run isolate, imperil and impoverish us," he said.

"We cannot, must not, dare not turn the clock back to 1930. We cannot be at once advocates and opponents of growth, expansion and competition. We cannot be at once political internationalists and economic nationalists."

One hundred and twenty-eight national and local organizations from the United States Chamber of Commerce to the Young Women's Christian Association were listed as sponsors.

Continued on Page 13, Column 3

$11,200 Left in Cab Awarded to Driver

By LAYHMOND ROBINSON

After months of frustration, Harold Petrie, a taxi driver, yesterday won possession of $11,200 in water-soaked bills that he found in the rear of his cab last July 24.

Justice Arthur G. Klein awarded the money to Mr. Petrie after throwing out a counterclaim by Walter Robinson, administrator of an estate. Mr. Robinson asserted in court that he had been ordered to claim the money by a "vision" of the owner, who died in 1929.

Carmine G. De Sapio, leader of Tammany, had been a passenger in the cab shortly before the money—wrapped in white paper—was found by the driver at Vanderbilt Avenue and Forty-second Street. Mr. De Sapio

Continued on Page 35, Column 2

U. S. Plans Moon Rockets; Initial Outlay Is 8 Million

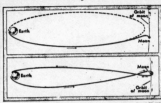

The New York Times March 28, 1958
The path of a rocket ejected from the earth's atmosphere with enough speed to coast to the moon would consist of segments of two elongated ellipses. One represents the path while the rocket is controlled by the earth's gravity. The other shows its route when moon gravity takes over. In the upper drawing the rocket would land on the moon. In the lower one it would circle and return to the earth. Charts are based on data from The Scientific American.

By JACK RAYMOND
Special to The New York Times.

WASHINGTON, March 27—The United States, with three artificial satellites circling the earth, announced plans today to explore space in the vicinity of the moon.

Four or more specially equipped unmanned vehicles will be hurled by powerful new rockets in an effort to get a "close look" at the moon.

The "lunar probes," as they were called in announcements at the White House and the Pentagon, are not intended to make an impact on the surface

—of the moon, although they "could," said James C. Hagerty, President Eisenhower's press secretary.

Officials gave no target date for the first attempt. A spokesman at the Defense Department, which will run the program, said:

"We are not in a race with the Russians."

The Soviet Union, the first nation to launch a satellite—it placed two in orbits around the

Continued on Page 8, Column 3

School Violence Reflects Instability in Adult World

This is the fifth of seven articles on the city's school students and their backgrounds and delinquency problems.

By HARRISON E. SALISBURY

No New Yorker needs to be told that it is in the city's schools the problem of "shook-up" adolescents reaches a stormy climax. Ever since the novel and film "Blackboard Jungle," New Yorkers have been increasingly aware of the impact of teen-age violence on the educational system. In recent weeks there has been a new series of tragic incidents.

It must be said at once that headlines about incidents are not necessarily a reliable barometer of conditions in general.

An enormous percentage of the 906,000 youngsters in the New York public schools are ordinary children, untouched by gang psychology. They are interested in their studies, enjoy an occasional skylark, but are a credit to their parents and the community. This goes for children of all races, colors and creeds.

Similar good marks must be given the city's teachers. By any objective criterion most of them do a first-rate job. The city has every reason to be proud of them.

Nonetheless, there is trouble in the schools, deep trouble.

Continued on Page 15, Column 2

REUTHER ADMITS ERROR ON KOHLER

But He Tells Inquiry That Union Acted in Setting of 'Modern Feudalism'

By JOSEPH A. LOFTUS
Special to The New York Times.

WASHINGTON, March 27—Walter P. Reuther conceded today that his union had erred in the four-year strike against the Kohler company. He contended, however, that the mistakes had been made in a setting of "modern industrial feudalism."

The president of the United Auto Workers told a Senate committee that the Wisconsin plumbing wares maker had "violated the spirit and the letter" of the law of collective bargaining, that its factory practices were "part of yesterday," and that it negotiated to avoid an agreement, not to make one.

Mr. Reuther's appearance before the Select Committee on Improper Activities in the Labor or Management Field attracted a turn-away crowd to the big caucus room. His long-billed bout with Senator Barry Goldwater, Republican of Arizona, however, was not spectacular. Only once was there audience participation.

Reuther Opposes Violence

The two political enemies, who have called each other "coward" at long distance, chose irony and icy politeness for close contact. The union leader was booked for a second appearance tomorrow.

Mr. Reuther cut some of the ground from under his adversaries by acknowledging again and again that pickets had no right to keep non-strikers from going to work. His longer statements aren't won in front of a man's home, a man's home is sacred," that "violence never settled anything," that the union man who beat up a non-striker without provocation did something "reprehensible."

He qualified all these with such remarks as "these things don't happen in a vacuum."

His concessions contrasted with the testimony yesterday of Herbert V. Kohler, president of the company, who declared his concern had done nothing illegal or improper.

Mr. Reuther, asked to list company activities he considered

Continued on Page 17, Column 4

SENATE APPROVES 5.5 BILLION PLAN FOR ROAD BUILDING

Passes Bill Aimed to Create Thousands of Jobs—Keeps Billboard Provision

By ALLEN DRURY
Special to The New York Times.

WASHINGTON, March 27—The Senate passed today an anti-recession highway construction bill. The measure is designed to pour $5,500,000,000 into the economy over the next two years and create thousands of new jobs.

Passage came on a roll-call vote of 84 to 4 after the measure had been before the Senate for four days. The bill caused a major controversy over a provision giving the Government authority to increase cash grants to states complying with Federal regulations for billboard advertising along the new 41,000-mile interstate system.

This provision was retained in a version that would give the Federal Government authority over approximately 65 per cent of the proposed system.

Bill Sent to House

The Labor Department, meanwhile, reported that nearly half of the nation's 149 major employment areas in mid-March were in the "substantial labor surplus" classification.

Senate approval of the highway bill sent it to the House. Leaders there hoped to by-pass floor debate and send it immediately to a Senate-House conference. The conference conceivably could complete work on the measure and forward it to President Eisenhower before the Easter recess, which starts April 4.

The House recently passed its own $2,000,000,000 version of a highway bill. It does not contain a billboard provision.

The possibility that the provision might still be stricken from the final version as it emerged from conference was seen in the choice of five Senate conferees. Three of the five voted against the provision yesterday when the Senate defeated an attempt to remove it from the Senate bill.

Second Anti-Recession Step

The highway bill is the second anti-recession measure passed so far by this session of Congress. A $1,850,000,000 housing bill is now at the White House awaiting President Eisenhower's signature.

The Senate version of the highway speed-up would pump $1,800,000,000 of Federal money into the highway program, and this with previous appropriations and matching state funds would bring the total money to be expended on highways to the $5,500,000,000 mark in the 1959, 1960 and 1961 fiscal years.

Estimates of the number of jobs that could be created by the bill ranged during debate

Continued on Page 15, Column 2

BOXING RECORDS SEIZED BY HOGAN

Office of Furrier Raided as 'Front' for Carbo—I.B.C. Data Are Subpoenaed

District Attorney Frank S. Hogan moved yesterday on two fronts in his investigation of illegal activities in professional boxing.

Detectives from the prosecutor's office, armed with search warrants, seized books and records from the offices of B. Wollman & Bros., Inc., furriers, of 352 Seventh Avenue.

One of the partners, Herman (Hymie the Mink) Wallman, is a fight manager described by Mr. Hogan's office as a "front man" for Frankie Carbo, an underworld hoodlum.

At the same time, a grand jury subpoena was served on Harry Markson, general manager of the International Boxing Club, calling for club records since 1956.

The seizure of the records from the Wollman offices resulted from an affidavit prepared by Assistant District Attorney John G. Bonomi and

Continued on Page 35, Column 2

Larger Summit Talk Role Seen for Soviet Chieftain

By JAY WALZ
Special to The New York Times.

WASHINGTON, March 27—United States observers commenting on the appointment of Nikita S. Khrushchev as Soviet Premier today leaned heavily to the view that he felt a need to become leader in name as well as in fact.

However, no evidence was readily apparent to officials that the move for broader authority by the First Secretary of the Soviet Communist party meant significant changes in Soviet foreign or domestic policy.

Official comment by the State Department noted that the development returned the Soviet Union to one-man control of the Government in Moscow for the first time since the death of Stalin in 1953.

But the statement suggested no conclusions to be drawn from that fact. It went on to say that the development "clarified" Mr. Khrushchev's standing at future meetings of heads of government.

Parley Stature Increased

In the past, he has been recognized as the "real spokesman" for the foreign and domestic policies of the Soviet Union. But, as one official put it, with only the title of Communist party secretary, he was actually an "interloper" at any top-level meeting.

Now, he will be the man with whom President Eisenhower, for example, must deal directly in any negotiations with the Soviet Union.

Senator Mike Mansfield, Democrat of Montana, expressed this thought in lighter vein with the remark:

"The only difference is that the guy who used to dictate the letters is now signing them."

For several months one of the few visible signs of the exercise of power by Marshal Nikolai A. Bulganin, former Premier, has been his signature to President Eisenhower and other heads of government. The letters have contained proposals and counter-proposals on the subjects of disarmament and atomic weapon controls.

Main Aims Called Obscure

There was widespread belief that Mr. Khrushchev was aiming at far more than the privilege of signing letters. But what his prime impulse might be was not clearly defined.

There was general agreement that as party chief he had no trouble getting his views accepted. And there was considerable doubt that as Premier he would have more "real power" than he held when Marshal Bulganin occupied that post.

However, some officials felt that the importance of making his exercise of power "legitimate" should not be discounted.

"There are practical advantages in driving a car to be in the driver's seat," said one official. Another observed that

Continued on Page 2, Column 3

KHRUSHCHEV TAKES FULL CONTROL, REPLACING BULGANIN AS PREMIER; U.S. EXPECTS NO CHANGE IN POLICY

Associated Press Radiophoto
VOTING FOR NEW SOVIET PREMIER: Raised hands in legislature signify approval of Nikita S. Khrushchev, head bowed, to replace Nikolai A. Bulganin, upper right, as Premier. Flanking Mr. Khrushchev are Anastas I. Mikoyan, left, and Marshal Kliment Y. Voroshilov. Others, from left, Averky B. Aristov, Nikolai I. Belyayev, Otto V. Kuusinen.

Some of the men in courtyard of a jail at Brownsville, Tex., after they were captured

U. S. Seizes 35 New Yorkers on Way to Join Castro

Associated Press Wirephoto
Some of the men in courtyard of a jail at Brownsville, Tex., after they were captured

Special to The New York Times.
BROWNSVILLE, Texas, March 27—Thirty-five Spanish-speaking New Yorkers bound for Cuba to join Fidel Castro, rebel leader, were arrested today by United States Coast Guardsmen who

—rammed and boarded their arms-laden trawler. The thirty-five men, as well as the captain and three crew members of the trawler and a Mexico City sporting goods store owner, who assertedly provided the arms, were held

in a total $307,500 bail by United States Commissioner Otto Reichert. All were charged with violating the United States Neutrality Act. The arms were confiscated. The

Continued on Page 8, Column 4

PARTY HELM KEPT

Moscow Chief Thus Unites Jobs Stalin Once Combined

By MAX FRANKEL
Special to The New York Times.

MOSCOW, March 27—Nikita Sergeyevich Khrushchev became Premier of the Soviet Union today. Thus he has emerged as the undisputed leader and chief spokesman of this nation in name as well as fact.

The Soviet legislature, the Supreme Soviet, dutifully and unanimously elected Mr. Khrushchev chairman of the Council of Ministers—the Premier—to succeed Marshal Nikolai A. Bulganin, who submitted his resignation.

The Supreme Soviet was told at once that the new Premier would remain First Secretary and therefore leader of the ruling Communist party.

Thus were joined again at the top the two hierarchies that direct the affairs of more than 200,000,000 Soviet citizens and lead the 1,000,000,000 persons of the Communist camp.

Advanced in 5 Years

They were united in the ebullient and energetic person of Mr. Khrushchev, the 63-year-old former mine mechanic, who in the five years since Stalin's death has emerged from the collective leadership and advanced to overwhelming responsibility and power.

Mr. Khrushchev has now succeeded to the posts that Stalin had formally combined. He is not only the acknowledged architect of all Soviet foreign and domestic policies but the leader of the disciplined party ranks and the extensive ministerial apparatus that administers and enforces the policies.

The momentous change in the Government was effected quickly and in strict forms of parliamentary procedure. There was no debate on the move and even before the full weight of the switch was apparent Premier Khrushchev began a two-hour-and-forty-minute dissertation on agricultural reforms.

He uttered only a few words of acceptance, words over which he appeared choked with emotion:

"With your decision," he told the 1,378 Deputies, "you have just expressed great confidence in me and have done me great honor. I shall do everything to justify your confidence and shall not spare strength, health or life to serve you."

His agricultural speech contained only one general comment that might be taken as an inaugural promise. "We shall conquer capitalism," Mr. Khrushchev declared, "with a high level of work and a higher standard of living."

Mr. Khrushchev was placed in nomination for the premiership by Marshal Kliment Y. Voroshilov only a few minutes after the marshal was elected

Continued on Page 2, Column 3

EISENHOWER SETS OIL IMPORT CURBS

He Lowers Ceiling and Acts to Deter Violators Under Voluntary Program

By RICHARD E. MOONEY
Special to The New York Times.

WASHINGTON, March 27—President Eisenhower today lowered the ceiling on imports of crude oil and set up procedures to discourage importers who would not respect it.

The lower ceiling means a 14.8 per cent reduction in imports by twenty-six importing companies from their current allowance of 771,400 barrels a day to a new ceiling of 713,000 barrels in April, May and June. The new ceiling includes an allocation of 55,900 barrels for fourteen companies not covered before.

The present ceiling forced a cutback when it was established last summer. All but three importers have complied so far and some have over-complied. The total of imports has been below the ceiling since fall in the program administered by Capt. Matthew Vaughan Carlson Jr.

A spokesman for the domestic producers, Russell B. Brown, general counsel of the Independent Petroleum Association of America, called the President's

Continued on Page 14, Column 3

French Rally to a G. I. Deserter Arrested After a 14-Year Tryst

By W. GRANGER BLAIR
Special to The New York Times.

PARIS, March 27—An avalanche of mail is pouring into the United States Embassy here asking clemency for an American deserter from World War II.

Pvt. Wayne Powers' fourteen-year idyl with a French village maid ended abruptly Saturday when the French police descended on the community of Montd'Origny. They took the Chilleothe, Mo., former soldier from Mlle. Yvette Beleuse and the couple's five children.

Powers was turned over to United States military authorities for court-martial.

This evening a spokesman at the United States Embassy said 43,000 letters had been received in the last two days asking President Eisenhower to grant clemency to the 37-year-old soldier, who—like Lieutenant

Henry in Ernest Hemingway's World War I novel "A Farewell to Arms"—made a "separate peace" and chose love to war. Among the letters received was one from Mlle. Beleuse.

Because he preferred life with Mlle. Beleuse to life with his transport outfit in the First Army, which was then engaging German forces in Belgium in November, 1944, Powers could be sentenced to death for desertion in time of war. Sentimental opinion here is that the combination of love and passage of time will spare Powers from a death sentence.

The deluge of mail on the embassy stems from a broadcast Tuesday night by the Saar-based Radio Station of Europe No. 1. The story of Wayne, Yvette and their four small sons

Continued on Page 4, Column 8

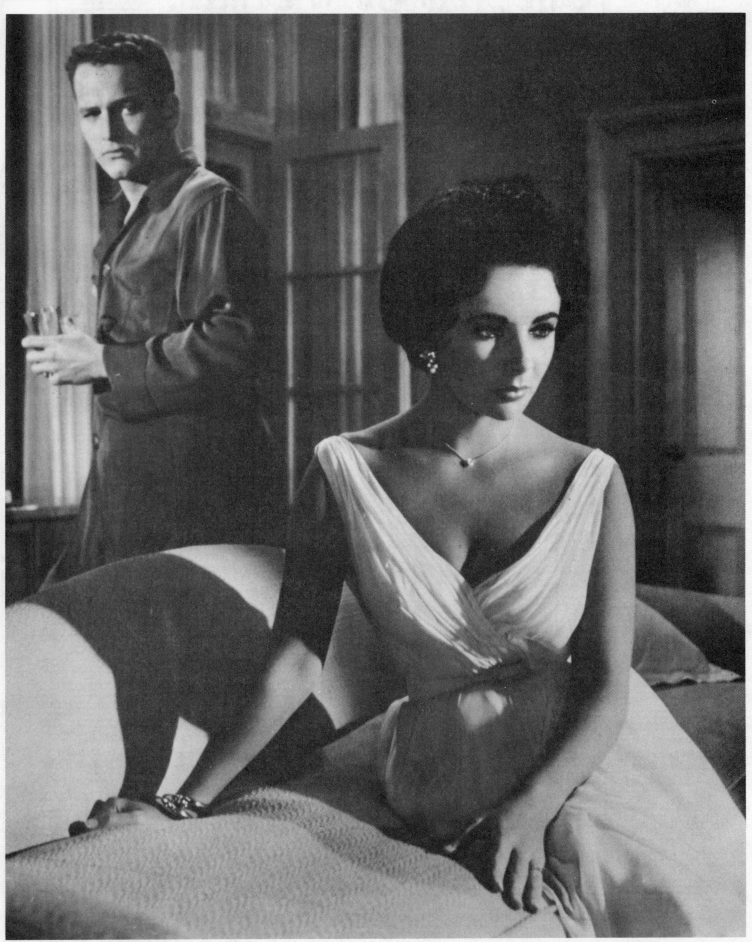

Elizabeth Taylor and Paul Newman starred in Cat on a Hot Tin Roof, *a film that expressed a more honest and explicit view of marital problems than had ever been presented by Hollywood.*

"All the News That's Fit to Print"

The New York Times.

LATE CITY EDITION
U. S. Weather Bureau Report (Page 65) forecasts: Mostly sunny today. Mostly fair and seasonably warm tomorrow.
Temp. range: 68—49. Yesterday: 66.3—52.

VOL. CVII . No. 36,635. | © 1958, by The New York Times Company, Times Square, New York 36, N. Y. | NEW YORK, WEDNESDAY, MAY 14, 1958. | 10c beyond 100-mile zone from New York City. Higher in air delivery cities. | FIVE CENTS

JUNTA TAKES ALGIERS RULE; FRANCE FEARS CIVIL WAR; PFLIMLIN IS NEW PREMIER

COTY MAKES PLEA

President Bids Army Obey Paris Orders —Massu Defiant

By ROBERT C. DOTY
Special to The New York Times.

PARIS, Wednesday, May 14—France had a new Government and a threat of civil war today.

The Government was headed by Pierre Pflimlin, a 51-year-old middle-of-the-road politician who was approved by the National Assembly early this morning by a vote of 274 to 129.

The threat of civil war was raised by a junta of senior French Army officers and European civilians in Algeria headed by Maj. Gen. Jacques Massu. They set up a "Committee of Public Safety" exercising power in Algiers. Its aim is to resist an anticipated effort by the Paris Government to seek negotiations with Moslem rebels to end the forty-three-month-old war in Algeria.

De Gaulle's Return Demanded

The return to power of Gen. Charles de Gaulle, wartime leader of the Free French and first post-war provisional President, was demanded by some Army elements in Algiers and by a fragmentary parliamentary party in France that proclaimed loyalty to the general.

The general himself was reported to have come to Paris from his rural retreat at Colombey-les-Deux-Eglises in eastern France.

At dawn, the Algerian radio, in the hands of insurgents, broadcast a statement by General Massu in which he "begged" General de Gaulle to break his silence and constitute a "Government of Public Safety" to save Algiers from the "Government of abandonment, which has just zeen installed with the complicity of Communist votes."

Franco's Action Recalled

General Massu "decreed" the mobilization of all French energies for support of the Committee of Peublic Safety, which he said would hold power "until the final victory."

Countering the insurgent's demand, President René Coty addressed an appeal to all ranks of the armed forces in Algeria, ordering them to remain loyal.

General Massu's action recalled ominously to some observers here the insurgency of another African colonial commander, General Francisco Franco, who launched his move-

Continued on Page 4, Column 6

Figures in Algerian Power Struggle

Gen. Raoul Salan

Associated Press
Gen. Jacques Massu

Army Group in Algeria Asks Power for de Gaulle

By Reuters.

ALGIERS, May 13—French troops seized control of Algeria tonight and demanded the return of Gen. Charles de Gaulle as Premier of France. The move was taken by many officials in Paris as a direct challenge to the French Government.

The army's intervention followed rioting by French settlers, who sacked French and United States official buildings during a protest against the confirmation of Pierre Pflimlin as Premier.

"We appeal to General de Gaulle to take the leadership of a government of public safety," said Gen. Jacques Massu, a former comrade of the wartime Free French leader.

Civilians on Committee

General Massu heads a newly-formed "Committee of Public Safety" here. He led a group of paratroopers who took control of the Algiers radio station and ousted the Government director earlier tonight.

Gen. Raoul Salan, the Commander in Chief, declared in a broadcast:

"I have provisionally taken into my hands the destinies of French Algeria.

"I ask you to put your trust in the army and its leaders and to show your calmness and your determination."

General Massu, in a statement read to approximately 30,000 demonstrators massed outside Government House, said General de Gaulle was "alone capable" of heading a French Government that would "ensure the everlastingness of French Algeria, an integral part of France."

The Massu committee, composed of three colonels and seven civilians, said it would "maintain order and avoid bloodshed" in the city.

There were conflicting reports

Continued on Page 3, Column 2

RIOTERS IN PARIS HALTED BY POLICE

Right-Wing Mob, Bitter Over Algeria, Is Blocked in March on Assembly

By W. GRANGER BLAIR
Special to The New York Times.

PARIS, May 13—A right-wing mob marched on the French National Assembly today but was stopped just short of its goal by armed security forces.

The march began as news of the riots in Algiers reached Paris and as Premier-designate Pierre Pflimlin went before the Assembly on the twenty-eighth day of the most serious political crisis under the Fourth Republic.

For almost three hours groups of rioters and the security forces clashed. The manifestations developed in various parts of the city but primarily along the broad avenue of Champs-Elysées and in the Place de la Concorde across the Seine River from the parliamentary building.

Students and War Veterans

The size of the mob, mostly university students and war veterans, was estimated to be between 2,000 and 5,000. At the end of the day three policemen and a sizable number of demonstrators were reported injured.

Traffic in the heart of Paris was paralyzed as the rioters dashed between cars screaming: "Algeria is French" and "The army to power." Buildings around and near the Place de la Concorde had shuttered windows and barred doors.

The march started at the Arch of Triumph at the opposite end of the Champs-Elysées from the Place de la Concorde. It boiled up as an aftermath of

Continued on Page 3, Column 1

KHRUSHCHEV SEEN EAGER FOR TALKS

Norwegians Report He Lays U. S. 'Delay' to Elections

By DREW MIDDLETON
Special to The New York Times.

OSLO, Norway, May 13—The Norwegian Government has learned that Soviet Premier Nikita S. Khrushchev believes the United States Administration wishes to postpone a summit meeting until after the Congressional elections in November.

The Soviet leader is said to think that the chances for a heads-of-government meeting this year are daily becoming more remote.

Mr. Khrushchev, according to Norwegians who have talked with him recently, wants very much to negotiate with President Eisenhower. The President, the Soviet leader insisted, is a man the Russians respect and trust.

Some tangible results would come from negotiation with President Eisenhower, Mr. Khrushchev told his visitors. He was less sanguine about the results of a foreign ministers' meeting. Most diplomats in the northern capitals think the foreign ministers' talks are about as far as East-West exchanges will go this year.

Norwegian sources support-

Continued on Page 6, Column 3

State Department Puts Curb on Press

By E. W. KENWORTHY
Special to The New York Times.

WASHINGTON, May 13—The State Department has taken measures to end individual contacts between its intelligence officers and newspaper men, and to require reports from other officials on their conversations with reporters.

These actions became public knowledge today as the State Department called "untrue" an Associated Press article that the department was drafting a directive to "regulate and limit" contacts between reporters and many officials.

Joseph W. Reap, State Department press officer, said that "no such directive is being drafted or is contemplated." Mr.

Continued on Page 16, Column 5

LEBANON CHARGES NASSER'S REGIME FOMENTS REVOLT

'Massive Interference' Is Cited by Malik—Protest to U. N. Considered

By FOSTER HAILEY
Special to The New York Times.

BEIRUT, Lebanon, May 13—Foreign Minister Charles Malik accused the United Arab Republic today of having instigated and aided the rebellion here against the pro-Western Government.

At a news conference Dr. Malik said:

"We have sent today a note of protest to the Government of the United Arab Republic. We interpret this massive interference from outside as having everything to do with the events now unrolling in Lebanon."

The Foreign Minister cited a number of incidents in the last two days to support his contention of direct intervention by Egypt and Syria, which make up the United Arab Republic under President Gamal Abdel Nasser.

Protest to U. N. Considered

He said the question of filing a complaint with the United Nations Security Council had been considered by the Cabinet but no decision had been taken.

[President Camille Chamoun called in the United States, British and French Ambassadors to report that the nation was under attack from abroad, The United Press said. One northern area of the country was reported to be in rebel hands and sharp fighting was under way elsewhere, but an American source said no request had been made for United States aid under the Eisenhower Doctrine.

[In Washington, Middle Eastern diplomats expected the Lebanese Government to protest to the United Nations against attacks organized by the United Arab Republic.]

Dr. Malik declined to answer a question as to whether Lebanon had considered invoking the Eisenhower Doctrine and asking the United States for military assistance. Such help is pledged by the United States Government to any Middle Eastern country faced with aggression from a country controlled by international communism, if the threatened country requests it.

U.S. Policy Backed by Beirut

Lebanon is the only one of the Arab lands that accepted the Eisenhower Doctrine.

The course of events in the Lebanese capital today indicated that the Government was coping with the insurrection, although there was scattered fighting and disturbances here and in other parts of the country.

Two attempted marches on the United States Embassy by several hundred young men were stopped by bayonet-wielding soldiers early this morning and the marchers were dispersed.

There were no further reports of attacks on the United States libraries here or on the homes

Continued on Page 4, Column 4

U. S. FLIES TROOPS TO CARIBBEAN AS MOBS ATTACK NIXON IN CARACAS; EISENHOWER DEMANDS HIS SAFETY

ROCKS SMASH CAR

Vice President Unhurt As Furious Crowds Halt Reception

By TAD SZULC
Special to The New York Times.

CARACAS, Venezuela, May 13—Hundreds of fury-spouting demonstrators attacked Vice President Richard M. Nixon's car with rocks and heavy sticks on his arrival today from Bogota.

About ten minutes later another mob, described as being in "lynching mood," tried to assault Army and Navy attachés of the United States Embassy at the National Pantheon. The Americans were there to attend the laying of a wreath by Mr. Nixon.

The ceremony never took place and two companies of helmeted infantry with poised bayonets were necessary to escort the two officers to safety.

Rocks Shatter Car Windows

In the first attack, three windows in the Vice President's closed limousine were smashed by melon-size rocks and Mr. Nixon was covered with shattered glass. Venezuelan Foreign Minister Oscar Garcia Lutin, riding next to the Vice President, was struck in the eye by a piece of glass.

[Later in the day mob violence broke out at the Government Palace as members of Venezuela's ruling junta returned from a meeting with Mr. Nixon, The Associated Press reported. The Government leaders' cars were stoned and two windows of one were smashed. Soldiers fired into the air and used tear gas to disperse the mob.]

The Vice President canceled all his scheduled visits in Caracas and said he would be seeing as many persons as possible at the Embassy residence. That building was the center of an armed camp tonight as more than 400 soldiers and military and civil policemen guarded Mr. Nixon.

Nixon Sees Red Direction

The Communist-led demonstrations appeared tonight to be turning into general manifestations against the Venezuelan armed forces and the governing junta.

Mr. Nixon, in a news conference, acknowledged that "a great majority of those who participated in the riots were not Communists." But he said "those who organized it were subject to central direction and are without a doubt Communist-dominated."

The Vice President's recognition of the fact that the presence in the United States of Venezuela's former dictator, Marcos Peréz Jiménez, and his police chief, Pedro Estrada, is one of the main irritants under-

Continued on Page 9, Column 1

Associated Press Radiophoto
DAMAGED CAR that carried Vice President Nixon is guarded by soldier after mobs' rocks shattered windows.

Goods and Services Total Off 4% From Peak in '57

By EDWIN L. DALE Jr.
Special to The New York Times.

WASHINGTON, May 13—Gross national product, the measure of the nation's output of goods and services, was even lower in the first quarter of the year than preliminary estimates had indicated, the Commerce Department reported today.

The annual rate of gross national product in the first quarter was $422,000,000,000, compared to $432,600,000,000 in the fourth quarter of 1957 and the record of $440,000,000,000 in the third quarter.

The preliminary estimate for the first quarter was $424,000,000,000. The drop of 4 per cent from the peak was still another proof that this qualifies as the worst of the three post-war recessions.

The decline in the 1948-49 recession was 3.2 per cent between its high and low points, and in the 1953-54 recession, it was 2.7 per cent.

At a Senate Finance Committee hearing, liberal and conservative Democrats opened separate attacks on a House-approved bill for supplementary unemployment benefits to jobless workers. The Secretary of Labor, James P. Mitchell, in his testimony, urged approval of the measure.

Inventory Drop Noted

The big item in the first quarter drop in national product—and the main change from the preliminary estimates—was liquidation of inventories. Businesses reduced their inventories at the record post-war rate of $9,000,000,000 a year in the first quarter. This was a faster rate than indicated by the preliminary figure of $7,500,000,000 and far faster than the $2,700,000,000 rate in the fourth quarter of 1957.

To the extent that consumer demand is met by the using up of stocks, production is cut back. Thus inventory liquidation is a "minus" figure in the

Continued on Page 18, Column 4

FOREIGN AID BILL WINS HOUSE TEST

Economic Assistance Curb Rejected After President's Plea to G.O.P. Leaders

By ALLEN DRURY
Special to The New York Times.

WASHINGTON, May 13—The Administration's foreign aid authorization survived its first major test in the House today.

Earlier, President Eisenhower had told Republican Congressional leaders he shuddered at what the impact abroad might be if the measure were subjected to further cuts.

In the first vote of a generally lackadaisical debate on the $1,958,000,000 measure, the House rejected, 102-59, an amendment to eliminate virtually all economic assistance. It was offered by Representative William M. Colmer, Democrat of Mississippi.

Martin Tells of Meeting

The President's opposition to further cuts in the bill—already trimmed by the House Foreign Affairs Committee to $339,000,000 below his request—was voiced at his regular Tuesday meeting with Republican Congressional leaders.

After the meeting the House minority leader, Joseph W. Martin Jr. of Massachusetts, told reporters:

"The President made it very clear that he already shudders at the idea of any further cuts.

Continued on Page 14, Column 4

WHITE HOUSE ACTS

Defense Agency Says Forces Will Be Used Only if Necessary

By RUSSELL BAKER
Special to The New York Times.

WASHINGTON, May 13—President Eisenhower sent four companies of marines and paratroopers into Caribbean bases tonight to back White House demands that Venezuela guarantee the safety of Vice President Richard M. Nixon.

While the troops were still airborne, James C. Hagerty, White House press secretary, said telephone reports from Caracas indicated that "the situation down there has gotten into much better shape" since mob attacks this morning on Mr. Nixon, his wife and his party.

A statement by the Department of Defense said that the combat-ready troops were being moved "as a precautionary measure" to be used "if assistance is requested" in case of further violence.

Afternoon Called Hectic

The announcement of troop movements was the high point of a hectic afternoon of swift and sharp responses to the mob attacks in Caracas. All bore the imprint of the President, who was described by some as angered and by Mr. Hagerty as "considerably concerned" over the assault on Mr. Nixon.

The troop elements involved are two companies of the 101st Airborne Division from Fort Campbell, Ky., and two companies of marines from Camp Lejeune, N. C. Altogether they total about 1,000 men.

To move the paratroopers—soldiers from the same division that was thrown into Little Rock, Ark., last fall during the school integration crisis—the Air Force used its new high-speed C-130 turboprop transports, which fly at 330 miles an hour.

Navy Planes Fly Marines

The marines were flown south by the Navy.

The Defense Department at first refused to announce their destinations. Later it said the airborne troops had been flown to the Ramey Air Force base in Puerto Rico, and the Marines to the United States naval base at Guantanamo, Cuba.

The official statement said:

"As a precautionary measure, two companies of airborne infantry and two companies of Marines are being moved to cer-

Continued on Page 8, Column 3

IVES WITHDRAWAL IS EXPECTED SOON

Health Is Cited—Hall and Rockefeller Slate Looms

By LEO EGAN

Senator Irving M. Ives has told friends that he will not seek re-election this year.

The 60-year-old Republican Senator, who is now completing his second term, said last night in Washington that his physician would have the final say on whether he would run again. He added that the "chances of getting an O. K. from the doctor aren't too good."

For more than five years he has been undergoing monthly tests for high blood pressure, he said. He said that his decision on whether to run would be made public today after a physical examination.

If Senator Ives withdraws, his action is expected to stimulate speculation about a Hall-Rockefeller or Rockefeller-Hall Republican ticket this fall. The top candidates on such a ticket would be Leonard W. Hall, former Republican national chairman, and Nelson A. Rockefeller, former Assistant Secretary of State. One would run for Governor and the other for Senator.

Mr. Hall edged nearer yesterday to a formal announcement that he wanted the Republican

Continued on Page 26, Column 3

Associated Press Radiophoto
PARIS PROTEST MARCHERS were met yesterday by club-swinging policemen as they surged toward the National Assembly to demonstrate against French policies in Algeria.

Stiff New City Code of Ethics Nearly Ready, Mayor Reports

By CHARLES G. BENNETT

A stiff new Code of Ethics for city officials, designed to avoid conflicts of interest in city government, has been nearly completed, Mayor Wagner made known yesterday.

The Mayor said that the new code would require "all municipal employes to comply with the highest standards of ethical conduct." It will be designed to replace the existing code contained generally in Section 886 of the City Charter.

In a letter to State Attorney General Louis J. Lefkowitz, the Mayor disclosed that S. Stanley Kreutzer, attorney for the City Council, had completed the projected new code in outline. The outline has been submitted to Mr. Wagner.

Soon after the Mayor's letter was made public, the City Council set a meeting of its Code Revision Committee for 1 P. M. Friday. At this meeting, Mr. Kreutzer's tentative code text is to be studied. Councilman Morris J. Stein, Democrat of Brooklyn, is chairman of the committee.

In his letter to Mr. Lefkowitz, Mayor Wagner wrote:

"Ours is a government that consciously seeks out bad spots, wherever they occur, and we shall act vigorously to get rid of corruption and dishonesty wherever they occur."

He said sweeping reorganizations under way in the Bureau

Continued on Page 27, Column 4

"All the News That's Fit to Print"

The New York Times.

LATE CITY EDITION
U. S. Weather Bureau Report (Page 45) forecasts:
Fair, breezy, less humid today; clear and cool tonight. Fair tomorrow.
Temp. range : 78.—60. Yesterday: 79.3—64.8.

VOL. CVII..No. 36,654.   © 1958, by The New York Times Company.
Times Square, New York 36, N. Y.   NEW YORK, MONDAY, JUNE 2, 1958.   10c beyond 100-mile zone from New York City.
Higher in air delivery cities.   FIVE CENTS

DE GAULLE NAMED PREMIER IN 329-224 VOTE; ASKS 6-MONTH DECREE RULE; LEFTISTS RIOT; ALGIERS IS DISPLEASED BY CABINET CHOICES

CRASHES KILL 344 ON 3-DAY HOLIDAY; RAIN CURBS TOLL

Auto Deaths Below Forecast — Temperature Climbs to 79.3 Degrees Here

By LAWRENCE O'KANE

Traffic fatalities climbed yesterday in the final, homebound hours of the Memorial Day week-end.

Bad weather over much of the nation dampened the outing spirits of many. But it also induced motorists to drive carefully.

By 2 A. M. today 344 persons had died in traffic accidents since 6 P. M. Thursday, according to The Associated Press. Altogether there were 554 accident deaths, including 122 drownings and eight-eight from miscellaneous causes.

In New York City, three persons were killed and 556 injured in 387 road accidents, according to Police Department figures covering the period from 8 A. M. Thursday to 4 P. M. yesterday. Only property was damaged in 487 other accidents.

Cautious Optimism

Late yesterday the National Safety Council began to express cautious optimism that traffic deaths would not exceed the peak three-day Memorial Day week-end toll of 369 recorded in 1955.

Last week the council had predicted 350 deaths for the 1958 holiday week-end, but after a series of multi-death accidents Saturday it began to voice fears of a new record.

The council said rain and slippery highways had restricted short-distance travel as picnics and beach outings were canceled. Showers and thunderstorms were reported sweeping from the Gulf states to southern New England. Squalls ranged the Great Lakes and tornado alerts were issued for parts of the South and Midwest.

Rain Avoids City

In New York City, the warmest day of the year sent hundreds of thousands to beaches and parks. Afternoon rains had been predicted, but failed to materialize. The threat kept crowds from swelling to record proportions, however, and chilly offshore winds kept most beachgoers out of the water.

The year's highest temperature here — 79.3 degrees — was registered at 4:20 P. M.

Today is expected to be fair, but not as warm or humid as yesterday. Afternoon temperatures are expected to be in the 70's. The prediction for Tuesday is fair with pleasant temperatures and low humidity.

As yesterday drew to a close, city-bound traffic increased on highways and bridges and in tunnels. Most reports described the flow as heavy, but moving freely.

A 22-year-old airman was injured fatally early yesterday when his automobile struck a

Continued on Page 15, Column 2

Mahoney Wins Upstate Support As G.O.P.'s Choice for Governor

By DOUGLAS DALES

Support for State Senator Walter J. Mahoney of Buffalo as the Republican nominee for Governor spread eastward over the week-end. Heretofore backing for the Senate leader was concentrated in western New York.

In a joint statement, county chairmen of four Hudson Valley - Catskill counties declared that no suggested candidate had Senator Mahoney's experience in state government or his capacity to present issues in a forthright and intelligent fashion.

The statement was issued by Neal Brandow of Greene, Dr. Ogden Bush of Delaware, Harold Cole of Sullivan and Kenneth L. Wilson of Ulster.

These counties, with six others whose leaders or party organizations have endorsed Mr. Mahoney, will have 181 of the 586 delegates needed for nomination at the convention Aug. 25 and 26 in Rochester.

Previously the Buffalo Senator has been assured publicly of the backing of Erie, Niagara, Chautauqua, Oneida, Madison and Herkimer Counties. In addition, he has received private assurances of support in at least ten other counties, according to close associates.

Neither of the two other potential candidates—Nelson A. Rockefeller and Leonard W. Hall—has received comparable delegate support. Mr. Hall

Ernst Report on Galindez Clears Dominican Dictator

Inquiry for Trujillo Hints That Missing Columbia Scholar May Be Alive— Anti-Franco Activities Cited

By PETER KIHSS

Morris L. Ernst has filed a report in effect clearing Generalissimo Rafael L. Trujillo and his Dominican dictatorship of any role in the two-year-old disappearance here of Jesús de Galindez, a Basque scholar.

The New York lawyer's report, made after a ten-month investigation for the Dominican Republic, implied that the anti-Trujillo writer might be alive. It suggested that Dr. Galindez' disappearance March 12, 1956, might be related "to his substantial and perhaps carefully confused fiscal operations and his profound interest in Spain after Franco."

Dr. Galindez, a Spanish exile, had reported to the Department of Justice a total of $1,024,118.24 in contributions he raised as agent for the anti-Franco Basque Government - in - exile from May, 1949, through January, 1956.

The Ernst report also rejected a theory that Gerald Lester Murphy, an American pilot who vanished in the Dominican Republic Dec. 3, 1956, might have flown Mr. Galindez to that country as a kidnap victim.

Mr. Ernst asserted that the Cuban Government had "reliable reports" that Mr. Murphy landed his plane in Cuba on March 13, 1956—before setting it down later that day in Miami.

The lawyer charged that Mr. Murphy had been "engaged in an illegal operation for hire." He recalled the pilot's reputed statements that he had flown arms and funds to Cuba for opponents of Cuban President Fulgencio Batista.

While formal comment by Government investigators in the United States was unavailable,

Continued on Page 14, Column 2

Hospital Deficits Increase With Advance in Medicine

By EMMA HARRISON

Voluntary hospitals in the New York area reported an operating loss of $23,500,000 for 1957, the United Hospital Fund disclosed yesterday. This is an increase of $3,550,000 over the 1956 figure of $19,950,000.

The operating loss for the seventy-four voluntary hospitals and convalescent homes is exclusive of the hospitals' receipts from philanthropic support and income from investment. But the figure also excludes hospital depreciation, interest on indebtedness and money spent on research and medical education, the fund noted.

The fund estimated the hospitals' net loss after all income at $6,000,000. This estimate includes an allowance of 5 per cent for plant depreciation.

However, operating income, including revenue from patients and from auxiliary activities such as nursing schools and cafeterias, went up 6.8 per cent to $176,000,000. Operating costs, meanwhile, climbed 8 per cent to $199,500,000.

Thus, with operating costs increasing partly because of better care for patients, the voluntary hospitals are faced with a paradox: The patients

Continued on Page 29, Column 2

187 MILLION URGED FOR CITY SCHOOLS

73 Projects Are Planned Over Three Budgets to House 74,740 Pupils

By GENE CURRIVAN

An extraordinary capital budget estimate of $187,600,000 for the city's school building program was announced yesterday. It would require financing in three successive budgets.

It includes seventy-three projects with an enrollment capacity of 74,740 pupils.

The proposed budget for next year is $108,200,000 for thirty-one projects.

Last year the Board of Education asked for $106,800,000 and received a little less than $96,000,000.

This year's unusual proposal was put forth by the Committee on Building and Sites headed by Charles J. Bensley. It may be predicated on the hope that a constitutional amendment giving the city the right to borrow $500,000,000 for spending on buildings will eventually be adopted. The amendment has been approved by the Legislature but must be reapproved at the next session and then submitted

Continued on Page 19, Column 4

Soviet Fishing Fleet Off Canada Causing Concern in Washington

Vessels Anchored Near Grand Banks — Each Departing Craft Always Replaced

By ALLEN DRURY

Special to The New York Times.

WASHINGTON, June 1—A half-dozen Soviet fishing ships riding at anchor 100 miles off the east coast of Canada have the United States Navy and Air Force puzzled.

The vessels, stationed near an area marked off with buoys flying small Soviet flags, are in international fishing waters near the Grand Banks.

Moscow recently lodged a vigorous protest with the United States Embassy, charging that a United States military plane had flown over one of the vessels at masthead height. The accusation has been denied by a high Washington official. He told newsmen that planes in the area normally flew at several thousand feet altitude.

This official said the presence of the Soviet ships and buoys did not constitute any violation of international law, but the knowledge that the number of ships seldom varies and the fact that a departing

Continued on Page 8, Column 4

JUNTA AIDE BITTER

'Not the Government We Hoped For,' Civil Leader Declares

By THOMAS F. BRADY

Special to The New York Times.

ALGIERS, June 1 — Léon Delbecque, vice president of the All-Algerian Committee of Public Safety, said tonight that the de Gaulle Cabinet was "not yet the Government of Public Safety we hoped for."

Looking at the list of ministers of Premier Charles de Gaulle, he said to reporters: "You call that a Government? Who is Minister of the Interior? A civil servant. Who is Minister of Foreign Affairs? A civil servant."

Emile Pelletier, the new Interior Minister, is a former Prefect. Maurice Couve de Murville, the Foreign Minister, is a career diplomat. Both are considered non-political "technicians."

Moderation Is Target

M. Delbecque was expressing the bitter disappointment that is felt among civilian insurgent leaders here at the liberal moderation shown thus far in General de Gaulle's assumption of power. No one associated with the Public Safety movement appears on the Cabinet list.

Although M. Delbecque did not appear to approve of career civil servants in the Cabinet, he expressed his confidence in Premier de Gaulle and said he regarded the Cabinet as a step toward the ultimate goal.

M. Delbecque denied a report that he had written Premier de Gaulle protesting against the make-up of the new Cabinet. The Algerian leader said he had written to the general every day for the last three days but did not indicate the contents except to say that he had informed General de Gaulle of the situation in Algeria. M. Delbecque added that he had not received any response.

Salan Aide Sees Victory

Col. Charles Lacheroy, spokesman for Gen. Raoul Salan, military ruler of Algeria, hailed General de Gaulle's assumption of power as a victory.

But outside the Government General Building, scene of regular mass demonstrations since the civil-military insurrection May 13, there was only a scattering of persons and no sign of rejoicing.

Asked why there was no celebration, Lucien Neuwirth, official spokesman for the Public Safety Committee, said: "Today is Sunday. People are at home." Last Sunday, however, the peo-

Continued on Page 5, Column 1

DE GAULLE STATES HIS TERMS: The general speaking in Paris yesterday in the French National Assembly before it approved the wartime leader as the nation's Premier.
Associated Press Radiophoto

U. S. IS 'GRATIFIED' AT FRENCH ACTION

White House Gives de Gaulle Warm Welcome—Capital Hopes He Can Visit Soon

By DANA ADAMS SCHMIDT

Special to The New York Times.

WASHINGTON, June 1—The White House welcomed Gen. Charles de Gaulle as Premier of France today in a warmly worded statement issued only two hours after the news of his investiture had reached Washington.

Administration officials said unofficially that they would be glad to see General de Gaulle visit the United States soon.

They said they assumed, however, that he would be too preoccupied with French internal affairs during his first six months to make such a trip unless it were required to prepare for a summit meeting with the Soviet Union.

The White House statement was issued from Gettysburg, where President Eisenhower is spending the week-end. It read as follows:

"We have been witnessing with sympathy and understanding the difficult days through which France has been passing, and we are gratified that the French crisis is now being resolved.

"General de Gaulle has assumed heavy responsibilities at a critical juncture in French history. Our thoughts go out to the great French nation, wish-

Continued on Page 6, Column 6

Supporters of Foreign Aid Hope For Senate Passage This Week

WASHINGTON, June 1—Administration supporters hope to see the $3,068,900,000 authorization for foreign aid safely through the Senate this week. They will then concentrate on getting the five-year foreign trade extension through the House of Representatives.

The prospects for the first appeared somewhat brighter today than prospects for the second. Passage of the aid bill without major change may come by Thursday.

Senate debate on the aid bill started last week with major speeches by the chairman of the Foreign Relations Committee, Senator Theodore Francis Green, Democrat of Rhode Island, and a top-ranking Republican, H. Alexander Smith of New Jersey. Much of the controversy, it was indicated, may center around an amendment authorizing aid to Communist-bloc nations.

This amendment would permit a broader interpretation of the Battle Act. That act now prohibits aid to Communist lands except when the President certifies to Congress that it is necessary for national de-

Continued on Page 16, Column 4

Red-Led Demonstrators Clash With Paris Police

By W. GRANGER BLAIR

Special to The New York Times.

PARIS, June 1—Communist-inspired riots erupted in Paris today a few hours before the National Assembly voted to install Gen. Charles de Gaulle as Premier. The outbreaks started at 3 P. M. in working-class quarters in northern, eastern and southern sections of the city.

At almost the same time the general rose to deliver his investiture speech in a jammed and tense Parliament ringed by armed security guards.

For the next three hours thousands of policemen, crowded into heavy vans, rushed to trouble spots to clash with about 10,000 demonstrators.

Many persons were injured—"several dozen," according to the police. The injured included twenty-five members of the security force. The police arrested 190 rioters.

Crowds Arrive From Suburbs

Besides Leftists ready for action in town, the mobs were replenished by Leftists from industrial suburbs. Even before they arrived, the police descended on key train, bus and subway exits to intercept them.

The first clash between security forces and rioters came in northern Paris near the Porte de Clignancourt. Several hundred demonstrators tried to force their way south toward the center of the city through four vanloads of policemen.

Both sides struck out with clubs. After fifteen minutes of confused fighting, the Leftists retreated northward.

These rioters, like their fellows elsewhere in the city, car-

Continued on Page 5, Column 1

DE GAULLE SHUNS ASSEMBLY DEBATE

Strides Out After He Makes Brief Statement — Anger and Fear Mark Session

By HENRY GINIGER

Special to The New York Times.

PARIS, June 1—In anger, defiance, fear and resignation, the National Assembly held today one of the last sessions of France's present parliamentary Government.

The French Republic may go on—many Deputies fear its end—but it will not be the same one that France has known since it began functioning in 1947.

This was the consensus of those who were able to fight their way into the Assembly building on the Left Bank of the Seine to witness the strangest and most memorable session the Assembly has ever had.

That France had turned a page of her history was evident in the way the session ran its course. It took the Assembly a little more than four hours to accept Gen. Charles de Gaulle by a vote of 329 to 224 and during that time the man the Deputies were debating was not present.

General Scorns System

In the past, lesser aspirants to the Premiership — those willing to work within the established system General de Gaulle has always scorned—have made the investiture speeches, then have sat down alone on the front-center benches of the semi-circular chamber to follow the debate, take notes and answer questions put to them.

When General de Gaulle, looking tired and slightly hunched in his gray, double-breasted suit, finished his seven-minute speech, he strode out and was not seen again. From about 3:45 P. M. to shortly after 7:30, the Deputies seemed to be addressing a phantom or to be arguing with each other.

It appeared to many that for General de Gaulle the dialogue between him and the Republic's representatives had ended with

Continued on Page 5, Column 4

GENERAL IS HEARD

Assembly Postpones Voting on Reforms Urged by Regime

Text of de Gaulle's speech to the Assembly, Page 4.

By ROBERT C. DOTY

Special to The New York Times.

PARIS, Monday, June 2—Gen. Charles de Gaulle has become Premier of France. The National Assembly voted last night, 329 to 224, to invest the 67-year-old leader of the wartime French liberation movement.

Approved at the same time was a fifteen-member Cabinet, including three former Premiers, representatives of seven parties on the Left, Right and Center, and five nonpolitical technicians. The most noteworthy of the latter was the choice of Maurice Couve de Murville, a career diplomat, as Foreign Minister.

General de Gaulle returns to power twelve years after renouncing the Provisional Presidency and at a moment when France faces the threat of civil war by civilians and military leaders dissatisfied with governmental efforts toward ending the rebellion in Algeria.

Terms Implicitly Accepted

By investing General de Gaulle as Premier, the Deputies implicitly accepted the terms he outlined in a seven-minute speech to the packed, breathless Assembly. He demanded:

¶Six months of full decree power, free from Parliamentary interference.

¶Immediate action to revise the Constitution in a manner to permit a popular referendum on sweeping reforms, transforming the Parliamentary regime into a Presidential one.

¶Authority to submit to a referendum reforms of the French Union, permitting a new basis of association with such overseas territories as Algeria and Central and West Africa. This was widely interpreted as opening the possibility even of full independence for some areas.

Breakdown of Vote

General de Gaulle had the almost solid support of the Center and Right wing, nearly half of the Socialist votes and more than half of the Radical votes. Voting against him were the Communists, the rest of the Socialists and Radicals, and scattered Deputies of other parties.

From Algiers came reports that the inclusion in the Cabinet of men of such liberal repute in colonial matters as former Premiers Antoine Pinay, an Independent, and Pierre Pflimlin, the Popular Republican who preceded General de Gaulle, had caused disappointment among ultra-colonialists in the dissident Committees of Public Safety there.

Soon after the Assembly vote was announced General de Gaulle met with President René Coty and the new Cabinet at Elysée Palace while a violent thunderstorm lashed the capital. During the meeting a bolt struck the palace. At the end of the meeting, the

Continued on Page 4, Column 6

Tunisian Units Fire At 3 French Planes

By Reuters.

TUNIS, June 1—Tunisian troops fired today on three French planes that "violated Tunisian air space" in the Gabès region, a Government spokesman said tonight.

No further details were given and there was no immediate comment by French sources here.

The Tunisians reported yesterday that their troops had "apparently" hit a French plane that flew over Tunisian positions in the Gabès area. Gabès, the site of a French air base, is on Tunisia's east coast about 200 miles south of Tunis.

Government sources still withheld official comment on French political developments. But the

Continued on Page 4, Column 5

The historic meeting of Communist leaders Nikita Khrushchev and Mao Tse-tung took place in Peiping in 1958.

After becoming premier, during the army's revolt against Algerian policies, General Charles de Gaulle arrived at the Elysee Palace to meet with President Rene Coty. In 1959, De Gaulle became the President of France.

"All the News That's Fit to Print"

The New York Times.

LATE CITY EDITION
U. S. Weather Bureau Report (Page 62) forecasts:
Mostly fair and continued warm today, tonight and tomorrow.
Temp. range: 86—68. Yesterday: 83.2—66.5.

VOL. CVII—No. 36,683.
© 1958 by The New York Times Company.
Times Square, New York, N. Y.

NEW YORK, TUESDAY, JULY 1, 1958.

10c beyond 100-mile zone from New York City.
Higher in air delivery cities.

K

FIVE CENTS

ALASKA TO JOIN UNION AS THE 49TH STATE; FINAL APPROVAL IS VOTED BY SENATE, 64-20; BILL SENT TO EISENHOWER, WHO WILL SIGN IT

2 MORE AMERICANS ABDUCTED IN CUBA BY REBEL FORCES

44 From U. S. and Canada Now Held — Officials of Nickel Plant Latest

Special to The New York Times.

HAVANA, June 30 — Two more Americans were kidnapped today by the Cuban rebels, bringing to forty-four the number of North American servicemen and civilians seized since last Thursday.

Those kidnapped today are officers of the Nicaro nickel plant, on the north coast of Oriente Province.

Oriente is the center of operations of the rebels, led by Fidel Castro and his brother Raul, against the Government of President Fulgencio Batista. The rebels say they have carried out the kidnappings to bring pressure on the United States Government to halt military aid and assistance to the Batista regime.

Among the United States citizens seized — three of the victims are Canadians — are twenty-eight sailors and marines from the United States Naval Base at Guantanamo Bay, on the south coast of Oriente.

U. S. Denies Rebel Charge

Replying to a rebel charge that the base had been used by Cuban military planes operating against the insurgents, the United States Ambassador, Earl E. T. Smith, issued a statement yesterday saying that the base was not open to planes on combat operations.

The rebels told a sailor whom they did not abduct that his kidnapped colleagues would be released today.

United States officials have been in contact with the rebels in an attempt to negotiate the release of the naval and marine personnel as well as the ten Americans and two Canadians seized last Thursday. All twelve are employes of the Moa Bay Mining Company, on the north coast of Oriente. Two civilians, an American and a Canadian, were kidnapped last night.

Mine Is Not Guarded

The Americans seized today are Sherman Avery White and J. Andrew Poll, assistant administrator general and assistant administrator general, respectively, of the Nickel Prospecting Company, which leases the Nicaro plant from the United States Government. They were carried off at 8:30 this morning by a group of eight rebels, according to the announcement of the United States Embassy.

No details are available, but it is supposed that the officials went to the mine, about twelve miles from the small town of Nicaro, where 6,000 workers and officials live, to check on operations. Presumably they were abducted there. The entrance of the town is guarded by an army detach-

Continued on Page 3, Column 6

Russians to Attend Geneva Talk Today

By JOHN W. FINNEY
Special to The New York Times.

GENEVA, June 30 — The Soviet Union agreed today to enter into technical talks with the West on the detection of tests of nuclear weapons. As a result, talks between scientists of four Western and four Communist nations will begin here tomorrow afternoon in a conference room in the Old League of Nations headquarters.

The Soviet agreement was announced by Dr. Yevgeni K. Fedorov, head of the Soviet delegation of scientists, following a two-hour conference with Dr. James B. Fisk, chairman of the Western scientific group.

Dr. Fedorov said at a news conference later it had been agreed that the talks would begin tomorrow and that discussions would be limited to

Continued on Page 5, Column 1

N. A. ROCKEFELLER ENTERS G.O.P. RACE FOR GOVERNORSHIP

Promises Strong Fight— Mahoney and Hall Top Him in Delegate Votes

Text of Rockefeller statement is printed on Page 36.

By CLAYTON KNOWLES

Nelson A. Rockefeller announced his candidacy for Governor yesterday. He said that if nominated he would "leave no stone unturned" to win election.

The announcement, expected for some weeks, brought the declared candidacies in Republican ranks to two.

Leonard W. Hall of Oyster Bay, L. I., former Republican national chairman, announced his candidacy several weeks ago and has been campaigning vigorously. State Senator Walter J. Mahoney of Buffalo has promised to announce his position "some time in August."

In promising an "aggressive campaign," Mr. Rockefeller declared that New York's status as the Empire State had been put in jeopardy by a "complacent administration" in Albany that evaded, rather than dealt with, serious fiscal and social problems.

New Approach Held Needed

His decision to make the race, he explained, was rooted in the "deep conviction that a new approach to government must be taken in New York State." He said "new energy and efficiency, vision, courage and imagination" would be needed to enable the state "to regain its traditional pre-eminence."

Mr. Rockefeller asserted that "a lifetime spent in administration, both in government and in private and philanthropic activities," qualified him to provide the "progressive, imaginative leadership" that state conditions required.

"If nominated, I will accept the challenge and wage an aggressive campaign on the issues," he said. "If elected, I shall serve with the full awareness of the responsibility such confidence places upon me."

A member of one of America's wealthiest families, the youthful-looking board chairman of Rockefeller Center, Inc., will celebrate his fiftieth birthday next Tuesday. He is the first Rockefeller to seek elective office.

A grandson of the late John D. Rockefeller, who founded the oil dynasty, he said his family

Continued on Page 36, Column 4

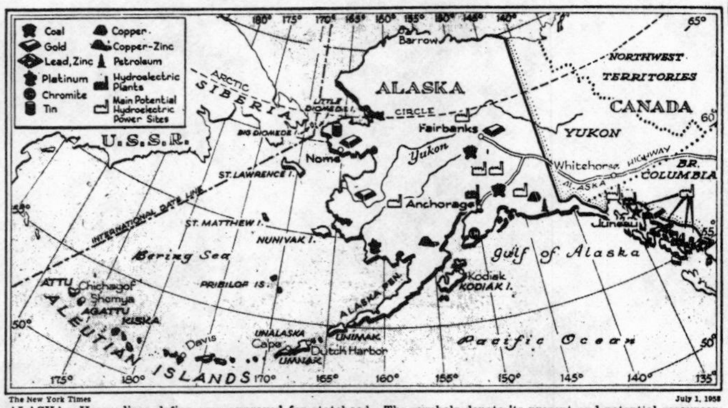

SEEKS NOMINATION: Nelson A. Rockefeller at news conference at which he discussed his candidacy for nomination for Governor of New York on Republican slate.

ALASKA: Heavy lines define area approved for statehood. The symbols denote its present and potential resources.

BEIRUT USES JETS TO CHECK REBELS

Bombards Force Imperiling Airport—U. N. Questions Suspected Syrians

By United Press International.

BEIRUT, Lebanon, June 30 — The Government sent rocket-firing jet fighters against rebels in the hills only seven miles from Beirut International Airport today. At the same time, the Tripoli command reported it had cut the main rebel supply line into that city.

On their side, the rebels declared they had cut the main highway between Beirut and Damascus.

Druse tribesmen under the leadership of rebel chieftain Kamal Jumblatt were in the hills overlooking the airport. Jumblatt's army of 500 to 1,000 men appeared also to be poised for a night attack on Chemlan, fifteen miles southeast of the capital, which had been emptied of civilians.

[At the United Nations, Secretary General Dag Hammarskjold said United Nations observers in Lebanon had begun to question prisoners, "said to be Syrians," on their possible connection with the Lebanese uprising.]

A rebel spokesman said the Druse forces were astride the main highway to Damascus. There was no Government confirmation, but former Premier

Continued on Page 6, Column 3

Soviet Offers Talk On Yugoslav Credit

By United Press International.

LONDON, Tuesday, July 1—The Soviet Union proposed negotiations with Yugoslavia today on $285,000,000 in credits that the Kremlin has suspended.

The Moscow radio said the proposal was contained in a Soviet note sent to Yugoslavia June 28 and published today in Moscow newspapers.

In the note the Soviet Union said an earlier note to Yugoslavia had suggested the postponement of one loan for several years. The Soviet Union received no reply to the suggestions, today's note said.

"The Soviet Government suggests that talks of representatives of both Governments should be held as soon as possible."

Continued on Page 2, Column 5

DISMISSAL RULING CURBS PRESIDENT

High Court Holds He Lacks Power to Oust Wiener of War Claims Agency

By RUSSELL BAKER
Special to The New York Times.

WASHINGTON, June 30— The Supreme Court tightened today the limitation on the President's power to remove officials of Federal quasi-judicial bodies.

Where Congress has not defined justifiable causes for dismissal, the court held, it must be assumed that Congress does not want to hang a "Damocles' sword" over these officials by permitting the President to remove them solely to substitute "men of his own choosing."

"Petitioner [the N. A. A. C. P.] has made an uncontroverted showing that on past occasions revelation of the identity of its rank-and-file members has exposed these members to economic reprisal, loss of employment, threat of physical coercion and other manifestations of public hostility."

1935 Ruling Recalled

The last significant Supreme Court ruling in the historic debate over Presidential power to dismiss was rendered in 1935. Then, in a case closely paralleling the Wiener case, the court ruled that the President could not dismiss an officer of a Federal regulatory agency for any reason except those stipulated in law.

In the 1935 case, Humphrey's Executor v. United States, President Roosevelt dismissed a member of the Federal Trade Commission on the ground that the "aims and purposes" of his Administration could be "carried out most effectively with personnel of my own selection."

The court overruled him, holding that a President could dismiss only for reasons speci-

Continued on Page 20, Column 2

Narcotics Agent Warns Inquiry Mafia Seeks to Invade Industry

By JOSEPH A. LOFTUS
Special to The New York Times.

WASHINGTON, June 30—An expert on the Mafia told Senators today that the secret criminal organization was making a "concerted effort" to penetrate unions and management.

They are "the same people who are active in the narcotics traffic," Martin F. Pera, a Federal narcotics agent, told the Select Committee on Improper Activities in the Labor or Management Field.

Mr. Pera was the second witness as the committee laid the groundwork for extensive hearings on what the chairman, Senator John L. McClellan said, "appears to be a close-knit, clandestine criminal syndicate."

The Arkansas Democrat, in his opening statement, said the committee "has become convinced that the relationship of

the national criminal syndicate with legitimate labor and business is far more critical than has heretofore been revealed."

The first witness was Sgt. Edgar D. Crosswell of the New York State police, who broke up a gangland meeting last Nov. 14 at the home of Joseph Barbara in Apalachin, N. Y. Barbara has a serious heart condition and will not testify.

Mr. Pera had barely touched on the labor-management angle when the committee recessed for the day. Photographs of him were barred because of the nature of his work.

The agent, who has worked on the narcotics problem in several foreign countries, told the committee about the origin of

Continued on Page 14, Column 6

Alabama Is Denied Access To Rolls of N. A. A. C. P.

Special to The New York Times.

WASHINGTON, June 30—A $100,000 contempt fine imposed by Alabama when the National Association for the Advancement of Colored People refused to disclose its list of members in the state was struck down today by the Supreme Court.

The court held unanimously that compulsory disclosure under the circumstances in Alabama would violate constitutional guarantees of free speech and association. Justice John Marshall Harlan, writing for the court, said:

"Inviolability of privacy in group association may in many circumstances be indispensable to preservation of freedom of

Text of the opinion will be found on Page 18.

association, particularly where a group espouses dissident beliefs.

A Major Victory

The decision was a major victory for the N. A. A. C. P. in a fight to continue operations in the South. Its activities include helping to bring suits to end school segregation.

Seven Southern states have passed legislation aimed at the association or have acted against it through state courts. Included are several statutes to require disclosure of members' names and others to restrict any financial help to Negro plaintiffs in lawsuits.

The organization has carried most of the legal burden of pushing for compliance with the Supreme Court's decision of 1954 holding school segregation unconstitutional.

In 1956 Alabama accused the N. A. A. C. P. of failing to obey a law requiring out-of-

Continued on Page 18, Column 1

ALASKANS APPEAR STUNNED BY NEWS

Civil Defense Whistles in Anchorage Signal Vote to Crowds in the Streets

By LAWRENCE E. DAVIES
Special to The New York Times.

ANCHORAGE, Alaska, June 30—Alaskans were stunned today by the realization that Congress had finally invited them to become "first class citizens."

Here in the territorial metropolis, the center of much of the agitation for statehood, it took them a while to get their bearings.

Long after the civil defense whistles had blown, signaling the Senate's action preparing the way for a forty-ninth star on the flag, unbelieving crowds almost silently walked the streets amid the tooting of automobile horns.

Texas Car Is 'Shot'

Stores did business as usual. A woman traffic policeman rode her motorcycle down Fourth Avenue putting tickets on cars that were parked overtime.

Some amateur photographers gleefully "shot" a passing car bearing a Texas license plate, emblematic of a state that would have to give up its much-loved stories of bigness as Alaska completes the transition to statehood.

Rita Martin, queen of the annual Fur Rendezvous, climbed a fire truck ladder and pinned a huge silver star—the bright ninth—to a 60-by-40-foot flag hurriedly draped over the front wall of the Federal Building. Miss Orah Dee Clark, 83 years old, who in 1915 was the first school principal here, stood watching the star-pinning ceremony on an automobile-jammed street.

It was an emotion-packed moment for her. She had come to the territory in 1906, and to

Continued on Page 16, Column 2

HIGH COURT BARS LITTLE ROCK PLEA

Suggests Appeals Bench Set Integration Stay Review Before School Term

Text of the opinion will be found on Page 19.

By ANTHONY LEWIS
Special to The New York Times.

WASHINGTON, June 30—The Supreme Court refused today to review on an emergency basis the order suspending school integration in Little Rock until January, 1961.

But the high court strongly suggested that the case be reviewed by the United States Court of Appeals for the Eighth Circuit before the next school term begins in September. That court has recessed for the summer.

"We have no doubt," the Supreme Court said in a short unsigned order, "that the Court of Appeals will recognize the vital importance of the time element in this litigation, and that it will act upon the application for a stay on the appeal in ample time to permit arrangements to be made for the next school year."

Summer Review Asked

Lawyers of the National Association for the Advancement of Colored People had asked the Supreme Court to by-pass the Eighth Circuit and hear the case this summer to assure early and final review.

A notice of appeal from District Judge Harry J. Lemley's suspension decision has been filed with the Eighth Circuit. So has an application for a stay of the decision pending its appeal. Judge Lemley denied a stay.

If the Eighth Circuit should grant the stay, the need for speed would be gone, from the N. A. A. C. P.'s viewpoint. Little Rock Central High School would open with a handful of Negro children among the whites, as this last year, when the appeal was argued.

Chief Justice Earl Warren read the order to a packed courtroom at the end of a busy and dramatic day—the last in the high court's 1957-58 term.

Twenty-one cases that had been argued earlier in the term were decided today—with forty opinions. The Chief Justice announced that the court had disposed of all its pending business before recess-

Continued on Page 19, Column 1

OPPOSITION WILTS

A Bipartisan Coalition Defeats All Efforts to Amend Plan

By C. P. TRUSSELL
Special to The New York Times.

WASHINGTON, June 30—The Senate approved tonight the admission of Alaska as the forty-ninth state in the Union. The vote was 64 to 20.

Only President Eisenhower's signature, which is assured, and approval in a territorial referendum remain before statehood is formally achieved. Test votes indicate that the issue will carry by an overwhelming majority.

The Senate accepted the statehood bill passed by the House of Representatives word for word, beating down every effort to change it. Thus the bill goes directly to the White House.

Any change in the language would have sent the bill back to the House and invited further delays and possible death.

Final Senate action came after five days and evenings of battle, some of it bitter. The vote crossed party lines. The South fought admission, but not solidly. Senators from other sections of the country were also divided.

Stepovich in Gallery

Thirty-three Republicans and thirty-one Democrats voted in favor of admission. Opposed were seven Republicans and thirteen Democrats.

Gov. Michael A. Stepovich of Alaska sat tensely in the Senate gallery while the vote was being taken. When the result was announced he shouted:

"Thank God."

As well-wishers surrounded him he made a prediction.

"I believe that we will show the United States of America that we will be one of the greatest states in the Union within the next fifty years," he said.

It is expected that Alaska will assume full statehood by autumn or early winter. Its two Senators and the member of the House of Representatives could take their Congressional posts when the Eighty-Sixth Congress convenes next January.

Amendments Defeated

Before the final vote tonight, the Senate rejected by a vote of 62—22 a point of order entered by Senator James O. Eastland, Democrat of Mississippi.

He noted that Alaska Constitution provided that in the election of the first two Senators, one be given a six-year term and the other two or four years, to permit the staggering of Senatorial incumbencies.

Mr. Eastland said that this violated the United States Constitution's provision that all Senators be elected for six years.

But the Senate decided that this was not a valid objection and overrode it.

Senator John Stennis, Democrat of Mississippi, moved that the bill be referred to the Sen-

Continued on Page 16, Column 1

Rayburn Bars G. O. P. Demand For Inquiry on Fox Testimony

By WILLIAM M. BLAIR
Special to The New York Times.

WASHINGTON, June 30—Speaker Sam Rayburn rejected today a Republican attempt to have the House of Representatives investigate the conduct of the subcommittee that has been investigating the relations of Sherman Adams and Bernard Goldfine.

The Democratic Speaker ruled out of order a resolution proposed by Representative Thomas B. Curtis, Republican of Missouri. Mr. Curtis argued that the testimony of John Fox of Boston, a lawyer and business man, should have been taken in executive session, in accordance with House rules.

His move was another effort by Republicans to smother the inquiry, which they contend has developed into a "smear" of Mr. Adams and others and to stem the political fears of Republican

candidates up for re-election. Mr. Adams is the assistant to President Eisenhower.

Meanwhile, Mr. Fox announced that he had instructed his lawyers to file libel suits against Mr. Adams and four other persons for what he called "scurrilous" statements about his veracity. He said he would ask $1,000,000 damages from each.

Besides Mr. Adams, he named Roger Robb of Washington and Samuel P. Sears of Boston, lawyers for Mr. Goldfine; Robert E. Choate, publisher of The Boston Herald and Boston Traveler; William J. Dempsey, counsel for the Boston Herald-Traveler Corporation, and the

Continued on Page 14, Column 4

"All the News That's Fit to Print"

The New York Times.

LATE CITY EDITION

U. S. Weather Bureau Report (Page 56) forecasts:
Afternoon thunder showers, warm,
humid today. Not so warm tomorrow,
Temp. range: 90—74. Yesterday: 88.2—71.5.

VOL. CVII—No. 36,698.

© 1958, by The New York Times Company.
Times Square, New York 36, N. Y.

NEW YORK, WEDNESDAY, JULY 16, 1958.

10c beyond 100-mile zone from New York City.
Higher in air delivery cities.

FIVE CENTS

EISENHOWER SENDS MARINES INTO LEBANON; CALLS FOR A U.N. FORCE TO REPLACE THEM; SOVIET CHARGES MOVE THREATENS NEW WAR

HARRIS HINTS LINK OF HIGH OFFICIALS TO ARMY CONTRACT

Says Administration Aides Appeared to Influence Textile Negotiation

By WILLIAM M. BLAIR
Special to The New York Times.

WASHINGTON, July 15 — Congressional investigators reported tonight that they had unearthed what they characterized as "political influence" by high Administration officials in an Army textile material contract.

Representative Oren Harris said that Bernard Goldfine, New England textile manufacturer, did not appear to be involved. But Mr. Harris declined to say the same for Sherman Adams, the Assistant to President Eisenhower.

Mr. Harris, Democrat of Arkansas, heads the House subcommittee investigating relations of Mr. Goldfine and Mr. Adams with Federal regulatory agencies. He reported the Army case after an executive session of more than four hours.

Informed subcommittee sources said, however, that information gathered by the House investigators linked Mr. Adams and other officials with a reversal by the Army last year of penalties assessed against a New England textile company for non-compliance with a 1940 contract.

Information in Documents

This information was understood to be in letters, other correspondence and memorandums found in the Pentagon. It was said to be from White House and other officials and others to the Army and the General Accounting Office.

It was further said by these subcommittee sources that the Army reversed itself last year and settled the case without penalties, which had been upheld in the United States Court of Claims, after Administration officials intervened.

Speaker Sam Rayburn of the House of Representatives was reported to be actively interested in the new case, indicating its importance. It was expected that the House Armed Services Committee or its subcommittee dealing with military contracts soon would begin an investigation.

Secretary of the Army Wilber M. Brucker was also said to have ordered an immediate inquiry.

Continued on Page 27, Column 2

GAIN IN ECONOMY SHOWN FOR JUNE

Production, Housing and Income Indexes Rise

By EDWIN L. DALE Jr.
Special to The New York Times.

WASHINGTON, July 15 — Significant improvement in June in three major indicators of the economy was reported by the Government today.

With other reports, they indicated that over-all activity in June increased over May by at least as much as May had increased over April.

Today's reports concerned industrial production, personal income and housing starts.

The Federal Reserve Board reported a two-point increase in June in industrial production over a May figure that had been revised upward a point. Thus the seasonally adjusted June level of 130 on the index (1947-1949 average is 100) was four points higher than the recession low in April.

This is a much more rapid increase than is customary in the early stages of a recovery. The rise is expected to halt or even be temporarily reversed in July, however, as plants shut down for vacation and model changeover.

The Department of Commerce reported an increase in June of $1,900,000,000 in the

Continued on Page 27, Column 2

Loyal Iraq Units Reported Marching on the Capital

Jordan Says Troops Stationed in the North Will Counterattack—Rebel Grip in Baghdad Held Shaky

By United Press International

AMMAN, Jordan, July 15 — A large force of Iraqi soldiers loyal to King Faisal is marching toward Baghdad to counterattack insurgents who captured the Iraqi capital yesterday, the Amman radio reported today.

The broadcast said the loyalist troops were of the Second Division of the Iraqi Army, stationed at Mosul, Kirkuk and Sulaimaniya in the extreme north of Iraq.

The northern provinces are about 150 miles north of Baghdad. The radio said the loyalist troops would reach the city in about a day.

[A Reuters dispatch from Ankara, Turkey, said King Faisal had been wounded and was under arrest and that Premier Nuri as-Said had been killed. Reuters also reported from London that the Iraqi insurgents had announced their withdrawal from the Arab Union of Jordan and Iraq.]

Baghdad radio broadcasts monitored in Amman indicated that the rebels had only shaky control of the capital. It issued continual appeals for calm in Baghdad.

A proclamation issued by the military governor general, Brig. Ahmed al-Abdi, warned against further demonstrations of "feeling you have expressed toward your sacred revolution."

"We are seeking to complete what we have started," the proclamation said. "Any unreasonable step taken to express this sentiment will give subversive elements a chance to disturb general order and peace."

The proclamation said "im-

Continued on Page 14, Column 2

Senate Gets Pentagon Bill; House Version Is Modified

By United Press International

WASHINGTON, July 15 — The Senate Armed Services Committee unanimously approved today a plan to reorganize the Defense Department after modifying some features that had drawn an attack from President Eisenhower.

Senator Richard B. Russell, Democrat of Georgia, committee chairman, said the group had not followed the Defense Department's recommendations but he said he did not believe it would find any "serious objections" to the measure.

Basically, the bill would give the President essentially what he had asked in the way of additional powers to provide more efficient defense in the nuclear-space age, including a vastly streamlined chain of command to units fighting in the field.

Seeks Action Next Week

"We tried to make it very clear that the Secretary of Defense is the supreme officer in the Department of Defense," Senator Russell said. He referred to complaints that interservice rivalries had hampered the missile program and other military projects.

He said he hoped that the Senate would be able to take up the bill next week. Once approved, it must go back to the House, which wrote in a series of provisions that the President labeled utterly unacceptable.

In moving to meet these objections, however, the Senate committee also sought to quiet fears of partisans of the Marine Corps, the Navy's air arm and the National Guard that these

Continued on Page 20, Column 5

SENATE APPROVES ATOM POWER BILL

President Is Rebuffed Again on 386 Million Measure— It Goes to Conference

By ALLEN DRURY
Special to The New York Times.

WASHINGTON, July 15 — The Senate passed and sent to conference with the House today a bill authorizing $386,679,000 for new atomic energy projects. This is almost twice as much as President Eisenhower requested.

The House voted the measure yesterday despite a letter from the President objecting to a number of the bill's major features. His views were similarly ignored in the Senate today.

Senator Leverett Saltonstall, Republican of Massachusetts, made a futile effort in behalf of the Administration to cut back several items in the bill to sums more nearly in line with the President's request.

Most of Mr. Saltonstall's amendments were vigorously opposed by Democratic Senate members of the Joint Congressional Atomic Energy Committee. These were defeated by voice votes. Final passage of the bill was also by voice vote.

One Amendment Accepted

One of Senator Saltonstall's amendments was accepted by the bill's managers and taken to conference with the House. This was designed to encourage private enterprise to build a proposed $51,000,000 gas-cooled reactor.

The bill would have required the reactor to be built either by a cooperative endeavor of private capital and the Government, or, if cooperative financing had not been obtained within sixty days from an announced date, by the Government alone.

The amendment provided that the reactor might be built by private capital if it is available.

The major argument today concerned Senator Saltonstall's attempt to cut back to $120,-000,000 from $145,000,000 an authorization for a plutonium reactor facility at Hanford, Wash., that could be converted to the production of power. The reduction would have prevented conversion of the plant.

Mr. Saltonstall, supported by

Continued on Page 15, Column 3

Meany Bids Labor Shun Exiled Unions

By A. H. RASKIN

George Meany prohibited yesterday alliances between affiliates of federated labor and the expelled International Brotherhood of Teamsters.

The bill would have required the reactor to be built either by a cooperative endeavor of private capital and the Government. The president becomes final, especially of the American Federation of Labor and Congress of Industrial Organizations indicated that he would press for the ouster of unions involved in pacts that helped strengthen the teamsters or other organizations exiled for corruption.

Mr. Meany's declaration of war on the spreading network of mutual assistance agreements between federation units and the giant truck union was made in a shipboard interview on the Cunard liner Queen Mary. He returned from a month-long visit to Europe, where he attended international labor conferences in Geneva

PLEDGE GIVEN U. N.

Marines to Stay Till It Can Act, Lodge Informs Council

Excerpts from U. N. debate and resolutions, Pages 4 and 5.

By THOMAS J. HAMILTON
Special to The New York Times.

UNITED NATIONS, N. Y., July 15 — The United States gave the Security Council a pledge today that United States Marines would remain in Lebanon only until the United Nations was able to insure her "continued independence."

Henry Cabot Lodge of the United States introduced tonight a resolution under which the Security Council would establish an international military force "to protect the territorial integrity and independence of Lebanon."

Earlier today the Soviet Union introduced a resolution calling on the United States to "cease its armed intervention" in the affairs of the peoples of the Arab states and to withdraw its troops forthwith.

Arkady A. Sobolev of the Soviet Union charged that the United States intervention "carries with it the threat of an acute deterioration of the international situation and can fling the world into the abyss of a new war."

Volunteers Mentioned

Several delegates said afterward that both his protest and that by Omar Loutfi of the United Arab Republic were milder than they had expected. However, a Soviet delegate told a correspondent today that the result might be the arrival of volunteers in the Middle East "not only from the Soviet Union but from many other countries."

The United States resolution would request the United Nations Observation Group in Lebanon, which was established a month ago, to "continue and develop" its activity.

However, it would direct the new international force to take over the same assignment, to "insure" against illegal infiltration of personnel or arms into Lebanon. It thus contained an implied rebuke to the Observation Group, if not to Secretary General Dag Hammarskjold, who appointed its three members and handed down its operating directive.

The operative part of the resolution is as follows:

"Requests the Secretary General

Continued on Page 6, Column 3

The New York Times (by Meyer Liebowitz)

A PLEDGE: Henry Cabot Lodge tells Security Council U. S. Marines will remain in Lebanon only until the U. N. can insure country's "continued independence."

A PROTEST: Arkady A. Sobolev of the Soviet Union calls on the United States to "cease its armed intervention" in the affairs of the peoples of the Arab states.

CAIRO DENOUNCES LANDINGS AS 'SUEZ'

United Arab Republic Aide Sees 'Greatest Mistake' of U. S. in Mideast

By OSGOOD CARUTHERS
Special to The New York Times.

CAIRO, July 15 — Officials of the United Arab Republic charged today that the landing of United States forces in Lebanon was "another Suez." They said the action was "a very serious one that would cause the United States to lose its friends and all of the Middle East."

Foreign Ministry officials gave no indication how the Government of President Gamal Abdel Nasser would react either in the area or in the United Nations. The United Arab Republic is composed of Egypt and Syria.

The officials said United States action might invite intervention by "volunteers" from the Soviet Union and other Communist nations.

"If this happens," said one highly placed Egyptian diplomat, "it will mean the beginning of an international war."

Officials said the landing of

Continued on Page 12, Column 6

Algerian Rebels Predict Victory With Their Hit-and-Run Tactics

Following is the first in a series of three dispatches from a correspondent of The New York Times who has been in camp with the insurgent forces in the Algerian hills:

By MICHAEL JAMES
Special to The New York Times.

WITH ALGERIAN REBELS, July 10 — A major difficulty of the United Nations forces in Korea and of the French Army in Indochina that heavily mechanized modern forces were fighting a lightly equipped enemy able to "evaporate" into the hills or the countryside.

The North Koreans and the Vietnamese Communists also enjoyed a privileged sanctuary just across the frontier.

The situation here is the same, and because of that, a recording to the rebels, victory will inevitably be theirs. To an observer here it is difficult to see just how, if the present situation is maintained, the French can win.

To one who recalls the mobile United States Army in Korea, or the somewhat less comfortable French military machine in Indochina, life among the Algerian rebels by contrast is Spartan.

These people are hospitable to a fault. This is reported to be one of their best-equipped bases and they insist on sharing what they have, which is little except for a plentiful supply of guns and ammunition.

Every member of the Army of the National Liberation Front theoretically wears the same uniform. It is manufactured in its own workshops in Tunisia out of stiff Italian cotton drill. Finer material came from France till Paris wondered why so much olive drab cotton was going to Tunisia.

The uniform consists of a pair of long underpants, fastened at the waist and ankles by tapes. Next comes a shirt much like the United States Army dark O.D. item familiar to millions of Americans. The uniform is completed with a pair of cotton trousers cut on the lines of British battle pants and a blouse patterned after the French copy of the United States battle blouse.

It is all topped off with a visored cap that the rebels are proud to note has been copied by the French. Shoes are the splendid French "patauges," ankle-high boots of heavy canvas or soft but tough suede leather with thick, heavily corrugated rubber soles. They are fine for climbing the hills of Algeria. Recently, however, the French have cut off exports of these boots to Tunisia or Mo-

Continued on Page 15, Column 4

Beirut Welcomes Marines; Second Contingent Ashore

By SAM POPE BREWER
Special to The New York Times.

BEIRUT, Lebanon, July 15 — United States Marines landed in Beirut at 3 P. M. today to back up the Lebanese Government of President Camille Chamoun against rebels or outsiders. The Beirut public received them like a circus coming to town.

The first move of the United States force was to occupy Beirut's International Airport at Khalde, just south of the city. The field had been closed to civil air traffic at 2 P. M. This afternoon, United States carrierborne planes were moving in there. Seven ships of the United States Sixth Fleet put ashore about 3,600 marines here during the afternoon.

[Another battalion of the marines went ashore early Wednesday, completing the force of about 5,000 announced by President Eisenhower, the Defense Department said.]

Chamoun Explains to Nation

The airport was reopened to normal traffic during the night.

President Chamoun in a radio broadcast to the nation in the evening said he had exhausted all other resources before asking for direct armed support.

Mr. Chamoun said he had asked for such direct armed help only after both the United Nations and the Arab League had failed to give effective response to his appeals. He said the United Nations observers sent here had been ineffective because of the limitations put on them both by the rebels and by their own organization.

In its first movement, the Sixth Fleet landed about 1,800 men

Continued on Page 12, Column 4

British Shift Units To Back U.S. Action

By DREW MIDDLETON
Special to The New York Times.

LONDON, July 15 — British land, sea and air forces were moving tonight from Malta, Kenya and the Persian Gulf to the support of their American allies in Lebanon.

Qualified military sources predicted late tonight that the most probable area of British military operations would be in Jordan, where King Hussein is supporting the cause of his cousin, King Faisal of Iraq.

Forces mentioned as "available" for this operation were a parachute brigade and the First Guards Brigade in Cyprus, totaling about 5,000 men.

There have been no British landings, the Ministry of Defense declared tonight. However, Foreign Secretary Selwyn Lloyd refused to give the Labor party assurance that forces would not be sent to Iraq, Lebanon or

Continued on Page 18, Column 4

RECOGNIZES RISKS

President Says More Troops Will Go if They Are Needed

Texts of President's statement, message to Congress, Page 2.

By FELIX BELAIR Jr.
Special to The New York Times.

WASHINGTON, July 15 — President Eisenhower dispatched more than 5,000 marines with supporting sea and air power to revolt-ridden Lebanon early today to protect American lives and help that Government defend its sovereignty and independence.

In a special message to Congress the President gave a detailed explanation of his action, saying the initial commitment of United States forces would be "augmented as required" and "withdrawn as rapidly as circumstances permit."

General Eisenhower recognized that "serious consequences" might follow the United States response to the urgent appeal for military assistance he received yesterday from President Camille Chamoun of Lebanon.

But he stressed that this country "could not in honor stand idly by in this hour of Lebanon's grave peril."

Necessary Despite Risks

"I have come to the considered and sober conclusion," said the President, "that despite the risks involved, this action is required to support the principles of justice and international law upon which peace and a stable international order depend."

In his separate statements during the day the President was at some pains to stress that "we wish to withdraw our forces as soon as the United Nations has taken further effective steps designed to safeguard Lebanese independence."

Meanwhile, General Eisenhower insisted, "we might be prepared to meet the situation, whatever the consequences."

There was more than a hint in the President's context that the United States and Lebanon would be the judges of what they would consider "effective steps" by the United Nations to maintain Lebanese sovereignty and territorial integrity.

The President's recitation of his reasons for committing United States forces in the Middle East failed to win unanimous bipartisan support in

Continued on Page 2, Column 3

U. S. FORCES MOVE TO BACK MARINES

Navy, Air and Army Units Affected—'Not War, but Like War,' Aide Says

By JACK RAYMOND
Special to The New York Times.

WASHINGTON, July 15 — United States naval, air and army units were ordered today into "improved readiness positions" in support of the United States Marines' landing in Lebanon.

A military authority at the Pentagon said the action by marines of the United States Sixth Fleet and the military movements to back it up were "not war, but like war" in that the consequences could not be foreseen.

This authority spoke gravely, even agitatedly, of the possibility that Americans might be shot at on foreign beaches, as the Defense Department issued short news reports in an atmosphere keynoted by his statement that "a lot of lives are at stake."

Transports Fly to Europe

An undisclosed number of Air Force C-124 Globemaster transport planes were dispatched from Donaldson Air Force Base, S. C., to Europe. They are for Army forces, already alerted in West Germany, should they be required for duty in the Middle East.

Also, the Pentagon reported late in the evening that more marines of the Second Division were being airlifted from Cherry Point, N. C., to reinforce the division's units that went ashore in Lebanon.

The new units of marines are bound "for an intermediate destination in the Mediterranean area where they will be in support of the Sixth Fleet landings in Lebanon," the Defense Department said.

Jet fighters and fighter bombers, constituting a composite air strike force, were sent from Langley Air Force Base, Va., to an undisclosed rendezvous in another move.

The Atlantic and Pacific Fleets were ordered on a four-hour alert. Leaves were canceled, men were told to report to their ships, and units were made ready for extended operations, it was reported from head-

Continued on Page 3, Column 1

CRITICS IN SENATE DEPLORE LANDING

Some Democrats Are Bitter but Leaders Back Move

By RUSSELL BAKER
Special to The New York Times.

WASHINGTON, July 15 — Despite backing from the Congressional leadership, President Eisenhower failed today to win solid bipartisan support for his decision to send troops into Lebanon.

Endorsements came from all segments of the Republican party in both houses as well as from Lyndon B. Johnson, Senate Democratic leader; Sam Rayburn, Democratic Speaker of the House, and Representative John W. McCormack of Massachusetts, House Democratic leader.

Dissent and criticism, however, were heard from the Democratic ranks in the Senate. Six Democratic members of the influential Foreign Relations Committee expressed opposition ranging from harsh criticism to worried doubt when the committee met in executive session this morning.

During the meeting the committee voted to request $300,000 for a long-range professional and scholarly examination of United States foreign policy. It also decided to seek $150,000 for an inquiry into the

Continued on Page 10, Column 5

Marlene Dietrich as Christine Vole in Witness for the Prosecution.

Brigitte Bardot starred in The Night Heaven Fell.

"All the News That's Fit to Print"

The New York Times.

LATE CITY EDITION
U. S. Weather Bureau Report (Page 34) forecasts: Warmer, more humid, brief showers today. Mostly fair tomorrow.
Temp. range: 82—67. Yesterday: 78—68.6.

VOL. CVII—No. 36,701. NEW YORK, SATURDAY, JULY 19, 1958. 10c beyond 100-mile zone from New York City. Higher in air delivery cities. FIVE CENTS

NASSER, IN MOSCOW, CAUTIONS KHRUSHCHEV TO AVOID ACTION IMPERILING WORLD PEACE; SOVIET VETOES U.S. BID FOR U.N. POLICE FORCE

EX-ARMY OFFICIAL CITES ADAMS NOTE IN CONTRACT CASE

But Says He Found Nothing Questionable in the Final Decision on Rebate

By WILLIAM M. BLAIR
Special to The New York Times.

WASHINGTON, July 18—A former Army official said today that he had protested vigorously last year against "pressure" in an Army contract case that involved Sherman Adams.

Roswell M. Austin, who retired last September as a member of the armed services Board of Contract Appeals, said he had written a "hot memorandum" against "unethical conduct" in the case turned up by Congressional investigators.

The communication that "sparked my resentment," he said, was a letter from Mr. Adams asking for information and enclosing a letter from someone either connected with or familiar with a New England textile company. The enclosed letter, he said, asked "help" from the Assistant to President Eisenhower.

Concern Was Penalized

The letters dealt with the now defunct Raylaine Worsted, Inc., of Manchester, N. H., which was penalized nearly $80,000 for late delivery on wartime cloth contracts but got back $41,284.21 last year on one contract.

Mr. Austin also said there had been a letter from a "member of Congress." He said he could not recall the name.

Mr. Austin said that as far as he knew there had been nothing questionable about the final decision although he did not participate in it. His only participation was in a decision to reopen the case. The final decision granting the company's appeal was made Nov. 27 of last year. Mr. Austin retired Sept. 30.

Col. Joseph A. Avery, president of the contract appeals board, declined to comment "at this time."

Hearings Start Monday

Mr. Austin was interviewed by telephone at his home in near-by Chevy Chase, Md. Colonel Avery talked from his home in near-by Arlington, Va.

A House Armed Services subcommittee will hold closed hearings Monday on the case.

It was first disclosed by the Special House Subcommittee on Legislative Oversight, which was investigating Bernard Goldfine and his relations with Mr. Adams and Federal regulatory agencies.

The District of Columbia police announced today an arrest in one phase of the New England industrialist's case, that of the alleged theft of Goldfine papers from a Sheraton-Carlton Hotel room.

The police named the suspect

Continued on Page 7, Column 4

British, U. S. and Soviet Delegates Vote at U. N.

Sir Pierson Dixon, center, and Henry Cabot Lodge vote with majority against the Soviet resolution calling on U. S. and Britain to "cease armed intervention" in Arab states.

The New York Times

Arkady A. Sobolev vetoes the U. S. proposal to send United Nations forces into Lebanon

Senate, 80 to 0, Approves Pentagon Reorganization

Special to The New York Times.

WASHINGTON, July 18—The Senate overwhelmingly passed a Pentagon reorganization bill tonight giving President Eisenhower many but not all of the changes in set-up he had requested. The vote was 80 to 0.

The measure faced no opposition and stirred none of the controversy that marked its passage through the House last month.

Of three critical changes sought by the President in the House bill, only one was fully granted by the Senate. This was a provision that would increase the administrative authority of the Secretary of Defense over the individual services.

The two other changes sought by the White House would have abolished the individual services' right to make complaints to Congress on their initiative and curb Congress' power to prevent merger, transfer or abolition of traditional service functions. Both were lost in committee.

Acceptable Substitute

The Administration has indicated, however, that it regards the Senate bill as an acceptable substitute for the more sweeping measure it sent to Congress in March. Differences between the House and Senate versions must be ironed out in conference between the two bodies and further changes are possible.

Senator Richard B. Russell of Georgia, Democratic chairman of the Armed Services Committee, assured the Senate that the continued existence of the National Guard and the Marine Corps was fully guaranteed under the bill.

The Senate committee wrote in specific safeguards against transfer or abolition of the Guard and spelled out the intent of Congress to maintain the Marine Corps as an effective combat force.

Aside from the three controversial issues, the bill gives the President virtually everything he asked.

Provisions Listed

Essential provisions are as follows:

¶The Secretary of Defense is given clear power to assign weapons to services of his choice.

¶Research and development is centralized under a new Director of Research and Engineering.

¶The size of the Joint Staff is increased from 210 men to 400, so that strategic and operational planning can be centralized under the Joint Chiefs of Staff.

¶The position of the chairman of the Joint Chiefs is enhanced, but the bill forbids establishment of a single Chief of Staff or an over-all armed

Continued on Page 7, Column 7

MAHONEY ENTERS REPUBLICAN RACE

Buffalo Senator Announces for Governorship in Bid to Halt Delegate Shift

By DOUGLAS DALES

State Senator Walter J. Mahoney took the spotlight yesterday in the battle for the Republican nomination for Governor.

In a surprise statement he said that if he were nominated at the party's convention in Rochester next month, he would accept.

Senator Mahoney had said repeatedly in recent weeks that he would not give his position on the gubernatorial race until just before the delegates convened on Aug. 25.

His announcement yesterday was widely interpreted as an effort to forestall defection of support that had been pledged to him by county leaders and organizations. It presumably was designed also to assure his supporters that they were not backing a candidate who would not be available to make the race.

The statement followed by a

Continued on Page 13, Column 4

DULLES DOUBTFUL OF SOVIET ACTION

Tells Senators Russia Won't Intervene Militarily—Asks More Aid Funds

By RUSSELL BAKER
Special to The New York Times.

WASHINGTON, July 18 — John Foster Dulles, Secretary of State, told a Senate committee today he doubted the Soviet Union would intervene militarily in the Middle East.

At the same time, both he and President Eisenhower made strong representations to Congress for strengthening the Administration's badly battered foreign aid bill.

The President invited eight Senate leaders from both parties to the White House tonight to discuss the foreign aid program amid speculation that he intended to ask for new funds for friendly Middle Eastern Governments.

Mr. Dulles, appearing before the Senate Appropriations Committee, argued that restoration of all funds cut out two weeks ago by the House of

Continued on Page 7, Column 2

COUNCIL HOBBLED

Soviet Plea to Recall Troops Also Beaten—Assembly Asked

Excerpts from U. N. debate are printed on Page 4.

By LINDESAY PARROTT
Special to The New York Times.

UNITED NATIONS, N. Y., July 18—The Soviet Union today vetoed a United States proposal to send United Nations troops to Lebanon.

Tonight, both the Soviet Union and the United States called for a special session of the General Assembly to take further steps in the Middle East crisis, for which the Security Council had failed to find a quick solution.

The Soviet veto came as a culmination of four days of debate set off Tuesday by the revolt in neighboring Iraq.

The Security Council, at the same session, voted down this afternoon two other draft resolutions, by the Soviet Union and by Sweden.

The Soviet resolution would have had the United States and Britain remove their troops from Lebanon and Jordan and "cease armed intervention in the domestic affairs of the Arab states."

Meeting Again Monday

Sweden had asked the Council to suspend the operations of the United Nations Observation Group in Lebanon following the arrival there of United States Marines.

After Japan had indicated that she intended to introduce a compromise resolution, the Council adjourned at 6:40 P. M. It will meet again Monday at 3 P. M.

In effect, the eleven-nation Council failed to agree on any further action in the Middle East crisis.

Henry Cabot Lodge, United States representative, immediately moved for an emergency session of the General Assembly. He asked that it "make appropriate recommendations" concerning Lebanon's complaint that the United Arab Republic, under President Gamal Abdel Nasser, continued to run men and arms across her frontiers, aiming at the overthrow of the Western-oriented Lebanese Government.

He withheld his resolution from a vote, however, pending a decision by the Council on the prospective move by Japan.

Koto Matsudaira, chief Japa-

Continued on Page 5, Column 2

Russians Assert 'Security' Will Guide Policy in Crisis

Renew Warning They Will Take Steps 'Necessary' to Meet Mideast Situation —Charge West Fights 'Liberation'

Special to The New York Times.

MOSCOW, July 18—The Soviet Government said tonight that it would "not remain indifferent to acts of unprovoked aggression in a region adjacent to its borders."

A statement about the situa-

Text of Soviet statement will be found on Page 2.

tion in the Middle East, reiterating a position set forth two days ago, added that Moscow "will have to take necessary measures dictated by the interest of the security of the Soviet Union and the preservation of general peace."

[The Soviet position was set forth in a Foreign Ministry statement delivered to the United States and British Ambassadors, United Press International reported.]

The official Soviet attitude as reflected in the statement appeared to be fairly moderate, more so than some observers here had expected.

The statement coincided with a brief visit here by President Gamal Abdel Nasser of the United Arab Republic. He conferred with Premier Nikita S. Khrushchev on Middle Eastern issues.

As it did two days ago, the Soviet Union urged again that steps to solve Middle Eastern problems be made the urgent business of the United Nations.

Among the measures mentioned in the statement that the Soviet Union presumably could take would be the strengthening of the country's defenses in the area closest to the Middle East, along the borders of

Continued on Page 2, Column 6

Embassy of U.S. Is Stoned By Thousands in Moscow

By WILLIAM J. JORDEN
Special to The New York Times.

MOSCOW, July 18—Tens of thousands of Moscow citizens vented their anger over United States action in the Middle East against the United States Embassy here today.

For several hours the embassy building on Tchaikowsky Street was besieged by shouting, whistling Muscovites who threw stones, bricks, metal pellets and ink bottles.

Inside the embassy, work was suspended and precautions were taken to minimize the damage and danger.

Two-thirds of the windows on the first floor of the building were broken and there was some damage to furniture and draperies. No one inside the building was injured.

[In Potsdam the offices of the United States and British military missions were attacked by East Germans.]

Soviet Police Watch Display

Soviet policemen and soldiers stood by while some of the crowd tossed missiles and ink bottles at will at the embassy. Only after more than an hour did they force the crowd back from the embassy and beyond throwing range.

Llewellyn E. Thompson Jr., United States Ambassador, was expected to register a strong protest against the attack and demand full compensation for all damage from the Soviet Government.

The day started quietly at the embassy. Several delegations arrived early to present petitions to Mr. Thompson urging the withdrawal of United States troops from Lebanon. The Ambassador received three representatives, answered their questions and remarked that the problem was being discussed at the United Nations, which he said was the "proper place" to consider such matters.

Written Protests Presented

Other petitioners handed in their written statements to embassy personnel at the gate on the first floor.

But by mid-afternoon the atmosphere changed considerably. A speakers' platform had been erected at a corner half a block from the embassy and loudspeakers were mounted along the street in preparation for the protest meeting. Groups with banners and placards denouncing the United States began converging on the area from all parts of the city.

By 4 P. M. the entire wide boulevard was a mass of screaming, fist-shaking, jeering people reaching as far as the eye could see down Tchaikowsky Street.

Twice embassy officials called the Soviet Foreign Ministry,

Continued on Page 3, Column 3

U. S. WARNS CAIRO ON MILITARY ACTS

Says Any Attacks on Forces in Mideast Could Bring 'Grave Consequences'

State Department's statement appears on Page 3.

By EDWIN L. DALE Jr.
Special to The New York Times.

WASHINGTON, July 18 — The United States has warned the United Arab Republic of Egypt and Syria that any attack by its military units on United States forces "could involve grave consequences."

This was revealed today by the State Department. The warning had been disclosed earlier at the United Nations by Omar Loutfi, Arab Republic delegate. It was delivered yesterday afternoon in Cairo by Raymond A. Hare, United States Ambassador, to Ali Sabu, acting Foreign Minister.

Mr. Hare's words, as outlined by Lincoln White, State Department spokesman, were that the United States "hoped to complete our military assignment

Continued on Page 3, Column 2

TRIP WAS SECRET

Arab Chief Also Asks What Help He Can Expect in Attack

Excerpts from Nasser speech are printed on Page 2.

By OSGOOD CARUTHERS
Special to The New York Times.

CAIRO, July 18—President Gamal Abdel Nasser has made an urgent secret flight to Moscow and, it is reported, appealed to Premier Nikita S. Khrushchev not to take any action in the Middle East that would threaten world peace.

The head of the United Arab Republic of Egypt and Syria was said by reliable informants to have asked the Soviet leader what help could be expected from the Soviet Union in the event the Western powers attacked the Syrian region or Iraq, where a pro-Nasser revolution has overthrown the monarchy.

The Middle East News Agency said President Nasser, who went to Moscow after a visit to President Tito of Yugoslavia, had two meetings yesterday with Mr. Khrushchev that lasted a total of eight hours.

Confers in Damascus

He was said to have left Moscow this morning. He then traveled to Damascus, where he went into conference with his ministers in the Syrian region.

[In a speech Friday in Damascus, President Nasser said, according to news agency accounts, that the Arab whole bloc would "fight" to defend the new regime in Iraq and Arab nationalism.]

President Nasser was described by informants as having been gravely concerned lest the landing of United States forces in Lebanon and British forces in Jordan might cause a Soviet reaction that would make the Middle East the starting arena for a third world war. He was said to have urged Soviet leaders to take no action unless he or his allies asked for it.

The Cairo regime's concern lest the tense situation explode into a final East-West struggle was voiced yesterday by Ali Sabry, acting Foreign Minister and President Nasser's chief aide, in meetings with the Ambassadors of India, Indonesia and Communist China.

U. S. Envoy Sees Cairo Aide

Mr. Sabry also saw the United States Ambassador, Raymond A. Hare, at an afternoon meeting and again at an unusual late night session.

Although embassy officials would not reveal what had been discussed, Egyptian sources said Mr. Sabry had reiterated his Government's fears that the United States and Britain might take some action that would invite Soviet intervention, either with "volunteers" or with regular forces.

The informants said Mr. Sabry had made no formal protest against the Western ac-

Continued on Page 2, Column 3

All Servicemen Freed in Cuba; Rebels Tie Act to Mideast Crisis

By PETER KIHSS
Special to The New York Times.

GUANTANAMO BAY, Cuba, July 18—Cuban rebels freed today the last fourteen kidnapped United States servicemen that they were holding. They told the men they had done so because of "the Lebanese situation."

Navy helicopters made four flights into the mountains, starting at 2:10 P.M. today. The last group of three servicemen arrived here at 6:20 P.M.

The rebels still held one Cuban civilian, Alberto Tito, an employe at the United States naval base at Guantanamo Bay. He had driven the liberty bus from which twenty-nine servicemen were kidnapped June 27.

Marine Pfc. Joseph J. Anderson Jr., 19 years old, of 170-34 118th Street, St. Albans, Queens, said a rebel commandant, whose name he did not know, had announced the decision to free all the men after the first helicopter had taken off with four men.

On Wednesday the rebels had set a daily limit of four releases.

The commandant, Private Anderson said, declared that the rebels "did not want to interfere" with the United States effort in Lebanon. Marines landed in Lebanon last Tuesday in an effort to insure the independence of that country.

Private Anderson also quoted the commandant as having told the servicemen "if the admiral wants to send us [the servicemen] into battle in Lebanon, they [the rebels] did not want to hold us back."

This version was confirmed by other servicemen returning

Continued on Page 36, Column 7

Beirut Pervaded by Tensions But Marines Find Hospitality

Travel at Night Forbidden

By ARNALDO CORTESI
Special to The New York Times.

BEIRUT, Lebanon, July 18—The traveler landing in this beautiful capital is immediately impressed by the contrast between the air of apparent peace and tranquillity and the very obvious tensions between sections of the population.

The prevailing strains and tensions are particularly evident at night, but also show up in some degree in the daytime.

This correspondent was driven yesterday in a Marine truck the four miles from the Beirut International Airport to a hotel. Two United States marines, armed with rifles, sat in front beside the driver and another rode in the back.

It was dusk, and the truck traveled at high speed to beat the curfew, which goes into effect at nightfall.

About two miles from the airport the truck was stopped by a Lebanese Army tank. Two soldiers conveyed in sign language the instruction that we were to await the arrival of an officer.

Meanwhile, a second tank lumbered up and stopped in front of the truck, with its gun

Continued on Page 6, Column 2

Airlift From Turkey On

By JAY WALZ
Special to The New York Times.

BEIRUT, Lebanon, July 18—United States marines, spread out along nine miles of the Lebanese coast, have the situation so well in hand that some of them began philosophizing today on why they were there.

Very few of the men who landed in and around Beirut have seen a rebel.

[A massive airlift from Turkey of United States paratroopers to Beirut began early Saturday to back up the marines, The Associated Press reported.]

At the latest count tonight, there have been no United States casualties; only "harassment," as a Marine public information officer put it.

These Americans abroad, most of them 18 and 19-year-olds on their first serious "landing" overseas, have experienced much more hospitality in Beirut than trouble.

One sentry, in a remarkable demonstration of the traditional discipline of his corps, turned down a free, cold beer because "I am on duty, sir."

But cola drinks and cookies were offered as freely as at a

Continued on Page 6, Column 3

U. S. Set to Call Advisers on Oil To Meet Emergency in Mideast

Special to The New York Times.

WASHINGTON, July 18—The United States Government is preparing to call in the committee of oil companies that formulated plans for the Suez oil lift in 1956 to consider plans for a possible new emergency.

Responsible officials have no information that there will be another emergency, but no assurance that there will not be. Today's Baghdad radio announcement of Iraq's intention to honor her oil obligations did not alter the feeling here that advance planning would be advisable

The Interior Department's Foreign Petroleum Supply Committee is a continuing body, created in 1953 as an outgrowth of the oil crisis in Iran, when that country's oil production was nationalized.

The committee advises the Secretary of the Interior. Its chairman is a government official, but the chair is not occupied at the moment. Its members are officials of fifteen oil companies in the United States.

As usual in arrangements of this sort, the antitrust question poses something of an obstacle. Twenty-nine oil companies were recently indicted by a Federal grand jury for having conspired to raise and fix crude oil and gasoline prices during the Suez crisis.

Though the United States Government's case has nothing to do with the industry cooperation on the oil lift itself, some companies are said to be using it as a ground for seeking assurances that they will be immune from antitrust action for any new emergency arrange-

Continued on Page 3, Column 5

1958

Conway Twitty's hit was It's Only Make Believe.

Cannonball *and* Ramrod *were two explosive hits for Duane Eddy.*

Neil Sedaka's successful career dates back to a song called The Diary, *which he recorded in 1958.*

"All the News
That's Fit to Print"

The New York Times.

LATE CITY EDITION
U.S. Weather Bureau Report (Page 32) forecast:
Fair and pleasant today;
fair tonight and tomorrow.
Temp. range: 83—67. Yesterday: 83.0—70.0.

VOL. CVII..No. 36,722.   © 1958, by The New York Times Company. Times Square, New York 36, N. Y.   NEW YORK, SATURDAY, AUGUST 9, 1958.   10c beyond 100-mile zone from New York City. Higher in air delivery cities.   FIVE CENTS

CHIEF OF U.N. GIVES A PLAN FOR MIDEAST

ASSEMBLY MEETS

Hears Call for Step-Up of Its Economic and Political Efforts

Hammarskjold and Munro statements are on Page 2.

By THOMAS J. HAMILTON
Special to The New York Times.

UNITED NATIONS, N. Y., Aug. 8—Secretary General Dag Hammarskjold proposed today that the United Nations step up its political and economic activities in the Middle East to stabilize the area.

Mr. Hammarskjold took the floor at the opening of the General Assembly's emergency special session on the Middle East to put forward his program. He had intended to present this proposal if there was a meeting of heads of government within the framework of the United Nations Security Council.

The principal provisions of his plan are:

¶A declaration by the Arab states reaffirming their adherence to the principles of mutual respect for each other's territory, non-aggression and non-interference in each other's internal affairs.

¶The continuation and extension of present United Nations activities in Lebanon and Jordan.

¶Joint action by the Arab states, with the support of the United Nations, in economic development. This would include arrangements for cooperation between "oil-producing and oil-transiting countries" and joint utilization of water resources.

Session Is Adjourned

Mr. Hammarskjold's statement was the outstanding development of the opening session, which lasted thirty-five minutes. The Assembly adjourned until 10:30 A. M. Wednesday to give foreign ministers of some of the eighty-one member nations time to get here.

Contrary to the general expectation, Arkady A. Sobolev, Soviet delegate, did not demand the admission of Chinese Communist representatives. However, he took the floor to repeat his denunciation of the presence of United States forces in Lebanon and British forces in Jordan, and again demanded their immediate withdrawal.

Henry Cabot Lodge Jr., the

Continued on Page 2, Column 2

The New York Times
CALL TO ACTION: Dag Hammarskjold addressing the General Assembly.

U.S. LEADERS SPLIT ON MIDEAST AIMS

Eisenhower Action May Be Needed to Fix Policy for Assembly Debate

By E. W. KENWORTHY
Special to The New York Times.

WASHINGTON, Aug. 8—High-level differences of opinion have developed within the Administration over the strategy and tactics to be used in the United Nations debate on the Middle East crisis, officials indicated today.

The differences are being argued out thoroughly and amicably, and a concerted position will almost certainly be arrived at during the week-end, these officials said. Nevertheless, it was considered possible that President Eisenhower might have to make the final decision on the United States approach.

Dulles Remark Recalled

The differences were said to have become apparent soon after Secretary of State Dulles' news conference a week ago Thursday. At that conference he made it clear that the United States intended to meet the Soviet charge of United States and British aggression in Lebanon and Jordan with a counter-arraignment against the Soviet Union and the United Arab Republic on "indirect aggression."

Until the problems of indirect aggression are met directly and dealt with, it will not be possible to create the atmosphere of political stability in the Middle East necessary for any attack on economic problems, Mr. Dulles said.

Almost immediately some

Continued on Page 2, Column 5

U. S. MAY REDUCE FORCE IN LEBANON

Token Removal of Marine Battalion Planned

By W. H. LAWRENCE
Special to The New York Times.

BEIRUT, Lebanon, Aug. 8—The United States tentatively plans to reload a marine battalion on ships next week in a "symbolic" gesture of withdrawal from Lebanon.

A responsible source said the decision to reduce the force on shore by about 2,000 men had been communicated to the Lebanese Government and to Gen. Fouad Chehab, armed forces commander and President-elect.

Before the marine unit is pulled out, a small detachment of Army engineers and truck personnel will be moved from Lebanon to the Turkish port of Iskenderun at the Atlantic alliance base at Adana, an important center of air striking power and supply for the United States operation in Lebanon.

The moves will have both political and military effects, it is believed. The political aims are both local and international.

Locally, leaders of the continuing insurrection against the Government of President Camille Chamoun have been insisting on speedy removal of United States troops as a condition for a cease-fire now that General Chehab has been elected. He will succeed Mr. Chamoun Sept.

Continued on Page 3, Column 2

HOUSE VOTES BILL TO AID EDUCATION IN SCIENCE FIELD

Student Loans Raised in Place of Scholarships by 900 Million Measure

By BESS FURMAN
Special to The New York Times.

WASHINGTON, Aug. 8—The House of Representatives adopted today a four-year, $900,000,000 bill to aid science education.

No money was shorn from the bill. But the scholarship provision, on which a compromise had already been made with President Eisenhower, was deleted.

The scholarship funds were shifted to the bill's loan provisions. This was accomplished in a standing vote of 109 to 78, on a motion offered by Representative Walter H. Judd, Republican of Minnesota.

The loan provisions of the bill were increased from $40,000,000 in the first year to $60,000,000 and from $60,000,000 in each of the three succeeding years to $80,000,000.

The final adoption was by voice vote, after a motion to kill the bill by sending it back to committee had been defeated in a roll-call vote of 233 to 139. The motion was offered by Representative Ralph W. Gwinn, Republican of Westchester.

The legislation now goes to the Senate, which has already scheduled to consider on Monday its own broader science-aid bill, sponsored by Senator Lister Hill, Democrat of Alabama.

Scholarships in Senate Bill

The Senate bill includes a four-year program totaling $70,000,000 for college scholarships. If that survives on the Senate floor, some compromise on scholarships will have to be worked out by House and Senate conferees.

As adopted, the House bill would cost an estimated total of $147,000,000 in the first year of operation.

It would provide:

¶Loans averaging $600 to more than 90,000 needy students, of which the Federal Government would pay a total of $60,000,000.

¶One thousand fellowships of $2,000 each to train college teachers, with reimbursement to universities for additional costs to expand graduate schools.

¶Grants to the states for scientific teaching equipment and laboratory improvement, totaling $60,000,000.

¶Grants to states to improve testing and guidance programs, $15,000,000, and $6,000,000 to set up teacher-training institutes in this field.

¶Grants to institutions to set up short-term institutes for foreign language teachers, to pay half the cost of permanent foreign language centers and stipends for those attending. This was estimated at a total of $4,500,000.

¶For research under the United States Office of Education on better educational use

Continued on Page 5, Column 3

Glennan, Ohio Educator, Named To Direct New U. S. Space Unit

Case Tech President Served on A.E.C. Under Truman— Dryden Picked as Aide

Special to The New York Times.

WASHINGTON, Aug. 8—T. Keith Glennan, a Cleveland educator and former member of the Atomic Energy Commission, is President Eisenhower's choice to head the new civilian space agency.

The President sent Mr. Glennan's nomination to the Senate today along with that of Dr. Hugh L. Dryden as Deputy Administrator of the agency.

Mr. Glennan is president of the Case Institute of Technology. Dr. Dryden is director of the National Advisory Committee for Aeronautics.

The National Aeronautics and Space Administration was created by an Act of Congress signed by the President ten days ago.

Mr. Glennan's appointment is believed to be noncontroversial. There may be some objection to the choice of Dr. Dryden, however, and this could delay Senate confirmation of the nominees.

Associated Press
T. Keith Glennan

before Congress adjourns, both can be installed under recess appointments.

Members of the House Space Committee have criticized Dr. Dryden as presenting a program for the conquest of space that lacked "boldness, imagina-

Continued on Page 6, Column 3

VETO THREATENED ON PENSIONS BILL

Social Security Rate Rise Backed by White House but State Plan Is Fought

By JOHN D. MORRIS
Special to The New York Times.

WASHINGTON, Aug. 8—The Eisenhower Administration raised the threat of a veto today against a bill to increase Social Security benefits.

The measure, approved by the House, calls for a 7 per cent increase in Old Age and Survivors Insurance benefits and higher Social Security taxes to finance it. Those provisions were endorsed by Arthur S. Flemming, Secretary of Health, Education and Welfare.

But the Administration is "strongly opposed," Mr. Flemming told the Senate Finance Committee, to provisions that would increase the Federal Government's share in the cost of state relief programs.

Would Recommend Veto

"Suppose we passed the House bill, would you recommend a veto?" asked Senator Paul H. Douglas, Democrat of Illinois.

"I would," Mr. Flemming replied.

Mr. Flemming was the first witness at the opening of two days of hearings on the measure, which is scheduled for Senate action before Congress adjourns. He told the Senators that his views were those of the Administration.

The bill calls for increases in monthly cash benefits under the insurance program starting

Continued on Page 5, Column 2

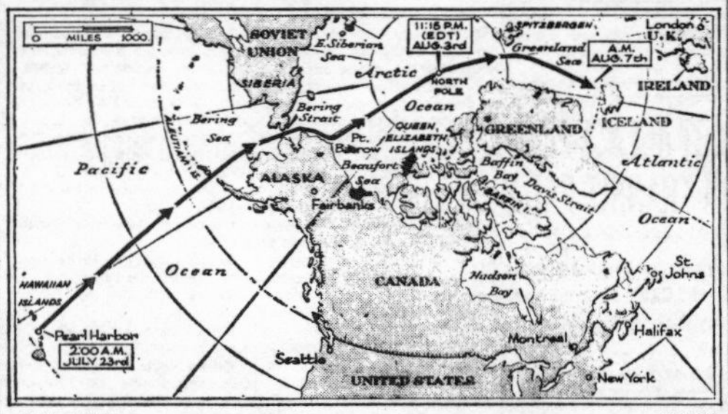

NAUTILUS SAILS UNDER THE POLE AND 1,830 MILES OF ARCTIC ICECAP IN PACIFIC-TO-ATLANTIC PASSAGE

TIME OF DECISION: Officers of the Nautilus choose a place to submerge below ice for undersea voyage across Arctic regions. Standing at the right in the conning tower of the submarine is her skipper, Comdr. W. R. Anderson.   U. S. Navy, from Associated Press

The New York Times   Aug. 9, 1958
NEW PASSAGE: Heavy line traces the Nautilus' route from Pacific to Atlantic Oceans

Hogan Is Expected To Enter the Race For Senate Monday

By DOUGLAS DALES

A statement circulated yesterday by the New York Young Democratic Club indicated that District Attorney Frank S. Hogan had made up his mind to enter the race for the Democratic Senate nomination nearly a month ago.

Mr. Hogan yesterday scheduled a news conference for Monday noon to "issue a statement."

If, as expected, he then announces his entry, he will become the fifth declared candidate in the field.

Mr. Hogan's intentions were forecast in a summary of an interview conducted by a committee of the Young Democratic Club with Mr. Hogan on July 17. The summary was submitted to Mr. Hogan for revisions before its circulation among club members.

The summary indicated that Mr. Hogan was already making plans for the future operation of his office and that he expected to have a say in the selection of a successor.

His views on this were given as follows:

"When queried as to the

Continued on Page 14, Column 4

Rackets Unit Asks Prosecution for 13

By ALLEN DRURY
Special to The New York Times.

WASHINGTON, Aug. 8—Senate rackets investigators voted unanimously today to ask the Senate to approve contempt-of-Congress citations against thirteen witnesses.

They include the president of the Carpenters Union and the reputed heir to Al Capone's gangland empire.

The action was taken by the Select Committee on Improper Activities in the Labor or Management Field. It acted in a closed meeting between morning and afternoon public sessions at which it heard witnesses give further testimony on associates of James R. Hoffa, president of the International Brotherhood of Teamsters.

Nine nuclear-powered submarines, each much larger than the Nautilus and each capable

Continued on Page 6, Column 8

POLAR TRIP OPENS DEFENSE FRONTIER

U.S. Strategic Advantage Is Seen as Temporary— Soviet Effort Expected

By HANSON W. BALDWIN

A new ocean—the frozen wastes of the Arctic—has been opened to navigation and hence to naval utilization.

This is the meaning of the transpolar, under-ice voyage from Alaska to the Greenland Sea of the nuclear-powered submarine Nautilus.

The newest achievement of the Nautilus, which had already broken all records in submarine history, has immense strategic implications.

Last year the Nautilus made a five-and-one-half-day, 1,000-mile trip under the Arctic ice pack and clearly foreshadowed the shape of things to come.

The Arctic ice pack has hitherto prevented penetration of the Arctic Ocean except, with great difficulty, by foot or by air.

Ships Skirt Land

In certain seasons of the year when the ice pack recedes from the land, or thins out, surface ships have skirted the land masses bordering the Arctic, but their cruises have been short and difficult and they have never penetrated deep into the pack.

The submerged navigation of the Nautilus under the Pole and from Pacific to Atlantic means that utilization of the Arctic Ocean for military purposes is now possible for the first time in history.

Three military capabilities for Arctic submarine operations are immediately foreseeable.

Potentially the most important—in a strategic sense—is the utilization of the Arctic for the launching of guided missiles from submarines. The fleet ballistic missile, Polaris, a two-stage, solid-fuel rocket with a range of 500 to 1,500 miles, and a powerful thermonuclear warhead, is now being developed. It has been designed for launching from a submerged submarine at considerable depths.

Continued on Page 6, Column 5

Nautilus' Skipper Helps to Mitigate A Snub to Rickover

By ANTHONY LEWIS
Special to The New York Times.

WASHINGTON, Aug. 8—The man largely responsible for construction of the world's first nuclear-powered submarine was not asked to the White House today to share her moment of triumph.

Some thought was given to inviting Rear Admiral Hyman G. Rickover to the ceremony for the Nautilus, White House officials said. But only "top brass" had been asked and it was decided no exception could be made for him.

The skipper of the Nautilus, Comdr. W. R. Anderson, proved in the circumstances to be as bold a navigator in Navy politics as in the waters under polar ice.

Commander Anderson went directly from the White House to Admiral Rickover's office in the Navy Building, a few blocks away. There he paid his personal respects on the slight, frail figure whose tough-minded drive made the Nautilus a reality.

For Admiral Rickover the of-

Continued on Page 6, Column 1

FOUR-DAY VOYAGE

New Route to Europe Pioneered—Skipper and Crew Cited

Text of Navy fact sheet, Page 6. The Citation, Page 7.

By FELIX BELAIR Jr.
Special to The New York Times.

WASHINGTON, Aug. 8—History's first undersea voyage across the top of the world, a distance of 1,830 miles under the polar icecap, was disclosed at the White House today.

The trip was made in four days by the Nautilus, the world's first atomic submarine. The voyage pioneered a new and shorter route from the Pacific to the Atlantic and Europe—a route that might be used by cargo submarines. It also added to man's knowledge of the subsurface of the Arctic basin.

The voyage took the Nautilus under the North Pole. The over-all trip began at Pearl Harbor July 23 and ended at Iceland Aug. 7.

Dives at Point Barrow

The Nautilus went under the icecap at Point Barrow, Alaska, and surfaced four days later at a point in the Atlantic between Spitzbergen and Greenland. She is now on her way to Western Europe.

The feat of the Nautilus, with 116 crewmen and scientific observers aboard, was revealed as President Eisenhower decorated the submarine's skipper, Comdr. W. R. Anderson, with the Legion of Merit. A Presidential Unit Citation—the first ever conferred in peacetime—went to the submarine, with a ribbon and special clasp in the form of a golden "N" to all who participated in the cruise.

The Presidential citation to Commander Anderson said that the Nautilus under his leadership had pioneered a submerged sea lane between the Eastern and Western Hemispheres. It added:

"This points the way for further exploration and possible use of this route by nuclear powered cargo submarines as a new commercial seaway between the major oceans of the world."

Skipper Tells Story

A few minutes after the award, Commander Anderson, admittedly "a little dazed" by the speed of events that brought him here overnight by helicopter and jet plane from Arctic waters, was telling his story of "Operation Northwest Passage."

News of the voyage reached the Capitol with electrifying effect. William F. Knowland of California, the Senate Republican leader, read a brief dispatch to the Senate and remarked:

"This should give us courage and remind us to have faith. It shows that this is no time to sell America short."

Senator Mike Mansfield of Montana, the Democratic acting

Continued on Page 7, Column 3

479 Get Jaywalking Summonses But Public Is Hailed on Response

By BERNARD STENGREN

Pedestrians waited for traffic lights and motorists waited for pedestrians yesterday as the police began enforcing New York's new safety law.

High officials of the Traffic and Police Departments said they were gratified at the extent of compliance by drivers and walkers.

Traffic Commissioner T. T. Wiley said:

"My hat is off to New York. My reaction is wonderful."

He spoke after a tour of midtown Manhattan during which turning trucks waited for pedestrians and cab drivers not only waited but also shouted warnings to pedestrians starting to cross against lights.

John J. King, assistant Chief Inspector and head of the Safety Division, said that although some persons had argued, most

There were, however, exceptions. Between 8 A. M., when enforcement began, and 4 P. M., when the police day shift ended, 479 summonses returnable for $2 were issued to pedestrians.

These included 255 in Manhattan, ninety-three in Brooklyn, ninety-eight in Queens, thirty-one in the Bronx and two in Richmond—where there is only one "Don't Walk" signal.

Twenty-two motorists who failed to give the right of way to pedestrians received summonses for that infraction, which was added Thursday to violations subject to "rigid enforcement."

In Manhattan, five were is-

Continued on Page 15, Column 8

Peronists Win Rule Of Argentine Labor

By JUAN de ONIS
Special to The New York Times.

BUENOS AIRES, Aug. 8—The Argentine Senate adopted today a controversial union organization law that virtually hands the labor movement back to Peronist control.

President Arturo Frondizi's Senate majority approved the text of a bill, passed by the Chamber of Deputies, without changing a word. It did so despite formal opposition to the measure by the Roman Catholic Church, business and professional organizations, nearly all of the press and the anti-Peronist labor unions.

The bill, which re-establishes the single General Labor Confederation, with the official right to speak for labor, awaits the President's signature only.

In eighteen of the bill's fifty-

Continued on Page 4, Column 7

The New York Times.

LATE CITY EDITION
U.S. Weather Bureau Report (Page 56) forecasts:
Mostly cloudy, slightly warmer today.
Fair and warmer tomorrow.
Temp. range: 73—54. Yesterday: 67.3—56.8.

VOL. CVII. No. 36,756. © 1958, by The New York Times Company. Times Square, New York 36, N. Y. — NEW YORK, FRIDAY, SEPTEMBER 12, 1958. — 10c beyond 100-mile zone from New York City. Higher in air delivery cities. — FIVE CENTS

HIGH COURT HEARS LITTLE ROCK PLEA; MAY RULE TODAY

FINAL ARGUMENTS

Justices Press School Board Attorney on Need for Delay

Excerpts from court hearing are on Pages 12 and 13.

By ANTHONY LEWIS
Special to The New York Times.

WASHINGTON, Sept. 11—The Supreme Court heard final argument today on the Little Rock school case, then recessed until noon tomorrow. Its decision is likely to come down at that time.

Richard C. Butler, attorney for the Little Rock School Board, pleaded, as he did two weeks ago in the first argument, that Little Rock must be allowed a "reasonable delay" in its plan to desegregate the schools.

Otherwise, he said, the school board would be "helpless" in the face of opposition from the public and the government of Arkansas.

One after the other the justices asked Mr. Butler what constructive purpose would be served by a delay, how the resulting injury to the constitutional rights of Negro children could be justified.

A Question by Harlan

Then Justice John Marshall Harlan put this question:

"If the Federal courts themselves are going to take a step to delay implementation of a decree, why isn't that delay going to spell even more hope on the part of the opposition that maybe this thing can be ultimately defeated?"

Mr. Butler answered: "That is a matter of opinion."

He went on to say that "mere delay may not be the answer." But he insisted—and he sounded this theme again and again—that some delay, allowing a return of "calm" to Little Rock, was a necessary prelude to any other moves toward acceptance of integration.

At the start of the historic session Chief Justice Earl Warren announced that the court had granted a formal writ of certiorari to review the issue that has been hanging over Little Rock and the rest of the South.

Problem Under Study

The question is: Does violent local opposition to school integration justify postponement of an integration plan? District Judge Harry J. Lemley granted Little Rock a postponement of two and one-half years. The Court of Appeals for the Eighth Circuit reversed him.

The Supreme Court met two weeks ago in special term to consider a request by lawyers of the National Association for the Advancement of Colored People to set aside a stay granted by the Eighth Circuit of its own order. This, in effect, would have required immediate resumption of integrated classes.

But the court decided, instead, to hear further argument today.

Continued on Page 13, Column 5

Boy Sent to Bellevue For Tests in Slaying

By PETER KIHSS

Eight-year-old Melvin Dean Nimer was remanded to Bellevue Hospital yesterday for further psychiatric examination. At the same time authorities continued to check his story that he had killed his mother and father in their Staten Island home Sept. 2.

District Attorney John M. Braisted Jr. and Deputy Chief Inspector Edward W. Byrnes emphasized that their investigation was still open.

Mr. Byrnes said that he had detectives "out of town" running down a new lead on "an avenue foreign to the boy." They were exploring the case, he said, from the angle of a different "possible motive."

The referral of the four-foot, slightly built boy to Bellevue was ordered by Domestic Relations Justice Charles E. Rams-

Continued on Page 15, Column 2

Rogers Builds Force For Duty at School

Special to The New York Times.

WASHINGTON, Sept. 11—The Justice Department announced tonight several more steps aimed at enforcement of integration in Little Rock, Ark., if the Supreme Court orders immediate resumption of the program.

Four Justice Department lawyers arrived in Little Rock today to help the local United States Attorney. The group was headed by an Assistant Attorney General, Malcolm R. Wilkey, chief of the Department's Office of Legal Counsel.

Mr. Rogers also sent a wire to Wayne Upton, president of

Continued on Page 14, Column 6

PORT AGENCY PLAN ON TRANSIT FAILS

Meyner and Tobin Agree Its Credit Can't Be Impaired by Risking Big Deficit

By GEORGE CABLE WRIGHT
Special to The New York Times.

TRENTON, Sept. 11—A proposal that the Port of New York Authority assume the task of integrating metropolitan rail facilities and of taking other steps to solve the region's rapid transit problems appeared doomed tonight.

Gov. Robert B. Meyner made this clear after a long conference with officials and others concerned with the transit situation. He said he had always preferred, and still desired, the creation of a metropolitan transit district to solve the commuter rail problem.

Mr. Meyner made his remarks at a press interview after the transit parley. In the presence of the Governor, Austin J. Tobin, executive director of the Port Authority, declared:

"The Port Authority cannot legally or financially involve itself in the transit problem, and would not under any circumstances do so."

Asserting that the bi-state agency's contract with its bond-

Continued on Page 20, Column 2

RECESSION BLAMED FOR MAJOR SHARE OF RECORD DEFICIT

U. S. Budget Head Also Cites High Outlays in Mid-Year Estimate of 12.2 Billion

By EDWIN L. DALE Jr.
Special to The New York Times.

WASHINGTON, Sept. 11—The Administration specified today why it faced a record peacetime deficit of $12,900,000,000 in the current fiscal year.

The annual mid-year budget review, bringing up to date the original estimates of last January, estimated expenditures at $79,300,000,000, up $5,300,000,000 from January, and receipts at $67,000,000,000, down $7,400,000,000 from January. In January, the two had been estimated as roughly in balance.

Maurice H. Stans, the Budget Director, told a news conference that he had some hope that the deficit might prove to be less than $12,200,000,000, if the economic recovery proved faster than expected. But he said the results could also be worse.

60% Laid to Recession

The review showed that 60 per cent of the big deficit was accounted for by the impact of the recession on receipts and 40 per cent by higher spending. It also showed that most of the higher spending was made up of items that had nothing to do with fighting the recession or improving defenses.

For the first time since records have been kept, the Government's "cash" deficit will be larger than its budget deficit. The cash figures include the transactions of the Government's trust funds, for such items as Social Security and unemployment compensation, and leave out certain intra-governmental transactions.

The cash budget is usually considered a more precise reflection of the economic impact of Government operations than the regular budget. It now shows estimated spending of $94,066,000,000, up $7,404,000,000 from the January estimate, and estimated receipts of $80,-357,000,000, down $6,929,000,000 from January.

Deficit in Trust Funds

The cash deficit is larger than the budget deficit because, for the first time, the trust funds as a whole will pay out more than they take in. This is only temporary, however. A further decline in unemployment is expected to swing the unemployment trust fund back into surplus, and Social Security tax increases voted by Congress will do the same for that fund starting in 1960.

Meanwhile, the cash deficit of $13,709,000,000 is a major factor leading to economic recovery—and possibly to inflation after the recovery.

Mr. Stans said the estimate of

Continued on Page 17, Column 4

U. S. TO HOLD BACK EXTRA ARMS FUND AND TRIM FORCES

Will Not Spend 1.1 Billion Voted by Congress Above White House Request

Special to The New York Times.

WASHINGTON, Sept. 11—The Administration disclosed today its intention to freeze $1,170,000,000 in extra defense funds that had been voted by Congress.

The disclosure came in the regular mid-year budget review published today and in supplementary remarks at a news conference by Maurice H. Stans, the Budget Director.

The freeze means that the money will be withheld and not spent. These were funds voted by Congress in addition to Administration requests.

The decision reflected a continuing Presidential determination to save money—a determination apparently not affected by the current crisis in Taiwan (Formosa).

Manpower Cuts to Stay

These are the main items affected:

¶Army manpower. Congress sought to avert a planned cut-back from 900,000 men to 870,000 men by the end of this fiscal year, June 30, 1959. The cutback will proceed.

¶Marine manpower. Here Congress tried to ward off a planned reduction from 200,000 to 175,000 men. Again the cutback will proceed.

¶Extra nuclear-missile submarines.

¶Polaris missiles to be fired from submarines.

¶More KC-135 jet tanker planes.

¶More planes for the Military Air Transport Service.

¶More funds for the Minuteman and Hound Dog missile programs. Minuteman is a proposed intercontinental ballistic missile using solid fuel. Hound Dog is an air-to-ground missile fired by bombers out of range of anti-aircraft interception.

Mr. Stans said the planned manpower cutbacks would save $220,000,000, all in the present fiscal year. The freeze on the other items, all procurement items, will save $950,000,000, of which only about $100,000,000 would have been spent this fiscal year, the rest later, he said.

The freeze action had been strongly hinted by Neil H. McElroy, Secretary of Defense.

Mr. Stans also disclosed that the Administration, out of necessity, would abide by a Congressional directive to maintain Army Reserve and National Guard forces at their present strength. Here Congress gave the force of law to its action adding to requested appropriations. The President strongly criticized this provision of the bill when he signed it.

Continued on Page 3, Column 3

REDS SHELL ISLE

Force a Nationalist Supply Fleet to Flee Without Unloading

By ROBERT TRUMBULL
Special to The New York Times.

TAIPEI, Taiwan, Friday, Sept. 12—Chinese Communist batteries subjected beaches on Quemoy Island to a record bombardment yesterday, forcing a vital Nationalist supply convoy to return to sea without unloading.

The convoy was carrying ammunition and other materials to the beleaguered Quemoy garrison.

The Nationalist vessels fled to the protection of the United States Seventh Fleet, which had escorted them to the three-mile limit of the international waters offshore. The Communist guns did not fire on the American warships, reports here indicated.

The Chinese Nationalist Ministry of Defense said the Communists on the near-by mainland hurled 57,746 shells onto the Quemoy complex, the group of small islands just outside the Communists' Amoy harbor, between 3:58 and 9:30 P. M. yesterday.

U. S. Gets Defense Role

This bombardment was the heaviest and most concentrated reported since the Chinese Reds renewed sustained artillery action against the Nationalist-held offshore islands three weeks ago.

[The 57,746 shells fired at Quemoy Thursday exceeded the initial assault, with 41,000, on Aug. 23 and even the 53,-314 shells fired last Monday.]

Earlier yesterday a spokesman for the United States Taiwan Defense Command and the United States Military Assistance Advisory Group announced that American air units on Taiwan had undertaken responsibility for night-time defense of Taiwan against attack.

This announcement and the news from Quemoy pointed up widely admitted serious deficiencies of the Nationalist Chinese armed forces in the protection of Taiwan and the offshore islands, which the Communists have been threatening to "liberate."

Dispatches from Quemoy indicated that the heaviest artillery fire yesterday landed on the beach where the Nationalist supply ships were attempting to unload cargo, including ammu-

Continued on Page 5, Column 3

West Tells Soviet Geneva Is Suitable For Atom Ban Talk

By E. W. KENWORTHY
Special to The New York Times.

WASHINGTON, Sept. 11—The United States and Britain have accepted a Soviet proposal to hold negotiations in Geneva on an agreement to suspend nuclear tests.

In communications to the Soviet Government Aug. 22, the two powers proposed that the tests suspension talks begin in New York Oct. 31. In a reply Aug. 30, the Soviet Union agreed to the date but expressed a preference for Geneva.

[In the field of peaceful uses of atomic energy the Geneva meeting studying this topic subscribed to the principle of cooperation with the Soviet Union but said Washington first must resolve political questions involved.]

Today the State Department made public a note delivered yesterday in Moscow. It said the United States agreed to Geneva. A note to the same effect was delivered by the British Ambassador in Moscow.

The State Department said that the United States delegation would be headed by James J. Wadsworth, United States

Continued on Page 7, Column 3

Hypnosis Therapy Backed by A.M.A.

The American Medical Association has endorsed the use of hypnosis by physicians and dentists, but condemned it for entertainment.

It has accepted a technique that since the days of Mesmer had been regarded by doctors with suspicion and hostility. Hypnosis was long considered the tool of charlatans and mystics.

Mesmer was run out of eighteenth-century Vienna. When he took refuge in Paris he was "tried" by a commission whose members included Benjamin Franklin. This report was unsympathetic, though it admitted he had achieved cures.

An association report, appearing in the issue of the A. M. A. Journal, out today, said hypnosis "has a recognized place" in the medical armory. It is applicable to use by surgeons.

Continued on Page 23, Column 2

IN CAPITAL FOR SPEECH: President Eisenhower follows two of his grandchildren, Barbara Anne, left, and Susan, down the ramp of Columbine III on his arrival from Newport, R. I. Behind the President are Capt. E. P. Aurand, his naval aide, and George E. Allen, a friend.
Associated Press Wirephoto

PRESIDENT SAYS NATION MUST FIGHT IF NECESSARY TO BAR QUEMOY FALL; SEES NO WAR; URGES NEGOTIATIONS

NO 'APPEASEMENT'

Eisenhower Asserts Situation Is Serious but Not Hopeless

Text of Eisenhower's speech will be found on Page 2.

By JAMES RESTON
Special to The New York Times.

WASHINGTON, Sept. 11—President Eisenhower told the American people tonight that he must fight, if need be, to prevent any conquest of the Quemoy and Matsu islands by Communist China.

In a nation-wide radio and television address from the White House the President emphasized that it would be "appeasement," probably leading to a major war, to allow the Chinese Communists to overwhelm the Chinese Nationalists, now under heavy shelling on the islands close to the China mainland.

"I do not believe," the President said, "that the United States can be lured or frightened into appeasement. I believe that in taking the position of opposing aggression by force, I am taking the only position which is consistent with the vital interests of the United States, and, indeed, with the peace of the world."

Dangers Stressed

While the President urged a solution of the crisis by negotiation, the general impression created by his speech was that General Eisenhower had emphasized, even more than Secretary of State Dulles did Tuesday at his news conference, the military dangers of the present situation.

The President described the present situation in the Taiwan Strait, where United States warships are convoying supplies for the Nationalists under the guns of the Communists from Taiwan to Quemoy, as "serious" but "by no means desperate or hopeless."

He insisted that "there is not going to be any appeasement" but he urged "negotiations" with the Chinese Communists on terms which he did not define. At the same time, he expressed his opinion that "there is not going to be any war."

Crisis Likened to 1939

The main thrust of the President's analysis of the Far Eastern crisis was as follows:

¶The nation faced a situation today very much like the crisis in Europe in the years immediately preceding the outbreak of the second World War in 1939.

¶Then, as now, the free nations were being tested by aggressive forces that sought to achieve their political objectives by force of arms.

¶"Appeasement" led to war then and would do so again. If the United States made concessions to the Chinese Communists now, as the Western democracies made concessions to Hitler

Continued on Page 2, Column 3

U. N. CHIEF URGES ARMS LIMIT TALKS

Hammarskjold Report Asks Study by Experts—Pact on Outer Space Sought

Text of introduction to report appears on Page 6.

By LINDESAY PARROTT
Special to The New York Times.

UNITED NATIONS, N. Y., Sept. 11—Secretary General Dag Hammarskjold suggested today a new approach to the disarmament problem: a series of talks among international scientific, military and legal experts.

In the introduction to his annual report to the General Assembly, made public here, he suggested that such "marginal" treatment of the main issue might serve at least to "improve the atmosphere and clarify many of the problems involved," thus preparing the ground for general discussions at a more propitious time.

The Secretary General coupled the proposals with an expression of hope that the Assembly, opening next Tuesday, might "move ahead" toward the internationalization of outer space. Such action by the United Nations already has been proposed by various delegates, among them Sir Leslie Munro of New Zealand, president of last year's Assembly.

Mr. Hammarskjold's report said that the eighty-one member countries might lay down the "basic rule that outer space and the celestial bodies therein are not considered as capable of appropriation by any state" and include "an assertion of the overriding interest of the community of nations in the peaceful and beneficial use of outer space."

"Such steps," he added, "would help to provide a basis for the future development in international cooperation of the use of outer space for the benefit of all."

The Secretary General's introduction, as in previous years, covered generally the fields of activity in which the United Nations had been active during the last twelve months.

Mr. Hammarskjold suggested the Assembly three other major reports, to be delivered during the forthcoming session.

Continued on Page 6, Column 5

India and Pakistan Ease Frontier Rift

By ELIE ABEL
Special to The New York Times.

NEW DELHI, India, Sept. 11—Pakistan and India have decided to exchange several small strips of land along the disputed eastern frontier "with a view to removing causes of tension."

A joint communiqué issued this evening has deliberately vague on the terms of an agreement worked out between the Prime Ministers of the two countries during their talks here yesterday and the day before. In fact the two leaders, Jawaharlal Nehru of India and Malik Firoz Khan Noon, agreed to very little more than a first step in the difficult and piece-meal process of drawing more natural boundaries between the countries.

The important thing, officials on both sides emphasize, is not the length of the stride but the

Continued on Page 9, Column 4

Columbia Named America's Cup Defender

Sears Sloop Outsails Vim and Will Race Britain's Sceptre

By JOSEPH M. SHEEHAN
Special to The New York Times.

NEWPORT, R. I., Sept. 11—Columbia, hailed as a yacht of destiny from the planning-board stage, earned the right today to pursue that destiny to the supreme goal.

The resplendent new 12-Meter sloop built to Olin Stephens' design for a six-man New York Yacht Club syndicate headed by Henry Sears of Greenwich, Conn., was named tonight as the seventeenth defender of the historic America's Cup.

With her nomination, she now is free to channel all her impressive energy into a relentless drive for her main objective.

That is to extend the stay on these shores of international yacht racing's most cherished prize, captured off England in 1851 by the schooner America.

In the first match since 1937 for the ornate $500 bottomless silver pitcher in pursuit of which millions have been spent, the American 12-Meter champion will oppose Britain's Royal Yacht Squadron challenger, Sceptre.

Ten miles to sea off here starting Sept. 20, those swift, stately seventy-foot, racing sloops will match speed of hull, soundness of equipment and skill of crew in a series that

Columbia, with right-of-way, forces Vim (foreground) to alter course to avoid a crash
Associated Press Wirephoto

will continue until one yacht has won four times.

Columbia's selection was announced some two hours after

Briggs Cunningham had guided her through champy Atlantic seas in a brisk northwesterly breeze to a thrilling twelve-

second victory over her sprightly nineteen - year - old sister sloop.

Continued on Page 30, Column 2

Gigi, starring Hermione Gingold, Louis Jourdan, Leslie Caron and Maurice Chevalier, was the winner of Academy Awards for best picture, direction, art direction, color, costumes, editing, scoring, song, and screenplay.

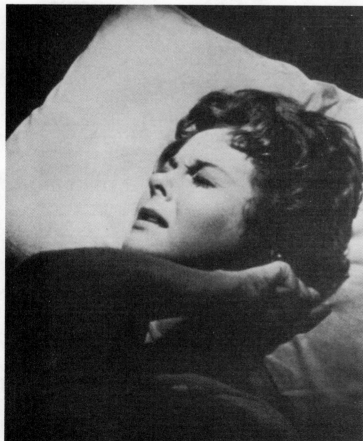

Susan Hayward in a dramatic scene from I Want to Live.

Although Elvis Presley was drafted by the U.S. Army during the filming of King Creole, which was based on Harold Robbins' A Stone for Danny Fisher, he was permitted to finish making the film.

"All the News That's Fit to Print"

The New York Times.

LATE CITY EDITION

U. S. Weather Bureau Report (Page 65) forecasts: Fair and warm today; mostly fair, mild tonight. Cloudy tomorrow. Temp. range: 75—60. Yesterday: 77.1—61.9.

VOL. CVIII . No. 36,767. © 1958, by The New York Times Company, Times Square, New York 36. N. Y. NEW YORK, TUESDAY, SEPTEMBER 23, 1958. 10c beyond 100-mile zone from New York City. Higher in air delivery cities. FIVE CENTS

SHERMAN ADAMS RESIGNS; SEES 'VILIFICATION' DRIVE; PRESIDENT VOICES SADNESS

Associated Press Wirephoto

CONFERENCE IN NEWPORT: President Eisenhower accompanies Sherman Adams to helicopter after talk at summer White House. The Assistant to the President had flown there early yesterday to confer on his resignation.

AIDE GOES ON TV

Tells Nation He Was Innocent of Wrong in Goldfine Case

Texts of Adams speech and President's letter, Page 18.

By RUSSELL BAKER
Special to The New York Times.

WASHINGTON, Sept. 22—Sherman Adams resigned his White House post today under heavy political pressure.

Mr. Adams, the Assistant to the President since early 1953, told a national radio and television audience that the decision had been forced upon him through a "campaign of vilification" calculated to destroy him and embarrass President Eisenhower and his Administration.

Rather than let this happen and endanger Republican chances for gaining control of Congress this November, Mr. Adams said, he decided to quit.

Resignation Accepted

President Eisenhower accepted the Adams resignation "with sadness." A letter from him to Mr. Adams was made public as the staff chief began speaking to the radio-TV audience.

In it the President deplored "the circumstances that have decided you to resign." Mr. Adams, he went on, showed "selfless and tireless devotion" to his White House job.

"Your total dedication to the nation's welfare," he wrote, "has been of the highest possible order."

The President called Mr. Adams' five-and-a-half-year performance in the White House "brilliant" and "unselfish."

"You will be sorely missed," he added.

Adams Defends Record

In his speech, Mr. Adams depicted himself as the innocent victim of elements—only partly identified—engaged in a "calculated and contrived effort" to discredit him.

Although he and the President earlier this year had both conceded that there might have been imprudence in his relationship with the New England textile magnate, Bernard Goldfine, Mr. Adams made no such concession tonight.

"I have done no wrong," he said.

He insisted that his own testimony and that of "every re-

Continued on Page 18, Column 5

U. S. SAYS PEIPING IS 'SHOOTING' AWAY TAIWAN SOLUTION

Holds Red China's Attacks on Offshore Island Bar Entry as U. N. Member

GROMYKO IN NEW THREAT

Asserts Washington Must Stop 'Playing With Fire' Before It Is Too Late

By THOMAS J. HAMILTON
Special to The New York Times.

UNITED NATIONS, N. Y., Sept. 22—The United States charged today that the Chinese Communists were "rapidly shooting themselves and shooting the world" out of a chance to settle the situation in the Taiwan Strait "as it should be settled."

Henry Cabot Lodge, United States representative, told the General Assembly that Communist China's bombardment of the offshore islands was "a further disqualification" for United Nations membership.

He added that "it would justify the United Nations in taking strong steps against that kind of behavior."

Andrei A. Gromyko, Soviet Foreign Minister, again demanded the withdrawal of United States forces from Taiwan and the area of Taiwan Strait.

Danger Is Stressed

"It remains only to hope that the United States Government will be able to correctly understand and duly evaluate this position of China and that it will cease playing with fire in the Far East, while it is not too late," he warned.

Officially, the Assembly was merely debating whether to place on its agenda the question of China's representation in the United Nations—in other words, whether the Peiping Government should take over China's seat from the Nationalist Government.

Some delegates hoped that the statements by Mr. Lodge and Mr. Gromyko would throw light on the possibility for a settlement of the entire problem of the Taiwan area.

Lodge Shields U. S. Terms

However, Mr. Lodge did not give any indication of the terms the United States was seeking in its negotiations with Communist China in Warsaw. Authoritative sources said the United States still hoped that these negotiations would result in a cease-fire.

Mr. Gromyko, who did not refer to the Warsaw negotiations in his speech last week, mentioned them today only as evidence that the United States itself "has been compelled to

Continued on Page 3, Column 1

U.N. Votes 61-10 to Debate Hungarian Killing of Nagy

Assembly Overrides Soviet's Protests —Budapest Minister Says Discussion Till 'Doomsday' Won't Alter Things

By KATHLEEN TELTSCH
Special to The New York Times.

UNITED NATIONS, N. Y., Sept. 22—The General Assembly voted over Soviet protests today to have a full airing of the situation in Hungary at its current session. The vote was 61 to 10, with 10 countries abstaining.

The Assembly decision opened the way for a debate on Communist Hungary's executions last June of former Premier Imre Nagy, Gen. Pal Maleter and others who led the 1956 revolt.

Only Yugoslavia sided with the nine Soviet bloc members in opposing inclusion of the item on Hungary in the agenda. The ten abstaining countries were India, Indonesia, Ir- , Nepal, Saudi Arabia, Finland, Ceylon, Yemen, Afghanistan and the United Arab Republic.

Yugoslavia's vote occasioned some interest, since Belgrade had protested strongly when former Premier Nagy was induced to leave asylum in the Yugoslav Embassy only to be arrested, tried in secret and executed.

However, Dobrivoje Vidic, a Yugoslav delegate, told the Assembly after the roll-call vote that his country felt that the Hungarian item would produce only a pointless debate that would not reduce world tensions. Ceylon expressed similar sentiments.

Inclusion of the Hungarian item was voted after another exchange of charges between United States and Soviet spokesman, typical of the harsh words used whenever the Hungarian

Continued on Page 6, Column 3

No Decision on Cease-Fire, New Warsaw Meeting Set

By A. M. ROSENTHAL
Special to The New York Times.

WARSAW, Sept. 22—United States and Chinese Communist diplomats held another negotiating session today without reaching any decision on fixing a cease-fire in the Strait of Taiwan. However, the talks have not reached the stage where either side is ready to suspend them as a lost cause. The negotiators met for an hour and forty-five minutes during the afternoon and will meet again Thursday.

The timing of the meetings illustrates the fact that the two Ambassadors, Jack D. Beam of the United States and Wang Ping-nan of Communist China, are getting every statement, every reply and every move approved in advance by their governments. Between each meeting there has been a gap of at least two days to allow for the transmission of fresh instructions.

Red Chinese Called Firm

Communist sources in this capital say the Chinese Communists remain determined not to agree to a cease-fire without winning tangible political benefits such as recognition of their right to take part in some great power consultations.

As the Chinese Communists have been telling it to their friends, this is a dispute that has the United States in a political corner. The Chinese Communists are said to believe that the United States is under pressure from its allies to reach

Continued on Page 5, Column 5

TAIWAN BIDS U. S. BACK AIR ATTACK

Chiang Said to Ask Approval for Raiding Red Guns— Effectiveness Doubted

By ROBERT TRUMBULL
Special to The New York Times.

TAIPEI, Taiwan, Tuesday, Sept. 23—Chinese Nationalist leaders conferring here with United States military commanders were reported yesterday to have argued for United States acquiescence in a Nationalist air attack on Communist coastal guns blockading Quemoy Island.

The same subject is expected to come up again today when Admiral Harry D. Felt, commander in chief of United States forces in the Pacific, meets with President Chiang Kai-shek.

[Admiral Felt and Generalissimo Chiang met later in the day, The Associated Press reported.]

Meets Military Chiefs

Yesterday Admiral Felt discussed the Taiwan Strait crisis with Vice President and Premier Chen Cheng and chiefs of the Nationalist armed services.

Gen. Laurence S. Kuter, commander of United States Air Forces in the Pacific, and Vice Admiral Roland N. Smoot, head of the newly reconstituted Taiwan Defense Command, also represented the United States side.

At least some United States authorities here doubt that the effectiveness of Nationalist air strikes against the heavily fortified and concealed Communist batteries would warrant the risks involved in possibly en-

Continued on Page 3, Column 3

GOV. COLLINS ASKS U.S.-STATE BOARDS FOR INTEGRATION

Tells Southern Governors Congress Should Move Quickly on Problem

By CLAUDE SITTON
Special to The New York Times.

LEXINGTON, Ky., Sept. 22—Gov. LeRoy Collins announced today a plan to speed school integration where feasible and protect against "improvident, forced desegregation."

The Florida Governor said legislation in this field should be "the first item of business" when Congress convened in January.

He suggested that one solution might be state desegregation commissions appointed by the President with the advice and concurrence of the Governors.

The commissions would be empowered to work with Federal District Courts in determining the pace of desegregation.

Key Southern Moderate

Mr. Collins, a leader among Southern moderates, is chairman of both the Southern and National Governors Conferences.

[In Little Rock, Ark., teachers conducted classes on television for students of the city's four high schools, closed to prevent integration.

[In Charlottesville, Va., two rival groups of parents prepared to establish temporary classes for students of schools closed under the state's massive resistance laws.

[In Washington, the integration dispute spurred a new anti-filibuster drive among Senators.]

Seeks New Approach

Asked whether he thought a school integration proposal should come from President Eisenhower, Governor Collins, a Democrat, replied:

"I haven't seen any initiative asserted from the White House for a new approach to a constructive solution. I sincerely hope there will be."

Governor Collins announced his plan in opening remarks at a three-day session of the Southern Governors. Later he discussed it with newsmen.

He said that he would ask the executive committee of the national organization to set up a planning session on the problem to include Governors, Congressional leaders and President Eisenhower or his representative.

The committee's next scheduled meeting will not be held until December, but Mr. Collins said that he was considering a special session because of the desegregation emergency.

The Florida Governor ignored tradition in bringing the prob-

Continued on Page 26, Column 7

CITY HALL AWAITS PUBLIC REACTION TO OFF-TRACK TAX

But Mayor Stresses Need for Funds—Talk of Sales Levy Rise 'Very General'

By CHARLES G. BENNETT

Whether the city administration will seek a tax on off-track betting on horse races is likely to depend in part on the public's reaction to the proposal.

Mayor Wagner indicated this in an interview at City Hall yesterday, discussing the city's probable need for $80,000,000 to $100,000,000 in additional funds in the fiscal year beginning July 1, 1959.

The Mayor suggested the possibility of an off-track betting tax at an executive session of the Board of Estimate last Friday, at which city finances were discussed.

The Sales Tax Question

At that meeting there was talk of a possible increase in the retail sales tax to 4 per cent from the present 3 per cent. Mayor Wagner emphasized yesterday that the board's entire discussion of possible new taxes had been "very general."

As to his personal view of an off-track betting tax, Mayor Wagner said he would withhold an opinion "until all of the facts for and against are in."

He added that he did not believe the betting levy would require a time-consuming state constitutional amendment, but could be authorized by state law. He also felt that "such a law would probably be passed" if the city asked for it.

Only one member of the Board of Estimate immediately expressed complete support of an off-track betting tax. Bronx Borough President James J. Lyons called the suggestion "a very excellent idea." He said it was a "mockery" to be able to bet at the track when it was "illegal to bet on the other side of the fence."

Others Are Noncommittal

Other members of the board were non-committal. City Council President Abe Stark said he had ordered an "independent study" of the question and would give his opinion when the study was finished.

John W. Hanes, president of the New York Racing Association, Inc., which operates the state thoroughbred racing tracks, said he would not comment on the city's tentative proposal to legalize and tax off-track betting until he had seen an operational plan.

The Board of Estimate's discussion Friday was described as the first of several meetings that will be necessary to prepare a city 1959-60 fiscal program for submission to the state Legislature next January. At

Continued on Page 24, Column 5

Birth Control Rule Says 2 Physicians Must Certify Need

By PETER KIHSS

The Department of Hospitals specified yesterday that two physicians would have to certify the need before birth control therapy could be given in any case.

Written consent of the woman involved, and if possible her husband, is also to be required. Instructions sent to the twenty-eight municipal hospitals further said the patient should be "advised to consult with her spiritual adviser" and family.

The new requirements were immediately labeled "strange" and "unique and superfluous" by Dr. Alan F. Guttmacher, chairman of the medical committee of the Planned Parenthood Federation of America.

Guttmacher Gives View

Dr. Guttmacher, who is also director of obstetrics and gynecology at Mount Sinai Hospital, said the new policy "puts the simple procedure of giving contraceptive advice in precisely the same rigid category as the much more formidable one of therapeutic abortion."

He expressed fear it "will create in the minds of decent and well-meaning patients the thought that they are doing something wrong if they accept contraception."

The Board of Hospitals saw nothing wrong in such treatment, he said.

The instructions were signed by Dr. Morris A. Jacobs, Commissioner of Hospitals, and Dr. Henry W. Kolbe, director of the bureau of medical and hospital services. The memorandum was the department's first move to carry out a policy voted by the Board of Hospitals last Wednes-

Continued on Page 30, Column 2

REPUBLICANS SEE GOVERNMENT LOSS

Nixon and Alcorn Extol Aide —Others Say Resignation Is for Good of Party

By United Press International.

WASHINGTON, Sept. 22—Top Republicans, led by Vice President Richard M. Nixon, called the resignation of Sherman Adams tonight a tragic loss to the Government.

In Mr. Adams' six years in the White House post he "established a standard of hard work and dedicated public service that few men in the nation's history have equaled," Mr. Nixon said.

"Because to do his job well he had to say no more often than yes, he has his share of critics," the Vice President asserted.

Meade Alcorn, G. O. P. national chairman, said "the nation is losing the services of the most talented, dedicated and conscientious man who ever served on a White House staff."

Simpson Backs Move

However, another high Republican said the resignation was the only step possible for the good of the party.

Representative Richard H. Simpson, chairman of the House G. O. P. Campaign Committee, declared that Mr. Adams "should have resigned earlier."

Democrats disputed Mr. Adams' contention that testimony before House influence investigators had proved that he had not sought favors for friends from Government agencies.

Representative John E. Moss, a member of the investigating subcommittee, said "it was my impression that the evidence

Continued on Page 18, Column 1

Van Buren Peaceful as Negroes Return to School

Associated Press Wirephoto

Three of the eight Negro students who returned to Van Buren High School enter building

Special to The New York Times.

VAN BUREN, Ark., Sept. 22—Eight Negro students returned today to Van Buren High School. Threats of a walkout by white students were not carried out. There were only minor taunts and hard looks as the Negroes went to school for the first time in more than two weeks. Four Negro students eligible to return failed to appear. At the near-by junior high school, three of five enrolled Negroes returned to class without incident. The return followed a Federal court order putting the community and its school board on their honor to restore integration. Federal Judge John E. Miller,

Continued on Page 27, Column 7

BEIRUT SEETHING ON EVE OF CHANGE

Chehab Takes Office Today —Shooting Erupts in City

By SAM POPE BREWER
Special to The New York Times.

BEIRUT, Lebanon, Sept. 22—Beirut, now living under an around-the-clock curfew that went into effect yesterday, was virtually a dead city today, except for feverish defense preparations being made in some sectors.

Only officials, diplomats and newspapermen could move about town as the Administration of President Camille Chamoun came to an end and preparations were made to inaugurate Gen. Fouad Chehab tomorrow as the new President.

[Shooting broke out in Beirut Monday night, The Associated Press said. Two persons were reported killed.]

The whole atmosphere of revolution, which had died down gradually since Parliament elected General Chehab July 31, has flamed up again. The immediate cause of tension was the kidnapping Friday of Fouad Haddad, an outspoken political commentator of a Christian newspaper here.

His disappearance is generally attributed to a biting article published in his paper that parodied the political speeches

Continued on Page 8, Column 3

Read S. & H. Green Stamps Message in Saturday Review. It's Important. Advt.

Israel Getting Arms From U.S. and Allies

By DANA ADAMS SCHMIDT
Special to The New York Times.

WASHINGTON, Sept. 22—Israel is beginning to receive a small but steady flow of weapons from Britain, France and the United States.

The Israeli Government is highly pleased, according to diplomatic informants, by the effect of its recent campaign to convince the Western capitals that Israel is entitled to a "deterrent" to the growing military strength of the United Arab Republic and its allies. This campaign followed the Iraqi revolution of July 14.

The smallest part of the flow of supplies to Israel is coming from the United States. Washington has made it unequivocally clear that the United States has never been, and is not now, a major supplier of arms to Israel.

This was specified by the

Continued on Page 9, Column 1

Mary Roberts Rinehart Is Dead; Author of Mysteries and Plays

Mrs. Mary Roberts Rinehart, the novelist, died in her sleep last night in her apartment at 635 Park Avenue. She was 82 years old and had been suffering from a heart ailment.

Ghosts and shadows, and strange night noises haunted Mrs. Rinehart from childhood. There was a touch of the unearthly in some of her mystery novels. But her literary distinction lies in the combination of love, humor and murder that she wove into tales. She helped the crime story to grow up, and earned a fortune on the way.

When she was 75, it was estimated that her books had sold more than 10,000,000 copies in regular editions and in thirteen translations. She had averaged a book a year for more than forty years.

Novels, humorous stories, plays and articles—her output was varied as well as tremendous. It was not easy, Mrs. Rinehart admitted.

"There is frightful discipline," she explained. "Writing is the hardest work in the world."

But whatever the effort entailed, she always placed her home and family interests first, and thought of herself as "fiercely a mother."

In later years, her three sons grown, her fortunes high, she had an eighteen-room apartment on Park Avenue furnished in rare Chinese Chippendale, Adams chairs and English portraits. She spent four months a year in Florida and Bar Harbor, Me. But during the other eight, she went to her desk every morning, pen in hand, as diligently as when she first turned to writing to rescue the family finances.

She was born in modest cir-

Continued on Page 33, Column 2

FOR everything in MUSIC G. Schirmer Inc., 3 E. 43d. MU 2-8100—Adv.

5 HOURS OF SCHOOL GIVEN ON TV HERE

State Starts Program Aimed at Classes and Homes

By LEONARD BUDER

Full-scale educational television became a reality here yesterday. Five hours and twenty minutes of special programs were beamed to schools and homes in the metropolitan area.

The programs—ranging from a Spanish lesson for elementary school pupils to a mathematics course for teachers—were presented by the State Education Department in cooperation with school systems in the area.

A total of twenty-eight hours and twenty minutes of telecasts will be provided this week and again next week. Beginning Oct. 6, and continuing to next June, about thirty-five hours will be offered weekly.

The project utilized the leased facilities and air time of WPIX (Channel 11). The programs can be received within a 100-mile radius of the station's transmitter in mid-Manhattan. About 60 per cent of the state's school children live in the area covered.

Schools in the city and the suburbs picked up the programs. Those with portable receivers generally arranged to have the sets moved from class to class to fit the offerings. Other schools, with fixed receivers, rescheduled classes so

Continued on Page 35, Column 4

1958

Peter Gunn, *a stylish private eye series, featured outstanding jazz theme music by Henry Mancini and starred Craig Stevens (in the title role), Lola Albright and Herschel Bernardi.*

Chuck Connors was The Rifleman *and Johnny Crawford played his son in this popular western series which aired for six seasons.*

The Thin Man, *a creation of Dashiell Hammett, was a sophisticated detective series based on the adventures of Nick and Nora Charles and their dog, Asta. Peter Lawford and Phyllis Kirk were the stars of the show.*

Althea Gibson is shown here in the 1958 Wimbledon finals where she defeated Angela Mortimer of England, 8-6 and 6-2.

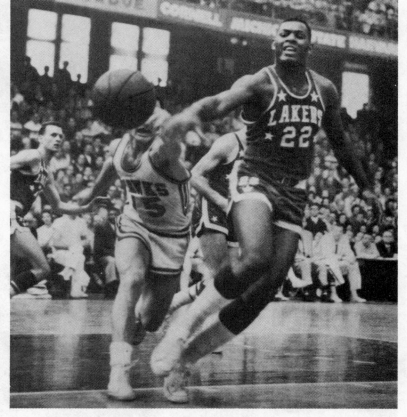

This great NBA forward, Elgin Baylor, joined the Lakers in 1958. He is seen here at the beginning of his career in a game against St. Louis.

George Romney gambled with the future prosperity of American Motors by developing and marketing the Rambler. By the end of the year the company's profits increased in accordance with the public's acceptance of the smaller car.

"All the News That's Fit to Print"

The New York Times.

LATE CITY EDITION
U. S. Weather Bureau Report (Page 73) forecast:
Partly cloudy and mild today and tomorrow.
Temp. range: 72—59. Yesterday: 68.5—52.5.

VOL. CVIII..No. 36,783.   © 1958 by The New York Times Company. Times Square, New York 36, N. Y.   NEW YORK, THURSDAY, OCTOBER 9, 1958.   10c beyond 100-mile zone from New York City. Higher in air delivery cities.   FIVE CENTS

YANKEES WIN, 4-3, IN TENTH AND TIE BRAVES IN SERIES

McDougald's Homer Ignites 2-Run Rally and Starts Spahn to Defeat

DUREN VICTOR IN RELIEF

But Turley Collects Final Out After Losers Score and Get Two Men On

By JOHN DREBINGER
Special to The New York Times.

MILWAUKEE, Oct. 8.—The Yankees kept going today in the 1958 world series. They did it by bringing down the Braves in ten innings to win the sixth game, 4 to 3.

Thus the Yankees, who only a few days ago trailed at three games to one, now are all square, with the seventh and deciding encounter coming up tomorrow.

Gil McDougald, with a home run in the tenth inning, brought to an end a heroic effort by the Milwaukee southpaw, Warren Spahn, to gain his third straight triumph of the series.

The blow broke a 2-all tie. In its wake the Bombers completed the rout of Spahn with singles by Elston Howard and Yogi Berra, a second tally coming home as Bill Skowron greeted the incoming Don McMahon with a single.

Braves Fight Back

The Yanks were ahead, 4—2, but the show was far from over for the crowd of 46,367. The Braves kicked up an uproar in the last of the tenth that just missed plunging the battle into another deadlock.

They routed Ryne Duren, whose blinding fast ball had baffled them in the four previous innings. They pushed across a run and got the tying run to third, with still another runner on first. But Casey Stengel, pulling out all the stops to maintain what was left of his firs lead, called on his other fireballing ace, Bob Turley.

Bullet Bob, who on Monday in New York had kept the Bombers in contention by winning the fifth game with a shutout, faced Frank Torre, a left-handed pinch hitter.

Torre sent a soft fly toward right and it looked every inch a single.

But McDougald, the Yankee second baseman and the hero apparent because of his homer, tore back on the grass. He leaped high in the air and pulled down the ball, which suddenly

Continued on Page 51, Column 5

MAN IN A BALLOON GIVES SPACE DATA

But Descends Prematurely After Going Up 19 Miles

By The Associated Press

ALAMOGORDO, N. M., Oct. 8—An Air Force balloon exploring the fringe of space returned to earth early tonight after it had carried its pilot, Lieut. Clifton McClure 3d, to 99,600 feet.

The balloon, launched today, began an unexpected and unexplained descent late this afternoon. A spokesman at Holloman Air Force Base said "it must be an emergency or they wouldn't be bringing him down."

The balloon landed on the desert ranges west of here, near the San Andres Mountains about thirty miles away.

The Air Force sent a helicopter to the site of the landing to pick up the pilot and the instruments the gondola carried to the stratosphere.

[Failure of the cooling system forced the balloon down, United Press International reported. Lieutenant McClure walked out of the gondola and was taken to an Air Force hospital for a physical examination.]

At 11:05 A. M. Mountain standard time (2:05 P. M., New York time) the balloon reached an altitude of 99,600 feet—just 400 feet short of the planned facilities. The balloon was launched at 6:50 A. M.

Lieutenant McClure started his descent about 4 P. M.

During his flight the 25-year-old jet pilot, who became a

Continued on Page 8, Column 3

Final Registration Is Starting Today

By LEO EGAN

The final registration period for this year's election starts today in New York City and Nassau and Westchester Counties. It will continue tomorrow and end on Saturday.

Democratic and Republican party officials are making strenuous efforts to persuade potential voters who have not registered yet to do so. Only those who have registered by Saturday night will be permitted to vote.

Those who registered for last year's municipal elections in New York City and Westchester are automatically registered for this year unless they have moved outside of their election districts. All others are required by law to register to qualify as voters.

In New York City 4,613

Continued on Page 31, Column 5

FAUBUS EXPANDS SCHOOL FUND PLEA

Letters With Seal of State Going Throughout Nation in Bid for Donations

Special to The New York Times.

LITTLE ROCK, Oct. 8—Gov. Orval E. Faubus opened a nation-wide appeal today for funds to help educate Little Rock's teen-agers in a system of private high schools.

The Governor said copies of a letter appealing for contributions would be mailed to persons who had written him pledging their support in his fight against school integration.

The letters will go out on official stationery bearing the official seal of the state. They will be signed by Governor Faubus and by Dr. T. J. Raney, president of the Little Rock Private School Corporation.

For the last ten days the corporation has been accepting donations for the operations of private high schools for Little Rock's white students.

No Date Announced

The corporation has not announced an opening date for its schools, although Dr. Raney has promised it would begin operation "as soon as we can get things rolling." The classes would be held in donated buildings.

Governor Faubus revealed the contents of his appeal letter in which he said donations would benefit "all freedom-loving citizens of this nation."

He said thousands of the letters would be printed. An extra staff of thirteen stenographers was at work filing addresses gleaned from the mail received by the Governor this fall. A secretary said there were between 20,000 and 30,000 pieces of mail and telegrams.

"If the state is going to discontinue public education in these localities," he added, "it must be a complete abandonment and not a pretext."

Judge Paul's decision was based on the doctrine—re-emphasized by the Supreme Court in its Little Rock opinion last week—that no institution that

Continued on Page 26, Column 5

The Governor's Letter

The appeal letter said:

"The plan set up by action of the extraordinary session of the General Assembly provided for the use of state funds, to be allocated on a per-student basis, for the student's education in whatever school he chose to attend.

"At the request of the N. A. A. C. P. (National Association for the Advancement of Colored People) and the Justice Department, the Federal courts have enjoined all public officials, including school teachers, from using the state funds, as provided by law.

"The acts have been challenged in the courts of the state, where they have already been upheld as constitutional. At the present time the schools are closed through the injunctive process of the Federal courts.

"For this reason it appears necessary that the Little Rock Private School Corporation should proceed with its plan to set up private schools in private facilities, to be operated by private funds.

"It is urgent that the students re-enter school at the earliest possible date. We would, therefore, appreciate your assistance in providing contributions to

Continued on Page 26, Column 6

'PRIVATE' CLASSES DIRECTED TO STOP USING VIRGINIA AID

U.S. Judge Paul Says White Units Must Drop Public Teachers or Integrate

By ANTHONY LEWIS
Special to The New York Times.

HARRISONBURG, Va., Oct. 8—Federal District Judge John Paul ruled today that "private" classes set up to replace closed Virginia schools must stop using public funds and teachers or else end segregation themselves.

"It is the opinion of the court," Judge Paul said, "that these so-called private schools are an obvious evasion of the mandate of the Supreme Court."

His order affects Charlottesville, where 1,700 children have been shut out of a high school and an elementary school, and Warren County, where 1,000 students are out of the county's only high school.

A state anti-integration law requires the closing of any public school where white and Negro children are enrolled.

Court to Rule on Norfolk

About 10,000 children are out of school in Norfolk. Judge Walter E. Hoffman will consider that case on Friday of this week.

In Charlottesville, public school teachers have been giving classes in private homes and churches and lodge halls. A similar plan for Warren County is scheduled to start tomorrow.

Attorneys of the National Association for the Advancement of Colored People asked Judge Paul in effect to make the two school boards reopen their schools. This was the burden of "motions for further relief" that they filed in the two cases.

Judge Paul said he did not think he had the right to direct the reopening of schools. He noted particularly that a suit to test the school closing law has been filed by state authorities in the Virginia Supreme Court of Appeals, and said he recognized the "propriety" of letting the issue be fought out there.

Asks State's Good Faith

But the judge said the state authorities, if they are in good faith, should not try to enforce the challenged acts until the results of the legal test are in.

"The state is not pursuing that course," he said. "It has closed these schools, and it is continuing to assist education in what are called private schools but are really public. All that has happened is that they've closed the school buildings but are continuing to operate the schools in other buildings.

Continued on Page 27, Column 1

U. S. ORDERS HALT IN QUEMOY ESCORT

Set to Resume Operations if Reds End Cease-Fire— Chiang Was Consulted

By E. W. KENWORTHY
Special to The New York Times.

WASHINGTON, Oct. 8—The United States announced today that its naval vessels in the Taiwan Strait had stopped escorting Chinese Nationalist convoys supplying Quemoy.

At the same time the United States made clear that it would resume the escort operations if the Chinese Communists resumed their artillery attacks on the Quemoy group.

Three days ago the Communists announced in a broadcast directed at the Nationalists that the bombardment had been ordered suspended for a week on condition that the United States stopped escorting Nationalist convoys.

Today the State Department said that the escort activity had been undertaken at the request of the Nationalist Government, and had been ordered "to the extent militarily neces-

Continued on Page 7, Column 5

POPE, 82, DIES AFTER 2D STROKE; MILLIONS OFFER THEIR PRAYERS; CARDINALS TO NAME SUCCESSOR

Announcement Of Pope's Death

By United Press International.

CASTEL GANDOLFO, Italy, Thursday, Oct. 9—Following is the official announcement of the death of the Pope:

The Supreme Pontiff, Pope Pius XII, is dead. Pius XII, the most esteemed and venerated man in the world, one of the greatest Pontiffs of the century, with sanctity at 3:52 A. M., Oct. 9, 1958.

Eugenio Pacelli was born March 2, 1876, and elected Pope on March 2, 1939, with the name of Pius XII. He was therefore 32 years 7 months 7 days, and his pontificate was nineteen years 7 months and 7 days.

The Catholic Church and the whole world, for whose profit he spent his brilliant, intellectual energies, his heart and his actions, now gather in mourning around his body and memory, grateful for the immense and valid work he carried out to re-establish among men, children of God, the force of justice, law and peace.

Let the unanimous prayers for the repose of his lofty soul, which today passed into eternal bliss, rise from the hearts of all faithful and the entire Christianity.

COLLEGE IS CALLED

55 Princes of Church Rule Pending Vote in 15 to 18 Days

Special to The New York Times.

ROME, Thursday, Oct. 9—The death of Pope Pius XII today opened the interregnum, or régime of the Holy See's vacancy. It will last until a new Pontiff is elected by the Cardinals in a secret conclave, to be convened not sooner than Oct. 24 or later than Oct. 27.

During the next few weeks the Church will be governed by the Sacred College of Cardinals. As dean of this body, Eugene Cardinal Tisserant immediately instructed the Vatican Secretariat of State to notify all his colleagues that the Apostolic See had become vacant, and to summon them to Rome.

Later today, the French-born, bearded Cardinal, who is 74 years old, is to make the first announcement of the Pope's death to the diplomats accredited to the Holy See and, through them or through apostolic nuncios in world capitals, to heads of state.

Fastest Travel Urged

Fifteen Cardinals were present in or near Rome early this morning. Of these, thirteen are Italians. The other two are Cardinal Tisserant and Gregory Peter XV, Cardinal Agagianian, a Russian-born Armenian who has risen to prominence in the Roman Curia, or central church administration.

Italian Cardinals heading Archdioceses in various parts of the country are due to reach the capital later today. Cardinals outside Italy are expected and indeed requested to come to Rome by the fastest possible means.

With aviation just entering the jet age, it may be foreseen that members of the Sacred College will gather here much quicker than after the death of Pius XI in 1939.

Will Meet Daily

As the "Senate of the Church," the Cardinals will hold a plenary meeting later today and will reconvene every day until they enter the conclave.

One of the first items on the agenda of the Cardinals' meeting later today will be the transfer of Pius XII's body from his death bed at Castel Gandolfo to Rome.

As if he had had a premonition, the late Pontiff in his apostolic constitution of 1945 concerning the vacancy of the Holy See inserted a provision contemplating the possibility of a Pope's death outside Rome. This had not occurred since the end of the eighteenth century. The provision was that the Cardinals must see to it 'that the dead Pontiff is moved to St. Peter's Basilica in Rome in a "decorous and dignified manner."

Some of the powers of the Sacred College will be wielded in its name by the Cardinal Camerlengo, or chamberlain of the church. This dignitary will be elected by the cardinals in their first plenary meeting later today.

Now 55 Cardinals

The Sacred College now has fifty-five members, fifteen short of its full complement of seventy. Fifteen are in Rome. Of the remaining forty will proceed here immediately for the exercise of the college's interim powers.

Most of these men are aged—in their seventies and eighties. Some are behind the Iron Curtain.

Jozsef Cardinal Mindszenty, Primate of Hungary, has been told that he will be allowed to go to Rome, but he has indicated that he probably will not do so, because he fears that the government might not readmit him.

The Cardinal is a refugee in the United States Legation in Budapest.

Others who may not reach Rome are Stefan Cardinal Wyszynski, Primate of Poland, and Aloysius Cardinal Stepinac, Primate of Yugoslavia. Cardinal

Continued on Page 24, Column 5

POPE PIUS XII

Associated Press

City Pays Homage On Receiving News Of Pontiff's Death

The news of the death of Pope Pius XII was received with varying manifestations in the New York area last night.

As the news became known in Times Square, many Roman Catholics paused and then continued on their way. A few inclined their heads briefly as they gave a prayer for the repose of the Pope's soul. Others made the sign of the cross unobtrusively.

Many Catholics entered the nearest Roman Catholic church, some of which had been kept open beyond their usual 10 P. M. closing, aware that the Pope's death was imminent. There, prayers were said and impromptu services were held informally as the communicants offered prayers to the effect that Pope Pius' soul reach Heaven.

Some Churches Reopened

As some of the Catholic churches reopened their doors and their lights streamed out onto the sidewalks, patrolling policemen, many of whom had not heard of the Pope's death, stopped to investigate. Some of them stayed to pray.

Some persons, not all of Catholic faith, felt the hard-to-describe emotion experienced when the news of the death of one of the great world figures comes to them.

The Pope's death found Cardinal Spellman, Archbishop of the Diocese of New York aboard the Greek liner, Olympia, bound for New York from Cannes, France. He had been accompanying a group of 450 Catholics visiting the Holy Places of Europe. He received an audience with the late Pope several days ago.

The Chancery, at 452 Madison Avenue, headquarters of the

Continued on Page 21, Column 4

3 Countries Named To Security Council

By KATHLEEN TELTSCH
Special to The New York Times.

UNITED NATIONS, N. Y., Oct. 8—Italy, Tunisia and Argentina were elected to Security Council membership today. They will fill the vacancies that occur when the terms of Sweden, Iraq and Colombia expire at the end of 1958.

The three new members were elected at a session of the General Assembly. The voting by secret ballot was a formality since the three nations were unchallenged candidates.

The six nonpermanent seats on the Council are traditionally allotted to nations of six broad geographic areas. The latest in this connection the six exceptions, the latest in the United States Legation in 1957, when Japan was elected to

Continued on Page 14, Column 5

ROME HEARS TOLL OF BELLS FOR PIUS

Some Citizens in Prayer Before St. Peter's Basilica as End Is Announced

By PAUL HOFMANN
Special to The New York Times.

ROME, Thursday, Oct. 9—When Rome's many church bells started tolling before dawn today to announce the death of Pius XII, a great number of persons were still praying in St. Peter's Square and in the city's churches that had remained open all night.

They had remained from the throngs gathered yesterday at the Square and at the churches. Some crossed themselves at the announcement and fell to their knees to pray for the dead Pontiff's soul. Many were tearful. One elderly woman was heard to exclaim, "A saint has left us."

Attention Concentrated

At midnight thousands had still been thronging in front of St. Peter's Basilica. Among them were a group of pilgrims who had come from Germany in a dozen buses.

Although the streets and open squares of Rome had gradually emptied about 2 A. M., many Romans stayed up at their homes to follow transmissions of the Vatican radio from Castel Gandolfo.

Listeners said they were deeply impressed and moved by the post-midnight mass said at the dying Pope's bedside by one of his former closest aides, Archbishop Domenico Tardini. The homely Roman accent with which the popular prelate church recited his Latin for once sounded solemn and grave as he recited the prayers of the dying.

After the end of the mass, the Vatican radio urged listeners to keep their sets tuned in and to pray for the Pontiff while waiting that "God's will be done."

The announcement to Rome of Pius XII's death was made in a brief bulletin by the Vatican radio at 3:56 A. M. (10:56 P. M., Wednesday, New York time.) Sacred music followed.

Pilgrims at Castel Gandolfo

CASTEL GANDOLFO, Italy, Oct. 8—Thousands of Romans and pilgrims gathered in this hill town today to be near the dying Pope and to pray for him.

With few exceptions they did not object to television cameras, batteries of klieg lights and clusters of newsmen in the narrow piazza in front of the pontifical palace.

The paraphernalia would have caused Pope Pius XII himself to smile indulgently and understandingly, a reporter told an officer when the Italian police attempted to clear part of

Continued on Page 24, Column 8

PONTIFF 19 YEARS

End Comes Quietly in Papal Bedroom at Summer Palace

By ARNALDO CORTESI
Special to The New York Times.

CASTEL GANDOLFO, Italy, Thursday, Oct. 9—Pope Pius XII, the 260th successor of the Apostle Peter on the Pontifical throne of Rome, died at 3:52 A. M. today (10:52 P. M., New York time, Wednesday).

The Pontiff's death came as millions prayed for him throughout the world.

The 82-year-old Pontiff did not regain consciousness after a cerebral stroke he suffered yesterday morning.

It was the second stroke he had suffered in forty-seven hours. The first occurred at 8:30 A. M. Monday and he seemed to be recovering from it.

The second stroke struck him at 7:30 A. M. yesterday. After it the Pope sank gradually until the moment of his death.

Death occurred in a simple and unadorned bedroom on the second floor at the back of the papal palace of Castel Gandolfo.

End Comes Quietly

The Pope was passing the summer there in the cooler atmosphere of the Alban Hills as he had done every year. He had planned to return to the Vatican at the end of November in time for the spiritual exercises before Christmas.

Pius XII had been Pope for nineteen years, seven months and seven days since his elevation to the pontificate March 2, 1939. He was born in Rome March 2, 1876. He was, therefore, elevated to the pontificate on his 63rd birthday and was a week more than 82 years and seven months of age when he died.

Since the Pope had been unconscious for many hours before his death he had left no last words in the generally accepted meaning of this term. The last recorded words that he uttered were: "Play, pray, pray that this unhappy situation for the Church may end."

At the moment of his death Pius XII was completely paralyzed and incapable of any movement. He had been un-

Continued on Page 21, Column 1

WASHINGTON SEES LEBANON SECURE

Plans to Recall All Troops —Karami Said to Quit

By DANA ADAMS SCHMIDT
Special to The New York Times.

WASHINGTON, Oct. 8—United States troops will be "totally withdrawn from Lebanon" by the end of this month, the State Department announced today.

The department said this decision was based on improvement in "international aspects of Lebanon's security situation" and progress toward "more stable international conditions in the area."

[Reports from Beirut said Premier Rashid Karami had resigned after thirty-one of the sixty-six Deputies in Parliament said they would not support him. United States tanks were patrolling Beirut after a disarmed three military policemen.]

State Department officials explained that Lebanon's security situation had improved mainly as a result of the election of a new President and the tapering off of Lebanon also has diminished against Lebanon.

Interference in the life of Lebanon by infiltration of arms and men has apparently ceased, they said. Inflammatory broadcasts against the Government of Lebanon also have diminished, although broadcasts against the Government of Jordan have tapered off only a little, the officials reported.

In this connection the officials

Continued on Page 5, Column 4

President Completes His Staff, Naming Counsel as No. 2 Aide

Gerald D. Morgan   David W. Kendall
Associated Press

By FELIX BELAIR Jr.
Special to The New York Times.

WASHINGTON, Oct. 8—President Eisenhower announced the reorganization of the White House staff today by designating Gerald D. Morgan as No. 2 man in the chain of command. Mr. Morgan, who is 49 years old, has been special counsel to the President since February, 1953. The announcement of the designation of Mr. Morgan was ac-

companied by the appointment of David W. Kendall, Washington attorney, to succeed Mr. Morgan as special counsel.

The promotion of another "old hand" on the White House staff served to emphasize President Eisenhower's continued main reliance on the staff system rather

Continued on Page 41, Column 1

"All the News That's Fit to Print"

The New York Times.

NEWS SUMMARY AND INDEX, PAGE 95

LATE CITY EDITION
U. S. Weather Bureau Report (Page 95) forecasts.
Mostly fair, cool today; fair tonight and tomorrow.
Temp. range: 56—44. Yesterday: 60.0—51.6.

SECTION ONE

VOL. CVIII—No. 36,786.   © 1958, by The New York Times Company.   Times Square. New York 36, N. Y.   NEW YORK, SUNDAY, OCTOBER 12, 1958.   35c outside New York city its suburban area and Long Island. Higher in air delivery cities   TWENTY-FIVE CENTS

DEMOCRATS SHOW LANDSLIDE TREND IN PENNSYLVANIA

Unemployment Issue Aids Leader and Lawrence, Team Survey Indicates

G. O. P. IS DISORGANIZED

Republicans May Lose Ten House Seats—Party Hurt by Shortage of Funds

A Times Team Report

This is a report from a New York Times team that surveyed political sentiment in Pennsylvania. Its members were Wayne Phillips, Edith Asbury, Stanley Levey, Joseph A. Loftus and William G. Weart. Before the elections, New York Times teams will survey other pivotal states.

By WAYNE PHILLIPS
Special to The New York Times.

HARRISBURG, Pa., Oct. 10—The Democrats in Pennsylvania are building up to a victory that could reach landslide proportions.

A team of New York Times reporters visited every corner of the state this week and talked to voters. The team emerged from its survey convinced that the Democrats would win the races for United States Senator and Governor and take at least two of the seventeen Congressional seats now held by Republicans.

The team found a Democratic tide running so strong that it created the possibility of victories in eight other Congressional districts that the Republican party had regarded as safe. This adds up to a potential Democratic gain of ten seats. Nowhere did the reporters find one of the thirteen Democratic Congressional seats in danger of being lost.

Although there is slightly more than three weeks until the election, all team members reported the Democrats running far ahead with the three essentials of a successful political campaign—an issue, an organization and money.

Republicans Lack Issue

The Republicans, they found, have yet to find an issue strong enough to swing many voters. The party is stumbling along with an organization that has apparently become inefficient and inept, and is paralyzed by a lack of contributions.

The team found there is only one issue in Pennsylvania—jobs —or the lack of them. The State is in a depression worse than anything since the Nineteen Thirties. Unemployment in seventeen key areas is more than 10 per cent of the labor force. In one section it is as high as 25 per cent. There is no sign yet of any "bottoming out." Between now and the election about 50,000 workers will exhaust their unemployment benefits and may have to go on relief.

"When the Republicans are in there is unemployment, when the Democrats are in there are jobs," was the way numerous steel workers in the Pittsburgh area summed it up. A farmer in Jefferson Boro said:

"I don't know how Ike's done

Continued on Page 72, Column 1

Major Sports News

FOOTBALL

Army defeated Notre Dame and Columbia downed Yale yesterday. Scores of major games:

Army	14	Notre Dame	2
Colgate	7	Bucknell	0
Columbia	13	Yale	0
Dartmouth	20	Brown	0
Duke	12	Baylor	7
Georgia T.	21	Tennessee	7
Harvard	20	Lehigh	0
Michigan St.	22	Pitt	8
Navy	20	Michigan	14
No. Carolina	6	S. Carolina	0
Ohio State	19	Illinois	13
Princeton	23	Penn'lv'nia	14
Rutgers	23	Richmond	13
Syracuse	55	Colgell	2
Texas	15	Oklahoma	14
Tenn. & S. M.	14	Maryland	10

HORSE RACING

First Landing took the $151,300 Champagne Stakes at Belmont. Round Table won the $172,850 Gold Cup at Hawthorne and surpassed Nashua's money-winning record.

Details in Section 5.

Eisenhower to Visit City 6 Hours Today

President Eisenhower's visit to New York City today will be fast-paced, precisely timed and crowded with activity.

In a six-hour stay the President will talk politics with Republican candidates, take part in the city's Columbus Day celebration, help to lay a cornerstone and greet welcomers from a motorcade.

The President is due at La Guardia Airport, Queens, at 10:30 A. M. after a helicopter and plane trip from his mountain retreat, Camp David, near Thurmont, Md.

From the airport, he will drive to the Waldorf-Astoria Hotel in a motorcade with a police escort. The route will follow the Grand Central Parkway to the Triborough Bridge, down the Franklin D. Roosevelt (East River) Drive.

Continued on Page 44, Column 3

CITY REGISTRATION EXCEEDS '54 MARK

Last-Day Rise Is Recorded —Total Is Far Short of '56 Presidential Figure

A big, last-day jump in voter registrations yesterday sent total voter enrollments in the city over the registration for 1954— the last comparable election year.

Enrollment fell far short, however, of that of 1956, the last Presidential election year, when 3,290,000 persons registered in the five boroughs.

Final figures from all of the city's sixty-five Assembly Districts showed registrations running generally four times above the average for each of the two previous days.

The total registration, including those previously enrolled under permanent registration, was 2,672,947.

The Bronx, which had recorded 11,427 new names the first day and 11,742 the second, reported 45,547 for yesterday in a final tabulation.

Added to those who had registered last year or earlier this year, the Bronx counted 514,491 registered voters. In 1954 the Bronx had 468,900 registered voters.

Complete figures from Brooklyn showed 79,743 new registrations yesterday. Added to the 24,296 who registered the first day and the 22,501 who registered Friday, the borough counted 126,540 new registrations. There are now 845,433 qualified voters in Brooklyn. Four years ago there were 790,700.

Final figures from the borough of Richmond produced the largest gains over the first two days. Richmond added 6,143 names yesterday. On the first day, 1,077 persons had registered, with 1,691 enrolling Friday. The borough now has 76,487 registered voters. In 1954 there were 61,600.

The registration proceeded

Continued on Page 35, Column 1

CARDINALS SEEK 'PASTORAL POPE' TO SUCCEED PIUS

Religious Traits Stressed— Rites Begin in St. Peters as Throngs Pass Bier

By PAUL HOFMANN
Special to The New York Times.

ROME, Oct. 11—A search for a "pastoral Pope" to succeed the "diplomatic Pope," Pius XII, appears to be a main trend within the Sacred College of Cardinals.

The Cardinals assembled in Rome were reported today to be already engaged in confidential soundings on possible candidacies for the conclave, which will begin meeting Oct. 25.

Meanwhile, hundreds of thousands of people began to file past the Pontiff's catafalque in St. Peter's Basilica while the first of nine solemn funeral masses was celebrated there. The burial will be Monday.

Sources close to the present interim regime of the Roman Catholic Church government agree that the field of choice is wide. No dominating personality seems to have emerged as far comparable to Eugenio Cardinal Pacelli, who became Pope Pius XII at the last conclave in 1939.

Plus Made No Choice

The late Pontiff made no recommendation to the Cardinals. Contrary to almost general expectation, he did not confer the red hat on the Archbishop of Milan, the Most Rev. Giovanni Battista Montini.

The Archbishop was his collaborator in the Vatican for many years. In the opinion of many, he would make an excellent Pope.

As the pious and successful head of one of the largest archdioceses in the world, Archbishop Montini would meet the requirements of a "pastoral Pope." However, it appears unlikely that the Sacred College would depart from an almost 500-year-old tradition by choosing a new Pope outside the college.

Autonomy Idea Disputed

The coming conclave, it is thought, will be not so much a contest of personalities as of ideas. Most of the non-Italian Cardinals are believed to be in favor of any Pope stressing the purely religious aspects of his lofty mission.

Giuseppe Cardinal Siri of Genoa, Giacomo Cardinal Lercaro of Bologna and Ernesto Cardinal Ruffini of Palermo are considered representative of this qualification. To a lesser degree, Paul-Emile Cardinal Leger of Montreal and Emmanuel Cardinal Goncalves Cerejeira of Lisbon also are so regarded.

If this trend prevails, it would exclude the Cardinals of the Curia from the Papacy. The fourteen Cardinals of this group reside permanently in Rome and serve in the church's central administration, known as the Curia.

Several candidates belonging to this group would find themselves at a disadvantage also if

Continued on Page 2, Column 3

U.S. ROCKET RISING 80,000 MILES, BUT WILL NOT CIRCLE THE MOON; MAY BE IN ORBIT AROUND EARTH

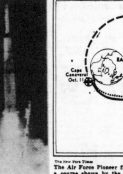

Associated Press Wirephoto

Service-line tower falls at right as the vehicle rises.

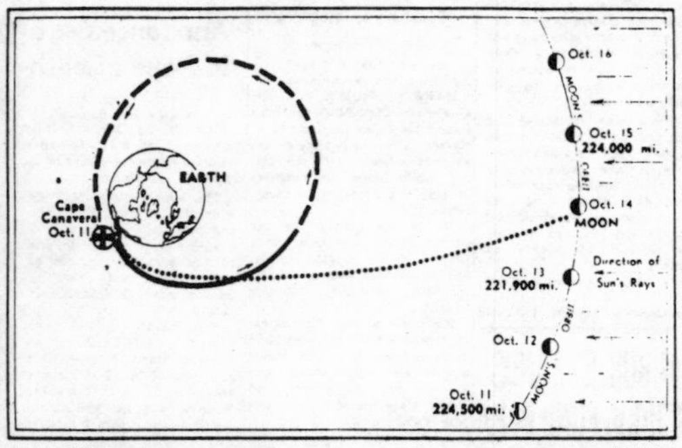

The New York Times   (Oct. 12, 1958)
The Air Force Pioneer fired yesterday at Cape Canaveral, Fla. (cross), traveled along a course shown by the solid line, instead of the projected path to the moon, about 222,000 miles away, as shown by the dotted line. The space vehicle is expected to circle back around the earth, as shown by the broken line. Although the dimensions of its orbit are not yet certain, it is thought that its maximum distance from the earth may reach 80,000 miles and that, when the Pioneer completes its first circuit, the low point may be only 250 miles above the earth. To increase the elevation of this perigee, or low point of orbit, the vehicle's retro-rocket may be fired by remote control from Hawaii.

DEMOCRATS URGE U.N. QUEMOY MOVE

Advisory Council Bids U. S. Submit Peiping's 'Breach of Peace' to World Body

Text of Democratic statement will be found on Page 26.

By E. W. KENWORTHY
Special to The New York Times.

WASHINGTON, Oct. 11—The Democratic Advisory Council proposed today that the United States submit to the United Nations "the breach of the peace" by Communist China in Taiwan Strait.

[Nationalist China, waiting out the final hours of the Communist-proclaimed cease-fire in the strait, was completing the evacuation of 6,000 of the civilians on Quemoy and Little Quemoy, The Associated Press said.]

In a foreign-policy statement approved by all of its twenty-four members, the Democratic Advisory Council said that the United States, in consultation with other governments, should ask the United Nations to work out recommendations for the Chinese situation along two lines.

These lines of action would be aimed (1) to stabilize the whole Taiwan Strait area in a way that would prevent aggression either by the Chinese

Continued on Page 26, Column 1

Lichtenberger Gets Top Episcopal Post

By GEORGE DUGAN
Special to The New York Times.

MIAMI BEACH, Oct. 11—The Right Rev. Arthur Carl Lichtenberger was elected Presiding Bishop of the Protestant Episcopal Church this morning.

The 58-year-old Bishop of Missouri was named to the highest post in his denomination at a closed meeting of the church's House of Bishops, in All Souls Episcopal Church.

While none of his colleagues would speak for quotation, it was learned the new Presiding Bishop won the election on the third ballot by a majority vote of the 150 Bishops present.

The church's 450-member House of Deputies later concurred with the Bishops in their choice. The two legislative arms

Continued on Page 52, Column 4

Britons Cheer Launching; Moscow Avoids Comment

Special to The New York Times.

LONDON, Oct. 11—Leading British scientists threw understatement to the wind today. They hailed the launching of the United States Pioneer rocket in superlatives despite late reports from the tracking station here that the missile was slightly off course.

Prof. A. C. B. Lovell, director of the world's most powerful radio telescope station at Jodrell Bank, Cheshire, declared a few hours after the launching:

"This is a most tremendous achievement on the part of the Americans. I should say success has already been achieved. If it blew up at this moment I would still say it was a tremendous success. It is terrific."

[In Moscow, Soviet newspapers printed a 350-word factual report of the Pioneer's firing. The Moscow radio, nearly eleven hours after the launching, finally broke the news to its listeners. Earlier, the Warsaw radio had reported the news without comment. In France the launching was greeted with satisfaction. In Italy it filled much of the front pages, which had been solidly devoted to the death of Pope Pius XII.]

Prof. H. S. W. Massey of the British International Geophysical Year Committee described the launching as "an amazing feat." The United States scientists and engineers responsible for the success have done "extraordinarily well," he said.

And Kenneth Gatland, vice chairman of the British Interplanetary Society, said that "the present epic journey of the Pioneer marks the beginning of a new age of enlightenment for mankind."

Prof. M. F. Mott, head of the radio astronomy section of the Cavendish Laboratory at Cambridge, exclaimed: "The whole thing is superb."

Prof. Richard Woolley, the

Continued on Page 58, Column 3

NEW JURY FORMED IN GALINDEZ CASE

Federal Panel Here to Study Kidnap Theory—Nature of Evidence Not Disclosed

By ROBERT ALDEN

A Federal grand jury has been impaneled here to investigate new evidence in the disappearance of Dr. Jesús de Galindez.

The nature of the evidence has not been made public. But it is understood that the investigation will center on the theory that Dr. Galindez was kidnapped by agents of the Dominican Republic.

Dr. Galindez was an outspoken opponent of Generalissimo Rafael L. Trujillo, dictator of the Dominican Republic. He was an instructor at Columbia University when he disappeared.

The kidnap theory has already been investigated by a Federal grand jury in Washington, which looked into the case for eighteen months before its tenure expired.

A source at the Justice Department in Washington said that the convening of the grand jury here did not mean that an indictment would be forthcoming. But, the source said, new evidence has been turned up in the case and the Justice Department does not want to leave any avenue unexplored.

Attorney General William P. Rogers has sent William G. Hundley, trial attorney for the Department of Justice, to New York to handle the case. It was Mr. Hundley who presented the Justice Department's case to the grand jury in Washington. The Washington jury handed

Continued on Page 36, Column 1

ASCENT TOO STEEP

Velocity Falls Short, but Vehicle Soars to Record Height

By RICHARD WITKIN
Special to The New York Times.

CAPE CANAVERAL, Fla., Oct. 11—The Air Force fired today a lunar rocket that may reach about 80,000 miles into space. This is a record feat, although far short of the ultimate objective of circling the moon.

The 82.7-pound space vehicle, named Pioneer, was reported to have traveled thirty times farther from the earth than any previous man-made object.

[At 12:47 A. M. Sunday, the Pioneer was about 77,740 miles above the earth, the Pentagon reported.]

Air Force calculations placed the Pioneer 71,750 miles in space at 10:45 P. M. today, Eastern daylight time.

At 7 o'clock tonight the Defense Department confirmed that the rocket would not reach the vicinity of the moon.

Too Steep an Angle

The rocket had taken off at a speed a little short of the required 23,870 miles an hour. A too-steep angle of climb deprived the rocket of the few hundred miles of velocity needed to reach the lunar region.

The speed dropped sharply as the rocket rose farther above the earth.

At 4:47 P. M. the Pioneer's speed was reported to be 3,000 miles an hour, which was about according to plan for the higher altitudes. Later altitudes attained indicated the rocket might be losing a little speed and inclining to a course more parallel to the earth.

The moon was to have been some 222,000 miles away at the time the Pioneer had been scheduled to go into an orbit around it.

The vehicle appeared, instead, to have become a far-ranging satellite of the earth—the nation's fifth and the world's eighth.

It was transmitting back to earth volumes of new data on the radiation that looms as a barrier to manned space flight, and on other spatial phenomena.

Firing Due Tonight

Unofficial calculations indicated that the new satellite's orbit would extend about 80,000 miles at its highest point, or apogee, and about 200 to 250 miles at lowest point, or perigee.

It was tentatively planned to attempt to improve the orbit by the remote firing of a final rocket, the last of four stages, to pierce the core of the vehicle.

It was hoped that the extra propulsion would raise the perigee from 250 to about 20,-000 miles and enable the satellite to stay in orbit indefinitely.

The firing of the last rocket was expected to take place about midnight Sunday, New York time, by remote control

Continued on Page 56, Column 1

PENTAGON CLAIMS A MAJOR SUCCESS

Rocket Sending Data That Indicate the Possibility of Putting a Man in Space

The texts of U. S. statements are printed on Page 56.

By JACK RAYMOND
Special to The New York Times.

WASHINGTON, Oct. 11—United States officials hailed today as a stunning success the launching of the lunar rocket, Pioneer, although the Air Force confirmed it would not reach the "near vicinity" of the moon.

A Pentagon announcement at 7 P. M. finally conceded that the space vehicle, launched shortly before dawn from Cape Canaveral, Fla., had gone too far off course to meet its planned goal within 50,000 miles of the moon's surface.

Officials said they were more satisfied by the achievements of the rocket shot. They pointed out that the Pioneer had ascended thousands of miles higher than any man-made vehicle.

Its delicate instruments, encased in the hurtling rocket, sent back a steady flow of scientific information about which scientists had only guessed until today.

Some signals, giving details of radiation and temperature, reinforced hopes of meeting the great challenge yet to come— launching a man into space.

For according to one Pentagon announcement, the radiation inside the Pioneer at more than 50,000 miles altitude was relatively light — about four roentgens an hour. This is more than a human being can be exposed to safely, but well within

Continued on Page 56, Column 8

Soviet Again Says U.S. Is Spying; Shows Balloon, Accuses Attache

By MAX FRANKEL
Special to The New York Times.

MOSCOW, Oct. 11—A growing campaign here against foreign "spies" culminated today in charges that the United States was using balloons to photograph Soviet military installations and that a United States officer stationed in Moscow was a thief.

An elaborate klieg-lighted news conference was called by the Foreign Ministry to exhibit a balloon and equipment that were said to have been brought down recently in Soviet territory.

The demonstration, similar to one held here in February, 1956, was described as evidence that United States balloons were still being used for aerial reconnaissance and photography to select Soviet "targets" for rockets.

"Several" balloons flying from

Continued on Page 11, Column 1

Sunday Times Now 35c Outside New York City, Suburbs and Long Island

The price of the Sunday Times beginning today is 35 cents to readers outside New York City, its suburban area (in a radius of about 50 miles) and all of Long Island.

The price remains 25 cents in New York City and its suburban communities in New York, New Jersey and Connecticut, and on all of Long Island.

This section consists of 144 pages divided into three parts. The news summary and the index will be found on Page 95. Society news begins on Page 88 and obituary articles are on Pages 83, 86 and 87.

PRAYERFUL PILGRIMAGE: Mourners passing the bier of Pope Pius XII yesterday in St. Peter's Basilica at Vatican, where the Pontiff will be buried tomorrow afternoon.
Associated Press Radiophoto

1959

1959

George C. Scott, Joseph N. Welch and Ben Gazzara starred in Otto Preminger's successful courtroom melodrama, Anatomy of a Murder.

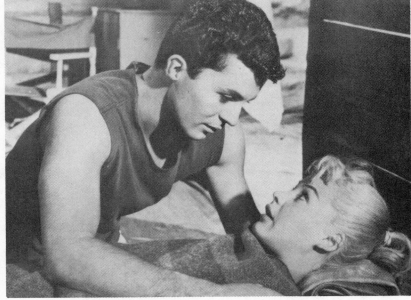

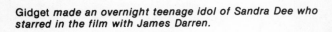

Gidget *made an overnight teenage idol of Sandra Dee who starred in the film with James Darren.*

Strangers When We Meet, *starring Kirk Douglas and Kim Novak, was one of the first films to deal with the extramarital affair.*

"All the News That's Fit to Print"

The New York Times.

LATE CITY EDITION
U.S. Weather Bureau Report (Page 44) Forecast:
Rainy and mild today. Cloudy, increasingly colder tomorrow.
Temp. range: 46—36. Yesterday: 41—27.8.

VOL. CVIII . No. 36,868.   © 1959, by The New York Times Company.
Times Square, New York 36, N. Y.   NEW YORK, FRIDAY, JANUARY 2, 1959.   10c beyond 100-mile zone from New York City.
Higher in air delivery cities.   FIVE CENTS

ROCKEFELLER BIDS STATE SHOW WAY TO BETTER WORLD

Scope of Inaugural Speech Intensifies Speculation on G.O.P. Nomination in '60

GOVERNOR LISTS GOALS

Pledges Increased Freedom of Opportunity—Scorns Ideological Labels

The text of the Rockefeller address is on Page 16.

By LEO EGAN
Special to The New York Times

ALBANY, Jan. 1—Nelson A. Rockefeller dedicated himself today to enlarging man's freedom of opportunity everywhere in a world of peace as he took office as New York's forty-ninth Governor.

In a fourteen-minute inaugural address delivered to an overflow crowd in the Assembly chamber, the new Governor, who is 50 years old, emphasized that New York's problems were closely related to those facing the nation and the world.

Mr. Rockefeller's discussion of national and international problems appeared likely to spur speculation that he was interested in the Republican party's Presidential nomination in 1960.

Mentions School Closings

His victory over Governor Harriman, whom he succeeded today, was the outstanding Republican bright spot in the national elections last year that saw the Democrats enlarge their majorities in both houses of Congress.

In his speech today Mr. Rockefeller referred to the closing of schools in some areas of the South to bar racial integration, the civil rights debate and the need for economic progress and expansion.

"We can serve—and save—freedom elsewhere only as we practice it in our lives," he warned.

"We cannot be impressively concerned with the needs of impoverished peoples in distant lands, if our own citizens are left in want.

"We cannot hope to spur economic progress and prosperity in the world unless such a state as New York can itself help to lead America herself toward new horizons of well-being and equal opportunity for all our citizens.

"We cannot pretend to help inspire new young nations in the ways of freedom and its institutions—if our schools do not enable our own youth to be enlightened citizens."

Notes Urgent Problems

Discussing the immediate problems facing New York, the new Governor said that the state must speed its economic growth and face realistically its transportation problems.

The Governor deplored the prevailing practice of placing ideological labels on public men. The program he is advancing, he said, is conservative, liberal and progressive, all at the same time.

His attack on the labeling practice appeared designed to reassure some of his Republican supporters, who were becoming concerned by the frequent description of Mr. Rockefeller as a "liberal."

Outlining his Administration's
Continued on Page 16, Column 1

Military Hints End Of Manned Planes

By JACK RAYMOND
Special to The New York Times

WASHINGTON, Jan. 1—The military budget prepared for the twelve-month period beginning next July 1 may close the era of manned military aircraft, defense officials indicated today.

Its chief impact on the United States military security program will be the integration, leading to eventual domination, of long-range missiles in the weapons inventory.

Piloted bombers and fighting planes, which have dominated military procurement for ten years, will still be a major item in the arsenal next year.

However, on the basis of the budget plan to be submitted to Congress by President Eisenhower this month, the forecast is that 1960 or 1961
Continued on Page 11, Column 6

I. G. Y. EMPHASIZED WEATHER STUDIES

4 Jet Streams Discovered—First Data Gathered on Antarctica's Winter

This is the second of a series of several articles on the achievements of the International Geophysical Year just ended.

By WALTER SULLIVAN

At exactly midnight, Greenwich Time, last Aug. 25, two Soviet scientists, looking something like divers with their moleskin face masks, special breathing apparatus and heavy furs, tried to launch a huge weather balloon.

At the same moment thousands of other weather men the world over were likewise engaged. At that hour, throughout the International Geophysical Year, they set loose special balloons designed to map the world's ocean of air up to eighteen miles in the sky.

For the Russians, however, this was a special day. The Diesel fuel that kept their little camp warm in the heart of Antarctica was thick as honey. The rubber-like covering of the balloon became brittle in the open air.

Lowest Reading Recorded

The temperature at their station, known as Vostok, had sunk to 125.3 degrees below zero. Fahrenheit—the lowest ever recorded on the face of the earth.

Probably the most thorough exploration carried out during the I. G. Y., an eighteen-month study that ended at midnight Wednesday, was that of the atmosphere. It only began the job, for weather is a four-dimensional problem.

The fourth dimension is time, a vital element, since it is the movement of air, sometimes gentle, sometimes destructive, that transports heat and produces weather.

The patterns of jet streams, seasonal wind reversals and other phenomena that were dis-
Continued on Page 3, Column 2

EISENHOWER FIRM ON BERLIN STAND; REBUKES MOSCOW

Swift Reply to Soviet Plea for End to 'Cold War' Bids Kremlin Show Good Faith

Exchange of the messages will be found on Page 2.

By The Associated Press.

GETTYSBURG, Pa., Jan. 1—President Eisenhower told the leaders of the Soviet Union today that "it seems to us critically important" that the Soviet Union work toward a peaceful solution of the Berlin situation.

The President, who is spending the holidays at his country home here, made the statement in a cabled reply to two top Russians who had voiced hope in a New Year's message that decisive action would be taken in 1959 toward removing "the dangers of a new war."

The exchange of messages was with Soviet Premier Nikita S. Khrushchev and Marshal Kliment Y. Voroshilov, titular chief of state, who sent President Eisenhower an expression of hope that the East-West "cold war" could be ended and the arms race slowed "with the aim of reducing dangerous tensions."

Although the Soviet message was signed by both Marshal Voroshilov and Premier Khrushchev, President Eisenhower addressed his reply to the marshal as a matter of protocol.

Discrepancy Is Seen

President Eisenhower expressed thanks for the message but at the same time voiced hope that the Russians would act according to their expressed sentiments.

"As of this moment it seems to us critically important to apply the sentiments expressed in your message to the Berlin situation," he said. "In this connection I cannot fail to recall your Government's declaration of intentions toward the people of Berlin. In my view they are not in accord with your expressed aspirations and hopes for peaceful coexistence."

The Berlin situation has been tense since Mr. Khrushchev on Nov. 10 demanded an end of the four-power occupation of the city. He hinted that the Soviet Union would no longer guarantee Western access to the city, which is situated within Communist East Germany.

Bars Soviet Coercion

President Eisenhower added in his message today:

"The United States Government regards that, in an atmosphere devoid of any kind of coercion and threat, it would welcome discussion on the question of Berlin in the wider framework of the whole German problem and European security.

"Positive progress in this specific problem would, I deeply believe, give real substance to the hope that 1959 would witness great advances toward the goal of a just and lasting peace."

Another New Year's message
Continued on Page 2, Column 7

BATISTA AND REGIME FLEE CUBA; CASTRO MOVING TO TAKE POWER; MOBS RIOT AND LOOT IN HAVANA

CASINOS WRECKED

Throngs Sack Hotels, Shops and a Paper During Vandalism

By HERBERT L. MATTHEWS
Special to The New York Times

HAVANA, Jan. 1—Years of pent-up emotion exploded in Havana today. The outbreak gathered momentum through the morning and accumulated ugliness as it went along.

[The Associated Press said thirteen persons had been killed in the Havana rioting. Rebel leaders issued warnings that looters would be treated harshly, and the violence eased off after nightfall.]

The earliest manifestations were excitement and joy—cars driving through the streets blowing their horns, excited youths waving flags and shouting, citizens coming to windows and balconies to cheer them on or just to see what was happening.

By 9 A. M. crowds of vandals and looters got going. Their first instinct was part destruction and part looting and it took the form of destroying hundreds of parking meters.

Symbols of Hated Regime

These had recently been installed by the Batista regime and were in that sense symbols of the hated men and of the Government whose leaders had fled. However, in most cases those who smashed the meters either took care to break them open and get the money out or took the top part away.

The next phase was one of demolishing the windows of shops, restaurants and hotels. Many shops were looted. Although the rioting seemed aimless, it was noteworthy that the places chosen were owned by known sympathizers of former President Fulgencio Batista.

The first victim was the Plaza Hotel on Calle Zulueta, which is connected on Cuban minds with the gangland figure Albert Anastasia, who was murdered in New York, and which is now run by an American named Joe Rogers Stassi.

Casinos Are Targets

The targets there and in another well-known hotel in the center of town on the Prado, the Sevilla Biltmore, were the casinos. Rightly or wrongly, the casinos and slot machines are connected in the public mind with gangsters, police protection and the corruption of the Batista regime and they have also been condemned by Fidel Castro's rebel movement. The newspaper El Tiempo, owned by a Batista supporter, was another victim.

A mob burst into the lobby
Continued on Page 5, Column 3

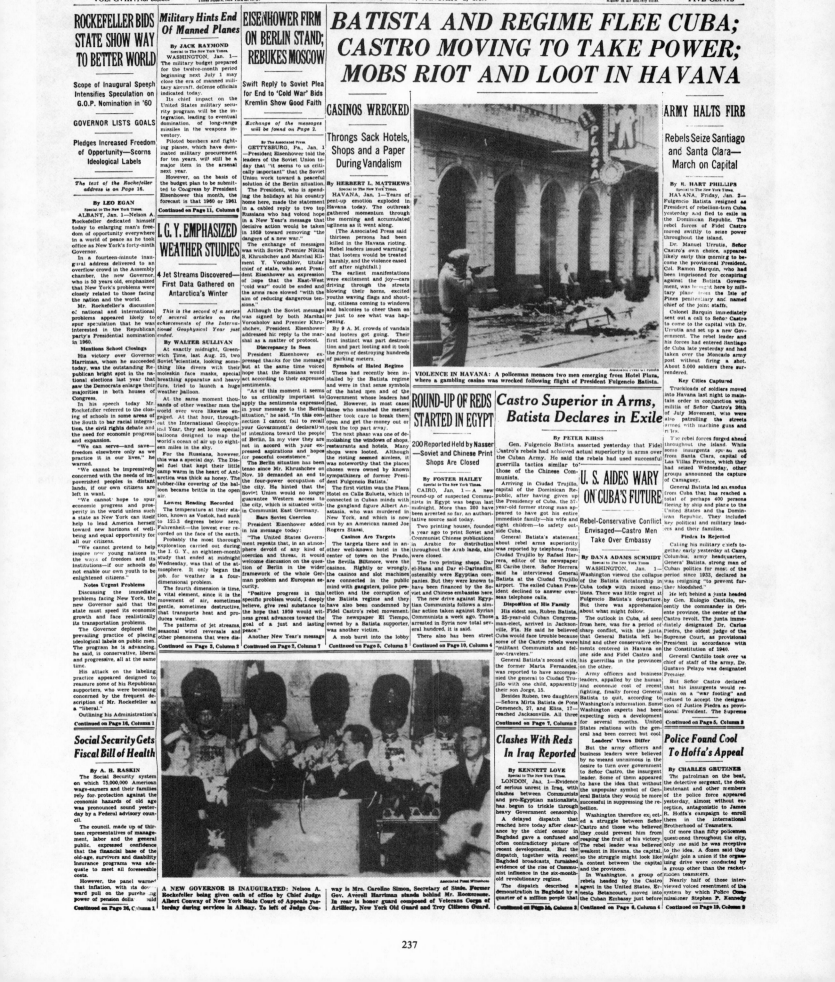

VIOLENCE IN HAVANA: A policeman menaces two men emerging from Hotel Plaza, where a gambling casino was wrecked following flight of President Fulgencio Batista.

ROUND-UP OF REDS STARTED IN EGYPT

200 Reported Held by Nasser —Soviet and Chinese Print Shops Are Closed

By FOSTER HAILEY
Special to The New York Times

CAIRO, Jan. 1—A new round-up of suspected Communists in Egypt was begun last night. More than 200 have been arrested so far, an authoritative source said today.

Two printing houses, founded a year ago to print Soviet and Communist Chinese publications in Arabic for distribution throughout the Arab lands, also were closed.

The two printing shops, Dar el-Hana and Dar el-Darinadim, ostensibly were Egyptian companies. But they were known to have been financed by the Soviet and Chinese embassies here.

The new drive against Egyptian Communists follows a similar action taken against Syrian Communists a week ago. Those arrested in Syria now total several hundred, it is said.

There also has been direct
Continued on Page 10, Column 4

Castro Superior in Arms, Batista Declares in Exile

By PETER KIHSS

Gen. Fulgencio Batista asserted yesterday that Fidel Castro's rebels had achieved actual superiority in arms over the Cuban Army. He said the rebels had used successful guerrilla tactics similar to those of the Chinese Communists.

Arriving in Ciudad Trujillo, capital of the Dominican Republic, after having given up the Presidency of Cuba, the 57-year-old former strong man appeared to have got his entire immediate family—his wife and eight children—to safety outside Cuba.

General Batista's statement about rebel arms superiority was reported by telephone from Ciudad Trujillo by Rafael Herrera, editor of the newspaper El Caribe there. Señor Herrera said he interviewed General Batista at the Ciudad Trujillo airport. The exiled Cuban President declined to answer overseas telephone calls.

Disposition of His Family

His eldest son, Ruben Batista, a 25-year-old Cuban Congressman-elect, arrived in Jacksonville, Fla. He said he believed Cuba would face trouble because some of the Castro rebels were "militant Communists and fellow-travelers."

General Batista's second wife, the former Marta Fernandez, was reported to have accompanied the general to Ciudad Trujillo with one child, apparently their son Jorge, 15.

Besides Ruben, two daughters—Señora Mirta Batista de Pons Domenech, 27, and Elisa, 17—reached Jacksonville. All three
Continued on Page 7, Column 2

U. S. AIDES WARY ON CUBA'S FUTURE

Rebel-Conservative Conflict Envisaged—Castro Men Take Over Embassy

By DANA ADAMS SCHMIDT
Special to The New York Times

WASHINGTON, Jan. 1—Washington viewed the collapse of the Batista dictatorship in Cuba today with mixed emotions. There was little regret at Fulgencio Batista's departure. But there was apprehension about what might follow.

The outlook in Cuba, as seen from here, was for a period of sharp conflict, with the junta that General Batista left behind and other conservative elements centered in Havana on one side and Fidel Castro and his guerrillas in the provinces on the other.

Army officers and business leaders, appalled by the human and economic cost of recent fighting, finally forced General Batista to quit, according to Washington's information. Some Washington experts had been expecting such a development for several months. United States relations with the general had been correct but cool.

Leaders' Views Differ

But the army officers and business leaders were believed by no means unanimous in the desire to turn over government to Señor Castro, the insurgent leader. Some of them appeared to have the idea that with the unpopular symbol of General Batista they would be more successful in suppressing the rebellion.

Washington therefore expected a struggle between Señor Castro and those who believed they could prevent him from reaping the fruit of his victory. The rebel leader was believed weakest in Havana, the capital, so the struggle might look like a contest between the capital and the provinces.

In Washington, a group of rebels headed by the Castro agent in the United States, Ernesto Betancourt, moved into the Cuban Embassy just before
Continued on Page 6, Column 4

ARMY HALTS FIRE

Rebels Seize Santiago and Santa Clara— March on Capital

By R. HART PHILLIPS
Special to The New York Times

HAVANA, Friday, Jan. 2—Fulgencio Batista resigned as President of rebellion-torn Cuba yesterday and fled to exile in the Dominican Republic. The rebel forces of Fidel Castro moved swiftly to seize power throughout the island.

Dr. Manuel Urrutia, Señor Castro's own choice, appeared likely early this morning to become the provisional President. Col. Ramon Barquin, who had been imprisoned for conspiring against the Batista Government, was brought here by military plane from the Isle of Pines penitentiary and named chief of the joint staffs.

Colonel Barquin immediately sent out a call to Señor Castro to come to the capital with Dr. Urrutia and set up a new Government. The rebel leader and his forces had entered Santiago de Cuba late yesterday and had taken over the Moncada army post without firing a shot. About 5,000 soldiers there surrendered.

Key Cities Captured

Truckloads of soldiers moved into Havana last night to maintain order in conjunction with militia of Señor Castro's 26th of July Movement, who were also patrolling the streets armed with machine guns and rifles.

The rebel forces forged ahead throughout the island. While some insurgents spread out from Santa Clara, capital of Las Villas Province, which they had seized Wednesday, other groups announced the capture of Camagüey.

General Batista led an exodus from Cuba that has reached a total of perhaps 400 persons fleeing by ship and plane to the United States and the Dominican Republic. They included key political and military leaders and their families.

Piedra Is Rejected

Calling his military chiefs together early yesterday at Camp Columbia, army headquarters, General Batista, strong man of Cuban politics for most of the period since 1933, declared he was resigning "to prevent further bloodshed."

He left behind a junta headed by Gen. Eulogio Cantillo, recently the commander in Oriente province, the center of the Castro revolt. The junta immediately designated Dr. Carlos Piedra, the oldest judge of the Supreme Court, as provisional President, in accordance with the Constitution of 1940.

General Cantillo took over as chief of staff of the army. Dr. Gustavo Pelayo was designated Premier.

But Señor Castro declared that his insurgents would remain on a "war footing" and refused to accept the designation of Justice Piedra as provisional President. The Supreme
Continued on Page 5, Column 2

Social Security Gets Fiscal Bill of Health

By A. H. RASKIN

The Social Security system on which 75,000,000 American wage-earners and their families rely for protection against the economic hazards of old age was pronounced sound yesterday by a Federal advisory council.

The council, made up of thirteen representatives of management, labor and the general public, expressed confidence that the financial base of the old-age, survivors and disability insurance programs was adequate to meet all foreseeable costs.

However, the council warned that inflation, with its downward pull on the purchasing power of pension dollars, could
Continued on Page 26, Column 1

Clashes With Reds In Iraq Reported

By KENNETT LOVE
Special to The New York Times

LONDON, Jan. 1—Evidence of serious unrest in Iraq, with clashes between Communists and pro-Egyptian nationalists, has begun to trickle through heavy Government censorship.

A delayed dispatch that reached here today after clearance by the chief censor in Baghdad gave a confused and often contradictory picture of recent developments. But the dispatch, together with recent Baghdad broadcasts, furnished evidence of the rise of Communist influence in the six-month-old revolutionary regime.

The dispatch described a demonstration in Baghdad a quarter of a million people that
Continued on Page 16, Column 3

A NEW GOVERNOR IS INAUGURATED: Nelson A. Rockefeller being given oath of office by Chief Judge Albert Conway of New York State Court of Appeals yesterday during services in Albany. To left of Judge Conway is Mrs. Caroline Simon, Secretary of State. Former Gov. Averell Harriman stands behind Mr. Rockefeller. In rear is honor guard composed of Veterans Corps of Artillery, New York Old Guard and Troy Citizens Guard.

Police Found Cool To Hoffa's Appeal

By CHARLES GRUTZNER

The patrolman on the beat, the detective sergeant, the desk lieutenant and other members of the police force appeared yesterday, almost without exception, antagonistic to James R. Hoffa's campaign to enroll them in the international Brotherhood of Teamsters.

Of more than fifty policemen questioned throughout the city, only one said he was receptive to the idea. A dozen said they might join a union if the organizing drive were conducted by a group other than the racket-ridden teamsters.

Nearly half of those interviewed voiced resentment of the system by which Police Commissioner Stephen P. Kennedy
Continued on Page 19, Column 2

1959

Shout *was an early hit song for the Isley Brothers.*

Bobby Darin's successful career included the #1 hit of 1959, Mack the Knife.

Brenda Lee sang Sweet Nothin's.

"All the News That's Fit to Print"

The New York Times.

LATE CITY EDITION
U. S. Weather Bureau Report (Page 95) forecasts: Mostly fair and mild today. Rain changing to snow early tomorrow. Temp. range: 45—36. Yesterday: 47.4—34.2.

NEWS SUMMARY AND INDEX, PAGE 95

SECTION ONE

VOL. CVIII . No. 36,870.

NEW YORK, SUNDAY, JANUARY 4, 1959.

35c outside New York City its suburban area and Long Island. Higher in air delivery cities.

TWENTY-FIVE CENTS

SOVIET SAYS ROCKET HAS PASSED MOON AND IS GOING INTO ORBIT AROUND SUN; INSTRUMENTS ON IT SEEK LUNAR DATA

Castro Heads Cuba's Armed Forces; Regime Is Sworn In

ROCKEFELLER SAYS HE IS CONSIDERING TAX WITHHOLDING

Notes Use of Plan Would Not Bar Rise in Levy on Income Earned in '59

By WARREN WEAVER Jr.
Special to The New York Times.

ALBANY, Jan. 3 — Governor Rockefeller revealed today that his administration was considering setting up a withholding system for paying state income taxes during 1959.

The Governor called a news conference to correct any possible misunderstanding resulting from a similar session yesterday. Then he had said that there would be no increase in the rates of taxes paid on 1958 income.

These taxes will be paid by returns due next April 15. They cover all income received during 1958. Mr. Rockefeller said it would be too difficult to change the rates, now that the forms have been printed and more than a million of them distributed.

Today, however, the Governor emphasized that he had not given any guarantee that the state's taxpayers would not have to make higher income-tax payments during 1959. Such payments could result if the rates were raised and a withholding system were established.

Wants It Understood

"I didn't want any misunderstanding about this," Mr. Rockefeller said. "If we should set up a 'pay-as-you-go' system during 1959, I wouldn't want any taxpayer to be able to say that I'd gone back on my word."

Under a withholding system, such as that used by the Federal Government, tax payments would be deducted from employes' earnings by employers and forwarded to the state. When the annual returns were filed, the employes would pay the balance, if not enough had been withheld, or get a refund if too much had been withheld.

The establishment of a withholding system for state taxes would mean that practically all taxpayers would have to meet two state taxes, or at least part of two, during a single year. During 1959 they would have to pay the tax on 1958 income, as

Continued on Page 69, Column 5

SPRING RULING SET ON SUBWAY FARES

Transit Authority Hopes No Rise Will Be Necessary

By STANLEY LEVEY

The next three or four months will determine the fate of the 15-cent subway fare.

By April or May the Transit Authority expects to know whether it will be able to hold the fare at 15 cents for the rest of the fiscal year that ends next June 30. The agency is hoping that no increase will be necessary until 1960.

The biggest single factor buoying the authority's hope is that it is doing far better this fiscal year that it thought it would.

Last July 1, when the year started, the expectation was that the deficit for the year would be $26,000,000. Now it appears that the loss will be nearer $17,000,000.

There are two reasons for the improved financial picture. One is that in the fall of 1958 there were no such mishaps as the 1957-58 influenza epidemic,

Continued on Page 41, Column 1

Alaska Becomes the 49th State

Associated Press Wirephoto

President Eisenhower talks to Speaker Sam Rayburn after proclaiming Alaska a state and revealing design of new flag, held by aide. Others at White House ceremony were Mike Stepovich, extreme right, and Waino Hendrickson, former officials of Alaska.

CONGRESS CHIEFS FORECAST GAINS

Johnson Says Session Will Be Constructive—Fight on Filibuster Looms

By JOHN D. MORRIS
Special to The New York Times.

WASHINGTON, Jan. 3—The Eighty-sixth Congress convenes Wednesday for a two-year stint that will test its ability to meet pressing domestic issues and new international challenges.

Leaders of the heavy Democratic majorities in both houses made pre-session predictions of a sound, constructive and responsible record.

Prospective differences with the Republican Administration over Federal spending for social welfare, defense and space programs were muffled as the leaders engaged in a series of preparatory conferences with key members.

The Senate Democratic leader, Lyndon B. Johnson of Texas, declared that the Soviet moon shot had placed in bold relief some of the new challenges faced by the new Congress.

Sees All Challenges Met

"I believe," he declared, "that this Congress will face up to all of the challenges, and I hope that when it is concluded the American people will be able to say that it was constructive, responsible and dedicated to increasing the strength and prosperity of the United States."

The practical housekeeping problems of organizing committees, procedures and machinery for the new Congress are likely, however, to force such long-range goals into the background during the early weeks of the 1959 session.

The Senate will plunge immediately into a battle over proposals to curb the filibuster—the tactic of dilatory debate to prevent a voting showdown on legislation opposed by a minority.

President Eisenhower will go over his plans for national defense and foreign policy legislation Monday with Congressional leaders of both parties.

On Friday he will deliver his annual State of the Union Mes-

Continued on Page 40, Column 1

New Flag Unveiled; 7 Staggered Rows Have 7 Stars Each

Texts of Alaska proclamation and flag order, Page 54.

By RICHARD E. MOONEY
Special to The New York Times

WASHINGTON, Jan. 3—Alaska became a state today.

By the clock on the mantel in the Cabinet Room at the White House, it was two minutes past noon. In Juneau, capital of the forty-ninth state, it was 9:02 A. M., Pacific Standard Time.

President Eisenhower signed the document of proclamation at the long table at which he meets his Cabinet. He used six pens to inscribe his name and the date. Then he took another handful of pens from the drawer in front of him and signed an Executive order setting a new design of forty-nine stars for the official flag of the United States.

The new design has seven staggered rows of stars, with seven stars in each row, and the traditional thirteen stripes. It was chosen a week or so ago by a four-man selection commission and formally approved by the President yesterday. It will become official on July 4.

President Eisenhower told

Continued on Page 54, Column 1

Police Search City For Abducted Baby

A city-wide police search failed yesterday to produce leads to the whereabouts of an infant girl who was kidnapped two hours after her birth Friday night in St. Peter's Hospital, Brooklyn.

The baby was believed to have been abducted from the nursery by a blond-haired woman who had been seen loitering in a stairwell and later had been observed leaving the hospital with a bundle under her arm.

Two unidentified boys, playing in the vicinity of Fifty-eighth Street and Third Avenue, Brooklyn, yesterday found a pink kimono, a pink blanket and a small white hospital

Continued on Page 55, Column 1

U. S. POLICY SHIFT ON LATINS URGED

Dr. Eisenhower Proposes Warmth for Democracies, Coolness to Dictators

Excerpts from the Eisenhower report are on Page 12.

By E. W. KENWORTHY
Special to The New York Times.

WASHINGTON, Jan. 3—Dr. Milton S. Eisenhower proposed today that the United States alter its policy in Latin America by making a distinction in official attitudes toward dictators and democratic leaders.

Dr. Eisenhower, president of Johns Hopkins University and a brother of President Eisenhower, suggested that the United States Government could do this subtly but effectively by giving the dictators merely "a formal handshake" and reserving the "abrazos" (embraces) for the democratic leaders.

This was but one of many recommendations contained in a report to President Eisenhower on measures for improving relations between the United States and the twenty Latin-American republics.

Fact-Finding Tour

The report is a result of a fact-finding trip that Dr. Eisenhower, a specialist in Latin-American affairs, made last July in company with several Government officials to five republics of Central America.

Dr. Eisenhower had made a similar report to the President in 1953 following a trip to ten South American republics. He has also served on the Inter-American Committee of Presidential Representatives.

Dr. Eisenhower's recommendation that Latin-American dictatbrs get a cold official hand had particular relevance, coming two days after the overthrow in Cuba of President Fulgencio Batista, one of the hemisphere's few remaining dictators.

Only three of the Latin-American countries are now ruled by dictators. These rulers

Continued on Page 10, Column 1

RIGHTS RESTORED

Rebel Chief Lifts Curb Batista Imposed—Gives Sugar Pledge

By R. HART PHILLIPS
Special to The New York Times

HAVANA, Jan. 3— Dr. Manuel Urrutia, Provisional President of Cuba, today named Fidel Castro head of the nation's armed forces. The President also administered oaths of office to five of seven ministers in the new Cabinet.

Señor Castro, leader of the successful Cuban rebellion, was reported en route from Santiago de Cuba to a victory celebration in Havana when Dr. Urrutia invested the Ministers in a night ceremony in Santiago. Señor Castro is expected to reach this city late tomorrow.

Dr. Urrutia had been proclaimed President by Señor Castro the night of Jan. 1. There was no formal inauguration of the President, who introduced each member of his Cabinet tonight to crowds gathered at the University of Oriente in Santiago.

Opposition to Dictators

Afterward, Dr. Urrutia addressed the crowd on the program of the new regime—essentially, to restore Cuba's economy, rebuild her democracy and oppose dictatorships throughout Latin America.

Señor Castro announced earlier that constitutional guarantees, suspended by Gen. Fulgencio Batista during the two-year rebellion, would be restored immediately.

The rebel leader said that complete freedom of press and radio would be re-established. He also promised that harvesting of the sugar crop would be started on schedule this month. Sugar brings the island $600,000,000 to $700,000,000 yearly.

Señor Castro was designated as Delegate of the President to the Armed Forces. The rebel leader's new post was evidently that of Commander in Chief.

Cabinet Aides Listed

The Cabinet members are:

Minister of State—Dr. Roberto Agramonte.
Justice—Dr. Angel Fernandez.
Treasury—Raul Chibas.
Commerce—Raul Cepero Bonilla.
Health—Dr. Martinez Paiz.
Labor—Manuel Fernandez.
Minister in charge of recovering stolen government property—Faustino Perez Hernandez.

Dr. Agramonte was presidential candidate in 1952 of the now non-existent but once powerful Orthodox party. He was a university professor. As head of a party that opposed the Batista regime he took political asylum in the Mexican Embassy in Havana in 1957.

The new Minister of the Treasury, Señor Chibas, is a

Continued on Page 3, Column 1

Path of the Soviet Lunar Vehicle

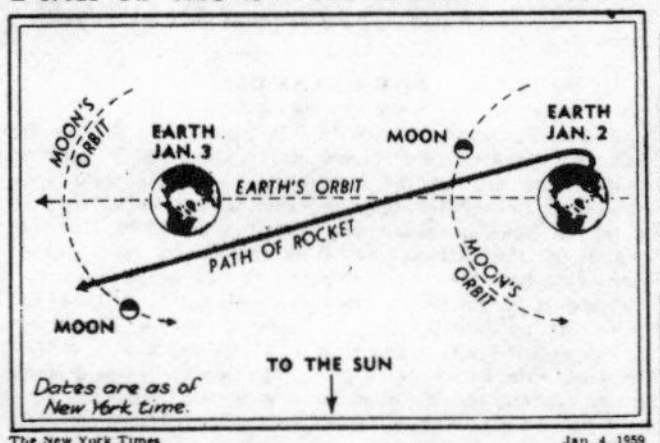

The New York Times — Jan. 4, 1959

Solid line shows the route traveled by the new Soviet satellite since it was fired toward moon on Friday.

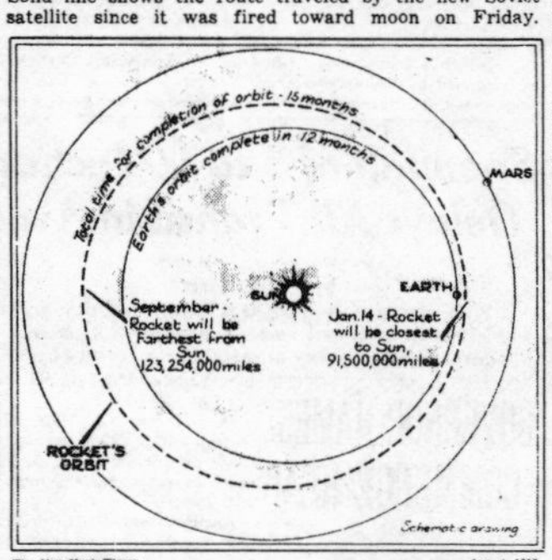

The New York Times — Jan. 4, 1959

Shown schematically are the orbits of Mars and earth and expected orbit of rocket, as plotted from Russian data.

Position of Moon Shaping the Orbit Of New 'Planet'

By RICHARD WITKIN

Krafft Ehricke, the rocket expert, said yesterday that the Soviet Union's lunar rocket was entering a solar orbit outside the earth's because of the moon's position at the time of launching.

His explanation went this way:

The moon was just about to start the last quarter of its monthly counter-clockwise turn around the earth when the rocket left its pad.

That meant that, if the sun's position was assumed to be at 12 o'clock in relation to the earth, the moon was just moving up toward 3 o'clock. The moon, therefore, was almost directly in the path of the earth's motion in its orbit, but just outside the orbit.

In firing a rocket toward the moon, the Russians fired in the direction of the earth's orbital path but slightly outward from the sun.

The rocket had a velocity equal to the orbital velocity of

Continued on Page 37, Column 1

65.6% Here Reported Affiliated With Churches or Synagogues

By GEORGE DUGAN

Nearly two-thirds of the more than 15,000,000 persons in the New York metropolitan area are members of a church or synagogue, it was brought out yesterday in a new statistical survey of religious affiliation.

The study disclosed that 15.9 per cent of the total population in the twenty-two county area is Protestant, 29.5 per cent Roman Catholic, 18 per cent Jewish and 2.2 per cent "other." The remaining 34.4 per cent was listed as unaffiliated.

Regarded as the most accurate compilation of religious statistics yet made of the New York area, the survey was prepared by the Rev. Leland Gartrell, executive secretary of the department of church planning and research of the Protestant Council of the City of New York.

In several instances, the figures obtained were mathematically projected to include the years 1957 and 1958 or to equate membership based on birth versus membership based on confirmation.

Mr. Gartrell's survey covered the five counties in New York City (the Bronx, Kings, New York, Queens and Richmond), seven upstate counties, nine New Jersey counties and Fairfield County in Connecticut.

Among the highlights of the survey were these findings:

¶In New York City's five

Continued on Page 44, Column 3

EISENHOWER HAILS SOVIET SPACE SHOT

Congratulates the Russians —Congress Wants U. S. to Spur Its Program

By JOHN W. FINNEY
Special to The New York Times.

WASHINGTON, Jan. 3—President Eisenhower congratulated the Soviet Union today on being first to send a rocket to the vicinity of the moon.

From Congress, meanwhile, came demands that the United States accelerate its program to overtake the Soviet Union in the race into space. Congress convenes on Wednesday.

These two reactions summed up the feelings within Congressional and Administration circles today as once again a Soviet technological feat in space caught the United States by surprise.

On the one hand, there was admiration for the Soviet ability to send a rocket to the moon and with an impressively larger scientific payload than in the four unsuccessful lunar probes by the United States.

This feeling of admiration, however, was offset by renewed concern over what steps should be taken by the United States to counter the Soviet Union's psychological and technological triumphs.

The President's statement was issued several hours before the Soviet rocket actually passed near the moon this evening and continued on, due to become an artificial planet.

From the time the launching announcement was first made yesterday, however, there had been little doubt among officials

Continued on Page 37, Column 3

This section consists of 122 pages, divided into three parts. The news summary and index will be found on Page 95. Society news begins on Page 90 and obituary articles are on Pages 87, 88 and 89.

PATH NEAR MOON

First Artificial Planet 4,600 Miles Away in Closest Approach

Texts of Moscow broadcasts on rocket are on Page 36.

By OSGOOD CARUTHERS
Special to The New York Times.

MOSCOW, Sunday, Jan. 4—The Soviet Union's mighty cosmic rocket soared past the moon this morning, it was officially announced.

The Moscow radio said the ton-and-a-half rocket was continuing on and would enter a great orbit around the sun as man's first artificial planet.

The announcement said the rocket had reached its nearest point of approach to the moon at 5:59 A. M., Moscow time (9:59 P. M., Saturday, New York time). At that time the moon was about 219,000 miles from the earth.

The distance from the rocket to the moon at the nearest point was not specified, but an earlier broadcast had estimated it at 7,500 kilometers (about 4,600 miles).

'Closest Look at Moon'

Tass, the Soviet press agency, said the close approach—about twice the diameter of the moon—would enable special telescopic equipment aboard the rocket to get the "closest look at the moon ever known to man and to transmit its sightings back to earth by radio."

Instruments and transmitters were reported continuing to work normally and sending valuable scientific material to earth receiving stations.

A Tass statement said that by 9 A. M. (1 A. M. Sunday, New York time) the rocket would be about 243,000 miles from the earth, or about 24,000 miles past the moon.

Soviet scientists said the rocket would enable man for the first time to determine whether the moon had a magnetic field and would facilitate a more precise check on the Einstein theory of gravitation.

At the end of the announcement of the successful shot near the moon the Moscow radio broadcast telemetric signals from the cosmic rocket.

"This, comrades, is the first radio signal ever heard on earth from the vicinity of the moon," the announcer said.

The broadcast said the

Continued on Page 36, Column 1

DULLES PREPARED TO MEET MIKOYAN

May Hold Early Talks With Soviet Leader, Due Today

By WILLIAM J. JORDEN
Special to The New York Times

WASHINGTON, Jan. 3—Secretary of State Dulles is prepared to meet with Anastas I. Mikoyan within twenty-four hours after Mr. Mikoyan's arrival in the United States, an authoritative source said today.

Mr. Mikoyan, a First Deputy Premier of the Soviet Union, is expected to arrive in New York tomorrow morning from Copenhagen, Denmark. He will come here a few hours later.

["I do not know the topics of our talks, which must be up to Mr. Dulles," Mr. Mikoyan said in Copenhagen Saturday.]

Mr. Dulles ended a two-week vacation in Jamaica today and flew to Washington. He will leave Monday afternoon for Ottawa for a meeting on Canadian-United States economic relations.

He will be prepared to see

Continued on Page 19, Column 1

The New York Times.

LATE CITY EDITION
U.S. Weather Bureau Report (Page 57) forecasts:
Partly cloudy, warmer today; cloudy
milder, chance of rain tomorrow.
Temp. range: 42—25. Yesterday: 31.3—27.9.

VOL. CVIII..No. 36,938.   © 1959, by The New York Times Company.
Times Square, New York 36, N. Y.   NEW YORK, FRIDAY, MARCH 13, 1959.   10 cents beyond 50-mile zone from New York City,
except on Long Island. Higher in air delivery cities.   FIVE CENTS

HAWAII IS VOTED INTO UNION AS 50TH STATE; HOUSE GRANTS FINAL APPROVAL, 323 TO 89; EISENHOWER'S SIGNATURE OF BILL ASSURED

ADENAUER IS FIRM AGAINST TROOP CUT IN MIDDLE EUROPE

Gets Assurance in Talks With Macmillan That the British Seek No Disengagement

By SYDNEY GRUSON
Special to The New York Times.

BONN, Germany, March 12 — Chancellor Konrad Adenauer restated to Prime Minister Harold Macmillan today West Germany's opposition to any reduction of Allied forces in Central Europe except within a general disarmament agreement.

The British leader came to Bonn today to give the Chancellor a personal report on his recent conversations in Moscow and to reassure the West Germans that Britain was not seeking the disengagement of Eastern and Western forces in Germany.

Nor, said a British Foreign Office spokesman, does London favor even a controlled limitation of forces if this would result in disequilibrium between the troops and armaments of East and West in Central Europe.

Trip Is Second of Three

Mr. Macmillan's trip here was the second of his three planned journeys to brief other Western leaders about his talks with Premier Nikita S. Khrushchev of the Soviet Union. Mr. Macmillan was in Paris earlier this week and he will cross the Atlantic for separate meetings with President Eisenhower and Prime Minister John Diefenbaker of Canada next week.

The first session between Mr. Macmillan and Dr. Adenauer, who were accompanied by their foreign ministers and two advisers each, lasted three hours. The talks were resumed tonight after a dinner in Mr. Macmillan's honor. They will continue tomorrow in the Chancellor's Palais Schaumburg offices.

The differences in outlook between the Prime Minister and the Chancellor were evident in their remarks at the airport on Mr. Macmillan's arrival.

Mr. Macmillan said the West was firm and united on the prin-

Continued on Page 3, Column 4

ROCKEFELLER ASKS A DRIVE ON CRIME

In Message to Legislature, He Urges Tighter Laws

By WARREN WEAVER Jr.
Special to The New York Times.

ALBANY, March 12 — Governor Rockefeller called on the Legislature today to join him in prosecuting a war against organized crime "more vigorously than ever before."

The Governor sent a special message to the lawmakers, with a dozen recommendations for tightening the existing criminal law and making law-enforcement organizations more powerful and better trained.

In his election campaign last fall, Mr. Rockefeller was outspoken in his criticism of the increase in criminal activity during the Harriman Administration. He pledged swift action against racketeers and law violators if he should be elected.

Mr. Rockefeller urged today that the Legislature:

¶Make it a misdemeanor to defy a subpoena from the State Commission of Investigation or engage in obstructive or contemptuous conduct before the crime panel.

¶Set up a municipal police training council that would establish minimum training standards for all members of police forces.

¶Increase the statute of limitations for prosecution of tax evasion from two to six years, thus giving the state more time

Continued on Page 16, Column 2

Governor Taking Charge Of Meeting City Tax Needs

Orders Report on Costs and Resources for Conference With Mayor Tomorrow — Wants an Agreement Next Week

By DOUGLAS DALES
Special to The New York Times.

ALBANY, March 12 — With his own program for higher state taxes out of the way, Governor Rockefeller has decided to take personal command of the Albany action needed to help New York City balance its budget for the fiscal year starting July 1.

The decision was made at a meeting with Republican legislative leaders today, called to discuss the conference to be held with Mayor Wagner Saturday morning on the city's budget problem.

The meeting will be held at the Executive Mansion and will be attended by Republican and Democratic legislative leaders.

In preparation for the meeting, Governor Rockefeller hastily named a task force to examine New York City's needs and the resources that might be tapped to meet them. A report has been asked by tomorrow night in time to be digested before the meeting with the Mayor.

The task force was designated at a meeting attended by Mr. Rockefeller, Tax Commissioner Joseph H. Murphy, Budget Director T. Norman Hurd, Majority Leader Walter J. Mahoney of the Senate and Majority Leader Joseph, F. Carlino of

Continued on Page 16, Column 4

Snowfall of 5 to 10 Inches Delays All Transit in Area

By PETER KIHSS

With spring only nine days away, the city got its heaviest snowfall of the season yesterday—5.3 inches. It was perhaps nature's way of marking the seventy-first anniversary of the famous blizzard of '88.

On March 12, 1888, that storm hurled 16.5 inches of snow on the city, and in two more days brought the total to 20.9 inches.

Rockland and Fairfield Counties reported ten inches of snow yesterday; Westchester, seven to nine; Bergen, six to seven; Long Island, five to six; Elizabeth, N. J., 5.4, and New Brunswick, N. J., two to three.

Rain and warming temperatures turned the snow into slush in the city. Temperatures dropped during the night, however, and turned the slush to ice on some roadways. The less heavily traveled roads in the suburbs and upstate were reported especially dangerous.

The forecast for today was for partly cloudy and warmer. The temperature may reach the low forties and cause the ice and snow to melt.

Yesterday's storm was caused by two low-pressure areas moving in from the Midwest and from the Virginia coast. Snow fell throughout the Northeast. Depths ranged up to fourteen inches in Chautauqua County on Lake Erie, the Schoharie Valley west of Albany and in western Maryland.

Seven deaths were attributed to the storm in New York, New Jersey and Ohio.

The city's public schools had only 70 per cent attendance. Radio station WOR, which gathers and broadcasts news of

Continued on Page 22, Column 1

GOVERNOR NAMES COMMERCE HEAD

Appoints McHugh, President of New York Telephone — Utility Picks Successor

Governor Rockefeller completed his Cabinet in Albany yesterday with the appointment of Keith S. McHugh to head the Department of Commerce.

Mr. McHugh, who is 64 years old, will retire as president of the New York Telephone Company on April 30 to accept the appointment.

Governor Rockefeller said he was looking to Mr. McHugh to "invigorate" the department so that its full potential to stimulate business in the state would be realized.

Mr. McHugh is leaving a $150,000-a-year job for one that pays $18,500. However, within a year, he will qualify for a company pension as a forty-year man. A company spokesman said a pension arrangement would be worked out by the board of directors.

Meanwhile, the directors of the telephone company elected Clifton W. Phalen to succeed

Continued on Page 16, Column 2

CITY VOTES DEAL ON POWER PLANTS WITH CON EDISON

But Contract Is Changed to Permit New Bids When Final Auction Is Held

By PAUL CROWELL

Contracts for the sale of the city's three rapid-transit power plants to the Consolidated Edison Company at a gross price of $125,840,000 were approved unanimously by the Board of Estimate last night.

The vote was taken after the language of the contracts had been changed slightly to make certain that bidders other than Consolidated Edison could submit offers when the power plants were disposed of at public auction, as required by the City Charter.

The changes were made after Harvey M. Spear, counsel for unidentified "substantial New York interests," had complained that his clients might not be able to submit bids technically admissible under the terms of the agreements.

Clients Not Identified

Mr. Spear declined to tell the board the names of his clients, saying that they would be disclosed when bids were received. Mr. Spear said his clients, while preferring to submit an offer to purchase the power plants for lease back to the Transit Authority, would also be prepared to submit a bid for purchase and operation.

The contracts approved by the board paved the way for transfer of the plants to Consolidated Edison by July 1, assuming that the company was the successful bidder.

The company's bid was for at least $99,382,871 in cash in addition to concessions that would bring the total minimum purchase price up to $125,840,000. The company also offered to supply the three divisions of the city subway system with power under a ten-year contract at uniform rates.

Company Supplies IND

The company now supplies all power for the IND division. The IRT and BMT divisions obtain power from the three city plants that are on Kent Avenue, Brooklyn, and West Fifty-ninth Street and East Thirty-seventh Street in Manhattan.

By its vote the Board of Estimate authorized the Mayor to execute, subject to specified conditions, a contract for selling the three plants and one for purchasing power for the three divisions of the city subway system now operated by the Transit Authority.

The board also authorized the Commissioner of Marine and Aviation, Vincent A. G. O'Connor, to execute waterfront leases in connection with the transfer

Continued on Page 15, Column 2

THE BIG NEWS: Chester Kahapea, 13, offering copies of The Honolulu Star-Bulletin yesterday in the Hawaiian capital. The flag on the front page contains fifty stars.
Associated Press Wirephoto

3 OF JOINT CHIEFS WILL BE RENAMED

Twining, Burke and White Slated for New Terms — Lemnitzer to Get Post

By HANSON W. BALDWIN
Special to The New York Times.

WASHINGTON, March 12 — The reappointments of three members of the Joint Chiefs of Staff will be announced soon.

Those who will be reappointed to new two-year terms starting this summer are Gen. Nathan F. Twining, chairman of the Joint Chiefs of Staff; Gen. Thomas D. White, Chief of Staff of the Air Force, and Admiral Arleigh A. Burke, Chief of Naval Operations.

Gen. Lyman L. Lemnitzer, Vice Chief of Staff of the Army, will succeed Gen. Maxwell D. Taylor, present Army Chief of Staff, whose second two-year term ends June 30. General Taylor is expected to retire.

The second two-year term of Gen. Randolph McC. Pate, as Commandant of the Marine Corps, does not expire until next Dec. 31, and as far as is known his successor has not yet been selected. General Pate also expects to retire.

The names of Lieut. Gen. Merrill B. Twining, a brother of the chairman of the Joint Chiefs, and of Lieut. Gen. Edwin A. Pollock have been mentioned

Continued on Page 4, Column 2

U.S. and Canada List Seaway Tolls, Effective on April 1

By RICHARD E. MOONEY
Special to The New York Times.

WASHINGTON, March 12 — The United States and Canada announced St. Lawrence Seaway tolls today, to take effect April 1.

They are identical to those proposed last June after negotiations by committees of both nations. The differences are primarily in definitions, mostly for the types of cargo that would qualify for the low rate applying, to "bulk" shipments.

[Opposition to the toll setup came from port, rail, shipping and civic interests. They called the rates unrealistically low and the estimated revenue too high. The Port of New York Authority feared a loss of 3,500 waterfront jobs because of "unfair competition" resulting from the tolls.]

Railroads Competing

The Seaway links the Great Lakes and the Atlantic for deepwater ships. Part of it was opened last summer, and the full length is scheduled to be working soon.

Interests that would benefit from the new water route and those against whom it would compete had been fighting over the toll issue.

The fight was moving into a new phase. Major railroads are considering a 20 to 25 per cent reduction of rates they charge for transporting grain for export. This would enable them better to compete with the price for shipping via the waterway.

Seaway tolls are intended to

Continued on Page 10, Column 2

HOUSE UNIT CUTS JOBLESS AID BILL

Restricts Extension of U. S. Assistance to 3 Months Instead of One Year

Special to The New York Times.

WASHINGTON, March 12 — The House Ways and Means Committee approved today a bill for a three-month tapering-off of emergency Federal aid to the unemployed.

The measure falls far short of earlier plans by Democratic leaders for a year's extension of the program beyond its present expiration date of March 31.

The effect would be to prevent an abrupt cut-off of payments to about 200,000 jobless workers expected to be drawing emergency benefits at the end of this month.

Instead, these workers would stay on the rolls until they had exhausted the benefits to which they would have been entitled in the absence of a March 31 termination date.

The committee acted in closed session by what was reported as a one-sided voice vote. The House is expected to pass the bill early next week.

Democratic sources reported that the one-year extension plan had been set aside in the interest of assuring quick enactment of a bill. President Eisenhower and House Republican leaders had voiced strong opposition to the earlier Democratic proposal.

Another factor was the apparent lack of enthusiasm with which the proposed one-year

Continued on Page 18, Column 4

HAWAIIANS START 2 DAYS' FESTIVITY

Alaska Sends First 'Aloha' to Celebrating Islanders

By LAWRENCE E. DAVIES
Special to The New York Times.

HONOLULU, March 12 — The kamaaina and the malihini celebrated today Congressional assurance that the nation was ready to welcome Hawaii as the fiftieth state.

That is to say, the oldtimer — the Hawaiian version of the Alaskan sourdough — joined with the newcomer — the Hawaiian counterpart of the Alaskan cheechako — in opening a two-day demonstration of gratitude over the prospective ending of territorial status for the islands.

The celebration got off to a restrained start. It picked up momentum as the day wore on toward a climax here on the island of Oahu with huge bonfire, aerial and offshore military pyrotechnics and hula dancing.

At the beginning everyone seemed to be waiting for someone else to show the way. Within a half-hour after word came from Washington of the action in the House of Representatives, however, the Waikiki area was clogged with horn-tooting automobiles. Bands and colorfully clad marchers took over at midafternoon.

Colored paper streamers were flung from downtown office buildings along King and Merchant Streets. Hands were thrust forward with a "happy statehood" salutation. Mayor Neal Blaisdell of Honolulu was

Continued on Page 13, Column 1

A Short-Cut Sends It Direct to President, Who Is 'Delighted'

By C. P. TRUSSELL
Special to The New York Times.

WASHINGTON, March 12 — The Territory of Hawaii was voted into the Union today as its fiftieth state.

The House of Representatives gave its approval by a vote of 323 to 89. Yesterday the Senate approved the Hawaii bill, 76 to 15.

President Eisenhower's approval is assured. The White House said today he was "delighted" and noted that "he has been urging it for some time."

Thus, after one of the fastest actions by Congress in years, only the mechanics of admitting a new state remain before Hawaii joins the Union.

The question arose as to whether the island territory some 2,000 miles from continental United States would seek to put its fiftieth star into the flag July 4 of this year when Alaska adds its forty-ninth. There is barely enough time to do so and island leaders doubted that it would be done.

Governor Gives Word

With the galleries filled, the House started its long roll-call in midafternoon. Among the spectators was the Governor of Hawaii, William F. Quinn. When the roll-call began he quietly left the gallery and went to the office of Sam Rayburn, Speaker of the House.

At the Speaker's office Governor Quinn telephoned Acting Gov. Edward E. Johnston at Honolulu and asked him to hold the line. When he was notified the roll-call had recorded 219 ayes—a majority of the House—Governor Quinn set off a celebration in the islands by shouting:

"Sound the sirens, close the schools and get going."

A little later he added a note of caution:

"Keep the lid on a little. Ed."

Before Hawaii can attain statehood it must hold a referendum on whether it wants to assume the burdens at this time. Besides agreeing at the polls with provisions of the new law,

Continued on Page 13, Column 2

Fulton Street Widening Dropped By Jack on Protest of Merchants

The highly controversial proposal to widen part of Fulton Street in lower Manhattan was withdrawn from further consideration yesterday by Borough President Hulan E. Jack of Manhattan.

The action by the Board of Estimate permitting Mr. Jack to drop the project constituted a victory for a group of Fulton Street merchants.

Opponents have fought the proposal as threatening hardship to "hundreds of business men and thousands of their employes." They have also argued that the widening would not materially relieve the area's traffic situation.

Mr. Jack said he favored studies of the possibility of both an eastbound and a westbound artery in lower Manhattan.

Pending such studies, he said, it would be better to withdraw the Fulton Street proposal. In the meantime, he added, he hoped all of those who have been involved in the widening dispute would have a better understanding of the problem.

The proposal that Mr. Jack withdrew called for widening Fulton Street on its south side from Broadway to Water Street. The project was intended as the first stage of an ultimate widening of Fulton Street from South Street to West Street.

Two major slum clearance cooperative housing projects totaling $61,000,000 in cost in the Rockaways, Queens, were approved by the board.

One was Hammels-Rockaway,

Continued on Page 22, Column 6

There Are Times When Bad Weather Brings Out the Best in a Man

It was such a time yesterday at Vesey St. and Broadway
And a man came forward to lend a gallant, helping hand
The New York Times (by Neal Boenzi)

Ben Hur, *which took five years to make, was the costliest film ever made. $15 million were expended for this movie, which consisted of a cast of 25,000. Actor Charleton Heston and Director William Wyler were among the recipients of the 9 Academy Awards this film won in 1959.*

Marilyn Monroe, Tony Curtis and Jack Lemmon starred in Some Like It Hot. *The two actors are seen here wearing women's clothing in this zany comedy.*

Simone Signoret and Laurence Harvey in a scene from Room at the Top, *the story of an ambitious young man, his swift rise to power and his love affair with an unhappy, older woman. Simone Signoret had the distinction of receiving the first Academy Award for Best Actress ever given to the star of a British film.*

1959

In 1959, NASA announced that seven experimental test pilots would commence training as spacemen, one of whom would eventually be thrust into space in a Mercury capsule intended to orbit the earth four times at 180,000 miles per hour. The projected date was 1961. Seen here are three pressure-suited astronauts experiencing a short duration of weightlessness, while a plane makes a parabolic curve.

The first ship entered the newly completed St. Lawrence Seaway in April, 1959. A joint project of the U.S. and Canadian governments, it opened to traffic officially in June.

Sir Laurence Olivier made his American TV debut in 1959 in The Moon and Sixpence, which also starred Hume Cronyn.

The New York Times.

NEWS SUMMARY AND INDEX, PAGE 95

VOL. CVIII—No. 36,982

© 1959, by the New York Times Company. Times Square, New York 36, N. Y.

NEW YORK, SUNDAY, APRIL 26, 1959.

35c outside New York City and Long Island. Higher in air delivery cities.

SECTION ONE

TWENTY-FIVE CENTS

LATE CITY EDITION

U. S. Weather Bureau Report (Page 95) forecasts.
Mild, chance of late showers today. Some cloudiness and cool tomorrow.
Temp. range: 70—55. Yesterday: 69.5—50.4.

KHRUSHCHEV BARS EISENHOWER PLAN ON ATOM-TEST BAN

Russian Endorses Instead a Proposal by Macmillan for Inspection Quotas

'UNFAIR DEAL' OPPOSED

Soviet Messages Reject U.S. Offer of Limited Curb as No Solution of Problem

Texts of Khrushchev letters are on Page 12.

By OSGOOD CARUTHERS
Special to The New York Times.

MOSCOW, April 25—Premier Nikita S. Khrushchev has bluntly rejected as "an unfair deal" President Eisenhower's proposal for an initial ban on all nuclear test explosions within a thirty-mile limit of the earth's atmosphere.

At the same, however, Mr. Khrushchev has accepted in principle a proposal by Prime Minister Harold Macmillan of Britain to set in advance a limited number of international inspections of atomic sites annually.

Mr. Khrushchev expressed his views in letters to President Eisenhower and Mr. Macmillan.

Demands Complete Ban

He was replying to the Western proposal of a phased ban of atomic tests starting with the prohibition of those up to thirty kilometers (about thirty miles). The letters of reply were made public today.

The Soviet Premier declared his Government's policy continued to be for a complete ban on tests "in the atmosphere, under ground, under water and at great altitudes."

He said people would be "justified in evaluating and condemning" President Eisenhower's proposal, which was introduced at the three-power test-ban negotiations in Geneva, as "an unfair deal."

President Asked First Step

President Eisenhower wrote to Mr. Khrushchev April 13, proposing that the nuclear powers—the United States, Britain and the Soviet Union—bypass the stumbling-block of setting up an international inspection system.

He suggested that the three powers "take the first and really attainable step of an agreed suspension of nuclear weapons tests in the atmosphere up to fifty kilometers while the political and technical problems associated with control of underground and outer-space tests are being resolved."

Such a proposal "does not solve the problem," Mr. Khrushchev replied in a letter dated April 23 and handed to the State Department through Ambassador Mikhail A. Menshikov.

"Should we sign such a

Continued on Page 12, Column 3

St. Lawrence Seaway Open to Ships

Associated Press Wirephoto

The icebreakers d'Iberville, lower left, and Montcalm entering the Seaway's St. Lambert Lock yesterday morning. At top right, beyond ships that are tied up, is the Simcoe, the first ship to enter the lock after the icebreakers.

Lake Vessels Show Way On Historic Voyage Inland

By RAYMOND DANIELL
Special to The New York Times.

MONTREAL, April 25—The St. Lawrence Seaway, after fifty years of talk and five years of building, opened for business this morning.

By nightfall nearly a score of salt-water ships had entered into the first of the series of locks that will eventually lift them 602 feet above sea level and into the fresh water of Lake Superior. That would be 2,342 miles deep into the heartland of North America.

Two Canadian icebreakers, the d'Iberville and Montcalm, led the ceremonial way today. They were not needed for their usual work, since there was little ice to bother ships.

Aboard the first icebreaker were George Hees, Canada's Minister of Transport, and D. J. Roberts, president of the Canadian Seaway Authority, and 250 members of Parliament and newspaper men.

Prime Minister John Diefenbaker, who had been expected to be aboard, found at the last moment that other business prevented his participation.

The ocean-going ships that entered the Seaway today were led by old lakers, which had wintered in Eastern ports. These ships were leading the way for hundreds of other vessels that will pass through the

Continued on Page 62, Column 5

PANAMA INVASION BY SEA REPORTED

Government Has Word of a Caribbean Coast Landing —President Calls Aides

By The Associated Press.

PANAMA, Sunday, April 26—The Government said early today it had reports that about thirty men had made a landing on Panama's Caribbean coast.

The Government said it had received word from the Commandant of the San Blas Indian Reservation that the landing had been made.

The commandant was quoted as saying that a beached ship had been found near the reported landing. The announcement added that a patrol of national guard troops had been dispatched to check the area.

Cabinet Is Summoned

President Ernesto de la Guardia Jr. and his Cabinet were in emergency session at the Presidential Palace as the report of the landing spread throughout the city.

An unconfirmed report was said to have been received at guard headquarters that a vessel was operating off the San Blas area, near Mandinga.

Ten days ago the Government declared that an invasion was being prepared for an attempt to overthrow the Administration.

Trouble broke into the open early this month, when three small bands fled into Panama's mountains, apparently trying to set up a base for an uprising patterned on the successful Cuban revolt led by Fidel Castro.

The bands had several brushes with the National Guard, army and police, but little has been heard of them lately.

Panamanian officials feared

Continued on Page 2, Column 5

RED CHINA PURGES 5 SINKIANG AIDES

Provincial Officials Ousted From Posts Because of Opposition to Peiping

By TILLMAN DURDIN
Special to The New York Times.

HONG KONG, April 25—Nationalist and religious opposition continues to be a serious problem for the Communists in Sinkiang, a Chinese province that borders on Tibet.

This was emphasized anew today in copies of the Sinkiang Daily News for March that have just arrived here.

The newspaper reported that five prominent oppositionists were recently relieved of official posts. More than 300 other persons were committed to the program of manual labor and further ideological re-education at the end of a six-and-a-half-month-long "rectification" conference at Urumchi, the provincial capital.

The Sinkiang Daily News of the conference had exposed "anti-party, anti-people, anti-Socialist elements" who had plotted "the overthrow of the leadership of the party, the overthrow of the people's state power and establishment of the reactionary government

Continued on Page 22, Column 1

ROCKEFELLER SIGNS BILL TO GIVE CITY 5 MORE JUSTICES

Rejects Mayor's Objections to Brooklyn Step—G.O.P. to Get Two of Posts

By WARREN WEAVER Jr.
Special to The New York Times.

ALBANY, April 25—Over the strong objection of Mayor Wagner, Governor Rockefeller has authorized the addition of five new City Court justices in Brooklyn.

In one of his last acts on legislation before the bill-signing period expired last midnight, the Governor signed a measure that is expected to result in the naming of two Republicans and three Democrats to the judicial posts.

In his memorandum of approval, Mr. Rockefeller made no mention of the fact that the court bill was the product of a political deal, under which the Republican Legislature and the Governor agreed to set up the new jobs in Democratic Brooklyn if their party was allowed to fill two of them.

Need for Justices Argued

The Governor confined himself to discussing the need for additional judicial manpower on the City Court bench in Brooklyn and weighing Mayor Wagner's objection that the extra seats would cost the city money it could not afford.

He quoted the Appellate Division, Second Department, in which Brooklyn is situated, to the effect that in the last two years undecided cases had been piling up in the court at the rate of 1,000 a month. This was the third bench still consisted of only five justices, as it had since 1930.

Cited as supporters of the measure were the Judicial Conference, the State Bar Association and the Kings County Bar Association. In addition to Mr. Wagner, a majority of the City Court justices outside Brooklyn opposed the bill.

Harriman Action Recalled

Mr. Rockefeller recalled that last year former Gov. W. Averell Harriman had been faced with similar opposition from the Mayor to a bill creating more Supreme Court justices in the Long Island area of Queens. But Mr. Harriman concluded that the added manpower was necessary, Governor Rockefeller noted.

"It is the responsibility of the executive and legislative branches of government to assure that an adequate and functioning judiciary is available to meet the needs of the people," he said. "The Legislature has accepted that responsibility. I can do no less."

When the measure setting up the new judgeships was being debated in the Legislature, it was reported that the leading Republican candidates for the new judgeships were Carmine Ventura, a former assistant United States attorney; George Nichola

Continued on Page 42, Column 3

Rise in Old-Age Pay Cutting Relief Rolls

By EDWIN L. DALE Jr.
Special to The New York Times.

WASHINGTON, April 25—The gradual rise in Social Security benefits for the aged has begun to cut significantly into the number of older persons required to seek relief.

An important result may be a downturn in the large item in the Federal budget for grants to the states for old-age assistance. This has been running at slightly more than $1,000,000,000 a year and is gradually rising. It is one of the biggest nondefense items in the budget. State spending would be reduced as well.

In February the number of persons receiving old-age assistance declined by 8,000, the largest decline for the month in six years. Moreover, the amount of money paid out in benefits declined by $1,300,000, the largest decline for any month in nine years.

The main reason for both declines was the same. In February the first checks went out containing the im-

Continued on Page 45, Column 1

LYNCH MOB SEIZES MISSISSIPPI NEGRO

Rape Suspect, Taken From Jail Cell, Is Feared Dead —F. B. I. Enters Case

By United Press International.

POPLARVILLE, Miss., April 25—A lynch mob of masked white men broke into the county jail here early today, beat an accused Negro rapist in his cell, and dragged him to a waiting car.

A trail of blood led from the third-floor cell where the mob had seized Mack C. Parker, 23-year-old truck driver, in the Pearl River County Jail. The victim was to have gone on trial Monday for the rape on Feb. 24 of a 24-year-old white woman. But authorities feared he would be found dead.

The Federal Bureau of Investigation sent a special squad here and pledged the use of all its detection facilities. Attorney General William P. Rogers sent the White House word being kept informed. Gov. J. P. Coleman called out six highway patrol units to aid six officers.

Governor Called F. B. I.

The Governor held a news conference in Jackson, the capital, that he had asked the F. B. I. to enter the case. He said he "never expected to see the day" when there would be new mob action in the state.

According to a highway patrolman, "the nine or ten men who did this knew what they were doing." He said, "They knew where the sheriff kept his keys, and they knew which cell Parker was in."

One of the six other Negro prisoners in the jail said nine men had broken in but that others waited in the courtroom. He said the mob arrived in five cars about 12:30 A. M.

[According to The Associated Press, there were fifteen to twenty abductors.]

C. J. Monday, a Negro charged with murder, was Mr. Parker's cell mate. He said the men "swarmed all over" the defendant, beating him with pistols and clubs. One hit him with a garbage can, the witness said.

"I heard them hitting him," he said. "Parker kept yelling 'Help. I didn't do it. I didn't do it.'"

"He was yelling to me the

Continued on Page 46, Column 3

LABOR BILL VOTED AS SENATE EASES 'RIGHTS' SECTION

Final Roll-Call Is 90-1, With Goldwater Opposing— House Fate in Doubt

KUCHEL PLAN ADOPTED

Vote Softening McClellan's Proposal Is 74-14—'Hot Cargo' Clause Stiffened

Text of Senate compromise appears on Page 52.

By JOSEPH A. LOFTUS
Special to The New York Times.

WASHINGTON, April 25—The Senate passed the Kennedy labor reform bill today with a compromise "bill of rights."

The vote was 90 to 1. Senator Barry M. Goldwater, Republican of Arizona, was the single dissenter.

The bill now goes to the House of Representatives and an uncertain future. The "rights" section was designed to protect union members from arbitrary discipline by their organizations and its leaders.

The compromise was offered by Senator Thomas H. Kuchel, Republican of California. It was not so hard and harassing in its potential as the original amendment of Senator John L. McClellan. But it appeared to be a stride toward making labor leaders responsive to the will of the membership.

Leaders Seen Unhappy

Top leaders of the united labor movement withheld comment. It is known that they are far from happy with the bill, but outright condemnation appeared unlikely.

With Senator McClellan, an Arkansas Democrat, agreeing, the Senate voted, 77 to 14, for adoption of the new "rights" version. Thirteen Republicans and one Democrat, Senator Frank J. Lausche of Ohio, voted no.

The Senate adopted several other amendments, including one that substantially hardened the ban on "hot cargo" clauses and provided for mandatory injunctions against union contracts where an employer complained that the union was seeking such a clause.

Standards Set Up

The Kennedy bill sets up standards for union financial operations and democracy through reporting and public disclosure. The Secretary of Labor has broad powers to investigate and enforce these standards.

Penalties of up to two years' imprisonment and $10,000 fines could be imposed on persons or organizations who interfered with the rights of members as set forth in the entire bill, including not only the right to vote and run for union office but also such rights as free

Continued on Page 52, Column 1

Major Sports News

BASEBALL

The Baltimore Orioles defeated the Yankees, 2—1, in eleven innings at the Stadium yesterday. Johnny Kucks, who pitched to only one batter, was the losing pitcher. In other games, the Chicago White Sox beat the Cleveland Indians, 8—6, with five unearned runs in the ninth, and the Cincinnati Reds downed the Milwaukee Braves, 7—6.

TRACK AND FIELD

Abilene Christian set records at the Penn Relays in the 440 and the 880 yard events, Bill Woodhouse of Abilene Christian also bettered the meet record for the 100-yard dash. In the Drake Relays at Des Moines, Ira Murchison defeated Bobby Morrow, the Olympic sprint champion, at 100 yards.

HORSE RACING

Whitly, 4 to 1, captured the $29,800 Excelsior Handicap by a length at Jamaica. Ridden by Sam Boulmetis, he earned $18,485 for his owner, W. Arnold Hanger. Mystic II was second and Grey Monarch third. The race was contested over the mile-and-a-sixteenth distance. Piano Jim, paying $4.40 for $2, scored a victory in the $26,975 Laurel Handicap. There were three other horses in the race.

Details in Section 5.

Ad Offers Bargain: Old Atom Smasher

By AUSTIN C. WEHRWEIN
Special to The New York Times.

CHICAGO, April 25—The following advertisement will appear tomorrow in a number of newspapers, including The New York Times:

FOR Sale. Fully equipped 100 Million Volt Electron accelerator in good operating order; built by General Electric Corp. Served as a fine instrument for basic research laboratory. Address Clement Mokstad, University of Chicago.

The advertisement was for the 200-ton atom smasher that the late Dr. Enrico Fermi, Nobel Prize winner and atomic pioneer, put into operation in 1950.

It cost $450,000 new. The way prices have risen it would cost twice that to build now, according to General Electric appraisers. The university's asking price is $100,000, f. o. b. Hyde

Continued on Page 6, Column 3

Major Mathematical Conjecture Propounded 177 Years Ago Is Disproved

The New York Times

Discussing their solution to problem, from left: Dr. E. T. Parker, Prof. S. S. Shrikhande and Prof. R. C. Bose.

By JOHN A. OSMUNDSEN

Another major mathematical problem—this one 177 years old—has been solved. Its solution was reported at the 557th meeting of the American Mathematical Association, which ended at the New Yorker Hotel yesterday.

It was the second such achievement to come out of the meeting, something attending mathematicians called "extremely rare." The solution to the first problem, known as Frobenius' conjecture, was reported by Prof.

John G. Thompson, a 26-year-old mathematician from De Paul University in Chicago. It dealt with so-called "group theory" and had puzzled mathematicians for more than fifty years. The second problem had resisted attempts at solution ever since Leonhard

Euler (pronounced "oiler") stated it in a memoir in 1782. It became famous for Euler's conjecture. The three mathematicians who finally cracked the problem are now known among their colleagues as

Continued on Page 42, Column 1

Clocks Put Ahead For Daylight Time

Clocks were set ahead one hour this morning over much of the United States as Daylight Saving Time went into effect for the forty-first year.

The lost hour will be regained in six months—on Oct. 25 when the period ends.

Daylight Saving Time is in effect in New York, New Jersey, all of New England, Washington, D. C., and most of Pennsylvania, Delaware, Indiana, Wisconsin, Nevada and California. Sections of many other states will also observe the fast time.

New timetables for daylight time are being issued by most public transportation facilities. Railroads, buses and other lines will operate on local time wherever practical.

Today's Sections

Section 1 (3 parts)	News
Section 2	Drama, Screen, Music, TV, Radio, Resorts, etc.
Section 3	Financial and Business
Section 4	Review of the Week
Section 5	Sports
Section 6 (2 parts)	Magazine and Men's Wear
Section 7	Book Review
Section 8	*Real Estate
Section 9	Employment Advertising
Section 10	Advertising
Section 11	Gardens

*Included in all copies in the New York metropolitan area and adjacent territory.

Index to Subjects

	Section	Page
Art	11	77, 84
Boats	5	16-17
Book Review	7	11-13
Bridge	2	
Dance	2	
Decorative Arts	6	72-73
Drama	2	1-5
Editorials	4	
Events Today	1	
Fashions	6	74-75
Financial and Business	3	76-77
Food	11	
Gardens	11	
Home Improvement	2	
Letters to Editor	4	
Men's Wear	6	(Part 2)
Music	2	
News Summary & Index	1	95
Obituaries	1	86-87
Photography	2	19
Puzzles	2	30
Real Estate	8	
Resorts	2	29-46
Review of Week	4	
Science	4	5-7
Screen	2	14-15
Ships & Aviation	5	88-117
Society	1	
Sports	5	
Television-Radio	2	18
Weather	1	95

While Solomon and Sheba was being filmed in 1959, Tyrone Power died of a heart attack. He was replaced by Yul Brynner. Power is seen here in a scene with George Sanders and Marisa Pavan, in the background.

James Shigeta and Emmanuelle Riva in Hiroshima, Mon Amour.

"All the News That's Fit to Print"

The New York Times.

LATE CITY EDITION
U. S. Weather Bureau Report (Page 46) forecasts:
Partly cloudy and warm today.
Warm, chance of showers tomorrow.
Temp. range: 80—68. Yesterday: 87.4—69.2.

VOL. CVIII..No. 37,015.

© 1959, by The New York Times Company.
Times Square, New York 36, N. Y.

NEW YORK, FRIDAY, MAY 29, 1959.

10 cents beyond 50-mile zone from New York City
except on Long Island. Higher in air delivery cities.

FIVE CENTS

BIG 4 MINISTERS CONFER IN PLANE; NEW PLAN HINTED

WEST SETS 4 AIMS

Seeks Geneva Accord on Principles as a Basis for Summit

By JAMES RESTON
Special to The New York Times.

WASHINGTON, May 28—The Big Four foreign ministers took their troubles above the clouds today in the first major airborne international conference in diplomatic history.

En route back to the Geneva conference after attending the funeral of former Secretary of State John Foster Dulles, the foreign chiefs of the United States, Britain, France and the Soviet Union agreed to confer this afternoon on the German problem before reaching their first stop at Ernest Harmon Air Force Base in Newfoundland.

This morning, they had met for thirty minutes with President Eisenhower at the White House. The President expressed the hope that future sessions at Geneva would provide a "measure of progress" to justify a summit session of the heads of government as "desirable and useful."

Meanwhile, it was reported that the Western foreign ministers had reached general agreement on the procedure and principles they planned to put before the Soviet Foreign Minister, Andrei A. Gromyko, as a means of winding up the Geneva conference and going on to a summit conference in Geneva later in the year.

Goal for Accord Outlined

According to this report, Secretary of State Christian A. Herter, Foreign Secretary Selwyn Lloyd of Britain and Foreign Minister Maurice Couve de Murville of France agreed to try to wind up the Geneva meeting, probably by the end of next week, with a communiqué that would do the following:

¶It would commit all four nations to the principle that they had the right to be in Berlin and that the status quo in Berlin could be changed only by agreement of all four nations.

¶It would obligate the four to settle their differences over Germany by peaceful means.

¶It would accept the reunification of East and West Germany as their objective and agree that free, secret, all-German elections at some time should be part of this process.

¶It would outline the subjects to be discussed at a summit meeting, including the future of Berlin and Germany, disarmament, and the means of giving international assistance to the under-developed nations.

It was conceded by a Western foreign minister that this procedure or writing general principles into a final communiqué would leave most of the basic East-West differences where they were.

He insisted, however, that the first task was to liquidate the Soviet threat to force the Western powers out of Berlin, Such a communiqué, he observed,

Continued on page 3, Column 2

City Schools Lose Red Informer Case

By WARREN WEAVER Jr.
Special to The New York Times.

ALBANY, May 28—The right of the State Education Commissioner to forbid the dismissal of New York City schoolteachers who refuse to inform on their fellows with respect to past Communist activity was upheld by the Court of Appeals today.

The state's highest court did not say that Commissioner James E. Allen Jr. had been right as a matter of principle in refusing to permit the dismissal of teachers who declined to inform. The tribunal said it had no right to overrule such a decision by the Commissioner unless it was "purely arbitrary."

Six of the seven judges

Continued on Page 10, Column 4

MONAGHAN BOLTS TRACK HEARINGS; CAFE TABS LISTED

Lawyer Cites Lack of Time to Prepare a Defense— Gifts Totaled $31,075

By RICHARD J. H. JOHNSTON

The State Commission of Investigation yesterday offered evidence that the Harness Racing Commissioner and his subordinates had accepted $31,075.55 worth of free liquor and food from operators of the Yonkers and Roosevelt Raceways in the last three years.

George P. Monaghan, the commissioner, made a brief appearance at the hearing but did not remain to hear these charges read into the record. He entered the hearing room with his lawyer, Emile Zola Berman, at 10 A. M.

Mr. Berman read a statement saying the Investigation Commission had not given him enough time to prepare Mr. Monaghan's defense. Five minutes later the two left the hearing chamber in the Criminal Courts Building.

'Will Not Be Back'

Outside Mr. Berman said: "Commissioner Monaghan will not be back unless he is subpoenaed."

As the hearing continued lawyers for the commission submitted in evidence waiters' tabs from the restaurants of the tracks in substantiation of the charges.

The accounting showed that Mr. Monaghan had accepted $2,735.75 worth of free entertainment; Thomas Burke, steward for the harness commission, $3,549.55; Samuel Rosenberg, chief accountant, $1,554.90; Leonard Levin, press representative, $632.75; Benjamin Rosenberg, assistant chief accountant, $599.40; Michael J. McGrath, $944.75; Violet Carnevale, executive assistant to Mr. Monaghan, $683.95, and racing judges, $20,374.50.

Admit Taking Gifts

Samuel Rosenberg and Miss Carnevale testified, under oath, during yesterday's session before the commission that they had accepted the gratuities. Both James S. Bell, the Yonkers Raceway head waiter, and Leo Dubin, the manager of the track restaurant, testified that they were aware of arrangements wherein Mr. Monaghan and his associates were to be "taken care of" by the management.

Mr. Rosenberg and Miss Carnevale also admitted under questioning by the investigation commission's assistant counsel, Carl Vergari, that on the dates covered by some of the checks for free meals they had submitted to the State Controller bills for dinner at $3.50, while "on state business."

At the close of the hearing, which lasted from 10 A. M. until 12:40 P. M., Goodman A. Sarachan, chairman of the commission, declared that the investigation could and would continue without Mr. Monaghan.

The hearings will be continued next Monday at 10 A. M.

Continued on Page 4, Column 4

CONDUCT UNDER STUDY: George P. Monaghan, State Harness Racing Commissioner, leaves hearing of Commission of Investigation.

JUKE BOX INQUIRY INDICTS 15 ON L. I.

O'Rourke, an Aide of Hoffa, in Group Charged With Coercion in Nassau

Special to The New York Times.

MINEOLA, L. I., Friday, May 29—John J. O'Rourke, vice president of the International Brotherhood of Teamsters, was arrested last night on indictments accusing him and fourteen others of juke box racketeering in Nassau County.

By 2:30 A. M. today, twelve men had been booked on charges of conspiracy, coercion, extortion and attempted extortion. The police moved quickly after the surprise indictments were returned by a Nassau grand jury.

Mr. O'Rourke, president of the Teamsters Joint Council of New York City and long a stalwart of James R. Hoffa, teamsters' international president, was arrested along with three officials of Local 266 of the teamsters.

Shortly after he was taken to Nassau County Jail at East Meadow, Mr. O'Rourke was released on $25,000 bail. The bail was set by Supreme Court Justice Howard Hogan. Mr. O'Rourke's attorney is Ed Neary, former District Attorney of Nassau County.

Says Arrest Is His First

"Why are you doing this to me?" Mr. O'Rourke asked the police as he was being booked. The 59-year-old union leader declared that it was the first time that he had ever been arrested. He gave his address as 41-50 Twentieth Street, Woodside, Queens.

The officers of the local who were arrested were Joseph DeGrandis, 53, president, of 3890 Victory Boulevard, Staten Island; Francis De Forte, 36, vice president, 1269 Forty-second Street, Brooklyn, and Ernest R. Zundel, 62, secretary-treasurer, 315 West 102d Street, Manhattan. After the indictments were returned, District Attorney Manuel J. Levine and Assist-

Continued on Page 9, Column 1

BRITAIN RELAXING CURBS ON IMPORTS

Quotas on Many Items From U. S. and Canada to be Ended or Increased

By WALTER H. WAGGONER
Special to The New York Times.

LONDON, May 28—Britain announced today a relaxation of curbs on imports of goods that must be paid for in dollars.

This will enable United States producers of scores of consumer items to compete on virtually an even basis with West European suppliers for the first time since World War II.

In a step made possible by Britain's good economic health, the Board of Trade ended quantitative restrictions, or quotas, on imports of about forty-five groups of consumer goods from dollar areas and increased the quotas for others. Tariff rates were not changed.

Auto Quota to Rise

The quota for automobiles will be increased from £600,000 ($1,680,000) to £1,500,000 ($4,200,000). Whether this will mean a proportionate rise in sales is problematical. It was permissible to import about 650 United States cars in 1958, but only about 200 were actually bought.

For most of the items, the effective date for the relaxation is June 8. For a smaller number, the date is next Jan. 1.

"The effect of these measures will be a further substantial reduction in discrimination in the operation of our import controls against Canada, the United States and the rest of the dollar area," the Board of Trade said.

"Over the range of goods

Continued on Page 4, Column 4

TREASURY TO ASK RISE OF 12 BILLION IN U.S. DEBT LIMIT

Seasonal Borrowing Needs Will Require 'Temporary' Ceiling of 295 Billion

By EDWIN L. DALE Jr.
Special to The New York Times.

WASHINGTON, May 28—The Treasury will soon ask Congress for an increase in the national debt limit, probably to $295,000,000,000. This would be $12,000,000,000 above the present "permanent" ceiling of $283,000,000,000.

Despite increasing hope that the budget will be balanced in the next fiscal year, beginning July 1, the Treasury's seasonal borrowing needs, plus allowance for emergencies, will require at least a "temporary" ceiling of $295,000,000,000.

The Treasury now expects it will have to borrow $6,000,000,000 to $7,000,000,000 in the period from July 1 to Dec. 31, when tax collections are lowest. This is an upward revision of some unofficial earlier estimates, despite optimism about the budget outlook.

A Technical Obstacle

The reason is a technical provision in the tax law that may keep corporation tax receipts unusually low next fall. Under the present outlook, all or nearly all of the $6,000,000,000 to $7,000,000,000 of borrowing will be paid off next spring, but the debt limit must be raised, meanwhile, to permit the borrowing.

The national debt is now $285,000,000,000. It is covered by a temporary ceiling of $288,000,000,000 that reverts to the permanent ceiling of $283,000,000,000 on June 30, the end of the present fiscal year.

The present expectation is that the debt will finish the fiscal year at about its present level. During June one large item of debt will be paid off but there will be increases in other items. At the same time, the Treasury is expected to enter the period of seasonal deficit with just an ordinary cash balance of about $4,000,000,000.

Thus it is all but certain that the debt will rise well above $290,000,000,000 temporarily. Given the need for a margin of error, the Treasury is expected to ask for a temporary ceiling during the year from July 1, 1959, to June 30, 1960, of $295,000,000,000.

Balanced Budget Likely

Some of the increase will be asked on a temporary basis and some will be requested as additional to the permanent debt ceiling. If the budget is balanced, as now seems a reasonably good prospect, the Treasury by a year from June 30 will have the debt down to about $285,000,000,000 again.

The main reason for the prospective heavy borrowing in the interim is related to corporation taxes.

Corporations are required to pay an increasing portion of their taxes in September and December as a sort of "advance" on their full tax liability due in the following March and June. However, the law gives them permission to base this "advance" payment on their earnings in the previous year.

Continued on Page 11, Column 4

House Unit Revises Defense-Fund Bill, Disputing President

By JACK RAYMOND
Special to The New York Times.

WASHINGTON, May 28—The House Appropriations Committee challenged President Eisenhower's defense planning today. It recommended more money for big missile programs than the President had requested and withheld money on other military projects.

The committee also cited differences among the highest military leaders who testified at its hearings and declared:

"The President, the Secretary of Defense, the Congress and the American people have a right to expect a better job from the Joint Chiefs of Staff in the way of military guidance."

Total Is Cut 1%

The House committee, in reporting the defense appropriations bill for floor debate next week, cut about 1 per cent—$399,861,000—from the President's request for $39,248,200,000 in new money for the fiscal year beginning July 1.

The committee recommended $38,848,339,000. If adopted, this sum would effect only a modest reduction in the President's plans for spending $40,945,000,000 for the military in the same period. Substantial time usually elapses between the appropriation of funds by Congress and actual expenditures.

But the committee clearly substituted its own military judgment for that of the Administration.

This was especially noticeable in continental air defense, in which the committee sided with the Army against the Air

Continued on Page 3, Column 7

Five City Tax Bills Fought at Hearing

By PAUL CROWELL

Five local bills designed to add $90,000,000 to the city's annual revenue from special taxes were assailed by business and civic groups yesterday at a day-long public hearing before the Finance Committee of the City Council.

The measures were sent to the Council by Mayor Wagner. They call for a 10-cent tax on taxicab rides, a tax of $25 a year on juke boxes, a levy of ½ of 1 per cent on real estate transfers, a doubling of the 1 per cent tax on gross receipts of public utilities and a 5¢ per cent rise in existing taxes on gross receipts of general and financial businesses.

All five bills set July 1 as their effective dates. The Fi-

Continued on Page 12, Column 3

2 MONKEYS SURVIVE FLIGHT INTO SPACE IN U. S. ROCKET AND ARE RETRIEVED AT SEA

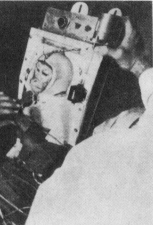

Associated Press Wirephoto (U. S. Army)
SPACE CADET: A rhesus monkey, born in the U. S., in apparatus like that used to send two monkeys into space and back. Monkey was one of those trained for the flight.

KILLIAN RESIGNS AS SCIENCE AIDE

Service Hailed by President —Harvard Man Named as Special Assistant

Eisenhower-Killian exchange of letters is on Page 2.

By JOHN W. FINNEY
Special to The New York Times.

WASHINGTON, May 28—Dr. James R. Killian Jr., the chief architect of the nation's scientific programs for the last eighteen months, resigned today as President Eisenhower's Special Assistant for Science and Technology.

To succeed Dr. Killian in the White House advisory post, the President named Dr. George Bogdan Kistiakowsky, a Russian-born scientist who is now Professor of Chemistry at Harvard University.

The resignation of Dr. Killian, to be effective in mid-July, was announced by the White House, which made public an exchange of letters between Dr. Killian and the President.

In a warmly worded "Dear Jim" letter, President Eisenhower accepted Dr. Killian's resignation with "very sincere regret" and praised his "highly significant contribution" in strengthening scientific and educational programs.

Returning to M. I. T.

Dr. Killian wrote the President that he was resigning "for compelling personal reasons" and to return to the Massachusetts Institute of Technology, from which he has been on a leave of absence. Dr. Killian was president of the institute when he left to become scientific adviser to the President in November, 1957. Last December he was named chairman of the M. I. T. Corporation.

Dr. Killian was called to Washington to help coordinate and strengthen the nation's scientific program following the launching of the first Soviet satellites.

In the new post of Presidential Assistant for Science and Technology, Dr. Killian has asserted a profound influence in the formulation of scientific programs to meet the Soviet satellites.

Dr. Killian has become the

Continued on Page 2, Column 6

A 1,700-MILE TRIP

10,000-Mile-an-Hour Speed Reached by Jupiter Cone

By RICHARD WITKIN
Special to The New York Times.

CAPE CANAVERAL, Fla., May 28—Two monkeys were rocketed 300 miles above the earth today and then were plucked alive from the ocean 1,700 miles down the Caribbean missile range. They reached a maximum speed of 10,000 miles an hour.

So far as is known they were the first animals to survive a long-distance flight through space.

The Russian dog Laika died after a week aboard Sputnik II, the orbit of which exceeded 1,000 miles in height. Two Russian dogs were sent to an altitude of 281 miles last year and were recovered unharmed. But that rocket trip was straight up and down.

If the Russians have accomplished anything comparable to today's exploit they are keeping it to themselves.

Ride In Nose Cone

The monkey astronauts, both females, took their awesome trip in the nose of a Jupiter, the intermediate-range ballistic missile developed by the Army team at Huntsville, Ala.

They were subjected to the ordeal to help answer questions that must be answered before this country will risk sending a human astronaut into space.

Dovetailing answers are to be sought by shooting four mice into orbit from Vandenberg Air Force Base in California. If possible, they will be returned safely to earth. The shot has been delayed two or three times. It is now scheduled for some time next week.

The first attempt by this country to send a human into orbit is not expected for about two years. Seven candidates for the mission have been picked. The National Aeronautics and Space Administration, the Federal agency that had jurisdiction over today's flight, also runs the man-in-space program.

Both Monkeys Wired

One of the primates on today's flight was a seven-pound reddish-brown rhesus monkey named Able.

She was wired so that readings on her physiological reactions could be transmitted to the ground. She was also trained to tap a switch, something like a telegraph key, when a red light flashed every one and a half to two seconds.

Most of the radio circuits provided good readings and showed that the monkey had taken the trip "remarkably well." But the transmitter from the "telegraph key" broke down before take-off. No one will ever know if Able performed her task under the stresses of space flight.

The passenger in the other space capsule was a one-pound brownish, goggle-eyed squirrel monkey named Baker. She was wired for physiological reac-

Continued on Page 2, Column 2

Benson Rules Out Subsidy for Eggs

By The Associated Press

WASHINGTON, May 28—The Agriculture Department has refused to subsidize the egg market.

This was disclosed today by Representative Harold D. Cooley, Democrat of North Carolina, who made public a letter from Clarence E. Miller, Assistant Agriculture Secretary. The department does not plan to purchase hens, broilers or eggs in shells to bolster failing prices.

Mr. Cooley, chairman of the House Agriculture Committee, termed this a callous approach to a problem that, he said, threatened disaster for the poultry industry.

"The Secretary stands idly by

Continued on Page 24, Column 3

WHITE HOUSE CONFERENCE: President Eisenhower chatting with Andrei A. Gromyko, right, Soviet Foreign Minister. Other visitors to his office are, from left, Secretary of State Herter, Maurice Couve de Murville, French Foreign Minister, and Selwyn Lloyd, British Foreign Minister. The four foreign ministers, who had gone to Washington to attend the funeral of former Secretary of State Dulles, returned to Geneva yesterday.

Associated Press Wirephoto

NEWS INDEX

	Page		Page
Books	31	Obituaries	31
Business	38-39	Real Estate	51
Buyers	39	Screen	13-15
Crossword	35	Ships and Air	44
Editorial	22	Society	27
Financial	38-46	Sports	28-35
Food	26	Theatres	13-15
Letters	22	TV and Radio	47
Man in the News	3	U. N. Proceedings	9
Music	13-15	Wash. Proceedings	11
		Weather	46

News Summary and Index, Page 25

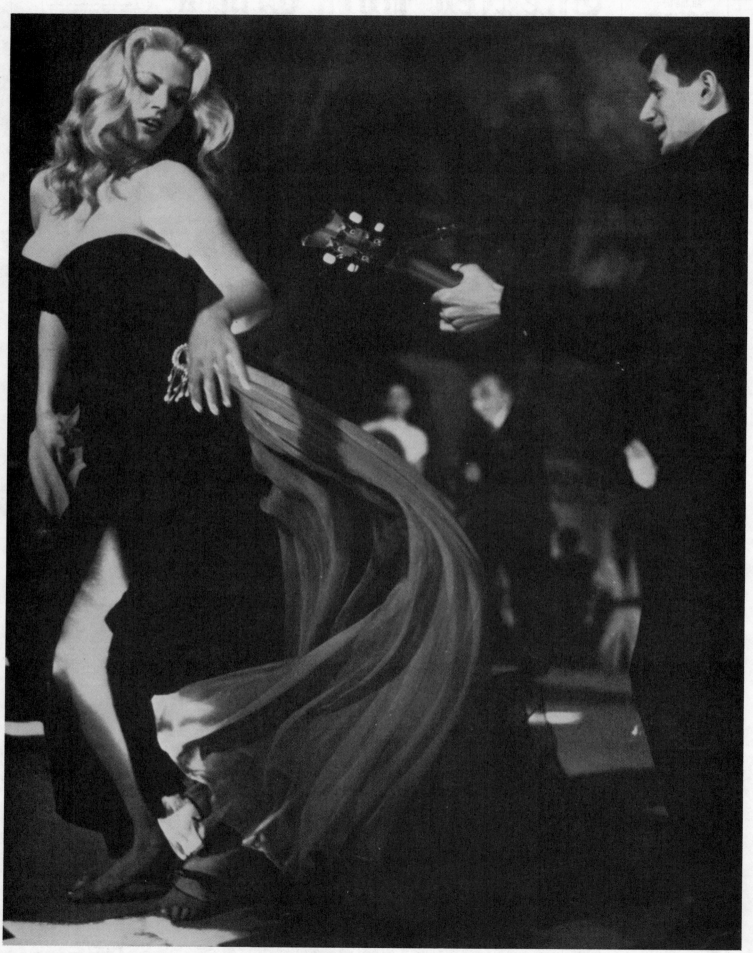

Federico Fellini's La Dolce Vita *caused a stir among American audiences.*

"All the News That's Fit to Print"

The New York Times.

LATE CITY EDITION
U. S. Weather Bureau Report (Page 58) forecasts: Fair and pleasant today; fair, cool tonight. Mostly fair tomorrow.
Temp. range: 75—56; yesterday: 77.0—57.6.

VOL. CVIII . . No. 37,123. NEW YORK, MONDAY, SEPTEMBER 14, 1959. 10 cents beyond 50-mile zone from New York City except on Long Island. Higher in air delivery cities. FIVE CENTS

SOVIET ROCKET HITS MOON AFTER 35 HOURS; ARRIVAL IS CALCULATED WITHIN 84 SECONDS; SIGNALS RECEIVED TILL MOMENT OF IMPACT

CONGRESS ENDING WITH EISENHOWER IN FIRM CONTROL

Early Democratic Initiative Gave Way to Moderation —Thrift the Key Issue

Record of voting during the session on Page 24

By JOHN D. MORRIS
Special to The New York Times.

WASHINGTON, Sept. 13—The Eighty-sixth Congress is bringing to a scheduled close tomorrow night a long session that produced substantial legislation shaped largely by a relatively conservative Republican Administration.

Its Democratic majorities, the largest in two decades, either compromised or yielded to a newly aggressive President Eisenhower on a broad range of economic and social issues.

The President was challenged on a few selected issues, but his free use of the veto and indirectly the veto threat forced frequent Democratic retreats and some surrenders.

In addition, the President was especially effective in rallying public opinion to his side. He did so with notable success in such major disputes as Federal spending and labor reform.

Appealed to Voters

With new-found vigor and articulation, he periodically sent strongly worded messages to Congress and repeatedly took his case directly to the voters in radio - television chats, speeches and news conferences.

At the Capitol, and particularly in the House of Representatives, the depleted Republican minorities fought his causes with effectiveness far beyond their numerical potential, often in coalition with conservative Democrats from the South.

When the new Congress came to Washington last January, fresh from a landslide victory for Democrats in the November elections, there were strong in-

Continued on Page 24, Column 1

SUSPECT IS SHOT AT PENN STATION

Youth Is Wounded in Chase —Bystander Is Grazed

A teen-aged suspect in a theft was shot and captured last night during a chase through Pennsylvania Station. One bystander was grazed in the neck by one of the five shots that were fired.

Two policemen pursued the suspect from the Greyhound Bus Terminal, on Thirty-third Street between Seventh and Eighth Avenues, across the street into the station. He was then chased along lower-level passageways to a railroad platform, where he was shot in the leg.

The station was not crowded when the chase started at 9:30 P. M., but about 200 persons in the station reacted with fear and consternation.

The pursuit began, the police said, with a telephone call from Robert E. Blackwell of 330 Oxford Street, Brooklyn. Mr. Blackwell, who phoned from the bus terminal, told the police that last Thursday a woman's pocketbook had been snatched in the terminal. He said that he had just spotted the thief.

When Patrolmen James Mierisch and Anthony Naglieri arrived in a radio car, Mr. Blackwell pointed to a man in the station. The police later identified him as Ronald Baxter, 19 years old, of 105 West 117th Street.

However, after questioning at the prison ward at Bellevue Hospital, the police said, Baxter admitted his name was James Talley, and he lived at 40-05 Twelfth Street, Astoria, Queens.

Continued on Page 58, Column 6

Schools Reopening In the City Today; 1,400,000 on Rolls

By LEONARD BUDER

After ten weeks of summer silence, school bells will signal the start of a new term here this morning.

Public, parochial and many private schools will reopen for more than 1,400,000 pupils.

The city's more than 800 public schools are expecting an enrollment of 985,000 youngsters, the largest number since 1941. Roman Catholic schools are expecting a record city-wide total of 369,950 pupils. Thousands of other pupils will attend Jewish and Protestant schools and nonsectarian private schools.

From kindergarten to senior high school, steps are being taken this year to improve what goes on in the classroom and to counteract some adverse influences that originate

Continued on Page 22, Column 4

STATE LABOR CUTS DEMOCRATIC TIES

Hollander Statement Praises G. O. P. Leaders but Also Bans All 'Entanglements'

Louis Hollander, chairman of the Committee on Political Education of the state A. F. L. - C. I. O., caustically criticized the Democratic leadership in Congress yesterday, while praising the records of Republican Governor Rockefeller and Senators Jacob K. Javits and Kenneth B. Keating.

The union chief, who headed the old state C. I. O. for ten years before the state merger last year, conceded that labor had been too close to the Democrats in past campaigns. He asserted that its future policy would be to shun entanglements with either party.

These views were given out after a joint meeting of the political education and executive committees of the state organization.

"I confess that the state C. I. O. made a mistake by allying itself solely with the Democrats," Mr. Hollander said in a statement. "They doublecrossed us, and the Republicans ignored us because they felt sure we would be on the other side anyway. This drove even the more enlightened Republicans into the arms of the Dixiecrats on labor legislation, civil

Continued on Page 19, Column 4

CAPITAL FINISHING ITS PREPARATIONS FOR KHRUSHCHEV

President to Discuss Plans with Herter and Dillon— Premier Due Tomorrow

By DANA ADAMS SCHMIDT
Special to The New York Times.

WASHINGTON, Sept. 13—Washington was engaged this week-end in the most painstaking preparations ever made for the reception of an official visitor to the United States.

The preparations are for Premier Nikita S. Khrushchev, who is due at 11:30 A. M. Tuesday at Andrews Air Force Base, fifteen miles from Washington. He will be met there by President Eisenhower.

The President will discuss his part in dealing with Mr. Khrushchev at a White House meeting tomorrow morning with Secretary of State Christian A. Herter and Under Secretary Douglas Dillon.

Mr. Herter returned to Washington today from a vacation in Massachusetts and spent the afternoon going over plans for Mr. Khrushchev's visit with his aides.

Herter Visits Nixon

This evening he dined with Vice President Richard M. Nixon who, on the strength of his recent tour of the Soviet Union, is considered among the Administration's leading authorities on how to handle the Soviet dictator.

Vice President Nixon said today that the Soviet Premier had approved of Chinese Communist aggression, perhaps in the hope of getting "more action" out of his visit here. On a New York State radio hook-up, Mr. Nixon said that the absence of any disapproving note in Soviet statements about intrusions into India and Laos "would seem to indicate that they are encouraging, or at least approve, that action."

Meanwhile, the State Department was completing arrangements for handling more than 100 Soviet visitors, including thirty-four journalists; at least 300 American and foreign reporters who want to follow the whole tour, and about 2,000 others who will cover parts of it.

Plans were made for deploying about 15,000 military men, policemen, detectives, National Guardsmen and security agents to protect the Russians in Washington. About 40,000 men will be used to maintain security during the thirteen-day tour.

Coordinating the operation is

Continued on Page 10, Column 3

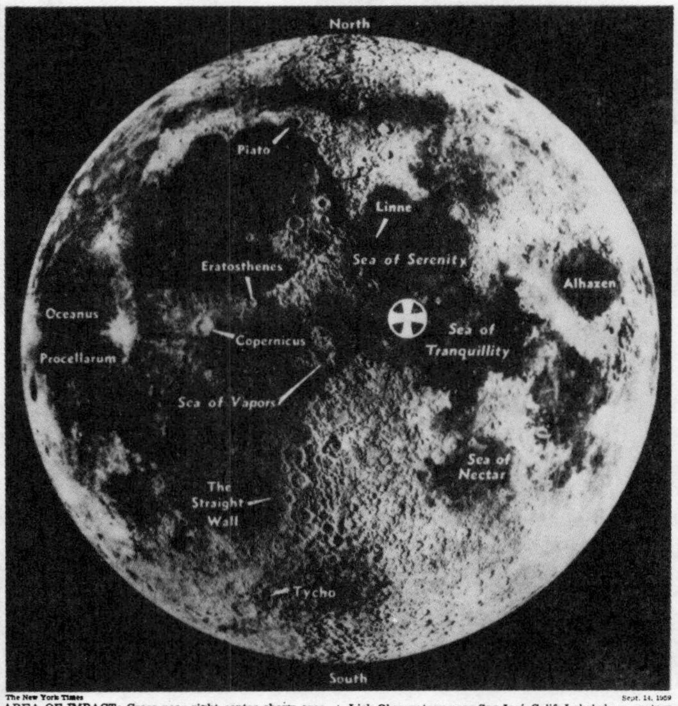

The New York Times Sept. 14, 1959

AREA OF IMPACT: Cross near right center shows area where Soviet rocket hit surface of moon. Photograph is a composite picture of face of moon taken by camera of Lick Observatory near San José, Calif. Labeled are craters such as Copernicus at left center and three seas in area of the landing, Tranquillity, Serenity and Vapors.

FLAGS IN VEHICLE

Sphere Rams Surface at 7,500 M.P.H.— Moscow Jubilant

Text of Soviet announcement is on Page 16.

By MAX FRANKEL
Special to The New York Times.

MOSCOW, Monday, Sept. 14—The Soviet Union hit the moon with a space rocket early this morning.

The first object sent by man from one cosmic body to another bore pennants and the hammer-and-sickle emblem of the Soviet Government.

The announcement said steps had been taken to prevent the destruction of the pennants by the impact.

The object was a sphere of unknown size weighing 858.4 pounds. It crashed into the moon at a speed of about 7,500 miles an hour at 2 minutes and 24 seconds after midnight Moscow time. This was 5:02:24 P. M. Sunday in New York.

The time of impact was only 84 seconds later than Soviet scientists had predicted.

Instrument Sphere

The success of the Soviet's moon shot was made known in a jubilant Government announcement at 35 minutes after midnight over the Moscow radio.

The sphere was a hermetically sealed instrument container that had been ejected from the last stage of a multi-stage rocket.

The rocket was launched from Soviet territory at about one o'clock Saturday afternoon Moscow time (6 A. M. in New York).

The container covered a distance of 236,875 miles in about 35 hours.

The impact was not visible from the earth, but the strike was signaled by the sudden end to radio transmissions that were being received here from the container during its space voyage.

[Jodrell Bank in England reported that it had received the signals up to the time the rocket hit the moon.]

Fate of Sphere Unknown

The sphere was able to reach the moon's surface because there is little or no atmosphere that would produce friction and burn it up.

It is not known whether it shattered on impact or penetrated the dust that is thought to blanket much of the moon's surface.

Soviet scientists had estimated before the final announcement that the container would hit at a point about 270 miles from the center of the face among three large depressions in the moon's surface known as the Seas of Tranquillity, Serenity and Vapors.

There was no word here on the fate of the last stage of the rocket, which had been flying in space near the container. The container was separated from the rocket segment after they had safely escaped from the

Continued on Page 16, Column 1

Red China Charges Indians Are Using 'Two-Faced' Policy

By TILLMAN DURDIN
Special to The New York Times.

HONG KONG, Sept. 13—Marshal Chen Yi, Foreign Minister of Communist China, said today that the Indian Government "used two-faced tactics" in the border dispute between the two countries.

He added that Indian troops and administrative personnel "should withdraw from Chinese territory" and that "there does not exist a question of Chinese troops' withdrawing from anywhere."

For the first time Marshal Chen brought the Dalai Lama into the dispute between New Delhi and Peiping over the Chinese-Indian boundary.

Marshal Chen said the Dalai Lama's political activities in India against China and his move to raise the Tibetan question in the United Nations exceeded "by far what is allowed under the international practice of asylum." The Mar-

Continued on Page 3, Column 2

14th U.N. Assembly Begins Tomorrow

Proposed agenda for the U. N. Assembly on Page 8.

By LINDESAY PARROTT
Special to The New York Times.

UNITED NATIONS, N. Y., Sept. 13—The eighty-two-nation General Assembly will begin its fourteenth annual session here Tuesday with sixty-nine items on the agenda before it.

Some of the items are comparatively routine, such as elections of members of councils and committees. Others are potentially explosive politically.

Some of the most strenuous discussion this year was expected to center on the issues of French North Africa and disarmament. But Communist aggression in Tibet and Laos also is sure to get an airing, in the

Continued on Page 8, Column 6

NIXON SAYS SOVIET FAILED IN 3 SHOTS

Reports Moscow Attempted to Hit Moon With Rocket 'in the Last Two Weeks'

Vice President Richard M. Nixon said here last night that the Soviet Union had "failed three times in the last two weeks" to hit the moon with a rocket.

Mr. Nixon said he could not reveal the source of his information.

The Soviet Union has made no mention of any failures. Neither have there been previous disclosures by the United States that any had occurred.

The Vice President made his statement as he arrived at La Guardia Airport from Washington.

He also took the occasion to caution against "hysterical" reactions to the apparent success of the Soviet Union's moon shot.

"In science, sometimes we're ahead and sometimes they're ahead," he said.

Told to Expect Shifts

The Vice President said that the country should learn to expect such shifts in a highly complex endeavor of taking the first steps into outer space.

"But over-all, we are way ahead," he said.

Moreover, Mr. Nixon said, the excited reactions to the Soviet effort should not become the occasion for renewed attacks on the state of this country's science and education.

"It's nothing to get excited about," he cautioned. "Scientifically and educationally we are way ahead of the Soviets and there is no reason to junk our educational programs."

What the country should do, he said, is to "redouble" its efforts in an area where "someone else may be ahead."

The Associated Press reported that the Vice President's press secretary, Herbert Klein, had said "there is no official proof yet" of the Soviet success.

The Vice President nodded

Continued on Page 18, Column 4

Washington Praises Feat; Hopes for Sharing of Data

By JOHN W. FINNEY
Special to The New York Times.

WASHINGTON, Sept. 13—The Soviet achievement of placing the first man-made object on the moon was greeted here today with admiration and congratulations. But the reaction was tinged with regrets that once again the United States had been bested in the space race.

Within official Washington there was none of the near-hysteria that prevailed nearly two years ago with the launching of the first artificial earth satellite by the Soviet Union.

Rather, the Russian feat was regarded as another, if important, step in the exploration of space, in which the Soviet Union had the good fortune and the necessary rocket power to be first.

Statement by Dryden

The principal official reaction came from Dr. Hugh L. Dryden, deputy administrator of the National Aeronautics and Space Administration.

"We have followed with interest the travel of the Soviet lunar probe to its impact with the moon," he said in a statement.

"We wish to congratulate our fellow scientists and engineers on their success in this forward step in the exploration of space. We hope that the scientific data obtained in this flight will soon be available for study by the scientists of all countries."

There was no tendency to minimize the scientific importance of the Soviet lunar rocket in extending the frontiers of man's knowledge of space. But it was generally agreed that the most immediate importance of the feat probably lay in the diplomatic and psychological realms.

The timing of the launching just prior to Premier Nikita S. Khrushchev's heralded visit to the United States confirmed a belief within official circles that the space experiment had been designed as much for a psychological impact on American and world opinion as for an impact on the lunar surface.

On the basis of past Soviet practice of using technological triumphs as a psychological lever in diplomacy, there was every expectation that Mr. Khrushchev, on his forthcoming trip to this country, would proudly point to the Soviet moon rocket as evidence that the Soviet Union was the technological match of the United States.

Coming as it did on a sunny, fall-like afternoon when official Washington was more en-

Continued on Page 16, Column 7

Khrushchev's Russia—7

Premier Tries a Pragmatic Approach Toward Soviet Arts and Literature

Following is the seventh of eight articles on the Soviet Union under Khrushchev by a correspondent who had extended tours of duty in Stalinist and post-Stalinist Russia and recently spent four months in the Soviet Union.

By HARRISON E. SALISBURY

Some people in Moscow are convinced that there was a plot last autumn in which a group of writers and editors allied themselves with powerful Communist party forces in an attempt to turn the ideological clock back to Stalin.

This, it is said, was an underlying reason for the savagery with which Boris Pasternak, Nobel Prize winner, and his novel "Doctor Zhivago" were attacked.

In the end Nikita S. Khrushchev turned against the cabal and repudiated the Stalinist implications of the literary-political intrigue and a new era of toleration in creative matters was decreed.

The Pasternak affair and its ramifications illustrate the dilemma of the Khrushchev regime in dealing with the intellectual. Mr. Khrushchev is deeply committed to greater creative freedoms. But Soviet writers, artists, musicians and poets move faster than the Communist party is prepared to go.

The ideological difficulties have been most severe in the realm of the printed word. In some artistic fields a quiet revolution has occurred with the aid and encouragement of Mr. Khrushchev. This is notably the case in architecture. Music is not far behind. Painting and sculpture are rapidly moving toward more modern Western concepts. Ballet stands on the threshold of new experimentation.

Only occasional echoes of the battles on the artistic front are heard in the West because the Soviet censorship often refuses to pass dispatches that touch on vital aspects of the controversies.

For example, the censors consistently eliminated all references to the fact that Mr. Khrushchev had sober second thoughts about the Pasternak case. The censorship also sup-

Continued on Page 14, Column 1

U.S Rejects Any Flag-Planting As Legal Claim to Rule Moon

By PETER KIHSS

The United States is taking the legal position that just planting flags on the moon as the Soviet Union says it has done will not give the Russians or anyone else any claim to rule over that body.

But John M. Raymond, deputy legal adviser to the State Department, said in Washington yesterday that the United States had "no views on how far you would have to go" to claim moon sovereignty, as yet. Mr. Raymond said one question was: "Is it subject to sovereignty?"

William A. Hyman, a New York international lawyer who has headed national and local bar association studies of space law and aeronautics, said here: "Since consistency is not one of the Soviets' virtues, it would not be surprising to hear them say that if the satellite made physical contact with the moon, they would then claim they had extended sovereignty to the lunar sphere. But this would be in violation of their own position taken in September, 1958."

Mr. Hyman noted that at that time, the Soviet legal journal Sovetskoye Gosudarstvo i Pravo, in an article by Miss A. Galina, had urged that no government be permitted to incorporate any portion of interplanetary space under its jurisdiction. This was in an argument that rockets could be launched into space without asking permission of any other government.

The hope that any Soviet claim to moon sovereignty might be in the name of the

Continued on Page 16, Column 5

NEWS INDEX

	Page		Page
Bills in Washington	25	Music	32-33
Books	27	Obituaries	29
Bridge	26	Real Estate	47
Business	42-43, 46	Screen	32-33
Buyers	42	Sermons	25
Crossword	27	Ships and Air	58
Editorial	28	Society	26
Fashions	34	Sports	35-41
Financial	42-46	TV and Radio	59
Food	34	Theatres	32-33
Man in the News	10	Weather	58

News Summary and Index, Page 31

The unpopular Cuban dictator, Fulgencio Batista, was overthrown by Fidel Castro.

Soviet Premier Nikita Khruschev visited President Eisenhower and toured the U.S. in 1959.

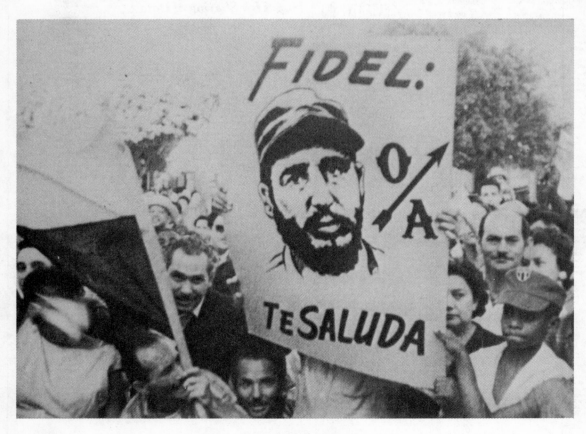

Enthusiastic Cubans congregated to hear the announcement that Fidel Castro would resume the premiership of Cuba.

The New York Times.

LATE CITY EDITION
U. S. Weather Bureau Report [Page 79] forecast:
Mostly cloudy and cool today and tomorrow.
Temp. range: 66–55; yesterday: 76,8–57.

VOL. CVIII—No. 37,125. © 1959, by The New York Times Company. Times Square, New York 36, N. Y. — NEW YORK, WEDNESDAY, SEPTEMBER 16, 1959. — 10 cents beyond 50-mile zone from New York City except on Long Island. Higher in air delivery cities. — FIVE CENTS

KHRUSHCHEV GETS BIG BUT QUIET WELCOME FROM 200,000 ON ARRIVAL IN WASHINGTON; HAS 'FRANK' 2-HOUR TALK WITH EISENHOWER

DE SAPIO IS VICTOR IN CLOSE PRIMARY AS KEY AIDES LOSE

Powell Winner in Harlem—Reform Group Jubilant—Clancy Is Nominated

By LEO EGAN

Carmine G. De Sapio retained his Greenwich Village Tammany district leadership by a razor-thin margin last night but found his leadership of the New York County Democratic organization materially weakened.

Three district leaders who had been stanch De Sapio allies fell before insurgents who had the backing of the Democratic reform faction headed by former Senator Herbert H. Lehman and Mrs. Franklin D. Roosevelt.

Three others upon whose support Mr. De Sapio had been able to count confidently succumbed to Harlem insurgents who had the support of Representative Adam Clayton Powell Jr. Mr. Powell won the leadership of the Twelfth District, South, from Elijah Crump, a De Sapio ally.

New Queens Leader Likely

The Harlem insurgents were not associated in any way with those supported by the reform faction.

In Queens, Borough President John T. (Pat) Clancy won in a three-way contest for the Democratic nomination for his present office. With his victory, Queens is expected to get any obligation to Mr. De Sapio.

Such a development could materially reduce Mr. De Sapio's stature as the top spokesman for the Democratic organization in New York City.

In a statement issued at Tammany Hall after he had reviewed the results of twenty contests for Tammany district leaderships up for election in yesterday's primaries, Mr. De Sapio said he expected to be re-elected county leader when the executive committee met to reorganize a week from tomorrow.

Able to Count on Votes

Police Commissioner Stephen P. Kennedy announced at 3 A. M. today that Charles E. McGuinness, who opposed Mr. De Sapio, had requested that the voting machines be guarded because of the close vote. Mr. McGuinness said there might have been some irregularities. The machines, which were placed under guard in forty districts, will be impounded in the morning, Mr. Kennedy said.

A source close to Mr. De Sapio calculated that he would be able to count on eleven of the sixteen votes in the Tammany executive committee even if all the reform leaders and the anti-De Sapio Harlem leaders banded together.

Mr. Lehman and George Backer, another leader in the anti-De Sapio movement, hailed the results as "a great victory for the reform forces."

The former Senator declared that Mr. McGuinness had made "an amazing showing" in his

Continued on Page 34, Column 5

Art Worth $600,000 Is Stolen in Toronto

Special to The New York Times

TORONTO, Sept. 15—The Toronto Art Gallery was looted of $600,000 worth of paintings last night.

Two Rembrandts, two Halses, a Renoir and a Rubens were cut from their frames in what was called the biggest art haul in Canadian history.

Alan Jarvis, retiring director of Canada's National Gallery, termed the theft "incredible and appalling." He said the stolen paintings were "all great works of art."

The robbery was discovered when the gallery opened this morning.

Paintings by Gainsborough and Vandyke were slashed, but the hurried thieves left the

Continued on Page 33, Column 3

Congress Adjourns; Extends Rights Unit

By RUSSELL BAKER

WASHINGTON, Sept. 15—The First Session of the Eighty-sixth Congress died with a yawn this morning just before breakfast.

Not, however, before the Senate had set forces in motion that could lead to an epic civil rights battle inflaming political emotionalism early in the 1960 Presidential election year.

Some Southerners, depressed by two crushing votes against a minor rights issue in the early morning, believed that 1960 might see a civil rights filibuster broken in the Senate for the first time in history.

The all-day, all-night endurance test, which finally crushed every last Senator's will to talk, was dominated by the civil rights issue, with

Continued on Page 23, Column 1

WHITE PUPILS END QUEENS BOYCOTT

5 Schools Quiet in Transfer Dispute—Demonstration in Riverdale Called Off

By LEONARD BUDER

White children returned to classes yesterday at five Queens public schools, ending a one-day boycott protesting the transfer of Negro and Puerto Rican pupils from Brooklyn.

With the exception of an unfounded bomb scare at one school and the brief appearance of two pickets at another, there were no demonstrations yesterday.

In another school development, a group of Negro parents from Harlem called off a demonstration scheduled for this morning at a junior high school in the Riverdale section of the Bronx.

The parents announced their decision after obtaining a court order requiring the Board of Education to show why the Harlem children should not be admitted to or to one in a predominantly white neighborhood in the northern part of Manhattan.

The school board was required to give its explanation tomorrow morning before Justice Henry Clay Greenberg in Supreme Court in Manhattan.

Paul B. Zuber, attorney for the Negro parents, asserted that his group—said to consist of about 200 parents and a

Continued on Page 33, Column 4

U.N. OPENS SESSION CALMLY AND PICKS PERUVIAN AS HEAD

Belaúnde, Assembly's New President, Sees Peace Hope —Soviet Silent on China

The text of Belaúnde speech is printed on Page 3.

By THOMAS J. HAMILTON

UNITED NATIONS, N. Y., Sept. 15—The General Assembly opened its 1959 session today in a tranquil atmosphere. Dr. Victor A. Belaúnde of Peru, who was elected president, told the Assembly that he wanted to express again "my unshakable faith in our organization."

"May God grant that this Assembly go down in history as the Assembly of peace," Dr. Belaúnde said.

Neither Dr. Belaúnde nor Rashid Karame, Premier of Lebanon, who presided during the election of the new president, referred to the arrival in the United States today of Premier Khrushchev. The Soviet leader's address before the Assembly Friday is expected to be the outstanding event of the session.

Dr. Belaúnde emphasized that the world faced the alternative of peace for all peoples or "war which will bring death and universal destruction."

Hope Voiced on Disarmament

He called on Assembly delegates to "remain confident that the great problems of disarmament will, under the auspices of the General Assembly and the Security Council, together with the determined cooperation of the great powers, start a process which will lead to a final solution."

Some Asian delegates saw an encouraging sign in the fact that the nine members of the Soviet bloc, which has never succeeded in electing one of its own delegates as president of the Assembly, voted for Dr. Belaúnde.

The vote was secret, with no nominating speeches, but the Peruvian received eighty-one of the eighty-two votes cast. One ballot was found invalid.

On some opening days in the past, the Soviet Union has interrupted normal procedure by demanding an immediate vote on the question of seating Chinese Communist representatives. However, no such attempt was made today.

The task of calling the Assembly into session fell to Premier Karame because Dr. Charles Malik, former Foreign

Continued on Page 3, Column 1

U. S. Turns Down Proposal by Soviet For Talks on Laos

By E. W. KENWORTHY

WASHINGTON, Sept. 15—The United States rejected today a Soviet proposal for an international conference to deal with the crisis in Laos.

The proposal was made last night, just before the departure of Premier Khrushchev for the United States.

The Soviet Government said the nations that attended the 1954 Geneva conference on Indochina should meet again and receive recommendations for normalizing the situation in Laos from the International Control Commission created by the conference.

Proposal Is Assailed

This morning the State Department issued a hastily composed statement just before the arrival of Mr. Khrushchev. The statement said that the solution of the situation in Laos "is not to be found in international conferences but in the cessation of intervention and subversion" by Laotian Communists, who have had the support of North Vietnam.

A second Geneva conference the United States declared, would be "unnecessary and disruptive," since the United Nations Security Council has already sent a fact-finding subcommittee to the Southeast Asian kingdom.

The Soviet Union cast a negative vote Sept. 7 when the Security Council approved a resolution submitted by the United States, Britain and France, calling for the creation of a subcommittee to study the situation in Laos.

However, Egidio Ortona of

Continued on Page 4, Column 5

Bomb Blast Kills 6 At Houston School

By The Associated Press

HOUSTON, Tex., Sept. 15—A man tossed a suitcase of explosives on a school playground today and killed three persons, himself and two other adults. The police identified one of the dead as the bomber's son.

The explosion sent at least nineteen children and the school principal to hospitals.

Miss Pat Johnston, a teacher, identified the bomber from a photograph as Paul Harold Orgeron, 49 years old, a tile contractor in suburban south Houston.

Police Chief Carl Shuptrine said positive identification of Orgeron as the bomber was established through fingerprints. The Poe Elementary School

Continued on Page 26, Column 1

U. S. AND SOVIET WEIGH ATOM POOL

Chiefs of Nuclear Agencies Discuss Exchanges in Peaceful Fields

Special to The New York Times

WASHINGTON, Sept. 13—The heads of the Soviet and United States atomic energy programs discussed today closer cooperation in the peaceful development of nuclear energy and the sharing of their research with the rest of the world.

John A. McCone, chairman of the Atomic Energy Commission, and Vasily S. Yemelianov, director of the Main Administration for Peaceful Uses of Atomic Energy, met for nearly two hours shortly after the arrival of Premier Khrushchev. Professor Yemelyanov is accompanying Mr. Khrushchev on his American trip.

Among the steps of closer nuclear cooperation discussed was an exchange of scientists as well as research findings in the field of controlled thermonuclear energy. Mr. McCone said he thought it possible that such an exchange of scientists and information could be arranged.

Reactors Discussed

A statement issued after the meeting said the two officials "discussed general ways and means of making available to interested nations the fruits of the unclassified research and development programs of their respective countries in the peaceful applications of atomic energy."

Among the areas discussed, the statement said, were research and power reactors, experiments in the development of processes to control the thermonuclear reactions for the production of electricity, and basic research in the physical and life sciences, including the field of high-energy physics.

United States officials said the discussions were still preliminary and no specific steps had been agreed upon to promote closer cooperation. Mr. McCone, said he would hold a further meeting with Professor Yemelyanov Sept. 24, following his return from a trip through the United States with Mr. Khrushchev.

The two officials discussed measures that could be taken to increase the prestige and functions of the International Atomic Energy Agency, particularly by making the agency an international center for atomic research.

The statement said that it was "agreed in principle" by the two officials that their two

Continued on Page 31, Column 5

INFORMAL: Premier Khrushchev, his black hat resting on a post, responds to President Eisenhower's welcome on his U. S. arrival. In background, from left: Henry Cabot Lodge, U. S. delegate to the United Nations; Mikhail A. Menshikov, Soviet Ambassador to the U. S., and Secretary of State Herter. The others in group are interpreters.

Khrushchev Sees Sights From Car and Helicopter

By DANA ADAMS SCHMIDT

WASHINGTON, Sept. 15—In his first ninety minutes in the United States, Premier Khrushchev saw a neat and white-washed air base, a verdant parkway, a new motel and apartment building, a Negro church, the Capitol clothed in scaffolding, massive government buildings and the White House.

These and the faces of 200,000 multiracial Americans were what may have caught his eye as he rode into the capital from Andrews Air Force Base, fifteen miles away.

Two Hours in Helicopter

About four hours later, he had another view of America. With President Eisenhower as his guide, he swung over the city and the Maryland and Virginia suburbs in a helicopter, glimpsing new housing developments, a marina on the Potomac, the President's favorite golf course and other country clubs, the National Institutes of Health at Bethesda and other landmarks.

The motorcade bearing the Soviet Premier and party and his American hosts swept into town over a route that is rarely taken by foreign visitors.

The giant Soviet TU-114 turbo-prop plane had to land at Andrews Base because the Na-

Continued on Page 18, Column 5

Mme. Khrushchev Is Beaming, Friendly and at Ease in Capital

Keeps State Department in Dark on Her Sight-Seeing Plans for U. S. Tour

By EDITH EVANS ASBURY

WASHINGTON, Sept. 15—Mme. Nina Petrovna Khrushchev beamed as she got her first view of the United States today, but she left the State Department uncertain as to what she wanted to see next.

The gray - haired, motherly-looking second wife of the Soviet Premier was friendly and at ease at the airport, in the car with President Eisenhower and on the steps of Blair House, where she posed for photographers.

After she entered Blair House, however, no word was forthcoming about her plans, and she did not emerge until it was time to cross the street for the state dinner in the White House.

Many places of interest she might like to visit here and during the rest of the tour were

Continued on Page 19, Column 6

PARLEYS ARE SET

President Voices Hope for Improved Basis to Meet Issues

Speeches and joint statement, Page 19; toasts, Page 20.

By HARRISON E. SALISBURY

Special to The New York Times

WASHINGTON, Sept. 15—Premier Khrushchev arrived today and received a big but undemonstrative welcome. He was greeted on landing by President Eisenhower.

The Soviet leader proclaimed immediately the desire of his people to live in peace with America.

Within three hours, Mr. Khrushchev, the first Soviet chief of state to visit the United States, was sitting in the President's oval office at the White House, discussing major issues in the presence of high Soviet and American officials.

A joint communiqué issued after the discussion, which lasted one hour and fifty minutes, said:

"The atmosphere of the talks was friendly and frank, with agreement that the discussions should continue in this spirit to achieve a better understanding."

Private Talk Follows

The talks touched in general terms on all of the major issues between the two countries. At their conclusion, President Eisenhower and Mr. Khrushchev spent about fifteen minutes talking face to face with only their interpreters present.

It was agreed that extended conversations would be held in an informal atmosphere at the President's Camp David retreat in Maryland Sept. 25, 26 and 27 after Mr. Khrushchev returns from his swing around the country.

Later, at a White House dinner, the President and Mr. Khrushchev exchanged toasts in champagne.

"Because of our importance in the world," the President said, "it is vital that we understand each other better. You and I have agreed on this."

The Premier agreed on the need for "improvement of our relations, because our countries are much too strong and we cannot quarrel with each other."

Mr. Khrushchev's great TU-

Continued on Page 18, Column 1

SOVIET SUSPENDS 'VOICE' JAMMING

Interference Is Halted for First Time in Ten Years

By JOHN W. FINNEY

Special to The New York Times

WASHINGTON, Sept. 15—The Soviet Union stopped jamming Voice of America broadcasts today for the first time in ten years. The jamming transmitters went off the air just about the time Premier Khrushchev left Moscow for Washington.

Voice of America officials were elated over the sudden silence of the persistent and powerful jamming network, for it meant that the United States had scored at least a temporary psychological victory in the propaganda war.

The Voice of America had virtually dared the Soviet Union to continue its jamming during Mr. Khrushchev's visit. Through diplomatic channels and in its broadcasts, the Voice had announced that it would carry some of the major speeches of Mr. Khrushchev during his tour.

The Soviet Government was

Continued on Page 18, Column 7

NEWS INDEX

	Page		Page
Art	42	Man in the News	15
Books	36–37	Music	44
Bridge	42	Obituaries	33
Business	52–54, 62	Real Estate	56
Buying Lines	62	Screen	44–45
Crossword	37	Ships and Air	76
Editorial	40	Society	47
Events Today	45	Sports	47–51
Fashions	47	TV and Radio	79
Financial	52–62, 44–46	Theatres	44
Food	44–46	U. N. Proceedings	11
Letters	40	Weather	79
		News Summary and Index, Page 41	

RIVALS: Charles E. McGuinness, opponent of Carmine G. De Sapio, turns from the Democratic leader, refusing to pose with him at polling place at 19 East Eighth Street.

249

"All the News That's Fit to Print"

The New York Times.

LATE CITY EDITION
U. S. Weather Bureau Report (Page 95) forecasts: Mostly fair, not so cool today and tonight. A little warmer tomorrow. Temp. range: 71—52; yesterday: 67.2—46.9.

NEWS SUMMARY AND INDEX, PAGE 95

SECTION ONE

VOL. CIX. No. 37,129. NEW YORK, SUNDAY, SEPTEMBER 20, 1959. 35c outside New York City, its suburban area and Long Island. Higher in air delivery cities. TWENTY-FIVE CENTS

KHRUSHCHEV THREATENS TO RETURN HOME; WARNS COAST AUDIENCE OF SOVIET ROCKETS; PUTS QUESTION OF WAR OR PEACE UP TO U. S.

EISENHOWER SAYS 'FAILURES' MARRED CONGRESS' RECORD

Deplores 'Net Effect' That Added to Spending—Cites New Long-Term Debt

Text of President's statement is printed on Page 62.

By FELIX BELAIR Jr.
Special to The New York Times.

GETTYSBURG, Pa., Sept. 19 — President Eisenhower described the recent Congressional session today as one of "many disappointing failures."

In a prepared statement, the President said:

"The most gratifying and most promising work of the session just ended" had been the way in which public demand "forced the majority to shelve at least temporarily its most lavish [spending] proposals."

The President blamed the Democratic majority in both the Senate and House of Representatives for the fact that a larger part of the Administration's program had not been passed.

Democrats React

Democrats reacted sharply to the President's charge. In Johnson City, Tex., Senator Lyndon

A table giving voting records of Senators during the 1959 session appears on Page 142. It corrects errors that were made in a table published last Monday.

B. Johnson, the majority leader, called it an attempt to start a "cold war" within the United States. Other Democratic leaders in Washington were also critical.

The President's blunt statement is expected to add heat to the 1960 election campaign and to sharpen partisan division in the Congressional session beginning in January.

President Eisenhower called the roll on what he considered the accomplishments as well as the "failures" of the first session of the Eighty-sixth Congress.

Among the session's achievements, President Eisenhower said, were passage of the labor reform bill, the Hawaiian statehood measure and a modification of the Administration's highway financing program.

He also spoke approvingly of the outcome of his personal campaign against "the big spenders" in Congress.

In connection with spending,

Continued on Page 62, Column 4

2 Democrats Assail G.O.P. On Moon Race and Inflation

Symington Tells Democratic Parley U. S. Won't Match Soviet Shot for Years—Gov. Williams Calls Foes 'Afraid'

Special to The New York Times.

WASHINGTON, Sept. 19—Two prominent Democrats tonight attacked the Eisenhower Administration's handling of a host of domestic issues ranging from education and conservation to moon shots.

Senator Stuart Symington of Missouri told a closing session of a conference of Democratic state chairmen that this country would not be able to duplicate the Soviet feat of landing a rocket on the moon "for many years."

The Soviet lunar shot again emphasized "how far the Russians are ahead of us in the conquest of outer space," the Senator said. And, he went on, this country will not be able to do the same thing for many years "even if everything goes exactly right."

"This delay will be extended even further because of recently decided upon additional heavy reductions in the budget," the Senator said without amplification.

Senator Symington is a former Secretary of the Air Force and is a member of the Senate Space and Armed Services Committees.

Gov. G. Mennen Williams of Michigan, meanwhile, told the party leaders that the Republicans were "brake-happy." He asserted that they were so "afraid of inflation, and they are so afraid the Democrats will get the economy going somewhere, that they overbrake, overcreep and overheat the economy into inflation."

"The Republicans are afraid to educate our children, clean up the slums, speed urban renewal, conserve our natural re-

Continued on Page 34, Column 1

Senate Unit Calls Science Vital Foreign Policy Tool

By JOHN W. FINNEY
Special to The New York Times.

WASHINGTON, Sept. 19—The Senate Foreign Relations Committee urged today that greater consideration be given in foreign policy to scientific developments. Such developments in the next decade will inevitably give rise to new problems or intensify existing problems in foreign policy, the committee report said.

Therefore, it said, "the national interest requires a more conscious direction of scientific activity in ways likely to assist in the achievement of America's international goals."

Among the report's specific recommendations was that the United States take the leadership in establishing an international development year—patterned after the International Geophysical Year—to deal with the problems of economic and social development in underprivileged countries.

The report was one of a series of studies being made by the Senate Foreign Relations Committee as part of an over-all review of the nation's foreign policy.

Entitled "Possible Nonmili-

Continued on Page 26, Column 1

A.F.L.-C.I.O. FACES 'JIM CROW' FIGHT

Porters Union Head Seeks Ouster of Two Groups for Ban on Negroes

By A. H. RASKIN
Special to The New York Times.

SAN FRANCISCO, Sept. 19—Discontent over the lag in the elimination of Jim Crow practices in many unions is scheduled to erupt in a floor fight next week at the convention of the American Federation of Labor and Congress of Industrial Organizations.

This became certain today when A. Philip Randolph, president of the Brotherhood of Sleeping Car Porters, announced that he would press for the ouster of two railroad unions for failure to drop prohibitions against Negro membership from their constitutions.

Mr. Randolph, who is the federation's only Negro vice president, disclosed that he would also demand the liquidation of segregated locals in all unions. Several major unions still maintain separate locals for white and Negro members,

Continued on Page 33, Column 1

FOREIGN AID PLAN WOULD INCREASE PURCHASES IN U.S.

Administration Weighs Curb on Use of Funds—Trade Deficit Major Factor

By EDWIN L. DALE Jr.
Special to The New York Times.

WASHINGTON, Sept. 19 — The Administration is seriously considering a plan to require that more foreign aid funds be spent on American goods.

The reason is the deficit in the United States balance of international payments, with its resulting outflow of gold and build-up of foreign assets in the United States.

No decision on expanded use of "tied" foreign aid has been reached. But there is a good chance that a decision will be made to require that considerably more, though not all, of the funds be spent in the United States.

The change would have a major impact on aid extended by the Development Loan Fund, whose operations are rapidly expanding. Some defense support aid might also be affected.

Opposed By Some

For years the Administration has resisted moves in Congress to require more "tied" aid. Now it is moving toward such a policy itself, though it will presumably continue to resist any fixed legal formula as a part of the foreign aid legislation.

Officials who are leaning toward a decision to tie more foreign aid to domestic purchases are centered in the financial agencies. There may be opposition to the plan from the State Department and the International Cooperation Administration.

A requirement that more foreign aid funds be spent in the United States would help the balance of payments because the outflow of aid dollars on one side of the balance would be matched by a rise in exports on the other side.

To the extent that foreign aid results in exports that would not otherwise be made, the dollars "come home," and there is no adverse effect on the balance of payments.

There are differing versions of the extent to which foreign aid dollars are already coming home and paying for United States exports. Some figures indicate that about 90 per cent

Continued on Page 19, Column 1

Associated Press Wirephoto

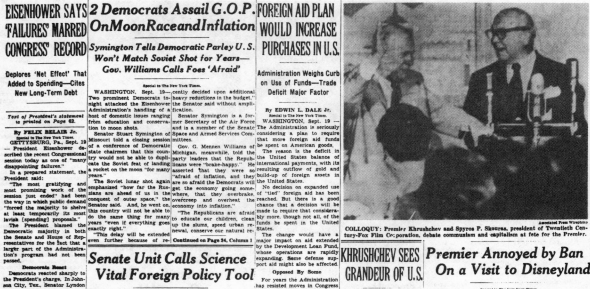

COLLOQUY: Premier Khrushchev and Spyros P. Skouras, president of Twentieth Century-Fox Film Corporation, debate communism and capitalism at fete for the Premier.

KHRUSHCHEV SEES GRANDEUR OF U.S.

Vast Continental Expanse Spreads Beneath Plane as Premier Flies West

Special to The New York Times.

LOS ANGELES, Sept. 19—Nikita S. Khrushchev got his first look today at the power and the majesty of America's continental expanse. It was a spectacle that would have moved almost anyone seeing it for the first time.

The Soviet Premier flew in a little more than five hours from the blue Atlantic seaboard, shimmering in morning sunlight, to the Pacific, which appeared gray under a light bank of clouds.

His flight in a silver Boeing 707 jet aircraft placed at his disposal by President Eisenhower was made at altitudes so great that an expanse of 150 to 200 miles in every direction was visible to him as he looked from the cabin window.

Mr. Khrushchev saw the great white cliffs of Manhattan's skyscrapers chiseled

Continued on Page 43, Column 1

Premier Annoyed by Ban On a Visit to Disneyland

Special to The New York Times.

LOS ANGELES, Sept. 19—Nikita S. Khrushchev's temper exploded today, not long after he arrived here from New York, when he was told that he could not go to Disneyland because security officials could not guarantee his safety.

"And I say, I would very much like to go and see Disneyland," Mr. Khrushchev shouted angrily. "But then, we cannot

Khrushchev-Skouras debate is printed on Page 41.

guarantee your security, they say. Then what must I do? Commit suicide?"

"What is it?" he asked. "Is there an epidemic of cholera there or something? Or have gangsters taken hold of the place that can destroy me?"

The incident probably was the first time that Disneyland had figured as a controversial subject in Soviet-United States relations. The 100-acre, $20,000,000 amusement park has been visited by some 15,000,000 persons in four years.

'Unsafe' Ruling Prevails

Chief William H. Parker of the Los Angeles police said the distance the Khrushchev motorcade would have to go to reach Disneyland—thirty miles of highway—and the complexity of the area made adequate security arrangements impossible.

Chief Parker said the Soviet security officers who planned arrangements with him had agreed it might be "unsafe" for the Premier to go to Disneyland.

Mr. Khrushchev arrived in Los Angeles at 12:10 P. M. (3:10 P. M., Eastern daylight time)

Continued on Page 40, Column 3

FILM STARS FETE RUSSIAN IN STUDIO

Movie Industry Goes All Out for Khrushchev—Luncheon Draws Hollywood Elite

By MURRAY SCHUMACH
Special to The New York Times.

HOLLYWOOD, Calif., Sept. 19—The movie industry dug into its bag of show tricks today to regale Nikita S. Khrushchev with an extraordinary welcome to the film capital.

From vodka to a can-can dance, the leaders of the movie world tried to amuse the Soviet Premier during the nearly four hours he spent at the studios of Twentieth Century-Fox.

A collection of Hollywood stars far beyond the means of any one studio turned out for the luncheon in honor of Mr. Khrushchev and his party.

It was at the studio luncheon that Premier Khrushchev engaged in a heated debate with Spyros P. Skouras, president of the Twentieth Century-Fox Film Corporation, on the respective merits of communism and capitalism.

Visits 'Can-Can' Set

The most important movie executives, who generally make a point of attacking communism, were on hand to pay their respects to Mr. Khrushchev.

As its pièce de résistance, following a program that included lunch and speeches, the industry staged part of a movie being made at Fox. With Mr. Khrushchev and his party in a sort of private box overlooking the floor of the sound stage, a section of "Can-Can," the movie version of the Broadway musical, was filmed for the visitor.

To bring special flavor to this performance, a departure was made from the usual procedure. Frank Sinatra acted as master of ceremonies to explain the proceedings—with the help of an interpreter in the Premier's box.

Mr. Sinatra, with his usual aplomb, grinned as he announced that the first number would be a song done by Louis Jourdan and Maurice Chevalier.

"It is called 'Live and Let Live,'" said Mr. Sinatra, "and I think it is a marvelous idea."

He told the Russians that the scene in which the song occurs is in "a movie about a lot of

Continued on Page 40, Column 4

PREMIER ANGERED

Flares Up as Mayor Cites 'Bury You' Gibe —Is Still Hopeful

Text of the speech appears on Pages 41 and 42.

By HARRISON E. SALISBURY
Special to The New York Times.

LOS ANGELES, Sept. 19—Nikita S. Khrushchev's trip to America took a critical turn late tonight that raised serious implications as to its outcome and its effect on relations between the two countries.

The Soviet Premier told a Los Angeles audience that he still had hope that he and President Eisenhower could find common ground. But he warned that the question as it stood today was one of "war or peace, life or death." He strongly implied that the choice must be made by the United States.

Mr. Khrushchev told a stunned audience that he had come to America in only twelve and a half hours by plane and that he could return in ten and a half. Calling out in the audience to A. A. Tupelov, son of the designer of the aircraft on which he arrived, he asked, "isn't that so?"

"Less than that," was Mr. Tupelov's laconic reply.

An Outburst of Temper

There was no mistaking the grave course that the Khrushchev trip had taken, arising originally in what had appeared to be a limited temper outburst by Mr. Khrushchev over the refusal of State Department and local authorities to set up security arrangements that would enable him to pay a visit to Disneyland.

A few hours later, however, he was warning his audience in terms of the greatest seriousness that if the United States really wanted to continue the "cold war" it was welcome to do so and that it would find in such a continuation that the Soviet Union was able to hold its own and then some.

"If you want to go on with the arms race, very well," Mr. Khrushchev said. "We accept that challenge. As for the output of rockets—well, they are on the assembly line. This is a most serious question. It is one of life or death, ladies and gentlemen. One of war and peace.

"If you don't understand—'" a voice from the audience

Continued on Page 40, Column 1

Sports News

BASEBALL

The Dodgers tied the Giants for the National League lead by beating San Francisco by 4—1 yesterday afternoon and 5—3 at night. The Braves routed the Phils, 9—3, and trail by half a game. The Tigers defeated the White Sox, 5—4. The Indians set back the Athletics, 13 to 7, in a night game. The Yanks beat the Red Sox, 3—1.

FOOTBALL

Navy trounced Boston College, 24—8. Dick Pariseau and Joe Bellino of the middies scored on long runs. Maryland turned back West Virginia, 27—7, on three scoring passes by Dick Novak. Louisiana State beat Rice, 26—3.

GOLF

Jack Nicklaus' birdie on the final hole beat Charley Coe in the United States amateur tournament final, 1 up.

HORSE RACING

Greentree Stable's Weatherwise, ridden by Eddie Arcaro, won the $143,220 Aqueduct Futurity, defeating the favored Udaipur by one and a quarter lengths. Round Table, piloted by Willie Shoemaker, captured the $100,000 United Nations Handicap at Atlantic City. Noureddin was the runner-up in the turf course race.

Details in Section 5

Steel Halt Causes Mounting Idleness

By EMANUEL PERLMUTTER

With steel negotiations in recess for the week-end, reports received here yesterday stressed the growing hardships caused by the ten-week-old strike.

Gov. David L. Lawrence of Pennsylvania announced that 220,000 workers, about 7 per cent of the state's population, were idle because of the strike.

He said that seventy-eight Pennsylvania plants had been closed for lack of steel or lack of orders from steel companies. Such closings would increase sharply unless the strike was settled soon, he added.

He said that the seventy-eight closings made 51,636 workers idle. The state has 166,600 steel workers on strike.

The families of 12,704 strikers were on public relief in the

Continued on Page 32, Column 1

Teacher Lures Plant as Tax Aid

Miss Louise Johnson with V. R. Bechtel, assistant to the executive vice president of American Cyanamid Company.

Her Plea for School in Jersey Attracts Cyanamid to Town

Special to The New York Times.

WAYNE, N. J., Sept. 19—A school teacher's interest in good schools and a letter she wrote to a large New York company are credited with bringing an $8,000,000 industrial project to this Passaic County township.

Miss Louise Johnson, a music teacher, wrote the letter last March after she had read that the American Cyanamid Company had been blocked in its plans to build administration offices in Alpine, N. J., which did not want to open its doors to industry.

She invited the company to locate in Wayne, declaring that towns where industries shared the tax burden had better schools.

The invitation was accepted. V. R. Bechtel, assistant to the executive vice president of American Cyanamid, said today the company expected to start construction in Wayne this fall.

A so-called campus arrangement of buildings connected by enclosed walkways or underground passages is planned. At the end of five years the com-

Continued on Page 80, Column 1

Russians Are Told Of Hostility in U.S.

By MAX FRANKEL
Special to The New York Times.

MOSCOW, Sept. 19 — Soviet readers received their first suggestion today that Premier Khrushchev had been encountering some stiff questioning and isolated picketing in the United States.

The opposition was characterized as a symptom of the "serious illness" of American politicians and business men, which Mr. Khrushchev was doing his best to "cure."

Moscow's two cultural papers concentrated on this aspect of the Premier's visit. Their correspondents, like most Russian writers, also complained about the architecture, hectic activity and traffic of New York.

However, all continued to celebrate Mr. Khrushchev's impact on ordinary Americans.

"What is taking place here

Continued on Page 46, Column 1

Today's Sections

Section	1 (3 parts)	News
Section	2	Drama, Screen, Music, TV, Radio, Gardens, Art
Section	3	Financial and Business
Section	4	Review of the Week
Section	5	Sports
Section	6	Magazine
		(Part 2) Home Furnishings
Section	7	Book Review
Section	8	*Real Estate
Section	9	*Employment Advertising
Section	10	Advertising
Section	11	Advertising
Section	12	Resorts & Travel

*Included in all copies in the New York metropolitan area and adjacent territory.

Index to Subjects

	Section.	Page.
Art	1	83
	2	17
Boats	5	17-18
Book Review	7	..
Bridge	2	23
Dance	2	13
Drama	2	1-7
Editorials	4	8
Education	4	9
Fashions	6	72-73
Financial and Business	3	..
Food	6	70-71
Gardens	2	25-32
Home Fashions (Part 2)	6	..
Home Improvement	2	24
Letters to Editor	4	8
Music	2	10-12
News Summary & Index	1	95
Obituaries	1	86-87
Photography	2	15
Puzzles	6	96
Real Estate	8	..
Records	2	13-14
Resorts	12	..
Review of Week	4	..
Science	4	9
Screen	2	8-10
Ships & Aviation	5	13-14
Society	1	88-124
Sports	5	..
Stamps, Coins	2	23
Television-Radio	2	18-22
Weather	1	95

Bonanza, *the continuing saga of the Cartwright family, came to television in 1959 and quickly became a Sunday night hit. Lorne Greene starred as Ben Cartwright; Dan Blocker, Pernell Roberts and Michael Landon played his sons, Hoss, Adam and Little Joe.*

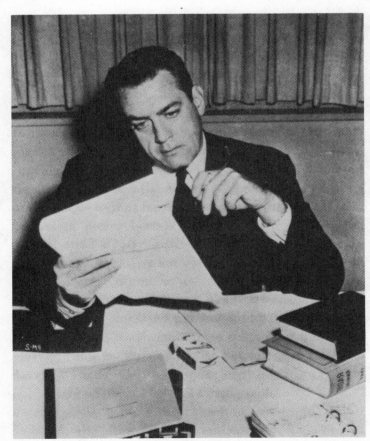

Perry Mason, *created by mystery writer Erle Stanley Gardner, starred Raymond Burr as the lawyer who never lost a case.*

The Untouchables, *a landmark police series starring Robert Stack as Eliot Ness, became notorious for its escalation of violence in prime time and for associating Italian names with the gangland crime of the Prohibition era.*

1959

The commencement of the jet transport era took place in 1959 when commercial service was initiated by Pan American World Airways with the Boeing 707. The jetliner could carry 175 passengers from New York City to Paris—3680 miles at 600 mph—in 7 hours.

The 1959 Cadillac.

Floyd Patterson lost his heavyweight title to Ingemar Johansson (standing).

"All the News That's Fit to Print"

The New York Times.

LATE CITY EDITION
U.S. Weather Bureau Report (Page 71) forecasts:
Cloudy, chance of rain today.
Fair and cool tomorrow.
Temp. range: 57—48; yesterday 59.8—49.

VOL. CIX..No. 37,166.   © 1959, by The New York Times Company. Times Square, New York 36, N. Y.   NEW YORK, TUESDAY, OCTOBER 27, 1959.   10 cents beyond 50-mile zone from New York City except on Long Island. Higher in air delivery cities.   FIVE CENTS

KAISER GIVES 22.5C AN HOUR IN STEEL PACT

CONTRACT SIGNED

Work Rules Issue Is Put to Labor and Industry Panel

Statements by McDonald and Kaiser are on Page 22.

By JOSEPH A. LOFTUS
Special to The New York Times.

WASHINGTON, Oct. 26—The Kaiser Steel Corporation and the United Steelworkers of America signed a new contract today. It cracked the united front of major steel companies.

The contract gives the union a package that is worth up to 22½ cents an hour in the next twenty months. The company said it was too early to talk about the effect the contract would have on steel prices.

The twelve major companies, headed by the United States Steel Corporation, have bargained with the union through a 104-day strike. The Kaiser strike, affecting about 7,500 employes at Fontana, Calif., was terminated.

[Kaiser immediately began recalling workers to fire up furnaces at its old home in but it is expected to take three or four weeks for the plant to get back into full production.

[In Pittsburgh, other steel producers informed the union and Government officials that the Kaiser settlement had made them more determined than ever to hold out.]

Kaiser and the union said they regarded the agreement as "a non-inflationary settlement."

Terms of Agreement

These were the principal terms:

¶In the first year, which has been whittled down to about eight months by the strike, wage rates will not be increased but take-home pay will rise as the company takes over the payments that employes have been making on group insurance. Improvements in pen-

Continued on Page 23, Column 1

NEW 'TROVATORE' OPENS 'MET' YEAR

Bing Sees Further Delay in Move to Lincoln Square

By ROSS PARMENTER

The Metropolitan Opera opened its seventy-fifth season last night at its old home on Broadway, and Rudolf Bing, the general manager, estimated that there would probably be at least three more such openings at the maroon and gold Victorian opera house.

The reprieve for the old era has been gained by delays in getting the new home started at the Lincoln Center for the Performing Arts. Because the ground for the new opera house has not yet been broken, the previously announced target date of 1961 has been abandoned, and already an opening there in 1962 is doubtful.

The opening of the Met is always one of the great "nights" of the New York year, and last night's opening, attended by 4,000 persons, had the traditional social fanfare, fashion display and general communal excitement. But there were also elements that distinguished it from other openings. They included a new production of Verdi's "Il Trovatore" (staged by Herbert Graf and designed by Motley), a lavish new program book and the serving of miniature Danish pastries to the standees.

The new program is being published by The Saturday Review in the size of that magazine. Its cover is a striking photograph that shows the interior of the opera house with its old gold glory in dazzling colors.

But the program's appearance caused a little consternation backstage. It had all the vital information about the new production of "Trovatore" ex-

Continued on Page 43, Column 4

TRUJILLO REGIME FOUND IMPERILED BY FISCAL CRISIS

Heavy Spending for Arms Severely Hurts Economy—Dictator Admits Danger

By TAD SZULC

The economic situation in the Dominican Republic is reported to have deteriorated so greatly in the last six months that diplomatic observers see in it a serious threat to the stability of that country's dictatorial regime.

In his anxiety to arm himself against possible invasions, Generalissimo Rafael Leonidas Trujillo Molina appears to have deeply injured the Dominican economy.

Heavy purchases of weapons have forced the Dominican Government to obtain loans ranging up to $40,000,000 abroad, mostly from Canadian banks, to help cover the growing deficit in the balance of payments.

Internal Outlook Bad

This is the first time in more than twenty years that the country is facing a deficit of that kind, and it will be the first time in twelve years that General Trujillo, known officially since 1947 as the "Financial Emancipator of the Nation," will owe money abroad.

Internally, the situation is reported to be just as unfavorable. On Oct. 17 the Generalissimo admitted publicly that there might not be enough money this year to pay the traditional Christmas bonuses to Government employes.

A week earlier the Government issued a decree canceling the implementation of a new tax structure that was to have gone into effect this month. Business and diplomatic observers interpreted the move as an admission that the nation could not afford any further economic strain to help finance General Trujillo's military effort.

Because of the deterioration in the Government's finances and of the retrenchment in business activities following the June invasions by Cuba-based Dominican exiles, the cost of living in Ciudad Trujillo was reported to have risen about 20 per cent between July and October. Prices had been stable for years.

Unrest in the Country

Diplomats familiar with the Dominican situation have reported that recent events may bring about the collapse of the economic prosperity that for the twenty-nine years of Trujillo rule has been the main pride of the regime.

At the same time, diplomatic sources have told of considerable unrest and anti-regime underground activities that followed the abortive invasions.

At least two fires of mysterious origin in government buildings were reported to have occurred in Ciudad Trujillo in recent months. The Ministry of Justice and the National Archives were damaged. Many police files are stored in these buildings.

But the consensus among business and diplomatic observers is that while General Trujillo can presumably cope with foreign attacks and domestic subversion, it is the economic problem that is causing him the most concern.

If economic prosperity deteriorates, these observers say, the regime's political foundations may collapse.

General Trujillo severely strained the Treasury with his

Continued on Page 6, Column 3

300,000 Rally to Back Castro; He Condemns 'Raids' From U.S.

By R. HART PHILLIPS
Special to The New York Times.

HAVANA, Oct. 26—Premier Fidel Castro, armed with a rifle, dropped out of the skies in a helicopter late this afternoon at the Presidential Palace, where between 300,000 and 400,000 persons had gathered to protest "aggression" from the United States.

The crowd gave him a ten-minute ovation when he stepped to the microphone.

Premier Castro attacked the United States bitterly, charging that it had permitted planes to take off from its territory last Wednesday to "bomb the defenseless population of Havana."

He said that two persons were killed and forty-five wounded in the raid.

The Premier then read a telegram from military authorities in Pinar del Rio province, charging that a sugar mill at Niagara was bombed by a plane today.

The telegram also declared that an incendiary bomb had been dropped on a house in the capital city of Pinar del Rio.

The plane also dropped subversive leaflets, according to the telegram. This is the second time the sugar mill has been reported bombed in three weeks.

Premier Castro asked the crowd if the Revolutionary military courts should be re-established to try traitors and counter-revolutionaries. Such courts

Continued on Page 5, Column 1

Lack of Steel Halts A Bridge Job Here

By JOSEPH C. INGRAHAM

A lack of steel has halted construction of the new lower deck of the George Washington Bridge.

In addition, a check showed yesterday, other projects in the vast arterial road-bridge program to ease snarls in the metropolitan area soon will be affected by the long steel strike.

The result, according to a consensus of highway officials, is that the construction timetable for about $800,000,000 of projects already in progress or scheduled to start soon will be set back by six months to a year.

The next casualty of the steel strike will be the Throgs Neck Bridge. Executives of the Triborough Bridge and Tunnel Authority said they

Continued on Page 23, Column 5

U. S. CALLS FOR END OF ALL TRADE BIAS

Dillon Warns GATT Parley Protectionism Will Grow if Nations Delay Action

By ROBERT TRUMBULL
Special to The New York Times.

TOKYO, Tuesday, Oct. 27—The United States demanded today that other nations take immediate steps to end trade barriers.

It noted that these barriers had contributed to a prospective $4,000,000,000 deficit this year in the United States balance of payments, which is the difference between spending abroad and income from abroad.

Economic recovery in other industrial countries has removed any justification for continued restrictions on purchases of American goods, said Douglas Dillon, Under Secretary of State.

He addressed representatives and observers from fifty countries at a meeting of the General Agreement on Tariffs and Trade, usually called GATT.

Retaliation Foreseen

Continued discrimination, especially against dollar goods, may lead to retaliatory protectionist measures, he warned.

Mr. Dillon also asked that restrictions be eased on imports from low-wage countries such as Japan.

Referring to the refusal of Britain and fourteen other countries to grant Japan the "most favored nation" treatment called for in the GATT convention, he said this was a matter of particular concern in Washington.

"We believe that the continuation of this situation for whatever reasons weakens the structure of the General Agreement and should be remedied as soon as possible," he said. "We strongly support Japan's hopes for full and equal treatment with other nations under the GATT."

Citing the "remarkable economic advance in many sectors of the economy of the free world," Mr. Dillon warned that,

Continued on Page 6, Column 3

City Crime Rising, Kennedy Declares; Youths' Part Cited

By GUY PASSANT

Police Commissioner Stephen P. Kennedy described the crime picture in New York City as "gloomy" yesterday and said major offenses continued to increase in the last nine months.

He said that a steady rise in murder, manslaughter, rape and other felonies emphasized that the Police Department's need for efficiency "is greater now than ever before."

He attributed the worsening crime situation in part to a step-up of youth violence in the last year, especially during the summer.

Commissioner Kennedy declared that youths under 16 years of age had committed ten more murders and "non-negligent" manslaughters this year than last. Those in the 16-to-20-year-old category, he said, committed thirty-one more of those crimes.

Fifty-one Police Promoted

The Commissioner made his remarks at a ceremony in headquarters after he had promoted fifty-one members of the force—four to the rank of captain, thirteen to lieutenant and thirty-four to sergeant.

"I don't know when there has ever a greater need for greater competence in the superior officers of this department," the Commissioner told those promoted.

"Today the crime picture is not improved. Hence, the responsibilities that rest upon you gentlemen are greater than ever.

"We have had increases in

Continued on Page 27, Column 3

BACK OF MOON 'SEEN' FIRST TIME; PHOTO BY SOVIET ROCKET SHOWS FEWER CRATERS THAN FACE HAS

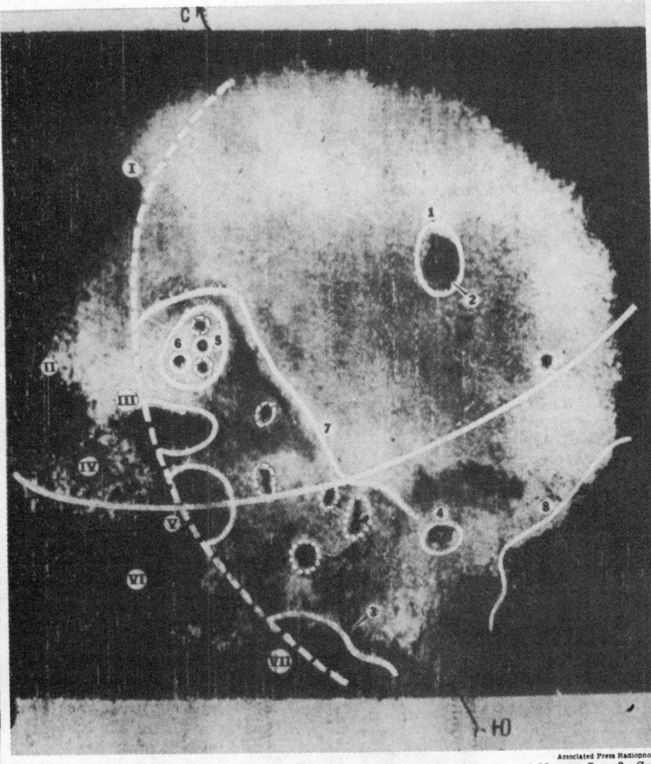

FAR SIDE OF THE MOON as photographed by equipment aboard Soviet vehicle. Picture, released by Tass, has not been retouched except for numerals and lines.

Soviet astronomers identify the long solid line as the moon's equator. Heavy broken line at left separates the part of the moon visible from the earth from the portion that cannot be seen. Solid lines surround objects absolutely identified; objects that need more clarity of form are enclosed in heavy dotted lines; fine-dotted lines are around objects now being classified.

The Arabic numerals, as given by Soviet astronomers, are as follows: 1—Moscow Sea, a crater 187 miles in diameter; 2—Astronauts' Bay of Moscow Sea; 3—Continuation of Southern Sea on the moon's face; 4—Crater of the main Tsiolkovsky Hill; 5—Crater of central Lomonosov Hill; 6—Joliot-Curie Crater; 7—Soviet Mountains; and 8—Sea of Dreams.

The Roman numerals designate areas visible from the earth: I—Humboldt's Sea; II—Sea of Crises; III—Marginal Sea; IV—Sea of Waves; V—Smyth's Sea; VI—Sea of Fertility; VII—Southern Sea.

Arrow indicates north pole (top), south pole (bottom). For those portions not designated by numerals or lines, further processing is now being done.

Associated Press Radiophoto

APALACHIN TRIAL OF 22 OPENS HERE

23d Defendant Wins Delay After Heart Attack

By EDWARD RANZAL

The selection of a jury in Federal Court began yesterday in the case of twenty-two men accused of conspiring to obstruct justice by concealing from a grand jury the true nature of the 1957 Apalachin meeting.

The trial of a twenty-third defendant was separated from that of the others because he had suffered a heart attack Sunday evening. He is Joseph Bonanno of Tucson, Ariz.

Of twenty-nine prospective jurors called before Judge Irving R. Kaufman, eight were excused because they said they had been prejudiced by newspaper and television accounts, two were excused for economic hardship and seven were challenged by the defense.

When court convened at 10:30 A. M. yesterday, Judge Kaufman was told that Bonanno had suffered a heart attack at 10:30 Sunday night while visiting friends in Brooklyn. He was rushed to St. Catherine's Hospital, where he was placed in an oxygen tent.

The selection of the jury was postponed until 2:30 P. M. to give a court-appointed physician an opportunity to examine Bonanno, who is 55 years old. The doctor was Dr. Simon Daub, head of the Department of Cardiology at Mount Sinai Hospital, whose name had been suggested to the court by Milton R.

Continued on Page 26, Column 5

AREAS ARE NAMED

Ground Switch Swung Lens Into Position— Picture Put on TV

By OSGOOD CARUTHERS
Special to The New York Times

MOSCOW, Tuesday, Oct 27 — The Soviet Union released today what it said was man's first picture of the hidden side of the moon.

Eight of the hazy dark spots shown in the single picture released were promptly given names by a specially appointed committee of the Soviet Academy of Sciences. One of the largest was a depression said to be 187 miles across. It was called the Moscow Sea.

The picture was transmitted by the official press agency, Tass, to its bureaus throughout the world, published in Moscow's two principal newspapers, Pravda and Izvestia, and shown to Soviet viewers over the Moscow television network.

Other Pictures Taken

The picture shown today was one of a "considerable number" that Tass said the Soviet Union's latest lunar rocket had taken during twenty days ago as it soared most the far side of the moon.

What does the other side of the moon look like? Here is what the photograph showed in part:

A vast white area with darker shadings covering most of the southern hemisphere and extending halfway up the western quarter of the northern hemisphere. The boundary of this shadow was named by the Soviet scientists the Soviet Mountains.

In the center of the huge, white area was a large irregular indentation, the one that was named the Moscow Sea. Scientists use the word sea to describe the dry depressions on the surface of the moon facing the earth, and the Russians apparently continued the practice for the far side.

In the western sector behind the Soviet Mountains is a group of four round spots, two of which were given names. The other two were said still to be under study for classification, as were ten other clearly defined spots on the unseen surface of the moon.

70 Per Cent Photographed

Photographs published by Pravda also showed the far lunar side was mostly covered by mountains.

[In a broadcast from Moscow Monday night, The Associated Press said, a Soviet scientist described the lunar discovery as follows:

["The unseen part of the moon is considerably more monotonous than the side turned toward the earth. It contains fewer seas and fewer contrasts."

[The scientist was Prof. Aleksandr A. Mikhailov, director of the Pulkovo Observatory.]

An earlier announcement said that the 600-pound cosmic vehicle had succeeded in photographing in bright sunlight 70

Continued on Page 4, Column 3

Soviet Terms Itself 'Greatest' of States

By MAX FRANKEL
Special to The New York Times

MOSCOW, Oct. 26—Whatever else Premier Khrushchev's trip to the United States accomplished, it has emboldened Soviet propagandists to describe their country without qualification as "the greatest power in the world."

This phrase has appeared twice in the last week, and such appearances are not accidental here. Both times it was used with the Premier's name, as a description of the country he heads.

The agitation and drum-beating over Mr. Khrushchev's American journey are almost as strong now as they were during the two weeks he spent in the United States last month. Above

Continued on Page 13, Column 2

Moon Photo Backs Theory Of a Smoother Far Side

By WALTER SULLIVAN

The seeming absence of craters and seas across much of the far side of the moon, as revealed yesterday in a Soviet photograph, was viewed here with interest, in view of a theory that predicted that the far side would be largely smooth.

It has been postulated in some scientific quarters that the formation of at least some of the lunar features resulted from the tug of the earth's gravity. The side of the moon facing the earth bulges roughly one mile in that direction, because of this tug.

This has been described as a "frozen tide" held permanently in the grip of the earth. The view that the stresses and strains of its formation created some of the lunar mountains and seas has been controversial.

A radio broadcast in Moscow quoted Prof. Aleksandr A. Mikhailov, director of Pulkovo Observatory, as saying that the topography of the far side was "considerably more monotonous" than that facing the earth. This, he said, was "beyond doubt associated with the

Continued on Page 5, Column 1

U. S. AIDE RELATES ORDEAL IN SOVIET

Langelle Says Reds Sought to 'Penetrate' Embassy

By WILLIAM J. JORDEN
Special to The New York Times

WASHINGTON, Oct. 26—A United States official who was expelled from the Soviet Union said today that Soviet efforts to "penetrate" the United States Embassy in Moscow increased in the last six months.

Russell A. Langelle, 37-year-old former security officer of the embassy, said he had repeatedly frustrated espionage efforts. He said he thought that was the principal reason the Soviet authorities wanted to get rid of him.

Mr. Langelle discussed his ouster at a news conference in the embassy. He vigorously denied Soviet charges that he had engaged in espionage.

Moscow accused Mr. Langelle of making contact with an

Continued on Page 14, Column 5

News conference excerpts will be found on Page 14.

NEWS INDEX

	Page		Page
Art	40-41	Music	40-41
Books	31	Obituaries	37
Bridge	41	Real Estate	39
Business	37-58	Screen	40-41
Buying		Ships and Air	71
Crossword	41	Society	30
Editorial	38	Sports	44-48
Events Today	41	Theatres	40-41
Fashions		TV and Radio	74-75
Financial	49-58	U. N. Proceedings	8
Food	31	U. S. Proceedings	
In the News	42	Washington	8
Letters		Weather	71

News Summary and Index, Page 39

253

Sidney Poitier and Dorothy Dandridge are shown here in a scene from Porgy and Bess.

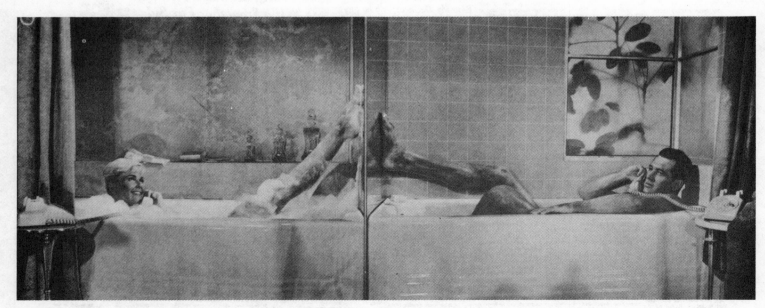

Doris Day and Rock Hudson are seen here in a scene from Pillow Talk, *which utilized a split-screen effect.*

"All the News
That's Fit to Print"

The New York Times.

LATE CITY EDITION
U. S. Weather Bureau Report (Page 63) forecast:
Mostly cloudy, mild, some rain today. Mostly cloudy tomorrow.
Temp. range: 50–37; yesterday: 41.6–34.5

SECTION ONE

NEWS SUMMARY AND INDEX, PAGE 63

VOL. CIX....No. 37,227.

© 1959 by The New York Times Company
Times Square, New York 36, N. Y.

NEW YORK, SUNDAY, DECEMBER 27, 1959.

10c outside New York City, its suburban area
and Long Island. Higher in air delivery cities.

TWENTY-FIVE CENTS

WEST TO CONFER SPEEDLY TO SET DATE OF SUMMIT

Mid-May Is Still Favored in Washington After Reply from Khrushchev

SWIFT AGREEMENT SEEN

President Must Also Act on the Expiration of Ban on Nuclear Weapons Tests

By JACK RAYMOND
Special to The New York Times

WASHINGTON, Dec. 26—A speedy round of consultations among the Western powers is in prospect today to set a date for summit talks in Paris with the Soviet Union.

New instructions are expected to be sent to the United States, British and French Ambassadors in Moscow some time next week to discuss the subject with Andrei A. Gromyko, the Soviet Foreign Minister.

A date in mid-May was still favored in the speculation here.

Much of the speculation centered on what President Eisenhower's preference might be, although no hint of his intentions was available. The President, who visited his grandchildren at his Gettysburg farm this morning, received no official visitors at the White House.

Two Urgent Issues at Hand

The summit talk is one of two urgent issues awaiting President Eisenhower's action. The other is the expiration Thursday night of the fourteen-month-old ban on nuclear-weapons testing.

The prevailing belief is that the President will order an extension of the prohibition, possibly for an indefinite period. Officials said no decision had been made.

Even if an extension is ordered, the President is expected to remind the Russians, who also have unilaterally suspended nuclear-weapons tests, that further observation of the moratorium by the United States would depend upon progress in the Geneva negotiations toward a formal agreement.

Inspection Is Obstacle

The United States, Britain and the Soviet Union have failed thus far in the talks that began at Geneva fourteen months ago to get over the stumbling block of an acceptable inspection system.

This undoubtedly will be a major matter for discussion at the projected summit meeting.

President Eisenhower joined with the British and French leaders this week in inviting Premier Khrushchev to meet them in Paris about April 27. The Soviet leader responded that the proposed date was inconvenient, apparently because of his expected presence at the traditional May Day celebration in Moscow. Mr. Khrushchev suggested April 21 or May 4 instead.

The Paris summit meeting, slated to be the forerunner of

Continued on Page 2, Column 4

Sports News

FOOTBALL

The New York Giants will play the Baltimore Colts in Baltimore's Memorial Stadium today in the National Football League championship play-off. The game will be seen by a sellout crowd of 57,557 and will be telecast and broadcast nationally. The Colts are favored by 3½ points. The Colts beat the Giants, 23 to 17, in the title game last year.

In college football, the Blue defeated the Gray, 20 to 8, yesterday in their annual all-star game at Montgomery, Ala. The North beat the South, 27 to 17, in their annual all-star contest at Miami. The passing of Joe Caldwell of Army was the major factor. The National All-Stars downed the Southwest All-Stars, 21 to 6, in the Copper Bowl at Tempe, Ariz.

BASKETBALL

Cincinnati trounced St. Bonaventure, 96 to 56, in the first round of the Holiday Festival tournament at Madison Square Garden. Oscar Robertson of Cincinnati scored 47 points. In other Festival games, New York University downed Dartmouth, 78 to 68; Iowa topped St. John's of Brooklyn, 91 to 84, and St. Joseph's of Philadelphia won from Manhattan College, 84 to 70.

Details in Section 5.

Soviet Party Orders Tightened Controls Over the Collectives

By MAX FRANKEL
Special to The New York Times

MOSCOW, Dec. 26—Tighter party control was decreed today for Soviet collective farms.

The Central Committee of the Communist party ordered the organizational changes to spur agricultural production, which it said had been good in 1959, but not good enough.

The committee's decrees were made public this evening after the close of a four-day meeting of the group devoted almost exclusively to agriculture. Although the final statement contained a serious indictment of the farm leadership in Kazakhstan, no high-level personnel changes were announced.

The party said the production of 62,000,000 tons of milk this year would exceed the gross milk output of the United States. It also expected

Continued on Page 2, Column 2

TRIBE WAR PERILS LIBERTY FOR CONGO

Barbaric Fighting Dismays Africans Who Seek Early Withdrawal by Belgians

By HOMER BIGART
Special to The New York Times

MUTOTO STATION, Belgian Congo, Dec. 26—A barbaric civil war in the heart of the Belgian Congo may wreck Congolese plans for speedy independence.

The savagery of the fighting has upset even some militant nationalists, who are beginning to dread what might happen if the restraining influence of Belgian authority were suddenly lifted.

Equally macabre has been the discovery by Belgian authorities of the mass poisoning of scores of members of the Bushongo tribe, which has been neutral in the fighting.

The Belgians say investigations revealed that 226 tribesmen were poisoned during a recent series of tachipapa, or occult ceremonial trials in which whole villages participate. Drinking bouts are held in which the contents of some cups are poisoned. Those who receive them are presumed to have been guilty of some offense.

Old Customs Revived

The Belgians have outlawed tachipapa. But the agitation for independence apparently has encouraged the Bushongo to revert to old customs. Cynics believe that the tschipapa are rigged by witch doctors who slip poison into the cups of tribesmen of whom the chief wants to be rid.

The war, cruder and more horrible than the tschipapa, involves two closely related tribes, the Lulua and the Baluba.

They are wrestling for control of Kasai Province, which is fertile, well populated and the world's biggest producer of industrial diamonds. Here the aggressive Lulua are trying to cast out the more docile and more advanced Baluba.

King Baudouin of the Belgians, who is touring the Congo, arrived this morning in Luluabourg, the provincial capital. He received a dignified, restrained

Continued on Page 8, Column 1

Deaths Exceed 350 In Holiday Driving

A rising toll of death on the highways marred celebration of the Christmas holiday during the long week-end.

By 2 o'clock this morning at least 355 persons had died in traffic accidents over the nation. In the city twelve persons were injured early today in an accident in the rain on the lower roadway of the Queensboro Bridge. Seven vehicles were involved.

Two tow trucks had responded after an accident between an automobile and a taxi, and three other cars crashed into the tow trucks.

The injured were taken to Grand Central Hospital. Their names were not immediately available. One was reported in critical condition.

Before the three-day holiday

Continued on Page 47, Column 2

MEYNER, RIBICOFF GET STUDY HITTING TAX BY NEW YORK

Levy Tied to Services Used Is Called Fairest System— Parley Set for Tuesday

Excerpts from report on tax will be found on Page 46.

By GEORGE CABLE WRIGHT
Special to The New York Times

TRENTON, Dec. 26—A report to Gov. Robert B. Meyner and Gov. Abraham A. Ribicoff said today that New York State should aim at taxing nonresidents only in proportion to the services it provided them.

It also suggested that nonresidents be permitted to deduct from their New York income taxes the levies they paid on residential properties in their home states.

If New York refuses to do this at present, the report continued, it should at least earmark 30 per cent of the nonresidents' taxes for aid to distressed commuter rail lines.

To Talk With Rockefeller

Governor Meyner of New Jersey and Governor Ribicoff of Connecticut will meet with Governor Rockefeller of New York on Tuesday in an attempt to solve the controversy over the taxing of out-of-state residents who work in New York.

The report was prepared by William C. Warren, interstate tax consultant to Mr. Meyner, and Roswell F. Magill, who acts in a similar capacity for Mr. Ribicoff. It comprised a detailed analysis of the effect on nonresidents of New York State's income tax.

Mr. Warren, who lives in Ridgewood, N. J., is Dean of the Columbia University Law School. Mr. Magill, a tax lawyer, lives in Westport, Conn.

The report argued that unless about $15,000,000 was cut annually from nonresident taxes there would be no equity among the states' taxpayers.

New York Plan Scored

It assailed the Rockefeller administration's plan for settling the thirty-year-old interstate tax dispute, characterizing the plan as "inherently defective and disparity" than under the present law.

The Rockefeller administration's proposal would permit nonresidents who worked in New York to take exemptions proportional to the share of their incomes earned in New York.

If approved by the New York Legislature, it would become effective only when neighboring states authorized their employers to withhold taxes on employees who live in New York or to furnish Albany with data

Continued on Page 46, Column 3

Police Drop a Historic Whistle

Order Here Scraps SOS Device That Dates to 1889

By IRA HENRY FREEMAN

Another bit of New York—the famous police whistle—is passing into history.

In an order dated Dec. 24, Police Commissioner Stephen P. Kennedy told his approximately 18,500 patrolmen and 1,500 sergeants that they would no longer be required to carry the tubular whistle.

The tubular whistle is a long, nickel-plated instrument with its own stimulating tone. It takes vigor to blow. Its sound can be heard for four or five blocks on a quiet night. For at least seventy years, it had been used by patrolmen and sometimes by civilians—to call other policemen on post to aid.

Today, Commissioner Kennedy's order said, the whistle is rarely used to call aid. The policeman uses the call-box telephone connected to his precinct, or the radio of his prowl car, or even a public telephone.

If there is no time to make telephone calls, the policeman in need can blow his traffic whistle, or bang his nightstick on the curb, or fire his revolver into the air, the Commissioner said.

The traffic whistle is that

Tubular whistle is dropped

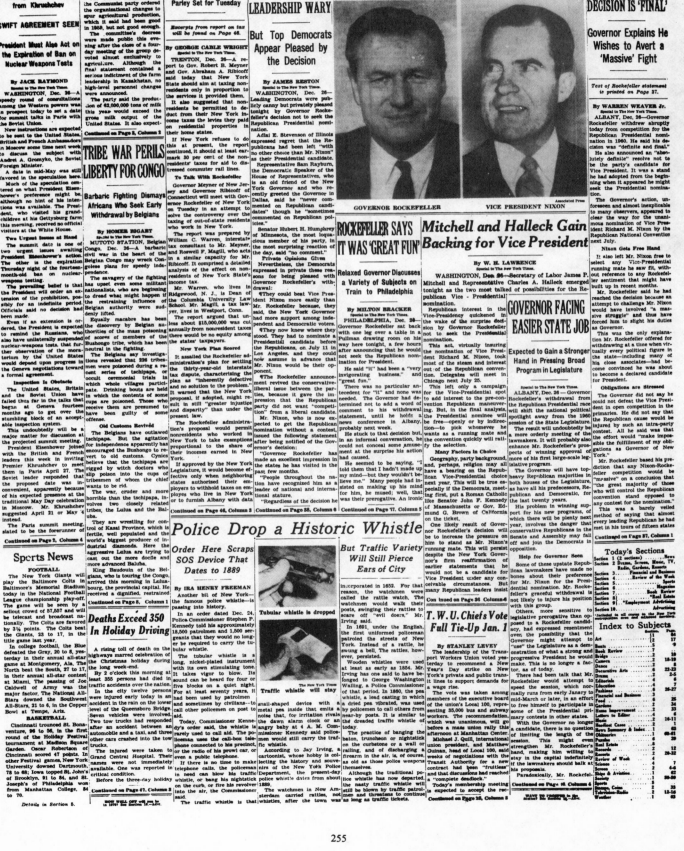

GOVERNOR ROCKEFELLER

VICE PRESIDENT NIXON

Associated Press

But Traffic Variety Will Still Pierce Ears of City

incorporated in 1652. For that reason, the watchmen were called the rattle watch. The watchmen would walk their posts, swinging their rattles to scare off "evil doers," Mr. Irving said.

In 1691, under the English, the first uniformed policeman patroled the streets of New York. Instead of a rattle, he swung a bell. The rattle, however, persisted.

Wooden whistles were used at least as early as 1854. Mr. Irving has one said to have belonged to George Washington Walling, a Police Commissioner of that period. In 1860, the pea whistle, a lead casting in which a dried pea vibrated, was used by policemen to call others from near-by posts. It is similar to the dreaded traffic whistle of today.

The practice of banging the baton, truncheon or nightstick on the curbstone or a wall or railing, and of discharging a firearm in the air, is, of course, as old as those police weapons themselves.

Although the traditional police whistle has now departed, the nasty traffic whistle will still be blown by traffic patrolmen and threatens to continue as long as traffic tickets.

Continued on Page 52, Column 2

The New York Times

Traffic whistle will stay

small-shaped device with a metal pea inside that emits a noise that, for irritation rivals the dawn alarm clock or an angry baby at 4 A. M. Commissioner Kennedy said policemen would still carry the traffic whistle.

According to Jay Irving, a cartoonist, whose hobby is collecting the history and souvenirs of the New York Police Department, the present-day police whistle dates from about 1889.

The watchmen in New Amsterdam carried rattles, not whistles, after the town was

ROCKEFELLER GIVES UP '60 RACE, CLEARING THE PATH FOR NIXON; DEMOCRATS' HOPES ARE BUOYED

LEADERSHIP WARY

But Top Democrats Appear Pleased by the Decision

By JAMES RESTON
Special to The New York Times

WASHINGTON, Dec. 26—Leading Democrats were publicly cautious but privately pleased tonight by Governor Rockefeller's decision not to seek the Republican Presidential nomination.

Adlai E. Stevenson of Illinois expressed regret that the Republicans had been left "with no other choice than Mr. Nixon" as their Presidential candidate.

Representative Sam Rayburn, the Democratic Speaker of the House of Representatives, who is an old friend of the New York Governor and who recently greeted the Governor in Dallas, said he "never commented on Republican candidates" though he "sometimes commented on Republican policies."

Senator Hubert H. Humphrey of Minnesota, the most loquacious member of his party, in the most surprising reaction of the day, said "no comment."

Private Opinions Given

Nevertheless, the Democrats expressed in private these reasons for being pleased with Governor Rockefeller's withdrawal:

¶They could beat Vice President Nixon more easily than Mr. Rockefeller because, they said, the New York Governor had more support among independent and Democratic voters.

¶They now knew where they stood. They had to nominate a Presidential candidate before the Republicans, on July 11 in Los Angeles, and they could now assume in advance that Mr. Nixon would be their opponent.

¶The Rockefeller announcement revived the conservative-liberal issue between the parties, because it gave the impression that the Republican party did not want "competition" from a liberal candidate.

Mr. Nixon, who is now expected to get the Republican nomination without a contest, issued the following statement after being notified of the Governor's decision:

"Governor Rockefeller has made an excellent impression in the states he has visited in the past few months.

"People throughout the nation have recognized him as a leader of national and international stature.

"Regardless of the decision he

Continued on Page 38, Column 6

ROCKEFELLER SAYS IT WAS 'GREAT FUN'

Relaxed Governor Discusses a Variety of Subjects on Train to Philadelphia

By MILTON BRACKER
Special to The New York Times

PHILADELPHIA, Dec. 26—Governor Rockefeller sat back with one leg over a table in his Pullman drawing room on his way here tonight, a few hours after announcing that he would not seek the Republican nomination for President.

He said "it" had been a "very invigorating business," and "great fun."

There was no particular antecedent for "it" and none was needed. The Governor had determined not to add a word of comment to his withdrawal statement, until his news conference in Albany, probably next week.

He stuck to that decision but, in an informal conversation, he could not conceal some amusement at the surprise his action had caused.

He seemed to be saying, "I told them that I hadn't made up my mind—but they wouldn't believe me." Many people had insisted on making up his mind for him, he mused; well, that was their prerogative. An ironic

Continued on Page 37, Column 3

Mitchell and Halleck Gain Backing for Vice President

By W. H. LAWRENCE
Special to The New York Times

WASHINGTON, Dec. 26—Secretary of Labor James P. Mitchell and Representative Charles A. Halleck emerged tonight as the two most talked of possibilities for the Republican Vice-Presidential nomination.

Republican interest in the Vice-Presidency quickened in the wake of the surprise decision by Governor Rockefeller not to seek the Republican Presidential nomination.

This act, virtually insuring the nomination of Vice President Richard M. Nixon, took most of the steam and interest out of the Republican convention. Delegates will meet in Chicago next July 25.

This left only a campaign for the Vice-Presidential spot to add interest to the pre-convention Republican maneuvering. But, in the final analysis, the Presidential nominee will be free—openly or by indirection—to pick whomever he wants as a running mate and the convention quickly will ratify the selection.

Many Factors in Choice

Geography, party background, and, perhaps, religion may all have a bearing on the Republican Vice-Presidential choice next year. This will be true especially if the Democrats, meeting first, put a Roman Catholic like Senator John F. Kennedy of Massachusetts or Gov. Edmund G. Brown of California on the ticket.

One likely result of Governor Rockefeller's decision will be to increase the pressure on him to stand as Mr. Nixon's running mate. This will persist despite the New York Governor's firm reaffirmation of earlier statements that he would not be a candidate for Vice President under any conceivable circumstances. But many Republican leaders insist

Continued on Page 36 Column 4

GOVERNOR FACING EASIER STATE JOB

Expected to Gain a Stronger Hand in Pressing Broad Program in Legislature

Special to The New York Times

ALBANY, Dec. 26—Governor Rockefeller's withdrawal from the Republican Presidential race will shift the national political spotlight away from the 1960 session of the State Legislature.

The result will undoubtedly be a more orderly meeting of the Legislature. It will probably also enhance Mr. Rockefeller's prospects of winning approval of more of his first large-scale legislative program.

His problem in winning support for his new programs, of which there will be plenty next year, involves the danger that conservative Republicans in the Senate and Assembly may fall off and join the Democrats in opposition.

Help for Governor Seen

Some of these upstate Republican lawmakers have made no bones about their preference for Mr. Nixon for the Presidential nomination. Mr. Rockefeller's graceful withdrawal is not likely to injure his position with this group.

Others, more sensitive to legislative prerogative than opposed to a Rockefeller candidacy, had expressed resentment over the possibility that the Governor might attempt to "use" the Legislature as a demonstration of what a strong and progressive President he would make. This is no longer a factor, as of today.

There had been talk that Mr. Rockefeller would attempt to speed the session, which normally runs from early Janary to mid-March or later, in an effort to free himself to participate in some of the Presidential primary contests in other states.

With the Governor no longer a candidate, there is no question of limiting the length of the session. This might even strengthen Mr. Rockefeller's hand, making him willing to stay in the capital indefinitely until the lawmakers dispose of his proposals.

Paradoxically, Mr. Rockefel-

Continued on Page 38, Column 6

DECISION IS 'FINAL'

Governor Explains He Wishes to Avert a 'Massive' Fight

Text of Rockefeller statement is printed on Page 37.

By WARREN WEAVER Jr.
Special to The New York Times

ALBANY, Dec. 26—Governor Rockefeller withdrew abruptly today from competition for the Republican Presidential nomination in 1960. He said his decision was "definite and final."

He also announced an "absolutely definite" resolve not to be the party's candidate for Vice President. It was a stand he had adopted from the beginning when it appeared he might seek the Presidential nomination.

The Governor's action, unforeseen and almost inexplicable to many observers, appeared to clear the way for the unanimous nomination of Vice President Richard M. Nixon by the Republican National Convention next July.

Nixon Gets Free Hand

It also left Mr. Nixon free to select any Vice-Presidential running mate he saw fit, without reference to any Rockefeller sentiment that might have built up in recent months.

Mr. Rockefeller said he had reached the decision because an attempt to challenge Mr. Nixon would have involved "a massive struggle" and thus have forced him to slight his duties as Governor.

This was the only explanation Mr. Rockefeller offered for withdrawing at a time when virtually every political figure in the state—including many of his close associates—had become convinced he was about to become a declared candidate for President.

Obligations Are Stressed

The Governor did not say he could not defeat the Vice President in open competition in the primaries. He said this, without saying that the Republican cause would be injured by such an intra-party contest. All he said was that the effort would "make impossible the fulfillment of my obligations as Governor of New York."

Mr. Rockefeller based his prediction that any Nixon-Rockefeller competition would be "massive" on a conclusion that "the great majority of those who will control the Republican convention stand opposed to any contest for the nomination."

This was a barely veiled method of saying that almost every leading Republican he had met in his tours of fifteen states

Continued on Page 37, Column 1

T. W. U. Chiefs Vote Full Tie-Up Jan. 1

By STANLEY LEVEY

The leadership of the Transport Workers Union voted yesterday to recommend a New Year's Day strike on New York's private and public transit lines to support demands for a wage rise.

The vote was taken among members of the executive board of the union's Local 100, representing 35,000 bus and subway workers. The recommendation, which was unanimous, will go before a mass union rally this afternoon at Manhattan Center.

Michael J. Quill, international union president, and Matthew Guinan, head of Local 100, said weeks of negotiations with the Transit Authority for a new contract had been "fruitless" and that discussions had reached a "complete deadlock."

Today's membership meeting is expected to accept the rec-

Continued on Page 52, Column 3

Today's Sections

Section 1 (2 sections) .... News
Section 2 ... Drama, Screen, Music, TV, Radio, Gardens, Resorts
Section 3 ..... Financial and Business
Section 4 .... Review of the Week
Section 5 .... Sports
Section 6 .... Magazine
Section 7 .... Book Review
Section 8 .... Real Estate
Section 9 .... 'Employment Advertising
Section 10 .... Advertising

Included in all copies in the New York metropolitan area and nearby points.

Index to Subjects

	Section	Page
Art	2	17
Boats	5	
Book Review	7	
Bridge	2	16
Business	3	
Churches	1	18-19
Decorative Arts	2	22-23
Drama	2	2-5
Editorials	4	8
Education	1	25-27
Fashions	6	
Financial and Business	3	
Food	2	34
Gardens	2	24
Home Improvement	2	32
Letters to Editor	4	8
Music	2	14-11
Obituaries	1	40-41
Puzzles	6	
Real Estate	8	
Records	2	12
Resorts	5	20-32
Review of Week	4	
Science	4	
Ships & Aviation	5	62
Society	1	39-40
Sports	5	
Television-Radio	2	11
Weather	1	63

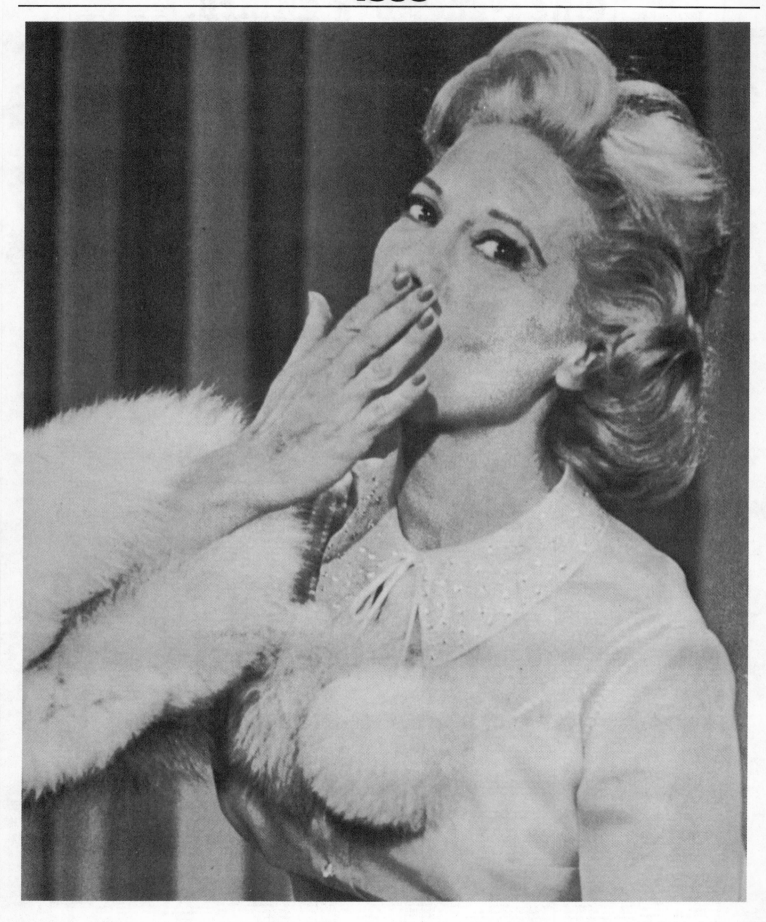